Educational Psychology

FOURTH EDITION

John W. Santrock

University of Texas at Dallas

McGraw Hill

Boston Burr Ridge, IL Dubuque, IA Madison, WI New York
San Francisco St. Louis Bangkok Bogotá Caracas Kuala Lumpur
Lisbon London Madrid Mexico City Milan Montreal New Delhi
Santiago Seoul Singapore Sydney Taipei Toronto

The McGraw-Hill Companies

Published by McGraw-Hill, an imprint of The McGraw-Hill Companies, Inc., 1221 Avenue of the Americas, New York, NY 10020. Copyright © 2009 by The McGraw-Hill Companies, Inc. All rights reserved. No part of this publication may be reproduced or distributed in any form or by any means, or stored in a database or retrieval system, without the prior written consent of The McGraw-Hill Companies, Inc., including, but not limited to, in any network or other electronic storage or transmission, or broadcast for distance learning.

Some ancillaries, including electronic and print components, may not be available to customers outside the United States.

This book is printed on acid-free paper.

Printed in China

2 3 4 5 6 7 8 9 0 CTP/CTP 11 10

ISBN: 978-0-07-128082-2
MHID: 0-07-128082-0

www.mhhe.com

About the Author

John W. Santrock received his Ph.D. from the College of Education and Human Development at the University of Minnesota. He taught at the University of Charleston and the University of Georgia before joining the faculty at the University of Texas at Dallas. He has worked as a school psychologist and currently teaches educational psychology at the undergraduate level. In 2006, John received the University of Texas at Dallas Excellence in teaching award. John's grandmother taught all grades in a one-room school for many years and his father was superintendent of a large school district. John's research has included publications in the *Journal of Educational Psychology* that focus on the contextual aspects of affectively toned cognition and children's self-regulatory behavior as well as teachers' perceptions of children from divorced families. He has been a member of

John Santrock, teaching in his undergraduate educational psychology class, in which he makes good use of small-group discussion.

the editorial boards of *Child Development* and *Developmental Psychology*. His publications include these leading McGraw-Hill texts: *Child Development* (12th ed.), *Adolescence* (12th ed.), *Life-Span Development* (12th ed.), and *Psychology* (7th ed.).

*For the educators in my family:
My wife, Mary Jo, a teacher; my father,
John F. Santrock, Jr., a teacher,
principal, and superintendent of
schools; my mother, Ruth Smith
Santrock, an administrative
assistant; my grandmother, Della
Karnes Santrock, who taught
all grades in a one-room
school; and John F. Santrock,
Sr., a principal.*

Brief Contents

Contents

CHAPTER 3

Social Contexts and Socioemotional Development 72

CHAPTER 4

Individual Variations 115

CHAPTER 5

Sociocultural Diversity   149

CHAPTER 8

The Information-Processing Approach 268

CHAPTER 12

Planning, Instruction, and Technology   419

CHAPTER 13

Motivation, Teaching, and Learning   458

CHAPTER 14

Managing the Classroom   500

CHAPTER 15

Standardized Tests and Teaching 539

CHAPTER 16

Classroom Assessment 574

List of Features

SELF-ASSESSMENT

TECHNOLOGY AND EDUCATION

CRACK THE CASE

DEVELOPMENTAL FOCUS

Expert Consultants for *Educational Psychology*, 4th Edition

Educational psychology has become an enormous, complex field—and no single author, or even several authors, can possibly keep up with the rapidly changing content in the many different areas of educational psychology. To solve this problem, author John Santrock sought the input of leading experts about content in numerous aspects of educational psychology. The experts provided detailed evaluations and recommendations for a chapter (or chapters) in their areas of expertise. The biographies and photographs of the experts, who literally represent a who's who in the field of educational psychology, follow.

Karen Harris

Dr. Harris is one of the world's leading experts on special education, teaching writing skills, and learning strategies. She received her D.Ed. from Auburn University and has worked in the field of education for over 30 years. Dr. Harris currently is Currey Ingram Professor of Special Education and Literacy at Vanderbilt University. She has taught kindergarten and fourth grade, as well as elementary and secondary students with ADHD, learning disabilities, and behavioral/emotional difficulties. Dr. Harris' research focuses on theoretical and intervention issues in the development of academic and self-regulation strategies among at-risk students and those with severe learning challenges such as learning disabilities and attention deficit hyperactivity disorder. Author of more than 100 publications, she contributes to the leading journals in special education, general education, and educational psychology. Dr. Harris is currently editor of the *Journal of Educational Psychology* and has served on numerous editorial boards. She is coauthor of several books, including *Powerful Writing Strategies for All Students* (with Steve Graham, Linda Mason, and Barbara Friedlander) (2008). Nationally, she has served as president of the Division for Research of the Council for Exceptional Children, as an officer for the American Educational Research Association, and as a consultant or officer for local, state, national, and international organizations. In 2001, she and Steve Graham received the Distinguished Researcher Award for special education research from the American Educational Research Association; in 2005, they received the Career Research Award from the International Council for Exceptional Children.

> The chapter (6, "Learners Who Are Exceptional") is well and clearly organized, and the book's structure includes many helpful features for learners. . . . I found the chapter to include a great deal of accurate and useful information, well presented to the reader. . . . I want to close by noting again how much good information there is here.
>
> —**Karen Harris**

Richard Mayer

Dr. Mayer is widely recognized as one of the world's leading experts on the application of cognitive psychology to children's education. Dr. Mayer is currently Professor of Psychology at the University of California–Santa Barbara (UCSB), where he has served since 1975. He obtained his Ph.D. at the University of Michigan. Dr. Mayer's current research involves the interaction of cognition, instruction, and technology with a special focus on multimedia learning and problem solving. He has served as president of the Division of Educational Psychology of the American Psychological Association, Vice-President of the American Educational Research Association, editor of *Educational Psychology*, co-editor of *Instructional Science*, and Chair of the UCSB Department of Psychology. He was the recipient of the E. L. Thorndike Award for career achievement in educational psychology and was the 2008 winner of the Distinguished Contribution of Applications of Psychology to Education and Training Award from the American Psychological Association. Dr. Mayer was ranked number one as the most productive educational psychologist (1991–2001) by *Contemporary Educational Psychology*. He is on the editorial boards of 11 journals, mainly in educational psychology, and has authored or edited 18 books and more than 250 articles and chapters, including *The Promise of Educational Psychology* (2002); *Multimedia Learning* (2001); *Learning and Instruction* (2nd ed., 2008); *E-Learning and the Science of Instruction* (with Ruth Clark) (2nd ed., 2008); and the *Cambridge Handbook of Multimedia Learning* (2005).

> I congratulate John Santrock on another successful edition. Reading this book is a pleasure because it is well written and engaging. It is clear, concise, and up-to-date. Prospective teachers will gain invaluable knowledge from reading this well-written book.
>
> —**Rich Mayer**

Donna Ford

Dr. Ford is a leading expert on the education of children who are gifted and on multicultural/urban education. She currently is Professor of Education and Human Development at Vanderbilt University, where she teaches in the Department of Special Education. Dr. Ford has been a faculty member at the Ohio State University, the University of Virginia, and the University of Kentucky, as well as a researcher with the National Research Center on the Gifted and Talented. Her research focuses on (1) recruiting and retaining culturally diverse students in gifted education, (2) multicultural and urban education, (3) minority student achievement and underachievement, and (4) family involvement. Dr. Ford has received numerous awards including the Early Career Award and the Career Award from the American Educational Research Association and the Early Scholar Award from the National Association of Gifted Children. She has written these books: *Reversing Underachievement Among Gifted Black Students*, *Multicultural Gifted Education*, *In Search of the Dream*, and *Teaching Culturally Diverse Students*. She also has published more than 100 articles and chapters. Dr. Ford is a board member of the National Association for Gifted Children and served on numerous editorial boards, including *Gifted Child Quarterly* and *Exceptional Children*.

> *I like the inclusion of PRAXIS™-type items, teachers' stories, and practical interventions.*
>
> **—Donna Ford**

Dale Schunk

Dr. Schunk is a leading expert on children's learning and motivation in educational settings. He is Dean of Education and Professor of Curriculum at the University of North Carolina at Greensboro. He received his Ph.D. from Stanford University. Previously, Dr. Schunk was a faculty member at the University of Houston, the University of North Carolina at Chapel Hill, and Purdue University (where he was head of the Department of Educational Studies). Dr. Schunk has published over 95 articles and chapters, is the author of *Learning Theories: An Educational Perspective* (5th ed., 2008), coauthor with Paul Pintrich and Judith Meece of *Motivation in Education* (3rd ed., 2008), and has edited several books on education and self-regulation. His awards include the Distinguished Service Award from Purdue University School of Education, the Early Contributions Award in Educational Psychology from the American Psychological Association, and the Albert J. Harris Research Award from the International Reading Association.

> *This continues to be one of the strongest educational psychology texts on the market. The content is clearly explained and exemplified extensively. The learning goals provide a clear framework for the chapter. The many other features, such as PRAXIS™ Practice items, Crack the Case, and Best Practices, make the chapter (7, "Behavioral and Social Cognitive Approaches") highly readable, interesting, and relevant to students. John Santrock has done a fine job in bridging the gap between theory, research, and practice. . . . There are no real weaknesses in the chapter. . . . My points in this chapter (13, "Motivation, Teaching, and Learning") are the same as for Chapter 7 ("Behavioral and Social Cognitive Approaches"). These are very strong chapters. They are well written, include the latest theory and research, and offer numerous practical applications of principles to teaching and learning settings. . . . I highly recommend this text for course adoption.*
>
> **—Dale Schunk**

Micki Chi

Dr. Chi is a leading expert on information processing, learning, and development. In 2008, she assumed her current position as Professor in the Division of Psychology and Education at Arizona State University. For many years, Dr. Chi was Professor in the Department of Psychology and Senior Scientist in the Learning Research and Development Center at the University of Pittsburgh. She also has been a Fellow at the Center for Advanced Study in the Behavioral Sciences at Stanford University. Her current research focuses on effective ways of learning, such as by self-explaining while reading a text, collaborating while solving problems, and observing tutorial dialogues collaboratively. Dr. Chi also studies how instructional intervention can overcome robust misconceptions, especially for emergent scientific processes. Her awards include the Boyd McCandless Young Scientist Award from the American Psychological Association and being the author of the top ten of the most widely cited studies in *Cognitive Science* and the author of the seventh most fascinating study in the field of child development for her work on expertise.

> *I really like the questions (under the PRAXIS™ Practice sections) that use everyday examples to ask about what concept it illustrates.*
>
> **—Micki Chi**

Barbara McCombs

Dr. McCombs is a leading expert on learner-centered psychological principles and school reform. She is a Senior Research Scientist at the University of Denver Research Institute and directs the Human Motivation, Learning, and Development Center at the Denver Research Institute, which focuses on professional development of educators, educational reform, and school violence prevention. Her current research is directed at new models of schooling and learning, including transformational teacher development approaches and the use of technology as a primary tool for empowering youth. Dr. McCombs is the author of numerous book chapters and journal articles. She is the primary author of the *Learner-Centered Psychological Principles (LCPPs)* being disseminated by the American Psychological Association's Task Force on Psychology in Education. Dr. McCombs has developed learner-centered models of teaching and learning that have been validated with 35,000 students and their teachers in grades K–3, 4–8, 9–12, and college level. She also has coauthored (with Jo Sue Whisler) *The Learner-Centered Classroom and School*. Dr. McCombs is also the primary editor for the American Psychological Association's *Psychology in the Classroom: A Series for Teachers and Teacher Educators*. She also inaugurated a series of books for teachers and school leaders with Corwin Press. The first two books in this series are *Learner-Centered Classroom Practices and Assessment* (with Lynda Miller) (2007) and *From Complexity to Simplicity: A School Leader's Guide to Creating Learner-Centered Education* (also coauthored with Linda Miller) (2008).

> *In general, the narrative has been updated with the latest and most important research. . . . I reviewed all 16 chapters in depth and my overall assessment is that this is a very well done and comprehensive book in terms of its coverage and organization.*
> —**Barbara McCombs**

David Sears

Dr. Sears is a leading expert on learning transfer and social aspects of learning. He received his Ph.D. in psychological studies in education from Stanford University and currently is a professor in Educational Psychology at Purdue University. His research interests focus on how to prepare students to apply and adapt what they learn to contexts outside of school and how or when social interaction may support these goals. Among the current questions Dr. Sears is exploring are what types of activities are naturally productive for collaborative groups and by what measures of learning. This work has included laboratory and classroom-based studies of students learning topics from third-grade science to college-level statistics.

> *I thought both chapters (9, "Complex Cognitive Processes," and 10, "Social Constructivist Approaches") provided a clear, comprehensive, and up-to-date description of their respective areas. . . . John Santrock did an outstanding job of covering many difficult concepts in a clear and interesting fashion in Chapter 9, "Complex Cognitive Processes."*
> —**David Sears**

Eric Anderman

Dr. Anderman is a leading expert on motivation and education. He received his Ph.D. in educational psychology from the University of Michigan and was a faculty member at the University of Kentucky from 1994 through 2007. His current position is Professor of Educational Psychology at Ohio State University. Dr. Anderman's research on adolescent motivation recently has focused on motivating adolescents to avoid engaging in risky behaviors and the role of motivation in academic cheating. He currently is associate editor of the *Journal of Educational Psychology* and president of Division 15 (Educational Psychology) of the American Psychological Association. He is the coauthor (with Lynley Anderman) (2008) of *Motivating Children and Adolescents in the Classroom* and coeditor of *Psychology of Academic Cheating* (with Tamera Murdock) (2007).

> *This is a very good chapter (13, "Motivation, Teaching, and Learning"). It covers a lot of relevant information, and the information is presented very clearly, so that teachers and teacher trainees will understand the information. The examples are good, and it is great that so many strategies are covered.*
> —**Eric Anderman**

Carlos F. Diaz

Carlos Diaz is a leading expert on diversity and education. His current position is Professor of Education at Florida Atlantic University, where he received his Ed.D. in curriculum and instruction. Dr. Diaz has been the Project Director for the Master of Education in Cultural Foundations with E.S.O.L. Endorsement program. He also has been a Visiting Professor at the University of Washington. Dr. Diaz has authored or coauthored a number of articles, chapters, and books, including these books: *Touch the Future: Teach!*, *Multicultural Education in the 21st Century*, and *Global Perspectives for Educators*. He has received numerous awards, including the Teaching Incentive Program Award, University Award for Excellence in Undergraduate Teaching, Notable American Men Award, and recognition in *Who's Who Among Hispanic Americans*, *Rising Americans*, and *American Education*. He is currently working on a book that contrasts the fields of multicultural and global education.

> *I looked carefully at the sources in the chapter (5, "Sociocultural Diversity") and noticed that the author has made a significant effort to update sources and research studies.*
> —**Carlos F. Diaz**

Carolyn Evertson

Dr. Evertson is widely recognized as one of the world's leading experts on classroom management. She is Professor of Education Emerita at Peabody College, Vanderbilt University, where she is Director of *COMP: Creating Conditions for Learning*, a nationally disseminated program for helping teachers to become more effective classroom managers. Her program has provided classroom management support for more than 70,000 teachers. Dr. Evertson received her Ph.D. from the University of Texas at Austin, and has published more than 100 articles and chapters on classroom management and supporting students' social and academic learning in school environments. She has coauthored two leading texts: *Classroom Management for Elementary Teachers* (8th ed., 2009) and *Classroom Management for Middle and High School Teachers* (8th ed., 2009). Dr. Evertson also coedited (with Carol Weinstein) the *Handbook of Classroom Management* (2006).

> *John Santrock's chapter on classroom management is the most current review I've seen . . . Best I've seen on how to create and support the classroom environment and set the stage.*
>
> —CAROLYN EVERTSON

James McMillan

Dr. McMillan is a leading expert on assessment. He is Professor and Chair, Department of Foundations of Education at Virginia Commonwealth University and Director of the Metropolitan Educational Research Consortium, a university/public school partnership that conducts and disseminates applied research. Dr. McMillan received his Ph.D. from Northwestern University. He is the author of *Educational Research* (5th ed., 2008), *Classroom Assessment* (4th ed., 2007), and *Assessment Essentials for Standards-Based Education* (2nd ed., 2008), and the editor of *Formative Assessment: Theory Into Practice* (2007). He has published extensively in leading education journals, including *Educational Measurement, Journal of Educational Psychology,* the *American Educational Research Journal,* and *Psychological Measurement.* Dr. McMillan is currently investigating links between classroom assessment, grading practices, and student motivation. For the past several years, he has been active in Virginia's state testing and accountability program.

> *The strengths of the chapter (15, "Standardized Tests and Teaching") include the presentation of many concepts in a nontechnical fashion, the emphasis on teacher use of standardized test scores, and the coverage of validity, reliability, and fairness.*
>
> —JAMES MCMILLAN

Karen Swan

Dr. Swan is one of the world's leading experts on technology and education. Her current position is Research Professor in the Research Center for Educational Technology at Kent State University and a faculty member in the Instructional Technology Program in the College and Graduate School of Education, Health, and Human Services. Dr. Swan's research focuses on media and learning. She has extensively published and presented nationally and internationally in this area. Dr. Swan also has authored several hypermedia programs and coedited two books. Her current research examines online learning, mobile computing, and ubiquitous computing environments. She was the 2006 recipient of the Sloan-C Award for Outstanding Achievement in Online Learning by an Individual. Dr. Swan is a member of the advisory board for the Sloan Consortium on Asynchronous Learning Networks, special issues editor for the *Journal of Educational Computing Research,* and editor of the *Journal of the Research Center for Educational Technology.* She serves on the editorial boards for several education and educational technology journals, and on the steering committees for three international conferences.

> *I think the real strength of John Santrock's text is the way it contextualizes educational psychology within a teaching context. Often it is hard to make teachers, or preservice teachers, see the relevance of learning principles they think are too abstract. This text makes abstract theory more concrete and more relevant for teachers. Especially useful are the application strategies and links to teaching portfolios for the PRAXIS™ exam.*
>
> —KAREN SWAN

Preface

It is gratifying that the first three editions of *Educational Psychology* have been so well received. Preparing the fourth edition has been both highly rewarding and challenging: rewarding because I continue to learn so much more about educating students and because the feedback from students and instructors has been consistently enthusiastic; challenging because of the need to continue meeting or exceeding instructors' expectations and keeping the material fresh and up-to-date.

One of my goals for each edition of *Educational Psychology* has been to write a book that students say this about:

> *"I love this book."*
>
> *"I am using many of the ideas from my educational psychology text in my teaching, and they are working great!"*
>
> *"I teach in the inner city, and my educational psychology text is a great resource for me. The focuses on diversity and technology have been extremely useful. I am enriched by the book."*

These comments come from Jennifer Holliman-McCarthy, Richard Harvell, and Greg Hill, who have used this text in their educational psychology course and gone on to become public school teachers.

Another goal I have had for each edition of *Educational Psychology* has been to write a book that instructors say this about:

> *"I wasn't prepared to like this text. In general, ed psych texts are all too predictable. While people claim to be innovative, in the end they are not. In contrast, John Santrock's text is a big WOW! His book is different. It is written for the prospective teacher and not the future educational psychologist."*
>
> *"Those who are not using Santrock have not seen it. Please communicate my sincere enjoyment of this quality text to John Santrock."*

These comments come from educational psychology instructors Randy Lennon, University of Northern Colorado, and Robert Brown, Florida Atlantic University—Boca Raton.

Finally, it is a goal of mine to keep each edition of *Educational Psychology* relevant and a resource that teachers can call upon in college and beyond. Here is what a school teacher with over two decades of teaching experience said about the fourth edition:

> *"I certainly found this edition of John's book interesting, clear, and very comprehensive. I'd urge teachers to continue using it as they go through their first decade; I would—even after 20+ years!"*

This comment comes from Keren Abra, a teacher at Convent of the Sacred Heart elementary school in San Francisco, California.

To continue to meet or exceed instructors' expectations, and to keep the material fresh and up-to-date, I created a new feature that examines how various topics covered in the book apply to children at different developmental levels, extensively revised and updated the content with the input of instructors and leading experts, and retained features to which instructors and reviewers gave high marks.

NEW FEATURE: DEVELOPMENTAL FOCUS

Each chapter now includes multiple inserts called *Developmental Focus*, providing classroom descriptions of teaching strategies at different grade levels by outstanding early childhood, elementary school, and secondary school teachers.

EMPHASIS ON PREPARING FOR PRACTICE AND PRAXIS™

The fourth edition of *Educational Psychology* includes many opportunities for students to prepare for their practice as teachers and for the PRAXIS II™ *Principles of Learning and Teaching (PLT)* test. Integrated into the new edition are many best practices that new teachers can adopt and numerous activities to help them do well on state standards-based tests, such as PRAXIS II™.

Best Practices. A number of times in each chapter, students will read *Best Practices*: Strategies for . . . interludes that provide extensive, detailed recommendations that students can use when they become teachers. Embedded in the *Best Practices* interludes, are comments from outstanding teachers about successful teaching strategies they have used in the classroom in *Through the Eyes of Teachers*.

PRAXIS™ and State Standards–Based Tests. The use of external standards-based tests to assess the competence of both students and teachers is one of the most dramatic educational reforms in decades. The fourth edition of *Educational Psychology* gives more attention to standards-based tests and No Child Left Behind legislation, beginning with an overview in Chapter 1 and then further integration into other chapters where appropriate.

To give prospective teachers an opportunity to practice answering PRAXIS™-type items, a PRAXIS™ Practice section appears in the Review, Reflect, and Practice. This feature is aligned with the text's B (second-level) headings in each chapter so that students answer a PRAXIS™-type item for each of these headings. PRAXIS™-type items also appear in many of the case studies at the end of each chapter.

The Practice and PRAXIS™ Package. Further integration of PRAXIS™ and state standards-based material into the package for *Educational Psychology,* fourth edition, involves an extensive array of media resources that will help students prepare for practice and a study guide for PRAXIS™. These are described further in the Ancillaries section of this Preface.

CONTENT AND CONTEMPORARY RESEARCH

Another important goal I have had for each edition of this text is to include solid content and research that is very up-to-date.

Recent Content and Research. The fourth edition of *Educational Psychology* presents the latest content and research, and includes more than 1,800 citations from the twenty-first century with more than 1,000 of these coming from 2006, 2007, 2008, and 2009. Later in the Preface, I will highlight the main content and research additions on a chapter-by-chapter basis.

Expert Content and Research Consultants. Educational psychology has become such an enormous, complex field that no single author, or even several authors, can possibly be an expert in many different areas. To solve this problem, beginning with the first edition, I have sought the input of leading experts in many different areas of educational psychology. The experts provided me with detailed evaluations of the first draft of the third edition and recommendations in their area of expertise. The expert consultants for *Educational Psychology,* fourth edition, are:

Karen Harris, *Vanderbilt University*

Dale Schunk, *University of North Carolina—Greensboro*

Micki Chi, *Arizona State University*

Richard Mayer, *University of California—Santa Barbara*

Donna Ford, *Vanderbilt University*

Carlos Diaz, *Florida Atlantic University*

Carolyn Evertson, *University of Tennessee*

David Sears, *Purdue University*

Barbara McCombs, *Denver Research Institute*

Eric Anderman, *Ohio State University*

Karen Swan, *Kent State University*

James McMillan, *Virginia Commonwealth University*

The biographies and photographs of the expert consultants appear on pages xix–xxii.

ACCESSIBILITY AND INTEREST

The new edition of this text should be accessible to students because of the extensive rewriting, organization, and learning system.

Writing and Organization. Every sentence, paragraph, section, and chapter of this book was carefully examined and when appropriate revised and rewritten. The result is a clearer, better-organized presentation of material in this new edition.

The Learning System. I strongly believe that students should not only be challenged to study hard and think more deeply and productively about educational psychology, but should also be provided with an effective learning system. Instructors and students have commented about how student-friendly this book has become.

Now more than ever, students struggle to find the main ideas in their courses, especially in courses like educational psychology, which include so much material. The learning system centers on learning goals that, together with the main text headings, keep the key ideas in front of the reader from the beginning to the end of the chapter. Each chapter has no more than six main headings and corresponding learning goals, which are presented side-by-side in the chapter-opening spread. At the end of each main section of a chapter, the learning goal is repeated in a feature called Review, Reflect, and Practice, which prompts students to review the key topics in the section and poses a question to encourage them to think critically about what they have read. In addition, as indicated earlier, the Review and Reflect section also includes multiple-choice PRAXIS™-type items that give students an opportunity to practice answering the types of questions that are on state standards-based tests. At the end of the chapter, under the heading Reach Your Learning Goals, the learning goals summary guides students through a chapter review. In addition to the verbal tools just described, maps that link up with the learning goals are presented at the beginning of each major section in the chapter. A visual presentation of the learning system is presented later in the Preface in a section titled To the Student.

Other Learning Features. A number of other learning features help students to learn about educational psychology and ways to become an effective teacher. These include:

- **Developmental Focus.** This new feature makes important connections between topics covered in the book and how those topics apply to the classroom at different developmental levels. Over 20 outstanding early childhood, elementary, and secondary school teachers provide commentary and strategies on how they deal with specific issues in the classroom. With this knowledge, students can see how teaching practices are adapted to children of different ages.

- **Best Practices Interludes.** This very important feature highlights the emphasis on translating theory/research for effective teaching in the classroom. This feature appears a number of times in each chapter. New to this edition is the integration of *Through the Eyes of Teachers*, which provides descriptions of best practices by outstanding teachers, into the *Best Practices* interludes at appropriate places.

- **Teaching Stories.** Each chapter opens with a high-interest story about one or more teachers related to the chapter's content.

- **Self-Assessments.** These encourage students to examine their characteristics and skills related to the content of the chapter.

- **Diversity and Education Interludes.** Diversity continues to be an important theme in the fourth edition. Chapter 5 is entirely devoted to sociocultural diversity, and each chapter has a *Diversity and Education* interlude, which is integrated into the text material, following immediately after material relevant to a diversity topic is presented.

- **Technology and Education Interludes.** In addition to the discussion of technology in the text of many chapters, each chapter has a *Technology and Education* interlude related to the chapter's content. A majority of the *Technology and Education* interludes are either new or have been significantly updated and expanded through the contributions of leading education technology expert Karen Swan of Kent State University.

- **Case Studies.** This full-page feature entitled *Crack the Case* presents high-interest case-study descriptions followed by a number of questions, including multiple-choice PRAXIS™-type questions. The *Crack the Case* studies were written by an outstanding educational psychology instructor, Nancy DeFrates-Densch of Northern Illinois University.

- **Portfolio Activities.** At the end of most chapters, four Portfolio Activities related to the chapter's content are presented. They are organized into three categories for instructors' ease of use: Independent Reflection, Collaborative Work, and Research/Field Experience. Most Portfolio Activities are coded to a specific INTASC standard.

- **Taking It to the Net.** An extensive effort was made to create Internet activities that will provide meaningful learning experiences for students.

- **Study, Practice, and Succeed.** This feature, which appears at the end of each chapter, reminds students of the extensive learning tools that can be found on the book's Online Learning Center: www.mhhe.com/santedu4e

- **Through the Eyes of Students.** These inserts that appear in most chapters give students an opportunity to see learning, teaching, and classroom experiences from the viewpoint of students.

CHAPTER-BY-CHAPTER CONTENT CHANGES

CHAPTER 1
Educational Psychology: A Tool For Effective Teaching

- Substantial research and citation updating
- New description of challenges faced by beginning teacher Amber Larkin and her journey to becoming an award-winning teacher (Wong Briggs, 2007)
- New updated coverage of ISTE's NETS standards (2007)
- Expanded and updated *Technology and Education* interlude, Schools and Communities, to include OneCommunity (2008) in Cleveland, Ohio, and the Exploratorium (2008)
- New coverage of focus groups in descriptive research methods discussion (Given, 2008)
- New section on personal journals and diaries in descriptive research methods discussion (Given, 2008)
- New addition to *Best Practices* related to being a teacher-researcher, recommending visiting the What Works Clearinghouse Web site
- New *Crack the Case,* The Case of the Classroom Decision

CHAPTER 2
Cognitive and Language Development

- Extensive research and citation updating throughout chapter

- Shortening of introductory section on the nature of development

- Considerable expansion and updated coverage of the increased interest in brain development, including a new image of myelination (Figure 2.2)

- Information about possible expanded functions of myelination to include energy to neurons and communication (Haynes & others, 2006)

- Important new section, Brain Development in Middle and Late Childhood, including recent research on changes in the prefrontal cortex and diffuse/focused activation in the brain, as well as the connection of these changes to cognitive functioning in areas such as cognitive control (Durston & Casey, 2006; Durston & others, 2006)

- Discussion of cortical thickening in children 5 to 11 years of age (Toga, Thompson, & Sowell, 2006)

- Extensive updating and revision of the development of the brain in adolescence, including new Figure 2.5 and new coverage of changes in the corpus collosum

- Revised discussion of brain plasticity illustrated by the remarkable recovery and changing brain of Michael Rehbein, including new Figure 2.7 showing brain images

- New coverage of the issue of whether changes in the brain are the result of biological changes or experience, including recent research on changes in the brain in adolescence and resistance to peer pressure (Paus & others, 2008)

- Expanded and updated discussion of what we know about applications of research on brain development to education, including four main conclusions (Coch, Dawson, & Fischer, 2007; Durston & others, 2006; Giedd, 2008; Steinberg, 2008)

- New final comments in section, The Brain and Children's Education, by leading experts Kurt Fischer and Mary Helen Immordino-Yang (2008) on the current state of links between neuroscience and education

- New *Diversity and Education* interlude, The Diverse Language Experiences Children Bring to School

- Updated and revised coverage of language development in middle and late childhood based on input from leading expert Jean Berko Gleason

- Updated *Technology and Education* interlude, Technology and Children's Vocabulary, to include Write: Outloud (2008), which can help students improve their vocabulary

CHAPTER 3
Social Contexts and Socioemotional Development

- Expanded coverage of parenting, including new material on ways that parents influence children's academic achievement and attitudes toward school

- Description of how parents can serve as gatekeepers in guiding children's academic and nonacademic activities

- Revised and updated section, Parents as Managers, describing important roles that parents play as managers of children's opportunities, monitors of their behavior, and social initiators and arrangers, including a recent research review of parental management in African American families (Eccles, 2007; Mandara, 2006)

- Updated and expanded discussion of television's influence on children's attention, creativity, and mental ability in the *Technology and Education* interlude, Communicating with Parents About Television and Children's Development (Roberts & Foehr, 2008; Schmidt & Vandewater, 2008)

- Description of recent research on maternal monitoring and a lower incidence of delinquency in Latino girls (Loukas, Suizzo, & Prelow, 2007)

- New section on coparenting, including a recent study on coparenting and children's effortful control (Karreman & others, 2008)

- New section on working parents, including recent research (Goldbert & Lucas-Thompson, 2008)

- Updated coverage of children in divorced families, including recent research (Ahrons, 2007; Amato, 2006)

- Inclusion of information about a recent study on increased depression in the adolescent daughters in divorced families (Oldehinkel & others, 2008)

- Added commentary that the problems children from divorced families experience often stem from active marital conflict in the predivorce period (Thompson, 2008)

- New section, Children in Stepfamilies

- Discussion of two longitudinal studies documenting long-term outcomes of peer relations in elementary school (Collins & van Dulmen, 2006; Huesmann & others, 2006)

- Coverage of recent research indicating the importance of friends' grade-point average in adolescent development (Cook, Deng, & Morgano, 2007)

- Inclusion of material on the positive aspect of girls' friendships with achievement-oriented best friends and how this is linked to taking math courses in high school (Crosnoe & others, 2008)

- Description of how not all developmentally appropriate programs show significant benefits for children and recent changes in the concept of developmentally appropriate education (Hyson, 2007; Hyson, Copple, & Jones, 2006)

- Updated material on Project Head Start, including information about it being the largest federally funded program for U.S. children (Hagen & Lamb-Parker, 2008)

- New discussion of the Reggio Emilia approach to early childhood education, including a photograph of children in a classroom in Reggio Emilia, Italy
- New material on the Montessori approach to early childhood education, including a photograph of two Montessori alumni, Larry Page and Sergey Brin
- Discussion of recent study on discipline problems in the transition to middle school (Cook & others, 2008)
- Updated statistics on school dropouts, including the substantial decrease in Latino dropouts since 2000 (National Center for Education Statistics, 2008)
- New coverage of the Bill and Melinda Gates Foundation's (2006, 2008) recent efforts to reduce school dropout rates, including the initiative to keep students with the same teacher through high school
- Updated and expanded discussion of the "I Have a Dream" Program, including recent data on its effectiveness ("I Have a Dream" Foundation, 2008)
- New coverage of the very positive role extracurricular activities play in secondary schools and positive adolescent outcomes (Fredricks, 2008; Parente & Mahoney, 2009)
- New material on two conditions that improve the likelihood that service learning will generate positive outcomes (Nucci, 2006)
- Updated and expanded coverage of service-learning outcomes, including recent research on different outcomes for adolescents depending on the type of service learning (Schmidt, Shumow, & Kackar, 2007)
- New *Through the Eyes of Students*, Jewel Cash, Teen Dynamo
- Inclusion of information about recent study linking low self-esteem in childhood with depression in adolescence and early adulthood (Orth & others, 2008)
- Coverage of recent study on a link between relationship authenticity and an increase in self-esteem during adolescence (Impett & others, 2008)
- Description of longitudinal study linking low self-esteem with a number of problems in adulthood (Trzesniewski & others, 2006)
- Inclusion of recent research on ethnic identity in Navajo adolescents (Jones & Galliher, 2007)
- New section on cheating, including recent research and information about why students cheat and strategies for preventing cheating (Anderman & Murdock, 2007; Stephens, 2008)
- Inclusion of recent information about 40 of 50 states now having mandates regarding character education (Nucci & Narváez, 2008)
- Coverage of recent acceptance of using a care perspective as part of character education (Noddings, 2008; Sherblom, 2008)

- Description of recent study on service learning and academic adjustment (Schmidt, Shumow, & Kackar, 2007)
- Inclusion of recent study of gender differences in service learning (Webster & Worrell, 2008)
- New section on moral education, An Integrative Approach, describing Darcia Narváez's (2006, 2008) recent perspective
- New section, Coping with Stress, including ways that teachers can help students cope with stressful events, such as terrorist attacks and hurricanes

CHAPTER 4
Individual Variations

- Reorganization of material on intelligence that now includes an introductory section on what intelligence is and a separate section on intelligence tests
- Considerable editing and updating of the discussion of intelligence based on feedback from expert consultant Robert J. Sternberg
- Revised description of what intelligence is, including variations on what Sternberg (2008a, b, c, 2009a, b) and Vygotsky might include in their definitions
- Update of the Stanford-Binet to include recent changes in the fifth edition (Bart & Peterson, 2008)
- Updated discussion of the Wechsler scales to include recently introduced composite indexes such as the Verbal Contribution Index, the Working Memory Index, and the Processing Speed Index
- New coverage of Sternberg's (2008a, 2009a, b) balance theory of wisdom and his recommendation that wisdom should be taught in schools
- Inclusion of new material on Sternberg's (2006) Rainbow assessment, reflecting his triarchic theory of intelligence, to improve the prediction of college students' grade-point average beyond the SAT
- Description of Gardner's consideration of including existential intelligence as a ninth intelligence (McKay, 2008)
- Much expanded and updated *Technology and Education* interlude, Technology and Multiple Intelligences, to include Web sites that can help students improve in a number of Gardner's multiple intelligences (Garage-Band, 2008; Knowledge Forum, 2008; Mathematica, 2008; Nintendo Wii, 2008; *Portals*, 2008; Zoo Cams Worldwide, 2008)
- Inclusion of recent research on assessment of emotional intelligence and its prediction of high school students' grades (Gil-Olarte Marquez, Palomera, & Brackett, 2007)
- New material on increased interest in emotional intelligence (Cox & Nelson, 2008), as well as criticism of the concept (Humphrey & others, 2008)

- Expanded and updated coverage of evaluating general tests of intelligence and the concept of *g* in comparison to the concept of multiple intelligencs, including Sternberg's (2008a, b, 2009a) most recent position on these topics

- New description of Sternberg and his colleagues (Sternberg & Grigrorenko, 2008; Zhang & Sternberg, 2008a) that there are no culture-fair tests, only culture-reduced tests

- Extensive updating and expansion of the key role that conscientiousness plays in child and adolescent adjustment and competence, including description of a number of recent research studies (Anderson & others, 2007; Noftie & Robins, 2007; Roberts & others, 2009)

- Inclusion of study on conscientiousness as a predictor of mortality risk from childhood through late adulthood (Martin, Friedman, & Schwartz, 2007)

- Coverage of Rothbart's (2007; Rothbart & Garstein, 2008) recent views on temperament categories and connection of these categories with the Big Five factors of personality

CHAPTER 5
Sociocultural Diversity

- Inclusion of recent description of what socioeconomic status means (Huston & Ripke, 2006)

- New Figure 5.1, illustrating environmental differences that children from poor and middle-income families experience

- New coverage of recent analysis by Carolyn Tamis-LeMonda and her colleagues (2008) that describes the importance of cultural values in parenting practices and how in many families children are reared in a context of individualistic and collectivistic values

- Inclusion of information about recent study linking neighborhood disadvantage, parenting behavior, and child outcomes (Kohen & others, 2008)

- Updated U.S. poverty statistics for U.S. children (Federal Interagency Forum on Child and Family Statistics, 2008)

- Description of recent research revealing cumulative effects of poverty on physiological indices of stress in children (Evans & Kim, 2007)

- Coverage of recent experimental study of a poverty intervention that resulted in positive outcomes for adolescents and their parents (Huston & others, 2006)

- Description of recent changes in the Quantum Opportunities Program and its expansion by the Eisenhower Foundation (2008)

- New Figure 5.2, showing the percentage of adolescents in various ethnic groups in 2000 and the projected figures for 2100

- Expanded and updated coverage of material on family duty and obligation in children and adolescents from different immigrant groups (Fuligni & Fuligni, 2007; Kim & others, 2009)

- Inclusion of recent studies linking discrimination of African American and Latino adolescents to more problems and lower-level academic achievement, including new Figure 5.3 showing types of racial hassles African American adolescents experience (DeGarmo & Martinez, 2006; Sellers & others, 2006)

- Description of recent research on discrimination of Chinese American children by their peers (Rivas-Drake, Hughes, & Way, 2008)

- Coverage of recent research review in which cognitive processes used in one language transfer more easily to learning a second language (Bialystok, 2007)

- Expanded and updated discussion of research indicating more complex conclusions about whether there are sensitive periods in learning a second language (Thomas & Johnson, 2008)

- Revised, expanded, and updated coverage of bilingual education, including description of variations in programs

- New coverage of James Banks' (2008) recent description of what characterizes a multicultural school

- Revised and updated definition of gender so as to not exclude biological factors based on input from leading expert Diane Halpern

- Inclusion of what gender-typing means

- Shortened, revised, and updated discussion of gender views

- Description of recent research on an increase in gender stereotyping from preschool through the fifth grade (Miller & others, 2008)

- Updating and movement of gender similarities and differences in the brain to the section on gender stereotyping, similarities, and differences

- Updating description of research on gender similarity in math, including a recent very large scale study of more than 7 million U.S. students (Hyde & others, 2008)

- New Figure 5.5 on consistently higher writing scores of girls on the National Assessment of Educational Progress from 1998 through 2007

- Description of recent research review on gender and visuospatial skills (Halpern & others, 2007)

- Updated and revised coverage of gender differences in school achievement (Halpern, 2006)

- Updating of discussion of relational aggression, including research that indicates relational aggression comprises a greater percentage of girls' total aggres-

- sion than is the case for boys (Putallaz & others, 2007)
- Revised coverage of gender-role classification, including updating
- Description of recent study on adolescent girls' experience of sexual harassment (Leaper & Brown, 2008)

CHAPTER 6
Learners Who Are Exceptional

- Extensive editing and shortening of chapter at the request of adopters and reviewers to allow for a better focus on different disabilities and special education issues
- Considerable editing of chapter based on expert consultant Karen Harris' recommendations
- Updated description of percentage of students with disabilities receiving special services (National Center for Education Statistics, 2008)
- Revised definition of learning disabilities to more closely approximate the U.S. government's definition
- Coverage of trends in percentage of students with learning disabilities who receive special services (National Center for Education Statistics, 2008)
- New description of variation that occurs across states and school systems in how learning disabilities are defined and diagnosed (Bender, 2008)
- Revised definition of dysgraphia
- New discussion of brain pathways that are involved in reading disabilities based on recent MRI brain scans (Shaywitz, Morris, & Shaywitz, 2008)
- New Figure 6.2, showing a 9-year-old boy with a learning disability undergoing an MRI to obtain a brain scan
- Description of recent intensive 16-week instruction program that increased reading skills of first-grade students with severe reading problems who had not responded adequately to reading instruction (Simos & others, 2007)
- Added description of how an ADHD diagnosis requires that the characteristics appear early in childhood and be debilitating for the child
- New description of how ADHD should not be diagnosed by school teams but rather by a specialist, such as a child psychiatrist (Bender, 2008)
- New material documenting a three-year delay in the thickening of the cerebral cortex in children with ADHD, including new Figure 6.3
- Updated coverage of new stimulant and nonstimulant drugs that are being evaluated in the treatment of ADHD (Bhatara & Aparasu, 2007; Faraone, 2007)

- New material on the important role the teacher plays in monitoring the effectiveness of an ADHD student's medication (Thompson, Moore, & Symons, 2007)
- New coverage of recent research linking autism spectrum disorders to genetic mutations on chromosome 16 in approximately 1 out of 100 cases of these disorders (Weiss & others, 2008).
- Revised and updated strategies for working with students with disabilities
- Change in terminology from collaborative consultation to the more widely used current term, collaborative teaming (Hallahan, Kauffman, & Pullen, 2009)
- New Figure 6.6, showing the percentage of U.S. students with disabilities who spent time in the regular classroom in a recent school year (National Center for Education Statistics, 2007)
- Much expanded and updated coverage of educating students who are gifted, including recent concerns that the No Child Left Behind legislation may be harming the education of children who are gifted (Clark, 2008; Cloud, 2007)
- New Through the Eyes of Teachers, featuring Margaret (Peg) Cagle, who is passionate about teaching math to students who are gifted (Wong Briggs, 2007)

CHAPTER 7
Behavioral and Social Cognitive Approaches

- Deleted Thorndike's early S-R view
- Updated coverage of punishment, including recent research studies on negative developmental outcomes of punishment (Alyahri & Goodman, 2008; Aucoin, Frick, & Bodin, 2006; Bender & others, 2007)
- Expanded description of strategies for effectively using time-out (Kazdin, 2008)
- Updated information about the percentage of male college students who plan to go into elementary and secondary education (Pryor & others, 2007)
- Expanded discussion of observational learning and modeling in the classroom (Schunk, 2008)
- Updated statistics on the percentage of African American and Latino teachers in relation to the percentage of African American and Latino students (National Center for Education Statistics, 2007)
- Description of Schunk and Zimmerman's (2007) recent emphasis on the effectiveness of using modeling to build self-regulatory skills and self-efficacy to improve students' reading and writing skills
- Expanded and updated coverage of self-regulation, including information about children's increased capacity for self-regulation in the elementary school

years and connection of increased self-regulation to the discussion of developmental advances in the brain's prefrontal cortex in Chapter 2, "Cognitive and Language Development" (Durston & others, 2007)

- Description of three recent studies that illustrate the importance of self-regulation in the development of academic skills (Blair & Razza, 2007; Glaser & Brunstein, 2007; McClelland & others, 2007)

- New emphasis on the importance of not only getting students to develop self-regulatory skills but also strategies (Harris & others, 2008)

- Expanded *Best Practices* interlude, Strategies for Encouraging Students to Be Self-Regulated Learners

CHAPTER 8
The Information-Processing Approach

- New description of recent research indicating that an increase in processing speed precedes an increase in working memory capacity (Kail, 2007)

- Much expanded and updated coverage of attention, including new material on divided attention, sustained attention, and executive attention (Rothbart & Gartstein, 2008)

- New discussion of multitasking and its possible harmful effects on children's and adolescents' allocation of attention, especially when engaging in a challenging task (Bauerlein, 2008; Begley & Interlandi, 2008)

- Connection of improved cognitive control of attention of elementary school children to increased focal activation in the prefrontal cortex (Durston & others, 2006)

- Updated discussion of the important role of attention in school readiness (NICHD Early Child Care Research Network, 2005; Posner & Rothbart, 2007)

- Coverage of recent study documenting a link between attentional problems in childhood and aspects of information processing in late adolescence (Friedman & others, 2007)

- Expanded coverage of strategies for improving students' attention, including attention exercises used in some European kindergartens (Mills & Mills, 2000; Posner & Rothbart, 2007)

- Expanded and updated discussion of roles of culture and gender in memory development (Bauer, 2006)

- Updated discussion of working memory and its link to a number of aspects of children's learning and development (Andersson & Lyxell, 2007; Baddeley, 2007a, b; Cowan & Alloway, 2009)

- Expanded and updated discussion of the importance of teachers being characterized by adaptive expertise (Gambrell, Malloy, & Anders-Mazzoni, 2007)

- Expanded and updated description of the young child's theory of mind (Harris, 2006; Rakoczy, Warneken, & Tomasello, 2007)

- Coverage of recent study linking young children's theory of mind competence with later metamemory skills (Lockl & Schneider, 2007)

- Expanded description of strategy instruction in the discussion of metacognition

- New online resources added in the *Best Practices* interlude, Strategies for Helping Students Use Strategies, that can help teachers learn how to effectively use strategy instruction in their classrooms

CHAPTER 9
Complex Cognitive Processes

- Expanded discussion of concepts, including new material on the importance of hierarchical categorization (Chi, 2008)

- Expanded and updated coverage of categories and concepts (Oakes, 2008; Quinn, Bhatt, & Hayden, 2008)

- Discussion of recent research study on children's intense concepts, including significant gender differences and new research Figure 9.1 (DeLoache, Simcock, & Macan, 2007)

- New coverage of Ellen Langer's concept of mindfulness and its role in students' critical thinking

- New commentary about research indicating that inductive reasoning skill often is a good predictor of academic achievement (Kinshuk & McNab, 2006)

- Coverage of the mounting concern that the No Child Left Behind legislation has harmed the development of students' creative-thinking skills (Burke-Adams, 2007; Kaufman & Sternberg, 2007)

- New section, Steps in the Creative Process, including Csikszentmihalyi's evaluation of this five-step process

- Inclusion of new strategies teachers can use to encourage students' creativity: (1) build students' self-confidence, (2) encourage students to take risks, and (3) guide students to be persistent and delay gratification

- Significantly expanded and updated *Technology and Education* interlude, Digital Mindtools, that now includes information about Web sites that focus on "mindtools" for critical thinking, inspiration for concept mapping, and WebQuest.Org for information about creating WebQuests

- Expanded *Self-Assessment 9.1*, How Good Am I at Thinking Creatively?, to include three new entries

- Expanded description of strategies for improving transfer, including recent research on self-explanation and transfer (Rittle-Johnson, 2006)

- Addition of a number of new strategies to improve transfer (Sears, 2008)

CHAPTER 10
Social Constructivist Approaches

- Significant updating of cooperative learning (Gillies, 2007; Johnson & Johnson, 2009)
- New discussion of how cooperative learning likely works better for more complex tasks than simple ones (Sears, 2006).
- Description of recent study, indicating that tutors' learning benefits most when they engage in reflective knowledge-building (Roscoe & Chi, 2008)
- Coverage of recent study of ClassWide Peer Tutoring, revealing the best outcomes for cooperative tutoring over competitive teaming and traditional teacher-led instruction (Madrid, Canas, & Ortega-Medina, 2007)
- Description of recent study of ClassWide Peer Tutoring in which it improved middle school students' grades on quizzes over a three-year period (Kamps & others, 2008)
- Inclusion of information about recent research analysis of the Reading Recovery program, indicating positive outcomes for the program especially in alphabet skills and general reading achievement (What Works Clearinghouse, 2007a)
- Updated figures on number of schools, states, and students involved in Slavin and Madden's Success for All (SFA) peer tutoring program
- Description of recent analysis of the Success for All tutoring program, indicating potentially positive outcomes for general reading achievement but mixed results for reading comprehension (What Works Clearinghouse, 2007b)
- Discussion of recent analysis of PALS, indicating it has potentially positive outcomes in reading achievement (What Works Clearinghouse, 2007c)
- Deletion of material on a cooperative school in Salt Lake City because it no longer exists

CHAPTER 11
Learning and Cognition in the Content Areas

- Expanded material on the importance of fluency in reading and which factors improve fluency (Mayer, 2008)
- Coverage of recent study focused on factors involved in a school in which students showed high achieve-

ment in reading and writing (Pressley & others, 2007b)
- New section on the importance of prior knowledge in reading (Mayer, 2008)
- Heightened emphasis on the importance of teachers in development of students' writing skills based on observations made by Michael Pressley and his colleagues (2007b)
- Discussion of recent meta-analysis of the most effective intervention factors in improving writing quality of fourth- through twelfth-grade students (Graham & Perin, 2007)
- Inclusion of specific writing strategies that research has shown benefit secondary school students (Graham & Perin, 2007)
- Discussion of recent rigorous analysis of math instruction programs in elementary school that found only one program (*Everyday Mathematics*) to have potentially positive effects on students' math achievement (What Works Clearinghouse, 2007)
- Description of recent study revealing that working memory and speed of processing information are linked to children's math performance (Swanson & Kim, 2007)
- Expanded and updated coverage of children's scientific thinking, including educational issues in teaching science to children (Gallagher, 2007; Martin & others, 2009)
- Description of recent research on more than 107,000 students in 41 countries linking family, economic, and cultural influences to science achievement (Chiu, 2007)
- Extensive updating and expansion of the *Technology and Education* interlude, Content Area Specific Technology Applications, to include a number of new Web sites that can be used by teachers and students

CHAPTER 12
Planning, Instruction, and Technology

- Shortening of chapter at the request of adopters and reviews by judicious editing, rewriting, and deletion of less central discussions and examples
- New discussion of cross-cultural comparisons of lesson planning in the United States and China, with recent studies revealing that Chinese teachers get far more time than U.S. teachers to engage in lesson planning during the school day and week (Shen, Zhen, & Poppink, 2007; Shen & others, 2007)
- New Figure 12.5 summarizing APA's fourteen learner-centered psychological principles in a manageable way

- Updated coverage of homework-achievement link, including recent research review and recent studies in Germany (Cooper, Robinson, & Patall, 2006; Trautwein, 2007; Trautwein & Ludtke, 2007)

- Description of recent study of teacher-centered and learner-centered instruction in a technology-enhanced ninth-grade classroom (Wu & Huang, 2007)

- Coverage of recent study comparing teacher-directed and problem-based learning in an eleventh-grade chemistry class (Tarhan & Acar, 2007)

- New *Technology and Education* interlude, The GenYes Program, emphasizing the collaboration of students and teachers in effectively integrating technology in the classroom (GenYes, 2008)

- New description of the International Society for Technology in Education (ISTE, 2007) revised standards for technology-literate students

- New Figure 12.6, which shows a sampling of ISTE's (2007) profiles for technology-literate students at different grade levels

- New coverage of high school students in Park City, Utah, who create their own TV broadcast daily at their school (ISTE, 2007)

- New description of the profound gap between technology knowledge and skills students learn in school and what they need in the twenty-first-century workplace (Partnership for 21st Century Skills, 2008)

CHAPTER 13
Motivation, Teaching, and Learning

- Extensive editing, rewriting, and updating of chapter to improve student learning and highlight central ideas

- Added description of how students don't have to adopt just one perspective on motivation

- Expanded *Best Practices* interlude, Strategies for Helping Students Achieve Flow

- Expanded discussion of how intrinsic and extrinsic motivation are simultaneously involved in students' motivation (Schunk, 2008)

- Substantially updated *Technology and Education* interlude—Technology Integration, Authentic Tasks, Curiosity, and Interest with new material on serious games, such as *Quest Atlantis*, that have been demonstrated to improve students' learning in multiple academic areas (Barab & others, 2008)

- New section, Mindset, describing Carol Dweck's (2006, 2007) most recent view on the important role of teachers in helping students develop a growth mindset

- Two new poignant descriptions of individuals—Patricia Miranda and Marva Collins—and their growth mindsets (Dweck, 2006)

- Inclusion of information about a recent study illustrating the importance of mastery goals in students' effort in mathematics (Chouinard, Karsenti, & Roy, 2007)

- New coverage that emphasizes how mastery and performance goal orientations are not always mutually exclusive and that for many students combining mastery and performance goal orientations benefits their success (Anderman, 2007; Schunk, Pintrich, & Meece, 2008)

- New material on observations of classrooms by Michael Pressley and his colleagues (2007a, b) that illustrates the importance of the teacher's role in helping students to develop strategies that will improve their achievement

- Coverage of recent study on academic profiles of adolescents with low and high self-efficacy (Bassi & others, 2007)

- Description of recent observation study of teachers in twelve classrooms to determine learning factors involved in classrooms in which teachers have high, average, or low expectations for students (Rubie-Davis, 2007)

- Important new main section, Values and Purpose, that focuses on the low percentage of parents and teachers who engage students in discussions of their purpose, highlighted by a summary of the recent book, *The Path to Purpose: Helping Our Children Find Their Calling in Life* by William Damon (2008)

- Discussion of recent study on teachers' and mothers' expectations and their link with students' achievement outcomes (Benner & Mistry, 2007)

- Coverage of recent study indicating that teachers' positive expectations help to protect students from the negative influence of low parental expectations (Wood, Kaplan, & McLoyd, 2007)

- Description of recent study that revealed a link between instructional and socioemotional support and first-grade students' achievement (Perry, Donohue, & Weinstein, 2007)

- Expanded coverage of social comparison, including more information about developmental changes in social comparison

- Inclusion of information about recent study of racial discrimination at school and its link to declines in grades and academic task values (Eccles, Wong, & Peck, 2006)

- New description of lack of resources to support learning in the home of students from low-income families (Schunk, Pintrich, & Meece, 2008)

- Coverage of recent research on factors linked to whether students engage in self-handicapping (Thomas & Gadbois, 2007)

- Linking of failure syndrome to low self-efficacy and fixed mindset

- Discussion of results from recent meta-analysis of studies on factors linked to procrastination (Steel, 2007)

CHAPTER 14
Managing the Classroom

- New section, Classroom Management and Diversity, including Geneva Gay's (2006) view on how to reduce cultural mismatches between teachers and students

- Updated coverage of many aspects of classroom management based on views of Carolyn Evertson and Edward Emmer (2009) and Carol Weinstein and Andrew Mignano (2007)

- Expanded coverage of technology and classroom management, including new description of how the wireless InterWrite Personal Response System is used at St. Francis Indian School in South Dakota

- Rewriting and editing of material on communication to focus more on the key points

- More focused coverage of bullying, allowing more attention to school programs and strategies for reducing bullying

- Description of recent research review of bullying interventions, indicating mixed outcomes for school-based intervention (Vreeman & Carroll, 2007)

- Coverage of recent research on links between bullying and negative developmental outcomes (Brunstein & others, 2007; Nylund & others, 2007)

- New description of cyberbullying and a Web site with information about ways to prevent it (Stop Cyberbullying, 2008)

CHAPTER 15
Standardized Tests and Teaching

- Important new section that describes criterion-referenced tests and compares them with norm-referenced tests (McMillan, 2007)

- At the request of adopters and reviewers, deletion of section on District and National Tests—deletion of these sections allowed for increased focus on high-stakes state-based tests and the No Child Left Behind legislation

- New coverage of required science assessments in No Child Left Behind in elementary, middle, and high schools in the 2007–2008 school year, a goal for 2014 that every U.S. child pass proficiency tests in math and literacy (Shaul, 2007)

- Inclusion of Nel Noddings' (2007) recent criticism of standardized testing and No Child Left Behind

- Description of leading expert Michael Pressley's (2007) observations in classrooms and interviews with teachers about too much emphasis and time being given to standardized testing and No Child Left Behind

- Inclusion of recent research showing considerable variation in states' standards of what constitutes a highly qualified teacher and material on which areas of education have the most unqualified teachers (Birman & others, 2007)

- Coverage of recent criticism by leading expert Linda Darling-Hammond that NCLB has failed to meet its goal of reducing the ethnic achievement gap and some reasons why it has failed

- Added new criticisms of No Child Left Behind that involve less attention to students who are gifted and students' creative thinking (Clark, 2008; Beghetto & Kaufman, 2009; Sternberg, 2009)

- Coverage of recent analysis of state-by-state standards required for passing NCLB tests, indicating that many states have low standards (King, 2007)

- Deleted material on T-scores because they are rarely if ever used by teachers

- New discussion of very recent trend of test publishers allowing teachers and schools to pull from an item bank to "test" students' progress toward meeting a state standard before students take the state standardized test (McMillan, 2007)

- New *Crack the Case*, The Case of the Standardized Test Pressure

CHAPTER 16
Classroom Assessment

- New coverage of increasing trend of using student self-assessment on a day-to-day basis in formative assessment in the classroom (McMillan & Hearn, 2008; Stiggins, 2008)

- Expanded and updated coverage of the importance of integrating high-stakes testing and tests mandated by No Child Left Behind legislation in teacher planning and classroom assessment (McMillan, 2007)

- Updated and expanded discussion of formative assessment, including role of positive feedback during formative assessment in increasing students' self-regulation of learning (Davis & McGowen, 2007; McMillan, 2008)

- Movement of multiple-choice items as first set of selected-response items and expansion of discussion of multiple-choice items and strategies for their use because of increase in high-stakes testing using these items (Center for Instructional Technology, 2006)

- Deletion of discussion of item discrimination index and item difficulty index at the recommendation of reviewers and adopters because these are rarely used as part of classroom assessment today

- Added student self-assessment and replaced affect with effort, motivation, and participation in *Self-Assessment 16.1*, My Classroom Assessment Practices

- At request of reviewers and adopters, deletion of last section on computers and assessment to make chapter a more manageable length
- Creation of new *Technology and Education* interlude, Web-Based Assessment, to go with section on trends in assessment toward the beginning of chapter
- Expanded and updated coverage of effort participation in grading (McMillan, 2007)

ACKNOWLEDGMENTS

I am deeply indebted to many people at McGraw-Hill who have provided outstanding guidance and support for this text. I especially thank David Patterson, Editor, who has brought a wealth of publishing knowledge and vision to bear on this edition. I also thank Beth Mejia, Publisher for education and psychology, for the superb guidance and support she has provided. Janice Wiggins, the Developmental Editor for this edition of the book, has been terrific to work with and did an excellent job in improving the manuscript. Beatrice Sussman once again proved what an indispensable, terrific copy editor she is. Marilyn Rothenberger did an excellent job orchestrating the page proofs of the book. Dr. Nancy DeFrates-Densch, Northern Illinois University, contributed extensively to the book by writing the case studies and the PRAXIS™ Practice items. I want to thank Deb Kalkman and Ronni Rowland for their outstanding work in writing the material for the book's Ancillaries.

On pages xix to xxii of the Preface, the numerous expert content and research consultants for the book are profiled. As stated earlier, their feedback was invaluable in helping me to make the book's content superior to what I could have accomplished alone.

Peer Reviewers for the Fourth Edition. In developing the fourth edition of *Educational Psychology*, we asked a number of educational psychology instructors to provide us with detailed information about the best ways to improve the text. Their recommendations were extremely helpful. Special thanks go to the following peer reviewers of the fourth edition:

Irene Aiken, *The University of North Carolina at Pembroke*
Christopher S. Boe, *Pfeiffer University*
Gypsy Denzine, *Northern Arizona University*
Beth Gallihue, *Towson University*
Patsy Garner, *Crowder College*
Felicia Hanesworth, *Medaille College*
Geoff Quick, *Lansing Community College*
Michael Slavkin, *University of Southern Indiana*
Beverly Klecker, *Morehead State University*
Elizabeth F. Wisner, *Florida Community College at Jacksonville*
Melissa Lorenson Barstow, *Community College of Rhode Island*
Jonathan Brown, *Clarion University*

Early Childhood, Elementary School, and Secondary School Teachers A number of outstanding teachers provided descriptions of their real-world experiences in the classroom for the Developmental Focus feature that appears one or more times in each chapter. The following teachers provided information for the Developmental Focus feature:

Keren Abra, *School of the Sacred Heart San Francisco CA*
Maureen "Missy" Dangler, *Suburban Hills School Chatham NJ*
Elizabeth J. Frascella, *Clinton Elementary Chatham NJ*
Janine Guida Poutre, *Clinton Elementary Chatham NJ*
Shane Schwarz, *Clinton Elementary South Orange NJ*
Susan M. Froelich, *Clinton School Maplewood NJ*
Karen L. Perry, *Cooper Mountain Elementary Portland OR*
Mark Fodness, *Bemidji Middle School Bemidji MN*
Esther Lindbloom, *Cooper Mountain Elementary Beaverton OR*
Craig Jensen, *Cooper Mountain Elementary Portland OR*
Casey Maass, *Edison Middle School West Orange NJ*
Jennifer Heiter, *Bremen High School Bremen IN*
Valerie Gorham, *Kiddie Quarters Union, NJ*
Heidi Kaufman, *Metro West YWCA Child Care and Educational Program Framingham MA*
Connie Christy, *Aynor Elementary School (Preschool Program) Aynor SC*
Dennis Peterson, *Deer River High School Bemidji MN*
Sandy Swanson, *Menomonee Falls High School Menomonee Falls WI*
Heather Zoldak, *Ridge Wood Elementary School Northville MI*
Felicia Peterson, *Pocantico Hills School Sleepy Hollow NY*

Expert Consultants for the Third Edition. A number of leading experts in the field of educational psychology provided detailed comments about chapters and topics in their areas of expertise. Special thanks go to the following expert consultants for the third edition:

Joyce Epstein, *Johns Hopkins University*
Dale Schunk, *University of North Carolina—Greensboro*
James Kauffman, *University of Virginia*
Barbara McCombs, *University of Denver*
Richard Mayer, *University of California—Santa Barbara*
Carolyn Evertson, *Vanderbilt University*
Carlos Diaz, *Florida Atlantic University*
Karen Swan, *Kent State University*
James McMillan, *Virginia Commonwealth University*
Gary Bitter, *Arizona State University*

Peer Reviewers for the Third Edition. In planning the third edition, we asked educational psychology instructors what improvements in the text and accompanying ancillaries they would like to see to help their students to learn and them to teach. Their suggestions received were incredibly helpful. A special thanks to:

Bambi Bailey, *Midwestern State University*
Richard Benedict, *Madonna University*
Ronald Dugan, *The College of St. Rose*
Audrey Edwards, *Eastern Illinois University*
Nancy Knapp, *University of Georgia*
William Lan, *Texas Tech University*
Edward Levinson, *Indiana University*
Julie Matuga, *Bowling Green State University*
Ron Mulson, *Hudson Valley Community College*
David Oxendine, *University of North Carolina—Pembroke*
Barbara Powell, *Eastern Illinois University*
James Rodriquez, *San Diego State University*
Susan Sawyer, *Southeastern Louisiana University*
Alison Shook, *Albright College*
Jenny Singleton, *University of Illinois—Urbana-Champaign*
Michael Steiff, *University of California—Davis*
David Tarver, *Angelo State University*
Libby Vesilind, *Bucknell University*
Ryan Wilke, *Florida State University*

Expert Consultants for the Second Edition. Beginning with the first edition, I have sought the input of leading experts in many different areas of educational psychology, who provided me with detailed evaluations and recommendations in their area of expertise. The expert consultants for *Educational Psychology, 2e,* were:

Albert Bandura, *Stanford University*
Gary Bitter, *Arizona State University*
Carlos Diaz, *Florida Atlantic University*
Eva Essa, *University of Nevada, Reno*
Carolyn Evertson, *Vanderbilt University*
Kenji Hakuta, *Stanford University*
Daniel Hallahan, *University of Virginia*
James McMillan, *Virginia Commonwealth University*
Valerie Pang, *San Diego State University*
Michael Pressley, *University of Notre Dame*
Dale Schunk, *University of North Carolina - Greensboro*
Robert Siegler, *Carnegie Mellon University*

Peer Reviewers for the Second Edition and Second Edition Classroom Update. An extensive number of educational psychology instructors gave me very detailed, helpful information about what they wanted in an ideal textbook for their course. Their ideas significantly influenced the content, organization, and pedagogy of the Second Edition and Classroom Update Edition of the book.

Eric Anderman, *University of Kentucky*
James M. Applefield, *University of North Carolina—Wilmington*
Jeffrey Baker, *Rochester Institute of Technology*
Dorothy A. Battle, *Georgia Southern University*
Douglas Beed, *University of Montana, Missoula*
Richard Benedict, *Madonna University*
John T. Binfet, *California State University—San Bernadino*

Joseph Braun, *California State University—Dominguez Hills*
Kathy Brown, *University of Central Oklahoma*
Robert G. Brown, *Florida Atlantic University*
Alison Bryant, *University of Missouri- Columbia*
Melva M. Burke, *East Carolina University*
Russell N. Carney, *Southwest Missouri State University*
Chuck Catania, *Miami University of Ohio*
John Newman Clark, *University of South Alabama*
Ellen Contopidis, *Keuka College*
Dorothy Valcarcel Craig, *Middle Tennessee University*
Rhoda Cummings, *University of Nevada – Reno*
Reagan Curtis, *Northwestern State University*
David Dalton, *Kent State University*
Nancy Defrates-Densch, *Northern Illinois University*
Gypsy Denzine, *Northern Arizona University*
Jesse Diaz, *Central Washington University*
Ronna Dillon, *Southern Illinois University—Carbondale*
Joseph DiMauro, *DeSales University*
Ruth Doyle, *Casper College*
Kenneth Durgans, *Xavier University*
Howard Epstein, *Miami University of Ohio*
Lena Ericksen, *Western Washington University*
Tsile Evers, *Miami University—Oxford*
Sheryl Feinstein, *Augusta College*
Aubrey Fine, *California Polytechnic University*
Ericka Fisher, *College of the Holy Cross*
William R. Fisk, *Clemson University*
M. Arthur Garmon, *Western Michigan University*
Alyssa Gonzalez, *Florida Atlantic University*
Caroline Gould, *Eastern Michigan University*
Charles R. Grah, *Austin Peay State University*
Kim Grilliot, *Bowling Green State University*
Lynne A. Hammann, *University of Akron*
Andrew Hanson, *California State University—Chico*
Walter Hapkiewicz, *Michigan State University*
Gregory Harper, *State University of New York—Fredonia*
Diane J. Harris, *San Francisco State University*
Jan Hayes, *Middle Tennessee State University*
William E. Herman, *State University of New York—Potsdam*
David Holliway, *Marshall University*
Sherri Horner, *University of Memphis*
Mara Huber, *State University of New York—Fredonia*
John H. Hummel, *Valdosta State University*
Judith Hughey, *Kansas State University*
Mona Ibrahim, *Concordia College*
Emilie Johnson, *Lindenwood University*
Steven Kaatz, *Bethel College*
Deborah Kalkman, *Northern Illinois University*
Susan Kelley, *Lycoming College*
Lee Kem, *Murray State University*
Elizabeth Kirk, *Miami University of Ohio*
Elaine Kisisel, *Calumet College of Saint Joseph*
Robert L. Kohn, *University of Kansas*
Becky Ladd, *Illinois State University*
Marvin Lee, *Shenandoah University*
Randy Lennon, *University of Northern Colorado*
Bernie Les, *Wayne State University*

Dov Liberman, *University of Houston*
Kim Loomis, *Kennesaw State University*
Catherine McCartney, *Bemidji State University*
John R. McClure, *Northern Arizona University*
Barbara F. Maestas, *Towson University*
P. Y. Mantzicopoulos, *Purdue University*
Julia M. Matuga, *Bowling Green State University*
Lisa Mehlig, *Northern Illinois University*
John K. Meis, *Flager College*
Dorothy D. Miles, *Saint Louis University*
Barbara Milligan, *Middle Tennessee State University*
Connie M. Moss, *Duquesne University*
Beverly Moore, *Auburn University*
Ronald Mulson, *Hudson Valley Community College*
Peter Myerson, *University of Wisconsin – Oshkosh*
Ernest Owen, *Western Kentucky University*
Joseph D. Nichols, *Indiana-Purdue University*
Nita A. Paris, *Kennesaw State University*
Jim Persinger, *Emporia State University*
Barbara M. Powell, *Eastern Illinois University*
Barbara L. Radigan, *Community College of Allegheny County*
Sandra Nagel Randall, *Saginaw Valley State University*
Marla Reese-Weber, *Illinois State University*
Robert Rice, *Western Oregon University*
Lynda Robinson, *University of the Ozarks*
Susan Rogers, *Columbus State Community College*
Lawrence R. Rogien, *Columbus State Community College*
Paul Rosenberg, *Muhlenberg College*
Deborah Salih, *University of Northern Iowa*
Jill Salisbury-Glennon, *Auburn University*
Ala Samarapungavan, *Purdue University*
Charles Jeff Sandoz, *University of Louisiana*
Rolando A. Santos, *California State University—Los Angeles*
Gayle Schou, *Grand Canyon University*
Marvin Seperson, *Nova Southeastern University*
Lisa Sethre-Hofstad, *Concordia College*
Patricia Slocum, *College of DuPage*
Brian G. Smith, *Moorhead State University*
Michael Smith, *Weber State University*
Daniel Stuempfig, *California State University – Chico*
Gabriele Sweidel, *Kutztown University of Pennsylvania*
David E. Tanner, *California State University, Fresno*
Sara Tannert, *Miami University of Ohio*
Karen Thierry, *Rutgers University*
Yuma I. Tomes, *Virginia Commonwealth University*
Donna Townsend, *Southwestern Assemblies of God University*
Julie Turner, *University of Notre Dame*
Atilano Valencia, *California State University—Fresno*
Eva G. Vandergiessen, *Fairmont State College*
David Vawter, *Wintrhop University*
Linda Veronie, *Slippery Rock University*
Libby Vesilind, *Bucknell University*
Penny Warner, *Winona State University*
Linda Weeks, *Lamar University*
Earl F. Wellborn, Jr., *Missouri Valley College*
David Wendler, *Martin Luther College*
Glenda Wilkes, *University of Arizona*

Patricia Willems, *Florida Atlantic University*
Victor Willson, *Texas A&M University*
Steven R. Wininger, *Western Kentucky University*
Betsy Wisner, *Sate University of New York—Cortland*
Patricia Whang, *California State University—Monterey Bay*
Jina Yoon, *Wayne State University*
Michael Young, *University of Connecticut*

Peer Reviewers for the First Edition. I am also indebted to the many reviewers of the first edition of the text who did an outstanding job in helping me to create the foundation for the book. These instructors and expert research consultants provided this feedback:

Frank Adams, *Wayne State College*
Robert R. Ayres, *Western Oregon University*
James Applefield, *University of North Carolina—Wilmington*
Elizabeth C. Arch, *Pacific University*
Roger Briscoe, *Indiana University of Pennsylvania*
Randy Brown, *University of central Oklahoma*
Kay Bull, *Oklahoma State University*
Mary D. Burbank, *University of Utah*
Sheryl Needle Cohn, *University of Central Florida*
Rayne Sperling Dennison, *Penn State*
Carlos F. Diaz, *Florida Atlantic University*
Ronna Dillon, *Southern Illinois University*
Peter Doolittle, *Virginia Polytechnic University*
David Dungan, *Emporia State University*
Gordon Eisenmann, *Augusta State University*
Vicky Farrow, *Lamar University*
William L. Franzen, *University of Missouri—St. Louis*
Susan Goldman, *Vanderbilt University*
Algea Harrison, *Oakland University*
Jan Hayes, *Middle Tennessee State University*
Alice S. Honig, *Syracuse University*
Kathryn W. Linden, emeritus, *Purdue University*
Richard E. Mayer *University of California—Santa Barbara*
Rita McKenzie, *Northern Arizona University*
James H. McMillan, *Virginia Commonwealth University*
Sharon McNeely, *Northeastern Illinois University*
Ann Pace, *University of Missouri*
Karen Menke Paciorek, *Eastern Michigan University*
Peggy Perkins, *University of Nevada—Las Vegas*
Nan Bernstein Ratner, *University of Maryland—College Park*
Gilbert Sax, *University of Washington*
Dale Schunk, *University of North Carolina—Greensboro*
Judith Stechly, *West Liberty State University*
O. Suthern Sims, Jr., *Mercer University*
David Wendler, *Martin Luther College*
Allan Wigfield, *University of Maryland—College Park*
Tony L. Williams, *Marshall University*
Ann K. Wilson, *Buena Vista University*
Peter Young, *Southern Oregon University*
Steven Yussen, *University of Minnesota*

Panel of Early Childhood, Elementary, Middle, and High School Teachers. A large panel of individuals who teach at the early childhood, elementary, middle, and high school levels provided me with the material about special teaching moments that they have experienced. These moments appear in the Teaching Stories and Best Practices boxes throughout the text. I owe these teachers a great deal of thanks for sharing the real world of their teaching experiences.

Karen Abra, *School of the Sacred Heart, San Francisco, CA*
Mrs. Lou Aronson, *Devils Lake High School, Devils Lake, ND*
Daniel Arnoux, *Lauderhill Middle Community School, Broward, FL*
Lynn Ayres, *East Middle School, Ypsilanti, MI*
Fay Bartley, *Bright Horizon Children Center, Bronx, NY*
Barbara M. Berry, *Ypsilanti High School, Ypsilanti, MI*
Kristen Blackenship, *Salem Church elementary, Midlothian, VA*
Wendy Bucci, *Sugar Creek Elementary School, Verona, WI*
Stella Cohen, *Hackley School, Tarrytown, NY*
Connie Christy, *Aynor Elementary, Aynor, SC*
Julie Curry, *Hubbard Elementary School, Forsyth, GA*
Alina Durso, *PS 59-Beekman Hill International School, New York, NY*
Andrea Fenton, *Cortez High School, Glendale Union, AZ*
Mark Fodness, *Bemidji Middle School, Bemidji, MN*
Kathy Fuchser, *St. Francis High School, Humphrey, NE*
Lawren Giles, *Baechtel Grove Middle School, Bibb County, GA*
Jerri Hall, *Miller Magnet Middle School, Bibb County, GA*
Jenny Heiter, *Bremen High School, Bremen, IN*
Anita Marie Hitchcock, *Holley Navarre Primary, Santa Rosa Schools, FL*
Laura Johnson-Brickford, *Nordhoff High School, Ojai, CA*
Heidi Kaufman, *Associate Executive Director of Childcare, MetroWest YMCA, Framingham, MA*
Juanita Kerton, *Gramercy School/New York League for Early Learning, New York, NY*
Chaille Lazar, *Hedgecoxe Elementary , Plano, TX*
Margaret Longworth, *St. Lucie West Middle School, St. Lucie, FL*
Adriane Lonzarich, *Heartwood, San Mateo, CA*
RoseMary Moore, *Angelo State University, Angelo, TX*
Therese Olejniczak, *Central Middle School, East Grand Forks, MN*
Dennis Peterson, *Deer River High School, Bemidji, MN*
Chuck Rawls, *Appling Middle School, Bibb County, GA*
Verna Brown Rollins, *West Middle School, Ypsilanti, MI*
Donna L. Shelhorse, *Short Pump Middle School, Henrico County, VA*
Michele Siegal, *Brockton High School, Brockton, MA*
Jason Stanley, *Syracuse Dunbar Avoca, Syracuse, NE*
Vicky Stone, *Cammack Middle School, Huntington, VA*
Sandy Swanson, *Menomonee Falls High School, Menomonee Falls, WI*
Tamela Varney, *Central City Elementary, Cabell County, WV*

Marlene Wendler, *St. Paul's Lutheran School, New Ulm, MN*
William Willford, *Perry Middle School, Perry, GA*
Yvonne Wilson, *North Elementary School, Deer River, MN*
Susan Youngblood, *Weaver Middle School, Bibb County, GA*
Heather Zoldak, *Ridge Wood Elementary, Northville, MI*

Special Features and Ancillary Authors. I also benefited enormously from the efforts of this outstanding group of educational psychology instructors who wrote material for special features in the text and the ancillaries.

Nancy Defrates-Densch, *Northern Illinois University,* author of Crack the Cases, OLC case studies, *The Educational Psychology Guide to Preparing for the PRAXIS II Exam*, the Theory into Practice modules, and the Enter the Debate features.
Deborah Kalkman, *Northern Illinois University,* author of the instructor's manual and the PowerPoint presentations.
Veronica Rowland, *University of California-Irvine,* author of Taking It to the Net, the Student OLC, and The Educational Psychology Guide to Preparing for the PRAXIS II Exam, as well as revising author of the student study guide and test bank.
Karen Swan, *Kent State University,* technology expert consultant and reviser of Technology and Education modules.

ANCILLARIES

The ancillaries listed here may accompany *Educational Psychology,* fourth edition. Please contact your McGraw-Hill representative for details concerning policies, prices, and availability.

Prepcenter

Prepcenter collects all of the faculty support materials—case studies, online activities, video segments, PowerPoints, instructor's manual sections—and integrates them into a single, on-demand resource. This concept-based archive allows you to access every resource related to a single concept or theory, regardless of where this material appears in the textbook. A professor preparing for a lecture on "attribution" can conduct a search on the term and collect every case study, instructor's manual page, PowerPoint slide, and video segment related to the topic—all suitable for use as part of an in-class lecture, or for posting to a course Web site.

To use *Prepcenter*, just visit the instructor's side of the Online Learning Center at www.mhhe.com/santedu4e. If this is your first time using a McGraw-Hill text, you'll need to get an instructor name and password first, so contact your local McGraw-Hill sales representative to get started.

Student's Online Learning Center (www.mhhe.com/santedu4e)

The online learning center includes:

- The Study Guide, containing study resources including multiple-choice, true/false, matching, short-answer, and essay quizzes

- Two additional Crack the Case studies for each chapter of the text
- Self-assessment exercises
- Observation activities
- The PRAXIS II study guide
- Bibliography Builder for easy and accurate citations and references

Instructor's Online Learning Center (www.mhhe.com/santedu4e)

All of the materials on the Online Learning Center can be sorted and downloaded through **Prepcenter**, or can be downloaded as complete documents. These include:

- The **Instructor's Manual**—authored by Deb Kalkman at Northern Illinois University—a flexible planner with teaching suggestions, learning objectives, extended chapter outlines, lecture/discussion suggestions, video and film recommendations,
- The **Test Bank**, with almost 1,000 questions specifically related to the main text, including multiple-choice, short-answer, critical thinking, and essay questions; many of which are applied assessment.
- **PowerPoint Slides** for every chapter and concept presented in the text.

CourseSmart
Learn Smart. Choose Smart.

CourseSmart is a new way for faculty to find and review eTextbooks. It's also a great option for students who are interested in accessing their course materials digitally and saving money. CourseSmart offers thousands of the most commonly adopted textbooks across hundreds of courses from a wide variety of higher education publishers. It is the only place for faculty to review and compare the full text of a textbook online, providing immediate access without the environmental impact of requesting a print exam copy. At CourseSmart, students can save up to 50% off the cost of a print book, reduce their impact on the environment, and gain access to powerful web tools for learning including full text search, notes and highlighting, and email tools for sharing notes between classmates.

Print Supplements and Related Texts

Cases in Child and Adolescent Development for Teachers, 1e Nancy Defrates-Densch, ISBN 0-07-352585-5

Containing more than 40 cases, *Case Studies in Child and Adolescent Development for Teachers* brings developmental issues to life. The reality-based cases address a variety of developmental issues, giving students an opportunity to think critically about the way development influences children everyday.

A Guide to Observation, Participation, and Reflection in the Classroom Arthea Reed and Verna Bergemann, ISBN 0-07-298553-4

This complete, hands-on guide to classroom observations provides detailed guides for observing the dynamics of the classroom, participating with the classroom teacher, and then reflecting on the experience. It also includes more than 50 practical blank forms that cover all aspects of observation, participation, and reflection, from the structured observation of a lesson to a checklist for determining teaching styles to reflections on small-group teaching.

Understanding Children: An Interview and Observation Guide for Educators Denise Daniels, Lorrie Beaumont, and Carol Doolin, ISBN 0-07-248185-4

This hands-on book is a guide for interviewing and observing children in educational settings. It includes practical tips for interviewing and observing children as a way to understand their behavior, learning, and development; makes connections to the work of major developmental theorists and educational researchers; and discusses the analysis of observational data and its uses for guiding educational practices (e.g., instruction, cooperative grouping, and parent conferences).

Teaching Portfolios: Presenting Your Professional Best, 2e Patricia Rieman and Jeanne Okrasinski, ISBN 0-07-287684-0

This portfolio handbook includes authentic, student-generated artifacts as well as insights from administrators, teachers, and parents. Issues of classroom management, diversity, communication, planning, standards-based education, and reflection are all addressed in the context of how to approach these important aspects within a teaching portfolio and during interviews. The materials are designed for continued use as the students become in-service educators.

Case Studies for Teacher Problem Solving Rita Silverman, William Welty, and Sally Lyon

Choose from an online menu of eighty cases addressing core curriculum areas in teacher education—development, classroom management, leadership, special education, diversity, teaching methods, educational psychology, and more. Visit www.mhhe.com/primis to preview the cases, then order a printed and bound copy for your consideration. If you like your case book, placing an order is easy. If you don't, make changes—there is no obligation.

Taking Sides and Annual Editions

Annual Editions: *Educational Psychology 09/10*, 24th Edition, Kathleen M Cauley and Gina Pannozzo ©2010, ISBN 0073516406

Taking Sides: Clashing Views in Educational Psychology, 6th Edition Leonard Abbeduto ©2010, ISBN 0078127548

Sources: Notable Selections in Educational Psychology Rhett Diessner and Stacy Simmons ©2000, ISBN 0072323345

To the Student

This book provides you with important study tools to help you more effectively learn about educational psychology. Especially important is the learning goals system that is integrated throughout each chapter. In the visual walk-through of features, pay special attention to how the learning goals system works.

ENCASING THE CHAPTER

The Learning Goals System

Using the learning goals system will help you to learn the material more easily. Key aspects of the learning goals system are the learning goals; chapter maps; Review, Reflect, and Practice; and Reach Your Learning Goals sections, which are all linked together.

At the beginning of each chapter, you will see a page that includes both a chapter outline and three to six learning goals that preview the chapter's main themes and underscore the most important ideas in the chapter. Then, at the beginning of each major section of a chapter, you will see a mini-chapter map that provides you with a visual organization of the key topics you are about to read in the section. At the end of each section is Review, Reflect, and Practice in which the learning goal for the section is restated, a series of review questions related to the mini-chapter map are asked, a question that encourages you to think critically about a topic related to the section appears, and PRAXIS™ Practice items are presented. At the end of the chapter, you will come to a section titled Reach Your Learning Goals. This includes an overall chapter map that visually organizes all of the main headings, a restatement of the chapter's learning goals, and a summary of the chapter's content that is directly linked to the chapter outline at the beginning of the chapter and the questions asked in the Review part of Review, Reflect, Practice within the chapter. The Reach Your Learning Goals summary essentially answers the questions asked in the within-chapter Review sections.

THE LEARNING GOALS SYSTEM

Chapter-Opening Outline and Learning Goals

This section previews the chapter's main themes and identifies the most important ideas. Each heading in the Outline appears later in the chapter as a mini chapter map.

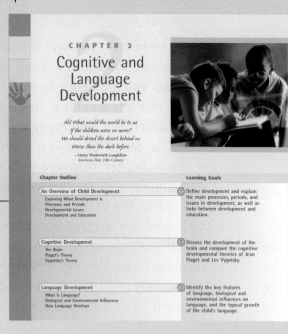

Mini–Chapter Map

Echoing the headings in the chapter-opening outline, these maps appear at the beginning of each major section in the chapter. The maps call your attention to the specific key topics that will be discussed in the upcoming text.

Think how important language is in children's everyday lives. They need language to speak with others, listen to others, read, and write. Their language enables them to describe past events in detail and to plan for the future. Language lets us pass down information from one generation to the next and create a rich cultural heritage. As you learned earlier, in Vygotsky's view, language plays a key role in children's cognitive development.

What Is Language?

Language is a form of communication—whether spoken, written, or signed—that is based on a system of symbols. Language consists of the words used by a community (vocabulary) and the rules for varying and combining them (grammar and syntax).

All human languages have some common characteristics (Berko Gleason, 2009). These include infinite generativity and organizational rules. *Infinite generativity* is the ability to produce an endless number of meaningful sentences using a finite set of words and rules.

When we say "rules," we mean that language is orderly and that rules describe the way language works (Berko Gleason & Ratner, 2009). Language involves five systems of rules: phonology, morphology, syntax, semantics, and pragmatics.

Phonology Every language is made up of basic sounds. **Phonology** is the sound system of a language, including the sounds used and how they may be combined (Menn & Stoel-Gammon, 2009). For example, English has the sounds *sp*, *ba*, and *ar*, but the sound sequences *zx* and *qp* do not occur.

Review, Reflect, and Practice

These sections are paired with the mini-chapter maps to summarize the key topics from the preceeding text and help you think critically about them. The *Practice* questions let you apply your understanding of the reading to answer questions of the kind typically found on state standards-based tests.

Reach Your Learning Goals

At the end of each chapter, this section presents the headings you saw in the chapter-opening outline. You will also find the *Learning Goals* restated in this section, along with a summary of the chapter content related to each goal.

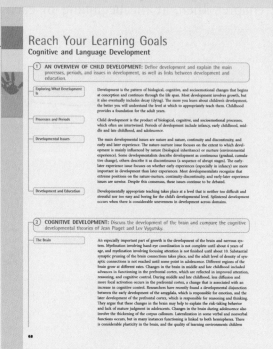

PRACTICE AND PRAXIS™

A number of learning features in the text will help you learn extensive strategies for becoming an effective teacher and preparing for state standards-based tests, such as PRAXIS™.

Teaching Stories

Each chapter opens with a high-interest teaching story that is linked to the chapter's content.

TEACHING STORIES   Donene Polson

In this chapter, you will study Lev Vygotsky's sociocultural cognitive theory of development. Donene Polson's classroom reflects Vygotsky's emphasis on the importance of collaboration among a community of learners. Donene teaches at Washington Elementary School in Salt Lake City, an innovative school that emphasizes the importance of people learning together (Rogoff, Turkanis, & Bartlett, 2001). Children as well as adults plan learning activities. Throughout the day at school, students work in small groups.

Donene loves working in a school in which students, teachers, and parents work as a community to help children learn (Polson, 2001). Before the school year begins, Donene meets with parents at each family's home to prepare for the upcoming year, getting acquainted and establishing schedules to determine when parents can contribute to classroom instruction. At monthly teacher-parent meetings, Donene and the parents plan the curriculum and discuss children's progress. They brainstorm about community resources that can be used to promote children's learning.

Many students come back to tell Donene that experiences in her classroom made important contributions to their development and learning. For example, Luisa Magarian reflected on how her experience in Donene's classroom helped her work with others in high school:

> From having responsibility in groups, kids learn how to deal with problems and listen to each other or try to understand different points of view. They learn how to help a group work smoothly and how to keep people interested in what they are doing. . . . As coeditor of the student news magazine at my high school, I have to balance my eagerness to get things done with patience to work with other students. (Rogoff, Turkanis, & Bartlett, 2001, pp. 84–85)

As Donene Polson's story shows, theories of cognitive development can form the basis of innovative instructional programs.

Crack the Case

This presents a full-page case study related to the chapter's content after the last Review, Reflect, and Practice section and before the chapter's summary. The case study gives you an opportunity to apply what you have learned in the chapter to a real-world teaching issue or problem. At the end of the case study, you are asked a series of questions—in some cases, PRAXIS™-type multiple-choice items—to reflect on and think critically about the case.

CRACK THE CASE
The Case of the Book Report

Mr. Johnson assigned his high school senior American government students to read two books during the semester that had "something, anything to do with government or political systems" and to write a brief report about each of their chosen books.

One student in the class, Cindy, chose to read *1984* and *Animal Farm*, both by George Orwell. *1984* is a book about what could happen in "the future" year of 1984, given certain earlier political decisions. In essence, the world turns into a terrible place in which "Big Brother" monitors all of one's actions via two-way television-like screens. Infractions of minor rules are punished severely. *Animal Farm* is a brief novel about political systems in which the characters are portrayed as various farm animals such as pigs and dogs. Cindy enjoyed both books and completed them both before midterm. Her reports were insightful, reflecting on the symbolism contained in the novels and the implications for present-day government.

Cindy's friend, Lucy, had put off reading her first book until the last minute. She knew Cindy enjoyed reading about government and had finished her reports. Lucy asked Cindy if she knew of a "skinny book" she could read to fulfill the assignment. Cindy gladly shared her copy of *Animal Farm* with her friend, but as Lucy began reading the book she wondered why Cindy had given her this book. It didn't seem to fit the requirements of the assignment at all.

The day before the first reports were due, Mr. Johnson overheard the girls talking. Lucy complained to Cindy, "I don't get it. It's a story about pigs and dogs."

Cindy responded, "They aren't really supposed to be farm animals. It's a story about the promises of communism and what happened in the Soviet Union once the communists took over. It's a great story! Don't you see? The pigs symbolize the communist regime that overthrew the czars during the Russian Revolution. They made all kinds of promises about equality for everyone. The people went along with them because they were sick and tired of the rich and powerful running everything while they starved. Once the czars were eliminated, the communists established a new government but didn't keep any of their promises, controlled everything. Remember in the book when the pigs moved into the house and started walking on two legs? That's supposed to be like when the communist leaders began acting just like the czars. They even created a secret police force—the dogs in the story. Remember how they bullied the other animals? Just like the secret police in the Soviet Union."

Lucy commented, "I still don't get it. How can a pig or a dog be a communist or a cop? They're just animals."

Cindy looked at her friend, dumbfounded. How could she *not* understand this book? It was so obvious.

1. Drawing on Piaget's theory, explain why Cindy understood the book.
2. Based on Piaget's theory, explain why Lucy didn't understand the book.
3. What could Mr. Johnson do to help Lucy understand?
4. How could Mr. Johnson have presented this assignment differently, so that Lucy did not need to rush through a book?
5. At which of Piaget's stages of cognitive development is Cindy operating?
   a. sensorimotor
   b. preoperational
   c. concrete operational
   d. formal operational
   Explain your choice.
6. At which of Piaget's stages of cognitive development is Lucy operating?
   a. sensorimotor
   b. preoperational
   c. concrete operational
   d. formal operational
   Explain your choice.

67

Best Practices: Strategies for . . . Interlude

Numerous times in each chapter, this important feature provides recommendations for effective ways to educate students related to the content that has just been discussed. Also, embedded in many *Best Practices* interludes are *Through the Eyes of Teachers* inserts that present the strategies used by outstanding, in many cases, award-winning teachers.

 BEST PRACTICES
Strategies for Applying Vygotsky's Theory to Children's Education

Vygotsky's theory has been embraced by many teachers and has been successfully applied to education (Gredler, 2008; Holtzman, 2009). Here are some ways Vygotsky's theory can be incorporated in classrooms:

1. *Assess the child's ZPD.* Like Piaget, Vygotsky did not think that formal, standardized tests are the best way to assess children's learning. Rather, Vygotsky argued that assessment should focus on determining the child's zone of proximal development (Camileri, 2005). The skilled helper presents the child with tasks of varying difficulty to determine the best level at which to begin instruction.

2. *Use the child's zone of proximal development in teaching.* Teaching should begin toward the zone's upper limit, so that the child can reach the goal with help and move to a higher level of skill and knowledge. Offer just enough assistance. You might ask, "What can I do to help you?" Or simply observe the child's intentions and attempts and provide support when needed. When the child hesitates, offer encouragement. And encourage the child to practice the skill. You may watch and appreciate the child's practice or offer support when the child forgets what to do. Next, you can read about John Mahoney's teaching practices that reflect Vygotsky's emphasis on the importance of the zone of proximal development.

John Mahoney, teaching math.

THROUGH THE EYES OF TEACHERS
Using Dialogue and Reframing Concepts to Find the Zone of Proximal Development

John Mahoney teaches mathematics at a high school in Washington, D.C. In Mahoney's view, guiding students' success in math is both collaborative and individual. He encourages dialogue about math during which he reframes concepts that help students subsequently solve problems on their own. Mahoney also never gives students the answers to math problems. As one student commented, "He's going to make you think." His tests always include a problem that students have not seen but have enough knowledge to figure out the problem's solution. (Source: Wong Briggs, 2005.)

3. *Use more-skilled peers as teachers.* Remember that it is not just adults that are important in helping children learn.

Children also benefit from the support and guidance of more-skilled children (John-Steiner, 2007; Wertsch, 2008). For example, pair a child who is just beginning to read with one who is a more advanced reader.

4. *Monitor and encourage children's use of private speech.* Be aware of the developmental change from externally talking to oneself when solving a problem during the preschool years to privately talking to oneself in the early elementary school years. In the elementary school years, encourage children to internalize and self-regulate their talk to themselves.

5. *Place instruction in a meaningful context.* Educators today are moving away from abstract presentations of material, instead providing students with opportunities to experience learning in real-world settings. For example, instead of just memorizing math formulas, students work on math problems with real-world implications.

6. *Transform the classroom with Vygotskian ideas.* Tools of the Mind is a curriculum that is grounded in Vygotsky's (1962) theory with special attention given to cultural tools and developing self-regulation, the zone of proximal development, scaffolding, private speech, shared activity, and play as important activity (Hyson, Copple, & Jones, 2006). Figure 2.16 illustrates how scaffolding was used in Tools of the Mind to improve a young child's writing skills. The Tools of the Mind curriculum was created by Elena Bodrova and Deborah Leong (2007) and has been implemented in more than 200 classrooms. Most of the children in the Tools of the Mind programs are at-risk because of their living circumstances, which in many instances involve poverty and other difficult conditions such as being homeless and having parents with drug problems.

In a Tools of the Mind classroom, dramatic play has a central role. Teachers guide children in creating themes based on the children's interests, such as treasure hunt, store, hospital, and restaurant. Teachers also incorporate field trips, visitor presentations, videos, and books in the development of children's play. They also help children develop a play plan, which increases the maturity of their play. Play plans describe what the children expect to do in the play period, including the imaginary context, roles, and props to be used. The play plans increase the quality of their play and self-regulation.

PRAXIS™-Type Multiple-Choice Questions in Review, Reflect, and Practice

At the end of each B-level head (second level heading) in every chapter in the feature titled Review, Reflect, and Practice you will get an opportunity to practice answering PRAXIS™-type multiple-choice questions related to the material you have just read.

Portfolio Items

Four activities related to the chapter's content are presented at the end of most chapters. Depending on your instructor's requirements, you may be asked to write about these educational circumstances in a portfolio and/or discuss them with other students.

Self-Assessment

This feature appears once in each chapter and is closely related to the content of the chapter. It is a powerful tool that helps you to evaluate and understand yourself in your efforts to become an outstanding teacher.

Developmental Focus

These inserts appear multiple times in each chapter and provide classroom strategies used by outstanding teachers at different grade levels.

OTHER LEARNING FEATURES

Diversity and Education

These interludes appear once in each chapter, immediately following a related discussion of sociocultural diversity in the text. These interludes focus on important cultural, ethnic, and gender issues related to education.

Technology and Education

These interludes appear once in each chapter, highlighting key issues involving how technology can be used to improve education.

Through the Eyes of Students

This feature provides stimulating comments by students about their attitudes and feelings related to the chapter's content.

Key Terms

Key terms are boldfaced in the text, and their definitions are provided in the margin next to where they are introduced in the text. All of the chapter's key terms are listed in the order in which they appear in the chapter, along with page numbers where they appeared. The key terms also are listed alphabetically, defined, and page-referenced in a Glossary at the end of the book.

Taking It to the Net

You are presented with questions related to the chapter that you can explore on the Internet. You will find links to the Web sites listed in the activities under Taking It to the Net on the Santrock *Educational Psychology*, fourth edition, Web site. These links will help you to think more deeply about the questions posed.

 TAKING IT TO THE NET

- Reflect on Vygotsky's concepts of "scaffolding" and "zone of proximal development" (ZPD). How do teachers identify what is within a child's ZPD? How do teachers determine the type of assistance to give, how much to give, and when a child can work independently? Provide an example of each of these concepts. http://naecs.crc.uiuc.edu/newsletter/volume3/number4.html
- Experts argue that enriched classroom and home environments produce improvements in brain functioning and learning. Describe an enriched school environment, including both physical (classroom arrangement) and nonphysical (instructional techniques) attributes. How could this environment con-

tribute to healthy brain development? www.atozteacherstuff.com/pages/1814.shtml
- Vocabulary is a critical component of reading comprehension; however, low-income students are exposed to far less written and oral language than their more affluent counterparts. Locate vocabulary games and activities on the Web, and devise a strategy for sharing these activities with parents to maximize students' contact with language. www.childdevelopmentinfo.com/learning/vocabulary.shtml

Connect to the Online Learning Center to explore possible answers.

 STUDY, PRACTICE, AND SUCCEED

Visit www.mhhe.com/santedu4e to review the chapter with self-grading quizzes and self-assessments, to apply the chapter material to two more Crack the Case studies, and for suggested activities to develop your teaching portfolio.

Study, Practice, and Succeed

This feature describes the various supplemental tools that you can use to manage each chapter's contents.

CHAPTER 1

Educational Psychology: A Tool for Effective Teaching

I touch the future. I teach.

—Christa McAuliffe
American Educator and Astronaut, 20th Century

Chapter Outline

Exploring Educational Psychology

Historical Background
Teaching: Art and Science

Effective Teaching

Professional Knowledge and Skills
Commitment and Motivation

Research in Educational Psychology

Why Research Is Important
Research Methods
Program Evaluation Research, Action Research,
   and the Teacher-as-Researcher

Learning Goals

1 Describe some basic ideas about the field of educational psychology.

2 Identify the attitudes and skills of an effective teacher.

3 Discuss why research is important to effective teaching, and how educational psychologists and teachers can conduct and evaluate research.

TEACHING STORIES   Margaret Metzger

Effective teachers know that principles of educational psychology and educational research will help them guide students' learning. Margaret Metzger has been an English teacher at Brookline High School, in Massachusetts, for more than 25 years. Here is some advice she gave to a student teacher she was supervising that incorporates her understanding of basic principles of educational psychology, such as teaching how to learn and the need to apply educational research to teaching practice:

> Emphasize *how* to learn, rather than what to learn. Students may never know a particular fact, but they always will need to know how to learn. Teach students how to read with a genuine comprehension, how to shape an idea, how to master difficult material, how to use writing to clarify thinking. A former student, Anastasia Korniaris, wrote to me, "Your class was like a hardware store. All the tools were there. Years later I'm still using that hardware store that's in my head. . . ."

> Include students in the process of teaching and learning. Every day ask such basic questions as, "What did you think of this homework? Did it help you learn the material? Was the assignment too long or too short? How can we make the next assignment more interesting? What should the criteria for assessment be?" Remember that we want students to take ownership of their learning. . . .

> Useful research has been conducted lately on learning styles and frames of intelligence. Read that research. The basic idea to keep in mind is that students should think for themselves. Your job is to teach them how to think and to give them the necessary tools. Your students will be endlessly amazed at how intelligent they are. You don't need to show them how intelligent you are. . . .

> In the early years of teaching you must expect to put in hours and hours of time. You would invest similarly long hours if you were an intern in medical school or an associate in a law firm. Like other professionals, teachers work much longer hours than outsiders know. . . .

> You have the potential to be an excellent teacher. My only concern is that you not exhaust yourself before you begin. Naturally, you will want to work very hard as you learn the craft. (Source: Metzger, 1996, pp. 346–351)

Preview

In the quotation that opens this chapter, twentieth-century teacher and astronaut Christa McAuliffe commented that when she touched the future, she taught. As a teacher, you will touch the future because children are the future of any society. In this chapter, we explore what the field of educational psychology is all about and how it can help you positively contribute to children's futures.

① EXPLORING EDUCATIONAL PSYCHOLOGY

Historical Background   Teaching: Art and Science

Psychology is the scientific study of behavior and mental processes. **Educational psychology** is the branch of psychology that specializes in understanding teaching and learning in educational settings. Educational psychology is a vast landscape that will take us an entire book to describe.

Historical Background

educational psychology The branch of psychology that specializes in understanding teaching and learning in educational settings.

The field of educational psychology was founded by several pioneers in psychology in the late nineteenth century just before the start of the twentieth century. Three pioneers—William James, John Dewey, and E. L. Thorndike—stand out in the early history of educational psychology.

William James   Soon after launching the first psychology textbook, *Principles of Psychology* (1890), William James (1842–1910) gave a series of lectures called "Talks to Teachers" (James, 1899/1993) in which he discussed the applications of psychology to educating children. James argued that laboratory psychology experiments often can't tell us how to effectively teach children. He emphasized the importance of observing teaching and learning in classrooms for improving education. One of his recommendations was to start lessons at a point just beyond the child's level of knowledge and understanding to stretch the child's mind.

John Dewey   A second major figure in shaping the field of educational psychology was John Dewey (1859–1952), who became a driving force in the practical application of psychology. Dewey established the first major educational psychology laboratory in the United States, at the University of Chicago in 1894. Later, at Columbia University, he continued his innovative work. We owe many important ideas to John Dewey (Berliner, 2006; Glassman, 2001). First, we owe to him the view of the child as an active learner. Before Dewey, it was believed that children should sit quietly in their seats and passively learn in a rote manner. In contrast, Dewey argued that children learn best by doing. Second, we owe to Dewey the idea that education should focus on the whole child and emphasize the child's adaptation to the environment. Dewey reasoned that children should not be just narrowly educated in academic topics but should learn how to think and adapt to a world outside school. He especially thought that children should learn how to be reflective problem solvers (Dewey, 1933). Third, we owe to Dewey the belief that all children deserve to have a competent education. This democratic ideal was not in place at the beginning of Dewey's career in the latter part of the nineteenth century, when quality education was reserved for a small portion of children, especially boys from wealthy families. Dewey pushed for a competent education for all children—girls and boys—as well as children from different socioeconomic and ethnic groups.

E. L. Thorndike   A third pioneer was E. L. Thorndike (1874–1949), who focused on assessment and measurement and promoted the scientific underpinnings of learning. Thorndike argued that one of schooling's most important tasks is to hone children's reasoning skills, and he excelled at doing exacting scientific studies of teaching and learning (Beatty, 1998). Thorndike especially promoted the idea that educational psychology must have a scientific base and should focus strongly on measurement (O'Donnell & Levin, 2001).

Diversity and Early Educational Psychology   The most prominent figures in the early history of educational psychology, as in most disciplines, were mainly White males, such as James, Dewey, and Thorndike. Prior to changes in civil rights laws and policies in the 1960s, only a few dedicated non-White individuals obtained the necessary degrees and broke through racial exclusion barriers to take up research in the field (Banks, 2008; Spring, 2008).

Two pioneering African American psychologists, Mamie and Kenneth Clark, conducted research on African American children's self-conceptions and identity (Clark & Clark, 1939). In 1971, Kenneth Clark became the first African American president of the American Psychological Association. In 1932, Latino psychologist George Sanchez conducted research showing that intelligence tests were culturally biased against ethnic minority children.

Like ethnic minorities, women also faced barriers in higher education and so have only gradually become prominent contributors to psychological research. One often overlooked person in the history of educational psychology is Leta Hollingworth. She was the first individual to use the term *gifted* to describe children who scored exceptionally high on intelligence tests (Hollingworth, 1916).

The Behavioral Approach   Thorndike's approach to the study of learning guided educational psychology through the first half of the twentieth century. In American psychology, B. F. Skinner's (1938) view, which built on Thorndike's ideas, strongly

William James

John Dewey

E. L. Thorndike

James, Dewey, and Thorndike created and shaped the field of educational psychology. *What were their ideas about educational psychology?*

George Sanchez   *Mamie and Kenneth Clark*   *Leta Hollingworth*

Like other disciplines, educational psychology had few ethnic minority individuals and women involved in its early history. These individuals were among the few people from such backgrounds to overcome barriers and contribute to the field.

influenced educational psychology in the middle of the century. Skinner's behavioral approach, which is described in detail in Chapter 7, involved attempts to precisely determine the best conditions for learning. Skinner argued that the mental processes proposed by psychologists such as James and Dewey were not observable and therefore could not be appropriate subject matter for a scientific study of psychology, which he defined as the science of observable behavior and its controlling conditions. In the 1950s, Skinner (1954) developed the concept of *programmed learning*, which involved reinforcing the student after each of a series of steps until the student reached a learning goal. In an early technological effort, he created a teaching machine to serve as a tutor and reinforce students for correct answers (Skinner, 1958).

The Cognitive Revolution   However, the objectives spelled out in the behavioral approach to learning did not address many of the actual goals and needs of classroom educators (Hilgard, 1996). In reaction, as early as the 1950s, Benjamin Bloom created a taxonomy of cognitive skills that included remembering, comprehending, synthesizing, and evaluating, which he suggested teachers should help students use and develop (Bloom & Krathwohl, 1956). A review chapter in the *Annual Review of Psychology* (Wittrock & Lumsdaine, 1977) stated, "A cognitive perspective implies that a behavioral analysis of instruction is often inadequate to explain the effects of instruction on learning." The cognitive revolution in psychology began to take hold by the 1980s and ushered in a great deal of enthusiasm for applying the concepts of cognitive psychology—memory, thinking, reasoning, and so on—to helping students learn. Thus, toward the latter part of the twentieth century, many educational psychologists returned to an emphasis on the cognitive aspects of learning advocated by James and Dewey at the beginning of the century (Byrnes, 2008).

Both cognitive and behavioral approaches continue to be a part of educational psychology today (Mayer, 2008; Schunk, 2008). We have much more to say about these approaches in Chapters 7 through 11.

More recently, educational psychologists have increasingly focused on the socioemotional aspects of students' lives. For example, they are analyzing the school as a social context and examining the role of culture in education (Gollnick & Chinn, 2009; Taylor & Whittaker, 2009). We explore the socioemotional aspects of teaching and learning in many chapters of the book.

Teaching: Art and Science

How scientific can teachers be in their approach to teaching? Both science and the art of skillful, experienced practice play important roles in a teacher's success (Oakes & Lipton, 2007).

Educational psychology draws much of its knowledge from broader theory and research in psychology. For example, the theories of Jean Piaget and Lev Vygotsky were not created in an effort to inform teachers about ways to educate children, yet in Chapter 2, "Cognitive and Language Development," you will see that both of these theories have many applications that can guide your teaching. The field also draws from theory and research more directly created and conducted by educational psychologists, and from teachers' practical experiences. For example, in Chapter 13, "Motivation, Teaching, and Learning," you will read about Dale Schunk's (2008; Schunk, Pintrich, & Meece, 2008) classroom-oriented research on self-efficacy (the belief that one can master a situation and produce positive outcomes). Educational psychologists also recognize that teaching sometimes must depart from scientific recipes, requiring improvisation and spontaneity (Palmer, 2008; Thompson, 2008).

As a science, educational psychology's aim is to provide you with research knowledge that you can effectively apply to teaching situations (Mayer, 2008; Schunk, 2008). But your teaching will still remain an art. In addition to what you can learn from research, you will also continually make important judgments in the classroom based on your personal skills and experiences, as well as the accumulated wisdom of other teachers (Hall, Quinn, & Gollnick, 2008).

First-grade teacher, Zakia Sims, guiding her students' learning at William Lloyd Elementary School in Washington, D.C. Recognized as an outstanding teacher, Zakia has a master's degree from Howard University and a coveted National Board certificate. *To what extent is her teaching success art, and to what extent is it science?*

Review, Reflect, and Practice

1 **Describe some basic ideas about the field of educational psychology.**

REVIEW

- How is educational psychology defined? Who were some key thinkers in the history of educational psychology, and what were their ideas?
- How would you describe the roles of art and science in the practice of teaching?

REFLECT

- John Dewey argued that children should not sit quietly in their seats and learn in a rote manner. Do you agree with Dewey? Why or why not?

PRAXIS™ PRACTICE

1. Mr. Smith believes that all children are entitled to an education and that this education should focus on the whole child. His views are most consistent with those of
   a. Benjamin Bloom.
   b. John Dewey.
   c. B. F. Skinner.
   d. E. L. Thorndike.

2. Four teachers are discussing influences on being an effective teacher. Which of their following four statements is likely to be most accurate?
   a. Applying information from scientific research is the most important factor in being an effective teacher.
   b. You can't beat a teacher's own personal experiences for becoming an effective teacher.
   c. Being an effective teacher is influenced by scientific research knowledge, teaching skills, and personal experiences.
   d. A teacher's innate skills trump all other factors in being an effective teacher.

Please see the answer key at the end of the book.

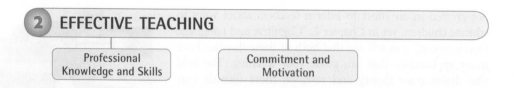

EFFECTIVE TEACHING

Professional Knowledge and Skills

Commitment and Motivation

Because of the complexity of teaching and individual variation among students, effective teaching is not "one size fits all" (Diaz, 1997). Teachers must master a variety of perspectives and strategies and be flexible in their application. This requires two key ingredients: (1) professional knowledge and skills, and (2) commitment and motivation.

Professional Knowledge and Skills

Effective teachers have good command of their subject matter and a solid core of teaching skills. They have excellent instructional strategies supported by methods of goal setting, instructional planning, and classroom management. They know how to motivate, communicate, and work effectively with students who have different levels of skills and come from culturally diverse backgrounds. Effective teachers also understand how to use appropriate levels of technology in the classroom.

Subject-Matter Competence   In their wish lists of teacher characteristics, secondary school students increasingly have mentioned "teacher knowledge of their subjects" (NAASP, 1997). Having a thoughtful, flexible, conceptual understanding of subject matter is indispensable for being an effective teacher. Of course, knowledge of subject matter includes more than just facts, terms, and general concepts. It also includes knowledge about organizing ideas, connections among ideas, ways of thinking and arguing, patterns of change within a discipline, beliefs about a discipline, and the ability to carry ideas from one discipline to another. Clearly, having a deep understanding of the subject matter is an important aspect of being a competent teacher (Bybee, Powell, & Trowbridge, 2008; Schwartz, 2008).

Instructional Strategies   At a broad level, two major approaches characterize how teachers teach: constructivist and direct instruction. The constructivist approach was at the center of William James' and John Dewey's philosophies of education. The direct instruction approach has more in common with E. L. Thorndike's view.

The **constructivist approach** is a learner-centered approach that emphasizes the importance of individuals actively constructing their knowledge and understanding with guidance from the teacher. In the constructivist view, teachers should not attempt to simply pour information into children's minds (Prawat, 2008). Rather, children should be encouraged to explore their world, discover knowledge, reflect, and think critically with careful monitoring and meaningful guidance from the teacher (Eby, Herrell, & Jordan, 2009). Constructivists argue that for too long children have been required to sit still, be passive learners, and rotely memorize irrelevant as well as relevant information (Sunal & Haas, 2008).

Today, constructivism may include an emphasis on *collaboration*—children working with each other in their efforts to know and understand (Holzman, 2009). A teacher with a constructivist instructional philosophy would not have children memorize information rotely but would give them opportunities to meaningfully construct knowledge and understand the material while guiding their learning (Bybee, Powell, & Trowbridge, 2008).

By contrast, the **direct instruction approach** is a structured, teacher-centered approach characterized by teacher direction and control, high teacher expectations for students' progress, maximum time spent by students on academic tasks, and efforts by the teacher to keep negative affect to a minimum. An important goal in

THROUGH THE EYES OF STUDENTS

A Good Teacher

Mike, Grade 2

A good teacher is a teacher that does stuff that catches your interest. Sometimes you start learning and you don't even realize it. A good teacher is a teacher that does stuff that makes you think (Nikola-Lisa & Burnaford, 1994).

constructivist approach A learner-centered approach to learning that emphasizes the importance of individuals actively constructing knowledge and understanding with guidance from the teacher.

direct instruction approach A structured, teacher-centered approach characterized by teacher direction and control, high teacher expectations for students' progress, maximum time spent by students on academic tasks, and efforts by the teacher to keep negative affect to a minimum.

the direct instruction approach is maximizing student learning time (Johnson & Street, 2008).

Some experts in educational psychology emphasize that many effective teachers use both a constructivist *and* a direct instruction approach rather than either exclusively (Darling-Hammond & Bransford, 2005). Further, some circumstances may call more for a constructivist approach, others for a direct instruction approach. For example, experts increasingly recommend an explicit, intellectually engaging direct instruction approach when teaching students with a reading or a writing disability (Berninger, 2006). Whether you teach more from a constructivist approach or more from a direct instruction approach, you can be an effective teacher.

Goal Setting and Instructional Planning   Whether constructivist or more traditional, effective teachers don't just "wing it" in the classroom. They set high goals for their teaching and organize plans for reaching those goals (Schunk, Pintrich, & Meece, 2008). They also develop specific criteria for success. They spend considerable time in instructional planning, organizing their lessons to maximize students' learning (Posner & Rudnitsky, 2006). As they plan, effective teachers reflect and think about how they can make learning both challenging and interesting. Good planning

What characterizes constructivist and direct instruction approaches to educating students?

> requires consideration of the kinds of information, demonstrations, models, inquiry opportunities, discussion, and practice students need over time to understand particular concepts and develop particular skills. Although research has found that all of these features can support learning, the process of instructional design requires that teachers figure out which things students should do when, in what order, and how. (Darling-Hammond & others, 2005, p. 186)

Chapter 12 addresses planning in detail.

Developmentally Appropriate Teaching Practices   Competent teachers have a good understanding of children's development and know how to create instruction materials appropriate for their developmental levels (Byrnes, 2008; Morrison, 2009). U.S. schools are organized by grade and to some degree by age, but these are not always good predictors of children's development.

At any grade level, there is usually a two- or three-year span of ages with an even wider span of skills, abilities, and developmental stages. Understanding developmental pathways and progressions is extremely important for teaching in ways that are optimal for each child (Henninger, 2009).

Throughout this text, we call attention to developmental aspects of educating children and provide examples of teaching and learning that take into account a child's developmental level. Chapter 2, "Cognitive and Language Development," and Chapter 3, "Social Contexts and Socioemotional Development," are devoted exclusively to development.

Classroom Management Skills   An important aspect of being an effective teacher is keeping the class as a whole working together and oriented toward classroom tasks. Effective teachers establish and maintain an environment in which learning can occur (Nissman, 2009). To create this optimal learning environment, teachers need a repertoire of strategies for establishing rules and procedures, organizing groups, monitoring and pacing classroom activities, and handling misbehavior (ASCD, 2009; Bloom, 2009).

Motivational Skills   Effective teachers have good strategies for helping students become self-motivated and take responsibility for their learning (Schunk, 2008; Schunk, Pintrich, & Meese, 2008). Educational psychologists increasingly stress that this is best accomplished by providing real-world learning opportunities of optimal difficulty and

"My mom told me to tell you that I am the educational challenge you were told about in college."

Reprinted by permission of Heiser Zedonek.

What are some effective strategies for managing the classroom and helping students become self-motivated?

novelty for each student (Brophy, 2004). Students are motivated when they can make choices in line with their personal interests. Effective teachers give them the opportunity to think creatively and deeply about projects (Blumenfeld, Kempler, & Krajcik, 2006).

In addition to guiding students to become self-motivated learners, the importance of establishing high expectations for students' achievement is increasingly recognized (Wigfield & others, 2006). High expectations for children's achievements need to come from teachers and parents. Too often children are rewarded for inferior or mediocre performance with the result that they do not reach their full potential. When high expectations are created, a key aspect of education is to provide children—especially low-achieving children—effective instruction and support to meet these expectations. Chapter 13 covers the topic of motivation in detail.

Communication Skills   Also indispensable to teaching are skills in speaking, listening, overcoming barriers to verbal communication, tuning in to students' non-verbal communication, and constructively resolving conflicts (Gamble & Gamble, 2009; Hybels & Weaver, 2009). Communication skills are critical not only in teaching but also in interacting with parents. Effective teachers use good communication skills when they talk "with" rather than "to" students, parents, administrators, and others; keep criticism at a minimum; and have an assertive rather than aggressive, manipulative, or passive communication style (Stewart, 2009). Effective teachers work to improve students' communication skills as well. This is especially important because communication skills have been rated as the skills most sought after by today's employers.

Paying More Than Lip Service to Individual Variations   Virtually every teacher knows that it is important to take individual variations into account when teaching, but this is not always easy to do. Your students will have varying levels of intelligence, use different thinking and learning styles, and have different temperaments and personality traits (Magliano & Perry, 2008). You also are likely to have some gifted students and others with disabilities of various types (Friend, 2008; Miller, 2008).

Consider Amber Larkin's challenges and experiences as a beginning teacher (Wong Briggs, 2007). Her classroom was a trailer, and her students included children who were homeless, non–English speaking, had disabilities, and refugees who had never worn shoes or experienced any type of formal education. After four years of teaching, she was named one of *USA Today*'s 2007 National All-Star Teach-

Amber Larkin, helping fifth-grade student Miya Kpa improve his academic skills. *What are some strategies for paying more than lip service to individual variation in students?*

ers. Almost all of her students pass state-mandated No Child Left Behind tests, but she is just as pleased about her students' socioemotional growth. Her principal described her in the following manner: "There's an unspoken aura that great things are going to happen, and that's how she goes about her day" (Wong Briggs, 2007, p. 6D).

Effectively teaching a class of students with such diverse characteristics requires much thought and effort. **Differentiated instruction** involves recognizing individual variations in students' knowledge, readiness, interests, and other characteristics, and taking these differences into account in planning curriculum and engaging in instruction (Tomlinson, 2006). Differentiated instruction emphasizes tailoring assignments to meet students' needs and abilities (Gibson & Hasbrouck, 2008). It is unlikely that a teacher can generate 20 to 30 different lesson plans to address the needs of each student in a classroom. However, differentiated instruction advocates discovering "zones" or "ball-

differentiated instruction   Involves recognizing individual variations in students' knowledge, readiness, interests, and other characteristics, and taking these differences into account when planning curriculum and engaging in instruction.

parks" in which students in a classroom cluster, thus providing three or four types/levels of instruction rather than 20 to 30. In Chapter 4, "Individual Variations," and Chapter 6, "Learners Who Are Exceptional," we provide strategies to help you guide students with different levels of skills and different characteristics to learn effectively.

Working Effectively with Students from Culturally Diverse Backgrounds   Today, one of every five children in the United States is from an immigrant family, and by 2040 one of every three U.S. children is projected to fit this description. Nearly 80 percent of the new immigrants are people of color from Latin America, Asia, and the Caribbean. Approximately 75 percent of the new immigrants are of Spanish-speaking origin, although children speaking more than 100 different languages are entering U.S. schools.

In today's world of increasing intercultural contact, effective teachers are knowledgeable about people from different cultural backgrounds and are sensitive to their needs (Gollnick & Chinn, 2009; Levine & McClosky, 2009). Effective teachers encourage students to have positive personal contact with diverse students and think of ways to create such settings. They guide students in thinking critically about cultural and ethnic issues, forestall or reduce bias, cultivate acceptance, and serve as cultural mediators (Nieto & Bode, 2008; Manning & Baruth, 2009). An effective teacher also needs to be a broker, or middle person, between the culture of the school and the culture of certain students, especially those who are unsuccessful academically (Banks, 2008; Taylor & Whittaker, 2009).

Here are cultural questions that competent teachers are sensitive to include (Pang, 2005):

- Do I recognize the power and complexity of cultural influences on students?
- Are my expectations for my students culturally based or biased?
- Am I doing a good job of seeing life from the perspective of my students who come from different cultures than mine?
- Am I teaching the skills students may need to talk in class if their culture is one in which they have little opportunity to practice "public" talking?

We explore diversity issues throughout the book and in *Diversity and Education* interludes. The first one, which follows, further explores the cultural aspects of schools.

What are some strategies effective teachers use regarding diversity issues?

DIVERSITY AND EDUCATION
The Cultural School

Valerie Pang (2005), an expert on cultural issues in schools, stresses that many teachers don't adequately take into account the cultural context of the school and cultural backgrounds students bring to the classroom. Teachers may not share their students' cultural experiences because they live in neighborhoods far from the school in which they teach. The teachers and students also may have grown up in very different cultures. Pang (2005) says teachers should become more familiar with the neighborhood in which the school is located if they live outside of it. They might shop at neighborhood stores, get to know the community leaders, and read community newspapers. In this way, teachers can become more in tune with their students' rhythm and culture. Pang also recommends that teachers bring examples from the children's lives into their teaching.

Valerie Pang is a professor of teacher education at San Diego State University and a former elementary school teacher. *What are some strategies she recommends that can increase teachers' awareness of their students' cultural backgrounds?*

An example of bringing local, cultural meaning to students involves a San Diego high school social studies class whose teacher invited Dr. Dorothy Smith—an African American college professor, community leader, and former chair of the San Diego School Board—to speak to her class. Dr. Smith talked about issues the students and parents were dealing with as citizens. She brought up many issues: What does it mean to be an African American? How important is it to go to college? How can I make a contribution to my neighborhood?

In preparation, the students developed interview questions to ask Dr. Smith. Also, one group of students videotaped her discussion so that the interview could be shown to other classes. Another group took notes and wrote an article about her talk for the student newspaper.

When students are given the opportunity to meet people like Dr. Smith, they are provided not only with important cultural role models but also with connections to the culture of their own neighborhood.

Assessment Skills Competent teachers also have good assessment skills. There are many aspects to effectively using assessment in the classroom (Gronlund & Waugh, 2009; Oosterof, 2009). You will need to decide what type of tests you want to use to document your students' performance after instruction. You also will need to use assessment effectively before and during instruction (Popham, 2008). For example, before teaching a unit on plate tectonics, you might decide to assess whether your students are familiar with terms like *continent, earthquake,* and *volcano.*

During instruction, you might want to use ongoing observation and monitoring to determine whether your instruction is at a level that challenges students and to detect which students need your individual attention (Brookhart & Nitko, 2008). You will need to develop a grading system that communicates meaningful information about your students' performance.

Other aspects of assessment you will be involved with include state-mandated tests to assess students' achievement and teachers' knowledge and skills. The federal government's No Child Left Behind (NCLB) legislation requires states to test students annually in mathematics, English/language arts, and science, and holds states accountable for the success and failure of their students (Yell, 2008).

Because of NCLB, the extent to which instruction should be tied to standards, or what is called *standards-based instruction,* has become a major issue in educational psychology and U.S. classrooms (Yell & Drasgow, 2009). This issue is all about standards of excellence and what it takes to get students to pass external, large-scale tests. Many educational psychologists stress that the challenge is to teach creatively within the structure imposed by NCLB (McMillan, 2007). Much more information about No Child Left Behind is provided in Chapter 15, "Standardized Tests and Teaching."

Before you become a teacher, your subject-matter knowledge and teaching skills are also likely to be assessed by the state in which you plan to teach. A large majority of states now use the PRAXIS™ test to determine whether prospective teachers are qualified to teach (Shorall, 2009). Because of the increasing use of the PRAXIS™ test, this text includes a number of resources to help you prepare for this test.

Technological Skills   Technology itself does not necessarily improve students' ability to learn, but it can support learning (Jonassen & others, 2008; Smaldino, Lowther, & Russell, 2008). Conditions that support the effective use of technology in education include vision and support from educational leaders; teachers skilled in using technology for learning; content standards and curriculum resources; assessment of effectiveness of technology for learning; and an emphasis on the child as an active, constructive learner (International Society for Technology in Education, [ISTE], 2007).

There is a profound gap between the technology knowledge and skills most students learn in school and those they need in the twenty-first-century workplace (Partnership for 21st Century Skills, 2008). Students will benefit from teachers who increase their technology knowledge and skills, and integrate computers appropriately into classroom learning (Forcier & Descy, 2008; Lever-Duffy & McDonald, 2008). This integration should match up with students' learning needs, including the need to prepare for tomorrow's jobs, many of which will require technological expertise and computer-based skills. In addition, effective teachers are knowledgeable about various assistive devices to support the learning of students with disabilities (Bitter & Legacy, 2008).

What are some assessment skills that characterize effective teachers?

National Educational Technology Standards (NETS) have been established by the ISTE (2001, 2007). The NETS standards include:

- Technology foundation standards for students, which describe what students should know about technology and be able to do with technology
- Standards for using technology in learning and teaching, which describe how technology should be used throughout the curriculum for teaching, learning, and instructional management
- Educational technology support standards, which describe systems, access, staff development, and support services needed to provide effective use of technology
- Standards for student assessment and evaluation of technology use, which describe various means of assessing student progress and evaluating the use of technology in learning and teaching

What are some important aspects of incorporating technology in the classroom?

To think further about schools, communities, and technology, see the *Technology and Education* interlude.

TECHNOLOGY AND EDUCATION

Schools and Communities

Not only is technology helping children learn more effectively in school, but it is also increasingly opening up schools to communities. For example, community-based organizations such as museums, zoos, and historical societies increasingly have educational Web sites. For example, One Community (2008) (www.onecleveland.org/) in Cleveland, Ohio, links schools with resources from local museums, the Cleveland Clinic (health), and public television stations. The Exploratorium (2008) (www.exploratorium.edu/educate/index/html) in San Francisco has extensive online resources for teachers and students. Also, in many districts, students and parents can communicate with teachers and administrators through e-mail. Teachers can post students' work on Web pages. Some schools provide students with laptop computers they can take home.

A special concern is to enable students from low-income backgrounds to have adequate access to computers. The Foshay Learning Center, a K–12 public school in Los Angeles, has created eight satellite learning centers in low-income apartment complexes. Without leaving their buildings, students in this school can use the computers to get help with homework, learn about technology, and participate in active learning experiences. Such programs are especially important because,

Cherokee Middle School students tackle LEGO robotic kit.

according to one survey, Americans earning less than $30,000 a year comprise only 18 percent of Internet users, despite comprising 28 percent of the population. Low-income youth are especially vulnerable, being eight times less likely to use computers at home than children in families earning $75,000 or more (Local Initiatives Support Corporation [LISC], 2005).

IBM recently created a Team Tech Volunteer program that will provide technology services to more than 2,500 health and human service agencies. The Team Tech program gives students opportunities to become volunteers in their community and provides technological services that can improve the education and learning of students. Another project was created by Steve Scott, an IBM employee in North Carolina, who recruited five IBM peers to hold a technology cap for 28 eighth-grade Native American students at Cherokee Middle School (IBM, 2006). The IBM employees discussed career opportunities and presented technical information in interesting, easy to understand ways. One project involves having teams of students work on LEGO robotic kits.

Do a thorough assessment of the businesses in your community. Like IBM, some might be willing to provide technological services and expertise for your classroom.

Commitment and Motivation

Being an effective teacher also requires commitment and motivation. This includes having a good attitude and caring about students.

Beginning teachers often report that the investment of time and effort needed to be an effective teacher is huge. Some teachers, even experienced ones, say they have "no life" from September to June. Even putting in hours on evenings and weekends, in addition to all of the hours spent in the classroom, might still not be enough to get things done.

In the face of these demands, it is easy to become frustrated or to get into a rut and develop a negative attitude. Commitment and motivation help get effective teachers through the tough moments of teaching. Effective teachers have confidence in their own self-efficacy, don't let negative emotions diminish their motivation, and bring a positive attitude and enthusiasm to the classroom (Schunk, Pintrich, & Meese, 2008). These qualities are contagious and help make the classroom a place where students want to be.

So, what is likely to nurture your own positive attitudes and continued enthusiasm for teaching? As in all fields, success breeds success. It's important to become aware of times when you've made a difference in an individual student's life. Consider the words of one of the expert consultants for this book, Carlos Diaz (1997), now a professor of education at Florida Atlantic University, about Mrs. Oppel, his high school English teacher:

> To this day, whenever I see certain words *(dearth, slake)* I recognize them fondly as some of Mrs. Oppel's vocabulary words. As a teacher, she was very calm and focused. She also was passionate about the power of language and the beauty of literature. I credit her, at least partially, for my determination to try to master the English language and become a professor and writer. I wish I could bottle these characteristics and implant them in all of my students.

The better teacher you become, the more rewarding your work will be. And the more respect and success you achieve in the eyes of your students, the better you will feel about your commitment to teaching.

With that in mind, stop for a moment and think about the images you have of your own former teachers. Some of your teachers likely were outstanding and left you with a very positive image. In a national survey of almost a thousand students 13 to 17 years of age, having a good sense of humor, making the class interesting, and having knowledge of the subject matter were the characteristics students listed as the most important for teachers to have (NAASP, 1997). Characteristics secondary school students most frequently attributed to their worst teachers were having a boring class, not explaining things clearly, and showing favoritism. These characteristics and others that reflect students' images of their best and worst teachers are shown in Figure 1.1.

Think about the roles that a good sense of humor and your own genuine enthusiasm are likely to play in your long-term commitment as a teacher. Also, notice other characteristics in Figure 1.1 that relate to the caring nature of outstanding teachers. Effective teachers care for their students, often referring to them as "my students." They really want to be with the students and are dedicated to helping them learn. At the same time, they keep their role as a teacher distinct from student roles. Beyond their own caring, effective teachers also look for ways to help their students consider others' feelings and care about each other.

To think about the best and worst characteristics of the teachers you have had, complete *Self-Assessment 1.1.* Use the self-assessment to further explore the attitudes behind your commitment to become a teacher.

Characteristics of best teachers	% Total		Characteristics of worst teachers	% Total
1. Have a sense of humor	79.2		1. Are dull/have a boring class	79.6
2. Make the class interesting	73.7		2. Don't explain things clearly	63.2
3. Have knowledge of their subjects	70.1		3. Show favoritism toward students	52.7
4. Explain things clearly	66.2		4. Have a poor attitude	49.8
5. Spend time to help students	65.8		5. Expect too much from students	49.1
6. Are fair to their students	61.8		6. Don't relate to students	46.2
7. Treat students like adults	54.4		7. Give too much homework	44.2
8. Relate well to students	54.2		8. Are too strict	40.6
9. Are considerate of students' feelings	51.9		9. Don't give help/individual attention	40.5
10. Don't show favoritism toward students	46.6		10. Lack control	39.9

FIGURE 1.1 Students' Images of Their Best and Worst Teachers

SELF-ASSESSMENT 1.1
The Best and Worst Characteristics of My Teachers

When you studied Figure 1.1, were you surprised by any of the characteristics listed by students to describe their best and worst teachers? Which of the top five characteristics students listed for the best teachers surprised you the most? Which of the top five characteristics of the worst teachers surprised you the most?

Now think about the top five characteristics of the best teachers you have had. Then think about the main five characteristics of the worst teachers you have had. In generating your lists, don't be constrained by the characteristics described in Figure 1.1. Also, after you have listed each characteristic, write down one or more examples of situations that reflected the characteristic.

Five Characteristics of the Best Teachers I Have Had

Characteristics	Examples of Situations That Reflected the Characteristic
1. _____	_____
2. _____	_____
3. _____	_____
4. _____	_____
5. _____	_____

Five Characteristics of the Worst Teachers I Have Had

Characteristics	Examples of Situations That Reflected the Characteristic
1. _____	_____
2. _____	_____
3. _____	_____
4. _____	_____
5. _____	_____

BEST PRACTICES
Strategies for Becoming an Effective Teacher

1. *Effective teaching requires teachers to wear many different hats.* It's easy to fall into the trap of thinking that if you have good subject-matter knowledge, excellent teaching will follow. Being an effective teacher requires many diverse skills. Next, you can read about how Susan Bradburn, who teaches fourth and sixth grades at West Marian Elementary School in North Carolina, brings many different skills to create effective lessons.

THROUGH THE EYES OF TEACHERS
The Turtle Lady

Susan created a school museum in which students conduct research and create exhibitions. She has put her school museum concept "on wheels" by having students take carts to other classes and into the community, and she has used the award money to spread the use of mobile museums to other North Carolina schools. Nicknamed "the turtle lady" because of her interest in turtles and other animals, Susan takes students on three-day field trips to Edisto Island, South Carolina, to search for fossils and study coastal ecology. Her students sell calendars that contain their original poetry and art, and they use the proceeds to buy portions of a rain forest so it won't be destroyed.

Susan Bradburn (left) with several students at West Marian Elementary School.

2. *Engage in perspective taking.* You want to be the very best teacher you can possibly be. Think about what your students need from you to improve their academic and life skills. Put your heart and mind into helping them construct these skills. Also think about how you perceive your students and how they perceive you. Here is how one teacher benefited from reflecting about how his perceptions of students' diversity were too stereotypical.

THROUGH THE EYES OF TEACHERS
Finding Individuality in Diversity

Paul August taught for 6 years in an integrated school but says that experience did not adequately prepare him, a non-Latino White, for teaching in an all African American

school. Initially, he perceived the African American students as looking alike. At the end of the school year, however, he realized how ridiculous this was, and individuality had bloomed in his classroom both on his part and his students'. He no longer was seen by his students as a White guy but as a teacher. Later, when Paul was transferred to teach in a predominantly Asian American school, he says that he regressed into the "they all look alike" stereotype. Once again, though, over time individuality trumped nationality and he "could see the differences in faces, names, and cultures of Chinese, Vietnamese, Cambodians, Laotions, Japanese, and Mien" (August, 2002, p. A29).

3. *Keep the list of characteristics of effective teachers we have discussed in this chapter with you through your teaching career.* Looking at the list and thinking about the different areas of effective teaching can benefit you as you go through your student teaching, your days as a beginning teacher, and even your years as an experienced teacher. By consulting it from time to time, you might realize that you have let one or two areas slip and need to spend time improving yourself.

Review, Reflect, and Practice

(2) **Identify the attitudes and skills of an effective teacher.**

REVIEW

- What professional knowledge and skills are required to be an effective teacher?
- Why is it important for teachers to be committed and motivated?

REFLECT

- What is most likely to make teaching rewarding for you in the long run?

PRAXIS™ PRACTICE

1. Suzanne spends a considerable amount of time writing lesson plans, developing criteria for student success, and organizing materials. Which professional skill is she demonstrating?
   a. classroom management
   b. communication
   c. developmentally appropriate teaching practices
   d. goal setting and instructional management

Review, Reflect, and Practice *continued*

2. Mr. Marcinello, who is midway through his first year of teaching, feels frustrated with his job. He is developing a negative attitude, and it is carrying over in his teaching. Which of the following areas does Mr. Marcinello need to work on the most at this point to become an effective teacher?
   a. classroom management and communication
   b. commitment and motivation
   c. technology and diversity
   d. subject-matter competence and individual variations

Please see the answer key at the end of the book.

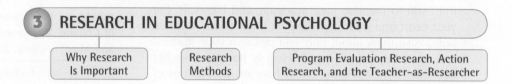

3 RESEARCH IN EDUCATIONAL PSYCHOLOGY

| Why Research Is Important | Research Methods | Program Evaluation Research, Action Research, and the Teacher-as-Researcher |

Research can be a valuable source of information about teaching. We will explore why research is important and how it is done, including how you can be a teacher-researcher.

Why Research Is Important

It sometimes is said that experience is the best teacher. Your own experiences and experiences that other teachers, administrators, and experts share with you will make you a better teacher. However, by providing you with valid information about the best ways to teach children, research also can make you a better teacher (Gay, Mills, & Airasian, 2009; Wiersma & Jurs, 2009).

We all get a great deal of knowledge from personal experience. We generalize from what we observe and frequently turn memorable encounters into lifetime "truths." But how valid are these conclusions? Sometimes we err in making these personal observations or misinterpret what we see and hear. Chances are, you can think of many situations in which you thought other people read you the wrong way, just as they might have felt that you misread them. When we base information only on personal experiences, we also aren't always totally objective because we sometimes make judgments that protect our ego and self-esteem (McMillan, 2008).

We get information not only from personal experiences but also from authorities or experts. In your teaching career, you will hear many authorities and experts spell out a "best way" to educate students. The authorities and experts, however, don't always agree, do they? You might hear one expert one week tell you about a reading method that is absolutely the best, yet the next week hear another expert tout a different method. One experienced teacher might tell you to do one thing with your students, while another experienced teacher tells you to do the opposite. How can you tell which one to believe? One way to clarify the situation is to look closely at research on the topic.

Research Methods

Collecting information (or data) is an important aspect of research. When educational psychology researchers want to find out, for example, whether regularly playing video games detracts from student learning, eating a nutritious breakfast improves alertness in class, or getting more recess time decreases absenteeism, they can choose from many methods of gathering research information (Leary, 2008; Rosnow & Rosenthal, 2008).

The three basic methods used to gather information in educational psychology are descriptive, correlational, and experimental.

Descriptive Research   Descriptive research has the purpose of observing and recording behavior. For example, an educational psychologist might observe the extent to which children are aggressive in a classroom or interview teachers about their attitudes toward a particular type of teaching strategy. By itself, descriptive research cannot prove what causes some phenomenon, but it can reveal important information about people's behavior and attitudes (Lammers & Badia, 2005).

Observation   We look at things all the time. Casually watching two students interacting, however, is not the same as the type of observation used in scientific studies. Scientific observation is highly systematic. It requires knowing what you are looking for, conducting observations in an unbiased manner, accurately recording and categorizing what you see, and effectively communicating your observations (McBurney & White, 2007).

A common way to record observations is to write them down, often using shorthand or symbols. In addition, tape recorders, video cameras, special coding sheets, one-way mirrors, and computers increasingly are being used to make observation more accurate, reliable, and efficient.

Observations can be made in laboratories or in naturalistic settings. A **laboratory** is a controlled setting from which many of the complex factors of the real world have been removed (Gall, Gall, & Borg, 2007). Some educational psychologists conduct research in laboratories at the colleges or universities where they work and teach. Although laboratories often help researchers gain more control in their studies, they have been criticized as being artificial (Beins, 2004).

In **naturalistic observation**, behavior is observed out in the real world. Educational psychologists conduct naturalistic observations of children in classrooms, at museums, on playgrounds, in homes, in neighborhoods, and in other settings (Given, 2008). Naturalistic observation was used in one study that focused on conversations in a children's science museum (Crowley & others, 2001). Parents were three times as likely to engage boys as girls in explanatory talk while visiting different exhibits at the science museum (see Figure 1.2). In another study, Mexican American parents who had completed high school used more explanations with their children as they were observed at a science museum than Mexican American parents who had not completed high school (Tennebaum & others, 2002).

Participant observation occurs when the observer-researcher is actively involved as a participant in the activity or setting (McMillan, 2008). The participant observer will often participate in a context and observe awhile, then take notes on what he or she has viewed. The observer usually makes these observations and writes down notes over a period of days, weeks, or months and looks for patterns in the observations (Glesne, 2007). For example, to study a student who is doing poorly in the class without apparent reason, the teacher might develop a plan to observe the student from time to time and record observations of the student's behavior and what is going on in the classroom at the time.

Interviews and Questionnaires   Sometimes the quickest and best way to get information about students and teachers is to ask them for it. Educational psychologists use interviews and questionnaires (surveys) to find out about children's and teachers' experiences, beliefs, and feelings. Most interviews take place face-to-face, although they can be done in other ways, such as over the phone or the Internet. Questionnaires usually are given to individuals in written form. They, too, can be transmitted in many ways, such as directly by hand, by mail, or via the Internet.

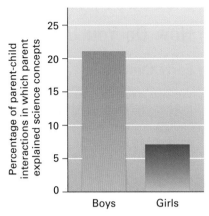

FIGURE 1.2 Parents' Explanations of Science to Sons and Daughters at a Science Museum

In a naturalistic observation study at a children's science museum, parents were three times more likely to explain science to boys than girls (Crowley & others, 2001). The gender difference occurred regardless of whether the father, the mother, or both parents were with the child, although the gender difference was greatest for fathers' science explanations to sons and daughters.

laboratory A controlled setting from which many of the complex factors of the real world have been removed.

naturalistic observation Observation outside of a laboratory in the real world.

participant observation Observation in which the observer-researcher is actively involved as a participant in the activity or setting.

DEVELOPMENTAL FOCUS 1.1

How Do You Use Participant Observation in Your Classroom?

Early Childhood

We take notes, observe, and record the activities of our young children throughout the day. Taking notes on children at the preschool level can be challenging because when children first notice that you are intently watching and taking notes, they may become curious and ask many questions, or become overly anxious and say things like, "Look at me!" to the teacher. As the year goes by, however, children get used to the recordings, and the questions are less frequent, allowing for a more accurate assessment of a child's needs.

—Valarie Gorham, *Kiddie Quarters, Inc.*

Elementary School: Grades K–5

I meet with leveled reading groups, typically ranging from three to five students. Materials and texts that are at the group's instructional level are used. As the lesson and activities are carried out, I take quick notes as I see the group or individuals grasping concepts, struggling in any way, or if a "teachable moment" presents itself. These notes help me later in my planning to make decisions about whether to reteach a certain lesson/concept, move on to new concepts/materials, or go to something other than originally planned because of a teachable moment or connection that has been discovered.

—Susan Froelich, *Clinton Elementary School*

Middle School: Grades 6–8

I once had a student who often came to class unprepared and late. Over time, I observed the student, took notes, and created a chart for myself that listed the times the student did not come to class prepared or on time. Because I kept good records, I was able to find out that when the student had a physical education class just before my class, he was late. I then worked with the student and phys. ed. teacher to come up with a solution so that the student had time to get to my class with the necessary classroom materials.

—Casey Maass, *Edison Middle School*

High School: Grades 9–12

In the lab portion of my class, I have a chart that identifies when students are off-task and a notation for what they are doing instead of the task, such as listening to an iPod, talking to their friends, and so on. After a pattern develops, I talk with the student and show them their pattern on the chart. High school students tend to understand graphs and data better than being reminded while they are being off-task. For me, charting provides a more positive environment than an interruption or reprimand.

—Sandy Swanson, *Menomonee Falls High School*

Good interviews and surveys involve concrete, specific, and unambiguous questions and some means of checking the authenticity of the respondents' replies (Rosnow & Rosenthal, 2008). Interviews and surveys, however, are not without problems. One crucial limitation is that many individuals give socially desirable answers, responding in a way they think is most socially acceptable and desirable rather than how they truly think or feel (Babbie, 2005). Skilled interviewing techniques and questions that increase forthright responses are crucial to obtaining accurate information. Another problem with interviews and surveys is that the respondents sometimes simply are untruthful.

standardized tests Tests with uniform procedures for administration and scoring. They assess students' performance in different domains and allow a student's performance to be compared with the performance of other students at the same age or grade level, often on a national basis.

Standardized Tests **Standardized tests** have uniform procedures for administration and scoring. They assess students' aptitudes or skills in different domains. Many standardized tests allow a student's performance to be compared with the performance of other students at the same age or grade level, in many cases on a national basis (Kingston, 2008). Students might take a number of standardized tests, including tests that assess their intelligence, achievement, personality, career interests, and other skills (Bart & Peterson, 2008). These tests can provide outcome measures for research studies, information that helps psychologists and educators make decisions about an individual student, and comparisons of students' performance across schools, states, and countries.

Standardized tests also play an important role in a major contemporary educational psychology issue—*accountability,* which involves holding teachers and students responsible for student performance (McNergney & McNergney, 2007). As we indicated earlier, both students and teachers increasingly are being given standardized tests in the accountability effort. The U.S. government's No Child Left Behind Act is at the centerpiece of accountability; it mandated that in 2005 every state had to give standardized tests to students in grades 3 through 8 in language arts and math, with testing for science achievement added in 2007.

Brandi Binder is evidence of the brain's hemispheric flexibility and resilience. Despite having the right side of her cortex removed because of a severe case of epilepsy, Brandi engages in many activities often portrayed as only "right-brain" activities. She loves music and art and is shown here working on one of her paintings.

Case Studies   A **case study** is an in-depth look at an individual. Case studies often are used when unique circumstances in a person's life cannot be duplicated, for either practical or ethical reasons. For example, consider the case study of Brandi Binder (Nash, 1997). She developed such severe epilepsy that surgeons had to remove the right side of her brain's cerebral cortex when she was 6 years old. Brandi lost virtually all control over muscles on the left side of her body, the side controlled by the right side of her brain. At age 17, however, after years of therapy ranging from leg lifts to mathematics and music training, Brandi is an A student. She loves music and art, which usually are associated with the right side of the brain. Her recuperation is not 100 percent—for example, she has not regained the use of her left arm—but her case study shows that if there is a way to compensate, the human brain will find it. Brandi's remarkable recovery also provides evidence against the stereotype that the left side (hemisphere) of the brain is solely the source of logical thinking and the right hemisphere exclusively the source of creativity. Brains are not that neatly split in terms of most functioning, as Brandi's case illustrates.

Although case studies provide dramatic, in-depth portrayals of people's lives, we need to exercise caution when interpreting them (Leary, 2008). The subject of a case study is unique, with a genetic makeup and set of experiences that no one else shares. For these reasons, the findings often do not lend themselves to statistical analysis and may not generalize to other people.

Ethnographic Studies   An **ethnographic study** consists of in-depth description and interpretation of behavior in an ethnic or a cultural group that includes direct involvement with the participants (Berg, 2007; Creswell, 2008). This type of study might include observations in naturalistic settings as well as interviews. Many ethnographic studies are long-term projects.

In one ethnographic study, the purpose was to examine the extent to which schools were enacting educational reforms for language minority students (U.S. Office of Education, 1998). In-depth observations and interviews were conducted in a number of schools to determine if they were establishing high standards and restructuring the way education was being delivered. Several schools were selected for intensive evaluation, including Las Palmas Elementary School in San Clemente, California. The study concluded that this school, at least, was making the necessary reforms for improving the education of language minority students.

Focus Groups   *Focus groups* involve interviewing people in a group setting, in most cases to obtain information about a particular topic or issue (Given, 2008). Focus groups typically consist of five to nine people in which a group facilitator asks a series of open-ended questions. Focus groups can be used to assess the value of a product, service, or program, such as a newly developed school Web site or the benefits of a recently instituted after-school program for middle school students.

case study An in-depth look at an individual.

ethnographic study In-depth description and interpretation of behavior in an ethnic or a cultural group that includes direct involvement with the participants.

What is an ethnographic study? Give an example of an ethnographic study.

correlational research Research that describes the strength of the relation between two or more events or characteristics.

experimental research Research that allows the determination of the causes of behavior; involves conducting an experiment, which is a carefully regulated procedure in which one or more of the factors believed to influence the behavior being studied is manipulated and all others are held constant.

independent variable The manipulated, influential, experimental factor in an experiment.

dependent variable The factor that is measured in an experiment.

Personal Journals and Diaries Individuals can be asked to keep personal journals or diaries to document quantitative aspects of their activities (such as how often the individual uses the Internet) or qualitiative aspects of their lives (such as their attitudes and beliefs about a particular topic or issue) (Given, 2008). Increasingly, researchers are providing digital audio or video recorders to participants in a study rather than have them write entries in a personal journal or diary.

Correlational Research In **correlational research**, the goal is to describe the strength of the relation between two or more events or characteristics. Correlational research is useful because the more strongly two events are correlated (related or associated), the more effectively we can predict one from the other (Kraska, 2008). For example, if researchers find that low-involved, permissive teaching is correlated with a student's lack of self-control, it suggests that low-involved, permissive teaching might be one source of the lack of self-control.

Correlation by itself, however, does not equal causation (Vogt, 2007). The correlational finding just mentioned does not mean that permissive teaching necessarily causes low student self-control. It could mean that, but it also could mean that the student's lack of self-control caused the teachers to throw up their arms in despair and give up trying to control the out-of-control class. It also could be that other factors, such as heredity, poverty, or inadequate parenting, caused the correlation between permissive teaching and low student self-control. Figure 1.3 illustrates these possible interpretations of correlational data.

Experimental Research **Experimental research** allows educational psychologists to determine the causes of behavior. Educational psychologists accomplish this task by performing an *experiment*, a carefully regulated procedure in which one or more of the factors believed to influence the behavior being studied is manipulated and all other factors are held constant. If the behavior under study changes when a factor is manipulated, we say that the manipulated factor causes the behavior to change. *Cause* is the event that is being manipulated. *Effect* is the behavior that changes because of the manipulation. Experimental research is the only truly reliable method of establishing cause and effect. Because correlational research does not involve manipulation of factors, it is not a dependable way to isolate cause (Mitchell & Jolley, 2007).

Experiments involve at least one independent variable and one dependent variable. The **independent variable** is the manipulated, influential, experimental factor. The label *independent* indicates that this variable can be changed independently of any other factors. For example, suppose we want to design an experiment to study the effects of peer tutoring on student achievement. In this example, the amount and type of peer tutoring could be an independent variable.

The **dependent variable** is the factor that is measured in an experiment. It can change as the independent variable is manipulated. The label *dependent* is used because the values of this variable depend on what happens to the participants in the experiment as the independent variable is manipulated. In the peer tutoring study, achievement is the dependent variable. This might be assessed in a number of ways. Let's say in this study it is measured by scores on a nationally standardized achievement test.

In experiments, the independent variable consists of differing experiences given to one or more experimental groups and one or more control groups. An

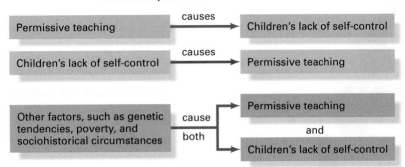

Observed correlation   **Possible explanations for this correlation**

FIGURE 1.3 Possible Explanations for Correlational Data

An observed correlation between two events cannot be used to conclude that one event caused the other. Some possibilities are that the second event caused the first event or that a third, unknown event caused the correlation between the first two events.

experimental group is a group whose experience is manipulated. A **control group** is a comparison group that is treated in every way like the experimental group except for the manipulated factor. The control group serves as the baseline against which the effects of the manipulated condition can be compared. In the peer tutoring study, we need to have one group of students who get peer tutoring (experimental group) and one group of students who don't (control group).

Another important principle of experimental research is **random assignment**: Researchers assign participants to experimental and control groups by chance. This practice reduces the likelihood that the experiment's results will be due to any preexisting differences between the groups (Mertler & Charles, 2008). In our study of peer tutoring, random assignment greatly reduces the probability that the two groups will differ on such factors as age, family status, initial achievement, intelligence, personality, health, and alertness.

To summarize the experimental study of peer tutoring and student achievement, each student is randomly assigned to one of two groups. One group (the experimental group) is given peer tutoring; the other (the control group) is not. The independent variable consists of the differing experiences (tutoring or no tutoring) that the experimental and control groups receive. After the peer tutoring is completed, the students are given a nationally standardized achievement test (dependent variable). Figure 1.4 illustrates the experimental research method applied to time management and students' grades.

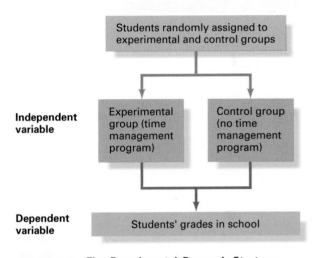

FIGURE 1.4 The Experimental Research Strategy Applied to a Study of the Effects of Time Management on Students' Grades

Program Evaluation Research, Action Research, and the Teacher-as-Researcher

In discussing research methods so far, we have referred mainly to methods used to improve our knowledge and understanding of general educational practices. The same methods also can be applied to research whose aim is more specific, such as determining how well a particular educational strategy or program is working (Creswell, 2008). This more narrowly targeted work often includes program evaluation research, action research, and the teacher-as-researcher.

experimental group The group whose experience is manipulated in an experiment.

control group In an experiment, a group whose experience is treated in every way like the experimental group except for the manipulated factor.

random assignment In experimental research, the assignment of participants to experimental and control groups by chance.

What methods can a teacher-as-researcher use to obtain information about students?

Program Evaluation Research **Program evaluation research** is research designed to make decisions about the effectiveness of a particular program (McMillan, 2008; Posavac & Carey, 2007). It often focuses on a specific location or type of program. Because program evaluation research often is directed at answering a question about a specific school or school system, its results are not intended to be generalized to other settings (Mertler & Charles, 2008). A program evaluation researcher might ask questions like these:

• Has a gifted program started two years ago had positive effects on students' creative thinking and academic achievement?

• Has a technology program in place for one year improved students' attitudes toward school?

• Which of two reading programs being used in this school system has improved students' reading skills the most?

Action Research **Action research** is used to solve a specific classroom or school problem, improve teaching and other educational strategies, or make a decision at a specific location (Holly, Arhar, & Kasten, 2009; Stringer, 2008). The goal of action research is to improve educational practices immediately in one or two classrooms, at one school, or at several schools. Action research is carried out by teachers and administrators rather than educational psychology researchers. The practitioners, however, might follow many of the guidelines of scientific research described earlier, such as trying to make the research and observations as systematic as possible to avoid bias and misinterpretation. Action research can be carried out school-wide or in more limited settings by a smaller group of teachers and administrators; it can even be accomplished in a single classroom by an individual teacher (Hendricks, 2009; Johnson, 2008).

The Teacher-as-Researcher The concept of **teacher-as-researcher** (also called "teacher-researcher") is the idea that classroom teachers can conduct their own studies to improve their teaching practices (Creswell, 2008). This is an important outgrowth of action research. Some educational experts believe that the increasing emphasis on the teacher-as-researcher reinvents the teacher's role, fuels school renewal, and improves teaching and learning (Flake & others, 1995; Gill, 1997). The most effective teachers routinely ask questions and monitor problems to be solved, then collect data, interpret them, and share their conclusions with other teachers (Cochran-Smith, 1995).

To obtain information, the teacher-researcher uses methods such as participant observation, interviews, and case studies (Glesne, 2007). One good, widely used technique is the clinical interview, in which the teacher makes the student feel comfortable, shares beliefs and expectations, and asks questions in a nonthreatening manner. Before conducting a clinical interview with a student, the teacher usually will put together a targeted set of questions to ask. Clinical interviews not only can help you obtain information about a particular issue or problem but also can provide you with a sense of how children think and feel.

In addition to participant observation, the teacher might conduct several clinical interviews with a student, discuss the student's situation with the child's parents, and consult with a school psychologist about the student's behavior. Based on this work as teacher-researcher, the teacher may be able to create an intervention strategy that improves the student's behavior.

Thus, learning about educational research methods not only can help you understand the research that educational psychologists conduct but also has another practical benefit. The more knowledge you have about research in educational psychology, the more effective you will be in the increasingly popular teacher-researcher role (Thomas, 2005).

program evaluation research
Research designed to make decisions about the effectiveness of a particular program.

action research   Research used to solve a specific classroom or school problem, improve teaching and other educational strategies, or make a decision at a specific level.

teacher-as-researcher   Also called teacher-researcher, this concept involves classroom teachers conducting their own studies to improve their teaching practice.

DEVELOPMENTAL FOCUS 1.2

How Has Research Influenced Your Teaching?

Early Childhood

Brain research has demonstrated the amazing amount of learning that takes place during the early years of life, in addition to the significant impact of high-quality early childhood education and care on the academic and long-term success of a child. Given the age of the children at our center—toddlers through pre–K—I find this research extremely motivating.

—Heidi Kaufman, *MetroWest YMCA Child Care and Educational Program*

Elementary School: Grades K–5

When adopting our new kindergarten reading curriculum, we conducted local assessments and collected data, read relevant research of best practices, and worked cooperatively to come up with the policies and practices that will work in collaboration with our state expectations as well as our school vision and mission.

—Heather Zoldak, *Ridge Wood Elementary School*

Middle School: Grades 6–8

I attend Learning and the Brain conferences, and read associated research papers and books. These materials have helped me understand brain development in middle school children, especially the considerable changes in early adolescence. This understanding has influenced my classroom management, enabled me to provide differentiated instruction, and helped me to appreciate and work with a range of students' learning styles and needs.

—Keren Abra, *Convent of the Sacred Heart School*

High School: Grades 9–12

The person who has most influenced my teaching is Nancie Atwell, a teacher who teaches teachers about teaching. Her lessons on how to get students to love reading are pragmatic and simple, yet extremely effective: Read what the students are reading, "sell" the books by talking about them to students, let students see you reading, read when they read, give time in class to read, make books easily available to students, and be excited and energetic when discussing new books in class. At the beginning of the year, nonreaders (who comprise the majority of the class) groan and roll their eyes when I say it is reading time. However, in just a few short weeks, students beg for daily reading time.

—Jennifer Heiter, *Bremen High School*

 BEST PRACTICES
Strategies for Becoming an Effective Teacher–Researcher

1. *As you plan each week's lessons, think about your students and which ones might benefit from your role as a teacher-researcher.* As you reflect on the past week's classes, you might notice that one student seemed to be sliding downhill in her performance and that another student seemed to be especially depressed. As you think about such students, you might consider using your observer participation and/or clinical interview skills in the following week in an effort to find out why they are having problems.

2. *Take a course in educational research methods.* This can improve your understanding of how research is conducted.

3. *Visit the What Works Clearinghouse Web site* (http://ies.ed.gov/ncee/wwe/). There you can read about a number of systematic assessments of research that provide conclusions about which programs and approaches work best in such areas as beginning reading, early childhood education, middle school math, and dropout prevention.

3. *Use the library or Internet resources to learn more about teacher-researcher skills.* This might include locating information about how to be a skilled clinical interviewer and a systematic, unbiased observer.

4. *Ask someone else (such as another teacher) to observe your class and help you develop some strategies for the particular research problem that you want to solve.*

Review, Reflect, and Practice

(3) Discuss why research is important to effective teaching, and how educational psychologists and teachers can conduct and evaluate research.

REVIEW

- Why is research important in educational psychology?
- What are some types of research? What is the difference between correlational research and experimental research?
- What are some kinds of research that relate directly to effective classroom practices? What tools might a teacher use to do classroom research?

REFLECT

- In your own K–12 education, can you remember a time when one of your teachers might have benefited from conducting action research regarding the effectiveness of his or her own teaching methods? What action research questions and methods might have been useful to the teacher?

PRAXIS™ PRACTICE

1. Which of the following is more scientific?
   a. systematic observation
   b. personal experience
   c. a person's opinion
   d. a book written by a journalist

2. Mr. McMahon wants to know how much time his students spend off-task each day. To determine this, he carefully watches the students in class, keeping a record of off-task behavior. Which research approach has he used?
   a. case study
   b. experiment
   c. laboratory experiment
   d. naturalistic observation

3. Ms. Simon has been hired to determine how effective a school's health education program has been in reducing adolescent pregnancies. Which type of research will she conduct?
   a. action research
   b. experimental research
   c. program evaluation
   d. teacher-as-researcher

Please see the answer key at the end of the book.

CRACK THE CASE
The Case of the Classroom Decision

Ms. Huang teaches fourth grade at King Elementary School. Her class is comprised of 26 students, 16 girls and 10 boys. They are an ethnically and economically diverse group. They are also diverse in terms of their achievement levels. She has two students who have been identified as being gifted and three students with diagnosed learning disabilities. Overall, they are a cooperative group with a desire to learn.

Ms. Huang's school district recently purchased a new math curriculum that emphasizes conceptual understanding and application of mathematical principles to real-life situations. While Ms. Huang appreciates this, she also has some concerns.

Many of Ms. Huang's students have not yet mastered their basic math facts. Ms. Huang fears that without knowing their basic math facts very well that understanding mathematical principles will be useless and that her students still won't be able to work on application of these principles. She also worries that this will cause her students undue frustration and may decrease their interest and motivation in math.

In the past, Ms. Huang has had her students work on developing mastery of math facts using drill-and-practice methods such as flashcards, worksheets filled with fact problems, and a computer game that is essentially an electronic version of flashcards with graphics. She is comfortable with this method and says that it has helped prior students to develop the mastery she believes they need.

She voices her concern to her principal, who responds that the publisher's representative provided the district with evidence that the new program also helps students to develop mastery of basic facts. However, Ms. Huang is still skeptical. She wants very badly to do the right thing for her students, but she isn't sure what that is. She decides that she needs to conduct some classroom research to determine which will benefit her students more—the new curricular approach or her more traditional approach.

1. What issues would need to be considered in conducting such a study?
2. What type of research would be most appropriate?
   a. case study
   b. correlational research
   c. experimental research
   d. naturalistic observation
3. Why?
4. If she compared the two different curricula and their outcomes, what would the independent variable be?
   a. student achievement relative to basic math facts
   b. the control group
   c. the experimental group
   d. which curricular approach was used
5. If Ms. Huang decided to conduct an experimental study in which she compared the two different curricula and their outcomes, what would the dependent variable be?
   a. student achievement relative to basic math facts
   b. the control group
   c. the experimental group
   d. which curricular approach was used
6. How should Ms. Huang go about conducting her study?

Reach Your Learning Goals
Educational Psychology: A Tool for Effective Teaching

(1) EXPLORING EDUCATIONAL PSYCHOLOGY: Describe some basic ideas about the field of educational psychology.

Historical Background

Educational psychology is the branch of psychology that specializes in understanding teaching and learning in educational settings. William James and John Dewey were important pioneers in educational psychology, as was E. L. Thorndike. William James emphasized the importance of classroom observation to improve education. Among the important ideas in educational psychology that we owe to Dewey are these: the child as an active learner, education of the whole child, emphasis on the child's adaptation to the environment, and the democratic ideal that all children deserve a competent education. E. L. Thorndike, a proponent of the scientific foundation of learning, argued that schools should sharpen children's reasoning skills. There were few individuals from ethnic minority groups and few women in the early history of educational psychology because of ethnic and gender barriers. Further historical developments included Skinner's behaviorism in the mid–twentieth century and the cognitive revolution that had taken hold by the 1980s. Also in recent years, there has been expanded interest in the socioemotional aspects of children's lives, including cultural contexts.

Teaching: Art and Science

Teaching is linked to both science and art. In terms of art, skillful, experienced practice contributes to effective teaching. In terms of science, information from psychological research can provide valuable ideas.

(2) EFFECTIVE TEACHING: Identify the attitudes and skills of an effective teacher.

Professional Knowledge and Skills

Effective teachers have subject-matter competence, use effective instructional strategies, pay more than lip service to individual variations, work with diverse ethnic and cultural groups, and have skills in the following areas: goal setting and planning, developmentally appropriate teaching practices, classroom management, motivation, communication, assessment, and technology.

Commitment and Motivation

Being an effective teacher also requires commitment and motivation. This includes having a good attitude and caring about students. It is easy for teachers to get into a rut and develop a negative attitude, but students pick up on this and it can harm their learning.

(3) RESEARCH IN EDUCATIONAL PSYCHOLOGY: Discuss why research is important to effective teaching, and how educational psychologists and teachers can conduct and evaluate research.

Why Research Is Important

Personal experiences and information from experts can help you become an effective teacher. The information you obtain from research also is extremely important. It will help you sort through various strategies and determine which are most and least effective. Research helps to eliminate errors in judgment that are based only on personal experiences.

Research Methods

Numerous methods can be used to obtain information about various aspects of educational psychology. Research data-gathering methods can be classified as descriptive, correlational, and experimental. Descriptive methods include observation, interviews and questionnaires, standardized tests, case studies, ethnographic studies, focus groups, and personal journals and diaries. In correlational research, the goal is to describe the strength of the relation between two or more events or characteristics. An important research principle is that correlation does not equal causation. Experimental research allows the causes of behavior to be determined and is the only truly reliable method of establishing cause and effect. Conducting an experiment involves examining the influence of at least one independent variable (the manipulated, influ-

| Program Evaluation Research, Action Research, and the Teacher-as-Researcher | ential, experimental factor) on one or more dependent variables (the measured factor). Experiments involve the random assignment of participants to one or more experimental groups (the groups whose experience is being manipulated) and one or more control groups (comparison groups treated in every way like the experimental group except for the manipulated factor). |

Program evaluation research is research designed to make decisions about the effectiveness of a particular program. Action research is used to solve a specific classroom or social problem, improve teaching strategies, or make a decision about a specific location. The teacher-as-researcher (teacher-researcher) conducts classroom studies to improve his or her educational practices.

 ## KEY TERMS

educational psychology 2	naturalistic observation 17	correlational research 20	control group 21
constructivist approach 6	participant observation 17	experimental research 20	random assignment 21
direct instruction approach 6	standardized tests 18	independent variable 20	program evaluation research 22
differentiated instruction 8	case study 19	dependent variable 20	action research 22
laboratory 17	ethnographic study 19	experimental group 21	teacher-as-researcher 22

 ## PORTFOLIO ACTIVITIES

Now that you have a good understanding of this chapter, complete these exercises to expand your thinking.

Independent Reflection

1. After some thinking, write a personal statement about the following. What kind of teacher do you want to become? What strengths do you want to have? What kinds of potential weaknesses might you need to overcome? Either place the statement in your portfolio or seal it in an envelope that you will open after your first month or two of teaching.

2. At the beginning of the chapter, you read teacher-astronaut Christa McAuliffe's quote: "I touch the future. I teach." Don your creative thinking hat and come up with one or more brief quotes that describe positive aspects of teaching.

3. Think about the grade level you are planning to teach. Consider at least one way your classroom at that grade level is

likely to be challenging. Write about how you will cope with this.

Research/Field Experience

4. Information about educational psychology appears in research journals and in magazines and newspapers. Find an article in a research or professional journal (such as *Contemporary Educational Psychologist, Educational Psychologist, Educational Psychology Review, Journal of Educational Psychology,* or *Phi Delta Kappan*) and an article in a newspaper or magazine on the same topic. How does the research/professional article differ from the newspaper or magazine account? What can you learn from this comparison? Write down your conclusions and keep copies of the articles.

Go to the Online Learning Center for downloadable portfolio templates.

 ## TAKING IT TO THE NET

- Begin building your network of support by subscribing to an education-related mailing list. Joining an e-mail list will keep you informed about the latest news in education and provide you with helpful instructional resources. Describe the mailing list you selected and what you hope to gain from it. www .educationworld.com/maillist.shtml

- The Internet offers educators unlimited resources for increasing their effectiveness in the classroom. Examine a Web site for educators. How could the available resources contribute

to your effectiveness in the classroom? www.educationworld .com

- Teachers can use student surveys in the classroom to improve their teaching practices. Select one of your ideas, and formulate a brief (eight to ten questions) sample survey that you could use for future classroom research. www.educationworld.com/ a_curr/curr364.shtml

Connect to the Online Learning Center to explore possible answers.

 ## STUDY, PRACTICE, AND SUCCEED

Visit **www.mhhe.com/santedu4e** to review the chapter with self-grading quizzes and self-assessments, to apply the chapter mate-

rial to two more Crack the Case studies, and for suggested activities to develop your teaching portfolio.

CHAPTER 2

Cognitive and Language Development

Ah! What would the world be to us
If the children were no more?
We should dread the desert behind us
Worse than the dark before.

—Henry Wadsworth Longfellow
American Poet, 19th Century

Chapter Outline	Learning Goals
An Overview of Child Development	**1** Define development and explain the main processes, periods, and issues in development, as well as links between development and education.
Exploring What Development Is	
Processes and Periods	
Developmental Issues	
Development and Education	
Cognitive Development	**2** Discuss the development of the brain and compare the cognitive developmental theories of Jean Piaget and Lev Vygotsky.
The Brain	
Piaget's Theory	
Vygotsky's Theory	
Language Development	**3** Identify the key features of language, biological and environmental influences on language, and the typical growth of the child's language.
What Is Language?	
Biological and Environmental Influences	
How Language Develops	

TEACHING STORIES   Donene Polson

In this chapter, you will study Lev Vygotsky's sociocultural cognitive theory of development. Donene Polson's classroom reflects Vygotsky's emphasis on the importance of collaboration among a community of learners. Donene teaches at Washington Elementary School in Salt Lake City, an innovative school that emphasizes the importance of people learning together (Rogoff, Turkanis, & Bartlett, 2001). Children as well as adults plan learning activities. Throughout the day at school, students work in small groups.

Donene loves working in a school in which students, teachers, and parents work as a community to help children learn (Polson, 2001). Before the school year begins, Donene meets with parents at each family's home to prepare for the upcoming year, getting acquainted and establishing schedules to determine when parents can contribute to classroom instruction. At monthly teacher-parent meetings, Donene and the parents plan the curriculum and discuss children's progress. They brainstorm about community resources that can be used to promote children's learning.

Many students come back to tell Donene that experiences in her classroom made important contributions to their development and learning. For example, Luisa Magarian reflected on how her experience in Donene's classroom helped her work with others in high school:

From having responsibility in groups, kids learn how to deal with problems and listen to each other or try to understand different points of view. They learn how to help a group work smoothly and how to keep people interested in what they are doing. . . . As coeditor of the student news magazine at my high school, I have to balance my eagerness to get things done with patience to work with other students. (Rogoff, Turkanis, & Bartlett, 2001, pp. 84–85)

As Donene Polson's story shows, theories of cognitive development can form the basis of innovative instructional programs.

Preview

Examining the shape of children's development allows us to understand it better. This chapter—the first of two on development—focuses on children's cognitive and language development. Before we delve into these topics, though, we need to explore some basic ideas about development.

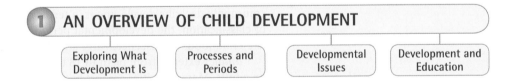

1 AN OVERVIEW OF CHILD DEVELOPMENT

| Exploring What Development Is | Processes and Periods | Developmental Issues | Development and Education |

Twentieth-century Spanish-born American philosopher George Santayana once reflected, "Children are on a different plane. They belong to a generation and way of feeling properly their own." Let's explore what that plane is like.

Exploring What Development Is

Why study children's development? As a teacher, you will be responsible for a new wave of children each year in your classroom. The more you learn about children's

PEANUTS: © United Features Syndicate, Inc.

development, the more you can understand at what level it is appropriate to teach them.

Just what do psychologists mean when they speak of a person's "development"? **Development** is the pattern of biological, cognitive, and socioemotional changes that begins at conception and continues through the life span. Most development involves growth, although it also eventually involves decay (dying).

Processes and Periods

The pattern of child development is complex because it is the product of several processes: biological, cognitive, and socioemotional. Development also can be described in terms of periods.

Children are the legacy we leave for the time we will not live to see.

—Aristotle
Greek Philosopher, 4th Century B.C.

Biological, Cognitive, and Socioemotional Processes *Biological processes* produce changes in the child's body and underlie brain development, height and weight gains, motor skills, and puberty's hormonal changes. Genetic inheritance plays a large part.

Cognitive processes involve changes in the child's thinking, intelligence, and language. Cognitive developmental processes enable a growing child to memorize a poem, imagine how to solve a math problem, come up with a creative strategy, or speak meaningfully connected sentences.

Socioemotional processes involve changes in the child's relationships with other people, changes in emotion, and changes in personality. Parents' nurturance toward their child, a boy's aggressive attack on a peer, a girl's development of assertiveness, and an adolescent's feelings of joy after getting good grades all reflect socioemotional processes in development.

Periods of Development   For the purposes of organization and understanding, we commonly describe development in terms of periods. In the most widely used system of classification, the developmental periods are infancy, early childhood, middle and late childhood, adolescence, early adulthood, middle adulthood, and late adulthood.

Infancy extends from birth to 18 to 24 months. It is a time of extreme dependence on adults. Many activities are just beginning, such as language development, symbolic thought, sensorimotor coordination, and social learning.

Early childhood (sometimes called the "preschool years") extends from the end of infancy to about 5 years. During this period, children become more self-sufficient, develop school readiness skills (such as learning to follow instructions and identify letters), and spend many hours with peers. First grade typically marks the end of early childhood.

Middle and late childhood (sometimes called the "elementary school years") extends from about 6 to 11 years of age. Children master the fundamental skills of reading, writing, and math, achievement becomes a more central theme, and self-control increases. In this period, children interact more with the wider social world beyond their family.

development The pattern of biological, cognitive, and socioemotional processes that begins at conception and continues through the life span. Most development involves growth, although it also eventually involves decay (dying).

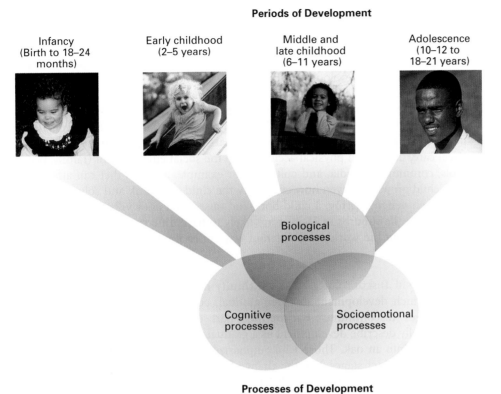

FIGURE 2.1 Periods and Processes of Development

Development moves through the infancy, early childhood, middle and late childhood, and adolescence periods. These periods of development are the result of biological, cognitive, and socioemotional processes.

Adolescence involves the transition from childhood to adulthood. It begins around ages 10 to 12 and ends around 18 to 21. Adolescence starts with rapid physical changes, including height and weight gains and development of sexual functions. Adolescents intensely pursue independence and seek their own identity. Their thought becomes more abstract, logical, and idealistic.

Adult developmental periods have been described, but we have confined our discussion to the periods most relevant for children's and adolescents' education (Birren, 2007). The child and adolescent periods of human development are shown in Figure 2.1 along with the processes of development (biological, cognitive, and socioemotional). The interplay of these processes produces the periods of human development.

Developmental Issues

Despite all of the knowledge that developmentalists have acquired, debate continues about the relative importance of factors that influence the developmental processes and about how the periods of development are related. The most important issues in the study of children's development include nature and nurture, continuity and discontinuity, and early and later experience.

Nature and Nurture   The **nature-nurture issue** involves the debate about whether development is primarily influenced by nature or by nurture (Buss, 2008; D'Onafrio, 2008). *Nature* refers to an organism's biological inheritance, *nurture* to its environmental experiences. Almost no one today argues that development can be explained by nature or nurture alone. But some ("nature" proponents) claim that the most important influence on development is biological inheritance, and others ("nurture" proponents) claim that environmental experiences are the most important influence.

According to the nature proponents, just as a sunflower grows in an orderly way—unless it is defeated by an unfriendly environment—so does a person. The

nature-nurture issue The issue regarding whether development is influenced primarily by nature (an organism's biological inheritance) or by nurture (an organism's environmental experiences). The "nature" proponents claim biological inheritance is the most important influence on development; the "nurture" proponents claim environmental experiences are the most important.

Children are busy becoming something they have not quite grasped yet, something which keeps changing.

Alastair Reid
American Poet, 20th Century

range of environments can be vast, but a genetic blueprint produces commonalities in growth and development. We walk before we talk, speak one word before two words, grow rapidly in infancy and less so in early childhood, and experience a rush of sexual hormones in puberty. Extreme environments—those that are psychologically barren or hostile—can stunt development, but nature proponents emphasize the influence of tendencies that are genetically wired into humans.

By contrast, other psychologists emphasize the importance of nurture, or environmental experiences, in development (Crane & Heaton, 2008; Parke & others, 2008). Experiences run the gamut from the individual's biological environment (nutrition, medical care, drugs, and physical accidents) to the social environment (family, peers, schools, community, media, and culture). For example, a child's diet can affect how tall the child grows and even how effectively the child can think and solve problems. Despite their genetic wiring, a child born and raised in a poor village in Bangladesh and a child in the suburbs of Denver are likely to have different skills, different ways of thinking about the world, and different ways of relating to people (Matsumoto & Juang, 2008).

Continuity and Discontinuity   The **continuity-discontinuity issue** focuses on the extent to which development involves gradual, cumulative change (continuity) or distinct stages (discontinuity). For the most part, developmentalists who emphasize nurture usually describe development as a gradual, continuous process, like the seedling's growth into an oak. Those who emphasize nature often describe development as a series of distinct stages, like the change from caterpillar to butterfly.

Consider continuity first. A child's first word, though seemingly an abrupt, discontinuous event, is actually the result of weeks and months of growth and practice. Puberty, another seemingly abrupt, discontinuous occurrence, is actually a gradual process occurring over several years.

Viewed in terms of discontinuity, each person is described as passing through a sequence of stages in which change is qualitatively rather than quantitatively different. A child moves at some point from not being able to think abstractly about the world to being able to. This is a qualitative, discontinuous change in development, not a quantitative, continuous change.

Early and Later Experience   The **early-later experience issue** focuses on the degree to which early experiences (especially in infancy) or later experiences are the key determinants of the child's development. That is, if infants experience harmful circumstances, can those experiences be overcome by later, positive ones? Or are the early experiences so critical—possibly because they are the infant's first, prototypical experiences—that they cannot be overridden by a later, better environment?

The early-later experience issue has a long history and continues to be hotly debated among developmentalists (Gottlieb, 2007; Posada, 2008). Some developmentalists argue that, unless infants experience warm, nurturing care during the first year or so of life, their development will never quite be optimal (Sroufe, 2007).

In contrast, later-experience advocates argue that children are malleable throughout development, and that later sensitive caregiving is just as important as earlier sensitive caregiving. A number of developmentalists who study adolescence, adult development, and aging stress that too little attention has been given to later experiences in development (Birren, 2007; Schaie, 2007). They accept that early experiences are important contributors to development but no more important than later experiences.

Evaluating the Developmental Issues   Most developmentalists recognize that it is unwise to take an extreme position on the issues of nature and nurture, continuity and discontinuity, and early and later experiences (Gottlieb, 2007; Rutter, 2007). Development is not all nature or all nurture, not all continuity or all discontinuity, and not all early or later experiences. However, there is still spirited debate about how

continuity-discontinuity issue The issue regarding whether development involves gradual, cumulative change (continuity) or distinct stages (discontinuity).

early-later experience issue The issue of the degree to which early experiences (especially infancy) or later experiences are the key determinants of the child's development.

strongly development is influenced by each of these factors (Sroufe, 2007).

Development and Education

In Chapter 1, we briefly described the importance of engaging in developmentally appropriate teaching practices (Henninger, 2009). Here we expand on this important topic and discuss the concept of splintered development.

Developmentally appropriate teaching takes place at a level that is neither too difficult and stressful nor too easy and boring for the child's developmental level (Morrison, 2009). One of the challenges of developmentally appropriate teaching is that you likely will have children with an age range of several years and a range of abilities and skills in the classes you teach (Horowitz & others, 2005). Competent teachers are aware of these developmental differences. Rather than characterizing students as "advanced," "average," and "slow," they recognize that their development and ability are complex, and children often do not display the same competence across different skills.

Splintered development refers to the circumstances in which development is uneven across domains (Horowitz & others, 2005). One student may have excellent math skills but poor writing skills. Within the area of language, another student may have excellent verbal language skills but not have good reading and writing skills. Yet another student may do well in science but lack social skills.

A special challenge are cognitively advanced students whose socioemotional development is at a level expected for much younger children. For example, a student may excel at science, math, and language but be immature emotionally. Such a child may not have any friends and be neglected or rejected by peers. This student will benefit considerably from having a teacher who helps him or her learn how to manage emotions and behave in more socially appropriate ways.

As we discuss development in this chapter and the next, keep in mind how the developmental changes we describe can help you understand the optimal level for teaching and learning. For example, it is not a good strategy to try to push children to read before they are developmentally ready—but when they are ready, reading materials should be presented at the appropriate level.

To what extent are early experiences, such as those involving relationships with parents, likely to be linked to later development, such as success in school?

Review, Reflect, and Practice

① Define development and explain the main processes, periods, and issues in development, as well as links between development and education.

REVIEW

- What is the nature of development?
- What three broad processes interact in a child's development? What general periods do children go through between birth and the end of adolescence?

(continued)

splintered development The circumstances in which development is uneven across domains.

Now that we have discussed some basic ideas about the nature of development, we will examine cognitive development at greater length. In examining different processes of development—biological, cognitive, and socioemotional—we indicated that these processes interact. In keeping with this theme, in our exploration of cognitive development, we will describe the physical development of the brain.

Review, Reflect, and Practice

REVIEW (CONTINUED)

- What are the main developmental issues? What conclusions can be reached about these issues?
- What implications does the concept of development have for the notion of "appropriate" learning?

REFLECT

- Give an example of how a cognitive process could influence a socioemotional process in the age of children you plan to teach. Then give an example of how a socioemotional process could influence a cognitive process in this age group.

PRAXIS™ PRACTICE

1. Mr. Huxtaby is giving a talk on development to a parent-teacher organization. In his talk, which of the following is he most likely to describe as not being an example of development?
   a. pubertal change
   b. improvement in memory
   c. change in friendship
   d. an inherited tendency to be shy
2. Ms. Halle teaches third grade. Which period of development is likely to be of most interest to her?
   a. infancy
   b. early childhood
   c. middle childhood and late childhood
   d. adolescence
3. Piaget argued that children progress through a series of cognitive development stages. In contrast, Skinner stressed that individuals simply learn more as time goes on. Which developmental issue is highlighted in their disagreement?
   a. continuity and discontinuity
   b. early and later experience
   c. nature and nurture
   d. biological and socioemotional development
4. Alexander's scores on standardized mathematics achievement tests are always very high—among the highest in the nation. In contrast, his scores on reading achievement tests indicate that he is about average. This is an example of
   a. developmentally appropriate teaching.
   b. early versus later development.
   c. nature versus nurture.
   d. splintered development.

Please see the answer key at the end of the book.

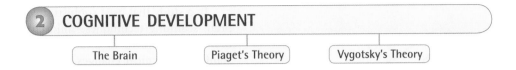

2 COGNITIVE DEVELOPMENT

| The Brain | Piaget's Theory | Vygotsky's Theory |

Twentieth-century American poet Marianne Moore said that the mind is "an enchanting thing." How this enchanting thing develops has intrigued many psychologists. First, we explore increasing interest in the development of the brain and then turn to two major cognitive theories—Piaget's and Vygotsky's.

The Brain

Until recently, little was known for certain about how the brain changes as children develop. Not long ago, scientists thought that genes determine how children's brains are "wired." Whatever brain children's heredity dealt them, they were essentially stuck with it. This view, however, turned out to be wrong. Instead, the brain has considerable *plasticity,* or the ability to change, and its development depends on experience (de Hann & Martinos, 2008; Nelson, 2008). What children do can change the development of their brain.

The old view of the brain in part reflected the fact that scientists did not have the technology to detect and map sensitive changes in the brain as it develops. Today, sophisticated brain-scanning techniques allow better detection of these changes (Casey, Jones, & Hare, 2008). Considerable progress is being made in charting developmental changes in the brain, although much is still unknown, and connections to children's education are difficult to make (Dubois & others, 2008; Fair & Schlagger, 2008).

Development of Neurons and Brain Regions   The number and size of the brain's nerve endings continue to grow at least until adolescence. Some of the brain's increase in size also is due to **myelination**, the process of encasing many cells in the brain with a myelin sheath (see Figure 2.2). This increases the speed at which information travels through the nervous system (Zalc, 2006). Myelination also may be involved in providing energy to neurons and in communication (Haynes & others, 2006). Myelination in the areas of the brain related to hand-eye coordination is not complete until about 4 years of age. Myelination in brain areas important in focusing attention is not complete until about 10 years of age (Tanner, 1978). The implications for teaching are that children will have difficulty focusing their attention and maintaining it for very long in early childhood, but their attention will improve as they move through the elementary school years. The most extensive increase in myelination, which occurs in the brain's frontal lobes, where reasoning and thinking occur, takes place during adolescence (Giedd, 2008; Shaw & others, 2008).

Another important aspect of the brain's development at the cellular level is the dramatic increase in connections between neurons (nerve cells). Synapses are tiny gaps between neurons where connections between neurons are made. Researchers have discovered an interesting aspect of synaptic connections. Nearly twice as many of these connections are made than ever will be used (Huttenlocher & Dabholkar, 1997; Huttenlocher & others, 1991). The connections that are used become strengthened and will survive, whereas the unused ones will be replaced by other pathways or disappear. That is, in the language of neuroscience, these connections will be "pruned." Figure 2.3 vividly shows the dramatic growth and later pruning of synapses in the visual, auditory, and prefrontal cortex areas of the brain. These areas are critical for higher-order cognitive functioning such as learning, memory, and reasoning. Notice that in the prefrontal cortex (where higher-level thinking and self-regulation take place) the peak of overproduction occurs at about 1 year of age. Notice also that it is not until middle to late adolescence that the adult density of the synapses is achieved.

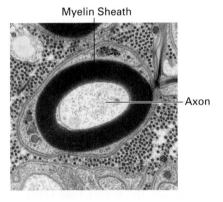

Myelin Sheath

Axon

FIGURE 2.2 A Myelinated Nerve Fiber

The myelin sheath, shown in brown, encases the axon (white), which is the part of the neuron (nerve cell) that transmits information away from the cell body. This image was produced by an electron microscope that magnified the nerve fiber 12,000 times. *What role does myelination play in the brain's development and children's cognition?*

myelination The process of encasing many cells in the brain with a myelin sheath, increasing the speed at which information travels through the nervous system.

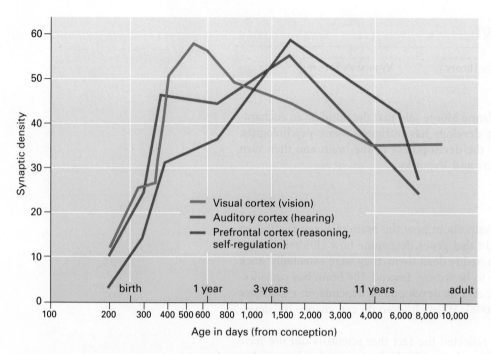

FIGURE 2.3 Synaptic Density in the Human Brain from Infancy to Adulthood

The graph shows the dramatic increase and then pruning of synaptic density for three regions of the brain: visual cortex, auditory cortex, and prefrontal cortex. Synaptic density is believed to be an important indication of the extent of connectivity between neurons.

In a study that used sophisticated brain-scanning techniques, children's brains were shown to undergo substantial anatomical changes between the ages of 3 and 15 (Thompson & others, 2000). By repeatedly obtaining brain scans of the same children for up to four years, researchers found that children's brains experience rapid, distinct growth spurts. The amount of brain material in some areas can nearly double within a year, followed by a drastic loss of tissue as unneeded cells are purged and the brain continues to reorganize itself. In this study, the overall size of the brain did not change from 3 to 15 years of age. However, rapid growth in the frontal lobes, especially areas related to attention, occurred from 3 to 6 years of age. Figure 2.4 shows the location of the brain's four lobes. Rapid growth in the temporal lobes (language processing) and parietal lobes (spatial location) occurred from age 6 through puberty.

Brain Development in Middle and Late Childhood The development of brain-imaging techniques, such as magnetic resonance imaging (MRI), has led to an increase in research on changes in the brain during middle and late childhood, and how these brain changes are linked to improvements in cognitive development (Toga, Thompson, & Sowell, 2006). Total brain volume stabilizes by the end of middle and late childhood, but significant changes in various structures and regions of the brain continue to occur. In particular, the brain pathways and circuitry involving the prefrontal cortex, the highest level in the brain, continue to increase in middle and late childhood (Durston & Casey, 2006). These advances in the prefrontal cortex are linked to children's improved attention, reasoning, and cognitive control (Anderson, Jacobs, & Harvey, 2005).

Changes also occur in the thickness of the cerebral cortex (cortical thickness) in middle and late childhood (Toga, Thompson, & Sowell, 2006). One study used brain scans to assess cortical thickness in 5- to 11-year-old children (Sowell & others, 2004). Cortical thickening across a two-year time period was observed in the temporal and frontal lobe areas that function in language, which may reflect improvements in language abilities such as reading.

FIGURE 2.4 The Brain's Four Lobes

Shown here are the locations of the brain's four lobes: frontal, occipital, temporal, and parietal.

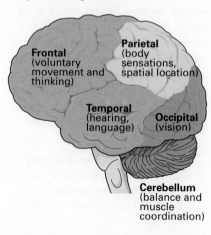

As children develop, activation of some brain areas increases while others decrease (Dowker, 2006). One shift in activation that occurs as children develop is from diffuse, larger areas to more focal, smaller areas (Turkeltaub & others, 2003). This shift is characterized by synaptic pruning in which areas of the brain not being used lose synaptic connections and those being used show an increase in connections. In a recent study, researchers found less diffusion and more focal activation in the prefrontal cortex from 7 to 30 years of age (Durston & others, 2006). The activation change was accompanied by increased efficiency in cognitive performance, especially in *cognitive control*, which involves flexible and effective control in a number of areas. These areas include controlling attention, reducing interfering thoughts, inhibiting motor actions, and being flexible in switching between competing choices (Munkata, 2006).

Brain Development in Adolescence   Along with the rest of the body, the brain is changing during adolescence, but the study of adolescent brain development is in its infancy. As advances in technology take place, significant strides will also likely be made in charting developmental changes in the adolescent brain (Casey, Jones, & Hare, 2008; McAnarney, 2008). What do we know now?

Using functional MRI (fMRI) brain scans, scientists have recently discovered that adolescents' brains undergo significant structural changes (Giedd & others, 2008). The **corpus callosum**, where fibers connect the brain's left and right hemispheres, thickens in adolescence, and this improves adolescents' ability to process information (Giedd & others, 2006). We described advances in the development of the **prefrontal cortex**—the highest level of the frontal lobes involved in reasoning, decision making, and self-control—earlier in this section. However, the prefrontal cortex doesn't finish maturing until the emerging adult years, approximately 18 to 25 years of age, or later, but the **amygdala**—the seat of emotions such as anger—matures earlier than the prefrontal cortex. Figure 2.5 shows the locations of the corpus callosum, prefrontal cortex, and amygdala. A recent study of 137 early adolescents revealed a positive link between the volume of the amygdala and the duration of adolescents' aggressive behavior during interactions with parents (Whittle & others, 2008).

Leading researcher Charles Nelson (2003; Nelson, Thomas, & de Haan, 2006) points out that although adolescents are capable of very strong emotions, their prefrontal cortex hasn't adequately developed to the point at which they can control these passions. This means that the brain region for putting the brakes on risky, impulsive behavior is still under construction during adolescence (Giedd, 2008). Or consider this interpretation of the development of emotion and cognition in adolescence: "early activation of strong 'turbo-charged' feelings with a relatively unskilled set of 'driving skills' or cognitive abilities to modulate strong emotions and motivations" (Dahl, 2004, p. 18). This developmental disjunction may account for increased risk taking and other problems in adolescence (Steinberg, 2008). "Some things just take time to develop and mature judgment is probably one of them" (Steinberg, 2004, p. 56).

Lateralization   The cerebral cortex (the highest level of the brain) is divided into two halves, or hemispheres (see Figure 2.6). **Lateralization** is the specialization of functions in each hemisphere of the brain (Bianco & others, 2008; Spironelli & Angrilli, 2008). In individuals with an intact brain, there is a specialization of function in some areas:

1. *Verbal processing.* The most extensive research on the brain's two hemispheres involves language. In most individuals, speech and grammar are localized to the left hemisphere. This does not mean, however, that all language processing is carried out in the brain's left hemisphere. For example, understanding such aspects of language as appropriate use of language in different contexts, evaluation of the emotional expressiveness of language, metaphor, and much of humor involves the right hemisphere (Imada & others, 2007). Also, when children lose much of their left hemisphere because of an accident, surgery for epilepsy, or other reasons, the right hemisphere in many cases can reconfigure itself for increased language processing (Liegeois & others, 2008).

2. *Nonverbal processing.* The right hemisphere is usually more dominant in processing nonverbal information such as spatial perception, visual recognition,

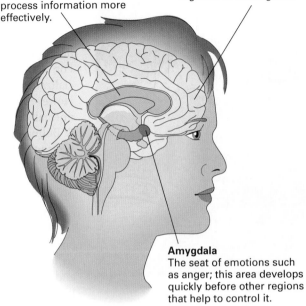

Corpus callosum
These nerve fibers connect the brain's two hemispheres; they thicken in adolescence to process information more effectively.

Prefrontal cortex
This "judgment" region reins in intense emotions but doesn't finish developing until at least age 20.

Amygdala
The seat of emotions such as anger; this area develops quickly before other regions that help to control it.

FIGURE 2.5 Changes in the Adolescent Brain

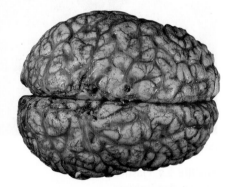

FIGURE 2.6 The Human Brain's Hemispheres

The two halves (hemispheres) of the human brain are clearly seen in this photograph.

corpus callosum Where fibers connect the brain's left and right hemispheres.

prefrontal cortex The highest level in the frontal lobes that is involved in reasoning, decision making, and self-control.

amygdala The seat of emotions in the brain.

lateralization The specialization of functions in each hemisphere of the brain.

(a)

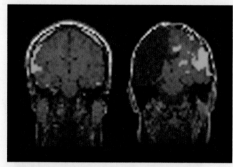

(b)

FIGURE 2.7 Plasticity in the Brain's Hemispheres

(*a*) Michael Rehbein at 14 years of age. (*b*) Michael's right hemisphere (*right*) has reorganized to take over the language functions normally carried out by corresponding areas in the left hemisphere of an intact brain (*left*). However, the right hemisphere is not as efficient as the left, and more areas of the brain are recruited to process speech.

and emotion (Demaree & others, 2005). For example, for most children the right hemisphere is mainly at work when they process information about people's faces (O'Toole, 2007). The right hemisphere also may be more involved when children express emotions or recognize others' emotions.

Because of the differences in functioning of the brain's two hemispheres, people commonly use the phrases "left-brained" and "right-brained" to say which hemisphere is dominant. Unfortunately, much of this talk is seriously exaggerated. For example, laypeople and the media commonly exaggerate hemispheric specialization by claiming that the left brain is logical and the right brain is creative. However, most complex functioning—such as logical and creative thinking—in normal people involves communication between both sides of the brain (Smith & Bulman-Fleming, 2005). Scientists who study the brain are typically very cautious with terms such as *left-brained* and *right-brained* because the brain is more complex than those terms suggest (Knect & others, 2001).

Plasticity   As we have seen, the brain has plasticity, and its development depends on context (Nelson, 2008; Reeb & others, 2008). What children do can change the development of their brain. Experts on learning argue that just as an enriched environment led to more advanced brain development in rats and other animals, so too can enriched environments produce improvements in brain functioning and learning (Bransford & others, 2006). By engaging students in optimal learning environments, you can stimulate the development of their brain (Fusaro & Nelson, 2009).

The remarkable case of Michael Rehbein illustrates the brain's plasticity. When Michael was 4½, he began to experience uncontrollable seizures—as many as 400 a day. Doctors said that the only solution was to remove the left hemisphere of his brain, where the seizures were occurring. Michael had his first major surgery at age 7 and another at age 10. Although recovery was slow, his right hemisphere began to reorganize and eventually took over functions, such as speech, that normally occur in the brain's left hemisphere (see Figure 2.7). Individuals like Michael are living proof of the growing brain's remarkable plasticity and ability to adapt and recover from a loss of brain tissue.

The Brain and Children's Education   What types of environments are the best for stimulating children's brains, and how much change can be expected? What do the new findings in "brain science" tell us? Unfortunately, too often statements about the implications of brain science for children's education have been speculative at best and often far removed from what neuroscientists know about the brain (Caviness, 2008; Fischer & Immordino-Yang, 2008). We don't have to look any further than the hype about "left-brained" individuals being more logical and "right-brained" individuals being more creative to see that links between neuroscience and brain education are incorrectly made (Sousa, 1995). Two leading experts on the development of the brain recently concluded that (Fischer & Immordino-Yang, 2008):

most of what is called "brain-based education" today has no grounding at all in brain or cognitive science. The only way that brains are involved in brain-based education is that the students have brains. . . . However, the good news is that the first glimmers of educational neuroscientific research are highly promising. For example, early research on reading difficulties such as dyslexia uses brain imaging to test how students learn to read and what methods can improve their learning (Szucs & Goswami, 2008). . . . Yet there will be no quick fix in educational neuroscience. Building a new field takes time.

Another commonly promoted link between neuroscience and brain education is that there is a critical, or sensitive, period—a biological window of opportunity—when learning is easier, more effective, and more easily retained than later in development. However, some experts on the development of the brain and learning conclude that the critical period view is exaggerated (Blakemore & Choudhury, 2006). One leading neuroscientist even told educators that although children's brains acquire a great deal of information during the early years, most learning likely takes place after synaptic formation stabilizes, which is after the age of 10 (Goldman-Rakic, 1996).

A major issue involving the development of the brain is which comes first, biological changes in the brain or experiences that stimulate these changes? (Lerner, Boyd, & Du, 2008). Consider a recent study in which the prefrontal cortex thickened and more brain connections formed when adolescents resisted peer pressure (Paus & others, 2008). Scientists have yet to determine whether the brain changes come first or whether the brain changes are the result of experiences with peers, parents, and others. Once again, we encounter the nature/nurture issue that is so prominent in examining children's and adolescents' development.

Given all of the hype and hyperbole about brain education in the media, what can we conclude about the current state of knowledge in applying the rapidly increasing research on the brain's development to education? Based on the current state of knowledge:

- *Both early and later experiences, including educational experiences, are very important in the brain's development.* Significant changes occur at the cellular and structural level in the brain through adolescence (Giedd, 2008).

- *Synaptic connections between neurons can change dramatically as a consequence of the learning experiences children and adolescents have* (Fusaro & Nelson, 2009). Connections between neurons that are used when children focus their attention, remember, and think as they are reading, writing, and doing math are strengthened; those that aren't used are replaced by other pathways or disappear.

- *Development at the highest level of the brain—the prefrontal cortex, where such important cognitive processes as thinking, reasoning, and decision making primarily occur—continues at least through the adolescent years* (Casey, Getz, & Galvan, 2008; Steinberg, 2008). This development in the prefrontal cortex moves from being more diffuse to more focal and involves increased efficiency of processing information (Durston & others, 2006). As activation in the prefrontal cortex becomes more focused, cognitive control increases. This is exemplified in children being able to focus their attention more effectively and ignore distractions while they are learning as they become older.

What are some applications of research on the brain's development to children's and adolescents' education?

- *Despite the increased focal activation of the prefrontal cortex as children grow older, changes in the brain during adolescence present a challenge to increased cognitive control.* In adolescence, the earlier maturation of the amygdala, which is involved in processing of emotions, and the more drawn-out development of the prefrontal cortex, provides an explanation of the difficulty adolescents have in controlling their emotions and their tendency to engage in risk taking (Steinberg, 2007).

- *Brain functioning occurs along specific pathways and involves integration of function.* According to leading experts Kurt Fischer and Mary Helen Immordino-Yang (2008),

  One of the lessons of educational neuroscience, even at this early point in its development, is that children learn along specific pathways, but they do not act or think in compartments. . . . On the one hand, they develop their learning along specific pathways defined by particular content, such as mathematics or history, but on the other hand they make connections between those pathways.

Reading is an excellent example of how brain functioning occurs along specific pathways and is integrated. Consider a child who is asked by a teacher to read aloud to the class. Input from the child's eyes is transmitted to the child's brain, then passed through many brain systems, which translate the patterns of black and white into codes for letters, words, and associations. The output occurs in the form of messages to the child's lips and tongue. The child's own gift of speech is possible because brain systems are organized in ways that permit language processing.

These conclusions suggest that education throughout the childhood and adolescent years can benefit children's and adolescents' learning and cognitive development (Fusaro & Nelson, 2009). Currently, there also are many research studies being conducted on the brain's role in a wide range of cognitive processes and educational activities, including memory, learning disabilities, attention deficit hyperactivity disorder, and others. Where appropriate throughout the rest of the book, we will describe research on the development of the brain and children's education.

Piaget's Theory

Poet Noah Perry once asked, "Who knows the thoughts of a child?" More than anyone, the famous Swiss psychologist Jean Piaget (1896–1980) knew.

Cognitive Processes   What processes do children use as they construct their knowledge of the world? Piaget stressed that these processes are especially important in this regard: schemas, assimilation and accommodation, organization, and equilibration.

Schemas   Piaget (1954) said that as the child seeks to construct an understanding of the world, the developing brain creates **schemas**. These are actions or mental representations that organize knowledge. In Piaget's theory, behavioral schemas (physical activities) characterize infancy, and mental schemas (cognitive activities) develop in childhood (Lamb, Bornstein, & Teti, 2002). A baby's schemas are structured by simple actions that can be performed on objects, such as sucking, looking, and grasping. Older children have schemas that include strategies and plans for solving problems. For example, a 6-year-old might have a schema that involves the strategy of classifying objects by size, shape, or color. By the time we have reached adulthood, we have constructed an enormous number of diverse schemas, ranging from how to drive a car, to how to balance a budget, to the concept of fairness.

Assimilation and Accommodation   To explain how children use and adapt their schemas, Piaget offered two concepts: assimilation and accommodation. **Assimilation** occurs when children incorporate new information into their existing schemas. **Accommodation** occurs when children adjust their schemas to fit new information and experiences.

Consider an 8-year-old girl who is given a hammer and nail to hang a picture on the wall. She has never used a hammer, but from observing others do this she realizes that a hammer is an object to be held, that it is swung by the handle to hit the nail, and that it usually is swung a number of times. Recognizing each of these things, she fits her behavior into this schema she already has (assimilation). But the hammer is heavy, so she holds it near the top. She swings too hard and the nail bends, so she adjusts the pressure of her strikes. These adjustments reflect her ability to slightly alter her conception of the world (accommodation). Just as both assimilation and accommodation are required in this example, so are they required in many of the child's thinking challenges (see Figure 2.8).

schemas In Piaget's theory, actions or mental representations that organize knowledge.

assimilation Piagetian concept of the incorporation of new information into existing knowledge (schemas).

accommodation Piagetian concept of adjusting schemas to fit new information and experiences.

Organization   To make sense out of their world, said Piaget, children cognitively organize their experiences. **Organization** in Piaget's theory is the grouping of isolated behaviors and thoughts into a higher-order system. Continual refinement of this organization is an inherent part of development. A boy with only a vague idea about how to use a hammer also may have a vague idea about how to use other tools. After learning how to use each one, he relates these uses, organizing his knowledge.

Equilibration and Stages of Development   **Equilibration** is a mechanism that Piaget proposed to explain how children shift from one stage of thought to the next. The shift occurs as children experience cognitive conflict, or disequilibrium, in trying to understand the world. Eventually, they resolve the conflict and reach a balance, or equilibrium, of thought. Piaget pointed out that there is considerable movement between states of cognitive equilibrium and disequilibrium as assimilation and accommodation work in concert to produce cognitive change. For example, if a child believes that the amount of a liquid changes simply because the liquid is poured into a container with a different shape—

Assimilation occurs when people incorporate new information into their existing schematic knowledge. *How might this 8-year-old girl first attempt to use the hammer and nail, based on her preexisting schematic knowledge about these objects?*

Accommodation occurs when people adjust their knowledge schemas to new information. *How might the girl adjust her schemas regarding hammers and nails during her successful effort to hang the picture?*

FIGURE 2.8 Assimilation and Accommodation

for instance, from a container that is short and wide into a container that is tall and narrow—she might be puzzled by such issues as where the "extra" liquid came from and whether there is actually more liquid to drink. The child will eventually resolve these puzzles as her thought becomes more advanced. In the everyday world, the child is constantly faced with such counterexamples and inconsistencies.

Assimilation and accommodation always take the child to a higher ground. For Piaget, the motivation for change is an internal search for equilibrium. As old schemas are adjusted and new schemas are developed, the child organizes and reorganizes the old and new schemas. Eventually, the organization is fundamentally different from the old organization; it is a new way of thinking.

Thus, the result of these processes, according to Piaget, is that individuals go through four stages of development. A different way of understanding the world makes one stage more advanced than another. Cognition is *qualitatively* different in one stage compared with another. In other words, the way children reason at one stage is different from the way they reason at another stage.

Piagetian Stages   Each of Piaget's stages is age-related and consists of distinct ways of thinking. Piaget proposed four stages of cognitive development: sensorimotor, preoperational, concrete operational, and formal operational (see Figure 2.9).

The Sensorimotor Stage   The **sensorimotor stage**, which lasts from birth to about 2 years of age, is the first Piagetian stage. In this stage, infants construct an understanding of the world by coordinating their sensory experiences (such as seeing and hearing) with their motor actions (reaching, touching)—hence the term sensorimotor. At the beginning of this stage, infants show little more than reflexive patterns to adapt to the world. By the end of the stage, they display far more complex sensorimotor patterns.

The Preoperational Stage   The **preoperational stage** is the second Piagetian stage. Lasting approximately from about 2 to 7 years of age, it is more symbolic than sensorimotor thought but does not involve operational thought. However, it is egocentric and intuitive rather than logical.

organization Piaget's concept of grouping isolated behaviors into a higher-order, more smoothly functioning cognitive system; the grouping or arranging of items into categories.

equilibration A mechanism that Piaget proposed to explain how children shift from one stage of thought to the next. The shift occurs as children experience cognitive conflict, or disequilibrium, in trying to understand the world. Eventually, they resolve the conflict and reach a balance, or equilibrium, of thought.

sensorimotor stage The first Piagetian stage, lasting from birth to about 2 years of age, in which infants construct an understanding of the world by coordinating sensory experiences with motor actions.

preoperational stage The second Piagetian stage, lasting from about 2 to 7 years of age; symbolic thought increase but operational thought is not yet present.

Sensorimotor Stage	Preoperational Stage	Concrete Operational Stage	Formal Operational Stage
The infant constructs an understanding of the world by coordinating sensory experiences with physical actions. An infant progresses from reflexive, instinctual action at birth to the beginning of symbolic thought toward the end of the stage.	The child begins to represent the world with words and images. These words and images reflect increased symbolic thinking and go beyond the connection of sensory information and physical action.	The child can now reason logically about concrete events and classify objects into different sets.	The adolescent reasons in more abstract, idealistic, and logical ways.
Birth to 2 Years of Age	*2 to 7 Years of Age*	*7 to 11 Years of Age*	*11 to 15 Years of Age Through Adulthood*

FIGURE 2.9 Piaget's Four Stages of Cognitive Development

FIGURE 2.10 Developmental Changes in Children's Drawings

(a) A 3½-year-old's symbolic drawing. Halfway into this drawing, the 3½-year-old artist said it was "a pelican kissing a seal." (b) This 11-year-old's drawing is neater and more realistic but also less inventive.

symbolic function substage The first substage of preoperational thought, occurring between about 2 to 4 years of age; the ability to represent an object not present develops and symbolic thinking increases; egocentrism is present.

intuitive thought substage The second substage of preoperational thought, lasting from about 4 to 7 years of age. Children begin to use primitive reasoning and want to know the answer to all sorts of questions. They seem so sure about their knowledge in this substage but are unaware of how they know what they know.

Preoperational thought can be subdivided into two substages: symbolic function and intuitive thought. The **symbolic function substage** occurs roughly between 2 and 4 years of age. In this substage, the young child gains the ability to represent mentally an object that is not present. This stretches the child's mental world to new dimensions. Expanded use of language and the emergence of pretend play are other examples of an increase in symbolic thought during this early childhood substage. Young children begin to use scribbled designs to represent people, houses, cars, clouds, and many other aspects of the world. Possibly because young children are not very concerned about reality, their drawings are fanciful and inventive (Winner, 1986). One 3½-year-old looked at the scribble he had just drawn and described it as a pelican kissing a seal (see Figure 2.10a). In the elementary school years, children's drawings become more realistic, neat, and precise (see Figure 2.10b).

Even though young children make distinctive progress in this substage, their preoperational thought still has an important limitation: egocentrism. *Egocentrism* is the inability to distinguish between one's own perspective and someone else's perspective. Piaget and Barbel Inhelder (1969) initially studied young children's egocentrism by devising the three mountains task (see Figure 2.11). The child walks around the model of the mountains and becomes familiar with what the mountains look like from different perspectives. The child also can see that there are different objects on the mountains. The child then is seated on one side of the table on which the mountains are placed. The experimenter moves a doll to different locations around the table. At each location, the child is asked to select from a series of photos the one that most accurately reflects the view the doll is seeing. Children in the preoperational stage often pick the view that reflects where they are sitting rather than the doll's view.

What further cognitive changes take place in the preoperational stage? The **intuitive thought substage** is the second substage of preoperational thought, starting at about 4 years of age and lasting until about 7 years of age. At this substage, children begin to use primitive reasoning and want to know the answers to all sorts of questions. Piaget called this substage "intuitive" because the children seem so sure about

Model of Mountains

   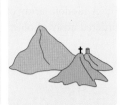

A
Child seated here

Photo 1 (View from A)   Photo 2 (View from B)   Photo 3 (View from C)   Photo 4 (View from D)

FIGURE 2.11 The Three Mountains Task

The mountain model on the far left shows the child's perspective from view A, where he or she is sitting. The four squares represent photos showing the mountains from four different viewpoints of the model—A, B, C, and D. The experimenter asks the child to identity the photo in which the mountains look as they would from position B. To identity the photo correctly, the child has to take the perspective of a person sitting at spot B. Invariably, a child who thinks in a preoperational way cannot perform this task. When asked what a view of the mountains looks like from position B, the child selects Photo 1, taken from location A (the child's own view at the time) instead of Photo 2, the correct view.

their knowledge and understanding yet are unaware of how they know what they know. That is, they say they know something but know it without the use of rational thinking.

An example of young children's limitation in reasoning ability is the difficulty they have putting things into correct categories. Look at the collection of objects in Figure 2.12a. You would probably respond to the direction "Put the things together that you believe belong together" by grouping the objects by size and shape. Your sorting might look something like that shown in Figure 2.12b. Faced with a similar collection of objects that can be sorted on the basis of two or more properties, preoperational children seldom are capable of using these properties consistently to sort the objects into appropriate groupings.

Many of these preoperational examples show a characteristic of thought called **centration**, which involves focusing (or centering) attention on one characteristic to the exclusion of all others. Centration is most clearly present in preoperational children's lack of **conservation**, the idea that some characteristic of an object stays the same even though the object might change in appearance. For example, to adults it is obvious that a certain amount of liquid stays the same regardless of a container's shape. But this is not obvious at all to young children. Rather, they are struck by the height of the liquid in the container. In this type of conservation task (Piaget's most famous), a child is presented with two identical beakers, each filled to the same level with liquid (see Figure 2.13). The child is asked if the beakers have the same amount of liquid. The child usually says yes. Then the liquid from one beaker is poured into a third beaker, which is taller and thinner. The child now is asked if the amount of liquid in the tall, thin beaker is equal to the liquid that remains in the second original beaker. Children younger than 7 or 8 usually say no. They justify their answer by referring to the differing height or width of the beakers. Older children usually answer yes. They justify their answers appropriately: If you poured the liquid back, the amount would still be the same.

In Piaget's view, failing the conservation of liquid task indicates that the child is at the preoperational stage of thinking. Passing the test suggests the child is at the concrete operational stage of thinking.

According to Piaget, preoperational children also cannot perform what he called *operations*. In Piaget's theory, operations are mental representations that are reversible.

centration Focusing, or centering, attention on one characteristic to the exclusion of all others; characteristic of preoperational thinking.

conservation The idea that some characteristic of an object stays the same even though the object might change in appearance; a cognitive ability that develops in the concrete operational stage, according to Piaget.

FIGURE 2.12 Arrays

(*a*) A random array of objects. (*b*) An ordered array of objects.

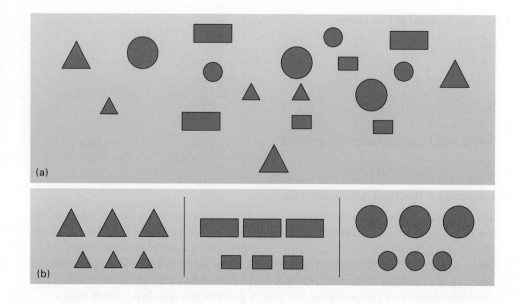

"I still don't have all the answers, but I'm beginning to ask the right questions."

© The New Yorker Collection 1989 Lee Lorenz from cartoonbank.com. All Rights Reserved.

FIGURE 2.13 Piaget's Conservation Task

The beaker test is a well-known Piagetian test to determine whether a child can think operationally—that is, can mentally reverse actions and show conservation of the substance. (*a*) Two identical beakers are presented to the child. Then, the experimenter pours the liquid from B into C, which is taller and thinner than A or B. (*b*) The child is asked if these beakers (A and C) have the same amount of liquid. The preoperational child says "no." When asked to point to the beaker that has more liquid, the preoperational child points to the tall, thin beaker.

As in the beaker task, preschool children have difficulty understanding that reversing an action brings about the original conditions from which the action began. These two examples should further help you understand Piaget's concepts of operations. A young child might know that 4 + 2 = 6 but not understand that the reverse, 6 − 2 = 4, is true. Or let's say a preschooler walks to his friend's house each day but always gets a ride home. If asked to walk home from his friend's house, he probably would reply that he didn't know the way because he never had walked home before.

Some developmentalists do not believe Piaget was entirely correct in his estimate of when conservation skills emerge. For example, Rochel Gelman (1969) trained preschool children to attend to relevant aspects of the conservation task. This improved their conservation skills.

Further, children show considerable variation in attaining conservation skills. Researchers have found that 50 percent of children develop conservation of mass at 6 to 9 years of age, 50 percent demonstrate conservation of length at 4 to 9 years of age, 50 percent show conservation of area at 7 to 9 years of age, and 50 percent of children don't attain conservation of weight until 8 to 10 years of age (Horowitz & others, 2005; Sroufe & others, 1992).

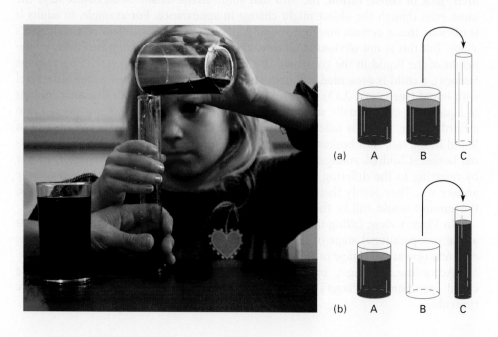

BEST PRACTICES
Strategies for Working with Preoperational Thinkers

1. *Ask children to make comparisons.* These might involve such concepts as bigger, taller, wider, heavier, and longer.

2. *Give children experience in ordering operations.* For example, have children line up in rows from tall to short and vice versa. Bring in various examples of animal and plant life cycles, such as several photographs of butterfly development or the sprouting of beans or kernels of corn.

3. *Have children draw scenes with perspective.* Encourage them to make the objects in their drawings appear to be at the same location as in the scene they are viewing. For example, if they see a horse at the end of a field,

they should place the horse in the same location in the drawing.

4. *Construct an inclined plane or a hill.* Let children roll marbles of various sizes down the plane. Ask them to compare how quickly the different-size marbles reach the bottom. This should help them understand the concept of speed.

5. *Ask children to justify their answers when they draw conclusions.* For example, when they say that pouring a liquid from a short, wide container into a tall, thin container makes the liquid change in volume, ask, "Why do you think so?" or "How could you prove this to one of your friends?"

Yet another characteristic of preoperational children is that they ask a lot of questions. The barrage begins around age 3. By about 5, they have just about exhausted the adults around them with "Why?" "Why" questions signal the emergence of the child's interest in figuring out why things are the way they are. Following is a sampling of 4- to 6-year-olds' questions (Elkind, 1976):

"What makes you grow up?"
"Who was the mother when everybody was a baby?"
"Why do leaves fall?"
"Why does the sun shine?"

The Concrete Operational Stage   The **concrete operational stage**, the third Piagetian stage of cognitive development, lasts from about 7 to about 11 years of age. Concrete operational thought involves using operations. Logical reasoning replaces intuitive reasoning, but only in concrete situations. Classification skills are present, but abstract problems go unsolved.

A concrete operation is a reversible mental action pertaining to real, concrete objects. Concrete operations allow the child to coordinate several characteristics rather than focus on a single property of an object. At the concrete operational level, children can do mentally what they previously could do only physically, and they can reverse concrete operations.

An important concrete operation is classifying or dividing things into different sets or subsets and considering their interrelationships. Reasoning about a family tree of four generations reveals a child's concrete operational skills (Furth & Wachs, 1975). The family tree shown in Figure 2.14 suggests that the grandfather (A) has three children (B, C, and D), each of whom has two children (E through J), and one of these children (J) has three children (K, L, and M). Concrete operational thinkers understand the classification. For example, they can reason that person J can at the same time be father, brother, and grandson. A preoperational thinker cannot.

Some Piagetian tasks require children to reason about relations between classes. One such task is **seriation**, the concrete operation that involves ordering stimuli along some quantitative dimension (such as length). To see if students can serialize, a teacher might place eight sticks of different lengths in a haphazard way on a table.

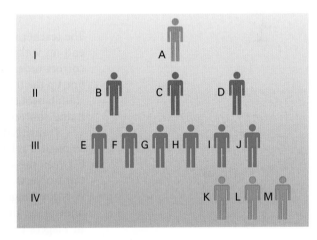

FIGURE 2.14 Classification

Classification is an important ability in concrete operational thought. When shown a family tree of four generations (I to IV), the preoperational child has trouble classifying the members of the four generations; the concrete operational child can classify the members vertically, horizontally, and obliquely (up and down and across).

> **concrete operational stage** Piaget's third cognitive developmental stage, lasting from about 7 to 11 years of age. At this stage, the child thinks operationally, and logical reasoning replaces intuitive thought but only in concrete situations; classification skills are present, but abstract problems present difficulties.

> **seriation** A concrete operation that involves ordering stimuli along some quantitative dimension.

BEST PRACTICES
Strategies for Working with Concrete Operational Thinkers

1. *Encourage students to discover concepts and principles.* Ask relevant questions about what is being studied to help them focus on some aspect of their learning. Refrain from telling students the answers to their questions outright. Try to get them to reach the answers through their own thinking.

2. *Involve children in operational tasks.* These include adding, subtracting, multiplying, dividing, ordering, seriating, and reversing. Use concrete materials for these tasks, possibly introducing math symbols later.

3. *Plan activities in which students practice the concept of ascending and descending classification hierarchies.* Have students list the following in order of size (such as largest to smallest): city of Atlanta, state of Georgia,

country of United States, Western Hemisphere, and planet Earth.

4. *Include activities that require conservation of area, weight, and displaced volume.* Realize that there is considerable variation in children's attainment of conservation across different domains.

5. *Create activities in which children order and reverse order.* Many third-graders have difficulty in reversing order, such as going from tall to short rather than short to tall.

6. *Continue to ask students to justify their answers when they solve problems.* Help them to check the validity and accuracy of their conclusions.

The teacher then asks the student to order the sticks by length. Many young children end up with two or three small groups of "big" sticks or "little" sticks rather than a correct ordering of all eight sticks. Another mistaken strategy they use is to evenly line up the tops of the sticks but ignore the bottoms. The concrete operational thinker simultaneously understands that each stick must be longer than the one that precedes it and shorter than the one that follows it.

Transitivity involves the ability to reason about and logically combine relationships. If a relation holds between a first object and a second object, and also holds between the second object and a third object, then it also holds between the first and third objects. For example, consider three sticks (A, B, and C) of differing lengths. A is the longest, B is intermediate in length, and C is the shortest. Does the child understand that if A is longer than B, and B is longer than C, then A is longer than C? In Piaget's theory, concrete operational thinkers do; preoperational thinkers do not.

The Formal Operational Stage The **formal operational stage**, which emerges at about 11 to 15 years of age, is Piaget's fourth and final cognitive stage. At this stage, individuals move beyond reasoning only about concrete experiences and think in more abstract, idealistic, and logical ways.

The abstract quality of formal operational thinking is evident in verbal problem solving. The concrete operational thinker needs to see the concrete elements A, B, and C to make the logical inference that if A = B and B = C, then A = C. In contrast, the formal operational thinker can solve this problem when it is verbally presented.

Accompanying the abstract nature of formal operational thought are the abilities to idealize and imagine possibilities. At this stage, adolescents engage in extended speculation about the ideal qualities they desire in themselves and others. These idealistic thoughts can merge into fantasy. Many adolescents become impatient with their newfound ideals and the problems of how to live them out.

At the same time as adolescents are thinking more abstractly and idealistically, they also are beginning to think more logically. As formal operational thinkers, they think more like scientists. They devise plans to solve problems and systematically test solutions. Piaget's term **hypothetical-deductive reasoning** embodies the concept that adolescents can develop hypotheses (best hunches) about ways to solve problems and systematically reach a conclusion. Formal operational thinkers test their hypotheses with judiciously chosen questions and tests. In contrast, concrete operational think-

transitivity The ability to reason and logically combine relationships.

formal operational stage Piaget's fourth cognitive developmental stage, which emerges between about 11 and 15 years of age; thought is more abstract, idealistic, and logical in this stage.

hypothetical–deductive reasoning Piaget's formal operational concept that adolescents can develop hypotheses to solve problems and systematically reach (deduce) a conclusion.

BEST PRACTICES
Strategies for Working with Formal Operational Thinkers

1. *Realize that many adolescents are not full-fledged formal operational thinkers.* Thus, many of the teaching strategies discussed earlier regarding the education of concrete operational thinkers still apply to many young adolescents. As discussed next, Jerri Hall, a math teacher at Miller Magnet High School, in Georgia, emphasizes that when a curriculum is too formal and too abstract, it will go over students' heads.

THROUGH THE EYES OF TEACHERS
Piaget as a Guide

I use Piaget's developmental theory as a guide in helping children learn math. In the sixth, seventh, and eighth grades, children are moving from the concrete to the abstract stage in their cognitive processes; therefore, when I teach, I try to use different methods to aid my students to understand a concept. For example, I use fraction circles to help students understand how to add, subtract, multiply, and divide fractions, and the students are allowed to use these until they become proficient with the algorithms. I try to incorporate hands-on experiences in which students discover the rules themselves, rather than just teaching the methods and having the stu-

dents practice them with drill. It is extremely important for students to understand the why behind a mathematical rule so they can better understand the concept.

2. *Propose a problem and invite students to form hypotheses about how to solve it.* For example, a teacher might say, "Imagine that a girl has no friends. What should she do?"

3. *Present a problem and suggest several ways it might be approached.* Then ask questions that stimulate students to evaluate the approaches. For example, describe several ways to investigate a robbery, and ask students to evaluate which is best.

4. *Develop projects and investigations for students to carry out.* Periodically ask them how they are going about collecting and interpreting the data.

5. *Encourage students to create hierarchical outlines when you ask them to write papers.* Make sure they understand how to organize their writing in terms of general and specific points. The abstractness of formal operational thinking also means that teachers with students at this level can encourage them to use metaphors.

---

ers often fail to understand the relation between a hypothesis and a well-chosen test of it, stubbornly clinging to ideas that already have been discounted.

A form of egocentrism also emerges in adolescence (Elkind, 1978). *Adolescent egocentrism* is the heightened self-consciousness reflected in adolescents' beliefs that others are as interested in them as they themselves are. Adolescent egocentrism also includes a sense of personal uniqueness. It involves the desire to be noticed, visible, and "on stage."

Egocentrism is a normal adolescent occurrence, more common in the middle school than in high school years. However, for some individuals, adolescent egocentrism can contribute to reckless behavior, including suicidal thoughts, drug use, and failure to use contraceptives during sexual intercourse. Egocentricity leads some adolescents to think that they are invulnerable.

Evaluating Piaget's Theory   What were Piaget's main contributions? Has his theory withstood the test of time?

Contributions   Piaget is a giant in the field of developmental psychology (Halford, 2008; Perret-Clermont & Barrelet, 2008). We owe to him the present field of children's cognitive development. We owe to him a long list of masterful concepts including assimilation and accommodation, object permanence, egocentrism,

Might adolescents' ability to reason hypothetically and to evaluate what is ideal versus what is real lead them to engage in demonstrations, such as this protest related to better ethnic relations? What other causes might be attractive to adolescents' newfound cognitive abilities of hypothetical-deductive reasoning and idealistic thinking?

DEVELOPMENTAL FOCUS 2.1

How Do Piaget's Stages of Cognition Apply to Your Classroom?

Early Childhood

When I teach songs to preschool students who are in the preoperational stage, I use PowerPoint slides projected on the board. The slides have either all the words of the song included, or just key words. I also include corresponding clip art and pictures on the page borders.

—Connie Christy, *Aynor Elementary School (Preschool Program)*

Elementary School: Grades K–5

In my second-grade science class, I use the following method to help students move from concrete thinking to more abstract thinking: Children are given tasks and asked to discuss what happened (for example, the object sank or floated; when something is added to a system, the outcome changes). Then a theory or idea is developed from the actual observations. When children observe an occurrence and explain what was seen, they can more easily move from the concrete to the more abstract. Although these methods and others like it work well with my students, I need to repeat them often.

—Janine Guida Poutre, *Clinton Elementary School*

Middle School: Grades 6–8

I challenge my seventh-grade students to share examples of how they've applied our classroom lessons to the real world. They can earn extra credit for doing so, but seem to care less about the points than they do about the opportunity to share their accomplishments. For example, after completing a unit on Progressivism, a student shared how he had gone online on his home computer and donated money to help Darfur refugees. He had previously planned to use this money to buy himself a new guitar. This student took the theory of social activism from the Progressive era 100 years ago and applied it to his life today. This student's actions clearly demonstrate Piaget's formal operational stage in action.

—Mark Fodness, *Bemidji Middle School*

High School: Grades 9–12

My high school art students take part in creativity competitions in which they build, create, explore, problem solve, and perform solutions to challenges presented to them. The competition—Destination Imagination—has challenged my students to brainstorm ideas and solutions to seemingly impossible tasks. As a result of their participation in this event, they have won regional and state titles along with the world championship.

—Dennis Peterson, *Deer River High School*

Many adolescent girls spend long hours in front of the mirror, depleting cans of hairspray, tubes of lipstick, and jars of cosmetics. *How might this behavior be related to changes in adolescent cognitive and physical development?*

conservation, and hypothetical-deductive reasoning. Along with William James and John Dewey, we also owe Piaget the current vision of children as active, constructive thinkers.

Piaget also was a genius when it came to observing children. His careful observations showed us inventive ways to discover how children act on and adapt to their world. Piaget showed us some important things to look for in cognitive development, such as the shift from preoperational to concrete operational thinking. He also showed us how children need to make their experiences fit their schemas (cognitive frameworks) yet simultaneously adapt their schemas to experience.

Criticisms   Piaget's theory has not gone unchallenged. Questions have been raised in the following areas:

- *Estimates of children's competence.* Some cognitive abilities emerge earlier than Piaget thought, others later (Bauer, 2008; Kuhn, 2008). Conservation of number has been demonstrated as early as age 3, although Piaget did not think it emerged until 7. Young children are not as uniformly "pre-" this and "pre-" that (precausal, preoperational) as Piaget thought (Flavell, Miller, & Miller,

Piaget is shown here with his family. Piaget's careful observations of his three children—Lucienne, Laurent, and Jacqueline—contributed to the development of his cognitive theory.

An outstanding teacher and education in the logic of science and mathematics are important cultural experiences that promote the development of operational thought. *Might Piaget have underestimated the roles of culture and schooling in children's cognitive development?*

2002). Other cognitive abilities can emerge later than Piaget thought. Many adolescents still think in concrete operational ways or are just beginning to master formal operations.

- *Stages.* Piaget conceived of stages as unitary structures of thought. Some concrete operational concepts, however, do not appear at the same time (Kuhn & Franklin, 2006). For example, children do not learn to conserve at the same time as they learn to cross-classify.
- *Training children to reason at a higher level.* Some children who are at one cognitive stage (such as preoperational) can be trained to reason at a higher cognitive stage (such as concrete operational). However, Piaget argued that such training is only superficial and ineffective, unless the child is at a maturational transition point between the stages (Gelman & Opfer, 2004).
- *Culture and education.* Culture and education exert stronger influences on children's development than Piaget envisioned (Maynard, 2008). For example, the age at which children acquire conservation skills is related to the extent to which their culture provides relevant practice (Cole, 2006). An outstanding teacher can guide students' learning experiences that will help them move to a higher cognitive stage.

Still, some developmental psychologists reason we should not throw out Piaget altogether (Carpendale, Muller, & Bibok, 2008). These **neo-Piagetians** argue that Piaget got some things right but that his theory needs considerable revision. In their revision of Piaget, neo-Piagetians emphasize how children process information through attention, memory, and strategies (Case, 2000). They especially stress that a more accurate vision of children's thinking requires more knowledge of strategies, how fast and how automatically children process information, the particular cognitive task involved, and the division of cognitive problems into smaller, more precise steps (Morra & others, 2008).

Despite such criticism, Piaget's theory is a very important one, and as we already have seen, information about his stages of development can be applied to teaching children. Here are some more ideas for applying Piaget's theory to children's education.

neo-Piagetians Developmental psychologists who argue that Piaget got some things right but that his theory needs considerable revision; emphasize how to process information through attention, memory, and strategies.

BEST PRACTICES
Strategies for Applying Piaget's Theory to Children's Education

1. *Take a constructivist approach.* In a constructivist vein, Piaget emphasized that children learn best when they are active and seek solutions for themselves. Piaget opposed teaching methods that treat children as passive receptacles. The educational implication of Piaget's view is that in all subjects students learn best by making discoveries, reflecting on them, and discussing them, rather than blindly imitating the teacher or doing things by rote.

2. *Facilitate rather than direct learning.* Effective teachers design situations that allow students to learn by doing. These situations promote students' thinking and discovery. Teachers listen, watch, and question students to help them gain better understanding. They ask relevant questions to stimulate students' thinking and ask them to explain their answers. As you will see next, Suzanne Ransleben creates imaginative classroom situations to facilitate students' learning.

THROUGH THE EYES OF TEACHERS
Stimulating Students' Thinking and Discovery

Suzanne Ransleben teaches ninth- and tenth-grade English in Corpus Christi, Texas. She designs classroom situations that stimulate students' reflective thinking and discovery. Suzanne created Grammar Football to make diagramming sentences more interesting for students and has students decipher song lyrics to help them better understand how to write poetry. When students first encounter Shakespeare, "They paint interpretations of their favorite line from *Romeo and Juliet*" (Source: Wong Briggs, 2004, p. 7D)

3. *Consider the child's knowledge and level of thinking.* Students do not come to class with empty heads. They have many ideas about the physical and natural world including concepts of space, time, quantity, and causality. These ideas differ from the ideas of adults. Teachers need to interpret what a student is saying and respond with discourse close to the student's level.

Suzanne Ransleben, teaching English.

4. *Promote the student's intellectual health.* When Piaget came to lecture in the United States, he was asked, "What can I do to get my child to a higher cognitive stage sooner?" He was asked this question so often here compared with other countries that he called it the American question. For Piaget, children's learning should occur naturally. Children should not be pushed and pressured into achieving too much too early in their development, before they are maturationally ready.

5. *Turn the classroom into a setting of exploration and discovery.* What do actual classrooms look like when the teachers adopt Piaget's views? Several first- and second-grade math classrooms provide some good examples (Kamii, 1985, 1989). The teachers emphasize students' own exploration and discovery. The classrooms are less structured than what we think of as a typical classroom. Workbooks and predetermined assignments are not used. Rather, the teachers observe the students' interests and natural participation in activities to determine what the course of learning will be. For example, a math lesson might be constructed around counting the day's lunch money or dividing supplies among students. Often games are prominently used in the classroom to stimulate mathematical thinking.

Vygotsky's Theory

According to Vygotsky, mental functions have external, or social, connections. Vygotsky argued that children develop more systematic, logical, and rational concepts as a result of *dialogue* with a skilled helper. Thus, in Vygotsky's theory, other people and language play key roles in a child's cognitive development (Gauvain, 2008; Holtzman, 2009).

The Zone of Proximal Development   Vygotsky's belief in the importance of social influences, especially instruction, on children's cognitive development is reflected in his concept of the zone of proximal development. **Zone of proximal development (ZPD)** is Vygotsky's term for the range of tasks that are too difficult for the child to master alone but that can be learned with guidance and assistance of adults or more-skilled children. Thus, the lower limit of the ZPD is the level of skill reached by the child working independently. The upper limit is the level of additional responsibility the child can accept with the assistance of an able instructor (see Figure 2.15). The ZPD captures the child's cognitive skills that are in the process of maturing and can be accomplished only with the assistance of a more-skilled person (Gredler, 2008; Levykh, 2008). Vygotsky (1962) called these the "buds" or "flowers" of development, to distinguish them from the "fruits" of development, which the child already can accomplish independently.

Teaching in the zone of proximal development reflects the concept of developmentally appropriate teaching we described earlier in the chapter. It involves being aware of "where students are in the process of their development and taking advantage of their readiness. It is also about teaching to enable developmental readiness, not just waiting for students to be ready" (Horowitz & others, 2005, p. 105).

Scaffolding   Closely linked to the idea of the ZPD is the concept of scaffolding. **Scaffolding** means changing the level of support. Over the course of a teaching session, a more-skilled person (a teacher or advanced peer) adjusts the amount of guidance to fit the child's current performance (Daniels, 2007). When the student is learning a new task, the skilled person may use direct instruction. As the student's competence increases, less guidance is given. Scaffolding is often used to help students attain the upper limits of their zone of proximal development (Horowitz & others, 2005).

Asking probing questions is an excellent way to scaffold students' learning and help them to develop more sophisticated thinking skills. A teacher might ask a student such questions as "What would an example of that be?" "Why do you think that is so?" "Now, what's the next thing you need to do?" and "How can you connect those?" Over time, students should begin internalizing these kinds of probes and improve monitoring their own work (Horowitz & others, 2005).

Many teachers who successfully use scaffolding circulate around the classroom, giving "just-in-time" assistance to individuals, or detecting a class-wide misconception and then leading a discussion to correct the problem. They also give "children time to grapple with problems" and guide them when they observe that the child can no longer make progress (Horowitz & others, 2005, pp. 106–107).

Language and Thought   In Vygotksy's view, language plays an important role in a child's development (Mercer, 2008). According to Vygotsky, children use speech not only for social communication, but also to help them solve tasks. Vygotsky (1962) further argued that young children use language to plan, guide, and monitor their behavior. This use of language for self-regulation is called *private speech*. For example, young children talk aloud to themselves about such things as their toys and the tasks they are trying to complete. Thus, when working on a puzzle, a child might say, "This piece doesn't go; maybe I'll try that one." A few minutes later she utters, "This is hard." For Piaget private speech is egocentric and immature, but for Vygotsky it is an important tool of thought during the early childhood years (John-Steiner, 2007; Wertsch, 2007).

Vygotsky said that language and thought initially develop independently of each other and then merge. He emphasized that all mental functions have external, or social, origins. Children must use language to communicate with others before they can focus inward on their own thoughts. Children also must communicate externally and use language for a long period of time before they can make the transition from external to internal speech. This transition period occurs between 3 and 7 years of age and involves talking to oneself. After a while, the self-talk becomes second nature to children, and they can act without verbalizing. When this occurs, children have

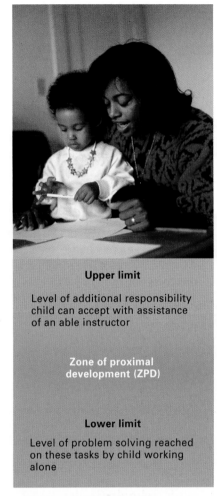

Upper limit

Level of additional responsibility child can accept with assistance of an able instructor

Zone of proximal development (ZPD)

Lower limit

Level of problem solving reached on these tasks by child working alone

FIGURE 2.15 Vygotsky's Zone of Proximal Development

Vygotsky's zone of proximal development has a lower limit and an upper limit. Tasks in the ZPD are too difficult for the child to perform alone. They require assistance from an adult or a more-skilled child. As children experience the verbal instruction or demonstration, they organize the information in their existing mental structures, so they can eventually perform the skill or task alone.

zone of proximal development (ZPD) Vygotsky's term for the range of tasks that are too difficult for children to master alone but that can be mastered with guidance and assistance from adults or more-skilled children.

scaffolding A technique that involves changing the level of support for learning. A teacher or more-advanced peer adjusts the amount of guidance to fit the student's current performance.

DEVELOPMENTAL FOCUS 2.2
How Does Vygotsky's Theory of Cognition Apply to Your Classroom?

Early Childhood

In teaching music to preschoolers, I use private speech to help children learn unfamiliar rhythms. When my young students are learning a new rhythm pattern on the African drums, for example, they don't count the eighth and quarter notes, because that is too difficult. Instead, I suggest certain words for them to repeat in rhythmic patterns to learn the beat, or they can come up with their own words to match the new rhythm. My guidance allows children to improve their understanding of musical rhythm.

—Connie Christy, *Aynor Elementary School (Preschool Program)*

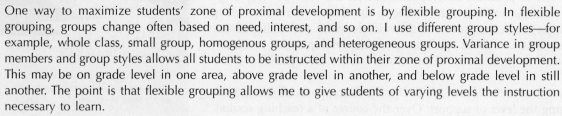

Elementary School: Grades K–5

One way to maximize students' zone of proximal development is by flexible grouping. In flexible grouping, groups change often based on need, interest, and so on. I use different group styles—for example, whole class, small group, homogenous groups, and heterogeneous groups. Variance in group members and group styles allows all students to be instructed within their zone of proximal development. This may be on grade level in one area, above grade level in another, and below grade level in still another. The point is that flexible grouping allows me to give students of varying levels the instruction necessary to learn.

—Susan Froelich, *Clinton Elementary School*

Middle School: Grades 6–8

When I teach my students a new skill, it is important that I stay close to them while they are working. This way if they need my assistance, I am there to help them master the new skill with some guidance. This practice works especially well when we are working on multistep projects.

—Casey Maass, *Edison Middle School*

High School: Grades 9–12

Advanced art students and independent-study students have always been an active part of my classroom, especially when it comes to helping other students maximize their zone of proximal development (and grow in their own skills as artists as well). In my ceramics class, for example, I have several advanced students—who have especially strong knowledge and skills on the ceramic wheel—help my first-year students, who are attempting to work on the wheel for the first time. This additional assistance from the advanced students allows me to help other students who need further instruction.

—Dennis Peterson, *Deer River High School*

internalized their egocentric speech in the form of *inner speech,* which becomes their thoughts.

Vygotsky argued that children who use private speech are more socially competent than those who don't (Santiago-Delefosse & Delefosse, 2002). He argued that private speech represents an early transition in becoming more socially communicative. For Vygotsky, when young children talk to themselves, they are using language to govern their behavior and guide themselves.

Piaget held that self-talk is egocentric and reflects immaturity. However, researchers have found support for Vygotsky's view that private speech plays a positive role in children's development (Winsler, Carlton, & Barry, 2000; Winsler, Diaz, & Montero, 1997). Researchers have found that children use private speech more when tasks are difficult, after they make mistakes, and when they are not sure how to proceed (Berk, 1994). They also have revealed that children who use private speech are more attentive and improve their performance more than children who do not use private speech (Berk & Spuhl, 1995).

SELF-ASSESSMENT 2.1
Applying Piaget and Vygotsky in My Classroom

The grade level at which I plan to teach is_____

Piaget

The Piagetian stage of the majority of children in my classroom will likely be

_____

The Piagetian concepts that should help me the most in understanding and teaching children at this grade level are

Concept	Example

Vygotsky

The concepts in Vygotsky's theory that should help me the most in understanding and teaching children at this grade level are

Concept	Example

We have discussed a number of ideas about both Piaget's and Vygotsky's theories and how the theories can be applied to children's education. To reflect on how you might apply their theories to your own classroom, complete *Self-Assessment 2.1.*

Evaluating Vygotsky's Theory How does Vygotsky's theory compare with Piaget's? Although both theories are constructivist, Vygotsky's is a **social constructivist approach**, which emphasizes the

Lev Vygotsky (1896–1934), shown here with his daughter, stressed that children's cognitive development is advanced through social interaction with more-skilled individuals embedded in a sociocultural backdrop. *How is Vygosky's theory different from Piaget's?*

social constructivist approach
Emphasizes the social contexts of learning and that knowledge is mutually built and constructed; Vygotsky's theory exemplifies this approach.

Vygotsky's theory has been embraced by many teachers and has been successfully applied to education (Gredler, 2008; Holtzman, 2009). Here are some ways Vygotsky's theory can be incorporated in classrooms:

1. *Assess the child's ZPD.* Like Piaget, Vygotsky did not think that formal, standardized tests are the best way to assess children's learning. Rather, Vygotsky argued that assessment should focus on determining the child's zone of proximal development (Camilleri, 2005). The skilled helper presents the child with tasks of varying difficulty to determine the best level at which to begin instruction.

2. *Use the child's zone of proximal development in teaching.* Teaching should begin toward the zone's upper limit, so that the child can reach the goal with help and move to a higher level of skill and knowledge. Offer just enough assistance. You might ask, "What can I do to help you?" Or simply observe the child's intentions and attempts and provide support when needed. When the child hesitates, offer encouragement. And encourage the child to practice the skill. You may watch and appreciate the child's practice or offer support when the child forgets what to do. Next, you can read about John Mahoney's teaching practices that reflect Vygotsky's emphasis on the importance of the zone of proximal development.

John Mahoney, teaching math.

THROUGH THE EYES OF TEACHERS
Using Dialogue and Reframing Concepts to Find the Zone of Proximal Development

John Mahoney teaches mathematics at a high school in Washington, D.C. In Mahoney's view, guiding students' success in math is both collaborative and individual. He encourages dialogue about math during which he reframes concepts that help students subsequently solve problems on their own. Mahoney also never gives students the answers to math problems. As one student commented, "He's going to make you think." His tests always include a problem that students have not seen but have enough knowledge to figure out the problem's solution. (Source: Wong Briggs, 2005.)

3. *Use more-skilled peers as teachers.* Remember that it is not just adults that are important in helping children learn.

Children also benefit from the support and guidance of more-skilled children (John-Steiner, 2007; Wertsch, 2008). For example, pair a child who is just beginning to read with one who is a more advanced reader.

4. *Monitor and encourage children's use of private speech.* Be aware of the developmental change from externally talking to oneself when solving a problem during the preschool years to privately talking to oneself in the early elementary school years. In the elementary school years, encourage children to internalize and self-regulate their talk to themselves.

5. *Place instruction in a meaningful context.* Educators today are moving away from abstract presentations of material, instead providing students with opportunities to experience learning in real-world settings. For example, instead of just memorizing math formulas, students work on math problems with real-world implications.

6. *Transform the classroom with Vygotskian ideas.* Tools of the Mind is a curriculum that is grounded in Vygotsky's (1962) theory with special attention given to cultural tools and developing self-regulation, the zone of proximal development, scaffolding, private speech, shared activity, and play as important activity (Hyson, Copple, & Jones, 2006). Figure 2.16 illustrates how scaffolding was used in Tools of the Mind to improve a young child's writing skills. The Tools of the Mind curriculum was created by Elena Bodrova and Deborah Leong (2007) and has been implemented in more than 200 classrooms. Most of the children in the Tools of the Mind programs are at-risk because of their living circumstances, which in many instances involve poverty and other difficult conditions such as being homeless and having parents with drug problems.

In a Tools of the Mind classroom, dramatic play has a central role. Teachers guide children in creating themes based on the children's interests, such as treasure hunt, store, hospital, and restaurant. Teachers also incorporate field trips, visitor presentations, videos, and books in the development of children's play. They also help children develop a play plan, which increases the maturity of their play. Play plans describe what the children expect to do in the play period, including the imaginary context, roles, and props to be used. The play plans increase the quality of their play and self-regulation.

BEST PRACTICES
Strategies for Applying Vygotsky's Theory to Children's Education

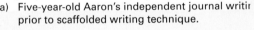

(a) Five-year-old Aaron's independent journal writing prior to scaffolded writing technique.

(b) Aaron's journal 2 months after using the Scaffolded Writing technique. He is now making the lines for himself and had no interaction with the story until he had completed it (a total of 4 pages of writing). The number of sentences and words per sentence continues to increase. He has become a prolific writer in a short period of time.

FIGURE 2.16 Writing Progress of a 5–Year–Old Boy over Two Months Using the Scaffolding Writing Technique in Tools of the Mind

social contexts of learning and the construction of knowledge through social interaction.

In moving from Piaget to Vygotsky, the conceptual shift is from the individual to collaboration, social interaction, and sociocultural activity (Holtzman, 2009; Yasnitsky & Ferrari, 2008). The endpoint of cognitive development for Piaget is formal operational thought. For Vygotsky, the endpoint can differ, depending on which skills are considered to be the most important in a particular culture. For Piaget, children construct knowledge by transforming, organizing, and reorganizing previous knowledge. For Vygotsky, children construct knowledge through social interaction (Gauvain, 2008). The implication of Piaget's theory for teaching is that children need support to explore their world and discover knowledge. The main implication of Vygotsky's theory for teaching is that students need many opportunities to learn with the teacher and more-skilled peers (Rogoff & others, 2007). In both Piaget's and Vygotsky's theories, teachers serve as facilitators and guides, rather than as directors and molders of learning. Figure 2.17 compares Vygotsky's and Piaget's theories.

Criticisms of Vygotsky's theory also have surfaced (Karpov, 2006). Some critics point out that Vygotsky was not specific enough about age-related changes (Gauvain, 2008). Another criticism focuses on Vygotsky not adequately describing how changes in socioemotional capabilities contribute to cognitive development (Gauvain, 2008).

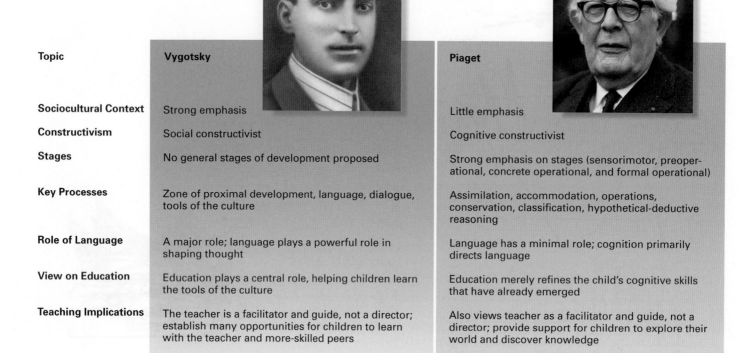

Topic	Vygotsky	Piaget
Sociocultural Context	Strong emphasis	Little emphasis
Constructivism	Social constructivist	Cognitive constructivist
Stages	No general stages of development proposed	Strong emphasis on stages (sensorimotor, preoperational, concrete operational, and formal operational)
Key Processes	Zone of proximal development, language, dialogue, tools of the culture	Assimilation, accommodation, operations, conservation, classification, hypothetical-deductive reasoning
Role of Language	A major role; language plays a powerful role in shaping thought	Language has a minimal role; cognition primarily directs language
View on Education	Education plays a central role, helping children learn the tools of the culture	Education merely refines the child's cognitive skills that have already emerged
Teaching Implications	The teacher is a facilitator and guide, not a director; establish many opportunities for children to learn with the teacher and more-skilled peers	Also views teacher as a facilitator and guide, not a director; provide support for children to explore their world and discover knowledge

FIGURE 2.17 Comparison of Vygotsky's and Piaget's Theories

Yet another criticism is that he overemphasized the role of language in thinking. Also, his emphasis on collaboration and guidance has potential pitfalls. Might facilitators be too helpful in some cases, as when a parent becomes too overbearing and controlling? Further, some children might become lazy and expect help when they might have done something on their own.

In our coverage of cognitive development, we have focused on the views of two giants in the field: Piaget and Vygotsky. However, information processing also has emerged as an important perspective in understanding children's cognitive development (Mayer, 2008). It emphasizes how information enters the mind, how it is stored and transformed, and how it is retrieved to perform mental activities such as problem solving and reasoning. It also focuses on how automatically and quickly children process information. Because information processing will be covered extensively in Chapters 8 and 9, we mention it only briefly here.

Review, Reflect, and Practice

(2) **Discuss the development of the brain and compare the cognitive developmental theories of Jean Piaget and Lev Vygotsky.**

REVIEW

- How does the brain develop, and what implications does this development have for children's education?
- What four main ideas did Piaget use to describe cognitive processes? What stages did he identify in children's cognitive development? What are some criticisms of his view?
- What is the nature of Vygotsky's theory? How can Vygotsky's theory be applied to education and his theory compared to Piaget's? What is a criticism of Vygotsky's theory?

REFLECT

- Do you consider yourself to be a formal operational thinker? Do you still sometimes feel like a concrete operational thinker? Give examples.

PRAXIS™ PRACTICE

1. Sander is a 16-year-old boy who takes many risks, such as driving fast and drinking while driving. Recent research on the brain indicates that a likely reason for this risk-taking behavior is that Sander's
   a. hippocampus is damaged.
   b. prefrontal cortex is still developing.
   c. brain lateralization is incomplete.
   d. myelination is complete.

2. Mrs. Gonzales teaches first grade. Which of her following strategies would Piaget most likely endorse?
   a. demonstrating how to perform a math operation and having students imitate her
   b. creating flash cards to teach vocabulary
   c. using a standardized test to assess students' reading skills
   d. designing contexts that promote student's thinking and discovery

3. Mr. Gould's fourth-grade students are learning about the relations among percentages, decimals, and fractions. Mr. Gould distributes an assignment requiring students to convert fractions to decimals and then to percentages. Christopher can do this assignment without help from Mr. Gould or his classmates. What would Vygotsky say about this task for Christopher?
   a. This task is appropriate for Christopher because it is within his zone of proximal development.
   b. This task is inappropriate for Christopher because it is above his zone of proximal development.
   c. This task is inappropriate for Christopher because it is below his zone of proximal development.
   d. This task is inappropriate for Christopher because it is within his zone of proximal development.

Please see the answer key at the end of the book.

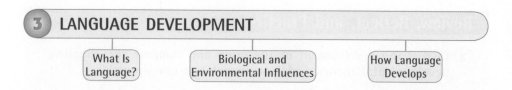

3 LANGUAGE DEVELOPMENT

| What Is Language? | Biological and Environmental Influences | How Language Develops |

Think how important language is in children's everyday lives. They need language to speak with others, listen to others, read, and write. Their language enables them to describe past events in detail and to plan for the future. Language lets us pass down information from one generation to the next and create a rich cultural heritage. As you learned earlier, in Vygotsky's view, language plays a key role in children's cognitive development.

What Is Language?

Language is a form of communication—whether spoken, written, or signed—that is based on a system of symbols. Language consists of the words used by a community (vocabulary) and the rules for varying and combining them (grammar and syntax).

All human languages have some common characteristics (Berko Gleason, 2009). These include infinite generativity and organizational rules. *Infinite generativity* is the ability to produce an endless number of meaningful sentences using a finite set of words and rules.

When we say "rules," we mean that language is orderly and that rules describe the way language works (Berko Gleason & Ratner, 2009). Language involves five systems of rules: phonology, morphology, syntax, semantics, and pragmatics.

Phonology   Every language is made up of basic sounds. **Phonology** is the sound system of a language, including the sounds used and how they may be combined (Menn & Stoel-Gammon, 2009). For example, English has the sounds *sp, ba,* and *ar,* but the sound sequences *zx* and *qp* do not occur.

A *phoneme* is the basic unit of sound in a language; it is the smallest unit of sound that affects meaning. A good example of a phoneme in English is /k/, the sound represented by the letter *k* in the word *ski* and the letter *c* in the word *cat.* The /k/ sound is slightly different in these two words, and in some languages such as Arabic these two sounds are separate phonemes.

Morphology   **Morphology** refers to the units of meaning involved in word formation. A *morpheme* is a minimal unit of meaning; it is a word or a part of a word that cannot be broken into smaller meaningful parts. Every word in the English language is made up of one or more morphemes. Some words consist of a single morpheme (for example, *help*), whereas others are made up of more than one morpheme (for example, *helper,* which has two morphemes, *help* + *er,* with the morpheme *-er* meaning "one who," in this case "one who helps"). Thus, not all morphemes are words by themselves—for example, *pre-, -tion,* and *-ing* are morphemes.

Just as the rules that govern phonology describe the sound sequences that can occur in a language, the rules of morphology describe the way meaningful units (morphemes) can be combined in words (Tager-Flusberg, 2009). Morphemes have many jobs in grammar, such as marking tense (for example, *she walks* versus *she walked*) and number (*she walks* versus *they walk*).

Syntax   **Syntax** involves the way words are combined to form acceptable phrases and sentences (Tager-Flusberg & Zukowski, 2009). If someone says to you, "Bob slugged Tom" or "Bob was slugged by Tom," you know who did the slugging and who was slugged in each case because you have a syntactic understanding of these sentence structures. You also understand that the sentence "You didn't stay, did you?" is a grammatical sentence but that "You didn't stay, didn't you?" is unacceptable and ambiguous.

language A form of communication, whether spoken, written, or signed, that is based on a system of symbols.

phonology A language's sound system.

morphology Refers to the units of meaning involved in word formation.

syntax The ways words are combined to form acceptable phrases and sentences.

FRANK & ERNEST © Thaves/Dist. by Newspaper Enterprise Association, Inc.

Semantics   **Semantics** refers to the meaning of words and sentences. Every word has a set of semantic features, or required attributes related to meaning. *Girl* and *women,* for example, share many semantic features, but they differ semantically in regard to age.

Words have semantic restrictions on how they can be used in sentences (Pan & Uccelli, 2009). The sentence *The bicycle talked the boy into buying a candy bar* is syntactically correct but semantically incorrect. The sentence violates our semantic knowledge that bicycles don't talk.

Pragmatics   A final set of language rules involves **pragmatics**, the appropriate use of language in different contexts. Pragmatics covers a lot of territory. When you take turns speaking in a discussion, you are demonstrating knowledge of pragmatics. You also apply the pragmatics of English when you use polite language in appropriate situations (for example, when talking to a teacher) or tell stories that are interesting.

Pragmatic rules can be complex, and they differ from one culture to another (Bryant, 2009). If you were to study the Japanese language, you would come face-to-face with countless pragmatic rules about conversing with individuals of various social levels and with various relationships to you.

Biological and Environmental Influences

Famous linguist Noam Chomsky (1957) argued that humans are prewired to learn language at a certain time and in a certain way. Some language scholars view the remarkable similarities in how children acquire language all over the world, despite the vast variation in language input they receive, as strong evidence that language has a biological basis.

Despite the influence of biology, children clearly do not learn language in a social vacuum (Goldfield & Snow, 2009; Meltzoff & Brooks, 2009). Enough variation occurs in language development when children's caregivers differ substantially in input styles to show that the environment plays a significant role in language development, especially in the acquisition of vocabulary. For example, in one study, by the time they were 3 years old, children living in poverty conditions showed vocabulary deficits, compared with their counterparts in middle-income families, and the deficits continued to be present when they entered school at 6 years of age (Farkas, 2001).

In sum, children are neither exclusively biological linguists nor exclusively social architects of language (Bohannon & Bonvillian, 2009; Berko Gleason & Ratner, 2009). No matter how long you converse with a dog, it won't learn to talk, because it doesn't have the human child's biological capacity for language. Unfortunately, though, some children fail to develop good language skills even in the presence of very good role models and interaction. An interactionist view emphasizes the contributions of both biology and experience in language development. That is, children are biologically prepared to learn language as they and their caregivers interact.

In or out of school, encouragement of language development, not drill and practice, is the key (Goldfield & Snow, 2008). Language development is not simply a matter of being rewarded for saying things correctly and imitating a speaker. Children

Both biological and environmental influences play important roles in children's language development.

semantics The meaning of words and sentences.

pragmatics The use of appropriate language in different contexts.

DIVERSITY AND EDUCATION
The Diverse Language Experiences Children Bring to School

Children vary enormously in their language skills and language experiences when they enter school. Some children have been exposed to preliteracy experiences, such as age-appropriate books and extensive conversational exchanges with literate adults, whereas others have not (Melzi & Ely, 2009). Some have had extensive exposure to the main language used in the school classroom; others have little exposure to it.

Socioeconomic status has been linked with how much parents talk to their children and with young children's vocabulary. In one study, the language environments of children whose parents were professionals and children whose parents were on welfare were observed (Hart & Risley, 1995). Compared with the professional parents, the parents on welfare talked much less to their young children, talked less about past events, and provided less elaboration. The children of the professional parents had a much larger vocabulary at 36 months of age than the children of the welfare parents.

Of course, not all children from low-income families have language deficiencies when they enter school. One study of young children living in low-income families found that the mother's language and literacy skills were positively related to the children's vocabulary development (Pan & others, 2005). For example, low-income mothers who used a more diverse vocabulary and frequently used pointing gestures when talking with their children had children with a larger vocabulary. Pointing usually occurs in concert with speech, and it may enhance the meaning of mothers' verbal input to their children.

An increasing number of children bring to school not only a language that is different, but also cultural ways of using language that differ, from the language used in the school classroom (Park & King, 2003). An important teaching skill is to discover the knowledge and skills children from diverse linguistic and cultural backgrounds bring to the classroom. Becoming aware of such differences can help

What are some strategies teachers can use to ease the transition to school for children from diverse language backgrounds?

DIVERSITY AND EDUCATION
The Diverse Language Experiences Children Bring to School

teachers to avoid underestimating or misinterpreting the language competence of these children.

Showing respect for the cultural and linguistic backgrounds of students and encouraging their parents to become involved in school activities can help to ease the transition to school (Echevarria, Voght, & Short, 2008). In addition to understanding how language systems and cultures of students vary, teachers can describe varied characteristics and styles of languages as part of classroom exercises, such as storytelling. Another effective strategy is to get students involved in research projects that draw on the expertise and experiences in their community (Park & King, 2003).

benefit when their parents and teachers actively engage them in conversation, ask them questions, and emphasize interactive rather than directive language. In the *Diversity and Education* interlude, we further explore how environmental experiences influence children's language development.

How Language Develops

What are some of the key developmental milestones in language development? We will examine these milestones in infancy, early childhood, middle and late childhood, and adolescence.

Infancy   Language acquisition advances past a number of milestones in infancy (Colombo, McCardle, & Freund, 2009; McGhee & Richgels, 2008; Sachs, 2009). Because the main focus of this text is on children and adolescents rather than infants, we will only describe several of the many language milestones in infancy. Babbling begins at about 3 to 6 months. Infants usually utter their first word at about 10 to 13 months. By 18 to 24 months, infants usually have begun to string two words together. In this two-word stage, they quickly grasp the importance of language in communication, creating phrases such as "Book there," "My candy," "Mama walk," and "Give Papa."

Early Childhood   As children leave the two-word stage, they move rather quickly into three-, four-, and five-word combinations. The transition from simple sentences expressing a single proposition to complex sentences begins between 2 and 3 years of age and continues into the elementary school years (Bloom, 1998).

Young children's understanding sometimes gets way ahead of their speech. One 3-year-old, laughing with delight as an abrupt summer breeze stirred his hair and tickled his skin, commented, "I got breezed!" Many of the oddities of young children's language sound like mistakes to adult listeners. From the children's point of view, however, they are not mistakes. They represent the way young children perceive and understand their world at that point in their development.

Let's explore the changes in the five rules systems we described earlier—phonology, morphology, syntax, semantics, and pragmatics—during early childhood. In terms of phonology, most preschool children gradually become sensitive to the sounds of spoken words (National Research Council, 1999). They notice rhymes, enjoy poems, make up silly names for things by substituting one sound for another (such as *bubblegum, bubblebum, bubbleyum*), and clap along with each syllable in a phrase.

As they move beyond two-word utterances, there is clear evidence that children know morphological rules. Children begin using the plural and possessive forms of

This is a wug.

Now there is another one.
There are two of them.
There are two _____.

FIGURE 2.18 Stimuli in Berko's Study of Young Children's Understanding of Morphological Rules

In Jean Berko's (1958) study, young children were presented cards such as this one with a "wug" on it. Then the children were asked to supply the missing word and say it correctly. "Wugs" is the correct response here.

nouns (*dogs* and *dog's*); putting appropriate endings on verbs (*-s* when the subject is third-person singular, *-ed* for the past tense, and *-ing* for the present progressive tense); and using prepositions (*in* and *on*), articles (*a* and *the*), and various forms of the verb *to be* ("I *was going* to the store"). In fact, they *overgeneralize* these rules, applying them to words that do not follow the rules. For example, a preschool child might say "foots" instead of "feet" or "goed" instead of "went."

Children's understanding of morphological rules was the subject of a classic experiment by children's language researcher Jean Berko (1958). Berko presented preschool and first-grade children with cards like the one shown in Figure 2.18. Children were asked to look at the card while the experimenter read the words on it aloud. Then the children were asked to supply the missing word. This might sound easy, but Berko was interested not just in the children's ability to recall the right word but also in their ability to say it "correctly" with the ending that was dictated by morphological rules. *Wugs* is the correct response for the card in Figure 2.18. Although the children were not perfectly accurate, they were much better than chance would dictate. Moreover, they demonstrated their knowledge of morphological rules not only with the plural forms of nouns ("There are two wugs") but also with the possessive forms of nouns and with the third-person singular and past-tense forms of verbs. Berko's study demonstrated not only that the children relied on rules, but also that they had *abstracted* the rules from what they had heard and could apply them to novel situations.

Preschool children also learn and apply rules of syntax (Tager-Flusberg & Zukuwski, 2009). After advancing beyond two-word utterances, the child shows a growing mastery of complex rules for how words should be ordered. Consider *wh*-questions, such as "Where is Daddy going?" or "What is that boy doing?" To ask these questions properly, the child must know two important differences between *wh*- questions and affirmative statements (for instance, "Daddy is going to work" and "That boy is waiting on the school bus"). First, a *wh*- word must be added at the beginning of the sentence. Second, the auxiliary verb must be inverted—that is, exchanged with the subject of the sentence. Young children learn quite early where to put the *wh*- word, but they take much longer to learn the auxiliary-inversion rule. Thus, preschool children might ask, "Where Daddy is going?" and "What that boy is doing?"

Children's knowledge of semantics or meanings also rapidly advances in early childhood (Pan & Uccelli, 2009). The speaking vocabulary of a 6-year-old child ranges from 8,000 to 14,000 words. Assuming that word learning began when the child was 12 months old, this translates into a rate of five to eight new word meanings a day between the ages of 1 and 6. To read about strategies for using technology to support children's vocabulary, see the *Technology and Education* interlude.

Substantial changes in pragmatics also occur during early childhood. A 6-year-old is simply a much better conversationalist than a 2-year-old. What are some of the changes in pragmatics that are made in the preschool years? At about 3 years of age, children improve in their ability to talk about things that are not physically present. That is, they improve their command of the characteristic of language known as *displacement*. Children become increasingly removed from the "here and now" and are able to talk about things not physically present, as well as things that happened in the past or may happen in the future. Preschoolers can tell you what they want for lunch tomorrow, something that would not have been possible at the two-word stage in infancy. Preschool children also become increasingly able to talk in different ways to different people.

Middle and Late Childhood Children gain new skills as they enter school that make it possible to learn to read and write: These include increased use of language to talk about things that are not physically present, learning what a word is, and learning how to recognize and talk about sounds (Berko Gleason, 2004). They also learn the *alphabetic principle,* that the letters of the alphabet represent sounds of the language.

TECHNOLOGY AND EDUCATION

Technology and Children's Vocabulary Development

Here are three ways to support children's vocabulary development using three types of technology (Miller, 2001).

Computers

CD-ROMs of stories, such as *Living Books*, can promote children's vocabulary development, especially when there is an option for students to find the meaning of unfamiliar words. Also, Write:Outloud (2008) can help students build their vocabulary (www.donjohnston.com/products/write_outloud/index.html). Further, using the computer for listening to and watching stories can be part of a student's reading center rotations, reading assignment, or an option during choice time. Learning new words can be enhanced if teachers plan a way for students to keep track of new words. For example, students can record new words in a portfolio for future reference.

An analysis of software products for children's vocabulary development offered the following guidelines (Wood, 2001):

1. *Relate the new to the known.* New vocabulary words are presented in a way that builds on students' previously acquired word knowledge; students are encouraged to map new word meanings onto their own experiences.

2. *Promote active, in-depth processing.* Students are motivated to construct the meanings of words rather than being taught through rote memorization of word meanings. This involves introducing a synonym for the new word or showing how it relates to a particular context; helping students apply their understanding of the word to a particular context; and challenging children to use the new word in a novel way to illustrate their understanding of its meaning.

3. *Encourage reading.* Reading promotes vocabulary development. It is important for software that promotes vocabulary development to motivate students to extend their learning through reading.

Audiobooks

Teachers can create listening centers to support vocabulary development. Listening centers should include tape recorders, headphones, audiobooks, and corresponding literature. Audiobooks can be used to supplement printed materials, listen to dramatization of stories, and pique student interest. Audiobooks may especially benefit students with special needs (Casbergue & Harris, 1996). For example, students whose primary language is not English can use tapes to improve vocabulary development, reading, and pronunciation. Weak readers can use the tapes to contribute to literature discussions in class even though they may be reading less-complex materials.

Educational Television

Educational television can be used to help children learn the alphabet, to see people using vocabulary in different contexts, and to hear stories that will motivate children to read these stories later (Comstock & Scharrer, 2006). One such program is *Reading Rainbow*. In one study, it was found that this program increases children's vocabulary and literacy (Wood & Duke, 1997). The show helps children to expand their vocabularies by introducing many potentially unfamiliar words per episode, linking the words by theme, creating rich contexts when using the words, clearly and directly explaining the meanings of new words, and linking new words in playful ways.

Vocabulary development continues at a breathtaking pace for most children during the elementary school years (Pan & Uccelli, 2009). After five years of word learning, the 6-year-old child does not slow down. According to some estimates, elementary school children in the United States are moving along at the awe-inspiring rate of 22 words a day! The average U.S. 12-year-old has developed a speaking vocabulary of approximately 50,000 words.

During middle and late childhood, changes occur in the way mental vocabulary is organized. When asked to say the first word that comes to mind when they hear a word, preschool children typically provide a word that often follows the word in a sentence. For example, when asked to respond to *dog* the young child may say "barks," or to the word *eat* respond with "lunch." At about 7 years of age, children begin to

DEVELOPMENTAL FOCUS 2.3
How Do You Expand or Advance Children's Language Development in Class?

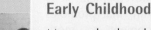

Early Childhood

My preschool students often listen to a piece of music and then describe what they heard in their own words. I use this opportunity to broaden their music vocabulary by expanding on what they've said. For example, a child listening to a recording might say, "I heard a low sound." I then respond by saying, "So what instrument do you think could have made that low *pitch*?"

—Connie Christy, *Aynor Elementary School (Preschool Program)*

Elementary School: Grades K–5

I often tell my fifth-grade students rich, vivid stories about my childhood experiences growing up in eastern Oregon. It is during these teaching moments that my students pay the most attention. I sometimes write these stories on a computer and project them onto a screen in the classroom. Then the students and I discuss the stories and the language used—for example, similes, metaphors, figures of speech. We revise and edit the stories as a group and discuss strengths and weaknesses. The students are then assigned a similar topic to write about. This transfer of knowledge is amazing as the students are entertained, exposed to a new way of writing as it happens—and they see how something can be improved on the spot.

—Craig Jensen, *Cooper Mountain Elementary School*

Middle School: Grades 6–8

During classroom discussions with my seventh-grade students, I intentionally incorporate unfamiliar words that will encourage them to ask, "What does that mean?" For example, when talking about John D. Rockefeller in class recently, I asked, "How many of you would like to become a philanthropist?" I urge students to use their newly learned word at home and to tell the class how they worked it into a conversation. This is a simple way to make vocabulary fun!

—Mark Fodness, *Bemidji Middle School*

High School: Grades 9–12

My high school students often use slang words that I am unfamiliar with. When this happens, I ask the students what the word means and politely tell them that I want to expand my vocabulary. This dialogue often results in conversations about more appropriate words that the students can use in the workplace, classroom, or at home (and I learn something too!)

—Sandy Swanson, *Menomonee Falls High School*

respond with a word that is the same part of speech as the stimulus word. For example, a child may now respond to the word *dog* with "cat" or "horse." To *eat*, they now might say "drink." This is evidence that children now have begun to categorize their vocabulary by parts of speech (Berko Gleason, 2004).

The process of categorizing becomes easier as children increase their vocabulary. Children's vocabulary increases from an average of about 14,000 words at age 6 to an average of about 40,000 words by age 11.

Children make similar advances in grammar (Tager-Flusberg & Zukowski, 2009). During the elementary school years, children's improvement in logical reasoning and analytical skills helps them understand such constructions as the appropriate use of comparatives *(shorter, deeper)* and subjectives ("If you were president . . ."). During the elementary school years, children become increasingly able to understand and use complex grammar, such as the following sentence: *The boy who kissed his mother wore a hat.* They also learn to use language in a more connected way, producing connected discourse. They become able to relate sentences to one another to produce

BEST PRACTICES
Strategies for Vocabulary Development

In the discussion of semantic development, we described the impressive gains in vocabulary that many children make as they go through the early childhood, middle and late childhood, and adolescent years. However, there are significant individual variations in children's vocabulary, and a good vocabulary contributes in important ways to school success (Pan & Uccelli, 2009). For example, a recent study found that vocabulary development was an important contributor to reading comprehension in second-grade students (Berninger & Abbott, 2005). Other research studies have also found that vocabulary plays an important role in reading comprehension and success in school (Paris & Paris, 2006; Snow & Kang, 2006). In addition to those described in the *Technology and Education* interlude, here are some further strategies for improving students' vocabularies:

Preschool and Kindergarten

1. *Explain new vocabulary in books that you read to young children.*

2. *Name and describe all of the things in the classroom.*

3. *In everyday conversation with children, introduce and elaborate on words that children are unlikely to know*

about. This activity can also be used at higher grade levels.

Elementary, Middle, and High School

1. *If students have severe deficits in vocabulary knowledge, provide intense vocabulary instruction.*

2. *As a rule, don't introduce more than 10 words at a time.*

3. *Give students an opportunity to use words in a variety of contexts.* These contexts might include read-aloud, fill-in-the-blank sentences, and read-and-respond activities (students read short, information articles about a topic that includes targeted vocabulary words and then respond to questions about the articles).

4. *Writing can help students process word meanings actively.* For example, assign students a topic to write about using assigned vocabulary words (Sources: Curtis & Longo, 2001; U.S. Department of Education, 2006).

---

descriptions, definitions, and narratives that make sense. Children must be able to do these things orally before they can be expected to deal with them in written assignments. In elementary school, defining words also becomes a regular part of classroom discourse, and children increase their knowledge of syntax as they study and talk about the components of sentences, such as subjects and verbs (Melzi & Ely, 2009).

These advances in vocabulary and grammar during the elementary school years are accompanied by the development of **metalinguistic awareness**, which is knowledge about language, such as knowing what a preposition is or the ability to discuss the sounds of a language. Metalinguistic awareness allows children "to think about their language, understand what words are, and even define them" (Berko Gleason, 2005, p. 4). It improves considerably during the elementary school years. Defining words becomes a regular part of classroom discourse, and children increase their knowledge of syntax as they study and talk about the components of sentences, such as subjects and verbs (Melzi & Ely, 2009).

Children also make progress in understanding how to use language in culturally appropriate ways—pragmatics. By the time they enter adolescence, most children know the rules for the use of language in everyday contexts—that is, what is appropriate and inappropriate to say.

Adolescence   Language development during adolescence includes increased sophistication in the use of words (Berko Gleason, 2009). As they develop abstract thinking,

What are some changes in language development in adolescence?

metalinguistic awareness Knowledge about language, such as knowing what a preposition is.

adolescents become much better than children at analyzing the function a word plays in a sentence.

Adolescents also develop more subtle abilities with words. They make strides in understanding *metaphor,* which is an implied comparison between unlike things. For example, individuals "draw a line in the sand" to indicate a nonnegotiable position; a political campaign is said to be a marathon, not a sprint. And adolescents become better able to understand and to use *satire,* which is the use of irony, derision, or wit to expose folly or wickedness. Caricatures are an example of satire. More advanced logical thinking also allows adolescents, from about 15 to 20 years of age, to understand complex literary works.

Most adolescents are also much better writers than children are. They are better at organizing ideas before they write, at distinguishing between general and specific points as they write, at stringing together sentences that make sense, and at organizing their writing into an introduction, body, and concluding remarks.

Everyday speech changes during adolescence "and part of being a successful teenager is being able to talk like one" (Berko Gleason, 2005, p. 9). Young adolescents often speak a dialect with their peers that is characterized by jargon and slang (Cave, 2002). A *dialect* is a variety of language distinguished by its vocabulary, grammar, or pronunciation. Nicknames that are satirical and derisive ("stilt," "refrigerator," "spaz") are part of the dialect of many young adolescents. They might use such labels to show that they belong to the group and to reduce the seriousness of a situation (Cave, 2002).

Review, Reflect, and Practice

(3) Identify the key features of language, biological and environmental influences on language, and the typical growth of the child's language.

REVIEW

- What is language? Describe these five features of spoken language: phonology, morphology, syntax, semantics, and pragmatics.
- What evidence supports the idea that humans are "prewired" for learning language? What evidence supports the importance of environmental factors?
- What milestones does a child go through in the course of learning language, and what are the typical ages of these milestones?

REFLECT

- How have teachers encouraged or discouraged your own mastery of language? What experiences have done the most to expand your language skills?

PRAXIS™ PRACTICE

1. Josh has developed a large vocabulary. Which of the following language systems does this reflect?
   a. semantics
   b. pragmatics
   c. syntax
   d. morphology
2. Children raised in isolation from human contact often show extreme, long-lasting language deficits that are rarely entirely overcome by later exposure to language. This evidence supports which aspect of language development?
   a. biological
   b. environmental
   c. interactionist
   d. pragmatic

Review, Reflect, and Practice

3. Tamara is discussing the birds she saw flying over her neighborhood. She says, "We saw a flock of gooses." If Tamara's language development is normal for her age, how old is Tamara likely to be?
   a. 2 years old
   b. 4 years old
   c. 6 years old
   d. 8 years old

   Please see the answer key at the end of the book.

CRACK THE CASE
The Case of the Book Report

Mr. Johnson assigned his high school senior American government students to read two books during the semester that had "something, anything to do with government or political systems" and to write a brief report about each of their chosen books.

One student in the class, Cindy, chose to read *1984* and *Animal Farm*, both by George Orwell. *1984* is a book about what could happen in "the future" year of 1984, given certain earlier political decisions. In essence, the world turns into a terrible place in which "Big Brother" monitors all of one's actions via two-way television-like screens. Infractions of minor rules are punished severely. *Animal Farm* is a brief novel about political systems in which the characters are portrayed as various farm animals such as pigs and dogs. Cindy enjoyed both books and completed them both before midterm. Her reports were insightful, reflecting on the symbolism contained in the novels and the implications for present-day government.

Cindy's friend, Lucy, had put off reading her first book until the last minute. She knew Cindy enjoyed reading about government and had finished her reports. Lucy asked Cindy if she knew of a "skinny book" she could read to fulfill the assignment. Cindy gladly shared her copy of *Animal Farm* with her friend, but as Lucy began reading the book she wondered why Cindy had given her this book. It didn't seem to fit the requirements of the assignment at all.

The day before the first reports were due, Mr. Johnson overheard the girls talking. Lucy complained to Cindy, "I don't get it. It's a story about pigs and dogs."

Cindy responded, "They aren't really supposed to be farm animals. It's a story about the promises of communism and what happened in the Soviet Union once the communists took over. It's a great story! Don't you see? The pigs symbolize the communist regime that overthrew the czars during the Russian Revolution. They made all kinds of promises about equality for everyone. The people went along with them because they were sick and tired of the rich and powerful running everything while they starved. Once the czars were eliminated, the communists established a new government but didn't keep any of their promises, controlled everything. Remember in the book when the pigs moved into the house and started walking on two legs? That's supposed to be like when the communist leaders began acting just like the czars. They even created a secret police force—the dogs in the story. Remember how they bullied the other animals? Just like the secret police in the Soviet Union."

Lucy commented, "I still don't get it. How can a pig or a dog be a communist or a cop? They're just animals."

Cindy looked at her friend, dumbfounded. How could she *not* understand this book? It was so obvious.

1. Drawing on Piaget's theory, explain why Cindy understood the book.
2. Based on Piaget's theory, explain why Lucy didn't understand the book.
3. What could Mr. Johnson do to help Lucy understand?
4. How could Mr. Johnson have presented this assignment differently, so that Lucy did not need to rush through a book?
5. At which of Piaget's stages of cognitive development is Cindy operating?
   a. sensorimotor
   b. preoperational
   c. concrete operational
   d. formal operational
   Explain your choice.
6. At which of Piaget's stages of cognitive development is Lucy operating?
   a. sensorimotor
   b. preoperational
   c. concrete operational
   d. formal operational
   Explain your choice.

Reach Your Learning Goals
Cognitive and Language Development

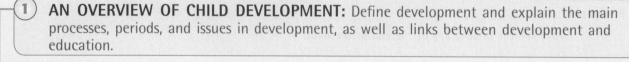

1 AN OVERVIEW OF CHILD DEVELOPMENT: Define development and explain the main processes, periods, and issues in development, as well as links between development and education.

Exploring What Development Is

Development is the pattern of biological, cognitive, and socioemotional changes that begins at conception and continues through the life span. Most development involves growth, but it also eventually includes decay (dying). The more you learn about children's development, the better you will understand the level at which to appropriately teach them. Childhood provides a foundation for the adult years.

Processes and Periods

Child development is the product of biological, cognitive, and socioemotional processes, which often are intertwined. Periods of development include infancy, early childhood, middle and late childhood, and adolescence.

Developmental Issues

The main developmental issues are nature and nature, continuity and discontinuity, and early and later experience. The nature-nurture issue focuses on the extent to which development is mainly influenced by nature (biological inheritance) or nurture (environmental experience). Some developmentalists describe development as continuous (gradual, cumulative change), others describe it as discontinuous (a sequence of abrupt stages). The early-later experience issue focuses on whether early experiences (especially in infancy) are more important in development than later experiences. Most developmentalists recognize that extreme positions on the nature-nurture, continuity-discontinuity, and early-later experience issues are unwise. Despite this consensus, these issues continue to be debated.

Development and Education

Developmentally appropriate teaching takes place at a level that is neither too difficult and stressful nor too easy and boring for the child's developmental level. Splintered development occurs when there is considerable unevenness in development across domains.

2 COGNITIVE DEVELOPMENT: Discuss the development of the brain and compare the cognitive developmental theories of Jean Piaget and Lev Vygotsky.

The Brain

An especially important part of growth is the development of the brain and nervous system. Myelination involving hand-eye coordination is not complete until about 4 years of age, and myelination involving focusing attention is not finished until about 10. Substantial synaptic pruning of the brain connections takes place, and the adult level of density of synaptic connections is not reached until some point in adolescence. Different regions of the brain grow at different rates. Changes in the brain in middle and late childhood included advances in functioning in the prefrontal cortex, which are reflected in improved attention, reasoning, and cognitive control. During middle and late childhood, less diffusion and more focal activation occurs in the prefrontal cortex, a change that is associated with an increase in cognitive control. Researchers have recently found a developmental disjunction between the early development of the amygdala, which is responsible for emotion, and the later development of the prefrontal cortex, which is responsible for reasoning and thinking. They argue that these changes in the brain may help to explain the risk-taking behavior and lack of mature judgment in adolescents. Changes in the brain during adolescence also involve the thickening of the corpus callosum. Lateralization in some verbal and nonverbal functions occurs, but in many instances functioning is linked to both hemispheres. There is considerable plasticity in the brain, and the quality of learning environments children experience influence the development of their brain. Too often links between neuroscience and education have been overstated. Based on recent research, what we do know indicates that educational experiences throughout childhood and adolescence can influence the brain's development.

Piaget's Theory

Jean Piaget proposed a major theory of children's cognitive development that involves these important processes: schemas, assimilation and accommodation, organization, and equilibration. In his theory, cognitive development unfolds in a sequence of four stages: sensorimotor (birth to about age 2), preoperational (from about ages 2 to 7), concrete operational (from about ages 7 to 11), and formal operational (from about ages 11 to 15). Each stage is a qualitative advance. In the sensorimotor stage, infants construct an understanding of the world by coordinating their sensory experiences with their motor actions. Thought is more symbolic at the preoperational stage, although the child has not yet mastered some important mental operations. Preoperational thought includes symbolic function and intuitive thought substages. Egocentrism and centration are constraints. At the concrete operational stage, children can perform operations, and logical thought replaces intuitive thought when reasoning can be applied to specific or concrete examples. Classification, seriation, and transitivity are important concrete operational skills. At the formal operational stage, thinking is more abstract, idealistic, and logical. Hypothetical-deductive reasoning becomes important. Adolescent egocentrism characterizes many young adolescents. We owe to Piaget a long list of masterful concepts as well as the current vision of the child as an active, constructivist thinker. Criticisms of his view focus on estimates of children's competence, stages, the training of children to reason at a higher cognitive level, and the neo-Piagetian criticism of not being precise enough about how children learn.

Vygotsky's Theory

Lev Vygotsky proposed another major theory of cognitive development. Vygotsky's view emphasizes that cognitive skills need to be interpreted developmentally, are mediated by language, and have their origins in social relations and culture. Zone of proximal development (ZPD) is Vygotsky's term for the range of tasks that are too difficult for children to master alone but that can be learned with the guidance and assistance of adults and more-skilled children. Scaffolding is an important concept in Vygotsky's theory. He also argued that language plays a key role in guiding cognition. Applications of Vygotsky's ideas to education include using the child's zone of proximal development and scaffolding, using more-skilled peers as teachers, monitoring and encouraging children's use of private speech, and accurately assessing the zone of proximal development. These practices can transform the classroom and establish a meaningful context for instruction. Like Piaget, Vygotsky emphasized that children actively construct their understanding of the world. Unlike Piaget, he did not propose stages of cognitive development, and he emphasized that children construct knowledge through social interaction. In Vygotsky's theory, children depend on tools provided by the culture, which determines which skills they will develop. Some critics say that Vygotsky overemphasized the role of language in thinking.

3 LANGUAGE DEVELOPMENT: Identify the key features of language, biological and environmental influences on language, and the typical growth of the child's language.

What Is Language?

Language is a form of communication, whether spoken, written, or signed, that is based on a system of symbols. Human languages are infinitely generative. All human languages also have organizational rules of phonology, morphology, syntax, semantics, and pragmatics. Phonology is the sound system of a language; morphology refers to the units of meaning involved in word formation; syntax involves the ways that words must be combined to form acceptable phrases and sentences; semantics refers to the meaning of words and sentences; and pragmatics describes the appropriate use of language in different contexts.

| Biological and Environmental Influences |

Children are biologically prepared to learn language as they and their caregivers interact. Some language scholars argue that the strongest evidence for the biological basis of language is that children all over the world reach language milestones at about the same age despite vast differences in their environmental experiences. However, children do not learn language in a social vacuum. Children benefit when parents and teachers actively engage them in conversation, ask them questions, and talk with, not just to, them. In sum, biology and experience interact to produce language development.

| How Language Develops |

Language acquisition advances through stages. Babbling occurs at about 3 to 6 months, the first word at 10 to 13 months, and two-word utterances at 18 to 24 months. As children move beyond two-word utterances, they can demonstrate that they know some morphological rules, as documented in Jean Berko's study. Children also make advances in phonology, syntax, semantics, and pragmatics. Vocabulary development increases dramatically during the elementary school years, and by the end of elementary school most children can apply appropriate rules of grammar. Metalinguistic awareness also advances in the elementary school years. In adolescence, language changes include more effective use of words; improvements in the ability to understand metaphor, satire, and adult literary works; and writing.

 ## KEY TERMS

development 30
nature-nurture issue 31
continuity-discontinuity
    issue 32
early-later experience
    issue 32
splintered development 33
myelination 35
corpus callosum 37
prefrontal cortex 37
amygdala 37

lateralization 37
schemas 40
assimilation 40
accommodation 40
organization 41
equilibration 41
sensorimotor stage 41
preoperational stage 41
symbolic function
    substage 42
intuitive thought substage 42

centration 43
conservation 43
concrete operational stage 45
seriation 45
transitivity 46
formal operational stage 46
hypothetical-deductive
    reasoning 46
neo-Piagetians 49
zone of proximal
    development (ZPD) 51

scaffolding 51
social constructivist
    approach 53
language 58
phonology 58
morphology 58
syntax 58
semantics 59
pragmatics 59
metalinguistic awareness 65

 ## PORTFOLIO ACTIVITIES

Now that you have a good understanding of this chapter, complete these exercises to expand your thinking.

Independent Reflection

1. Select the general age of the child you expect to teach one day. Make a list of that child's characteristic ways of thinking according to Piaget's theory of cognitive development. List other related characteristics of the child based on your own childhood. Then make a second list of your own current ways of thinking. Compare the lists. In what important cognitive ways do you and the child differ? What adjustments in thinking will you need to make when you set out to communicate with the child? Summarize your thoughts in a brief essay.

2. How might thinking in formal operational ways rather than concrete operational ways help students develop better study skills?

3. What is the most useful idea related to children's language development that you read about in this chapter? Write the idea down in your portfolio and explain how you will implement this idea in your classroom.

Research/Field Experience

4. Find an education article in a magazine or on the Internet that promotes "left-brained" and "right-brained" activities for learning. In a brief report, criticize the article based on what you read in this chapter about neuroscience and brain education.

Go to the Online Learning Center for downloadable portfolio templates.

TAKING IT TO THE NET

- Reflect on Vygotsky's concepts of "scaffolding" and "zone of proximal development" (ZPD). How do teachers identify what is within a child's ZPD? How do teachers determine the type of assistance to give, how much to give, and when a child can work independently? Provide an example of each of these concepts. **http://naecs.crc.uiuc.edu/newsletter/volume3/number4.html**

- Experts argue that enriched classroom and home environments produce improvements in brain functioning and learning. Describe an enriched school environment, including both physical (classroom arrangement) and nonphysical (instructional techniques) attributes. How could this environment contribute to healthy brain development? **www.atozteacherstuff.com/pages/1814.shtml**

- Vocabulary is a critical component of reading comprehension; however, low-income students are exposed to far less written and oral language than their more affluent counterparts. Locate vocabulary games and activities on the Web, and devise a strategy for sharing these activities with parents to maximize students' contact with language. **www.childdevelopmentinfo.com/learning/vocabulary.shtml**

Connect to the Online Learning Center to explore possible answers.

STUDY, PRACTICE, AND SUCCEED

Visit **www.mhhe.com/santedu4e** to review the chapter with self-grading quizzes and self-assessments, to apply the chapter material to two more Crack the Case studies, and for suggested activities to develop your teaching portfolio.

CHAPTER 3

Social Contexts and Socioemotional Development

In the end, the power behind development is life.

—Erik Erikson
European-born American Psychotherapist, 20th Century

Chapter Outline		Learning Goals
Contemporary Theories Bronfenbrenner's Ecological Theory Erikson's Life-Span Development Theory	**1**	Describe two contemporary perspectives on socioemotional development: Bronfenbrenner's ecological theory and Erikson's life-span development theory.
Social Contexts of Development Families Peers Schools	**2**	Discuss how the social contexts of families, peers, and schools are linked with socioemotional development.
Socioemotional Development The Self Moral Development Coping with Stress	**3**	Explain these aspects of children's socioemotional development: self-esteem, identity, moral development, and coping with stress.

TEACHING STORIES Keren Abra

The socioemotional contexts of children's lives influence their ability to learn. Keren Abra teaches fifth grade in San Francisco. A student in her class, Julie, was very quiet, so quiet that in classroom discussions she whispered her responses. Her parents, who had gone through a bitter divorce, agreed that Julie needed a good therapist.

Julie was significantly underachieving, doing minimal work and scoring low on tests. A crisis of low grades and incomplete work brought her mother to school one evening, and her father to school the next morning, to talk with Keren. Later that week, Keren spoke with Julie, who looked terrified. Following are Keren's comments about her talk with Julie:

> I kept some objectives in mind. This child needed to know that she was a good student, that she was loved, that adults could be consistent and responsible, and that she didn't have to hide and keep secrets. I told her that her parents

had come in because we all were concerned about her and knew we needed to help her. I told her that her parents loved her very much and asked if she knew this (she and I agreed that nobody's perfect, least of all adults with their own problems). I explained that a tutor was going to help her with her work . . . I talked with Julie about how much I liked her and about coming forward more in class.

> Change did not happen overnight with Julie, but she did begin to increasingly look me in the eye with a more confident smile. She spoke out more in class, and improved her writing efforts. Her best months were when she was seeing both a therapist and a tutor, although her grades remained a roller coaster. At the end of the school year, she commented that she and her mother both noticed that her best work was when she felt supported and confident. For an 11-year-old, that is a valuable insight.

Preview

Divorce is just one of the many aspects of children's social contexts that can have profound effects on children's performance in school. Later in the chapter, we will examine the topic of divorce and provide further teaching strategies for helping students cope with the divorce of their parents. In this chapter, we will explore how parents cradle children's lives as well as how children's development is influenced by successive waves of peers, friends, and teachers. Children's small worlds widen as they become students and develop relationships with many new people. In this second chapter on development, we will study these social worlds and examine children's socioemotional development.

1 CONTEMPORARY THEORIES

Bronfenbrenner's Ecological Theory   Erikson's Life–Span Development Theory

A number of theories address children's socioemotional development. In this chapter, we will focus on two main theories: Bronfenbrenner's ecological theory and Erikson's life-span development theory. These two theories were chosen for the comprehensive way they address the social contexts in which children develop (Bronfenbrenner) and major changes in children's socioemotional development (Erikson). In Chapter 7, we will discuss other theories (behavioral and social cognitive) that also are relevant to socioemotional development.

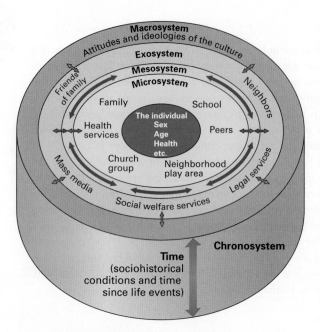

FIGURE 3.1 Bronfenbrenner's Ecological Theory of Development

Bronfenbrenner's ecological theory consists of five environmental systems: microsystem, mesosystem, exosystem, macrosystem, and chronosystem.

Urie Bronfenbrenner developed ecological theory, a perspective that is receiving increased attention. *What is the nature of ecological theory?*

ecological theory Bronfenbrenner's theory that consists of five environmental systems: microsystem, mesosystem, exosystem, macrosystem, and chronosystem.

Bronfenbrenner's Ecological Theory

The ecological theory developed by Urie Bronfenbrenner (1917–2005) primarily focuses on the social contexts in which children live and the people who influence their development.

Five Environmental Systems Bronfenbrenner's (1995, 2004; Bronfenbrenner & Morris, 1998, 2006) **ecological theory** consists of five environmental systems that range from close interpersonal interactions to broad-based influences of culture. The five systems are the microsystem, mesosystem, exosystem, macrosystem, and chronosystem (see Figure 3.1).

A *microsystem* is a setting in which the individual spends considerable time, such as the student's family, peers, school, and neighborhood. Within these microsystems, the individual has direct interactions with parents, teachers, peers, and others. For Bronfenbrenner, the student is not a passive recipient of experiences but is someone who reciprocally interacts with others and helps to construct the microsystem.

The *mesosystem* involves linkages between microsystems. Examples are the connections between family experiences and school experiences and between family and peers. For example, consider one important mesosystem, the connection between schools and families. In one study of a thousand eighth-graders, the joint impact of family and classroom experiences on students' attitudes and achievement was examined as the students made the transition from the last year of middle school to the first year of high school (Epstein, 1983). Students who were given greater opportunities for communication and decision making, whether at home or in the classroom, showed more initiative and earned better grades.

In another mesosystem study, middle school and high school students participated in a program that was designed to connect their families, peers, schools, and parents' work (Cooper, 1995). This outreach program (administered by a university) targeted Latino and African American students in low-income areas. The students commented that the outreach program helped them to bridge the gaps across their different social worlds. Many of the students saw their schools and neighborhoods as contexts in which people expected them to fail, become pregnant and leave school, or behave delinquently. The outreach program provided students with expectations and moral goals to do "something good for your people," such as working in the community and encouraging siblings to go to college. We will have more to say about family-school connections later in the chapter.

The *exosystem* is at work when experiences in another setting (in which the student does not have an active role) influence what students and teachers experience in the immediate context. For example, consider the school and park supervisory boards in a community. They have strong roles in determining the quality of schools, parks, recreation facilities, and libraries. Their decisions can help or hinder a child's development.

The *macrosystem* involves the broader culture. *Culture* is a very broad term that includes the roles of ethnicity and socioeconomic factors in children's development. It's the broadest context in which students and teachers live, including the society's values and customs (Kagitcibasi, 2007; Matsumoto, 2008). For example, some cultures (such as rural China and Iran) emphasize traditional gender roles. Other cultures (such as found in the United States) accept more varied gender roles. In many Middle Eastern countries, educational systems promote male dominance. In the United States, schools increasingly have endorsed the value of equal opportunities for females and males (Matlin, 2008).

Socioeconomic status, an important aspect of culture, can have important effects on students' school performance (Coltrane & others, 2008; Crane & Heaton, 2008).

For example, poverty can overwhelm children's development and impair their ability to learn, although some children in impoverished circumstances are remarkably resilient (Eccles, 2007). We will say much more about poverty and education in Chapter 5, "Sociocultural Diversity."

The *chronosystem* includes the sociohistorical conditions of students' development. For example, the lives of children today are different in many ways from when their parents and grandparents were children (Schaie, 2007). Today's children are more likely to be in child care, use computers, live in a divorced or remarried family, have less contact with relatives outside their immediate family, and grow up in new kinds of dispersed, deconcentrated cities that are not quite urban, rural, or suburban.

Evaluating Bronfenbrenner's Theory   Bronfenbrenner's theory has gained popularity in recent years. It provides one of the few theoretical frameworks for systematically examining social contexts on both micro and macro levels, bridging the gap between behavioral theories that focus on small settings and anthropological theories that analyze larger settings. His theory has been instrumental in showing how different contexts of children's lives are interconnected. As we have just discussed, teachers often need to consider not just what goes on in the classroom but also what happens in students' families, neighborhoods, and peer groups.

Critics of Bronfenbrenner's theory say that it gives too little attention to biological and cognitive factors in children's development. They also point out that the theory does not address the step-by-step developmental changes that are the focus of theories such as Piaget's and Erikson's.

Erikson's Life–Span Development Theory

Complementing Bronfenbrenner's analysis of the social contexts in which children develop and the people who are important in their lives, the theory of Erik Erikson (1902–1994) presents a developmental view of people's lives in stages. Let's take a journey through Erikson's view of the human life span.

Eight Stages of Human Development   In Erikson's (1968) theory, eight stages of development unfold as people go through the human life span (see Figure 3.2). Each stage consists of a developmental task that confronts individuals with a crisis. For Erikson, each crisis is not catastrophic but a turning point of increased vulnerability and enhanced potential. The more successfully an individual resolves each crisis, the more psychologically healthy the individual will be. Each stage has both positive and negative sides.

Trust versus mistrust is Erikson's first psychosocial stage. It occurs in the first year of life. The development of trust requires warm, nurturing caregiving. The positive outcome is a feeling of comfort and minimal fear. Mistrust develops when infants are treated too negatively or are ignored.

Autonomy versus shame and doubt is Erikson's second psychosocial stage. It occurs in late infancy and the toddler years. After gaining trust in their caregivers, infants begin to discover that their behavior is their own. They assert their independence and realize their will. If infants are restrained too much or punished too harshly, they develop a sense of shame and doubt.

Initiative versus guilt is Erikson's third psychosocial stage. It corresponds to early childhood, about 3 to 5 years of age. As young children experience a widening social world, they are challenged more than they were as infants. To cope with these challenges, they need to engage in active, purposeful behavior that involves initiative. Children develop uncomfortable guilt feelings if they are irresponsible or are made to feel too anxious.

Industry versus inferiority is Erikson's fourth psychosocial stage. It corresponds approximately with the elementary school years, from 6 years of age until puberty or early adolescence. As they move into the elementary school years, they direct their energy toward mastering knowledge and intellectual skills. The danger in the

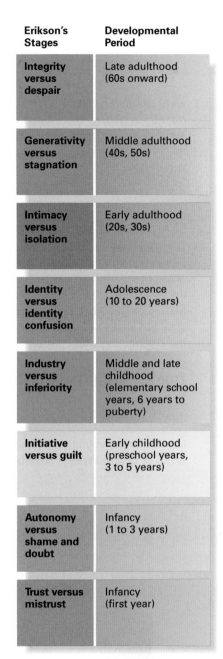

Erikson's Stages	Developmental Period
Integrity versus despair	Late adulthood (60s onward)
Generativity versus stagnation	Middle adulthood (40s, 50s)
Intimacy versus isolation	Early adulthood (20s, 30s)
Identity versus identity confusion	Adolescence (10 to 20 years)
Industry versus inferiority	Middle and late childhood (elementary school years, 6 years to puberty)
Initiative versus guilt	Early childhood (preschool years, 3 to 5 years)
Autonomy versus shame and doubt	Infancy (1 to 3 years)
Trust versus mistrust	Infancy (first year)

FIGURE 3.2 Erikson's Eight Life-Span Stages

Like Freud, Erikson proposed that individuals go through distinct, universal stages of development. Thus, in terms of the continuity-discontinuity issue both favor the discontinuity side of the debate. Notice that the timing of Erikson's first four stages is similar to that of Freud's stages. *What are implications of saying that people go through stages of development?*

BEST PRACTICES
Strategies for Educating Children Based on Bronfenbrenner's Theory

1. *Think about the child as embedded in a number of environmental systems and influences.* These include schools and teachers, parents and siblings, the community and neighborhood, peers and friends, the media, religion, and culture.

2. *Pay attention to the connection between schools and families.* Build these connections through formal and informal outreach.

3. *Recognize the importance of the community, socioeconomic status, and culture in the child's development.* These broader social contexts can have powerful influences on the child's development (Kagitcibasi, 2007; Matsumoto, 2008). Next, Juanita Kirton, an assistant principal at Gramercy Preschool in New York City, describes the community's value for her students.

THROUGH THE EYES OF TEACHERS
The Community Is Full of Learning Opportunities and Supports for Students

Use of the community is very important. New York City is full of opportunities. I have been able to work closely

with the Disabled Library in the neighborhood. They have been great at supplying the school with audiobooks for the children and lending special equipment for their use. The local fire department has been used for numerous trips. The firemen have been especially attentive to the students because of their various disabilities. The fire department has also come to visit the school, which was very exciting for the children. It was amazing to see how patient the firefighters were with the students. I am also encouraged to see many colleges and universities sending items and student teachers visiting the school. Donations from the Hasbro toy company during the holidays make a big difference in the way some students and families get to spend their holiday vacation. Our students are very visible in the New York City community, where we are located. This helps our neighbors get to know the staff and children and creates a safer environment.

Erik Erikson with his wife, Joan, an artist. Erikson generated one of the most important developmental theories of the twentieth century. *Which stage of Erikson's theory are you in? Does Erikson's description of this stage characterize you?*

elementary school years is developing a sense of inferiority, unproductiveness, and incompetence.

Identity versus identity confusion is Erikson's fifth psychosocial stage. It corresponds to the adolescent years. Adolescents try to find out who they are, what they are all about, and where they are going in life. They are confronted with many new roles and adult statuses (such as vocational and romantic). Adolescents need to be allowed to explore different paths to attain a healthy identity. If adolescents do not adequately explore different roles and don't carve out a positive future path, they can remain confused about their identity.

Intimacy versus isolation is Erikson's sixth psychosocial stage. It corresponds to the early adult years, the twenties and thirties. The developmental task is to form positive close relationships with others. The hazard of this stage is that one will fail to form an intimate relationship with a romantic partner or friend and become socially isolated.

Generativity versus stagnation is Erikson's seventh psychosocial stage. It corresponds to the middle adulthood years, the forties and fifties. Generativity means transmitting something positive to the next generation. This can involve such roles as parenting and teaching, through which adults assist the next generation in developing useful lives. Erikson described stagnation as the feeling of having done nothing to help the next generation.

Integrity versus despair is Erikson's eighth and final psychosocial stage. It corresponds to the late adulthood years, the sixties until death. Older adults review their lives, reflecting on what they have done. If the retrospective evaluations are positive, they develop a sense of integrity. That is, they view their life as positively integrated and worth living. In contrast, older adults become despairing if their backward glances are mainly negative.

DEVELOPMENTAL FOCUS 3.1

How Does Erikson's Life-Span Theory Apply to Your Classroom?

Early Childhood

The initiative versus guilt stage of Erikson's theory characterizes my classroom as students are expected to become more responsible throughout the year. Children are assigned "jobs" to do for the day, such as being the door-holder, line leader, or messenger. The children are also expected to follow through with classroom and school rules. Uncomfortable, guilty feelings may arise if the children feel irresponsible as a result of breaking classroom rules or not fulfilling their responsibilities.

—Missy Dangler, *Suburban Hills School*

Elementary School: Grades K–5

The industry versus inferiority stage of Erikson's theory most applies to my second-grade students. As children enter this stage, there is an energy to learn; however, the dangers at this stage are that children may feel incompetent if they are unsuccessful in their work. As a teacher of students at this developmental stage, it is important to give students opportunities to be successful. For example, if a second-grader is reading at a kindergarten level, and second-grade-level materials are given to this student, the student will develop feelings of incompetence. I use leveled reading materials in my classroom in reading and spelling. Each student is reading and being instructed with material at his or her reading level, which fosters feelings of confidence.

—Susan Froelich, *Clinton Elementary School*

Middle School: Grades 6–8

Erikson's identity versus identity confusion stage is evident in my sixth-grade students. At this stage, so many of my students experience a decline in self-esteem. To address these negative feelings, I often have them become the teacher. That is, under my guidance, a student will conduct different classroom activities. Many times I select students who need to be recognized by their peers to be teacher for a day. Other times, I ask students—especially those most reluctant to participate in class—to have lunch with me. During lunch, I give them steps on how to overcome any fears or apprehensions they may have about taking part in class.

—Margaret Reardon, *Pocantico Hills School*

High School: Grades 9–12

As high school teachers, dealing with students in the identity versus identity confusion stage, we need to especially value adolescents as human beings. I know of so many teachers who roll their eyes at their students' petty squabbles and emotional curves. However, we need to remember that we went through the very same things, and these struggles helped to define who we are as adults. This came to me so vividly during my student teaching. The building was so similar in design to my own school. As I walked in the door, I immediately experienced every pimple on my chin and every tear shed in the girls' bathroom. Suddenly, I was the insecure girl listening to Lionel Richie at the dance, longing for John to ask me out.

—Jennifer Heiter, *Bremen High School*

Evaluating Erikson's Theory   Erikson's theory captures some of life's key socio-emotional tasks and places them in a developmental framework (Adams, 2008). His concept of identity is especially helpful in understanding older adolescents and college students. His overall theory was a critical force in forging our current view of human development as lifelong rather than being restricted only to childhood.

Erikson's theory is not without criticism (Kroger, 2007). Some experts point out that his stages are too rigid. Bernice Neugarten (1988) says that identity, intimacy, independence, and many other aspects of socioemotional development are not like

BEST PRACTICES
Strategies for Educating Children Based on Erikson's Theory

1. *Encourage initiative in young children.* Children in pre-school and early childhood education programs should be given a great deal of freedom to explore their world. They should be allowed to choose some of the activities they engage in. If their requests for doing certain activities are reasonable, the requests should be honored. Provide exciting materials that will stimulate their imagination. Children at this stage love to play. It not only benefits their socioemotional development but also is an important medium for their cognitive growth. Especially encourage social play with peers and fantasy play. Help children assume responsibility for putting toys and materials back in place after they have used them. Children can be given a plant or flower to care for and be assisted in caring for it. Criticism should be kept to a minimum so that children will not develop high levels of guilt and anxiety. Young children are going to make lots of mistakes and have lots of spills. They need good models far more than harsh critics. Structure their activities and environment for successes rather than failures by giving them developmentally appropriate tasks. For example, don't frustrate young children by having them sit for long periods of time doing academic paper-and-pencil tasks.

2. *Promote industry in elementary school children.* Teachers have a special responsibility for children's development of industry. It was Erikson's hope that teachers could provide an atmosphere in which children become passionate about learning. In Erikson's words, teachers should mildly but firmly coerce children into the adventure of finding out that they can learn to accomplish things that they themselves would never have thought they could do. In elementary school, children thirst to know. Most arrive at elementary school steeped in curiosity and a motivation to master tasks. In Erikson's view, it is important for teachers to nourish this motivation for mastery and curiosity. Challenge students, but don't overwhelm them. Be firm in requiring students to be productive, but don't be overly critical. Especially be tolerant of honest mistakes and make sure that every student has opportunities for many successes.

3. *Stimulate identity exploration in adolescence.* Recognize that the student's identity is multidimensional. Aspects include vocational goals; intellectual achievement; and interests in hobbies, sports, music, and other areas. Ask adolescents to write essays about such dimensions, exploring who they are and what they want to do with their lives. Encourage adolescents to think independently and to freely express their views. This stimulates self-exploration. Also encourage adolescents to listen to debates on religious, political, and ideological issues. This will stimulate them to examine different perspectives.

Many adolescents in middle schools are just beginning to explore their identity, but even at this time exposing them to various careers and life options can benefit their identity development. Encourage adolescents to talk with a school counselor about career options as well as other aspects of their identity. Have people from different careers come and talk with your students about their work regardless of the grade you teach. Next, Therese Olejniczak, a teacher at Central Middle School in East Grand Forks, Minnesota, describes how she encourages students to think about their identity on the first day of school.

THROUGH THE EYES OF TEACHERS
Using Art to Explore Adolescents' Identities

My seventh-grade art students come to class the first day to read a list of classroom rules. I surprise them by passing out sheets of art paper, old magazines, and glue with the verbal directions to tell me about themselves—build a self-portrait—with torn paper. The students are inventive, enthusiastic, and excited to focus on their identities, and waste no time beginning. . . . After the opening project, my students are at ease knowing their creative expression is allowed and encouraged, and I am better able to understand their many changing attitudes and need to express them.

4. *Examine your life as a teacher through the lens of Erikson's eight stages* (Gratz & Bouton, 1996). For example, you might be at the age at which Erikson says the most important issue is identity versus identity confusion or intimacy versus isolation. Erikson stressed that one of identity's most important dimensions is vocational. Your successful career as a teacher could be a key aspect of your overall identity. Another important aspect of development for young adults is to have positive, close relationships with others. Your identity will benefit from having a positive relationship with a partner and with one or more friends. Many teachers develop strong camaraderie with other teachers or their mentors, which can be very rewarding.

5. *Benefit from the characteristics of some of Erikson's other stages.* Competent teachers trust, show initiative, are industrious and model a sense of mastery, and are motivated to contribute something meaningful to the next generation. In your role as a teacher, you will actively meet the criteria for Erikson's concept of generativity.

beads on a string that appear in neatly packaged age intervals. Rather, they are important issues throughout most of our lives. Although much research has been done on some of Erikson's stages (such as identity), the overall scope of his theory (such as whether the eight stages always occur in the order he proposed) has not been scientifically documented. For example, for some individuals (especially females), intimacy concerns precede identity or develop simultaneously.

Review, Reflect, and Practice

(1) **Describe two contemporary perspectives on socioemotional development: Bronfenbrenner's ecological theory and Erikson's life-span development theory.**

REVIEW

- What are Bronfenbrenner's five environmental systems? What are some criticisms of his theory?
- What are the eight Eriksonian stages? What are some criticisms of his theory?

REFLECT

- How well do you think your own socioemotional development can be described using Erikson's theory?

PRAXIS™ PRACTICE

1. Which of the following is the best example of the mesosystem?
   a. Ike's parents monitor his behavior closely. They know where he is and with whom at all times.
   b. Ike's parents express concern about his grades. They attend parent-teacher conferences and belong to the PTA, as does John's teacher. They chaperone field trips.
   c. Ike attends church regularly, goes to religious school each week, and is preparing for his confirmation.
   d. Ike is quite adept with technology. His parents often ask him to program their electronic devices because of their lack of experience with these things when they were children.

2. Ms. Koslowsky teaches fourth grade. Understanding that it is important for her students to do well on the state-mandated achievement tests, she has high expectations for their daily work. Often her lessons frustrate some of her students because they don't understand the material. Rather than helping them to understand, she forges ahead. She is then frustrated by their performance on homework, often making caustic remarks on their papers. How would Ms. Rogers' teaching style be described from Erikson's perspective?
   a. Ms. Rogers' teaching style is closely aligned with the need to promote industry in elementary school children. Her high expectations will motivate the children to succeed.
   b. Ms. Rogers' teaching style is closely aligned with elementary-school-age children's need to discover who they are and establish an identity.
   c. Ms. Rogers' teaching style is unlikely to promote industry in elementary-school-age children. Instead, it is likely to make them feel inferior.
   d. Ms. Rogers' teaching style is likely to increase students' initiative. They will respond to her high expectations by taking initiative in their work.

Please see the answer key at the end of the book.

How do parents' values and decisions influence students' education and activities?

In Bronfenbrenner's theory, the social contexts in which children live are important influences on their development. Let's explore three of the contexts in which children spend much of their time: families, peers, and schools.

Families

Although children grow up in diverse families, in virtually every family parents play an important role in supporting and stimulating children's academic achievement and attitudes toward school (Epstein, 2007a, b; Schader, 2008). The value parents place on education can mean the difference in whether children do well in school. Parents not only influence children's in-school achievement, but they also make decisions about children's out-of-school activities. Whether children participate in such activities as sports, music, and other activities is heavily influenced by the extent to which parents sign up children for such activities and encourage their participation (Simpkins & others, 2006).

Parenting Styles   There can be times when you as a teacher will be asked to give parents advice. There also might be times when it is helpful for you to understand how parents are rearing their children and the effects this has on the children (Bornstein & Zlotnik, 2008).

Is there a best way to parent? Diana Baumrind (1971, 1996), a leading authority on parenting, thinks so. She states that parents should be neither punitive nor aloof. Rather, they should develop rules for children while at the same time being supportive and nurturing. Hundreds of research studies, including her own, support her view (Collins & Steinberg, 2006). Baumrind says that parenting styles come in four main forms:

- **Authoritarian parenting** is restrictive and punitive. Authoritarian parents exhort children to follow their directions and respect them. They place firm limits and controls on their children and allow little verbal exchange. For example, an authoritarian parent might say, "Do it my way or else. There will be no discussion!" Children of authoritarian parents often behave in socially incompetent ways. They tend to be anxious about social comparison, fail to initiate activity, and have poor communication skills.

- **Authoritative parenting** encourages children to be independent but still places limits and controls on their actions. Extensive verbal give-and-take is allowed, and parents are nurturant and supportive. Children whose parents are authoritative often behave in socially competent ways. They tend to be self-reliant, delay gratification, get along with their peers, and show high self-esteem. Because of these positive outcomes, Baumrind strongly endorses authoritative parenting.

- **Neglectful parenting** is a parenting style in which parents are uninvolved in their children's lives. Children of neglectful parents develop the sense that other aspects of their parents' lives are more important than they are. Children of neglectful parents often behave in socially incompetent ways. They tend to have poor self-control, don't handle independence well, and aren't achievement motivated.

- **Indulgent parenting** is a parenting style in which parents are highly involved with their children but place few limits or restrictions on their behaviors. These parents often let their children do what they want and get their way because

authoritarian parenting A restrictive and punitive parenting style in which there is little verbal exchange between parents and children; associated with children's social incompetence.

authoritative parenting A positive parenting style that encourages children to be independent but still places limits and controls on their actions; extensive verbal give-and-take is allowed; associated with children's social competence.

neglectful parenting A parenting style of uninvolvement in which parents spend little time with their children; associated with children's social incompetence.

indulgent parenting A parenting style of involvement but few limits or restrictions on children's behavior; linked with children's social incompetence.

they believe the combination of nurturant support and lack of restraints will produce a creative, confident child. The result is that these children usually don't learn to control their own behavior. These parents do not take into account the development of the whole child.

Do the benefits of authoritative parenting transcend the boundaries of ethnicity, socioeconomic status, and household composition? Although some exceptions have been found, evidence links authoritative parenting with competence on the part of the child in research across a wide range of ethnic groups, social strata, cultures, and family structures (Collins & Steinberg, 2006; Shea & Coyne, 2008).

Nonetheless, researchers have found that in some ethnic groups, aspects of the authoritarian style may be associated with more positive child outcomes than Baumrind predicts. Elements of the authoritarian style may take on different meanings and have different effects depending on the context (Parke & others, 2008).

For example, Asian American parents often continue aspects of traditional Asian child-rearing practices sometimes described as authoritarian. Many Asian American parents exert considerable control over their children's lives. However, Ruth Chao (2005, 2007) argues that the style of parenting used by many Asian American parents is distinct from the domineering control of the authoritarian style. Instead, Chao argues that the control reflects concern and involvement in children's lives and is best conceptualized as a type of training. The high academic achievement of Asian American children may be a consequence of the "training" provided by their parents.

According to Ruth Chao, what type of parenting style do many Asian American parents use?

An emphasis on requiring respect and obedience is also associated with the authoritarian style. However, in many African American and Latino families, especially in low-income, dangerous neighborhoods, this type of child rearing may have positive outcomes. In these contexts, requiring obedience to parental authority may be an adaptive strategy to keep children from engaging in antisocial behavior that can have serious consequences for the victim or the perpetrator (Dixon, Graber, & Brooks-Gunn, 2008; McLoyd, Aikens, & Burton, 2006).

In addition to parenting styles, ethnic groups vary on many other factors, including their socioeconomic status (SES) (Harris & Graham, 2007; Patterson & Hastings, 2007). More children in African American and Latino families live in lower-SES circumstances than non-Latino children, and there are socioeconomic status differences in the way that parents think about education (Gonzales & others, 2007; Hernandez & others, 2007). Middle-SES parents more often think of education as something that should be mutually encouraged by parents and teachers. Lower-SES parents are more inclined to view education as the teacher's job. In the *Diversity and Education* interlude, we will explore educational concerns about America's fastest-growing female minority population—Latinas.

Coparenting   *Coparenting* is the support that parents provide one another in jointly raising a child. Poor coordination between parents, undermining of the other parent, lack of cooperation and warmth, and disconnection by one parent are conditions that place children at risk for problems (Feinberg & Kan, 2008). For example, a recent study revealed that coparenting influenced children's effortful control above and beyond maternal and paternal parenting by themselves (Karreman & others, 2008).

The Changing Family in a Changing Society   Increasing numbers of children are being raised in divorced families, stepparent families, and families in which both parents work outside the home. As divorce has become epidemic, a staggering number of children have been growing up in single-parent families. The United States has a higher percentage of single-parent families than virtually any other industrialized country (see Figure 3.3). Today, about one in every four children in the United States have lived a portion of their lives in a stepfamily by age 18. Also, more than two of every three mothers with a child from 6 to 17 years of age are in the labor force.

DIVERSITY AND EDUCATION
Are America's Schools Leaving Latinas Behind?

What educational challenges do Latinas face?

The high school graduation rate of Latinas is lower than for girls in any other ethnic group, and they are the least likely to go to college (National Center for Education Statistics, 2006). Despite the importance of education to the Latino community, family needs and peer pressure often clash with Latinas' school expectations (Montero-Sieburth & Melendez, 2007). For example, many Latinas face pressure about going to college from boyfriends and fiancés who expect their girlfriends or future wives to not be "too educated."

Contrary to stereotypes about Latino communities, most Latino parents hope that their children will excel in school. However, many Latino families face economic and social problems that defer the realization of those dreams for their children (Rodriguez-Galindo, 2006).

Latino girls and boys face similar educational challenges and experience stereotyping and other obstacles that discourage their success in school. Some obstacles, though, are different for Latinas than Latinos (Lara, 2006). Latinas are three times as likely to fear for their personal safety in schools as other girls, and too often Latinos are assumed to be gang members by teachers and counselors simply because they speak Spanish (Ginorio & Huston, 2000).

Recommendations for improving the education of Latinas and Latinos include the following:

- *All adults need to encourage academic success.* Latinas and Latinos need to hear from all the adults in their lives that college and professional careers are rewarding options and ones that they can achieve.

- *Involve the whole family in the process of college preparation.* Teachers and counselors need to work with Latino families to demystify college requirements and the long-term benefits of college.

- *Deal meaningfully with stereotypes and challenges such as adolescent pregnancy that impact school performance.* This includes offering child care and alternative scheduling and recognizing that being a young mother and completing one's education are not incompatible.

FIGURE 3.3 Single-Parent Families in Various Countries

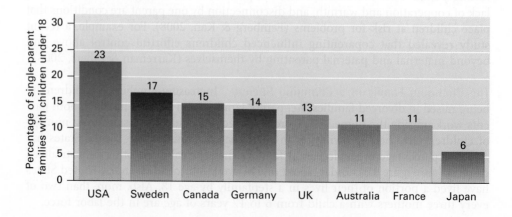

Working Parents   Work can produce positive and negative effects on parenting (Crouter & McHale, 2005). Recent research indicates that what matters for children's development is the nature of parents' work rather than whether one or both parents works outside the home (Clarke-Stewart, 2006). Ann Crouter (2006) recently described how parents bring their experiences at work into their homes. She concluded that parents who have poor working conditions, such as long hours, overtime work, stressful work, and lack of autonomy at work, are likely to be more irritable at home and engage in less effective parenting than their counterparts who have better work conditions in their jobs. A consistent finding is the children (especially girls) of working mothers engage in less gender stereotyping and have more egalitarian views of gender (Goldberg & Lucas-Thompson, 2008).

Children in Divorced Families   Children from divorced families show poorer adjustment than their counterparts in nondivorced families (Hetherington, 2006; Pham & Carlson, 2008) For example, a longitudinal study revealed that when individuals experienced the divorce of their parents in childhood or adolescence, it was linked to having unstable romantic or marital relationships and low levels of education in adulthood (Amato, 2006). A recent study revealed that adolescent girls with divorced parents were especially vulnerable to developing depressive symptoms (Oldehinkel & others, 2008). Nonetheless, keep in mind that a majority of children in divorced families do not have significant adjustment problems (Ahrons, 2007).

What concerns are involved in whether parents should stay together for the sake of the children or become divorced?

Note that marital conflict may have negative consequences for children in the context of marriage or divorce (Cox & others, 2008). Indeed, many of the problems children from divorced homes experience begin during the predivorce period, a time when parents are often in active conflict with other. Thus, when children from divorced homes show problems, the problems may not be due only to the divorce, but the marital conflict that led to it (Thompson, 2008).

The effects of divorce on children are complex, depending on such factors as the child's age, the child's strengths and weaknesses at the time of the divorce, the type of custody, socioeconomic status, and postdivorce family functioning (Kelly, 2007; Wallerstein, 2008). The use of support systems (relatives, friends, housekeepers), an ongoing positive relationship between the custodial parent and the ex-spouse, the ability to meet financial needs, and quality schooling help children adjust to the stressful circumstances of divorce (Huurre, Junkkari, & Aro, 2006).

E. Mavis Hetherington's (1995, 2006) research documents the importance of schools when children grow up in a divorced family. Throughout elementary school, children in divorced families had the highest achievement and fewest problems when both the parenting environment and the school environment were authoritative (according to Baumrind's categorization). In the divorced families, when only one parent was authoritative, an authoritative school improved the child's adjustment. The most negative parenting environment occurred when neither parent was authoritative. The most negative school environment was chaotic and neglecting.

Children in Stepfamilies   As in divorced families, children in stepfamilies show more adjustment problems than children in nondivorced families (Hetherington, 2006). The adjustment problems are similar to those found among children of divorced parents—academic problems and lower self-esteem, for example. However, it is important to recognize that like in divorced families, a majority of children in stepfamilies do not have problems. In one analysis, 25 percent of children from stepfamilies showed adjustment problems compared with 10 percent in intact, never-divorced families (Hetherington & Kelly, 2002). Adolescence is an especially difficult time for the formation of a stepfamily (Anderson & others, 1999). This may occur because becoming part of a stepfamily exacerbates normal adolescent concerns about identity, sexuality, and autonomy.

How is parental management and involvement linked to students' achievement?

School–Family Linkages In Bronfenbrenner's theory, linkages between the family and the school are an important mesosystem (Fiese, Eckert, & Spagnola, 2006). Also, in Hetherington's study, which we just discussed, an authoritative school environment benefited children from divorced families. Two aspects of family-school linkages are parents as managers and parental involvement, which we discuss next.

Parents as Managers Parents can play important roles as managers of children's opportunities, as monitors of their behavior, and as social initiators and arrangers (Parke & Buriel, 2006). Mothers are more likely than fathers to engage in a managerial role in parenting. For example, parental monitoring of adolescents is especially important in determining whether an adolescent becomes a delinquent (Laird & others, 2008). A recent study revealed that maternal monitoring was linked to a lower incidence of delinquency in Latino girls (Loukas, Suizzo, & Prelow, 2007).

Researchers have found that family management practices are positively related to students' grades and self-responsibility, and negatively to school-related problems (Eccles, 2007; Taylor & Lopez, 2005). Among the most important family management practices in this regard are maintaining a structured and organized family environment, such as establishing routines for homework, chores, bedtime, and so on, and effectively monitoring the child's behavior. A recent research review of family functioning in African American students' academic achievement found that when African American parents monitored their son's academic achievement by ensuring that homework was completed, restricted time spent on nonproductive distractions (such as video games and TV), and participated in a consistent, positive dialogue with teachers and school officials, their son's academic achievement benefited (Mandara, 2006).

Parental Involvement and School-Family-Community Connections Even though parents typically spend less time with their children as the children go through elementary and secondary school, they continue to have a strong influence on children's development. Parents can serve as gatekeepers and provide guidance as children assume more responsibility for themselves (Huston & Ripke, 2006). Parents especially play an important role in supporting and stimulating children's academic achievement. The value parents place on education can mean the difference in whether children do well in school. Parents not only influence children's in-school achievement,

DEVELOPMENTAL FOCUS 3.2
How Do You Get Parents/Guardians Involved in the Schooling of Their Child?

Early Childhood

Parents are an integral part of our classroom community; teachers cannot be successful without parental cooperation and participation. We engage parents through ongoing conversation, home phone calls when needed, weekly newsletters, e-mails, parent-teacher conferences, and workshops every month where dinner is served.

—Valarie Gorham, *Kiddie Quarters, Inc.*

Elementary School: Grades K–5

Not all parents are available to volunteer in the classroom. For that reason, I provide alternative ways for parents to participate in their child's schooling. For example, I sometimes ask parents to prepare materials at home that will be used in a classroom lesson. Additionally, each month we have a monthly homework calendar that parents complete with their child and fill out a response form on the back letting me know what the parent learned about their child, as well as how they helped their child complete the tasks.

—Heather Zoldak, *Ridge Wood Elementary School*

Middle School: Grades 6–8

My team uses technology to communicate with parents daily. We post grades, homework, and daily announcements online. We also require our students to use planners to write down assignments, missing work, and so on. We contact parents if there are concerns, but we also contact parents with positive news about their child.

—Mark Fodness, *Bemidji Middle School*

High School: Grades 9–12

I teach 15 miles from my home in a small community, but I make it a point to be visible—this may mean shopping at the grocery or drugstore in my school's community rather than frequenting the one closer to my home. When I shop within the vicinity of the school, I often see my students working and parents shopping, which makes me more approachable. I also try to go to school plays, competitions, and athletic events so that when parent-teacher conferences roll around, parents who have grown familiar with my face may be more inclined to attend the conference.

—Jennifer Heiter, *Bremen High School*

but they also make decisions about children's out-of-school activities (Eccles, 2007). Whether children participate in such activities as sports, music, and other activities is heavily influenced by the extent to which parents sign up children for such activities and encourage their participation.

Experienced teachers know the importance of getting parents involved in children's education. All parents, even those with considerable education, need yearly guidance from teachers in how to remain productively involved in their children's education. For one thing, education expert Joyce Epstein (2001, 2005, 2007a, b) explains that almost all parents want their children to succeed in school, but need clear and useful information from their children's teachers and from other school and district leaders in order to help their children develop their full potential. For example, sometimes parents ask their child, "How was school today?" We know that may end with the child responding, "Fine" or "Okay" and not much more. Parents should be guided, instead, to ask their child, "Would you read to me something you wrote today?" or "Could you show me something you learned in math today?" or similar

TECHNOLOGY AND EDUCATION

Communicating with Parents About Television and Children's Development

Many children spend more time in front of the television set than they do with their parents. U.S. 8- to 18-year-olds average more than 21 hours a week watching television (Roberts & Foehr, 2008). Amazingly, the 20,000 hours of television, on average, that children watch by the time they graduate from high school represents more hours than they have spent in the classroom!

How does television influence children's attention, creativity, and mental ability? Media use has not been found to cause attention deficit hyperactivity disorder but there is a small link between heavy television watching and nonclinical attention levels in children (Schmidt & Vanderwater, 2008). In general, television has not been shown to influence children's creativity but is negatively related to their mental ability (Comstock & Scharrer, 2006).

The more children watch TV, the lower their school achievement (Comstock & Scharrer, 2006). Why might watching TV be negatively related to children's achievement? Three possibilities are interference, displacement, and self-defeating tastes/preferences. In terms of interference, having a TV on can distract children while they are doing cognitive tasks such as homework. In terms of displacement, TV can take time away from engaging in achievement-related tasks, such as homework, reading, writing, and mathematics. Researchers have found that children's reading achievement is negatively linked to the amount of time they watch TV (Comstock & Scharrer, 2006). In terms of self-defeating tastes and preferences, TV attracts children to entertainment, sports, commercials, and other activities that capture their interest more than school achievement. Children who are heavy TV watchers tend to view books as dull and boring (Comstock & Scharrer, 2006).

Here are some recommendations that you can communicate to parents about reducing TV's negative impact and increasing its positive impact on their children's development (Singer & Singer, 1987):

- Monitor children's viewing habits and plan what they will watch, instead of letting them view TV randomly. Be active with young children between planned programs.

"Mrs. Horton, could you stop by school today?"

Copyright © Martha Campbell.

- Look for children's programs that feature children in the child's age group.
- Make sure that television is not a substitute for other activities.
- Develop discussions about sensitive television themes with children. Give them the opportunity to ask questions about the programs.
- Balance reading and television activities. Children can "follow up" on interesting television programs by checking out the library books from which some programs have been adapted and by pursuing additional stories by the authors of those books.
- Point out positive examples of females performing competently both in professions and at home, and positive examples that show how various ethnic and cultural groups contribute to a better society.

direct questions about work and projects in other content areas. Conversations or homework assignments that enable students to share ideas and celebrate successes are likely to promote positive school-related parent-child interactions.

A low level of parental involvement concerns educators because it is linked with students' low achievement (Anguiano, 2004). By contrast, in a study of more than 16,000 students, the students were more likely to get *A*s and less likely to repeat a grade or be expelled if both parents were highly involved in their schooling (National Center for Education Statistics, 1997). In this study, high involvement was defined as the parent participating in three or four of the following: school meetings, a teacher

BEST PRACTICES
Strategies for Forging School–Family–Community Linkages

Joan Epstein has developed six types of involvement that can be implemented to develop comprehensive school, family, and community partnerships in any elementary, middle, or high school. These goal-oriented and age-appropriate activities include the following:

1. *Provide assistance to families.* Schools can provide parents with information about child-rearing skills, the importance of family support, child and adolescent development, and home contexts that enhance learning at each grade level. Teachers are an important contact point between schools and families and can become aware of whether the family is meeting the child's basic physical and health needs. Next, Juanita Kirton, who earlier described the importance of involving the community in children's education, talks about the importance of involving parents in children's schooling.

THROUGH THE EYES OF TEACHERS
Connecting with Parents

Parents are the primary ingredient of the classroom team at the Gramercy Preschool. Many parents of preschool children have no idea as to how or if their child will develop. It becomes the job of educators and other professionals to assist parents in their child's development. We then become partners. We have ongoing parent training groups, support groups, and parents can spend time in school with a therapist at any time. The Gramercy Preschool has an open-door policy. . . . When a family faces a very challenging situation, I might meet with them or I might call in the psychologist to assist with specific issues. We have on occasion asked parents to assist other parents or to be a resource for others. This is powerful and gives support to families.

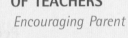

This mother is working with her son at a Saturday math workshop in Oakland, California, sponsored by Family Math.

2. *Communicate effectively with families about school programs and their child's progress.* This involves both school-to-home and home-to-school communication. Encourage parents to attend parent-teacher conferences and other school functions (Eagle & Oeth, 2008; Glasgow & Whitney, 2009). Their attendance conveys to their children that they are interested in their school performance. Set up times for parent meetings that are convenient for them to attend. Most parents cannot come to meetings during the school day because of other obligations. One option is "work nights" for parents and children to come to school and work on various projects to improve the school's physical appearance, mount artwork, and so on. Also, work on developing activities in which parents can get to know each other, not just know the teacher.

3. *Encourage parents to be volunteers.* Try to match the skills of volunteers to classroom needs. Remember from the opening teaching story in Chapter 2 that in some schools parents are extensively involved in educational planning and assisting teachers. Parents have different talents and abilities, just like children, which is reflected in the following comments by Heather Zoldak, a teacher at Ridge Wood Elementary School in Michigan.

THROUGH THE EYES OF TEACHERS
Encouraging Parent Involvement

Understanding that parents come with different levels of comfort with the school environment is important when encouraging parent support for the classroom. Prepare a variety of opportunities for parents to become involved both inside the classroom and to support the classroom in other ways. Due to busy schedules, work restrictions, or comfort level based on their own experiences with school, some parents may be more involved if they can help outside the classroom on field trips or even prepare items at home for an upcoming project. Taking steps to build the comfort level and relationship with parents is a key factor in encouraging parents to be volunteers.

4. *Involve families with their children in learning activities at home.* This includes homework and other curriculum-linked activities and decisions (Epstein, 2007b). Epstein (1998) coined the term *interactive homework* and designed a program that encourages students to go to their parents for help. In one elementary school that uses Epstein's approach, a weekly teacher's letter informs parents about the objective of each assignment, gives directions, and asks for comments.

(continued)

BEST PRACTICES
Strategies for Forging School–Family–Community Linkages

5. *Include families as participants in school decisions.* Parents can be invited to be on PTA/PTO boards, various committees, councils, and other parent organizations. At Antwa Elementary School in a rural area of Wisconsin, potluck supper parent-teacher organization meetings involve discussions with parents about school and district educational goals, age-appropriate learning, child discipline, and testing performance.

6. *Coordinate community collaboration.* Help interconnect the work and resources of community businesses, agencies, colleges and universities, and other groups to strengthen school programs, family practices, and student learning (Epstein, 2007a, 2009). Schools can alert families to community programs and services that will benefit them.

conference, a class meeting, or volunteering. Other studies have found that students' grades and academic achievement are linked to parental involvement (Epstein, 2005; Sheldon & Epstein, 2005). For information about getting parents involved in their children's television viewing habits, see the *Technology and Education* interlude.

For ways to develop effective school-family-community partnerships and programs, see the Web site of the National Network of Partnership Schools at Johns Hopkins University (NNPS): www.partnershipschool.org. Especially look at the section titled "In the Spotlight."

Peers

In addition to families and teachers, peers also play powerful roles in children's development (Allen & Antonishak, 2008). Just what are peers?

In the context of child development, *peers* are children of about the same age or maturity level. One of the most important functions of the peer group is to provide a source of information and comparison about the world outside of the family.

Peer relations are linked to whether children do well in school and later in life (Bukowski, Brendgen, & Vitaro, 2007; Song & Siegel, 2008). Consider the results of these two longitudinal studies that illustrate the positive long-term influence that peer relations in childhood can have:

- Competence in peer relations during elementary school was linked to work success and satisfaction in romantic relationships in early adulthood (Collins & van Dulmen, 2006). Competence in peer relations was assessed by teacher ratings of children's social contact with peers, popularity, friendship, and social skills and leadership.
- Popularity with peers and a low level of aggression at age 8 foreshadowed a higher occupational status at age 48 (Huesmann & others, 2006).

Peer Statuses Developmentalists have pinpointed five types of peer status: popular children, average children, neglected children, rejected children, and controversial children.

Many children worry about whether or not they are popular (McElhaney & others, 2008). *Popular children* are frequently nominated as a best friend and are rarely disliked by their peers. Popular children give out reinforcements, listen carefully, maintain open lines of communication with peers, are happy, act like themselves, show enthusiasm and concern for others, and are self-confident without being conceited (Hartup, 1983). *Average children* receive an average number of both positive and negative nominations from their peers. *Neglected children* are infrequently nominated as a best friend but are not disliked by their peers. *Rejected children* are infrequently

What are some statuses that children have with their peers?

nominated as someone's best friend and are often actively disliked by their peers. *Controversial children* are frequently nominated both as someone's best friend and as being disliked.

Rejected children often have more serious adjustment problems than do neglected children. A social-skills intervention program was successful in increasing social acceptance and self-esteem and decreasing depression and anxiety in peer-rejected children (DeRosier & Marcus, 2005). Students participated in the program once a week (50 to 60 minutes) for eight weeks. The program included instruction in how to manage emotions, how to improve prosocial skills, how to become better communicators, and how to compromise and negotiate.

A special peer relations problem involves bullying. We will discuss bullying in Chapter 14, "Managing the Classroom," where we will provide strategies for dealing with bullies.

Friendship   The importance of friendship was underscored in a two-year longitudinal study (Wentzel, Barry, & Caldwell, 2004). Sixth-grade students who did not have a friend engaged in less prosocial behavior (cooperation, sharing, helping others), had lower grades, and were more emotionally distressed (depression, low well-being) than their counterparts with one or more friends. Two years later, in the eighth grade, the students who did not have a friend in the sixth grade were still more emotionally distressed.

Having friends can be a developmental advantage, but keep in mind that friendships are not all alike (Lindsey & Stopp, 2008; Rubin, Fredstrom, & Bowker, 2008). Having friends who are academically oriented, socially skilled, and supportive is a developmental advantage. For example, a recent study revealed that friends' grade-point averages were an important positive attribute (Cook, Deng, & Morgano, 2007). Friends' grade-point averages were consistent predictors of positive school achievement and also were linked to a lower level of negative behavior in areas such as drug abuse and acting out. Another recent study found that taking math courses in high school, especially for girls, was strongly linked to the achievement of their best friends (Crosnoe & others, 2008). And having delinquent peers and friends greatly increases the risk of becoming delinquent (Brown & others, 2008; Dishion, Piehler, & Myers, 2008). It sometimes is disadvantageous to a child or an adolescent to be friends with someone who is several years older. Students with older friends engage in more deviant behaviors than their counterparts who have same-age friends (Poulin & Peterson, 2007). Early-maturing adolescents are especially vulnerable in this regard.

What are some aspects of friendship that might influence a student's schooling and achievement?

Schools

In school, children spend many years as members of a small society that exerts a tremendous influence on their socioemotional development. How does this social world change as children develop?

Schools' Changing Social Developmental Contexts   Social contexts vary through the early childhood, elementary school, and adolescent years (Kellough & Carjuzaa, 2009; Minuchin & Shapiro, 1983). The early childhood setting is a protected environment whose boundary is the classroom. In this limited social setting, young children interact with one or two teachers, usually female, who are powerful figures in their lives. Young children also interact with peers in dyads or small groups.

The classroom still is the main context in elementary school, although it is more likely to be experienced as a social unit than is the early childhood classroom. The teacher symbolizes authority, which establishes the climate of the classroom, the conditions of social interaction, and the nature of group functioning. Peer groups are more important now, and students have an increased interest in friendship.

BEST PRACTICES
Strategies for Improving Children's Social Skills

In every class you teach, some children will likely have weak social skills. One or two might be rejected children. Several others might be neglected. Are there things you can do to help these children improve their social skills? As you think about this, keep in mind that improving social skills is easier when children are 10 years of age or younger (Malik & Furman, 1993). In adolescence, peer reputations become more fixed as crowds and peer groups take on more importance. Here are some good strategies for improving children's social skills:

1. *Help rejected children learn to listen to peers and "hear what they say" instead of trying to dominate peers.*

2. *Help neglected children attract attention from peers in positive ways and hold their attention.* They can do this by asking questions, listening in a warm and friendly way, and saying things about themselves that relate to the peers' interests. Also work with neglected children on entering groups more effectively.

3. *Provide children low in social skills with knowledge about how to improve these skills.* In one study of sixth- and seventh-graders, knowledge of both appropriate and inappropriate strategies for making friends was related positively to peer acceptance (Wentzel & Erdley, 1993).

Knowledge of Appropriate Strategies Includes Knowing:

• How to initiate interaction, such as asking someone about his or her favorite activities and asking the other child to do things together

• That it is important to be nice, kind, and considerate

• That it is necessary to show respect for others by being courteous and listening to what others have to say

Knowledge of Inappropriate Strategies Includes Knowing:

• That it is not a good idea to be aggressive, show disrespect, be inconsiderate, hurt others' feelings, gossip, spread rumors, embarrass others, or criticize others

• Not to present yourself negatively, be self-centered, care only about yourself, or be jealous, grouchy, or angry all the time

• Not to engage in antisocial behavior, such as fighting, yelling at others, picking on others, making fun of others, being dishonest, breaking school rules, or taking drugs

4. *Read and discuss appropriate books on peer relations with students, and devise supportive games and activities.* Include these as thematic units in your curriculum for young children. Make books on peer relations and friendship available to older children and adolescents.

As children move into middle and junior high school, the school environment increases in scope and complexity (Eccles, 2007). The social field is now the whole school rather than the classroom. Adolescents interact with teachers and peers from a broader range of cultural backgrounds on a broader range of interests. More of the teachers are male. Adolescents' social behavior becomes weighted more strongly toward peers, extracurricular activities, clubs, and the community. Secondary school students are more aware of the school as a social system and might be motivated to conform to it or challenge it.

Early Childhood Education   There are many variations in how young children are educated (Driscoll & Nagel, 2008; Henninger, 2009). However, an increasing number of education experts advocate that this education be developmentally appropriate (Hyson, 2007; Morrison, 2009).

developmentally appropriate education Education based on knowledge of the typical development of children within an age span (age-appropriateness) as well as the uniqueness of the child (individual-appropriateness).

Developmentally Appropriate Education   In Chapters 1 and 2, we described the importance of engaging in developmentally appropriate teaching practices. Here we expand on this topic in our discussion of developmentally appropriate education for children from birth to 8 years of age. **Developmentally appropriate education** is based on knowledge of the typical development of children within an age span (age-appropriateness) as well as the uniqueness of the child (individual-appropriateness). Here are some of the themes of developmentally appropriate education (Bredekamp & Copple, 1997):

- *Domains of children's development—physical, cognitive, and socioemotional—are closely linked and development in one domain can influence and be influenced by development in other domains.* Recognition of the connections across domains can be used to plan children's learning experiences.

- *Development occurs in a relatively orderly sequence with later abilities, skills, and knowledge building on those already acquired.* Knowledge of typical development within the age range served by the program provides a general framework to guide teachers in preparing the learning environment.

- *Individual variation characterizes children's development.* Each child is a unique individual, and all children have their own strengths, needs, and interests. Recognizing this individual variation is a key aspect of being a competent teacher.

- *Development is influenced by multiple social and cultural contexts.* Teachers need to understand how sociocultural contexts—such as poverty and ethnicity—affect children's development.

- *Children are active learners and should be encouraged to construct an understanding of the world around them.* Children contribute to their own learning as they strive to make meaning out of their daily experiences.

- *Development advances when children have opportunities to practice newly acquired skills as well as when they experience a challenge just beyond their present level of mastery.* In tasks that are just beyond the child's independent reach, the adult and more-competent peers can provide scaffolding that allows the child to learn.

- *Children develop best in the context of a community where they are safe and valued, their physical needs are met, and they feel psychologically secure.* Children benefit from having caring teachers who genuinely want to help them learn and develop in positive ways.

Do developmentally appropriate educational practices improve young children's development? Some researchers have found that young children in developmentally appropriate classrooms are likely to have less stress, be more motivated, be more skilled socially, have better work habits, be more creative, have better language skills, and demonstrate better math skills than children in developmentally inappropriate classrooms (Hart & others, 1996, 2003; Sherman & Mueller, 1996; Stipek & others, 1995). However, not all studies show significant positive benefits for developmentally appropriate education (Hyson, Copple, & Jones, 2006). Among the reasons it is difficult to generalize about research on developmentally appropriate education is that individual programs often vary, and developmentally appropriate education is an evolving concept. Recent changes in the concept have given more attention to sociocultural factors, the teacher's active involvement and implementation of systematic intentions, as well as how strong academic skills should be emphasized and how they should be taught.

The Reggio Emilia Approach   The Reggio Emilia approach, which was developed in the northern Italian city of Reggio Emilia, reflects a developmentally appropriate approach to early childhood education. The children are encouraged to learn by investigating and exploring topics that interest them. A wide range of stimulating media and materials is available for children to use as they learn music, movement,

A Reggio Emilia classroom in which young children explore topics that interest them.

Larry Page and Sergey Brin, founders of the highly successful Internet search engine, Google, recently said that their early years at Montessori schools were a major factor in their success (International Montessori Council, 2006). During an interview with Barbara Walters, they said they learned how to be self-directed and self-starters at Montessori (ABC News, 2005). They commented that Montessori experiences encouraged them to think for themselves and allowed them the freedom to develop their own interests.

What is the curriculum controversy in early childhood education?

Montessori approach An educational philosophy in which children are given considerable freedom and spontaneity in choosing activities and are allowed to move from one activity to another as they desire.

drawing, painting, sculpting, collages, puppets and disguises, and photography, for example (Strong-Wilson & Ellis, 2007). At the core of the Reggio Emilia approach is the image of children who are competent and have rights, especially the right to outstanding care and education. Parent participation is considered essential, and cooperation is a major theme in the schools. Many early childhood education experts point out that the Reggio Emilia approach provides a supportive, stimulating context in which children are motivated to explore their world in a competent and confident manner (New, 2005, 2007).

The Montessori Approach Montessori schools are patterned after the educational philosophy of Maria Montessori (1870–1952), an Italian physician-turned-educator, who crafted a revolutionary approach to young children's education at the beginning of the twentieth century. Her approach has been widely adopted in private schools, especially those with early childhood programs, in the United States.

The **Montessori approach** is a philosophy of education in which children are given considerable freedom and spontaneity in choosing activities. They are allowed to move from one activity to another as they desire. The teacher acts as a facilitator rather than a director. The teacher shows the child how to perform intellectual activities, demonstrates interesting ways to explore curriculum materials, and offers help when the child requests it (Cossentino, 2008). A special emphasis in Montessori schools is to encourage children to make decisions at an early age and become self-regulated problem solvers who manage time effectively (Hyson, Copple, & Jones, 2006). The number of Montessori schools in the United States has expanded dramatically in recent years, from one school in 1959 to 355 schools in 1970 to approximately 4,000 in 2005 (Whitescarver, 2006).

Some developmentalists favor the Montessori approach, but others hold that it neglects children's social development. For example, although Montessori fosters independence and the development of cognitive skills, it deemphasizes verbal interaction between the teacher and child and peer interaction. Montessori's critics also argue that it restricts imaginative play and that its heavy reliance on self-corrective materials may not adequately allow for creativity and for a variety of learning styles (Goffin & Wilson, 2001).

Controversy in Early Childhood Education A current controversy in early childhood education involves what the curriculum for early childhood education should be (Hyson, 2007). On one side are those who advocate a child-centered, constructivist approach much like that emphasized by the National Association for the Education of Young Children (NAEYC), along the lines of developmentally appropriate practice. On the other side are those who advocate an academic, direct instruction approach.

In reality, many high-quality early childhood education programs include both academic and constructivist approaches. Many education experts like Lilian Katz (1999), though, worry about academic approaches that place too much pressure on young children to achieve and don't provide any opportunities to actively construct knowledge. Competent early childhood programs also should focus on cognitive development *and* socioemotional development, not exclusively on cognitive development (Kagan & Scott-Little, 2004; NAEYC, 2002).

Early Childhood Education for Children from Low-Income Families   Beginning in the 1960s, *Project Head Start* was designed to provide young children from low-income families opportunities to acquire the skills and experiences that are important for success in school. Funded by the federal government, Project Head Start continues to serve children who are disadvantaged today. Project Head Start is the largest federally funded program for U.S. children (Hagen & Lamb-Parker, 2008).

In high-quality Head Start programs, parents and communities are involved in positive ways (Thurgood, 2001). The teachers are knowledgeable about children's development and use developmentally appropriate practices. Researchers have found that when young children from low-income families experience a quality Head Start program, there are substantial long-term benefits (Allen, 2008). These include being less likely to drop out of school, to be in a special education class, or to be on welfare than their low-income counterparts who did not attend a Head Start program (Lazar & others, 1982; Schweinhart, 1999). However, Head Start programs are not all created equal. One estimate is that 40 percent of the 1,400 Head Start programs are inadequate (Zigler & Finn-Stevenson, 1999).

The Transition to Elementary School   As children make the transition to elementary school, they interact and develop relationships with new and significant others. School provides them with a rich source of ideas to shape their sense of self.

A special concern about early elementary school classrooms is that they not proceed primarily on the basis of negative feedback. I (your author) vividly remember my first-grade teacher. Unfortunately, she never smiled; she was a dictator in the classroom, and learning (or lack of learning) progressed more on the basis of fear than of enjoyment and passion. Fortunately, I experienced some warmer, more student-friendly teachers later on.

Children's self-esteem is higher when they begin elementary school than when they complete it (Blumenfeld & others, 1981). Is that because they experienced so much negative feedback and were criticized so much along the way? We will say more about the roles of reinforcement and punishment in children's learning in Chapter 7 and about managing the classroom in Chapter 14.

The Schooling of Adolescents   Three special concerns about adolescent schooling are (1) the transition to middle or junior high school, (2) effective schooling for young adolescents, and (3) the quality of high schools. How might the transition to middle or junior high school be difficult for many students?

The Transition to Middle or Junior High School   This transition can be stressful because it coincides with many other developmental changes (Anderman & Mueller, 2008; Eccles, 2007). Students are beginning puberty and have increased concerns about their body image. The hormonal changes of puberty stimulate increased interest in sexual matters. Students are becoming more independent from their parents and want to spend more time with peers. They must make the change from a smaller, more personalized classroom to a larger, more impersonal school. Achievement becomes more serious business, and getting good grades becomes more competitive (Kellough & Carjuzaa, 2009).

The transition from elementary to middle or junior high school occurs at the same time as a number of other developmental changes. *What are some of these other developmental changes?*

As students move from elementary to middle or junior high school, they experience the *top-dog phenomenon*. This refers to moving from the top position (in elementary school, being the oldest, biggest, and most powerful students in the school) to the lowest position (in middle or junior high school, being the youngest, smallest, and least powerful students in the school). A recent study in North Carolina schools revealed that sixth-grade students attending middle schools were far more likely to be cited for discipline problems than their counterparts who were attending elementary schools (Cook & others, 2008). Schools that provide more support, less anonymity, more stability, and less complexity improve student adjustment during this transition (Fenzel, Blyth, & Simmons, 1991).

There can also be positive aspects to the transition to middle or junior high school. Students are more likely to feel grown up, have more subjects from which to select, have more opportunities to spend time with peers and locate compatible friends, and enjoy increased independence from direct parental monitoring. They also may be more challenged intellectually by academic work.

Effective Schools for Young Adolescents Educators and psychologists worry that junior high and middle schools have become watered-down versions of high schools, mimicking their curricular and extracurricular schedules. Critics argue that these schools should offer activities that reflect a wide range of individual differences in biological and psychological development among young adolescents. The Carnegie Foundation (1989) issued an extremely negative evaluation of our nation's middle schools. It concluded that most young adolescents attended massive, impersonal schools; were taught from irrelevant curricula; trusted few adults in school; and lacked access to health care and counseling. It recommended that the nation should develop smaller "communities" or "houses" to lessen the impersonal nature of large middle schools, have lower student-to-counselor ratios (10 to 1 instead of several-hundred-to-1), involve parents and community leaders in schools, develop new curricula, have teachers team teach in more flexibly designed curriculum blocks that integrate several disciplines, boost students' health and fitness with more in-school programs, and help students who need public health care to get it. Twenty-five years later, experts are still finding that middle schools throughout the nation need a major redesign if they are to be effective in educating adolescents (Eccles, 2007).

Improving America's High Schools Just as there are concerns about U.S. middle school education, so are there concerns about U.S. high school education (Borman,

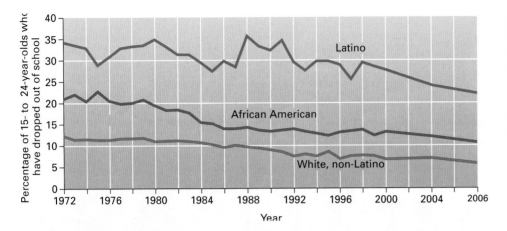

FIGURE 3.4 Trends in High School Dropout Rates

From 1972 through 2006, the school dropout rate for Latinos remained very high (22.1 percent of 16- to 24-year-olds in 2006). The African American dropout rate was still higher (10.9 percent) than the White non-Latino rate (5.8 percent) in 2006.

Cahill, & Cotner, 2007; Gonsalves & Leonard, 2007). Critics stress that in many high schools expectations for success and standards for learning are too low. Critics also argue that too often high schools foster passivity and that schools should create a variety of pathways for students to achieve an identity. Many students graduate from high school with inadequate reading, writing, and mathematical skills—including many who go on to college and have to enroll in remediation classes there. Other students drop out of high school and do not have skills that will allow them to obtain decent jobs, much less to be informed citizens.

In the last half of the twentieth century and the first several years of the twenty-first century, U.S. high school dropout rates declined (National Center for Education Statistics, 2008) (see Figure 3.4). In the 1940s, more than half of U.S. 16- to 24-year-olds had dropped out of school; by 2006, this figure had decreased to 9.3 percent. The dropout rate of Latino adolescents remains high, although it is decreasing in the twenty-first century (from 28 percent in 2000 to 22.1 percent in 2006). The highest dropout rate in the United States, though, likely occurs for Native American youth—less than 50 percent finish their high school education.

Students drop out of schools for many reasons (Christenson & Thurlow, 2004). In one study, almost 50 percent of the dropouts cited school-related reasons for leaving school, such as not liking school or being expelled or suspended (Rumberger, 1995). Twenty percent of the dropouts (but 40 percent of the Latino students) cited economic reasons for leaving school. One-third of the female students dropped out for personal reasons such as pregnancy or marriage.

According to a research review, the most effective programs to discourage dropping out of high school provide early reading programs, tutoring, counseling, and mentoring (Lehr & others, 2003). They also emphasize the creation of caring environments and relationships, use block scheduling, and offer community-service opportunities.

Early detection of children's school-related difficulties, and getting children engaged with school in positive ways, are important strategies for reducing the dropout rate. Recently the Bill and Melinda Gates Foundation (2006, 2008) has funded efforts to reduce the dropout rate in schools where dropout rates are high. One strategy that is being emphasized in the Gates' funding is keeping students at risk for dropping out of school with the same teachers through their high school years. The hope is that the teachers will get to know these students much better, their relationship with the students will improve, and they will be able to monitor and guide the students toward graduating from high school.

Participation in extracurricular activities also is linked to reduced school dropout rates (Fredricks, 2008). Adolescents in U.S. schools usually have a wide array of extracurricular activities they can participate in beyond their academic courses. These adult-sanctioned activities typically occur in the after-school hours and can be sponsored either by the school or the community. They include such diverse activities as sports, academic clubs, band, drama, and service groups. In addition to lower school

These adolescents participate in the "I Have a Dream" (IHAD) Program, a comprehensive, long-term dropout prevention program that has been very successful.

How is participation in extracurricular activities linked to secondary school students' development?

dropout rates, researchers have found that participation in extracurricular activities is linked to higher grades, school engagement, improved likelihood of going to college, higher self-esteem, and lower rates of depression, delinquency, and substance abuse (Fredricks, 2008). Adolescents benefit from a breadth of extracurricular activities more than focusing on a single extracurricular activity (Morris & Kalil, 2006). Also, the more years adolescents spend in extracurricular activities, the stronger the link is with positive developmental outcomes (Fredricks & Eccles, 2006).

Of course, the quality of the extracurricular activities matters (Fredricks, 2008; Parente & Mahoney, 2009). High-quality extracurricular activities that are likely to promote positive adolescent development include competent, supportive adult mentors, opportunities for increasing school connectedness, challenging and meaningful activities, and opportunities for improving skills (Fredricks & Eccles, 2006).

Review, Reflect, and Practice

2 Discuss how the social contexts of families, peers, and schools are linked with socioemotional development.

REVIEW

- What four parenting styles did Baumrind propose, and which is likely to be the most effective? How do aspects of families such as working parents, divorce, and stepfamilies affect children's development and education? In what ways can school-family linkages be fostered?
- What are peers and the five peer statuses? What risks are attached to certain peer statuses? How do friendships matter?
- What are some characteristics and key aspects of schools at different levels of education—early childhood education, the transition to elementary school, and the schooling of adolescents?

REFLECT

- What parenting style(s) have you witnessed and experienced? What effects did they have?

Review, Reflect, and Practice

PRAXIS™ PRACTICE

1. Which of the following teachers is most likely to encourage appropriate parental involvement in their children's education?
   a. Mr. Bastian sends home weekly progress notes to the parents who request them. He invites each parent to a conference at the end of the first grading period, and contacts parents if a child is in serious trouble at school.
   b. Ms. Washington contacts parents before the school year begins. She holds a meeting for parents to discuss her expectations for both children and parents and to answer questions. She requests volunteers to help in the classroom and chaperone field trips. She sends home weekly progress reports that include academic and social information.
   c. Ms. Jefferson tells parents that their children need to develop independence, which won't happen if they hover around at school and interfere with the educational process.
   d. Ms. Hernandez holds two parent-teacher conferences each year and e-mails parents if children fall behind in their work or present any problems in class. She occasionally e-mails a parent when a child has made marked improvement or accomplished something special.

2. Samuel is in fourth grade. He is large for his age, but not very mature. He is extremely sensitive to any kind of criticism—constructive or not. He cries when somebody teases him, which is often. Samuel often elicits teasing from his peers by engaging in it himself. Which peer status is most likely for Samuel?
   a. controversial
   b. neglected
   c. popular
   d. rejected

3. Which of the following is the best example of a developmentally appropriate unit on pioneer life for third-graders?
   a. Mr. Johnson's class has read about the daily lives of pioneers and is now constructing log cabins that demonstrate their understanding of the typical cabin of the period. Mr. Johnson moves around the room, giving help when needed, asking students why they are including certain features, and ensuring that all stay on task.
   b. In Ms. Lincoln's class, each student has read a different book about pioneer life and is now writing a book report. The students work quietly at their desks on their reports. She occasionally chastises students for talking or for daydreaming.
   c. Mr. Roosevelt's class is taking turns reading aloud a book about pioneer life. Each student reads a paragraph of the book in turn. When they are finished with the book, they will be tested on the content.
   d. Ms. Silver is lecturing to her students about pioneer life. She has gone over reasons for the westward migration, modes of transportation, and clearing the land and building a cabin. She will give them a test about pioneer life on Friday.

Please see the answer key at the end of the book.

3 SOCIOEMOTIONAL DEVELOPMENT

The Self | Moral Development | Coping with Stress

So far we have discussed three important social contexts that influence students' socioemotional development: families, peers, and schools. In this section, we focus more on the individual students themselves, as we explore the development of the self, morality, and coping with stress.

The Self

According to twentieth-century Italian playwright Ugo Betti, when children say "I," they mean something unique, not to be confused with any other. Psychologists often refer to that "I" as the self. Two important aspects of the self are self-esteem and identity.

Self-Esteem **Self-esteem** refers to an individual's overall view of himself or herself. Self-esteem also is referred to as *self-worth,* or *self-image.* For example, a child with high self-esteem might perceive that she is not just a person but a *good* person.

For many students, periods of low self-esteem come and go. But for some students, persistent low self-esteem translates into other, more serious problems. Persistent low self-esteem is linked with low achievement, depression, eating disorders, and delinquency (Harter, 2006). A New Zealand longitudinal study assessed self-esteem at 11, 13, and 15 years of age and adjustment and competence of the same individuals when they were 26 years old (Trzesniewski & others, 2006). The results revealed that adults characterized by poorer mental and physical health, worse economic prospects, and higher levels of criminal behavior were more likely to have low self-esteem in adolescence than their better-adjusted, more competent adult counterparts.

The seriousness of the problem depends not only on the nature of the student's low self-esteem but on other conditions as well. When low self-esteem is compounded by difficult school transitions (such as the transition to middle school) or family problems (such as divorce), the student's problems can intensify.

Researchers have found that self-esteem changes as children develop (Galambos, Barker, & Krahn, 2006). In one study, both boys and girls had high self-esteem in childhood but their self-esteem dropped considerably in early adolescence (Robins & others, 2002). The self-esteem of girls dropped about twice as much as that of boys during adolescence (see Figure 3.5). Other researchers have found that the self-esteem of girls drops more than that of boys during adolescence (Kling & others, 1999; Major & others, 1999). Among the reasons given for the self-esteem decline in both boys and girls are the upheaval in physical changes of puberty, increased achievement demands and expectations, and inadequate support from schools and parents. Among the reasons given for the gender disparity in the decline of self-esteem are the high expectations for physical attractiveness in girls, which becomes more pronounced with pubertal change, and motivation for social relationships that is not rewarded by society (Crawford & Unger, 2004). However, note in Figure 3.5 that despite the drop in self-esteem among adolescent girls, their average self-esteem score (3.3) was still higher than the neutral point on the scale (3.0). A recent study examined why some adolescent girls recover and develop healthy self-esteem but others don't (Impett & others, 2008). In this study, both self-esteem and relationship authenticity (a consistency between what one thinks and feels, and what one says and does in relational contexts) increased from the eighth through the twelfth grade. Also, the self-esteem of girls who scored high on relationship authenticity in the eighth grade increased over the course of adolescence more than girls who scored low on this measure in the eighth grade.

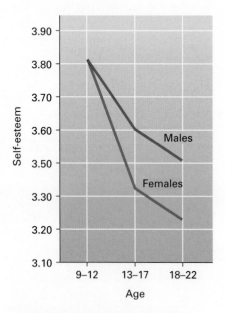

FIGURE 3.5 The Decline of Self-Esteem in Adolescence

In one study, the self-esteem of both boys and girls declined during adolescence, but it declined considerably more for girls than boys (Robins & others, 2002). The self-esteem scores represent the mean self-esteem scores on a 5-point scale, with higher scores reflecting higher self-esteem.

self-esteem Also called self-image and self-worth, the individual's overall conception of himself or herself.

DEVELOPMENTAL FOCUS 3.3

How Do You Promote Self-Esteem in Your Classroom?

Early Childhood

Our preschoolers feel really great when they receive stickers, stamps, and reward certificates for good behavior and work. In addition, each week children are asked to come to school with one special item from home to discuss in class and say why the item is important to them.

—Missy Dangler, *Suburban Hills School*

Elementary School: Grades K–5

To help my second-graders improve self-esteem I focus on what they are doing correctly as opposed to what they are doing incorrectly. I steer them to the correct answer rather than saying, "No, that's not right." Repeating or rephrasing the question also gives them another chance to try again in a nonthreatening environment. I also get on their eye level physically, sitting or bending down, so I can look them straight in the eyes, not down over them. These strategies help my young students feel important, valued, and part of the class, not just as a learner, but as a person.

—Janine Guida Poutre, *Clinton Elementary School*

Middle School: Grades 6–8

I once had a student that did poorly on tests and quizzes. Every time there was a test, he would break down and start calling himself names because he could not answer the questions. However, this student was very good at drawing, and I used that skill to bolster his self-esteem. For example, I made sure that every time I needed some kind of diagram for a class assignment, I called on him for help. I would tell him that he had amazing artistic ability and tell him that everyone has strengths and weaknesses, and that it was important to work on his test-taking issues in order to improve them. I also told him about a few of my own weaknesses and what I do to improve them. And, I created review games that included drawing to help him study for quizzes. This did not help his self-esteem overnight, but over the course of the school year, he became prouder of his work and did not put himself down as much.

—Casey Maass, *Edison Middle School*

High School: Grades 9–12

With my high school students, I make praise loud and clear, and I love to take the kids who have been labeled "loser" and relabel them as "reader" or "grammar princess" or "best arguer in the school." Although these labels may seem silly, my high school students blossom under the praise. I also remember that the praise I give to one of my students may be the only praise that he or she has heard—indeed, that student may not get any praise at home. Praise not only improves self-esteem for students' in-class performance, but it also gives them *permission* to succeed and do well in general.

—Jennifer Heiter, *Bremen High School*

Variations in self-esteem have been linked with many aspects of development (Harter, 2006). A recent study found that low self-esteem in childhood was linked with depression in adolescence and early adulthood (Orth & others, 2008). Another recent study found that adolescents who had low self-esteem had lower levels of mental health, physical health, and economic prospects as adults than adolescents with high self-esteem (Trzesniewski & others, 2006). However, much of the research on self-esteem is *correlational* rather than experimental. Recall from Chapter 1 that correlation does not equal causation. Thus, if a correlational study finds an association between children's low self-esteem and low academic achievement, low academic achievement could cause the low self-esteem as much as low self-esteem causes low academic achievement (Bowles, 1999).

BEST PRACTICES
Strategies for Improving Children's Self-Esteem

A current concern is that too many of today's children and adolescents grow up receiving empty praise and as a consequence have inflated self-esteem (Graham, 2005; Stipek, 2005). Too often they are given praise for mediocre or even poor performance. They may have difficulty handling competition and criticism. The title of a book, *Dumbing Down Our Kids: Why American Children Feel Good About Themselves But Can't Read, Write, or Add* (Sykes, 1995), vividly captures the theme that many U.S. children's, adolescents', and college students' academic problems stem from unmerited praise as part of an effort to prop up their self-esteem. Instead, it is possible to raise children's self-esteem through four strategies (Bednar, Wells, & Peterson, 1995; Harter, 2006):

1. *Identify the causes of low self-esteem and the areas of competence important to the self.* This is critical. Is the child's low self-esteem due to poor school achievement? Family conflict? Weak social skills? Students have the highest self-esteem when they perform competently in areas that they themselves feel are important. Thus, find out from students with low self-esteem what areas of competence they value.

2. *Provide emotional support and social approval.* Virtually every class has children who have received too many negative evaluations. These children might come from an abusive and demeaning family that constantly puts them down, or they might have been in prior classrooms that delivered too much negative feedback. Your emotional support and social approval can make a big difference in helping them value themselves more. The following comments by Judy Logan, a middle school teacher in San Francisco, underscore the importance of providing emotional support.

Through The Eyes of Teachers
Listening, Explaining, and Supporting

I believe that a good teacher should passionately be on the side of her students. That does not mean I support them in everything I do. It means I demand the best of them and am willing to help them be their best selves. It means I listen, explain, support, and allow without judgment, sarcasm, or the need to impose the truth from the outside. The passage from childhood to adulthood we call adolescence is a very vulnerable journey. It is often a difficult time for students and for their families. It is an adolescent's "job" to rebel at times and to question the family environment that was such a comfortable cocoon during childhood. No matter how wonderful the parents, how loving the family, each adolescent needs to have other adults in whom to confide. . . .

3. *Help children achieve.* Achieving can improve children's self-esteem. Straightforward teaching of real academic skills often improves children's achievement, and subsequently their self-esteem. Often it is not enough to tell children they can achieve something; you also have to help them develop their academic skills.

4. *Develop children's coping skills.* When children face a problem and cope with it rather than avoid it, their self-esteem often improves. Students who cope rather than avoid are likely to face problems realistically, honestly, and nondefensively, which can help raise their self-esteem. On the other hand, for students with low self-esteem, their unfavorable self-evaluations trigger denial, deception, and avoidance. This type of self-generated disapproval makes a student feel personally inadequate.

In fact, there are only moderate correlations between school performance and self-esteem, and these correlations do not suggest that high self-esteem produces better school performance (Baumeister & others, 2003). Efforts to increase students' self-esteem have not always led to improved school performance (Davies & Brember, 1999).

Students' self-esteem often varies across different domains, such as academic, athletic, physical appearance, social skills, and so on (Harter, 1999, 2006). Thus, a student might have high self-esteem in regard to his or her schoolwork but have low self-esteem in the areas of athletic skills, physical appearance, and social skills. Even within the academic domain, a student might have high esteem in some subjects (math, for example) and low self-esteem in others (English, for example).

Also, as students age their self-esteem becomes more differentiated (Harter, 2006; Horowitz & others, 2005). For example, Susan Harter (1999) added three new self-perception domains in her assessment of adolescents' self-perceptions (close friendship, romantic appeal, and job competence) to the five she assesses with children (scholastic competence, athletic competence, social acceptance, physical appearance, and behavioral conduct).

Identity Development   Another important aspect of the self is identity. Earlier in the chapter, we indicated that Erik Erikson (1968) argued that the most important issue in adolescence involves identity development—searching for answers to questions like these: Who am I? What am I all about? What am I going to do with my life? Not usually considered during childhood, these questions become nearly universal concerns during the high school and college years (Davis, 2008; Kroger, 2007).

		Has the person made a commitment?	
		Yes	**No**
Has the person explored meaningful alternatives regarding some identity question?	**Yes**	Identity Achievement	Identity Moratorium
	No	Identity Foreclosure	Identity Diffusion

FIGURE 3.6 Marcia's Four Identity Statuses

Identity Statuses   Canadian researcher James Marcia (1980, 1998) analyzed Erikson's concept of identity and concluded that it is important to distinguish between exploration and commitment. *Exploration* involves examining meaningful alternative identities. *Commitment* means showing a personal investment in an identity and staying with whatever that identity implies.

The extent of an individual's exploration and commitment is used to classify him or her according to one of four identity statuses (see Figure 3.6).

- **Identity diffusion** occurs when individuals have not yet experienced a crisis (that is, they have not yet explored meaningful alternatives) or made any commitments. Not only are they undecided about occupational and ideological choices, but they are also likely to show little interest in such matters.
- **Identity foreclosure** occurs when individuals have made a commitment but have not yet experienced a crisis. This occurs most often when parents hand down commitments to their adolescents, more often than not in an authoritarian manner. In these circumstances, adolescents have not had adequate opportunities to explore different approaches, ideologies, and vocations on their own.
- **Identity moratorium** occurs when individuals are in the midst of a crisis, but their commitments are either absent or only vaguely defined.
- **Identity achievement** occurs when individuals have undergone a crisis and have made a commitment.

To further consider identity, complete *Self-Assessment 3.1.* There you will be able to apply Marcia's identity statuses to a number of different areas of identity in your own life.

Ethnic Identity   *Ethnic identity* is an enduring aspect of the self that includes a sense of membership in an ethnic group, along with the attitudes and feelings related to that membership (Phinney, 2006). The indicators of identity often differ for each succeeding generation of immigrants (Phinney & Ong, 2007). First-generation immigrants are likely to be secure in their identities and unlikely to change much; they may or may not develop a new identity. The degree to which they begin to feel "American" appears to be related to whether or not they learn English, develop social networks beyond their ethnic group, and become culturally competent in their new country. Second-generation immigrants are more likely to think of themselves as "American" possibly because citizenship is granted at birth. For second-generation immigrants, ethnic identity is likely to be linked to retention of their ethnic language and social networks. In the third and later generations, the issues become more complex. Broad social factors may affect the extent to which members of this generation retain their ethnic identities. For example, media images may either discourage or encourage

identity diffusion The identity status in which individuals have neither explored meaningful alternatives nor made a commitment.

identity foreclosure The identity status in which individuals have made a commitment but have not explored meaningful alternatives.

identity moratorium The identity status in which individuals are in the midst of exploring alternatives but their commitments are absent or vaguely defined.

identity achievement The identity status in which individuals have explored meaningful alternatives and made a commitment.

SELF-ASSESSMENT 3.1

Where Are You Now? Exploring Your Identity

Your identity is made up of many different parts, and so too will your students' identities be comprised of many different dimensions. By completing this checklist, you should gain a better sense of your own identity and the different aspects of your future students' identities. For each component, check your identity status as diffused, foreclosed, in a moratorium, or achieved.

Identity Component	Identity Status			
	Diffused	Foreclosed	Moratorium	Achieved
Vocational identity				
Religious identity				
Achievement/intellectual identity				
Political identity				
Sexual identity				
Gender identity				
Relationship identity				
Lifestyle identity				
Ethnic and cultural identity				
Personality characteristics				
Interests				

If you checked "Diffused" or "Foreclosed" for any areas, take some time to think about what you need to do to move into a "Moratorium" identity status in those areas, and write about this in your portfolio.

THROUGH THE EYES OF STUDENTS

Identity Exploring

Michelle Chin, age 16, reflecting on her identity, commented, "Parents do not understand that teenagers need to find out who they are, which means a lot of experimenting, a lot of mood swings, a lot of emotions and awkwardness. Like any teenager, I am facing an identity crisis. I am still trying to figure out whether I am a Chinese American or an American with Asian eyes."

members of an ethnic group from identifying with their group or retaining parts of its culture. Discrimination may force people to see themselves as cut off from the majority group and encourage them to seek the support of their own ethnic culture.

The immediate contexts in which ethnic minority youth live also influence their identity development (Spencer, 2006). In the United States, many ethnic minority youth live in pockets of poverty, are exposed to drugs, gangs, and crime, and interact with youth and adults who have dropped out of school or are unemployed. Support for developing a positive identity is scarce. In such settings, programs for youth can make an important contribution to identity development.

Researchers are also increasingly finding that a positive ethnic identity is related to positive outcomes for ethnic minority adolescents (Umana-Taylor, 2006). For example, one study revealed that ethnic identity was linked with higher school engagement and lower aggression (Van Buren & Graham, 2003). And in a recent study, Navajo adolescents' affirmation and belonging to their ethnic heritage was linked to higher self-esteem, school connectedness, and social functioning (Jones & Galliher, 2007).

Moral Development

As children develop a sense of self and an identity, they also develop a sense of morality. Moral development has important implications in the classroom. For example, a strong moral sense may increase the likelihood that students will consider others' feelings or not cheat on a test. In one survey of 8,600 U.S. high school students, 70 percent admitted that they had cheated on at least one school exam in the current school year, up from 60 percent in 1990 (*Upfront,* 2000). In this survey, almost 80 percent said they had lied to a teacher at least once.

Domains of Moral Development   **Moral development** concerns rules and conventions about just interactions between people. These rules can be studied in three domains: cognitive, behavioral, and emotional. In the cognitive domain, the key issue is how students reason or think about rules for ethical conduct. In the behavioral domain, the focus is on how students actually behave rather than on the morality of their thinking. In the emotional domain, the emphasis is on how students morally feel. For instance, do they associate strong enough guilt feelings with an immoral action to resist performing that action? Do they show empathy toward others?

Kohlberg's Theory   Lawrence Kohlberg (1976, 1986) stressed that moral development primarily involves moral reasoning and occurs in stages. Kohlberg arrived at his theory after interviewing children, adolescents, and adults (primarily males) about their views on a series of moral dilemmas.

Kohlberg's Levels and Stages of Moral Development   Kohlberg constructed a theory of moral development that has three main levels with two stages at each of the levels. A key concept in understanding Kohlberg's theory is *internalization*, which refers to the developmental change from externally controlled behavior to internally controlled behavior.

   Preconventional reasoning is the lowest level of moral development in Kohlberg's theory. At this level, the child shows no internalization of moral values. Moral reasoning is controlled by external rewards and punishment.

   Conventional reasoning is the second, or intermediate, level in Kohlberg's theory. At this level, the child's internalization is intermediate. The child abides internally by certain standards, but they are essentially the standards imposed by other people, such as parents, or by society's laws.

   Postconventional reasoning is the highest level in Kohlberg's theory. At this level, morality is completely internalized and not based on external standards. The student recognizes alternative moral courses, explores options, and then decides on the moral code that is best for him or her. A summary of Kohlberg's three levels and six stages, along with examples of each of the stages, is presented in Figure 3.7.

   In studies of Kohlberg's theory, longitudinal data show a relation of the stages to age, although few people ever attain the two highest stages, especially stage 6 (Colby & others, 1983). Before age 9, most children reason about moral dilemmas at a preconventional level. By early adolescence, they are more likely to reason at the conventional level.

   Kohlberg stressed that underlying changes in cognitive development promote more advanced moral thinking. He also said that children construct their moral thoughts as they pass through the stages—that they do not just passively accept a cultural norm for morality. Kohlberg argued that a child's moral thinking can be advanced through discussions with others who reason at the next higher stage.

Lawrence Kohlberg, the architect of a provocative cognitive developmental theory of moral development. *What is the nature of his theory?*

moral development Development with respect to the rules and conventions of just interactions between people.

preconventional reasoning In Kohlberg's theory, the lowest level of moral development; at this level, the child shows no internalization of moral values, and moral reasoning is controlled by external rewards and punishments.

conventional reasoning In Kohlberg's theory, the middle level of moral development; at this level, internalization is intermediate in the sense that individuals abide by certain standards (internal), but these essentially are the standards of others (external).

postconventional reasoning In Kohlberg's theory, the highest level of moral development; at this level, moral development is internalized and not based on external standards.

LEVEL 1 Preconventional Level No Internalization	**LEVEL 2** Conventional Level Intermediate Internalization	**LEVEL 3** Postconventional Level Full Internalization
Stage 1 Heteronomous Morality *Children obey because adults tell them to obey. People base their moral decisions on fear of punishment.*	**Stage 3** Mutual Interpersonal Expectations, Relationships, and Interpersonal Conformity *Individuals value trust, caring, and loyalty to others as a basis for moral judgments.*	**Stage 5** Social Contract or Utility and Individual Rights *Individuals reason that values, rights, and principles undergird or transcend the law.* **Stage 6** Universal Ethical Principles *The person has developed moral judgments that are based on universal human rights. When faced with a dilemma between law and conscience, a personal, individualized conscience is followed.*
Stage 2 Individualism, Purpose, and Exchange *Individuals pursue their own interests but let others do the same. What is right involves equal exchange.*	**Stage 4** Social Systems Morality *Moral judgments are based on understanding of the social order, law, justice, and duty.*	

FIGURE 3.7 Kohlberg's Three Levels and Six Stages of Moral Development
Kohlberg argued that people everywhere develop their moral reasoning by passing through these age-based stages.

Carol Gilligan (*center*) is shown with some of the students she has interviewed about the importance of relationships in a female's development. *What is Gilligan's view of moral development?*

justice perspective A moral perspective that focuses on the rights of the individual; Kohlberg's theory is a justice perspective.

care perspective A moral perspective that focuses on connectedness and relationships among people; Gilligan's approach reflects a care perspective.

Kohlberg thought that the mutual give-and-take of peer relations promotes more advanced moral thinking because of the role-taking opportunities they provide children.

Kohlberg's Critics   Kohlberg's provocative theory has not gone unchallenged (Lapsley, 2008; Sherblom, 2008). One powerful criticism centers on the idea that moral thoughts don't always predict moral behavior. The criticism is that Kohlberg's theory places too much emphasis on moral thinking and not enough on moral behavior. Moral reasons sometimes can be a shelter for immoral behavior. Bank embezzlers and U.S. presidents endorse the loftiest of moral virtues, but their own behavior can prove to be immoral. No one wants a nation of stage-6 Kohlberg thinkers who know what is right yet do what is wrong.

Another line of criticism is that Kohlberg's theory is too individualistic. Carol Gilligan (1982, 1998) distinguishes between the justice perspective and the care perspective. Kohlberg's is a **justice perspective** that focuses on the rights of the individual, who stands alone and makes moral decisions. The **care perspective** views people in terms of their connectedness. Emphasis is placed on relationships and concern for others. According to Gilligan, Kohlberg greatly underplayed the care perspective—possibly because he was a male, most of his research was on males, and he lived in a male-dominant society.

In extensive interviews with girls from 6 to 18 years of age, Gilligan found that they consistently interpret moral dilemmas in terms of human relationships, not in terms of individual rights. Gilligan (1996) also has argued that girls reach a critical juncture in their development in early adolescence. At about 11 or 12 years of age, they become aware of how much they prize relationships yet come to realize this interest is not shared by the male-dominant society. The solution, says Gilligan, is to give relationships and concern for others a higher priority in our society. Gilligan does not recommend totally throwing out Kohlberg's theory. She argues the highest level of moral development occurs when individuals combine the care and justice perspectives in positive ways. Controversy exists over whether the gender difference in moral judgment is as strong as Gilligan says (Hyde, 2007; Saltzstein, 2008).

Cheating   A moral development concern of teachers is whether students cheat and how to handle the cheating if they discover it (Anderman & Murdock, 2007). Academic cheating can take many forms including plagiarism, using "cheat sheets" during an exam, copying from a neighbor during a test, purchasing papers, and falsifying lab results. A 2006 survey revealed that 60 percent of secondary school students said they had cheated on a test in school during the past year and one-third of the students reported that they had plagiarized information from the Internet in the past year (Josephson Institute of Ethics, 2006).

Why do students cheat? Among the reasons students give for cheating include the pressure for getting high grades, time pressures, poor teaching, and lack of interest (Stephens, 2008). In terms of poor teaching, "students are more likely to cheat when they perceive their teacher to be incompetent, unfair, and uncaring" (Stephens, 2008, p. 140).

A long history of research also implicates the power of the situation in determining whether students cheat or not (Hartshorne & May, 1928–1930; Murdock, Miller, & Kohlbhardt, 2004). For example, students are more likely to cheat when they are not being closely monitored during a test, when they know their peers are cheating, whether they know if another student has been caught cheating, and when student scores are made public (Anderman & Murdock, 2007; Carrell, Malmstrom, & West, 2008).

Why do students cheat? What are some strategies teachers can adopt to prevent cheating?

Among the strategies for decreasing academic cheating are preventive measures such as making sure students are aware of what constitutes cheating, what the consequences will be if they cheat, closely monitoring students' behavior while they are taking tests, and the importance of being a moral, responsible individual who engages in academic integrity. In promoting academic integrity, many colleges have instituted an honor code policy that emphasizes self-responsibility, fairness, trust, and scholarship (Narváez & others, 2008). However, few secondary schools have developed honor code policies. The Center for Academic Integrity (www.academicintegrity.org) has extensive materials available to help schools develop academic integrity policies.

Moral Education   Is there a best way to educate students so they will develop better moral values? Moral education is hotly debated in educational circles (Holter & Narváez, 2008). We will study one of the earliest analyses of moral education, then turn to some contemporary views.

The Hidden Curriculum   Recall from Chapter 1 that John Dewey was one of educational psychology's pioneers. Dewey (1933) recognized that even when schools do not have specific programs in moral education, they provide moral education through a "hidden curriculum." The **hidden curriculum**—conveyed by the moral atmosphere that is a part of every school—is created by school and classroom rules, the moral orientation of teachers and school administrators, and text materials. Teachers serve as models of ethical or unethical behavior (Mayhew & King, 2008; Sanger, 2008). Classroom rules and peer relations at school transmit attitudes about cheating, lying, stealing, and consideration for others. Through its rules and regulations, the school administration infuses the school with a value system.

Character Education   Currently 40 of 50 states have mandates regarding **character education**, a direct approach to moral education that involves teaching students basic moral literacy to prevent them from engaging in immoral behavior and doing harm to themselves or others (Arthur, 2008; Carr, 2008; Nucci & Narváez, 2008). The argument is that behaviors such as lying, stealing, and cheating are wrong, and that students should be taught this throughout their education (Berkowitz, Battistich, & Bier, 2008; Davidson, Lickona, & Khmelkov, 2008). According to the character education approach, every school should have an explicit moral code that is clearly communicated to students. Any violations of the code should be met with sanctions. Instruction in moral concepts with respect to specific behaviors, such as cheating, can take the form of example and definition, class discussions and role-playing, or

hidden curriculum Dewey's concept that every school has a pervasive moral atmosphere, even if it does not have a specific program of moral education.

character education A direct approach to moral education that involves teaching students basic moral literacy to prevent them from engaging in immoral behavior and doing harm to themselves or others.

DEVELOPMENTAL FOCUS 3.4

How Do You Advance Children's Moral Development, Values, and Prosocial Behavior in the Classroom?

Early Childhood

One prosocial rule that we establish with our preschoolers is zero tolerance for fighting. However, this is a difficult concept to teach some young children because when they are angry, the first thing they want to do is hit. A way to address hitting is to constantly teach children self-control. For example, we say things to children like "When we are walking in the hallway, we have control of own body and can make it walk a certain way." Our goal is to make self-control second nature in our children.

—Valarie Gorham, *Kiddie Quarters, Inc.*

Elementary School: Grades K–5

My fifth-graders take on at least two community-service projects a year. This year, we went on a field trip to the Oregon Food Bank. My students learned about hungry families in Oregon, what each child can do to help, and were given a task to do at the food bank. We bagged around 1,600 pounds of carrots, and this equated to feeding about 57 families. It was hard work, but my students saw the results and felt good about themselves.

—Craig Jensen, *Cooper Mountain Elementary School*

Middle School: Grades 6–8

As my seventh-graders study history, I like to present them with discussion questions in the form of moral dilemmas: "What would you do if ..." types of questions. A teacher can ask an endless number of questions that relate to a students' everyday life. For instance, Robert E. Lee had to decide if he would be loyal to his state or his country. In this lesson, I ask students questions such as: "Is your loyalty ever tested? If so, how did you make your decision?" These questions make for great discussions and get students thinking about their own values and morals.

—Mark Fodness, *Bemidji Middle School*

High School: Grades 9–12

I sometimes discuss my own moral dilemmas with my students and tie them to classroom topics so that they have a role model. For example, I once told them the story of when my infant daughter and I were in Walmart and she somehow grabbed a jar of baby food off the shelf and tucked it into her car seat. I didn't notice the jar until I lifted her out of the car when we arrived home. Although the value of the jar of food was only 37 cents, I returned it to the store. I share this story with my students when we discuss plagiarism and Modern Language Association (MLA) citation style to emphasize the importance of being honest.

—Jennifer Heiter, *Bremen High School*

---

rewards to students for proper behavior. More recently, an emphasis on the importance of encouraging students to develop a care perspective has been accepted as a relevant aspect of character education (Noddings, 2008; Sherblom, 2008). Rather than just instructing adolescents in refraining from engaging in morally deviant behavior, a care perspective advocates educating students in the importance of engaging in prosocial behaviors, such as considering others' feelings, being sensitive to others, and helping others. Critics argue that some character education programs encourage students to be too passive and noncritical.

Values Clarification **Values clarification** means helping people to clarify what their lives are for and what is worth working for. In this approach, students are

values clarification An approach to moral education that emphasizes helping people clarify what their lives are for and what is worth working for; students are encouraged to define their own values and understand the values of others.

encouraged to define their own values and to understand others' values. Values clarification differs from character education in not telling students what their values should be. In values clarification exercises, there are no right or wrong answers. The clarification of values is left up to the individual student. Advocates of values clarification say it is value-free. Critics, however, argue that its controversial content offends community standards. They also say that because of its relativistic nature, values clarification undermines accepted values and fails to stress morally correct behavior.

Cognitive Moral Education   **Cognitive moral education** is an approach based on the belief that students should learn to value ideals such as democracy and justice as their moral reasoning develops. Kohlberg's theory has been the basis for a number of cognitive moral education programs (Hult, 2008). In a typical program, high school students meet in a semester-long course to discuss a number of moral issues. The instructor acts as a facilitator rather than as a director of the class. The hope is that students will develop more advanced notions of such concepts as cooperation, trust, responsibility, and community. Toward the end of his career, Kohlberg (1986) recognized that the school's moral atmosphere is more important than he initially envisioned. For example, in one study, a semester-long moral education class based on Kohlberg's theory was successful in advancing moral thinking in three democratic schools but not in three authoritarian schools (Higgins, Power, & Kohlberg, 1983). The hope is that students will develop more advanced notions of such concepts as cooperation, trust, responsibility, and community (Enright & others, 2008; Power & Higgins-D'Alessandro, 2008).

THROUGH THE EYES OF STUDENTS

Jewel Cash, Teen Dynamo

Jewel Cash, seated next to her mother, is participating in a crime watch meeting at a community center. A junior at Boston Latin Academy, Jewel was raised in one of Boston's housing projects by her mother, a single parent. Today she is a member of the Boston Student Advisory Council, mentors children, volunteers at a women's shelter, manages and dances in two troupes, and is a member of a neighborhood watch group—among other activities. Jewel told an interviewer from the *Boston Globe,* "I see a problem and I say, 'How can I make a difference?' . . . I can't take on the world, even though I can try. . . . I'm moving forward but I want to make sure I'm bringing people with me" (Silva, 2005, pp. B1, B4).

Service Learning   **Service learning** is a form of education that promotes social responsibility and service to the community. In service learning, students engage in activities such as tutoring, helping older adults, working in a hospital, assisting at a child-care center, or cleaning up a vacant lot to make a play area. An important goal of service learning is for students to become less self-centered and more strongly motivated to help others (Catalano, Hawkins, & Toumbourou, 2008; Hart, Matsuba, & Atkins, 2008). Service learning is often more effective when two conditions are met (Nucci, 2006): (1) giving students some degree of choice in the service activities in which they participate, and (2) providing students opportunities to reflect about their participation.

Service learning takes education out into the community (Enfield & Collins, 2008; Nelson & Eckstein, 2008). Adolescent volunteers tend to be extraverted, committed to others, and have a high level of self-understanding (Eisenberg & Morris, 2004). Also, a recent study revealed that adolescent girls participated in service learning more than adolescent boys (Webster & Worrell, 2008).

Researchers have found that service learning benefits adolescents in a number of ways (Hart, Matsuba, & Atkins, 2008; Reinders & Youniss, 2006). These improvements in adolescent development related to service learning include higher grades in school, increased goal setting, higher self-esteem, an improved sense of being able to make a difference for others, and an increased likelihood that they will serve as volunteers in the future (Benson & others, 2006; Hart, Atkins, & Donnelly, 2006). A recent study of more than 4,000 high school students revealed that those who worked directly with

cognitive moral education An approach to moral education based on the belief that students should value things such as democracy and justice as their moral reasoning develops; Kohlberg's theory has served as the foundation for many cognitive moral education programs.

service learning A form of education that promotes social responsibility and service to the community.

individuals in need were better adjusted academically, whereas those who worked for organizations had better civic outcomes (Schmidt, Shumow, & Kacar, 2007).

An Integrative Approach Darcia Narváez (2006, 2008) emphasizes an *integrative approach* to moral education that encompasses both the reflective moral thinking and commitment to justice advocated in Kohlberg's approach, and developing a particular moral character as advocated in the character education approach. She highlights the Child Development Project as an excellent example of an integrative moral education approach. In the Child Development Project, students are given multiple opportunities to discuss other students' experiences, which encourages empathy and perspective taking, and they participate in exercises that encourage them to reflect on their own behaviors in terms of such values as fairness and social responsibility (Battistich, 2008; Berkowitz, Battistich, & Bier, 2008). Adults coach students in ethical decision making and guide them in becoming more caring individuals. Students experience a caring community, not only in the classroom, but also in after-school activities and through parental involvement in the program. Research evaluations of the Child Development Project indicate that it is related to an improved sense of community, an increase in prosocial behavior, better interpersonal understanding, and an increase in social problem solving (Battistich, 2008; Solomon, Watson, & Battistich, 2002).

Coping with Stress

In service learning and integrative ethical education, an important theme is getting students to help others. There are times, though, when students need help, especially when they experience stressful events (Mayer & others, 2009; Taylor & Stanton, 2007). As children get older, they more accurately appraise a stressful situation and determine how much control they have over it. Older children generate more coping alternatives to stressful conditions and use more cognitive coping strategies (Saarni & others, 2006). They are better than younger children at intentionally shifting their thoughts to something that is less stressful; and at reframing, or changing one's perception of a stressful situation. For example, a younger child may be very disappointed that a teacher did not say hello when the child arrived in the classroom. An older child may reframe the situation and think, "My teacher may have been busy with other things and just forgot to say hello."

By 10 years of age, most children are able to use these cognitive strategies to cope with stress (Saarni, 1999). However, in families that have not been supportive and are characterized by turmoil or trauma, children may be so overwhelmed by stress that they do not use such strategies (Frydenberg, 2008; Klingman, 2006).

The terrorist attacks on the World Trade Center in New York City and the Pentagon in Washington, D.C., on September 11, 2001, and Hurricane Katrina in August 2005, raised special concerns about how to help children cope with such stressful events (Osofsky, 2007). Following are some strategies teachers can use to help students cope with stressful events (Gurwitch & others, 2001, pp. 4–11):

- Reassure children (numerous times, if necessary) of their safety and security.
- Allow children to retell events and be patient in listening to them.
- Encourage children to talk about any disturbing or confusing feelings, reassuring them that such feelings are normal after a stressful event.
- Protect children from reexposure to frightening situations and reminders of the trauma—for example, by limiting discussion of the event in front of the children.

What are some effective strategies teachers can use to help children cope with traumatic events, such as the terrorist attacks on the United States on 9/11/2001 and Hurricane Katrina in August 2005?

- Help children make sense of what happened, keeping in mind that children may misunderstand what took place. For example, young children "may blame themselves, believe things happened that did not happen, believe that terrorists are in the school, etc. Gently help children develop a realistic understanding of the event" (p. 10).

In Chapters 2 and 3 we have examined how students develop, focusing mainly on the general pattern. In Chapter 4, we will explore how individual students vary with regard to intelligence and other personal characteristics.

Review, Reflect, and Practice

(3) **Explain these aspects of children's socioemotional development: self-esteem, identity, moral development, and coping with stress.**

REVIEW
- What is self-esteem, and what are some ways to increase students' self-esteem? What is the nature of identity development, and what are the four statuses of identity?
- What is moral development? What levels of moral development were identified by Kohlberg, and what are two criticisms of his theory? Contrast the justice and care perspectives. What characterizes academic cheating? What are some forms of moral education?
- How can children be helped to cope with stress?

REFLECT
- What is the level of moral development likely to be among the children you intend to teach? How might this affect your approach to how you manage students' relations with others in class?

PRAXIS™ PRACTICE
1. Teachers can have the most positive impact on students' self-esteem and achievement by
   a. making academic tasks easy.
   b. having children who often receive negative feedback from peers work in groups with these peers to foster social approval.
   c. helping children succeed by teaching them appropriate learning strategies.
   d. intervening in children's problems so that they don't get frustrated.

2. Marika sees Jamal take Yosuke's snack. Soon afterward, she sees Yosuke retaliate by taking Jamal's favorite pen. Marika does not report these incidents to the teacher, because they involve equal exchanges. According to Kohlberg, which stage of moral development has Marika reached?
   a. stage 1
   b. stage 2
   c. stage 3
   d. stage 4

(continued)

Review, Reflect, and Practice

3. Ms. Delgado teaches third grade in a community in which a gunman opened fire on the patrons of a store in the local mall. Her students are understandably upset by the news and by the fact that the gunman has not, as of yet, been apprehended. According to Gurwitch and colleagues (2001), which of the following would be the *least* appropriate thing for Ms. Delgado to do?
   a. Allow her students to talk about what happened and their fears that it could happen at the school.
   b. Disallow conversation about the shootings so that the students do not get upset.
   c. Reassure her students that they are safe at school, incuding a brief discussion of appropriate emergency procedures.
   d. Listen to the students' accounts to ensure that they have no misconceptions regarding having caused the shootings.

   Please see the answer key at the end of the book.

CRACK THE CASE
The Case of the Fight

Many schools, including the one in which Miss Mahoney teaches, emphasize character education as a strategy for preventing violence. The basic idea is to promote empathy among students and to disallow behaviors such as teasing, name-calling, and threats of any kind. Miss Mahoney has included character education in the curriculum of her fifth-grade class. However, many of her students, especially the boys, continue to display the very behaviors she is trying to eliminate.

Two students in Miss Mahoney's class, Santana and Luke, are on the same club soccer team and often get into verbal conflicts with each other, although they appreciate each other's talents on the field. Tuesday night at practice, in violation of the team's rules, Santana told Luke that he "sucks." Luke decides to let it go. He doesn't want Santana to suffer a one-game suspension, recognizing Santana's value to the team in light of facing a tough opponent that weekend.

Thursday in class, Luke accuses Santana of stealing the cards he was using to organize a project. Luke is very angry. Santana also gets infuriated, claiming he did not steal them. He then finds them on the floor and hands them to Luke. "Here's your dumb cards, Luke," he says. "See, I didn't steal them."

In anger, Luke says, "Fine. Then how come they're all crinkled? You know, I could beat you up and maybe I just will."

"Yeah, right. You and who else?" asks Santana with a sneer.

Two other boys working nearby overheard the altercation and begin contributing their perspectives.

"Yeah, Santana, Luke would kick your rear," says Grant.

"I think Santana would win," chimes in Peter.

"Meet me at the park tomorrow after school and let's just see!" demands Santana.

"No problem," retorts Luke.

Thursday evening, they are both at soccer practice. Nothing is said about the fight that was to take place the next day after school.

Friday morning, Santana's mother calls Miss Mahoney to tell her that Santana is afraid to come to school because Luke has threatened to beat him up. Obviously, Miss Mahoney is concerned and realizes she must address the situation. Luke's mother also talks to the principal about the situation. However, all Santana's mother told either of them is that Luke had threatened to beat up her son. She didn't know why and did not think the reason mattered in the least. She wanted her son protected and the other boy punished.

That morning, Luke's mother was in the school for another purpose. The principal stopped her to talk about the situation, telling her that Santana had told his mother he was afraid to come to school because Luke was going to beat him up. Luke's mother asked for more information. On hearing Santana's side of the story, which was simply that Luke had threatened him, she told the principal that this didn't sound right—that Luke was impulsive enough that if he'd wanted to beat up Santana, he probably would have just hit him, not planned a fight for a later date. She wanted to talk to Luke before she jumped to any conclusions and asked that Miss Mahoney and the principal talk to both of the boys and any other children involved.

Both Miss Mahoney and the principal did as Luke's mother asked. The story that came out is the one you read. They decided that Luke should serve an in-school suspension the following day and miss recess all week "because it is the third 'incident' we've had with him this year." Santana received no punishment and walked away from the meeting, grinning.

- What are the issues in this case?
- At what stage of moral development would you expect these boys to be, based on the information you have? What predictions can you make regarding each boy's sense of self and emotional development?
- What can you say about the boys' mothers?
- What do you think about the punishment that Luke received? How would you have handled this situation?
- What impact do you think this will have on the boys' future relationship? What impact on their attitudes toward school?

Reach Your Learning Goals
Social Contexts and Socioemotional Development

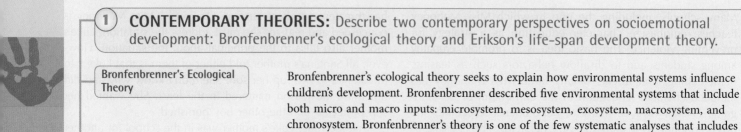

① CONTEMPORARY THEORIES: Describe two contemporary perspectives on socioemotional development: Bronfenbrenner's ecological theory and Erikson's life-span development theory.

Bronfenbrenner's Ecological Theory

Bronfenbrenner's ecological theory seeks to explain how environmental systems influence children's development. Bronfenbrenner described five environmental systems that include both micro and macro inputs: microsystem, mesosystem, exosystem, macrosystem, and chronosystem. Bronfenbrenner's theory is one of the few systematic analyses that includes both micro and macro environments. Critics say the theory lacks attention to biological and cognitive factors. They also point out that it does not address step-by-step developmental changes.

Erikson's Life-Span Development Theory

Erikson's life-span development theory proposes eight stages, each centering on a particular type of challenge or dilemma: trust versus mistrust, autonomy versus shame and doubt, initiative versus guilt, industry versus inferiority, identity versus identity confusion, intimacy versus isolation, generativity versus stagnation, and integrity versus despair. Erikson's theory has made important contributions to understanding socioemotional development, although some critics say the stages are too rigid and that their sequencing lacks research support.

② SOCIAL CONTEXTS OF DEVELOPMENT: Discuss how the social contexts of families, peers, and schools are linked with socioemotional development.

Families

Baumrind proposed four parenting styles: authoritarian, authoritative, neglectful, and indulgent. Authoritative parenting is associated with children's social competence and is likely to be the most effective. Greater numbers of children are growing up in diverse family structures than at any other point in history. A special concern is the number of children of divorce. The nature of parents' work can affect their parenting quality. When both the parenting and school environment are authoritative, children in divorced families benefit. Children benefit when parents engage in coparenting. As in divorced families, children living in stepparent families have more adjustment problems than their counterparts in nondivorced families. However, a majority of children in stepfamilies do not have adjustment problems. Two important aspects of school-family linkages are parents as managers and parental involvement. Fostering school-family partnerships involves providing assistance to families, communicating effectively with families about school programs and student progress, encouraging parents to be volunteers, involving families with their children in learning activities at home, including families in school decisions, and coordinating community collaboration.

Peers

Peers are children of about the same age or maturity level. Children can have one of five peer statuses: popular, average, rejected, neglected, or controversial. Rejected children often have more serious adjustment problems than do neglected children. Friendship is an important aspect of students' social relations. Students who have friends engage in more prosocial behavior, have higher grades, and are less emotionally distressed.

Schools

Schools involve changing social developmental contexts from preschool through high school. The early childhood setting is a protected environment with one or two teachers, usually female. Peer groups are more important in elementary school. In middle school, the social field enlarges to include the whole school, and the social system becomes more complex. Controversy characterizes early childhood education curricula. On the one side are the developmentally appropriate, child-centered, constructivist advocates; on the other are those who advocate an instructivist, academic approach. Two increasingly popular early childhood programs are the Reggio Emilia and Montessori approaches. Head Start has provided early childhood education for children from low-income families. High-quality Head Start programs are effective educational interventions, but up to 40 percent of these programs may be ineffective. A special concern is that many early elementary school classrooms rely mainly on negative feedback. The transition to middle or junior high is stressful for many students because it coincides with so many physical, cognitive, and socioemotional changes. It involves going from the top-dog position to the lowest position in a school hierarchy. Effective schools for young adolescents adapt to individual variations in students, take seriously what is known about the development of young adolescents, and give as much emphasis to socioemotional as to cognitive development. An increasing number of educational experts also believe that substantial changes need to be made in U.S. high school education. Participation in extracurricular activities has a number of positive outcomes for adolescents.

---

③ SOCIOEMOTIONAL DEVELOPMENT: Explain these aspects of children's socioemotional development: self-esteem, identity, moral development, and coping with stress.

| The Self | Self-esteem, also referred to as *self-worth* or *self-image,* is the individual's overall conception of himself or herself. Self-esteem often varies across domains and becomes more differentiated in adolescence. Four keys to increasing students' self-esteem are to (1) identify the causes of low self-esteem and the domains of competence important to the student, (2) provide emotional support and social approval, (3) help students achieve, and (4) develop students' coping skills. Marcia proposed that adolescents have one of four identity statuses (based on the extent to which they have explored or are exploring alternative paths and whether they have made a commitment): identity diffusion, identity foreclosure, identity moratorium, identity achievement. Ethnic identity is an important dimension of identity for ethnic minority students. |

| Moral Development | Moral development concerns rules and conventions about just interactions between people. These rules can be studied in three domains: cognitive, behavioral, and emotional. Kohlberg stressed that the key to understanding moral development is moral reasoning and that it unfolds in stages. Kohlberg identified three levels of moral development (preconventional, conventional, and postconventional), with two stages at each level. As individuals go through the three levels, their moral thinking becomes more internalized. Two main criticisms of Kohlberg's theory are (1) Kohlberg did not give enough attention to moral behavior, and (2) Kohlberg's theory gave too much power to the individual and not enough to relationships with others. In this regard, Gilligan argued that Kohlberg's theory is a male-oriented justice perspective. She argues that what is needed in moral development is a female-oriented care perspective. Academic cheating is pervasive and can occur in many ways. A long history of research indicates the power of the situation in influencing whether students cheat or not. The hidden curriculum is the moral atmosphere that every school has. Three types of moral education are character education, values clarification, and cognitive moral education. Service learning is becoming increasingly important in schools. A recently developed perspective is integrative moral education. |

| Coping with Stress | As children get older, they use a greater variety of coping strategies and more cognitive strategies. Teachers can guide students in developing effective strategies—for example, providing reassurance, encouraging children to talk about disturbing feelings, and helping children make sense of what happened—for coping with stressful events, such as terrorist attacks and hurricanes. |

113

KEY TERMS

 PORTFOLIO ACTIVITIES

Now that you have a good understanding of this chapter, complete these exercises to expand your thinking.

Independent Reflection

Meeting the Socioemotional Needs of Students. Think about the age of students you intend to teach. Which of Erikson's stages is likely to be central for them? What, if anything, does Bronfenbrenner's theory suggest about important resources for students at that age? Does his system suggest particular challenges to students or ways that you as a teacher might facilitate their success? Write down your ideas in your portfolio.

Collaborative Work

The Role of Moral Education in Schools. Which approach to moral education (character education, values clarification, or cog-nitive moral education) do you like the best? Why? Should schools be in the business of having specific moral education programs? Get together with several other students in this class and discuss your perspectives. Then write a brief statement that reflects your own perspective on moral education.

Research/Field Experience

Foster Family-School Linkages. Interview several teachers from local schools about how they foster family-school linkages. Try to talk with a kindergarten teacher, an elementary teacher, a middle school teacher, and a high school teacher. Summarize your discoveries.

Go to the Online Learning Center for downloadable portfolio templates.

 TAKING IT TO THE NET

- How can teachers help children and youth successfully resolve the challenges of the different stages of psychosocial development? Describe a teaching strategy that could be used to foster independence, confidence, and risk taking in students. **www.extension.umn.edu/distribution/youthdevelopment/DA6715.html**

- Research shows that family involvement greatly influences student attitudes, attendance, and academic achievement. Develop an action plan for involving families in your classroom in a variety of ways. What are some of the challenges to involving families, and how do you plan to overcome these? **www.ncrel.org/sdrs/areas/issues/envrnmnt/famncomm/pa300.htm**

- Do you believe that helping students develop good character is just as important as teaching reading, writing, and math? Or should families solely be in control of character and moral instruction? Why? In what ways do teachers inherently impact students' character development through their daily interactions? **http://chiron.valdosta.edu/whuitt/col/morchr/morchr.html**

Connect to the Online Learning Center to explore possible answers.

 STUDY, PRACTICE, AND SUCCEED

Visit **www.mhhe.com/santedu4e** to review the chapter with self-grading quizzes and self-assessments, to apply the chapter material to two more Crack the Case studies, and for suggested activities to develop your teaching portfolio.

CHAPTER 4

Individual Variations

Individuals play out their lives in different ways.

—Thomas Huxley
English Biologist, 19th Century

Learning Goals

1 Discuss what intelligence is, how it is measured, theories of multiple intelligences, and some controversies and issues about its use by educators.

2 Describe learning and thinking styles.

3 Characterize the nature of personality and temperament.

TEACHING STORIES Shiffy Landa

Shiffy Landa, a first-grade teacher at H. F. Epstein Hebrew Academy in St. Louis, Missouri, uses the multiple-intelligences approach of Howard Gardner (1983, 1993) in her classroom. Gardner argues that there is not just one general type of intelligence but at least eight specific types.

Landa (2000, pp. 6–8) believes that the multiple-intelligences approach is the best way to reach children because they have many different kinds of abilities. In Landa's words:

> My role as a teacher is quite different from the way it was just a few years ago. No longer do I stand in front of the room and lecture to my students. I consider my role to be one of a facilitator rather than a frontal teacher. The desks in my room are not all neatly lined up in straight rows . . . students are busily working in centers in cooperative learning groups, which gives them the opportunity to develop their interpersonal intelligences.

Students use their "body-kinesthetic intelligence to form the shapes of the letters as they learn to write. . . . They also use this intelligence to move the sounds of the vowels that they are learning, blending them together with letters, as they begin to read."

Landa believes that "intrapersonal intelligence is an intelligence that often is neglected in the traditional classroom." In her classroom, students "complete their own evaluation sheets after they have concluded their work at the centers. They evaluate their work and create their own portfolios," in which they keep their work so they can see their progress.

As she was implementing the multiple-intelligences approach in her classroom, Landa recognized that she needed to educate parents about it. She created "a parent education class called the Parent-Teacher Connection," which meets periodically to view videos, talk about multiple intelligences, and discuss how they are being introduced in the classroom. She also sends a weekly newsletter to parents, informing them about the week's multiple-intelligences activities and students' progress.

Preview

Shiffy Landa's classroom techniques build on Howard Gardner's multiple-intelligences theory, one of the theories of intelligence that we will explore in this chapter. You will see that there is spirited debate about whether people have a general intelligence or a number of specific intelligences. Intelligence is but one of several main topics in this chapter. We also will examine learning and thinking styles, as well as personality and temperament. For each of these topics, an important theme is students' individual variations and the best strategies for teachers to use related to these variations.

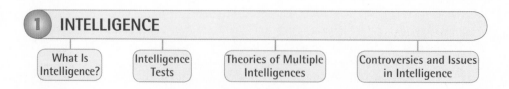

1 INTELLIGENCE

What Is Intelligence? — Intelligence Tests — Theories of Multiple Intelligences — Controversies and Issues in Intelligence

Intelligence is one of our most prized possessions. However, even the most intelligent people have not been able to agree on how to define and measure the concept of intelligence.

What Is Intelligence?

What does the term *intelligence* mean to psychologists? Some experts describe intelligence as the ability to solve problems. Others describe it as the capacity to adapt and learn from experience. Still others argue that intelligence includes characteristics such as creativity and interpersonal skills.

The problem with intelligence is that—unlike height, weight, and age—intelligence cannot be directly measured. We can't peel back a person's scalp and see how much intelligence he or she has. We can evaluate intelligence only *indirectly* by studying and comparing the intelligent acts that people perform.

The primary components of intelligence are similar to the cognitive processes of memory and thinking that we will discuss in Chapters 8 and 9. The differences in how these cognitive processes are described, and how we will discuss intelligence, lie in the concepts of individual differences and assessment. *Individual differences* are the stable, consistent ways in which people are different from one another. Individual differences in intelligence generally have been measured by intelligence tests designed to tell us whether a person can reason better than others who have taken the test (Christ & Thorndike, 2008).

We will use as our definition of **intelligence** the ability to solve problems and to adapt and learn from experiences. But even this broad definition doesn't satisfy everyone. As you will see shortly, Robert Sternberg (2008a, b, c, 2009a, b) proposes that practical know-how should be considered part of intelligence. In his view, intelligence involves weighing options carefully and acting judiciously, as well as developing strategies to improve shortcomings. Also, a definition of intelligence based on a theory such as Lev Vygotsky's, which we discussed in Chapter 2, would have to include the ability to use the tools of the culture with help from more-skilled individuals. Because intelligence is such an abstract, broad concept, it is not surprising that there are so many different ways to define it.

Alfred Binet constructed the first intelligence test after being asked to create a measure to determine which children would benefit from instruction in France's schools.

Intelligence Tests

Robert Sternberg (1997) had considerable childhood anxieties about intelligence tests. Because he got so stressed out about taking the tests, he did very poorly on them. Fortunately, a fourth-grade teacher worked with Robert and helped instill the confidence in him to overcome his anxieties. He not only began performing better on them, but when he was 13, he devised his own intelligence test and began using it to assess classmates—until the school principal found out and scolded him. Sternberg became so fascinated by intelligence that he made its study a lifelong pursuit, and later in this chapter we will discuss his theory of intelligence. In this section, we will first describe individual intelligence tests, then examine group intelligence tests.

Individual Intelligence Tests   The two main intelligence tests that are administered to children on an individual basis today are the Stanford Binet test and the Wechsler scales. As you will see next, an early version of the Binet was the first intelligence test that was devised.

The Binet Tests   In 1904, the French Ministry of Education asked psychologist Alfred Binet to devise a method of identifying children who were unable to learn in school. School officials wanted to reduce crowding by placing in special schools students who did not benefit from regular classroom teaching. Binet and his student Theophile Simon developed an intelligence test to meet this request. The test is called the 1905 Scale. It consisted of 30 questions, ranging from the ability to touch one's ear to the abilities to draw designs from memory and define abstract concepts.

Binet developed the concept of **mental age (MA)**, an individual's level of mental development relative to others. In 1912, William Stern created the concept of **intelligence quotient (IQ)**, which refers to a person's mental age divided by chronological age (CA), multiplied by 100. That is, MA/CA × 100.

intelligence Problem-solving skills and the ability to adapt to and learn from experiences.

mental age (MA) An individual's level of mental development relative to others.

intelligence quotient (IQ) A person's mental age (MA) divided by chronological age (CA), multiplied by 100.

FIGURE 4.1 The Normal Curve and Standard-Binet IQ Scores

The distribution of IQ scores approximates a normal curve. Most of the population falls in the middle range of scores. Notice that extremely high and extremely low scores are very rare. Slightly more than two-thirds of the scores fall between 84 and 116. Only about 1 in 50 individuals has an IQ of more than 132, and only about 1 in 50 individuals has an IQ of less than 68.

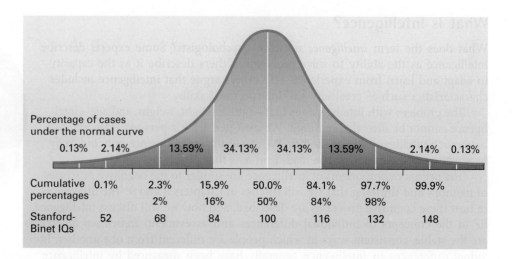

	Percentage of cases under the normal curve							
	0.13%	2.14%	13.59%	34.13%	34.13%	13.59%	2.14%	0.13%
Cumulative percentages	0.1%	2.3%	15.9%	50.0%	84.1%	97.7%	99.9%	
		2%	16%	50%	84%	98%		
Stanford-Binet IQs	52	68	84	100	116	132	148	

If mental age is the same as chronological age, then the person's IQ is 100. If mental age is above chronological age, then IQ is more than 100. For example, a 6-year-old with a mental age of 8 would have an IQ of 133. If mental age is below chronological age, then IQ is less than 100. For example, a 6-year-old with a mental age of 5 would have an IQ of 83.

The Binet test has been revised many times to incorporate advances in the understanding of intelligence and intelligence testing. These revisions are called the *Stanford-Binet tests* (because the revisions were made at Stanford University). By administering the test to large numbers of people of different ages from different backgrounds, researchers have found that scores on a Stanford-Binet test approximate a normal distribution (see Figure 4.1). As described more fully in Chapter 15, "Standardized Tests and Teaching," a **normal distribution** is symmetrical, with a majority of the scores falling in the middle of the possible range of scores and few scores appearing toward the extremes of the range.

The current Stanford-Binet test is administered individually to people aged 2 through adult. It includes a variety of items, some of which require verbal responses, others nonverbal responses. For example, items that reflect a typical 6-year-old's level of performance on the test include the verbal ability to define at least six words, such as *orange* and *envelope*, as well as the nonverbal ability to trace a path through a maze. Items that reflect an average adult's level of performance include defining such words as *disproportionate* and *regard*, explaining a proverb, and comparing idleness and laziness.

The current version of the Stanford-Binet is the fifth edition. An important addition to the fourth edition that has been continued and expanded on in the fifth edition is analysis of five aspects of cognitive ability (fluid reasoning, knowledge, quantitative reasoning, visual-spatial reasoning, and working memory) and two aspects of intelligence (Bart & Peterson, 2008). The five aspects of cognitive ability are fluid reasoning (abstract thinking), knowledge (conceptual information), quantitative reasoning (math skills), visual-spatial reasoning (understanding visual forms and spatial layouts), and working memory (recall of new information). The two aspects of intelligence assessed by the fifth edition of the Stanford-Binet are verbal intelligence and nonverbal intelligence. A general composite score is still obtained to reflect overall intelligence. The Stanford-Binet continues to be one of the most widely used tests to assess students' intelligence.

The Wechsler Scales Another set of tests widely used to assess students' intelligence is called the *Wechsler scales,* developed by psychologist David Wechsler. They include the Wechsler Preschool and Primary Scale of Intelligence–Third Edition (WPPSI-III) to test children from 2 years 6 months to 7 years 3 months of age; the Wechsler

normal distribution A symmetrical distribution, with a majority of scores falling in the middle of the possible range of scores and few scores appearing toward the extremes of the range.

Verbal Subscales

Similarities

A child must think logically and abstractly to answer a number of questions about how things might be similar.

Example: "In what way are a lion and a tiger alike?"

Comprehension

This subscale is designed to measure an individual's judgment and common sense.

Example: "What is the advantage of keeping money in a bank?"

Nonverbal Subscales

Block Design

A child must assemble a set of multicolored blocks to match designs that the examiner shows. Visual-motor coordination, perceptual organization, and the ability to visualize spatially are assessed.

Example: "Use the four blocks on the left to make the pattern on the right."

FIGURE 4.2 Sample Subscales of the *Wechsler Intelligence Scale for Children–Fourth Edition.* (WISC–IV)

Simulated items similar to those in the *Wechsler Intelligence Scale for Children–Fourth Edition.* Copyright © 2003 by NCS Pearson, Inc. Reproduced with permission. All rights reserved.

Intelligence Scale for Children–Fourth Edition (WISC-IV) for children and adolescents 6 to 16 years of age; and the Wechsler Adult Intelligence Scale–Third Edition (WAIS-III).

The Wechsler scales not only provide an overall IQ score and scores on a number of subtests but also yield several composite indexes (for example, the Verbal Comprehension Index, the Working Memory Index, and the Processing Speed Index). The subtest and composite scores allow the examiner to quickly determine the areas in which the child is strong or weak. Three of the Wechsler subscales are shown in Figure 4.2.

Intelligence tests such as the Stanford-Binet and Wechsler are given on an individual basis. A psychologist approaches an individual assessment of intelligence as a structured interaction between the examiner and the student. This provides the psychologist with an opportunity to sample the student's behavior. During the testing, the examiner observes the ease with which rapport is established, the student's enthusiasm and interest, whether anxiety interferes with the student's performance, and the student's degree of tolerance for frustration.

Group Intelligence Tests Students also may be given an intelligence test in a group. Group intelligence tests include the Lorge-Thorndike Intelligence Tests, the Kuhlman-Anderson Intelligence Tests, and the Otis-Lennon School Ability Test (OLSAT). Group intelligence tests are more convenient and economical than individual tests, but they do have their drawbacks. When a test is given to a large group, the examiner cannot establish rapport, determine the student's level of anxiety, and so on. In a large-group testing situation, students might not understand the instructions or might be distracted by other students.

Because of such limitations, when important decisions are made about students, a group intelligence test should always be supplemented with other information about the student's abilities. For that matter, the same strategy holds for an individual intelligence test, although it usually is wise to have less confidence in the accuracy of group intelligence test scores. Many students take tests in large groups at school, but a decision to place a student in a class for students who have mental retardation, a special education class, or a class for students who are gifted should not be based on

BEST PRACTICES
Strategies for Interpreting Intelligence Test Scores

Psychological tests are tools (Anastasi & Urbino, 1997). Like all tools, their effectiveness depends on the user's knowledge, skill, and integrity. A hammer can be used to build a beautiful kitchen cabinet or to break down a door. Similarly, psychological tests can be well used or badly abused. Here are some cautions about IQ that can help teachers avoid using information about a student's intelligence in negative ways:

1. *Avoid unwarranted stereotypes and negative expectations about students based on IQ scores.* Too often, sweeping generalizations are made on the basis of an IQ score. Imagine that you are in the teachers' lounge on the second day of school in the fall. You mention one of your students, and another teacher remarks that she had him in her class last year. She says that he was a real dunce and that he scored 83 on an IQ test. How hard is it to ignore this information as you go about teaching your class? Probably difficult. But it is important that you not develop the expectation that because Johnny scored low

on an IQ test, it is useless to spend much time teaching him (Weinstein, 2004). An IQ test should always be considered a measure of current performance. It is not a measure of fixed potential. Maturational changes and enriched environmental experiences can advance a student's intelligence.

2. *Don't use IQ tests as the main or sole characteristic of competence.* A high IQ is not the ultimate human value. Teachers need to consider not only students' intellectual competence in areas such as verbal skills, but also their creative and practical skills (Drefs & Saklofske, 2008).

3. *Especially be cautious in interpreting the meaningfulness of an overall IQ score.* It is wiser to think of intelligence as consisting of a number of domains. Many educational psychologists stress that it is important to consider the student's strengths and weaknesses in different areas of intelligence. Intelligence tests such as the Wechsler scales can provide information about those strengths and weaknesses.

Robert J. Sternberg, who developed the triarchic theory of intelligence.

triarchic theory of intelligence Sternberg's view that intelligence comes in three main forms: analytical, creative, and practical.

a group test alone. In such instances, an extensive amount of relevant information about the student's abilities should be obtained outside the testing situation (Neukrug & Fawcett, 2006).

Theories of Multiple Intelligences

Is it more appropriate to think of a student's intelligence as a general ability or as a number of specific abilities? Psychologists have thought about this question since early in the twentieth century and continue to debate the issue.

Sternberg's Triarchic Theory According to Robert J. Sternberg's (1986, 2004, 2006, 2007a, b, 2008a, b, c, 2009a, b) **triarchic theory of intelligence**, intelligence comes in three forms: analytical, creative, and practical. Analytical intelligence involves the ability to analyze, judge, evaluate, compare, and contrast. Creative intelligence consists of the ability to create, design, invent, originate, and imagine. Practical intelligence focuses on the ability to use, apply, implement, and put into practice.

To understand what analytical, creative, and practical intelligence mean, let's look at examples of people who reflect these three types of intelligence:

- Consider Latisha, who scores high on traditional intelligence tests such as the Stanford-Binet and is a star analytical thinker. Latisha's *analytical intelligence* approximates what has traditionally been called intelligence and what is commonly assessed by intelligence tests. In Sternberg's view, analytical intelligence consists of several components: the ability to acquire or store information; to retain or retrieve information; to transfer information; to plan, make decisions, and solve problems; and to translate thoughts into performance.

- Todd does not have the best test scores but has an insightful and creative mind. Sternberg calls the type of thinking at which Todd excels *creative intel-*

ligence. According to Sternberg, creative people have the ability to solve new problems quickly, but they also learn how to solve familiar problems in an automatic way so their minds are free to handle other problems that require insight and creativity.

- Finally, consider Emanuel, a person whose scores on traditional IQ tests are low but who quickly grasps real-life problems. He easily picks up knowledge about how the world works. Emanuel's "street smarts" and practical know-how are what Sternberg calls *practical intelligence.* Practical intelligence includes the ability to get out of trouble and a knack for getting along with people. Sternberg describes practical intelligence as all of the important information about getting along in the world that you are not taught in school.

Sternberg (2002; Sternberg & Grigorenko, 2008; Sternberg, Jarvin, & Grigorenko, 2008) says that students with different triarchic patterns look different in school. Students with high analytic ability tend to be favored in conventional schools. They often do well in classes in which the teacher lectures and gives objective tests. These students typically get good grades, do well on traditional IQ tests and the SAT, and later gain admission to competitive colleges.

Students high in creative intelligence often are not in the top rung of their class. Creatively intelligent students might not conform to teachers' expectations about how assignments should be done. They give unique answers, for which they might get reprimanded or marked down.

Like students high in creative intelligence, students who are practically intelligent often do not relate well to the demands of school. However, these students frequently do well outside the classroom's walls. Their social skills and common sense may allow them to become successful managers or entrepreneurs, despite undistinguished school records.

Sternberg (2008a, b; Sternberg & Grigorenko, 2008) stresses that few tasks are purely analytic, creative, or practical. Most tasks require some combination of these skills. For example, when students write a book report, they might analyze the book's main themes, generate new ideas about how the book could have been written better, and think about how the book's themes can be applied to people's lives. Sternberg argues that it is important for classroom instruction to give students opportunities to learn through all three types of intelligence.

Sternberg (1998, 2008c, d, 2009a, b) argues that *wisdom* is linked to both practical and academic intelligence. In his view, academic intelligence is a necessary but in many cases insufficient requirement for wisdom. Practical knowledge about the realities of life also is needed for wisdom. For Sternberg, balance between self-interest, the interests of others, and context produces a common good. Thus, wise individuals don't just look out for themselves—they also need to consider others' needs and perspectives, as well as the particular context involved. Sternberg assesses wisdom by presenting problems to individuals that require solutions which highlight various intrapersonal, interpersonal, and contextual interests. He also emphasizes that such aspects of wisdom should be taught in schools (Sternberg, 2008 c, d, 2009, a, b; Sternberg, Jarvin, & Reznitskaya, 2009).

Sternberg (1993; Sternberg & others, 2001a) developed the Sternberg Triarchic Abilities Test (STAT) to assess analytical, creative, and practical intelligence. The three kinds of abilities are examined through verbal items and essays, quantitative items, and drawings with multiple-choice items. The goal is to obtain a more complete assessment of intelligence than is possible with a conventional test.

The analytical section of STAT is much like a conventional test, with individuals required to provide the meanings of words, complete number series, and complete matrices. The creative and practical sections are different from conventional tests. For example, in the creative section, individuals write an essay on designing an ideal school. The practical section has individuals solve practical everyday problems such as planning routes and purchasing tickets to an event.

"You're wise, but you lack tree smarts."
© The New Yorker Collection, 1988, Donald Reilly from cartoonbank.com. All Rights Reserved.

Howard Gardner, here working with a young child, developed the view that intelligence comes in the forms of these eight kinds of skills: verbal, mathematical, spatial, bodily-kinesthetic, musical, intrapersonal, interpersonal, and naturalist.

An increasing number of studies are investigating the effectiveness of the STAT in predicting such important aspects of life as success in school. For example, in one study of 800 college students, scores on the STAT were effective in predicting college grade-point average (Sternberg & others, 2001a). More research, however, is needed to determine the validity and reliability of the STAT.

Recently, Sternberg and the Rainbow Project Collaborators (2006) modified the STAT in an attempt to develop an assessment to augment the SAT in predicting college achievement. The results indicated that the Rainbow assessment that reflects Sternberg's triarchic intelligence concept enhanced the prediction of college students' grade-point average beyond the SAT.

Gardner's Eight Frames of Mind As we indicated in the *Teaching Stories* introduction to this chapter, Howard Gardner (1983, 1993, 2002) says there are many specific types of intelligence, or frames of mind. They are described here along with examples of the occupations in which they are reflected as strengths (Campbell, Campbell, & Dickinson, 2004):

- *Verbal skills:* The ability to think in words and to use language to express meaning (authors, journalists, speakers)
- *Mathematical skills:* The ability to carry out mathematical operations (scientists, engineers, accountants)
- *Spatial skills:* The ability to think three-dimensionally (architects, artists, sailors)
- *Bodily-kinesthetic skills:* The ability to manipulate objects and be physically adept (surgeons, craftspeople, dancers, athletes)
- *Musical skills:* A sensitivity to pitch, melody, rhythm, and tone (composers, musicians, and music therapists)
- *Intrapersonal skills:* The ability to understand oneself and effectively direct one's life (theologians, psychologists)
- *Interpersonal skills:* The ability to understand and effectively interact with others (successful teachers, mental health professionals)
- *Naturalist skills:* The ability to observe patterns in nature and understand natural and human-made systems (farmers, botanists, ecologists, landscapers)

Gardner argues that each form of intelligence can be destroyed by a different pattern of brain damage, that each involves unique cognitive skills, and that each shows up in unique ways in both the gifted and idiot savants (individuals who have mental retardation but have an exceptional talent in a particular domain, such as drawing, music, or numerical computation).

At various times, Gardner has considered including *existential intelligence*, which involves concern and reasoning about meaning in life, as a ninth intelligence (McKay, 2008). However, as yet, he has not added it as a different form of intelligence.

Although Gardner has endorsed the application of his model to education, he has also witnessed some misuses of the approach. Here are some cautions he gives about using it (Gardner, 1998):

- There is no reason to assume that every subject can be effectively taught in eight different ways to correspond to the eight intelligences, and attempting to do this is a waste of effort.
- Don't assume that it is enough just to apply a certain type of intelligence. For example, in terms of bodily-kinesthetic skills, random muscle movements have nothing to do with cultivating cognitive skills.
- There is no reason to believe that it is helpful to use one type of intelligence as a background activity while children are working on an activity related to a different type of intelligence. For example, Gardner points out that playing music in the background while students solve math problems is a misapplication of his theory.

DEVELOPMENTAL FOCUS 4.1

How Does Gardner's Theory of Multiple Intelligences Apply to Your Classroom?

Early Childhood

Since each one of my preschoolers is different, I recognize that they have different skills and different needs. For example, we had a child who was very good at physical activities, such as bouncing a ball and tossing it into a net, but who struggled with learning how to count. To improve her counting skills, we had her count the number of times she bounced the ball and how many times the ball went into the net.

—Heidi Kaufman, *Metro West YMCA Child Care and Educational Program*

Elementary School: Grades K–5

Students need choices. Some need to move around regularly in the classroom, sit on the floor, or write on the board. Some need a nondistracting, edge of the room seat. If instruction is given, or a question is asked, partner-talk can help to reinforce learning, but some students need a quiet, personal prompt from the teacher. I also provide choices for final assignments—for example, oral presentation, graphic representation, an essay or poem, and PowerPoint slides.

—Keren Abra, *Convent of the Sacred Heart Elementary School*

Middle School: Grades 6–8

Group projects offer great opportunities to incorporate Gardner's theory into the classroom. I try to develop group projects that require participants to read, do artwork, do math, think creatively, speak in public, and so on. By including these various skills, group members are able to express their knowledge in a way that meets their individual style of learning.

—Casey Maass, *Edison Middle School*

High School: Grades 9–12

I often give my students the power of choice when it comes to how a project can be completed. For example, they can complete a project as an artistic piece, a written project, or a demonstration so that students can choose the mode that best fits their comfort level.

— Jennifer Heiter, *Bremen High School*

The Key School, a K–6 elementary school in Indianapolis, immerses students in activities that involve a range of skills that closely correlate with Gardner's eight frames of mind (Goleman, Kaufman, & Ray, 1993). Each day every student is exposed to materials designed to stimulate a range of human abilities, including art, music, language skills, math skills, and physical games. In addition, students devote attention to understanding themselves and others.

The Key School's goal is to allow students to discover their natural curiosity and talent, then let them explore these domains. Gardner underscores that if teachers give students the opportunities to use their bodies, imaginations,

These children attend the Key School, which has "pods" where they can pursue activities of special interest to them. Every day, each child can choose from activities that draw on Gardner's eight frames of mind. The school's pods include gardening, architecture, gliding, and dancing.

TECHNOLOGY AND EDUCATION
Technology and Multiple Intelligences

Technology can be used to facilitate learning in each area of intelligence:

- *Verbal skills.* Computers encourage students to revise and rewrite compositions; this should help them to produce more competent papers. "Learning keyboarding is as important today as learning to write with a pencil, and learning to use a word processor is as important as learning to type." Also, many aspects of computer-mediated communication, such as e-mail, chat, and text messaging, provide students with opportunities to practice and expand their verbal skills.

- *Logical/mathematical skills.* "Students of every ability can learn effectively through interesting software programs that provide immediate feedback and go far beyond drill-and-practice exercises." These programs challenge students to use their thinking skills to solve math problems. Formula manipulation software such as *Mathematica* (2008) (www.wolfram.com/products/mathematica/index.html) and Flash mathematics applets can help students improve their logical/mathematics skills.

- *Spatial skills.* Computers allow students to see and manipulate material. They can create many different forms before they make final copies of a written project. Virtual-reality technology can provide students with opportunities to exercise their visual-spatial skills while spatial games such as *Portals* (2008) (www.newgrounds.com/portal/view/404612) also can be used to improve students' spatial skills.

- *Bodily-kinesthetic skills.* "Computers rely mostly on eye-hand coordination for their operation—keyboarding and the use of a mouse or touch-screen. This kinesthetic activity . . . makes the student an active participant in the learning." Nintendo Wii (2008) (http://www.nintendo.com/wii) can be used to improve students' bodily-kinesthetic skills.

- *Musical skills.* "The development of musical intelligence can be enhanced by technology in the same way that verbal fluency is enhanced by word processors. . . . The Musical Instrument Digital Interface (MIDI) makes it possible to compose for and orchestrate many different instruments through the computer." Apple Computer's GarageBand (2008) (www.apple.com/ilife/garageband) software is a good musical skills source.

- *Interpersonal skills.* "When students use computers in pairs or small groups, their comprehension and learning are facilitated and accelerated. Positive learning experiences can result as students share discoveries, support each other in solving problems, and work collaboratively on projects." Knowledge Forum (2008) is a good Web site for students to learn more about and practice collaboration skills (www.knowledgeforum.com).

- *Intrapersonal skills.* "Technology offers the means to explore a line of thought in great depth" and to have extensive access to a range of personal interests. "The opportunity for students to make such choices is at the heart of giving them control over their own learning and intellectual development."

- *Naturalist skills.* Electronic technologies can "facilitate scientific investigation, exploration, and other naturalist activities. Telecommunications technologies help students to understand the world beyond their own environments." For example, National Geographic Online allows students to go on expeditions with famed explorers and photographers. Zoo Cams Worldwide (2008) provides excellent material for learning more about animals (www.zoos-worldwide.de/zoocams.html). (Source: Dickinson, 1998, 1–3).

and different senses, almost every student finds that he or she is good at something. Even students who are not outstanding in any single area will still find that they have relative strengths.

For nine-week time periods, the school emphasizes different themes, such as the Renaissance in sixteenth-century Italy and "Renaissance Now" in Indianapolis. Students develop projects related to the theme. The projects are not graded. Instead, students present them to their classmates, explain them, and answer questions. Collaboration and teamwork are emphasized in the theme projects and in all areas of learning.

The *Technology and Education* interlude describes how technology can be used in Gardner's eight types of intelligence.

We have discussed a number of ideas about Gardner's eight types of intelligence. To evaluate your strengths and weaknesses in these areas, complete *Self-Assessment 4.1.*

BEST PRACTICES
Strategies for Implementing Each of Gardner's Multiple Intelligences

Applications of Gardner's theory of multiple intelligences to children's education continue to be made (Campbell, 2008; Hirsh, 2004; Weber, 2005). Following are some strategies that teachers can use related to Gardner's eight types of intelligence (Campbell, Campbell, & Dickinson, 2004):

1. *Verbal skills*. Read to children and let them read to you, visit libraries and bookstores with children, and have children summarize and retell a story they have read.

2. *Mathematical skills*. Play games of logic with children, be on the lookout for situations that can inspire children to think about and construct an understanding of numbers, and take children on field trips to computer labs, science museums, and electronics exhibits.

3. *Spatial skills*. Have a variety of creative materials for children to use, take children to art museums and hands-on children's museums, and go on walks with children. When they get back, ask them to visualize where they have been and then draw a map of their experiences.

4. *Bodily-kinesthetic skills*. Provide children with opportunities for physical activity and encourage them to participate, provide areas where children can play indoors and outdoors (if this is not possible, take them to a park), and encourage children to participate in dance activities.

5. *Musical skills*. Give children an opportunity to play musical instruments, create opportunities for children to make music and rhythms together using voices and instruments, and take children to concerts.

6. *Intrapersonal skills*. Encourage children to have hobbies and interests, listen to children's feelings and give them sensitive feedback, and have children keep a journal or scrapbook of their ideas and experiences.

7. *Interpersonal skills*. Encourage children to work in groups, help children to develop communication skills, and provide group games for children to play.

8. *Naturalist skills*. Create a naturalist learning center in the classroom, engage children in outdoor naturalist activities, such as taking a nature walk or adopting a tree, and have children make collections of flora or fauna and classify them.

Next, Joanna Smith, a high school English teacher, describes how she implements Gardner's multiple intelligences into her classroom.

THROUGH THE EYES OF TEACHERS
Giving Students a Choice of Which Type of Intelligence They Want to Use for a Project

I try to draw on Gardner's eight frames of mind throughout the year by giving a variety of assignments. My students sometimes have a choice about which "type of intelligence" to use, depending on their project. For example, at the end of the first semester, students do an outside reading project based on a self-selected book. They create a project based on the book's themes and characters. For example, students might give a monologue from a character's perspective, create a family tree, make a CD of thematic songs, or give a "tour" of the book's setting live or on tape. This type of project is always successful because it allows students to choose in what mode, in what frame of mind, they will present their knowledge.

Emotional Intelligence   Both Gardner's and Sternberg's theories include one or more categories related to the ability to understand one's self and others and to get along in the world. In Gardner's theory, the categories are interpersonal intelligence and intrapersonal intelligence; in Sternberg's theory, practical intelligence. Other theorists who emphasize interpersonal, intrapersonal, and practical aspects of intelligence focus on what is called *emotional intelligence*, which was popularized by Daniel Goleman (1995) in his book *Emotional Intelligence.*

The concept of emotional intelligence was initially developed by Peter Salovey and John Mayer (1990). They conceptualize **emotional intelligence** as the ability to perceive and express emotion accurately and adaptively (such as taking the perspective of others), to understand emotion and emotional knowledge (such as understanding the roles that emotions play in friendship and other relationships), to use feelings to facilitate thought (such as being in a positive mood, which is linked to creative thinking), and to manage emotions in oneself and others (such as being able to control one's anger).

emotional intelligence The ability to perceive and express emotion accurately and adaptively, to understand emotion and emotional knowledge, to monitor one's own and others' emotions and feelings, to discriminate among them, and to use this information to guide one's thinking and action.

SELF-ASSESSMENT 4.1

Evaluating Myself on Gardner's Eight Types of Intelligence

Read these items and rate yourself on a 4-point scale. Each rating corresponds to how well a statement describes you: 1 = not like me at all, 2 = somewhat unlike me, 3 = somewhat like me, and 4 = a lot like me.

	1	2	3	4

Verbal Thinking

1. I do well on verbal tests, such as the verbal part of the SAT.

2. I am a skilled reader and read prolifically.

3. I love the challenge of solving verbal problems.

Logical/Mathematical Thinking

4. I am a very logical thinker.

5. I like to think like a scientist.

6. Math is one of my favorite subjects.

Spatial Skills

7. I am good at visualizing objects and layouts from different angles.

8. I have the ability to create maps of spaces and locations in my mind.

9. If I had wanted to be, I think I could have been an architect.

Bodily-Kinesthetic Skills

10. I have great hand-eye coordination.

11. I excel at sports.

12. I am good at using my body to carry out an expression, as in dance.

Musical Skills

13. I play one or more musical instruments well.

14. I have a good "ear" for music.

15. I am good at making up songs.

Insightful Skills for Self-Understanding

16. I know myself well and have a positive view of myself.

17. I am in tune with my thoughts and feelings.

18. I have good coping skills.

Insightful Skills for Analyzing Others

19. I am very good at "reading" people.

20. I am good at collaborating with other people.

21. I am a good listener.

Naturalist Skills

22. I am good at observing patterns in nature.

23. I excel at identifying and classifying objects in the natural environment.

24. I understand natural and human-made systems.

SELF-ASSESSMENT 4.1

Scoring and Interpretation

Total your score for each of the eight types of intelligence and place the total in the blank that follows the label for each kind of intelligence. Which areas of intelligence are your strengths? In which are you the least proficient? It is highly unlikely that you will be strong in all eight areas or weak in all eight areas. By being aware of your strengths and weaknesses in different areas of intelligence, you can get a sense of which areas of teaching students will be the easiest and most difficult for you. If I (your author) had to teach musical skills, I would be in big trouble because I just don't have the talent. However, I do have reasonably good movement skills and spent part of my younger life playing and coaching tennis. If you are not proficient in some of Gardner's areas and you have to teach students in those areas, consider getting volunteers from the community to help you. For example, Gardner says that schools need to do a better job of calling on retired people, most of whom likely would be delighted to help students improve their skills in the domain or domains in which they are competent. This strategy also helps to link communities and schools with a sort of "intergenerational glue."

The Mayer-Salovey-Caruso Emotional Intelligence Test (MSCEIT) measures the four aspects of emotional intelligence just described: perceiving emotions, understanding emotions, facilitating thought, and managing emotions (Mayer, Salovey, & Caruso, 2002, 2004, 2007). The test consists of 141 items, can be given to individuals 17 years of age and older, and takes about 30 to 45 minutes to administer. In one recent study, the MSCEIT predicted high school students' final grades in their courses (Gil-Olarte Marquez, Palomera, & Brackett, 2007).

There continues to be considerable interest in the concept of emotional intelligence (Chan, 2008; Cox & Nelson, 2008: Ghee & Johnson, 2008; Kingston, 2008). Critics argue that emotional intelligence broadens the concept of intelligence too far and has not been adequately assessed and researched (Humphrey & others, 2007).

Do Children Have One Intelligence or Many Intelligences?   Figure 4.3 provides a comparison of Gardner's, Sternberg's, and Salovey/Mayer's views. Notice that Gardner includes a number of types of intelligence not addressed by the other views, and that Sternberg is unique in emphasizing creative intelligence. These theories of multiple intelligences have much to offer. They have stimulated us to think more broadly about what makes up people's intelligence and competence (Moran & Gardner, 2006). And they have motivated educators to develop programs that instruct students in different domains (Winner, 2006).

Theories of multiple intelligences also have many critics. They conclude that the research base to support these theories has not yet developed. In particular, some argue that Gardner's classification seems arbitrary. For example, if musical skills represent a type of intelligence, why don't we also refer to chess intelligence, prizefighter intelligence, and so on?

A number of psychologists still support the concept of *g* (general intelligence) (Johnson, 2008; Johnson, te Nijenhouse, & Bouchard,

FIGURE 4.3 Comparing Gardner's, Sternberg's, and Salovey/Mayer's Intelligences

Gardner	Sternberg	Salovey/Mayer
Verbal Mathematical	Analytical	
Spatial Movement Musical	Creative	
Interpersonal Intrapersonal	Practical	Emotional
Naturalistic		

2008; Reeve & Lamb, 2007). For example, one expert on intelligence, Nathan Brody (2007), argues that people who excel at one type of intellectual task are likely to excel at other intellectual tasks. Thus, individuals who do well at memorizing lists of digits are also likely to be good at solving verbal problems and spatial layout problems. This general intelligence includes abstract reasoning or thinking, the capacity to acquire knowledge, and problem-solving ability (Brody, 2007; Carroll, 1993).

Advocates of the concept of general intelligence point to its success in predicting school and job success (Deary & others, 2007). For example, scores on tests of general intelligence are substantially correlated with school grades and achievement test performance, both at the time of the test and years later (Brody, 2007; Colomb & Florez-Mendoza, 2007; Strentze, 2007).

Intelligence tests are moderately correlated with job performance (Lubinski, 2000). Individuals with higher scores on tests designed to measure general intelligence tend to get higher-paying, more prestigious jobs (Zagorsky, 2007). However, general IQ tests predict only about one-fourth of the variation in job success, with most variation being attributable to other factors such as motivation and education (Wagner & Sternberg, 1986). Further, the correlations between IQ and achievement decrease the longer people work at a job, presumably because as they gain more job experience they perform better (Hunt, 1995).

Some experts who argue for the existence of general intelligence conclude that individuals also have specific intellectual abilities (Brody, 2007; Chiappe & MacDonald, 2005). In sum, controversy still characterizes whether it is more accurate to conceptualize intelligence as a general ability, specific abilities, or both (Brody, 2007; Dai, 2008; Horn, 2007; Sternberg, 2007a, b, 2008a, b, 2009a). Sternberg (2007a) actually accepts that there is a *g* for the kinds of analytical tasks that traditional IQ tests assess but thinks that the range of tasks those tests measure is far too narrow.

Controversies and Issues in Intelligence

The topic of intelligence is surrounded by controversy. Is nature or nurture more important in determining intelligence? Are intelligence tests culturally biased? Should IQ tests be used to place children in particular schooling tracks?

Nature and Nurture   The **nature-nurture issue** involves the debate about whether development is primarily influenced by nature or by nurture. *Nature* refers to a child's biological inheritance, *nurture* to environmental experiences.

"Nature" proponents argue that intelligence is primarily inherited and that environmental experiences play only a minimal role in its manifestation (Davis, Arden, & Plomin, 2008; Jensen, 2008; Plomin, DeFries, & Fulker, 2007). The emerging view of the nature-nurture issue is that many complicated qualities, such as intelligence, probably have some genetic loading that gives them a propensity for a particular developmental trajectory, such as low, average, or high intelligence. The actual development of intelligence, however, requires more than just heredity.

Most experts today agree that the environment also plays an important role in intelligence (Campbell, 2007; Preiss & Sternberg, 2009; Sternberg, Kaufman, & Grigorenko, 2008). This means that improving children's environments can raise their intelligence (Tong & others, 2007). It also means that enriching children's environments can improve their school achievement and the acquisition of skills needed for employment. Craig Ramey and his associates (1988) found that high-quality early educational child care (through 5 years of age) significantly raised the tested intelligence of young children from impoverished backgrounds. Positive effects of this early intervention were still evident in the intelligence and achievement of these students when they were 13 and 21 years of age (Campbell, 2007; Ramey, Ramey, & Lanzi, 2001, 2006).

Another argument for the importance of environment in intelligence involves the increasing scores on IQ tests around the world. Scores on these tests have been

nature–nurture issue Issue that involves the debate about whether development is primarily influenced by nature (an organism's biological inheritance) or nurture (environmental experiences).

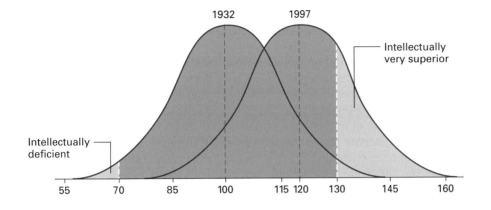

FIGURE 4.4 The Increase in IQ Scores from 1932 to 1997

As measured by the Stanford-Binet intelligence test, American children seem to be getting smarter. Scores of a group tested in 1932 fell along a bell-shaped curve with half below 100 and half above. Studies show that if children took that same test today, half would score above 120 on the 1932 scale. Very few of them would score in the "intellectually deficient" end, on the left side, and about one-fourth would rank in the "very superior" range.

increasing so fast that a high percentage of people regarded as having average intelligence in the early 1900s would be considered below average in intelligence today (Flynn, 1999, 2007a, b) (see Figure 4.4). If a representative sample of today's children took the Stanford-Binet test used in 1932, about one-fourth would be defined as very superior, a label usually accorded to less than 3 percent of the population. Because the increase has taken place in a relatively short period of time, it can't be due to heredity but, rather, might result from such environmental factors as the explosion in information people are exposed to and the much higher percentage of the population receiving education. This worldwide increase in intelligence test scores over a short time frame is called the *Flynn effect,* after the researcher who discovered it—James Flynn (1999, 2007a, b).

Studies of schooling also reveal effects on intelligence (Ceci & Gilstrap, 2000; Gustafsson, 2007; Sternberg, Jarvin, & Grigorenko, 2008). The biggest effects occurred when large groups of children were deprived of formal education for an extended period, resulting in lower intelligence. In one study, the intellectual functioning of ethnic Indian children in South Africa, whose schooling was delayed by four years because of the unavailability of teachers, was investigated (Ramphal, 1962). Compared

Students in an elementary school in South Africa. *How might schooling influence the development of children's intelligence?*

These children live in a slum area of a small Vermont town where the unemployment rate is very high because of a decline in industrial jobs. They are experiencing an environment that is far from optimal for the development of intelligence. *What types of programs and support services might be needed to increase such children's intelligence?*

with children in nearby villages who had teachers, the Indian children whose entry into school was delayed by four years experienced a drop of 5 IQ points for each year of delay.

One analysis of studies on schooling and intelligence concluded that schooling and intelligence influence each other (Ceci & Williams, 1997). For example, individuals who finish high school are more intelligent than those who drop out of school. This might be because brighter individuals stay in school longer, or because the environmental influence of schooling contributes to their intelligence.

Further, intelligence test scores tend to rise during the school year and decline during the summer months (Ceci & Gilstrap, 2000). Also, children whose birthdays just make the cutoff point for school entrance temporarily have higher intelligence scores than those born just slightly later, who are a year behind them in school (Ceci & Gilstrap, 2000).

Researchers increasingly are interested in manipulating the early environment of children who are at risk for impoverished intelligence (Campbell, 2007; Ramey, Ramey, & Lanzi, 2006; Sternberg, 2008b). The emphasis is on prevention rather than remediation. Many low-income parents have difficulty providing an intellectually stimulating environment for their children. Programs that educate parents to be more sensitive caregivers and better teachers, as well as support services such as quality child-care programs, can make a difference in a child's intellectual development.

It is extremely difficult to tease apart the effects of nature or nurture, so much so that psychologist William Greenough (1997, 2000) says that asking which is more important is like asking what's more important to a rectangle, its length or its width. We still do not know what, if any, specific genes actually promote or restrict a general level of intelligence. If such genes exist, they certainly are found both in children whose families and environments appear to promote the development of children's abilities and in children whose families and environments do not appear to be as supportive. Regardless of one's genetic background, growing up "with all the advantages" does not guarantee high intelligence or success, especially if those advantages are taken for granted. Nor does the absence of such advantages guarantee low intelligence or failure, especially if the family and child can make the most of whatever opportunities are accessible to them.

Ethnicity and Culture Are there ethnic differences in intelligence? Are conventional tests of intelligence biased, and if so, can we develop culture-fair tests?

Ethnic Comparisons In the United States, children from African American and Latino families score below children from White families on standardized intelligence tests. On the average, African American schoolchildren score 10 to 15 points lower on standardized intelligence tests than White American schoolchildren do (Brody, 2000; Lynn, 1996). These are *average scores,* however. About 15 to 25 percent of African American schoolchildren score higher than half of White schoolchildren do, and many Whites score lower than most African Americans. The reason is that the distribution of scores for African Americans and Whites overlap.

As African Americans have gained social, economic, and educational opportunities, the gap between African Americans and Whites on standardized intelligence tests has begun to narrow (Ogbu & Stern, 2001). This gap especially narrows in college, where African American and White students often experience more similar environments than in the elementary and high school years (Myerson & others, 1998). Also, when children from disadvantaged African American families are adopted into more-advantaged middle-socioeconomic-status families, their scores on intelligence tests more closely resemble national averages for middle-socioeconomic-status children than for lower-socioeconomic-status children (Scarr & Weinberg, 1983).

Cultural Bias and Culture-Fair Tests Many of the early tests of intelligence were culturally biased, favoring urban children over rural children, children from middle-

How might stereotype threat be involved in ethnic minority students' performance on standardized tests?

income families over children from low-income families, and white children over minority children (Miller-Jones, 1989). The standards for the early tests were almost exclusively based on White, middle-socioeconomic-status children. Also, some of the items were obviously culturally biased. For example, one item on an early test asked what you should do if you find a 3-year-old in the street. The "correct" answer was "Call the police." However, children from impoverished inner-city families might not choose this answer if they have had bad experiences with the police, and children living in rural areas might not have police nearby. Contemporary intelligence tests attempt to reduce such cultural bias (Merenda, 2004).

One potential influence on intelligence test performance is **stereotype threat**, the anxiety that one's behavior might confirm a negative stereotype about one's group (Hollis-Sawyer & Sawyer, 2008; Kellow & Jones, 2008; Steele & Aronson, 2004). For example, when African Americans take an intelligence test, they may experience anxiety about confirming the old stereotype that Blacks are "intellectually inferior." Some studies have confirmed the existence of stereotype threat (Beilock, Rydell, & McConnell, 2007; Brown & Day, 2006). For example, African American students do more poorly on standardized tests if they perceive that they are being evaluated. If they think the test doesn't count, they perform as well as White students (Aronson, 2002). However, critics argue that the extent to which stereotype threat explains the testing gap has been exaggerated (Sackett, Hardison, & Cullen, 2005).

The *Diversity and Education* interlude further explores possible IQ test bias.

Culture-fair tests are intelligence tests that aim to avoid cultural bias. Two types of culture-fair tests have been developed. The first includes questions familiar

stereotype threat The anxiety that one's behavior might confirm a negative stereotype about one's group.

culture-fair tests Tests of intelligence that are intended to be free of cultural bias.

FIGURE 4.5 Sample Item from the Raven's Progressive Matrices Test

Individuals are presented with a matrix arrangement of symbols, such as the one at the top of this figure, and must then complete the matrix by selecting the appropriate missing symbol from a group of symbols, such as the ones at the bottom.

Simulated item similar to those found in the Raven's Progressive Matrices. Copyright © 1976, 1958, 1938 by NCS Pearson, Inc. Reproduced with permission. All rights reserved.

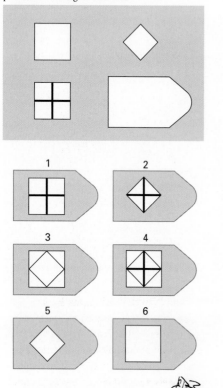

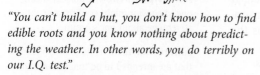

"You can't build a hut, you don't know how to find edible roots and you know nothing about predicting the weather. In other words, you do terribly on our I.Q. test."

© ScienceCartoonsPlus.com. Reprinted by permission of Sidney Harris.

DIVERSITY AND EDUCATION
The Controversy over Cultural Bias in IQ Tests

Larry P. is African American and poor. When he was 6 years old, he was placed in a class for the "educable mentally retarded" (EMR), which is supposed to mean that Larry learns much more slowly than average students. The primary reason Larry was placed in the EMR class was his very low score of 64 on an intelligence test.

Is there a possibility that the intelligence test Larry took was culturally biased? This question continues to be debated. The controversy has been the target of various lawsuits challenging the use of standardized IQ tests to place African American students in EMR classes. The initial lawsuit, filed on Larry P.'s behalf in California, claimed that the IQ test underestimated his true learning ability. His lawyers argued that IQ tests place too much emphasis on verbal skills and fail to account for the backgrounds of African American students from low-income families, and that Larry P. was incorrectly labeled as mentally retarded and might be burdened with that stigma forever.

As part of the lengthy court battle involving Larry P., six African American EMR students were independently retested by psychologists. The psychologists made sure that they established good rapport with the students and made special efforts to overcome the students' defeatism and distraction. For example, items were reworded in terms more consistent with the students' social background, and recognition was given to nonstandard answers that showed a logical, intelligent approach to problems. This modified testing approach produced scores of 79 to 104—17 to 38 points higher than the students received when initially tested. In every case, the scores were above the ceiling for placement in an EMR class.

In Larry's case, the judge ruled that IQ tests are culturally biased and should not be used in decisions about placing students in EMR classes. However, in subsequent rulings, such as *Pase* v. *Hannon* in Illinois, judges have ruled that IQ tests are not culturally biased. Also, a task force established by the American Psychological Association concluded that IQ tests are not culturally biased (Neisser & others, 1996). The controversy continues.

to people from all socioeconomic and ethnic backgrounds. For example, a child might be asked how a bird and a dog are different, on the assumption that virtually all children are familiar with birds and dogs. The second type of culture-fair test contains no verbal questions. Figure 4.5 shows a sample question from the Raven's Progressive Matrices Test. Even though tests such as the Raven's Progressive Matrices are designed to be culture-fair, people with more education still score higher than those with less education do (Shiraev & Levy, 2007).

Why is it so hard to create culture-fair tests? Most tests tend to reflect what the dominant culture thinks is important (Gregory, 2007; Matsumoto & Juang, 2008). If tests have time limits, that will bias the test against groups not concerned with time. If languages differ, the same words might have different meanings for different language groups. Even pictures can produce bias because some cultures have less experience with drawings and photographs (Anastasi & Urbina, 1997). Within the same culture, different groups could have different attitudes, values, and motivation, and this could affect their performance on intelligence tests. Items that ask why buildings should be made of brick are biased against children with little or no experience with brick houses. Questions about railroads, furnaces, seasons of the year, distances between cities, and so on can be biased against groups who have less experience than others with these contexts. Because of such difficulties in creating culture-fair tests, Robert Sternberg and his colleagues (Sternberg, 2008e; Sternberg & Grigorenko, 2008; Zhang & Sternberg, 2008a) conclude that there are no culture-fair tests, only *culture-reduced tests*.

Ability Grouping and Tracking Another controversial issue is whether it is beneficial to use students' scores on an intelligence test to place them in ability groups. Two types of ability grouping have been used in education: between-class and within-class.

Between-Class Ability Grouping (Tracking) **Between-class ability grouping (tracking)** consists of grouping students based on their ability or achievement. Tracking has long been used in schools as a way to organize students, especially at the secondary level (Gustafson, 2007; Slavin, 1995). The positive view of tracking is that it narrows the range of skill in a group of students, making it easier to teach them. Tracking is said to prevent less-able students from "holding back" more talented students.

A typical between-class grouping involves dividing students into a college preparatory track and a general track. Within the two tracks, further ability groupings might be made, such as two levels of math instruction for college preparatory students. Another form of tracking takes place when a student's abilities in different subject areas are taken into account. For example, the same student might be in a high-track math class and a middle-track English class.

Critics of tracking argue that it stigmatizes students who are consigned to low-track classes (Banks & others, 2005). For example, students can get labeled as "low-track" or "the dummy group." Critics also say that low-track classrooms often have less-experienced teachers, fewer resources, and lower expectations (Wheelock, 1992). Further, critics stress that tracking is used to segregate students according to ethnicity and socioeconomic status because higher tracks have fewer students from ethnic minority and impoverished backgrounds (Banks, 2008). In this way, tracking can actually replay segregation within schools. The detractors also argue that average and above-average students do not get substantial benefits from being grouped together.

Does research support the critics' contention that tracking is harmful to students? Researchers have found that tracking harms the achievement of low-track students (Hallinan, 2003; Kelly, 2008; Slavin, 1990). However, tracking seems to benefit high-track students (such as those in a gifted program). Also, researchers have found that "students who are 'tracked-up' or who are exposed to a more rigorous curriculum learn more than the same ability students who are 'tracked-down' or offered a less challenging course of study (Gamaron, 1990; Hallinan, 2003) . . ." (Banks & others, 2005, p. 239).

One variation of between-class ability grouping is the **nongraded (cross-age) program**, in which students are grouped by their ability in particular subjects regardless of their age or grade level (Fogarty, 1993). This type of program is used far more in elementary than in secondary schools, especially in the first three grades. For example, a math class might be composed of first-, second-, and third-graders grouped together because of their similar math ability. The **Joplin plan** is a standard nongraded program for instruction in reading. In the Joplin plan, students from

(*Top*) The intelligence of the Iatmul children of Papua New Guinea involves the ability to remember the names of many clans. (*Bottom*) On the 680 Caroline Islands in the Pacific Ocean, east of the Philippines, the intelligence of their inhabitants includes the ability to navigate by the stars. *Why might it be difficult to create a culture-fair intelligence test for the Iatmul children, Caroline Islands children, and U.S. children?*

between–class ability grouping (tracking) Grouping students based on their ability or achievement.

nongraded (cross-age) program A variation of between-class ability grouping in which students are grouped by their ability in particular subjects, regardless of their age or grade level.

Joplin plan A standard nongraded program for instruction in reading.

second, third, and fourth grade might be placed together because of their similar reading level.

We mentioned that tracking has negative effects on low-track students. When tracks are present, it is especially important to give low-achieving students an opportunity to improve their academic performance and thus change tracks. In the San Diego County Public Schools, the Advancement Via Individual Determination (AVID) program provides support for underachieving students. Instead of being placed in a low track, they are enrolled in rigorous courses but are not left to achieve on their own. A comprehensive system of support services helps them succeed. For example, a critical aspect of the program is a series of workshops that teach students note-taking skills, question-asking skills, thinking skills, and communication skills. The students also are clustered into study groups and urged to help each other clarify questions about assignments. College students, many of them AVID graduates, serve as role models, coaches, and motivators for the students. At each AVID school, a lead teacher oversees a team of school counselors and teachers from every academic discipline. In recent years, the dropout rate in AVID schools has declined by more than one-third, and an amazing 99 percent of the AVID graduates have enrolled in college.

In sum, tracking is a controversial issue, especially because of the restrictions it places on low-track students. Too often, scores on a single-group IQ test are used to place students in a particular track. Researchers have found that group IQ tests are not good predictors of how well students will do in a particular subject area (Garmon & others, 1995).

Within-Class Ability Grouping **Within-class ability grouping** involves placing students in two or three groups within a class to take into account differences in students' abilities. A typical within-class ability grouping occurs when elementary school teachers place students in several reading groups based on their reading skills. A second-grade teacher might have one group using a third-grade, first-semester reading program; another using a second-grade, first-semester program; and a third group using a first-grade, second-semester program. Such within-class grouping is far more common in elementary than in secondary schools. The subject area most often involved is reading, followed by math. Although many elementary school teachers use some form of within-class ability grouping, there is no clear research support for this strategy.

within-class ability grouping Placing students in two or three groups within a class to take into account differences in students' abilities.

These students participate in the Advancement Via Individual Determination (AVID) program is San Diego. Rather than being placed in a low track, they are enrolled in rigorous courses and provided support to help them achieve success. *What types of support are they provided?*

BEST PRACTICES
Strategies for the Use of Tracking

1. *Use other measures of student knowledge and potential in particular subject areas to place students in ability groups rather than a group-administered IQ test.*

2. *Avoid labeling groups as "low," "middle," and "high."* Also avoid comparisons of groups.

3. *Don't form more than two or three ability groups.* You won't be able to give a larger number of groups adequate attention and instruction.

4. *Consider the students' placements in various ability groups as subject to review and change.* Carefully mon- itor students' performance, and if a low-track student progresses adequately, move the student to a higher group. If a high-track student is doing poorly, evaluate whether the high track is the right one for the student and decide what supports the student might need to improve performance.

5. *Especially consider alternatives to tracking for low- achieving students.* Throughout this book, we will describe instructional strategies and support services for low-achieving students, such as those being used in the AVID program.

Review, Reflect, and Practice

(1) Discuss what intelligence is, how it is measured, theories of mul- tiple intelligences, and some controversies and issues about its use by educators.

REVIEW

- What does the concept of intelligence mean?
- What did Binet and Wechsler contribute to the field of intelligence? What are some pros and cons of individual versus group tests of intelligence?
- What is Sternberg's triarchic theory of intelligence? What is Gardner's system of "frames of mind"? What is Mayer, Salovey, and Goleman's concept of emotional intelligence? How is each theory relevant to education? What are some aspects of the controversy about whether intelligence is better conceptualized as general intelligence or multiple intelligences?
- What are three controversies related to intelligence?

REFLECT

- Suppose that you were about to teach a particular group of children for the first time and were handed intelligence test scores for every child in the class. Would you hesitate to look at the scores? Why or why not?

PRAXIS™ PRACTICE

1. Which of the following is the best indicator of high intelligence?
   a. scoring 105 on an IQ test
   b. reciting the Gettysburg Address from memory
   c. not making the same mistakes twice when given the opportunity to repeat a task after receiving feedback
   d. earning high grades

(continued)

Review, Reflect, and Practice

2. Susan took the Otis-Lennon School Ability Test to determine if she qualified for her school's gifted program. Based on her score of 125, she did not qualify for the program. Which of the following is a valid statement regarding this screening procedure?
   a. Because this was an individual test, the psychologist was able to ensure that rapport had been established and that anxiety did not interfere with her performance. Thus, the decision should stand.
   b. Because this was a group test, the psychologist was unable to ensure that rapport had been established and anxiety did not interfere with her performance. Thus, the decision should not stand. More information is needed.
   c. Because her score was well above average, she should be included in the gifted program.
   d. Because her score is just average, she should not be included in the gifted program.

3. Which of these students best exemplifies Sternberg's practical intelligence?
   a. Jamal, who writes wonderful science fiction stories
   b. Chandra, who is able to understand *The Great Gatsby*'s symbolism at a complex level
   c. Mark, who is the most talented athlete in the school
   d. Susan, who gets along well with others and is good at "reading" others' emotions

4. Which of these statements is most consistent with current research on the nature-nurture issue in intelligence?
   a. Because intelligence in mainly inherited, there is little room to improve students' intelligence.
   b. Because intelligence is influenced by both heredity and environment, providing students with an enriched classroom environment might have a positive influence on their intelligence.
   c. Students who delay schooling tend to score higher on intelligence tests than those who do not, which suggests that environment is more important for intelligence than heredity.
   d. Recent steep increases in intelligence indicate that intelligence is mainly determined by heredity.

Please see the answer key at the end of the book.

(2) LEARNING AND THINKING STYLES

> Impulsive/Reflective Styles   Deep/Surface Styles

Intelligence refers to ability. **Learning and thinking styles** are not abilities but, rather, preferred ways of using one's abilities (Dunning, 2008; Zhang & Sternberg, 2008b). In fact, teachers will tell you that children approach learning and thinking in an amazing variety of ways. Teachers themselves also vary in their styles of learning and thinking. None of us has just a single learning and thinking style; each of us has a profile of

learning and thinking styles Individuals' preferences in how they use their abilities.

DEVELOPMENTAL FOCUS 4.2
How Do You Influence Students' Learning/Thinking Skills?

Early Childhood

Preschoolers can be very eager to answer a question or take part in an activity, which means they often talk over others so that they can be heard by the teacher. While we are always happy to have enthusiastic students, we also teach them to wait to be called on and to take their time before answering a question.

—Missy Dangler, *Suburban Hills School*

Elementary School: Grades K–5

We use a "think time" procedure in which students think and respond to a question on signal after an adequate time for reflection. And we incorporate a think-pair-share procedure that gives all students an opportunity to think about a question, pair up with a partner, and then share their ideas. I also ask students what their partner said to encourage listening skills.

—Heather Zoldak, *Ridge Wood Elementary School*

Middle School: Grades 6–8

I try to provide differentiated learning opportunities to suit all of my students' learning styles. For example, the students who are gifted can work on extensive independent research projects, and students who enjoy technology are allowed to complete a research project using a PowerPoint presentation. I give hands-on projects to students who enjoy drawing or developing creative projects.

—Felicia Peterson, *Pocantico Hills School*

High School: Grades 9–12

As an art teacher, I foster an attitude of openness and acceptance in my classroom, which helps to promote my students' learning. When students feel that their ideas will be respected and heard, they are not afraid to try something different.

—Dennis Peterson, *Deer River High School*

---

many styles. Individuals vary so much that literally hundreds of learning and thinking styles have been proposed by educators and psychologists. Our coverage of learning and thinking styles is not meant to be exhaustive but introduces two widely discussed sets of styles: impulsive/reflective and deep/surface.

Impulsive/Reflective Styles

Impulsive/reflective styles, also referred to as *conceptual tempo*, involve a student's tendency either to act quickly and impulsively or to take more time to respond and reflect on the accuracy of an answer (Kagan, 1965). Impulsive students often make more mistakes than reflective students.

Research on impulsivity/reflection shows that reflective students are more likely than impulsive students to do well at these tasks (Jonassen & Grabowski, 1993): remembering structured information; reading comprehension and text interpretation; and problem solving and decision making.

Reflective students also are more likely than impulsive students to set their own learning goals and concentrate on relevant information. Reflective students usually have higher standards for performance. The evidence is strong that reflective students learn more effectively and do better in school than impulsive students.

impulsive/reflective styles Also referred to as *conceptual tempo*, they involve a student's tendency either to act quickly and impulsively or to take more time to respond and reflect on the accuracy of the answer.

BEST PRACTICES
Strategies for Working with Impulsive Children

1. *Monitor students in the class to determine which ones are impulsive.*

2. *Talk with them about taking their time to think through an answer before they respond.*

3. *Encourage them to label new information as they work with it.*

4. *Model the reflective style as a teacher.*

5. *Help students set high standards for their performance.*

6. *Recognize when impulsive students start to take more time to reflect. Compliment them on their improvement.*

7. *Guide students in creating their own plan to reduce impulsivity.*

In thinking about impulsive and reflective styles, keep in mind that although most children learn better when they are reflective rather than impulsive, some children are simply fast, accurate learners and decision makers. Reacting quickly is a bad strategy only if you come up with wrong answers. Also, some reflective children ruminate forever about problems and have difficulty finishing tasks. Teachers can encourage these children to retain their reflective orientation but arrive at more timely solutions. In Chapter 7, "Behavioral and Social Cognitive Approaches," we will discuss a number of other strategies for helping students self-regulate their behavior.

Deep/Surface Styles

Deep/surface styles involve how students approach learning materials. Do they do this in a way that helps them understand the meaning of the materials (deep style) or as simply what needs to be learned (surface style) (Marton, Hounsell, & Entwistle, 1984)? Students who approach learning with a surface style fail to tie what they are learning into a larger conceptual framework. They tend to learn in a passive way, often rotely memorizing information. Deep learners are more likely to actively construct what they learn and give meaning to what they need to remember. Thus, deep learners take a constructivist approach to learning. Deep learners also are more likely to be self-motivated to learn, whereas surface learners are more likely to be motivated to learn because of external rewards, such as grades and positive feedback from the teacher (Snow, Corno, & Jackson, 1996).

deep/surface styles Involve the extent to which students approach learning materials in a way that helps them understand the meaning of the materials (deep style) or as simply what needs to be learned (surface style).

Review, Reflect, and Practice

2 **Describe learning and thinking styles.**

REVIEW

- What is meant by learning and thinking styles? Describe impulsive/reflective styles.
- How can deep/surface styles be characterized?

REFLECT

- Describe yourself or someone else you know well in terms of the learning and thinking styles presented in this section.

Review, Reflect, and Practice

PRAXIS™ PRACTICE

1. Ms. Garcia has her students read passages from a novel and then gives them 30 minutes to describe the gist of what they have read. Which students are likely to do well on this task?
   a. students with an impulsive style of thinking
   b. students with a reflective style of thinking
   c. students with practical intelligence
   d. students with average intelligence

2. Which question encourages a deep style of thinking?
   a. What is the inverse of one-half?
   b. What is the lowest prime number?
   c. How much flour would you use to make half of the cookie recipe?
   d. What does it mean to say that addition is the opposite of subtraction?

   Please see the answer key at the end of the book.

BEST PRACTICES
Strategies for Helping Surface Learners Think More Deeply

1. *Monitor students to determine which ones are surface learners.*

2. *Discuss with students the importance of not just rotely memorizing material.* Encourage them to connect what they are learning now with what they have learned in the past.

3. *Ask questions and give assignments that require students to fit information into a larger framework.* For example, instead of just asking students to name the capital of a particular state, ask them if they have visited the capital and what their experiences were, what other cities are located in that section of the United States, or how large or small the city is.

4. *Be a model who processes information deeply rather than just scratching the surface.* Explore topics in depth, and talk about how the information you are discussing fits within a larger network of ideas.

5. *Avoid using questions that require pat answers.* Instead, ask questions that require students to deeply process information. Connect lessons more effectively with children's existing interests.

Next, East Grand Forks, Minnesota, middle school teacher Therese Olejniczak describes how she gets students to slow down so they won't gloss over important material.

THROUGH THE EYES OF TEACHERS
Paying Attention to the Details

Seventh-graders are in a hurry, no matter which intelligences they favor or use. I often teach study skills to students to help them slow down and gather details they might miss in their haste to complete assignments.

One method I use is to have the entire class silently read an article on a topic I've selected with their interests in mind. Then I ask the students to list details of the article on the blackboard. I call on students one at a time as they raise their hands enthusiastically, and each student—in his or her adolescent need to belong—participates by contributing details to the list.

Afterward, the students and I review the details, marveling at the depth of information they have found. Unplanned peer-tutoring occurs when students discover obscure items that others have skimmed past, revealing to one another their need to slow down. Small groups then create final reports that include a written summary and illustration.

3 PERSONALITY AND TEMPERAMENT

Personality — Temperament

We have seen that it is important to be aware of individual variations in children's cognition. It also is important to understand individual variations in their personality and temperament.

Personality

We make statements about personality all the time and prefer to be around people with certain types of personality. Let's examine just what the term *personality* means.

Personality refers to distinctive thoughts, emotions, and behaviors that characterize the way an individual adapts to the world. Think about yourself for a moment. What is your personality like? Are you outgoing or shy? Considerate or caring? Friendly or hostile? These are some of the characteristics involved in personality. As we see next, one view stresses that five main factors make up personality.

The "Big Five" Personality Factors As with intelligence, psychologists are interested in identifying the main dimensions of personality (Engler, 2009; Roberts & Mroczek, 2008). Some personality researchers argue that they have identified the **"Big Five" factors of personality**, the "supertraits" thought to describe personality's main dimensions: openness, conscientiousness, extraversion, agreeableness, and neuroticism (emotional stability) (see Figure 4.6). (Notice that if you create an acronym from these trait names, you get the word *OCEAN*.)

Much of the research on the Big Five factors has used adults as the participants in studies (McCrae & Costa, 2006). However, an increasing number of studies involving the Big Five factors focus on children and adolescents (Heaven & Ciarrochi, 2008; Hendriks & others, 2008; Soto & others, 2008).

The major finding in the study of the Big Five factors in childhood and adolescence is the emergence of conscientiousness as a key predictor of adjustment and competence (Anderson & others, 2008; Roberts & others, 2009). Following is a sampling of recent research documenting this link:

- A study of the Big Five factors revealed that conscientiousness was the best predictor of both high school and college grade-point average (Noftie & Robins, 2007). In this study, openness was the best predictor of SAT verbal scores.
- A study of fifth- to eighth-graders found that conscientiousness was linked to better interpersonal relationships: higher-quality friendships, better acceptance by peers, and less victimization by peers (Jensen-Campbell & Malcolm, 2007).
- A longitudinal study of more than 1,200 individuals across seven decades revealed that the Big Five personality factor of conscientiousness predicted higher mortality risk from childhood through late adulthood (Martin, Friedman, & Schwartz, 2007).

The Big Five factors can give you a framework for thinking about your students' personality traits. Your students will differ in their emotional stability, how extraverted or introverted they are, how open to experience, how agreeable, and how conscientious they are.

Person–Situation Interaction In discussing learning and thinking styles, we indicated that a student's style can vary according to the subject matter the student is learning or thinking about. The same is true for personality characteristics. According to the concept of **person-situation interaction**, the best way to characterize an

An adolescent with a high level of conscientiousness organizes his daily schedule and plans how to use his time effectively. *What are some characteristics of conscientiousness? How is it linked to adolescents' competence?*

personality Distinctive thoughts, emotions, and behaviors that characterize the way an individual adapts to the world.

Big Five factors of personality Openness, conscientiousness, extraversion, agreeableness, and neuroticism (emotional stability).

person–situation interaction The view that the best way to conceptualize personality is not in terms of personal traits or characteristics alone, but also in terms of the situation involved.

Openness	**C**onscientiousness	**E**xtraversion	**A**greeableness	**N**euroticism (emotional stability)
• Imaginative or practical	• Organized or disorganized	• Sociable or retiring	• Softhearted or ruthless	• Calm or anxious
• Interested in variety or routine	• Careful or careless	• Fun-loving or somber	• Trusting or suspicious	• Secure or insecure
• Independent or conforming	• Disciplined or impulsive	• Affectionate or reserved	• Helpful or uncooperative	• Self-satisfied or self-pitying

FIGURE 4.6 The "Big Five" Factors of Personality

Each column represents a broad "supertrait" that encompasses more narrow traits and characteristics. Using the acronym *OCEAN* can help you to remember the Big Five personality factors (openness, conscientiousness, and so on).

individual's personality is not in terms of personal traits or characteristics alone, but also in terms of the situation involved. Researchers have found that students choose to be in some situations and avoid others (Burger, 2008; Schultz & Schultz, 2009).

Suppose you have an extravert and an introvert in your class. According to the theory of person-situation interaction, you can't predict which one will show the best adaptation unless you consider the situation they are in. The theory of person-situation interaction predicts that the extravert will adapt best when asked to collaborate with others and that the introvert will adapt best when asked to carry out tasks independently. Similarly, the extravert likely will be happier when socializing with lots of people at a party, the introvert when in a more private setting alone or with a friend.

In sum, don't think of personality traits as always dooming a student to behave in a particular way across all situations. The context or situation matters (Berecz, 2009). Monitor situations in which students with varying personality characteristics seem to feel most comfortable and provide them with opportunities to learn in those situations. If a particular personality trait is detrimental to the student's school performance (perhaps one student is so introverted that he or she fears working in a group), think of ways you can support the student's efforts to change.

Temperament

Temperament is closely related to personality and to learning and thinking styles. **Temperament** is a person's behavioral style and characteristic ways of responding. Some students are active; others are calm. Some respond warmly to people; others fuss and fret. Such descriptions involve variations in temperament.

Scientists who study temperament seek to find the best ways to classify temperaments (Rothbart & Garstein, 2008). The most well-known classification was proposed by Alexander Chess and Stella Thomas (Chess & Thomas, 1977; Thomas & Chess, 1991). They conclude that there are three basic styles, or clusters, of temperament:

- An **easy child** is generally in a positive mood, quickly establishes regular routines in infancy, and adapts easily to new experiences.
- A **difficult child** reacts negatively and cries frequently, engages in irregular daily routines, and is slow to accept change.
- A **slow-to-warm-up child** has a low activity level, is somewhat negative, and displays a low intensity of mood.

In their longitudinal investigation, Chess and Thomas found that 40 percent of the children they studied could be classified as easy, 10 percent as difficult, and 15 percent as slow to warm up. Notice that 35 percent did not fit any of the three patterns. Researchers have found that these three basic clusters of temperament are

temperament A person's behavioral style and characteristic ways of responding.

easy child A temperament style in which the child is generally in a positive mood, quickly establishes regular routines, and easily adapts to new experiences.

difficult child A temperament style in which the child tends to react negatively, cries frequently, engages in irregular routines, and is slow to accept new experiences.

slow-to-warm-up child A temperament style in which the child has a low activity level, is somewhat negative, and displays a low intensity of mood.

moderately stable across the childhood years. A difficult temperament, or a temperament that reflects a lack of control, can place a student at risk for problems.

Another way of classifying temperament focuses on the differences between a shy, subdued, timid child and a sociable, extraverted, bold child. Jerome Kagan (2002, 2006, 2008) regards shyness with strangers (peers or adults) as one feature of a broad temperament category called *inhibition to the unfamiliar*.

Mary Rothbart and John Bates (Rothbart, 2007; Rothbart and Bates, 2006) emphasize that three broad dimensions best represent what researchers have found to characterize the structure of temperament. Here are descriptions of these three temperament dimensions (Rothbart, 2004, p. 495):

- *Extraversion/surgency* includes "positive anticipation, impulsivity, activity level, and sensation seeking." Kagan's uninhibited children fit into this category.
- *Negative affectivity* consists of "fear, frustration, sadness, and discomfort." These children are easily distressed; they may fret and cry often. Kagan's inhibited children fit this category.
- *Effortful control (self-regulation)* involves "attentional focusing and shifting, inhibitory control, perceptual sensitivity, and low-intensity pleasure." Children high on effortful control show an ability to keep their arousal from getting too high and have strategies for soothing themselves. By contrast, children low on effortful control are often unable to control their arousal; they become easily agitated and intensely emotional.

From Rothbart's perspective (2004, 2007), early views of temperament emphasized that children's behavior is energized by their positive and negative emotions or arousal level. The more recent emphasis on effortful control, however, stresses that children can engage in a more cognitive, flexible approach to stressful circumstances.

In a recent research review, Rothbart (2007) concluded that temperament is linked to the Big Five factors of personality. Extraversion/surgency is connected with extraversion, neuroticism maps onto negative affectivity, and conscientiousness is related to effortful control.

This chapter has been about individual variations. Because individual variations are so important in effectively teaching children, we will address them throughout the book. For example, in Chapter 6, we will focus on teaching students who are exceptional, including those with a learning disability and those who are gifted. Also, in Chapter 5, we will explore individual variations in students' culture, ethnicity, socioeconomic status, and gender.

What are some different categories that have been used to classify children's temperament? How would you classify your temperament? What are some good strategies for working with students with different temperaments?

BEST PRACTICES
Strategies for Teaching Children with Different Temperaments

Here are some teaching strategies related to students' temperaments (Keogh, 2003; Sanson & Rothbart, 1995):

1. *Show attention to and respect for individuality* (Sanson & Rothbart, 1995). Teachers need to be sensitive to the student's signals and needs. The goal of good teaching might be accomplished in one way with one student, in another way with another student, depending on the students' temperaments.

2. *Consider the structure of the students' environment* (Sanson & Rothbart, 1995). Crowded, noisy classrooms often pose greater problems for a "difficult" child than for an "easy" child. Fearful, withdrawn students often benefit from slower entry into new contexts.

3. *Be aware of problems that can emerge by labeling a child "difficult" and packaged programs for "difficult children"* (Sanson & Rothbart, 1995). Some books and programs for parents and teachers focus specifically on the child's temperament (Cameron, Hansen, & Rosen, 1989). Most of these focus on the difficult child. Acknowledging that some children are harder to teach than others often is helpful. Advice on how to handle a particular temperament also can be useful. However, whether a particular characteristic is truly "difficult" depends on its fit with the environment, so the problem does not necessarily rest with the child. As with labeling a child as more or less intelligent, labeling the child as "difficult" has the danger of becoming a self-fulfilling prophecy. Also keep in mind that temperament can be modified to some degree (Sanson & Rothbart, 2002).

Here are some effective strategies for dealing with difficult children in the classroom (Keogh, 2003):

- Try to avoid confrontations and power struggles by anticipating problem situations for the student; if the student engages in disruptive behavior, intervene at the first instance of the disruption.

- Evaluate the physical context of the classroom, such as where the difficult child sits, who sits near him or

her, and so on for clues about reducing disruptive behavior.

- Minimize delay times between activities and standing in line, which gives a difficult child less time to be disruptive.

4. *Use effective strategies with shy and slow-to-warm-up students.* Keep in mind that it is easy to overlook shy, slow-to-warm-up children because they are unlikely to cause problems in the classroom. Following are some strategies for helping these children (Keogh, 2003):

- Don't place this type of student immediately into group activities, and let the student become involved in groups at his or her own pace initially. If over time, shy students are still reluctant to actively participate in groups, encourage them but don't push them.

- Assign students' work partners with their temperaments in mind; for example, don't pair an intense, difficult child with a shy, slow-to-warm-up child.

- Help shy, slow-to-warm-up students get started on activities that they appear hesitant about beginning, and be available to provide help during these activities.

5. *Help children with problems controlling their emotions to regulate their behavior.* In this regard, you can:

- Control your emotions when interacting with students. By observing how you handle difficult situations, students may model your calm behavior.

- Recognize that you are an important person in being able to guide children to regulate their emotions. Instruct children to talk to themselves in ways that may help to reduce their frustration and arousal. For example, if children have difficulty controlling their anger, they can learn to distract themselves from arousing events or stop and take a series of deep breaths.

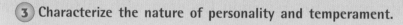

Review, Reflect, and Practice

③ Characterize the nature of personality and temperament.

REVIEW

- What is meant by the concept of personality? What are the Big Five factors of personality? What does the idea of person-situation interaction suggest about personality?

- How is temperament different from personality? Describe an easy child, a difficult child, and a slow-to-warm-up child. What are other categorizations of temperament? What are some good teaching strategies related to children's temperament?

REFLECT

- Describe yourself in terms of the Big Five personality factors. In your K–12 education, how aware do you think your teachers were of your personality strengths and weaknesses? Might things have been different if they had known you better?

PRAXIS™ PRACTICE

1. Maria is an outgoing, agreeable, fun-loving child. According to the concept of person-situation interaction, which of the following is likely to characterize Maria?
   a. Maria enjoys working independently on detail-oriented tasks.
   b. Maria likes to work on tasks that involve interaction with other students.
   c. Maria prefers to read by herself in a corner.
   d. Maria needs to be taught to control her impulses.

2. Stanton has been a challenging student. His frustration tolerance is low, and when he gets frustrated he often disrupts the class with angry outbursts. His teacher has difficulty handling him. What advice is most likely to help her deal with Stanton?
   a. She should show her frustration in dealing with him because once he realizes the impact of his behavior on others, he will learn to control his behavior.
   b. She should be calm with Stanton so he can observe a more adaptive response to frustration.
   c. She should send him out of the classroom every time he gets angry.
   d. She should separate him from his classmates and make him do his classwork by himself so that they don't imitate his behavior.

Please see the answer key at the end of the book.

CRACK THE CASE
The Case of the Workshops

Mr. Washington and his colleague, Ms. Rosario, had just attended a workshop on adapting instruction to children's learning styles. Ms. Jacobson and her colleague, Mr. Hassan, had just attended a workshop on adapting instruction to cover multiple intelligences. The four met in the teachers' workroom and were discussing what they had learned.

"Well," said Mr. Washington, "this certainly explains why some students seem to want to sit and listen to me talk, while others like to be more actively involved. Joe's obviously an executive type. He likes lectures. Martha, on the other hand, must be legislative. She just loves to work on projects and can't stand it when I tell her how to do things."

"No, I don't think so," Ms. Jacobson replies. "I think Joe's high in verbal intelligence. That's why he can make sense out of your lectures. He writes well, too. Martha likes to do things with her hands. She's higher in spatial and bodily-kinesthetic intelligence."

Mr. Washington responds, "No, no, no. Learning styles explain their differences much better. Here, look at this."

At this point, Mr. Washington shows Ms. Jacobson the handouts from the workshop he and Ms. Rosario had attended. Mr. Hassan gets out the handouts from the workshop he and Ms. Jacobson had attended as well. They begin comparing notes. They all recognize students in each of the schemes in the handouts. In fact, they can recognize the same student in both sets of handouts.

At this point, two other teachers—Mrs. Peterson and Mrs. Darby—walk into the room. They are very excited about a graduate class they are taking at a nearby university.

Mrs. Peterson says, "You know, I never thought about personality when considering teaching methods. It's no wonder Martha doesn't behave terribly well in my class. She's just too impulsive for the kind of structure I have."

Ms. Jacobson is dismayed. "You mean they're telling you we have to adapt our classrooms to the students' personalities now, too?" she asks.

Mr. Hassan is also upset. "Gee," he says, "just when I thought I had it all figured out. Used to be we just had to consider IQ. Now all this. We have 25 kids in our classes. How can we possibly adapt to all these differences? What are we supposed to do, have 25 different lesson plans? Maybe we should do some kind of profile on them and then group them by profile. What do you think, guys?"

1. What are the issues in this case?

2. To what extent should teachers adapt their instruction to the strengths, learning styles, and personalities of their students? Why?

3. What will you do in your classroom to accommodate individual differences such as students' strengths, learning styles, and personalities?

4. What other individual differences do you think you might have to accommodate? How will you do this?

5. On which theory is Ms. Jacobson basing her comments regarding Joe and Martha?
   a. Gardner's eight frames of mind
   b. general intelligence
   c. Sternberg's triarchic theory of intelligence
   d. Vygotsky's sociocultural theory

6. What type of grouping is Mr. Adams most likely discussing?
   a. between-class ability grouping
   b. Joplin plan
   c. nongraded program
   d. within-class ability grouping

Reach Your Learning Goals
Individual Variations

(1) INTELLIGENCE: Discuss what intelligence is, how it is measured, theories of multiple intelligences, and some controversies and issues about its use by educators.

What Is Intelligence?

Intelligence consists of problem-solving skills and the ability to adapt to and learn from experiences. Interest in intelligence often focuses on individual differences and assessment.

Intelligence Tests

Binet and Simon developed the first intelligence test. Binet developed the concept of mental age, and Stern created the concept of IQ as MA/CA × 100. The Stanford-Binet scores approximate a normal distribution. The Wechsler scales also are widely used to assess intelligence. They yield an overall IQ plus scores on a number of subscales and composite indexes. Group tests are more convenient and economical than individual tests, but group tests have a number of drawbacks (lack of opportunities for the examiner to establish rapport, distraction from other students). A group intelligence test should always be supplemented with other relevant information when decisions are made about students. This also holds for an individual intelligence test.

Theories of Multiple Intelligences

According to Sternberg's triarchic theory of intelligence, intelligence comes in three forms: analytical, creative, and practical. Gardner argues there are eight types of intelligence, or frames of mind: verbal, mathematical, spatial, bodily-kinesthetic, musical, intrapersonal, interpersonal, and naturalist. Project Spectrum and the Key School involve educational applications of Gardner's theory of multiple intelligences. The concept of emotional intelligence was initially developed by Salovey and Mayer. Goleman popularized the concept of emotional intelligence in his book, *Emotional Intelligence*. Mayer, Salovey, and Goleman stress that emotional intelligence is an important aspect of being a competent person. These approaches have much to offer, stimulating teachers to think more broadly about what makes up a student's competencies. However, they have been criticized along the lines of including some skills that should not be classified under intelligence and for the lack of a research base to support the approaches. Also, advocates of the general concept of intelligence argue that general intelligence is a reasonably good predictor of school and job performance.

Controversies and Issues in Intelligence

Three controversies and issues related to intelligence are (1) the nature-nurture question of how heredity and environment interact to produce intelligence, (2) how fairly intelligence testing applies across cultural and ethnic groups, and (3) whether students should be grouped according to ability (tracking). It is especially important to recognize that intelligence tests are an indicator of current performance, not fixed potential.

② LEARNING AND THINKING STYLES: Describe learning and thinking styles.

Impulsive/Reflective Styles

Styles are not abilities but, rather, preferred ways of using abilities. Each individual has a number of learning and thinking styles. Impulsive/reflective styles also are referred to as *conceptual tempo*. This dichotomy involves a student's tendency to act quickly and impulsively or to take more time to respond and reflect on the accuracy of an answer. Impulsive students typically make more mistakes than reflective students.

Deep/Surface Styles

Deep/surface styles involve the extent to which students approach learning in a way that helps them understand the meaning of materials (deep style) or as simply what needs to be learned (surface style). Deep learners are more likely to be self-motivated to learn and take a constructivist approach to learning; surface learners are more likely to be motivated to learn because of external rewards.

③ PERSONALITY AND TEMPERAMENT: Characterize the nature of personality and temperament.

Personality

Personality refers to distinctive thoughts, emotions, and behaviors that characterize the way an individual adapts to the world. Psychologists have identified the Big Five personality factors as openness, conscientiousness, extraversion, agreeableness, and neuroticism (emotional stability). The Big Five factors give teachers a framework for thinking about a student's personality characteristics. The Big Five factor of conscientiousness has increasingly been shown to be an important factor in children's and adolescents' development. The concept of person-situation interaction states that the best way to characterize an individual's personality is not in terms of traits alone but also in terms of both the traits and the situations involved.

Temperament

Temperament refers to a person's behavioral style and characteristic way of responding. Chess and Thomas maintain that there are three basic temperament styles, or clusters: an easy child (generally in a positive mood), a difficult child (reacts negatively and cries easily), and a slow-to-warm-up child (low activity level, somewhat negative). A difficult temperament places a child at risk for problems. Other temperament categorizations have been proposed by Kagan (inhibition to the unfamiliar) and Rothbart and Bates (extraversion/surgency, negative affectivity, and effortful control [self-regulation]). In education involving students' temperaments, teachers can show attention to, and respect for, individuality; consider the structure of a student's environment; be aware of the problems involved when labeling a student as "difficult"; and use effective classroom strategies with difficult children, shy, slow-to-warm up children, and children who have difficulty regulating their emotions.

KEY TERMS

PORTFOLIO ACTIVITIES

Now that you have a good understanding of this chapter, complete these exercises to expand your thinking.

Independent Reflection

Your Multiple Intelligences. Evaluate your own intelligence profile according to Gardner. In what frames of mind do you come out strongest? In which of Sternberg's three areas do you feel you are the strongest? Write about your self-evaluation. (INTASC: Principles *2, 3*)

Collaborative Work

Personality Profiles. Form a group of five or six students from your class, and have one person identify his or her personality and temperament traits. Have other members do the same, in turn. After all have presented, discuss how the individuals in

your group are similar or different. How will your personalities and temperaments translate into teaching styles? Write about this experience. (INTASC: Principles *2, 3*)

Research/Field Experience

Learning Styles in the Classroom. Interview several teachers about students' different learning and thinking styles. Ask them what teaching strategies they use to accommodate these differences in students. Write a synopsis of your interviews. (INTASC: Principles *2, 3, 4, 9*)

Go to the Online Learning Center for downloadable portfolio templates.

 TAKING IT TO THE NET

- How could you conduct a lesson about Howard Gardner's theory of multiple intelligences in your classroom? Why do you think it is important for students to be aware of this theory and its implications for education and society? How could you involve students in planning lessons and projects that utilize many learning styles? http://school.discovery.com/lesson plans/programs/multipleintelligences/index.html

- What is your learning style? Take an online test to discover if you are more active or reflective? Visual or verbal? Sequential or global? In what ways do you think your learning style will impact your teaching style in the classroom? www. engr.ncsu .edu/learningstyles/ilsweb.html

- Reflect on what it means to be emotionally intelligent. How can a teacher's emotional intelligence impact the classroom? How can a student's emotional intelligence impact his or her academic performance and social relationships? Describe a classroom activity or routine that can help students increase their capacity for emotional intelligence and for "knowing themselves, choosing themselves, and giving themselves." www.6seconds .org/modules.php?name=News&file=article&sid=2

Connect to the Online Learning Center to explore possible answers.

 STUDY, PRACTICE, AND SUCCEED

Visit www.mhhe.com/santedu4e to review the chapter with self-grading quizzes and self-assessments, to apply the chapter material to two more Crack the Case studies, and for suggested activities to develop your teaching portfolio.

CHAPTER 5

Sociocultural Diversity

*We need every human gift and cannot afford
to neglect any gift because of artificial barriers
of sex or race or class or national origin.*

—Margaret Mead
American Anthropologist, 20th Century

Learning Goals

1 Discuss how variations in culture, socioeconomic status, and ethnic background need to be taken into account in educating children.

2 Describe some ways to promote multicultural education.

3 Explain various facets of gender, including similarities and difference in boys and girls; discuss gender issues in teaching.

149

TEACHING STORIES   Margaret Longworth

Margaret Longworth taught high school for a number of years and was a Teacher of the Year. She recently moved to the middle school level and currently teaches language arts at West Middle School in St. Lucie, Florida. When considering sociocultural diversity, she believes it is important for teachers to make schools "user friendly" for parents. In her words:

> Many parents—especially ethnic minority parents of color—are very intimidated by schools. They think teachers know everything. Principals know everything. And God forbid that they ever would need to approach the school board. To combat this intimidation, I became "user friendly." Many students and parents center their lives around the church in my community. So, to break the barriers between school and home, my Haitian paraprofessional began setting up meetings for me at the Haitian churches. The churches gave me their Sunday evening services. After they completed their preliminaries, they turned the service over to me. Through the assistance of an interpreter, I presented opportunities to help parents develop academic and life skills through edu-

cation. I talked with them about special education classes, gifted classes, language programs, and scholarships, and encouraged them to keep their children in school. In turn, they felt confident enough to ask me about different happenings at school. Because of the parent-school-church connections that I was able to build up, I rarely had a discipline problem. If I did have to call parents, they would leave work or whatever they were doing and show up in my classroom. Many of these parents developed a relationship with the principal and guidance counselor and felt free to talk with school officials.

Margaret Longworth believes that in the classroom the key to improving children's interethnic relations is understanding. She comments:

> Understanding other persons' points of view requires spending time with them and getting to know them—how they think and feel. As students talk with each other and begin to appreciate each other, they soon learn that in many ways they aren't that different after all.

Preview

Ours is a multicultural world of diverse backgrounds, customs, and values. Margaret Longworth's Teaching Story shows how teachers can improve students' lives and educational orientation by building bridges to their community. In this chapter, we will explore many ways teachers have found to educate children from diverse cultural, socioeconomic, and ethnic backgrounds, including ways to make the classroom relevant for these children. We will also examine gender in schools, including ways in which teachers interact differently with boys and girls.

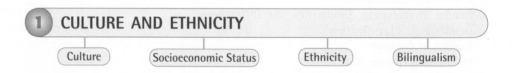

1 CULTURE AND ETHNICITY

Culture   Socioeconomic Status   Ethnicity   Bilingualism

The students in the schools of Fairfax County, Virginia, near Washington, D.C., come from 182 countries and speak more than a hundred languages. Although the Fairfax County schools are a somewhat extreme example, they are harbingers of what is coming to America's schools. By the year 2025, 50 percent of all public school students are predicted to be from backgrounds that are currently classified as "minority." This challenges current definitions of the term. It also points to an important educational goal of helping students develop respect for people from different cultural and ethnic backgrounds (Banks, 2008; Nieto & Bode, 2008).

In this section, we will explore diversity in terms of cultures, socioeconomic status, and ethnicity. We'll also examine language issues, including the debate about bilingual education.

Culture

Culture refers to the behavior patterns, beliefs, and all other products of a particular group of people that are passed on from generation to generation. These products result from the interactions among groups of people and their environments over many years (Kitayama & Cohen, 2007; Shiraev & Levy, 2007). A cultural group can be as large as the United States or as small as an isolated Amazon tribe. Whatever its size, the group's culture influences the behavior of its members (Matsumoto & Juang, 2008).

Psychologist Donald Campbell and his colleagues (Brewer & Campbell, 1976; Campbell & LeVine, 1968) found that people in all cultures often believe that what happens in their culture is "natural" and "correct" and what happens in other cultures is "unnatural" and "incorrect," behave in ways that favor their cultural group, and feel hostility toward other cultural groups.

Psychologists and educators who study culture often are interested in comparing what happens in one culture with what happens in one or more other cultures (Chiu & Hong, 2007; Matsumoto & Huang, 2008). **Cross-cultural studies** involve such comparisons, providing information about the degree to which people are similar and to what degree certain behaviors are specific to certain cultures.

Individualist and Collectivist Cultures   One way that differences in cultures have been described involves individualism and collectivism (Triandis, 2007). **Individualism** refers to a set of values that give priority to personal goals rather than to group goals. Individualist values include feeling good, personal distinction, and independence. **Collectivism** consists of a set of values that support the group. Personal goals are subordinated to preserve group integrity, interdependence of the group's members, and harmonious relationships. Many Western cultures such as those of the United States, Canada, Great Britain, and the Netherlands are described as individualist. Many Eastern cultures such as those of China, Japan, India, and Thailand are labeled collectivist. Mexican culture also has stronger collectivist characteristics than U.S. culture. However, the United States has many collectivist subcultures, such as Chinese American and Mexican American.

A recent analysis proposed four values that reflect parents' beliefs in individualistic cultures about what is required for children's effective development of autonomy: (1) *personal choice,* (2) *intrinsic motivation,* (3) *self-esteem,* and (4) *self-maximization,* which consists of achieving one's full potential (Tamis-LeMonda & others, 2008). The analysis also proposed that three values reflect parents' beliefs in collectivistic cultures: (1) *connectectness to the family and other close relationships,* (2) *orientation to the larger group,* and (3) *respect and obedience.*

Critics of the individualistic and collectivistic cultures concept argue that these terms are too broad and simplistic, especially with globalization increasing (Kagitcibasi, 2007). Regardless of their cultural background, people need both a positive sense of self and connectedness to others to develop fully as human beings. The analysis by Carolyn Tamis-LeMonda and her colleagues (2008, p. 204) emphasizes that in many families, children are not reared in environments that uniformly endorse individualistic or collectivistic values, thoughts, and actions. Rather, in many families, children are "expected to be quiet, assertive, respectful, curious, humble, self-assured, independent, dependent, affectionate, or reserved depending on the situation, people present, children's age, and social-political and economic circles."

What are some differences in individualist and collectivist cultures? What are some teaching strategies for working with students from these cultures?

culture The behavior patterns, beliefs, and all other products of a particular group of people that are passed on from generation to generation.

cross-cultural studies Studies that compare what happens in one culture with what happens in one or more other cultures; they provide information about the degree to which people are similar and to what degree behaviors are specific to certain cultures.

individualism A set of values that give priority to personal rather than to group goals.

collectivism A set of values that support the group.

How do East Asian and U.S. adolescents spend their time differently?

Cross-Cultural Comparisons of Adolescents' Time Use In addition to examining whether cultures are individualist or collectivist, another important cross-cultural comparison involves how children and adolescents spend their time. Reed Larson and Suman Verma (Larson, 2001, 2007; Larson & Verma, 1999) have studied how adolescents in the United States, Europe, and East Asia spend their time in work, play, and developmental activities such as school. U.S. adolescents spent about 60 percent as much time on schoolwork as East Asian adolescents did, mainly because U.S. adolescents did less homework. U.S. adolescents also spent more time in paid work than their counterparts in most developed countries. And what U.S. adolescents had more of than adolescents in other industrialized countries was free time. About 40 to 50 percent of U.S. adolescents' waking hours (not counting summer vacations) was spent in discretionary activities, compared with 25 to 35 percent in East Asia and 35 to 45 percent in Europe. Whether this additional discretionary time is a liability or an asset for U.S. adolescents, of course, depends on how they use it.

The largest amounts of U.S. adolescents' free time were spent using the media and engaging in unstructured leisure activities, often with friends. U.S. adolescents spent more time in voluntary structured activities—such as sports, hobbies, and organizations—than East Asian adolescents.

According to Reed Larson (2001, 2007), U.S. adolescents may have too much unstructured time for optimal development. When adolescents are allowed to choose what they do with their time, they typically engage in unchallenging activities such as hanging out and watching TV. Although relaxation and social interaction are important aspects of adolescence, it seems unlikely that spending large numbers of hours per week in unchallenging activities fosters development. Structured voluntary activities may provide more promise for adolescent development than unstructured time, especially if adults give responsibility to adolescents, challenge them, and provide competent guidance in these activities (Larson & Sheeber, 2008; Larson & Wilson, 2004).

Socioeconomic Status

Socioeconomic status (SES) refers to the grouping of people with similar occupational, educational, and economic characteristics. Socioeconomic status implies certain inequalities. Generally, members of a society have (1) occupations that vary in prestige, and some individuals have more access than others to higher-status occupations; (2) different levels of educational attainment, and some individuals have more access than others to better education; (3) different economic resources; and (4) different levels of power to influence a community's institutions. These differences in the ability to control resources and to participate in society's rewards produce unequal opportunities. Socioeconomic differences are a "proxy for material, human, and social capital within and beyond the family" (Huston & Ripke, 2006, p. 425). In the United States, SES has important implications for education. Low-SES individuals often have less education, less power to influence a community's institutions (such as schools), and fewer economic resources.

A parent's SES is likely linked to the neighborhoods and schools in which children live and the schools they attend (Coltrane & others, 2008; Hutson, 2008). Such variations in neighborhood settings can influence children's adjustment (Conger & Conger, 2008). For example, a recent study revealed that neighborhood disadvantage (involving such characteristics as low neighborhood income and unemployment) was linked to less consistent, less stimulating, and more punitive parenting, and ultimately

socioeconomic status (SES) A grouping of people with similar occupational, educational, and economic characteristics.

to negative child outcomes (low verbal ability and behavioral problems) (Kohen & others, 2008).

The Extent of Poverty in America   In a report on the state of America's children, the Children's Defense Fund (1992) described what life is like for all too many children. When sixth-graders in a poverty-stricken area of St. Louis were asked to describe a perfect day, one boy said that he would erase the world, then sit and think. Asked if he wouldn't rather go outside and play, the boy responded, "Are you kidding, out there?"

Children who grow up in poverty represent a special concern (Conger & Conger, 2008; Crane & Heaton, 2008). In 2006, approximately 17 percent of U.S. children were living in families below the poverty line (Federal Interagency Forum on Child and Family Statistics, 2008). The 17 percent figure represents an increase from 2001 (16.2 percent) but reflects a drop from a peak of 22.7 percent in 1993. The U.S. figure of 17 percent of children living in poverty is much higher than those from other industrialized nations. For example, Canada has a child poverty rate of 9 percent and Sweden has a rate of 2 percent.

Poverty in the United States is demarcated along family structure and ethnic lines (Federal Interagency Forum on Child and Family Statistics, 2008). In 2006, 42 percent of female-headed families lived in poverty compared with only 8 percent of married-couple families. In 2006, 33 percent of African American families and 27 percent of Latino families lived in poverty, compared with only 10 percent of non-Latino White families. Compared with White children, ethnic minority children are more likely to experience persistent poverty over many years and live in isolated poor neighborhoods where social supports are minimal and threats to positive development abundant.

Vonnie McLoyd (right) has conducted a number of important investigations of the roles of poverty, ethnicity, and unemployment in children's and adolescents' development. She has found that economic stressors often diminish children's and adolescents' belief in the utility of education and their achievement strivings.

Educating Students from Low-SES Backgrounds   Children in poverty often face problems at home and at school that compromise their learning (Children's Defense Fund, 2008; Conger & Conger, 2008). A review of the environment of childhood poverty concluded that compared with their economically more-advantaged counterparts, poor children experience these adversities (Evans, 2004): more family conflict, violence, chaos, and separation from their families; less social support; less intellectual stimulation; more TV viewing; inferior schools and child-care facilities, as well as parents who are less involved in their school activities; more pollution and crowded, noisy homes; and more dangerous, deteriorating neighborhoods. Figure 5.1 shows the results of one study that illustrates these types of environmental differences that children from poor families and middle-income families experience (Evans & English, 2002). A recent study also revealed that the more years children spent living in poverty, the more their physiological indices of stress were elevated (Evans & Kim, 2007).

The schools that children from impoverished backgrounds attend often have fewer resources than schools in higher-income neighborhoods (Ballentine & Hammock, 2009; Liu & Hernandez, 2008). In low-income areas, students tend to have lower achievement test scores, lower graduation rates, and lower rates of college attendance. School buildings and classrooms are often old, crumbling, and poorly maintained. They are also more likely to be staffed by young teachers with less experience than schools in higher-income neighborhoods (Liu & Hernandez, 2008). Schools in low-income areas also are more likely to encourage rote learning, whereas schools in higher-income areas are more likely to work with children to improve their thinking skills (Spring, 2008). In sum, far too many schools in low-income

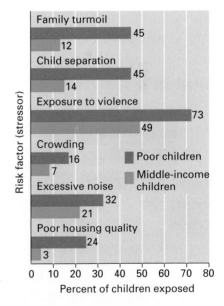

FIGURE 5.1 Exposure to Six Stressors Among Poor and Middle-Income Children

One recent study analyzed the exposure to six stressors among poor children and middle-income children (Evans & English, 2002). Poor children were much more likely to face each of these stressors.

In *The Shame of the Nation,* Jonathan Kozol (2005) criticized the inadequate quality and lack of resources in many U.S. schools, especially those in the poverty areas of inner cities, that have high concentrations of ethnic minority children. Kozol praises teachers like Angela Lively (right), who keeps a box of shoes in her Indianapolis classroom for students in need.

neighborhoods provide students with environments that are not conducive to effective learning (Hutson, 2008; Leventhal, Brooks-Gunn, & Kamerman, 2008).

In *Savage Inequalities,* Jonathan Kozol (1991) vividly described some of the problems that children of poverty face in their neighborhood and at school. Here are some of Kozol's observations in one inner-city area. East St. Louis, Illinois, which is 98 percent African American, has no obstetric services, no regular trash collection, and few jobs. Blocks upon blocks of housing consist of dilapidated, skeletal buildings. Residents breathe the chemical pollution of nearby Monsanto Chemical Company. Raw sewage repeatedly backs up into homes. Child malnutrition is common. Fear of violence is real. The problems of the streets spill over into the schools, where sewage also backs up from time to time. Classrooms and hallways are old and unattractive, athletic facilities inadequate. Teachers run out of chalk and paper, and the science labs are 30 to 50 years out of date. Kozol says that anyone who visits places like East St. Louis, even for a brief time, comes away profoundly shaken.

Another message from Kozol's observations is that although children in low-income neighborhoods and schools experience many inequities, these children and their families also have many strengths, including courage. Parents in such impoverished circumstances may intensely pursue ways to get more effective teachers and better opportunities for their children.

One trend in antipoverty programs is two-generational intervention (McLoyd, Aikens, & Burton, 2006). This involves providing both services for children (such as educational child care or preschool education) and services for parents (such as adult education, literacy training, and job skills training).

Two boys who live in a poverty section of the South Bronx in New York City. *How does poverty affect the development of children like these? What types of experiences might they need to counter living in poverty circumstances?*

BEST PRACTICES
Strategies for Working with Children in Poverty

1. *Improve thinking and language skills.* If you teach in a school in a low-income neighborhood, adopt the goal of helping children improve their thinking and language skills. As described next, this is an important goal in the classroom of Jill Nakamura, a first-grade teacher in Fresno, California.

THROUGH THE EYES OF TEACHERS
Daily After-School Reading Club for Students in a High-Poverty School

Jill Nakamura teaches in a school located in a high-poverty area. She visits students at home early in the school year in a effort to connect with them and develop a partnership with their parents. "She holds daily after-school reading clubs for students reading below grade level . . . ; those who don't want to attend must call parents to tell them. In a recent school year (2004), she "raised the percent of students reading at or above grade level from 29 percent to 76 percent" (Wong, 2004, p. 6D).

Jill Nakamura, teaching in her first-grade classroom.

2. *Don't overdiscipline.* Where poverty and other factors make it difficult to maintain safety and discipline, recognize the right, workable tradeoff between discipline and children's freedom. We will say more about classroom discipline in Chapter 14, "Managing the Classroom."

3. *Make student motivation a high priority.* Because many children from low-income backgrounds might come to your class not having experienced high parental standards for achievement, and thus might lack the motivation to learn, pay special attention to motivating these children to learn. We will address this topic further in Chapter 13, "Motivation, Teaching, and Learning."

4. *Think about ways to support and collaborate with parents.* Recognize that many parents in poor areas are not able to provide much academic supervision or assistance to their children. Look for ways to support the parents

who can be trained and helped to do so. One study found that when low-income parents had high educational aspirations, it was linked to more positive educational outcomes in youth (Schoon, Parsons, & Sacker, 2004).

5. *Look for ways to involve talented people from impoverished communities.* Recognize that parents in poor areas can be quite talented, caring, responsive people in ways that teachers might not expect. Most impoverished communities have people whose wisdom and experience defy stereotypes. Find these people and ask them to volunteer their services to help support children's learning in your classroom, accompany children on field trips, and make the school more attractive.

6. *Observe the strengths of children from low-income backgrounds.* Many children from these circumstances come to school with considerable untapped knowledge, and teachers can access such richness (Pang, 2005). For example, these children may have substantial knowledge about how to use mass transit, whereas children in higher-income families are simply transported in cars.

In a recent experimental study, Aletha Huston and her colleagues (2006; Gupta, Thornton, & Huston, 2007) evaluated the effects of New Hope, a program designed to increase parental employment and reduce family poverty, on adolescent development. They randomly assigned families with 6- to 10-year old children living in poverty to the New Hope program and to a control group. New Hope offered poor adults who were employed 30 or more hours a week benefits that were designed to increase family income (a wage supplement which ensured that net income increased as parents earned more) and provide work supports through subsidized child care (for any child under age 13) and health insurance. Management services were provided to New Hope participants to assist them in job searches and other needs. The New Hope program was available to the experimental-group families for three years (until the children were 9 to 13 years old). Five years after the program began and two years after it had ended, the program's effects on the children were examined when they were 11 to 16 years old. Compared with adolescents in the control group, New Hope adolescents were more competent at reading, had better school performance, were less likely to be in special education classes, had more positive social skills, and were more likely to be in formal after-school arrangements. New Hope parents reported better psychological well-being and a greater sense of self-efficacy in managing their adolescents than control-group parents did. To read about another program that benefited youth living in poverty, see the *Diversity and Education* interlude.

Ethnicity

The word *ethnic* comes from the Greek word that means "nation." **Ethnicity** refers to a shared pattern of characteristics such as cultural heritage, nationality, race, religion, and language. Everyone is a member of one or more ethnic groups, and relations between people from different ethnic backgrounds, not just in the United States but in virtually every corner of the world, are often charged with bias and conflict.

Nowhere is the changing tapestry of American culture more apparent than in the changing ethnic balances among America's citizens (Liu & others, 2009; Tewari & Alvarez, 2009). At the onset of the twenty-first century, one-third of all school-age children fell into the category now loosely referred to as "children of color" (principally African Americans, Latinos, Asian Americans, and Native Americans). Relatively high rates of minority immigration have contributed to the growth in the proportion of ethnic minorities in the U.S. population (Kim & others, 2009; Merali, 2008). And this growth of ethnic minorities is expected to continue throughout the twenty-first century (Healey, 2009). Asian Americans are expected to be the fastest-growing ethnic group of adolescents, with a growth rate of almost 600 percent by 2100. Latino adolescents are projected to increase almost 400 percent by 2100. Figure 5.2 shows the actual numbers of adolescents in different ethnic groups in the year 2000, as well as the numbers projected through 2100. Notice that by 2100, Latino adolescents are expected to outnumber non-Latino White adolescents.

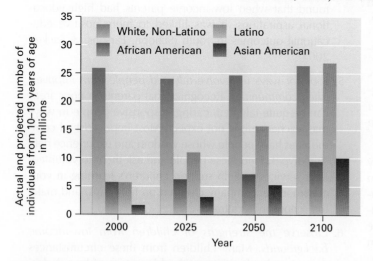

FIGURE 5.2 Actual and Projected Number of U.S. Adolescents Aged 10 to 19, 2000–2100.

In 2000, there were more than 25 million White non-Latino adolescents 10 to 19 years of age in the United States, whereas the numbers for ethnic minority groups were substantially lower. However, projections for 2025 through 2100 reveal dramatic increases in the number of Latino and Asian American adolescents to the point at which in 2100 it is projected that there will be more Latino than White non-Latino adolescents in the United States and more Asian American than African American adolescents.

ethnicity A shared pattern of characteristics such as cultural heritage, nationality, race, religion, and language.

An important point about any ethnic group is that it is diverse (Hayashino & Chopra, 2009; Quijada, 2008; Suyemoto, 2009). There are many ready examples: Mexican Americans and Cuban Americans are Latinos, but they had different reasons for migrating to the United States, come from varying socioeconomic backgrounds, and experience different rates and types of employment in the United States. Individuals born in Puerto Rico are distinguished from Latino individuals who have immigrated to the United States in that they are born U.S. citizens and are therefore not immigrants, regardless of where they live in the United States. The U.S. government currently recognizes 511 different Native American tribes, each having a unique ancestral background with differing values and characteristics. Asian Americans include individuals of Chinese, Japanese, Filipino, Korean, and Southeast Asian origin, each group having distinct ancestries and languages. The diversity of Asian

DIVERSITY AND EDUCATION
The Quantum Opportunities Program

Children participating in the Quantum Opportunities Program at the Carver Center in Washington, D.C.

A downward trajectory is not inevitable for children and adolescents living in poverty (Burchinal & others, 2008; Philipsen, Johnson, & Brooks-Gunn, 2009). One potential positive path for such youth is to become involved with a caring mentor. The Quantum Opportunities Program, funded by the Ford Foundation, was a four-year, year-round mentoring effort (Carnegie Council on Adolescent Development, 1995). The students were entering the ninth grade at a high school with high rates of poverty, were minorities, and came from families that received public assistance. Each day for four years, mentors provided sustained support, guidance, and concrete assistance to their students.

The Quantum program required students to participate in (1) academic-related activities outside school hours, including reading, writing, math, science, and social studies, peer tutoring, and computer skills training; (2) community-service projects, including tutoring elementary school students, cleaning up the neighborhood, and volunteering in hospitals, nursing homes, and libraries; and (3) cultural enrichment and personal development activities, including life skills training, and college and job planning. In exchange for their commitment to the program, students were offered financial incentives that encouraged participation, completion, and long-range planning. A stipend of $1.33 was given to students for each hour they participated in these activities. For every 100 hours of education, service, or development activities, students received a bonus of $100. The average cost per participant was $10,600 for the four years, which is one-half the cost of one year in prison.

An evaluation of the Quantum project compared the mentored students with a nonmentored control group. Sixty-three percent of the mentored students graduated from high school, but only 42 percent of the control group did; 42 percent of the mentored students are currently enrolled in college, but only 16 percent of the control group are. Furthermore, control-group students were twice as likely as the mentored students to receive food stamps or welfare, and they had more arrests. Such programs clearly have the potential to overcome the intergenerational transmission of poverty and its negative outcomes.

The original Quantum Opportunities Program no longer exists, but the Eisenhower Foundation (2008) recently began replicating the Quantum program in Alabama, South Carolina, New Hampshire, Virginia, Mississippi, Oregon, Maryland, and Washington, D.C.

Americans is reflected in their educational attainment. Some achieve a high level of education; many others have little education. For example, 90 percent of Korean American males graduate from high school, but only 71 percent of Vietnamese males do.

Many of the families that have immigrated in recent decades to the United States, such as Mexican Americans and Asian Americans, come from collectivist cultures in which family obligation and duty to one's family are strong (Fuligni & Fuligni, 2007; Kim & others, 2009). The family obligation and duty may take the form of assisting

Latino immigrants in the Rio Grande Valley, Texas. *What are some cultural adaptations and educational challenges these immigrant children from Guadalajara, Mexico, might face in the United States?*

parents in their occupations and contributing to the family's welfare (Parke & others, 2008). This often occurs in service and manual labor jobs, such as those in construction, gardening, cleaning, and restaurants. Many immigrant students serve as translators and negotiators for their families with the outside English-speaking world. Asian American and Latino families place a greater emphasis on family duty and obligation than do non-Latino White families (Fuligni & Fuligni, 2007).

Ethnicity and Schools Educational segregation is still a reality for children of color in the United States (Banks, 2008). Almost one-third of African American and Latino students attend schools in which 90 percent or more of the students are from minority groups, typically their own minority group. The school experiences of students from different ethnic groups also depart in other ways (Koppelman & Goodhart, 2008; Okagki, 2006). For example, African American and Latino students are much less likely than non-Latino White or Asian American students to be enrolled in academic, college preparatory programs and much more likely to be enrolled in remedial and special education programs. Asian American students are far more likely than students from other ethnic minority groups to take advanced math and science courses in high school. African American students are twice as likely as Latinos, Native Americans, or Whites to be suspended from school. Ethnic minorities of color constitute the majority in 23 of the 25 largest school districts in the United States, a trend that is increasing (Banks, 1995). However, 90 percent of the teachers in America's schools are non-Latino White, and the percentage of minority teachers is projected to be even lower in coming years.

Further, just as the schools of students from low-income backgrounds have fewer resources than those of students from higher-income backgrounds, so too do the schools of students from ethnic minority backgrounds have fewer resources than the schools of their counterparts from largely non-Latino White backgrounds (Banks, 2008; Engle & Black, 2008). For example, studies have found that students in California's predominantly minority schools had less access to every instructional resource surveyed, including textbooks, supplies, and computers, and were five times more likely to have uncertified teachers than students in predominantly non-Latino White schools (Oakes & Saunders, 2002; Shields & others, 2001).

In *The Shame of the Nation*, Jonathan Kozol (2005) described his visits to 60 U.S. schools in low-income areas of cities in 11 states. He saw many schools in which the minority population was 80 to 90 percent, concluding that school segregation is still

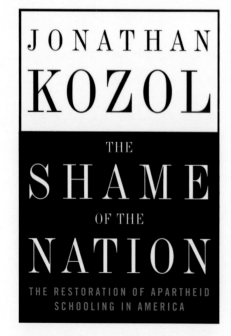

What is the nature of Jonathan Kozol's (2005) book, The Shame of the Nation?

present for many poor minority students. Kozol saw many of the inequities just summarized—unkempt classrooms, hallways, and restrooms; inadequate textbooks and supplies; and lack of resources. He also saw teachers mainly instructing students to rotely memorize material, especially as preparation for mandated tests, rather than engage in higher-level thinking. Kozol also frequently observed teachers using threatening disciplinary tactics to control the classroom.

Prejudice, Discrimination, and Bias   The negative schooling experiences of many ethnic minority children that Kozol described may involve prejudice, discrimination, and bias (Heiphetz & Vescio, 2008; Rowley, Kurtz-Costes, & Cooper, 2009). **Prejudice** is an unjustified negative attitude toward an individual because of the individual's membership in a group. The group toward which the prejudice is directed might be defined by ethnicity, sex, age, or virtually any other detectable difference (Chavous & others, 2008; Rivas-Drake, Hughes, & Way, 2008). Our focus here is prejudice against ethnic groups of color.

People who oppose prejudice and discrimination often have contrasting views (Brewer, 2007). Some value and praise the strides made in civil rights in recent years. Others criticize American schools and other institutions because they conclude that many forms of discrimination and prejudice still exist there (Smalls & others, 2007).

American anthropologist John Ogbu (1989; Ogbu & Stern, 2001) asserts that ethnic minority students are placed in a position of subordination and exploitation in the American educational system. He argues that students of color, especially African American and Latino students, have inferior educational opportunities, are exposed to teachers and school administrators who have low academic expectations for them, and encounter negative stereotypes of ethnic minority groups.

Recent studies provide insight into the discrimination experienced by ethnic minority adolescents. In one study, discrimination of seventh- to tenth-grade African American students was related to their lower level of psychological functioning, including perceived stress, symptoms of depression, and lower perceived well-being; more positive attitudes toward African Americans were associated with more positive psychological functioning in adolescents (Sellers & others, 2006). Figure 5.3 shows the percentage of African American adolescents who reported experiencing different types of racial hassles in the past year. Also, in a study of Latino youth, discrimination was negatively linked and social and parental support were positively related to their academic success (DeGarmo & Martinez, 2006). A recent study of sixth-grade students in the United States revealed that Chinese American children experienced discrimination from their peers that was comparable to discrimination faced by African American children (Rivas-Drake, Hughes, & Way, 2008).

Diversity and Differences   Historical, economic, and social experiences produce both prejudicial and legitimate differences among various ethnic groups (Taylor & Whittaker, 2009). Individuals who live in a particular ethnic or cultural group adapt to that culture's values, attitudes, and stresses (Suyemoto, 2009). Their behavior might be different from one's own yet be functional for them. Recognizing and respecting these differences is an important aspect of getting along in a diverse, multicultural world (Cooper & McLoyd, 2008; Cooper & others, 2008). One study revealed that when teachers were "color-blind" (that is, they did not recognize ethnic differences in students), they suspended African American male students at a disproportionately high rate and did not integrate multicultural education into their classrooms (Schofield, 2003). "A well-meaning statement such as 'I don't see color' fails to legitimize" ethnic "identifications that often define the experiences of people of color" (Banks & others, 2005, p. 267).

Type of racial hassle	Percent of adolescents who reported the racial hassle in the past year
Being accused of something or treated suspiciously	71.0
Being treated as if you were "stupid," being "talked down to"	70.7
Others reacting to you as if they were afraid or intimidated	70.1
Being observed or followed while in public places	69.1
Being treated rudely or disrespectfully	56.4
Being ignored, overlooked, not given service	56.4
Others expecting your work to be inferior	54.1
Being insulted, called a name, or harassed	52.2

FIGURE 5.3 African American Adolescents' Reports of Racial Hassles in the Past Year

prejudice An unjustified negative attitude toward an individual because of the individual's membership in a group.

A first- and second-grade bilingual English-Cantonese teacher instructing students in Chinese in Oakland, California. *What is the nature of bilingual education?*

Unfortunately, when differences between ethnic minority groups and the White majority were emphasized, it was damaging to ethnic minority individuals. For too long, virtually all differences were thought of as deficits or inferior characteristics on the part of the ethnic minority group (Meece & Kurtz-Costes, 2001).

Recall also the point made earlier that another important dimension of every ethnic group is its diversity (Payne, 2008; Tewari & Alvarez, 2009). Not only is U.S. culture diverse—so is every ethnic group within the U.S. culture.

Bilingualism

Throughout the world, many children speak more than one language (Gort, 2008). *Bilingualism*—the ability to speak two languages—has a positive effect on children's cognitive development. Children fluent in two languages perform better than their single-language counterparts on tests of control of attention, concept formation, analytical reasoning, cognitive flexibility, and cognitive complexity (Bialystok, 1999, 2001). They also are more conscious of the structure of spoken and written language and better at noticing errors of grammar and meaning, skills that benefit their reading ability (Bialystok, 1997).

Some aspects of children's ability to learn a second languge are transferred more easily to the second language than others (Pena & Bedore, 2009). A recent research review indicated that in learning to read, phonological awareness is rooted in general cognitive processes and thus transfers easily across languages; however, decoding is more language specific and needs to be relearned with each language (Bialystok, 2007).

Learning a Second Language U.S. students are far behind their counterparts in many developed countries in learning a second language. For example, in Russia, schools have 10 grades, called *forms,* which roughly correspond to the 12 grades in American schools. Children begin school at age 7 in Russia and begin learning English in the third form. Because of this emphasis on teaching English, most Russian citizens under the age of 40 today are able to speak at least some English.

Are there sensitive periods in learning a second language? That is, if individuals want to learn a second language, how important is the age at which they begin to learn it? For many years, it was claimed that if individuals did not learn a second language prior to puberty they would never reach native-language-learners' proficiency in the second language (Johnson & Newport, 1991). However, recent research indicates a more complex conclusion: Sensitive periods likely vary across different language systems (Thomas & Johnson, 2008). Thus, for late language learners, such as adolescents and adults, new vocabulary is easier to learn than new sounds or new grammar (Neville, 2006; Werker & Tees, 2005). For example, children's ability to pronounce words with a nativelike accent in a second language typically decreases with age, with an especially sharp drop occurring after the age of about 10 to 12. Also adults tend to learn a second language faster than children, but their final level of second-language attainment is not as high as children's. And the way children and adults learn a second language differs somewhat. Compared with adults, children are less sensitive to feedback, less likely to use explicit strategies, and more likely to learn a second language from large amounts of input (Thomas & Johnson, 2008).

BEST PRACTICES
Strategies for Working with Linguistically and Culturally Diverse Children

Here are some classroom recommendations for working with linguistically and culturally diverse children:

1. *"Recognize that all children are cognitively, linguistically, and emotionally connected to the language and culture of their home."*

2. *"Acknowledge that children can demonstrate their knowledge and capacity in many ways.* Whatever language children speak, they should be able to show their capabilities and feel appreciated and valued." Next, Verna Rollins, a middle-school language-arts teacher in Ypsilanti, Michigan, describes her experience with a Romanian student.

THROUGH THE EYES OF TEACHERS
Helping a 12-Year-Old Romanian Student to Become Proficient in English

Christina, a 12-year-old Romanian student, has been in America for about 15 months and is developing proficiency in English. Knowing she needs to learn to speak, read, and write standard English to be a successful, contributing member of American society, I looked for strengths that she brought to our community. Christina attended school in Romania and was able to read and write in her first language at an age-appropriate level. To take into account the context of language learning, I've altered many assignments I've given to Christina, and I've used gestures and my knowledge of other Romance languages to help her understand writing tasks. I've also encouraged Christina to accompany her writing with drawings that were unhampered by language deficiencies.

3. *"Understand that without comprehensible input, second-language learning can be difficult.* It takes time to be linguistically competent in any language."

4. *"Model appropriate use of English, and provide the child with opportunities to use newly acquired vocabulary and language."* Learn at least a few words in the child's first language to demonstrate respect for the child's culture.

5. *"Actively involve parents and families in the early learning program and setting."* Encourage and assist parents in becoming knowledgeable about the value for children of knowing more than one language. Provide parents with strategies to support and maintain home language learning.

6. *"Recognize that children can and will acquire the use of English even when their home language is used and respected."* Next, Daniel Arnoux, a middle school English teacher in Broward, Florida, describes how he seeks to make a difference in the lives of students whose natural first language is not English.

THROUGH THE EYES OF TEACHERS
Giving Students a Sense of Pride

For the past seven years, I have been teaching ESOL (English for speakers of other languages) in addition to other middle-school subjects. I believe that I've made a difference in my students' lives by giving them a sense of pride in their heritage and by providing a learning environment in which they can grow.

To achieve equality, the educational system must recognize students' ethnic background and gender. The student's home culture isn't to be discarded but instead used as a teaching tool. What works best in improving children's interethnic problems is to confront the problem head-on. I create lessons that teach empathy and tolerance toward others. I've used my free time to talk to classes about human rights and prejudice toward students of different nationalities and cultures—in particular Haitian students, who are continually harassed and sometimes beaten in school.

Try always to know your students as human beings, and they will surely open up to you and learn. Tell them that you believe in them. If you believe they can achieve, they will.

7. *"Collaborate with other teachers to learn more about working with linguistically and culturally diverse children."*

Source: National Association for the Education of Young Children, 1996, pp. 7–11

Bilingual Education   A current controversy related to bilingualism involves the millions of U.S. children who come from homes in which English is not the primary language (Gonzales, 2009; Lessow-Hurley, 2009). **English as a second language (ESL)** has now become a widely used term for bilingual education programs and classes that teach English to students whose native language is not English (Diaz-Rico, 2008a, b; Peregoy & Boyle, 2009). What is the best way to teach these children, who are referred to as *English-language learners (ELL)*?

The main ways that English-language learners are taught are (1) English immersion, in which English-language learners are taught mainly or exclusively in English; (2) transitional bilingual education, in which ELL students are taught reading or other subjects in their native language for several years and then moved into English classes; and (3) two-way or dual bilingual education, in which both native English-speaking students and ELL students are integrated in a bilingual classroom. In two-way or dual bilingual education, a minimum of 30 percent of the students generally need to be ELL students.

Advocates of bilingual education argue that if children who do not know English are taught only in English, they will fall behind in academic subjects. How, they ask, can 7-year-olds learn arithmetic or history taught only in English when they do not speak the language?

Those who oppose bilingual education argue that students in the programs don't become proficient in English. Supporting this argument, the states of California, Arizona, and Massachusetts have significantly reduced access to bilingual education programs. However, most states continue to implement bilingual education programs.

Drawing general conclusions about the effectiveness of bilingual education is difficult—programs vary considerably in the number of years they are in effect, type of instruction, qualities of schooling other than bilingual education, teachers, school population, and other factors. Further, no effectively conducted experiments comparing bilingual to English-only education in the United States have been performed (Snow & Kang, 2006). Some experts argue that the quality of instruction is more important in determining outcomes than the language in which it is delivered (Lesaux & Siegel, 2003).

Some researchers have reported support for bilingual education in that children have difficulty learning a subject when it is taught in a language they do not understand, and when both languages are integrated in the classroom, children learn the second language more readily and participate more actively (Hakuta, 2000, 2001, 2005; Horowitz, 2008).

Researchers have found that it takes English-language learners approximately three to five years to develop speaking proficiency and seven years to develop reading proficiency in English (Hakuta, Butler, & Witt, 2000). However, many bilingual education programs do not last this long. It is important to note that immigrant children vary in their ability to learn English (Levine & McCloskey, 2009; Quiocho & Ulanoff, 2009). For example, children from lower-socioeconomic backgrounds have more difficulty than those from higher-socioeconomic backgrounds (Hakuta, 2001; Rueda & Yaden, 2006). Thus, especially for low-SES immigrant children, more years of bilingual education may be needed than they currently receive.

English as a second language (ESL)
A widely used term for bilingual education programs and classes that teach English to students whose native language is not English.

Review, Reflect, and Practice

1 Discuss how variations in culture, socioeconomic status, and ethnic background need to be taken into account in educating children.

REVIEW

- What is culture? How do individualistic and collectivistic cultures differ? How do U.S. adolescents spend their time compared with adolescents in Europe and East Asia?
- What is socioeconomic status? In what ways are children from impoverished backgrounds likely to have difficulty in school?
- How is ethnicity involved in children's schooling?
- What is the nature of second-language learning? What characterizes bilingual education?

REFLECT

- In the context of education, are all ethnic differences negative? Come up with some differences that might be positive in U.S. classrooms.

PRAXIS™ PRACTICE

1. Mr. Austin, who grew up in the midwestern United States, teaches math in a high school with students who have immigrated from Mexico, Korea, Vietnam, India, Pakistan, Poland, and the Czech Republic. He often uses competitive games as class activities, many of which involve individual races to solve problems on the whiteboard at the front of the classroom. Some of his students seem to immensely enjoy the games, but some students get upset because they are unable to solve a problem. They become even more upset when Mr. Austin constructively criticizes them during the game. The most plausible explanation is that students who do *not* enjoy the games
   a. are not good athletes.
   b. have low self-esteem.
   c. grew up in a collectivist culture.
   d. grew up in an individualist culture.

2. Sally is a third-grade student at an economically diverse school. Sally lives in poverty, as do about one-fourth of her class. Another one-fourth of the class come from upper-middle-income families, and another half come from middle-income families. Sally's teacher, Ms. Roberts, has assigned a diorama (a scenic representation with sculpted figures and lifelike objects) project in lieu of a standard book report on *Charlotte's Web*.

(continued)

Review, Reflect, and Practice

PRAXIS™ PRACTICE (CONTINUED)

Kanesha, one of the more affluent children in the class, has created an elaborate diorama in a large shoe box. She placed plastic animals and small dolls in the diorama. The inside of her box is paneled with craft sticks to look like barn siding, and she used fine fishing line to create a web.

Although Sally read, understood, and enjoyed the book, her diorama does not compare favorably to Kanesha's. First, she did not have a shoe box to use, so she used an old box she found at a grocery store. She made her animals out of paper because she could not afford plastic animals. She made her web out of an old shoelace.

When Sally looked at her diorama next to Kanesha's, she almost cried. She did cry when Ms. Roberts gushed over how lovely Kanesha's diorama looked. What should Ms. Roberts have done differently?

a. She should have explained the income differences to the students before they began their project.

b. She should have had the students write traditional book reports.

c. She should have provided the materials and then had the students create the dioramas.

d. She should have praised Sally's diorama more than Kanesha's.

3. Robert teaches at an ethnically diverse elementary school. Since he decided to become a teacher, his goal has been to teach in a school like this one because he wants to help ethnic minority children. In his class, he makes considerable effort to ensure that all of his students are successful and feel part of the larger group. He is warm and caring toward his students, sometimes even providing lunch for those who forget to bring one or don't have enough money for the cafeteria. He often praises minority students for work that he would find only average from his majority students. What is Robert doing wrong?

a. He is substituting nurturance for academic standards.

b. He should provide a more nurturing environment for all students.

c. He should provide lunch for all of his students or none of them.

d. He is setting standards for minority students that are too high.

4. Mr. Williams teaches first grade and thinks his students will benefit from learning a second language, so he labels many of the items in his classroom in both English and Spanish. He chose Spanish because that is the second most common language in the area in which he teaches. What research supports Mr. Williams' approach?

a. First-graders are the right age to learn to read a second language but aren't too old to learn to speak a second language.

b. Because students in most countries do not learn to read a second language, Mr. Williams is giving his students an important advantage.

c. Children learn a second language better and more easily at this age than they will when they get older.

d. Mr. Williams should select a second language that is unfamiliar to most of his class.

Please see the answer key at the end of the book.

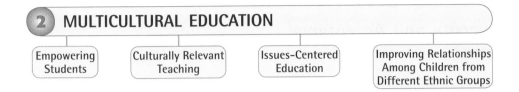

In 1963, President John Kennedy said, "Peace is a daily, a weekly, a monthly process, of gradually changing opinions, slowly eroding old barriers, quietly building new structures." Cultural and ethnic tensions regularly threaten this fragile peace. The hope is that multicultural education can contribute to making our nation more like what the late civil rights leader Martin Luther King, Jr., dreamed of: a nation where children will be judged not by the color of their skin but by the quality of their character.

Multicultural education is education that values diversity and includes the perspectives of a variety of cultural groups on a regular basis. Its proponents believe that children of color should be empowered and that multicultural education benefits all students (Cano, 2008). An important goal of multicultural education is equal educational opportunity for all students. This includes closing the gap in academic achievement between mainstream students and students from underrepresented groups (Gollnick & Chinn, 2009; King & Cardwell, 2008; Manning & Baruth, 2009).

Multicultural education grew out of the civil rights movement of the 1960s and the call for equality and social justice for women and people of color (Spring, 2008). As a field, multicultural education includes issues related to socioeconomic status, ethnicity, and gender. Because social justice is one of the foundational values of the field, prejudice reduction and equity pedagogy are core components (Banks, 2008). *Prejudice reduction* refers to activities teachers can implement in the classroom to eliminate negative and stereotypical views of others. *Equity pedagogy* refers to the modification of the teaching process to incorporate materials and learning strategies appropriate to both boys and girls and to various ethnic groups.

You and your students will benefit if you take a course or have some type of preparation involving multicultural education. For example, a study of math and science teachers revealed that their students' achievement was enhanced when their "teachers had a degree in the field in which they were teaching *and* had had preparation regarding multicultural education, special education, and English language development (Wenglinksy, 2002)" (Banks & others, 2005, p. 233).

Multicultural education expert James Banks (2008) recently described what characterizes a multicultural school. Following are some characteristics he thinks should be present if a school practices multicultural education:

- *The school staff's attitudes, beliefs, and actions.* The school's staff has high expectations for all students and are passionate about helping them learn.
- *The curriculum.* Multicultural education reforms the course of study so that students perceive events, concepts, and issues from the diverse views of different ethnic and socioeconomic groups.
- *Instructional materials.* Many biases are present in textbooks and learning materials. Among these biases are marginalizing the experiences of people of color, second-language minorities, women, and low-income individuals. In a multicultural school, instructional materials represent the backgrounds and experiences of diverse ethnic and cultural views.
- *The school culture and the hidden curriculum.* The hidden curriculum is the curriculum that is not explicitly taught but that nevertheless is present and learned by students. The school's attitudes toward diversity can appear in subtle ways, such as the types of photographs that are present on school bulletin boards, the ethnic composition of the school's staff, and the fairness by which students from diverse backgrounds are disciplined or suspended. In

multicultural education Education that values diversity and includes the perspectives of a variety of cultural groups on a regular basis.

DEVELOPMENTAL FOCUS 5.1

How Do You Promote Diversity and Acceptance of Others in the Classroom?

Early Childhood

In all areas of my classroom, multicultural books in several languages, posters, and other items—for example, garments, dolls, and music—that speak to diversity are displayed. The foods served to children during meal and snack times come from various cuisines and ethnic groups. At story time, books are read in different languages by parents and interpreted for the children to understand. Our philosophy is that we don't have to teach diversity, it already exists.

—Valarie Gorham, *Kiddie Quarters, Inc.*

Elementary School: Grades K–5

I teach the second-grade integrated ESL (English as a second language) class. At the beginning of the school year, as we are establishing our classroom community, we take time to recognize each student by creating a bulletin board with a poster of the world at the center. The display is entitled: "We are the children . . . We are the World." Each child's photo is taken and then displayed with a string designating his or her country of origin. We use this map throughout the year as a springboard for many geography and social studies lessons as we explore and learn about the world and each other's cultural backgrounds.

—Elizabeth Frascella, *Clinton Elementary School*

Middle School: Grades 6–8

I sometimes hear students call each other names in the halls and in the cafeteria. Instead of ignoring this behavior, I make sure I use these incidents as teaching moments and explain to the students why it is wrong to call others names. I also use my classroom time to educate students on the beliefs and customs of different religions and cultural groups. And I am the advisor of our school's Unity Club, which celebrates the diversity within our school by showcasing different cultures. For example, the club recently created a special bulletin board—displaying the flags from each country represented within our school.

—Casey Maass, *Edison Middle School*

High School: Grades 9–12

One-third of my school's population is Native American. As an art teacher, I present information on Native American art forms including pottery, beading, birchbark baskets, quillwork, and black ash baskets. All students learn what a Native American medicine wheel is (a circle of life) and what the various symbols—colors, directions, and animals—mean. Students make a medicine wheel for themselves and their own personal culture, whether they are Native American or not. Each piece is unique, which speaks to the diversity within the school.

—Dennis Peterson, *Deer River High School*

a multicultural school, the school's contexts are revised so that the hidden curriculum's message reflects positive aspects of diversity.

- *The counseling program.* A multicultural school's counseling program guides students from diverse backgrounds toward effective career choices and helps students take the appropriate courses that will enable them to pursue these choices. The school's counselors challenge diverse students to dream and provide them with strategies to reach those dreams.

Empowering Students

The term **empowerment** refers to providing people with the intellectual and coping skills to succeed and make this a more just world. In the 1960s to 1980s, multicultural education was concerned with empowering students and better representing minority and cultural groups in curricula and textbooks. Empowerment continues to be an important theme of multicultural education today (Cooper, 2008; Cushner, McClelland, & Safford, 2009). In this view, schools should give students the opportunity to learn about the experiences, struggles, and visions of many different ethnic and cultural groups (Banks, 2008). The hope is that this will raise minority students' self-esteem, reduce prejudice, and provide more-equal educational opportunities. The hope also is that it will help White students become more knowledgeable about minority groups and that both White students and students of color will develop multiple perspectives within their curricula.

Banks (2006, 2008) suggests that future teachers can benefit from writing a brief essay about a situation in which they felt marginalized (being excluded) by another group. Virtually everyone, whether from a minority or majority group, has experienced this type of situation at some point in their life. Banks emphasizes that you should be in a better position to understand the issues of sociocultural diversity after writing such an essay.

Sonia Nieto (2005), a Puerto Rican who grew up in New York City, says that her education made her feel that her cultural background was somehow deficient. She provides these recommendations:

- The school curriculum should be openly antiracist and antidiscriminatory. Students should feel free to discuss issues of ethnicity and discrimination.
- Multicultural education should be a part of every student's education. This includes having all students become bilingual and study different cultural perspectives. Multicultural education should be reflected everywhere in the school, including bulletin boards, lunchrooms, and assemblies.
- Students should be trained to be more conscious of culture. This involves getting students to be more skillful at analyzing culture and more aware of the historical, political, and social factors that shape their views of culture and ethnicity. The hope is that such critical examination will motivate students to work for political and economic justice.

Culturally Relevant Teaching

Culturally relevant teaching is an important aspect of multicultural education (Gollnick & Chinn, 2009). It seeks to make connections with the learner's cultural background (Pang, 2005).

Multicultural education experts stress that effective teachers are aware of and integrate culturally relevant teaching into the curriculum because it makes teaching more effective (Manning & Baruth, 2009). Some researchers have found that students from some ethnic groups behave in ways that may make some educational tasks more difficult than others. For example, Jackie Irvine (1990) and Janice Hale-Benson (1982) observed that African American students are often expressive and high in energy. They recommended that, when students behave in this way, giving them opportunities to make presentations rather than always being required to perform on a written exam might be a good strategy. Other researchers have found that many Asian American students prefer visual learning more than their European American peers (Litton, 1999; Park, 1997). Thus, with these students, teachers might want to use more three-dimensional models, graphic organizers, photographs, charts, and writing on the board.

Going into the community where your students live and their parents work can improve your understanding of their ethnic and cultural backgrounds (Banks & others, 2005). The *funds of knowledge approach* emphasizes that teachers should

empowerment Providing people with intellectual and coping skills to succeed and make this a more just world.

Culturally relevant teaching is an important aspect of multicultural education. One aspect of culturally relevant teaching involves going in to the community where parents live and work. Here a teacher visits a home of students who attend the Susan B. Anthony Elementary School in Sacramento.

visit students' households to develop social relationships with their students' family members to learn more about their cultural and ethnic background so that they can incorporate this knowledge into their teaching (Moll & Gonzáles, 2004). Through this approach, teachers can learn more about the occupations, interests, and community characteristics of their students' families. Examples of the funds of knowledge approach include guiding students to understand how their parents' carpentry skills relate to geometry and how the type of language students encounter outside of the classroom might help teachers in teaching students in English classes in school. Researchers have found that when the funds of knowledge approach is used, Latino students' academic performance improves (Gonzáles, Moll, & Amanti, 2005). The funds of knowledge approach acts as a bridge between the student's school and community.

Teachers need to have high achievement expectations for students from ethnic minority and low-income backgrounds and engage them in rigorous academic programs (Cooper & Huh, 2008; Graves & Graves, 2008). When high achievement expectations and rigorous academic programs are combined with culturally relevant teaching and community connections, students from ethnic minority and low-income backgrounds benefit enormously. In one study of California students, a four-year evaluation found that Latino students who participated in a rigorous academic program that included community-based writing and study, academic advising, and time with community leaders were almost twice as likely to apply to and attend universities as their counterparts who did not participate in the program (Gandara, 2002).

Issues-Centered Education

Issues-centered education also is an important aspect of multicultural education. In this approach, students are taught to systematically examine issues that involve equity and social justice. They not only clarify their values but also examine alternatives and consequences if they take a particular stance on an issue. Issues-centered education is closely related to moral education, which we discussed in Chapter 3, "Social Contexts and Socioemotional Development."

Consider the circumstance when some students were concerned with the lunch policy at a high school (Pang, 2005). The students who were on federally subsidized programs were forced to use a specific line in the cafeteria, which "labeled" them

What are some features of a jigsaw classroom?

poor. Many of these low-income students felt humiliated and embarrassed to the point that they went without lunch. The students alerted teachers to what had happened to them, and together, the students and teachers developed a plan of action. They presented the plan to the school district, which revised its lunch line policy at the ten high schools affected by it.

Improving Relations Among Children from Different Ethnic Groups

A number of strategies and programs are available to improve relationships among children from different ethnic groups. To begin, we will discuss one of the most powerful strategies.

The Jigsaw Classroom   When social psychologist Elliot Aronson was a professor at the University of Texas at Austin, the school system contacted him for ideas to reduce the increasing racial tension in classrooms. Aronson (1986) developed the concept of the **jigsaw classroom**, which involves having students from different cultural backgrounds cooperate by doing different parts of a project to reach a common goal. Aronson used the term *jigsaw* because he saw the technique as much like a group of students cooperating to put different pieces together to complete a jigsaw puzzle.

How might this work? Consider a class of students, some White, some African American, some Latino, some Native American, and some Asian American. The lesson concerns the life of Joseph Pulitzer. The class might be broken up into groups of six students each, with the groups being as equally mixed as possible in terms of ethnic composition and achievement level. The lesson about Pulitzer's life is divided into six parts, and one part is assigned to each member of each six-person group. The parts might be passages from Pulitzer's biography, such as how the Pulitzer family came to the United States, Pulitzer's childhood, his early work, and so on. All students in each group are given an allotted time to study their parts. Then the groups meet, and each member works to teach his or her part to the group. Learning depends on the students' interdependence and cooperation in reaching the same goal.

Sometimes the jigsaw classroom strategy is described as creating a superordinate goal or common task for students. Team sports, drama productions, and music performances are additional examples of contexts in which students cooperatively and often very enthusiastically participate to reach a superordinate goal.

jigsaw classroom A classroom in which students from different cultural backgrounds cooperate by doing different parts of a project to reach a common goal.

TECHNOLOGY AND EDUCATION
Technology Connections with Students Around the World

Traditionally, students have learned within the walls of their classroom and interacted with their teacher and other students in the class. With advances in telecommunications, students can learn with and from teachers and students around the world.

For example, in the Global Laboratory Project, an international, telecommunication-based project, students investigated local and global environments (Schrum & Berenfeld, 1997). After sharing their findings, students collaboratively identified various aspects of environments, discussed research plans, and conducted distributed studies using the same methods and procedures. Students from such diverse locations as Moscow, Russia; Warsaw, Poland; Kenosha, Wisconsin; San Antonio, Texas; Pueblo, Colorado; and Aiken, South Carolina, participated. As their data collection and evaluation evolved, students continued to communicate with their peers worldwide and to learn more, not only about science, but also about the global community.

New advances in telecommunication make it possible for students around the world to communicate through videoconferencing over the Internet. For example, at the Research Center for Educational Technology (RCET) at Kent State University, Ohio elementary students and their teachers are collaborating with their peers at the Instituto Thomas Jefferson in Mexico City on a variety of projects including studies of plant biology, climate, and biography, using both Internet-based videoconferencing and e-mail (Swan & others, 2006). RCET researchers have found that projects that share common understandings but highlight local differences are especially productive.

An increasing number of schools are also using Internet-based videoconferencing for foreign language instruction. Instead of simulating a French café in a typical French lan-

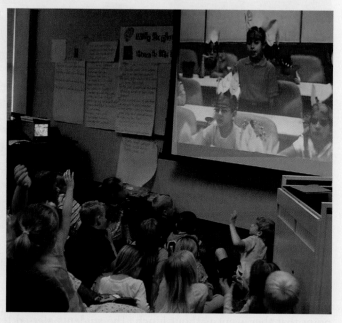

Students in the Research Center for Educational Technology's AT&T classroom at Kent State University, studying plant biology with students at the Instituto Thomas Jefferson in Mexico City.

guage class, American students might talk with French students in a real café in France.

Such global technology projects can go a long way toward reducing American students' ethnocentric beliefs. The active building of connections around the world through telecommunications gives students the opportunity to experience others' perspectives, better understand other cultures, and reduce prejudice.

Positive personal contact that involves sharing doubts, hopes, ambitions, and much more is one way to improve interethnic relations.

Positive Personal Contact with Others from Different Cultural Backgrounds   Contact by itself does not always improve relationships. For example, busing ethnic minority students to predominantly White schools, or vice versa, has not reduced prejudice or improved interethnic relations (Frankenberg & Orfield, 2007). What matters is what happens after students arrive at a school.

Relations improve when students talk with each other about their personal worries, successes, failures, coping strategies, interests, and so on. When students reveal personal information about themselves, they are more likely to be perceived as individuals than simply as members of a group. Sharing personal information frequently produces this discovery: People from different backgrounds share many of the same hopes, worries, and feelings. Sharing personal information can help break down in-group/out-group and we/they barriers.

Perspective Taking   Exercises and activities that help students see other people's perspectives can improve interethnic relations. In one exercise, students learn certain proper behaviors of two distinct cultural groups (Shirts, 1997). Subsequently, the two groups interact with each other in accordance with those behaviors. As a result, they experience feelings of anxiety and apprehension. The exercise is designed to help students understand the culture shock that comes from being in a cultural setting with people who behave in ways that are very different from what one is used to. Students also can be encouraged to write stories or act out plays that involve prejudice or discrimination. In this way, students "step into the shoes" of students who are culturally different from themselves and feel what it is like to not be treated as an equal (Cushner, 2006).

Studying people from different parts of the world also encourages students to understand different perspectives (Mazurek, Winzer, & Majorek, 2000). In social studies, students can be asked why people in certain cultures have customs different from their own. Teachers can also encourage students to read books on many different cultures. To read further about bringing the global community into American students' classrooms, see the *Technology and Education* interlude.

Critical Thinking and Emotional Intelligence Students who learn to think deeply and critically about interethnic relations are likely to decrease their prejudice and stereotyping of others. Students who think in narrow ways are often prejudiced. However, when students learn to ask questions, think first about issues rather than respond automatically, and delay judgment until more complete information is available, they become less prejudiced.

Emotional intelligence benefits interethnic relations. Recall from Chapter 4 that being emotionally intelligent means having emotional self-awareness, managing your emotions, reading emotions, and handling relationships. Consider how the following emotionally intelligent skills can help students to improve their relations with diverse others: understanding the causes of one's feelings, being good at managing one's own anger, being good at listening to what other people are saying, and being motivated to share and cooperate.

Reducing Bias Louise Derman-Sparks and the Anti-Bias Curriculum Task Force (1989) created a number of tools to help young children reduce, handle, or even eliminate their biases. The antibias curriculum argues that although differences are good, discriminating against someone is not. It encourages teachers to confront troublesome bias issues rather than covering them up.

These are some of the antibias strategies recommended for teachers:

Cover of the spring 2007 issue of *Teaching Tolerance* magazine, which includes numerous resources for improving interethnic relationships.

- Display images of children from a variety of ethnic and cultural groups. Select books for students that also reflect this diversity.
- Choose play materials and activities that encourage ethnic and cultural understanding. Use dramatic play to illustrate nonstereotypic roles and families from diverse backgrounds.
- Talk with students about stereotyping and discriminating against others. Make it a firm rule that no child is allowed to be teased or excluded because of their ethnicity or race.
- Engage parents in discussions of how children develop prejudice, and inform parents about your efforts to reduce ethnic bias in your classroom.

Increasing Tolerance The "Teaching Tolerance Project" provides schools with resources and materials to improve intercultural understanding and relationships between White children and children of color (Heller & Hawkins, 1994). The biannual magazine *Teaching Tolerance* is distributed to every public and private school in the United States (you can obtain a free copy by contacting Teaching Tolerance through www.tolerance.org). The magazine's purpose is to share views on and provide resources for teaching tolerance. For elementary school teachers, the "Different and Same" videos and materials (available through www.fci.org) can help children become more tolerant.

BEST PRACTICES
Strategies for Multicultural Education

We already have discussed many ideas that will benefit children's relations with people from different ethnic and cultural backgrounds. Further guidelines for multicultural teaching include these recommendations from leading multicultural education expert James Banks (2006, 2008):

1. *Be sensitive to racist content in materials and classroom interactions.* A good source for learning more about racism is Paul Kivel's (1995) book, *Uprooting Racism.*

2. *Learn more about different ethnic groups.* According to diversity expert Carlos Diaz (2005), only when you consider yourself "multiculturally literate" will you likely encourage students to think deeply and critically about diversity. Otherwise, says Diaz, teachers tend to see diversity as a "can of worms" that they don't want to open because they lack the background to explain it. To increase your multicultural literacy, read at least one major book on the history and culture of American ethnic groups. Two of Banks' books that include historical descriptions of these groups are *Cultural Diversity and Education* (2006) and *Teaching Strategies for Ethnic Studies* (2003).

3. *Be aware of students' ethnic attitudes.* Respond to students' cultural views in sensitive ways. Next, Kathy Fucher, a high school teacher in Humphrey, Nebraska, describes some strategies for reducing students' prejudice.

THROUGH THE EYES OF TEACHERS
Seeking to Reduce Prejudice Toward Latino Students in Nebraska

The meatpacking industry in Nebraska has brought many Latinos to our area. I find my students have a definite negative attitude toward them, usually as a result of their parents' influence. My effort to help them realize their prejudice is to teach David Gutterson's *Snow Falling on Cedars* to senior-level students. Though the fictional novel takes place off Puget Sound and deals with Japanese immigrants during World War II, I take students through discussion questions that provide striking similarity to their prejudice against Latinos. I have no way to measure the degree of prejudice, but I feel that education and awareness are key steps in decreasing the problem.

4. *Use trade books, films, videotapes, and recordings to portray ethnic perspectives.* Banks's (2003) book, *Teaching Strategies for Ethnic Studies,* describes a number of these. Next, Marlene Wendler, a fourth-grade teacher in New Ulm, Minnesota, describes her teaching strategies in this regard.

THROUGH THE EYES OF TEACHERS
Using Literature to Show How Minorities Have Been Treated

I use literature to help students understand other people and how they have sometimes been treated unfairly. During January, I focus on the southeastern United States in our social studies class and integrate language arts by having the whole class read *Meet Addy* and *Mississippi Bridge.* On Martin Luther King Day we read his biography. We get a little overview of how the Jews were treated in World War II through *Number the Stars.* We also get interested in learning more about Anne Frank. When the children read how these minorities were treated, they understand more fully that all people are more similar to them than different.

5. *Take into account your students' developmental status when you select various cultural materials.* In early childhood and elementary school classrooms, make the learning experience specific and concrete. Banks stresses that fiction and biographies are especially good choices for introducing cultural concepts to these students. Banks recommends that students at these levels can study such concepts as similarities, differences, prejudice, and discrimination but are not developmentally ready to study concepts such as racism.

6. *Perceive all students in positive ways and have high expectations for them regardless of their ethnicity.* All students learn best when their teachers have high achievement expectations for them and support their learning efforts. We will have much more to say about the importance of high expectations for students' achievement in Chapter 13, "Motivation, Teaching, and Learning."

7. *Recognize that most parents, regardless of their ethnicity, are interested in their children's education and want them to succeed in school.* However, understand that many parents of color have mixed feelings about schools because of their own experiences with discrimination. Think of positive ways to get parents of color more involved in their children's education and view them as partners in their children's learning.

The School and Community as a Team   Yale psychiatrist James Comer (1988, 2004, 2006) stresses that a community team approach is the best way to educate children. Three important aspects of the Comer Project for Change are (1) a governance and management team that develops a comprehensive school plan, assessment strategy, and staff development program; (2) a mental health or school support team; and (3) a parents' program. The Comer program emphasizes no-fault (the focus should be on solving problems, not blaming), no decisions except by consensus, and no paralysis (that is, no naysayer can stand in the way of a strong majority decision). Comer says the entire school community should have a cooperative rather than an adversarial attitude. The Comer program is currently operating in more than 600 schools in 82 school districts in 26 states.

One of the first schools to implement the Comer approach was the Martin Luther King, Jr., Elementary School in New Haven, Connecticut. When the Comer program began there, its students were an average of 19 months below grade level in language arts and 18 months below grade level in math. After 10 years of the Comer program, the students' national achievement test scores were at grade level, and after 15 years they were 12 months above grade level. Even though no socioeconomic changes had taken place in this predominantly African American, low-income, inner-city area over this period, school absenteeism dropped dramatically, serious behavior problems decreased, parent participation increased substantially, and staff turnover was almost nil.

James Comer (left) is shown with some inner-city African American students who attend a school where Comer has implemented his community team approach.

In his latest book, *Leave No Child Behind,* Comer (2004) agrees with the increased emphasis on higher standards and accountability in U.S. schools but argues that the emphasis on test scores and curriculum alone is inadequate. Comer says that children's socioemotional development and relationships with caregivers also need to be improved if educational reform is to be successful.

Review, Reflect, and Practice

(2) Describe some ways to promote multicultural education.

REVIEW

- What is multicultural education? What is the aim of "empowering" students?
- What is culturally relevant teaching?
- What is issues-centered education?
- How can teachers improve relationships among children from different ethnic groups?

REFLECT

- In terms of multicultural education, what do you hope to do differently as a teacher than what your former teachers did?

PRAXIS™ PRACTICE

1. According to Sonia Nieto, which of these is the best educational practice for empowering students?
   a. avoiding discussion of prejudice and discrimination
   b. teaching a second language to all White students
   c. having separate weekly classes on multicultural topics
   d. encouraging all students to study culture critically

(continued)

Review, Reflect, and Practice

PRAXIS™ PRACTICE (CONTINUED)

2. Which teacher's practice best exemplifies the concept of culturally relevant education?
   a. Mr. Lincoln, who does not allow any discussion of race or ethnicity in his class, deeming it irrelevant to his students' education
   b. Mr. Peters, who has differing expectations of his students based on gender, ethnicity, and SES
   c. Mr. Welch, who displays favoritism to members of ethnic minority groups
   d. Mr. Patterson, who recognizes that he comes from a different background than his students, but spends time in the community to help him to understand their culture

3. Which of the following is the best example of issues-centered education?
   a. As Mr. DeRosa's students study their history text, they look at events in terms of fairness to all groups and long-term social impact.
   b. Ms. Pang's students discuss historical facts and their impact on mainstream culture.
   c. Ms. Broadhouse's students are encouraged to debate issues, but debate winners always share the same views as Ms. Broadhouse.
   d. Mr. Taha's students are having a culture fair this Friday.

4. Middlesborough High School is an ethnically diverse school with considerable racial tension and conflict. When possible, the students self-select single-ethnicity groups. When forced to work in ethnically diverse groups, the students often argue and fail to cooperate. Several racially motivated violent episodes have occurred during this school year. Based on information in the text, which of these practices is most likely to improve relationships among the students from different ethnic groups?
   a. Assign the students to read books about various ethnic groups' history and contributions and discuss them in class in mixed ethnic groups.
   b. Keep putting students of mixed ethnicity together in classes and project groups so that they get to know each other and the conflict will decrease.
   c. Allow the students to stay in single-ethnicity groups because they are old enough to make these choices for themselves.
   d. Ignore ethnicity altogether so that students gradually become less aware of ethnic differences.

Please see the answer key at the end of the book.

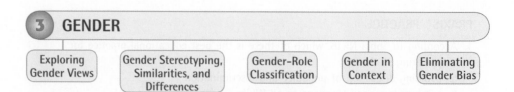

3 GENDER

Exploring Gender Views | Gender Stereotyping, Similarities, and Differences | Gender-Role Classification | Gender in Context | Eliminating Gender Bias

Gender is a term that is extensively used throughout our everyday lives, including schools and education. Among the questions related to gender that we will explore are: What exactly do we mean by gender? How extensive is gender stereotyping and what are the real gender differences, especially those involving children's educa-

tion? How extensively do gender influences vary according to the contexts in children's lives? What is meant by
gender-role classification? What are some strategies
for eliminating gender bias?

Exploring Gender Views

Gender refers to the characteristics of people as males
and females. A **gender role** is a set of expectations
that prescribe how females and males should act,
think, and feel. **Gender-typing** is the process by which
children acquire the thoughts, feelings, and behaviors
that are considered appropriate for their gender in a
particular culture.

There are various ways to view gender development.
Some views stress biological factors in the behavior of males
and females; others emphasize social or cognitive factors (Blakemore, Berenbaum, &
Liben, 2009; Burge & Filer, 2008). Even gender experts with a strong environmental
orientation acknowledge that girls and boys are treated differently because of their
physical differences and their different roles in reproduction. What is at issue is the
directness or indirectness of biological and environmental influences. For example,
androgen is the predominant sex hormone in males. If a high androgen level directly
influences brain functioning, which in turn increases some behavior such as aggression or activity level, then the biological effect is direct. If a child's high androgen
level produces strong muscle development, which in turn causes others to expect the
child to be a good athlete and, in turn, leads the child to participate in sports, then
the biological effect on behavior is more indirect.

Social views of gender especially highlight the importance of the various social
contexts in which children develop, especially families, peers, schools, and the media
(Blakemore, Berenbaum, & Liben, 2009). Many parents encourage boys and girls to
engage in different types of play and activities (Bronstein, 2006). Girls are more likely
to be given dolls and, when old enough, are more likely to be assigned baby-sitting
duties. Girls are encouraged to be more nurturant than boys. Fathers are more likely
to engage in aggressive play with their sons than with their daughters. Parents allow
their adolescent sons to have more freedom than their adolescent daughters.

The playground in elementary school
is like going to "gender school," as boys
prefer to interact with boys and girls
choose to interact with girls.

Peers also extensively reward and punish gender-related behavior (Rubin,
Bukowski, & Parker, 2006). After extensive observations of elementary school classrooms, two researchers characterized the play settings as "gender school" (Luria &
Herzog, 1985). In elementary school, boys usually hang out with boys and girls with
girls. It is easier for "tomboy" girls to join boys' groups than for "feminine" boys
to join girls' groups, because of our society's greater sex-typing pressure on boys.
Developmental psychologist Eleanor Maccoby (1998, 2002, 2007), who has studied
gender for a number of decades, concludes that peers play an especially important
gender-socializing role, teaching each other what is acceptable and unacceptable gender behavior.

Schools and teachers have important gender-socializing influences on boys and
girls. Shortly, we will explore such topics as the gender differences related to schools
and students interactions with teachers, educational achievement, and gender bias
in classrooms.

The media also play a gender-socializing role, portraying females and males in
particular gender roles (Dubow, Huesmann, & Greenwood, 2007). Even with the
onset of more diverse programming in recent years, researchers still find that television presents males as more competent than females (Strasburger, Wilson, & Jordan,
2008). In one analysis of rap videos on TV, teenage girls were primarily shown as
concerned with dating, shopping, and their appearance (Campbell, 1988). They were
rarely depicted as interested in school or career plans. Attractive girls were mainly
pictured as "airheads," unattractive girls as intelligent.

gender The characteristics of people as
males and females.

gender role The set of expectations that
prescribe how males and females should
think, act, and feel.

gender-typing The process by which
children acquire the thoughts, feelings,
and behaviors that are considered
appropriate for their gender in a
particular culture.

In addition to biological and social factors, cognitive factors also contribute to children's gender development (Blakemore, Berenbaum, & Liben, 2009; Zosuls, Lurye, & Ruble, 2008). **Gender schema theory**, currently the most widely accepted cognitive theory of gender, states that gender-typing emerges as children gradually develop gender schemas of what is gender-appropriate and gender-inappropriate in their culture. A *schema* is a cognitive structure, a network of associations that guides an individual's perceptions. A *gender schema* organizes the world in terms of female and male. Children are internally motivated to perceive the world and to act in accordance with their developing schemas. Bit by bit, children pick up what is gender-appropriate and gender-inappropriate in their culture, and develop gender schemas that shape how they perceive the world and what they remember. Children are motivated to act in ways that conform with these gender schemas.

Gender Stereotyping, Similarities, and Differences

What are the real differences between boys and girls? Before attempting to answer that question, let's consider the problem of gender stereotypes.

Gender Stereotypes   **Gender stereotypes** are broad categories that reflect impressions and beliefs about what behavior is appropriate for females and males. All stereotypes—whether they relate to gender, ethnicity, or other categories—refer to an image of what the typical member of a category is like. Many stereotypes are so general that they become ambiguous. Consider the categories of "masculine" and "feminine." Diverse behaviors can be assigned to each category, such as scoring a touchdown or growing facial hair for "masculine," playing with dolls or wearing lipstick for "feminine." Stereotyping students as "masculine" or "feminine" can have significant consequences (Matlin, 2008). Labeling a male "feminine" or a female "masculine" can diminish his or her social status and acceptance in groups.

Gender stereotyping changes developmentally (Zosuls, Lurye, & Ruble, 2008). A recent study revealed that children's gender stereotyping increased from preschool through the fifth grade (Miller & others, 2008). In this study, preschoolers tended to stereotype dolls and appearance as characteristic of girls' interests and toys and behaviors (such as action heroes and hitting) as the province of boys. During middle and late childhood, children expanded the range and extent of their gender stereotyping in such areas as occupations, sports, and school tasks. Researchers also have found that boys' gender stereotypes are more rigid than girls' (Zosuls, Lurye, & Ruble, 2008).

Stereotypes are often negative and can be wrapped in prejudice and discrimination. **Sexism** is prejudice and discrimination against an individual because of the person's sex. A person who says that women cannot be competent engineers is expressing sexism. So is a person who says that men cannot be competent early childhood teachers. Later in this chapter, when we discuss gender in the schools, we will describe some strategies for creating a nonsexist classroom.

Gender Similarities and Differences in Academically Relevant Domains   Many aspects of students' lives can be examined to determine how similar or different girls and boys are.

The Brain   Does gender matter when it comes to brain structure and activity? Human brains are much alike, whether the brain belongs to a male or a female (Halpern, 2006; Hyde, 2007). However, researchers have found some differences (Hofer & others, 2007a, b). Among the differences that have been discovered are as follows:

- Female brains are smaller than male brains, but female brains have more folds; the larger folds (called *convolutions*) allow more surface brain tissue within the skulls of females than in males (Luders & others, 2004).

gender schema theory States that gender-typing emerges as children gradually develop gender schemas of what is gender-appropriate and gender-inappropriate in their culture.

gender stereotypes Broad categories that reflect impressions and beliefs about what behavior is appropriate for females and males.

sexism Prejudice and discrimination against an individual because of the person's sex.

- An area of the parietal lobe that functions in visuospatial skills tends to be larger in males than in females (Frederikse & others, 2000).
- The areas of the brain involved in emotional expression tend to show more metabolic activity in females than in males (Gur & others, 1995).

Similarities and differences in the brains of males and females could be due to evolution and heredity, as well as social experiences.

Physical Performance   Because physical education is an integral part of U.S. educational systems, it is important to address gender similarities and differences in physical performance. In general, boys outperform girls in athletic skills such as running, throwing, and jumping. In the elementary school years, the differences often are not large; they become more dramatic in the middle school years (Smoll & Schutz, 1990). The hormonal changes of puberty result in increased muscle mass for boys and increased body fat for girls. This leads to an advantage for boys in activities related to strength, size, and power. Nonetheless, environmental factors are involved in physical performance even after puberty. Girls are less likely to participate in activities that promote the motor skills necessary to do well in sports (Thomas & Thomas, 1988).

Activity level is another area of physical performance in which gender differences occur. From very early in life, boys are more active than girls are in terms of gross motor movements (Ruble, Martin, & Berenbaum, 2006). In the classroom, this means that boys are more likely than girls to fidget and move around the room, and they are less likely to pay attention. In physical education classes, boys expend more energy through movement than girls do.

Math and Science Skills   In the National Assessment of Educational Progress in the United States, fourth- and eighth-grade boys continued to slightly outperform girls in math through 2007 (National Assessment of Educational Progress, 2005, 2007). However, not all recent studies have shown differences. A recent very large scale study of more than 7 million U.S. students in grades 2 through 11 revealed no differences in math scores for boys and girls (Hyde & others, 2008).

One area of math that has been examined for possible gender differences is visuospatial skills, which include being able to rotate objects mentally and determine what they would look like when rotated. These types of skills are important in courses such as plane and solid geometry and geography. A recent research review revealed that boys have better visuospatial skills than girls (Halpern & others, 2007). For example, despite equal participation in the National Geography Bee, in most years all ten finalists are boys (Liben, 1995). However, some experts argue that the gender difference in visuospatial skills is small (Hyde, 2007).

What about science? Are there gender differences? In one recent national study of science achievement, boys did slightly better in science than girls in the fourth, eighth, and twelfth grades (National Assessment of Educational Progress, 2005) (see Figure 5.4). In another study focused on eighth- and tenth-graders, boys scored higher than girls on science tests, especially among average- and high-ability students (Burkham, Lee, & Smerdon, 1997). In science classes that emphasized hands-on lab activities, girls' science test scores improved considerably. This suggests the importance of active involvement of students in science classrooms, which may promote gender equity.

Verbal Skills   A major review of gender similarities and differences conducted in the 1970s concluded that girls have better verbal skills than boys do (Maccoby & Jacklin, 1974). However, more recent analyses suggest that in some instances there may be little or no differences in girls' and boys' verbal skills. For example, today boys score as high as girls on the verbal portion of the SAT test (Educational Testing Service, 2002).

During the elementary and secondary school years, however, girls outperform boys in reading and writing. In recent national studies, girls had higher reading

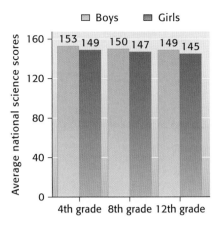

FIGURE 5.4 National Science Scores for Boys and Girls

In the National Assessment of Educational Progress, data collected in 2005 indicated that boys had slightly higher scores than girls in the fourth, eighth, and twelfth grades (Grigg, Lauko, & Brockway, 2006). The science scores could range from 0 to 300.

"So according to the stereotype, you can put two and two together, but I can read the handwriting on the wall."

Joel Pett, *The Lexington Herald-Leader,* Cartoon-Arts International/CWS.

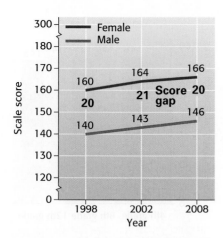

FIGURE 5.5 Trends in U.S. Eighth-Grade Boys' and Girls' Average Writing Scores on the National Assessment of Educational Progress

achievement than boys in grades 4, 8, and 12, with the gap widening as students progressed through school (Coley, 2001; National Assessment of Educational Progress, 2007). Girls also have performed substantially better than boys in grades 4, 8, and 12 in writing skills (National Assessment of Educational Progress, 2007). Figure 5.5 shows the consistently higher writing scores of eighth-grade girls.

Educational Attainment   With regard to school achievement, girls earn better grades and complete high school at a higher rate than boys (Halpern, 2006). Boys are more likely than girls to be assigned to special/remedial education classes. Girls are more likely to be engaged with academic material, be attentive in class, put forth more academic effort, and participate more in class than boys are (DeZolt & Hull, 2001).

Relationship Skills   Sociolinguist Deborah Tannen (1990) says that boys and girls grow up in different worlds of talk—parents, siblings, peers, teachers, and others talk to boys and girls differently. In describing this talk, Tannen distinguishes between rapport talk and report talk:

- **Rapport talk** is the language of conversation and a way of establishing connections and negotiating relationships. Girls enjoy rapport talk and conversation that is relationship-oriented more than boys do.
- **Report talk** is talk that gives information. Public speaking is an example of report talk. Boys hold center stage through report talk with such verbal performances as storytelling, joking, and lecturing with information.

Some researchers criticize Tannen's ideas as being overly simplified and view communication between males and females as more complex (Edwards & Hamilton, 2004; Hyde, 2005, 2007; MacGeorge, 2004). For example, a meta-analysis confirmed the criticism that Tannen overemphasizes the size of gender differences in communication (Leaper & Smith, 2004). Gender differences did occur, but they were small, with girls only slightly more talkative and engaging in more affiliative speech than boys, and boys being more likely to use self-assertive speech.

Prosocial Behavior   Are there gender differences in prosocial behavior? Girls view themselves as more prosocial and empathic (Eisenberg & Morris, 2004). Across childhood and adolescence, girls engage in more prosocial behavior (Hastings, Utendale, & Sullivan, 2007). The biggest gender difference occurs for kind and considerate behavior with a smaller difference in sharing.

Aggression   One of the most consistent gender differences is that boys are more physically aggressive than girls (Dodge, Coie, & Lynam, 2006). The difference is especially pronounced when children are provoked—this difference occurs across all cultures and appears very early in children's development (Ostrov, Keating, & Ostrov, 2004). Both biological and environmental factors have been proposed to account for gender differences in physical aggression (Blakemore, Berenbaum, & Liben, 2009). Biological factors include heredity and hormones; environmental factors include cultural expectations, adult and peer models, and the rewarding of physical aggression in boys.

Although boys are consistently more physically aggressive than girls, might girls show as much or more verbal aggression, such as yelling, than boys? When verbal aggression is examined, gender differences typically either disappear or are sometimes even more pronounced in girls (Eagly & Steffen, 1986). Recently, increased interest has been shown in relational aggression, which involves harming someone by manipulating a relationship (Coyne & others, 2008; Crick, Ostrov, & Kawabata, 2007; Soenens & others, 2008). Researchers have found mixed results regarding gender and relational aggression, with some studies showing girls engaging in more relational aggression and others revealing no differences between boys and girls (Young, Boye, & Nelson, 2006). One consistency in findings is that relational aggression comprises

rapport talk The language of conversation and a way of establishing connections and negotiating relationships; more characteristic of females than males.

report talk Talk that gives information; more characteristic of males than females.

a greater percentage of girls' overall aggression than is the case for boys (Putallaz & others, 2007).

Emotion and Its Regulation   Beginning in the elementary school years, boys are more likely to hide their negative emotions, such as sadness, and girls are less likely to express emotions such as disappointment that might hurt others' feelings (Eisenberg, 1986). Beginning in early adolescence, girls say they experience more sadness, shame, and guilt, and report more intense emotions; boys are more likely to deny that they experience these emotions (Ruble, Martin, & Berenbaum, 2006). An important skill is to be able to regulate and control one's emotions and behavior. Boys usually show less self-regulation than girls (Eisenberg, Spinrad, & Smith, 2004). This low self-control can translate into behavior problems. In one study, children's low self-regulation was linked with greater aggression, teasing of others, over-reaction to frustration, low cooperation, and inability to delay gratification (Block & Block, 1980).

Gender Controversy   The previous sections revealed some substantial differences in physical performance, writing skills, aggression, self-regulation, and prosocial behavior but small or nonexistent differences in communication, math, and science. Controversy swirls about such similarities and differences. Evolutionary psychologists such as David Buss (2008) argue that gender differences are extensive and caused by the adaptive problems faced across evolutionary history. Alice Eagly (2001, 2008) also concludes that gender differences are substantial but reaches a very different conclusion about their cause. She emphasizes that gender differences are due to social conditions that have resulted in women having less power and controlling fewer resources than men.

What gender differences characterize aggression?

By contrast, Janet Shibley Hyde (2005, 2007; Hyde & others, 2008) concludes that gender differences have been greatly exaggerated, especially fueled by popular books such as John Gray's (1992) *Men Are from Mars, Women Are from Venus* and Deborah Tannen's (1990) *You Just Don't Understand*. She argues that the research shows that females and males are similar on most psychological factors.

Gender-Role Classification

Not very long ago, it was accepted that boys should grow up to be masculine and girls to be feminine. In the 1970s, however, as both females and males became dissatisfied with the burdens imposed by their stereotypic roles, alternatives to femininity and masculinity were proposed. Instead of describing masculinity and femininity as a continuum in which more of one means less of the other, it was proposed that individuals could have both masculine and feminine traits.

This thinking led to the development of the concept of **androgyny**, the presence of positive masculine and feminine characteristics in the same person (Bem, 1977; Spence & Helmreich, 1978). The androgynous boy might be assertive (masculine) and nurturant (feminine). The androgynous girl might be powerful (masculine) and sensitive to others' feelings (feminine). Recent studies confirmed that societal changes are leading girls to be more assertive (Spence & Buckner, 2000) and that sons were more androgynous than their fathers (Guastello & Guastello, 2003).

Gender experts such as Sandra Bem argue that androgynous individuals are more flexible, competent, and mentally healthy than their masculine or feminine counterparts. To some degree, though, which gender-role classification is best depends on context. For example, in close relationships, feminine and androgynous orientations might be more desirable. One study found that children high in femininity showed a stronger interest in caring than did children high in masculinity (Karniol, Groz, & Schorr, 2003). However, masculine and androgynous orientations might be

androgyny The presence of positive masculine and feminine characteristics in the same individual.

more desirable in traditional academic and work settings because of the achievement demands in these contexts.

Despite talk about the "sensitive male," William Pollack (1999) argues that little has been done to change traditional ways of raising boys. He says that the "boy code" tells boys that they should show little if any emotion and should act tough. Boys learn the boy code in many contexts, especially peer contexts—sandboxes, playgrounds, schoolrooms, camps, hangouts. The result, according to Pollack, is a "national crisis of boyhood." Pollack and others suggest that boys would benefit from being socialized to express their anxieties and concerns and to better regulate their aggression. To think about your gender-role classification, see *Self-Assessment 5.1*.

Gender in Context

Earlier we said that the concept of gender-role classification involves categorizing people in terms of personality traits. However, recall from our discussion of personality in Chapter 4, "Individual Variations," that it is beneficial to think of personality in terms of person-situation interaction rather than personality traits alone (Engler, 2009; Schultz & Schultz, 2009). Let's now further explore gender in context.

Helping Behavior and Emotion   The stereotype is that females are better than males at helping. But it depends on the situation (Ruble, Martin, & Berenbaum, 2006). Females are more likely than males to volunteer their time to help children with personal problems and engage in caregiving behavior. However, in situations where males feel a sense of competence or that involve danger, males are more likely to help (Eagly & Crowley, 1986). For example, a male is more likely than a female to stop and help a person stranded by the roadside with a flat tire.

She is emotional; he is not. That's the master emotional stereotype. However, like helping behavior, emotional differences in males and females depend on the particular emotion involved and the context in which it is displayed (Shields, 1991). Males are more likely to show anger toward strangers, especially male strangers, when they feel they have been challenged. Males also are more likely to turn their anger into aggressive action. Emotional differences between females and males often show up in contexts that highlight social roles and relationships. For example, females are more likely to discuss emotions in terms of relationships. They also are more likely to express fear and sadness.

Culture   The importance of considering gender in context is most apparent when examining what is culturally prescribed behavior for females and males in different countries around the world (Shiraev & Levy, 2007). In the United States, there is now more acceptance of similarities in male and female behavior, but in many other countries roles have remained gender-specific. For example, in many Middle Eastern countries the division of labor between males and females is dramatic. In Iraq and Iran, males primarily are socialized and schooled to work in the public sphere; females are mainly socialized to remain in the private world of home and child rearing. Any deviations from this traditional masculine and feminine behavior are severely disapproved of. Likewise, in rural China, although women have made some strides, the male role is still dominant.

Cultural and ethnic backgrounds also influence how boys and girls will be socialized in the United States. One study indicated that Latino and Latina adolescents were socialized differently as they were growing up (Raffaelli & Ontai, 2004). Latinas experienced far greater restrictions than Latinos in curfews, interacting with members of the other sex, getting a driver's license, getting a job, and involvement in after-school activities.

Eliminating Gender Bias

How gendered are social interactions between teachers and students? What can teachers do to reduce or eliminate gender bias in their classrooms?

A school in the Middle East with boys only. Many adolescents in the Middle East are not allowed to interact with the other sex, even in school. Although in the United States there now is more acceptance of similarities in schooling and work opportunities for males and females, many countries around the world remain more gender-specific.

SELF-ASSESSMENT 5.1

What Gender–Role Orientation Will I Present to My Students?

The items below inquire about what kind of person you think you are. Place a check mark in the column that best describes you for each item: 1 = Not like me at all, 2 = Somewhat unlike me, 3 = Somewhat like me, and 4 = Very much like me.

Item	1	2	3	4
1. I'm independent.				
2. My emotional life is important to me.				
3. I provide social support to others.				
4. I'm competitive.				
5. I'm a kind person.				
6. I'm sensitive to others' feelings.				
7. I'm self-confident.				
8. I'm self-reflective.				
9. I'm patient.				
10. I'm self-assertive.				
11. I'm aggressive.				
12. I'm willing to take risks.				
13. I like to tell secrets to my friends.				
14. I like to feel powerful.				

Scoring and Interpretation

Items 1, 4, 7, 10, 11, 12, 14 are masculine items. Items 2, 3, 5, 6, 8, 9, and 13 are feminine items. Look at the pattern of your responses. If you mainly checked 3 and 4 for the masculine items and mainly 1 and 2 for the feminine items, you likely are characterized by masculinity. If you mainly checked 3 and 4 for the feminine items and 1 and 2 for the masculine items, you likely are characterized by femininity. If you mainly checked 3 and 4 for both the masculine items and the feminine items, you likely are characterized by androgyny. If you mainly checked 1 and 2 for both the masculine and feminine items, your gender-role classification is likely undifferentiated.

Teacher–Student Interaction   Gender bias is present in classrooms (Burge & Filer, 2008; Clerkin, 2008). Teachers interact more with boys and girls at all levels of schooling (Ruble, Martin, & Berenbaum, 2006). What evidence is there that this interaction is biased against boys? Here are some factors to consider (DeZolt & Hull, 2001):

- Complying, following rules, and being neat and orderly are valued and reinforced in many classrooms. These are behaviors that are typically associated with girls rather than boys.
- A large majority of teachers are females, especially in the elementary school. This may make it more difficult for boys than for girls to identify with their teachers and model their teachers' behavior.
- Boys are more likely than girls to be identified as having learning problems.
- Boys are more likely than girls to be criticized.
- School personnel tend to stereotype boys' behavior as problematic.

What are some of the ways that teachers interact with students on the basis of gender?

What evidence is there that the classroom is biased against girls? Consider the following factors (Sadker & Sadker, 1994, 2005):

- In a typical classroom, girls are more compliant, boys more rambunctious. Boys demand more attention; girls are more likely to quietly wait their turn. Educators worry that girls' tendency to be compliant and quiet comes at a cost: diminished assertiveness.

- In many classrooms, teachers spend more time watching and interacting with boys, whereas girls work and play quietly on their own. Most teachers don't intentionally favor boys by spending more time with them, yet somehow the classroom frequently ends up with this type of gendered profile.

- Boys get more instruction than girls and more help when they have trouble with a question. Teachers often give boys more time to answer a question, more hints at the correct answer, and further tries if they give the wrong answer.

- Girls and boys enter first grade with roughly equal levels of self-esteem, yet by the middle school years, girls' self-esteem is significantly lower than boys' (Robins & others, 2002).

- Although girls are identified for gifted programs more than boys in elementary school, by high school there are more boys than girls in gifted programs (U.S. Office of Education, 1999). There especially is a low number of African American and Latino girls in gifted programs (Banks & others, 2005).

Thus, there is evidence of gender bias against both boys and girls in schools (DeZolt & Hull, 2001; Halpern, 2006; Thornton & Goldstein, 2006). Many school personnel are not aware of their gender-biased attitudes. These attitudes are deeply entrenched in, and supported by, the general culture. Increasing awareness of gender bias in schools is clearly an important strategy in reducing such bias.

Might same-sex education be better for children than co-ed education? The research evidence related to this question is mixed (Ruble, Martin, & Berenbaum, 2006). Some research indicates that same-sex education has positive outcomes for girls' achievement; other research does not show any improvements in achievement for girls or boys in same-sex education (Mael, 1998; Warrington & Younger, 2003).

Curriculum Content and Athletics Content Schools have made considerable progress in reducing sexism and sex stereotyping in books and curriculum materials largely in response to Title IX of the Educational Amendment Act of 1972, which states that schools must treat females and males equally (Eisenberg, Martin, & Fabes, 1996). As a result, today's textbooks and class materials are more gender-neutral. Also, schools now offer girls far more opportunities to take vocational educational courses and participate in athletics than was the case when their parents and grandparents went to school (Gill, 2001). In 1972, 7 percent of high school athletes were girls. Today, that figure has risen to nearly 40 percent. In addition, schools no longer can expel, or eliminate services for, pregnant adolescents.

Nonetheless, bias still remains at the curricular level. For example, school text adoptions occur infrequently, and therefore many students still are studying outdated, gender-biased books.

Sexual Harassment Girls can encounter sexual harassment in many different forms—ranging from sexist remarks and covert physical contact (patting, brushing against bodies) to blatant propositions and sexual assaults (Martin, 2008; Rauscher, 2008). Literally millions of girls experience such sexual harassment each year in educational settings. A recent study of 12- to 18-year-old U.S. girls revealed that 90 percent of the girls reported having been sexually harassed at least once, with the likelihood increasing with age (Leaper & Brown, 2008). In another study of eighth- to eleventh-graders by the American Association of University Women (1993), 83

DEVELOPMENTAL FOCUS 5.2

How Do You Prevent Gender Bias in Your Classroom?

Early Childhood

The books we have in the classroom showcase men and women in various roles—for example, some of our books have female doctors and male nurses. We also encourage boys to cook and girls to build. However, we often have concern from parents when their son expresses interest in playing with dolls or playing "dress up" with the girls. We had a parent workshop about these concerns in which we told parents that at this developmental stage, children are experimenting with roles and working out situations through play. This was a difficult workshop because although they listened, parents were not interested in breaking traditions.

—Valarie Gorham, *Kiddie Quarters, Inc.*

Elementary School: Grades K–5

To get my fifth-grade students to recognize gender bias, I do a short unit using old books I've collected over the years that are very gender biased. We talk about the historical aspect of these books and how roles have changed for both men and women. In addition to discussing how women's roles have changed, I also point out that men now have opportunities they didn't have in the past such as being nurses and early childhood education teachers.

—Craig Jensen, *Cooper Mountain Elementary School*

Middle School: Grades 6–8

To prevent my sixth-grade students from sitting together by gender—that is, boys with boys and girls with girls—I have them sit in mixed, cooperative groups with each group consisting of two boys and two girls. Another strategy I use in class is to never randomly pick students to participate. Instead, I go down my class list so that everyone gets a chance or I choose students in a boy-girl order.

—Casey Maass, *Edison Middle School*

High School: Grades 9–12

I love to do exactly the opposite of what is traditional in my class when it comes to gender. For example, I ask girls to help me move heavy books, or boys to help clean up a spill. Recently, I was telling my students how to address formal business letters, and we were talking about using "Miss," "Mr.," "Mrs.," or "Ms." I told them that I think it is silly that women are defined by marital status, whereas men are "Mr." regardless. Several students, boys and girls alike, had a faraway look that said, "I hadn't thought of that before." I may have planted a seed that will grow into their questioning the traditions that have very little merit in our modern world.

—Jennifer Heiter, *Bremen High School*

percent of the girls and 60 percent of the boys said that they had been sexually harassed. Girls reported being more severely harassed than boys. Sixteen percent of the students said they had been sexually harassed by a teacher. And a recent survey of 2,000 college women by the American Association of University Women (2006) revealed that 62 percent of them reported that they had experienced sexual harassment while attending college. Most of the college women said that the sexual harassment involved noncontact forms such as crude jokes, remarks, and gestures. However, almost one-third said that the sexual harassment was physical in nature.

The U.S. Office for Civil Rights (2008) publishes a guide on sexual harassment. In this guide, a distinction is made between quid pro quo and hostile environment sexual harassment:

BEST PRACTICES
Strategies for Reducing Gender Bias

Every student, female or male, deserves an education free of gender bias. Here are some strategies for attaining this desirable educational climate (Derman-Sparks & the Anti-Bias Curriculum Task Force, 1989; Sadker & Sadker, 1994):

1. *If you are given textbooks that are gender-biased, discuss this with your students.* By talking with your students about stereotyping and bias in the texts, you can help them think critically about such important social issues. If these textbooks are not gender-fair, supplement them with other materials that are. Many schools, libraries, and colleges have gender-fair materials that you can use.

2. *Make sure that school activities and exercises are not gender-biased.* Assign students projects in which they find articles about nonstereotypical males and females, such as a female engineer or a male early childhood education teacher. Invite people from the community who have nonstereotypical jobs (such as a male flight attendant or a female construction worker) to come to your class and talk with your students. Next, Judy Logan, who has taught language arts and social studies for many years in San Francisco, describes one way that she helps students understand the contributions of females.

THROUGH THE EYES OF TEACHERS
The Inclusive Quilt

In my 25 years of teaching middle school, one of my goals has been for my classroom to be a blend of some of the things I know and some of the things my students know. The quilt experience serves as an example. My idea was to have the students feel connected not only to the women in the fields of science, politics, art, social reform, music, sports, literature, journalism, space, law, civil rights, education, humor, and so on, but also to the women in their own families.

I put a big piece of butcher paper on the blackboard, with the word *inclusive* at the top and asked the students to develop a list of what was needed to make our quilt truly inclusive. Hands popped up, and students volunteered categories first. We should have women in medicine. Sports. Civil rights. The list grew.

What else? How else can we make this quilt inclusive? What else do we know about diversity? Hands popped up again to create a second list. We should have Native American women. European American women. Latino women. Asian American women. Lesbian women. Again, our list grew. . . . We began to brainstorm a third list of individual women who were potential subjects for

Judy Logan, in front of the inclusive quilt in her classroom.

quilt squares. We created a long list of possibilities like Nancy Reagan, Jackie Kennedy, and Martha Washington, who did not end up on the final quilt itself, because the students decided they didn't want to have a lot of presidents' wives on the quilt. They ended up honoring Eleanor Roosevelt and Abigail Adams, who fit other categories on our list, such as social reform. . . .

I gave some thought to whom I wanted to honor on my patch. I decided to honor Brenda Collins, who is also named Eagle Woman. She is a member of the Bird Clan of the Cherokee Nation. She is a medicine woman, the first woman of her clan to get a Ph.D. and a teacher at Santa Rosa Junior College. She is also a friend and mentor. I have heard her speak several times, and I remember her saying that to be an educated Indian woman is like having a foot in each of two canoes, in rapid waters, always balancing two cultures. I decided to put two canoes and rapid water on her patch, with an eagle's wing by one canoe, and her doctoral degree by the other canoe. . . .

The finished quilt is colorful and diverse. No two patches are the same. I have provided the outline, the framework for the assignment, but each participant has created something uniquely their own. . . . (Source: Logan, 1997, pp. 1–23)

---

3. *Be a nonsexist role model as a teacher. Help students learn new skills and share tasks in a nonsexist manner.*

4. *Analyze the seating chart in your classroom and determine whether there are pockets of gender segregation.* When your students work in groups, monitor whether the groups are balanced by gender.

BEST PRACTICES
Strategies for Reducing Gender Bias

5. *Enlist someone to track your questioning and reinforcement patterns with boys and girls.* Do this on several occasions to ensure that you are giving equal attention and support to girls and boys.

6. *Use nonbiased language.* Don't use the pronoun *he* to refer to inanimate objects or unspecified persons. Replace words such as fireman, policeman, and mailman with words such as firefighter, police officer, and letter carrier. To improve your use of nonsexist language, consult

The Nonsexist Word Finder: A Dictionary of Gender-Free Usage (Maggio, 1987). Also ask students to suggest fair terminology (Wellhousen, 1996).

7. *Keep up-to-date on sex equity in education.* Read professional journals on this topic. Be aware of your own rights as a female or male and don't stand for sexual inequity and discrimination.

8. *Be aware of sexual harassment in schools and don't let it happen.*

- **Quid pro quo sexual harassment** occurs when a school employee threatens to base an educational decision (such as a grade) on a student's submission to unwelcome sexual conduct. For example, a teacher gives a student an *A* for allowing the teacher's sexual advances, or the teacher gives the student an *F* for resisting the teacher's approaches.
- **Hostile environment sexual harassment** occurs when students are subjected to unwelcome sexual conduct that is so severe, persistent, or pervasive that it limits the students' ability to benefit from their education. Such a hostile environment is usually created by a series of incidents, such as repeated sexual overtures.

Quid pro quo and hostile environment sexual harassment are illegal in educational settings, but potential victims are often not given access to a clear reporting and investigation mechanism where they can make a complaint.

Sexual harassment is a form of power and dominance of one person over another, which can result in harmful consequences for the victim. Sexual harassment can be especially damaging when the perpetrators are teachers who have considerable power and authority over students (Ormerod, Collinsworth, & Perry, 2008).

Review, Reflect, and Practice

(3) **Explain various facets of gender, including similarities and differences in boys and girls; discuss gender issues in teaching.**

REVIEW
- What is gender, and what do the concepts of gender roles and gender-typing mean? How have psychologists attempted to explain gender from biological, social, and cognitive perspectives?
- What are gender stereotypes? What problems are created by gender stereotypes? How are boys and girls similar and different?
- What characterizes gender-role classification?
- How might looking at behaviors in context reduce gender stereotyping?
- What evidence is there of gender bias in the classroom? What progress have schools made in reducing bias?

(continued)

quid pro quo sexual harassment
Occurs when a school employee threatens to base an educational decision (such as a grade) on a student's submission to unwelcome sexual conduct.

hostile environment sexual harassment Occurs when students are subjected to unwelcome sexual conduct that is so severe, persistent, or pervasive that it limits the students' ability to benefit from their education.

Review, Reflect, and Practice

REFLECT

- From your own K–12 education, come up with at least one instance in which your school or teacher favored either boys or girls. As a teacher, how would you try to correct that gender bias?

PRAXIS™ PRACTICE

1. In Jack's family, the person who does the cooking does not do the dishes. Since Jack's mother generally cooks, his father generally does the dishes. One day in the "housekeeping" area of his kindergarten class, Jack was pretending to be the father of the family. His "wife" Emily pretended to cook dinner on the toy stove. After the family ate, Emily started to pretend to wash the dishes. Jack gasped and cried, "Hey, I'm the dad!"

   This example best supports which theory of gender development?
   a. biological
   b. cognitive developmental
   c. social cognitive
   d. psychoanalytic

2. Which teacher's opinion about gender differences is best supported by current research?
   a. Mr. Kain, who believes that girls are more talkative than boys
   b. Ms. Nash, who believes that boys are better at math than girls
   c. Ms. Kim, who believes that boys are more physically aggressive than girls
   d. Ms. Walter, who believes that boys are generally fairer and more law-abiding than girls

3. Which student would best be described as androgynous?
   a. Alex, who is sensitive to others' feelings, shares secrets with friends, and provides social support to others
   b. Chris, who is independent, competitive, patient, self-reflective, and provides social support to others
   c. Pat, who is kind, sensitive, self-reflective, and likes to tell secrets to friends
   d. Terry, who is independent, competitive, self-confident, aggressive, and willing to take risks

4. A male is most likely to display helping behavior in which situation?
   a. A friend's car battery has died and needs a jump.
   b. A small child needs help with writing a poem for language arts class.
   c. A family member is ill and needs someone to provide care.
   d. A friend needs advice about a personal problem.

5. Ms. Vandt teaches fifth grade. Her class is comprised of approximately equal numbers of boys and girls. She often wonders why the boys can't behave more like the girls. The girls sit quietly, follow rules, and work well together. The boys have problems sitting still. They are rowdy and loud. Ms. Vandt tries to treat all of her students the same, but she often needs to reprimand the boys. What should she do?
   a. Allow the children time and space to move around and blow off steam. This will help the boys to attend better in class and the girls to socialize.
   b. Continue to reprimand the boys when they behave inappropriately. They will learn to sit quietly and be compliant.
   c. Divide the children into gender-specific groups so that the boys don't interfere with the girls' work.
   d. Point out the girls' compliant behavior as a model for the boys, so that they will understand what is expected of them.

Please see the answer key at the end of the book.

CRACK THE CASE
The Case of These Boys

Imagine that Larry is a 9-year-old boy in the fourth-grade class in which you are student teaching. You have heard him and a number of other students complaining about gender bias on the part of their teacher, Mrs. Jones. One day you overhear Larry being reprimanded by Mrs. Jones for an altercation he had with Annie, a female classmate.

"It isn't fair, Mrs. Jones," Larry says. "Annie took my homework and ripped it, and I get in trouble for taking it back."

"Now, Larry," admonishes Mrs. Jones. "You know Annie would never do that. You go apologize to her. I'll see you after school."

Larry walks away with a very angry look on his face, muttering, "The girls *never* get in trouble. It's always the boys."

You have heard this from students of Mrs. Jones in the past but have never really believed it. Over the course of the next three weeks you pay much closer attention to Mrs. Jones's behavior with a special sensitivity to gender bias. You notice that girls receive higher grades than do boys, except in math. Boys are required to stay after school several times, girls not at all. When Mrs. Jones is on recess duty and there are altercations between boys and girls on the playground, the boys end up standing against the wall, while the girls walk away, smiling. In class, the girls are used as models of behaviors much more frequently than the boys. Their work receives more praise as well. You examine what students have been reading over the course of the year. Their required reading thus far consists of *Little House on the Prairie, Charlotte's Web,* and *Little Women.*

The only thing you notice that appears to favor the boys is that they receive more of Mrs. Jones's attention. On further examination, however, you see that much of the attention is disciplinary in nature.

At one point, you overhear Mrs. Jones as she is walking down the hall, saying to a colleague, "These boys, I just don't know what I am going to do with them."

1. What are the issues in this case?

2. Based on the ideas and information presented in your text to this point, discuss what you believe to be happening in this classroom and the possible influences on Mrs. Jones's ideas of gender. Cite research and theories of gender development.

3. What influence do you believe Mrs. Jones's behavior will have on her students? Why?

4. What should Mrs. Jones do at this point? Why? What sort of outside assistance might help her?

5. If you were a student teacher in this classroom, what, if anything, would you do? Why?

6. What will you do in your own classroom to minimize gender bias?

Reach Your Learning Goals

Sociocultural Diversity

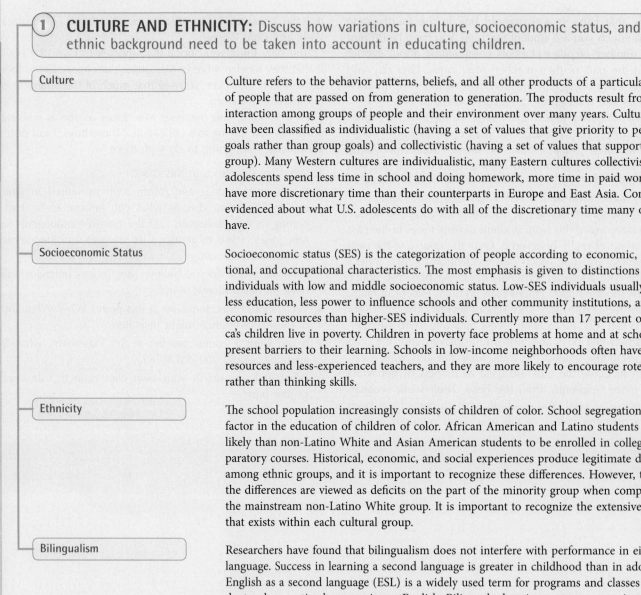

1   **CULTURE AND ETHNICITY:** Discuss how variations in culture, socioeconomic status, and ethnic background need to be taken into account in educating children.

Culture

Culture refers to the behavior patterns, beliefs, and all other products of a particular group of people that are passed on from generation to generation. The products result from the interaction among groups of people and their environment over many years. Cultures have been classified as individualistic (having a set of values that give priority to personal goals rather than group goals) and collectivistic (having a set of values that support the group). Many Western cultures are individualistic, many Eastern cultures collectivistic. U.S. adolescents spend less time in school and doing homework, more time in paid work, and have more discretionary time than their counterparts in Europe and East Asia. Concern is evidenced about what U.S. adolescents do with all of the discretionary time many of them have.

Socioeconomic Status

Socioeconomic status (SES) is the categorization of people according to economic, educational, and occupational characteristics. The most emphasis is given to distinctions between individuals with low and middle socioeconomic status. Low-SES individuals usually have less education, less power to influence schools and other community institutions, and fewer economic resources than higher-SES individuals. Currently more than 17 percent of America's children live in poverty. Children in poverty face problems at home and at school that present barriers to their learning. Schools in low-income neighborhoods often have fewer resources and less-experienced teachers, and they are more likely to encourage rote learning rather than thinking skills.

Ethnicity

The school population increasingly consists of children of color. School segregation is still a factor in the education of children of color. African American and Latino students are less likely than non-Latino White and Asian American students to be enrolled in college preparatory courses. Historical, economic, and social experiences produce legitimate differences among ethnic groups, and it is important to recognize these differences. However, too often the differences are viewed as deficits on the part of the minority group when compared with the mainstream non-Latino White group. It is important to recognize the extensive diversity that exists within each cultural group.

Bilingualism

Researchers have found that bilingualism does not interfere with performance in either language. Success in learning a second language is greater in childhood than in adolescence. English as a second language (ESL) is a widely used term for programs and classes for students whose native language is not English. Bilingual education programs vary in terms of whether English-language learners (ELL) are taught primarily in English or in a two-way, dual immersion approach. Becoming proficient in English for ELL students is usually a very lengthy process.

(2) MULTICULTURAL EDUCATION: Describe some ways to promote multicultural education.

Empowering Students

Multicultural education is education that values diversity and includes the perspectives of a variety of cultural groups on a regular basis. Empowerment, which consists of providing people with the intellectual and coping skills to succeed and make this a more just world, is an important aspect of multicultural education today. It involves giving students the opportunity to learn about the experiences, struggles, and visions of many different ethnic and cultural groups. The hope is that empowerment will raise minority students' self-esteem, reduce prejudice, and provide more-equal educational opportunities.

Culturally Relevant Teaching

Culturally relevant teaching is an important aspect of multicultural education. It seeks to make connections with the learner's cultural background.

Issues-Centered Education

Issues-centered education also is an important aspect of multicultural education. In this approach, students are taught to systematically examine issues that involve equity and social justice.

Improving Relationships Among Children from Different Ethnic Groups

Among the strategies/related ideas for improving relationships between children from different ethnic groups are these: the jigsaw classroom (having students from different cultural backgrounds cooperate by doing different parts of a project to reach a common goal), positive personal contact, perspective taking, critical thinking and emotional intelligence, reduced bias, increased tolerance, and development of the school and community as a team.

(3) GENDER: Explain various facets of gender, including similarities and differences in boys and girls; discuss gender issues in teaching.

Exploring Gender Views

Gender refers to the characteristics of people as males and females. Key aspects of gender include gender roles (expectations that prescribe how males and females should think, feel, and act) and gender-typing (the process by which children acquire the thoughts, feelings, and behaviors that are considered appropriate for their gender by a particular culture). Biological, social, and cognitive views of gender have been proposed. Some views stress biological factors; other views emphasize social or cognitive factors. The most widely accepted cognitive view today is gender schema theory.

Gender Stereotyping, Similarities, and Differences

Gender stereotypes are broad categories that reflect impressions and beliefs about what behavior is appropriate for females and males. All stereotypes involve an image of what the typical member of a category is like. Some gender stereotypes can be harmful for children, especially those that involve sexism (prejudice and discrimination against a person because of the person's sex). Psychologists have studied gender similarities and differences in physical performance, the brain, math and science skills, verbal skills, school attainment, relationship skills (rapport talk and report talk), aggression/self-regulation, and prosocial behavior. In some cases, gender differences are substantial (as in physical performance, reading and writing skills, school attainment, physical aggression, and prosocial behavior); in others they are small or nonexistent (as in communication, math, and science). Today, controversy still swirls about how common or rare such differences really are.

Gender-Role Classification

Gender-role classification focuses on how masculine, feminine, or androgynous an individual is. In the past, competent males were supposed to be masculine (powerful, for example), females feminine (nurturant, for example). The 1970s brought the concept of androgyny, the idea that the most competent individuals have both masculine and feminine positive characteristics. A special concern involves adolescents who adopt a strong masculine role.

Gender in Context

Evaluation of gender-role categories and gender similarities and differences in areas such as helping behavior and emotion suggest that the best way to think about gender is not in terms of personality traits but instead in terms of person-situation interaction (gender in context). Although androgyny and multiple gender roles are often available for American children to choose from, many countries around the world still are male-dominant.

Eliminating Gender Bias

There is gender bias in schools against boys and girls. Many school personnel are unaware of these biases. An important teaching strategy is to attempt to eliminate gender bias. Schools have made considerable progress in reducing sexism and sex stereotyping in books and curriculum materials, but some bias still exists. Sexual harassment is a special concern in schools and is more pervasive than once believed. Recently, a distinction has been made between quid pro quo sexual harassment and hostile environment sexual harassment.

KEY TERMS

culture 151
cross-cultural studies 151
individualism 151
collectivism 151
socioeconomic status
   (SES) 152
ethnicity 157

prejudice 159
English as a second language
   (ESL) 162
multicultural education 165
empowerment 167
jigsaw classroom 169
gender 175

gender roles 175
gender-typing 175
gender schema theory 176
gender stereotypes 176
sexism 176
rapport talk 178

report talk 178
androgyny 179
quid pro quo sexual
   harassment 185
hostile environment sexual
   harassment 185

PORTFOLIO ACTIVITIES

Now that you have a good understanding of this chapter, complete these exercises to expand your thinking.

Independent Reflection

Fostering Cultural Understanding in the Classroom. Imagine that you are teaching a social studies lesson about the westward movement in U.S. history and a student makes a racist, stereotyped statement about Native Americans, such as "The Indians were hot-tempered and showed their hostility toward the White settlers." How would you handle this situation? (Banks, 1997). Describe the strategy you would adopt. (INTASC: Principles *1, 2, 4, 6, 7*)

Collaborative Work

Planning for Diversity. With three or four other students in the class, come up with a list of specific diversity goals for your future classrooms. Also brainstorm and come up with some innovative activities to help students gain positive diversity experiences, such as the inclusive quilt discussed in this chapter. Summarize the diversity goals and activities. (INTASC: Principles *3, 4, 5, 6*)

Research/Field Experience

Equity in Action. Observe lessons being taught in several classrooms that include boys and girls and students from different ethnic groups. Did the teachers interact with females and males differently? If so, how? Did the teachers interact with students from different ethnic groups in different ways? If so, how? Describe your observations. (INTASC: Principles *3, 6, 9*)

Go to the Online Learning Center for downloadable portfolio templates.

TAKING IT TO THE NET

- How does your state measure up in the area of children's socio-economic status and school resources? Offer some evidence as to why you think your state ranks low/average/high compared with other states. How can conditions be improved? **www.aecf.org/kidscount/sld/databook.jsp**

- What is your position on the debate about multicultural education? Do you believe that multicultural perspectives should be integrated into academic subjects? Or do you think that multicultural education dilutes the rigor of "regular" curriculum and that many subjects do not lend themselves well to this

approach? Why? **http://www.tolerance.org/teach/magazine/features.jsp?p=0&is=17&ar=174**

- Analyze a curriculum activity at the Teaching Tolerance Web site. Discuss how conducting this kind of lesson could help reduce gender, racial, or cultural bias in the classroom. **www.tolerance.org/teach/index.jsp**

Connect to the Online Learning Center to explore possible answers.

 STUDY, PRACTICE, AND SUCCEED

Visit **www.mhhe.com/santedu4e** to review the chapter with self-grading quizzes and self-assessments, to apply the chapter material to two more Crack the Case studies, and for suggested activities to develop your teaching portfolio.

CHAPTER 6

Learners Who Are Exceptional

Only the educated are free.

—Epicurus
Greek Philosopher, 4th Century B.C.

Chapter Outline	Learning Goals

Children with Disabilities

Learning Disabilities
Attention Deficit Hyperactivity Disorder
Mental Retardation
Physical Disorders
Sensory Disorders
Speech and Language Disorders
Autism Spectrum Disorders
Emotional and Behavioral Disorders

1 Describe the various types of disabilities and disorders.

Educational Issues Involving Children with Disabilities

Legal Aspects
Technology

2 Explain the legal framework and technology advances for children with disabilities.

Children Who Are Gifted

Characteristics
Life Course of the Gifted
Educating Children Who Are Gifted

3 Define what gifted means and discuss some approaches to teaching children who are gifted.

192

TEACHING STORIES Verna Rollins

Verna Rollins teaches language arts at West Middle School in Ypsilanti, Michigan, and has developed a reputation for effectively dealing with so-called hard to teach or difficult students. She has found that the best strategy to use with these students is to find out what they need, decide how to provide it, provide it, and constantly evaluate whether it is working. A challenge for many regular education classroom teachers is how to effectively teach children with disabilities. In many instances, the education of children with disabilities in the regular education classroom is carried out in coordination with a special education teacher or staff. Here is Verna Rollins' description of her contribution in the coordinated effort to teach a student with a severe disability:

> Jack was in a special education classroom for children with physical disabilities. He has twisted legs, cerebral palsy, seizures, and some other brain damage from birth. He also has a comparatively short attention span. Since he drools, speaks in a loud monotone, stutters when he is excited, and has so little motor control that his penmanship is unreadable, people often think he is mentally retarded.
>
> My strategies included making sure that he had all the equipment he needed to succeed. I gave him tissues for the drooling and mutually agreed-upon reminders to wipe his mouth. I found that he could speak softly and without stuttering if he calmed down. We developed a signaling plan in which I would clear my throat when he talked too loudly and I would prompt him with the phrase "slow speech" when he was too excited to speak in a smooth voice.
>
> He used a computer to take quizzes and needed a little more time to complete any task, but he was so excited about being "out in the real world" that his attention span improved, as did his self-worth. In fact, his mother wrote a letter to me expressing her gratitude for the "most positive influence you have been on him! You have re-instilled and greatly increased his love of reading and writing. You have given my child a wonderful gift."

Preview

Verna Rollins was challenged to find the best way to teach a child with multiple disabilities in her classroom and to coordinate this teaching with Jack's special education teacher. Like Verna Rollins, when you teach you will likely work with children with disabilities if you teach in a regular classroom. In the past, public school did little to educate these children. Today, however, children with disabilities must have a free, appropriate education—and increasingly they are educated in regular classrooms. In this chapter, we will study children with many different types of disabilities, as well as another group of children who are exceptional, those who are gifted.

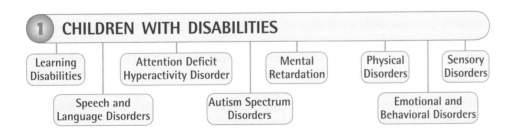

1 CHILDREN WITH DISABILITIES

Learning Disabilities | Attention Deficit Hyperactivity Disorder | Mental Retardation | Physical Disorders | Sensory Disorders

Speech and Language Disorders | Autism Spectrum Disorders | Emotional and Behavioral Disorders

Approximately 14 percent of all children from 3 to 21 years of age in the United States received special education or related services in the 2006–2007 school year (National Center for Education Statistics, 2008). Figure 6.1 shows the four largest groups of

Disability	Percentage of All Children in U.S. Public Schools
Learning disabilities	5.6
Speech and language impairments	3.0
Mental retardation	1.1
Emotional disturbance	0.9

FIGURE 6.1 The Four Highest Percentages of Students with a Disability Served by a Federal Program as a Percentage of All Students Enrolled in U.S. Public Schools (National Center for Education Statistics, 2008)

students with a disability who were served by federal programs in the 2006–2007 school year (National Center for Education Statistics, 2008). As indicated in Figure 6.1, students with a learning disability were the largest group of students with a disability to be given special education.

Educators increasingly speak of "children with disabilities" rather than "disabled children" to emphasize the person, not the disability. Also, children with disabilities are no longer referred to as "handicapped," although the term *handicapping conditions* is still used to describe the impediments to the learning and functioning of individuals with a disability that have been imposed by society. For example, when children who use a wheelchair do not have adequate access to a bathroom, transportation, and so on, this is referred to as a handicapping condition.

Learning Disabilities

Bobby's second-grade teacher complains that his spelling is awful. Eight-year-old Tim says reading is really hard for him, and a lot of times the words don't make much sense. Alisha has good oral language skills but has considerable difficulty in computing correct answers to arithmetic problems. Each of these students has a learning disability.

Characteristics and Identification The U.S. government created a definition of learning disabilities in 1997 and then reauthorized the definition with a few minor changes in 2004. Following is a description of the government's definition of what determined whether a child should be classified as having a learning disability. A child with a **learning disability** has difficulty in learning that involves understanding or using spoken or written language and the difficulty can appear in listening, thinking, reading, writing, and spelling. A learning disability also may involve difficulty in doing mathematics. To be classified as a learning disability, the learning problem is not primarily the result of visual, hearing, or motor disabilities; mental retardation; emotional disorders; or due to environmental, cultural, or economic disadvantage.

From the mid-1970s through the early 1990s, there was a dramatic increase in the percentage of U.S. students receiving special education services (from 1.8 percent in 1976–1977 to 12.2 percent in 1994–1995) (National Center for Education Statistics, 2008). Some experts say that the dramatic increase reflected poor diagnostic practices and overidentification. They argue that teachers sometimes are too quick to label children with the slightest learning problem as having a learning disability, instead of recognizing that the problem may rest in their ineffective teaching. Other experts say the increase in the number of children being labeled with a "learning disability" is justified (Bender, 2008; Hallahan, Kaufmann, & Pullen, 2009).

About three times as many boys as girls are classified as having a learning disability. Among the explanations for this gender difference are a greater biological vulnerability among boys and *referral bias* (that is, boys are more likely to be referred by teachers for treatment because of their behavior) (Liederman, Kantrowitz, & Flannery, 2005).

Most learning disabilities are lifelong. Compared with children without a learning disability, children with a learning disability are more likely to show poor academic performance, high dropout rates, and poor employment and postsecondary education records (Berninger, 2006). Children with a learning disability who are taught in the regular classroom without extensive support rarely achieve the level of competence of even children who are low achieving and do not have a disability (Hocutt, 1996). Still, despite the problems they encounter, many children with a learning disability grow up to lead normal lives and engage in productive work.

Diagnosing whether a child has a learning disability is often a difficult task (Bender, 2008; Fritschmann & Solari, 2008). Because federal guidelines are just that, guidelines, it is up to each state, or in some cases school systems within a state, to determine how to define and implement diagnosis of learning disabilities. The same

learning disability A child with a learning disability has difficulty in learning that involves understanding or using spoken or written language and the difficulty can appear in listening, thinking, reading, writing, and spelling. A learning disability also may involve difficulty in doing mathematics. To be classified as a learning disability, the learning problem is not primarily the result of visual, hearing, or motor disabilities; mental retardation; emotional disorders; or due to environmental, cultural, or economic disadvantage.

child might be diagnosed as having a learning disability in one school system and receive services but not be diagnosed and not receive services in another school system. In such cases, parents sometimes will move to either obtain or avoid the diagnosis.

Initial identification of a possible learning disability usually is made by the classroom teacher. If a learning disability is suspected, the teacher calls on specialists. An interdisciplinary team of professionals is best suited to verify whether a student has a learning disability. Individual psychological evaluations (of intelligence) and educational assessments (such as current level of achievement) are required (Hallahan, Kauffman, & Pullen, 2009). In addition, tests of visual-motor skills, language, and memory may be used.

"Your feelings of insecurity seem to have started when Mary Lou Gumblatt said, 'Maybe I don't have a learning disability—maybe you have a teaching disability.'"

Tony Saltzman, from *Phi Delta Kappan* (1975). Reprinted by permission of Tony Saltzman.

Reading, Writing, and Math Difficulties   The most common academic areas in which children with a learning disability have problems are reading, writing, and math (Bursuck & Damer, 2007).

Dyslexia   The most common problem that characterizes children with a learning disability involves reading, which affects approximately 80 percent of children with a learning disability (Shaywitz, Gruen, & Shaywitz, 2007). Such children have difficulty with phonological skills, which involve being able to understand how sounds and letters match up to make words, and also can have problems in comprehension. **Dyslexia** is a category reserved for individuals with a severe impairment in their ability to read and spell (Mathes & Fletcher, 2008; Reid & others, 2009).

Dysgraphia   **Dysgraphia** is a learning disability that involves difficulty in handwriting (Adi-Japha & others, 2007). Children with dysgraphia may write very slowly, their writing products may be virtually illegible, and they may make numerous spelling errors because of their inability to match up sounds and letters.

Dyscalculia   **Dyscalculia**, also known as developmental arithmetic disorder, is a learning disability that involves difficulty in math computation (Soltesz & others, 2007). It is estimated to characterize 2 to 6 percent of U.S. elementary school children (National Center for Learning Disabilities, 2006). Researchers have found that children with difficulties in math computation often have cognitive and neuropsychological deficits, including poor performance in working memory, visual perception, and visuospatial abilities (Shalev, 2004). A child may have both a reading and a math disability, and there are cognitive deficits that characterize both types of disabilities, such as poor working memory (Siegel, 2003).

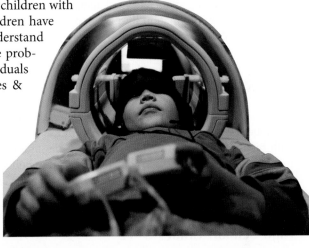

FIGURE 6.2 Brain Scans and Learning Disabilities

An increasing number of studies are using MRI brain scans to examine the brain pathways involved in learning disabilities. Shown here is 9-year-old Patrick Price, who has dyslexia. Patrick is going through an MRI scanner disguised by drapes to look like a child-friendly castle. Inside the scanner, children must lie virtually motionless as words and symbols flash on a screen and they are asked to identify them by clicking different buttons.

Causes and Intervention Strategies   The precise causes of learning disabilities have not yet been determined. However, some possible causes have been proposed. Learning disabilities tend to run in families with one parent having a disability such as dyslexia or dyscalculia, although the specific genetic transmission of learning disabilities is not known (Astrom, Wadsworth, & DeFries, 2007). Also, some learning disabilities are likely caused by problems during prenatal development or delivery. For example, a number of studies have found that learning disabilities are more prevalent in low birth weight infants (Litt & others, 2005).

Researchers also use brain-imaging techniques, such as magnetic resonance imaging (MRI), to reveal any regions of the brain that might be involved in learning disabilities (Shaywitz, Morris, & Shaywitz, 2008) (see Figure 6.2). This research indicates that it is unlikely learning disabilities reside in a single, specific brain location. More likely learning disabilities are due to problems in integrating

dyslexia A severe impairment in the ability to read and spell.

dysgraphia A learning disability that involves difficulty in handwriting.

dyscalculia Also known as developmental arithmetic disorder, this learning disability involves difficulty in math computation.

DEVELOPMENTAL FOCUS 6.1

How Do You Work with Students with a Learning Disability?

Early Childhood

To accommodate our children with learning disabilities, we have them sit close to teachers during work time at craft tables, use more transition warnings so all students clearly know when we are moving to a different activity, and prepare lessons that are visual and hands-on. Having children of different abilities in our school not only benefits the learning of children with disabilities, but it immensely helps their "typically" developing peers to accept others who are not like them.

—Valarie Gorham, *Kiddie Quarters, Inc.*

Elementary School: Grades K–5

Learning disabilities come in all shapes and sizes and require adaptations to ensure that all students reach their full potential. An adaptation that helps a student with ADHD is not an adaptation that will help a student with dyslexia. Some of the adaptations and modifications I use in my class are visuals, modeling, graphic organizers, and mnemonic devices. Many students with learning disabilities have trouble learning information through one sense. Therefore, the more senses you engage while teaching, the more likely the children will learn.

—Shane Schwarz, *Clinton Elementary School*

Middle School: Grades 6–8

When working with students with learning disabilities, I offer assistance with organization (by providing a notebook with color-coded individual folders for each subject); provide a structured classroom setting with high expectations; have private, open discussions concerning specific disabilities with the student; maintain a consistent classroom routine and schedule (students with learning challenges often have difficulty with change); and provide a daily overview of the day.

—Felicia Peterson, *Pocantico Hills School*

High School: Grades 9–12

With high school students, I find it extremely effective to pair the student with a learning disability with a concerned, helpful peer. Sometimes it is necessary to let the peer know what to expect or how to help the other student. However, there is a fine line to walk as you do not want other students to be aware of the student's disability. I also find that books on tape help students with a learning disability master information as does providing extra time to complete tests and quizzes.

—Sandy Swanson, *Menomonee Falls High School*

information from multiple brain regions or subtle difficulties in brain structures and functions (National Institutes of Health, 1993). Using MRI brain scans, researchers have found that two neural pathways in the brain's left hemisphere are among the brain's neural circuitry involved in reading; children with dyslexia have deficiencies in these pathways (Shaywitz, Lyon, & Shaywitz, 2006): (1) in the back of the brain, in the parietal/temporal lobe region of the cerebral cortex, is a sort of phonological module where words are broken down into phonemes before they can be processed by the rest of the brain's language areas; and (2) in the back of the brain, where the occipital and temporal lobes converge, is a second pathway, used by skilled readers, that functions in reading whole words.

Many interventions have focused on improving the child's reading ability (Bender, 2008). Intensive instruction over a period of time by a competent teacher can help

BEST PRACTICES
Strategies for Working with Children Who Have Learning Disabilities

Nancy Downing, teaching in her classroom in Little Rock, Arkansas.

1. *Take the needs of the child with a learning disability into account during instructional time.* Clearly state the objective of each lesson. Present it visually on the board or with an overhead projector as well. Be sure directions are explicit. Explain them orally. Use concrete examples to illustrate abstract concepts.

2. *Provide accommodations for testing and assignments.* This refers to changing the academic environment so that these children can demonstrate what they know. An accommodation usually does not involve altering the amount of learning the child has to demonstrate. Common accommodations include reading instructions to children, highlighting important words (such as underline, or answer two of the three questions), using/giving untimed tests, and extra time on assignments.

3. *Make modifications.* This strategy changes the work itself, making it different from other children's work in an effort to encourage children's confidence and success. Asking a child with dyslexia to give an oral report while other children give written reports is an example of a modification.

4. *Improve organizational and study skills.* Many children with a learning disability do not have good organizational skills. Teachers and parents can encourage them to keep long-term and short-term calendars and create "to-do" lists each day. Projects should be broken down

into their elements, with steps and due dates for each part.

5. *Work with reading and writing skills.* As we indicated earlier, the most common type of learning disability involves reading problems. Children with a reading problem often read slowly, so they need more advance notice of outside reading assignments and more time for in-class reading. Many children with a learning disability that involves writing deficits find that a word processor helps them compose their writing projects more quickly and competently. Next, you can read about how two teachers improved the classroom experiences of students with a learning disability.

THROUGH THE EYES OF TEACHERS
*Creating a Character Named Uey Long
and Using a Team Approach*

Nancy Downing, a second-grade teacher at McDermott Elementary School in Little Rock, Arkansas, takes a multisensory approach to education, which she developed while working with her own child, who has learning difficulties. She created Downfeld Phonics using phonics, sign language, and lively jingles to make learning fun for students. She developed the character Uey Long (a uey is the sign over a short vowel) to demonstrate vowel rules.

6. *Challenge children with a learning disability to become independent and reach their full potential.* It is not only important to provide support and services for children with a learning disability but to also guide them toward becoming responsible and independent. Teachers need to challenge children with a learning disability to become all they can be. We will have more to say about the importance of challenging children with disabilities to reach their potential later in the chapter.

Using these seven main teaching strategies we have described is not meant to give children with a learning disability an unfair advantage, just an equal chance to learn. Balancing the needs of children with learning disabilities and those of other children is a challenging task.

many children (Shaywitz, Morris, & Shaywitz, 2008). For example, a recent brain-imaging study of 15 children with severe reading difficulties who had not shown adequate progress in response to reading instruction in the first grade were given an intensive eight weeks of instruction in phonological decoding skills and then another

Many children with ADHD show impulsive behavior, such as this child who is jumping out of his seat and throwing a paper airplane at other children. *How would you handle this situation if you were a teacher and this were to happen in your classroom?*

intensive eight weeks of word recognition skills (Simos & others, 2007). Significant improvement in a majority of the children's reading skills and changes in brain regions involved in reading occurred as a result of the intensive instruction.

Attention Deficit Hyperactivity Disorder

Matthew has attention deficit hyperactivity disorder, and the outward signs are fairly typical. He has trouble attending to the teacher's instructions and is easily distracted. He can't sit still for more than a few minutes at a time, and his handwriting is messy. His mother describes him as very fidgety.

Characteristics **Attention deficit hyperactivity disorder (ADHD)** is a disability in which children consistently show one or more of these characteristics over a period of time: (1) inattention, (2) hyperactivity, and (3) impulsivity. For an ADHD diagnosis, onset of these characteristics early in childhood is required, and the characteristics must be debilitating for the child.

Inattentive children have difficulty focusing on any one thing and may get bored with a task after only a few minutes. One study found that problems in sustaining attention were the most common type of attentional problem in children with ADHD (Tsal, Shalev, & Mevorach, 2005). Hyperactive children show high levels of physical activity, almost always seeming to be in motion. Impulsive children have difficulty curbing their reactions and don't do a good job of thinking before they act. Depending on the characteristics that children with ADHD display, they can be diagnosed as (1) ADHD with predominantly inattention, (2) ADHD with predominantly hyperactivity/impulsivity, or (3) ADHD with both inattention and hyperactivity/impulsivity.

Diagnosis and Developmental Status The number of children diagnosed and treated for ADHD has increased substantially, by some estimates doubling in the 1990s. A recent national survey found that 7 percent of U.S. children 3 to 17 years of age had ADHD (Bloom & Dey, 2006). The disorder occurs as much as four to nine times more in boys than in girls. There is controversy about the increased diagnosis of ADHD, however (Sciutto & Eisenberg, 2007; Zentall, 2006). Some experts attribute the increase mainly to heightened awareness of the disorder. Others are concerned that many children are being diagnosed without undergoing extensive professional evaluation based on input from multiple sources.

Unlike learning disabilities, ADHD is not supposed to be diagnosed by school teams because ADHD is a disorder that appears in the classification of psychiatric disorders (called DSM-IV) with specific diagnostic criteria (Bender, 2008). Although some school teams may diagnose a child as having ADHD, this is incorrectly done and can lead to legal problems for schools and teachers. One reason that is given as to why a school team should not do the diagnosis for ADHD is that ADHD is difficult to differentiate from other childhood disorders, and accurate diagnosis requires the evaluation by a specialist in the disorder, such as a child psychiatrist.

Although signs of ADHD are often present in the preschool years, children with ADHD are not usually classified until the elementary school years (Zentall, 2006). The increased academic and social demands of formal schooling, as well as stricter standards for behavioral control, often illuminate the problems of the child with ADHD (Daley, 2006). Elementary school teachers typically report that this type of child has difficulty in working independently, completing seat work, and organizing work. Restlessness and distractibility also are often noted. These problems are more likely to be observed in repetitive or difficult tasks, or tasks the child perceives to be boring (such as completing worksheets or doing homework).

It used to be thought that children with ADHD improved during adolescence, but now it appears this often is not the case. Estimates suggest symptoms of ADHD decrease in only about one-third of adolescents. Increasingly, it is being recognized that these problems may continue into adulthood (Miller, Nigg, & Faraone, 2007).

attention deficit hyperactivity disorder (ADHD) A disability in which children consistently show one or more of the following characteristics over a period of time: (1) inattention, (2) hyperactivity, and (3) impulsivity.

DEVELOPMENTAL FOCUS 6.2

How Do You Work with Students with ADHD?

Early Childhood

Our preschoolers who have been diagnosed with ADHD work well within a very structured environment. Although our ADHD students are treated just like any other student in the classroom, we take care to give them ample physical activity and sometimes receive extra time to gather their thoughts and calm down by taking a few deep breaths. If necessary, medication is given as prescribed by a pediatrician.

—Missy Dangler, *Suburban Hills School*

Elementary School: Grades K–5

I find that frequent breaks (such as asking the student to bring something to the school secretary or to put something away) helps give the child an opportunity to move a bit and then refocus. In second grade, we play a lot of singing and movement games (such as "Simon Says") in the room between lessons, or when I see at lot of "itchiness." All of these games/songs allow standing up, moving, and singing or laughing and provide stretching and body awareness, which can help a child with ADHD to focus. Also, I don't have a problem with a child lying on the floor to work or standing at a desk, if that is how the child needs to focus. This is okay as long as the child is not bothering anyone else and completing the task at hand.

—Janine Guida Poutre, *Clinton Elementary School*

Middle School: Grades 6–8

Working with ADHD students requires organization and planning. My ADHD students sit in a strategic location in the room. I usually pick a spot that allows them freedom to get up and move around if necessary. I also make sure that these students sit where I can easily access them. And I give directions clearly and ask the ADHD students to repeat the directions to me to make sure that they not only are listening but also understand.

—Casey Maass, *Edison Middle School*

High School: Grades 9–12

One of my biggest challenges in teaching is working with untreated ADHD students. One thing I do with my ADHD students is to sit them in the front row. I may touch the student's shoulder as I walk by or gently knock on the desk to refocus the student's attention. When I am walking about the room, I will "loop" back to the student's desk or quietly ask for directions to be repeated back to me. I often check their assignment books to make sure that homework assignments are written down correctly. Of course, communication with parents also is very important.

—Jennifer Heiter, *Bremen High School*

Causes and Treatment   Definitive causes of ADHD have not been found. However, a number of causes have been proposed (Biederman, 2007; Stein & others, 2007). Some children likely inherit a tendency to develop ADHD from their parents (Goos, Ezzatian, & Schachar, 2007; Lasky-Su & others, 2007). Other children likely develop ADHD because of damage to their brain during prenatal or postnatal development (Banerjee, Middleton, & Faraone, 2007; Thompson, Moore, & Symons, 2007). Among early possible contributors to ADHD are cigarette and alcohol exposure during prenatal development and low birth weight (Greydanus, Pratt, & Patel, 2007; Neuman & others, 2007).

As with learning disabilities, the development of brain-imaging techniques is leading to a better understanding of the brain's role in ADHD (Shaw & others, 2007).

Prefrontal Cortex   Prefrontal Cortex

□ Greater than 2 years delay

□ 0 to 2 years delay

FIGURE 6.3 Regions of the Brain in Which Children with ADHD Had a Delayed Peak in the Thickness of the Cerebral Cortex

Note: The greatest delays occurred in the prefrontal cortex.

A recent study revealed that peak thickness of the cerebral cortex occurred three years later (10.5 years) in children with ADHD than children without ADHD (peak at 7.5 years) (Shaw & others, 2007). The delay was more prominent in the prefrontal regions of the brain that especially are important in attention and planning (see Figure 6.3).

Stimulant medication such as Ritalin or Adderall is effective in improving the attention of many children with ADHD, but it usually does not improve their attention to the same level as children who do not have ADHD (Barbaresi & others, 2006; Pliszka, 2007). Researchers have often found that a combination of medication (such as Ritalin) and behavior management improves the behavior of children with ADHD better than medication alone or behavior management alone, although not in all cases (Chronis & others, 2004; Jensen & others, 2007). Other drugs, such as the stimulant called mixed amphetamine salts extended release (MAS XR) and the nonstimulant Strattera, are currently being studied in the treatment of children with ADHD, and early findings involving these drugs are promising (Bhatara & Aparasu, 2007; Faraone, 2007).

Teachers play an important role in monitoring whether ADHD medication has been prescribed at the right dosage level. For example, it is not unusual for a student on ADHD medication to complete academic tasks in the morning, but in the afternoon, when the dosage has worn off, to be inattentive or hyperactive (Thompson, Moore, & Symons, 2007).

Critics argue that many physicians are too quick to prescribe stimulants for children with milder forms of ADHD (Marcovitch, 2004). Also, in 2006, the U.S. government issued a warning about the cardiovascular risks of stimulant medication to treat ADHD.

BEST PRACTICES
Strategies for Working with Children Who Have ADHD

1. *Monitor whether the child's stimulant medication is working effectively.*

2. *Repeat and simplify instructions about in-class and home-work assignments.*

3. *Involve a special education resource teacher.*

4. *State clear expectations and give the child immediate feedback.*

5. *Use behavior management strategies, especially providing positive feedback for progress.* We will discuss these approaches in considerable detail in Chapter 7, "Behavioral and Social Cognitive Approaches."

6. *Provide structure and teacher-direction.* In many instances, a structured learning environment benefits children with ADHD. Next, Joanna Smith, a high school English teacher, describes how she arranges her classroom to accommodate students with ADHD.

THROUGH THE EYES OF TEACHERS
*Structuring the Classroom
to Benefit Students with ADHD*

I have found success with these students when I seat them in the front row, make instructions explicit, break down larger tasks into smaller ones, write necessary information on the board and point out exactly where it is, allow extra time on tests (as specified on his or her plan), and check in with the students frequently. This frequent contact allows me to know how the student is doing, how much he understands, and gives him a welcomed opportunity to chat.

7. *Provide opportunities for students to get up and move around.*

8. *Break assignments into shorter segments.*

Mental Retardation

Increasingly, children with mental retardation are being taught in the regular classroom (Hodapp & Dykens, 2006). The most distinctive feature of mental retardation is inadequate intellectual functioning (Friend, 2008). Long before formal tests were developed to assess intelligence, individuals with mental retardation were identified by a lack of age-appropriate skills in learning and in caring for themselves. Once intelligence tests were created, numbers were assigned to indicate how mild or severe the retardation was. A child might be only mildly retarded and able to learn in the regular classroom or severely retarded and unable to learn in that setting.

In addition to low intelligence, deficits in adaptive behavior and early onset also are included in the definition of mental retardation (Copeland & Luckasson, 2008). Adaptive skills include skills needed for self-care and social responsibility such as dressing, toileting, feeding, self-control, and peer interaction. By definition, **mental retardation** is a condition with an onset before age 18 that involves low intelligence (usually below 70 on a traditional individually administered intelligence test) and difficulty in adapting to everyday life. For an individual to be given a diagnosis of mental retardation, the low IQ and low adaptiveness should be evident in childhood, not following a long period of normal functioning that is interrupted by an accident or other type of assault on the brain.

Classification and Types of Mental Retardation   As indicated in Figure 6.4, mental retardation is classified as mild, moderate, severe, or profound. Approximately 89 percent of students with mental retardation fall into the mild category. By late adolescence, individuals with mild mental retardation can be expected to develop academic skills at approximately the sixth-grade level. In their adult years, many can hold jobs and live on their own with some supportive supervision or in group homes. Individuals with more severe mental retardation require more support.

If you have a student with mental retardation in your classroom, the degree of retardation is likely to be mild. Children with severe mental retardation are more likely to also show signs of other neurological complications, such as cerebral palsy, epilepsy, hearing impairment, visual impairment, or other metabolic birth defects that affect the central nervous system (Terman & others, 1996).

Most school systems still use the classifications mild, moderate, severe, and profound. However, because these categorizations based on IQ ranges aren't perfect predictors of functioning, the American Association on Mental Retardation (1992) developed a new classification system based on the degree of support children require to function at their highest level (Hallahan & Kauffman, 2006). As shown in Figure 6.5, the categories used are intermittent, limited, extensive, and pervasive.

Determinants   Genetic factors, brain damage, and environmental factors are key determinants of mental retardation. Let's explore genetic causes first.

Genetic Factors   The most commonly identified form of mental retardation is **Down syndrome**, which is genetically transmitted. Children with Down syndrome have an extra (47th) chromosome (Tartaglia, Hansen, & Hagerman, 2007). They have a round face, a flattened skull, an extra fold of skin over the eyelids, a protruding tongue, short limbs, and retardation of motor and mental abilities. It is not known why the extra chromosome is present, but the health of the male sperm or female ovum might be involved (Nokelainen & Flint, 2002). Women between the ages of 18 and 38 are far less likely than younger or older women to give birth to a child with Down syndrome. Down syndrome appears in about 1 in every 700 live births. African American children are rarely born with Down syndrome.

With early intervention and extensive support from the child's family and professionals, many children with Down syndrome can grow into independent adults (Taylor, Brady, & Richards, 2005). Children with Down syndrome can fall into the mild to severe retardation categories (Terman & others, 1996).

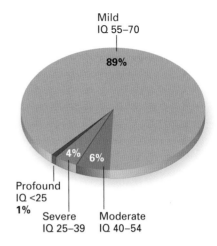

FIGURE 6.4 Classification of Mental Retardation Based on IQ

A child with Down syndrome. *What causes a child to develop Down syndrome?*

mental retardation A condition with an onset before age 18 that involves low intelligence (usually below 70 on a traditional individually administered intelligence test) and difficulty in adapting to everyday life.

Down syndrome A genetically transmitted form of mental retardation due to an extra (47th) chromosome.

FIGURE 6.5 Classification of Mental Retardation Based on Levels of Support

Intermittent	Supports are provided "as needed." The individual may need episodic or short-term support during life-span transitions (such as job loss or acute medical crisis). Intermittent supports may be low- or high-intensity when provided.
Limited	Supports are intense and relatively consistent over time. They are time-limited but not intermittent. They require fewer staff members and cost less than more-intense supports. These supports likely will be needed for adaptation to the changes involved in the school-to-adult period.
Extensive	Supports are characterized by regular involvement (for example, daily) in at least some setting (such as home or work) and are not time-limited (for example, extended home-living support).
Pervasive	Supports are constant, very intense, and are provided across settings. They may be of a life-sustaining nature. These supports typically involve more staff members and intrusiveness than the other support categories.

Brain Damage and Environmental Factors Brain damage can result from many different infections and environmental hazards (Hodapp & Dykens, 2006). Infections in the pregnant mother-to-be, such as rubella (German measles), syphilis, herpes, and AIDS, can cause retardation in the child. Meningitis and encephalitis are infections that can develop in childhood. They cause inflammation in the brain and can produce mental retardation. Environmental hazards that can result in mental retardation include blows to the head, malnutrition, poisoning, birth injury, and alcoholism or heavy drinking on the part of the pregnant woman (Berine-Smith, Patton, & Kim, 2006).

BEST PRACTICES
Strategies for Working with Children Who Are Mentally Retarded

During the school years, the main goals often are to teach children with mental retardation basic educational skills such as reading and mathematics, as well as vocational skills (Boyles & Contadino, 1997). Here are some positive teaching strategies for interacting with children who have mental retardation:

1. *Help children who are mentally retarded to practice making personal choices and to engage in self-determination when possible.*

2. *Always keep in mind the child's level of mental functioning.* Children who have mental retardation will be at a considerably lower level of mental functioning than most other students in your class. If you start at one level of instruction, and the child is not responding effectively, move to a lower level.

3. *Individualize your instruction to meet the child's needs.*

4. *As with other children with a disability, make sure that you give concrete examples of concepts.* Make your instructions clear and simple.

5. *Give these children opportunities to practice what they have learned.* Have them repeat steps a number of times and overlearn a concept to retain it.

6. *Have positive expectations for the child's learning.* It is easy to fall into the trap of thinking that the child with mental retardation cannot achieve academically. Set a goal to maximize his or her learning.

7. *Look for resource support.* Use teacher aides and recruit volunteers such as sensitive retirees to help you educate children with mental retardation. They can assist you in increasing the amount of one-on-one instruction the child receives.

8. *Consider using applied behavior analysis strategies.* Some teachers report that these strategies improve children's self-maintenance, social, and academic skills. If you are interested in using these strategies, consult a resource such as *Applied Behavior Analysis for Teachers*, by Paul Alberto and Anne Troutman (2006). The precise steps involved in applied behavior analysis can especially help you use positive reinforcement effectively with children who have mental retardation.

Physical Disorders

Physical disorders in children include orthopedic impairments, such as cerebral palsy, and seizure disorders. Many children with physical disorders require special education and related services, such as transportation, physical therapy, school health services, and psychological services (Gargiulo, 2009; Heller & others, 2009).

Orthopedic Impairments **Orthopedic impairments** involve restricted movement or lack of control over movement due to muscle, bone, or joint problems. The severity of problems ranges widely. Orthopedic impairments can be caused by prenatal or perinatal problems, or they can be due to disease or accident during the childhood years. With the help of adaptive devices and medical technology, many children with orthopedic impairments function well in the classroom (Hallahan, Kauffman, & Pullen, 2009).

Cerebral palsy is a disorder that involves a lack of muscular coordination, shaking, or unclear speech. The most common cause of cerebral palsy is lack of oxygen at birth. Special computers especially can help children with cerebral palsy to learn.

Seizure Disorders The most common seizure disorder is **epilepsy**, a neurological disorder characterized by recurring sensorimotor attacks or movement convulsions. Children who experience seizures are usually treated with one or more anticonvulsant medications, which often are effective in reducing the seizures but do not always eliminate them. When they are not having a seizure, students with epilepsy show normal behavior. If you have a child in your class who has a seizure disorder, become well acquainted with the procedures for monitoring and helping the child during a seizure (Heller & others, 2009).

Sensory Disorders

Sensory disorders include visual and hearing impairments. Visual impairments include the need for corrective lenses, low vision, and being educationally blind. Children who are hearing impaired can be born deaf or experience a loss in hearing as they develop.

Visual Impairments A small portion of students (about 1 in every 1,000 students) have very serious visual problems and are classified as visually impaired. This includes students who have low vision and students who are blind. Children with *low vision* have a visual acuity of between 20/70 and 20/200 (on the familiar Snellen scale, in which 20/20 vision is normal) with corrective lenses. Children with low vision can read large-print books or regular books with the aid of a magnifying glass. Children who are *educationally blind* cannot use their vision in learning and must rely on their hearing and touch to learn. Approximately 1 in every 3,000 children is educationally blind. Many children who are educationally blind have normal intelligence and function very well academically with appropriate supports and learning aids.

An important task in working with a child who has visual impairments is to determine the modality (such as touch or hearing) through which the child learns best. Seating in the front of the class often benefits the child with a visual impairment.

THROUGH THE EYES OF STUDENTS

It's Okay to Be Different

Why me? I often ask myself, why did I have to be the one? Why did I get picked to be different? It took more than ten years for me to find answers and to realize that I'm not *more* different than anyone else. My twin sister was born with no birth defects, but I was born with cerebral palsy.

People thought I was stupid because it was hard for me to write my own name. So when I was the only one in the class to use a typewriter, I began to feel I was different. It got worse when the third-graders moved on to the fourth grade and I had to stay behind. I got held back because the teachers thought I'd be unable to type fast enough to keep up. Kids told me that was a lie and the reason I got held back was because I was a retard. It really hurt to be teased by those I thought were my friends. . . .

I have learned that no one was to blame for my disability. I realize that I can do things and that I can do them very well. Some things I can't do, like taking my own notes in class or running in a race, but I will have to live with that. . . .

There are times when I wish I had not been born with cerebral palsy, but crying isn't going to do me any good. I can only live once, so I want to live the best I can. . . . Nobody else can be the Angela Marie Erickson who is writing this. I could never be, or ever want to be, anyone else.

Angie Erickson
Ninth-Grade Student
Wayzata, Minnesota

orthopedic impairments Restricted movements or lack of control of movements, due to muscle, bone, or joint problems.

cerebral palsy A disorder that involves a lack of muscle coordination, shaking, or unclear speech.

epilepsy A neurological disorder characterized by recurring sensorimotor attacks or movement convulsions.

BEST PRACTICES
Strategies for Working with Children Who Have a Hearing Impairment

1. *Be patient.*

2. *Speak normally (not too slowly or too quickly).*

3. *Don't shout, because this doesn't help.* Speaking distinctly is more helpful.

4. *Reduce distractions and background noises.*

5. *Face the student to whom you are speaking, because the student needs to read your lips and see your gestures.*

THROUGH THE EYES OF STUDENTS

Eyes Closed

In kindergarten, children truly begin to appreciate, not fear or think strange, each other's differences. A few years ago, a child in my kindergarten class was walking down the hall with his eyes closed and ran into the wall. When I asked him what he was doing, he said, "I was just trying to do like Darrick. How come he does it so much better?" Darrick is his classmate who is legally blind. He wanted to experience what it was like to be blind. In this case, imitation truly was the greatest form of flattery.

Anita Marie Hitchcock
Kindergarten Teacher
Holle Navarre Primary
Santa Rosa County, Florida

For over half a century, recorded textbooks from Recording for the Blind & Dyslexic have contributed to the educational progress of students with visual, perceptual, or other disabilities. More than 90,000 volumes of these audio and computerized books are available at no charge (phone: 1-866-732-3585).

Hearing Impairments   A hearing impairment can make learning very difficult for children (Soukup & Feinstein, 2007). Children who are born deaf or experience a significant hearing loss in the first several years of life usually do not develop normal speech and language. You also might have some children in your class who have hearing impairments that have not yet been detected (Gargiulo, 2009). If you have students who turn one ear toward a speaker, frequently ask to have something repeated, don't follow directions, or frequently complain of earaches, colds, and allergies, consider having the student's hearing evaluated by a specialist, such as an audiologist.

Many children with hearing impairments receive supplementary instruction beyond the regular classroom. Educational approaches to help students with hearing impairments learn fall into two categories: oral and manual. *Oral approaches* include using lip reading, speech reading (a reliance on visual cues to teach reading), and whatever hearing the student has. *Manual approaches* involve sign language and finger spelling. Sign language is a system of hand movements that symbolize words. Finger spelling consists of "spelling out" each word by signing each letter of a word. Oral and manual approaches are increasingly used together for students who are hearing impaired (Hallahan & Kauffman, 2006). Medical and technological advances, such as cochlear implants and tubes placed in the child's ears, hearing aids, and telecommunication devices (such as a teletypewriter-telephone) also have improved the learning of children with hearing impairments.

Speech and Language Disorders

Speech and language disorders include a number of speech problems (such as articulation disorders, voice disorders, and fluency disorders) and language problems (difficulties in receiving information and expressing language) (Norbury, Tomblin, & Bishop, 2008). Approximately 17 percent of all children who receive special education services have a speech or language impairment (National Center for Education Statistics, 2006).

Articulation Disorders   **Articulation disorders** are problems in pronouncing sounds correctly. A child's articulation at 6 or 7 years is still not always error-free, but it should be by age 8. A child with an articulation problem might find communication with peers and the teacher difficult or embarrassing. As a result, the child might avoid asking questions, participating in discussions, or communicating

speech and language disorders A number of speech problems (such as articulation disorders, voice disorders, and fluency disorders) and language problems (difficulties in receiving information and expressing language).

articulation disorders Problems in pronouncing sounds correctly.

with peers. Articulation problems can usually be improved or resolved with speech therapy, though it might take months or years (Dunkelberger, 2008).

Voice Disorders   **Voice disorders** are reflected in speech that is hoarse, harsh, too loud, too high-pitched, or too low-pitched. Children with cleft palate often have a voice disorder that makes their speech difficult to understand. If a child speaks in a way that is consistently difficult to understand, refer the child to a speech therapist.

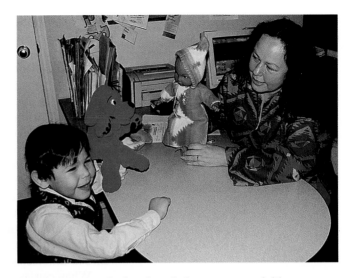

Speech therapist Sharla Peltier, helping a young child improve her language and communication skills. *What are some different types of speech problems children can have?*

Fluency Disorders   **Fluency disorders** often involve what is commonly called "stuttering." Stuttering occurs when a child's speech has a spasmodic hesitation, prolongation, or repetition (Ratner, 2005). The anxiety many children feel because they stutter often just makes their stuttering worse. Speech therapy is recommended (Kuder, 2009).

Language Disorders   **Language disorders** include a significant impairment in a child's receptive or expressive language. **Receptive language** involves the reception and understanding of language. **Expressive language** involves using language for expressing one's thoughts and communicating with others. Language disorders can result in significant learning problems (Kuder, 2009; Skarakis-Doyle, 2008). Treatment by a language therapist generally produces improvement in the child with a language disorder, but the problem usually is not eradicated. Language disorders include difficulties in phrasing questions properly to get the desired information, following oral directions, following conversation, especially when it is rapid and complex, and understanding and using words correctly in sentences.

Specific Language Impairment   **Specific language impairment (SLI)** involves language development problems with no other obvious physical, sensory, or emotional difficulties (Conti-Ramsden, 2008; Monaco, 2008). In some cases, the disorder is referred to as *developmental language disorder.*

Children with SLI have problems in understanding and using words in sentences (Pennington & Bishop, 2009). One indicator of SLI in 5-year-old children is their incomplete understanding of verbs (Leonard, 2007; Proctor-Williams & Fey, 2007). They typically drop the *–s* from verb tenses (such as "She walk to the store" instead of "She walks to the store") and ask questions without "be" or "do" verbs (rather than saying "Does he live there?" the child will say "He live there?"). (Marinis & van der Lely, 2007). These characteristics make children with specific language impairment sound like children who are approximately two years younger than they are.

Early identification of SLI is important and can usually be accurately accomplished by 5 years of age and in some cases earlier. Intervention includes modeling correct utterances, rephrasing the child's incorrect utterances during conversation, and reading instruction (Ratner, 2009; Snowling, 2008). Parents may also wish to send a child with SRI to a speech or language pathologist (Kuder, 2009).

Autism Spectrum Disorders

Autism spectrum disorders (ASD), also called pervasive developmental disorders, range from the severe disorder labeled *autistic disorder* to the milder disorder called *Asperger syndrome.* Autism spectrum disorders are characterized by problems in social interaction, problems in verbal and nonverbal communication, and repetitive behaviors (Boucher, 2009; Hall, 2009; Simpson & LaCava, 2008).

voice disorders Disorders producing speech that is hoarse, harsh, too loud, too high-pitched, or too low-pitched.

fluency disorders Disorders that often involve what is commonly referred to as "stuttering."

language disorders Significant impairments in a child's receptive or expressive language.

receptive language The reception and understanding of language.

expressive language The ability to use language to express one's thoughts and communicate with others.

specific language impairment (SLI) Involves problems in language development that are not accompanied by other obvious physical, sensory, or emotional problems; in some cases, the disorder is called developmental language disorder.

autism spectrum disorders (ASD) Also called pervasive developmental disorders, they range from the severe disorder labeled autistic disorder to the milder disorder called Asperger syndrome. Children with these disorders are characterized by problems in social interaction, verbal and nonverbal communication, and repetitive behaviors.

The boy sitting on the sofa has autistic disorder. *What are some characteristics of children with autistic disorder?*

autistic disorder A severe developmental autism spectrum disorder that has its onset in the first three years of life and includes deficiencies in social relationships, abnormalities in communication, and restricted, repetitive, and stereotyped patterns of behavior.

Asperger syndrome A relatively mild autism spectrum disorder in which the child has relatively good verbal language, milder nonverbal language problems, a restricted range of interests and relationships, and often engages in repetitive routines.

emotional and behavioral disorders Serious, persistent problems that involve relationships, aggression, depression, fears associated with personal or school matters, and other inappropriate socioemotional characteristics.

Children with these disorders may also show atypical responses to sensory experiences. Autism spectrum disorders can often be detected in children as early as 1 to 3 years of age.

Autistic disorder is a severe developmental autism spectrum disorder that has its onset in the first three years of life and includes deficiencies in social relationships, abnormalities in communication, and restricted, repetitive, and stereotyped patterns of behavior. Estimates indicate that approximately 2 to 5 of every 10,000 young children in the United States have an autistic disorder. Boys are about four times more likely to have an autistic disorder than girls.

Asperger syndrome is a relatively mild autism spectrum disorder in which the child has relatively good verbal language, milder nonverbal language problems, and a restricted range of interests and relationships (Bennett & others, 2008; Lewis, Murdoch, & Woodyatt, 2007). Children with Asperger syndrome often engage in obsessive repetitive routines and preoccupations with a particular subject (South, Ozofnoff, & McMahon, 2005). For example, a child may be obsessed with baseball scores or railroad timetables.

What causes the autism spectrum disorders? The current consensus is that autism is a brain dysfunction with abnormalities in brain structure and neurotransmitters (Boucher, 2009). Genetic factors likely play a role in the development of the autism spectrum disorders (Herman & others, 2007; Katzov, 2007). A recent study revealed that mutations—missing or duplicated pieces of DNA on chromosome 16—can raise a child's risk of developing autism 100-fold (Weiss & others, 2008). Estimates are that approximately 1 million U.S. children have an autistic disorder, so about 10,000 of them have this genetic mutation. There is no evidence that family socialization causes autism (Rutter & Schopler, 1987). Mental retardation is present in some children with autism; others show average or above-average intelligence (McCarthy, 2007).

Children with autism benefit from a well-structured classroom, individualized instruction, and small-group instruction (Pueschel & others, 1995). As with children who are mentally retarded, behavior modification techniques are sometimes effective in helping autistic children learn (Alberto & Troutman, 2006; Hall, 2009).

Emotional and Behavioral Disorders

Most children have emotional problems sometime during their school years. A small percentage have problems so serious and persistent that they are classified as having an emotional or a behavioral disorder (Gargiulo, 2009; Kauffman & Landrum, 2009). **Emotional and behavioral disorders** consist of serious, persistent problems that involve relationships, aggression, depression, fears associated with personal or school matters, and other inappropriate socioemotional characteristics. Approximately 7 percent of children who have a disability and require an individualized education plan fall into this classification. Boys are three times as likely as girls to have these disorders (National Center for Education Statistics, 2003).

Various terms have been used to describe emotional and behavioral disorders, including *emotional disturbances, behavior disorders,* and *maladjusted children.* The term *emotional disturbance (ED)* recently has been used to describe children with these types of problems for whom it has been necessary to create individualized learning plans. However, critics argue that this category has not been clearly defined (Council for Exceptional Children, 1998).

Aggressive, Out-of-Control Behaviors Some children classified as having a serious emotional disturbance engage in disruptive, aggressive, defiant, or dangerous behaviors and are removed from the classroom. These children are much more likely to be boys than girls and more likely to come from low-income than from middle- or high-income families (Dodge, Coie, & Lynam, 2006). When these children are returned to the regular classroom, both the regular classroom teacher and a special education teacher or consultant must spend a great deal of time helping them adapt and learn effectively.

In Chapter 3, we discussed rejected students and improving students' social skills (Rubin, Bukowski, & Parker, 2006). Many of the comments and recommendations we made there apply to children with a serious emotional disturbance. In Chapter 7, "Behavioral and Social Cognitive Approaches," and Chapter 14, "Managing the Classroom," we will discuss more strategies and plans for effectively dealing with children who show emotional and behavioral problems.

Depression, Anxiety, and Fears   Some children turn their emotional problems inward. Their depression, anxiety, or fears become so intense and persistent that their ability to learn is significantly compromised. All children feel depressed from time to time, but most get over their despondent, down mood in a few hours or a few days. For some children, however, the negative mood is more serious and longer lasting. *Depression* is a type of mood disorder in which the individual feels worthless, believes that things are not likely to get better, and behaves lethargically for a prolonged period of time. When children show these signs for two weeks or longer, they likely are experiencing depression. Having a poor appetite and not being able to sleep well also can be associated with depression.

Depression is much more likely to appear in adolescence than in childhood and has a much higher incidence in girls than in boys (Nolen-Hoeksema, 2007). Experts on depression say that this gender difference is likely due to a number of factors. Females tend to ruminate on their depressed mood and amplify it, whereas males tend to distract themselves from the negative mood; girls' self-images are often more negative than those of boys during adolescence; and societal bias against female achievement might be involved (Nolen-Hoeksema, 2007).

Because it is turned inward, depression is far more likely to go unnoticed than aggressive, acting-out behaviors. If you think that a child has become depressed, have the child meet with the school counselor (Kauffman & Landrum, 2009).

Anxiety involves a vague, highly unpleasant feeling of fear and apprehension. It is normal for children to be concerned or worried when they face life's challenges, but some children have such intense and prolonged anxiety that it substantially impairs their school performance (Rapee, Hudson, & Schniering, 2009). Some children also have personal or school-related fears that interfere with their learning. If a child shows marked or substantial fears that persist, have the child see the school counselor. More information about anxiety appears in Chapter 13, "Motivation, Teaching, and Learning."

At this point, we have explored many different disabilities and disorders. To evaluate your experiences with people who have these disabilities and disorders, complete *Self-Assessment 6.1.*

What are some characteristics of students who show aggressive, out-of-control behaviors?

What are some characteristics of students who are depressed?

SELF-ASSESSMENT 6.1

Evaluating My Experiences with People Who Have Various Disabilities and Disorders

Read each of these statements and place a check mark next to the ones that apply to you.

1. Learning Disabilities

_____ I know someone who has a learning disability and have talked with him or her about the disability.

_____ I have observed students with learning disabilities in the classroom and talked with teachers about their strategies for educating them.

2. Attention Deficit Hyperactivity Disorder

_____ I know someone with ADHD and have talked with him or her about the disability.

_____ I have observed students with ADHD in the classroom and talked with teachers about their strategies for educating them.

3. Mental Retardation

_____ I know someone who has mental retardation and have talked with his or her parents about their child's disability.

_____ I have observed students with mental retardation in the classroom and talked with their teachers about their strategies for educating them.

4. Physical Disorders

_____ I know someone with a physical disorder and have talked with him or her about the disability.

_____ I have observed students with physical disorders in the classroom and talked with their teachers about strategies for educating them.

5. Sensory Disorders

_____ I know someone with a sensory disorder and have talked with him or her about the disability.

_____ I have observed students with sensory disorders in the classroom and talked with their teachers about their strategies for educating them.

6. Speech and Language Disorders

_____ I know someone with a speech and language disorder and have talked with him or her about the disability.

_____ I have observed students with a speech and language disorder in the classroom and talked with their teacher about strategies for educating them.

7. Autism Spectrum Disorders

_____ I know someone with an autism spectrum disorder.

_____ I have observed students with an autism spectrum disorder in the classroom and talked with their teachers about strategies for educating them.

8. Emotional and Behavioral Disorders

_____ I know someone with an emotional and behavioral disorder and have talked with him or her about the disorder.

_____ I have observed students with emotional and behavioral disorders and talked with their teachers about strategies for educating them.

For those disabilities that you did not place a check mark beside, make it a point to get to know and talk with someone who has the disability and observe students with the disability in the classroom. Then talk with their teachers about their strategies for educating them.

Review, Reflect, and Practice

① **Describe the various types of disabilities and disorders.**

REVIEW

- What is the definition of a learning disability? What are some common learning disabilities? How are they identified? How are they best treated?
- What is attention deficit hyperactivity disorder? What are some important aspects of attention deficit hyperactivity disorder for teachers to know?
- What is the nature of mental retardation?
- What types of physical disorders in children are teachers likely to see?
- What are some common visual and hearing sensory disorders in children?
- What are the differences among articulation, voice, fluency, and language disorders?
- What characterizes autism spectrum disorders?
- What are the main types of emotional and behavioral disorders?

REFLECT

- Considering the age group of children and the subject that you plan to teach, which of the disabilities that we have discussed do you think will present the most difficulty for your teaching? Where should you focus your attention in learning more about this disability?

PRAXIS™ PRACTICE

1. Marty is in the fourth grade. Intelligence tests indicate that he is of average to above-average intelligence. However, his grades in reading, social studies, spelling, and science are very low. His math grades, on the other hand, are quite high and his writing skills are adequate. Achievement tests indicate that he reads at the first-grade level. When he reads aloud, it is apparent that he has difficulty matching sounds and letters. Marty most likely has
   a. ADHD.
   b. dyscalculia.
   c. dyslexia.
   d. dysgraphia.

2. Which of the following classroom environments is most likely to help students with ADHD achieve?
   a. Ms. Caster's class, which is very loosely structured so that students will only have to attend to something for a short period of time.
   b. Ms. Dodge's class, which is tightly structured and has explicit expectations. Student learning is often supplemented with computer games and physical activity.
   c. Ms. Ebert's class, in which students are expected to sit still for extended periods of time, working independently on seatwork.
   d. Ms. Fish's class, in which students work at their own pace on self-selected tasks and receive sporadic feedback regarding their progress and behavior.

3. Marci is a White non-Latino with mild mental retardation. In addition to cognitive deficits, she has poor motor skills. Her legs and arms are shorter than average. She has a round face, with an extra fold of skin over her eyelids. Her tongue protrudes. What is most likely the cause of Marci's mental retardation?
   a. Down syndrome
   b. fetal alcohol spectrum disorders
   c. fragile X syndrome
   d. maternal illness during pregnancy

(continued)

Review, Reflect, and Practice

PRAXIS™ PRACTICE (CONTINUED)

4. Mark is a middle school student in Ms. Walsh's language-arts class. She observes that Mark often stares out the window. Sometimes calling his name redirects his attention to her; at times he continues to stare out the window for several seconds and appears oblivious to Ms. Walsh's reprimands. Mark's grades are suffering as a result of his inattention. What is the most likely explanation for Mark's inattention?
   a. ADHD
   b. absence seizure disorder
   c. tonic-clonic epilepsy
   d. cerebral palsy

5. Amiel's first-grade teacher notices that he squints a lot and holds books close to his face. Amiel most likely has which of the following disorders?
   a. physical disorder
   b. speech and language disorder
   c. sensory disorder
   d. autism spectrum disorder

6. Carrie's third-grade teacher, Ms. Brown, often gets frustrated when Carrie tries to answer questions in class. Carrie takes a long time to answer. Her sentence structure is not as good as that of other students in her class, and she often presents ideas in what sounds like a random manner. Ms. Brown should suspect that Carrie has
   a. articulation disorder.
   b. expressive language disorder.
   c. receptive language disorder.
   d. specific language impairment.

7. Mike is a seventh-grade boy of above-average intelligence. He has good language skills but does not interact well with other young adolescents. He has one friend and responds well to his mother and to the aide who works with him, although he shies away from contact with other people. He does fairly well in school, as long as his routine is not disrupted. He especially enjoys math and anything to do with numbers. He has memorized the batting averages of the starting line-up of all major league baseball teams. Mike most likely has
   a. autistic disorder.
   b. Asperger syndrome.
   c. behavioral disorder.
   d. specific language disorder.

8. Which middle school student is at greatest risk of developing a serious emotional disturbance?
   a. Jill, the most popular girl in the seventh grade, who sometimes says demeaning things to less popular girls
   b. Kevin, an eighth-grader who gets good grades in most subjects, has difficulty interacting with classmates, and has memorized all of Shakespeare's sonnets
   c. Harriet, a sixth-grade girl whose ADHD symptoms are controlled well by medication
   d. Mark, a seventh-grade boy who gets poor grades in many classes and frequently acts out in angry, violent ways

Please see the answer key at the end of the book.

② EDUCATIONAL ISSUES INVOLVING CHILDREN WITH DISABILITIES

```
        ┌─────────────┐      ┌──────────────┐
        │ Legal Aspects │      │  Technology   │
        └─────────────┘      └──────────────┘
```

Public schools are legally required to serve all children with disabilities in the least restrictive environment possible. We will explore the legal aspects of working with children who have a disability and examine the role of technology in educating children with a disability.

Legal Aspects

Beginning in the mid-1960s to mid-1970s, legislatures, the federal courts, and the U.S. Congress laid down special educational rights for children with disabilities. Prior to that time, most children with disabilities were either refused enrollment or inadequately served by schools. In 1975, Congress enacted **Public Law 94-142**, the Education for All Handicapped Children Act, which required that all students with disabilities be given a free, appropriate public education and which provided the funding to help implement this education.

Individuals with Disabilities Education Act (IDEA)   In 1990, Public Law 94-142 was recast as the **Individuals with Disabilities Education Act (IDEA).** IDEA was amended in 1997 and then reauthorized in 2004 and renamed the Individuals with Disabilities Education Improvement Act. IDEA spells out broad mandates for services to all children with disabilities (Hallahan, Kauffman, & Pullen, 2009). These include evaluation and eligibility determination, appropriate education and an individualized education plan (IEP), and education in the least restrictive environment (LRE) (Taylor, Smiley, & Richards, 2009).

Children who are thought to have a disability are evaluated to determine their eligibility for services under IDEA. Schools are prohibited from planning special education programs in advance and offering them on a space-available basis. In other words, schools must provide appropriate education services to all children who are determined to need them (Bryant, Smith, & Bryant, 2008).

Children must be evaluated and diagnosed with a disability or other health impairment before a school can begin providing special services. However, because an assessment can take a long time, variations of prereferral interventions are in place in many schools. Parents must be invited to participate in the evaluation process. Reevaluation is required at least every three years (sometimes every year), when requested by parents, or when conditions suggest a reevaluation is needed. A parent who disagrees with the school's evaluation can obtain an independent evaluation, which the school is required to consider in providing special education services. If the evaluation finds that child has a disability and requires special services, the school must provide the child with appropriate services.

IDEA requires that students with disabilities have an **individualized education plan (IEP)**. An IEP is a written statement that spells out a program specifically tailored for the student with a disability. In general, the IEP should be (1) related to the child's learning capacity, (2) specially constructed to meet the child's individual needs and not merely copy what is offered to other children, and (3) designed to provide educational benefits.

IDEA has many other specific provisions that relate to the parents of a child with a disability (Smith & others, 2008). These include requirements that schools send notices to parents of proposed actions, that parents be allowed to attend meetings regarding the child's placement or individualized education plan, and that parents have the right to appeal school decisions to an impartial evaluator.

Public Law 94–142 The Education for All Handicapped Children Act, which required that all students with disabilities be given a free, appropriate public education and which provided the funding to help implement this education.

Individuals with Disabilities Education Act (IDEA) This act spells out broad mandates for services to all children with disabilities, including evaluation and determination of eligibility, appropriate education and an individualized education plan (IEP), and education in the least restrictive environment (LRE).

individualized education plan (IEP) A written statement that spells out a program specifically tailored for the student with a disability.

Increasingly, children with disabilities are being taught in the regular classroom, as is this child with mild mental retardation.

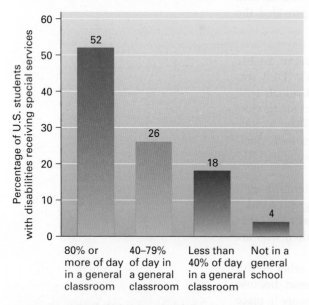

FIGURE 6.6 Percentage of U.S. Students with Disabilities 6 to 21 Years of Age Receiving Special Services in the General Classroom

Note: Data for 2004–2005 school year; National Center for Education Statistics (2007).

least restrictive environment (LRE)
A setting that is as similar as possible to the one in which children who do not have a disability are educated.

inclusion Educating children with special education needs full-time in the regular classroom.

Amendments were made to IDEA in 1997. Two of these involve positive behavioral support and functional behavioral assessment.

Positive behavioral support focuses on culturally appropriate application of positive behavioral interventions to attain important behavior changes in children (Thompson, Moore, & Symons, 2007). "Culturally appropriate" refers to considering the unique and individualized learning histories of children (social, community, historical, gender, and so on). Positive behavioral support especially emphasizes supporting desirable behaviors rather than punishing undesirable behaviors in working with children with a disability or disorder.

Functional behavioral assessment involves determining the consequences (what purpose the behavior serves), antecedents (what triggers the behavior), and setting events (in which contexts the behavior occurs) (Heller & others, 2009). Functional behavioral assessment emphasizes understanding behavior in the context in which it is observed and guiding positive behavioral interventions that are relevant and effective.

A major aspect of the 2004 reauthorization of IDEA involved aligning it with the government's No Child Left Behind (NCLB) legislation, which was designed to improve the educational achievement of all students, including those with disabilities (Keys & others, 2008; Turnbull, Huerta, & Stowe, 2009). Both IDEA and NCLB mandate that most students with disabilities be included in general assessments of educational progress. This alignment includes requiring most students with disabilities "to take standard tests of academic achievement and to achieve at a level equal to that of students without disabilities. Whether this expectation is reasonable is an open question" (Hallahan & Kauffman, 2006, pp. 28–29). Alternative assessments for students with disabilities and funding to help states improve instruction, assessment, and accountability for educating students with disabilities are included in the 2004 reauthorization of IDEA.

Least Restrictive Environment (LRE) Under IDEA, the child with a disability must be educated in the **least restrictive environment (LRE)**. This means a setting as similar as possible to the one in which children who do not have a disability are educated. And schools must make an effort to educate children with a disability in the regular classroom. The term **inclusion** means educating a child with special educational needs full-time in the regular classroom. Figure 6.6 indicates that in a recent school year slightly more than 50 percent of U.S. students with a disability spent more than 80 percent of their school day in a general classroom.

What is least restrictive likely depends to some degree on the child's disability (Carter, Prater, & Dyches, 2009). Some children with a learning disability or a speech impairment can be educated in the regular classroom, but children with severe hearing or vision impairments may need to be educated in separate classes or schools (Friend, 2008).

In the last two decades, collaborative teaming has been increasingly advocated in educating children with disabilities (Hallahan, Kauffman, & Pullen, 2009). In *collaborative teaming*, people with diverse expertise interact to provide services for children. Researchers have found that collaborative teaming often results in gains for children, as well as improved skills and attitudes for teachers (Snell & Janney, 2005).

BEST PRACTICES
Strategies for Working with Children with Disabilities as a Regular Teacher

1. *Carry out each child's individualized education plan (IEP).*

2. *Encourage your school to provide increased support and training in how to teach children with disabilities.* Next, Michelle Evans, a sixth-grade teacher, describes her relationship with resource personnel and some strategies that worked for her students.

THROUGH THE EYES OF TEACHERS
Strategies for Working with Children Who Have a Disability

Support and resource personnel are invaluable. Communication with parents, student, and with anyone involved is essential. Make certain that you communicate with your entire class, too. . . . Because I want each student to feel successful, I create different levels of mastery or participation in learning objectives.

One student with cerebral palsy had difficulty standing, mental impairments, and other problems. She had little and often no short-term memory. As we sat together and talked, I found that her strength was that she loved to copy words, stories, and other things. Her hands were weak, but writing helped them. Her parents wanted her to do anything she could. By capitalizing on her fondness for copying and writing, she eventually learned math facts and spelling words. I assigned a poem about having a positive attitude as a memorization for everyone in the class. A few kids complained that the poem would be too hard to memorize when I presented it. She copied that poem so many times that three days after the assignment she stood and delivered it flawlessly to the class. I could see the complainers melt away as we all realized that she was the first to recite the poem. Her parents came to witness her accomplishment. There wasn't a dry eye in the room by the time she finished. She taught us a great deal.

3. *Become more knowledgeable about the types of children with disabilities in your classroom.* Read education jour-nals, such as *Exceptional Children, Teaching Exceptional Children,* and *Journal of Learning Disabilities,* to keep up-to-date on the latest information about these children. Look into taking a class at a college or university or a continuing education course on topics such as exceptional children, mental retardation, learning disabilities, and emotional and behavioral disorders.

4. *Be cautious about labeling children with a disability.* It is easy to fall into the trap of using the label as an explanation of the child's learning difficulties. For example, a teacher might say, "Well, Larry has trouble with reading because he has a learning disability," when, in fact, the teacher really knows only that for some unknown reason Larry is having trouble with reading. Also, labels have a way of remaining after the child has improved considerably. Remember that terms such as *mental retardation* and *learning disability* are descriptive labels for disorders. Always think of children with disabilities in terms of what the best conditions are for improving their learning and how they can be helped to make progress rather than in terms of unchanging labels.

5. *Remember that children with disabilities benefit from many of the same teaching strategies that benefit children without disabilities and vice versa.* These include being caring, accepting, and patient; having positive expectations for learning; helping children with their social and communication skills as well as academic skills; and challenging children with disabilities to reach their full potential.

6. *Help children without a disability to understand and accept children with a disability.* Provide children without a disability information about children with a disability and create opportunities for them to interact with each other in positive ways. Peer tutoring and cooperative learning activities can be used to encourage positive interaction between children without a disability and children with a disability (Fuchs, Fuchs, & Burish, 2000). We will discuss these activities further in Chapter 10, "Social Constructivist Approaches."

Ideally, collaborative teaming encourages shared responsibility in planning and decision making. It also enables educators with diverse expertise to construct effective alternatives to traditional educational approaches. When collaborative teaming is used, many children remain in the regular classroom, and the regular classroom teacher is actively involved in planning the child's education.

Many legal changes regarding children with disabilities have been extremely positive. Compared with several decades ago, far more children today are receiving competent, specialized services. For many children, inclusion in the regular classroom,

DIVERSITY AND EDUCATION
Minority Students in Special Education

The U.S. Department of Education (2000) has three concerns about the over-representation of minority students in special education programs and classes: (1) students may be unserved or receive services that do not meet their needs, (2) students may be misclassified or inappropriately labeled, and (3) placement in special education classes may be a form of discrimination.

African American students are overrepresented in special education—15 percent of the U.S. student population is African American, but 20 percent of special education students are African American (National Center for Education Statistics, 2008). In some disabilities, the discrepancies are even greater. For example, African American students represent 32 percent of the students in programs for mild mental retardation, 29 percent in programs for moderate mental retardation, and 24 percent in programs for serious emotional disturbance.

However, it is not just a simple matter of overrepresentation of certain minority groups in special education. Latino children may be underidentified in the categories of mental retardation and emotional disturbance.

More appropriate inclusion of minority students in special education is a complex problem and requires the creation of a successful school experience for all students (Hick & Thomas, 2009; Skidmore, 2009). Recommendations for reducing disproportionate representation in special education include the following (Burnette, 1998):

- Reviewing school practices to identify and address factors that might contribute to school difficulties
- Forming policy-making groups that include community members and promote partnerships with service agencies and cultural organizations
- Helping families get social, medical, mental health, and other support services
- Training more teachers from minority backgrounds and providing all teachers with more extensive course work and training in educating children with disabilities and diversity issues

with modifications or supplemental services, is appropriate (Friend, 2008). However, some leading experts on special education argue that the effort to use inclusion to educate children with disabilities has become too extreme in some cases. For example, James Kauffman and his colleagues (Kauffman & Hallahan, 2005; Kauffman, McGee, and Brigham, 2004) state that inclusion too often has meant making accommodations in the regular classroom that do not always benefit children with disabilities. They advocate a more individualized approach that does not always involve full inclusion but rather allows for options such as special education outside the regular classroom. Kauffman and his colleagues (2004, p. 620) acknowledge that children with disabilities "*do* need the services of specially trained professionals to achieve their full potential. They *do* sometimes need altered curricula or adaptations to make their learning possible." However,

> we sell students with disabilities short when we pretend that they are not different from typical students. We make the same error when we pretend that they must *not* be expected to put forth extra effort if they are to learn to do some things—or learn to do something in a different way.

Like general education, an important aspect of special education should be to challenge students with disabilities "to become all they can be."

One concern about special education involves disproportionate representation of students from minority backgrounds in special education programs and classes

(Klingner, Blanchett, & Harry, 2007). The *Diversity and Education* interlude addresses this issue.

Technology

The Individuals with Disabilities Education Act (IDEA), including its 1997 amendments, requires that technology devices and services be provided to students with disabilities if they are necessary to ensure a free, appropriate education (Ulman, 2005).

Two types of technology that can be used to improve the education of students with disabilities are instructional technology and assistive technology (Blackhurst, 1997). *Instructional technology* includes various types of hardware and software, combined with innovative teaching methods, to accommodate students' learning needs in the classroom. Examples include videotapes, computer-assisted instruction, and complex hypermedia programs in which computers are used to control the display of audio and visual images stored on videodisc.

Assistive technology consists of various services and devices to help students with disabilities function within their environment. Examples include communication aids, alternative computer keyboards, and adaptive switches. To locate such services, educators can use computer databases such as the Device Locator System (Academic Software, 1996). To read further about instructional and assistive technologies, see the *Technology and Education* interlude.

Review, Reflect, and Practice

(2) **Explain the legal framework and technology advances for children with disabilities.**

REVIEW

- What is IDEA? How is it related to IEPs and LREs? What is the current thinking about inclusion?
- What is the difference between instructional and assistive technology?

REFLECT

- What do you think will present the greatest challenges to you in teaching children with a disability?

PRAXIS™ PRACTICE

1. Jenny has a moderate learning disability. She is educated in the special education classroom of her school, as she has been for the past two years. She and her classmates eat lunch in the resource room as well. Each of the students in the resource room works on different things, due to their very different abilities and disabilities. This placement was made because the regular education teachers in Jenny's school do not have the necessary skills to teach Jenny. Therefore, she was placed in the resource room with the school's sole special educator. What is the legal issue with this placement?
   a. Jenny's IEP does not specify a diagnosis.
   b. Jenny is not being educated in the least restrictive environment.
   c. Jenny's placement needs to be reconsidered at least every six months.
   d. The functional behavior assessment did not consider the use of technology.

2. Azel has cerebral palsy. His teacher has found an alternative computer keyboard to facilitate his learning. What type of technology is the teacher using?
   a. instructional technology
   b. computer-assisted instruction
   c. assistive technology
   d. complex hypermedia

Please see the answer key at the end of the book.

TECHNOLOGY AND EDUCATION

Technology and Special Needs Students

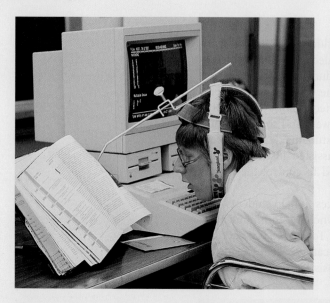 

These special input devices can help students with physical disabilities use computers more effectively. (a) A student uses a special input device attached to the student's head to send signals to the computer. (b) Many students with physical disabilities such as cerebral palsy cannot use a conventional keyboard and mouse. Many can use alternative keyboards effectively.

Technology can be used to help students with special needs. Next, we distinguish between instructive and assistive technologies that serve these purposes (Roblyer, Edwards & Havriluk, 1997).

Instructional Applications

Software and hardware designed for use with traditional students are also being used with considerable success with students who have special needs, especially in inclusion classes. Word prediction software can be used to help children with physical disabilities write on a computer. Word processing has helped many children with disabilities make progress in their written language skills (Holberg, 1995). Talking word processors such as *Write: Outloud, IntelliTalk II, Kids Works 2,* and *The Amazing Writing Machine* can be especially helpful in the education of children with speech problems. On request, these programs read text aloud.

Mobile computers also hold great promise for use with special needs students. Preliminary research provides evidence that the use of mobile computing devices in inclusive classes can improve the engagement of special needs students and help lessen the achievement gap between special needs and regular students (Swan & others, 2005).

Assistive Technologies

Assistive technologies are software and hardware designed specifically to help students with special needs. For example, software and special hardware such as closed-circuit television can enlarge computer images and text for children with a visual impairment. Printers can produce large print or Braille. Tactile devices that scan a page and translate the text into vibrating, tactile displays also can be used with children who are visually impaired. Captioned video provides subtitles for television and other video presentations so that children who are hearing impaired can read what others are saying.

Telecommunication technologies for the deaf allow children with hearing impairments to communicate with people over the phone. The Internet gives children with a disability who are homebound access to educational opportunities. Many children with physical disabilities (such as cerebral palsy) cannot use traditional devices such as a keyboard and a mouse. Touch screens, touch tablets, optical pointers, alternative keyboards, and voice-controlled devices are alternatives that allow them to use a computer.

3 CHILDREN WHO ARE GIFTED

Characteristics | Life Course of the Gifted | Educating Children Who Are Gifted

The final type of exceptionality we will discuss is quite different from the disabilities and disorders that we have described so far. **Children who are gifted** have above-average intelligence (usually defined as an IQ of 130 or higher) and/or superior talent in some domain such as art, music, or mathematics. Admissions standards for children who are gifted in schools are typically based on intelligence and academic aptitude, although there is increasing call to widen the criteria to include such factors as creativity and commitment (Chart, Grigorenko, & Sternberg, 2008; Jarvin & others, 2008; Makel & Plucker, 2008). The U.S. government has described five areas of giftedness: intellectual, academic, creative, visual and performing arts, and leadership.

Some critics argue that too many children in "gifted programs" aren't really gifted in a particular area but are just somewhat bright, usually cooperative, and, usually, non-Latino White (Kaufman & Sternberg, 2007, 2008). They say the mantle of brilliance is cast on many children who are not that far from simply being "smart normal."

Although general intelligence as defined by an overall IQ score still remains as a key criterion in many states' decision of whether a child should be placed in a gifted program, changing conceptions of intelligence increasingly include ideas such as Gardner's multiple intelligences, and placement criteria are likely to move away from an IQ criterion in the future (Miller, 2008; Pfeiffer & Blei, 2008).

Characteristics

Ellen Winner (1996), an expert on creativity and giftedness, described three criteria that characterize children who are gifted:

1. *Precocity.* Children who are gifted are precocious when given the opportunity to use their gift or talent. They begin to master an area earlier than their peers. Learning in their domain is more effortless for them than for children who are not gifted. In most instances, children who are gifted are precocious because they have an inborn high ability in a particular domain or domains, although this inborn precocity has to be identified and nourished.

2. *Marching to their own drummer.* Children who are gifted learn in a qualitatively different way than children who are not gifted. One way they march to a different drummer is that they require less support, or scaffolding (discussed in Chapter 2), from adults to learn than their nongifted peers do. Often they resist explicit instruction. They also often make discoveries on their own and solve problems in unique ways within their area of giftedness. They can be normal or below normal in other areas.

3. *A passion to master.* Children who are gifted are driven to understand the domain in which they have high ability. They display an intense, obsessive interest and an ability to focus. They are not children who need to be pushed by their parents. They frequently have a high degree of internal motivation.

A fourth area in which children who are gifted excel involves information-processing skills. Researchers have found that children who are gifted learn at a faster pace, process information more rapidly, are better at reasoning, use better strategies, and monitor their understanding better than their nongifted counterparts (Davidson & Davidson, 2004; Sternberg & Clinkenbeard, 1995).

At 2 years of age, art prodigy Alexandra Nechita colored in coloring books for hours and took up pen and ink. She had no interest in dolls or friends. By age 5 she was using watercolors. Once she started school, she would start painting as soon as she got home. At the age of 8, in 1994, she saw the first public exhibit of her work. In succeeding years, working quickly and impulsively on canvases as large as 5 feet by 9 feet, she has completed hundreds of paintings, some of which sell for close to $100,000 apiece. As a teenager, she continues to paint—relentlessly and passionately. It is, she says, what she loves to do. *What are some characteristics of children who are gifted?*

children who are gifted Children with above-average intelligence (usually defined as an IQ of 130 or higher) and/or superior talent in some domain such as art, music, or mathematics.

DEVELOPMENTAL FOCUS 6.3
How Do You Work with Students Who Are Gifted?

Early Childhood

Our preschoolers who are considered gifted are given more challenging projects to complete and given more responsibilities throughout the day. Parents are also contacted and given strategies and suggestions about extracurricular activities that will stimulate their child's strengths.

—Missy Dangler, *Suburban Hills School*

Elementary School: Grades K–5

When working with students who are gifted, it is important to remember that they don't need *more* work, but they do need work that will challenge them. Also, no matter how gifted students are, their work needs to always be checked to make sure that they haven't misunderstood something.

—Esther Lindbloom, *Cooper Mountain Elementary School*

Middle School: Grades 6–8

It is important that you not bore students who are gifted in your classroom. For example, if children who are gifted are learning about the causes and effects of the Civil War, and they already know the information being covered, I would have them apply what they already know by having them create a journal about someone who lived during that time period.

—Casey Maass, *Edison Middle School*

High School: Grades 9–12

Students who are gifted have a unique set of issues. They need to be challenged at a higher level, but they also need to accept the fact that other students who are not as gifted as they are also have worth. My homeroom is a prime example. Among the 18 students I have, one is the number-one student who never found a math or science problem that he couldn't solve; one is learning disabled with a seizure disorder; and three students have missed school time for jail. In the three years that we have been together, we have worked on respecting differences in each other and on teamwork activities, and have won homeroom competitions. Relationships are key in getting students of all abilities to work together and feel part of a school or classroom community. Teachers need to build trust in order for this to happen.

—Sandy Swanson, *Menomonee Falls High School*

Life Course of the Gifted

Is giftedness a product of heredity or environment? Likely both. Individuals who are gifted recall that they had signs of high ability in a particular area at a very young age, prior to or at the beginning of formal training (Howe & others, 1995). This suggests the importance of innate ability in giftedness. However, researchers also have found that individuals with world-class status in the arts, mathematics, science, and sports all report strong family support and years of training and practice (Bloom, 1985). Deliberate practice is an important characteristic of individuals who become experts in a particular domain. *Deliberate practice* is practice that occurs at an appropriate level of difficulty for the individual, provides corrective feedback, and allows opportunities for repetition (Ericsson, 2006). In one study, the best musicians engaged in twice as much deliberate practice over their lives as the least successful ones did (Ericsson, Krampe, & Tesch-Romer, 1993).

Do children who are gifted become gifted and highly creative adults? In Terman's research on children with superior IQs, the children typically became experts in a well-established domain, such as medicine, law, or business. However, most did not become major creators (Winner, 2000). That is, they did not create a new domain or revolutionize an old domain.

One reason that some children who are gifted do not become gifted adults is that they have been pushed too hard by overzealous parents (Thomas, Ray, & Moon, 2007). As a result, they lose their intrinsic (internal) motivation (Winner, 1996, 2006). However, as we will discuss next, many children who are gifted have not been adequately challenged in school to develop their talent.

Educating Children Who Are Gifted

Increasingly, experts argue that the education of children who are gifted in the United States requires a significant overhaul (Clark, 2008; Cloud, 2007; Karnes & Stephens, 2008; Kaufman & Sternberg, 2008). Such concerns are registered in the titles of these books and reports: *Genius Denied: How to Stop Wasting Our Brightest Young Minds* (Davidson & Davidson, 2004) and *A Nation Deceived: How Schools Hold Back America's Brightest Students* (Colangelo, Assouline, & Gross, 2004).

Underchallenged children who are gifted can become disruptive, skip classes, and lose interest in achieving. Sometimes these children just disappear into the woodwork, becoming passive and apathetic toward school (Moon, 2008). Teachers must challenge children who are gifted to reach high expectations (Tassell-Baska & Stambaugh, 2006; Webb & others, 2007; Winner, 2006).

Four program options for children who are gifted follow (Hertzog, 1998):

- *Special classes.* Historically, this has been the common way to educate children who are gifted. The special classes during the regular school day are called "pullout" programs. Some special classes also are held after school, on Saturdays, or in the summer.

- *Acceleration and enrichment in the regular classroom setting.* This could include early admission to kindergarten, grade skipping (also known as double promotion), telescoping (completing two grades in one year), advanced placement, subject-matter acceleration, and self-paced instruction (Cloud, 2007; Johnsen, 2005). Curriculum compacting is a variation of acceleration in which teachers skip over aspects of the curriculum that they believe children who are gifted do not need.

- *Mentor and apprenticeship programs.* Some experts stress these are important, underutilized ways to motivate, challenge, and effectively educate children who are gifted (Pleiss & Feldhusen, 1995).

- *Work/study and/or community-service programs.*

Educational reform has brought into the regular classroom many strategies that once were the domain of separate gifted programs. These include an emphasis on

THROUGH THE EYES OF STUDENTS

Children Who Are Gifted Speak

James Delisle (1987) interviewed hundreds of elementary school children who are gifted. Here are some of their comments.

In response to: Describe Your Typical School Day

Oh what a bore to sit and listen,
To stuff we already know.
Do everything we've done and done again,
But we must still sit and listen.
Over and over read one more page
Oh bore, oh bore, oh bore.

Girl, Age 9, New York

I sit there pretending to be reading along when I'm really six pages ahead. When I understand something and half the class doesn't, I have to sit there and listen.

Girl, Age 10, Connecticut

In response to: What Makes a Teacher a Gifted Teacher?

She is capable of handling our problems and has a good imagination to help us learn.

Girl, Age 10, Louisiana

Will challenge you and let the sky be your limit.

Boy, Age 11, Michigan

Opens your mind to help you with your life.

A young Bill Gates, founder of Microsoft and now the world's richest person. Like many highly gifted students, Gates was not especially fond of school. He hacked a computer security system at 13 years of age, and as a high school student, he was allowed to take some college math classes. He dropped out of Harvard University and began developing his plan for creating what was to become Microsoft Corporation. *What are some ways that schools can enrich the education of such highly talented students as Gates to make it a more challenging and meaningful experience?*

problem-based learning, having children do projects, creating portfolios, and critical thinking. Combined with the increasing emphasis on educating all children in the regular classroom, many schools now try to challenge and motivate children who are gifted in the regular classroom. Some schools also include after-school or Saturday programs or develop mentor apprenticeship, work/study, or community-service programs. Thus, an array of in-school and out-of-school opportunities is provided (Van-Tassel-Baska & Stambaugh, 2008).

The Schoolwide Enrichment Model (SEM), developed by Joseph Renzulli (1998), is a program for children who are gifted that focuses on total school improvement. Renzulli says that when enrichment has a school-wide emphasis, positive outcomes are likely to occur, not only for children who are gifted but also for children who are not gifted and for classroom and resource teachers. When school-wide enrichment is emphasized, "us" versus "them" barriers often decrease, and classroom teachers are more willing to use curriculum compacting with their children who are most gifted. Instead of feeling isolated, resource teachers begin to feel more like members of a team, especially when they work with regular classroom teachers on enriching the entire classroom. Thus, important goals of SEM are to improve outcomes for both students who are gifted and those who are not gifted and to improve the contributions and relationships of classroom and resource teachers.

Research evaluation of acceleration and enrichment programs has not revealed which approach is best (Winner, 1997). Some researchers have found support for acceleration programs (Kulik, 1992), although critics say a potential problem of grade skipping is that it places children with others who are physically more advanced and socioemotionally different. Other researchers have found support for enrichment programs (Renzulli & Reis, 1997).

A number of experts argue that too often children who are gifted are socially isolated and underchallenged in the classroom (Robinson, 2008). It is not unusual for them to be ostracized and labeled "nerds" or "geeks." A child who is truly gifted often is the only such child in the room who does not have the opportunity to learn with students of like ability. Many eminent adults report that school was a negative experience for them, that they were bored and sometimes knew more than their teachers (Bloom, 1985). Winner (2006) points out that American education will benefit when standards are raised for all children. When some children are still underchallenged, she recommends that they be allowed to attend advanced classes in their domain of exceptional ability such as allowing some especially precocious middle school students to take college classes in their area of expertise. For example, Bill Gates, founder of Microsoft, took college math classes and hacked a computer security system at 13; Yo-Yo Ma, famous cellist, graduated from high school at 15 and attended Juilliard School of Music in New York City.

Some educators conclude that the inadequate education of children who are gifted has been compounded by the federal government's No Child Left Behind policy that seeks to raise the achievement level of students who are not doing well in school at the expense of enriching the education of children who are gifted (Clark, 2008; Cloud, 2007). In the era of No Child Left Behind policy, some individuals concerned

BEST PRACTICES
Strategies for Working with Children Who Are Gifted

Here are some recommended strategies for working with children who are gifted (Colangelo, Assouline, & Gross, 2004, pp. 49–50):

1. *Recognize that the child is academically advanced.*

2. *Guide the child to new challenges and ensure that school is a positive experience.* To read about some ways a talented teacher accomplishes this, see *Through the Eyes of Teachers.*

THROUGH THE EYES OF TEACHERS
Passionate About Teaching Math
to Students Who Are Gifted

Margaret (Peg) Cagle teaches gifted seventh- and eighth-grade math students at Lawrence Middle School in Chatsworth, California. She especially advocates challenging students who are gifted to take intellectual risks. To encourage collaboration, she often has students work together in groups of four, and frequently tutors students during lunch hour. As 13-year-old Madeline Lewis

commented, "If I don't get it one way, she'll explain it another and talk to you about it and show you until you do get it." Peg says it is important to be passionate about teaching math and open up a world for students that shows them how beautiful learning math can be. (*Source:* Wong Briggs, 2007, p. 6D)

___

3. *Monitor the accurate evaluation of the child's readiness to be accelerated.*

4. *Discuss with parents ways to appropriately challenge the child.*

5. *Learn about and use resources for children who are gifted.* Among these are National Research Center on Gifted and Talented Education at the University of Connecticut and the Belin-Blank Center at the University of Iowa; *Gifted Child Quarterly* and *Gifted Child Today* journals; books on children who are gifted: *Genius Denied* by Jan Davidson and Bob Davidson (2004); *A Nation Deceived* by Nicholas Colangelo, Susan Assouline, and Miraca Gross (2004); and *Handbook of Gifted Education,* third edition, by Nicholas Colangelo and Gary Davis (2003).

Margaret (Peg) Cagle with her seventh- and eighth-grade math students who are gifted at Lawrence Middle School in Chatsworth, California.

about the neglect of students who are gifted argue that schools spend far more time identifying students' deficiencies than cultivating students' talents (Cloud, 2007). For example, U.S. schools spend approximately $8 billion a year educating students who are mentally retarded and only $800 million educating students who are gifted. In many cases, say the critics, U.S. education squanders the potential contributions of America's most talented young minds (Cloud, 2007).

This concludes our coverage of children who are exceptional learners. From time to time in this chapter, we described some behavioral strategies for changing children's behavior. For example, we indicated that children who are mentally retarded often benefit from the use of precise steps in using positive reinforcement to change their behavior. In Chapter 7, we will explore many aspects of positive reinforcement and other learning strategies.

Review, Reflect, and Practice

(3) Define what gifted means and discuss some approaches to teaching children who are gifted.

REVIEW

- What is the definition of being gifted? What are some criticisms of gifted programs? What characteristics does Winner ascribe to children who are gifted?
- How can the life course of the gifted be described?
- What are some options for educating students who are gifted?

REFLECT

- Suppose that you had several students in your class who were strikingly gifted. Might this lead to problems? Explain. What might you do to prevent such problems from developing?

PRAXIS™ PRACTICE

1. Ms. Larson has a student in her kindergarten class who continuously surprises her. He requested that she allow him to play with a puzzle of the United States that no children had played with in years. She observed him expertly put each state in place, saying its name as he did so. Soon he was teaching the other students in the class each state's name, its capitol, and where it belonged in the puzzle. On a recent trip to the school learning center, he asked to check out a book of international flags that was written at an eighth-grade level. Her first instinct was to deny his request, but instead she asked him about the book. He told her "I know I can't read *all* of it, but I can read the names of the countries, and I want to learn more flags. See how many I already know?" He then flipped through the book, correctly identifying most of the flags. Which characteristics of giftedness is this student showing?
   a. numerical ability, highly developed social skills, and precocity
   b. verbal ability, intensity, and a passion to master
   c. high reading level, marching to his own drummer, and stubbornness
   d. precocity, marching to his own drummer, and a passion to master

2. Research suggests that the best way to encourage children who are gifted to succeed in school is to
   a. promote a love of learning for its own sake.
   b. remind them of their parents' high expectations.
   c. promote a spirit of competition for rewards.
   d. employ them as peer teachers as much as possible.

Review, Reflect, and Practice

PRAXIS™ PRACTICE (CONTINUED)

3. The kindergarten student in Ms. Larson's class (item 1) continued to progress in school. In fourth grade, he finished third in his K–8 school's geography bee. He finished first in the next two years. In seventh grade, he finally took his first course in geography. He received C's. He often complained to his parents that he already knew the material being taught, that he wanted to learn "new stuff, not just listen to the same old junk." His teacher put a great deal of emphasis on completing map worksheets, which he completed very quickly and sloppily. He often became disruptive in class. How should the geography teacher handle this situation?

   a. The teacher should punish the student for disrupting class. The student should continue to do the same assignments as the other students, because he needs to understand that not all work is fun.

   b. The teacher should consider curriculum compacting, because the student has already mastered the course content. Once challenged, his disruptive behavior is likely to diminish.

   c. The teacher should ask this student to become a co-teacher.

   d. The teacher should use the student's sloppy work as a negative example to the rest of the class.

   Please see the answer key at the end of the book.

CRACK THE CASE
The Case of Now What

Before the school year starts, Ms. Inez always holds a "get acquainted meeting" with the parents of her incoming kindergartners. She does this so that she can explain what the children will be doing in kindergarten, her educational philosophy and expectations, the procedure for dropping students off at school the first day, and of course, to allow parents to ask any questions and share any concerns they might have. Inevitably, parents do have concerns and questions they would like addressed.

Here are some typical things she hears from parents:

"Joey still naps in the afternoon; can we have him changed to the morning class?"

"Ashley has severe asthma. She will need to have her nebulizer close in case she has an asthma attack. Do you know how to use one?"

"I just know that Steve won't be able to sit still for very long. Do you let the kids move a lot?"

"I hope you give the kids lots of active time. Bill won't be able to sit still for long either."

"Alex is very advanced for his age. What can you do to challenge him?"

"Amanda is advanced, too."

"So is my Timmy."

"Well, Peter seems to be behind. He doesn't speak very well."

Ms. Inez listens respectfully to each concern or question and assures the parents, "I'll do everything I can to ensure your children have a good year in my class. All children are different and learn at different rates, so don't be too worried about your child being a little bit behind or ahead. I think we'll all do fine together." As she is leaving for the evening, she chuckles at the number of parents who think their children are very advanced. It's the same every year—about a third of the parents are convinced that their child is the next Einstein.

The school year begins uneventfully. Ms. Inez uses the children's free-play time to observe them. Although there are obvious differences between the children, she doesn't notice that any of the children are truly exceptional, except perhaps for Harman and Rowan. Their lack of attention and inability to sit still during story time is beginning to be a bit disruptive. Ms. Inez makes a note to herself to talk to their parents about the possibility that they might have ADHD and recommend testing. Some other students might be candidates for this as well, including Alex. Although Ms. Inez has learned how to use Ashley's nebulizer, she hasn't needed to use it thus far.

Each day at the beginning of class, Ms. Inez marks off the day of the month on the calendar with a large X. She then writes a statement on the blackboard, describing the day's weather. On the tenth day of school she writes on the board, "Today is sunny and hot." She then reads the statement to the students so that they can begin to make word associations. "Today is sunny and warm." Alex shouts out, "That isn't what you wrote. You wrote today is sunny and hot." Ms. Inez is astounded. Later, during free-play time she asks Alex to sit with her. Alex looks longingly at the puzzles, but grudgingly complies. "Alex, will you read this book to me?"

"Sure," replies Alex, and he does so flawlessly.

Ms. Inez queries, "Do you have this book at home?"

Alex: "Yep. Lots of others, too."

Ms. Inez: "How about this one? Do you have it?"

Alex: "Nope."

Ms. Inez: "Well then, suppose you try to read this one to me."

Alex: "OK, but then can I go play with the puzzles?"

Ms. Inez: "Certainly."

Alex reads the book to Ms. Inez, missing only a few words, and then rushes off to play with the puzzles, build towers of blocks and knock them down, and play with trucks. The next day during calendar time, Ms. Inez asks the class, "If today is the fifteenth day of the month and there are thirty days in the month, how could we find out how many days are left?"

The children call out, "We could count the days that don't have X's on them."

"Very good," replies Ms. Inez.

Alex looks puzzled. "What's wrong, Alex?" asks Ms. Inez.

"Why don't we just subtract?" he asks.

1. What are the issues in this case?

2. Why do you suppose Ms. Inez makes light of parents' perceptions of their children's strengths?

3. How should Ms. Inez approach the parents of the students she thinks might have ADHD?

4. Is it appropriate for her to recommend testing of any of the children? Why or why not? Would it be appropriate for her to recommend a particular doctor for this testing? Why or why not?

5. If Alex can already read and subtract, are there other skills he has likely mastered? If so, what might they be? How might this impact his experiences in kindergarten?

6. How should Ms. Inez address this?

7. Which of the following is most likely true about Alex?
   a. Alex has a fluency disorder.
   b. Alex has a learning disability.
   c. Alex has ADHD.
   d. Alex is gifted.

Reach Your Learning Goals
Learners Who Are Exceptional

1 CHILDREN WITH DISABILITIES: Describe the various types of disabilities and disorders.

Learning Disabilities

A child with a learning disability has difficulty in learning that involves understanding or using spoken or written language, and the difficulty can appear in listening, thinking, reading, writing, and spelling. A learning disability also may involve difficulty in doing mathematics. To be classified as a learning disability, the learning problem is not primarily the result of visual, hearing, or motor disabilities; mental retardation; emotional disorders; or due to environmental, cultural, or economic disadvange. An estimated 14 percent of U.S. children between 3 and 21 years of age receive special education or related services. The term "children with disabilities" is now used rather than "disabled children," and children with disabilities are no longer referred to as handicapped children. About three times as many boys as girls have a learning disability. The most common academic problems for children with a learning disability are reading, writing, and math. Dyslexia is a severe impairment in the ability to read and spell. Dysgraphia is a learning disability that involves having difficulty in handwriting. Dyscalculia is a learning disability that involves difficulties in math computation. Controversy surrounds the "learning disability" category; some critics believe it is overdiagnosed; others argue that it is not. Diagnosis is difficult, especially for mild forms. Initial identification of children with a possible learning disability often is made by the classroom teacher, who then asks specialists to evaluate the child. Various causes of learning disabilities have been proposed. Many interventions targeted for learning disabilities focus on reading ability and include such strategies as improving decoding skills. The success of even the best-designed interventions depends on the training and skills of the teacher.

Attention Deficit Hyperactivity Disorder

Attention deficit hyperactivity disorder (ADHD) is a disability in which children consistently show problems in one or more of these areas: inattention, hyperactivity, and impulsivity. For an ADHD diagnosis, the characteristics must appear early in childhood and be debilitating for the child. Although signs of ADHD may be present in early childhood, diagnosis of ADHD often doesn't occur until the elementary school years. Many experts recommend a combination of academic, behavioral, and medical interventions to help students with ADHD learn and adapt. ADHD is not supposed to be diagnosed by school teams because accurate diagnosis requires evaluation by a specialist, such as a psychiatrist. It is important for teachers to monitor whether ADHD medication has been prescribed at the right dosage, to involve a special education resource teacher, to use behavior management strategies, to supply immediate feedback to the child for clearly stated expectations, and to provide structure and teacher-direction.

Mental Retardation

Mental retardation is a condition with an onset before age 18 that involves low intelligence (usually below 70 on an individually administered intelligence test) and difficulty in adapting to everyday life. Mental retardation has been classified in terms of four categories based mainly on IQ scores: mild, moderate, severe, and profound. More recently, a classification system based on degree of support required has been advocated. Determinants of mental retardation include genetic factors (as in Down syndrome), brain damage (which can result from many different infections, such as AIDS), and environmental hazards.

Physical Disorders

Among the physical disorders that students might have are orthopedic impairments (such as cerebral palsy) and seizure disorders (such as epilepsy).

Sensory Disorders

Sensory disorders include visual and hearing impairments. Visual impairments include having low vision and being educationally blind. A child with low vision can read large-print books or regular books with a magnifying glass. An educationally blind child cannot use vision in learning, instead relying on hearing and touch. An important task is to determine which modality (such as touch or hearing) the student who is visually impaired learns best in. A number of technological devices help these students learn. Educational strategies for students with hearing impairments fall into two main categories: oral and manual. Increasingly, both approaches are used with the same student in a total-communication approach.

Speech and Language Disorders

Speech and language disorders include a number of speech problems (such as articulation disorders, voice disorders, and fluency disorders) and language problems (difficulties in receiving and expressing language). Articulation disorders are problems in pronouncing words correctly. Voice disorders are reflected in speech that is too hoarse, loud, high-pitched, or low-pitched. Children with cleft palate often have a voice disorder. Fluency disorders often involve what we commonly call "stuttering." Language disorders involve significant impairments in children's receptive or expressive language. Receptive language involves the reception and understanding of language. Expressive language involves using language for expressing one's thoughts and communicating with others. Specific language impairment (SLI) is another type of speech and language disorder that children may have and involves problems in understanding and using words in sentences.

Autism Spectrum Disorders

Autism spectrum disorder (ASD) is an increasingly popular term that refers to a broad range of autism disorders including the classical, severe form of autism, as well as Asperger syndrome. Autism is a severe autism spectrum disorder with an onset in the first three years of life, and it involves abnormalities in social relationships and communications. It also is characterized by repetitive behaviors. The current consensus is that autism involves an organic brain dysfunction.

Emotional and Behavioral Disorders

Emotional and behavioral disorders consist of serious, persistent problems that involve relationships, aggression, depression, fears associated with personal or school matters, and other inappropriate socioemotional characteristics. The term emotional disturbance (ED) recently has been used to describe this category of disorders, although it is not without criticism. In severe instances of aggressive, out-of-control behaviors, students are removed from the classroom. The problems are far more characteristic of boys than of girls. Problems involving depression, anxiety, and fear, involving turning problems inward, are much more likely to appear in girls than in boys.

② EDUCATIONAL ISSUES INVOLVING CHILDREN WITH DISABILITIES: Explain the legal framework and technology advances for children with disabilities.

Legal Aspects

The educational rights for children with disabilities were laid down in the mid-1960s. In 1975, Congress enacted Public Law 94-142, the Education for All Handicapped Children Act, which mandated that all children be given a free, appropriate public education. Public Law 94-142 was recast in 1990 as the Individuals with Disabilities Education Act (IDEA), which spells out broad requirements for services to all children with disabilities. Children who are thought to have a disability are evaluated to determine their eligibility for services. The IDEA has many provisions that relate to the parents of children with disabilities. IDEA was amended in 1997 and then reauthorized in 2004 and renamed the Individuals with Disabilities Improvement Act. The 2004 version especially focuses on its alignment with No Child Left Behind legislation, which has raised questions about whether students with disabilities can be expected to meet the same general education standards and achievement as students without disabilities. The IEP is a written plan of the program specifically tailored for the child with a disability. The plan should (1) relate to the child's learning capacity, (2) be individualized and not a copy of a plan that is offered to other children, and (3) be designed to provide educational benefits. The concept of least restrictive environment (LRE) is contained in the IDEA. It states that children with disabilities must be educated in a setting that is as similar as possible to the one in which children without disabilities are educated. This provision of IDEA has given a legal basis to making an effort to educate children with disabilities in the regular classroom. The term inclusion means educating children with disabilities full-time in the regular classroom. The trend is toward using inclusion more. Children's academic and social success is affected more by the quality of instruction they receive than by where they are placed.

| Technology | Instructional technology includes various types of hardware and software, combined with innovative teaching methods, to accommodate children's needs in the classroom. Assistive technology consists of various services and devices to help children with disabilities function within their environment. |

3 **CHILDREN WHO ARE GIFTED:** Define what gifted means and discuss some approaches to teaching children who are gifted.

| Characteristics | Children who are gifted have above-average intelligence (usually defined as an IQ of 130 or higher) and/or superior talent in some domain, such as art, music, or mathematics. Some critics argue that gifted programs include too many children who are just somewhat bright, usually cooperative, and, usually, non-Latino White. Winner described children who are gifted as having three main characteristics: precocity, marching to the tune of a different drummer, and a passion to master. |

| Life Course of the Gifted | Giftedness likely involves a combination of heredity and environment. Deliberate practice is often important in the achievement of the gifted. In Terman's study, many gifted children became successful achievers in adulthood, but most did not become major creators. |

| Educating Children Who Are Gifted | Educational programs available for children who are gifted include special classes ("pullout" programs), acceleration, enrichment, mentor and apprenticeship programs, as well as work/study or community-service programs. Debate focuses on whether acceleration or enrichment programs most benefit children who are gifted. Children who are gifted increasingly are being educated in the regular classroom. Some experts recommend that increasing the standards in the regular classroom will help children who are gifted, although programs such as mentoring and additional instruction might be needed for children who are still underchallenged. One concern is that the No Child Left Behind legislation has harmed the education of students who are gifted by focusing attention on students' deficiencies. |

 KEY TERMS

learning disability 194
dyslexia 195
dysgraphia 195
dyscalculia 195
attention deficit hyperactivity disorder (ADHD) 198
mental retardation 201
Down syndrome 201
orthopedic impairments 203
cerebral palsy 203

epilepsy 203
speech and language disorders 204
articulation disorders 204
voice disorders 205
fluency disorders 205
language disorders 205
receptive language 205
expressive language 205

specific language impairment (SLI) 205
autism spectrum disorders (ASD) 205
autistic disorder 206
Asperger syndrome 206
emotional and behavioral disorders 206
Public Law 94-142 211

Individuals with Disabilities Education Act (IDEA) 211
individualized education plan (IEP) 211
least restrictive environment (LRE) 212
inclusion 212
children who are gifted 217

PORTFOLIO ACTIVITIES

Now that you have a good understanding of this chapter, complete these exercises to expand your thinking.

Independent Reflection

Fostering Positive School-Home Linkages for Children with Disabilities. Place yourself in the role of a parent. Imagine that the school has just notified you that your child has a learning disability. Write down answers to these questions: (1) What feelings are you likely to be having as a parent? (2) As a parent, what questions do you want to ask the teacher? (3) Now put yourself in the role of the teacher. How would you respond to these questions? (INTASC: Principles *3, 10*)

Collaborative Work

Technology Resources for Gifted Students. Together with three or four other students in your class, come up with a list and

description of software programs that you think would benefit gifted children. One good source of information on such software is the *Journal of Electronic Learning.* Write down the list and descriptions. (INTASC: Principles *3, 4, 9*)

Research/Field Experience

Inclusion in Action. Interview elementary school, middle school, and high school teachers about their impressions of inclusion and other aspects of educating children with disabilities. Ask them what their most successful strategies are in working with children who have disabilities. Also ask what the biggest challenges are. Write a summary of the interviews. (INTASC: Principle *9*)

Go to the Online Learning Center for downloadable portfolio templates.

 TAKING IT TO THE NET

- Teachers who work with special needs children typically develop an individualized education plan (IEP) for each child. What is an IEP? Review sample IEPs online, and discuss how all students could benefit from receiving the type of feedback present in an IEP. How could you use an IEP as a model for tailoring your instruction to the special needs of all students? **www.bced.gov.bc.ca/specialed/iepssn**

- You recommend that a student be assessed for possible entry into your school's gifted program, but the school psychologist informs you that the child is a *C* student. Is it possible to be a "gifted underachiever"? Explain. **www.ericec.org/digests/darchives/e478.html**

- Imagine that you have two students in your classroom who have been diagnosed with ADHD. What are some strategies for helping these children succeed in the classroom? Why is family support so important, and what specific actions will you take to maintain ongoing communication with them? **www.ldonline .org/ld_indepth/add_adhd/tec_home_school_ collab.html**

Connect to the Online Learning Center to explore possible answers.

 STUDY, PRACTICE, AND SUCCEED

Visit **www.mhhe.com/santedu4e** to review the chapter with self-grading quizzes and self-assessments, to apply the chapter material to two more Crack the Case studies, and for suggested activities to develop your teaching portfolio.

CHAPTER 7

Behavioral and Social Cognitive Approaches

To learn is a natural pleasure.
—Aristotle
Greek Philosopher, 4th Century, B.C.

TEACHING STORIES Ruth Sidney Charney

Ruth Sidney Charney has been a teacher for more than 35 years. She has developed the responsive classroom approach to teaching and learning, a method that emphasizes positive reinforcement of students' good behavior. Following are some of her thoughts about reinforcing students' learning (Charney, 2005, pp. 1–2):

> We reinforce children when we notice. We notice the personal detail our children bring to school and we notice their efforts to behave and learn. . . . We applaud the five correct answers on the math paper (when last week there were only two), the extra sentence in writing, the crisp adjectives, the ten minutes of fair play in a game. . . .
>
> We reinforce by noticing the positive attempts children make to follow the rules and meet class expectations. We reinforce when children are practicing new skills or when they demonstrate behaviors recently modeled. . . .
>
> Examples of noticing and reinforcing students include:
>
> - "Today's the day, isn't it?" the teacher whispers to Hector. He smiles at her and they share a quick high-

five salute, acknowledging Hector's impending solo performance in the church choir.

- "Snazzy new boots?" the teacher asks Leila as she struts into class. . . .
- "Thanks for helping Tessa with her spelling. I notice you gave her good hints so she could spell some of the words herself."
- "I noticed it took much less time today to get in line. What did you notice . . . ?"
- "I noticed you got your math done this morning with no interruption. That took lots of concentration. . . ."
- "Thank you for your very efficient clean-up today. I noticed caps back on markers, pencils with points down in cans, paper off the floor. . . ."
- "You really found an interesting way to solve the problem and complete the project together."

Preview

Virtually everyone agrees that helping students learn is an important function of schools. However, not everyone agrees on the best way to learn. We begin this chapter by examining just what learning involves, then turn to the main behavioral approaches to learning. Next, we explore how behavioral principles are applied to educating students. In the final section, we will discuss the social cognitive approaches to learning.

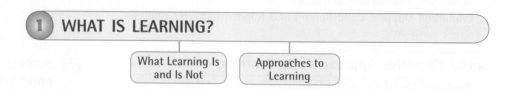

Learning is a central focus of educational psychology. When people are asked what schools are for, a common reply is "To help children learn."

What Learning Is and Is Not

When children learn how to use a computer, they might make some mistakes along the way, but at a certain point they will get the knack of the behaviors required to use the computer effectively. The children will change from being individuals who cannot operate a computer into being individuals who can. Once they have learned how, they don't lose those skills. It's like learning to drive a car. Once you have learned how, you don't have to learn all over again. Thus, **learning** can be defined as a relatively permanent influence on behavior, knowledge, and thinking skills, which comes about through experience.

Not everything we know is learned. We inherit some capacities—they are inborn or innate, not learned. For example, we don't have to be taught to swallow, to flinch at loud noises, or to blink when an object comes too close to our eyes. Most human behaviors, however, do not involve heredity alone. When children use a computer in a new way, work harder at solving problems, ask better questions, explain an answer in a more logical way, or listen more attentively, the experience of learning is at work.

The scope of learning is broad (Hergenhahn & Olson, 2009; Klein, 2009; Weiss, 2008). It involves academic behaviors and nonacademic behaviors. It occurs in schools and everywhere else that children experience their world.

Approaches to Learning

A number of approaches to learning have been proposed. Next we explore behavioral and cognitive approaches to learning.

Behavioral   The learning approaches that we discuss in the first part of this chapter are called *behavioral*. **Behaviorism** is the view that behavior should be explained by observable experiences, not by mental processes. For the behaviorist, behavior is everything that we do, both verbal and nonverbal, that can be directly seen or heard: a child creating a poster, a teacher explaining something to a child, one student picking on another student, and so on. **Mental processes** are defined by psychologists as the thoughts, feelings, and motives that each of us experiences but that cannot be observed by others. Although we cannot directly see thoughts, feelings, and motives, they are no less real. Mental processes include children thinking about ways to create the best poster, a teacher feeling good about children's efforts, and children's inner motivation to control their behavior.

For the behaviorist, these thoughts, feelings, and motives are not appropriate subject matter for a science of behavior because they cannot be directly observed (Shanks, 2009). Classical conditioning and operant conditioning, two behavioral views that we will discuss shortly, adopt this stance. Both of these views emphasize **associative learning**, which consists of learning that two events are connected or associated (Olson & Hergenhahn, 2009). For example, associative learning occurs when a student associates a pleasant event with learning something in school, such as the teacher smiling when the student asks a good question.

Cognitive   Cognition means "thought," and psychology became more cognitive or began focusing more on thought in the last part of the twentieth century. The cognitive emphasis continues today and is the basis for numerous approaches to learning (Mayer, 2008; Sternberg, 2008, 2009a, b, c). We discuss four main cognitive approaches to learning in this book: social cognitive; information processing; cognitive constructivist; and social constructivist. The *social cognitive* approaches, which emphasize how behavior, environment, and person (cognitive) factors interact to influence learning, will be covered later in this chapter (Bandura, 2006, 2007a, b, 2008, 2009). The second set of approaches, *information processing*, focuses on how children process information through attention, memory, thinking, and other cognitive processes (Galotti, 2008). The third set of approaches, *cognitive constructivist*, emphasizes the child's cognitive construction of knowledge and understanding (Halford, 2008). The fourth set of cognitive approaches, *social constructivist*, focuses on collaboration with others to produce knowledge and understanding (Holzman, 2009).

learning A relatively permanent influence on behavior, knowledge, and thinking skills, which comes about through experience.

behaviorism The view that behavior should be explained by observable experiences, not by mental processes.

mental processes Thoughts, feelings, and motives that cannot be observed by others.

associative learning Learning that two events are connected (associated).

What are five main approaches to learning?

Adding these four cognitive approaches to the behavioral approaches, we arrive at five main approaches to learning that we discuss in this book: behavioral, social cognitive, information processing, cognitive constructivist, and social constructivist. All contribute to our understanding of how children learn. A summary of the five approaches is presented in Figure 7.1.

As you read Chapters 7 through 11 on learning and cognition, keep in mind that students are more likely to learn in optimal ways in appropriate learning environments. Students learn best when learning environments are tailored to specific learning goals, to the students' backgrounds and prior knowledge, and to the contexts in which learning will occur. Thus teachers not only need to understand the basic principles of learning but must also know how to use them judiciously to meet diverse learning goals in contexts where students' needs differ (Bransford & others, 2005, p. 78).

Review, Reflect, and Practice

① **Define learning and describe five approaches to studying it.**

REVIEW

- What is learning? Are there any behaviors that don't reflect learning?
- What essentially is behaviorism? What are four main cognitive approaches to learning?

REFLECT

- How do you learn? Think of a behavior you engage in and describe how you learned it.

PRAXIS™ PRACTICE

1. According to the psychological definition of learning, all of the following are examples of learning *except*
   a. writing.
   b. sneezing.
   c. swimming.
   d. washing dishes.
2. Mr. Zeller does not believe his students have learned anything unless they demonstrate it to him. This demonstration could be through assignments they turn in to him, answering questions in class, or the way they behave. Which approach to learning is most consistent with Mr. Zeller's ideas?
   a. cognitive
   b. behavioral
   c. social cognitive
   d. conditioning

Please see the answer key at the end of the book.

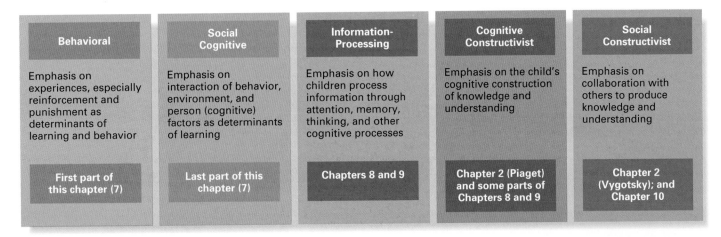

FIGURE 7.1 Approaches to Learning

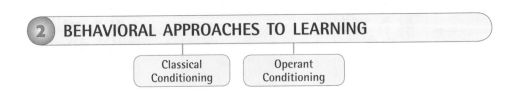

② BEHAVIORAL APPROACHES TO LEARNING

The behavioral approaches emphasize the importance of children making connections between experiences and behavior. The first behavioral approach we will examine is classical conditioning.

Classical Conditioning

Classical conditioning is a type of learning in which an organism learns to connect, or associate, stimuli. In classical conditioning, a neutral stimulus (such as the sight of a person) becomes associated with a meaningful stimulus (such as food) and acquires the capacity to elicit a similar response. Classical conditioning was the brainchild of Ivan Pavlov (1927). To fully understand Pavlov's theory of classical conditioning, we need to understand two types of stimuli and two types of responses: unconditioned stimulus (UCS), unconditioned response (UCR), conditioned stimulus (CS), and conditioned response (CR).

Figure 7.2 summarizes the way classical conditioning works. An *unconditioned stimulus (UCS)* is a stimulus that automatically produces a response without any prior learning. Food was the UCS in Pavlov's experiments. An *unconditioned response (UCR)* is an unlearned response that is automatically elicited by the UCS. In Pavlov's experiments, the dog's salivation in response to food was the UCR. A *conditioned stimulus (CS)* is a previously neutral stimulus that eventually elicits a conditioned response after being associated with the UCS. Among the conditioned stimuli in Pavlov's experiments were various sights and sounds that occurred prior to the dog's actually eating the food, such as the sound of the door closing before the food was placed in the dog's dish. A *conditioned response (CR)* is a learned response to the conditioned stimulus that occurs after UCS-CS pairing.

Classical conditioning can be involved in both positive and negative experiences of children in the classroom (Lippman, 2008). Among the things in the child's schooling that produce pleasure because they have become classically conditioned are a favorite song and feelings that the classroom is a safe and fun place to be. For example, a song could be neutral for the child until the child joins in with other classmates to sing it with accompanying positive feelings.

Ivan Pavlov (1849–1936), the Russian physiologist who developed the concept of classical conditioning.

classical conditioning A form of associative learning in which a neutral stimulus becomes associated with a meaningful stimulus and acquires the capacity to elicit a similar response.

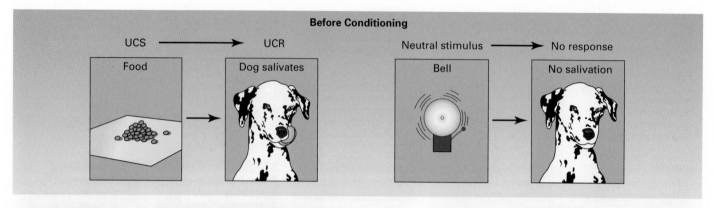

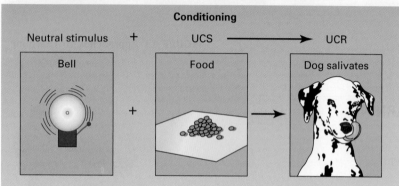

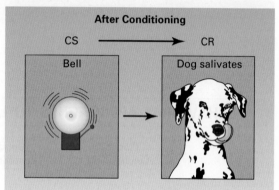

FIGURE 7.2 Pavlov's Classical Conditioning

In one experiment, Pavlov presented a neutral stimulus (bell) just before an unconditioned stimulus (food). The neutral stimulus became a conditioned stimulus by being paired with the unconditioned stimulus. Subsequently, the conditioned stimulus (bell) by itself was able to elicit the dog's salivation.

FIGURE 7.3 Classical Conditioning Involved in Teachers' Criticism of Children and Tests

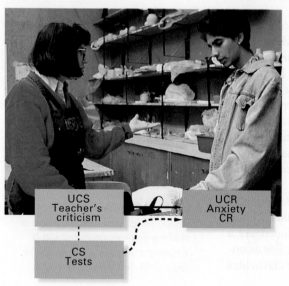

Children can develop fear of the classroom if they associate the classroom with criticism, so the criticism becomes a CS for fear. Classical conditioning also can be involved in test anxiety. For example, a child fails and is criticized, which produces anxiety; thereafter, the child associates tests with anxiety, so they then can become a CS for anxiety (see Figure 7.3).

Some children's health problems also might involve classical conditioning. Certain physical complaints—asthma, headaches, and high blood pressure—might be partly due to classical conditioning. We usually say that such health problems can be caused by stress. Often what happens, though, is that certain stimuli, such as a parent's or teacher's heavy criticism, are conditioned stimuli for physiological responses. Over time, the frequency of the physiological responses can produce a health problem. A teacher's persistent criticism of a student can cause the student to develop headaches, muscle tension, and so on. Anything associated with the teacher, such as classroom learning exercises and homework, might trigger the student's stress and subsequently be linked with headaches or other physiological responses.

Generalization, Discrimination, and Extinction   In studying a dog's responses to various stimuli, Pavlov rang a bell before giving meat powder to the dog. By being paired with the UCS (meat), the bell became a CS and elicited the dog's salivation. After a time, Pavlov found that the dog also responded to other sounds, such as a whistle. The more bell-like the noise, the stronger the dog's response. *Generalization* in classical conditioning involves the tendency of a new stimulus similar to the original conditioned stimulus to produce a similar response (Pearce & Hall, 2009). Let's consider a classroom example. A student is criticized for poor performance on a biology test. When the student begins to prepare for a chemistry test, she also becomes very nervous because these two subjects are closely related in the sciences. Thus, the student's anxiety generalizes from taking a test in one subject to taking a test in another.

Discrimination in classical conditioning occurs when the organism responds to certain stimuli but not others. To produce discrimination, Pavlov gave food to the dog only after ringing the bell, not after any other sounds. Subsequently, the dog responded only to the bell. In the case of the student taking tests in different classes, she doesn't become nearly as nervous about taking an English test or a history test because they are very different subject areas.

Extinction in classical conditioning involves the weakening of the conditioned response (CR) in the absence of the unconditioned stimulus (UCS). In one session, Pavlov rang the bell repeatedly but did not give the dog any food. Eventually the dog stopped salivating at the sound of the bell. Similarly, if the student who gets nervous while taking tests begins to do much better on tests, her anxiety will fade.

Systematic Desensitization   Sometimes the anxiety and stress associated with negative events can be eliminated by classical conditioning (Kelly & Forsyth, 2007; Maier & Seligman, 2009). **Systematic desensitization** is a method based on classical conditioning that reduces anxiety by getting the individual to associate deep relaxation with successive visualizations of increasingly anxiety-producing situations. Imagine that you have a student in your class who is extremely nervous about talking in front of the class. The goal of systematic desensitization is to get the student to associate public speaking with relaxation, such as walking on a quiet beach, rather than anxiety. Using successive visualizations, the student might practice systematic desensitization two weeks before the talk, then a week before, four days before, two days before, the day before, the morning of the talk, on entering the room where the talk is to be given, on the way to the podium, and during the talk.

Desensitization involves a type of counterconditioning. The relaxing feelings that the student imagines (UCS) produce relaxation (UCR). The student then associates anxiety-producing cues (CS) with the relaxing feelings. Such relaxation is incompatible with anxiety. By initially pairing a weak anxiety-producing cue with relaxation and gradually working up the hierarchy (from two weeks before the talk to walking up to the podium to give the talk), all of the anxiety-producing cues should generate relaxation (CR).

Chances are you will have students who fear speaking in front of the class or have other anxieties, and there may be circumstances in your own life where you might benefit from replacing anxiety with relaxation. For example, it is not unusual for some teachers to feel comfortable when talking in front of their students but to get very nervous if asked to give a presentation at a teaching conference. Counselors and mental health professionals have been very successful at getting individuals to overcome their fear of public speaking using systematic desensitization. Should you be interested in adopting this strategy, do it with the help of a school psychologist rather than on your own.

How might systematic desensitization be used with students who have a fear of giving a talk in class?

Evaluating Classical Conditioning   Classical conditioning helps us understand some aspects of learning better than others (Brown & Jenkins, 2009). It excels in explaining how neutral stimuli become associated with unlearned, involuntary responses (Rescorla, 2009). It is especially helpful in understanding students' anxieties and fears (Klein, 2008). However, it is not as effective in explaining voluntary behaviors, such as why a student studies hard for a test or likes history better than geography. For these areas, operant conditioning is more relevant.

systematic desensitization A method based on classical conditioning that reduces anxiety by getting the individual to associate deep relaxation with successive visualizations of increasingly anxiety-provoking situations.

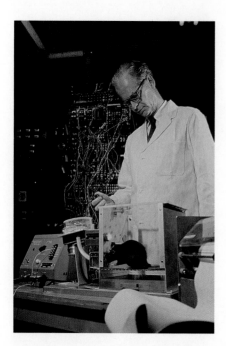

B. F. Skinner conducting an operant conditioning study in his behavioral laboratory. The rat being studied is in a Skinner box.

Operant Conditioning

Operant conditioning (also called *instrumental conditioning*) is a form of learning in which the consequences of behavior produce changes in the probability that the behavior will occur. Operant conditioning is at the heart of B. F. Skinner's (1938) behaviorial view. Consequences—rewards and punishments—are contingent on the organism's behavior.

Reinforcement and Punishment **Reinforcement (reward)** is a consequence that increases the probability that a behavior will occur. In contrast, **punishment** is a consequence that decreases the probability a behavior will occur. For example, you might tell one of your students, "Congratulations. I'm really proud of the story that you wrote." If the student works harder and writes an even better story the next time, your positive comments are said to reinforce, or reward, the student's writing behavior. If you frown at a student for talking in class and the student's talking decreases, your frown is said to punish the student's talking.

To reinforce behavior means to strengthen the behavior (Donahue, 2008). Two forms of reinforcement are positive reinforcement and negative reinforcement. In **positive reinforcement**, the frequency of a response increases because it is followed by a rewarding stimulus, as in the example in which the teacher's positive comments increased the student's writing behavior. Similarly, complimenting parents on being at a parent-teacher conference might encourage them to come back again.

Conversely, in **negative reinforcement**, the frequency of a response increases because it is followed by the removal of an aversive (unpleasant) stimulus. For example, a father nags at his son to do his homework. He keeps nagging. Finally, the son gets tired of hearing the nagging and does his homework. The son's response (doing his homework) removed the unpleasant stimulus (nagging).

One way to remember the distinction between positive and negative reinforcement is that in positive reinforcement something is added (Eagle, 2008). In negative reinforcement, something is subtracted, or removed. It is easy to confuse negative reinforcement and punishment. To keep these terms straight, remember that negative reinforcement *increases* the probability a response will occur, whereas punishment *decreases* the probability it will occur. Figure 7.4 summarizes and presents examples of the concepts of positive reinforcement, negative reinforcement, and punishment.

Generalization, Discrimination, and Extinction In our coverage of classical conditioning, we discussed generalization, discrimination, and extinction. These processes also are important dimensions of operant conditioning (Martin & Pear, 2007). Remember that in classical conditioning, generalization is the tendency of a stimulus similar to the conditioned stimulus to produce a response similar to the conditioned response. *Generalization* in operant conditioning means giving the same response to similar stimuli. Especially of interest is the extent to which behavior generalizes from one situation to another. For example, if a teacher praises the student for asking good questions related to English, will this generalize to harder work in history, math, and other subjects?

Remember that in classical conditioning, discrimination means responding to certain stimuli but not others. *Discrimination* in operant conditioning involves differentiating among stimuli or environmental events. For example, a student knows that the tray on the teacher's desk labeled "Math" is where she is supposed to place today's math work, whereas another tray labeled "English" is where today's English assignments are to be put. This might sound overly simple, but it is important because students' worlds are filled with such discriminative stimuli. Around school these discriminative stimuli might include signs that say "Stay Out," "Form a Line Here," and so on.

In operant conditioning, *extinction* occurs when a previously reinforced response is no longer reinforced and the response decreases. In the classroom, the most common use of extinction is for the teacher to withdraw attention from a behavior that

operant conditioning Also called instrumental conditioning, this is a form of learning in which the consequences of behavior produce changes in the probability that the behavior will occur.

reinforcement (reward) A consequence that increases the probability that a behavior will occur.

punishment A consequence that decreases the probability that a behavior will occur.

positive reinforcement Reinforcement based on the principle that the frequency of a response increases because it is followed by a rewarding stimulus.

negative reinforcement Reinforcement based on the principle that the frequency of a response increases because an aversive (unpleasant) stimulus is removed.

Positive Reinforcement

Negative Reinforcement

Punishment

BEHAVIOR		
Student asks a good question	Student turns homework in on time	Student interrupts teacher

CONSEQUENCE		
Teacher praises student	Teacher stops criticizing student	Teacher verbally reprimands student

FUTURE BEHAVIOR		
Student asks more good questions	Student increasingly turns homework in on time	Student stops interrupting teacher

Remember that reinforcement comes in positive and negative forms. In both forms, the consequences increase behavior. In punishment, behavior is decreased.

FIGURE 7.4 Reinforcement and Punishment

the attention is maintaining. For example, in some cases a teacher's attention inadvertently reinforces a student's disruptive behavior, as when a student pinches another student and the teacher immediately talks with the perpetrator. If this happens on a regular basis, the student might learn that pinching other students is a good way to get the teacher's attention. If the teacher withdraws his or her attention, the pinching might extinguish.

Review, Reflect, and Practice

② **Compare classical conditioning and operant conditioning.**

REVIEW

- What is classical conditioning? What are the UCS, UCR, CS, and CR? In the context of classical conditioning, what is generalization, discrimination, extinction, and systematic desensitization?
- What is operant conditioning? Explain the different types of reinforcement and punishment. In the context of operant conditioning, what is generalization, discrimination, and extinction?

REFLECT

- Do you think that your emotions are the result of classical conditioning, operant conditioning, or both? Explain.

(continued)

Review, Reflect, and Practice

PRAXIS™ PRACTICE

1. Sylvia is participating in a class spelling bee. The teacher asks her to spell the word *mortgage*. "Don't forget the *t*, don't forget the *t*," Sylvia says to herself. "M-O-R-T-A-G-E," says Sylvia. "I'm sorry, that's incorrect, Sylvia," says her teacher. One of the students in the back of the class snickers and comments, "Gee, about time Miss Smarty-pants got one wrong. See, she's not so smart." Some other students join in the laughter. Sylvia begins to cry and runs out of the room. After that, Sylvia becomes very anxious about spelling bees. According to classical conditioning theory, what is the conditioned stimulus in this scenario?
   a. the teacher telling her she is incorrect
   b. the other students' laughter
   c. the word *mortgage*
   d. spelling bees

2. Tyler is a fourth-grade student. He loves to crack jokes, often at his teacher's expense. One day he called his teacher, Ms. Bart, "Ms. Fart." Ms. Bart quickly admonished him for his behavior and told him that name-calling was unacceptable. She made him stay after school to discuss his behavior. The other students in the class thought Tyler's nickname for Ms. Bart was hilarious, laughing along with Tyler and later telling him what a good name that was for Ms. Bart. The next day, Tyler again called Ms. Bart by the insulting nickname. According to operant conditioning theory, Tyler continued to use this name in spite of having to stay after school the day before because
   a. the behavior had continued for a lengthy period of time.
   b. he was positively reinforced by his classmates for the behavior.
   c. he was negatively reinforced by his teacher for his behavior.
   d. he was punished by his teacher for his behavior.

Please see the answer key at the end of the book.

3 APPLIED BEHAVIOR ANALYSIS IN EDUCATION

What Is Applied Behavior Analysis?	Increasing Desirable Behaviors	Decreasing Undesirable Behaviors	Evaluating Operant Conditioning and Applied Behavior Analysis

Many applications of operant conditioning have been made outside of research laboratories in the wider worlds of classrooms, homes, business settings, hospitals, and other real-world settings (Miltenberger, 2008; Scarlett, Ponte, & Singh, 2009). This section describes how teachers can use applied behavior analysis to improve students' behavior and learning.

What Is Applied Behavior Analysis?

applied behavior analysis Application of the principles of operant conditioning to change human behavior.

Applied behavior analysis involves applying the principles of operant conditioning to change human behavior. Three uses of applied behavior analysis are especially important in education: increasing desirable behavior, using prompts and shaping, and decreasing undesirable behavior (Alberto & Troutman, 2006; Gortmaker & others, 2007). Applications of applied behavior analysis often use a series of steps (Madle, 2008). These often begin with some general observations and then turn to determining the specific target behavior that needs to be changed, as well as observing its antecedent conditions. Behavioral goals are then set, particular reinforcers or punish-ers are selected, a behavior management program is carried out, and the success or failure of the program is evaluated (Kerr & Nelson, 2006).

Increasing Desirable Behaviors

Six operant conditioning strategies can be used to increase a child's desirable behaviors: choose effective reinforcers; make reinforcers contingent and timely; select the best schedule of reinforcement; consider contracting; use negative reinforcement effectively; and use prompts and shaping.

Choose Effective Reinforcers Not all reinforcers are the same for every child. Applied behavior analysts recommend that teachers find out what reinforcers work best with which children—that is, individualize the use of particular reinforcers (Scarlett, Ponte, & Singh, 2009). For one student it might be praise, for another it might be getting to spend more time participating in a favorite activity, for another it might involve being a hall monitor for a week, and for yet another it could be getting to surf the Internet. To find out the most effective reinforcers for a child, you can examine what has motivated the child in the past (reinforcement history), what the student wants but can't easily or frequently get, and the child's perception of the reinforcer's value. Some applied behavior analysts recommend asking children which reinforcers they like best. Another recommendation is to consider novel reinforcers to reduce the child's boredom. Natural reinforcers such as praise and privileges are generally recommended over material rewards such as candy, stars, and money.

Activities are some of the most common reinforcers that teachers use. Named after psychologist David Premack, the **Premack principle** states that a high-probability activity can serve as a reinforcer for a low-probability activity. The Premack principle is at work when an elementary school teacher tells a child, "When you complete your writing assignment, you can play a game on the computer" (but only effective if playing games on a computer is more desirable for the student than writing). The Premack principle also can be used with the entire class. A teacher might tell the class, "If all of the class gets their homework done by Friday, we will take a field trip next week."

Make Reinforcers Contingent and Timely For a reinforcer to be effective, the teacher must give it only after the child performs the particular behavior. Applied behavior analysts often recommend that teachers make "If . . . then" statements to children—for example, "Tony, if you finish ten math problems, then you can go out to play." This makes it clear to Tony what he has to do to get the reinforcer. Applied behavior analysts say that it is important to make the reinforcer contingent on the child's behavior. That is, the child has to perform the behavior to get the reward. If Tony does not complete ten math problems and the teacher still lets him go out to play, the contingency has not been established.

Reinforcers are more effective when they are given in a timely way, as soon as possible after the child performs the target behavior (Umbreit & others, 2007). This helps children see the contingency connection between the reward and their behavior. If the child completes the target behavior (such as doing ten math problems by midmorning) and the teacher doesn't give the child playtime until late afternoon, the child might have trouble making the contingency connection.

Select the Best Schedule of Reinforcement Most of the examples given so far assume continuous reinforcement—that is, the child is reinforced every time he or she makes a response. In continuous reinforcement, children learn very rapidly, but when the reinforcement stops (the teacher stops praising), extinction also occurs

Premack principle The principle that a high-probability activity can serve as a reinforcer for a low-probability activity.

"Once it became clear to me that, by responding correctly to certain stimuli, I could get all the bananas I wanted, getting this job was a pushover."

rapidly. In the classroom, continuous reinforcement is rare. A teacher with a classroom of twenty-five or thirty students can't praise a child every time he or she makes an appropriate response.

Partial reinforcement involves reinforcing a response only part of the time. Skinner (1957) developed the concept of **schedules of reinforcement**, which are partial reinforcement timetables that determine when a response will be reinforced. The four main schedules of reinforcement are fixed-ratio, variable-ratio, fixed-interval, and variable-interval.

On a *fixed-ratio schedule,* a behavior is reinforced after a set number of responses. For example, a teacher might praise the child only after every fourth correct response, not after every response. On a *variable-ratio schedule,* a behavior is reinforced after an average number of times, but on an unpredictable basis. For example, a teacher's praise might average out to being given every fifth response but be given after the second correct response, after eight more correct responses, after the next seven correct responses, and after the next three correct responses.

Interval schedules are determined by the amount of time elapsed since the last behavior was reinforced. On a *fixed-interval schedule,* the first appropriate response after a fixed amount of time is reinforced. For example, a teacher might praise a child for the first good question the child asks after two minutes have elapsed or give a quiz every week. On a *variable-interval schedule,* a response is reinforced after a variable amount of time has elapsed. On this schedule, the teacher might praise the child's question-asking after three minutes have gone by, then after fifteen minutes have gone by, after seven minutes have gone by, and so on. Giving a pop quiz at uneven intervals is another example of a variable-interval schedule.

What is the effect of using these schedules of reinforcement with children? Initial learning is usually faster with continuous rather than partial reinforcement. In other words, when students are first learning a behavior, continuous reinforcement works better. However, partial reinforcement produces greater persistence and greater resistance to extinction than continuous reinforcement does. Thus, once children master a response, partial reinforcement works better than continuous reinforcement.

Children on fixed schedules show less persistence and faster response extinction than children on variable schedules. Children show the most persistence on a variable-interval schedule. This schedule produces slow, steady responding because children don't know when the reward will come. As we mentioned earlier, giving pop quizzes at uneven intervals is a good example of the variable-interval schedule. If the teacher starts making the quizzes more predictable (for example, once a week on Fridays), children will begin to show the stop-start work pattern that characterizes the fixed-interval schedule. That is, they won't work hard for most of the week; then toward the end of the week they will start cramming for the quiz. Thus, if your goal as a teacher is to increase children's persistence after the behavior has been established, variable schedules work best, especially the variable-interval schedule. Figure 7.5 shows the different response patterns associated with the different schedules of reinforcement.

Consider Contracting **Contracting** involves putting reinforcement contingencies in writing. If problems arise and children don't uphold their end of the bargain, the teacher can refer the children to the contract they agreed to. Applied behavior analysts suggest that a classroom contract should be the result of input from both the teacher and the student. Classroom contracts have "If . . . then" statements

schedules of reinforcement Partial reinforcement timetables that determine when a response will be reinforced.

contracting Putting reinforcement contingencies into writing.

and are signed by the teacher and child, then dated. A teacher and child might agree on a contract that states that the child agrees to be a good citizen by doing _____, _____, and _____. As part of the contract, the teacher agrees to _____ if the student behaves in this manner. In some instances, the teacher asks another child to sign the contract as a witness to the agreement.

Use Negative Reinforcement Effectively Remember that in *negative reinforcement,* the frequency of response increases because the response removes an aversive (unpleasant) stimulus (Alberto & Troutman, 2006). A teacher who says, "Thomas, you have to stay in your seat and finish writing your story before you join the other students in making a poster," is using negative reinforcement. The negative condition of being left in his seat while the other children are doing something enjoyable will be removed if Thomas finishes the story he should have completed earlier.

Using negative reinforcement has some drawbacks. Sometimes when teachers try to use this behavioral strategy, children throw a tantrum, run out of the room, or destroy materials. These negative outcomes happen most often when children don't have the skills or capabilities to do what the teacher asks of them.

Use Prompts and Shaping Earlier in our discussion of operant conditioning, we indicated that discrimination involves differentiating among stimuli or environmental events. Students can learn to discriminate among stimuli or events through differential reinforcement. Two differential reinforcement strategies available to teachers are prompts and shaping (Alberto & Troutman, 2006).

Prompts A **prompt** is an added stimulus or cue that is given just before a response that increases the likelihood that the response will occur. A reading teacher who holds up a card with the letters *w-e-r-e* and says, "Not was, but . . . " is using a verbal prompt. An art teacher who places the label "Watercolors" on one group of paints and "Oils" on another also is using prompts. Prompts help get behavior going. Once the students consistently show the correct responses, the prompts are no longer needed.

Instructions can be used as prompts (Alberto & Troutman, 2006). For example, as the art period is drawing to a close, the teacher says, "Let's get started on reading." If the students keep doing art, the teacher adds the prompt, "Okay, put away your art materials and come with me over to the reading area." Some prompts come in the form of hints, as when the teacher tells students to line up "quietly." Bulletin boards are common locations for prompts, frequently displaying reminders of class rules, due dates for projects, the location of a meeting, and so on. Some prompts are presented visually, as when the teacher places her hand on her ear when a student is not speaking loudly enough.

Shaping When teachers use prompts, they assume that students can perform the desired behaviors. But sometimes students do not have the ability to perform them. In this case, shaping is required (Peterson, 2008). **Shaping** involves teaching new behaviors by reinforcing successive approximations to a specified target behavior. Initially, you reinforce any response that in some way resembles the target behavior. Subsequently, you reinforce a response that more closely resembles the target, and so on until the student performs the target behavior, and then you reinforce it (Wildman, 2008).

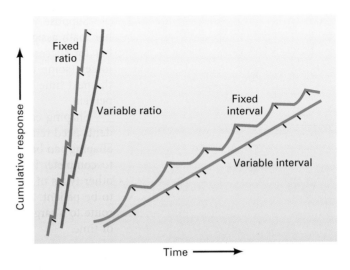

FIGURE 7.5 Schedules of Reinforcement and Different Patterns of Responding

In this figure, each hash mark indicates the delivery of reinforcement. Notice that ratio schedules (reinforcement is linked with number of responses) produce higher rates of responding than interval schedules (reinforcement is linked with the amount of time elapsed). The predictability of a reward also is important in that a predictable (fixed) schedule produces a higher response rate than an unpredictable (variable) schedule.

prompt An added stimulus or cue that is given just before a response that increases the likelihood the response will occur.

shaping Teaching new behaviors by reinforcing successive approximations to a specified target behavior.

Suppose you have a student who has never completed 50 percent or more of her math assignments. You set the target behavior at 100 percent, but you reinforce her for successive approximations to the target. You initially might provide a reinforcer (some type of privilege, for example) when she completes 60 percent, then the next time only when she completes 70 percent, then 80, then 90, and finally 100 percent.

Shaping can be an important tool for the classroom teacher because most students need reinforcement along the way to reaching a learning goal (Peterson, 2008). Shaping can be especially helpful for learning tasks that require time and persistence to complete. However, when using shaping, remember to implement it only if the other types of positive reinforcement and prompts are not working. Also remember to be patient. Shaping can require the reinforcement of a number of small steps en route to a target behavior, and these might take place only over an extended period of time.

Decreasing Undesirable Behaviors

When teachers want to decrease children's undesirable behaviors (such as teasing, hogging a class discussion, or smarting off to the teacher), what are their options? Applied behavior analysts Paul Alberto and Anne Troutman (2006) recommend using these steps in this order:

1. Use differential reinforcement.
2. Terminate reinforcement (extinction).
3. Remove desirable stimuli.
4. Present aversive stimuli (punishment).

Thus, the teacher's first option should be differential reinforcement. Punishment should be used only as a last resort and always in conjunction with providing the child information about appropriate behavior.

Use Differential Reinforcement In *differential reinforcement,* the teacher reinforces behavior that is more appropriate or that is incompatible with what the child is doing. For example, the teacher might reinforce a child for doing learning activities on a computer rather than playing games with it, for being courteous rather than interrupting, for being seated rather than running around the classroom, or for doing homework on time rather than late.

Terminate Reinforcement (Extinction) The strategy of terminating reinforcement involves withdrawing positive reinforcement from a child's inappropriate behavior. Many inappropriate behaviors are inadvertently maintained by positive reinforcement, especially the teacher's attention. Applied behavior analysts point out that this can occur even when the teacher gives attention to an inappropriate behavior by criticizing, threatening, or yelling at the student. Many teachers find it difficult to determine whether they are giving too much attention to inappropriate behavior. A good strategy is to get someone to observe your classroom on several occasions and chart the patterns of reinforcement you use with your students (Alberto & Troutman, 2006). If you become aware that you are giving too much attention to a student's inappropriate behavior, ignore that behavior and give attention to the student's appropriate behavior. Always combine taking attention away from inappropriate behavior with giving attention to appropriate behavior. For instance, when a student stops monopolizing the conversation in a group discussion after you withdraw your attention, compliment the student on the improved behavior.

This second-grade student has been placed in "time-out" for misbehaving. *What is the nature of time-out?*

Remove Desirable Stimuli Suppose you have tried the first two options, and they haven't worked. A third option is to remove desirable stimuli from the student. Two strategies for accomplishing this are "time-out" and "response cost."

DEVELOPMENTAL FOCUS 7.1

How Do You Use Applied Behavior Analysis in the Classroom?

Early Childhood

We use applied behavior analysis with our preschoolers by giving time-out to students who are misbehaving. For example, if a child throws a toy across the room during free play, hits another student, or speaks disrespectfully, we explain why this behavior is inappropriate and give time-out. The child has to sit in a chair, away from other students, and misses five minutes of free-play time. As a result, the child learns that negative behavior will not be tolerated.

—Missy Dangler, *Suburban Hills School*

Elementary School: Grades K–5

For my second-grade students, tangible or implied (a smile from me or attention) rewards work best. I also find that a combination of individual and group rewards work well in my classroom. For example, I give each student a "Compliment Sheet" at the beginning of the school year. When I see behavior that I want to encourage, I tell the student publicly that he or she may have a compliment. The student fills in one of the circles on the compliment page, and the others in the class—seeing that this student's particular behavior has been rewarded—imitate the student's behavior almost immediately. The rules are that no compliment may be removed and that a student may not ask for a compliment. When the Compliment Sheet is completed, a big deal is made of it, and the student can go the prize box and choose a small token such as stickers. At first this is an external way of conditioning behavior, but the children seem to move rapidly from wanting the "thing" to wanting the compliment to wanting the positive attention to doing the right thing.

—Janine Guida Poutre, *Clinton Elementary School*

Middle School: Grades 6–8

I'm not big on rewards for my sixth-grade students. I think students who act inappropriately in class need to learn how to cope and deal with controlling their behavior without expecting to receive something in return. Instead of rewards, I give students who turn from negative behavior to positive behavior more responsibility in the classroom. For example, students who engage in good behavior are given classroom jobs—for example, handing out pencils and paper, checking my mail box in the main office, and turning on/shutting off computers. Students love responsibility and are happy when I depend on them to perform important duties in the classroom.

—Felicia Peterson, *Pocantico Hills School*

High School: Grades 9–12

I set clear expectations for my high school students. For example, it is a classroom expectation that students are in my classroom, ready to work, when the bell rings. Students soon learn that walking in late results in not knowing what is going on in class and may lower their grade if they cannot complete an activity. It is important to start class on time and not let the stragglers determine when class will start.

—Sandy Swanson, *Menomonee Falls High School*

Time-Out   The most widely used strategy that teachers use to remove desirable stimuli is **time-out**. In other words, take the student away from positive reinforcement (Kazdin, 2008).

Response Cost   A second strategy for removing desirable stimuli involves **response cost**, which refers to taking a positive reinforcer away from a student, as when the student loses certain privileges. For example, after a student misbehaves, the teacher might take away 10 minutes of recess time or the privilege of being a class monitor. Response cost typically involves some type of penalty or fine. As with time-out,

time-out Removing an individual from positive reinforcement.

response cost Taking a positive reinforcer away from an individual.

243

BEST PRACTICES
Strategies for Using Time-Out

In using time-out, you have several options:

1. *Keep the student in the classroom, but deny the student access to positive reinforcement.* This strategy is most often used when a student does something minor. The teacher might ask the student to put his or her head down on the desk for a few minutes or might move the student to the periphery of an activity so the student can still observe other students experiencing positive reinforcement. Next, kindergarten teacher Rosemary Moore describes an innovative use of time-out.

THROUGH THE EYES OF TEACHERS
The Peace Place

Resolving conflicts is always difficult for children. When my kindergartners engaged in power struggles, they often turned to me to referee. I thought it would be much more beneficial if they could arrive at their own compromise. Ownership of the plan would make it more acceptable to all parties. To accomplish this, I put two small chairs in a corner of the room. Above the chairs was a sign that said, "Peace Place." Then when I heard a struggle begin, I would send the parties to this corner. There they sat facing each other with their knees almost touching. Their task was to negotiate a "peace plan." When the plan was agreed upon, they were to come to me. I would listen to their plan and either approve it or send them back for another try. Initially, this took some time, but as the children began to realize that the time they spent arguing was time away from the activity they were arguing about, they arrived at their plan much more quickly. It was a pleasure to watch them grow in their negotiating abilities.

2. *For time-out to be effective, the setting from which the student is removed has to be positively reinforcing, and the setting in which the student is placed has to not be positively reinforcing.* For example, if you seat a student in the hall outside your classroom and students from other classes come down the hall and talk with the student, the time-out is clearly not going to serve its intended purpose.

3. *If you use time-out, be sure to identify the student's behaviors that resulted in time-out.* For example, say to the student, "You tore up Corey's paper, so go to time-out right now for five minutes." Don't get into an argument with the student or accept lame excuses as to why the student should not get a time-out. If necessary, take the student to the time-out location. If the misbehavior occurs again, reidentify it and place the student in a time-out again. If the student starts yelling, knocking over furniture, and so on, when you assess time-out, add time to time-out. Be sure to let the student out of time-out when the designated time away from positive reinforcement is up. Don't comment on how well the student behaved during time-out; just return the student to the prior activity.

4. *Positively reinforce the student's positive behavior when he or she is not in time-out* (Kazdin, 2008). A good strategy is to reinforce the opposite behavior of the one being punished. For example, if the student got time-out for disruptive behavior, the teacher can praise the student for working on an assignment during regular class time.

5. *Keep records of each time-out session, especially if a time-out room is used.* This will help you monitor effective and ethical use of time-outs.

response cost should always be used in conjunction with strategies for increasing the student's positive behaviors.

Present Aversive Stimuli (Punishment)   Most people associate the presentation of aversive (unpleasant) stimuli with punishment, as when a teacher yells at a student or a parent spanks a child. However, in accordance with the definition of punishment given earlier in the chapter, an aversive stimulus is punishment only if it decreases the undesirable behavior. All too often, though, aversive stimuli are not effective punishments, in that they do not decrease the unwanted behavior and indeed sometimes increase the unwanted behavior over time (de Zoysa, Newcombe, & Rajapakse, 2008). One study found that when parents used spanking to discipline 4- to 5-year-old children, the problem behavior increased over time (McLoyd & Smith, 2002). Another study revealed that children whose parents hit or slapped them in the prior two weeks showed more emotional and adjustment problems than children who had not been hit or slapped by parents in the same time frame (Aucoin, Frick, & Bodin, 2006). A recent study discovered that a history of harsh physical discipline was linked to adolescent depression and externalized problems, such as juvenile delinquency (Bender & others, 2007). And another recent study found that harsh corporal punishment by parents was linked to poor school performance (Alyahri & Goodman, 2008).

The most common types of aversive stimuli that teachers use are verbal reprimands. These are more effectively used when the teacher is near the student rather than across the room and when used together with a nonverbal reprimand such as a frown or eye contact (Van Houten & others, 1982). Reprimands are more effective when they are given immediately after unwanted behavior and when they are short and to the point. Such reprimands do not have to involve yelling and shouting, which often just raise the noise level of the classroom and present the teacher as an uncontrolled model for students. Instead, a firmly stated "stop doing that" with eye contact is often sufficient to stop unwanted behavior. Another strategy is to take the student aside and reprimand the student in private rather than in front of the entire class.

Many countries, such as Sweden, have banned the physical punishment of schoolchildren (which usually involves school paddling) by principals and teachers (Durrant, 2008). However, in 2003, 23 U.S. states still allowed it with the greatest prevalence in southern states. A study of college students in 11 countries found that the United States and Canada have more favorable attitudes toward corporal punishment than many other countries (Curran & others, 2001; Hyman & others, 2001) (see Figure 7.6). Use of corporal punishment by parents is legal in every state in America, and it is estimated that 70 to 90 percent of American parents have spanked their children (Straus, 1991). A national survey of U.S. parents with 3- and 4-year-old children found that 26 percent of parents reported spanking their children frequently, and 67 percent of the parents reported yelling at their children frequently (Regaldo & others, 2004).

In U.S. schools, male minority students from low-income backgrounds are the most frequent recipients of physical punishment. Most psychologists and educators argue that physical punishment of students should not be used in any circumstance.

Physical or otherwise, numerous problems are associated with using aversive stimuli as intended punishment (Durrant, 2008; Gracia & Herrero, 2008):

- Especially when you use intense punishment such as yelling or screaming, you are presenting students with an out-of-control model for handling stressful situations (Sim & Ong, 2005).
- Punishment can instill fear, rage, or avoidance in students. Skinner's biggest concern was this: What punishment teaches is how to avoid something. For example, a student who experiences a punitive teacher might show a dislike for the teacher and not want to come to school.
- When students are punished, they might become so aroused and anxious that they can't concentrate clearly on their work for a long time after the punishment has been given.
- Punishment tells students what not to do rather than what to do (Kazdin, 2008). If you make a punishing statement, such as "No, that's not right," always accompany it with positive feedback, such as "but why don't you try this."
- What is intended as punishment can turn out to be reinforcing. A student might learn that misbehaving will not only get the teacher's attention but put the student in the limelight with classmates as well.
- Punishment can be abusive. When parents discipline their children, they might not intend to be abusive, but they might become so aroused when they are punishing the child that they become abusive.

A final lesson in all of this is to spend a lot more class time monitoring what students do right rather than what they do wrong (Maag, 2001). Too often disruptive

Country	Mean score (5 point scale)	
Canada	3.14	
United States	3.13	
South Korea	3.00	
Malaysia	2.90	
Great Britian	2.68	
Finland	2.34	
Greece	2.26	
Germany	2.13	
Spain	2.05	
Argentina	1.96	
Sweden	1.35	

FIGURE 7.6 Attitudes About Corporal Punishment in Different Countries

A 5-point scale was used to assess attitudes toward corporal punishment, with scores closer to 1 indicating an attitude against its use and scores closer to 5 suggesting an attitude for its use.

When used effectively, what are ways that operant conditioning and applied behavior analysis can be used to help teachers manage the classroom? What are some criticisms that have been leveled at these approaches?

behavior, not competent behavior, grabs a teacher's attention. Every day make it a point to scan your classroom for positive student behaviors that you ordinarily would not notice and give students attention for them.

Evaluating Operant Conditioning and Applied Behavior Analysis

Operant conditioning and applied behavior analysis have made contributions to teaching practice (Crimmins & others, 2007; McGoey & Rezzetano, 2008). Reinforcing and punishing consequences are part of teachers' and students' lives. Teachers give grades, praise and reprimand, smile and frown. Learning about how such consequences affect students' behavior improves your capabilities as a teacher. Used effectively, behavioral techniques can help you manage your classroom (Miltenberger, 2008). Reinforcing certain behaviors can improve some students' conduct and—used in conjunction with the time-out—can increase desired behaviors in some incorrigible students (Charles, 2008; Charles & Senter, 2008).

Critics of operant conditioning and applied behavior analysis argue that the whole approach places too much emphasis on external control of students' behavior—a better strategy is to help students learn to control their own behavior and become internally motivated (Eisenberger, 2009). Some critics argue that it is not the reward or punishment that changes behavior but, rather, the belief or expectation that certain actions will be rewarded or punished (Schunk, 2008). In other words, the behavioral theories do not give adequate attention to cognitive processes involved in learning (Anderson, 2009). Critics also point to potential ethical problems when operant conditioning is used inappropriately, as when a teacher immediately resorts to punishing students instead of first considering reinforcement strategies, or punishes a student without also giving the student information about appropriate behavior. Another criticism is that when teachers spend a lot of time using applied behavior analysis, they might focus too much on student conduct and not enough on academic learning. We will have much more to say about student conduct in Chapter 14, "Managing the Classroom."

Review, Reflect, and Practice

③ Apply behavior analysis to education.

REVIEW

- What is applied behavior analysis?
- What are six ways to increase desirable behaviors?
- What are four ways to decrease undesirable behaviors?
- What are some effective and ineffective uses of operant conditioning and applied behavior analysis?

REFLECT

- Come up with your own example in an educational setting for each of the six ways to increase desirable behavior.

Review, Reflect, and Practice

PRAXIS™ PRACTICE

1. The uses of applied behavior analysis in education include all of the following *except*
   a. asking a child to reflect about undesirable behavior.
   b. increasing desirable behavior.
   c. using prompts and shaping.
   d. decreasing undesirable behavior.

2. Ms. Sanders wants her students to be quiet and ready to learn as soon as possible after coming in from recess. Sometimes the children are so excited that they have difficulty quieting down. To help remind them that it is time to be quiet and listen, Ms. Sanders flicks the light switch on and off several times. The children immediately quiet and listen to her instructions. According to applied behavioral analysis, what is Ms. Sanders doing when she turns the lights on and off?
   a. prompting
   b. punishing
   c. coercing
   d. shaping

3. Sid is a real handful in class. He talks when he should be working quietly. He gets out of his seat without permission. He often disrupts class. His third-grade teacher, Ms. Marin, sends him out into the hall when he misbehaves as a form of time-out. However, Sid continues to misbehave. At one point, Ms. Marin checks on Sid in the hall and finds him quietly tossing a ball back and forth with a child from another class.
   Why has time-out been ineffective with Sid?
   a. Ms. Marin did not present an aversive enough stimulus to Sid.
   b. Ms. Marin did not use differential reinforcement effectively.
   c. Sid finds being in class to be reinforcing.
   d. Sid finds being in the hallway to be reinforcing.

4. Critics of applied behavior analysis techniques often point out that when these techniques are used in the classroom they
   a. lead to physical abuse of students.
   b. do not work effectively.
   c. take time away from academics.
   d. emphasize external control of behavior.

Please see the answer key at the end of the book.

④ SOCIAL COGNITIVE APPROACHES TO LEARNING

Bandura's Social Cognitive Theory	Observational Learning	Cognitive Behavior Approaches and Self-Regulation	Evaluating the Social Cognitive Approaches

Because students' thoughts affect their behavior and learning, a number of cognitive approaches to learning have been proposed. In this section, we will explore several social cognitive approaches, beginning with social cognitive theory. This theory evolved out of behavioral theories but has become increasingly more cognitive (Schunk, 2008).

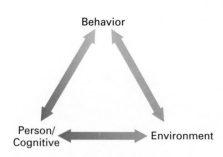

FIGURE 7.7 Bandura's Social Cognitive Theory

Bandura's social cognitive theory emphasizes reciprocal influences of behavior, environment, and person/cognitive factors.

Albert Bandura, who developed social cognitive theory.

social cognitive theory Bandura's theory that social and cognitive factors, as well as behavior, play important roles in learning.

self-efficacy The belief that one can master a situation and produce positive outcomes.

Bandura's Social Cognitive Theory

Social cognitive theory states that social and cognitive factors, as well as behavior, play important roles in learning. Cognitive factors might involve the student's expectations for success; social factors might include students' observing their parents' achievement behavior. Social cognitive theory is an increasingly important source of classroom applications (Denzine, 2008; Gredler, 2009; Hirt & Reilly, 2008).

Albert Bandura (1986, 1997, 2001, 2006, 2007a, b, 2008, 2009) is the main architect of social cognitive theory. He says that when students learn, they can cognitively represent or transform their experiences. Recall that in operant conditioning, connections occur only between environmental experiences and behavior.

Bandura developed a *reciprocal determinism model* that consists of three main factors: behavior, person/cognitive, and environment. As shown in Figure 7.7, these factors can interact to influence learning: Environmental factors influence behavior, behavior affects the environment, person (cognitive) factors influence behavior, and so on. Bandura uses the term *person*, but I have modified it to *person/cognitive* because so many of the person factors he describes are cognitive. The person factors Bandura describes that do not have a cognitive bent are mainly personality traits and temperament. Recall from Chapter 4, "Individual Variations," that such factors might include being introverted or extraverted, active or inactive, calm or anxious, and friendly or hostile. Cognitive factors include expectations, beliefs, attitudes, strategies, thinking, and intelligence.

Consider how Bandura's model might work in the case of the achievement behavior of a high school student we will call Sondra:

- *Cognition influences behavior.* Sondra develops cognitive strategies to think more deeply and logically about how to solve problems. The cognitive strategies improve her achievement behavior.
- *Behavior influences cognition.* Sondra's studying (behavior) has led her to achieve good grades, which in turn produce positive expectancies about her abilities and give her self-confidence (cognition).
- *Environment influences behavior.* The school Sondra attends recently developed a pilot study-skills program to help students learn how to take notes, manage their time, and take tests more effectively. The study-skills program improves Sondra's achievement behavior.
- *Behavior influences environment.* The study-skills program is successful in improving the achievement behavior of many students in Sondra's class. The students' improved achievement behavior stimulates the school to expand the program so that all students in the high school participate in it.
- *Cognition influences environment.* The expectations and planning of the school's principal and teachers made the study-skills program possible in the first place.
- *Environment influences cognition.* The school establishes a resource center where students and parents can go to check out books and materials on improving study skills. The resource center also makes study-skills tutoring services available to students. Sondra and her parents take advantage of the center's resources and tutoring. These resources and services improve Sondra's thinking skills.

In Bandura's learning model, person/cognitive factors play important roles. The person/cognitive factor that Bandura (2006, 2008, 2009) has emphasized the most in recent years is **self-efficacy**, the belief that one can master a situation and produce positive outcomes. Bandura says that self-efficacy has a powerful influence over behavior. For example, a student who has low self-efficacy might not even try to study for a test because he doesn't believe it will do him any good. We will have much more to say about self-efficacy in Chapter 13, "Motivation, Teaching, and Learning."

Next, we discuss the important learning process of observational learning, which is another of Bandura's main contributions. As you read about observational learning, note how person/cognitive factors are involved.

Observational Learning

Observational learning is learning that involves acquiring skills, strategies, and beliefs by observing others. Observational learning involves imitation but is not limited to it. What is learned typically is not an exact copy of what is modeled but rather a general form or strategy that observers often apply in creative ways. The capacity to learn behavior patterns by observation eliminates tedious trial-and-error learning. In many instances, observational learning takes less time than operant conditioning.

Bandura (1986) describes four key processes in observational learning: attention, retention, production, and motivation (see Figure 7.8):

- *Attention*. Before students can produce a model's actions, they must attend to what the model is doing or saying. Attention to the model is influenced by a host of characteristics. For example, warm, powerful, atypical people command more attention than do cold, weak, typical people. Students are more likely to be attentive to high-status models than to low-status models. In most cases, teachers are high-status models for students.

- *Retention*. To reproduce a model's actions, students must code the information and keep it in memory so that they retrieve it. A simple verbal description or a vivid image of what the model did assists students' retention. For example, the teacher might say, "I'm showing the correct way to do this. You have to do this step first, this step second, and this step third," as she models how to solve a math problem. A video with a colorful character demonstrating the importance of considering other students' feelings might be remembered better than if the teacher just tells the students to do this. Such colorful characters are at the heart of the popularity of *Sesame Street* with children. Students' retention will be improved when teachers give vivid, logical, and clear demonstrations.

- *Production*. Children might attend to a model and code in memory what they have seen—but, because of limitations in their motor ability, not be able to reproduce the model's behavior. A 13-year-old might watch basketball player Lebron James and golfer Michelle Wie execute their athletic skills to perfection, or observe a famous pianist or artist, but not be able to reproduce their motor actions. Teaching, coaching, and practice can help children improve their motor performances.

- *Motivation*. Often children attend to what a model says or does, retain the information in memory, and possess the motor skills to perform the action but are not motivated to perform the modeled behavior. This was demonstrated in Bandura's (1965) classic Bobo doll study when children who saw the model being punished did not reproduce the punished model's aggressive actions (see Figure 7.9). However, when they subsequently were given a reinforcement or incentive (stickers or fruit juice), they did imitate the model's behavior.

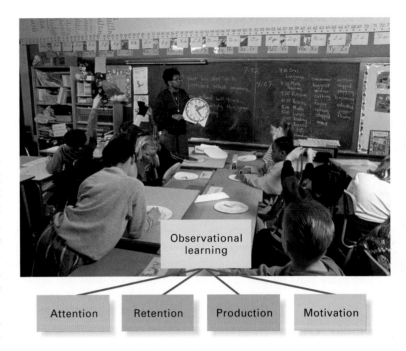

FIGURE 7.8 Bandura's Model of Observational Learning

In Bandura's model of observational learning, four processes need to be considered: attention, retention, production, and motivation. *How might these processes be involved in this classroom situation in which a teacher is demonstrating how to tell time?*

observational learning Learning that involves acquiring skills, strategies, and beliefs by observing others.

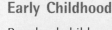

DEVELOPMENTAL FOCUS 7.2

How Do You Use Observational Learning in Your Classroom?

Early Childhood

Preschool children spend a lot of time doing informal observation and may try to imitate what someone else has done to see if they can get similar results. For example, when a teacher tells a group of children to walk down the hall instead of running and praises those students who are walking, children who are running often slow down and walk, hoping they will be praised by the teacher.

—Heidi Kaufman, *Metro West YMCA Child Care and Educational Program*

Elementary School: Grades K–5

My basic assumption with my elementary school students is that they learn appropriate behavior by observation and experience. Class rules are established and agreed upon at the beginning of the school year. I model effective learning behaviors, identify them when students use them, teach study skills, and end every class by stating one or two behavioral skills that were done well.

—Keren Abra, *Convent of the Sacred Heart Elementary School*

Middle School: Grades 6–8

I use observational learning with my sixth-grade students all the time. I make sure that they understand my expectations by not only discussing them but also showing them what I expect. For example, I create checklists for my students at the beginning of the year so they can assess their work and monitor their progress. We then go over the checklists one-on-one and as a group and discuss ways that they can improve their work or behavior in order to reach their desired goals.

—Casey Maass, *Edison Middle School*

High School: Grades 9–12

As a high school art teacher, I am fortunate to work in an area that is visual, hands-on, and creative. Through one-on-one demonstrations, small-group and sometimes total class lectures/demonstrations, my students observe and learn artistic skills.

—Dennis Peterson, *Deer River High School*

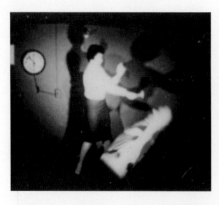

FIGURE 7.9 Bandura's Classic Bobo Doll Study: The Effects of Observational Learning on Children's Aggression

In the top frame, an adult model aggressively attacks the Bobo doll. In the bottom frame, a kindergarten-age girl who has observed the model's aggressive actions follows suit. *In Bandura's experiment, under what conditions did the children reproduce the model's aggressive actions?*

Bandura argues that reinforcement is not always necessary for observational learning to take place. But if the child does not reproduce the desired behaviors, four types of reinforcement can help do the trick: (1) reward the model; (2) reward the child; (3) instruct the child to make self-reinforcing statements such as "Good, I did it!" or "Okay, I've done a good job of getting most of this right; now if I keep trying I will get the rest"; or (4) show how the behavior leads to reinforcing outcomes.

As you can see, you will be an important model in students' lives. Your students will be observing your behavior countless times every day of the school year. An intentional way that teachers can use observational learning is through *modeled demonstrations*, in which the teacher describes and shows students how to solve problems and succesfully complete academic tasks (Schunk, 2008). For example, a teacher might demonstrate how to create an outline for a paper or do a PowerPoint presentation.

In addition to being a key model yourself for children to observe and learn from, students learn from observing many other models, including parents, mentors, and peers. Students especially are likely to attend to and attempt to learn the behaviors of individuals who are competent and have prestige (Schunk, 2008). For example, a teacher might invite a well-known professional athlete to come to her class and talk about how important reading and doing well in school is. Because of the athlete's prestige, the students are likely to attend to what the athlete says and be motivated to adopt the behaviors he or she recommends.

Peers also can be important models in the classroom (Schunk, 2008). By observing peers successfully do school tasks, especially peers that a student likes or admires, the student's self-efficacy for performing well in school likely increases.

To evaluate the roles that models and mentors have played in your own life and can play in your students' lives, complete *Self-Assessment 7.1*. To explore the lack of male and minority role models and mentors in children's education, read the *Diversity and Education* interlude.

Volunteer Edna Wharf serves as a reading tutor for first-grade students at Claxton Elementary School in Asheville, North Carolina. One strategy to improve students' learning is to look around the community and invite competent individuals to mentor students in your classroom. Mentors can serve as important models for students and help teachers give more individual attention to students.

To read about applications of observational learning in the popular children's television show *Sesame Street*, see the *Technology and Education* interlude.

Cognitive Behavior Approaches and Self-Regulation

Operant conditioning spawned applications and other real-world settings, and the interest in cognitive behavior approaches has also produced such applications. In the fifth century B.C., the Chinese philosopher Confucius said, "If you give a man a fish, you feed him for a day. If you teach a man to fish, you feed him for a lifetime." As you read about the cognitive behavior approaches and self-regulation, you will discover that they reflect Confucius' simple expression.

Cognitive Behavior Approaches In the **cognitive behavior approaches**, the emphasis is on getting students to monitor, manage, and regulate their own behavior rather than letting it be controlled by external factors. In some circles, this has been called *cognitive behavior modification* (Soares & Vannest, 2008). Cognitive behavior approaches stem from both cognitive psychology, with its emphasis on the effects of thoughts on behavior, and behaviorism, with its emphasis on techniques for changing behavior. Cognitive behavior approaches try to change students' misconceptions, strengthen their coping skills, increase their self-control, and encourage constructive self-reflection (Watson & Tharp, 2007).

Self-instructional methods are cognitive behavior techniques aimed at teaching individuals to modify their own behavior. Self-instructional methods help people alter what they say to themselves.

cognitive behavior approaches
Changing behavior by getting individuals to monitor, manage, and regulate their own behavior rather than letting it be controlled by external factors.

self-instructional methods Cognitive behavior techniques aimed at teaching individuals to modify their own behavior.

SELF-ASSESSMENT 7.1
Models and Mentors in My Life and My Students' Lives

Having positive role models and mentors can make an important difference in whether individuals develop optimally and reach their full potential. First, evaluate the role models and mentors who have played an important part in your life. Second, think about the type of role model you want to be for your students. Third, give some thought to how you will incorporate other models and mentors into your students' lives. Fourth, explore who your education mentor might be.

My Models and Mentors

List the most important role models and mentors in your life. Then describe what their positive modeling and mentoring have meant to your development.

Role Models and Mentors	Their Contributions
1. _____	_____
2. _____	_____
3. _____	_____
4. _____	_____
5. _____	_____

The Type of Role Model I Want to Be for My Students

Describe which characteristics and behaviors you believe are the most important for you to model for your students.

1. _____

2. _____

3. _____

4. _____

5. _____

How I Will Incorporate Models and Mentors in My Classroom?

Describe a systematic plan for bringing models and mentors into your students' lives in one or more domain(s) you plan to teach, such as math, English, science, and music.

_____

_____

Who Will Be My Education Mentor? What Would My Ideal Education Mentor Be Like?

Do you have someone in mind who might serve as an education mentor when you become a teacher? If so, describe the person.

_____

What would your ideal education mentor be like?

_____

_____

DIVERSITY AND EDUCATION
Male and Minority Role Models and Mentors

As students in U.S. schools have become more ethnically diverse in recent decades, their teachers are overwhelmingly non-Latino White females. In 2004, approximately 15 percent of U.S. public school students were African American, but just over 7 percent of their teachers were African American (National Center for Education Statistics, 2007). Only a small percentage of the African American teachers were males. In the same year, Latinos made up more than 19 percent of U.S. public school students, but just over 6 percent of their teachers were Latino. A majority of U.S. public schools still do not have a single ethnic minority teacher.

Men comprise about 10 percent of elementary school teachers but comprise nearly half of middle and high school teachers (many of whom are lured by additional incentives for coaching athletic teams). The situation is likely to get worse. In a recent national survey of college students, only 1 percent of males said their probable career would be as an elementary school teacher or administrator, and only 4.7 percent indicated that a similar career in secondary education was likely to be in their future (Pryor & others, 2007).

The education program at Livingstone College in Salisbury, North Carolina, is trying to do something about the shortage of male teachers of color. They developed a special program to recruit men of color into the teaching profession. One of the program's graduates, Nakia Douglas, teaches kindergarten. He says he wants to eliminate negative stereotypes about African American males—that they are poor role models, aren't responsible, and shouldn't be teaching young children. Another graduate, Mistor Williams, teaches history to eighth-graders in a school with a large percentage of ethnic minority students. He says that he feels the responsibility to provide a role model and support for ethnic minority students.

If you are a White female, think about ways you can bring women and men of color into your classroom to talk with students and demonstrate their work skills. This is especially important when you have a number of students of color in your class.

Regardless of your ethnic background, look around the community for possible mentors for students, especially students who come from low-income backgrounds and who lack positive role models. For example, the aim of the 3-to-1 mentoring program is to surround each ethnic minority male student with three positive ethnic minority role models. The program began when several African American men were challenged by a sermon delivered by Zach Holmes at the St. Luke's Methodist Church in Dallas. In the sermon, Reverend Holmes urged his congregation to become more involved with

Dr. Leonard Berry is a mentor in the 3-to-1 program in Dallas. He is shown here with Brandon Scarbough, 13 (front), and his own son, Leonard, 12 (back). Brandon not only has benefited from Dr. Berry's mentoring but also has become friends with his son.

DIVERSITY AND EDUCATION
Male and Minority Role Models and Mentors

children, both their own and children in the community who don't have good role models. The 3-to-1 mentoring program has signed up more than 200 men and 100 boys (ages 4 to 18). That's far short of the goal of three mentors for each boy, but the men are working on increasing the number of mentors in the program. Some of the men in the mentoring program have their own children, like Dr. Leonard Berry, a physician, who has two sons and a daughter. He heeded the minister's challenge and regularly participates in the mentoring program, which involves academic tutoring as well as outings to activities such as sporting and cultural events. The mentors also take the students to visit the Johnson Space Center in Houston.

As a teacher, you do not have to wait for someone in the community to bring mentors to your students. Look around the community in which you teach and evaluate who would be good candidates for mentoring your students or starting a mentoring program. Contact them and get the program started. Clearly, mentoring programs can benefit all students, male or female, of any ethnic background.

In the present educational climate that emphasizes reflection and critical thinking, it is easy to overlook the power of observational learning in educating children, yet observational learning remains one of the most common and effective means of learning (Schunk, 2008). The *Best Practices* interlude can help you to use this powerful form of learning in your classroom.

Imagine a situation in which a high school student is extremely nervous about taking standardized tests, such as the SAT. The student can be encouraged to talk to himself in positive ways. Following are some self-talk strategies that students and teachers can use to cope more effectively with such stressful situations (Meichenbaum, Turk, & Burstein, 1975):

- Prepare for anxiety or stress.
  "What do I have to do?"
  "I'm going to develop a plan to deal with it."
  "I'll just think about what I have to do."
  "I won't worry. Worry doesn't help anything."
  "I have a lot of different strategies I can use."

- Confront and handle the anxiety or stress.
  "I can meet the challenge."
  "I'll keep on taking just one step at a time."
  "I can handle it. I'll just relax, breathe deeply, and use one of the strategies."
  "I won't think about my stress. I'll just think about what I have to do."

- Cope with feelings at critical moments.
  "What is it I have to do?"
  "I knew my anxiety might increase. I just have to keep myself in control."
  "When the anxiety comes, I'll just pause and keep focusing on what I have to do."

- Use reinforcing self-statements.
  "Good, I did it."
  "I handled it well."
  "I knew I could do it."
  "Wait until I tell other people how I did it!"

1. *Think about what type of model you will present to students.* Every day, hour after hour, students will watch and listen to what you say and do. Just by being around you, students will absorb a great deal of information. They will pick up your good or bad habits, your expectations for their high or low achievement, your enthusiastic or bored attitude, your controlled or uncontrolled manner of dealing with stress, your learning style, your gender attitudes, and many other aspects of your behavior.

2. *Demonstrate and teach new behaviors.* Demonstrating means that you, the teacher, are a model for your students' observational learning. Demonstrating how to do something, such as solve a math problem, read, write, think, control anger, and perform physical skills, is a common teacher behavior in classrooms. For example, a teacher might model how to diagram a sentence, develop a strategy for solving algebraic equations, or shoot a basketball. When demonstrating how to do something, you need to call students' attention to the relevant details of the learning situation. Your demonstrations also should be clear and follow a logical sequence.

3. *Think about ways to use peers as effective models.* The teacher is not the only model in the classroom. As with teachers, children can pick up their peers' good and bad habits, high or low achievement orientations, and so on through observational learning. Remember that students are often motivated to imitate high-status models. Older peers usually have higher status than same-age peers. Thus, a good strategy is to have older peers from a higher grade model how to engage in the behaviors you want your students to perform. For students with low abilities or who are not performing well, a low-achieving student who struggles but puts considerable effort into learning and ultimately performs the behaviors can be a good model. More will be said in Chapter 10, "Social Constructivist Approaches," about peer collaboration and peers as tutors.

4. *Think about ways that mentors can be used as models.* Students and teachers benefit from having a mentor— someone they look up to and respect, someone who serves as a competent model, someone who is willing to work with them and help them achieve their goals. As a teacher, a potential mentor for you is a more experienced teacher, possibly someone who teaches down the hall and has had a number of years of experience in dealing with some of the same problems and issues you will have to cope with.

In the Quantum Opportunities Program that we described in Chapter 5, "Sociocultural Diversity," students from low-income backgrounds significantly benefited from meeting with a mentor over a four-year period (Carnegie Council on Adolescent Development, 1995; Eisenhower Foundation, 2008). These mentors modeled appropriate behavior and strategies, gave sustained support, and provided guidance. Just spending a few hours a week with a mentor can make a difference in a student's life, especially if the student's parents have not been good role models.

5. *Evaluate which classroom guests will provide good models for students.* Who else would be beneficial models for your students? To change the pace of classroom life for you and your students, invite guests who have something meaningful to talk about or demonstrate. Recall what we said in Chapter 4 about Gardner's theory of multiple intelligences: There likely are some domains (physical, musical, artistic, or other) in which you don't have the skills to serve as a competent model for your students. When you need to have such skills demonstrated to your students, spend some time locating competent models in the community. Invite them to come to your classroom to demonstrate and discuss their skills. If this can't be arranged, set up field trips in which you take students to see them where they are working or performing. Next, fourth-grade teacher Marlene Wendler describes a positive role model her school brings to teachers' classrooms.

THROUGH THE EYES OF TEACHERS
Here Comes the Judge

Our local judge has taken a proactive role in trying to eliminate teen behavioral problems. With a half dozen adults from the community, he comes to the fourth-grade classrooms in our areas and puts on skits about bullying. They show the whole group picking on a student in a bus situation. Then they do the skit again with someone in the group stopping the bullying. The students then role-play bullying situations, learning what to do if they are bullied and how to help someone who is bullied. Having the judge come to our school has made a lasting impression on our students.

6. *Consider the models children observe on television, videos, and computers.* Students observe models when they watch television programs, videos, films, or computer screens in your classroom. The principles of observational learning we described earlier apply to these media. For example, the extent to which the students perceive the media models as high or low in status, intriguing or boring, and so on will influence the extent of their observational learning. And as we indicated in Chapter 3, "Social Contexts and Socioemotional Development," it is important to monitor children's TV watching to ensure that they are not being exposed to too many negative models, especially violent ones.

TECHNOLOGY AND EDUCATION
Educational Lessons from *Sesame Street*

One of television's major programming attempts to educate young children is *Sesame Street,* which is designed to teach both cognitive and social skills (Bryant, 2007). The program began in 1969 and is still going strong. A fundamental message of *Sesame Street* is that education and entertainment work well together (Lesser, 1972). On *Sesame Street,* learning is exciting and entertaining. One study found that preschool children who watched *Sesame Street* were more likely to positively resolve conflicts, make positive comments about others, and engage in less stereotyping than their counterparts who did not watch the TV show (Cole & others, 2003).

Sesame Street also illustrates the point that teaching can be done in both direct and indirect ways. Using the direct way, a teacher tells children exactly what they are going to be taught and then actually teaches it to them. This method is often used on *Sesame Street* to teach cognitive skills. But social skills usually are communicated in indirect ways on the show. Thus, rather than telling children "You should cooperate with people," a sequence of events is shown to help children figure out what it means to be cooperative and what the advantages are.

Should the world be shown to children as it is, or as it ought to be? The *Sesame Street* advisory board of educators and psychologists decided that the real world should be shown—but with an emphasis on what the world would be like if everyone treated each other with decency and kindness. To show the world as it really is, the program might show an adult doing something unjustifiably inconsiderate

What educational lessons can be learned from Sesame Street?

to another adult, with alternative ways of coping with this acted out. Finally, the program would portray the happy outcomes when people stop acting inconsiderately.

Some of the attentional techniques used on *Sesame Street* are worthwhile to consider in the classroom. These involve first *catching* the child's attention, then directing it, and finally *sustaining* it. Music and sound are very effective in eliciting children's attention. For example, in teaching children to discriminate sounds, an automobile horn might be sounded or a computer's keyboard repeatedly pressed. Music is especially useful because it leads children to become actively involved in what they are watching or listening to. It is not unusual for children watching *Sesame Street* to get up out of their seats and start dancing and singing along with the jingles. Once the child's attention has been captured, it should be directed to something. Surprise and novelty are especially helpful in this regard. They make children work hard to figure out what is going to happen. Their attention is directed because they begin to anticipate what is going to happen next.

Once attention is directed, it then needs to be maintained. *Sesame Street* especially uses humor to accomplish this. Humor is judiciously placed: Ernie outsmarts Bert; the Cookie Monster annoyingly interrupts a lecture given by Kermit the Frog. For young children, physical gags often are funnier than verbal ones, and much of the humor that is effective involves physical acts that are surprising and incongruous.

In many instances, the strategy is to replace negative self-statements with positive ones. For example, a student might say to herself, "I'll never get this work done by tomorrow." This can be replaced with positive self-statements such as these: "This is going to be tough but I think I can do it." "I'm going to look at this as a challenge rather than a stressor." "If I work really hard, I might be able to get it done." Or in having to participate in a class discussion, a student might replace the negative thought "Everyone else knows more than I do, so what's the use of saying anything" with positive self-statements such as these: "I have as much to say as anyone else." "My ideas may be different, but they are still good." "It's okay to be a little nervous; I'll relax and start talking." Figure 7.10 shows posters that students in one fifth-grade class developed to help them remember how to talk to themselves while listening, planning, working, and checking.

Talking positively to oneself can help teachers and students reach their full potential (Kendall & Treadwell, 2007; Watson & Tharp, 2007). Uncountered negative thinking has a way of becoming a self-fulfilling prophecy. You think you can't do it, and

self-regulatory learning The self-generation and self-monitoring of thoughts, feelings, and behaviors in order to reach a goal.

so you don't. If negative self-talk is a problem for you, at random times during the day ask yourself, "What am I saying to myself right now?" Moments that you expect will be potentially stressful are excellent times to examine your self-talk. Also monitor your students' self-talk. If you hear students saying, "I can't do this" or "I'm so slow I'll never get this done," spend some time getting them to replace their negative self-talk with positive self-talk.

Cognitive behaviorists recommend that students improve their performance by monitoring their own behavior (Schunk, 2008; Watson & Tharp, 2007). This can involve getting students to keep charts or records of their behavior. When I (your author) wrote this book, I had a chart on my wall with each of the chapters listed. I planned how long it would take me to do each of the chapters, and then as I completed each one I checked it off and wrote down the date of completion. Teachers can get students to do some similar monitoring of their own progress by getting them to keep records of how many assignments they have finished, how many books they have read, how many homework papers they have turned in on time, how many days in a row they have not interrupted the teacher, and so on. In some cases, teachers place these self-monitoring charts on the walls of the classroom. Alternatively, if the teacher thinks that negative social comparison with other students will be highly stressful for some students, then a better strategy might be to have students keep private records (in a notebook, for example) that are periodically checked by the teacher.

Self-monitoring is an excellent strategy for improving learning, and one that you can help students learn to do effectively (Soares & Vannest, 2008; Watson & Tharp, 2007). By completing *Self-Assessment 7.2,* you should get a sense of the benefits of self-monitoring for your students.

Self-Regulatory Learning   Educational psychologists increasingly advocate the importance of self-regulatory learning (Schunk, 2008; Schunk & Zimmerman, 2006; Weinstein & Acee, 2008). **Self-regulatory learning** consists of the self-generation and self-monitoring of thoughts, feelings, and behaviors in order to reach a goal. These goals might be academic (improving comprehension while reading, becoming a more organized writer, learning how to do multiplication, asking relevant questions) or they might be socioemotional (controlling one's anger, getting along better with peers).

As children become older, their capacity for self-regulation increases (Thompson, Meyer, & Jochem, 2008). The increased capacity in self-regulation is linked to developmental advances in the brain's prefrontal cortex, which was discussed in Chapter 2, "Cognitive and Language Development" (Durston & others, 2007).

What are some of the characteristics of self-regulated learners? Self-regulatory learners do the following (Winne, 2001, 2005):

- Set goals for extending their knowledge and sustaining their motivation
- Are aware of their emotional makeup and have strategies for managing their emotions
- Periodically monitor their progress toward a goal
- Fine-tune or revise their strategies based on the progress they are making
- Evaluate obstacles that may arise and make the necessary adaptations.

Researchers have found that high-achieving students are often self-regulatory learners (Schunk, 2008; Schunk, Pintrich, & Meece, 2008). For example, compared with low-achieving students, high-achieving students set more specific learning goals, use more strategies to learn, self-monitor their learning more, and more systematically evaluate their progress toward a goal. Results of the following recent research reveal the importance of self-regulation in children's development of academic skills:

- Improvement in 3- to 5-year-old children's ability to regulate their behavior predicted advances in literacy, vocabulary, and math skills across a school year (McClelland & others, 2007).

Poster 1
While listening

1. Does this make sense?
2. Am I getting this?
3. I need to ask a question before I forget.
4. Pay attention.
5. Can I do what the teacher is saying to do?

Poster 2
While planning

1. Do I have everything together?
2. Do I have my friends tuned out so I can get this done?
3. I need to get organized first.
4. What order can I do this in?
5. I know this stuff.

Poster 3
While working

1. Am I working fast enough?
2. Stop staring at my girlfriend (boyfriend) and get back to work.
3. How much time is left?
4. Do I need to stop and start all over?
5. This is hard for me but I can manage it.

Poster 4
While checking

1. Did I finish everything?
2. What do I need to recheck?
3. Am I proud of this work?
4. Did I write all of the words?
5. I think I'm finished. I organized myself. Did I daydream too much, though?

FIGURE 7.10 Some Posters Developed by a Fifth-Grade Class to Help Them Remember How to Effectively Talk to Themselves

From Brenda H. Manning and Beverly D. Payne, *Self-Talk for Teachers and Students: Metacognitive Strategies for Personal and Classroom Use.* Published by Allyn and Bacon, Boston, MA. Copyright © 1996 by Pearson Education. Reprinted by permission of the publisher.

SELF-ASSESSMENT 7.2
Self-Monitoring

Self-monitoring can benefit you as well as your students. Many successful learners regularly self-monitor their progress to see how they are doing in their effort to complete a project, develop a skill, or perform well on a test or other assessment. For the next month, self-monitor your study time for this course you are taking in educational psychology. To achieve high grades, most instructors recommend that students spend two or three hours out of class studying, doing homework, and working on projects for every hour they are in class in college (Santrock & Halonen, 2009). The experience of self-monitoring your own study time should give you a sense of how important such skills are for your students to develop. You might adapt this form for students' homework, for example. Remember from our discussion of Bandura's social cognitive theory that self-efficacy involves your belief that you can master a situation and produce positive outcomes. One way to evaluate self-efficacy is your expectancy for attaining a particular score on an upcoming quiz or test. Determine what score or grade you want to achieve on your next quiz or test. Then each day you study, rate your self-efficacy for achieving the score you desire on a 3-point scale: 1 = not very confident, 2 = moderately confident, and 3 = very confident.

Form for Self-Monitoring Study Time

| Date | Assignment | Time Started | Time Finished | Study Context | | | Self-Efficacy |
				Where?	With Whom?	Distractions	

- The ability of 3- to 5-year-old children from low-income families to regulate their behavior was linked to their development of early math and reading skills (Blair & Razza, 2007).
- Teaching fourth-grade students self-regulation skills in addition to composition strategies resulted in more complete and better stories at the end of the instruction and five weeks later (Glaser & Brunstein, 2007). The self-regulation skills that students were taught included self-monitoring of planning what to write, self-assessment that included how to review and assess the quality of a story, and self-monitoring of revision.

FIGURE 7.11 A Model of Self-Regulatory Learning

Note that in this last study students were taught strategies in addition to self-regulation skills. Researchers have found that teaching students strategies as well as self-regulation skills is critical in many academic areas. For example, most students with writing problems don't have adequate writing strategies to review and assess the quality of a story. Thus, to become better writers they not only need to learn self-regulation skills but also need training in writing strategy instruction (Harris & others, 2008).

Teachers, tutors, mentors, counselors, and parents can help students become self-regulatory learners (Schunk, 2008; Schunk, Pintrich, & Meece, 2008). Barry Zimmerman, Sebastian Bonner, and Robert Kovach (1996) developed a model for turning low-self-regulatory students into students who engage in these multistep strategies: (1) self-evaluation and monitoring, (2) goal setting and strategic planning, (3) putting a plan into action and monitoring it, and (4) monitoring outcomes and refining strategies (see Figure 7.11).

Zimmerman and colleagues describe a seventh-grade student who is doing poorly in history and apply their self-regulatory model to her situation. In step 1, she self-evaluates her studying and test preparation by keeping a detailed record of them. The teacher gives her some guidelines for keeping these records. After several weeks, the student turns the records in and traces her poor test performance to low comprehension of difficult reading material.

In step 2, the student sets a goal, in this case of improving reading comprehension, and plans how to achieve the goal. The teacher assists her in breaking the goal into components, such as locating main ideas and setting specific goals for understanding a series of paragraphs in her textbook. The teacher also provides the student with strategies, such as focusing initially on the first sentence of each paragraph and then scanning the others as a means of identifying main ideas. Another support the teacher might offer the student is adult or peer tutoring in reading comprehension if it is available.

In step 3, the student puts the plan into action and begins to monitor her progress. Initially, she may need help from the teacher or tutor in identifying main ideas in the reading. This feedback can help her monitor her reading comprehension more effectively on her own.

In step 4, the student monitors her improvement in reading comprehension by evaluating whether it has had any impact on her learning outcomes. Most importantly, has her improvement in reading comprehension led to better performance on history tests?

Self-evaluations reveal that the strategy of finding main ideas has only partly improved her comprehension, and only when the first sentence contained the paragraph's main idea, so the teacher recommends further strategies. Figure 7.12 describes how teachers can apply the self-regulatory model to homework.

The development of self-regulation is influenced by many factors, among them modeling and self-efficacy (Bandura, 2008, 2009; Schunk, 2008). A recent analysis described Zimmerman's four-phase model and how modeling can be an effective strategy for building self-regulatory skills and self-efficacy in improving reading and

FIGURE 7.12 Applying the Self–Regulatory Model to Homework

1. Self-evaluation and monitoring

- The teacher distributes forms so that students can monitor specific aspects of their studying.
- The teacher gives students daily assignments to develop their self-monitoring skills and a weekly quiz to assess how well they have learned the methods.
- After several days, the teacher begins to have students exchange their homework with their peers. The peers are asked to evaluate the accuracy of the homework and how effectively the student engaged in self-monitoring. Then the teacher collects the homework for grading and reviews the peers' suggestions.

2. Goal setting and strategic planning

- After a week of monitoring and the first graded exercise, the teacher asks students to give their perceptions of the strengths and weaknesses of their study strategies. The teacher emphasizes the link between learning strategies and learning outcomes.
- The teacher and peers recommend specific strategies that students might use to improve their learning. Students may use the recommendations or devise new ones. The teacher asks students to set specific goals at this point.

3. Putting a plan into action and monitoring it

- The students monitor the extent to which they actually enact the new strategies.
- The teacher's role is to make sure that the new learning strategies are openly discussed.

4. Monitoring outcomes and refining strategies

- The teacher continues to give students opportunities to gauge how effectively they are using their new strategies.
- The teacher helps students summarize their self-regulatory methods by reviewing each step of the self-regulatory learning cycle. She also discusses with students the hurdles the students had to overcome and the self-confidence they have achieved.

writing (Schunk & Zimmerman, 2006). Among the self-regulatory skills that models can engage in are planning and managing time effectively, attending to and concentrating, organizing and coding information strategically, establishing a productive work environment, and using social resources. For example, students might observe a teacher engage in an effective time management strategy and verbalize appropriate principles. By observing such models, students can come to believe that they also can plan and manage time effectively, which creates a sense of self-efficacy for academic self-regulation and motivates students to engage in those activities.

Self-efficacy can influence a student's choice of tasks, effort expended, persistence, and achievement (Bandura, 1997, 2008, 2009; Schunk, 2008). Compared with students who doubt their learning capabilities, those with high self-efficacy for acquiring a skill or performing a task participate more readily, work harder, persist longer in the face of difficulty, and achieve at a higher level. Self-efficacy can have a strong effect on achievement, but it is not the only influence. High self-efficacy will not result in competent performance when requisite knowledge and skills are lacking. We will further explore self-efficacy, goal setting, planning, and self-regulation in Chapter 13, "Motivation, Teaching, and Learning."

Teachers who encourage students to be self-regulatory learners convey the message that students are responsible for their own behavior, for becoming educated, and for becoming contributing citizens to society (Lajoie & Azevedo, 2006). Another message conveyed by self-regulatory learning is that learning is a personal experience that requires active and dedicated participation by the student (Zimmerman, Bonner, & Kovach, 1996).

BEST PRACTICES
Strategies for Encouraging Students to Be Self-Regulated Learners

Following are some effective strategies for guiding students to engage in self-regulated learning:

1. *Gradually guide students to become self-regulated learners.* It is not a good strategy to just assume that you can all of a sudden give students the independence to self-regulate their learning. Helping students become self-regulated learners takes time and requires considerable monitoring, guidance, and encouragement on your part (Cooper, Horn, & Strahan, 2005).

2. *Make the classroom learning experience challenging and interesting for students.* When students are bored and uninterested in learning, they are less likely to become self-regulated learners. Instead of just giving students a particular book to read, providing students with a variety of interesting books is likely to encourage their motivation to read (Gutherie & others, 2004). Giving students choices increases students' personal investment in their learning and increases their self-regulation (Blumenfeld, Kempler & Krajcik, 2006).

3. *Provide tips about thoughts and actions that will help students engage in self-regulation.* These might include giving specific guidelines as needed, such as "Planning for 30 minutes will help you . . ." and "Every day stop and monitor where you are in what you want to accomplish." Other suggestions include encouraging students to reflect on their strengths and weaknesses in a learning situation and encouraging them to search for help

and ways to use help effectively (All Kinds of Minds, 2005).

4. *Give students opportunities to experience the type of activities recommended by Zimmerman and his colleagues* (1996). That is, create projects for students in which they self-evaluate their current learning, set a goal to improve their learning and plan how to reach the goal, put the plan into action and monitor their progress toward the goal, and monitor the outcome and refine their strategies. Monitor students' progress through these steps and encourage their ability to engage in these learning activities independently.

5. *Especially pay attention to low-achieving students.* High-achieving students are more likely to already be self-regulated learners than low-achieving students. All students can benefit from practicing their self-regulated learning skills, but recognize that low-achieving students will need more instruction and time to develop these skills.

6. *Model self-regulated learning.* Verbalize effective self-regulation strategies for students, and tell students how you use self-regulation in your learning.

7. *Make sure that students don't just self-regulate but combine self-regulation with effective strategies for learning.* Students can self-regulate all they want but if they don't have the "know-how" their self-regulation is unlikely to be beneficial.

Evaluating the Social Cognitive Approaches

The social cognitive approaches have made important contributions to educating children. While keeping the behaviorists' scientific flavor and emphasis on careful observation, they significantly expanded the emphasis of learning to include social and cognitive factors. Considerable learning occurs through watching and listening to competent models and then imitating what they do. The emphasis in the cognitive behavior approach on self-instruction, self-talk, and self-regulatory learning provides an important shift from learning controlled by others to responsibility for one's own learning (Watson & Tharp, 2007). These self-enacted strategies can significantly improve students' learning.

Critics of the social cognitive approaches come from several camps. Some cognitive theorists point out that the approaches still focus too much on overt behavior and external factors and not enough on the details of how cognitive processes such as thinking, memory, and problem solving actually take place. Some developmentalists criticize them for being nondevelopmental, in the sense that they don't specify age-related, sequential changes in learning. It is true that social cognitive theory does not address development in great depth because it is mainly a theory of learning and social behavior. But labeling it as nondevelopmental is not accurate. Also, humanistic theorists fault social cognitive theorists for not placing enough attention on self-esteem and caring, supportive relationships. All of these criticisms also have been leveled at the behavioral approaches, such as Skinner's operant conditioning.

Review, Reflect, and Practice

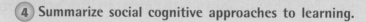

④ Summarize social cognitive approaches to learning.

REVIEW

- How does Figure 7.7 help to summarize Bandura's social cognitive theory? What does he mean by self-efficacy?
- What is Bandura's model of observational learning?
- What is the focus of self-instructional methods? What does self-regulatory learning involve?
- What are some contributions and criticisms of the social cognitive approaches?

REFLECT

- Give some examples of how you use self-instructional and self-regulatory methods in your personal life. How effective are these methods? Should you use them more than you do? Explain.

PRAXIS™ PRACTICE

1. Macy sits staring at her math homework. She has not attempted a single problem. "What's the use?" she sighs, "I'll never get it right." According to Bandura's social cognitive theory, what is the most plausible explanation for Macy's response?
   a. Macy does not have the requisite language skills to do her homework.
   b. Macy has low self-efficacy.
   c. Macy has too much math anxiety.
   d. Macy's teacher has not provided enough negative feedback about her math homework.

2. Matt is the star of his high school's basketball team. The team is doing very well this year, in large part because of Matt's performance. This makes him a very popular student. About halfway through basketball season, Matt decides to shave his head. Soon other members of the basketball team shave their heads. Then the trend spreads to the rest of the school. By the end of February, 30 percent of the male students in the school have shaved heads. According to Bandura's social cognitive theory, what is the most plausible explanation for the students' behavior?
   a. Matt is a high-status role model.
   b. Matt was not punished.
   c. Matt was positively reinforced.
   d. Matt's self-efficacy was raised.

3. Marsha, a junior in high school, has debilitating test anxiety. She is particularly anxious about high-stakes tests, such as final exams. She often becomes so anxious that she "blanks out" and forgets everything that she has studied. What would a teacher using a cognitive behavior modification approach do to help her with her test anxiety?
   a. Help Marsha to develop anxiety management strategies and use self-instructions.
   b. Give her a study-skills book to read.
   c. Encourage her to think more about the consequences if she does do better on the tests.
   d. Tell Marsha to study until she has overlearned the material.

4. An important way in which social cognitive theory builds on behavioral theory is its emphasis on
   a. personality.
   b. self-efficacy.
   c. attitudes.
   d. careful observation.

Please see the answer key at the end of the book.

CRACK THE CASE
The Case of Consequences

Adam, a student in Mr. Potter's fourth-grade class, is disruptive from time to time, although he is very bright. One day during language arts, Adam began talking loudly to other students in his area. He was also laughing and telling jokes. Mr. Potter chose to ignore Adam's behavior, hoping he would stop on his own. But Adam didn't stop. Instead, his behavior became more raucous. Still Mr. Potter ignored it. Soon Adam was making enough noise that Mr. Potter was afraid that students in the neighboring classrooms would be disturbed, so he verbally reprimanded Adam.

Adam was a bit quieter for the next few minutes. After that, however, he once again became loud and disruptive. Again Mr. Potter verbally reprimanded him. This time he also told Adam that if he continued with his disruptive behavior, he would have to go to the office. Adam's behavior became even more disruptive, so Mr. Potter sent him to the office. When Adam arrived at the office it was full of people—teachers getting their mail and making copies, volunteers signing in, students who were ill, students sent on errands, and other students who had been sent for disciplinary reasons. The school secretary told Adam to have a seat, which he did. He conversed with every person who entered the office as well as those who were there when he arrived. Half an hour after his arrival, he was sent back to class. He behaved quite well for the rest of the day, to Mr. Potter's relief.

The next day when students were assigned to write a paragraph, Adam once again became disruptive. He loudly told jokes to his classmates, laughed until tears were streaming down his face, and threw a paper airplane across the room. Mr. Potter reprimanded him and asked him to stop. When Adam didn't comply, Mr. Potter sent him to the office, which was once again bustling with activity.

Over the course of the next two weeks, Adam was sent to the office for disrupting class each day, always during a writing assignment. Mr. Potter was perplexed. Even more perplexing was that within three school days other children were becoming disruptive as well, requiring that they too be sent to the office.

1. What are the issues in this case?

Answer the following questions using principles of behavioral learning theories and correct terminology:

2. Why did Adam continue to disrupt class despite the consequences?

3. What has Adam learned?

4. Why did the other students join Adam in his disruptive behavior?

5. What should Mr. Potter do now?

6. What was Mr. Potter most likely trying to do when he initially ignored Adam's disruptive behavior?
   a. He was trying to extinguish the behavior by not reinforcing it.
   b. He was trying to negatively reinforce the behavior.
   c. He was trying to positively reinforce the behavior.
   d. He was trying to punish the behavior.

7. If Adam's goal was to escape writing assignments, which of the following best explains the consequences in operant conditioning terms?
   a. Adam was negatively reinforced for his behavior. An aversive stimulus was removed.
   b. Adam was positively reinforced for his behavior. A pleasant stimulus was presented.
   c. Adam was punished for his behavior. A pleasant stimulus was removed.
   d. Adam was punished for his behavior. An aversive stimulus was presented.

Reach Your Learning Goals
Behavioral and Social Cognitive Approaches

---

(1) WHAT IS LEARNING? Define learning and describe five approaches to studying it.

What Learning Is and Is Not

Learning is a relatively permanent change in behavior, knowledge, and thinking skills that occurs through experience. Learning is not involved in inborn, innate behaviors, such as blinking or swallowing.

Approaches to Learning

Behaviorism is the view that behavior should be explained by experiences that can be directly observed, not by mental processes. Classical conditioning and operant conditioning are behavioral views that emphasize associative learning. Psychology became more cognitive in the last part of the twentieth century, and the cognitive emphasis continues today. This is reflected in four cognitive approaches to learning we discuss in this book: social cognitive, information processing, cognitive constructionist, and social constructivist. Social cognitive approaches emphasize the interaction of behavior, environment, and person (cognition) in explaining learning. Information-processing approaches focus on how children process information through attention, memory, thinking, and other cognitive processes. Cognitive constructivist approaches emphasize the child's cognitive construction of knowledge and understanding. Social constructivist approaches focus on collaboration with others to produce knowledge and understanding.

---

(2) BEHAVIORAL APPROACHES TO LEARNING: Compare classical conditioning and operant conditioning.

Classical Conditioning

In classical conditioning, the organism learns to connect, or associate, stimuli. A neutral stimulus (such as the sight of a person) becomes associated with a meaningful stimulus (such as food) and acquires the capacity to elicit a similar response. Classical conditioning involves these factors: unconditioned stimulus (UCS), conditioned stimulus (CS), unconditioned response (UCR), and conditioned response (CR). Classical conditioning also involves generalization, discrimination, and extinction. Generalization is the tendency of a new stimulus similar to the original conditioned stimulus to produce a similar response. Discrimination occurs when the organism responds to certain stimuli and not to others. Extinction involves the weakening of the CR in the absence of the UCS. Systematic desensitization is a method based on classical conditioning that reduces anxiety by getting the individual to associate deep relaxation with successive visualizations of increasingly anxiety-producing situations. Classical conditioning is better at explaining involuntary behavior than voluntary behavior.

Operant Conditioning

In operant conditioning (also called instrumental conditioning), the consequences of behavior produce changes in the probability that the behavior will occur. Operant conditioning's main architect was B. F. Skinner. Reinforcement (reward) is a consequence (either positive or negative) that increases the probability that a behavior will occur; punishment is a consequence that decreases the probability that a behavior will occur. In positive reinforcement, a behavior increases because it is followed by a rewarding stimulus (such as praise). In negative reinforcement, a behavior increases because the response removes an aversive (unpleasant) stimulus. Generalization, discrimination, and extinction also are involved in operant conditioning. Generalization means giving the same response to similar stimuli. Discrimination is differentiating among stimuli or environmental events. Extinction occurs when a previously reinforced response is no longer reinforced and the response decreases.

What Is Applied Behavior Analysis?

Applied behavior analysis involves applying the principles of operant conditioning to change human behavior.

Increasing Desirable Behaviors

Strategies to increase desirable behaviors include choosing effective reinforcers, making reinforcers timely and contingent, selecting the best schedule of reinforcement, contracting, using negative reinforcement effectively, and using prompts and shaping. Find out which reinforcers work best with which students. The Premack principle states that a high-probability activity can be used to reinforce a low-probability activity. Applied behavior analysts recommend that a reinforcement be contingent—that is, be given in a timely manner and only if the student performs the behavior. "If . . . then" statements can be used to make it clear to students what they have to do to get a reward. Skinner described a number of schedules of reinforcement. Most reinforcement in the classroom is partial. Skinner described four schedules of partial reinforcement: fixed-ratio, variable-ratio, fixed-interval, and variable-interval. Contracting involves putting reinforcement contingencies in writing. Although negative reinforcement can increase some students' desirable behavior, exercise caution with students who don't have good self-regulatory skills. A prompt is an added stimulus or cue that increases the likelihood that a discriminative stimulus will produce a desired response. Shaping involves teaching new behaviors by reinforcing successive approximations to a specified target behavior.

Decreasing Undesirable Behaviors

Strategies for decreasing undesirable behaviors include using differential reinforcement, terminating reinforcement, removing desirable stimuli, and presenting aversive stimuli. In differential reinforcement, the teacher might reinforce behavior that is more appropriate or that is incompatible with what the student is doing. Terminating reinforcement (extinction) involves taking reinforcement away from a behavior. Many inappropriate behaviors are maintained by teacher attention, so taking away the attention can decrease the behavior. The most widely used strategy for removing desirable stimuli is time-out. A second strategy for removing desirable stimuli involves response cost, which occurs when a positive reinforcer, such as a privilege, is taken away from the student. An aversive stimulus becomes a punisher only when it decreases behavior. The most common forms of punisher in the classroom are verbal reprimands. Punishment should be used only as the last option and in conjunction with reinforcement of desired responses. Physical punishment should not be used in the classroom.

Evaluating Operant Conditioning and Applied Behavior Analysis

Used effectively, behavioral techniques can help you manage your classroom. Critics say that these approaches place too much emphasis on external control and not enough on internal control. They also argue that ignoring cognitive factors leaves out much of the richness of students' lives. Critics warn about potential ethical problems when operant conditioning is used inappropriately. And some critics say that teachers who focus too much on managing the classroom with operant techniques may place too much emphasis on conduct and not enough on academic learning.

4 **SOCIAL COGNITIVE APPROACHES TO LEARNING:** Summarize social cognitive approaches to learning.

Bandura's Social Cognitive Theory

Albert Bandura is the main architect of social cognitive theory. His reciprocal determinism model of learning includes three main factors: person/cognition, behavior, and environment. The person (cognitive) factor given the most emphasis by Bandura in recent years is self-efficacy, the belief that one can master a situation and produce positive outcomes.

Observational Learning

Observational learning is learning that involves acquiring skills, strategies, and beliefs by observing others. Bandura describes four key processes in observational learning: attention, retention, production, and motivation.

Cognitive Behavior Approaches and Self-Regulation

Self-instructional methods are cognitive behavior techniques aimed at teaching individuals to modify their own behavior. In many cases, it is recommended that students replace negative self-statements with positive ones. Cognitive behaviorists argue that students can improve their performance by monitoring their behavior. Self-regulatory learning consists of the self-generation and self-monitoring of thoughts, feelings, and behaviors to reach a goal. High-achieving students are often self-regulatory learners. One model of self-regulatory learning involves these components: self-evaluation and monitoring, goal setting and strategic planning, putting a plan into action, and monitoring outcomes and refining strategies. Self-regulatory learning gives students responsibility for their learning.

Evaluating the Social Cognitive Approaches

The social cognitive approaches have significantly expanded the scope of learning to include cognitive and social factors, in addition to behavior. A considerable amount of learning occurs by watching and listening to competent models and then imitating what they do. The cognitive behavior emphasis on self-instruction, self-talk, and self-regulatory learning provides an important shift from learning controlled by others to self-management of learning. Critics of the social cognitive approaches say that they still place too much emphasis on overt behavior and external factors and not enough on the details of how cognitive processes such as thinking occur. They also are criticized for being nondevelopmental (although social cognitive advocates argue this label is not justified) and not giving enough attention to self-esteem and warmth.

 KEY TERMS

PORTFOLIO ACTIVITIES

Now that you have a good understanding of this chapter, complete these exercises to expand your thinking.

Independent Reflection

Design a Self-Regulation Plan. Letitia is a high school student who doesn't have adequate self-regulatory skills, and this is causing her to have serious academic problems. She doesn't plan or organize, has poor study strategies, and uses ineffective time management. Using Zimmerman's four-step strategy, design an effective self-regulation program for Letitia. (INTASC: Principle 5)

Collaborative Work

Decreasing Undesirable Behaviors. Together with three or four other students in your class, consider the following students' undesirable behaviors. You want to decrease the behaviors. What is the best strategy for each? Discuss and compare your strategies with the group. (1) Andrew, who likes to utter profanities every now and then; (2) Sandy, who tells you to quit bugging her when you ask her questions; (3) Matt, who likes to mess up other students' papers; and (4) Rebecca, who frequently talks with other students around her while you are explaining or demonstrating something. (INTASC: Principles 2, 5)

Research/Field Experience

***Sesame Street* and Social Cognitive Learning.** *Sesame Street* uses many effective techniques to increase children's attention and help them learn. Watch an episode. Analyze the show. How were these techniques used on the show you watched? Describe any additional techniques you observed that you might be able to use in your classroom. (INTASC: Principles 2, 7, 9)

Go to the Online Learning Center for downloadable portfolio templates.

 TAKING IT TO THE NET

- Make a list of specific classroom activities that foster student self-regulation. Which of the activities would be most effective in helping students become more responsible for their learning and developing metacognitive skills? Explain why. Develop a brief action plan for implementing your chosen activity. www.ncrel.org/sdrs/areas/issues/students/learning/lr200.htm

- An important principle of Bandura's social cognitive theory is that exposure to positive role models can alter students' attitudes. How do you think a teacher's behavior and attitude in the classroom influences students' behaviors and attitudes? What kind of student behavior would you expect to find in a classroom with an authoritarian teacher? Authoritative teacher?

Permissive teacher? http://chiron.valdosta.edu/whuitt/col/soccog/soclrn.html

- Develop a system of classroom rewards/consequences for a particular age/grade level. Does your system utilize intrinsic motivators, extrinsic motivators, or a combination of both? Provide examples of student rewards and explain why you selected those specific items. Discuss the benefits and challenges of implementing your rewards system. www.education-world.com/a_curr/curr301.shtml

Connect to the Online Learning Center to explore possible answers.

 STUDY, PRACTICE, AND SUCCEED

Visit www.mhhe.com/santedu4e to review the chapter with self-grading quizzes and self-assessments, to apply the chapter material to two more Crack the Case studies, and for suggested activities to develop your teaching portfolio.

CHAPTER 8

The Information-Processing Approach

The mind is an enchanting thing.

—Marianne Moore
American Poet, 20th Century

Chapter Outline	Learning Goals
The Nature of the Information-Processing Approach Information, Memory, and Thinking Cognitive Resources: Capacity and Speed of Processing Information Mechanisms of Change	**1** Describe the information-processing approach.
Attention What Is Attention? Developmental Changes	**2** Characterize attention and summarize how it changes during development.
Memory What Is Memory? Encoding Storage Retrieval and Forgetting	**3** Discuss memory in terms of encoding, storage, and retrieval.
Expertise Expertise and Learning Acquiring Expertise Expertise and Teaching	**4** Draw some lessons about learning from the way experts think.
Metacognition Developmental Changes The Good Information-Processing Model Strategies and Metacognitive Regulation	**5** Explain the concept of metacognition and identify some ways to improve children's metacognition.

TEACHING STORIES   Laura Bickford

Laura Bickford chairs the English Department at Nordoff High School in Ojai, California. She recently spoke about how she encourages students to think:

> I believe the call to teach is a call to teach students how to think. In encouraging critical thinking, literature itself does a good bit of work for us, but we still have to be guides. We have to ask good questions. We have to show students the value in asking their own questions, in having discussions and conversations. In addition to reading and discussing literature, the best way to move students to think critically is to have them write. We write all the time in a variety of modes: journals, formal essays, letters, factual reports, news articles, speeches, or other formal oral presentations. We have to show students where they merely scratch the surface in their thinking and writing. I call these moments "hits and runs." When I see this "hit and run" effort, I draw a window on the paper. I tell them it is a "window of opportunity" to go deeper, elaborate, and clarify. Many students don't do this kind of thinking until they are prodded to do so.
>
> I also use metacognitive strategies all the time—that is, helping students know about knowing. These include:

asking students to comment on their learning after we have finished particular pieces of projects and asking them to discuss in advance what we might be seeking to learn as we begin a new project or activity. I also ask them to keep reading logs so they can observe their own thinking as it happens. For example, they might copy a passage from a reading selection and comment on it. Studying a passage from J. D. Salinger's *The Catcher in the Rye,* a student might write: "I've never thought about life the way that Holden Caulfield does. Maybe I see the world differently than he does. He always is so depressed. I'm not depressed. Salinger is good at showing us someone who is usually depressed. How does he manage to do that?" In addition, I ask students to comment on their own learning by way of grading themselves. This year a student gave me one of the most insightful lines about her growth as a reader that I have ever seen from a student. She wrote, "I no longer think in a monotone when I'm reading." I don't know if she grasps the magnitude of that thought or how it came to be that she made that change. It is magic when students see themselves growing like this.

Preview

In the opening story, teacher Laura Bickford tells how she uses meta-cognitive strategies, one of the important aspects of cognitive learning and a major topic of this chapter. In addition to metacognition, we'll explore what it means to take an information-processing approach in teaching and examine three important aspects of cognition: attention, memory, and expertise.

---

1   THE NATURE OF THE INFORMATION-PROCESSING APPROACH

| Information, Memory, and Thinking | Cognitive Resources: Capacity and Speed of Processing Information | Mechanisms of Change |

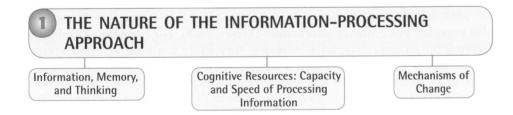

How capable are children? Proponents of the information-processing approach to learning believe they are highly capable. Children attend to information being presented and tinker with it. They develop strategies for remembering. They form concepts. They reason and solve problems. These important skills are the topics of this section.

Information, Memory, and Thinking

The **information-processing approach** emphasizes that children manipulate information, monitor it, and strategize about it. Central to this approach are the processes of memory and thinking. According to the information-processing approach, children develop a gradually increasing capacity for processing information, which allows them to acquire increasingly complex knowledge and skills (Halford, 2008).

Behaviorism and its associative model of learning was a dominant force in psychology until the 1950s and 1960s, when many psychologists began to acknowledge that they could not explain children's learning without referring to mental processes such as memory and thinking. The term *cognitive psychology* became a label for approaches that sought to explain behavior by examining mental processes. Although a number of factors stimulated the growth of cognitive psychology, none was more important than the development of computers. The first modern computer, developed by John von Neumann in the late 1940s, showed that inanimate machines could perform logical operations. This suggested that some mental operations might be carried out by computers, possibly telling us something about the way human cognition works. Cognitive psychologists often draw analogies to computers to help explain the relation between cognition and the brain (Robinson-Riegler & Robinson-Riegler, 2008). The physical brain is compared with the computer's hardware, cognition with its software. Although computers and software aren't perfect analogies for brains and cognitive activities, nonetheless, the comparison contributed to our thinking about the child's mind as an active information-processing system.

Cognitive Resources: Capacity and Speed of Processing Information

As children grow and mature, and as they experience the world, their information-processing abilities increase. These changes are likely influenced by increases in both capacity and speed of processing (Frye, 2004). These two characteristics are often referred to as *cognitive resources,* which are proposed to have an important influence on memory and problem solving.

Both biology and experience contribute to growth in cognitive resources. Think about how much faster you can process information in your native language than in a second language. The changes in the brain we described in Chapter 2 provide a biological foundation for increased cognitive resources. As children grow and mature, important biological developments occur both in brain structures, such as changes in the frontal lobes, and at the level of neurons, such as the blooming and pruning of connections between neurons that produces fewer but stronger connections (Kuhn, 2008; Nelson, 2009). Also, as we discussed in Chapter 2, myelination (the process that covers the axon with a myelin sheath) increases the speed of electrical impulses in the brain. Myelination continues through childhood and adolescence (Spear, 2007).

Most information-processing psychologists argue that an increase in capacity also improves processing of information (Mayer, 2008). For example, as children's information-processing capacity increases, they likely can hold in mind several dimensions of a topic or problem simultaneously, whereas younger children are more prone to focus on only one dimension. Adolescents can discuss how the varied experiences of the Founding Fathers influenced the Declaration of Independence and Constitution. Elementary-age children are more likely to focus on simple facts about the founders' lives.

What is the role of processing speed? How fast children process information often influences what they can do with that information. If an adolescent is trying to add up mentally the cost of items he is buying at the grocery store, he needs to be able to compute the sum before he has forgotten the price of the individual items. Children's speed in processing information is linked with their competence in thinking (Bjorklund, 2005). For example, how fast children can articulate a series of words

information–processing approach
A cognitive approach in which children manipulate information, monitor it, and strategize about it. Central to this approach are the cognitive processes of memory and thinking.

affects how many words they can store and remember. Generally, fast processing is linked with good performance on cognitive tasks. However, some compensation for slower processing speed can be achieved through effective strategies.

Researchers have devised a number of ways for assessing processing speed. For example, it can be assessed through a *reaction-time task* in which individuals are asked to push a button as soon as they see a stimulus such as a light. Or individuals might be asked to match letters or numbers with symbols on a computer screen.

There is abundant evidence that the speed with which such tasks are completed improves dramatically across the childhood years (Kail, 2007; Luna & others, 2004; Mabbott & others, 2006). Processing speed continues to improve in early adolescence. For example, in one study, 10-year-olds were approximately 1.8 times slower at processing information than young adults on such tasks as reaction time, letter matching, mental rotation, and abstract matching (Hale, 1990). Twelve-year-olds were approximately 1.5 times slower than young adults, but 15-year-olds processed information on the tasks as fast as the young adults. Also, a recent study of 8- to 13-year-old children revealed that processing speed increased with age, and further that the developmental change in processing speed preceded an increase in working memory capacity (Kail, 2007).

How does speed of processing information change during childhood and adolescent years?

There is controversy about whether the increase in processing speed is due to experience or biological maturation. Experience clearly plays an important role. Think how much faster you could process the answer to a simple arithmetic problem as an adolescent than as a child. Also think about how much faster you can process information in your native language than in a second language. The role of biological maturation likely involves myelination.

Mechanisms of Change

According to Robert Siegler (1998), three mechanisms work together to create changes in children's cognitive skills: encoding, automaticity, and strategy construction.

Encoding is the process by which information gets stored in memory. Changes in children's cognitive skills depend on increased skill at encoding relevant information and ignoring irrelevant information. For example, to a 4-year-old, an *s* in cursive writing is a shape very different from an *s* that is printed. But a 10-year-old has learned to encode the relevant fact that both are the letter *s* and to ignore the irrelevant differences in their shape.

Automaticity refers to the ability to process information with little or no effort. Practice allows children to encode increasing amounts of information automatically. For example, once children have learned to read well, they do not think about each letter in a word as a letter; instead, they encode whole words. Once a task is automatic, it does not require conscious effort. As a result, as information processing becomes more automatic, we can complete tasks more quickly and handle more than one task at a time (Mayer, 2008; Schraw, 2006). Imagine how long it would take you to read this page if you did not encode words automatically but instead focused your attention on each letter in each word.

Strategy construction is the creation of new procedures for processing information. For example, children's reading benefits when they develop the strategy of stopping periodically to take stock of what they have read so far. Developing an effective repertoire of strategies and selecting the best one to use on a learning task is a critical aspect of becoming an effective learner (Pressley, 2007; Pressley & Harris, 2006).

In addition to these mechanisms of change, children's information processing is characterized by *self-modification* (Siegler, 1998, 2007; Siegler & Chen, 2008). That is, children learn to use what they have learned in previous circumstances to adapt their responses to a new situation. For example, a child who is familiar with dogs and cats goes to the zoo and sees lions and tigers for the first time. She then modifies her concept of "animal" to include her new knowledge. Part of this self-modification draws on **metacognition**, which means "knowing about knowing" (Dunlosky & Metcalfe,

encoding The process by which information gets into memory.

automaticity The ability to process information with little or no effort.

strategy construction Creation of a new procedure for processing information.

metacognition Cognition about cognition, or "knowing about knowing."

2009, Harris & others, 2009). One example of metacognition is what children know about the best ways to remember what they have read. Do they know that they will remember what they have read better if they can relate it to their own lives in some way? Thus, in Siegler's application of information processing to development, children play an active role in their cognitive development when they develop metacognitive strategies.

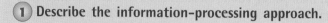

Review, Reflect, and Practice

① **Describe the information-processing approach.**

REVIEW

- What view does the information-processing approach take of children as learners?
- What are two important cognitive resources and how do they contribute to developmental changes in children's information processing?
- What are some key mechanisms of change in the information-processing approach?

REFLECT

- In terms of your ability to learn, are there ways that you wish you were more like a computer? Or are you better than any computer in all aspects of processing information? Explain.

PRAXIS™ PRACTICE

1. Information processing is most closely aligned with
   a. behaviorism.
   b. cognitive psychology.
   c. social cognitive theory.
   d. ecological theory.

2. According to the information-processing approach, a 15-year-old can compute faster than a 10-year-old because the
   a. 15-year-old's brain has had more time to develop, and the 15-year-old has had more experience working with numbers.
   b. 15-year-old has had more experiences of both positive and negative reinforcement.
   c. 15-year-old's brain has lost many of its original connections and undergone demyelinization.
   d. 15-year-old has had much more time to develop rote memory skills.

3. Ms. Parks wants her students to know their basic math facts without having to stop to think about them. Therefore, Ms. Parks plays many math games with her second-grade students, such as addition and subtraction bingo, math bees, and card games. What is Ms. Parks' goal in playing these games with her students?
   a. to help her students to develop automaticity in knowing their math facts
   b. to encourage strategy construction
   c. to foster encoding skills
   d. to improve metacognitive skills, such as self-awareness

Please see the answer key at the end of the book.

2 ATTENTION

What Is Attention?   Developmental Changes

The world holds a lot of information that we need to perceive. What is attention and what effect does it have? How does it change developmentally?

What Is Attention?

Attention is the focusing of mental resources. Attention improves cognitive processing for many tasks, from hitting a baseball, reading a book, or adding numbers (Kane & others, 2007; Knudsen, 2007). At any one time, though, children, like adults, can pay attention to only a limited amount of information. They allocate their attention in different ways. Psychologists have labeled these types of allocation as selective attention, divided attention, sustained attention, and executive attention.

What attentional demands does multitasking place on children and adolescents?

- **Selective attention** is focusing on a specific aspect of experience that is relevant while ignoring others that are irrelevant. Focusing on one voice among many in a crowded room or a noisy restaurant is an example of selective attention.
- **Divided attention** involves concentrating on more than one activity at the same time. If you are listening to music while you are reading this, you are engaging in divided attention.
- **Sustained attention** is the ability to maintain attention over an extended period of time. Sustained attention is also called vigilance. Staying focused on reading this chapter from start to finish without interruption is an example of sustained attention. Recall from our discussion in Chapter 6 that in one study difficulties in sustaining attention were the most common type of attentional problem characterizing children with ADHD (Tsal, Shalev, & Mevorach, 2005).
- **Executive attention** involves action planning, allocating attention to goals, error detection and compensation, monitoring progress on tasks, and dealing with novel or difficult circumstances. An example of executive attention is effectively deploying attention to effectively engage in the aforementioned cognitive tasks while writing a 10-page paper for a history course.

One trend involving divided attention is children's and adolescents' multitasking, which in some cases involves not just dividing attention between two activities, but even three or more (Bauerlein, 2008). A major influence on the increase in multitasking is availability of multiple electronic media. Many children and adolescents have a range of electronic media at their disposal. It is not unusual for adolescents to simultaneously divide their attention by working on homework, while engaging in an instant messaging conversation, surfing the Web, and looking at an iTunes playlist.

Is this multitasking beneficial or distracting? It may have possible harmful effects—multitasking expands the information children and adolescents attend to and forces the brain to share processing resources, which can distract attention from what might be most important at the moment (Begley & Interlandi, 2008).

Sustained and executive attention also are very important aspects of cognitive development. As children and adolescents are required to engage in larger, increasingly complex tasks that require longer time frames to complete, their ability to sustain attention is critical for succeeding on the tasks. An increase in executive attention supports the rapid increase in effortful control required to effectively engage in these complex academic tasks (Rothbart & Gartstein, 2008).

attention The focusing of mental resources.

selective attention Focusing on a specific aspect of experience that is relevant while ignoring others that are irrelevant.

divided attention Concentrating on more than one activity at a time.

sustained attention Maintaining attention over an extended period of time; also called vigilance.

executive attention Involves action planning, allocating attention to goals, error detection and compensation, monitoring progress on tasks, and dealing with novel or difficult circumstances.

What are some developmental changes in attention?

What are some good strategies teachers can use to get students' attention?

Developmental Changes

Some important changes in attention occur during childhood (Courage & Richards, 2008; Posner & Rothbart, 2007). Much of the research on attention has focused on selective attention. One study of 5- to 7-year-old children found that the older children and more socially advantaged children in a sample resisted the interference of competing demands and focused their attention better than the younger children and more socially disadvantaged children (Mezzacappa, 2004).

The length of time children can pay attention increases as they get older. The toddler wanders around, shifts attention from one activity to another, and seems to spend little time focused on any one object or event. In contrast, the preschool child might watch television for half an hour at a time. One study that observed 99 families in their homes for 4,672 hours found that visual attention to television dramatically increased in the preschool years (Anderson & others, 1985).

Preschool children's ability to control and sustain their attention is related to school readiness (Posner & Rothbart, 2007). For example, a study of more than 1,000 children revealed that their ability to sustain their attention at 54 months of age was linked to their school readiness (which included achievement and language skills) (NICHD Early Child Care Research Network, 2005). And a recent study revealed that sustained attention improved from 5 to 6 years to 11 to 12 years of age, and the increased attention was linked to better performance on cognitive tasks (Betts & others, 2006).

Control over attention shows important changes during childhood (Posner & Rothbart, 2007). External stimuli are likely to determine the target of the preschooler's attention; what is salient, or obvious, grabs the preschooler's attention. For example, suppose a flashy, attractive clown presents the directions for solving a problem. Preschool children are likely to pay attention to the clown and ignore the directions, because they are influenced strongly by the salient features of the environment. After the age of 6 or 7, children pay more attention to features relevant to performing a task or solving a problem, such as the directions. Thus, instead of being controlled by the most striking stimuli in their environment, older children can direct their attention to more important stimuli. This change reflects a shift to *cognitive control* of attention, so that children act less impulsively and reflect more. Recall from Chapter 2, "Cognitive and Language Development," that the increase in cognitive control during the elementary school years is linked to changes in the brain, especially more focal activation in the prefrontal cortex (Durston & others, 2006).

Attention to relevant information increases steadily through the elementary and secondary school years (Davidson, 1996). Processing of irrelevant information decreases in adolescence.

As children grow up, their abilities both to direct selective attention and to divide attention also improve. Older children and adolescents are better than younger children at tasks that require shifts of attention. For example, writing a good story requires shifting attention among many competing tasks—spelling the words, composing grammar, structuring paragraphs, and conveying the story as a whole. Children also improve in their ability to do two things at once. For example, in one investigation, 12-year-olds were markedly better than 8-year-olds and slightly worse than 20-year-olds at allocating their attention in a situation involving two tasks (divided attention) (Manis, Keating, & Morrison, 1980). These improvements in divided attention might be due to an increase in cognitive resources (through increased processing speed or capacity), automaticity, or increased skill at directing resources.

As we saw in Chapter 6, "Learners Who Are Exceptional," individual variations also characterize children, with some children having such significant attention problems that they are classified as having attention deficit hyperactivity disorder (ADHD). A recent study revealed that such attention problems in childhood are linked to information-processing difficulties in late adolescence (Friedman & others, 2007). In the study, 7- to 14-year-old children with attention problems

DEVELOPMENTAL FOCUS 8.1

How Do You Help Your Students Focus Their Attention in Class?

Early Childhood

Very young children are just developing their attention span. To help them along, we often use songs or instruments for transitions from play time to work time. When material is introduced, we call out the children's names and ask questions, thus engaging them with the newly introduced item. During story time, we use exaggerated physical gestures and take on the voices of characters in the book to keep children motivated and listening.

—Valarie Gorham, *Kiddie Quarters, Inc.*

Elementary School: Grades K–5

One strategy I use to keep my fourth-grade students focused is to get into a role. For example, when I read *Bubba, the Cowboy Prince,* I put on a cowboy hat and create an accent. I also find that saying, "You will see this on your homework tonight" and "This will be on your test" also grab their attention.

—Shane Schwarz, *Clinton Elementary School*

Middle School: Grades 6–8

My students especially stay focused when I let them teach each other—that is, I let them take turns playing the role of teacher.

—Casey Maass, *Edison Middle School*

High School: Grades 9–12

High school students stay more focused when they know how events and information presented in class relate to their own lives. For example, the topic of food-borne illness is boring to most of my students, but when I tell them about how I got salmonella poisoning from a plate of chicken salad at a local restaurant, and the intense suffering I went through for many days, they become more intrigued with the topic of salmonella, its causes, prevention, and symptoms.

—Sandy Swanson, *Menomonee Falls High School*

(including inattention, disorganization, impulsivity, and hyperactivity) had difficulty inhibiting responses and working memory difficulties at 17 years of age (Friedman & others, 2007).

Review, Reflect, and Practice

2 Characterize attention and summarize how it changes during development.

REVIEW

- What is attention? What are four ways attention can be allocated?
- How does attention develop in childhood and adolescence?

REFLECT

- Imagine that you are an elementary school teacher and a child is having difficulty sustaining attention on a learning task. What strategies would you try to use to help the child sustain attention?

(continued)

1. *Encourage students to pay close attention and minimize distraction.* Talk with children about how important it is to pay attention when they need to remember something. Give them exercises with opportunities to give their undivided attention to something. In Central European countries, such as Hungary, kindergarten children participate in exercises designed to improve their attention (Mills & Mills, 2000; Posner & Rothbart, 2007). For example, in one eye-contact exercise, the teacher sits in the center of a circle of children, and each child is required to catch the teacher's eye before being permitted to leave the group. In other exercises created to improve attention, teachers have children participate in stop-go activities during which they have to listen for a specific signal, such as as drumbeat or an exact number of rhythmic beats, before stopping the activity.

2. *Use cues or gestures to signal that something is important.* This might involve raising your voice, repeating something with emphasis, and writing the concept on the board or on a transparency.

3. *Help students generate their own cue or catch phrase for when they need to pay attention.* Possibly vary this from month to month. Give them a menu of options to select from, such as "Alert," "Focus," or "Zero in." Teach them to say their word or pet phrase quietly but firmly to themselves when they catch their minds wandering.

4. *Make learning interesting.* Boredom can set in quickly for students, and when it does their attention wanes. Relating ideas to students' interests increases their attention. So does infusing the classroom with novel, unusual, or surprising exercises. Just starting off a biology exercise on heredity and aging with a question such as "Can you live to be 100?" or "Might someone be able to live to be even 400 some day?" is sure to capture students' attention. Think of dramatic questions such as these to introduce various topics.

5. *Use media and technology effectively as part of your effort to vary the pace of the classroom.* Video and television programs have built-in attention-getting formats, such as zooming in on an image; flashing a vivid, colorful image on the screen; and switching from one setting to another. Look for relevant videos and television programs that can help you vary the classroom's pace and increase students' attention. Unfortunately, too many teachers show videos only to keep students quiet, which does not promote learning. Also, if the curriculum is dull, it doesn't matter what kinds of "tricks" or "splashes" the teacher uses—students will not learn effectively. Make sure that the media and technology you use captures students' attention in meaningful ways that promote effective learning.

6. *Focus on active learning to make learning enjoyable.* A different exercise, a guest, a field trip, and many other activities can be used to make learning more enjoyable, reduce student boredom, and increase attention. Next, middle school English and drama teacher Lynn Ayres describes how games can add interest at all grade levels.

THROUGH THE EYES OF TEACHERS
Turning Boring Exercises into Active Learning Games

I have found that the most boring exercises (such as the kind you find on worksheets and textbooks) can be turned into an active learning game. One favorite game in my seventh-grade English class was "sit-set, rise-raise." I'd put two students in chairs next to tables and place a book on each table. If I said "rise," they were to stand. If I said "raise," they were to raise the book. They were to seat themselves if I said "sit," and they were to place the book on the table if I said "set." If I said "rise," and one of them stood up and the other student lifted the book, the student with the book held up was out and was replaced by a teammate. Or if they both stood up, the one who stood up first stayed, and the other student was replaced by a teammate. The students loved that game, and they really learned the difference between those two commonly confused pairs of verbs in the process.

That game taught me the effectiveness of getting students physically involved. I developed dozens of other games involving bells and timers and teams that had students running around the room, ringing bells, trying to beat a member of the opposing team in telling me if a word was a noun or an adjective. Almost any workbook or textbook exercise can be turned into a physical activity game if you put some thought into it, and middle school students learn so much more from doing an exercise that is both physical and mental.

7. *Don't overload students with too much information.* We live in an information society where sometimes the tendency is to feel like you have to get students to learn everything quickly. However, students who are given too much information too fast often have difficulty focusing their attention.

8. *Be aware of individual differences in students' attentional skills.* Some students have severe problems in paying attention. You will need to take this into account when presenting material. Before you begin an exercise, look around the room for potential distractions, such as an open window to a playground where students are being noisy. Close the window and draw the shade to eliminate the distraction.

Review, Reflect, and Practice

PRAXIS™ PRACTICE

1. Ms. Samson teaches first grade. Often while she is working with one group of children, she must monitor the behavior of the rest of the class, occasionally intervening in some manner. Sometimes she has three or four students at her desk, each needing something different from her. This does not seem to faze her in the least. She can talk to one student while tying another's shoes and monitoring the behavior of the rest with no problem. What skill has Ms. Samson mastered?
   a. divided attention
   b. selective attention
   c. sustained attention
   d. personal attention

2. Mark shifts his attention very quickly from one thing to another. The more colorful and noisy the thing, the more likely it is to draw his attention. He rarely attends to any one thing for more than a few minutes. From this description, Mark is most likely to be a
   a. toddler.
   b. preschooler.
   c. elementary-school-age child.
   d. adolescent.

Please see the answer key at the end of the book.

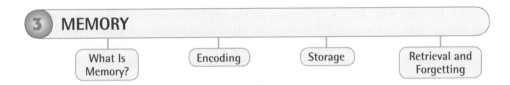

Twentieth-century playwright Tennessee Williams once commented that life is all memory except for that one present moment that goes by so quickly that you can hardly catch it going. But just what is memory?

What Is Memory?

Memory is the retention of information over time. Educational psychologists study how information is initially placed or encoded into memory, how it is retained or stored after being encoded, and how it is found or retrieved for a certain purpose later. Memory anchors the self in continuity. Without memory you would not be able to connect what happened to you yesterday with what is going on in your life today. Today, educational psychologists emphasize that it is important not to view memory in terms of how children add something to it but rather to underscore how children actively construct their memory (Schacter, 2001).

The main body of our discussion of memory will focus on encoding, storage, and retrieval. Thinking about memory in terms of these processes should help you to understand it better (see Figure 8.1). For memory to work, children have to take information in, store it or represent it, and then retrieve it for some purpose later.

As you learned earlier, *encoding* is the process by which information gets into memory. *Storage* is the retention of information over time. *Retrieval* means taking

memory The retention of information over time, which involves encoding, storage, and retrieval.

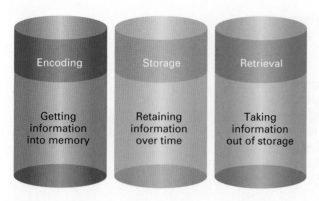

FIGURE 8.1 Processing Information in Memory

As you read about the many aspects of memory in this chapter, think about the organization of memory in terms of these three main activities.

information out of storage. Let's now explore each of these three important memory activities in greater detail.

Encoding

In everyday language, encoding has much in common with attention and learning. When a student is listening to a teacher, watching a movie, listening to music, or talking with a friend, he or she is encoding information into memory. In addition to attention, which we just discussed, encoding consists of a number of processes: rehearsal, deep processing, elaboration, constructing images, and organization.

Rehearsal **Rehearsal** is the conscious repetition of information over time to increase the length of time information stays in memory. For example, when you make a date to meet your best friend for lunch, you are likely to repeat, or rehearse, the date and time: "OK—Wednesday at 1:30." Rehearsal works best when you need to encode and remember a list of items for a brief period of time. When you must retain information over long periods of time, as when you are studying for a test you won't take until next week, other strategies usually work better than rehearsal. Rehearsal does not work well for retaining information over the long term because it often involves just rote repetition of information without imparting any meaning to it. When you construct your memory in meaningful ways, you remember better. As we will see next, you also remember better when you process material deeply and elaborate it.

Deep Processing Following the discovery that rehearsal is not an efficient way to encode information for long-term memory, Fergus Craik and Robert Lockhart (1972) proposed that we can process information at a variety of levels. Their theory, **levels of processing theory**, states that the processing of memory occurs on a continuum from shallow to deep, with deeper processing producing better memory. Shallow processing means analyzing a stimuli's sensory, or physical, features at a shallow level. This might involve detecting the lines, angles, and contours of a printed word's letters or a spoken word's frequency, duration, and loudness. At an intermediate level of processing, you recognize the stimulus and give it a label. For example, you identify a four-legged, barking object as a dog. Then, at the deepest level, you process information semantically, in terms of its meaning. For example, if a child sees the word *boat*, at the shallow level she might notice the shapes of the letters, at the intermediate level she might think of the characteristics of the word (for instance, that it rhymes with *coat*), and at the deepest level she might think about the last time she went fishing with her dad on a boat and the kind of boat it was. Researchers have found that individuals remember information better when they process it at a deep level (Otten, Henson, & Rugg, 2001).

Elaboration Cognitive psychologists soon recognized, however, that there is more to good encoding than just depth of processing. They discovered that when individuals use elaboration in their encoding of information, their memory benefits (Terry, 2006). **Elaboration** is the extensiveness of information processing involved in encoding. Thus, when you present the concept of democracy to students, they likely will remember it better if they come up with good examples of it. Thinking of examples is a good way to elaborate information. For instance, self-reference is an effective way to elaborate information. If you are trying to get students to remember the concept of fairness, the more they can generate personal examples of inequities and equities they have personally experienced, the more likely they are to remember the concept.

The use of elaboration changes developmentally (Nelson, 2006; Schneider, 2004). Adolescents are more likely to use elaboration spontaneously than children are. Ele-

rehearsal The conscious repetition of information over time to increase the length of time information stays in memory.

levels of processing theory The theory that processing of memory occurs on a continuum from shallow to deep, with deeper processing producing better memory.

elaboration The extensiveness of information processing involved in encoding.

mentary school children can be taught to use elaboration strategies on a learning task, but they are less likely than adolescents to use the strategies on other learning tasks in the future. Nonetheless, verbal elaboration can be an effective memory strategy even with young elementary school children. In one study, the experimenter told second- and fifth-grade children to construct a meaningful sentence for a keyword (such as "The postman carried a letter in his cart" for the keyword *cart*). As shown in Figure 8.2, both second- and fifth-grade children remembered the keywords better when they constructed a meaningful sentence containing the word than when the keyword and its definition were told to the child (Pressley, Levin, & McCormick, 1980).

One reason elaboration works so well in encoding is that it adds to the distinctiveness of memory code (Hunt & Ellis, 2004). To remember a piece of information, such as a name, an experience, or a fact about geography, students need to search for the code that contains this information among the mass of codes in their long-term memory. The search process is easier if the memory code is unique (Hunt & Kelly, 1996). The situation is not unlike searching for a friend at a crowded airport—if your friend is 6 feet 3 inches tall and has flaming red hair, it will be easier to find him in the crowd than if he has more common features. Also, as a student elaborates information, more information is stored. And as more information is stored, it becomes easier to differentiate the memory from others. For example, if a student witnesses another student being hit by a car that speeds away, the student's memory of the car will be far better if she deliberately encodes her observations that the car is a red 2005 Pontiac with tinted windows and spinners on the wheels than if she observes only that it is a red car.

Constructing Images   When we construct an image of something, we are elaborating the information. For example, how many windows are there in the apartment or house where your family has lived for a substantial part of your life? Few of us ever memorize this information, but you probably can come up with a good answer, especially if you reconstruct a mental image of each room.

Allan Paivio (1971, 1986) argues that memories are stored in one of two ways: as verbal codes or as image codes. For example, you can remember a picture by a label (*The Last Supper*, a verbal code) or by a mental image. Paivio says that the more detailed and distinctive the image code, the better your memory of the information will be.

Researchers have found that encouraging children to use imagery to remember verbal information works better for older children than for younger children (Schneider, 2004). In one study, experimenters presented twenty sentences to first- through sixth-grade children to remember (such as "The angry bird shouted at the white dog" and "The policeman painted the circus tent on a windy day") (Pressley & others, 1987). Children were randomly assigned to an imagery condition (make a picture in your head for each sentence) and a control condition (children were told just to try hard). Figure 8.3 shows that the imagery instructions improved memory more for the older children (grades 4 through 6) than for the younger children (grades 1 through 3). Researchers have found that young elementary school children can use imagery to remember pictures better than they can verbal materials, such as sentences (Schneider & Pressley, 1997).

THROUGH THE EYES OF STUDENTS

The Cobwebs of Memory

I think the point of having memories is to share them, especially with close friends or family. If you don't share them, they are just sitting inside your brain getting cobwebs. If you have a great memory of Christmas and no one to share it with, what's the point of memories?

Seventh-Grade Student
West Middle School
Ypsilanti, Michigan

FIGURE 8.2 Verbal Elaboration and Memory

Both second- and fifth-grade children remembered words better when they constructed a meaningful sentence for the word (verbal elaboration group) than when they merely heard the word and its definition (control group). The verbal elaboration worked better for the fifth-graders than the second-graders.

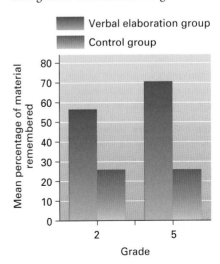

Frank and Ernest

FRANK & ERNEST © Thaves/Dist. by Newspaper Enterprise Association, Inc.

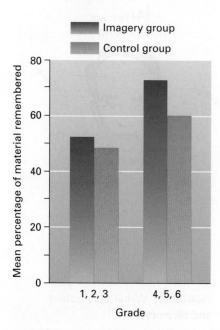

FIGURE 8.3 Imagery and Memory of Verbal Information

Imagery improved older elementary school children's memory for sentences more than younger elementary school children's memory for sentences.

chunking Grouping, or "packing," information into "higher-order" units that can be remembered as single units.

sensory memory Memory that holds information from the world in its original form for only an instant.

short-term memory A limited-capacity memory system in which information is retained for as long as 30 seconds, unless the information is rehearsed, in which case it can be retained longer.

Organization If students organize information when they are encoding it, their memory benefits. To understand the importance of organization in encoding, complete the following exercise: Recall the 12 months of the year as quickly as you can. How long did it take you? What was the order of your recall? Your answers are probably a few seconds and in natural order (January, February, March, and so on). Now try to remember the months in alphabetical order. Did you make any errors? How long did it take you? There is a clear distinction between recalling the months in natural order and recalling alphabetically. This exercise is a good one to use with your students to help them understand the importance of organizing their memories in meaningful ways.

The more you present information in an organized way, the easier your students will remember it. This is especially true if you organize information hierarchically or outline it. Also, if you simply encourage students to organize information, they often will remember it better than if you give them no instructions about organizing (Mandler, 1980).

Chunking is a beneficial organizational memory strategy that involves grouping, or "packing," information into "higher-order" units that can be remembered as single units. Chunking works by making large amounts of information more manageable and more meaningful. For example, consider this simple list of words: *hot, city, book, forget, tomorrow, smile.* Try to hold these in memory for a moment, then write them down. If you recalled all six words, you succeeded in holding 30 letters in your memory. But it would have been much more difficult to try to remember those 30 letters. Chunking them into words made them meaningful.

Storage

After children encode information, they need to retain, or store, the information. Memory storage involves three types of memory with different time frames: sensory memory, working (or short-term) memory, and long-term memory.

Memory's Time Frames Children remember some information for less than a second, some for about half a minute, and other information for minutes, hours, years, even a lifetime. The three types of memory, which correspond to these different time frames, are *sensory memory* (which lasts a fraction of a second to several seconds); *short-term memory* (also called *working memory;* lasts about 30 seconds), and *long-term memory* (which lasts up to a lifetime).

Sensory Memory **Sensory memory** holds information from the world in its original sensory form for only an instant, not much longer than the brief time a student is exposed to the visual, auditory, and other sensations.

Students have a sensory memory for sounds for up to several seconds, sort of like a brief echo. However, their sensory memory for visual images lasts only for about one-fourth of a second. Because sensory information lasts for only a fleeting moment, an important task for the student is to attend to the sensory information that is important for learning quickly, before it fades.

Short-Term Memory **Short-term memory** is a limited-capacity memory system in which information is retained for as long as 30 seconds, unless the information is rehearsed or otherwise processed further, in which case it can be retained longer. Compared with sensory memory, short-term memory is limited in capacity but relatively longer in duration. Its limited capacity intrigued George Miller (1956), who described this in a paper with a catchy title: "The Magical Number Seven, Plus or Minus Two." Miller pointed out that on many tasks, students are limited in how much information they can keep track of without external aids. Usually the limit is in the range of 7 +/− 2 items.

The most widely cited example of the 7 +/− 2 phenomenon involves **memory span**, the number of digits an individual can report back without error from a single presentation. How many digits individuals can report back depends on how old they are. In one study, memory span increased from two digits in 2-year-olds, to five digits in 7-year-olds, to six to seven digits in 12-year-olds (Dempster, 1981) (see Figure 8.4). Many college students can handle lists of eight or nine digits. Keep in mind that these are averages and that individuals differ. For example, many 7-year-olds have a memory span of fewer than six or seven digits; others have a memory span of eight or more digits.

Related to short-term memory, British psychologist Alan Baddeley (1993, 2000, 2006, 2007a, b) proposed that **working memory** is a three-part system that temporarily holds information as people perform tasks. Working memory is a kind of mental "workbench" where information is manipulated and assembled to help us make decisions, solve problems, and comprehend written and spoken language. Notice that working memory is not like a passive storehouse with shelves to store information until it moves to long-term memory. Rather, it is a very active memory system (Schraw, 2006; Yen, 2008).

Figure 8.5 shows Baddeley's view of working memory and its three components: phonological loop, visuospatial working memory, and central executive. Think of them as an executive (central executive) with two assistants (phonological loop and visuospatial working memory) to help do your work.

- The *phonological loop* is specialized to briefly store speech-based information about the sounds of language. The phonological loop contains two separate components: an acoustic code, which decays in a few seconds, and rehearsal, which allows individuals to repeat the words in the phonological store.
- *Visuospatial working memory* stores visual and spatial information, including visual imagery. Like the phonological loop, visuospatial working memory has a limited capacity. The phonological loop and visuospatial working memory function independently. You could rehearse numbers in the phonological loop while making spatial arrangements of letters in visuospatial working memory.
- The *central executive* integrates information not only from the phonological loop and visuospatial working memory but also from long-term memory. In Baddeley's view, the central executive plays important roles in attention, planning, and organizing behavior. The central executive acts much like a supervisor who monitors which information and issues deserve attention and which should be ignored. It also selects which strategies to use to process information and solve problems. As with the other two components of working memory—the phonological loop and visuospatial working memory—the central executive has a limited capacity.

Working memory is linked to many aspects of children's development (Cowan & Alloway, 2009; Imbo & Vandierendonck, 2007). For example, children who have better working memory are more advanced in reading comprehension, math skills, and problem solving than their counterparts with less effective working memory (Andersson & Lyxell, 2007; Demetriou & others, 2002).

Is the working memory of adolescents better than the working memory of children? One study found that it was (Swanson, 1999). Investigators examined the performances of children and adolescents on both verbal and visuospatial working memory tasks. As shown in Figure 8.6, working memory increased substantially from 8 through 24 years of age no matter what the task. Thus, the adolescent years are likely to be an important developmental period for improvement in working memory.

"Can we hurry up and get to the test? My short-term memory is better than my long-term memory."

© 2006; reprinted courtesy of Bunny Hoest and *Parade.*

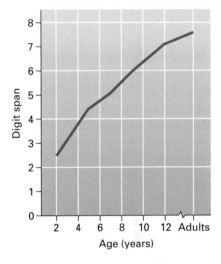

FIGURE 8.4 Developmental Changes in Memory Span

In one study, memory span increased about 3 digits from 2 years of age to 5 digits at 7 years of age (Dempster, 1981). By 12 years of age, memory span had increased on average another 1½ digits.

memory span The number of digits an individual can report back without error in a single presentation.

working memory A three-part system that holds information temporarily as a person performs a task. A kind of "mental workbench" that lets individuals manipulate, assemble, and construct information when they make decisions, solve problems, and comprehend written and spoken language.

FIGURE 8.5 Working Memory

In Baddeley's working memory model, working memory is like a mental workbench where a great deal of information processing is carried out. Working memory consists of three main components: The phonological loop and visuospatial working memory serve as assistants, helping the central executive do its work. Input from sensory memory goes to the phonological loop, where information about speech is stored and rehearsal takes place, and visuospatial working memory, where visual and spatial information, including imagery, are stored. Working memory is a limited-capacity system, and information is stored there for only a brief time. Working memory interacts with long-term memory, using information from long-term memory in its work and transmitting information to long-term memory for longer storage.

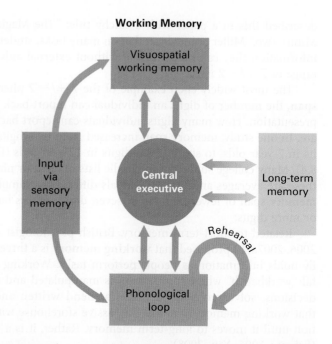

FIGURE 8.6 Developmental Changes in Working Memory

Note: The scores shown here are the means for each age group and the age also represents a mean age. Higher scores reflect superior working memory performance.

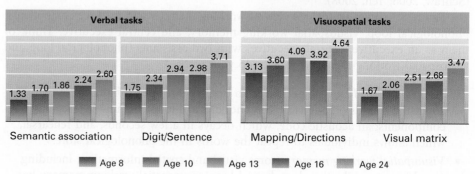

long-term memory A type of memory that holds enormous amounts of information for a long period of time in a relatively permanent fashion.

Atkinson-Shiffrin model A model of memory that involves a sequence of three stages: sensory memory, short-term memory, and long-term memory.

Long-Term Memory **Long-term memory** is a type of memory that holds enormous amounts of information for a long period of time in a relatively permanent fashion. A typical human's long-term memory capacity is staggering, and the efficiency with which individuals can retrieve information is impressive. It often takes only a moment to search through this vast storehouse to find the information we want. Think about your own long-term memory. Who wrote the Gettysburg Address? Who was your first-grade teacher? You can answer thousands of such questions instantly. Of course, not all information is retrieved so easily from long-term memory.

A Model of the Three Memory Stores This three-stage concept of memory we have been describing was developed by Richard Atkinson and Richard Shiffrin (1968). According to the **Atkinson-Shiffrin model**, memory involves a sequence of sensory memory, short-term memory, and long-term memory stages (see Figure 8.7). As we have seen, much information makes it no further than the sensory memories of sounds and sights. This information is retained only for a brief instant. However, some information, especially that to which we pay attention, is transferred to short-term memory, where it can be retained for about 30 seconds (or longer with the aid of rehearsal). Atkinson and Shiffrin claimed that the longer information is retained in short-term memory through the use of rehearsal, the greater its chance is of getting into long-term memory. Notice in Figure 8.7 that information in long-term memory also can be retrieved back into short-term memory.

Some contemporary experts on memory believe that the Atkinson-Shiffrin model is too simple (Bartlett, 2008). They argue that memory doesn't always work in a neatly packaged three-stage sequence, as Atkinson and Shiffrin proposed. For exam-

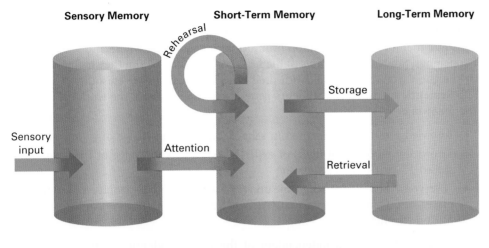

FIGURE 8.7 Atkinson and Shiffrin's Theory of Memory

In this model, sensory input goes into sensory memory. Through the process of attention, information moves into short-term memory, where it remains for 30 seconds or less, unless it is rehearsed. When the information goes into long-term memory storage, it can be retrieved over the lifetime.

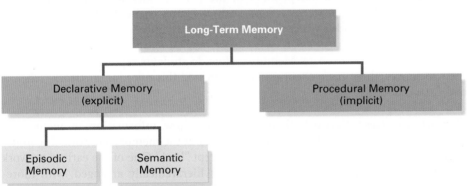

FIGURE 8.8 Classification of Long-Term Memory's Contents

ple, these contemporary experts stress that *working memory* uses long-term memory's contents in more flexible ways than simply retrieving information from it. Despite these problems, the model is useful in providing an overview of some components of memory.

Long–Term Memory's Contents   Just as different types of memory can be distinguished by how long they last, memory can be differentiated on the basis of its contents (Schraw, 2006). For long-term memory, many contemporary psychologists accept the hierarchy of contents described in Figure 8.8 (Bartlett, 2008; Squire, 1987). In this hierarchy, long-term memory is divided into the subtypes of declarative and procedural memory. Declarative memory is subdivided into episodic memory and semantic memory.

Declarative and Procedural Memory   **Declarative memory** is the conscious recollection of information, such as specific facts or events that can be verbally communicated. Declarative memory has been called "knowing that" and more recently has been labeled "explicit memory." Demonstrations of students' declarative memory could include recounting an event they have witnessed or describing a basic principle of math. However, students do not need to be talking to be using declarative memory. If students simply sit and reflect on an experience, their declarative memory is involved.

Procedural memory is nondeclarative knowledge in the form of skills and cognitive operations. Procedural memory cannot be consciously recollected, at least not in the form of specific events or facts. This makes procedural memory difficult, if not impossible, to communicate verbally. Procedural memory is sometimes called "knowing how," and recently it also has been described as "implicit memory" (Schacter, 2000). When students apply their abilities to perform a dance, ride a bicycle, or type on a computer keyboard, their procedural memory is at work. It also is at work when they speak grammatically correct sentences without having to think about how to do it.

declarative memory The conscious recollection of information, such as specific facts or events that can be verbally communicated.

procedural memory Nondeclarative knowledge in the form of skills and cognitive operations. Procedural memory cannot be consciously recollected, at least not in the form of specific events or facts.

Episodic and Semantic Memory   Cognitive psychologist Endel Tulving (1972, 2000) distinguishes between two subtypes of declarative memory: episodic and semantic. **Episodic memory** is the retention of information about the where and when of life's happenings. Students' memories of the first day of school, whom they had lunch with, or the guest who came to talk with their class last week are all episodic.

Semantic memory is a student's general knowledge about the world. It includes the following:

- Knowledge of the sort learned in school (such as knowledge of geometry)
- Knowledge in different fields of expertise (such as knowledge of chess, for a skilled 15-year-old chess player)
- "Everyday" knowledge about meanings of words, famous people, important places, and common things (such as what the word *pertinacious* means or who Nelson Mandela is)

Semantic memory is independent of the person's identity with the past. For example, students might access a fact—such as "Lima is the capital of Peru"—and not have the foggiest idea when and where they learned it.

Representing Information in Memory   How do students represent information in their memory? Three main theories have addressed this question: network, schema, and fuzzy trace.

Network Theories   **Network theories** describe how information in memory is organized and connected. They emphasize nodes in the memory network. The nodes stand for labels or concepts. Consider the concept "bird." One of the earliest network theories described memory representation as hierarchically arranged, with more-concrete concepts ("canary," for example) nestled under more abstract concepts (such as "bird"). However, it soon became clear that such hierarchical networks are too neat to accurately portray how memory representation really works. For example, students take longer to answer the question "Is an ostrich a bird?" than to answer the question "Is a canary a bird?" Thus, today memory researchers envision the memory network as more irregular and distorted (Schraw, 2006). A typical bird, such as a canary, is closer to the node, or center, of the category "bird" than is the atypical ostrich.

Schema Theories   Long-term memory has been compared with a library of books. The idea is that our memory stores information just as a library stores books. In this analogy, the way students retrieve information is said to be similar to the process they use to locate and check out a book. The process of retrieving information from long-term memory, however, is not as precise as the library analogy suggests. When we search through our long-term memory storehouse, we don't always find the exact "book" we want, or we might find the "book" we want but discover that only "several pages" are intact—we have to reconstruct the rest.

Schema theories state that when we reconstruct information, we fit it into information that already exists in our mind. A **schema** is information—concepts, knowledge, information about events—that already exists in a person's mind. Unlike network theories, which assume that retrieval involves specific facts, schema theory claims that long-term memory searches are not very exact. We often don't find precisely what we want, and we have to reconstruct the rest. Often when asked to retrieve information, we fill in the gaps between our fragmented memories with a variety of accuracies and inaccuracies.

We have schemas for all sorts of information (Elliott & Chandler, 2008; Solso, MacLin, & MacLin, 2008). If you tell virtually any story to your class and then ask the students to write down what the story was about, you likely will get many different versions. That is, your students won't remember every detail of the story you told and will reconstruct the story with their own particular stamp on it. Suppose you tell your class a story about two men and two women who were involved in a train crash

episodic memory The retention of information about the where and when of life's happenings.

semantic memory An individual's general knowledge about the world, independent of the individual's identity with the past.

network theories Theories that describe how information in memory is organized and connected; they emphasize nodes in the memory network.

schema theories Theories that when we construct information, we fit it into information that already exists in our mind.

schema Information—concepts, knowledge, information about events—that already exists in a person's mind.

DEVELOPMENTAL FOCUS 8.2

How Do You Help Your Students Improve Their Memory Skills?

Early Childhood

Repetition often helps preschoolers remember. For example, as a weekly theme, we focus on a letter of the week. Children are asked to write the same letter throughout the week. They also hear stories related to just that one letter and are asked to bring in something for "show and tell" that starts with the letter being highlighted that week.

—Missy Dangler, *Suburban Hills School*

Elementary School: Grades K–5

One strategy that works well with my students is to play the game *Jeopardy!* and use categories like math, grammar, science, social studies, and famous stories. The game keeps them excited and focused on the topics. Students receive bonus points for correct answers, which they can trade in for certain classroom privileges.

—Craig Jensen, *Cooper Mountain Elementary School*

Middle School: Grades 6–8

I use self-tests to help my seventh-graders improve their memory. Based on notes taken in class, students create their own quizzes and tests. Questions are on one side of the paper, answers on the other. When they study, they are seeing the questions, not the answers. This approach not only helps them remember, but also helps eliminate test anxiety for many students because they know what the test looks like before they get to class.

—Mark Fodness, *Bemidji Middle School*

High School: Grades 9–12

I find that mnemonic devices, silly little rhymes, and dances work best when helping my students remember information. Amazingly, as goofy as this may sound, my high school students remember information using these techniques.

—Jennifer Heiter, *Bremen High School*

---

in France. One student might reconstruct the story by saying the characters died in a plane crash, another might describe three men and three women, another might say the crash was in Germany, and so on. The reconstruction and distortion of memory is nowhere more apparent than in the memories given by courtroom witnesses. In criminal court trials such as that of O. J. Simpson, the variations in people's memories of what happened underscores how we reconstruct the past rather than take an exact photograph of it.

In sum, schema theory accurately predicts that people don't always coldly store and retrieve bits of data in a computer-like fashion (Reysen 2008; Schacter, 2001; Schraw, 2006). The mind can distort an event as it encodes and stores impressions of reality.

A **script** is a schema for an event. Scripts often have information about physical features, people, and typical occurrences. This kind of information is helpful when teachers and students need to figure out what is happening around them. In a script for an art activity, students likely will remember that you will instruct them on what to draw, that they are supposed to put on smocks over their clothes, that they must get the art paper and paints from the cupboard, that they are to clean the brushes when they are finished, and so on. For example, a student who comes in late to the art activity likely knows much of what to do because he has an art activity script.

script A schema for an event.

"Why? You cross the road because it's in the script—that's why!"

Fuzzy Trace Theory Another variation of how individuals reconstruct their memories is **fuzzy trace theory**, which states that when individuals encode information it creates two types of memory representations: (1) a *verbatim memory trace*, which consists of precise details; and (2) a *fuzzy trace*, or gist, which is the central idea of the information (Brainerd & Reyna, 2004; Brainerd & others, 2006; Reyna, 2004; Reyna & Rivers, 2008). For example, consider a child who is presented with information about a pet store that has 10 birds, 6 cats, 8 dogs, and 7 rabbits. Then the child is asked two different types of questions: (1) verbatim questions, such as "How many cats are in the pet store, 6 or 8?" and (2) gist questions, such as "Are there more cats or more dogs in the pet store?" Researchers have found that preschool children tend to remember verbatim information better than gist information, but elementary-school-aged children are more likely to remember gist information (Brainerd & Gordon, 1994). According to Brainerd and Reyna, the increased use of gist information by elementary-school-aged children accounts for their improved memory, because fuzzy traces are less likely to be forgotten than verbatim traces.

Retrieval and Forgetting

After students have encoded information and then represented it in memory, they might be able to retrieve some of it but might also forget some of it. What factors influence whether students can retrieve information?

Retrieval When we retrieve something from our mental "data bank," we search our store of memory to find the relevant information. Just as with encoding, this search can be automatic or it can require effort. For example, if you ask your students what month it is, the answer will immediately spring to their lips. That is, the retrieval will be automatic. But if you ask your students to name the guest speaker who came to the class two months earlier, the retrieval process likely will require more effort.

An item's position on a list also affects how easy or difficult it will be to remember it. In the **serial position effect**, recall is better for items at the beginning and end of a list than for items in the middle. Suppose that when you give a student directions about where to go to get tutoring help, you say, "Left on Mockingbird, right on Central, left on Balboa, left on Sandstone, and right on Parkside." The student likely will remember "Left on Mockingbird" and "Right on Parkside" better than "Left on Balboa." The *primacy effect* is that items at the beginning of a list tend to be remembered. The *recency effect* is that items at the end of the list also tend to be remembered.

Figure 8.9 shows a typical serial position effect with a slightly stronger recency effect than primacy effect. The serial position effect applies not only to lists but also to events. If you spread out a history lesson over a week and then ask students about it the following Monday, they likely will have the best memory for what you told them on Friday of last week and the worst memory for what you told them on Wednesday of last week.

Another factor that affects retrieval is the nature of the cues people use to prompt their memory (Homa, 2008). Students can learn to create effective cues. For example, if a student has a "block" about remembering the name of the guest who came to class two months ago, she might go through the alphabet, generating names with each letter. If she manages to stumble across the right name, she likely will recognize it.

Another consideration in understanding retrieval is the **encoding specificity principle**: that associations formed at the time of encoding or learning tend to be

fuzzy trace theory States that memory is best understood by considering two types of memory representations: (1) verbatim memory trace and (2) fuzzy trace, or gist. In this theory, older children's better memory is attributed to the fuzzy traces created by extracting the gist of information.

serial position effect The principle that recall is better for items at the beginning and the end of a list than for items in the middle.

encoding specificity principle The principle that associations formed at the time of encoding or learning tend to be effective retrieval cues.

effective retrieval cues. For example, imagine that a 13-year-old child has encoded this information about Mother Teresa: She was born in Albania, lived most of her life in India, became a Roman Catholic nun, was saddened by seeing people sick and dying in Calcutta's streets, and won a Nobel Prize for her humanitarian efforts to help the poor and suffering. Later, when the child tries to remember details about Mother Teresa, she can use words such as *Nobel Prize, Calcutta,* and *humanitarian* as retrieval cues. The concept of encoding specificity is compatible with our earlier discussion of elaboration: The more elaboration children use in encoding information, the better their memory of the information will be. Encoding specificity and elaboration reveal how interdependent encoding and retrieval are (Robinson-Riegler & Robinson-Riegler, 2008).

Yet another aspect of retrieval is the nature of the retrieval task itself. *Recall* is a memory task in which individuals must retrieve previously learned information, as students must do for fill-in-the-blank or essay questions. *Recognition* is a memory task in which individuals only have to identify ("recognize") learned information, as is often the case on multiple-choice tests. Many students prefer multiple-choice items because they provide good retrieval cues, which fill-in-the-blank and essay items don't do.

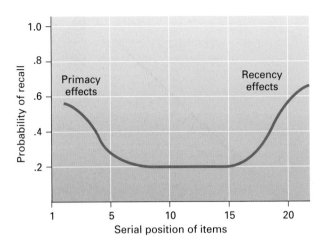

FIGURE 8.9 The Serial Position Effect
When a person is asked to memorize a list of words, the words memorized last usually are recalled best, those at the beginning next best, and those in the middle least efficiently.

Forgetting   One form of forgetting involves the cues we just discussed. **Cue-dependent forgetting** is retrieval failure caused by a lack of effective retrieval cues. The notion of cue-dependent forgetting can explain why a student might fail to retrieve a needed fact for an exam even when he is sure he "knows" the information. For example, if you are studying for a test in this course and are asked a question about a distinction between recall and recognition in retrieval, you likely will remember the distinction better if you possess the cues "fill-in-the-blank" and "multiple-choice," respectively.

The principle of cue-dependent forgetting is consistent with **interference theory**, which states that we forget not because we actually lose memories from storage but rather because other information gets in the way of what we are trying to remember. For a student who studies for a biology test, then studies for a history test, and then takes the biology test, the information about history will interfere with remembering the information about biology. Thus, interference theory implies that, if you have more than one test to study for, you should study last what you are going to be tested on next. That is, the student taking the biology test would have benefited from studying history first and studying biology afterward. This strategy also fits with the recency effect we described earlier.

Another source of forgetting is memory decay. According to **decay theory**, new learning involves the creation of a neurochemical "memory trace," which will eventually disintegrate. Thus, decay theory suggests that the passage of time is responsible for forgetting. Leading memory researcher Daniel Schacter (2001) now refers to forgetting that occurs with the passage of time as *transience*.

Memories decay at different speeds. Some memories are vivid and last for long periods of time, especially when they have emotional ties. We can often remember these "flashbulb" memories with considerable accuracy and vivid imagery. For example, consider a car accident you were in or witnessed, the night of your high school graduation, an early romantic experience, and where you were when you heard about the destruction of the World Trade Center towers. Chances are, you will be able to retrieve this information many years after the event occurred.

In their study of memory, researchers have not extensively examined the roles that sociocultural factors such as culture and gender might play in memory. In the *Diversity and Education* interlude, we will explore these topics.

cue-dependent forgetting Retrieval failure caused by a lack of effective retrieval cues.

interference theory The theory that we forget not because we actually lose memories from storage but because other information gets in the way of what we are trying to remember.

decay theory The theory that new learning involves the creation of a neurochemical "memory trace," which will eventually disintegrate. Thus, decay theory suggests that the passage of time is responsible for forgetting.

DIVERSITY AND EDUCATION
Culture, Gender, and Memory

A culture sensitizes its members to certain objects, events, and strategies, which in turn can influence the nature of memory (Fivush, 2009; Matsumoto & Juang, 2008). In schema theory, a person's background, which is encoded in schemas, is revealed in the way the person reconstructs a story. This effect of cultural background on memory is called the *cultural specificity hypothesis*. It states that cultural experiences determine what is relevant in a person's life and, thus, what the person is likely to remember. For example, imagine that you live on a remote island in the Pacific Ocean and make your livelihood by fishing. Your memory about how weather affects fishing is likely to be highly developed. By contrast, a Pacific Islander might be hard-pressed to encode and recall the details of one hour of MTV. The culture specificity hypothesis also refers to subgroups within a culture. For example, many basketball fans in the United States can recount an impressive array of National Basketball Association (NBA) statistics. A devout gardener might know the informal and Latin names of all plants seen on a garden tour. Our specific interests in our culture and subculture shape the richness of our memory stores and schemas on any given topic.

As we indicated earlier in this chapter, *scripts* are schemas for an event. In one study, individuals in the United States and Mexico remembered according to script-based knowledge (Harris, Schoen, & Hensley, 1992). In line with common practices in their respective cultures, individuals in the United States remembered information about a dating script better when no chaperone was present on a date, whereas individuals in Mexico remembered the information better when a chaperone was present. American children, especially American girls, describe autobiographical narratives

that are longer, more detailed, more specific, and more "personal" (both in terms of mention of self, and mention of internal states), than narratives by children from China and Korea. The pattern is consistent with expectations derived from the finding that in their conversations about past events, American mothers and their children are more elaborative and more focused on autonomous themes . . . and that Korean mothers and their children have

Students in a classroom in Nairobi, Kenya. *How might schooling influence memory?*

DIVERSITY AND EDUCATION
Culture, Gender, and Memory

less frequent and less detailed conversations about the past. . . . (Bauer, 2006, p. 411)

Gender is another aspect of sociocultural diversity that has been given little attention in memory research until recently (Aarston, Martin, & Zimprich, 2003; Bauer, 2006; Gerstorf, Herlitz, & Smith, 2006). Researchers have found these gender differences in memory:

- Females are better at episodic memory, which is memory for personal events that include the time and place the event occurred (Halpern, 2006).

- Females are better than males at emotion-linked memory, such as memory for an emotional film (Cahill & others, 2001). In childhood and adulthood, females' memory narratives include more emotional language and emotional experiences than those of males (Bauer, 2006).

- Males are better than females on tasks that require transformations in visuospatial working memory (Halpern, 2006). These tasks include mental rotation, which involves the imagined motion of stationary objects (such as what a shape would look like if it were rotated in space).

- Females may process information more elaborately and in greater detail, whereas males may be more likely to use schemas or focus on overall information (Guillem & Mograss, 2005).

On many memory tasks, though, researchers do not find gender differences, or when differences occur they are small (Hyde, 2005, 2007).

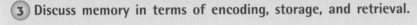

Review, Reflect, and Practice

(3) Discuss memory in terms of encoding, storage, and retrieval.

REVIEW
- What is memory? What is necessary for it to work?
- How are these five processes—rehearsal, deep processing, elaboration, constructing images, and organization—involved in encoding?
- What are the three time frames of memory? How are long-term memory's contents described? What are three theories about how they might they be represented in memory?
- What makes a memory easier or harder to retrieve? What are some theories about why we forget?

REFLECT
- Which principles and strategies in our discussion of memory are likely to be useful for the subjects and grade levels at which you plan to teach?

PRAXIS™ PRACTICE
1. Natalie is playing a game called "memory" at a birthday party. A covered tray with 15 objects is brought into the room. The cover is removed, and the children have 30 seconds to memorize the objects. They will then write down the objects they remember. The child who correctly remembers the most objects wins the

(continued)

BEST PRACTICES
Strategies for Helping Students Improve Their Memory

1. *Motivate children to remember material by understanding it rather than by memorizing it.* Children will remember information better over the long term if they understand the information rather than just rehearse and memorize it. Rehearsal works well for encoding information into short-term memory, but when children need to retrieve the information from long-term memory, it is much less efficient. For most information, encourage children to understand it, give it meaning, elaborate on it, and personalize it. Give children concepts and ideas to remember and then ask them how they can relate the concepts and ideas to their own personal experiences and meanings. Give them practice on elaborating a concept so they will process the information more deeply.

2. *Assist students in organizing what they put into their memory.* Children will remember information better if they organize it hierarchically. Give them some practice arranging and reworking material that requires some structuring.

3. *Teach mnemonic strategies.* Mnemonics are memory aids for remembering information. Mnemonic strategies can involve imagery and words (Homa, 2008). Here are some different types of mnemonics:

   • *Method of loci.* In the *method of loci,* children develop images of items to be remembered and mentally store them in familiar locations. Rooms of a house and stores on a street are common locations used in this memory strategy. For example, if children need to remember a list of concepts, they can mentally place them in the rooms of their house, such as entry foyer, living room, dining room, and kitchen. Then when they need to retrieve the information, they can imagine the house, mentally go through the rooms, and retrieve the concepts. Next, teacher Rosemary Moore describes a similar idea for teaching spelling words.

THROUGH THE EYES OF TEACHERS
Seeing Words in the Mind's Eye

Many children memorize spelling words quite easily, but a few struggle with this. I wanted to help these stu-

dents as much as I could, so I would write the spelling words on index cards and place them in random order and various positions (vertical, diagonal, upside down) across the front of the room. As we did spelling assignments, exercises, and games throughout the week, the words were there for the students to refer to if they got "stuck." The index cards were taken down before the test on Friday, but as I called out each of the spelling words I would notice students turning their eyes to the place where that particular word had been displayed. I believe they were seeing the word in their "mind's eye." My students' spelling scores improved dramatically.

FIGURE 8.10 The Keyword Method
To help children remember the state capitals, the keyword method was used. A special component of the keyword method is the use of mental imagery, which was stimulated by presenting the children with a vivid visual image, such as two apples being married. The strategy is to help the children associate *apple* with Annapolis and *marry* with Maryland.

   • *Rhymes.* Examples of mnemonic rhymes are the spelling rule "*i* before *e* except after *c*," the month rule "Thirty days hath September, April, June, and November," the bolt-turning rule "Right is tight, left is loose," and the alphabet song.

   • *Acronyms.* This strategy involves creating a word from the first letters of items to be remembered. For example, *HOMES* can be used as a cue for remembering the five original Great Lakes: *Huron, Ontario, Michigan, Erie,* and *Superior.*

   • *Keyword method.* Another mnemonic strategy that involves imagery is the *keyword method,* in which vivid imagery is attached to important words. This method has been used to practical advantage in teaching students how to rapidly master new information such as foreign vocabulary words, the states and capitals of the United States, and the names of U.S. presidents. For example, in teaching children that Annapolis is the capital of Maryland, you could ask them to connect vivid images of Annapolis and Maryland, such as two apples getting married (Levin, 1980) (see Figure 8.10).

Some educators argue against teaching children to use mnemonics because they involve rote memorization. Clearly, as we said earlier, remembering for understanding is preferred over rote memorization. However, if children need to learn lists of concepts, mnemonic devices can do the trick. Think of mnemonic devices as a way for children to learn some specific facts that they might need to know to solve problems.

Review, Reflect, and Practice

game. Natalie notices that five of the objects are hair-related items—a comb, a brush, shampoo, a barrette, and a ponytail holder. She notices that another five objects are school supplies—a pencil, a pen, a ruler, a marker, and a glue stick. The final five objects appear to be random. Natalie has no problem remembering the items that she was able to group by type. She only remembers two of the other items. What memory strategy is Natalie using?

a. chunking
b. constructing images
c. elaboration
d. rehearsal

2. To test his students' memory skills, Mr. Watkins reads lists of nonsense words to them and asks them to recall as many as they can. Veronica can recall five words. If she performs as is expected for age, how old is Veronica most likely to be?

a. 4
b. 7
c. 12
d. 17

3. When asked to describe in detail how to make a peanut-butter-and-jelly sand-wich, Maria skips several steps. When asked to make a sandwich, Maria does so flawlessly. Why is it that although Maria knows how to make a sandwich, she is unable to describe the process in detail?

a. It is difficult to translate procedural memory into words.
b. Maria has not encoded the process into long-term memory.
c. It is difficult to translate episodic memory into semantic memory.
d. Maria's episodic memory is faulty.

4. Mr. Madison wants his students to know the names of all of the states in the United States. To help them, he teaches them a song in which each state name is sung in alphabetical order. Most of his students learn the song with relative ease. They even sing the song to themselves when he gives them a quiz that requires them to write down the name of each state. However, when he gives them blank U.S. maps to fill in with state names, his students cannot complete them successfully. Why were they able to remember the names of the states, but not their locations?

a. Mnemonic devices, such as the song Mr. Madison taught his students, are not effective for memorizing material.
b. Mnemonic devices, such as the song Mr. Madison taught his students, increase the likelihood of cue-dependent forgetting.
c. Mnemonic devices, such as the song Mr. Madison taught his students, increase the serial position effect.
d. Mnemonic devices, such as the song that Mr. Madison taught his students, involve rote memorization and do not generalize to other memory tasks.

Please see the answer key at the end of the book.

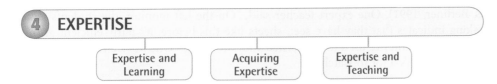

4 **EXPERTISE**

Expertise and Learning | Acquiring Expertise | Expertise and Teaching

In the last section, we considered various aspects of memory. Our ability to remember new information about a subject depends considerably on what we already know about it (Ericsson, Krampe, & Tesch-Romer, 2009). For example, a student's ability

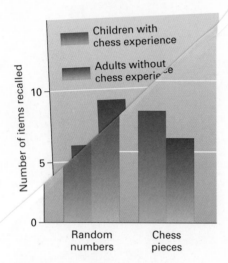

FIGURE 8.11 Memory for Numbers and Chess Pieces

to recount what she saw when she was at the library is largely governed by what she already knows about libraries, such as where books on certain topics are likely to be and how to check books out. If she knew little about libraries, the student would have a much harder time recounting what was there.

The contribution of prior content knowledge to our ability to remember new material is especially evident when we compare the memories of experts and novices in a particular knowledge domain. An expert is the opposite of a novice (someone who is just beginning to learn a content area). Experts demonstrate especially impressive memory in their areas of expertise. One reason that children remember less than adults is that they are far less expert in most areas.

Expertise and Learning

Studying the behavior and mental processes of experts can give us insights into how to guide students in becoming more effective learners (Ericsson, Krampe, & Tesch-Romer, 2009). What is it, exactly, that experts do? According to the National Research Council (1999), they are better than novices at the following:

- Detecting features and meaningful patterns of information
- Accumulating more content knowledge and organizing it in a manner that shows an understanding of the topic
- Retrieving important aspects of knowledge with little effort
- Adapting an approach to new situations
- Using effective strategies

In this section, we will consider various ways that you can help your students learn and remember these skills that experts use so effortlessly.

Detecting Features and Meaningful Patterns of Organization   Experts are better at noticing important features of problems and contexts that novices may ignore (Bransford & others, 2006). Thus, the attentional advantage of experts starts them off at a more advantageous level than novices in a learning context. Experts also have superior recall of information in their area of expertise. The process of chunking, which we discussed earlier, is one way they accomplish this superior recall. For example, "Chess masters perceive chunks of meaningful information, which affects their memory of what they see. . . . Lacking a hierarchical, highly organized structure for the domain, novices cannot use this chunking strategy" (National Research Council, 1999, p. 21).

In areas where children are knowledeable and competent, their memory is often extremely good. In fact, it often exceeds that of adults who are novices in that content area. This was documented in a study of 10-year-old chess experts (Chi, 1978). These children were excellent chess players but not especially brilliant in other ways. As with most 10-year-olds, their memory spans for digits were shorter than an adult's. However, they remembered the configurations of chess pieces on chessboards far better than did the adults who were novices at chess (see Figure 8.11).

Expert teachers recognize features and patterns that are not noticed by novice teachers (National Research Council, 1999, pp. 21, 25). For example, in one study, expert and novice teachers had a very different understanding of the events in a videotaped classroom lesson, in which three screens showed simultaneous events taking place throughout the classroom (left, center, and right areas) (Sabers, Cushing, & Berliner, 1991). One expert teacher said, "On the left monitor, the students' note taking indicates that they have seen sheets like this before; it's fairly efficient at this point because they're used to the format they are using." One novice teacher sparsely responded, "It's a lot to watch."

Organization and Depth of Knowledge   Experts' knowledge is organized around important ideas or concepts more than novices' knowledge is (National Research Council, 1999). This provides experts with a much deeper understanding of knowledge than novices have (Bransford & others, 2006).

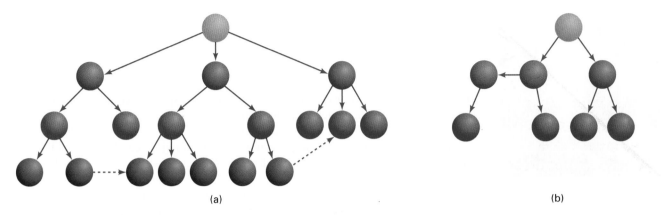

(a)

(b)

Experts in a particular area usually have far more elaborate networks of information about that area than novices do (see Figure 8.12). The information they represent in memory has more nodes, more interconnections, and better hierarchical organization.

The implications for teaching are that too often a curriculum is designed in a way that makes it difficult for students to organize knowledge in meaningful ways. This especially occurs when there is only superficial coverage of facts before moving on to the next topic. In this context, students have little time to explore the topic in depth and get a sense of what the important, organizing ideas are. This type of shallow presentation can occur in any subject area but is common in history and science texts that emphasize facts (National Research Council, 1999).

Fluent Retrieval Retrieval of relevant information can range from taking a lot of effort to being fluent and almost effortless (Gluck & Bower, 2009; National Research Council, 1999). Experts retrieve information in an almost effortless, automatic manner, whereas novices expend a great deal of effort in retrieving information (Posner & Rothbart, 2007).

Effortless retrieval places fewer demands on conscious attention. Since the amount of information a student can attend to at one time is limited, ease of processing information in some aspects of a task frees up capacity to attend to other aspects of a task.

Consider expert and novice readers. Expert readers can quickly scan the words of a sentence and paragraph, which allows them to devote attention to understanding what they are reading. However, novice readers' ability to decode words is not yet fluent, so they have to allocate considerable attention and time to this task, which restricts the time they can give to understanding a passage. An important aspect of teaching is to help students develop the fluency they need to competently perform cognitive tasks (Beck & others, 1991).

Adaptive Expertise An important aspect of expertise "is whether some ways of organizing knowledge are better" than others for helping people to be "flexible and adaptive to new situations" (National Research Council, 1999, p. 33). Adaptive experts are able to approach new situations flexibly rather than always responding in a rigid, fixed routine (Bransford & others, 2006; Gambrell, Malloy, & Anders-Mazzoni, 2007; Hatano & Oura, 2003). An important theme in a recent book, *Preparing Teachers for a Changing World* (Darling-Hammond & Bransford, 2005, p. 3), was to "help teachers become 'adaptive experts' who are prepared for effective lifelong learning that allows them to continually add to their knowledge and skills." Thus, teachers characterized by adaptive expertise are flexible and open to rethinking important ideas and practices to improve their students' learning (Hammerness & others, 2005).

Indeed, innovation *and* efficiency are the two main dimensions of one model of adaptive expertise (Bransford & others, 2006; Schwartz, Bransford, & Sears, 2005). Experts characterized by *efficiency* can quickly retrieve and apply information in skillful ways to explain something or solve a problem. Experts characterized by *innovation*

FIGURE 8.12 An Example of How Information Is Organized in the Mind of an Expert and a Novice

(a) An expert's knowledge is based on years of experience in which small bits of information have been linked with many other small pieces, which together are placed in a more general category. This category is in turn placed in an even more general category of knowledge. The dotted lines are used as pointers, associations between specific elements of knowledge that connect the lower branches and provide mental shortcuts in the expert's mind. *(b)* The novice's knowledge shows far fewer connections, shortcuts, and levels than an expert's knowledge.

What are some characteristics of teachers who are adaptive experts?

are able to move away from efficiency, at least on a short-term basis, and unlearn previous routines. Innovation occurs when individuals "let go" and rethink their routine way of doing something.

In this model, adaptive experts possess a balance of efficiency and innovation (Bransford & others, 2006; Schwartz, Bransford, & Sears, 2005). For example, efficiency is at work when a teacher teaches students to speedily complete math computations, but this efficiency may limit the students' competence when they face new math problems. When this efficiency-oriented teacher adapts and adds teaching for understanding and application, innovation is taking place. The new skills she teaches are likely to increase the students' competence when they encounter new math problems.

Adaptive experts are motivated to learn from others (Hammerness & others, 2005). This may not be that difficult when the learning involves making a teacher's existing routines and practices more efficient. However, as we just indicated, adaptive expertise also includes innovation that requires sometimes replacing or transforming prior routines and practices, which is often not easy to do. Your teaching likely will benefit if you seek feedback from other competent teachers, even if their approaches are different than yours. This might occur when you watch a videotape of your teaching with other teachers who provide feedback about your teaching or invite a colleague to come to your classroom to observe your teaching.

In sum, adaptive expertise is a critical aspect of being an outstanding teacher. Teachers who are knowledgeable and adept at adapting different methods, practices, and strategies to meet the needs of different students are most likely to guide students to higher levels of learning and achievement (Gambrell, Malloy, & Anders-Mazzoni, 2007).

Strategies Experts use effective strategies in understanding the information in their area of expertise and in advancing it (Ornstein, Haden, & Elischberger, 2006; Pressley & Harris, 2006). Earlier in the chapter we described a number of strategies that students can use to remember information, and later in the chapter we will further examine strategies in our discussion of metacognition. Let's now explore some effective strategies that students can develop to become competent at learning and studying.

Patricia Alexander (2003) uses the label *acclimation* to describe the initial stage of expertise in a particular domain (such as English, biology, or mathematics). At this stage, students have limited and fragmented knowledge that restricts their ability to detect the difference between accurate and inaccurate and relevant and tangential information. To help students move beyond the acclimation stage, teachers need to guide students in determining what content is central and what is peripheral, as well as what is accurate and well supported and what is inaccurate and unsupported. In Alexander's (2003) view, students don't come to the classroom equipped with the strategies they need to move beyond the acclimation stage. Teachers must help students learn effective strategies and practice them in relevant situations before students can experience their value. Students also need to be encouraged to change and combine strategies to solve the problem at hand.

Spreading Out and Consolidating Learning Students' learning benefits when teachers talk with them about the importance of regularly reviewing what they learn. Children who have to prepare for a test will benefit from distributing their learning over a longer period rather than cramming for the test at the last minute. Cramming tends to produce short-term memory that is processed in a shallow rather than deep manner. A final, concentrated tune-up before the test is better than trying to learn everything at the last minute.

Asking Themselves Questions When children ask themselves questions about what they have read or about an activity, they expand the number of associations with the information they need to retrieve. At least as early as the middle of elementary school, the self-questioning strategy can help children to remember. For example, as children read, they can be encouraged to stop periodically and ask themselves questions such as "What is the meaning of what I just read?" "Why is this important?" and "What is an example of the concept I just read?" Students can use the same self-questioning strategy when they listen to you conduct a lesson, hear a guest give a talk, or watch a video. If you periodically remind children to generate questions about their experiences, they are more likely to remember the experiences.

Taking Good Notes   Taking good notes from either a lecture or a text benefits learning. When children are left to take notes without being given any strategies, they tend to take notes that are brief and disorganized. When they do write something down, it often is a verbatim record of what they have just heard. Give children some practice in taking notes and then evaluate their note taking. Encourage children not to write down everything they hear when they take notes. It is impossible to do this, anyway, and it can prevent them from getting the big picture of what the speaker is saying. Here are some good note-taking strategies:

What are some good study strategies?

- *Summarizing.* Have the children listen for a few minutes and then write down the main idea that a speaker is trying to get across in that time frame. Then have the child listen for several more minutes and write down another idea, and so on.
- *Outlining.* Show the children how to outline what a speaker is saying, using first-level heads as the main topics, second-level heads as subtopics under the first-level heads, and third-level heads under the second-level heads.
- *Using concept maps.* Help the children practice drawing concept maps, which are similar to outlines but visually portray information in a more spiderlike format (see Chapter 9).

All three note-taking strategies described so far—summarizing, outlining, and using concept maps—help children evaluate which ideas are the most important to remember. Outlining and concept maps also help children arrange the material hierarchically, which underscores an important theme of learning: It works best when it is organized.

Using a Study System   Various systems have been developed to help people to remember information that they are studying from a book. One of the earliest systems was called *SQ3R,* which stands for *Survey, Question, Read, Recite,* and *Review.* A more recently developed system is called *PQ4R,* which stands for *Preview, Question, Read, Reflect, Recite,* and *Review.* Thus, the PQ4R system adds an additional step, "Reflect," to the SQ3R system. From the later elementary school years on, students will benefit from practicing the PQ4R system (Adams, Carnine, & Gersten, 1982). The system benefits students by getting them to meaningfully organize information, ask questions about it, reflect on it, and review it. Here are more details about the steps in the PQ4R system:

- *Preview.* Tell your students to briefly survey the material to get a sense of the overall organization of ideas—to look at the headings to see the main topics and subtopics that will be covered.
- *Question.* Encourage the children to ask themselves questions about the material as they read it.
- *Read.* Now tell the children to read the material. Encourage your students to be active readers—to immerse themselves in what they are reading and strive to understand what the author is saying. This helps students to avoid being empty readers whose eyes just track the lines of text but whose minds fail to register anything important.
- *Reflect.* By occasionally stopping and reflecting on the material, students increase its meaningfulness. Encourage the children to be analytic at this point in studying. After they have read something, challenge them to break open the ideas and scratch beneath their surface. This is a good time for them to think out applications and interpretations of the information, as well as connecting it with other information already in their long-term memory.

Yo-Yo Ma is an expert cellist. He gave a public cello performance at 5 years of age, performed with Leonard Bernstein at 8, and graduated from high school at 15. He has recorded more than 75 albums and won 15 Grammy Awards. *To what extent is Ma's expertise likely due to practice and motivation? To talent?*

- *Recite.* This involves children self-testing themselves to see if they can remember the material and reconstruct it. At this point, encourage the children to make up a series of questions about the material and then try to answer them.
- *Review.* Tell your students to go over the material and evaluate what they know and don't know. At this point, they should reread and study the material they don't remember or understand well.

We will further explore strategies later in the chapter in our discussion of metacognition. To evaluate the extent to which you use good memory and study strategies, complete *Self-Assessment 8.1.*

Acquiring Expertise

What determines whether or not someone becomes an expert? Can motivation and practice get someone to expert status? Or does expertise also require a great deal of talent (Sternberg & Ben-Zeev, 2001)?

Practice and Motivation   One perspective is that a particular kind of practice—*deliberate practice*—is required to become an expert (Schraw, 2006). Deliberate practice involves practice that is at an appropriate level of difficulty for the individual, provides corrective feedback, and allows opportunities for repetition (Ericsson, 2006; Ericsson, Krampe, & Tesch-Romer, 2009; Rosenzweig & Bennett, 2009).

In one study of violinists at a music academy, the extent to which children engaged in deliberate practice distinguished novices and experts (Ericsson, Krampe, & Tesch-Romer, 1993). The top violinists averaged 7,500 hours of deliberate practice by age 18, the good violinists only 5,300 hours. Many individuals give up on becoming an expert because they won't put forth the effort it takes to engage in extensive deliberate practice over a number of years.

Such extensive practice requires considerable motivation. Students who are not motivated to practice long hours are unlikely to become experts in a particular area. Thus, a student who complains about all of the work, doesn't persevere, and doesn't extensively practice solving math problems over a number years is not going to become an expert in math.

Talent   A number of psychologists who study expertise stress that it requires not only deliberate practice and motivation but also talent (Bloom, 1985; Hunt, 2006; Sternberg, 2009).

A number of abilities—music and athletic, for example—seem to have a heritable component (Plomin, DeFries, & Fulker, 2007). For example, is it likely that Mozart could have become such an outstanding musical composer just because he practiced long hours? Is it likely that Tiger Woods became such a fantastic golfer just because he was motivated to do so? Many talented individuals have attempted to become as great as Mozart or Woods but have given up trying after only mediocre performances. Clearly, heredity matters. Nonetheless, Mozart and Woods would not have developed expertise in their fields without being highly motivated and engaging in extensive deliberate practice. Talent alone does not make an expert (Hunt, 2006; Winner, 2006).

Expertise and Teaching

Being an expert in a particular domain—such as physics, history, or math—does not mean that the expert is good at helping others learn it (Bransford & others, 2006). Indeed, "expertise can sometimes hurt teaching because many experts forget what is easy and what is difficult for students" (National Research Council, 1999, p. 32).

Some educators have distinguished between the content knowledge required for expertise and the pedagogical content knowledge necessary to effectively teach it. *Pedagogical content knowledge* includes ideas about common difficulties that students have as they try to learn a content area; typical paths students must take to understand the area; and strategies for helping students overcome the difficulties they experience.

Expert teachers are good at monitoring students' learning and assessing students' progress. They also know what types of difficulties students are likely to encounter, are aware of students' existing knowledge, and use this awareness to teach at the right level and to make new information meaningful. Some educational psychologists argue that in the absence of expert pedagogical awareness of their own students, inexpert teachers simply rely on textbook publishers' materials, which, of course, contain no information about the particular pedagogical needs of students in the teacher's classroom (Brophy, 2004). To read further about expertise, see the *Technology and Education* interlude.

An expert teacher monitoring a student's learning. *What are some characteristics of expert teachers?*

TECHNOLOGY AND EDUCATION
Experts and Technology

As described by the National Research Council (1999), experts in many fields are using new technologies to represent information in new ways. For example, three-dimensional models of the surface of Venus or of a molecular structure can be electronically created and viewed from any angle.

One of the characteristics of expertise we have discussed involves organizing knowledge meaningfully around important ideas. The Belvedere computer technology system is designed to help students who lack a deep understanding of many areas of science, have difficulty zeroing in on the key issues in a scientific debate, and have trouble recognizing connections of ideas in scientific theories (Suthers & others, 1995). Belvedere uses graphics with specialized boxes to represent connections of ideas in an effort to support students' reasoning about scientific issues. An online advisor gives students hints to help them improve their understanding and reasoning.

The Belvedere system can also help students in nonscientific studies such as analyzing social policies. This system helps students by (1) giving arguments a concrete, diagram-like form and providing tools for focusing on particular problems encountered in the construction and evaluation of complex arguments; (2) providing access to online information resources; and (3) supporting students working in small groups to construct documents to be shared with others.

Review, Reflect, and Practice

 Draw some lessons about learning from the way experts think.

REVIEW

- What do experts do that novices often don't do in the process of learning?
- What does it take to become an expert?
- Is subject experience enough to make a good teacher? What else is needed?

REFLECT

- Choose an area in which you feel at least somewhat of an expert. Compare your ability to learn in that field with the ability of a novice.

PRAXIS™ PRACTICE

1. The case studies in this text are designed to help educational psychology students learn the material and begin to develop expertise. The first question of each case study asks students to identify the issues in the case. The author most likely included this question for each case because he understood that
   a. it is important for students to consolidate their learning.
   b. it is important for students to learn to determine what content is central and what is peripheral.
   c. in learning, it is important to strike a balance between efficiency and innovation.
   d. students need a great deal of help in developing fluid retrieval skills.

2. Ryan is the best player on his soccer team. His coach thinks of him as a coach's dream player because he works so hard. It is rare for Ryan to perform a skill better than his teammates when it is initially introduced, but by the time the next practice comes, he will have mastered the skill. At one point, Ryan decided that he wanted to be able to score from a corner kick. He gathered up all the soccer balls he could find and kicked them one after another from the corner, trying to curl them into the goal. When he had finished, he gathered the balls and did it again. He continued this for an entire afternoon, and thereafter for at least an hour after school each day. His coach was very happily surprised when, in

Review, Reflect, and Practice

the next game, Ryan scored a goal from a corner kick. Why has Ryan developed expertise in soccer?

a. He engages in extensive deliberative practice.

b. He is relying on an inborn talent.

c. He has an excellent teacher in his coach.

d. He uses the PQ4R method 3.

3. Mr. Williams is a former college history professor who is now teaching high school American history. He discusses his research and writing with his students and tries to make history come alive by telling them about how historians find out about the past. After a month of teaching, he finds that his students seem confused during class discussions and perform poorly on tests of factual knowledge. The most likely explanation is that Mr. Williams lacks

a. content expertise.

b. pedagogical content knowledge.

c. metacognition.

d. cue-dependent knowledge.

Please see the answer key at the end of the book.

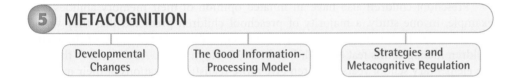

5 METACOGNITION

| Developmental Changes | The Good Information-Processing Model | Strategies and Metacognitive Regulation |

So far in this chapter, we have examined a number of ways that you help students improve their ability to process information as they learn, including how to improve their attention and memory, as well as strategies that can increase the likelihood that they will make the transition from being a novice to being an expert. Another way that you can help children process information more effectively is by encouraging them to examine what they know about how their mind processes information (Harris & others, 2009; Zabrucky & Agler, 2008). As you read at the beginning of this chapter, this involves metacognition, which involves cognition about cognition, or "knowing about knowing" (Flavell, 1999, 2004). A distinction can be made between metacognitive knowledge and metacognitive activity. *Metacognitive knowledge* involves monitoring and reflecting on one's current or recent thoughts. This includes both factual knowledge, such as knowledge about the task, one's goals, or oneself, and strategic knowledge, such as how and when to use specific procedures to solve problems. *Metacognitive activity* occurs when students consciously adapt and manage their thinking strategies during problem solving and purposeful thinking.

Metacognitive skills have been taught to students to help them solve problems (Hacker, Dunlosky, & Graesser, 2009). In one study, in which each of thirty daily lessons involved math story problems, a teacher guided low-achieving students in learning to recognize when they did not know the meaning of a word, did not have all of the information necessary to solve a problem, did not know how to subdivide the problem into specific steps, or did not know how to carry out a computation (Cardelle-Elawar, 1992). After the thirty daily lessons, the students who were given this metacognitive training had better math achievement and better attitudes toward math.

One expert on children's thinking, Deanna Kuhn (1999; Kuhn & Franklin, 2006), argues that metacognition should be a stronger focus of efforts to help children become better critical thinkers, especially at the middle school and high school levels. She distinguishes between first-order cognitive skills, which enable children to know about the world (and have been the main focus of critical-thinking programs), and second-order cognitive skills—meta-knowing skills—which involve knowing about one's own (and others') knowing.

Developmental Changes

How does metacognition change in childhood? Are there further changes in meta-cognition during adolescence?

Childhood   Many studies have focused on children's metamemory, or knowledge of how memory works. In the last several decades, there has been extensive interest in children's theories about how the human mind works.

Metamemory   By 5 or 6 years of age, children usually know that familiar items are easier to learn than unfamiliar ones, that short lists are easier than long ones, that recognition is easier than recall, and that forgetting becomes more likely over time (Lyon & Flavell, 1993). In other ways, however, young children's metamemory is limited. They don't understand that related items are easier to remember than unrelated ones or that remembering the gist of a story is easier than remembering information verbatim (Kreutzer & Flavell, 1975). By fifth grade, students understand that gist recall is easier than verbatim recall.

Preschool children also have an inflated opinion of their memory abilities. For example, in one study, a majority of preschool children predicted that they would be able to recall all ten items of a list of ten items. When tested, none of the young children managed this feat (Flavell, Friedrichs, & Hoyt, 1970). As they move through the elementary school years, children give more realistic evaluations of their memory skills (Schneider & Pressley, 1997).

Preschool children also have little appreciation for the importance of memory cues, such as "It helps when you can think of an example of it." By 7 or 8 years of age, children better appreciate the importance of cueing for memory. In general, children's understanding of their memory abilities and their skill in evaluating their performance on memory tasks is relatively poor at the beginning of the elementary school years but improves considerably by age 11 or 12 (Bjorklund & Rosenblum, 2000).

Theory of Mind   Even young children are curious about the nature of the human mind. They have a **theory of mind**, which refers to awareness of one's own mental processes and the mental processes of others. Studies of theory of mind view the child as "a thinker who is trying to explain, predict, and understand people's thoughts, feelings, and utterances" (Harris, 2006, p. 847). Researchers are increasingly discovering that children's theory of mind is linked to cognitive processes and disabilities (Doherty, 2009; Schick & others, 2007). For example, theory of mind competence at age 3 is related to a higher level of metamemory at age 5 (Lockl & Schneider, 2007). Researchers also have found that autistic children have difficulty in developing a theory of mind, especially in understanding others' beliefs and emotions (Boucher, 2009). Sometimes this has been referred to as "mindblindness" (Jurecic, 2006).

Children's theory of mind changes as they develop through childhood (Doherty, 2009; Flavell, 2004). The main changes occur at 2 to 3 years of age, 4 to 5 years of age, middle and late childhood, and adolescence.

- *Two to Three Years of Age.* In this time frame, children begin to understand three mental states: (1) perceptions, (2) emotions, and (3) desires. *Perceptions:* The child realizes that another person sees what is in front of her eyes and not necessarily what is in front of the child's eyes. *Emotions:* The child can distin-

theory of mind Awareness of one's own mental processes and the mental processes of others.

guish between positive (for example, happy) and negative (sad, for example) emotions. A child might say, "Tommy feels bad." *Desires:* The child understands that if someone wants something, he or she will try to get it. A child might say, "I want my mommy." Children refer to desires earlier and more frequently than they refer to cognitive states such as thinking, knowing, and beliefs (Harris, 2006; Rakoczy, Warneken, & Tomasello, 2007). Two- to three-year-olds understand the way that desires are related to actions and to simple emotions (Harris, 2006). For example, they understand that people will search for what they want and that if they obtain it, they are likely to feel happy, but if they don't they will keep searching for it and are likely to feel sad or angry (Hadwin & Perner, 2001; Wellman & Woolley, 1990).

- *Four to Five Years of Age.* Children come to understand that the mind can represent objects and events accurately or inaccurately. The realization that people can have *false beliefs*—beliefs that are not true—develops in a majority of children by the time they are 5 years old (Wellman, Cross, & Watson, 2001) (see Figure 8.13) In one study of false beliefs, young children were shown a Band-Aids box and asked what was inside (Jenkins & Astington, 1996). To the children's surprise, the box actually contained pencils. When asked what a child who had never seen the box would think was inside, 3-year-olds typically responded "pencils." However, the 4- and 5-year-olds, grinning at the anticipation of the false beliefs of other children who had not seen what was inside the box, were more likely to say "Band-Aids."

  Children's understanding of thinking has some limitations in early childhood (Harris, 2006; Siegler & Alibali, 2005). They often underestimate when mental activity is likely occurring. For example, they fail to attribute mental activity to someone who is sitting quietly, reading, or talking (Flavell, Green & Flavell, 1995).

- *Middle and Late Childhood.* It is only beyond the early childhood years that children have a deepening appreciation of the mind itself rather than just an understanding of mental states (Wellman, 2004). Not until middle and late childhood do children see the mind as an active constructor of knowledge or processing center (Flavell, Green, & Flavell, 1998). In middle and late childhood, children move from understanding that beliefs can be false to an understanding of beliefs and mind as "interpretive," exemplified in an awareness that the same event can be open to multiple interpretations (Carpendale & Chandler, 1996).

- *Adolescence.* Important changes in metacognition also take place during adolescence (Kuhn & Franklin, 2006). Compared with children, adolescents have an increased capacity to monitor and manage cognitive resources to effectively meet the demands of a learning task. This increased metacognitive ability results in more effective cognitive functioning and learning.

Adolescents have more resources available to them than children (through increased processing speed, capacity, and automaticity), and they are more skilled at directing the resources. Further, adolescents have a better meta-level understanding of strategies—that is, knowing the best strategy to use and when to use it in performing a learning task (Kuhn, 2008).

Keep in mind, though, that there is considerable individual variation in adolescents' metacognition. Indeed, some experts argue that individual variation in metacognition is much more pronounced in adolescence than in childhood (Kuhn & Franklin, 2006). Thus, some adolescents are quite good at using metacognition to improve their learning, others far less effective.

The Good Information-Processing Model

Michael Pressley and his colleagues (Pressley, Borkowski, & Schneider, 1989; Schneider & Pressley, 1997) developed a metacognitive model called the *Good*

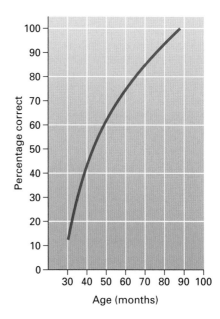

FIGURE 8.13 Developmental Changes in False-Belief Performance

False-belief performance dramatically increases from 2½ years of age through the middle of the elementary school years. In a summary of the results of many studies, 2½-years-olds gave incorrect responses about 80 percent of the time (Wellman, Cross, & Watson, 2001). At 3 years, 8 months, they were correct about 50 percent of the time, and after that, gave increasingly correct responses.

Information-Processing model. It emphasizes that competent cognition results from a number of interacting factors. These include strategies, content knowledge, motivation, and metacognition. They argue that children become good at cognition in three main steps:

1. *Children are taught by parents or teachers to use a particular strategy.* With practice, they learn about its characteristics and advantages for learning *specific knowledge.* The more intellectually stimulating children's homes and schools are, the more specific strategies they will encounter and learn to use.

2. *Teachers may demonstrate similarities and differences in multiple strategies in a particular domain, such as math, which motivates students to see shared features of different strategies.* This leads to better *relational knowledge.*

3. *At this point, students recognize the general benefits of using strategies, which produces general strategy knowledge.* They learn to attribute successful learning outcomes to the efforts they make in evaluating, selecting, and monitoring strategy use *(metacognitive knowledge and activity).*

Strategies and Metacognitive Regulation

In the view of Pressley and his colleagues (Pressley, 1983; Pressley & Harris, 2006; Pressley & Hilden, 2006), the key to education is helping students learn a rich repertoire of strategies that results in solutions of problems. Good thinkers routinely use strategies and effective planning to solve problems. Good thinkers also know when and where to use strategies (metacognitive knowledge about strategies). Understanding when and where to use strategies often results from the learner's monitoring of the learning situation.

Pressley and his colleagues argue that when students are given instruction about effective strategies, they often can apply strategies that they previously have not used on their own. They emphasize that students benefit when the teacher models the appropriate strategy and overtly verbalizes its steps. Then, students subsequently practice the strategy, guided and supported by the teacher's feedback until the students can use it autonomously. When instructing students about employing a strategy, it also is a good idea to explain to them how using the strategy will benefit them. However, there are some developmental limitations to this approach. For instance, young children often cannot use mental imagery competently.

Just having students practice the new strategy is usually not enough for them to continue to use the strategy and transfer it to new situations. For effective maintenance and transfer, encourage students to monitor the effectiveness of the new strategy relative to their use of old strategies by comparing their performance on tests and other assessments (Harris & others, 2008). Pressley says that it is not enough to say, "Try it, you will like it"; you need to say, "Try it and compare."

An important aspect of metacognition is monitoring how well one is performing on a task (Graham & Olinghouse, 2008; Harris & others, 2009). This might involve becoming aware that one has not studied enough for a test or needs to reread a particular section of a chapter to understand it better. Mismonitoring is common. For example, elementary school students often think they are better prepared for a test than they actually are and think they understand text material better than they do. One strategy is to encourage students who mismonitor to create practice tests and questions to assess how complete their understanding is.

Learning how to use strategies effectively often takes time (Bjorklund, Dukes, & Brown, 2009). Initially, it takes time to learn to execute the strategies, and it requires guidance and support from the teacher. With practice, students learn to execute strategies faster and more competently. *Practice* means that

What are some strategies for improving metacognitive regulation?

BEST PRACTICES
Strategies for Helping Students Use Strategies

The following strategies are based on the recommendations of Michael Pressley and his colleagues (McCormick & Pressley, 1997; Pressley, 1983, 2007; Pressley & McCormick, 2007):

1. *Recognize that strategies are a key aspect of solving problems.* Monitor students' knowledge and awareness of strategies for effective learning outcomes. Many students do not use good strategies and are unaware that strategies can help them learn. And after students learn a strategy, they tend to shorten and reduce it, in the process losing important components. Thus, be sure to monitor students who modify strategies in ways that make the strategies less effective.

2. *Model effective strategies for students.*

3. *Give students many opportunities to practice the strategies.* As students practice the strategies, provide guidance and support to the students. Give them feedback until they can use the strategies independently. As part of your feedback, inform them about where and when the strategies are most useful.

4. *Encourage students to monitor the effectiveness of their new strategy in comparison to the effectiveness of old strategies.*

5. *Remember that it takes students a considerable amount of time to learn how to use an effective strategy.* Be patient and give students continued support during this tedious learning experience. Keep encouraging students to use the strategy over and over again until they can use it automatically.

6. *Understand that students need to be motivated to use the strategies.* Students are not always going to be motivated to use the strategies. Especially important to students' motivation is their expectations that the strategies

will lead to successful learning outcomes. It can also help if students set goals for learning effective strategies. And when students attribute their learning outcomes to the effort they put forth, their learning benefits.

7. *Encourage children to use multiple strategies.* Most children benefit from experimenting with multiple strategies, finding out what works well, when, and where.

8. *Read more about strategy instruction.* Two good resources are *Best Practices in Literacy Instruction* (Gambrell, Morrow, & Pressley, 2007) and a chapter by Michael Pressley and Karen Harris (2006) titled "Cognitive strategies instruction: From basic research to classroom instruction," both of which include numerous helpful ideas about how to improve children's use of strategies.

9. *Ask questions that help to guide students' thinking in various content areas.* These might include, "How can proofreading help me in writing a paper?" "Why is it important periodically to stop when I'm reading and try to understand what is being said so far?" and "What is the purpose of learning this formula?"

10. *Recognize that low-achieving students and students with disabilities often need more support and time to become effective in independently using strategies.*

11. *Read about strategy instruction online.* Especially good sources are (a) http://shop.ascd.org/ProductDisplay .cfm?ProductID=402086 (strategy instruction is shown in a video focusing on teaching in elementary and middle school classrooms), (b) http://iris.peabody.van derbilt.edu/index.html (a free online interactive tutorial on strategy instruction), and (c) www.unl.edu/csi (Robert Reid's excellent Web site that is devoted to strategy instruction).

students use the effective strategy over and over again until they perform it automatically. To execute the strategies effectively, they need to have the strategies in long-term memory, and extensive practice makes this possible. Learners also need to be motivated to use the strategies. Thus, an important implication for helping students develop strategies such as organization is that once a strategy is learned, students usually need more time before they can use it efficiently (Schneider, 2004). Further, it is important for teachers to be aware that students may drop an effective strategy or continue to use a strategy that does not help them (Miller, 2000).

Do children use one strategy or multiple strategies in memory and problem solving? They often use more than one strategy (Bjorklund, Dukes, & Brown, 2009). Most children benefit from generating a variety of alternative strategies and experimenting with different approaches to a problem and discovering what works well, when, and where (Schneider & Bjorklund, 1998). This is especially true for children from the middle elementary school grades on, although some cognitive psychologists argue that even young children should be encouraged to practice varying strategies (Siegler & Alibali, 2005).

Pressley and his colleagues (Pressley & others, 2001, 2003, 2004) have spent considerable time in recent years observing the use of strategy instruction by teachers and strategy use by students in elementary and secondary school classrooms. They conclude that teachers' use of strategy instruction is far less complete and intense than what is needed for students to learn how to use strategies effectively. They argue that education needs to be restructured so that students are provided with more opportunities to become competent strategic learners.

A final point about strategies is that many strategies depend on prior knowledge (Pressley & Harris, 2006; Pressley & Hilden, 2006). For example, students can't apply organizational strategies to a list of items unless they know the correct categories into which the items fall. The point about the importance of prior knowledge in strategy use coincides with the emphasis in our discussion earlier in the chapter of how experts use more effective strategies than novices.

Review, Reflect, and Practice

(5) **Explain the concept of metacognition and identify some ways to improve children's metacognition.**

REVIEW

- How do young children compare with older children in their metacognitive abilities?
- According to Pressley and colleagues' Good Information-Processing model, competent cognition results from what interacting factors?
- How can children be helped to learn metacognitive strategies and self-regulation?

REFLECT

- How might the three steps in the Good Information-Processing model be part of teaching a topic to children? Select a topic that you might teach one day and try working through it as an example.

PRAXIS™ PRACTICE

1. Sharmala's uncle has just played a trick on her. He presented her with a can that looked like a can of peanuts. However, when she opened the can, a cloth snake sprang out at her. Sharmala thought the trick was very funny and could hardly wait to play it on her brother. When her uncle asked her what she thought her brother would expect to be in the can, she giggled and responded, "Peanuts, but won't he be surprised." This is an example of Sharmala's development of
   a. the ability to allocate attention to different aspects of a problem.
   b. problem-solving expertise.
   c. metamemory skills.
   d. theory of mind.

2. Marvel has learned to use strategies to solve math problems but does not use them to study for history exams or spelling quizzes. According to the Good Information-Processing model, the next step for Marvel's metacognitive development would most likely be to
   a. ask his teacher for specific strategies for studying history.
   b. ask his parents about the benefits of using strategies for math.

Review, Reflect, and Practice

    c. understand shared features of many different strategies.

    d. learn to attribute successful learning to use of strategies.

3. Mr. Quinton has taught his students the PQ4R strategy for reading textbooks, in hopes that it will help them on their next history test. The majority of his class improves their scores. Mr. Quinton is disappointed when in spite of improved performance, many of his students don't continue using the PQ4R strategy. What is the most plausible explanation for the students' behavior?

    a. They did not compare the results of using the PQ4R with their prior strategies.

    b. They don't have the requisite background knowledge to use the PQ4R strategy effectively.

    c. They have not had enough practice to use the strategy effectively.

    d. They have not yet developed expertise in using the strategy.

Please see the answer key at the end of the book.

CRACK THE CASE
The Case of the Test

George has a test next week in his eighth-grade history class. He is having considerable difficulty remembering terms, names, and facts. On his last test, he identified General Sherman as a Vietnam War hero and Saigon as the capital of Japan. Historical dates are so confusing to him that he does not even try to remember them. In addition, George has difficulty spelling.

The test will consist of fifty objective test items (multiple-choice, true/false, and fill-in-the-blank) and two essay items. In general, George does better on essay items. He purposely leaves out any names about which he is uncertain and always omits dates. Sometimes he mixes up his facts, though, and often loses points for misspelled words. On objective items he has real problems. Usually, more than one answer will appear to be correct to him. Often he is "sure" he is correct, only to discover later that he was mistaken.

Before the last test, George tried to design some mnemonic devices to help him understand. He used acronyms, such as *HOMES* (for *H*uron, *O*ntario, *M*ichigan, *E*rie, and *S*uperior). Although he remembered his acronyms quite well, he could not recall what each letter stood for. The result was a test paper filled with acronyms. Another time a classmate suggested that George try using concept maps. This classmate lent George the concept maps she had designed for her own use. George looked at them and found them to be very busy and confusing—he couldn't figure out what they even meant. They were not at all useful to him.

George has decided he is in need of some serious help if he is to pass this class. He has sought you out for his help.

1. What are the issues in this case?

2. With what type of learning is George having difficulty?

3. What type of learning is easier for George?

4. Design a study-skills program for George drawing on principles of the cognitive information-processing approach.

Reach Your Learning Goals
The Information-Processing Approach

(1) THE NATURE OF THE INFORMATION-PROCESSING APPROACH: Describe the information-processing approach.

Information, Memory, and Thinking

The information-processing approach emphasizes that children manipulate information, monitor it, and strategize about it. Central to this approach are the processes of memory and thinking.

Cognitive Resources: Capacity and Speed of Processing Information

Capacity and speed of processing information, often referred to as cognitive resources, increase across childhood and adolescence. Changes in the brain serve as biological foundations for developmental changes in cognitive resources. In terms of capacity, the increase is reflected in older children being able to hold in mind several dimensions of a topic simultaneously. A reaction-time task has often been used to assess speed of processing. Processing speed continues to improve in early adolescence.

Mechanisms of Change

According to Siegler, three important mechanisms of change are encoding (how information gets into memory), automaticity (ability to process information with little or no effort), and strategy construction (creation of new procedures for processing information). Children's information processing is characterized by self-modification, and an important aspect of this self-modification involves metacognition—that is, knowing about knowing.

(2) ATTENTION: Characterize attention and summarize how it changes during development.

What Is Attention?

Attention is focusing mental resources. Four ways that children and adolescents can allocate their attention are selective attention (focusing on a specific aspect of experience that is relevant while ignoring others that are irrelevant), divided attention (concentrating on more than one activity at the same time), sustained attention (maintaining attention over an extended period of time), and executive attention (involves action planning, allocating attention to goals, error detection and compensation, monitoring progress on tasks, and dealing with novel or difficult circumstances). Multitasking is an example of divided attention, and it can have possible harmful effects on children's and adolescents' attention when they are engaging in a challenging task.

Developmental Changes

Salient stimuli tend to capture the attention of the preschooler. After 6 or 7 years of age, there is a shift to more cognitive control of attention. Selective attention improves through childhood and adolescence.

(3) MEMORY: Discuss memory in terms of encoding, storage, and retrieval.

What Is Memory?

Memory is the retention of information over time and involves encoding, storage, and retrieval.

Encoding

In everyday language, encoding has much to do with attention and learning. Rehearsal, deep processing, elaboration, constructing images, and organization are processes involved in encoding, which is the mechanism by which information gets into memory. Rehearsal increases the length of time that information stays in memory. In deep processing, information is processed semantically, in terms of its meaning. Elaboration involves the extensiveness of information processing. Constructing images helps to elaborate the information, and the more information is presented in an organized way, the easier it is to remember.

Storage

One way that memory varies involves its time frames: sensory memory, short-term memory, and long-term memory. There is increasing interest in working memory, a kind of mental workbench. The Atkinson-Shiffrin model states that memory involves a sequence of three stages: sensory, short-term, and long-term memory. Long-term memory includes different types of content. Many contemporary psychologists accept this hierarchy of long-term memory's contents: division into declarative and procedural memory, with declarative memory further subdivided into episodic and semantic memory. Declarative memory (explicit memory) is the conscious recollection of information, such as specific facts or events. Procedural memory (implicit memory) is knowledge of skills and cognitive operations about how to do something; it is hard to communicate verbally. Episodic memory is the retention of information about the where and when of life's happenings; semantic memory is a general knowledge about the world.

Three major approaches to how information is represented are network theories (which focus on how information is organized and connected, with emphasis on nodes in the memory network); schema theories (which stress that students often reconstruct information and fit it into an existing schema); and fuzzy trace theory (which states that memory is best understood by considering two types of memory representation: (1) verbatim memory trace and (2) fuzzy trace, or gist. In this theory, older children's better memory is attributed to the fuzzy traces created by extracting the gist of information. A script is a schema for an event.

Retrieval and Forgetting

Retrieval is influenced by the serial position effect (memory is better for items at the beginning and end of a list than for items in the middle), the effectiveness of retrieval cues, encoding specificity, and the retrieval task (such as recall versus recognition). Forgetting can be explained in terms of cue-dependent forgetting (failure to use effective retrieval cues), interference theory (because information gets in the way of what we are trying to remember), and decay (losing information over time).

(4) EXPERTISE: Draw some lessons about learning from the way experts think.

Expertise and Learning

Five important characteristics of experts are that they (1) notice features and meaningful patterns of information that novices don't, (2) have acquired a great deal of content knowledge that is organized in a manner that reflects deep understanding of the subject, (3) can retrieve important aspects of their knowledge with little effort, (4) are adaptive in their approach to new situations, and (5) use effective strategies.

Acquiring Expertise

Becoming an expert usually requires deliberate practice, motivation, and talent.

Expertise and Teaching

Being an expert in a particular area does not mean that the expert is good at helping others learn it. Pedagogical content knowledge is required to effectively teach a subject.

METACOGNITION: Explain the concept of metacognition and identify some ways to improve children's metacognition.

Developmental Changes	Children's metamemory improves considerably through the elementary school years. At 5 years of age, a majority of children understand that people can have false beliefs, and in middle and late childhood they understand that people actively construct knowledge. Adolescents have an increased capacity to monitor and manage resources to effectively meet the demands of a learning task, although there is considerable individual variation in metacognition during adolescence.
The Good Information-Processing Model	Developed by Michael Pressley and his colleagues, the Good Information-Processing model stresses that competent cognition results from several interacting factors including strategies, content knowledge, motivation, and metacognition.
Strategies and Metacognitive Regulation	In the view of Pressley and his colleagues, the key to education is helping students learn a rich repertoire of strategies that result in solutions to problems. Most children benefit from using multiple strategies and exploring which ones work well, when, and where. For example, teachers can model strategies for students and ask questions that help guide students' thinking in various content areas.

KEY TERMS

information-processing
    approach 270
encoding 271
automaticity 271
strategy construction 271
metacognition 271
attention 273
selective attention 273
divided attention 273
sustained attention 273

executive attention 273
memory 277
rehearsal 278
levels of processing
    theory 278
elaboration 278
chunking 280
sensory memory 280
short-term memory 280
memory span 281

working memory 281
long-term memory 282
Atkinson-Shiffrin model 282
declarative memory 283
procedural memory 283
episodic memory 284
semantic memory 284
network theories 284
schema theories 284
schema 284

script 285
fuzzy trace theory 286
serial position effect 286
encoding specificity
    principle 286
cue-dependent
    forgetting 287
interference theory 287
decay theory 287
theory of mind 300

PORTFOLIO ACTIVITIES

Now that you have a good understanding of this chapter, complete these exercises to expand your thinking.

Independent Reflection

Developing Expert Knowledge. Think about the experts you know. Are your parents or instructors considered experts in their fields? How do you think they came to become experts and how long did it take? Based on what you know about how experts process information, which strategies do you think these experts use to organize, remember, and utilize their knowledge and skills? (INTASC: Principles *2, 4, 9*)

Collaborative Work

Strategies to Enhance Memory. Get together with three or four other students in the class and brainstorm about the best ways to guide students in developing better memory and study strategies. Discuss how you might do this differently for children and adolescents at different grade levels. For example, at what age should students start learning effective note-taking strategies? For children too young to be taking elaborate notes, are there gamelike activities that might help them begin to learn the concept and value of taking notes or keeping running records of some event? Write your conclusions. (INTASC: Principles *2, 4*)

Research/Field Experience

Capturing Students' Attention. Observe a kindergarten, elementary, middle school, and high school classroom and focus on how the teacher maintains students' attention. How effective are each teacher's strategies? Would you do things differently to capture the students' attention? (INTASC: Principles *2, 9*)

Go to the Online Learning Center for downloadable portfolio templates.

TAKING IT TO THE NET

- Information-processing theorists emphasize that learning results from interaction between the environment and the learner's prior knowledge. Describe teaching techniques that help students connect new information with previous experiences and learning. Why are these connections so critical for learning to occur? **www.ncrel.org/sdrs/areas/issues/students/learning/lr100.htm**

- Take a moment to reflect upon your own study strategies, and describe your typical study routine. In relation to memory research, how could you improve your study techniques? Design a classroom activity that you could use to help students develop effective study skills. **www.mtsu.edu/~studskl/mem.html**

- Plan a classroom project for a particular grade level and subject area. First, describe the strategies you will use to capture student attention. Then outline how you intend to maintain student attention throughout the project. Explain how your strategies are appropriate for your students' age group based on what you've learned about brain development. **www.teachers.ab.ca/Quick+Links/Publications/Other+Publications/Teaching+Students+with+Learning+Disabilities/c.htm**

Connect to the Online Learning Center to explore possible answers.

STUDY, PRACTICE, AND SUCCEED

Visit **www.mhhe.com/santedu4e** to review the chapter with self-grading quizzes and self-assessments, to apply the chapter material to two more Crack the Case studies, and for suggested activities to develop your teaching portfolio.

CHAPTER 9

Complex Cognitive Processes

I think, therefore I am.

—René Descartes
French Philosopher and Mathematician, 17th Century

Chapter Outline

Conceptual Understanding

What Are Concepts?
Promoting Concept Formation

Thinking

What Is Thinking?
Reasoning
Critical Thinking
Decision Making
Creative Thinking

Problem Solving

Steps in Problem Solving
Obstacles to Solving Problems
Developmental Changes
Problem-Based Learning and Project-Based Learning

Transfer

What Is Transfer?
Types of Transfer

Learning Goals

1 Discuss conceptual understanding and strategies for teaching concepts.

2 Describe several types of thinking and ways that teachers can foster them.

3 Take a systematic approach to problem solving.

4 Define transfer and explain how to enhance it as a teacher.

TEACHING STORIES   Marilyn Whirry

Marilyn Whirry is a twelfth-grade English teacher at Mira Costa High School in Manhattan Beach, California. In 1999, she was named Teacher of the Year in the United States and honored at a White House Reception. The following description of Marilyn's teaching appeared in a report by the Council of Chief State School Officers (2005, pp. 1–3).

> Marilyn's enthusiasm for life carries over into the classroom. Marilyn says about her life: "It is a canvas with swirling brush strokes that depict the motifs of my experience." According to Marilyn, teachers may never know how many students' lives they changed for the better because of their sense of responsibility and excitement for life.
>
> Marilyn's teaching philosophy centers around embracing and celebrating the act of learning. She says that teachers need to help students become motivated to search for knowledge and to discover answers to questions of why and how. One of Marilyn's most important goals as a teacher is to get students to think deeply as they read and write. . . . Her teaching strategies include getting students to become aware of writing techniques in literary works that "promote dialogue and debate in group discussions."

One of Marilyn's former students, Mary-Anna Rae, said that Marilyn's "intellectual engagement and her passion for life make her a powerful role model for students. In everything she does, she makes it clear that she is listening, attending to the students' deepest thinking." Mary-Anna, who now teaches herself, adds that Marilyn "enriched and expanded her world." Mary-Anna also says that Marilyn helped her to "grow more confident in what I had to say, finding my writer's voice and discovering that I could give my life purpose."

Preview

One of Marilyn Whirry's major goals is to get her students to think deeply, an important emphasis in this chapter. In addition to exploring many aspects of thinking, we examine how teachers can guide students to engage in these other complex cognitive processes: understanding concepts, solving problems, and transferring what they learn to other settings.

1 CONCEPTUAL UNDERSTANDING

(What Are Concepts?)   (Promoting Concept Formation)

Conceptual understanding is a key aspect of learning (Chi, 2008; Goodman & others, 2008; Slotta & Chi, 2008). An important teaching goal is to help students understand the main concepts in a subject rather than just memorize isolated facts (Chiu, Guo, & Treagust, 2007; Morse & Jutras, 2008). In many cases, conceptual understanding is enhanced when teachers explore a topic in depth and give appropriate, interesting examples of the concepts involved. As you will see, concepts are the building blocks of thinking.

What Are Concepts?

To understand what concepts are, we first have to define **categories** They group objects, events, and characteristics on the basis of common properties. **Concepts** are ideas about what categories represent, or said another way, the sort of thing we think category members are. Concepts and categories help us to simplify and summarize information (Oakes, 2008; Quinn, Bhatt, & Hayden, 2008).

Imagine a world in which we had no concepts: We would see each object as unique and would not be able to make any generalizations. If we had no concepts, we would find the most trivial problems difficult to formulate and even impossible to solve. Indeed, concepts help students make sense of the world (Nersessian, 2007). Consider the concept of "book." If a student were not aware that a book is made of sheets of paper of uniform size, all bound together along one edge, and full of printed words and pictures in some meaningful order, each time the student encountered a new book she would have to figure out what it was. In a way, then, concepts keep us from "reinventing the wheel" each time we come across a new piece of information.

Concepts also aid the process of remembering, making it more efficient. When students group objects to form a concept, they can remember the concept, then retrieve the concept's characteristics. Thus, when you assign math homework, you probably won't have to go through the details of what math is or what homework is. Students will have embedded in their memory a number of appropriate associations. In ways such as this, concepts not only help to jog memory but also make communication more efficient. If you say, "It's time for art," students know what you mean. You don't have to go into a lengthy explanation of what art is. Thus, concepts help students to simplify and summarize information, as well as improve the efficiency of their memory, communication, and use of time.

Students form concepts through direct experiences with objects and events in their world. For example, in constructing a sophisticated concept of "cartoons," children might initially experience TV cartoon shows, then read comic strips, and eventually look at some political caricatures. Students also form concepts through experience with symbols (things that stand for, or represent, something else). For example, words are symbols. So are math formulas, graphs, and pictures.

Some concepts are relatively simple, clear, and concrete, whereas others are more complex, fuzzy, and abstract. The former are easier to agree on. For example, most people can agree on the meaning of "baby." But we have a harder time agreeing on what is meant by "young" or "old." We agree on whether something is an apple more readily than on whether something is a fruit. Some concepts are especially complex, fuzzy, and abstract, like the concepts involved in theories of economic collapse or string theory in physics.

Promoting Concept Formation

In a number of ways, teachers can guide students to recognize and form effective concepts. The process begins with becoming aware of the features of a given concept.

Learning About the Features of Concepts   An important aspect of concept formation is learning the key features, attributes, or characteristics of the concept (Solso, MacLin, & MacLin, 2008). These are the defining elements of a concept, the dimensions that make it different from another concept. For example, in our earlier example of the concept of "book," the key features include sheets of paper, being bound together along one edge, and being full of printed words and pictures in some meaningful order. Other characteristics such as size, color, and length are not key features that define the concept of "book." Consider also these critical features of the concept of "dinosaur": extinct and reptilian. Thus, in the case of the concept of "dinosaur," the feature "extinct" is important.

categories They group objects, events, and characteristics on the basis of common properties.

concepts Ideas about what categories represent, or said another way, the sort of thing we think category members are.

Defining Concepts and Providing Examples An important aspect of teaching concepts is to clearly define them and give carefully chosen examples. The *rule-example strategy* is an effective way to do this (Tennyson & Cocchiarella, 1986). The strategy consists of four steps:

1. *Define the concept.* As part of defining it, link it to a superordinate concept and identify its key features or characteristics. A *superordinate* concept is a larger class into which it fits. Thus, in specifying the key features of the concept of *dinosaur,* you might want to mention the larger class into which it fits: reptiles.

2. *Clarify terms in the definition.* Make sure that the key features or characteristics are well understood. Thus, in describing the key features of the concept of *dinosaur,* it is important for students to know what a reptile is—usually an egg-laying vertebrate with an external covering of scales or horny plates that breathes by means of lungs.

3. *Give examples to illustrate the key features or characteristics.* With regard to dinosaurs, one might give examples and descriptions of different types of dinosaurs, such as a triceratops, an apatosaur, and a stegosaur. The concept can be further clarified by giving examples of other reptiles that are not dinosaurs, such as snakes, lizards, crocodiles, and turtles. Indeed, giving nonexamples of a concept as well as examples is often a good strategy for teaching concept formation. More examples are required when you teach complex concepts and when you work with less-sophisticated learners (Jonassen, 2007).

4. *Provide additional examples.* Ask students to categorize concepts, explain their categorization, or have them generate their own examples of the concept. Give examples of other dinosaurs, such as *Tyrannosaurus, Ornitholestes,* and *Dimetrodon,* or ask students to find more examples themselves. Also ask them to think up other nonexamples of dinosaurs, such as dogs, cats, and whales.

Do some children develop an intense, passionate interest in a particular category of objects or activities? A recent study of 11-month-old-to 6-year-old children confirmed that they do (DeLoache, Simcock, & Macari, 2007). A striking finding was the large gender difference in categories with an extreme intense interest in particular categories stronger for boys than girls. Categorization of boys' intense interests focused on vehicles, trains, machines, dinosaurs, and balls; girls' intense interests were more likely to involve dress-ups and books/reading (see Figure 9.1).

Hierarchical Categorization and Concept Maps Categorization is important because once a concept is categorized it can take on characteristics and features from being a member of a category (Chi, 2008). For example, students can infer that a triceratops is a reptile even if they have never been told that fact as long as they know that dinosaurs are reptiles and a triceratops is a dinosaur. Knowing that a triceratops is a type of dinosaur lets students infer that a triceratops assumes the characteristics of dinosaurs (that they are reptiles).

A **concept map** is a visual presentation of a concept's connections and hierarchical organization. Getting students to create a map of a concept's features or characteristics can help them to learn the concept (Nesbit & Hadwin, 2006; Wang & Dwyer, 2007). The concept map also might embed the concept in a superordinate category and include examples and nonexamples of the concept. The visual aspects of the concept map relate to our Chapter 8 discussion of the use of imagery in memory. You might create a concept map with students' help, or let them try to develop it individually or in small groups. Figure 9.2 shows an example of a concept map for the concept of "reptile."

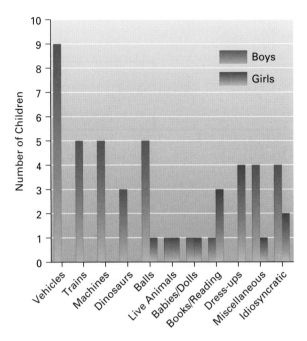

FIGURE 9.1 Categorization of Boys' and Girls' Intense Interests

Source: DeLoache, Simcock, & Macari (2007), Fig. 2.1 p 1583, *Developmental Psychology*, vol 43.

concept map A visual presentation of a concept's connections and hierarchical organization.

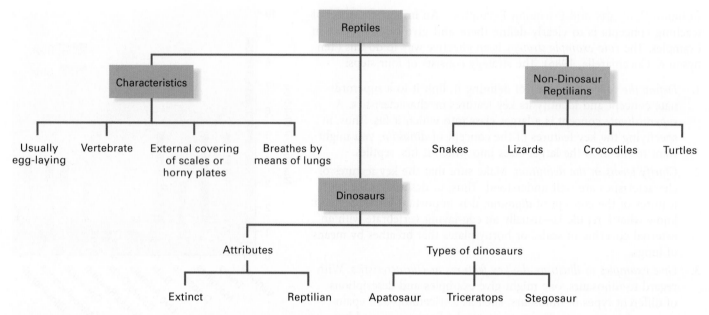

FIGURE 9.2 Example of a Concept Map for the Concept of *Reptile*

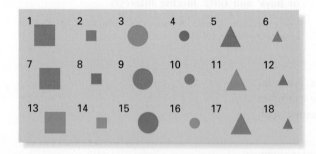

FIGURE 9.3 Getting Students to Generate Hypotheses About a Concept

Hypothesis Testing *Hypotheses* are specific assumptions and predictions that can be tested to determine their accuracy. Students benefit from the practice of developing hypotheses about what a concept is and is not. One way to develop a hypothesis is to come up with a rule about why some objects fall within a concept and others do not. Here is an example of how you can give your students practice in developing such hypotheses: Present your students with the picture of geometric forms shown in Figure 9.3. Then silently select the concept of one of those geometric forms (such as "circle" or "green circle") and ask your students to develop hypotheses about what concept you have selected. They zero in on your concept by asking you questions related to the geometric forms and eliminating nonexamples. You might also let the students take turns selecting a concept and answering questions

The concept of birds includes many different types of birds. *Which of these birds is likely to be viewed as the most typical bird?*

BEST PRACTICES
Strategies for Helping Students Form Concepts

1. *Use the rule-example strategy.* Remember that this involves four steps: (a) define the concept; (b) clarify the terms in the definition; (c) give examples to illustrate the key features or characteristics; and (d) provide additional examples and ask students to categorize these and explain their categorization, or have students generate their own examples of the concepts.

2. *Help students learn not only what a concept is but also what it is not.* Let's return to the concept "cartoon." Students can learn that even though they are humorous, jokes, clowns, and funny poems are not cartoons. If you are teaching the concept of "triangle," ask students to list the characteristics of "triangle" such as "three-sided," "geometric shape," "can be of any size," "can be of any color," "sides can vary in length," "angles can be different," and so on; also ask them to list examples of things that are not triangles, such as circles, squares, and rectangles.

3. *Make concepts as clear as possible and give concrete examples.* Spend some time thinking about the best way to present a new concept, especially an abstract one. Make it as clear as possible. If you want students to understand the concept "vehicle," ask them to come up with examples of it. They probably will say "car" and maybe "truck" or "bus." Show them photographs of other vehicles, such as a sled and a boat, to illustrate the breadth of the concept.

4. *Help students relate new concepts to concepts they already know.* In Chapter 8, we discussed the strategy of outlining for taking notes. Once students have learned this procedure, it is easier for them to learn how to construct concept maps, because you can show them

how concept maps are linked with outlining in terms of hierarchical organization. As another example of helping students to relate a new concept to concepts they already know, they might know what gold and silver are but not be aware of what platinum and plutonium are. In this case, build on their knowledge of gold and silver to teach the concepts of platinum and plutonium.

5. *Encourage students to create concept maps.* Getting students to visually map out the hierarchical organization of a concept can help them learn it. The hierarchical arranging can help students understand the concept's characteristics from more general to more specific. Hierarchical organization benefits memory.

6. *Ask students to generate hypotheses about a concept.* Generating hypotheses encourages students to think and develop strategies. Work with students on developing the most efficient strategies for determining what a concept is.

7. *Give students experience in prototype matching.* Think of different concepts and then ask students what the prototypes of the concepts are. Then ask them for nonprototypical examples of the concept.

8. *Check for students' understanding of a concept and motivate them to apply the concept to other contexts.* Make sure that students don't just rotely memorize a concept. Ask students how the concept can be applied in different contexts. For example, in learning the concept of fairness, ask students how fairness can make life smoother, not only at school but also at play, at home, and at work.

from the other students. Work with your students on developing the most efficient strategies for identifying the correct concept.

Prototype Matching   In **prototype matching**, individuals decide whether an item is a member of a category by comparing it with the most typical item(s) of the category (Rosch, 1973). The more similar the item is to the prototype, the more likely it is that the individual will say the item belongs to the category; the less similar, the more likely the person will judge that it doesn't belong in the category. For example, a student's concept of a football player might include being big and muscular like an offensive lineman. But some football players, such as many field goal kickers, are not so big and muscular. An offensive lineman is a more prototypical example of a football player than a field goal kicker. When students consider whether someone belongs in the category "football player," they are more likely to think of someone who looks like an offensive lineman than to think of someone who looks like a field goal kicker. Similarly, robins are viewed as being more typical birds than ostriches or penguins. Nonetheless, members of a category can vary greatly and still have qualities that make them a member of that category (Verbeemen & others, 2007).

prototype matching Deciding if an item is a member of a category by comparing it with the most typical item(s) of the category.

Review, Reflect, and Practice

1 Discuss conceptual understanding and strategies for teaching concepts.

REVIEW

- What are concepts and why are they indispensable to thinking?
- What are some ways that students can be guided to construct effective concepts?

REFLECT

- What might the concept "art" mean to a 3-year-old? To a 10-year-old? To a 16-year-old? To a professional artist? How do such changes come about?

PRAXIS™ PRACTICE

1. Which of the following is the best example of a superordinate concept?
   a. collie
   b. dog
   c. German shepherd
   d. poodle
2. Ms. Peloti wants her students to learn about the concept "bird." She discusses the characteristics of birds with her students, including a defining characteristic: feathers. She then discusses irrelevant characteristics, such as flying—insects and bats fly too, but they are not birds; ostriches don't fly, but they are birds. Finally, the class discusses what a typical bird looks like. They finally agree that the most typical bird is a robin. Ms. Peloti then gives the children a list of animals and asks them to determine if they are birds by comparing them to the robin. What strategy of concept formation does this task represent?
   a. concept mapping
   b. hypothesis testing
   c. prototype matching
   d. relating concepts

Please see the answer key at the end of the book.

2 THINKING

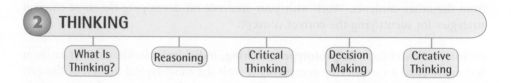

What does it mean to think? How can teachers help students to become better thinkers? In this section, we will attempt to answer these important questions.

What Is Thinking?

Thinking involves manipulating and transforming information in memory. We think to form concepts, reason, think critically, make decisions, think creatively, and solve problems. Students can think about the concrete, such as a vacation at the beach or

thinking Manipulating and transforming information in memory, which often is done to form concepts, reason, think critically, make decisions, think creatively, and solve problems.

how to win at a video game. They can also think about more abstract subjects, such as the meaning of freedom or identity. They can think about the past (such as what happened to them last month) and the future (what their life will be like in the year 2020). They can think about reality (such as how to do better on the next test) and fantasy (what it would be like to meet Elvis Presley or land a spacecraft on Mars).

Reasoning

Reasoning is logical thinking that uses induction and deduction to reach a conclusion. We begin by focusing on inductive reasoning.

Inductive Reasoning **Inductive reasoning** involves reasoning from the specific to the general. That is, it consists of drawing conclusions (forming concepts) about all members of a category based on observing only some of its members (Heit, 2008; Varzi, 2008). Researchers have found that inductive reasoning skill is often a good predictor of academic achievement (Kinshuk & McNab, 2006).

What are some examples of the use of inductive reasoning in classrooms? When a student in English class reads only a few Emily Dickinson poems and is asked to draw conclusions from them about the general nature of Dickinson's poems, inductive reasoning is being requested. When a student is asked whether a concept in a math class applies to other contexts, such as business or science, again, inductive reasoning is being called for. Educational psychology research is inductive when it studies a sample of participants to draw conclusions about the population from which the sample is drawn. It is also inductive in that scientists rarely take a single study as strong evidence to reach a conclusion about a topic, instead requiring a number of studies on the same topic to have more confidence in a conclusion.

Indeed, an important aspect of inductive reasoning is repeated observation. Through repeated observation, information about similar experiences accumulates to the point that a repetitive pattern can be detected and a more accurate conclusion drawn about it. To study this aspect of inductive reasoning, researchers have examined whether inductive inferences are justified based on evidence about a single instance of two co-occurring events (Kuhn, Katz, & Dean, 2004). When two events occur together in time and space, we often conclude that one has caused the other, despite the possibility that other factors are involved. For example, a parent might conclude, "Harry is a bad influence on my daughter; Sharon didn't drink before she met him." The boy might be the cause, but the event may have been a coincidence. Of course, if there is repeated evidence (for example, every girl Harry has ever gone out with develops a drinking problem), then the argument becomes more persuasive.

Consider also a child who observes a black snake and concludes "All snakes are black." The child's cousin sends him an e-mail about a pet snake she recently bought, and the child concludes that the pet snake must be black. However, the child clearly has not observed all of the snakes in the world—actually only one in this case—so he has seen only a small sample of the world's snake population. Of course, he would be forced to change his mind if he saw a gray snake or a white snake. The conclusions drawn as a result of inductive reasoning are never finally certain, only more or less probable. But induction can provide conclusive *negative* results—for example, seeing a yellow snake proves that the assertion "All snakes are black" is *false.*

Notice that inductive conclusions are never entirely certain—that is, they may be inconclusive. An inductive conclusion may be very likely, but there always is a chance that it is wrong, just as a sample does not perfectly represent its population (Kuhn & Franklin, 2006). Teachers can help students improve their inductive reasoning by encouraging them to consider that the conclusion they reach depends on the quality

inductive reasoning Reasoning from the specific to the general.

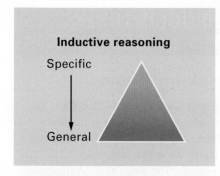

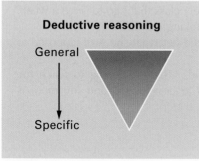

FIGURE 9.4 Inductive and Deductive Reasoning

The pyramid at the top (right side up) represents inductive reasoning—going from specific to general. The pyramid or triangle at the bottom (upside down) represents deductive reasoning—going from general to specific.

analogy A correspondence in some respects between otherwise dissimilar things.

deductive reasoning Reasoning from the general to the specific.

critical thinking Thinking reflectively and productively and evaluating the evidence.

mindfulness Means being alert, mentally present, and cognitively flexible while going through life's everyday activities and tasks. Mindful students maintain an active awareness of the circumstances in their lives.

and the quantity of the information available (Constantinos & Papageorgiou, 2007). Students often overstate a conclusion, making it more definitive than the evidence indicates.

Let's now consider another aspect of inductive reasoning: It is basic to analogies (Glynn, 2007). An **analogy** is a correspondence between otherwise dissimilar things. Analogies can be used to improve students' understanding of new concepts by comparing them with already learned concepts (Oliva, Azcarate, & Navarrete, 2007; Tunteler & Resing, 2007).

One type of analogy involves formal reasoning and has four parts, with the relation between the first two parts being the same as, or very similar to, the relation between the last two. For example, solve this analogy: Beethoven is to music as Picasso is to _____. To answer correctly ("art"), you had to induce the relation between Beethoven and music (the former created the latter) and apply this relationship to Picasso (what did he create?).

How good are children and adolescents at inductive reasoning? Adolescents are better at many aspects of inductive reasoning than are children, including analogies and false inclusion when generalizing from a single event, but not as good as young adults (Kuhn & Franklin, 2006).

Deductive Reasoning In contrast to inductive reasoning, **deductive reasoning** is reasoning from the general to the specific. Figure 9.4 provides a visual representation of the difference between inductive and deductive reasoning.

When you solve puzzles or riddles, you are engaging in deductive reasoning. When you learn about a general rule and then understand how it applies in some situations but not others, you are engaging in deductive reasoning (Johnson-Laird, 2008). Deductive reasoning is always certain in the sense that if the initial rules or assumptions are true, then the conclusion will be correct. When educators and psychologists use theories and intuitions to make predictions, then evaluate these predictions by making further observations, they are using deductive reasoning.

Many aspects of deductive reasoning have been studied, including the occasions when knowledge and reasoning conflict (Csapo, 2007; Kuhn & Franklin, 2006; Stalnaker, 2008). During adolescence, individuals are increasingly able to reason deductively even when the premises being reasoned about are false. Consider this deductive inference problem:

All basketball players are motorcycle drivers.
All motorcycle drivers are women.

Assuming that these two statements are true, decide if the following statement is true or false:

All basketball players are women.

Children rarely conclude that such conclusions are valid deductions from the premises. From early adolescence through early adulthood, individuals improve in their ability to make accurate conclusions when knowledge and reasoning conflict. That is, they can "reason independently of the truth status of the premises" (Kuhn & Franklin, 2006).

Critical Thinking

Currently, there is considerable interest in critical thinking among psychologists and educators, although it is not an entirely new idea (Bernard & others, 2008; Nieto & Saiz, 2008; Willingham, 2008). **Critical thinking** involves thinking reflectively and productively and evaluating the evidence. Many of the "Reflect" questions that appear in every section of this book call for critical thinking.

Mindfulness According to Ellen Langer (1997, 2000, 2005), mindfulness is a key to critical thinking. **Mindfulness** means being alert, mentally present, and cognitively flexible while going through life's everyday activities and tasks. Mindful students maintain an active awareness of the circumstances in their lives.

Mindful students create new ideas, are open to new information, and are aware of more than one perspective. In contrast, mindless students are entrapped in old ideas, engage in automatic behavior, and operate from a single perspective. Mindless students accept what they read or hear without questioning the accuracy of the information. Mindless students become trapped in rigid mindsets, not taking into account possible variations in contexts and perspectives. Langer emphasizes that asking good questions is an important ingredient of mindful thinking. She also stresses that it is important to focus on the process of learning rather than the outcome. For example, Trisha didn't do well on her math test earlier this week. All she can think about is how poorly she did. If she were engaging in mindfulness, Trisha would evaluate why she did so poorly and think about what changes she can adopt to do better on the next test.

"For God's sake, think! Why is he being so nice to you?"

© The New Yorker Collection. 1998 Sam Gross from cartoonbank.com. All Rights Reserved.

Critical Thinking in Schools   Here are some ways teachers can consciously build critical thinking into their lesson plans:

- Ask not only what happened but also "how" and "why."
- Examine supposed "facts" to determine whether there is evidence to support them.
- Argue in a reasoned way rather than through emotions.
- Recognize that there is sometimes more than one good answer or explanation.
- Compare various answers to a question and judge which is really the best answer.
- Evaluate and possibly question what other people say rather than immediately accept it as the truth.
- Ask questions and speculate beyond what we already know to create new ideas and new information.

Jacqueline and Martin Brooks (1993, 2001) lament that few schools really teach students to think critically. In their view, schools spend too much time on getting students to give a single correct answer in an imitative way rather than encouraging students to expand their thinking by coming up with new ideas and rethinking earlier conclusions. They believe that too often teachers ask students to recite, define, describe, state, and list rather than to analyze, infer, connect, synthesize, criticize, create, evaluate, think, and rethink.

One way to encourage students to think critically is to present them with controversial topics or articles that present both sides of an issue to discuss. Some teachers shy away from having students engage in these types of critical-thinking debates or discussions because it is not "polite" or "nice" (Winn, 2004). However, critical thinking is promoted when students encounter conflicting accounts of arguments and debates, which can motivate them to delve more deeply into a topic and attempt to resolve an issue (Kuhn, 2008a; Toulmin, 2008). In these circumstances, students often benefit when teachers refrain from stating their own views, allowing students to more freely explore different sides of issues and multiple perspectives on topics.

Getting students to think critically is not always an easy task (Mayer, 2008; Willingham, 2008). Many students come into a class with a history of passive learning, having been encouraged to recite the correct answer to a question, rather than put forth the intellectual effort to think in more complex ways (Noddings, 2008). By using more assignments that require students to focus on an issue, a question, or a problem, rather than just reciting facts, teachers stimulate students' ability to think critically. To read about ways to use technology to stimulate students' critical thinking, see the *Technology and Education* interlude.

What are some good strategies for nurturing children's critical thinking?

DEVELOPMENTAL FOCUS 9.1

How Do You Help Your Students Improve Their Critical-Thinking Skills?

Early Childhood

One of the techniques we use to develop our preschoolers' critical-thinking skills is to have them put a favorite item into a mystery box. The child then tells the class three clues about what is in the box, and the rest of the class guesses until they figure out what is inside the box. This game is rotated so that each child has a chance to put something in the box.

—Missy Dangler, *Suburban Hills School*

Elementary School: Grades K–5

One trait that is essential to critical thinking is intellectual courage. I teach this trait by asking my second-graders to consider such questions as "If everyone around you believes in 'such and such,' why is it hard to disagree?" or "When is it good to disagree?" or "Why do people get mad when they are questioned or doubted?" These questions help my students to think outside the box.

—Elizabeth Frascella, *Clinton Elementary School*

Middle School: Grades 6–8

I always have the question: "What is the significance . . . ?" written on the classroom whiteboard. When we are covering any topic in sixth-grade social studies class, I point to that question. I also have students write in a journal reflecting on a historical event and have them discuss what would be different today if the event never took place.

—Casey Maass, *Edison Middle School*

High School: Grades 9–12

We have our psychology students compile a "personality scrapbook" that includes completed personality tests along with reflective journals about the results as they relate to the student. Students then write a final paper entitled: "Who am I?" in which they "rethink" their own assumptions about themselves and their personality development. Students can also criticize and evaluate the effectiveness of personality tests in general.

—Joseph Maley, *South Burlington High School*

Critical Thinking in Adolescence If a solid basis of fundamental skills (such as literacy and math skills) is not developed during childhood, critical-thinking skills are unlikely to mature in adolescence. For those adolescents who lack fundamental skills, potential gains in adolescent thinking are not likely. For other adolescents, this time is an important transitional period in the development of critical thinking (Kuhn, 2008b; Reyna & Rivers, 2008). Several cognitive changes occur during adolescence that allow improved critical thinking, including the following (Keating, 1990):

- Increased speed, automaticity, and capacity of information processing, which frees cognitive resources for other purposes (See Chapter 8.)
- More knowledge in a variety of domains
- An increased ability to construct new combinations of knowledge
- A greater range and more spontaneous use of strategies or procedures such as planning, considering alternatives, and cognitive monitoring

In one study of fifth-, eighth-, and eleventh-graders, critical thinking increased with age but still occurred in only 43 percent of the eleventh-graders (Klaczynski & Narasimham, 1998). Many adolescents showed self-serving biases in their reasoning.

TECHNOLOGY AND EDUCATION
Digital Mindtools

David Jonassen (1996) argues that one of the best uses of technology in education involves computer applications that encourage students to think critically about the content they are studying. He calls such applications "mindtools," and sees them as constructivist tools that scaffold student creation of knowledge and reasoning about subject content. Jonassen distinguishes several categories of mindtools, including semantic organization tools, dynamic modeling tools, information interpretation tools, and conversation and collaboration tools. To read further about mindtools, go to this Web site: www.coe.missouri.edu/%Ejonassen/courses/mindtool/mindtools.html. The examples and software sections are especially helpful. Perhaps you might want to select one mindtool and create a lesson plan that you can use in your teaching.

Semantic organization tools, such as concept mapping tools, help students organize, analyze, and visualize information they are studying. For example, students studying climate can query global databases to test their hypotheses concerning links between climate and population. Inspiration and Kidspiration are concept mapping tools for K–12 students that are relatively inexpensive and easy to use. At www.inspiration.com you can download free trial versions of these tools. Consider using the free trial version of one of the programs at this Web site to explore how you might use it in your classroom.

Dynamic modeling tools help students explore connections between concepts. These include spreadsheets, expert systems, systems modeling tools, and microworlds. For example, spreadsheets have been used in mathematics classes to help students explore mathematical relations between numbers. Microworlds simulate real-world phenomena, such as genetic combinations.

Information interpretation tools help learners access and interpret information. For example, visualization tools create visual models of complex phenomena that make them more comprehensible. Knowledge construction tools, such as hypermedia, video editing or web design programs, scaffold student construction of knowledge in various forms.

WebQuests are Web sites that have a specific educational objective and are typically created by teachers. WebQuest.Org (http://webquest.org/index.php) explains the concept of WebQuests, has numerous resources to help teachers create their own WebQuests, and also has a number of WebQuests created by teachers that others can use. You might choose one of the WebQuests teachers have already developed on the Web site and explore how you can use it in your teaching.

Finally, a variety of digital *conversation and collaboration tools,* such as e-mail, online discussion, chat, videoconferencing, and blogs, make it possible for students to interact and collaborate with experts and other students around the world. For example, students studying foreign languages can converse with native speakers using computer-mediated communication.

The photographs in this *Technology and Education* interlude portray educational settings designed to stimulate students to think critically.

Students in the Research Center for Educational Technology's AT&T classroom at Kent State University studying energy by designing an energy-efficient home using *Better Homes and Gardens Home Designer* software.

Kindergarten students in the Research Center for Educational Technology's AT&T classroom at Kent State University exploring patterns by programming the Logo Robotic Turtle.

BEST PRACTICES
Strategies for Improving Children's Thinking

Twentieth-century German dictator Adolph Hitler once remarked that it was such good fortune for people in power that most people do not think. Education should help students become better thinkers. Every teacher would agree with that goal, but the means for reaching it are not always in place in schools. Here are some guidelines for helping students to become better thinkers.

1. *Be a guide in helping students to construct their own thinking.* You can't and shouldn't do students' thinking for them. However, you can and should be an effective guide in helping students construct their own thinking. Teachers who help students construct their own thinking (Brooks & Brooks, 1993, 2001)

Do

- Highly value students' questions.
- View students as thinkers with emerging theories about the world.
- Seek students' points of view.
- Seek elaboration of students' initial responses.
- Nurture students' intellectual curiosity.

Don't

- View students' minds as empty or see their role as a teacher as simply pouring information into students' minds.
- Rely too heavily on textbooks and workbooks.
- Simply seek the correct answer to validate student learning.

2. *Use thinking-based questions.* One way to analyze your teaching strategies is to see whether you use a lecture-based approach, fact-based questioning, or thinking-based questioning (Sternberg & Spear-Swirling, 1996). In the lecture-based approach, the teacher presents information in the form of a lecture. This is a helpful approach for quickly presenting a body of information, such as factors that led to the French Revolution. In fact-based questioning, the teacher asks questions primarily designed to get students to describe factual information. This is best used for reinforcing newly acquired information or testing students' content knowledge. For example, the teacher might ask, "When did the French Revolution occur? Who were the king and queen of France at that time?" In thinking-based questioning, the teacher asks questions that stimulate thinking and discussion. For

Alan Haskvitz with middle school students Simon Alarcon and Tracy Blozis, examining bones and trying to figure out where in the animal kingdom they belong.

example, the teacher might ask, "Compare the French and American revolutions. How were they similar? How were they different?"

Make a point to include thinking-based questions in your teaching. They will help your students construct a deeper understanding of a topic. Next, two teachers describe how they get students to think more productively and the importance of having high expectations for higher-level thinking.

THROUGH THE EYES OF TEACHERS
Challenging Students to Be Intellectual Risk-Takers

Alan Haskvitz, who teaches social studies at Suzanne Middle School in Walnut, California, believes in learning by doing and the importance of motivating students to improve the community. His students have rewritten voting instructions adopted by Los Angeles County, lobbied for a law requiring state government buildings to have rough-resistant landscaping, and created measures to reduce the city's graffiti. Alan has compiled thousands of teacher resources on this Web site: www.reacheverychild.com. He challenges students to be independent thinkers and intellectual risk-takers. He has students create an ideal island and discuss what everything from government to geography would be like on the island. (Sources: Briggs, 1999; Educational Cyber Playground, 2006).

THROUGH THE EYES OF TEACHERS
Use the Word Explain *Often and Have High Expectations*

Donna Shelhorse, a teacher at Short Pump Middle School in Virginia, says: "I use the word *explain* a lot. I do not accept an answer without asking the student to explain. This gets the students to think about their answers and provide support for their answers."

De Tonack, a high school math teacher, recommends having high expectations for students to engage in higher-level learning. She especially advocates getting students to do independent research projects. In her words, "What better educational challenge and poten-

BEST PRACTICES
Strategies for Improving Children's Thinking

tial for growth than doing a primary research, not just a report on someone's findings. This is a struggle. Students are conditioned to do reports, not research. Encourage visiting the state historical society, museums, doing interviews, conducting surveys, doing experiments. The hardest challenge is probably coming up with a question to investigate, but perhaps that is what an educated person must know how to do. Students in our program have investigated local light pollution; the development of Omaha's Boystown; the North Platte, Nebraska, World War II canteen; the orphan train through the Midwest."

3. *Provide positive role models for thinking.* Look around your community for positive role models who can demonstrate effective thinking, and invite them to come to your classroom and talk with your students. Also think about contexts in the community, such as museums, colleges and universities, hospitals, and businesses, where

you can take students and they can observe and interact with competent thinkers.

4. *Be a thinking role model for students as a teacher.* Have an active and inquiring mind yourself. Examine what we have said about thinking in this chapter. Work on being a positive thinking model for students by practicing these strategies.

5. *Keep up-to-date on the latest developments in thinking.* Continue to learn actively about new developments in teaching students to become more effective thinkers after you have become a teacher. Over the next decade, there likely will be new technology programs through which you can improve students' thinking skills. Go to libraries now and then to read educational journals, and attend professional conferences that include information about thinking.

Decision Making

Think of all the decisions you have to make in your life. Which grade level and subject should I teach? Should I go to graduate school right after college or get a job first? Should I establish myself in a career before settling down to have a family? Should I buy a house or rent? **Decision making** involves thinking in which individuals evaluate alternatives and make choices among them.

In deductive reasoning, people use clear-cut rules to draw conclusions (Rips, 2008). When we make decisions, the rules are seldom clear-cut and we may have limited knowledge about the consequences of the decisions (Gerrard & others, 2008). In addition, important information might be missing, and we might not trust all of the information we have (Matlin, 2005).

In one type of decision-making research, investigators have studied how people weigh the costs and benefits of various outcomes (Redelmeier, 2005). They have found that people choose the outcome with the highest expected value (Smyth & others, 1994). For example, in choosing a college, a high school student might list the pluses and minuses of going to different colleges (related to such factors as cost, quality of education, and social life), then make a decision based on how the colleges fared on these criteria. In making a decision, the student might have weighted some of these factors more heavily than others (such as cost 3 points, quality of education 2 points, and social life 1 point).

Another fruitful subject of decision-making research is the biases and flawed heuristics (rules of thumb) that affect the quality of decisions (Pretz, 2008; Shah & Oppenheimer, 2008). In many cases, our decision-making strategies are well adapted to deal with a variety of problems (Nisbett & Ross, 1980). However, we are prone to certain flaws in our thinking (Stanovich, 2007). Common flaws involve confirmation bias, belief perseverance, overconfidence bias, hindsight bias, and the availability and representativeness heuristics (Ricco, 2007). Decision making is improved when we become aware of these potential flaws.

"You take all the time you need, Larry—this certainly is a big decision."

© The New Yorker Collection 1990, Eric Teitelbaum, from cartoonbank.com. All Rights Reserved.

decision making Evaluating alternatives and making choices among them.

Confirmation Bias **Confirmation bias** is the tendency to search for and use information that supports our ideas rather than refutes them. Thus, in making a decision, a student might have an initial belief that a certain approach is going to work. He tests out the approach and finds out that it does work some of the time. He concludes that his approach is right rather than further exploring the fact that in a number of cases it doesn't work.

We tend to seek out and listen to people whose views confirm our own rather than listen to dissenting views (Bilalic, McLeod, & Gobet, 2008; Kerschreiter & others, 2008). Thus, you might have a particular teaching style, such as lecturing, that you like to use. If so, you probably have a tendency to seek advice from other teachers who use that style rather than from teachers who prefer other styles, such as collaborative problem solving by students.

In one study, Deanna Kuhn and her colleagues (1994) had participants listen to an audiotaped reenactment of an actual murder trial. Then, they were asked what their verdict would be and why. Rather than considering and weighing possibilities drawing on all the evidence, many participants hurriedly composed a story that drew only from evidence that supported their view of what happened. These participants showed a confirmation bias by ignoring evidence that ran counter to their version of events. Be aware of how easy it is for you and your students to become trapped by confirmation bias.

Belief Perseverance Closely related to confirmation bias, **belief perseverance** is the tendency to hold on to a belief in the face of contradictory evidence. People have a difficult time letting go of an idea or a strategy once they have embraced it (Stanovich & West, 2008). Consider Madonna. We might have a hard time thinking of her in a maternal role because of the belief perseverance that she is a wild, fun-loving rock star.

Another example of belief perseverance gives some college students trouble. They may have gotten good grades in high school by using the strategy of cramming for tests the night before. The ones who don't adopt a new strategy—spacing their study sessions more evenly through the term—often do poorly in college.

Overconfidence Bias **Overconfidence bias** is the tendency to have more confidence in judgments and decisions than we should based on probability or past experience. People are overconfident about how long those with a fatal disease will live, which businesses will go bankrupt, whether a defendant is guilty in a court trial, and which students will do well in college (Kahneman & Tversky, 1995). People consistently have more faith in their judgments than predictions based on statistically objective measures indicate they should (Finn, 2008).

In one study, college students were asked to make predictions about themselves in the coming academic year (Vallone & others, 1990). They were asked to predict whether they would drop any courses, vote in an election, and break up with their girlfriend or boyfriend. At the end of the year, the accuracy of their predictions was examined. The results: They were more likely to drop a class, not vote in an election, and break up with a girlfriend or a boyfriend than they had predicted.

Hindsight Bias People not only are overconfident about what they predict will happen in the future (overconfidence bias), but also tend to overrate their past performances at prediction (Asa & Wiley, 2008; Blank & others, 2008). **Hindsight bias** is our tendency to falsely report, after the fact, that we accurately predicted an event.

As I write this chapter, baseball season is just beginning. Lots of people in different cities are predicting that their teams are going to make it to the World Series. Come October, after almost all of the teams have fallen by the wayside, many of the same people will say, "I told you our team wasn't going to have a good season."

confirmation bias The tendency to search for and use information that supports our ideas rather than refutes them.

belief perseverance The tendency to hold on to a belief in the face of contradictory evidence.

overconfidence bias The tendency to have more confidence in judgment and decisions than we should based on probability or past experience.

hindsight bias The tendency to falsely report, after the fact, that we accurately predicted an event.

Creative Thinking

An important aspect of thinking is to be able to think creatively (Beghetto & Kaufman, 2009; Sternberg, 2009a, b, c). **Creativity** is the ability to think about something in novel and unusual ways and come up with unique solutions to problems.

J. P. Guilford (1967) distinguished between **convergent thinking**, which produces one correct answer and is characteristic of the kind of thinking required on conventional intelligence tests, and **divergent thinking**, which produces many answers to the same question and is more characteristic of creativity. For example, a typical convergent item on a conventional intelligence test is "How many quarters will you get in return for 60 dimes?" The question has only one right answer. In contrast, divergent questions have many possible answers. For example, consider these questions: "What image comes to mind when you sit alone in a dark room?" and "What are some unique uses for a paper clip?"

Are intelligence and creativity related? Although most creative students are quite intelligent (as measured by high scores on conventional intelligence tests), in other respects the reverse is not necessarily true. Many highly intelligent students are not very creative (Md-Yunus, 2007; Sternberg, 2009a, b, c).

What do you mean, "What is it?" It's the spontaneous, unfettered expression of a young mind not yet bound by the restraints of narrative or pictorial representation.

Sydney Harris. www.ScienceCartoons Plus.com.

Steps in the Creative Process   The creative process is often described as a five-step sequence:

1. *Preparation.* Students become immersed in a problem issue that interests them and their curiosity is aroused.

2. *Incubation.* Students churn ideas around in their head, a point at which they are likely to make some unusual connections in their thinking.

3. *Insight.* Students experience the "Aha!" moment when all pieces of the puzzle seem to fit together.

4. *Evaluation.* Now students must decide whether the idea is valuable and worth pursuing. They need to think, "Is the idea novel or is it obvious?"

5. *Elaboration.* This final step often covers the longest span of time and involves the hardest work. This step is what famous twentieth-century American inventor Thomas Edison was thinking about when he said that creativity is 1 percent inspiration and 99 percent perspiration.

creativity The ability to think about something in novel and unusual ways and come up with unique solutions to problems.

convergent thinking Thinking with the aim of producing one correct answer. This is usually the type of thinking required on conventional intelligence tests.

divergent thinking Thinking with the aim of producing many answers to the same question. This is characteristic of creativity.

What are some good strategies teachers can use to guide children in thinking more creatively?

Mihaly Csikszentmihalyi (pronounced ME-hihg CHICK-sent-me-high-ee) (1996) argues that this five-step sequence provides a helpful framework for thinking about how to develop creative ideas. However, he emphasizes that creative people don't always go through the steps in a linear sequence. For example, elaboration is often interrupted by periods of incubation. Fresh insights may appear during incubation, evaluation, and elaboration. And insight might take years or only a few hours. Sometimes the creative idea consists of one deep insight. At other times, it is a series of small insights.

Teaching and Creativity An important teaching goal is to help students become more creative (Beghetto & Kaufman, 2009; Sternberg, 2009a, b, c; Sternberg, Kaufman, & Grigorenko, 2008). Teachers need to recognize that students will show more creativity in some domains than others (Grigorenko & others, 2008; Plucker & Beghetto, 2008). A student who shows creative-thinking skills in mathematics may not exhibit these skills in art, for example.

The design of schools and classrooms may influence the creativity of students (Beghetto & Kaufman, 2009). School environments that encourage independent work, are stimulating but not distracting, and make resources readily available are likely to encourage students' creativity (Hasirci & Demirkan, 2003).

Recall our discussion in Chapter 6, "Learners Who Are Exceptional," that a current concern is the education of children who are gifted in the face of standards-based

Bill Gates, the highly creative founder of Microsoft Corporation, talking with fifth-grade students from Dearborn Park Elementary School at the Seattle Art Museum before touring the museum. Two good strategies for encouraging students' creative thinking are to provide them with environments that stimulate creativity and to introduce them to creative people. Museums are especially good settings for stimulating students' creative thinking. You probably won't be able to find someone as famous as Bill Gates to talk with your students, but a good strategy is look around your community and identify its creative thinkers and either invite them to come to your classroom or take your students to where the creative thinkers work.

DEVELOPMENTAL FOCUS 9.2
How Do You Help Your Students Develop Creative-Thinking Skills?

Early Childhood

When teaching music to my preschool students, I have them suggest an instrument from our instrument library to make the sound of a character in the book. Students also have to give a reason for why they selected the particular instrument.

—Connie Christy, *Aynor Elementary School (Preschool Program)*

Elementary School: Grades K–5

When I teach social studies, I have my students construct a mock travel agency. We start out by talking about traveling around the world, which emphasizes geography. We then discuss the business of travel agencies. The students brainstorm about what the travel agent's job entails and what would be found at a real travel agency. Students then become the travel agent, create travel brochures, book trips, and so on. This social studies project is fun and involves reading, writing, research, art, and marketing.

—Craig Jensen, *Cooper Mountain Elementary School*

Middle School: Grades 6–8

When telling stories to my students, I often leave the last part of the story blank and have them create an ending. There is no right or wrong answer—just an opportunity for students to expand their creative thinking.

—Margaret Reardon, *Pocantico Hills School*

High School: Grades 9–12

By providing an environment of freedom and safety, teachers can foster students' creative thinking. In particular, I find that having students brainstorm about various topics makes the creative juices flow.

—Dennis Peterson, *Deer River High School*

education such as the No Child Left Behind legislation. So too is their mounting concern that this legislation has harmed the development of students' creative thinking by focusing attention on memorization of materials to do well on standardized tests (Burke-Adams, 2007; Kaufman & Sternberg, 2007).

Following are a number of strategies that teachers can use to guide students' development of creative thinking.

Encourage Creative Thinking on a Group and Individual Basis *Brainstorming* is a technique in which people are encouraged to come up with creative ideas in a group, play off each other's ideas, and say practically whatever comes to mind that seems relevant to a particular issue. Participants are usually told to hold off from criticizing others' ideas at least until the end of the brainstorming session.

Provide Environments That Stimulate Creativity Some classrooms nourish creativity, others inhibit it (Beghetto & Kaufman, 2009; Piggott, 2007). Teachers who encourage creativity often rely on students' natural curiosity. They provide exercises and activities that stimulate students to find insightful solutions to problems, rather than ask a lot of questions that require rote answers. Teachers also encourage creativity by taking students on field trips to locations where creativity is valued. Howard Gardner (1993) emphasizes that science, discovery, and children's museums offer rich opportunities to stimulate creativity.

Don't Overcontrol Students Teresa Amabile (1993) says that telling students exactly how to do things leaves them feeling that originality is a mistake and exploration

THROUGH THE EYES OF STUDENTS

The Eight-Year-Old Filmmaker and Oozy Red Goop

Steven was 12-years-old when he got his filmmaking badge in the Boy Scouts. He started imagining what he needed to do to make a movie and his father bought him a super-8 movie camera. Steven made a film called "The Last Gunfight."

His mother game him free reign of the house, letting him virtually turn it into a movie studio. When he was 16-years-old, as part of making the movie, "The Firelight," he needed some "red, bloody-looking goop to ooze from the kitchen cabinets," so he got his mother to buy 30 cans of cherries. Steven dumped the cherries "into the pressure cooker and produced an oozy red goop."

Steven is Steven Spielberg, whose mother supported his imagination and passion for film making. Of course, Spielberg went on to become one of Hollywood's greatest directors with such films as E.T., Jurassic Park, and Schindler's List. (Source: Goleman, Kaufman, & Ray, 1993, p.70.)

is a waste of time. If, instead of dictating which activities they should engage in, you let your students select their interests and you support their inclinations, you will be less likely to destroy their natural curiosity. Amabile also emphasizes that when teachers hover over students all of the time, they make them feel that they are constantly being watched while they are working. When students are under constant surveillance, their creative risk-taking and adventurous spirit diminish. Students' creativity also is diminished when teachers have grandiose expectations for their performance and expect perfection from them, according to Amabile.

Encourage Internal Motivation Excessive use of prizes, such as gold stars, money, or toys, can stifle creativity by undermining the intrinsic pleasure students derive from creative activities. Creative students' motivation is the satisfaction generated by the work itself. Competition for prizes and formal evaluations often undermine intrinsic motivation and creativity (Amabile & Hennesey, 1992). However, this is not to rule out material rewards altogether. We will say more about internal and external motivation in Chapter 13, "Motivation, Teaching, and Learning."

Guide Students to Help Them Think in Flexible Ways Creative thinkers are flexible in the way they approach problems in many different ways rather than getting locked into rigid patterns of thought. Give students opportunities to exercise this flexibility in their thinking (Sternberg, 2009a, b, c).

Build Students' Self-Confidence To expand students' creativity, it helps when teachers encourage students to believe in their own ability to create something innovative and worthwhile. Building students' confidence in their creative skills aligns with Bandura's (2007a, b, 2008, 2009a, b, c) concept of *self-efficacy*, the belief that one can master a situation and produce positive outcomes. We will have much more to say about self-efficacy in Chapter 13, "Motivation, Teaching, and Learning."

Guide Students to Be Persistent and Delay Gratification Most highly successful creative products take years to develop. Most creative individuals work on ideas and projects for months and years without being rewarded for their efforts (Sternberg & Williams, 1996). As we discussed in Chapter 6, "Learners Who Are Exceptional," children don't become experts at sports, music, or art overnight. It usually takes many years working at something to become an expert at it; so it is with being a creative thinker who produces a unique, worthwhile product.

Encourage Students to Take Risks Creative individuals take risks and seek to discover or invent something never before discovered or invented (Sternberg, 2009c). They risk spending a lot of time on an idea or project that may not work. Creative people are not afraid of failing or getting something wrong (Sternberg, Jarvin, & Grigorenko, 2009). They often see failure as an opportunity to learn. They might go down twenty dead-end streets before they come up with an innovative idea.

Introduce Students to Creative People A good strategy is to identify the most creative people in your community and ask them to come to your class and describe what helps them become creative or to demonstrate their creative skills. A writer, a poet, a craftsperson, a musician, a scientist, and many others can bring their props and productions to your class.

To evaluate how good you are at thinking creatively, complete *Self-Assessment 9.1.*

SELF-ASSESSMENT 9.1

How Good Am I at Thinking Creatively?

Rate each of these activities as they apply to you in terms of how often you engage in them: 1 = never, 2 = rarely, 3 = sometimes, and 4 = a lot.

	1	2	3	4
1. I come up with new and unique ideas.				
2. I brainstorm with others to creatively find solutions to problems.				
3. I am internally motivated.				
4. I'm flexible about things and like to play with my thinking.				
5. I read about creative projects and creative people.				
6. I'm surprised by something and surprise others every day.				
7. I wake up in the morning with a mission.				
8. I search for alternative solutions to problems rather than giving a pat answer.				
9. I have confidence in my ability to create something innovative and worthwhile.				
10. I delay gratification and persist until I have developed creative ideas and products.				
11. I take risks in developing creative thoughts.				
12. I spend time around creative people.				
13. I spend time in settings and activities that stimulate me to be creative.				

Examine your overall pattern of responses. What are your strengths and weaknesses in creativity? Keep practicing your strengths and work on improving your weaknesses to provide students with a creative role model.

Review, Reflect, and Practice

Describe several types of thinking and ways that teachers can foster them.

REVIEW
- What is thinking?
- How do inductive and deductive reasoning differ?
- What is the focus of critical thinking? Do most schools teach students to think critically?
- What is decision making? What are some flaws that can hinder effective decision making?
- What is creative thinking? How can teachers foster creative thinking?

REFLECT
- Some experts lament that few schools teach students to think critically. Does your own experience support this view? If you agree with the experts, why is critical thinking not more widely or effectively taught?

(continued)

Review, Reflect, and Practice

PRAXIS™ PRACTICE

1. Ms. McDougal has a pet rabbit in her classroom. One day while Amari is petting the rabbit, it bites her. Amari decides that all rabbits are mean. This is an example of what kind of reasoning?
   a. analogy
   b. critical thinking
   c. deductive
   d. inductive

2. Which teaching strategy is most likely to foster the development of critical-thinking skills in social studies?
   a. having students create timelines of important historical dates
   b. presenting students with worksheets that require them to recall the facts presented in their textbooks
   c. presenting students with statements such as "Lincoln was our greatest president" to defend or refute
   d. giving a multiple-choice test

3. Many students enter their educational psychology courses believing that when an authority figure presents an aversive stimulus to a child, and the child's misbehavior diminishes, the authority figure has negatively reinforced the child's behavior. Of course, we know that the authority figure has punished the child's behavior. Many of the students who entered your class with this misconception will get questions incorrect that test this idea on the final exam and will still have this misconception when they leave the class. What is the best explanation for this phenomenon?
   a. belief perseverance
   b. confirmation bias
   c. hindsight bias
   d. none of the above

4. All fifth-grade classes at Central School have just read *The Jungle Book*. Which assignment is most likely to foster creativity?
   a. The students write a story about how their lives would have been different if they had grown up in the wild like Mowgli.
   b. The students complete a story diagram, in which they describe the setting, characters, plot, climax, and theme of the book.
   c. The students create models of the temple where the monkeys lived, following a prototype that the teacher constructed.
   d. The students complete worksheets containing questions about the plot and characters of the book.

Please see the answer key at the end of the book.

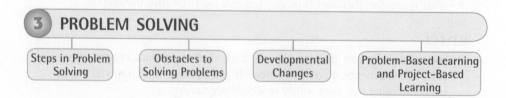

3 PROBLEM SOLVING

| Steps in Problem Solving | Obstacles to Solving Problems | Developmental Changes | Problem-Based Learning and Project-Based Learning |

Let's examine problem solving as a cognitive process, including the steps it involves, the obstacles to it, and how best to teach it.

Problem solving involves finding an appropriate way to attain a goal. Consider these tasks that require students to engage in problem solving: creating a project for a science fair, writing a paper for an English class, getting a community to be more environmentally responsive, and giving a talk on the factors that cause people to be prejudiced. Although they seem quite different, each involves a similar series of steps.

Steps in Problem Solving

Efforts have been made to specify the steps that individuals go through in effectively solving problems (Solso, MacLin, & MacLin, 2008). Following are four such steps (Bransford & Stein, 1993):

1. Find and Frame Problems   Before you can solve a problem, you must recognize that it exists (Mayer, 2008). In the past, most problem-solving exercises in school involved well-defined problems that lent themselves to specific, systematic operations that produced a well-defined solution. Today, educators increasingly recognize the need to teach students the real-world skill of identifying problems instead of just offering clear-cut problems to be solved (Robinson-Riegler & Robinson-Riegler, 2008).

Consider a student whose broad goal is to create a science-fair project. What branch of science would it be best for her to present—biology, physics, computer science, psychology? Then, she'll have to narrow the problem even more. For example, which domain within psychology—perception, memory, thinking, personality? Within the domain of memory, she might pose this question: How reliable are people's memories of traumatic events they have experienced? Thus, it may take considerable exploration and refinement for the student to narrow the problem down to a point of generating specific solutions. Exploring such alternatives is an important part of problem solving.

2. Develop Good Problem–Solving Strategies   Once students find a problem and clearly define it, they need to develop strategies for solving it (Quiamzade, Mugny, & Darnon, 2008). Among the effective strategies are setting subgoals and using algorithms, heuristics, and means-end analysis.

Subgoaling involves setting intermediate goals that put students in a better position to reach the final goal or solution. Students might do poorly in solving problems because they don't generate subproblems or subgoals. Let's return to the science-fair project on the reliability of people's memory for traumatic events they have experienced. What might be some subgoaling strategies? One might be locating the right books and research journals on memory; another might be interviewing people who have experienced traumas in which basic facts have been recorded. At the same time as the student is working on this subgoaling strategy, she likely will benefit from establishing further subgoals in terms of what she needs to accomplish along the way to her final goal of a finished science project. If the science project is due in three months, she might set the following subgoals: finishing the first draft of the project two weeks before the project is due; having the research completed a month before the project is due; being halfway through the research two months before the project is due; having three trauma interviews completed two weeks from today; and starting library research tomorrow.

Notice that in establishing the subgoals, we worked backward in time. This is often a good strategy. Students first create a subgoal closest to the final goal and then work backward to the subgoal closest to the beginning of the problem-solving effort.

Algorithms are strategies that guarantee a solution to a problem. Algorithms come in different forms, such as formulas, instructions, and tests of all possible solutions (Robinson-Riegler & Robinson-Riegler, 2009).

problem solving Finding an appropriate way to attain a goal.

subgoaling The process of setting intermediate goals that place students in a better position to reach the final goal or solution.

algorithms Strategies that guarantee a solution to a problem.

If a student wants to do a science-fair project on the reliability of people's memories for traumatic events, such as the 9/11/01 terror attack, what might be some subgoaling strategies the students could adopt?

When students solve a multiplication problem by a set procedure, they are using an algorithm. When they follow the directions for diagramming a sentence, they are using an algorithm. Algorithms are helpful in solving clear-cut problems. But since many real-world problems aren't so straightforward, looser strategies also are needed.

Heuristics are strategies or rules of thumb that can suggest a solution to a problem but don't ensure it will work. Heuristics help us to narrow down the possible solutions and help us find one that works (Pretz, 2008; Shah & Oppenheimer, 2008). Suppose that you go out on a day hike and find yourself lost in the mountains. A common heuristic for getting "unlost" is simply to head downhill and pick up the nearest tiny stream. Small streams lead to larger ones, and large streams often lead to people. Thus, this heuristic usually works, although it could bring you out on a desolate beach.

In the face of a multiple-choice test, several heuristics could be useful. For example, if you are not sure about an answer, you could start by trying to eliminate the answers that look most unlikely and then guess among the remaining ones. Also, for hints about the answer to one question, you could examine the statements or answer choices for other questions on the test.

A **means-end analysis** is a heuristic in which one identifies the goal (end) of a problem, assesses the current situation, and evaluates what needs to be done (means) to decrease the difference between the two conditions. Another name for means-end analysis is *difference reduction*. Means-end analysis also can involve the use of subgoaling, which we described earlier. Means-end analysis is commonly used in solving problems. Consider a student who wants to do a science-fair project (the end) but has not yet found a topic. Using means-end analysis, she could assess her current situation, in which she is just starting to think about the project. Then she maps out a plan to reduce the difference between her current state and the goal (end). Her "means" might include talking to several scientists in the community about potential projects, going to the library to study the topic she chooses, and exploring the Internet for potential projects and ways to carry them out.

3. Evaluate Solutions Once we think we have solved a problem, we might not know whether our solution is effective unless we evaluate it. It helps to have in mind a clear criterion for the effectiveness of the solution. For example, what will be the student's criterion for effectively solving the science-fair problem? Will it be simply getting it completed? Receiving positive feedback about the project? Winning an award? Winning first place? Gaining the self-satisfaction of having set a goal, planned for it, and reached it?

4. Rethink and Redefine Problems and Solutions over Time An important final step in problem solving is to continually rethink and redefine problems and solutions over time (Bereiter & Scardamalia, 2006). People who are good at problem solving are motivated to improve on their past performances and to make original contributions. Thus, the student who completed the science-fair project can look back at the project and think about ways the project can be improved. The student might use feedback from judges or others who attended the fair in order to fine-tune the project for presentation again in some other venue.

Obstacles to Solving Problems

Some common obstacles to solving problems are fixation and a lack of motivation and persistence. We'll also discuss inadequate emotional control, which is another stumbling block to effective problem solving.

Fixation It is easy to fall into the trap of becoming fixated on a particular strategy for solving a problem. **Fixation** involves using a prior strategy and failing to look at a problem from a fresh, new perspective. *Functional fixedness* is a type of fixation in

heuristics Strategies or rules of thumb that can suggest a solution to a problem but don't ensure that it will work.

means-end analysis A heuristic in which one identifies the goal (end) of a problem, assesses the current situation, and evaluates what needs to be done (means) to decrease the difference between the two conditions.

fixation Using a prior strategy and thereby failing to examine a problem from a fresh, new perspective.

which an individual fails to solve a problem because he or she views the elements involved solely in terms of their usual functions. A student who uses a shoe to hammer a nail has overcome functional fixedness to solve a problem.

A **mental set** is a type of fixation in which an individual tries to solve a problem in a particular way that has worked in the past. I (your author) had a mental set about using a typewriter rather than a computer to write my books. I felt comfortable with a typewriter and had never lost any sections I had written. It took a long time for me to break out of this mental set. Once I did, I found that books are much easier to write using a computer. You might have a similar mental set against using the new computer and video technology available for classroom use. A good strategy is to keep an open mind about such changes and monitor whether your mental set is keeping you from trying out new technologies that can make the classroom more exciting and more productive.

Lack of Motivation and Persistence Even if your students already have great problem-solving abilities, that hardly matters if they are not motivated to use them (Perry, Turner, & Meyer, 2006). It is especially important for students to be internally motivated to tackle a problem and persist at finding a solution. Some students avoid problems or give up too easily.

An important task for teachers is to devise or steer students toward problems that are meaningful to them and to encourage and support them in finding solutions. Students are far more motivated to solve problems that they can relate to their personal lives than textbook problems that have no personal meaning for them. Problem-based learning takes this real-world, personal approach (Schmidt & others, 2007).

Inadequate Emotional Control Emotion can facilitate or restrict problem solving. At the same time that they are highly motivated, good problem solvers are often able to control their emotions and concentrate on a solution to a problem (Kuhn & Franklin, 2006). Too much anxiety or fear can especially restrict a student's ability to solve a problem. Individuals who are competent at solving problems are usually not afraid of making mistakes.

Developmental Changes

One way that developmental changes in problem solving have been studied is called the *rule-assessment approach*, which focuses on children's increasing ability to effectively use rules to solve problems as they get older (Siegler, 2006; Siegler & Alibali, 2005). Even young children begin to use rules to solve problems. During early childhood, the relatively stimulus-driven toddler is transformed into a child capable of more flexible, goal-directed problem solving (Zelazo & Müller, 2004). Consider a problem in which children must sort stimuli using the rule of *color*. In the course of the color sorting, a child may describe a red rabbit as a *red one* to solve the problem. However, in a subsequent task, the child may need to discover a rule that describes the rabbit as just a *rabbit* to solve the problem. If young children fail to understand that it is possible to provide multiple descriptions of the same stimulus, they persist in describing the stimulus as a red rabbit. Researchers have found that at about 4 years of age, children acquire the concept of perspectives, which allows them to appreciate that a single thing can be described in different ways (Frye, 1999).

Young children, however, have some drawbacks that prevent them from solving many problems effectively. Especially notable is their lack of planning, which improves during the elementary and secondary school years. Among the reasons for the poor planning skills of young children is their tendency to try to solve problems too quickly at the expense of accuracy and their inability to inhibit an activity. Planning often requires inhibiting a current behavior to stop and think; preschool children often have difficulty inhibiting an ongoing behavior, especially if it is enjoyable (Bjorklund, 2005). Another drawback of young children's problem-solving ability is that even though they may know a rule they fail to use it.

mental set A type of fixation in which an individual tries to solve a problem in a particular way that has worked in the past.

What are some developmental changes in problem solving?

Other reasons that older children and adolescents become better problem solvers than young children involve *knowledge* and *strategies* (Pressley, 2007). The problems that older children and adolescents must solve are often more complex than those young children face, and solving these problems accurately usually requires accumulated knowledge. The more children know about a particular topic, the better they will be able to solve a problem related to the topic. The increase in accumulated knowledge about a topic ties in with our discussion of experts and novices in Chapter 8.

Older children and adolescents also are more likely than young children to have effective strategies that help them solve problems (Kuhn & Franklin, 2006; Pressley, 2007). Recall our extensive discussion of metacognition and strategies in Chapter 8, in which we discussed how children's use of strategies improves as they get older. Especially important in using strategies to solve problems is to have a range of strategies from which to select, and this increases during the elementary and secondary school years. Adolescents have an increased capacity to monitor and manage their resources to effectively meet the demands of a problem-solving task (Kuhn & Franklin, 2006). Adolescents also are better than children at screening out information irrelevant to solving a problem (Kail, 2002; Kuhn & Franklin, 2006).

Problem–Based Learning and Project–Based Learning

Now that we have discussed many aspects of problem solving, we turn our attention to two types of learning involving problems. First, we will describe problem-based learning and then explain project-based learning.

Problem–Based Learning **Problem-based learning** emphasizes solving authentic problems like those that occur in daily life (Bereiter & Scardamalia, 2006; ChanLin & Chan, 2007; Massa, 2008; Park & Ertmer, 2008). Problem-based learning is used in a program called YouthALIVE! at the Children's Museum of Indianapolis (Schauble & others, 1996). There, students solve problems related to conceiving, planning, and installing exhibits; designing videos; creating programs to help visitors understand and interpret museum exhibits; and brainstorming about strategies for reaching the wider community.

Project–Based Learning In **project-based learning**, students work on real, meaningful problems and create tangible products (Baumgartner & Zabin, 2008; Harado, Kirio, & Yamamoto, 2008). Project-based learning and problem-based learning are sometimes treated as synonymous. However, while still emphasizing the process of learning in a constructivist manner, project-based learning gives more attention to the end product than problem-based learning (Bereiter & Scardamalia, 2006). The types of problems explored in project-based learning are similar to those studied by scientists, mathematicians, historians, writers, and other professionals (ChanLin, 2008).

Project-based learning environments are characterized by five main features (Krajcik & Blumenfeld, 2006):

1. *A driving question.* The learning process begins with a key question or problem that needs to be solved.
2. *Authentic, situated inquiry.* As students examine the key question, they learn about the problem-solving process engaged in by experts in the discipline in relevant contexts.
3. *Collaboration.* Students, teachers, and community participants collaborate to find solutions to the problem.
4. *Scaffolding.* Learning technologies are used to challenge students to go beyond what they normally would in a problem-solving context.

problem–based learning Learning that emphasizes authentic problems like those that occur in daily life.

project–based learning Students work on real, meaningful problems and create tangible products.

SELF-ASSESSMENT 9.2

How Effective Are My Thinking and Problem-Solving Strategies?

Teachers who practice good thinking and problem-solving strategies themselves are more likely to model and communicate these to their students than teachers who don't use such strategies. Candidly respond to these items about your own thinking and problem-solving strategies. Rate yourself: 1 = very much unlike me, 2 = somewhat unlike me, 3 = somewhat like me, and 4 = very much like me; then total your points.

1	2	3	4

1. I am aware of effective and ineffective thinking strategies.

2. I periodically monitor the thinking strategies I use.

3. I am good at reasoning.

4. I use good strategies for forming concepts.

5. I am good at thinking critically and deeply about problems and issues.

6. I construct my own thinking rather than just passively accepting what others think.

7. I like to use technology as part of my effort to think effectively.

8. I have good role models for thinking.

9. I keep up-to-date on the latest educational developments in thinking.

10. I use a system for solving problems, such as the four-step system described in the text.

11. I am good at finding and framing problems.

12. I make good decisions and monitor biases and flaws in my decision making.

13. When solving problems, I use strategies such as subgoaling and working backward in time.

14. I don't fall into problem-solving traps such as fixating, lacking motivation and persistence, and not controlling my emotions.

15. When solving problems, I set criteria for my success and evaluate how well I have met my problem-solving goals.

16. I make a practice of rethinking and redefining problems over an extended period of time.

17. I love to work on problem-solving projects.

18. I am good at creative thinking.

Total _____

Scoring and Interpretation

If you scored 66–72 points, your thinking strategies likely are very good. If you scored 55–65 points, you likely have moderately good thinking strategies. If you scored below 54 points, you likely would benefit from working on your thinking strategies.

5. *End product.* Students create tangible end products that address the key, driving question.

To evaluate your thinking and problem-solving skills, complete *Self-Assessment 9.2.*

BEST PRACTICES
Strategies for Improving Students' Problem Solving

1. *Give students extensive opportunities to solve real-world problems.* Make this a part of your teaching. Develop problems that are relevant to your students' lives. Such real-world problems are often referred to as "authentic," in contrast to textbook problems that too often do not have much meaning for students.

2. *Monitor students' effective and ineffective problem-solving strategies.* Keep the four problem-solving steps in mind when you give students opportunities to solve problems. Also keep in mind such obstacles to good problem solving as becoming fixated, harboring biases, not being motivated, and not persisting. Next, Lawren Giles, who teaches at Baechtel Grove Middle School in Willits, California, describes the different strategies she encourages students to use.

THROUGH THE EYES OF TEACHERS
A Toolbox of Strategies

In teaching math, I use such problem-solving strategies as working backward, making a similar but simpler problem, drawing a diagram, making a table, and looking for patterns. We talk about what strategies make the most sense with different types of problems. When students successfully solve a problem, we look to see what methods were used, often finding more than one. I talk about multiple strategies in terms of carpenters having more than one kind of hammer in their toolboxes.

3. *Involve parents in children's problem solving.* A program of parental involvement has been developed at the University of California at Berkeley (Schauble & others, 1996). It is called Family Math (Matematica Para la Familia, in Spanish) and helps parents experience math with their children in a positive, supportive way. In the program, Family Math classes are usually taught by grade levels (K–2, 3–5, and 6–8). Many of the math activities require teamwork and communication between parents and children, who come to better understand not only the math but also each other. Family Math programs have served more than 400,000 parents and children in the United States.

4. *Work with children and adolescents to improve their use of rules, knowledge, and strategies in solving problems.* Recognize that young children may know a rule that enables them to solve a problem but not use it, so you may need to encourage them to use the rules they know. Encourage children to build up their knowledge base and to improve their knowledge of effective strategies that will help them solve problems.

5. *Use technology effectively.* Be motivated to incorporate multimedia programs into your classroom. Such programs can significantly improve your students' thinking and problem-solving skills.

Review, Reflect, and Practice

3 Take a systematic approach to problem solving.

REVIEW
- What is problem solving? What are the main steps in problem solving?
- What are three obstacles to problem solving?
- What are some developmental changes in problem solving?
- What is problem-based learning? What is project-based learning?

REFLECT
- When you tackle a difficult problem, do you follow the four steps we described? What might you do to become a better model of a problem solver for your students?

PRAXIS™ PRACTICE

1. Which of the following is the best example of the use of a heuristic?
   a. Betina needs to compute the average of a series of numbers. First she determines their sum and then divides the sum by the number in the series.

Review, Reflect, and Practice

    b. Anders becomes separated from his mother at the store. He goes to a cashier and tells her that he is lost. The cashier takes him to the service counter and his mother is paged.

    c. Samarie needs to remember all five of the Great Lakes. He uses the acronym HOMES.

    d. Marjorie needs to know how much carpet she needs to cover the floor of her room. She uses the formula for the area of a rectangle and converts square feet to square yards.

2. Which of the following is the best example of functional fixedness?

    a. Zack needs to screw in a screw, but he has no screwdriver. He has some change in his pocket, but he does not try to use a dime instead.

    b. Xavier continues to use the strategy of adding a number multiple times rather than learning his multiplication facts.

    c. Maria uses the formula for the area of a rectangle when solving a problem requiring her to find the area of a triangle.

    d. Sol is lost in the woods. He remembers his mother telling him that if he gets lost like this, he should "hug a tree." He stays in one spot and within 30 minutes his family finds him.

3. Jackson is 16 years old and is much better at problem solving than when he was younger. Which of the following is most likely to explain his improved problem solving as a teenager?

    a. His hormones are settling down better since he is no longer in puberty.

    b. He is better at monitoring the demands of a problem-solving task.

    c. He is more stimulus-driven, and that helps him to sort through more stimuli when he is given a problem to solve.

    d. He uses a minimum number of strategies that he knows well.

4. Which of the following is the best example of problem-based learning?

    a. Ms. Christian's science students use a shoe box to protect a raw egg from breaking when dropped off the school roof.

    b. Ms. Kohler's students solve word problems to help them see the application of math facts to everyday life.

    c. Ms. Kringle's students solve a series of addition and multiplication problems of increasing difficulty.

    d. Ms. Randall's students answer the questions at the end of the chapter in their history book.

Please see the answer key at the end of the book.

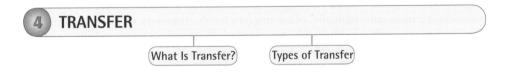

4 **TRANSFER**

What Is Transfer?   Types of Transfer

An important complex cognitive goal is for students to be able to apply what they learn in one situation to new situations (Schwartz, Varma, & Martin, 2008; Vosniadou, 2007). An important goal of schooling is that students learn things that they can apply outside the classroom. Schools are not functioning effectively if students do well on tests in language arts but can't write a competent letter as part of a job application. Schools also are not effectively educating students if the students do well on math tests in the classroom but can't solve arithmetic problems on a job.

"I don't get it! They make us learn reading, writing and arithmetic to prepare us for a world of videotapes, computer terminals and calculators!"

Harley Schwadron from *Phi Delta Kappan.* Reprinted by permission of Harley Schwadron.

transfer Applying previous experiences and knowledge to learning or problem solving in a new situation.

near transfer The transfer of learning to a situation that is similar to the one in which the initial learning took place.

far transfer The transfer of learning to a situation that is very different from the one in which the initial learning took place.

low-road transfer The automatic, often unconscious, transfer of learning to another situation.

high-road transfer The transfer of learning from one situation to another that is conscious and effortful.

What Is Transfer?

Transfer occurs when a person applies previous experiences and knowledge to learning or problem solving in a new situation (Mayer, 2008). Thus, if a student learns a concept in math and then uses this concept to solve a problem in science, transfer has occurred. It also has occurred if a student reads and studies about the concept of fairness in school and subsequently treats others more fairly outside the classroom.

Some experts argue that the best way to ensure transfer is to "teach for it" (Schwartz, Bransford, & Sears, 2005). They stress that transfer problems virtually are eliminated when teaching occurs in contexts where individuals need to perform. By preparing students so that the problems they are likely to encounter in real life are at worst near-transfer problems, the gap between students' present learning level and learning goals is significantly reduced (Bransford & others, 2005). Some other strategies that can improve transfer include giving two or more examples of a concept because one often is not enough; giving students representations or models, such as matrices, that help them structure a problem-solving activity; and encouraging students to generate more information themselves, which increases the likelihood they will remember what needs to be transferred (Sears, 2008). Yet another strategy to increase transfer is to give students well-structured contrasting cases and have them try to invent solutions for them before being given a lecture on the expert solution. The idea is that by first inventing a solution, students bring their prior knowledge to bear on the problem and make connections to the features of the problem. When they see the expert solution and how it relates the key features to each other, the students should be able to better understand how it works and thus transfer it better in the future.

Types of Transfer

What are some different types of transfer? Transfer can be characterized as (1) near or far and, (2) low-road or high-road (Schunk, 2008).

Near or Far Transfer   **Near transfer** occurs when the classroom learning situation is similar to the one in which the initial learning took place. For example, if a geometry teacher instructs students in how to logically prove a concept, and then tests the students on this logic in the same setting in which they learned the concept, near transfer is involved. Another example of near transfer occurs when students who have learned to type on a typewriter transfer this skill to typing on a computer keyboard.

Far transfer means the transfer of learning to a situation very different from the one in which the initial learning took place. For instance, if a student gets a part-time job in an architect's office and applies what he learned in geometry class to helping the architect analyze a spatial problem different from any problem the student encountered in geometry class, far transfer has occurred.

Low-Road or High-Road Transfer   Gabriel Salomon and David Perkins (1989) distinguished between low-road and high-road transfer. **Low-road transfer** occurs when previous learning automatically, often unconsciously, transfers to another situation. This occurs most often with highly practiced skills in which there is little need for reflective thinking. For example, when competent readers encounter new sentences in their native language, they read them automatically.

By contrast, **high-road transfer** is conscious and effortful. Students consciously establish connections between what they learned in a previous situation and the new situation they now face. High-road transfer is mindful—that is, students have to be aware of what they are doing and think about the connection between contexts. High-road transfer implies abstracting a general rule or principle from previous experience and then applying it to the new problem in the new context. For example, students might learn about the concept of subgoaling (setting intermediate goals) in math

DEVELOPMENTAL FOCUS 9.3

How Do You Help Your Students Transfer Classroom Knowledge to the Outside World?

Early Childhood

One way that we connect classroom knowledge with the outside world is to have instruments in class that make sounds similar to the music children hear when they are at home. For example, we have children from different cultures, and the music they and their families listen to features congas, steel drums, and guitars; we have these instruments in class and encourage children to play them.

—Valarie Gorham, *Kiddie Quarters, Inc.*

Elementary School: Grades K–5

When discussing immigration with my second-graders, I begin by asking them to think of a time when they moved to a new place, such as a new classroom or school, a new house or community, or a new country. I them ask them how they felt (for example, happy, sad, nervous) when they moved to this new place and why they felt this way. Then I ask them to take these thoughts and draw a picture of this time in their lives. This exercise helps students transfer information they have learned in class about immigration to similar experiences in their own lives.

—Elizabeth Frascella, *Clinton Elementary School*

Middle School: Grades 6–8

When teaching social studies, I often have my students read newspaper articles about a particular topic and then write their own newspaper article that responds to what they have read. This gets them more personally involved in the topic.

—Casey Maass, *Edison Middle School*

High School: Grades 9–12

High school students, especially juniors and seniors, are particularly interested in future careers. As a career and technical education teacher, I find that my students especially enjoy the unit on career awareness in which they identify personal skills and interests and identify careers in which those skills and interests would be best served.

—Sandy Swanson, *Menomonee Falls High School*

class. Several months later, one of the students thinks about how subgoaling might help him complete a lengthy homework assignment in history. This is high-road transfer.

Salomon and Perkins (1989) subdivide high-road transfer into forward-reaching and backward-reaching transfer. **Forward-reaching transfer** occurs when students think about how they can apply what they have learned to new situations (from their current situation, they look "forward" to apply information to a new situation ahead). For forward-reaching transfer to take place, students have to know something about the situations to which they will transfer learning. **Backward-reaching transfer** occurs when students look back to a previous ("old") situation for information that will help them solve a problem in a new context.

To better understand these two types of high-road transfer, imagine a student sitting in English class who has just learned some writing strategies for making sentences and paragraphs come alive and "sing." The student begins to reflect on how she could use those strategies to engage readers next year, when she plans to become a writer for the school newspaper. That is forward-reaching transfer. Now consider a student who is at his first day on the job as editor of the school newspaper. He is trying to figure out how to construct the layout of the pages. He reflects for a few

forward-reaching transfer Occurs when the individual looks to apply learned information to a future situation.

backward-reaching transfer Occurs when the individual looks back to a previous situation for information to solve a problem in a new context.

DIVERSITY AND EDUCATION
Transfer and Cultural Practices

Prior knowledge includes the kind of knowledge that learners acquire through cultural experiences, such as those involving ethnicity, socioeconomic status, and gender (National Research Council, 1999). In some cases, this cultural knowledge can support children's learning and facilitate transfer, but in others it may interfere (Cole, 2006; Greenfield & others, 2006).

For children from some cultural backgrounds, there is a minimal fit or transfer between what they have learned in their home communities and what is required or taught by the school. For example, consider the language skill of storytelling. Euro-American children use a linear style that more closely approximates the linear expository style of writing and speaking taught in most schools (Lee & Slaughter-Defoe, 1995). This may involve recounting a series of events in a rigidly chronological sequence. By contrast, in some ethnic groups—such as Asian Pacific Island or Native American—a nonlinear, holistic/circular style is more common in telling a story, and Euro-American teachers may consider their discourse to be disorganized (Clark, 1993). Also, in African American children, a nonlinear, topic-associative storytelling approach is common (Michaels, 1986).

Methods of argumentation in support of certain beliefs also differ across cultures. Chinese speakers prefer to present supporting evidence first, leading up to a major point or claim (in contrast to a topic sentence followed by supporting details). Non-Chinese listeners sometimes judge this style as "beating around the bush" (Tsang, 1989).

Rather than perceiving such variations in communication styles as being chaotic or as necessarily inferior to Euro-American styles, teachers need to be sensitive to them and aware of cultural differences. This is especially important in the early elementary school grades, when students are making the transition from the home environment to the school environment.

moments and thinks about some geography and geometry classes he has previously taken. He draws on those past experiences for insights into constructing the layout of the student newspaper. That is backward-reaching transfer.

Cultural practices may be involved in how easy or difficult transfer is. The *Diversity and Education* interlude explores this topic.

BEST PRACTICES
Strategies for Helping Students Transfer Information

1. *Think about what your students need for success in life.*
   We don't want students to finish high school with a huge data bank of content knowledge but no idea how to apply it to the real world. One strategy for thinking about what students need to know is to use the "working-backward" problem-solving strategy we discussed earlier in this chapter. For example, what do employers want high school and college graduates to be able to do? In a national survey of employers of college students, the three skills that employers most wanted graduates

   to have were (1) oral communication skills, (2) interpersonal skills, and (3) teamwork skills (Collins, 1996). Thus, the three most desired skills for students to have all involved communication. The employers also wanted students to be proficient in their field, have leadership abilities, have analytical skills, be flexible, and be able to work with computers. By thinking about and practicing the competencies that your students will need in the future and working with them to improve these skills, you will be guiding them for positive transfer.

(continued)

BEST PRACTICES
Strategies for Helping Students Transfer Information

2. *Give students many opportunities for real-world learning.* Too often, learning in schools has been artificial, with little consideration for transfer beyond the classroom or textbook. This will be less true for your students if you give them as many real-world problem-solving and thinking challenges as possible. In general, the more similar two situations are, the easier it will be for students to transfer information learned in one to the other. You can bring the real world into your classroom by inviting people from varying walks of life to come and talk with your students. Or you can take your students to the real world by incorporating visits to museums, businesses, colleges, and so on in the curriculum. Such learning opportunities should increase transfer. Next, we describe how Chris Laster, an outstanding teacher, instructs students in ways that help them transfer what they learn to the world outside the classroom.

THROUGH THE EYES OF TEACHERS
Bringing Science Alive and Connecting Students to the Community

Chris Laster's students say that he brings science alive. Among Laster's innovative real-world teaching strategies that help students transfer their knowledge and understanding beyond the classroom are the following:

1. *Science Blasters.* Students write, direct, and produce short videos for the school's closed-circuit TV station.
2. *Sci-Tech Safari.* Over the summer, students get hands-on experience on field trips to intriguing places such as the Okefenokee Swamp.
3. *Intrepid.* Students engage in vigorous training to prepare for a simulated 27-hour space mission aboard a realistic-looking space shuttle built by Laster and other teachers with parts from local businesses and a nearby air force base. (Copeland, 2003)

---

3. *Root concepts in applications.* The more you attempt to pour information into students' minds, the less likely it is that transfer will occur. When you present a concept, also define it (or get students to help you define it), and then ask students to generate examples. Challenge them to apply the concept to their personal lives or to other contexts.

4. *Teach for depth of understanding and meaning.* Teaching for understanding and meaning transfers more than does teaching for the retention of facts. And students' understanding improves when they actively construct meaning and try to make sense out of material.

Chris Laster working with a student on the flight deck of the space shuttle that Laster and other teachers built.

5. *Use prompts to encourage students to engage in self-explanation.* Researchers have found that generating explanations for oneself increases transfer (Chi, 2000; Siegler, 2002). For example, a recent study revealed that encouraging third- to fifth-grade students engaging in math problem-solving exercises to explain how they arrived at their answers was linked with improved transfer to new types of math problems (Rittle-Johnson, 2006).

6. *Teach strategies that will generalize.* Transfer involves not only skills and knowledge but also strategies (Schunk, 2008). Too often students learn strategies but don't understand how to apply them in other contexts. They might not understand that the strategy is appropriate for other situations, might not know how to modify it for use in another context, or might not have the opportunity to apply it (Pressley, 2007).

One model for teaching strategies that will generalize was developed by Gary Phye (1990; Phye & Sanders, 1994). He described three phases for improving transfer. In an initial acquisition phase, students are given information about the importance of the strategy and how to use it as well as opportunities to rehearse and practice using it. In the second phase, called retention, students get more practice in using the strategy, and their recall of how to use the strategy is checked out. In the third phase, transfer, students are given new problems to solve. These problems require them to use the same strategy, but on the surface the new problems appear to be different. Phye also emphasizes that motivation is an important aspect of transfer. He recommends that teachers increase students' motivation for transfer by showing them examples of how to use knowledge in their real lives.

Review, Reflect, and Practice

(4) Define transfer and explain how to enhance it as a teacher.

REVIEW

- What is transfer? Why should teachers think about it?
- What are some different types of transfer?

REFLECT

- Are there experiences from your own formal education that don't seem to transfer to outside of school? What do you think is going on in such situations?

PRAXIS™ PRACTICE

1. Which of the following is *not* an example of transfer?
   a. Maria reads a novel written in the eighteenth century and uses the information she gleans about marriage customs to answer a question in history class.
   b. Frank studies hard and learns an algorithm in math class.
   c. Danielle learns about endangered amphibians in science class and uses the information to research a science-fair project.
   d. Emma learns to use a dictionary in language-arts class and uses it to look up a social studies term.

2. Which of the following is the best example of far transfer?
   a. Cory uses the techniques she was taught in statistics class to analyze the data for a research project.
   b. Debbie drives her sister's car with little thought because of her experience driving her own car.
   c. Jason uses the trouble-shooting process that he was taught with regard to computers to successfully diagnose the problem with his car.
   d. Mike is able to read the Spanish word for television (televisión) because it looks like the English word.

Please see the answer key at the end of the book.

CRACK THE CASE
The Case of the Statistics Test

Cassandra has a test in her math class this Friday. She has spent the last several evenings studying the statistical formulas for measures of central tendency and variability, as she knows they will be covered on the test. To do this she has quizzed herself repeatedly. In the beginning, she got them confused, but after repeated tries, she can now recite the formulas for each without fail. She is certain that she will have no problems on the test.

When she receives her test on Friday, the first thing she does is write down all of the formulas before she can forget them, certain that will be all she will need to do well on the exam. After writing down the formulas, she begins reading the test. The first question gives a list of scores and asks for the mean, median, mode, variance, and standard deviation.

Cassandra anxiously looks at her list of formulas. She knows which formula goes with which measure—for instance, she knows that the formula for the mean is $\Sigma x/n$. The problem is that she doesn't know what Σx means. She is reasonably sure that "/n" means she is to divide by n, but what is n? When looking at the rest of the formulas, she realizes that she has similar problems. She stares at the test in dismay. After all that studying and careful memorization, she can't complete a single problem on the test.

1. What are the issues in this case?
2. What went wrong for Cassandra?
3. What should she do differently if she wants to do better on her next test?
4. If you were the teacher of Cassandra's class, how would you help your students to prepare for this type of test?
5. Which of the following strategies is most likely to help Cassandra on her next statistics test?
   a. Concentrate on learning only one formula at a time.
   b. Forget about memorizing the formulas.
   c. Learn the definitions of *mean, median, mode, variance,* and *standard deviation.*
   d. Work practice problems of each type.
6. Which of the following teaching strategies would be most likely to help students to do well on this type of test?
   a. Make certain that students understand what the formulas mean by working many example problems in class.
   b. Quiz students on the definitions of *mean, median, mode, variance,* and *standard deviation.*
   c. Quiz students on the formulas.
   d. Teach students a mnemonic device to help them remember the formulas.

Reach Your Learning Goals
Complex Cognitive Processes

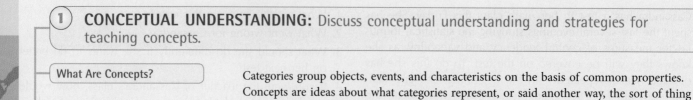

(1) CONCEPTUAL UNDERSTANDING: Discuss conceptual understanding and strategies for teaching concepts.

What Are Concepts?	Categories group objects, events, and characteristics on the basis of common properties. Concepts are ideas about what categories represent, or said another way, the sort of thing we think category members are. Concepts also improve memory, communication, and time use.
Promoting Concept Formation	In teaching concept formation to children, it is helpful to discuss with them the key features of concepts, definitions and examples of concepts (using the rule-example strategy), hierarchical categorization and concept maps, hypothesis testing, and prototype matching.

(2) THINKING: Describe several types of thinking and ways that teachers can foster them.

What Is Thinking?	Thinking involves manipulating and transforming information in memory. Types of thinking include forming concepts, reasoning, thinking critically, making decisions, thinking creatively, and solving problems.
Reasoning	Inductive reasoning involves reasoning from the specific to the general. Analogies draw on inductive reasoning. Deductive reasoning is reasoning from the general to the specific. Both inductive and deductive reasoning improve during adolescence.
Critical Thinking	Critical thinking involves thinking reflectively and productively and evaluating evidence. Mindfulness is a concept that reflects critical thinking. Brooks and Brooks argue that too few schools teach students to think critically and deeply. They stress that too often schools give students a correct answer instead of encouraging them to expand their thinking by coming up with new ideas.
Decision Making	Decision making is thinking that involves evaluating alternatives and making choices among them. One type of decision making involves weighing the costs and benefits of various outcomes. Numerous biases (confirmation bias, belief perseverance, overconfidence bias, and hindsight bias) can interfere with good decision making.
Creative Thinking	Creativity is the ability to think about something in novel and interesting ways and come up with unique solutions to problems. Guilford distinguished between convergent thinking (which produces one correct answer and is characteristic of the type of thinking required on conventional intelligence tests) and divergent thinking (which produces many answers to the same question and is characteristic of creativity). Although most creative students are quite intelligent, the reverse is not necessarily true. The creative process often involves five steps, although they don't always follow the same sequence. Here are some ways teachers can foster creativity in students: encourage creative thinking on a group and individual basis, provide environments that stimulate creativity, don't overcontrol students, encourage internal motivation, foster flexible thinking, build students' self-confidence, encourage students to take risks, guide students to be persistent and delay gratification, and introduce students to creative people.

3 PROBLEM SOLVING: Take a systematic approach to problem solving.

Steps in Problem Solving

Problem solving involves finding an appropriate way to attain a goal. Four steps in problem solving are (1) finding and framing problems; (2) developing good problem-solving strategies (such as using subgoaling, heuristics, algorithms, and means-end analysis); (3) evaluating solutions; and (4) rethinking and redefining problems and solutions over time.

Obstacles to Solving Problems

Obstacles to solving problems include fixedness (functional fixedness and mental set), lack of motivation and persistence, and not controlling one's emotions.

Developmental Changes

Developmental changes in problem solving occur. Even young children begin to use rules to solve problems, including their failure to enact rules they know and their poor planning skills. Accumulated knowledge and effectively using strategies improve older children's and adolescents' problem-solving ability.

Problem–Based Learning and Project–Based Learning

Problem-based learning emphasizes solving authentic problems like those that occur in daily life. In project-based learning, students work on real, meaningful problems and create tangible products.

4 TRANSFER: Define transfer and explain how to enhance it as a teacher.

What Is Transfer?

Transfer occurs when a person applies previous experiences and knowledge to learning or problem solving in a new situation. Students especially benefit when they can apply what they learn in the classroom to situations in their lives outside of the classroom.

Types of Transfer

Types of transfer include near and far and low-road and high-road. Near transfer occurs when situations are similar; far transfer occurs when situations are very different. Low-road transfer occurs when previous learning automatically transfers to another situation. High-road transfer is conscious and effortful. High-road transfer can be subdivided into forward-reaching and backward-reaching transfer.

 KEY TERMS

PORTFOLIO ACTIVITIES

Now that you have a good understanding of this chapter, complete these exercises to expand your thinking.

Independent Reflection

Evaluate Your Decision-Making Skills. Reflect on the ways that you make decisions. Are you able to make good-quality decisions regardless of opposition from others? Discuss to what extent your decisions are influenced by confirmation bias, belief perseverance, overconfidence bias, and hindsight bias. What can you do to strengthen your decision-making skills? (INTASC: Principles 4, 9)

Collaborative Work

Create a Problem-Based Learning Project. In the discussion of problem-based learning, the text describes *Jasper* series prob-

lem-solving adventures in math. Thinking creatively, get together with three or four other students in the class and devise a problem-solving adventure in a subject area other than math, such as science, social science, or literature. Write it down. (INTASC: Principles 1, 4)

Research/Field Experience

Creativity Research. Read work by one of the leading researchers in the field of creativity, such as Teresa Amabile or Mark Runco. What are the key findings about creativity discussed in the research? To what extent can this research be implemented in the classroom? (INTASC: Principles 4, 9)

Go to the Online Learning Center for downloadable portfolio templates.

 TAKING IT TO THE NET

- Describe the characteristics of a person who is an effective problem solver. How does open-ended problem solving lead to knowledge and skills that are transferable? Why is the transfer of knowledge so critical to our changing and increasingly complex society? http://www.nwrel.org/msec/nwteacher/spring2000/open.html

- Implementing critical-thinking activities in the classroom can help students take charge of their own learning and take responsibility for their own behavior. Select an online lesson plan (www.lessonplanspage.com), and "remodel" it as a critical-thinking activity. Identify elements of the remodeled lesson

that will develop and reinforce students' critical-thinking skills. www.criticalthinking.org/resources/articles/#Teaching

- Evaluate an online lesson plan for its creative value. Discuss aspects of the lesson that foster students' creative and divergent thinking. What role would you play in supporting students' creativity? How would your classroom environment support creative thinking? Explain how you think the lesson could be improved to increase its creative value. www.artsedge.kennedy-center.org/teach/les.cfm

Connect to the Online Learning Center to explore possible answers.

 STUDY, PRACTICE, AND SUCCEED

Visit www.mhhe.com/santedu4e to review the chapter with self-grading quizzes and self-assessments, to apply the chapter material to two more Crack the Case studies, and for suggested activities to develop your teaching portfolio.

CHAPTER 10

Social Constructivist Approaches

The human being is by nature a social animal.

—Aristotle
Greek Philosopher, 4th Century B.C.

Chapter Outline

Learning Goals

Social Constructivist Approaches to Teaching

Social Constructivism in the Broader Constructivist Context
Situated Cognition

1 Compare the social constructivist approach with other constructivist approaches.

Teachers and Peers as Joint Contributors to Students' Learning

Scaffolding
Cognitive Apprenticeship
Tutoring
Cooperative Learning

2 Explain how teachers and peers can jointly contribute to children's learning.

Structuring Small-Group Work

Composing the Group
Team-Building Skills
Structuring Small-Group Interaction

3 Discuss effective decisions in structuring small-group work.

Social Constructivist Programs

Fostering a Community of Learners
Schools for Thought

4 Describe two social constructivist programs.

TEACHING STORIES   Chuck Rawls

Chuck Rawls teaches language arts at Appling Middle School in Macon, Georgia. He provides this teaching story about peer tutoring, a social constructivist approach to instruction:

I was tricked into trying something different my first year of teaching. It was peer teaching in the guise of a school-wide activity known as "Switch Day." This consists of having selected students switch places with members of the faculty and staff. Each student who wants to switch is required to choose a faculty or staff member and then write an essay explaining why he or she wants to switch with that particular person. To my surprise, Chris wrote a very good essay and was selected to switch with me.

It worked wonderfully. Chris delivered the lesson very professionally, and the students were engaged because it was something new and different. It was a riot to watch because Chris, both intentionally and unintentionally, used many of my pet phrases and mannerisms. He really did know his stuff, though, and demonstrated this as he helped students with their seatwork.

As the saying goes, "I didn't know he had it in him." Chris became my resident expert on subject-verb agreement, as that was the topic of the lesson and the students remembered what he taught them.

I learned two lessons that day: (1) don't be afraid to try something different, and (2) peer tutoring works. However, it has to be the right student teaching the right material in the right setting.

Preview

Children do some of their thinking by themselves, but because we are social beings, as Chuck Rawls' teaching story indicates, effective learning can also take place when children collaborate. Because of our American emphasis on the individual rather than the group, collaborative thinking only recently emerged as an important theme in American education. This chapter focuses on the collaborative thinking advocated by social constructivist approaches.

1   SOCIAL CONSTRUCTIVIST APPROACHES TO TEACHING

Social Constructivism in the Broader Constructivist Context

Situated Cognition

The social constructivist approaches involve a number of innovations in classroom learning. Before we study these innovations, let us first consolidate our knowledge about various constructivist perspectives and where the social constructivist approaches fit in the overall constructivist framework.

Social Constructivism in the Broader Constructivist Context

Recall from Chapter 1 that *constructivism* emphasizes how individuals actively construct knowledge and understanding. Early in this book (Chapter 2, "Cognitive and Language Development"), we described Piaget's and Vygotsky's theories of development, both of which are constructivist. In Chapters 8 and 9, our main focus was on the information-processing approaches to learning, which included some ideas about

What is the social constructivist approach to education?

how the individual child uses information-processing skills to think in constructivist ways. According to all of these constructivist approaches, students author their own knowledge.

In general, a **social constructivist approach** emphasizes the social contexts of learning and that knowledge is mutually built and constructed (Bodrova & Leong, 2007; Gauvain, 2008). Involvement with others creates opportunities for students to evaluate and refine their understanding as they are exposed to the thinking of others and as they participate in creating shared understanding (Gauvain & Perez, 2007). In this way, experiences in social contexts provide an important mechanism for the development of students' thinking (Johnson & Johnson, 2009).

Vygotsky's social constructivist theory is especially relevant for the current chapter. Vygotsky's model is a social child embedded in a sociohistorical context. Moving from Piaget to Vygotsky, the conceptual shift is from the individual to collaboration, social interaction, and sociocultural activity (Cole & Gajdamaschko, 2007; Gredler, 2008). In Piaget's cognitive constructivist approach, students construct knowledge by transforming, organizing, and reorganizing previous knowledge and information. Vygotsky's social constructivist approach emphasizes that students construct knowledge through social interactions with others. The content of this knowledge is influenced by the culture in which the student lives, which includes language, beliefs, and skills (Holzman, 2009).

Piaget emphasized that teachers should provide support for students to explore and develop understanding. Vygotsky emphasized that teachers should create many opportunities for students to learn by coconstructing knowledge along with the teacher and with peers (Gauvain, 2008; Gredler, 2008). In both Piaget's and Vygotsky's models, teachers serve as facilitators and guides rather than directors and molders of children's learning.

Notice that we speak about emphasis rather than a clear-cut distinction. Often there are not clear-cut distinctions between social constructivist and other constructivist approaches. For example, when teachers serve as guides for students in discovering knowledge, there are social dimensions to the construction. And the same is true for processing information. If a teacher creates a brainstorming session for students to come up with good memory strategies, social interaction is clearly involved.

Some sociocultural approaches, such as Vygotsky's, emphasize the importance of culture in learning—for example, culture can determine what skills are important (such as computer skills, communication skills, teamwork skills) (Gredler & Shields,

social constructivist approach
Approach that emphasizes the social contexts of learning and that knowledge is mutually built and constructed.

2007). Other approaches focus more exclusively on the immediate social circumstances of the classroom, as when students collaborate to solve a problem.

In one study of collaborative learning, pairs of children from two U.S. public schools worked together (Matusov, Bell, & Rogoff, 2001). One member of each pair was from a traditional school that provided only occasional opportunities for children to work together as they learned. The other member of the pair was from a school that emphasized collaboration throughout the school day. The children with the collaborative schooling background more often built on the partner's ideas in a collaborative way than the children with traditional schooling experience. The traditional school children predominately used a "quizzing" form of guidance based on asking known-answer questions and withholding information to test the partner's understanding. Researchers also have found that collaborative learning often works best in classrooms with well-specified learning goals (Gabriele & Montecinos, 2001).

An increasing number of efforts are being made to connect collaborative learning and technology in the classroom (Rummel & Spada, 2005; Yang & Liu, 2005). For example, one program, Computer-Supported Collaborative Learning (CSCL), attempts to increase peer interaction and joint construction of knowledge through technology (Kapur & others, 2008; Solimeno & others, 2008).

Situated Cognition

Situated cognition is an important assumption in the social constructivist approaches. It refers to the idea that thinking is located (situated) in social and physical contexts, not within an individual's mind. In other words, knowledge is embedded in, and connected to, the context in which the knowledge developed (Gauvain, 2008; Greeno, 2006; Roth, 2007). If this is so, it makes sense to create learning situations that are as close to real-world circumstances as possible. For example, to expand students' knowledge and understanding of volcanos, some students are placed in the role of scientists studying an active volcano, while other students are given the task of reporting what to expect to an emergency evacuation team (PSU, 2006). Using Internet resources, the "scientist" students examine news stories about active volcanos; the "evacuation team" students search for information about the impact that volcanos have on inhabitants and how they can be removed from the danger of an erupting volcano. Our discussion of problem-based learning and project-based learning in Chapter 9 demonstrated a similar emphasis on situated cognition.

Review, Reflect, and Practice

(1) Compare the social constructivist approach with other constructivist approaches.

REVIEW
- Although they overlap, what is the basic difference between Piaget's and Vygotsky's approach?
- What is situated cognition?

REFLECT
- From what you learned in Chapter 2, do you think you would feel more at home with Piaget or Vygotsky? How might that be reflected in your own approach to classroom teaching?

PRAXIS™ PRACTICE

1. Which of the following is an example of a social constructivist approach?
   a. In Mr. Hanratty's class, students work together on social studies projects.
   b. In Ms. Baker's class, students work independently to discover basic principles of science.

situated cognition The idea that thinking is located (situated) in social and physical contexts, not within an individual's mind.

Review, Reflect, and Practice

    c. In Ms. Rinosa's class, students are assigned one hour of homework a day.

    d. In Mr. Francois' class, students engage in silent reading of their self-chosen books.

2. Which of the following best reflects situated cognition?

    a. Students read a book about the role of a justice of the peace in the legal system.

    b. The teacher arranges for students to visit a local justice of the peace office, talk with the justice of the peace, and observe a justice of the peace session.

    c. Students are given an assignment to collaborate with each other and write a report on the role of the justice of the peace in the legal system.

    d. The teacher assigns students the task of searching for articles about what a justice of the peace does and to do an oral report on what they have found.

Please see the answer key at the end of the book.

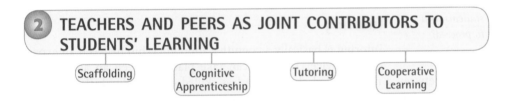

2 TEACHERS AND PEERS AS JOINT CONTRIBUTORS TO STUDENTS' LEARNING

Scaffolding   Cognitive Apprenticeship   Tutoring   Cooperative Learning

Social constructivist approaches emphasize that teachers and peers can contribute to students' learning. Four tools for making this happen are scaffolding, cognitive apprenticeship, tutoring, and cooperative learning.

Scaffolding

In Chapter 2, we described *scaffolding* as the technique of changing the level of support over the course of a teaching session; a more-skilled person (teacher or more-advanced peer of the child) adjusts the amount of guidance to fit the student's current performance. When the task the student is learning is new, the teacher might use direct instruction. As the student's competence increases, the teacher provides less guidance (Pawan, 2008). Think of scaffolding in learning like the scaffolding used to build a bridge. The scaffolding provides support when needed, but it is gradually removed as the bridge approaches completion. Researchers have found that when teachers and peers use scaffolding in collaborative learning, students' learning benefits (Belland, Glazewski, & Richardson, 2008; Perry, Turner, & Meyer, 2006).

Look for situations to use scaffolding in the classroom (John-Steiner, 2007; Wertsch, 2007). For instance, good tutoring involves scaffolding, as we will see shortly. Also, scaffolding is increasingly used when technology is involved in learning (Fund, 2007; Kapur & others, 2008; Prinsen, Volman, & Terwei, 2007; Solimeno & others, 2008). Work on giving just the right amount of assistance. Don't do for students what they can do for themselves. But do monitor their efforts and give them needed support and assistance.

Cognitive Apprenticeship

Developmental psychologist Barbara Rogoff (1990, 2003; Rogoff & others, 2007) stresses that an important tool of education is **cognitive apprenticeship**, a technique in which an expert stretches and supports a novice's understanding and use of a culture's skills. The term *apprenticeship* underscores the importance of active learning and highlights

cognitive apprenticeship A relationship in which an expert stretches and supports a novice's understanding and use of a culture's skills.

When teachers think of their relationship with students as a cognitive apprenticeship, how is teaching likely to proceed?

the situated nature of learning. In a cognitive apprenticeship, teachers often model strategies for students. Then, teachers or more-skilled peers support students' efforts at doing the task. Finally, they encourage students to continue their work independently.

To illustrate the importance of cognitive apprenticeships in learning, Rogoff describes the contrasting experiences of students from middle-income and poverty backgrounds. Many middle- and upper-income American parents involve their children in cognitive apprenticeships long before they go to kindergarten or elementary school. They read picture books with young children and bathe their children in verbal communication. In contrast, American parents living in poverty are less likely to engage their children in a cognitive apprenticeship that involves books, extensive verbal communication, and scaffolding (Heath, 1989).

Cognitive apprenticeships are important in the classroom (Charney & others, 2007; Vosniadou, 2007). Researchers have found that students' learning benefits from teachers who think of their relationship with a student as a cognitive apprenticeship, using scaffolding and guided participation to help the student learn (Grindstaff & Richmond, 2008).

Tutoring

Tutoring is basically a cognitive apprenticeship between an expert and a novice. Tutoring can take place between an adult and a child or between a more-skilled child and a less-skilled child. Individual tutoring is an effective strategy that benefits many students, especially those who are not doing well in a subject (Chi, Mauguerite, & Hausmann, 2008; Slavin & others, 2009).

Classroom Aides, Volunteers, and Mentors It is frustrating to find that some students need more individual help than you as their teacher can give them and still meet the needs of the class as a whole. Classroom aides, volunteers, and mentors can help reduce some of this frustration. Monitor and evaluate your class for students you believe could benefit from one-on-one tutoring. Scour the community for individuals with skills in the areas in which these students need more individual attention than you are able to give. Some parents, college students, and retirees might be interested in filling your classroom tutoring needs.

Several individual tutoring programs have been developed. The Reading Recovery program offers daily half-hour one-on-one tutorial sessions for students who are having difficulty learning to read after one year of formal instruction (Sensenbaugh, 1995). Evaluations of the Reading Recovery program have found that students who participated in the program in the first grade were still performing better in reading in third grade than their counterparts who did not participate (Sensenbaugh, 1995). However, some researchers have found that the key to whether a program like Reading Recovery is effective is the extent to which phonological-processing skills are included (Chapman, Tunmer, & Prochnow, 2001). A recent analysis with strict criteria for research success revealed that Reading Recovery has positive effects on students' alphabet skills and general reading achievement, and also has potentially positive outcomes for reading fluency and comprehension (What Works Clearinghouse, 2007a).

Another program that uses tutoring is Success for All (SFA). Developed by Robert Slavin and his colleagues (1996; Slavin, Daniels, & Madden, 2005; Slavin & others, 2009), this comprehensive program includes the following:

- A systematic reading program that emphasizes phonics, vocabulary development, and story telling and retelling in small groups

- A daily 90-minute reading period with students in the first through third grades being regrouped into homogeneous cross-age ability groups
- One-on-one tutoring in reading by specially trained certified teachers who work individually with students who are reading below grade level
- Assessments every eight weeks to determine students' reading progress, adjust reading group placement, and assign tutoring if needed
- Professional development for teachers and tutors, which includes three days of in-service training and guidelines at the beginning of the school year, and follow-up training throughout the year
- A family support team designed to provide parenting education and support family involvement in the school

Participants in the Success for All middle school program. *What is the nature of the Success for All program?*

First implemented during the 1987–1988 school year in five inner-city schools in Baltimore, Maryland, SFA has expanded to over 475 schools in 31 states. Some studies have found that students who have participated in the program have better reading skills and are less likely to be in special education classes than disadvantaged students who have not been involved in the program (Slavin & others, 2009; Weiler, 1998). A recent analysis with strict criteria for evidence of research support revealed that Success for All potentially has positive effects in general reading achievement but more mixed results in reading comprehension (What Works Clearinghouse, 2007b).

Mentors can play an important role in improving some students' learning. Usually viewed as older and wiser, mentors guide, teach, and support younger individuals, who are sometimes called *mentees* or *protégés* (Linley, 2009; Weingartner, 2009; Wilkins & Clift, 2007).

> The guidance is accomplished through demonstration, instruction, challenge, and encouragement on a more or less regular basis over an extended period of time. In the course of this process, the mentor and the young person develop a special bond of mutual commitment. In addition, the younger person's relationship to the mentor takes on an emotional character of respect, loyalty, and identification. (Hamilton & Hamilton, 2004, p. 396, based on a personal communication with ecological theorist Urie Bronfenbrenner)

The majority of mentoring programs are outside the school and include such organizations as Big Brothers and Big Sisters, the largest formal mentoring program in the United States, as well as Boys and Girls Clubs of America and YMCA and YWCA. Recently, schools have been the location of an increasing number of mentoring efforts, both for students and for beginning teachers who are mentored by experienced teachers (Dingus, 2008; Randolf & Johnson, 2008). The mentor comes to the school and works with the student, in many cases for an hour each week. Schools can be helpful in identifying students who might benefit from mentoring. A good strategy is to select not only high-risk, underachieving students for mentoring, but other students as well (DuBois & Karcher, 2006). Also, some mentoring relationships are more effective than others, and the matching of a student with a mentor requires careful selection and monitoring (Kilburg & Hancock, 2007; Spencer, 2007).

Peer Tutors   Fellow students also can be effective tutors (Roscoe & Chi, 2008; Slavin & others, 2009). In peer tutoring, one student teaches another. In *cross-age* *peer tutoring,* the peer is older. In *same-age peer tutoring,* the peer is a classmate. Cross-age peer tutoring usually works better than same-age peer tutoring. An older peer is more likely to be skilled than a same-age peer, and being tutored by a same-age classmate is more likely to embarrass a student and lead to negative social comparison.

Peer tutoring engages students in active learning and allows the classroom teacher to guide and monitor student learning as she or he moves around the classroom. Researchers have found that peer tutoring often benefits students' achievement (O'Donnell, 2006: Slavin & others, 2009). In some instances, the tutoring benefits the tutor as well as the tutee, especially when the older tutor is a low-achieving student. Teaching something to someone else is one of the best ways to learn, although researchers have found that tutees' learning benefits more than tutors' learning (Roscoe & Chi, 2008).

A recent study revealed that tutors learned most effectively when they engaged in *reflective knowledge-building,* in which they monitored their own behavior, generated inferences to correct misunderstandings, and elaborated on source materials (Roscoe & Chi, 2008). However, in this study, tutors more often were characterized by *knowledge-telling bias,* which was characterized by summarizing source materials with little elaboration. In most instances, reflective knowledge-building on the part of tutors most often occurred when tutees asked questions that included an inference or required an inferential answer.

In a study that won the American Educational Research Association's award for best research study, the effectiveness of a class-wide peer tutoring program in reading was evaluated for three learner types: low-achieving students with and without disabilities and average-achieving students (Fuchs & others, 1997). Twelve elementary and middle schools were randomly assigned to experimental (peer tutoring) and control (no peer tutoring) groups. The peer tutoring program was conducted in 35-minute sessions during regularly scheduled reading instruction three days a week. It lasted for 15 weeks. The training of peer tutors emphasized helping students get practice in reading aloud from narrative text, reviewing and sequencing information read, summarizing large amounts of reading material, stating main ideas, predicting and checking story outcomes, and other reading strategies. Pretreatment and post-treatment reading achievement data were collected. Irrespective of the type of learner, students in the peer tutoring classrooms showed greater reading progress over the 15 weeks than their counterparts who did not receive peer tutoring.

The peer tutoring program used in the study just described is called Peer-Assisted Learning Strategies (PALS). PALS was created by the John F. Kennedy Center and the Department of Special Education at Peabody College at Vanderbilt University. In PALS, teachers identify which children require help on specific skills and who the most appropriate children are to help other children learn those skills. Using this information, teachers pair children in the class so that partners work simultaneously and productively on different activities that address the problems they are experiencing. Pairs are changed regularly so that as students work on a variety of skills, all students have the opportunity of being "coaches" and "players."

PALS is a 25- to 35-minute activity that is used two to four times a week. Typically it creates thirteen to fifteen pairs in a classroom. It has been designed for use in the areas of reading and mathematics for kindergarten through sixth grade. It is not designed to replace existing curricula.

In PALS Math, students work on a sheet of problems in a skill area, such as adding, subtracting, number concepts, or charts and graphs. PALS Math involves pairing students as a coach and a player. The coach uses a sheet with a series of questions designed to guide the player and provides feedback to the player. Students then exchange papers and score each others' practice sheets. Students earn points for cooperating and constructing good explanations during coaching and for doing problems correctly during practice. PALS Math and PALS Reading are effective in

DEVELOPMENTAL FOCUS 10.1
How Do You Use Peer Tutors and Mentors in the Classroom?

Early Childhood

We often have children lead various activities in the classroom—such as "show and tell"—giving them the opportunity to learn from each other.

—Missy Dangler, *Suburban Hills School*

Elementary School: Grades K–5

I use peer tutors in a variety of ways with my second-graders: "Buddy Readers" pairs strong readers with struggling readers; "Resident Experts" gives students showing full understanding of new skills in math, science, and social studies the opportunity to work with students who need extra help in these areas. In "Ask Three, Before Me," students who finish a writing task are expected to confer with three other students about their work (and make revisions as suggested) before sharing with me.

—Elizabeth Frascella, *Clinton Elementary School*

Middle School: Grades 6–8

We first identify students who likely will be successful peer tutors and students who likely would benefit from having a tutor. We then have peer tutors go through a training session; without this training, tutoring is much less likely to be successful. Tutoring not only helps the student who needs extra help, but also benefits the tutor because one of the best ways to learn a concept is by teaching it to someone else.

—Mark Fodness, *Bemidji Middle School*

High School: Grades 9–12

Students in my food service class are mentors to first-graders at the elementary school next door. My students do reading activities, including acting out and making "Stone Soup" with the younger children. While these activities help the first-graders, it also reinforces important social skills for my high school students.

—Sandy Swanson, *Menomonee Falls High School*

developing students' mathematical and reading skills (Fuchs, Fuchs, & Burish, 2000; Mathes, Torgesen, & Allor, 2001).

The PALS program is highly effective with at-risk students, especially students in the early elementary grades, ethnic minority students, students in urban schools, and possibly low-income students (Rohrbeck & others, 2003). In one recent study, the reading comprehension of third- through sixth-grade native Spanish-speaking English language learners improved more when they were taught in a PALS format than in other reading instruction formats (Saenz, Fuchs, & Fuchs, 2005). A recent analysis involving strict criteria for evidence of research support revealed that PALS has potentially positive outcomes for reading achievement (What Works Clearinghouse, 2007c).

Two other peer tutoring programs are Reciprocal Peer Tutoring (RPT) and ClassWide Peer Tutoring (CWPT) (Ginsburg-Block, 2005). RPT was

Students Participating in the PALS program.

DIVERSITY AND EDUCATION
The Valued Youth Program

In 24 cities in the United States and Brazil, the Valued Youth program (now jointly sponsored by the Intercultural Development Research Association and Coca-Cola, and called the Coca-Cola Valued Youth program) gives secondary school students who are not achieving well or are at risk for school-related problems the responsibility of tutoring elementary school children (IDRA, 2008; Simons, Finlay, & Yang, 1991). The Valued Youth program began in 1984 and continues to expand today, with more than 450,000 students having participated in the program. The hope is that the tutoring experience will improve not only the achievement of the students being tutored but also the achievement of the tutors (Anderson, 2007). Over the course of its existence, less than 2 percent of students who participated in the Valued Youth program dropped out of school (IDRA, 2008).

In one school's Valued Youth program, four days a week participants walk or ride a bus to tutor for one class period at a nearby elementary school. Each tutor works with three children on subjects such as math or reading, and tutors work with the same children for the entire school year. On the fifth day of the week, the tutors work with their teacher at their own school, discussing tutoring skills, reflecting on how the week has gone, and brushing up on their own literacy skills. For their work, the tutors receive course credit and minimum-wage pay.

One of the Valued Youth program tutors said, "Tutoring makes me want to come to school because I have to come and teach the younger kids." He also said that he did not miss many days of school, as he used to, because when he had been absent the elementary school children always asked him where he was and told him that they missed him. He said that he really liked the kids he taught, and that if he had not been a tutor he probably would have dropped out of school already.

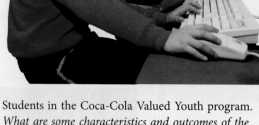

Students in the Coca-Cola Valued Youth program. *What are some characteristics and outcomes of the program?*

initially developed for use with low-achieving urban elementary school students and provides opportunities for students to alternate in tutor and tutee roles. CWPT includes tutor training, reciprocal teaching, and motivational strategies such as team competition (Struckman, 2005). A recent study using CWPT revealed that both team competition and team cooperation resulted in higher achievement by bilingual children; cooperative tutoring resulted in the highest achievement (Madrid, Canas, & Ortega-Medina, 2007). Another recent study found that over a three-year period CWPT was effective in improving middle school students' grades on weekly quizzes (Kamps & others, 2008).

The *Diversity and Education* interlude includes more information about the effectiveness of peer tutoring.

BEST PRACTICES
Strategies for Using Peer Tutoring

Here are some suggestions for how to use peer tutoring (Goodlad & Hirst, 1989; Jenkins & Jenkins, 1987):

1. *Use cross-age tutoring rather than same-age tutoring when possible.* Set aside specific times of the day for peer tutoring and communicate the learning assignment clearly and precisely to the peer tutor—for example, "Today from 9 to 9:30 I would like you to work with Jimmy on the following math problem-solving exercises: _____, _____, and _____."

THROUGH THE EYES OF TEACHERS
Cross-Age Peer Teaching at the Zoo

In Lincoln, Nebraska, several high school science teachers use the Folsum Zoo and Botanical Gardens as a context for guiding students' learning. The science classes are taught in two trailers at the zoo. The teachers emphasize the partnership of students, teachers, zoo, and community. One highlight of the program is the "Bug Bash," when the high school students teach fourth-grade students about insects.

2. *Let students participate in both tutor and tutee roles.* This helps students learn that they can both help and be helped. Pairing of best friends often is not a good strategy because they have trouble staying focused on the learning assignment. Next, you can read about how elementary school teacher Julie Curry in Macon, Georgia, uses cross-age peer interaction in reading instruction.

THROUGH THE EYES OF TEACHERS
Cross-Age Peer Interaction in Reading Instruction

Students with a learning disability in the area of reading often feel a lack of self-worth from years of struggling to read. When remediating a reading disability, it is important to address the emotional as well as the academic deficit. Working with younger peers has proven to be a successful strategy with my students who have a learning disability.

Once my students have mastered a critical skill, I encourage them to create a short student-made book covering the skills mastered (short vowel sounds, for example). Students have created beautiful, informative

Lincoln zoo crew: clockwise from back left, teachers Beth Briney, Amy Vanderslice, De Tonack, Sara LeRoy-Toren, and James Barstow.

books related to phonetic awareness skills, reading comprehension, and consonant/vowel blending.

Once students have completed their books, the books are presented to a small group and the project is celebrated. Students then read and discuss their book with a younger child, who views them as a hero. It's not embarrassing to make an alphabet book in the fourth grade if your audience is a kindergarten class. Student-made books are then placed on display in the media center.

3. *Don't let tutors give tests to tutees.* This can undermine cooperation between the students.

4. *Spend time training tutors.* For peer tutoring to be successful, you will have to spend some time training the tutors. To get peer tutors started off right, discuss competent peer tutoring strategies. Demonstrate how scaffolding works. Give the tutors clear, organized instructions and invite them to ask questions about their assignments. Divide the group of peer tutors into pairs and let them practice what you have just demonstrated. Let them alternately be tutor and tutee.

5. *Don't overuse peer tutoring.* It is easy to fall into the trap of using high-achieving students as peer tutors too often. Be sure that these students get ample opportunities to participate in challenging intellectual tasks themselves.

6. *Let parents know that their child will be involved in peer tutoring.* Explain to them the advantages of this learning strategy and invite them to visit the classroom to observe how the peer tutoring works.

Cooperative Learning

Cooperative learning occurs when students work in small groups to help each other learn. Cooperative learning groups vary in size, although four is a typical number of students. In some cases, cooperative learning is done in dyads (two students). When students are assigned to work in a cooperative group, the group usually stays together for weeks or months, but cooperative groups usually occupy only a portion of the student's school day or year. In a cooperative learning group, each student typically learns a part of a larger unit and then teaches that part to the group (Gillies, 2007; Stevens, 2008). When students teach something to others, they tend to learn it more deeply.

Research on Cooperative Learning   Researchers have found that cooperative learning can be an effective strategy for improving achievement, especially when two conditions are met (Slavin, 1995):

- *Group rewards are generated.* Some type of recognition or reward is given to the group so that the group members can sense that it is in their best interest to help each other learn.
- *Individuals are held accountable.* Some method of evaluating a student's individual contribution, such as an individual quiz or report, needs to be used. Without this individual accountability, some students might do some "social loafing" (let other students do their work), and some might be left out because others believe that they have little to contribute. When the conditions of group rewards and individual accountability are met, cooperative learning improves achievement across different grades and in tasks that range from basic skills to problem solving (Johnson & Johnson, 2005).

Motivation   Increased motivation to learn is common in cooperative groups (Blumenfeld, Kempler, & Krajcik, 2006). In one study, fifth- and sixth-grade Israeli students were given a choice of continuing to do schoolwork or going out to play (Sharan & Shaulov, 1990). Only when students were in cooperative groups were they likely to forgo going out to play. Positive peer interaction and positive feelings about making their own decisions were motivating factors behind students' choice to participate in the cooperative groups. In another study, high school students made greater gains and expressed more intrinsic motivation to learn algebraic concepts when they were in cooperative rather than individualistic learning contexts (Nichols & Miller, 1994).

Interdependence and Teaching One's Peers   Cooperative learning also promotes increased interdependence and connection with other students (Blumenfeld, Kempler, & Krajcik, 2006). In one study, fifth-graders were more likely to move to a correct strategy for solving decimal problems if their partners clearly explained their ideas and considered each other's proposals (Ellis, Klahr, & Siegler, 1994).

Types of Tasks in Which Cooperative Learning Works Best   Do some types of tasks work better in cooperative, collaborative efforts and others better on an individual basis? Researchers have found that cooperative learning implemented without rewards has little benefit on simple tasks such as rote learning, memorization, or basic mathematics but produces better results with more complex tasks (Sears, 2006).

Cooperative Learning Approaches   A number of cooperative learning approaches have been developed. They include STAD (Student-Teams-Achievement Divisions), the jigsaw classroom (I and II), learning together, group investigation, and cooperative scripting. To read about these approaches, see Figure 10.1.

Creating a Cooperative Community   The school community is made up of faculty, staff, students, parents, and people in the neighborhood. More broadly, the

cooperative learning Learning that occurs when students work in small groups to help each other learn.

STAD (Student-Teams-Achievement Divisions)

STAD involves team recognition and group responsibility for learning in mixed-ability groups (Slavin, 1995). Rewards are given to teams whose members improve the most over their past performances. Students are assigned to teams of four or five members. The teacher presents a lesson, usually over one or two class periods. Next, students study worksheets based on material presented by the teacher. Students monitor their team members' performance to ensure that all members have mastered their material.

Teams practice working on problems together and study together, but the members take quizzes individually. The resulting individual scores contribute to the team's overall score. An individual's

contribution to the team score is based on that individual's improvement, not on an absolute score, which motivates students to work hard because each contribution counts. In some STAD classrooms, a weekly class newsletter is published that recognizes both team and individual performances.

The STAD approach has been used in a variety of subjects (including math, reading, and social studies) and with students at different grade levels. It is most effective for learning situations that involve well-defined objectives or problems with specific answers or solutions. These include math computation, language use, geography skills, and science facts.

The Jigsaw Classroom

In Chapter 5, "Sociocultural Diversity," we described the jigsaw classroom, which involves having students from different cultural backgrounds cooperate by doing different parts of a project to reach a common goal. Here we elaborate on the concept.

Developed by Elliot Aronson and his colleagues (1978), *jigsaw I* is a cooperative learning approach in which six-member teams work on material that has been broken down into parts. Each team member is responsible for a part. Members of different teams who have studied the same part convene, discuss their part, and then return to their teams, where they take turns teaching their part to other team members.

Robert Slavin (1995) created *jigsaw II,* a modified version of *jigsaw I.* Whereas *jigsaw I* consists of teams of six, *jigsaw II* usually has teams of four or five. All team members study the entire lesson rather than one part, and individual scores are combined to form an overall team score, as in STAD. After they have studied the entire lesson, students become expert on one aspect of the lesson; then students with the same topics meet in expert groups to discuss them. Subsequently, they return to their teams and help other members of the team learn the material.

Learning Together

Created by David and Roger Johnson (1994), this approach has four components: (1) face-to-face interaction, (2) positive interdependence, (3) individual accountability, and (4) development of interpersonal group skills. Thus, in addition to Slavin's interest in achievement, the Johnsons' cooperative learning approach also

focuses on socioemotional development and group interaction. In learning together, students work in four- or five-member heterogeneous groups on tasks with an emphasis on discussion and team building (Johnson & Johnson, 2009).

Group Investigation

Developed by Shlomo Sharan (1990; Sharan & Sharan, 1992), this approach involves a combination of independent learning and group work in two- to six-member groups), as well as a group reward for individual achievement. The teacher chooses a problem for the class to study, but students decide what they want to study in exploring the problem. The work is divided among the

group's members, who work individually. Then the group gets together, integrating, summarizing, and presenting the findings as a group project. The teacher's role is to facilitate investigation and maintain cooperative effort. Students collaborate with the teacher to evaluate their effort. In Sharan's view, this is the way many real-world problems are solved in communities around the world.

Cooperative Scripting

Students work in reciprocal pairs, taking turns summarizing information and orally presenting it to each other (Dansereau, 1988; McDonald and others, 1985). One member of the pair presents the material. The other member listens, monitors the

presentation for any mistakes, and gives feedback. Then the partner becomes the teacher and presents the next set of material while the first member listens and evaluates it.

FIGURE 10.1 Cooperative Learning Approaches

school community also includes central administrators, college admissions officers, and future employers. To create an effective learning community, David and Roger Johnson (2002, pp. 144–146) conclude that cooperation and positive interdependence needs to occur at a number of different levels: the learning group of children within a classroom (which we just discussed), the classroom, between classrooms, school, school-parent, and school-neighborhood:

- *Class cooperation.* There are many ways to create cooperation and interdependence for the whole class. Class goals can be generated and class rewards given. This can be accomplished by adding bonus points to all class members' academic scores when all class members attain a goal "or by giving nonacademic rewards, such as extra free time, extra recess time, stickers, food, T-shirts, or a class party." Classroom cooperation can be promoted by "putting teams in charge of daily class cleanup, running a class bank or business, or engaging in other activities that benefit the class as a whole. Classroom interdependence may also be structured through dividing resources, such as having the class publish a newsletter in which each cooperative group contributes one article . . . one class was studying geography." The ceiling was turned into a large world map. "The class was divided into eight cooperative groups. Each group was assigned a geographical location on which to do a report. The class then planned an itinerary for a trip to visit all eight places. Yarn was used to mark their journey. As they arrived at each spot, the appropriate group presented its report" about the location.

- *Interclass cooperation.* An interdisciplinary team of teachers may organize their classes into a "neighborhood" or "school within a school" in which classes work together on joint projects.

- *School-wide cooperation.* Cooperation at the level of the entire school can be attained in a number of ways. "The school mission statement may articulate the mutual goals shared by all members of the school and be displayed on the school walls" and highlighted on a school Web page. "Teachers can work in a variety of cooperative teams . . . and faculty/staff can meet weekly in teaching teams and/or study groups. . . . Teachers may be assigned to task forces to plan and implement solutions to school-wide issues. . . . Finally, school interdependence may be highlighted in a variety of school-wide activities, such as the weekly student-produced school news broadcast, . . . all-school projects, and regular school assemblies."

- *School-parent cooperation.* Cooperation is promoted between the school and parents "by involving parents in establishing mutual goals and strategic plans to attain the goals, . . . in sharing resources to help the school achieve its goals," and in creating activities that improve the likelihood that parents will develop a positive attitude toward the school.

- *School-neighborhood cooperation.* If the school is embedded in a neighborhood, a positive interdependence between the school and the neighborhood can benefit both. The school's mission "can be supported by neighborhood merchants who provide resources and financing for various events. Classes can perform neighborhood service projects, such as cleaning up a park."

Evaluating Cooperative Learning Among the positive aspects of cooperative learning are increased interdependence and interaction with other students, enhanced motivation to learn, and improved learning by teaching material to others (Johnson

DEVELOPMENTAL FOCUS 10.2

How Do You Use Cooperative Learning in Your Classroom?

Early Childhood

We often have our preschoolers work together by creating art projects or by cooking together. In these tasks, children are assigned different responsibilities and learn how to work together to reach a common goal.

—Missy Dangler, *Suburban Hills School*

Elementary School: Grades K–5

I use base groups with learning partners on an ongoing basis in my classroom. These groups consist of four children who have established a feeling of trust with each other, work well together, and are balanced by gender, ability, and interest. The idea of learning partners is introduced as struggling readers are placed in these groups with students who are able to be supportive readers and empathetic to their classmates' needs.

—Elizabeth Frascella, *Clinton Elementary School*

Middle School: Grades 6–8

The best group projects have a role for every participant; they all need to feel like they bring something to the table. I develop group projects that require participants to read, do artwork, think creatively, speak in public, and so on. By including these skills, group members should be able to express their knowledge in a way that meets their style of learning.

—Mark Fodness, *Bemidji Middle School*

High School: Grades 9–12

I have learned that it is better not to have groups in which students select who will be included. Instead, I use a deck of cards for random groups and change them for each project. Also, many students have had experiences with cooperative learning—and unfortunately some have learned to sit back and let others in the group do all the work. Teachers need to monitor the groups to make sure all students make an effort to contribute in the group.

—Sandy Swanson, *Menomonee Falls High School*

& Johnson, 2009; Williams, 2007). The possible drawbacks of cooperative learning are that some students prefer to work alone; low-achieving students may slow down the progress of high-achieving students; a few students may do most or all of the cognitive work while others do little (called "social loafing"); some students may become distracted from the group's task because they enjoy socializing; and many students lack the skills needed to collaborate effectively with others, engage in productive discussions, and explain their ideas or evaluate others' ideas effectively (Blumenfeld, Kempler, & Krajcik, 2006). Teachers who implement cooperative learning in their classrooms need to be attentive to these drawbacks and work to reduce them (King & Behnke, 2005).

Review, Reflect, and Practice

(2) Explain how teachers and peers can jointly contribute to children's learning.

REVIEW

- What is scaffolding?
- What is a cognitive apprenticeship?
- Is tutoring effective? What are some alternative sources of tutors?
- What is cooperative learning and how might it benefit students? What are some ways to structure it?

REFLECT

- How would you handle the situation if parents became angry that, because of time allotted to cooperative learning, their children were being allowed less time to learn on an individual basis?

PRAXIS™ PRACTICE

1. Which of the following is the best example of scaffolding?
   a. Steve gives his friend Vlade the answers to today's homework.
   b. Steve helps his friend Vlade complete today's homework by giving him the least amount of assistance he needs for each question.
   c. Steve helps his friend Vlade complete today's homework by giving him hints to each answer.
   d. Steve tells his friend Vlade that he has to do his homework on his own.

2. Which of the following is an example of a cognitive apprenticeship?
   a. Ms. Notwitzki asks her students lots of questions. If a student does not know the answer to a question, she moves on to another student because she does not want her students to be embarrassed.
   b. Ms. Edgar pays attention to both the verbal and nonverbal cues her students give her regarding their understanding of her lessons. If she asks a student a question, she can determine if the student is thinking or confused. She often gives her students hints to help them answer.
   c. Ms. Lindell asks her students lots of questions. If a student does not respond immediately to her query, she gives the student the correct answer.
   d. Ms. Samuel lectures her class and they take notes. She answers any questions that they have at the end of the lesson.

3. Which teacher is using peer tutoring in the most positive way for both the tutor and the student?
   a. Ms. Gasol uses sixth-grade students to tutor her third-grade students in math for 30 minutes, four times each week. She gives each tutor explicit instructions.
   b. Ms. Mathews uses the buddy system in her class. Children choose who they would like to tutor them and what they would like to learn. Generally, they pick a close friend.
   c. Ms. Rankowski selects lower-achieving students from the higher grades to come to her class at least once per week to work with her students. She generally has them do things such as administer spelling.
   d. Ms. Taylor likes to use peer tutoring with her students, especially in math. She has found that often other students can explain things to her students more easily than she can. Therefore, she uses more advanced students in her class to teach those who are struggling with math concepts.

Review, Reflect, and Practice

4. Mr. Kotter has assigned the students to work cooperatively on a project about the Civil War. He puts the students into heterogeneous groups of four and gives each group the project guidelines. They are to turn in one project on which they will receive a group grade. He is surprised when some students contribute little to their group's effort. What is Mr. Kotter doing *wrong?*
   a. Mr. Kotter did not include any individual accountability in his assessment.
   b. Mr. Kotter should not give the students a group grade.
   c. Mr. Kotter should not have used heterogeneous groups.
   d. Mr. Kotter should not use cooperative learning in history.

   Please see the answer key at the end of the book.

3 STRUCTURING SMALL-GROUP WORK

Composing the Group | Team-Building Skills | Structuring Small-Group Interaction

We have seen that group work has many benefits for students. It requires careful planning on the teacher's part, however. When you structure students' work in small groups, you have to make decisions about how to compose the group, build team skills, and structure group interaction.

Composing the Group

Teachers often ask how they should assign students to small groups in their class. The cooperative learning approaches featured in Figure 10.1 generally recommend heterogeneous groups with diversity in ability, ethnic background, socioeconomic status, and gender (Johnson & Johnson, 2009). The reasoning behind heterogeneous grouping is that it maximizes opportunities for peer tutoring and support, improves cross-gender and cross-ethnic relations, and ensures that each group has at least one student who can do the work (Kagan, 1992).

Heterogeneous Ability   One of the main reasons for using heterogeneous ability groups is that they benefit low-ability students, who can learn from higher-ability students. However, some critics argue that such heterogeneous groupings hold back high-ability students. In most studies, though, high-achieving students perform equally well on achievement tests after working in heterogeneous groups or homogeneous groups (Hooper & others, 1989). In heterogeneous groups, high-ability students often assume the role of "teacher" and explain concepts to other students. In homogeneous groups, high-ability students are less likely to assume this teaching role.

One problem with heterogeneous groups is that when high-ability, low-ability, and medium-ability students are included, the medium-ability students get left out to some extent; high-ability and low-ability students form teacher-student relationships, excluding medium-ability students from group interaction. Medium-ability students might perform better in groups where most or all of the students have medium abilities.

What are some guidelines for forming groups that involve students from different ethnic and socioeconomic backgrounds?

Ethnic, Socioeconomic, and Gender Heterogeneity   Some of the initial reasons that cooperative learning groups were formed was to improve interpersonal relations among students from different ethnic and socioeconomic backgrounds. The hope was that interaction under conditions of equal status in cooperative groups would reduce prejudice. However, getting students to interact on the basis of equal status has been more difficult than initially envisioned.

When forming ethnically and socioeconomically heterogeneous groups, it is important to pay attention to a group's composition. One recommendation is to not make the composition too obvious. Thus, you might vary different social characteristics (ethnicity, socioeconomic status, and gender) simultaneously, such as grouping together a middle-income African American female, a White male from a low-income family, and so on. In this way, for example, the White males would not all be from high-income families. Another recommendation is to avoid forming groups that have only one minority student, if at all possible; this avoids calling attention to the student's "solo status."

In mixed-gender groups, males tend to be more active and dominant. Thus, when mixing females and males, an important task for teachers is to encourage girls to speak up and boys to allow girls to express their opinions and contribute to the group's functioning. A general strategy is to have an equal number of girls and boys. In groups of five or six children in which only one member is a girl, the boys tend to ignore the girl (Webb, 1984).

Team-Building Skills

Good cooperative learning in the classroom requires that time be spent on team-building skills. This involves thinking about how to start team building at the beginning of the school year, helping students become better listeners, giving students practice in contributing to a team product, getting students to discuss the value of a team leader, and working with team leaders to help them deal with problem situations.

Structuring Small-Group Interaction

One way to facilitate students' work in small groups is to assign students different roles. For example, consider these roles that students can assume in a group (Kagan, 1992):

- Encourager—brings out reluctant students and is a motivator
- Gatekeeper—equalizes participation of students in the group
- Coach—helps with academic content

BEST PRACTICES
Strategies for Developing Students' Team-Building Skills

Here are some guidelines (Aronson & Patnoe, 1997):

1. *Don't begin the year with cooperative learning on a difficult task.* Teachers report that academic cooperative learning often works best when students have previously worked together on team-building exercises. A short period each day for several weeks is usually adequate for this team building.

2. *Do team building at the level of the cooperative group (two to six students) rather than at the level of the entire class.* Some students on the team will be more assertive; others will be more passive. The team-building goal is to give all members some experience in being valuable team members, as well as to get them to learn that being cooperative works more effectively than being competitive.

3. *In team building, work with students to help them become better listeners.* Ask students to introduce themselves by name all at the same time to help them see that they have to take turns and listen to each other instead of hogging a conversation. You also can ask students to come up with behavioral descriptions of how they can show others that they are listening. These might include looking directly at the speaker, rephrasing what she just said, summarizing her statement, and so on.

4. *Give students some practice in contributing to a common product as part of team building.* Ask each student to participate in drawing a group picture by passing paper and pen from student to student. Each student's task is to add something to the picture as it circulates several times through the team. When the picture is finished, discuss each student's contribution to the team. Students will sense that the product is not complete unless each member's contribution is recognized. Next, you can read about how a ninth-grade history teacher uses this strategy effectively.

THROUGH THE EYES OF TEACHERS
An Eye-Level Meeting of the Minds

Jimmy Furlow has groups of students summarize textbook sections and put them on transparencies to help the entire class prepare for a test. Furlow lost both legs

Ninth-grade history teacher Jimmy Furlow converses with a student in his class.

in Vietnam but he rarely stays in one place, moving his wheelchair around the room and communicating with students at eye level. When the class completes their discussion of all the points on the overhead, Furlow edits their work to demonstrate concise, clear writing and help students zero in on an important point (Marklein, 1998).

5. *During team building, you may want to discuss the value of having a group leader.* You can ask students to discuss the specific ways a leader should function to maximize the group's performance. Their brainstorming might come up with such characteristics as "helps get the group organized," "keeps the group on task," "serves as liaison between the teacher and the group," "shows enthusiasm," "is patient and polite," and "helps the group deal with disagreements and conflicts." The teacher may select the group leader or students may be asked to elect one.

6. *Work with team leaders to help them deal with problem situations.* For example, some members might rarely talk, one member might dominate the group, members might call each other names, some members might refuse to work, one member might want to work alone, and everyone might talk at once. You can get group leaders together and get them to role-play such situations and discuss effective strategies for handling the problem situation.

- Checker—makes sure the group understands the material
- Taskmaster—keeps the group on task
- Recorder—writes down ideas and decisions
- Quiet captain—monitors the group's noise level
- Materials monitor—obtains and returns supplies

SELF-ASSESSMENT 10.1
Evaluating My Social Constructivist Experiences

What experiences have you already had with social constructivist thinking and learning? You may have had such experiences in school or in other settings. For each of these settings that you have experienced, record at least one instance in which you can look back and see social constructivist principles at work.

1. Your family:

_____

_____

2. A club or program such as the Scouts:

_____

_____

3. Your K–12 school experince:

_____

_____

4. College:

_____

_____

How do those experiences shape your judgment regarding these ideas for classroom teaching?

1. That thinking should be viewed as located (situated) in social and physical contexts, not only within an individual's mind:

_____

_____

2. Vygotsky's sociocultural cognitive theory:

_____

_____

3. Scaffolding:

_____

_____

4. Peer tutoring:

_____

_____

5. Cooperative learning:

_____

_____

6. Small-group work:

_____

_____

Such roles help groups to function more smoothly and give all members of the group a sense of importance. Note that although we just described nine different roles that can be played in groups, most experts, as we noted earlier, recommend that groups not exceed five or six members to function effectively. Some members can fill multiple roles, and all roles do not always have to be filled.

Another way roles can be specialized is to designate some students as "summarizers" and others as "listeners." Researchers have consistently found that summarizing benefits learning more than listening, so if these roles are used, all members should get opportunities to be summarizers (Dansereau, 1988).

To evaluate your attitudes toward social constructivist approaches and whether you are likely to use such strategies when you teach, complete *Self-Assessment 10.1.*

Review, Reflect, and Practice

③ Discuss effective decisions in structuring small-group work.

REVIEW
- What are some important considerations in placing students in small groups?
- What can teachers do to build team skills within groups?
- What types of role assignments can improve a group's structure?

REFLECT
- Suppose you and five other students have decided to form a group to study for a final exam in educational psychology. How would you structure the group? What roles would you want the group to assign?

PRAXIS™ PRACTICE

1. Which of the following represents the best practice for forming work groups?
   a. one White, high-achieving girl; three African American, middle-achieving boys
   b. one African American, high-achieving boy; two White, middle-achieving girls; one Asian American, low-achieving boy
   c. two Asian American, high-achieving boys; two White, low-achieving boys
   d. two African American, high-achieving girls; one African American, middle-achieving boy; one African American, low-achieving girl

2. Mr. Fandango decides to work on team building at the beginning of the school year. To this end, he takes his entire class outside and has them create a human knot. They then must work together to untie the "knot." Several students become frustrated and angry during the activity. Mr. Fandango intervenes by encouraging the students to elect a leader and to listen to each other. According to *Best Practices:* "Strategies for Developing Students' Team-Building Skills," what did Mr. Fandango do *incorrectly*?
   a. He did not emphasize the importance of listening skills.
   b. He did not have enough students in the group.
   c. He did not use heterogeneous grouping.
   d. He started with the whole class and a difficult task.

3. George, John, Paul, Cassie, and Mackenzie are working together on a group project involving the Civil War. George is the resident expert on the Civil War. As they work on the project, he answers the other students' questions. John volunteers to get all the supplies that the group needs. The project goes smoothly and each of the students participates, because Cassie reminds them that everyone's contribution is valuable. During one group work session, the group starts discussing last weekend's football game. Paul says, "Hey guys, we're supposed to be working on this project, you know." After this, the group gets back on task. They

(continued)

Review, Reflect, and Practice

become so engrossed in their discussion that they become rather noisy. At this point, Mackenzie reminds her peers to quiet down.

Which student took the gatekeeper role?

a. George
b. John
c. Mackenzie
d. Cassie

Please see the answer key at the end of the book.

4 SOCIAL CONSTRUCTIVIST PROGRAMS

Fostering a Community of Learners

Schools for Thought

Let's explore two programs that systematically incorporate social constructivist philosophies in their efforts to challenge students to solve real-world problems and develop a deeper understanding of concepts. These programs can show you some ways to successfully use social constructivist ideas and techniques in your classroom.

Fostering a Community of Learners

Ann Brown and Joe Campione (1996; Brown, 1997; Campione, 2001) have developed a program called **Fostering a Community of Learners (FCL)**, which focuses on literacy development and biology. As currently established, it is set in inner-city elementary schools and is appropriate for 6- to 12-year-old children. Reflection and discussion are key dimensions of the program. In FCL, constructive commentary, questioning, querying, and criticism are the norm rather than the exception. Many of the class activities occur in small groups in which students talk with, try to convince, and challenge each other. Although teachers guide topic selection, an important goal is to gradually turn over responsibility for learning to students (Lehrer & Schauble, 2006).

The FCL program emphasizes three strategies that encourage reflection and discussion: (1) the use of adults as role models, (2) children teaching children, and (3) online computer consultation.

Adults as Role Models   Visiting experts and classroom teachers introduce the big ideas and difficult principles at the beginning of a unit. The adult demonstrates how to think and self-reflect in the process of identifying topics within a general area of inquiry or reasoning with given information. The adults continually ask students to justify their opinions and then to support them with evidence, to think of counterexamples of rules, and so on.

For example, one area of biological inquiry used in the FCL program is "Changing Populations." Outside experts or teachers introduce this topic and ask students to generate as many questions about it as possible. The teacher and the students categorize the questions into subtopics such as extinct, endangered, artificial, assisted, and urbanized populations. About six students make up a learning group, and each group takes responsibility for one of the subtopics.

Fostering a Community of Learners (FCL) A social constructivist program that focuses on literacy development and biology. FCL encourages reflection and discussion through the use of adults as role models, children teaching children, and online computer consultation.

A Fostering a Community of Learners (FCL) classroom. *What is the nature of this approach to education?*

Children Teaching Children Brown (1997) says that children as well as adults enrich the classroom learning experience by contributing their particular expertise. Cross-age teaching, in which older students teach younger students, is used. This occurs both face-to-face and via e-mail. Older students often serve as discussion leaders. Cross-age teaching provides students with invaluable opportunities to talk about learning, gives students responsibility and purpose, and fosters collaboration among peers.

FCL uses **reciprocal teaching**, in which students take turns leading a small-group discussion. Reciprocal teaching requires students to discuss complex passages, collaborate, and share their individual expertise and perspectives on a particular topic. Reciprocal teaching can involve a teacher and a student as well as interaction between students.

A modified version of the jigsaw classroom (which was described in Chapter 5 and Figure 10.1) also is used. As students create preliminary drafts of reports, they participate in "crosstalk" sessions. These are whole-class activities in which groups periodically summarize where they are in their learning activity and get input from the other groups. "Mini-jigsaws" (small groups) also are used. At both the whole-class level and mini-jigsaw level, if group members can't understand what a student is saying or writing about, the student must revise a product and present it again later. Students are then grouped into reciprocal teaching seminars in which each student is an expert on one subtopic, teaches that part to the others, and participates in constructing test questions based on the subunit (Rico & Shulman, 2004).

Online Computer Consultation As just noted, FCL classrooms also use e-mail to build community and expertise. Through e-mail, experts provide coaching and advice, as well as commentary about what it means to learn and understand. Online experts function as role models of thinking. They wonder, query, and make inferences based on incomplete knowledge.

At the heart of FCL is a culture of learning, negotiating, sharing, and producing work that is displayed to others. Products of students' work are often in the form of text or talk that include posters, presentations, written reports, or teaching ideas for working with younger children (Lehrer & Schauble, 2006). The educational experience involves an interpretive community that encourages active exchange and reciprocity. This approach has much in common with what Jerome Bruner (1996)

reciprocal teaching A learning arrangement used by FCL in which students take turns leading a small-group discussion.

"Blueprint for Success"

Christina and Marcus, two students from Trenton, visit an architectural firm on Career Day. While learning about the work of architects, Christina and Marcus hear about a vacant lot being donated in their neighborhood for a playground. This is exciting news because there is no place in their downtown neighborhood for children to play. Recently, several students have been hurt playing in the street. The challenge is for students to help Christina and Marcus design a playground and ballfield for the lot.

"The Big Splash"

Jasper's young friend Chris wants to help his school raise money to buy a new camera for the school TV station. His idea is to have a dunking booth in which teachers would be dunked when students hit a target. He must develop a business plan for the school principal in order to obtain a loan for his project. The overall problem centers on developing this business plan, including the use of a statistical survey to help him decide if this idea would be profitable.

FIGURE 10.2 Problem–Solving Adventures in the *Jasper* Series

Schools for Thought (SFT) A social constructivist program that combines aspects of The Jasper Project, Fostering a Community of Learners, and CSILE.

recommended for improving the culture of education. Research evaluation of the Fostering a Community of Learners approach suggests that it benefits students' understanding and flexible use of content knowledge, resulting in improved achievement in reading, writing, and problem solving. FCL is being increasingly implemented in a number of classrooms (Schoenfeld, 2004; Sherin, Mendez, & Louis, 2004; Shulman & Shulman, 2004; Whitcomb, 2004).

In a recent description, science education experts Richard Lehrer and Laura Schauble (2006) called FCL "a landmark in developmental science education." That said, they also raised several questions about its effectiveness. First, even though many educators might agree that shared discourse is an important aspect of classrooms, it is not clear how to implement this and difficult to know if it is successful or not. Second, in regard to science education, is too much emphasis placed on reading about science, integrating text information, and learning *about* science in FCL and too little emphasis on *doing* science?

Schools for Thought

Schools for Thought (SFT) is another formal program of social constructivist teaching. Too often students emerge from instruction with only a fragile understanding of the material (Segal, 1996). For example, students might be able to repeat various scientific principles they have been taught in science, but they run into difficulties when they have to explain everyday scientific phenomena. Similarly, in math, students might be good at plugging numbers into formulas but when confronted with variations of these problems be unable to solve them. Thus, many students acquire enough information to pass tests in school but gain no deep understanding of concepts.

In one effort, Schools for Thought (Lamon & others, 1996) has combined aspects of The Jasper Project, Fostering a Community of Learners (FCL), and Computer-Supported Intentional Learning Environments (CSILE) in a school learning environment. The project is named after John Bruer's (1993) award-winning book, *Schools for Thought*. The Jasper Project, FCL, and CSILE share certain features that allow them to be combined in a school learning environment.

What are the three components of Schools for Thought like? The Jasper Project focuses on *The Adventures of Jasper Woodbury,* a multimedia set of twelve math problem-solving adventures, and is an example of problem-based learning (Cognition and Technology Group at Vanderbilt, 1997) (see Figure 10.2). *Jasper*-related projects also have been created for students in science, history, and social studies. We already have described FCL. To learn about CSILE, read the *Technology and Education* interlude.

Curriculum The three core programs of Schools for Thought stress the importance of getting students to think about real-world problems. Problem-based and project-based activities are at the heart of the curriculum. Extended in-depth inquiry in domains such as science, math, and social studies are emphasized. All three programs also incorporate cross-disciplinary inquiry across traditional boundaries. For example, exploring what it means for an animal to be endangered could involve examining problems related to estimating populations, sampling, and other issues usually restricted to mathematics. In the Schools for Thought project, curricula are being developed that integrate geography, geology, environmental and physical science, ancient and American history, and language arts and reading.

Instruction All three SFT programs involve a change in the classroom instructional climate. In a traditional classroom, students are receivers of information dispensed

TECHNOLOGY AND EDUCATION
Computer-Supported Intentional Learning Environments (Knowledge Forum)

In the early 1990s, researchers at the Centre for Applied Cognitive Science, in the Ontario Institute for Studies in Education, began applying their work on intentional learning to the development of computer applications to support knowledge building communities (Scardamalia & Bereiter, 1994). Their work led to the development of CSILE (Computer-Supported Intentional Learning Environments), an evolving database application that allows students to collaboratively develop a knowledge base, enter their views and questions, compare perspectives, and reflect on their joint understanding of ideas.

CSILE helped students understand how knowledge is socially constructed and gave them opportunities to reflect on, revise, and transform their thinking. In addition, students in CSILE classrooms performed better on standardized achievement tests of language and mathematics, gave deeper explanations of concepts, were better problem solvers, and had a more positive attitude toward learning than students in traditional classrooms (Scardamalia, Bereiter, & Lamon, 1994).

More recently, CSILE has morphed into a commercial enterprise known as Knowledge Forum (www.knowledge forum. com) and expanded from a K–12 focus to incorporate all kinds of education and training (Bruckman, 2006; Scardamalia & Bereiter, 2006). Knowledge Forum includes knowledge building tools for collaboration, constructing, storing, retrieving, referencing, quoting, and tracking notes, identifying gaps or advances in knowledge, building idea networks, and viewing ideas and idea networks from multiple perspectives.

Knowledge Forum is essentially CSILE online. It provides users with structures and tools to create a knowledge building community via a local area network, through Internet communications, or using the World Wide Web. Each community creates its own knowledge base in which it can store notes, connect ideas, and build on previous thinking. Users start with an empty knowledge base to which they submit ideas, share information, reorganize the knowledge, and ultimately build understandings. Knowledge Forum makes information accessible from multiple perspectives and from multiple entry points. With it, any number of individuals and groups can share information, launch collaborative investigations, and build networks of new ideas . . . together.

by teachers, textbooks, and other media; the teacher's role is to give information and mold students' learning. In many traditional schools, what students mainly do is listen, watch, and mimic what teachers and texts tell them to do (Greeno, 1993, 2006). In contrast, all three SFT programs provide students with many opportunities to plan and organize their own learning and problem solving. They also encour-

A Schools for Thought science classroom at Compton-Drew School in St. Louis.

age students to work collaboratively as they learn and think. Students explore ideas, evaluate information, and consider others' ideas in an ongoing reciprocal interchange with peers, teachers, and experts.

The Schools for Thought environments are not simply freewheeling discovery environments. They involve a considerable amount of structure. Teachers and community experts keep learning focused on key principles in the domains being studied, such as mathematics, science, or social science. They monitor and reframe students' self-generated questions and exploration to keep them within the perspective of the key principles. In this manner, they guide the direction of students' inquiry so that students discover the deep concepts of the domain. Still, there is considerable flexibility in how this understanding is achieved and the nature of the projects undertaken.

Community   In many schools, classrooms and teachers operate in isolation, not just from each other but from the outside community as well. The Jasper Project, FCL, and CSILE all emphasize the importance of giving students and teachers opportunities to see themselves as part of a team and as members of a larger community. Problems often have a community focus, to encourage students to think about how learning and problem solving can be used to better understand and improve the world in which we live.

Technology   The Jasper Project, FCL, and CSILE all use technology to break the isolation of the traditional classroom. They encourage students to communicate electronically with a community of learners beyond the classroom's walls.

Assessment   The goals in creating The Jasper Project, FCL, and CSILE were not to improve students' achievement test scores. Assessment in the three programs focuses on achieving authentic performances (such as reading for the purpose of answering research questions, writing to build new knowledge), making assessment coordinate smoothly with learning and instruction, and encouraging students to engage in self-assessment.

Review, Reflect, and Practice

(4) Describe two social constructivist programs.

REVIEW

- What three strategies are embedded in the Fostering a Community of Learners program?
- What programs are combined in Schools for Thought? What do these programs have in common?

REFLECT

- Which of the two social constructivist programs appeals to you the most? Why?

PRAXIS™ PRACTICE

1. Which of the following is the best example of Fostering a Community of Learners?
   a. Marks Middle School brings students together to work on math projects. They bring in community members to act as mentors to the students and try to make connections between mathematics and the world in which these rural teens live.

Review, Reflect, and Practice

  b. Lincoln Elementary School uses small-group discussions in which students challenge each other's perspectives. They bring in community members to act as mentors to the students. When outside mentors lack the expertise needed, students e-mail outside experts. Older students help younger ones.
  c. Johnson High School uses a hands-on approach to teaching biology. Students complete experiments, dissections, and involve themselves in an environmental project. Students work in small groups on these projects under the guidance of an adult role model.
  d. Luther High School uses a flexible, modular approach to teaching science with extensive opportunities for students to engage in projects that they construct themselves. Students are encouraged to engage in self-reflection and cooperative learning.

2. Mr. Patrick, the principal at Johnson High School, wants to implement Schools for Thought. He works with his teachers to integrate various aspects of the curriculum so that students will understand their interdependence. The teachers develop interdisciplinary units that revolve around projects. In addition, the teachers alter the way in which they teach to become facilitators of learning rather than dispensers of knowledge. What aspect of Schools for Thought has Mr. Patrick neglected?
  a. community
  b. curriculum
  c. discipline
  d. instruction

Please see the answer key at the end of the book.

CRACK THE CASE
The Case of the Social Constructivist Classroom

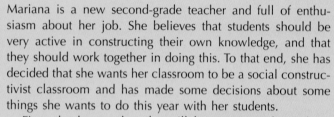

Mariana is a new second-grade teacher and full of enthusiasm about her job. She believes that students should be very active in constructing their own knowledge, and that they should work together in doing this. To that end, she has decided that she wants her classroom to be a social constructivist classroom and has made some decisions about some things she wants to do this year with her students.

First, she knows that she will have to provide students with scaffolding when material is new and gradually adjust the amount of help her students receive. She wants to use peer tutoring for this in her class, because she believes that children can often learn more from each other than they can from an adult. So she sets up a system in which the more-advanced students in her class help those who are less advanced.

Mariana also likes the idea of cooperative learning. She creates student groups so that they are heterogeneous with regard to ability, gender, ethnicity, and SES. She then assigns roles to each student in a group. Sometimes these roles are things such as coach, encourager, checker, taskmaster, recorder, and materials monitor. She uses this approach for many content areas. Sometimes she uses a jigsaw approach in which each student is responsible for becoming an expert in a particular area and then sharing that expertise with his or her group members. She uses this approach in science and in social studies.

In math, Mariana feels very fortunate that her school has adopted the Everyday Mathematics curriculum. This program makes connections with the real world that she thinks is so important in math instruction. Group work is also stressed.

Mariana hopes that her students and their parents will share her excitement as they "all learn together." However, she soon becomes disappointed. When she groups students, she hears groans of "Not again." "Why do I have to work with

her? She doesn't know anything." "He's too bossy." "I always have to be with him, and then I end up doing everything." "She never lets me do anything but sit there and watch." Parents have gotten in on the act too. She has received calls and letters from parents who don't understand what she's trying to do. They all seem concerned about test scores and grades rather than what their children are learning together. One parent asked that her child no longer be grouped with another child who is "holding back" her child's learning.

1. What are the issues in this case?
2. What do you think Mariana did incorrectly?
3. What should she do now to recover her constructivist classroom?
4. How can she elicit the cooperation of the parents?
5. Which of the following suggestions would you make to Mariana regarding peer tutoring?
   a. Allow children to choose their partners.
   b. Insist that the more-advanced students help those who are less advanced, regardless of parental feelings.
   c. Use cross-age peer tutoring rather than same-age peer tutoring.
   d. Use peer tutors who don't like each other so they won't be tempted to goof around instead of working.
6. Which of the following suggestions would you make to Mariana regarding her use of student groups?
   a. Compose gender-segregated groups to make students more comfortable.
   b. Compose racially segregated groups to make students more comfortable.
   c. Give leadership roles to students who are shy to help draw them out.
   d. Mix up the group composition from time to time, so that middle-ability-level students don't get left out.

Reach Your Learning Goals
Social Constructivist Approaches

(1) SOCIAL CONSTRUCTIVIST APPROACHES TO TEACHING: Compare the social constructivist approach with other constructivist approaches.

Social Constructivism in the Broader Constructivist Context

Piaget's and Vygotsky's theories are constructivist. Piaget's theory is a cognitive constructivist theory, whereas Vygotsky's is social constructivist. The implication of Vygotsky's model for teaching is to establish opportunities for students to learn through social interactions with others—with the teacher and peers—in constructing knowledge and understanding. In Piaget's view, students construct knowledge by transforming, organizing, and reorganizing previous knowledge and information. In both Piaget's and Vygotsky's models, teachers are facilitators, not directors. Distinctions between cognitive and social constructivist approaches are not always clear-cut. All social constructivist approaches emphasize that social factors contribute to students' construction of knowledge and understanding.

Situated Cognition

Situated cognition is the idea that thinking is located (situated) in social and physical contexts, not within an individual's mind.

(2) TEACHERS AND PEERS AS JOINT CONTRIBUTORS TO STUDENTS' LEARNING: Explain how teachers and peers can jointly contribute to children's learning.

Scaffolding

Scaffolding is the technique of providing changing levels of support over the course of a teaching session, with a more-skilled individual—a teacher or a more-advanced peer of the child—providing guidance to fit the student's current performance.

Cognitive Apprenticeship

A cognitive apprenticeship involves a novice and an expert, who stretches and supports the novice's understanding of and use of a culture's skills.

Tutoring

Tutoring involves a cognitive apprenticeship between an expert and a novice. Tutoring can take place between an adult and a child or a more-skilled child and a less-skilled child. Individual tutoring is effective. Classroom aides, volunteers, and mentors can serve as tutors to support teachers and classroom learning. Reading Recovery and Success for All are examples of effective tutoring programs. In many cases, students benefit more from cross-age tutoring than from same-age tutoring. Tutoring can benefit both the tutee and the tutor.

Cooperative Learning

Cooperative learning occurs when students work in small groups to help each other learn. Researchers have found that cooperative learning can be an effective strategy for improving students' achievement, especially when group goals and individual accountability are instituted. Cooperative learning works better for complex than simple tasks. Cooperative learning often improves intrinsic motivation, encourages student interdependence, and promotes deep understanding. Cooperative learning approaches include STAD (Student-Teams-Achievement Divisions), the jigsaw classroom (I and II), learning together, group investigation, and cooperative scripting. Cooperative learning approaches generally recommend heterogeneous groupings with diversity in ability, ethnicity, socioeconomic status, and gender. Creating a cooperative community involves developing positive interdependence at a number of levels: a small group within a classroom, the class as a whole, between classrooms, the entire school, between parents and the school, and between the school and the neighborhood. Cooperative learning has a number of strengths, but there also are some potential drawbacks to its use.

3 **STRUCTURING SMALL-GROUP WORK:** Discuss effective decisions in structuring small-group work.

| Composing the Group | Two strategies in composing a small group are to assign children to heterogeneous groups and to have the group membership reflect diversity in ability, ethnic background, socioeconomic status, and gender. |

| Team-Building Skills | Structuring small-group work also involves attention to team-building skills. A good strategy is to spend several weeks at the beginning of the school year on building team skills, helping students become better listeners, and giving them practice in contributing to a team product. Assigning one student in each small group to be a team leader can help to build the team. |

| Structuring Small-Group Interaction | A group also can benefit when students are assigned different roles—for example, encourager, gatekeeper, taskmaster, quiet captain, and materials monitor—that are designed to help the group function more smoothly. |

4 **SOCIAL CONSTRUCTIVIST PROGRAMS:** Describe two social constructivist programs.

| Fostering a Community of Learners | Fostering a Community of Learners emphasizes (1) using adults as role models, (2) children teaching children, and (3) online computer consultation. |

| Schools for Thought | Schools for Thought combines activities from three programs: (1) The Jasper Project, (2) Fostering a Community of Learners, and (3) Computer-Supported Intentional Learning Environments. Extended in-depth inquiry is fostered. Teachers guide students in becoming architects of their knowledge. |

 KEY TERMS

social constructivist
    approach 349
situated cognition 350
cognitive apprenticeship 351

cooperative learning 358
Fostering a Community of
    Learners (FCL) 368

reciprocal teaching 369
Schools for Thought
    (SFT) 370

PORTFOLIO ACTIVITIES

Now that you have a good understanding of this chapter, complete these exercises to expand your thinking.

Independent Reflection

Evaluating Social Constructivist Experiences. To what extent have you experienced various social constructivist approaches in your education? Think about your different levels of schooling (early childhood, elementary, middle, high school, and college), and evaluate your experience (or lack of experience) with scaffolding, cognitive apprenticeship, tutoring, and cooperative learning. (INTASC: Principles *2, 3, 4, 5, 9*)

Collaborative Work

Balancing Individual and Group Activities. With four or five other students in the class, discuss how much of the curriculum should include group activities and how much should involve individual activities at the early childhood, elementary, middle, high school, and college levels. Describe your group's thoughts. Also discuss whether some subject areas might lend themselves better than others to group activities. (INTASC: Principles *1, 3, 4, 5*)

Research/Field Experience

Practical Applications of Social Constructivism. Beyond a teacher and a room full of students, what resources do the two social constructivist programs that were described in the chapter require? How practical is it to use these programs on a widespread basis? Write your responses. (INTASC: Principles *4, 5, 7*).

Go to the Online Learning Center for downloadable portfolio templates.

 TAKING IT TO THE NET

- Imagine that you typically give students frequent opportunities to engage in collaborative group work. What questions should you ask yourself when deciding how to organize the groups and structure the work? Why is collaborative group work an important educational experience for students? **www.netc.org/classrooms%40work/classrooms/peter/working/grouping.htm**
- Multimedia projects offer numerous opportunities for students to engage in social learning. Explore the ThinkQuest Library and evaluate one of the student-created Web projects. In what ways does your selected project employ social constructivist principles of learning? **www.thinkquest.org/library/index.html**

- Work with a partner, and browse the Web to find a high-quality resource that could serve as a "cognitive apprenticeship" for students, and describe its merits as a teaching tool. For example, a student can be an apprentice to astronauts in training by accessing their electronic journals, photos, and interviews. Why is the Web such a powerful tool for implementing social constructivist approaches in the classroom? **www.nasa.gov/audience/foreducators/9-12/features/ F_Astronaut_Journals.html**

Connect to the Online Learning Center to explore possible answers.

 STUDY, PRACTICE, AND SUCCEED

Visit **www.mhhe.com/santedu4e** to review the chapter with self-grading quizzes and self-assessments, to apply the chapter material to two more Crack the Case studies, and for suggested activities to develop your teaching portfolio.

CHAPTER 11

Learning and Cognition in the Content Areas

Meaning is not given to us but by us.

—Eleanor Duckworth
Contemporary American Educator

Learning Goals

1 Distinguish between expert knowledge and pedagogical content knowledge.

2 Explain how reading develops and discuss some useful approaches to teaching reading.

3 Describe how writing develops and discuss some useful approaches to teaching writing.

4 Characterize how mathematical thinking develops and identify some issues related to teaching mathematics.

5 Identify some challenges and strategies related to teaching children how to think scientifically.

6 Summarize how learning in social studies is becoming more constructivist.

TEACHING STORIES   Wendy Nelson Kauffman

Wendy Nelson Kauffman teaches social studies to tenth- and twelfth-grade students at a Bloomfield, Connecticut, high school. Wendy turned to teaching after a career in journalism that left her feeling unfulfilled. Among the many activities she has students do to improve their thinking and writing skills are:

- Writing autobiographies each fall
- Keeping journals all year and writing position papers on historical questions
- Participating in dramatic role-playing
- Carrying out debates and holding "town meetings" to discuss contentious issues such as racial problems
- Interpreting political cartoons and songs
- Making posters

- Engaging in real-world learning experiences—these have included a visit to Ellis Island, after which students acted out immigrant experiences in a school-wide performance, and interviews with retirement home residents about the Great Depression and World War II for an oral history book

In Wendy's words, "Certain skills they have to learn: writing, critical thinking, class participation. If you mix that with something that's fun for them and plays to their strengths, I think it makes it easier for them to do the hard work in class." Wendy also mentors new teachers, about whom she says, "I want them to feel safe, I want them to take risks, I want them to become who they want to be." (*Source: USA Today*, October 16, 2003)

Preview

In previous chapters, we described the basic principles of children's learning and cognition. In this chapter, we will apply these principles to learning and cognition in five content areas: reading, writing, mathematics, science, and social studies. We begin the chapter by revisiting the concept of expertise and exploring the distinction between expert knowledge and pedagogical content knowledge, the kind of knowledge that teachers like Wendy Nelson Kauffman use to teach effectively.

 1   EXPERT KNOWLEDGE AND PEDAGOGICAL CONTENT KNOWLEDGE

In Chapter 8, we discussed the distinction between experts and novices. We saw that sometimes individuals who are experts in the content of a particular area, such as mathematics or biology, aren't good at teaching it in ways that others can effectively learn. These individuals have *expert knowledge* but lack *pedagogical content knowledge*. Let's examine the difference between the two types of knowledge.

Expert knowledge, sometimes referred to as *subject matter knowledge*, means excellent knowledge about the content of a particular discipline. Clearly, expert knowledge is important—how can teachers teach students something that they don't understand themselves (Grossman, Schoenfeld, & Lee, 2005)? However, some individuals with expert knowledge about a particular subject area, such as reading, math, or science, have difficulty understanding the subject matter in a way that allows them to teach it effectively to others. The term *expert blind spots* has been used to describe the gap between what an expert knows and what students know (Nathan & Petrosino, 2003). Too often experts (teachers) don't communicate all of the information and steps necessary for students (novices) to learn something (Bransford, Darling-Hammond, & LePage, 2005).

> **expert knowledge** Also called *subject matter knowledge;* means excellent knowledge about the content of a particular discipline.

What is pedagogical content knowledge? How is it different from expert knowledge?

What teachers need in addition to expert knowledge is **pedagogical content knowledge**—knowledge about how to effectively teach a particular discipline (Schoenfeld, 2006). Both expert knowledge and pedagogical content knowledge are required for being an expert teacher. *Expert teachers* know the structure of their disciplines, and this knowledge gives them the ability to create cognitive road maps that guide the assignments they give to students, the assessments they use to evaluate students' progress, and the types of questions and answers they generate in class (National Research Council, 2005). Being an expert teacher in a particular discipline also involves being aware of which aspects of the discipline are especially difficult or easy for students to learn.

In previous chapters, we explored general teaching strategies that are effective across all disciplines. For example, a good teacher in any discipline asks questions that stimulate students' curiosity, encourages students to go beyond the surface of a topic and gain a depth of understanding about a topic, and pays attention to individual variations in students' learning. However, pedagogical content knowledge about particular disciplines goes beyond these general teaching strategies. We will examine five content areas—reading, writing, mathematics, science, and social studies—and point out effective teaching strategies in each one.

Review, Reflect, and Practice

1 Distinguish between expert knowledge and pedagogical content knowledge.

REVIEW

- How is expert knowledge different from pedagogical content knowledge?

REFLECT

- Have you ever had a teacher who was clearly an expert in his or her discipline but not a good teacher? What pedagogical content knowledge was missing?

pedagogical content knowledge
Knowledge about how to effectively teach a particular discipline.

Review, Reflect, and Practice

PRAXIS™ PRACTICE

1. Maria is frustrated with her calculus teacher, a former university math professor. He knows his math but has a difficult time communicating his knowledge to his students. In fact, half the time in class, Maria has no idea what he is talking about. When she asks for help, he is willing to meet with her, but his explanations are no clearer than they are in class. Which statement best characterizes Maria's calculus teacher?
   a. He has both expert knowledge in calculus and pedagogical content knowledge.
   b. He has expert knowledge in calculus but lacks pedagogical content knowledge.
   c. He lacks expert knowledge in calculus but has pedagogical content knowledge.
   d. He lacks both expert knowledge in calculus and pedagogical content knowledge.

   Please see the answer key at the end of the book.

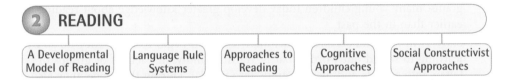

2 READING

| A Developmental Model of Reading | Language Rule Systems | Approaches to Reading | Cognitive Approaches | Social Constructivist Approaches |

Reading expert Steve Stahl (2002) argues that the three main goals of reading instruction should be to help children (1) automatically recognize words, (2) comprehend text, and (3) become motivated to read and appreciate reading. These goals are interrelated. If children cannot recognize words automatically, their comprehension suffers. If they cannot comprehend the text, they are unlikely to be motivated to read it.

Recent analyses by Rich Mayer (2004, 2008) focused on the cognitive processes a child needs to go through in order to read a printed word. In his view, the three processes are as follows:

1. *Being aware of sound units in words,* which consists of recognizing phonemes
2. *Decoding words,* which involves converting printed words into sounds
3. *Accessing word meaning,* which consists of finding a mental representation of a word's meaning

How do children develop the reading skills that Stahl and Mayer describe? What is the best way to teach children to read? How can children construct their reading skills? These are among the main questions that we will examine in our coverage of reading. As we discuss these questions, you will see that teachers play a key role in the development of children's reading skills (Reutzel & Cooter, 2009; Vacca & others, 2009).

A Developmental Model of Reading

In one view, reading skills develop in five stages (Chall, 1979). The age boundaries are approximate and do not apply to every child. For example, some children learn to read before they enter first grade. Nonetheless, Chall's stages convey a general sense of the developmental changes involved in learning to read:

What are some developmental changes in reading?

- *Stage 0.* From birth to first grade, children master several prerequisites for reading. Many learn the left-to-right progression and order of reading, how to identify the letters of the alphabet, and how to write their names. Some learn to read words that commonly appear on signs. As a result of watching TV shows such as *Sesame Street* and attending preschool and kindergarten programs, many young children today develop greater knowledge about reading earlier than in the past.

- *Stage 1.* In first and second grade, many children begin to read. They do so by learning to sound out words (that is, translate individual letters or groups of letters into sounds and blend sounds into words). During this stage, they also complete their learning of letter names and sounds.

- *Stage 2.* In second and third grade, children become more fluent at retrieving individual words and other reading skills. However, at this stage, reading is still not used much for learning. The mechanical demands of learning to read are so taxing at this point that children have few resources left over to process the content.

- *Stage 3.* In fourth through eighth grade, children become increasingly able to obtain new information from print. The change from stage 2 to stage 3 involves a shift from "learning to read" to "reading to learn." In stage 3, children still have difficulty understanding information presented from multiple perspectives within the same story. For children who haven't yet learned to read, a downward spiral begins that leads to serious difficulties in many academic subjects.

- *Stage 4.* In the high school years, many students become fully competent readers. They develop the ability to understand material written from many different perspectives. This allows them to engage in sometimes more sophisticated discussions of literature, history, economics, and politics. It is no accident that great novels are not presented to students until high school, because understanding the novels requires advanced reading.

Keep in mind that the age boundaries in Chall's model are approximate and do not apply to every child. However, the stages convey a sense of the developmental changes involved in becoming a competent reader.

Language Rule Systems

As the previous discussion has implied, *reading* is the ability to understand written discourse. Children cannot be said to read if all they can do is respond to flash

This teacher is helping a student sound out words. Researchers have found that phonics instruction is a key aspect of teaching students to read, especially beginning readers and students with weak reading skills.

cards. Good readers have mastered the basic language rules of phonology, morphology, syntax, and semantics that we discussed in Chapter 2, "Cognitive and Language Development."

Phonology   *Phonology* is the sound system of a language, including the sounds that are used and how they may be combined. Phonology plays a critical role in the early development of reading skills (Cunningham, 2009; Menn & Stoel Gammon, 2009; Newton, Podak, & Rasinski, 2008). Recall Mayer's (2004, 2008) conclusion that a child is unlikely to be able to read a printed word if he or she does not become aware of the sound units in words. Providing direct instruction in phonemic awareness improves reading achievement (Ehri & others, 2001). If students don't develop good phonological skills in the first several years of elementary school, they are unlikely to develop automaticity in decoding words, which means they will have to spend more time in decoding, leaving less time for reading comprehension (Stanovich, 1994). A likely outcome of poor phonological skills is a weak vocabulary, which, as we will discuss shortly, is linked to deficiencies in reading comprehension. As little as 5 to 18 hours of direct instruction in phonological awareness can help put students on the path to becoming proficient readers (Ehri & others, 2001; Mayer, 2008).

Morphology   *Morphology* refers to the units of meaning involved in word formation (Tager Flusberg & Zukowski, 2009). Every word in the English language is made up of one or more morphemes. A *morpheme* is a minimal unit of meaning, such as the *-ed* that turns *help* into *helped*. "Morphology is what turns a relatively simple word like *heal* into *health*" (Rutter, 2005, p. 6). Morphology begins to become important in reading around the third and fourth grades when students increasingly encounter words that contain multiple syllables. Readers who are not proficient at morphology often have difficulty recognizing suffixes such as *-tion* and pronouncing words with these suffixes (Rutter, 2005). Many students from the mid-elementary school grades through college who are problem readers do not have good morphological awareness (Berninger, 2006).

Syntax   *Syntax* involves the way words are combined to form acceptable sentences. Syntax especially focuses on grammar skills (Tager Flusberg & Zukowski, 2009). Good grammatical skills play an important role in reading comprehension. A child who has poor grammatical skills for speech and listening and does not understand what is meant by "The car was pushed by a truck" when it is spoken will not understand its meaning in print either. Likewise, a child who cannot determine what pronouns refer to (as in "John went to the store with his dog. It was closed.") will not do well in reading comprehension.

Semantics *Semantics* refers to the meaning of words and sentences. Good semantic skills are involved in becoming a proficient reader (Pan & Uccelli, 2008). An important aspect of semantics is vocabulary. Recall that in Mayer's definition of reading (2004, 2008), accessing word meaning is a key cognitive process in reading. Having a good vocabulary helps readers access word meaning effortlessly, and researchers have found that vocabulary development is an important aspect of reading (Snow & Kang, 2006). For example, a recent study found that a good vocabulary was linked to reading comprehension in second-grade students (Berninger & Abbott, 2005). Other research studies have also found that vocabulary plays an important role in reading comprehension (Paris & Paris, 2006).

Two main ways to increase children's vocabulary involve direct instruction and immersion (Mayer, 2008). Direct instruction involves teaching students the definitions of words. Immersion consists of students engaging in activities such as reading, listening, and producing prose. Some experts on reading argue that students learn most of their vocabulary words through immersion (Nagy & Scott, 2000).

Approaches to Reading

What are some approaches to teaching children how to read? Education and language experts continue to debate how children should be taught to read. Currently, debate focuses on the phonics approach versus the whole-language approach (Beaty, 2009; Cunningham, 2009).

The **phonics approach** emphasizes that reading instruction should focus on phonics and basic rules for translating written symbols into sounds. Early reading instruction should involve simplified materials. Only after they have learned the correspondence rules that relate spoken phonemes to the alphabet letters that represent them should children be given complex reading materials, such as books and poems (Cunningham & Hall, 2009; Hall & Cunningham, 2009).

By contrast, the **whole-language approach** stresses that reading instruction should parallel children's natural language learning. Reading materials should be whole and meaningful. That is, children should be given material in its complete form, such as stories and poems, so that they learn to understand language's communicative function. Reading should be connected with listening and writing skills. Although there are variations in whole-language programs, most share the premise that reading should be integrated with other skills and subjects, such as science and social studies, and that it should focus on real-world material. Thus, a class might read newspapers, magazines, or books, and then write about and discuss them. In some whole-language classes, beginning readers are taught to recognize whole words or even entire sentences, and to use the context of what they are reading to guess at unfamiliar words.

Which approach is better? Children can benefit from both approaches, but instruction in phonics needs to be emphasized especially in kindergarten and the first grade (Mayer, 2008; Mraz, Padak, & Rasinski, 2008). A recent study revealed that in a school in which students showed high achievement in reading both phonics and whole language were emphasized (Pressley & others, 2007a). In this study, intensive instruction in phonics improved the reading achievement of students with weak reading skills, whereas more holistic instruction was linked with higher achievement for students with stronger reading skills.

phonics approach An approach that emphasizes that reading instruction should teach phonics and its basic rules for translating written symbols into sounds; early reading instruction should use simplified materials.

whole-language approach An approach that stresses that reading instruction should parallel children's natural language learning. Reading materials should be whole and meaningful.

As Mayer (2004, 2008) and an increasing number of experts in the field of reading now conclude, direct instruction in phonological training is a key aspect of learning to read (Cunningham, 2009; Melzi & Ely, 2009). Effective training for phonological awareness includes two main techniques:

- *Blending,* which involves listening to a series of separate spoken sounds and blending them, such as /g/ /o/
- *Segmentation,* which consists of tapping out or counting out the sounds in a word, such as /g/ /o/ = *go,* which is two sounds

In addition, researchers have found that the best training for phonological awareness has three characteristics: the phonological training is integrated with reading and writing, is simple, and it is conducted in small groups rather than with a whole class (Stahl, 2002).

Conclusions reached by the National Reading Panel (2000) suggest that children benefit from *guided oral* reading—that is, from reading aloud with guidance and feedback. Learning strategies for reading comprehension—such as monitoring one's own reading progress and summarizing—also help children (Fisher, Frey, & Berkin, 2009).

In one study, Michael Pressley and his colleagues (2001) examined literacy instruction in five U.S. classrooms. Based on academic and classroom literacy performance of students, the effectiveness of classrooms was analyzed. In the most effective classrooms, teachers exhibited excellent classroom management based on positive reinforcement and cooperation; balanced teaching of skills, literature, and writing; scaffolding and matching of task demands to students' skill level; encouragement of student self-regulation; and strong connections across subject areas. In general, the extensive observations did not support any particular reading approach (such as whole-language or phonics); rather, excellent instruction involved multiple, well-integrated components. An important point in this study is that effective reading instruction involves more than a specific reading approach—it also includes effective classroom management, encouragement of self-regulation, and other components.

Reading, like other important skills, takes time and effort (Ogle & Beers, 2009). In a national assessment, children in the fourth grade had higher scores on a national reading test when they read 11 or more pages daily for school and homework (National Assessment of Educational Progress, 2000) (see Figure 11.1). Teachers who required students to read a great deal on a daily basis had students who were more proficient at reading than teachers who required little reading by their students.

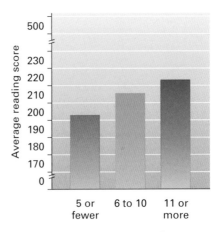

FIGURE 11.1 The Relation of Reading Achievement to Number of Pages Read Daily

In the recent analysis of reading in the fourth grade in the National Assessment of Educational Progress (2000), reading more pages daily in school and as part of homework assignments was related to higher scores on a reading test in which scores ranged from 0 to 500.

Cognitive Approaches

Cognitive approaches to reading emphasize decoding and comprehending words, prior knowledge, and developing expert reading strategies.

Decoding and Comprehending Words   At the beginning of our discussion of reading, we described Mayer's (2004, 2008) view that decoding words is a key cognitive process in learning to read. The cognitive approach emphasizes the cognitive processes involved in decoding and comprehending words. Important in this regard are certain metacognitive skills and increasing automaticity that is characterized by fluency.

Metacognition is involved in reading in the sense that good readers develop control of their own reading skills and understand how reading works. For example, good readers know that it is important to comprehend the "gist" of what an author is saying.

Teachers can help students develop good metacognitive strategies for reading by getting them to monitor their own reading, especially when they run into difficulties in their reading (Fisher, Frey, & Berkin, 2009). Here are some metacognitive strategies that teachers can help students use to improve their reading (Pressley & Harris, 2006; Pressley & Hilden, 2006):

- Overview text before reading.
- Look for important information while reading and pay more attention to it than other information; ask yourself questions about the important ideas or relate them to something you already know.
- Attempt to determine the meaning of words not recognized (use the words around a word to figure out its meaning, use a dictionary, or temporarily ignore it and wait for further clarification).
- Monitor text comprehension.
- Understand relationships between parts of text.
- Recognize when you might need to go back and reread a passage (you didn't understand it, to clarify an important idea, it seemed important to remember, or to underline or summarize for study).
- Adjust pace of reading depending on the difficulty of the material.

When students process information automatically, they do so with little or no conscious effort. When word recognition occurs rapidly, meaning also often follows in a rapid fashion (Stanovich, 1994). Many beginning or poor readers do not recognize words automatically. Their processing capacity is consumed by the demands of word recognition, so they have less capacity to devote to comprehension of groupings of words as phrases or sentences. As their processing of words and passages becomes more automatic, it is said that their reading becomes more fluent (Kuhn, 2009; Wolsey, & Fisher, 2009). Students' fluency often improves when they (Mayer, 2008) (1) hear others read a passage before and after they read it, which is called assisted practice; (2) spend considerable time at reading various passages; and (3) speak with appropriate expression and rhythm in oral reading.

Prior Knowledge Another emphasis in the cognitive approach to reading is that students' prior knowledge about a topic is related to what they remember from reading about the topic and their ability to make correct inferences about the material they read (Mayer, 2008). If teachers detect that students don't have adequate knowledge about a topic they are going to read about, what needs to be done? For one, they need to evaluate whether the reading material is too difficult for students. If so, then passages that are more appropriate for the students' reading level can be chosen. Also, teachers can provide prereading activities for students related to the topic.

Developing Expert Reading Strategies In the cognitive approach, researchers have searched for the underlying cognitive processes that explain reading. This search has led to an interest in strategies, especially the strategies of expert readers compared with those of novice readers (Allington, 2009; Fisher, Frey, & Berkin, 2009). Researchers advise teachers to guide students in developing good reading strategies.

Michael Pressley and his colleagues (1992) developed the **transactional strategy instruction approach**, a cognitive approach to reading that emphasizes instruction in strategies (especially metacognitive strategies). In their view, strategies control students' abilities to remember what they read. It is especially important to teach students metacognitive strategies to monitor their reading progress. Summarizing is also thought to be an important reading strategy. In the strategy approach, authors of teachers' manuals for subjects other than reading per se are encouraged to include information about the importance of reading strategies, how and when to use particular strategies, and prompts to remind students about using strategies.

Social Constructivist Approaches

The social constructivist approaches bring the social aspects of reading to the forefront (Hiebert & Raphael, 1996). The contribution of the social context in helping

transactional strategy instruction approach A cognitive approach to reading that emphasizes instruction in strategies, especially metacognitive strategies.

DEVELOPMENTAL FOCUS 11.1
How Do You Help Students Read More Effectively?

Early Childhood

With very young children, it is essential to have a print-rich environment in which they can see words and phrases everywhere. Our classroom is filled with storybooks, picture dictionaries, magazines, and so on. Also, every object in the classroom is labeled—for example, doors, chairs, windows, and bookshelves, so children associate the word printed on the label with the object. And children's names are printed in many places so that they get used to seeing it in print.

—Valarie Gorham, *Kiddie Quarters, Inc.*

Elementary School: Grades K–5

I help my second-graders read more effectively by stressing reading for comprehension. That said, I incorporate prereading, during-reading, and postreading comprehension strategies. In prereading, I state the purpose of the reading and preview pictures, titles, headings, boldface words, and so on. During reading we check the selection for meaning (Does it make sense? Any confusing words?) and reread for understanding. In postreading, we check to see if we know what was read, summarize, and reflect.

—Elizabeth Frascella, *Clinton Elementary School*

Middle School: Grades 6–8

One of the best ways to become a better reader is to read! Every time I cover a historical era with my seventh-graders, I also make them aware of the related books that are available in our school library. Our librarian will pull corresponding books off the shelves and display them for students. Even the most ardent "nonreader" has a book he or she likes; the trick is to find the right book!

—Mark Fodness, *Bemidji Middle School*

High School: Grades 9–12

With the way we teach reading in America, it is no wonder many students hate it. We teachers make reading so painful and serious—for example, we pick apart novels, we quiz and test to death. Teachers need to show students that reading is fun—they should read what students are reading; "sell" the books to students by talking about the most interesting parts; let students see them reading; and be excited and energetic when discussing new books in class.

—Jennifer Heiter, *Bremen High School*

children learn to read includes such factors as how much emphasis the culture places on reading, the extent to which parents have exposed their children to books before they enter formal schooling, the teacher's communication skills, the extent to which teachers give students opportunities to discuss what they have read, and the district-mandated reading curriculum (Jalongo, 2007; McGee & Richgels, 2008). Whereas cognitive constructivists emphasize the student's construction of meaning, social constructivists stress that meaning is *socially negotiated.* In other words, meaning involves not only the reader's contribution but also the social context and the purpose for reading. Social constructivist approaches emphasize the importance of giving students opportunities for engaging in meaningful dialogue about their reading. One way of doing this is through reciprocal teaching.

Reciprocal Teaching   In our discussion of the Fostering a Community of Learners program in Chapter 10, we described **reciprocal teaching** in terms of students taking turns leading a small-group discussion. Reciprocal teaching also can involve a teacher and a student. In reciprocal teaching, teachers initially explain the strategies and model how to use them to make sense of the text. Then they ask students to

> **reciprocal teaching** A learning arrangement in which students take turns leading a small-group discussion; can also involve teacher-scaffolded instruction.

What are some important aspects of social contexts that influence children's reading?

demonstrate the strategies, giving them support as they learn them. As in scaffolding, the teacher gradually assumes a less active role, letting the student assume more initiative. For example, Annemarie Palincsar and Ann Brown (1984) used reciprocal teaching to improve students' abilities to enact certain strategies to improve their reading comprehension. In this teacher-scaffolded instruction, teachers worked with students to help them generate questions about the text they had read, clarify what they did not understand, summarize the text, and make predictions. Research on reciprocal teaching suggests that it is a very effective strategy for improving reading comprehension (Webb & Palincsar, 1996).

School/Family/Community Connections   From the social constructivist perspective, schools are not the only sociocultural context that is important in reading. Families and communities are also important (Vukelich, Christie, & Enz, 2008).

Of special concern are the language experiences of students from low-income families (Garcia & Willis, 2001). In Chapter 5, "Sociocultural Diversity," we discussed research findings that, on average, young children in welfare homes heard about 600 words an hour, whereas young children in professional families heard about 2,100 words an hour (Hart & Risley, 1995). These researchers also found that, on average, children in welfare homes received only half as much language experience in their early years as children in middle-income families. They also revealed that children in high-income families had twice as much language experience as even children in middle-income families. At-risk students who do not read outside of school fall further behind as they go through the elementary school years (Rowe, 1994). Most students who are avid readers report that they have at least one other person to talk with about their reading and about what to read next (Fielding, Wilson, & Anderson, 1986). Many parents of at-risk students have their own reading difficulties, as well as problems in obtaining books (Gunning, 2000).

Review, Reflect, and Practice

(2) **Explain how reading develops and discuss some useful approaches to teaching reading.**

REVIEW

- What happens at each stage in Chall's developmental model of reading?
- How are language rule systems involved in reading?
- What are some differences between the whole-language approach and the phonics approach to teaching reading? Which approach is better?
- What are the key ideas in cognitive approaches to reading?
- What are the important features of social constructivist approaches to reading?

REFLECT

- What would be some of the key considerations in a balanced view of teaching reading?

PRAXIS™ PRACTICE

1. Kareem is reading his science text. He is taking notes as he reads to help him remember the information. He has learned much about science from his text this year. For instance, he learned that there are many different kinds of rocks that vary in how they were formed, their hardness, and their color. However, when presented with conflicting views on a scientific matter, Kareem is easily confused. Which of Chall's (1979) developmental stages of reading best characterizes Kareem?
   a. stage 1
   b. stage 2
   c. stage 3
   d. stage 4

2. Which of the following is the best example of a student struggling with phonemic awareness?
   a. Keeshan, who often misorders the words in a sentence
   b. Katrina, who does not recognize that *television* is made up of two units of meaning: *tele*, meaning across, and *vision*
   c. Sam, who struggles to sound out words he doesn't recognize immediately
   d. Tasha, who has a limited vocabulary

3. Which of the following is the best example of the use of the whole-language approach to teaching reading?
   a. Ms. Tillman uses flash cards to help her students develop their sight vocabulary.
   b. Ms. Muhammad's students are immersed in literature. They read various types of literature and write about what they have read.
   c. Ms. Orton uses a phonics workbook to help her students develop their decoding skills.
   d. Ms. Wade's students use a computer game to practice their reading skills. A character says a word, and the student clicks on the correct printed word.

4. Which of the following is the best example of a teacher using a cognitive approach to teaching reading?
   a. Ms. Beckham uses flashcards to help students learn new words and reinforces them with candy for correct responses.
   b. Ms. Gomes has her students choose from a variety of books to read. Those students who read a particular book then meet to discuss the book on a regular basis.

(continued)

Review, Reflect, and Practice

    c. Ms. Owen emphasizes the importance of using context clues to help determine the meaning of new words.

    d. Ms. Ronaldo has her students write each word they miss on a spelling pretest five times to help them remember the word.

5. Which of the following is the best example of a teacher using a social constructivist approach to teaching reading?

    a. Ms. Beckham uses flashcards to help students learn new words and reinforces them with candy for correct responses.

    b. Ms. Gomes has her students choose from a variety of books to read. Those students who read a particular book then meet to discuss the book on a regular basis.

    c. Ms. Owen emphasizes the importance of using context clues to help determine the meaning of new words.

    d. Ms. Ronaldo has her students write each word they miss on a spelling pretest five times to help them remember the word.

Please see the answer key at the end of the book.

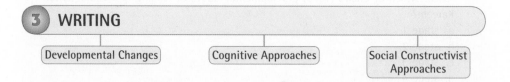

3 WRITING

Developmental Changes — Cognitive Approaches — Social Constructivist Approaches

Major concerns about students' writing competence are increasingly being voiced (Harris, Graham, & Mason, 2008; Harris & others, 2009). One study revealed that 70 to 75 percent of U.S. students in grades 4 through 12 are low-achieving writers (Persky, Daane, & Jin, 2003). College instructors report that 50 percent of high school graduates are not prepared for college-level writing (Achieve, Inc., 2005). Two-thirds of U.S. students indicate that their writing assignments total less than one hour per week (Applebee & Langer, 2006).

As with reading, teachers play a critical role in students' development of writing skills. The observations of classrooms made by Michael Pressley and his colleagues (2007b) revealed that students became good writers when teachers spent considerable time on writing instruction and were passionate about teaching students to write. Their observations also indicated that classrooms with students who scored high on writing assessments had walls that overflowed with examples of effective writing, whereas it was much harder to find such examples on the walls of classrooms that had many students who scored low on writing assessments.

Our further coverage of writing focuses on these questions: How do writing skills develop? What are cognitive and social constructivist approaches to writing?

Developmental Changes

Children's writing emerges out of their early scribbles, which appear at around 2 to 3 years of age. In early childhood, children's motor skills usually become well enough developed for them to begin printing letters and their name (Morrow, 2009). In the United States, most 4-year-olds can print their first name. Five-year-olds can reproduce letters and copy several short words. As they develop their printing skills, children gradually learn to distinguish between the distinctive characteristics of letters, such as whether the lines are curved or straight, open or closed, and so on. Through the early elementary grades, many children still continue to reverse letters such as *b* and *d* and *p* and *q*. At this point in development, if other aspects of the child's development are normal, these letter reversals are not a predictor of literacy problems.

As they begin to write, children often invent spellings of words (Soderman & Farrell, 2008). They usually do this by relying on the sounds of words they hear as clues for how to spell. Teachers and parents should encourage children's early writing without being overly concerned about the proper formation of letters or correct conventional spelling. Such printing errors should be viewed as a natural part of the young child's growth, not scrutinized and criticized. Spelling and printing corrections can be made in positive ways and judiciously enough to avoid dampening early enjoyment and spontaneity in writing (Vukelich, Christie, & Enz, 2008).

Like becoming a good reader, becoming a good writer takes many years and lots of practice (Melzi & Ely, 2009). Children should be given many writing opportunities in the elementary and secondary school years. As their language and cognitive skills improve with good instruction, so will their writing skills (Smith & Reud, 2009). For example, developing a more sophisticated understanding of syntax and grammar serves as an underpinning for better writing (Irvin, Buehl, & Kiemp, 2007).

So do such cognitive skills as organization and logical reasoning (Deshler & Hock, 2007; Perin, 2007). Through elementary, middle, and high school, students develop increasingly sophisticated methods of organizing their ideas. In early elementary school, they narrate and describe or write short poems. In late elementary and middle school, they move to projects such as book reports that combine narration with more reflection and analysis. In high school, they become more skilled at forms of exposition that do not depend on narrative structure (Conley, 2008; McKeough & others, 2007). A recent meta-analysis (use of statistical techniques to combine the results of studies) revealed that the following interventions were the most effective in improving fourth- through twelfth-grade students' writing quality: (1) strategy instruction, (2) summarization, (3) peer assistance, and (4) setting goals (Graham & Perin, 2007).

Cognitive Approaches

Cognitive approaches to writing emphasize many of the same themes that we discussed with regard to reading, such as constructing meaning and developing strategies (Graham & Olinghouse, 2009; Harris & Graham, 2008). Planning, problem solving, revising, and metacognitive strategies are thought to be especially important in improving students' writing.

Planning   Planning, which includes outlining and organizing content information, is an important aspect of writing (Graham, 2008; Graham & Harris, 2008; Mayer,

THROUGH THE EYES OF STUDENTS

The Devl and the Babe Goste

Anna Mudd is the 6-year-old author of "The Devl and the Babe Goste." Anna has been writing stories for at least 2 years. Her story includes poetic images, sophisticated syntax, and vocabulary that reflect advances in language development.

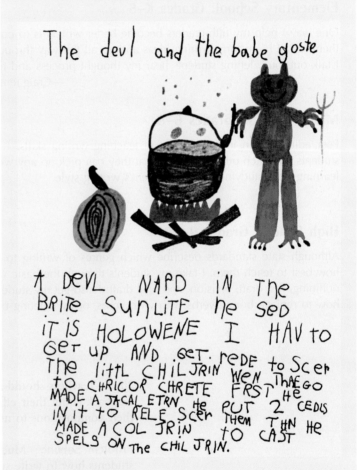

(Source: From Jean Berko Gleason, *The Development of Language*, 3/e. Published by Allyn and Bacon, Boston, MA. Copyright © 1993 by Pearson Education. Reprinted by permission of the publisher.)

DEVELOPMENTAL FOCUS 11.2

How Do You Help Students Improve Their Writing Skills?

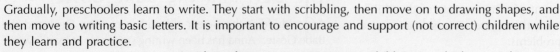

Early Childhood

Gradually, preschoolers learn to write. They start with scribbling, then move on to drawing shapes, and then move to writing basic letters. It is important to encourage and support (not correct) children while they learn and practice.

—Heidi Kaufman, *Metro West YMCA Child Care and Educational Program*

Elementary School: Grades K–5

One way I help my fifth-graders become better writers is to compose a story myself. I start by showing them how I brainstorm writing ideas and go all the way through to writing the final copy. As I do this, I talk out loud, letting students hear my thought process and thus learn effective writing strategies.

—Craig Jensen, *Cooper Mountain Elementary School*

Middle School: Grades 6–8

Peer editing is an important part of teaching writing skills. I find it especially important to have my students edit each other's work so that they can pick up any writing errors in a classmate's paper, while learning from studying another student's writing style.

—Casey Maass, *Edison Middle School*

High School: Grades 9–12

Although state standards describe which genres of writing to teach, it is up to the teacher to decide how best to teach them. I take my students through the basic writing phases: brainstorming, prewriting, outlining, first draft, revision, and final draft. I also get my students to think about style by showing them how to replace boring verbs with vivid verbs, or by deleting unnecessary adverbs and adjectives.

—Jennifer Heiter, *Bremen High School*

2008). Teachers should show students how to outline and organize a paper and give feedback about their efforts. Figure 11.2 provides a model for helping students plan their compositions to meet a deadline.

Problem Solving Much of the instruction in writing in schools involves teaching students how to write sentences and paragraphs properly. However, there is more to writing than avoiding run-on sentences or making sure that paragraphs support topic sentences (Harris & others, 2009). More fundamentally, writing is a broader sort of problem solving (Mayer, 2008). One psychologist called the problem-solving process in writing "the making of meaning" (Kellogg, 1994).

As problem solvers, writers need to establish goals and work to attain them. It also is helpful to think of writers as constrained by their need for integrated understanding of the subject, knowledge of how the language system works, and the writing problem itself. The writing problem includes the purpose of the paper, the audience, and the role of the writer in the paper to be produced (Flower & Hayes, 1981). A student who is having a problem may be having difficulty with any one of these aspects of writing. Identifying the specific difficulty is the first step in helping the student become a better writer.

Revising Revising is a major component of successful writing (Gunning, 2008). Revising involves writing multiple drafts, getting feedback from individuals who are knowledgeable about writing, and learning how to use the critical feedback to improve the writing. It also includes detecting and correcting errors (Ogle & Beers, 2009). Researchers have found that older and more-skilled writers are more likely to revise their writing than younger and less-skilled writers (Hayes & Flower, 1986).

Metacognition and Strategies When we emphasize knowledge of writing strategies, we move into the area of metacognition, which we discussed in Chapter 8. Monitoring one's writing progress is especially important in becoming a good writer (Harris & Graham, 2008; Harris & others, 2009). This includes being receptive to feedback and applying what one learns in writing one paper to making the next paper better (Tompkins, 2009).

A recent research review revealed that the following are effective writing strategies that should be taught to secondary school students (Graham & Perin, 2007):

- *Prewriting.* A good strategy is to have students engage in prewriting activities that involve generating or organizing ideas for their composition.

- *Planning, revising, and editing.* These are critical skills in becoming a good writer, and students need considerable practice in developing and using them.

- *Summarization.* Teachers need to explicity and systematically teach students how to summarize the text they write.

- *Sentence combining.* Students need to practice constructing more complex, sophisticated sentences.

One to two months before the deadline	Select topic. Map ideas. Develop writing plan. Begin to develop a thesis statement. Start research.
Two weeks before the deadline	Develop individual sections of paper. Revise with vigor. Complete research. Finalize thesis statement.
The week before the deadline	Polish the individual sections of the paper. Create an interesting title. Check references for accuracy. Get some feedback.
The night before the deadline	Combine the parts of the paper. Print the final draft. Proofread the paper. Assemble the paper.

FIGURE 11.2 A Sample Timetable for a Writing Deadline

Social Constructivist Approaches

As in reading, social constructivist approaches emphasize that writing is best understood as being culturally embedded and socially constructed rather than being internally generated.

The Social Context of Writing The social constructivist perspective focuses on the social context in which writing is produced. Students need to participate in a writing community to understand author/reader relationships and learn to recognize how their perspective might differ from that of others (Hiebert & Raphael, 1996).

Some students bring a rich background of writing experiences and encouragement to write to the classroom; others have little writing experience and have not been encouraged to write extensively. In some classrooms the teacher places a high value on writing; in others the teacher treats writing as being less important. A recent study revealed that in a school in which students showed high achievement in writing and reading, language arts were given a high priority by the principal

PEANUTS © United Features Syndicate, Inc.

THROUGH THE EYES OF STUDENTS

Writing Self-Evaluations

San Francisco fifth-grade teacher Keren Abra periodically asks her students to evaluate their writing for their writing portfolios. Here are several of her students' comments toward the end of the school year.

I am in fifth grade right now and I love writing. Anytime that I get to write I will; as far as I can remember I have loved writing. I feel that my writing has developed since fourth grade and I am pleased with my writing. Some authors might not like their writing unlike me; I have *never* thrown away any of my writing. I love to share my writing and give and get ideas from other writers. . . . If I could describe myself as a writer I would say (not to brag) that I was a descriptive, imaginative, captivating writer.

Michelle

I think writing a story is easy because there is so much to write about and if I have to write about a certain thing there are also more things to do with the story. . . . If someone read my writing they would think I probably am a happy and energetic kid. They will think this because most of my stories are upbeat.

Sarah

I feel that when I'm writing I could do better. I could do better especially on spelling. When I was in kindergarten we did not do a lot of writing. When I was in third grade I did not like writing. It was scary learning new things about writing. I'm in fifth grade and I love to write but sometimes it annoys me that I can't spell that well. One thing I like about my writing is the way I put action into all of my work because I love to get excited! I think that if someone were to read my writing uncorrected they would not be able to read it. If it was corrected I think the person would really like my story.

Janet

and teachers (Pressley & others, 2007b). The principal directed resources toward reading and writing instruction, including a considerable expansion of the number of books in the school's library and encouragement of field trips related to languge arts.

Meaningful Writing and Student-Teacher Writing Conferences   According to the social constructivist approach, students' writing should include opportunities to create "real" texts, in the sense of writing about personally meaningful situations. For example, consider Anthony, whose teacher frequently asks students to write about personal experiences. He wrote about his grandmother's life and death, and his teacher gave him considerable support for writing about this emotional experience. Student-teacher writing conferences play an important support role in helping students become better writers.

Peer Collaboration and Editing   While working in groups, writers experience the processes of inquiry, clarification, and elaboration that are important in good writing (Webb & Palincsar, 1996). Also, students often benefit from editing other students' writing.

Students often bring diverse experiences to bear when they collaborate and coauthor papers. Such rich, shared collaboration can produce new insights into what to write about and how (Harris & others, 2009). By contrast, writing simply to meet the teacher's expectations often produces constrained, imitative, and conforming results. In peer writing groups, teacher expectations are often less apparent. In addition to peer collaboration in writing, students' writing often improves when they edit other students' writing.

School-Community Connections   In the social constructivist approach, it is important to connect students' experiences at school with the world outside the classroom. A good strategy is to involve the writing community in your class. Look around your community and think about expert writers you could invite to your classroom to discuss their work. Most communities have such experts, such as journalists and other authors and editors. One of the four most successful middle schools in the United States identified by Joan Lipsitz (1984) built a special Author's Week into its curriculum. Based on students' interest, availability, and diversity, authors are invited to discuss their craft with students. Students sign up to meet individual authors. Before they meet the author, they are required to read at least one of the author's books. Students prepare questions for their author sessions. In some cases, authors come to the class for several days to work with students on their writing projects.

In the course of our discussion of reading and writing, we have described a number of ideas that can be used in the classroom. To evaluate your reading and writing experiences, complete *Self-Assessment 11.1.*

SELF-ASSESSMENT 11.1
Evaluating My Reading and Writing Experiences

Regardless of the academic subject or grade you teach, one of your goals should be to help students not only become competent at reading and writing but also enjoy these activities. Think about your own past and current experiences in reading and writing:

1. What made learning to read enjoyable for you?

_____

_____

2. What made learning to read difficult or unenjoyable?

_____

_____

3. How do you feel about reading now?

_____

_____

4. Do you enjoy libraries? Why or why not?

_____

_____

5. Are there reading skills that you still need to improve?

_____

_____

6. What made learning to write enjoyable for you?

_____

_____

7. What made learning to write difficult or unenjoyable?

_____

_____

8. How do you feel about writing now?

_____

_____

9. Are there writing skills that you still need to improve?

_____

_____

Based on your own experience and ideas in this chapter, how could you make learning to read and write more successful and enjoyable for your students?

BEST PRACTICES
Strategies for Incorporating Writing into the Curriculum

You will have many opportunities to incorporate writing into the curriculum. Here are some examples (Bruning & Horn, 2001; Halonen, 2008):

1. *Nurture positive attitudes toward writing.* This can be done by making sure that many writing tasks ensure student success and by displaying the way that teachers write personally. Give students choices about what they will write.

2. *Foster student engagement through authentic writing tasks and contexts.* Encourage students to write about topics of personal interest, have students write for different audiences, and integrate writing into instruction in other disciplines, such as science, mathematics, and social studies.

3. *Provide a supportive context for writing.* Encourage students to set writing goals, plan how to reach the goals, and monitor their progress toward the goals. Assist students in creating goals that are neither too challenging nor too simple. Teach writing strategies and monitor their use by students. Give students feedback on their progress toward their writing goals. Use peers as writing partners in literacy communities.

4. *Have students write to learn.* This can work in any subject area. For example, in biology, after students have studied the adaptation of different species, ask them to write a summary of the main ideas and generate examples not described in class or the text.

5. *Use free-writing assignments.* In free writing, students write whatever they think about a subject. Such assignments are usually unstructured but have time limits. For example, one free-writing assignment in American history might be "Write about the American Revolution for five minutes." Free writing helps students discover new ideas, connections, and questions they might not have generated if they had not had this free-writing opportunity.

6. *Give students creative writing assignments.* These assignments give students opportunities to explore themselves and their world in creative, insightful ways. They might include poetry, short stories, or essays reflecting personal experiences.

THROUGH THE EYES OF TEACHERS
Imagine the Possibilities

Beverly Gallagher, a third-grade teacher at Princeton Day School, in New Jersey, created the Imagine the Pos-

Beverly Gallagher, working with students to stimulate their interest in reading and writing.

sibilities program, which brings nationally known poets and authors to her school. She phones each student's parents periodically to describe their child's progress and new interests. She invites students from higher grades to work with small groups in her class so that she can spend more one-on-one time with students. Beverly also created poetry partnerships between eleventh-graders and her third-graders in which the older and younger students collaborate to create poems. Each of her students keeps a writer's notebook to record thoughts, inspirations, and special words that intrigue them. Students get special opportunities to sit in an author's chair, where they read their writing to the class. (Source: *USA Today*, 2000).

7. *Require formal writing assignments.* These involve giving students opportunities to express themselves using an objective point of view, precise writing style, and evidence to support their conclusions. Formal writing helps students learn how to make formal arguments. For example, high school students might construct a major paper on topics such as "Global Warming: Real Fears or Hype?" or "An In-Depth Examination of Faulkner's Writing Style," or "Why People Are Prejudiced." Such writing projects stimulate students to think analytically, learn how to use resources, and cite references. Work with students on generating topics for a paper, structuring the paper, using planning and time management skills for completing the paper in a timely manner, drafting and revising, and overcoming spelling and grammatical errors.

Review, Reflect, and Practice

(3) **Describe how writing develops and discuss some useful approaches to teaching writing.**

REVIEW
- What skills are acquired in writing? At what ages are they commonly acquired?
- What cognitive processes are essential to effective writing?
- What are the key ideas in social constructivist approaches to writing?

REFLECT
- For the age group and subject you plan to teach, in what ways will the writing assignments you give to students likely be highly structured and specific? In what ways might they be flexible and open-ended?

PRAXIS™ PRACTICE

1. Which of the following is the best example of developmentally appropriate writing instruction for first-graders?
   a. Ms. Balboa's students are learning how to spell through the use of drill and practice of specific words.
   b. Ms. Donovan carefully corrects students' grammar and spelling errors on their papers and is critical of their errors.
   c. Ms. Figo's students use invented spelling in their work, and she provides them with correct spelling but she does not criticize their efforts.
   d. Ms. Lalas's students practice writing by copying stories that she has written on the blackboard.

2. Ms. Williams emphasizes the importance of prewriting activities to her students. Which aspect of the cognitive approach to writing does she emphasize?
   a. metacognitive strategies
   b. planning
   c. problem solving
   d. revising

3. Which of the following is the best example of a social constructivist approach to writing?
   a. Ms. Reddick's students write reports on various subjects, based on research they have completed.
   b. Ms. Duhon's students write about their own personal experiences and meet with her regularly to discuss their work.
   c. Ms. Williams's students write responses to essay questions about material in their social studies text.
   d. Ms. Randolph's students choose the books they want to read and write book reports about each book that they complete.

Please see the answer key at the end of the book.

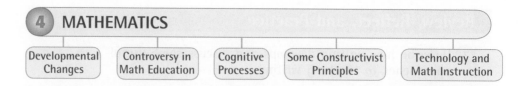

4 MATHEMATICS

| Developmental Changes | Controversy in Math Education | Cognitive Processes | Some Constructivist Principles | Technology and Math Instruction |

What are some developmental changes in the way children think about mathematics and their math abilities at different grade levels? What is the biggest controversy in mathematics education today?

Developmental Changes

The National Council of Teachers of Mathematics (NCTM, 2000) has described the basic principles and standards for school mathematics at different grade levels. We will survey these for all grade levels, beginning with prekindergarten through grade 2.

Prekindergarten Through Grade 2 Children already have a substantial understanding of numbers before they enter first grade (Smith, 2006). Most kindergartners from middle-income families can count past 20, and many can count beyond 100; most can accurately count the number of objects in a set, can add and subtract single digits, and know the relative magnitudes of single-digit numbers (for example, that 8 is greater than 6) (Siegler & Robinson, 1982).

Children are likely to enter elementary school with different levels of mathematical understanding. Some children will need additional support for math learning (Van de Walle, 2007). Early assessments should be used to obtain information for teaching and for potential early interventions.

Understanding basic aspects of number and geometry are critical in kindergarten through the second grade (NCTM, 2000). For example, at these grade levels, children need to learn the base-10 numeration system. They must recognize that the word *ten* may represent a single entity or 10 separate units (10 ones) and that these representations can be interchanged.

When they go to school, children learn many higher numerical skills (NCTM, 2007a). It is important to be aware that they are often doing something more than simply learning to calculate in a standard way. In fact, what children learn about mathematics and how to solve mathematical problems often reflects independent thinking as well as what they are being "taught" (Tolchinsky, 2002). This can be true even in the case of learning the basic "facts" of addition and subtraction, which most of us ultimately memorize.

Grades 3 Through 5 Three key themes of mathematics in grades 3 through 5 are as follows:

- *Multiplicative reasoning.* The emphasis on multiplicative reasoning develops knowledge that children build on as they move to the middle grades, where the focus is on proportional reasoning. In multiplicative reasoning, children need to develop their understanding of fractions as part of a whole and as division.

- *Equivalence.* The concept of *equivalence* helps students to learn different mathematical representations and provides an avenue for exploring algebraic ideas.

What are some developmental changes in the basic mathematics principles children need to learn in elementary school?

What are some developmental changes in the math principles students need to learn in middle school and high school?

- *Computational fluency.* Students need to learn efficient and accurate methods of computing that are based on well-understood properties and number relationships. For example, 298×42 can be thought of as $(300 \times 42) - (2 \times 42)$, or 41×16 is computed by multiplying 41×8 to get 328 and then doubling 328 to obtain 656.

Grades 6 Through 8 In middle school, students benefit from a balanced mathematics program that includes algebra and geometry. Teachers can help students understand how algebra and geometry are connected. Middle school mathematics also should prepare students to deal with quantitative solutions in their lives outside of school.

Students develop far more powerful mathematical reasoning when they learn algebra. A single equation can represent an infinite variety of situations. Even many students who get *A*'s and *B*'s in algebra classes, however, do so without understanding what they are learning—they simply memorize the equations. This approach might work well in the classroom, but it limits these students' ability to use algebra in real-world contexts (NCTM, 2007c).

Grades 9 Through 12 The NCTM (2000) recommends that all students study mathematics in each of the four years of high school. Because students' interests may change during and after high school, they will likely benefit from taking a range of math classes. They should experience the interplay of algebra, geometry, statistics, probability, and discrete mathematics (which involves the mathematics of computers). They should become adept at visualizing, describing, and analyzing situations in mathematical terms. They also need to be able to justify and prove mathematically based ideas (Brahier, 2009; Huetinck & Munshin, 2008).

Controversy in Math Education

Educators currently debate whether math should be taught using a cognitive, conceptual, and constructivist approach or a practice, computational approach. Some proponents of the cognitive approach argue against memorization and practice in teaching mathematics. Instead, they emphasize constructivist mathematical problem solving. Others assume that speed and automaticity are fundamental to effective mathematics achievement and argue that such skills can be acquired only through extensive practice and computation. In recent years, the constructivist approach has become increasingly popular. In this approach, effective instruction focuses on

DEVELOPMENTAL FOCUS 11.3
What Are Your Best Strategies for Teaching Math?

Early Childhood

For preschoolers, math is a natural. They constantly want to know how much, how long, or is it finished yet. We build on this inquisitiveness by helping children find the answers for themselves. In the classroom, we have scales for measuring blocks, liquid, counting bears, and more. We measure how tall they are throughout the year and show them in inches and centimeters. We sharpen their counting skills by having them count the number of steps to the bathroom, and have clocks, timers, rulers, calculators, and numbers in numerous places.

—Valarie Gorham, *Kiddie Quarters, Inc.*

Elementary School: Grades K–5

I find that math manipulatives (physical objects used to represent or model a problem situation) are extremely helpful in teaching my second-graders because they help bring students from concrete thinking to more abstract thinking. Instead of simply memorizing, manipulatives allow students to understand complicated mathematical concepts. This understanding helps them to apply mathematical knowledge to other problems and areas.

—Susan Froelich, *Clinton Elementary School*

Middle School: Grades 6–8

Math skills can be taught through any number of academic disciplines. In social studies, for example, I apply math skills by having students create timelines, placing historical events in chronological order. Graphing skills are also used when we locate different places on a map.

—Casey Maass, *Edison Middle School*

High School: Grades 9–12

As a career and technical education teacher, I make it a point to show students how mathematical skills are applied to real-world situations. For example, I have my food services students create a gingerbread house in which they use rulers, measurements, and protractors—things some of them have not used since middle school. They also multiply and divide recipes. Having my students develop recipes that sometimes work and sometimes fail (often because of incorrect measurements or division) helps them to see the importance of mastering mathematical skills.

—Sandy Swanson, *Menomonee Falls High School*

involving children in solving a problem or developing a concept and in exploring the efficiency of alternative solutions (Van de Walle & Lovin, 2006).

A recent rigorous analysis of research on math instruction programs in elementary schools revealed that only one program had potentially positive effects on math achievement (What Works Clearinghouse, 2007). The program is *Everyday Mathematics* (Wright Group, 2004, 2007), which includes a comprehensive set of instructions and activities that involve basic math processes and computation as well as critical thinking and problem solving.

Cognitive Processes

In our discussion of developmental changes and the controversy in math education, we mentioned several cognitive processes that help children learn math, such as problem-solving skills, understanding how math concepts are linked, and exploring alternative solutions. The National Research Council (2005) concluded that conceptual understanding, procedural fluency, effective organization of knowledge, and metacognitive strategies are important processes in learning math. A recent study also revealed that working memory and speed of processing information were linked to children's math performance (Swanson & Kim, 2007).

In our discussion of the controversy in math education, we saw that debate flourishes about whether conceptual understanding or procedural competences should be the main focus in math education. The National Research Council's (2005) conclusion is that both are important. Teaching math with only an emphasis on procedural competency results in students having too little conceptual understanding, and when students have too little knowledge of procedures they often do not solve math problems competently.

As students move through elementary and secondary school and take increasingly complex math courses, new knowledge and competencies must build on, and be integrated with, previous knowledge (Schwartz, 2008). By the time students begin solving algebra problems, they must have a network of organized knowledge that they can engage to support new algebraic understanding. "The teacher's challenge, then, is to help students build and consolidate prerequisite competencies, understand new concepts in depth, and organize both concepts and competencies in a network of knowledge" (Fuson, Kalchman, & Bransford, 2005, p. 232).

Math instruction that supports students' use of metacognitive strategies also is recommended by the National Research Council (2005). Students can engage in metacognitive self-monitoring to determine their progress in solving individual math problems and their progress in a math course. "Metacognitive functioning is also facilitated by shifting from a focus on answers as just right or wrong to a more detailed focus on 'debugging' a wrong answer, that is, finding where the error is, why it is an error, and correcting it" (Fuson, Kalchman, & Bransford, 2005, p. 239).

Developing some effective general problem-solving strategies can also help students' math learning (Fuson, Kalchman, & Bransford, 2005; National Research Council, 2005). Two of these are making a drawing of a situation and asking one's self questions. Students can learn to use these strategies as part of their self-monitoring in math.

Gary Piercey, who teaches math to high school students in Houston, Texas, makes the classroom an exciting place to be for students. He sometimes dresses up for skits, as in the case shown here in which he plays Freeze, whose evil plans can be foiled only by students being able a successfully solve algebra problems.

Some Constructivist Principles

From a constructivist perspective, the principles discussed next can be followed when teaching math (Middleton & Goepfert, 1996). These include strategies for making math realistic and interesting, the need to consider the students' prior knowledge, and how the math curriculum can be socially interactive.

Make Math Realistic and Interesting   Build your teaching of math around realistic and interesting problems. These problems might involve some kind of conflict, suspense, or crisis that motivates students' interest. The math problem-solving activities might center on the student, community issues, scientific discoveries, or historical events. Math games can provide a motivating context for learning math. Connecting math with other subject areas, such as science, geography, reading, and writing, also is recommended.

Consider the Students' Prior Knowledge   In our discussion of cognitive processes, we indicated that building on the student's knowledge is an important aspect of math education (National Research Council, 2005). Evaluate what knowledge the students bring to the unit and the context in which instruction takes place. Make enough

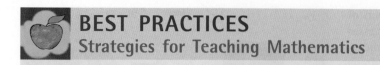

BEST PRACTICES
Strategies for Teaching Mathematics

We have discussed many strategies for teaching mathematics. Here are some of the key ones:

1. *Teach students to become both procedurally and conceptually competent in math.* Students need to develop good computational skills, and they also need to understand math concepts.

2. *Help students to develop good math problem-solving skills.*

3. *Encourage students to use metacognitive strategies.* Guide students to monitor their progress in solving math problems and becoming more competent at math.

4. *Make math interesting for students.* For example, using real-world contexts and games can improve many students' motivation for spending more time on math, especially students who are not doing well in math.

Henry Brown.

THROUGH THE EYES OF TEACHERS
Never See Failure as Failure

An at-risk student, Henry Brown's life was turned around by middle school teacher Cora Russell, and the experience inspired him to teach. Brown, a recent Florida Teacher of the Year, teaches math at Hallandale Adult Alternative High School. In Brown's view, "Never see failure as failure." Half of the students enter this school with math skills below the fifth-grade level. He believes

it is important to teach real-world math skills. In one project, Brown devised a dummy corporation and had students play different roles in it, learning important math skills as they worked and made decisions in the corporation. He also created Helping Hands, which involves senior citizens in the classroom. (Source: *USA Today,* 2001)

5. *Use technology effectively.* As indicated earlier, some research indicates that use of calculators and computers in math may be best for students if delayed until the middle school years.

6. *Connect with parents.* In Chapter 9, we described Family Math, a program that helps parents experience math with their children in a positive, supportive way. In addition to telling parents about Family Math, consider having Family Math nights, especially at the beginning of the school year. At the Family Math night, offer resources that parents can use at home to help their children learn math more effectively.

7. *If you teach math, one good active step is to join the NCTM and use its resources.* The NCTM has annual conferences, publishes an annual yearbook with stimulating chapters on recent developments in math education, and publishes journals such as *Mathematics Teacher*. For more information about the NCTM, call (703) 620-9840 or go to www.nctm.org.

information available for students to be able to come up with a method for solving math problems but withhold enough information so that students must stretch their minds to solve the problems.

Make the Math Curriculum Socially Interactive Develop math projects that require students to work together to come up with a solution (NCTM, 2007b). Build into the math curriculum opportunities for students to use and improve their communication skills. Generate math projects that engender discussion, argument, and compromise.

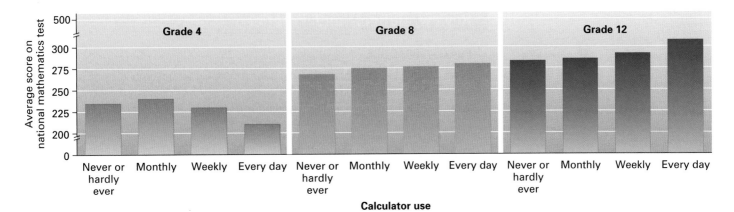

FIGURE 11.3 Frequency of Calculator Use at Different Grade Levels and National Mathematics Achievement Test Scores

Note: Scores on the National Mathematics Achievement Test can range from 0 to 500.

Technology and Math Instruction

One issue in math education is how technology intensive it should be (De Corte & Verschafell, 2006; NCTM, 2007c). The NCTM's *Curriculum and Evaluation Standards* recommends that calculators be used at all levels of mathematics instruction and that some access to computers is also necessary if students are to be adequately educated for future careers. In many school systems, adequate funds for computers is a major issue.

In contrast to U.S. teachers, Japanese and Chinese teachers do not allow the everyday use of calculators or computers in mathematics classes, because they want the students to understand the concepts and operations required to solve problems. Some critics argue that the American emphasis on the early use of these technology aids prevents students from gaining experience in manipulating concrete objects—that they need to learn mathematical concepts (Stevenson, 2001). Only at the high school level, after students have developed a clear understanding of mathematical concepts, are East Asian students allowed to use calculators for solving mathematical problems. In the recent National Assessment of Educational Progress, in the fourth grade, frequent calculator use was associated with lower national achievement test scores in mathematics, whereas in the eighth and twelfth grades, more frequent use of calculators was linked with higher national test scores (see Figure 11.3).

Review, Reflect, and Practice

4 **Characterize how mathematical thinking develops and identify some issues related to teaching mathematics.**

REVIEW

- What are some developmental changes in mathematical skills?
- What is the main controversy in math education?
- What are some cognitive processes involving math?
- What are some constructivist principles in learning math?
- What role can technology play in math instruction?

REFLECT

- Do you think that teachers in Asia are wise not to allow young students to use calculators? Should the United States follow this example?

(continued)

Review, Reflect, and Practice

PRAXIS™ PRACTICE

1. Ms. Carpenter's students are working on developing an understanding of place value. They are most likely in grade
   a. K–2.
   b. 3–5.
   c. 6–8.
   d. 9–12.

2. Malavi is very fast and accurate at doing multiplication and division. In the controversy on math education, he could be cited as an example of the importance of adopting which of these approaches?
   a. constructivist
   b. practice, computational
   c. conceptual
   d. cognitive

3. Joan is going over her math exam. She is examining her mistakes in an effort to find out what she did wrong. Then she corrects her mistakes and resubmits the exam. Her teacher, Mr. Ewing, allows students to receive credit for going through this process because he believes it helps students to learn from their errors. This is an example of
   a. algebraic reasoning.
   b. algorithms.
   c. debugging.
   d. rote memorization.

4. Which of the following is the best example of application of constructivist principles to math teaching?
   a. Ms. Carmichael's students complete timed tests of basic math facts.
   b. Ms. Dodge's students play store, which allows them to add up their purchases, pay for them, and make change.
   c. Ms. Luker's students solve word problems but do not work on computation.
   d. Mr. Pinks's students complete problems on the board so he can determine if they have grasped the concepts.

5. Based on the results of research on calculator use and math achievement, at which of the following grade levels should Ingrid start using a calculator in doing math?
   a. first
   b. third
   c. fifth
   d. eighth

Please see the answer key at the end of the book.

5 SCIENCE

Science Education   Constructivist Teaching Strategies

What are some key ideas in educating students about science? What are some constructivist strategies for teaching science?

Science Education

Scientists typically engage in certain kinds of thinking and behavior. For example, they regularly make careful observations; collect, organize, and analyze data; measure, graph, and understand spatial relations; pay attention to and regulate their own thinking; and know when and how to apply their knowledge to solve problems (Chapman, 2000).

These skills, which are essential to the practice of science, are not routinely taught in schools, especially elementary schools. As a result, many students are not competent at them. Many scientists and educators argue that schools need to increasingly guide students in learning how to use these skills (Bass, Contant, & Carrin, 2009; Martin & others, 2009).

Children have many misconceptions that are incompatible with science and reality (Bransford & Donovan, 2005). They may go through mental gymnastics trying to reconcile seemingly contradictory new information with their new beliefs (Miller, 2000). For example, after learning about the solar system, children sometimes conclude that there are two Earths—the seemingly flat world in which they live and the round ball floating in space that their teacher just described.

Good teachers perceive and understand a child's underlying concepts, then use the concepts as a scaffold for learning (Bybee, Powell, & Trowbridge, 2008). Effective science teaching helps children distinguish between fruitful errors and misconceptions, and detect plainly wrong ideas that need to be replaced by more accurate conceptions (Bransford & Donovan, 2005).

How might experiences in families, economic conditions, and culture be linked to children's science achievement? A recent study of more than 107,000 students in 41 countries examined this question (Chiu, 2007). Students had higher science achievement scores when they lived in two-parent families, experienced more family involvement, lived with fewer siblings, their schools had more resources, and they lived in wealthier countries or lived in countries with more equal distribution of household income.

Constructivist Teaching Strategies

Many science teachers help their students construct their knowledge of science through guided discovery (Bass, Contant, & Carrin, 2009). Constructivist teaching emphasizes that children have to build their own scientific knowledge and understanding with guidance from the teacher. At each step in science learning, they need to interpret new knowledge in the context of what they already understand. Rather than putting fully formed knowledge into children's minds, in the constructivist approach teachers serve as guides and consultants as children construct scientifically valid interpretations of the world and provide them with feedback to help them correct their scientific misconceptions (Martin & others, 2009).

Critics of constructivist approaches argue that too much attention is given to inquiry skills and not enough is given to discipline-specific information. In response, advocates of the constructivist approach to biology argue that it creates more scientifically literate citizens who know how to think in scientific ways rather than just memorize scientific facts (Gallagher, 2007).

Keep in mind, though, that it is important that students not be left completely on their own to construct scientific knowledge independent of *science content*. Students' inquiry should be guided (Magnusson & Palincsar, 2005). Teachers at a minimum should initially scaffold students' science learning, extensively monitor their progress, and ensure that they are learning science content. Thus, in pursuing science investigations, students need to "learn inquiry skills *and* science content" (Lehrer & Schauble, 2006).

Pete Karpyk, who teaches chemistry in Weirton, West Virginia, uses an extensive array of activities that bring science alive for students. Here he has shrink-wrapped himself to demonstrate the effects of air pressure. He has some students give chemistry demonstrations at elementary schools and has discovered that in some cases students who don't do well on tests excel when they teach children. He also adapts his teaching based on feedback from former students and incorporates questions from their college chemistry tests as bonus questions on the tests he gives his high school students. (Source: Briggs, 2005. p. 6D)

BEST PRACTICES
Strategies for Teaching Science

A summary of important strategies to use when teaching science include:

1. *Helping students learn how to think like scientists.* Create settings in which students are required to make careful observations, work effectively with data, and solve scientific problems.

2. *Monitoring students' misconceptions about science and working with them to develop more accurate conceptions.*

3. *Guiding students in developing inquiry skills.* When teaching inquiry skills, don't leave students completely to their own devices; use guided inquiry.

4. *Teaching science content.* Students not only need to develop inquiry skills, they also need to learn science content.

5. *Making science interesting by giving students opportunities to explore everyday science problems.* Next, you can read about how Peggy Schweiger, a physics teacher at Klein Oak High School in Katy, Texas, does this.

Peggy Schweiger with a student who is learning how to think and discover how physics works in people's everyday lives.

THROUGH THE EYES OF TEACHERS
Dropping an Egg on a Teacher's Head

Peggy Schweiger uses hands-on projects, such as wiring a doll house and making replicas of a boat for a regatta, to improve students' understanding of physics. She especially works hard to create projects that will interest both female and male students. According to former student Alison Arnett, 19, "She taught us how to think and learn, not how to succeed in physics class. We were encouraged to stand on desks, tape things to the ceiling, and even drop an egg on her head to illustrate physics—anything to make us discover that we live with physics every day." (Source: *USA Today,* 2001, p. 6)

Review, Reflect, and Practice

5 Identify some challenges and strategies related to teaching children how to think scientifically.

REVIEW
- What are key ideas in science education?
- What are some constructivist approaches to teaching science?

REFLECT
- How effectively did your elementary, middle, and high school teach science to the typical student? If less than perfectly, how could their approach have been improved?

Review, Reflect, and Practice

PRAXIS™ PRACTICE

1. Which of the following teachers is most likely to be successful in helping students to overcome scientific misconceptions?
   a. Ms. Coster finds out what her students' misconceptions are by carefully asking them questions and then explicitly combats their misconceptions via direct instruction.
   b. Ms. Quigley uses a science text and carefully tests her students over the content in the text.
   c. Mr. Jones sets up situations in which the students explore materials themselves to discover their misconceptions.
   d. Mr. Foster designs experiences that demonstrate to the students that their misconceptions are incorrect and point out the correct principles.

2. Which of the following is the best example of constructivist teaching strategies in science?
   a. Mr. Ricardo's students study the material in their science tests and take quizzes over each chapter.
   b. Mr. Bunker's students have a "science bee" every Friday. He asks questions and the students respond. Students who answer wrong are out of the competition.
   c. Ms. Mertz's students perform carefully designed experiments in a few areas that demonstrate scientific principles, helping them to learn in depth and to learn the process of scientific inquiry.
   d. Ms. O'Connor's students keep science notebooks in which they take notes on her presentations, and she gives periodic tests on the material in the notebooks.

Please see the answer key at the end of the book.

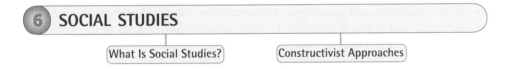

6 SOCIAL STUDIES

What Is Social Studies?   Constructivist Approaches

What is the nature of social studies? What key themes characterize teaching and learning in social studies? How can constructivist approaches be applied to social studies?

What Is Social Studies?

In general, the field of **social studies**, also called social sciences, seeks to promote civic competence. The goal is to help students make informed and reasoned decisions for the public good as citizens of a culturally diverse, democratic society in an interdependent world (Drake & Nelson, 2009). In schools, social studies draws from disciplines such as anthropology, economics, geography, history, law, philosophy, political science, psychology, religion, and sociology.

Social studies is taught in kindergarten through grade 12 in the United States. In elementary school, children often learn social studies that are integrated across several disciplines (Savage & Armstrong, 2008; Zarillo, 2008). This often takes the

social studies The field that seeks to promote civic competence with the goal of helping students make informed and reasoned decisions for the public good as citizens of a culturally diverse, democratic society in an interdependent world.

form of units constructed around broad themes that are examined in terms of time, continuity, and change (Parker, 2009). In middle schools and high schools, courses may be interdisciplinary—such as a history course drawing from geography, economics, and political science—or focused more on a single discipline, such as just history itself (Chapin, 2009; Sunal & Haas, 2008).

The National Council for the Social Sciences (2000) emphasizes that ten themes should be stressed in social sciences:

- *Time, continuity, and change.* Students need to understand their historical roots and locate themselves in time. Knowing how to effectively read about and construct the past helps students to explore questions such as "How am I connected to the past?" and "How can my personal experience be viewed as part of the larger human story across time?" This theme typically appears in history courses. Rather than simply teaching history as lists of facts to be memorized, expert history teachers guide students in analyzing and reflecting about historical events, especially encouraging students to think about possible alternative meanings of events and how they might be interpreted in different ways. A number of expert history teachers also get students to engage in debate about the evidence pertaining to a particular historical circumstance.

- *People, places, and environments.* The study of these topics helps students to develop spatial and geographic perspectives on the world. This helps students make informed and competent decisions about the relationship of humans to their environment. In schools, this theme usually appears in units and courses linked to geography.

- *Individual development and identity.* A student's personal identity is shaped by culture, groups, and institutions. Students can explore such questions as "Who am I?" "How do people learn, think, and develop?" and "How do people meet their needs in a variety of contexts?" In schools, this theme usually appears in units and courses focused on psychology and anthropology.

- *Individuals, groups, and institutions.* Students need to learn about the ways in which schools, churches, families, government agencies, and the courts play integral roles in people's lives. Students can explore the roles of various institutions in the United States and other countries. In schools, this theme typically appears in units and courses on sociology, anthropology, psychology, political science, and history.

- *Power, authority, and governance.* Understanding the development of power, authority, and governance in the United States and other parts of the world is essential for developing civic competence. In this theme, students explore such topics as the following: What is power and what forms does it take? How do people gain power, use it, and justify it? How can people keep their government responsive to their needs and interests? How can conflicts within a nation and between nations be resolved? This theme typically appears in units and courses focused on government, political science, history, and other social sciences.

- *Production, distribution, and consumption.* People have needs and desires that sometimes exceed the limited resources that are available to them. As a result, questions such as these are raised: What is to be produced? How is production to be organized? How are goods and services distributed? What is the most effective allocation of production (land, capital, and management)? Increasingly, these questions are global in scope. In schools, this theme typically appears in units and courses focused on economics.

- *Science, technology, and society.* Modern life as we know it would be impossible without technology and the science that supports it. However, technology raises many questions: Is new technology always better? How can people effectively cope with rapid technological advances? How are values related to tech-

What knowledge and perspectives do courses in geography help students to develop?

nology? This theme appears in units and courses involving history, geography, economics, civics, and government

- *Global connections.* The realities of increasing interdependence among nations requires understanding nations and cultures around the world. Conflicts between national and global priorities can involve health care, economic development, environmental quality, universal human rights, and other agendas. This theme typically appears in units and courses involving geography, culture, economics, and other social sciences.

- *Civic ideals and practices.* Understanding civic ideals and the practices of citizenship is important for full participation in society. Students focus on such questions as these: What is civic participation and how can I be involved? What is the balance between individual needs and community responsibilities? In schools, this theme typically appears in units and courses involving history, political science, and anthropology.

- *Culture.* The study of culture prepares students to ask and answer such questions as these: How are cultures similar and different? What is the best way to interact with people who are from cultures that are different from your own? How does religion influence the beliefs of people in different cultures? In schools, the theme of culture typically appears in units and courses that focus on geography, history, and anthropology, as well as multicultural topics that cut across the curriculum. In the *Diversity and Education* interlude, you can read further about teaching culture and cultural diversity in social studies.

Constructivist Approaches

Many social studies classes continue to be taught in a traditional manner of using a single textbook, with the teacher lecturing and controlling question-and-answer strategies. However, some educators conclude that learning about social studies would benefit from constructivist strategies, such as using varied sources of information, student-generated questions to guide inquiry, and peer collaboration—the strategy used in the UN peacekeeping unit we just discussed. In the constructivist view, students should form their own interpretation of evidence and submit it for review. Allowing them to do so should encourage greater reflection and deeper understanding of social issues (Chapin, 2009; Zarillo, 2008).

   Constructivist approaches also emphasize the meaningfulness of social studies (Beal, Mason-Bolik, & Martorella, 2009; Sunal & Haas, 2008). Students benefit when

DIVERSITY AND EDUCATION
UN Peacekeeping: A Constructivist Approach

One Canadian middle school social studies teacher developed a project on UN peacekeeping to encourage students to think more deeply and productively about respecting citizens in their own country and about the hardships that people in many countries continue to experience (Welshman, 2000). During the last 50 years, the United Nations has been involved in separating adversaries, maintaining cease-fires, delivering humanitarian relief, helping refugees, and creating conditions that promote democracy. Studying the UN initiatives became a way for students to examine various prosocial values such as kindness, empathy, cooperation, loyalty, equality, and responsibility. In this project, students used a variety of resources, including books and the Internet, over the course of several class periods.

In introducing the UN peacekeeping topic, the teacher asked if any of the students ever had a disagreement with a friend or classmate at school. Students contributed comments and the teacher said that in many instances it takes a third party to sort things out and help solve the problem. The teacher then shifted attention to how such conflicts also characterize world politics between countries and different ethnic groups. Nations, regions, and small groups of people have disagreements, and there is no teacher present to help cool things down. This is where UN peacekeepers often step in to help solve a particular problem.

Then, students brainstormed about UN peacekeeping, during which they recalled any information they had previously learned about the topic and discussed their ideas with each other. The classroom had a world map on which to identify regions of the world where peacekeeping was taking or had taken place.

Next, the students were organized into five small groups of five students each to explore questions they had about UN peacekeeping. The first group of students focused on the history of peacekeeping. Questions explored included where the first peacekeeping mission occurred and how peacekeeping has changed since the end of the Cold War. Group two expressed an interest in the personal side of peacekeeping. Their questions included how much force peacekeepers can use in a mission and some of the dangers they face. The third group wanted to know about the organization of peacekeeping missions and asked questions such as these: Who provides funding for the mission? How are peacekeepers selected? The fourth group was interested in Canada's role in UN peacekeeping, asking these questions: When did Canada get involved in this? Have any Canadians commanded UN peacekeeping missions? The fifth group was intrigued by why peacekeeping occurs and asked questions such as these: What is the decision-making process like in determining when to form a UN peacekeeping mission? How do people decide on which world problems should be dealt with and which should not? After generating these questions, students researched and presented answers.

they find that what they learned in social studies classes is useful both in and outside of school. Meaningful learning often takes place when classroom interaction focuses on sustained examination of a few important topics rather than superficial coverage of many.

Constructivist approaches to social studies also stress the importance of thinking critically about values. Ethical dimensions of topics and controversial issues provide an arena for reflective thinking and understanding. Effective teachers recognize opposing points of view, respect for well-supported positions, sensitivity to cultural

In the History Alive! program of the Teacher's Curriculum Institute, students work in cooperative groups of four to prepare one student to be the actor in a lively panel debate.

similarities and differences, and a commitment to social responsibility. From the constructivist perspective, teachers guide students to consider ethical dimensions of topics and address controversial issues rather than directly telling students what is ethical.

To close our coverage of social studies education, the following comments by former high school history teacher Robert Bain (2005, p. 209) capture many of the themes emphasized in this chapter, not only about social science education but also about education in other content areas:

> When my high school students began to study history, they tended to view the subject as a fixed entity, a body of facts that historians retrieved and placed in textbooks (or in the minds of history teachers) for students to memorize. The purpose of history, if it had one, was to somehow inoculate students from repeating past errors. The process of learning history was straightforward and, while not always exciting, relatively simple. Ironically, when I first entered a school to become a history teacher over 30 years ago, I held a similar view, often supported by my education and history courses. . . . I no longer hold such innocent and naïve views of learning or teaching history, and I try to disabuse my students of these views as well. Indeed, our experiences in my history courses have taught us that, to paraphrase Yogi Berra, it's not what we know that's the issue, it's what we know for sure that isn't so. . . . Learning and teaching history demands complex thinking by both teachers and students. It centers around interesting, generative, and organizing problems; critical weighing of evidence and accounts; suspension of our views to understand those of others; use of facts, concepts, and interpretations to make judgments; and later, if the evidence persuades, to changes in our views and judgments.

In this chapter, we have explored effective strategies for educating students in a number of content areas. To read about some of the best ways to use technology in these and other content areas, see the *Technology and Education* interlude.

TECHNOLOGY AND EDUCATION

Content Area–Specific Technology Applications

There are a wealth of content-specific technology resources available for teachers, some of which are commercial products, some of which are free.

In English language arts, there are many good programs for beginning readers, such as the *Reader Rabbit* or *Living Books* series. The latter provides software versions of children's literature classics with which young students can read along and interact. For older students, Google Lit Trips (http://web .mac.com/jburg/GoogleLit/Home.html) has sources developed by teachers that allow students to explore many places referenced in literature for all ages. The Gutenberg Project (www.gutenberg.org) gives the full texts of thousands of books whose copyright has expired. Many children's authors have Web sites that provide supplementary information about the authors and their books (see, for example, www.judy blume.com). There are good supports for writing in most word processors, as well as programs that read written text back to students, such as *Write:OutLoud,* and so help improve their writing.

There are many commercial programs for giving students practice in arithmetic and algebra as well as interesting applications that support geometry explorations, such as the *Geometric Supposer.* Symbol manipulation programs, like Mathematica (www.wolfram.com/products/mathematica/ index.html) or Maple (www.maplesoft.com), allow students to explore algebra and calculus in multiple representations. There are also large repositories of mathematics learning objects (see www.walterfendt.de/ml4e/or www.merlot.org/ artifact/BrowseArtifacts.po?catcode=223&browsecat=223& sort=rating) for supporting the learning of specific mathematical concepts. Also, the Sim Calc projects (www.sim calc.umassd.edu) provide simulations and activities that run on calculators, computers, and handheld devices; these are designed to help students explore change and variation. And the National Council for Teachers of Mathematics (www .nctm.org) provides a variety of digital objects for illustrating mathematical concepts for its members called *Illuminations.*

Technology support for inquiry-based science includes the use of science probes, online access to science expeditions, online interactive activities for students (for example, www .exploratorium.edu), and virtual science laboratories such as those freely available at www.sciencecourseware.org. The WISE Web site (http://wise-demo.berkeley.edu) provides a free online science learning environment with inquiry modules on such topics as global climate change, population genetics, and recycling. Vernier (www.vernier.com) and Pasco (www .pasco.com) offer a wide variety of hardware and software for supporting hands-on science activities. Online access to science expeditions can be found at Web sites such as the Jason Project (www.jason.org/public/home/aspx). There are also good online repositories of learning objects for teaching science including the National Science Foundation's *Digital Library* (http://nsdl.org) and the National Science Teachers Association's *SciLinks* (www.nsta.org/scilinks).

In social studies, Tom Snyder Productions (www.tom snyder.com) offers a variety of role-playing simulations that introduce students to decision making among competing stakeholders as do *SimCity* and *Civilization* from Aspyr (www .aspyr.com) on a grander and more complex scale. My World GIS (www.myworldgis.org) is a geographic information system designed for use in educational settings that allows students to explore and analyze geographic data from around the world. There are also incredible sources of original documents (for example, see the Library of Congress *American Memory Collection* [http://memory.loc.gov/ammem] or the *Congressional Record,* [www.gpoaccess.gov/crecord]), virtual tours of cities all over the world, world newspapers, and collections of maps, including the David Rumsey historical map collection (www.davidrumsey.com). Another terrific social studies application is Google Earth (http://earth.google.com), which allows students to bring up aerial views of landscapes all over the world at varying degrees of resolution.

There are also good resources for specialized content areas. For example, the *WebMuseum* is a good source of reproductions for teaching art history, especially the Impressionists. Indeed, museums around the world have good reproductions available. The *Afropop Worldwide* site has a wealth of information about African and world music including music downloads.

And there is much, much more available over the Internet. For example, the WebQuests created by teachers available at http://webquest.org can be sorted by topic as can the digital objects available in the MERLOT (www.merlot.org) library. In addition, many publishers provide CD-ROMs and online sites for teachers using their texts. A good source for selected commercial software is KidsClick (www.Kidsclick.com).

Review, Reflect, and Practice

6 **Summarize how learning in social studies is becoming more constructivist.**

REVIEW

- What does social studies instruction aim to accomplish? What themes are emphasized by the National Council for the Social Sciences?
- What are some constructivist approaches to teaching social studies?

REFLECT

- Think about a specific community in which you might teach one day. How might you tailor social studies instruction specifically for those children? How could you make it constructivist?

PRAXIS™ PRACTICE

1. Mr. Chen wants his students to understand that not all people live in the same way that they do. His students study the ways of life of different people around the world. Which theme of social studies does Mr. Chen emphasize?
   a. culture
   b. civic ideals and practice
   c. power, authority, and governance
   d. production, distribution, and consumption

2. Which is the best example of a constructivist approach to social studies?
   a. Mr. Ewing's students listen to his lectures and take notes on the content covered.
   b. Ms. Drexler's students color and label detailed maps to help them learn geography.
   c. Ms. Byrd's students learn the material in their textbooks and take tests covering the content on a regular basis.
   d. Mr. Jordan presents his students with a controversial issue, which they discuss and debate.

Please see the answer key at the end of the book.

CRACK THE CASE
The Case of the Constructivist Math Curriculum

Connie teaches fourth grade in a middle-SES school district. Her district has adopted a new K–6 math curriculum for this year, based on constructivist principles. In attending the in-service devoted to training teachers in implementing the new curriculum, Connie discovers that many differences exist between what she has been teaching for the past 20 years and this new curriculum. The new curriculum focuses on the use of math in "real life." Instead of endless speed drills, the problems ask the students to think and make connections between their lives at home and what they are doing in math. What drill and practice there is takes place in the context of various games the children play together. Students are allowed, and even taught, to approach problems in a variety of ways rather than focusing on a single algorithm for a particular type of problem. Many of these approaches are completely alien to Connie and, she guesses, to other teachers and parents. "This is going to be a lot of work," she thinks. "I'm going to have to relearn math myself in order to teach this way."

As the school year begins, other teachers begin expressing their concerns over the new curriculum. It is just so different from anything they have ever done in the past. Most of the teachers are managing to stay just a lesson or two ahead of the students. The children in first and second grade seem to love the new math program. They are actively involved during math period, and many of them have said that math is fun. The students in fourth through sixth grade don't appear to be as enthusiastic about the new curriculum, however. Many of them are unable to complete their homework. They can't seem to grasp how to complete problems using the techniques taught in the new curriculum. They constantly fall back on the old algorithms they were taught when they were younger. This is frustrating Connie and her colleagues, as they have worked very hard to master the alternate ways of approaching problems themselves.

To make matters worse, parents are complaining. They can't help their children with their homework because they don't know how to use the new approaches, either. This has caused many parents to become angry. Several have threatened to remove their children from the school and take them "somewhere where they teach normal math." A group of parents will be addressing the board of education regarding this at their next meeting.

Adding fuel to the fire is one of the middle school math teachers, who insists that this new curriculum won't give the students the foundation they need for algebra. "They need to develop automaticity with their math facts. That just isn't going to happen with this program. It takes them in too many directions. They'll never make it back to normal in time for algebra."

Proponents answer the middle school teacher by indicating that the new curriculum will actually better prepare the students for higher math because they will have a better conceptual understanding of *why* they are doing things and how the traditional algorithms work. Connie feels caught in the middle. She understands what the curriculum is supposed to do. She even believes it might actually benefit the students in the long run. However, every day she has students in tears in her class because they don't understand what she is asking them to do. She has fielded her share of phone calls from angry parents as well.

1. What are the issues in this case?

2. The students in first and second grade seem to be flourishing in this curriculum, whereas the older students are struggling. Why might this be? Tie your answer to a constructivist principle.

3. How should the teachers address parental concerns regarding the new curriculum?

4. How should they address the concerns of the algebra teacher?

5. What can the teachers do to help their students at this point?

Reach Your Learning Goals
Learning and Cognition in the Content Areas

(1) EXPERT KNOWLEDGE AND PEDAGOGICAL CONTENT KNOWLEDGE: Distinguish between expert knowledge and pedagogical content knowledge.

Expert knowledge, also called *subject matter knowledge,* involves being an expert regarding the content of a discipline. Pedagogical content knowledge involves knowledge of how to effectively teach a particular discipline. Both are required for being an expert teacher.

(2) READING: Explain how reading develops and discuss some useful approaches to teaching reading.

A Developmental Model of Reading	Chall's model proposes five stages in reading development: (0) from birth to first grade, identify letters of the alphabet and learn to write one's name; (1) in first and second grade, learn to sound out words and complete learning of letter names and sounds; (2) in second and third grade, become more fluent at retrieving individual words and other reading skills; (3) in fourth through eighth grade, increasingly obtain new information from print and shift from "learning to read" to "reading to learn"; and (4) in high school, become a fully competent reader and understand material from different perspectives.
Language Rule Systems	The language rules systems of phonology, morphology, syntax, and semantics play important roles in reading. Phonological awareness, which involves becoming aware of the sound units in words, is especially important in early reading development. Morphological awareness—referring to the units of meaning in word formation—begins to become important in the middle of elementary school when students increasingly encounter multisyllabic words. Syntax is involved in reading because students who have poor grammar skills have difficulty detecting the way words are combined in sentences. Good semantic skills are involved in becoming a proficient reader because a good vocabulary helps readers to access word meaning effortlessly and is linked to reading comprehension.
Approaches to Reading	Current debate focuses on the phonics approach versus the whole-language approach. The phonics approach emphasizes that reading instruction should focus on phonics and basic rules for translating written symbols into sounds and give children simplified materials for early reading instruction. The whole-language approach stresses that reading instruction should parallel children's natural language learning and give children whole-language materials, such as books and poems. Although both approaches can benefit children, the phonics approach needs to be emphasized especially in kindergarten and first grade. Research indicates that phonological awareness instruction is especially effective when it is combined with letter training and as part of a total literacy program. Effective phonological awareness training mainly involves two skills: blending and segmentation. Children's reading also benefits from guided oral reading and instruction in reading strategies.
Cognitive Approaches	Cognitive approaches to reading emphasize decoding and comprehending words, prior knowledge, and developing expert reading strategies. Metacognitive strategies and automatic processes are involved in decoding and comprehending words. Prior knowledge about a topic can help students make correct inferences about material they read. Transactional strategy instruction is one approach to helping students learn to read.

| Social Constructivist Approaches | Social constructivist approaches to reading stress that the social context plays an important part in helping children learn to read and that meaning is socially negotiated. Reciprocal teaching is a valuable technique in helping students improve their reading. School/family/community connections also reflect the social constructivist perspective. |

(3) WRITING: Describe how writing develops and discuss some useful approaches to teaching writing.

| Developmental Changes | Children's writing follows a developmental timetable, emerging out of scribbling. Most 4-year-olds can print their name. Most 5-year-olds can reproduce letters and copy several short words. Advances in children's language and cognitive development provide the foundation for improved writing. |

| Cognitive Approaches | Cognitive approaches to writing emphasize many of the same themes as for reading, such as constructing meaning and developing strategies. Planning, problem solving, revising, and metacognitive strategies are thought to be especially important. |

| Social Constructivist Approaches | Social constructivist approaches to writing focus on the social context in which writing is produced. This social context includes the importance of students participating in a writing community to understand author/reader relationships and taking perspectives of others. Social constructivist approaches to writing include writing of "real texts" about meaningful experiences, teacher-student writing conferences, peer collaboration in writing, and school-community connections. |

(4) MATHEMATICS: Characterize how mathematical thinking develops and identify some issues related to teaching mathematics.

| Developmental Changes | Children have a substantial understanding of numerical concepts before they enter first grade. When they go to school, children learn many more advanced kinds of numerical skills. The National Council of Teachers of Mathematics has developed standards for learning mathematics at these grade levels: kindergarten through grade 2 (base-10 numeration system, for example); grades 3 through 5 (multiplicative reasoning, equivalence, and computational fluency); grades 6 through 8 (mathematical reasoning—algebra and geometry); and grades 9 through 12 (interplay of algebra, geometry, statistics, probability, and discrete mathematics). |

| Controversy in Math Education | Currently, there is controversy in math education about whether math should be taught using a cognitive, conceptual, and constructivist approach, or a practice, computational approach. Students need to develop both a conceptual understanding of math and procedural competency in math. |

| Cognitive Processes | Among the cognitive processes involved in math are conceptual understanding, knowledge of math procedures, effective organization of knowledge, and metacognitive strategies. |

| Some Constructivist Principles | Some constructivist principles include making math education more realistic and interesting, making connections to students' prior knowledge, and making the math curriculum socially interactive. |

| Technology and Math Instruction | The NTCM's *Curriculum and Evaluation Standards* recommends that calculators be used at all levels of mathematical instruction and that students' access to computers also is necessary. However, some education experts argue that, as in East Asia, calculators should not be used prior to high school to improve students' ability to learn math concepts. |

5 SCIENCE: Identify some challenges and strategies related to teaching children how to think scientifically.

| Science Education | Too often, the skills scientists use, such as careful observation, graphing, self-regulatory thinking, and knowing when and how to apply one's knowledge to solve problems, are not routinely taught in schools. Children have many misconceptions that are incompatible with science and reality. Good teachers perceive and understand a child's underlying concepts, then use the concepts as a scaffold for learning. |

| Constructivist Teaching Strategies | Constructivist teaching strategies include an emphasis on discovery learning—however, teachers need to supply guidance and feedback, and be consultants as children construct scientifically valid interpretations of the world. Effective science education emphasizes inquiry and science content knowledge. |

6 SOCIAL STUDIES: Summarize how learning in social studies is becoming more constructivist.

| What Is Social Studies? | The field of social studies seeks to promote civic competence. In schools, social studies draws from disciplines such as anthropology, economics, geography, history, law, philosophy, political science, psychology, religion, and sociology. Ten themes are recommended to be used for units and courses in social studies by the National Council for the Social Sciences: time, continuity, and change; people, places, and environments; individual development and identity; individuals, groups, and institutions; power, authority, and governance; production, distribution, and consumption; science, technology, and society; global connections; civic ideals and practices; and culture. |

| Constructivist Approaches | Many social studies classes continue to be taught in a traditional lecture format, but there is increasing interest in teaching these classes from a constructivist perspective. This perspective emphasizes using varied sources of information, the importance of greater reflection, understanding, meaning, critical thinking about values, and sustained examination of a few important topics rather than superficial coverage of many topics. |

KEY TERMS

expert knowledge 379
pedagogical content
   knowledge 380

phonics approach 384
whole-language
   approach 384

transactional strategy
   instruction approach 386

reciprocal teaching 387
social studies 407

PORTFOLIO ACTIVITIES

Now that you have a good understanding of this chapter, complete these exercises to expand your thinking.

Independent Reflection

The Cognitive and Socially Constructive Classroom. For the grade level you plan to teach, create a summary of good ideas for making learning both cognitive and socially constructive. Draw ideas from this and other chapters. Add further ideas of your own. (INTASC: Principles 4, 5)

Collaborative Work

Taking a Stand in the Math Controversy. There is controversy in math education about whether math should be taught in a constructivist manner or in a more traditional manner. There is also controversy about whether calculators and computers should be used in math instruction in the elementary school years. Get together with several students and evaluate these controversies. Summarize your discussion. (INTASC: Principles 1, 2, 4)

Research/Field Experience

Researching the Nuts and Bolts of Reading. Read about current trends in teaching children to read. Evaluate these trends based on what you've learned in this chapter. Compare current trends with how you were taught to read. Which method do you think is most effective? Why? What do you think accounts for persistent low reading scores on nationwide standardized tests? (INTASC: Principles 1, 7)

Go to the Online Learning Center for downloadable portfolio templates.

TAKING IT TO THE NET

- The social constructivist approach to writing emphasizes students' participation in a writing community. Explore an educational, electronic pen pals Web site, and develop an action plan for integrating this resource into your content area. Describe the kinds of opportunities students will have to write "real" texts, collaborate with peers, and share diverse perspectives. **www.epals.com**

- Online exhibits designed by science museums such as The Exploratorium (**www.exploratorium.edu**) and The Franklin Institute Science Museum (**www.fi.edu**) offer a gold mine of hands-on science projects that emphasize discovery and exploration. Visit a science museum online and discuss how its resources can enrich science learning in the classroom. **www.exploratorium.edu/sports/index.html**

- Evaluate a Web site that could be used in a social studies classroom. Illustrate how the resource could help you portray events from several different perspectives. Describe historical documents and artifacts provided by the resource. How could you use this information to challenge students to think critically about past events or current social issues? Develop a lesson or project using this resource. **http://memory.loc.gov**

Connect to the Online Learning Center to explore possible answers.

STUDY, PRACTICE, AND SUCCEED

Visit **www.mhhe.com/santedu4e** to review the chapter with self-grading quizzes and self-assessments, to apply the chapter material to two more Crack the Case studies, and for suggested activities to develop your teaching portfolio.

CHAPTER 12

Planning, Instruction, and Technology

Education is the transmission of civilization.

—Ariel and Will Durant
American Authors and Philosophers, 20th Century

Chapter Outline

Planning
Instructional Planning
Time Frames and Planning

Teacher-Centered Lesson Planning and Instruction
Teacher-Centered Lesson Planning
Direct Instruction
Teacher-Centered Instructional Strategies
Evaluating Teacher-Centered Instruction

Learner-Centered Lesson Planning and Instruction
Learner-Centered Principles
Some Learner-Centered Instructional Strategies
Evaluating Learner-Centered Strategies

Technology and Education
The Technology Revolution and the Internet
Standards for Technology-Literate Students
Teaching, Learning, and Technology

Learning Goals

1 Explain what is involved in classroom planning.

2 Identify important forms of teacher-centered instruction.

3 Discuss important forms of learner-centered instruction.

4 Summarize how to effectively use technology to help children learn.

TEACHING STORIES   Lois Guest and Kevin Groves

In Lois Guest's fifth-grade classroom at Hesperian Elementary School in San Lorenzo, California, 30 students are working on their new laptop computers provided by the school district. A month after the computers arrived, outdated encyclopedias sit on shelves, and students no longer have to compete for time in the school's computer lab.

The new laptops mark a monumental shift in Guest's career. She has taught for 35 years at Hesperian Elementary and remembers when slide projectors were the height of high tech. Now, she is building a Web site for her class and learning how to use a digital camera and an optical scanner. Guest says that she is learning a lot about technology and that her students are also teaching her how to do things on the computer. Ten-year-old Bianca Guitierrez said that she

enjoys working on her new laptop computer so much that it makes her look forward to coming to school.

When Kevin Groves took his fifth-grade class on a field trip to a botanical garden, his students insisted that they be allowed to bring their laptops. One of his students, Salvador Mata, spread out on the grass with his mother and explained to her how to make a PowerPoint presentation. His mother is pleased about Salvador learning how to use a computer at such an early age, believing that it will help him get a good job later in his life. Groves commented that he researches every link he puts on his Web site to make sure it is educational and won't lead to something bad for his students. (*Source*: May, 2001, pp. A1, A24)

Preview

This chapter builds on the learning and cognitive processes we discussed in Chapters 7 through 11 and addresses instructional planning at the level of the overall lesson plan or unit. We explore teacher-centered lesson planning, building on the behavioral principles covered in Chapter 7, and learner-centered lesson planning, building on material covered in Chapters 8 through 11. Finally, we explore important classroom applications of technology, such as use of the Internet.

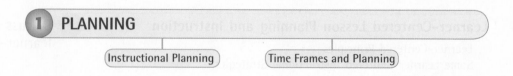

It has been said that when people fail to plan, they plan to fail. Many successful people attribute their accomplishments to effective planning. Our introduction to planning describes what instructional planning is and the different time frames of planning.

Instructional Planning

Planning is a critical aspect of being a competent teacher (Glasgow & Hicks, 2009; Wiles, 2009). **Instructional planning** involves developing a systematic, organized strategy for lessons. Teachers need to decide what and how they are going to teach before they do it. Although some wonderful instructional moments are spontaneous, lessons still should be carefully planned (Eby, Herrell, & Jordan, 2009).

instructional planning A systematic, organized strategy for planning lessons.

FRANK AND ERNEST © Thaves/Dist. by Newspaper Enterprise Association Inc.

Instructional planning might be mandated by the school in which you teach. Many principals and instructional supervisors require teachers to keep written plans, and you may be asked to submit lesson plans several weeks in advance. When observing classroom teachers, supervisors check to see if the teacher is following the plan. If a teacher is absent, a substitute teacher can follow the plan.

Expectations for teacher planning have increased with the promulgation of state learning standards that specify what students need to know and be able to do (Guillaume, 2008; Joyce & Weil, 2009). However, these standards usually do not state what the teacher should do in the classroom to reach these standards. When standards are in place, teachers must figure out how to plan and organize their curriculum around the most important dimensions implied by the standards and create a "sequence and set of learning activities for the particular students they teach" (Darling-Hammond & others, 2005, p. 184).

Many planning strategies are organized around four elements: "the nature of the subject matter, the learners, the context, and the teacher's role" (Darling-Hammond & others, 2005, p. 184). One effective planning strategy that many teachers use is *mapping backward* from "goals to desired performances to activities and elements of scaffolding needed to support student progress." Indeed, a good strategy is to begin your planning by thinking about what goals you want your students to reach by the end of the school year and then map backward from that point. In one analysis, many experienced teachers described how in the early years of their teaching they lacked a long-term vision in their curriculum planning and strongly urged beginning teachers to think more about the big picture—the key things they want their students to learn this year—and how they can guide their students to get there (Kunzmann, 2003).

Linda Darling-Hammond and her colleagues (2005, pp. 185–186) recently described some important aspects of curriculum planning:

> Teachers must decide what is important to include, given their goals, and know how to make it accessible to a particular group of students. This requires thinking about how to give students a schema or conceptual map of the domain to be studied (National Research Council, 2000) as well as planning specific activities in light of students' levels of readiness for various kinds of learning experiences. It also requires consideration of the kinds of information, demonstrations, models, inquiry opportunities, discussion, and practice students need over time to understand particular concepts and develop particular skills. . . .

In sum, teachers need to "figure out which things students should do when, in what order, and how" to implement the big picture of their curricular vision.

Time Frames and Planning

As we just indicated, developing systematic time plans involves knowing what needs to be done and when to do it, or focusing on "task" and "time."

You will need to plan for different time spans, ranging from yearly to daily planning (Eby, Herrell, & Jordan, 2009). If school-wide planning or your own career

DEVELOPMENTAL FOCUS 12.1

What Are Some Planning Strategies That Help You Teach More Effectively?

Early Childhood

Lesson planning for our preschoolers is done by a team of two at the beginning of the month. The team determines what will be covered by reviewing skills that need to be mastered and implementing appropriate activities. We also incorporate the children's interests in building our plans.

—Valarie Gorham, *Kiddie Quarters, Inc.*

Elementary School: Grades K–5

To prepare for my second-grade classes, I plan each week's (and sometimes two weeks') lessons the Thursday before. This way I can have all copies made, have the necessary materials, and be sure additional materials are available (library books, for example). I then map out the week and check that time is set aside to reteach and reinforce material.

—Janine Guida Poutre, *Clinton Elementary School*

Middle School: Grades 6–8

When planning my lessons, I use the backward design method: I make a list of essential questions that I want my students to know when they finish the activity. These essential questions go on my whiteboard so that the students are aware of what they are going to learn. By knowing exactly what I want the students to learn, I can plan a successful lesson.

—Casey Maass, *Edison Middle School*

High School: Grades 9–12

I get to school by 6:00 A.M. to plan and lay out what I need for the day. I need quiet time without others around and access to copy machines without a line. By 7:00 A.M. I have my activities for the day laid out and ready to go. Of course, I am a morning person!

—Sandy Swanson, *Menomonee Falls High School*

FIGURE 12.1 Five Time Spans of Teacher Planning and Their Occurrence over the School Year

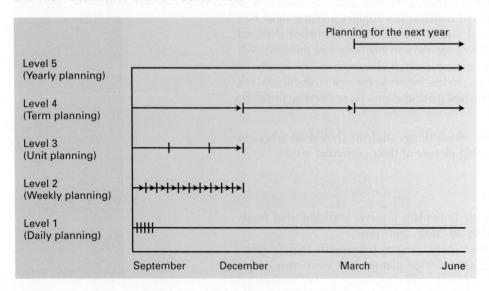

planning is involved, the time frame likely will be a number of years. Robert Yinger (1980) identified five time spans of teacher planning: yearly planning, term planning, unit planning, weekly planning, and daily planning. Figure 12.1 illustrates these time frames and shows planning for them. Yinger also recommends that teachers attend to four areas when planning: goals, sources of information, the form of the plan, and criteria for the effectiveness of the planning.

Although planning is a key dimension of successful teaching, don't overplan to the point of becoming an automaton. Develop organized plans and try to carry them out, but be flexible; as a year, month, week, or day unfolds, adapt to changing circumstances. A controversial current

How does time allotted to lesson planning differ in Chinese and American schools?

event or necessary topic might emerge that you did not originally include. Monitor and rework your plans as the school year goes by to suit these changing circumstances (Cruickshank, Metcalf, & Jenkins, 2009).

A final comment needs to be made about planning. It is increasingly understood that teachers need to monitor and evaluate their curriculum planning in terms of how well students are making progress toward learning goals as they go through the term (Darling-Hammond & others, 2005). Thus, time for assessment and feedback to students needs to be built into the planning process. We will explore different types of assessment in Chapters 15 and 16.

A final consideration involves how much time schools allot to lesson planning in the United States compared with other countries. Recent cross-cultural comparisons reveal that lesson planning is given a much higher priority in Chinese than American schools (Shen, Zhen, & Poppink, 2007; Shen & others, 2007). Many American teachers' teaching schedules allow little time for lesson planning, in many cases 30 minutes or less, during the school day. By contrast, Chinese teachers teach only one or two hours a day, in a core subject area, and they spend extensive time on lesson planning: on average about two hours a week of formal collaboration and two hours a week of informational collaboration with colleagues in one core subject area. They also have one to two hours a day to correct homework and classwork, and 30 minutes a day for homework feedback to students.

Review, Reflect, and Practice

1 **Explain what is involved in classroom planning.**

REVIEW

- What is instructional planning? Why does instruction need to be planned?
- What planning needs to be done related to the use of time?

REFLECT

- In your own K–12 experiences, did you ever have a teacher who did not put enough effort into planning? What was that like for students?

(continued)

Review, Reflect, and Practice

PRAXIS™ PRACTICE

1. Ms. Swenson is planning for the school year. Which of the following strategies should she follow?
   a. Plan forward, starting with plans for the first week of school.
   b. Map backward, determining the goals she wants her students to reach by the end of the school year.
   c. Not spend too much time in planning but rather get a sense of where her students are in the first month of school.
   d. Engage in circular planning.

2. In planning, Mr. Tomasello considers the objectives established by the district and state-mandated standards and aligns his curriculum to them. After doing this, he considers what he wants to teach when, based on the sequence that makes the most sense. Finally, he reserves the necessary equipment and requests the appropriate materials to carry out his plans. At what level of planning is Mr. Tomasello most likely to be engaging?
   a. daily
   b. weekly
   c. term
   d. yearly

Please see the answer key at the end of the book.

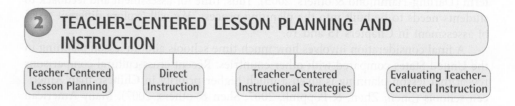

2 · TEACHER-CENTERED LESSON PLANNING AND INSTRUCTION

| Teacher-Centered Lesson Planning | Direct Instruction | Teacher-Centered Instructional Strategies | Evaluating Teacher-Centered Instruction |

Traditionally, the focus in schools has been on teacher-centered lesson planning and instruction. In this approach, planning and instruction are highly structured and the teacher directs students' learning.

Teacher-Centered Lesson Planning

Three general tools are especially useful in teacher-centered planning. These are behavioral objectives, task analysis, and instructional taxonomies (classifications), which we explore next.

Behavioral Objectives **Behavioral objectives** are statements about changes that the teacher wishes to see in students' performance. In Robert Mager's (1962) view, behavioral objectives should be very specific. Mager stresses that behavioral objectives should have three parts:

- *Student's behavior.* Focus on what the student will learn or do.
- *Conditions under which the behavior will occur.* State how the behavior will be evaluated or tested.
- *Performance criteria.* Determine what level of performance will be acceptable.

behavioral objectives Statements that communicate proposed changes in students' behavior to reach desired levels of performance.

For example, a teacher might develop a behavioral objective around the idea that the student will describe five causes of the decline of the British Empire (student's behavior). The teacher plans to give the student an essay test on this topic (conditions under which the behavior will occur). And the teacher decides that explaining four or five causes will be acceptable performance (performance criterion).

Task Analysis   Another tool of teacher-centered planning is **task analysis**, which focuses on breaking down a complex task that students are to learn into its component parts (Alberto & Troutman, 2006; Miller, 2006). The analysis can proceed in three basic steps (Moyer & Dardig, 1978):

1. Determine what skills or concepts the student needs to have to learn the task.
2. List any materials that will be required in order to perform the task, such as paper, pencil, and calculator.
3. List all of the components of the task in the order in which they must be performed.

Instructional Taxonomies   Instructional taxonomies also aid teacher-centered approaches (Eby, Herrell, & Jordan, 2009). A **taxonomy** is a classification system. **Bloom's taxonomy** was developed by Benjamin Bloom and his colleagues (1956). It classifies educational objectives into three domains: cognitive, affective, and psychomotor. Bloom's taxonomy has been used by many teachers in their lesson planning to create goals and objectives (Bart, 2008; Hanna, 2007; Lord & Baviskar, 2007).

The Cognitive Domain   Bloom's cognitive taxonomy has six objectives (Bloom & others, 1956):

- *Knowledge.* Students have the ability to remember information. For example, an objective might be to list or describe four main advantages of using a computer for word processing.
- *Comprehension.* Students understand the information and can explain it in their own words. For example, an objective might be to explain or discuss how a computer can effectively be used for word processing.
- *Application.* Students use knowledge to solve real-life problems. For example, an objective might be to apply what has been learned about using a computer for word processing to how this could be used in various careers.
- *Analysis.* Students break down complex information into smaller parts and relate information to other information. For example, an objective might be to compare one type of word-processing program with another for doing term papers.
- *Synthesis.* Students combine elements and create new information. For example, an objective might be to organize all that has been learned about the use of computers for writing.
- *Evaluation.* Students make good judgments and decisions. For example, an objective might be to critique different word-processing programs or to judge the strengths and weaknesses of a particular word-processing program.

The Affective Domain   The affective taxonomy consists of five objectives related to emotional responses to tasks (Krathwohl, Bloom, & Masia, 1964). Each of the following five objectives requires the student to show some degree of commitment or emotional intensity:

- *Receiving.* Students become aware of or attend to something in the environment. For example, a guest comes to class to talk with students about reading. An objective might be for students to listen carefully to the speaker.

task analysis Breaking down a complex task that students are to learn into its component parts.

taxonomy A classification system.

Bloom's taxonomy Developed by Benjamin Bloom and colleagues; classifies educational objectives into three domains—cognitive, affective, and psychomotor.

Imagine you are a teacher in the three educational settings shown above. *What instructional taxonomies and objectives might be involved in each of these settings?*

- *Responding.* Students become motivated to learn and display a new behavior as a result of an experience. An objective might be for students to become motivated to become better readers as a result of the guest speaker's appearance.
- *Valuing.* Students become involved in, or committed to, some experience. An objective might be for students to value reading as an important skill.
- *Organizing.* Students integrate a new value into an already existing set of values and give it proper priority. An objective might be to have students participate in a book club.
- *Value characterizing.* Students act in accordance with the value and are firmly committed to it. An objective might be that over the course of the school year, students increasingly value reading.

The Psychomotor Domain Most of us link motor activity with physical education and athletics, but many other subjects, such as handwriting and word processing, also involve movement. In the sciences, students have to manipulate complex equipment; the visual and manual arts require good hand-eye coordination. Bloom's psychomotor objectives include these:

- *Reflex movements.* Students respond involuntarily without conscious thought to a stimulus—for example, blinking when an object unexpectedly hurtles their way.
- *Basic fundamentals.* Students make basic voluntary movements that are directed toward a particular purpose, such as grasping a microscope knob and correctly turning it.
- *Perceptual abilities.* Students use their senses, such as seeing, hearing, or touching, to guide their skill efforts, such as watching how to hold an instrument in science, like a microscope, and listening to instructions on how to use it.
- *Physical abilities.* Students develop general skills of endurance, strength, flexibility, and agility, such as running long distances or hitting a softball.
- *Skilled movements.* Students perform complex physical skills with some degree of proficiency, such as effectively sketching a drawing.
- *Nondiscussive behaviors.* Students communicate feelings and emotions through bodily actions, such as doing pantomimes or dancing to communicate a musical piece.

Teachers can use Bloom's taxonomies for the cognitive, affective, and psychomotor domains to plan instruction. In the past, instructional planning has generally focused on cognitive or behavioral objectives. Bloom's taxonomy provides for a more expansive consideration of skills by also including affective and psychomotor domains.

A group of educational psychologists updated Bloom's knowledge and cognitive process dimensions in light of recent theory and research (Anderson & Krathwohl, 2001). In the update, the knowledge dimension has four categories, which lie along a continuum from concrete (factual) to abstract (metacognition):

- *Factual:* The basic elements students must know to be acquainted with a discipline or solve problems in it (technical vocabulary, sources of information)

- *Conceptual:* The interrelationships among the basic elements within a larger structure that allow them to function together (periods of geological time, forms of business ownership)

- *Procedural:* How to do something, methods of inquiry, and criteria for using skills (skills used in painting with watercolors, interviewing techniques)

What are some objectives in Bloom's original cognitive taxonomy? How have these been modified in the update of Bloom's taxonomy?

- *Metacognitive:* Knowledge of cognition and awareness of one's own cognition (knowledge of outlining and strategies for remembering)

In the update of the cognitive process dimension, six categories lie along a continuum from less complex (remember) to more complex (create):

- *Remember.* Retrieve relevant knowledge from long-term memory. (Recognize the dates of important events in U.S. history.)
- *Understand.* Construct meaning from instruction that includes interpreting, exemplifying, classifying, summarizing, inferring, comparing, and explaining. (Explain the causes of important eighteenth-century events in France.)
- *Apply.* Carry out or use a procedure in a given situation. (Use a law in physics in situations in which it is appropriate.)
- *Analyze.* Break material into its component parts and determine how the parts relate to each other and to overall structure or purpose. (Distinguish between relevant and irrelevant numbers in a math word problem.)
- *Evaluate.* Make judgments based on criteria and standards. (Detect inconsistencies or fallacies in a product.)
- *Create.* Put elements together to form a coherent or functional whole; reorganize elements into a new pattern or structure. (Generate hypotheses to account for an observed phenomenon.)

Direct Instruction

As we indicated in Chapter 1, **direct instruction** is a structured, teacher-centered approach that is characterized by teacher direction and control, high teacher expectations for students' progress, maximum time spent by students on academic tasks, and efforts by the teacher to keep negative affect to a minimum. The focus of direct instruction is academic activity; nonacademic materials (such as toys, games, and puzzles) tend not to be used; also deemphasized is nonacademically oriented teacher-student interaction (such as conversations about self or personal concerns) (Johnson & Street, 2008).

Teacher direction and control take place when the teacher chooses students' learning tasks, directs students' learning of the tasks, and minimizes the amount of nonacademic talk. The teacher sets high standards for performance and expects students to reach these levels of excellence.

direct instruction Structured, teacher-centered approach focused on academic activity; characterized by teacher direction and control, high teacher expectations for student progress, and keeping negative affect to a minimum.

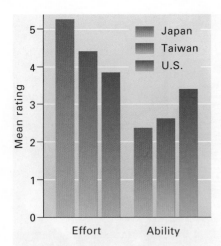

FIGURE 12.2 Mothers' Beliefs About the Factors Responsible for Children's Math Achievement in Three Countries

In one study, mothers in Japan and Taiwan were more likely to believe that their children's math achievement was due to effort rather than innate ability, whereas U.S. mothers were more likely to believe their children's math achievement was due to innate ability (Stevenson, Lee, & Stigler, 1986). If parents believe that their children's math achievement is due to innate ability and their children are not doing well in math, the implication is that they are less likely to think their children will benefit from putting forth more effort.

Reprinted with permission from "Mathematics Achievement of Chinese, Japanese, and American Children" by H.W. Stevenson, S. Lee, and J.W. Stigler in *Science*, Vol. 231 (1986), pp. 693–699, Figure 6. Copyright © 1986 AAAS.

DIVERSITY AND EDUCATION
Cross-Cultural Comparions in Math Education

Harold Stevenson is one of the leading experts on children's learning and conducted research on this topic for five decades. In the 1980s and 1990s, he turned his attention to discovering ways to improve children's learning by conducting cross-cultural comparisons of children in the United States with children in Asian countries, especially Japan, China, and Taiwan (Stevenson, 1992, 1995, 2000; Stevenson & Hofer, 1999; Stevenson & others, 1990). In Stevenson's research, Asian students consistently outperformed American students in mathematics. Also, the longer students were in school, the wider the gap became—the lowest difference was in first grade, the highest in eleventh grade (the highest grade studied).

To learn more about the reasons for these cross-cultural differences, Stevenson and his colleagues spent thousands of hours observing in classrooms, as well as interviewing and surveying teachers, students, and parents. They found that Asian teachers spent more of their time teaching math than American teachers did. For example, in Japan more than one-fourth of the total classroom time in first grade was spent on math instruction, compared with only one-tenth of the time in U.S. first-grade classrooms. Also, Asian students were in school an average of 240 days a year, compared with 178 days in the United States.

In addition, differences were found between the Asian and American parents. American parents had much lower expectations for the children's education and achievement than did the Asian parents. Also, the American parents were more likely to say that their children's math achievement was due to innate ability; the Asian parents were more likely to say that their children's math achievement was the consequence of effort and training (see Figure 12.2). The Asian students were more likely to do math homework than the American students, and the Asian parents were far more likely to help their children with their math homework than were the American parents (Chen & Stevenson, 1989).

In Stevenson's research, Asian students scored considerably higher than U.S. students on math achievement tests. *What are some possible explanations for these findings?*

An important goal in the direct-instruction approach is maximizing student learning time (Hollingsworth & Yberra, 2009). Time spent by students on academic tasks in the classroom is called *academic learning time*. Learning takes time. The more academic learning time students experience, the more likely they are to learn the material and achieve high standards. The premise of direct instruction is that the best way to maximize time on academic tasks is to create a highly structured, academically oriented learning environment. The *Diversity and Education* interlude describes cross-cultural research about the amount of time students spend on math in different countries, as well as other comparisons across countries.

Yet another emphasis in the direct-instruction approach is keeping negative affect to a minimum. Researchers have found that negative affect interferes with learning (Merrell, Parisi, & Whitcomb, 2007; Merrell & others, 2007). Advocates of direct instruction underscore the importance of keeping an academic focus and avoiding negative affect, such as the negative feelings that can often arise in both the teacher and students when a teacher overcriticizes.

Teacher-Centered Instructional Strategies

Many teacher-centered strategies reflect direct instruction. Here we will talk about orienting students to new material; lecturing, explaining, and demonstrating; questioning and discussing; mastery learning; seatwork; and homework.

Orienting   Before presenting and explaining new material, establish a framework for the lesson and orient students to the new material: (1) review the previous day's activities; (2) discuss the lesson's objective; (3) provide clear, explicit instructions about the work to be done; and (4) give an overview of today's lesson.

Advance organizers are teaching activities and techniques that establish a framework and orient students to material before it is presented. You can use advance organizers when you begin a lesson to help students see the "big picture" of what is to come and how information is meaningfully connected.

Advance organizers come in two forms: expository and comparative. **Expository advance organizers** provide students with new knowledge that will orient them to the upcoming lesson. The chapter-opening outline and learning goals in each chapter of this book are expository advance organizers. Another way to provide an expository advance organizer is to describe the lesson's theme and why it is important to study this topic. For example, in orienting students to the topic of exploring the Aztec civilization in a history class, the teacher says that they are going to study the Spanish invasion of Mexico and describes who the Aztecs were, what their lives were like, and their artifacts. To heighten student interest, she also says that they will study worlds in collision as Spain's conquistadors were filled with awe at sights of a spectacular Western civilization. There are Mexican American students in her class, and the teacher emphasizes how this information can help everyone in the class understand these students' personal and cultural identity.

A high school math teacher lecturing his class. *What are some good strategies for teachers to use when they lecture?*

Comparative advance organizers introduce new material by connecting it with what students already know. For example, in the history class just mentioned, the teacher says that the Spanish invasion of Mexico continued the transatlantic traffic that changed two worlds: Europe and the Americas. She asks students to think about how this discussion of the Aztecs connects with Columbus' journey, which they examined last week.

Lecturing, Explaining, and Demonstrating   Lecturing, explaining, and demonstrating are common teacher activities in the direct-instruction approach (Milner-Bolotin, Kotlicki, & Rieger, 2007). Researchers have found that effective teachers spend more time explaining and demonstrating new material than their less-effective counterparts do (Rosenshine, 1971).

advance organizers Teaching activities and techniques that establish a framework and orient students to material before it is presented.

expository advance organizers Organizers that provide students with new knowledge that will orient them to the upcoming lesson.

comparative advance organizers Organizers that introduce new material by connecting it with the students' prior knowledge.

BEST PRACTICES
Strategies for Lecturing

These are some good strategies to use when lecturing:

1. *Be prepared.* Don't just "wing" a lecture. Spend time preparing and organizing what you will present.

2. *Keep lectures short and intersperse them with questions and activities.* For example, lecture for 10 or 15 minutes to provide the background information and framework for a topic, then place students in small discussion groups.

3. *Make the lecture interesting and exciting.* Think about what you can say that will motivate students' interest in a topic. Vary the pace of the lecture by interlacing it with related video clips, demonstrations, handouts, and/or activities for students.

4. *Follow a designated sequence and include certain key components:*
   - Begin with advance organizers or previews of the topic.

- Verbally and visually highlight any key concepts or new ideas (like the boldfaced key terms in this book). Use the blackboard, an overhead projector, or another large-display device.
- Present new information in relation to what students already know about the topic.
- Periodically elicit student responses to ensure that they understand the information up to that point and to encourage active learning.
- At the end of the lecture, provide a summary or an overview of the main ideas.
- Make connections to future lectures and activities.

On some occasions we sit through boring lectures, yet on other occasions we have been captivated by a lecturer and learned a great deal from the presentation. Let's explore some guidelines for when lecturing is a good choice and some strategies for delivering an effective lecture. Here are some goals that lecturing can accomplish (Henson, 1988):

1. Presenting information and motivating students' interest in a subject
2. Introducing a topic before students read about it on their own, or giving instructions on how to perform a task
3. Summarizing or synthesizing information after a discussion or inquiry
4. Providing alternative points of view or clarifying issues in preparation for discussion
5. Explaining materials that students are having difficulty learning on their own

Questioning and Discussing It is necessary but challenging to integrate questions and discussion in teacher-centered instruction (Gray & Madson, 2007; Weinstein, 2007). Teachers should respond to each student's learning needs while maintaining the group's interest and attention. It also is important to distribute participation widely while also retaining the enthusiasm of eager volunteers. An additional challenge is allowing students to contribute while still maintaining the focus on the lesson (Kellough & Jarolimek, 2008).

Mastery Learning **Mastery learning** involves learning one concept or topic thoroughly before moving on to a more difficult one. A successful mastery learning approach involves these procedures (Bloom, 1971; Carroll, 1963):

- Specify the learning task or lesson. Develop precise instructional objectives. Establish mastery standards (this typically is where *A* students perform).

mastery learning Involves learning one topic or concept thoroughly before moving on to a more difficult one.

Let's examine some effective strategies for using questions in the classroom:

1. *Use fact-based questions as entreés into thinking-based questions.* For example, in teaching a lesson on environmental pollution, the teacher might ask the fact-based question: "What are three types of environmental pollution?" Then she could follow with this thinking-based question: "What strategies can you think of for reducing one of these types of environmental pollution?" Don't overuse fact-based questions, because they tend to produce rote learning rather than learning for understanding.

2. *Avoid yes/no and leading questions.* Yes/no questions should be used only as a segue into more probing questions. For example, avoid questions like "Was environmental pollution responsible for the dead fish in the lake?" Keep these questions to a minimum, only occasionally using them as a warm-up for questions such as these: "How did the pollution kill the fish?" "Why do you think companies polluted the lake?" "What can be done to clean up environmental pollution?"

   Also avoid asking leading questions such as "Don't you agree?" or other rhetorical questions such as "You do want to read more about environmental pollution, don't you?" These types of questions don't produce meaningful responses and simply hand the initiative back to the teacher.

4. *Leave enough time for students to think about answers.* Too often when teachers ask questions, they don't give students enough time to think. In one study, teachers waited less than one second, on the average, before calling on a student to respond (Rowe, 1986)! In the same study, teachers waited only about one second, on the average, for the student to respond before supplying the answer themselves. Such intrusions don't give students adequate time to construct answers. In the study just mentioned, teachers were subsequently instructed to wait three to five seconds to allow students to respond to questions. The increased wait time led to considerable improvements in responses, including better inferences about the materials and more student-initiated questions. Waiting three to five seconds or more for students to respond is not as easy as it might seem; it takes practice. But your students will benefit considerably from having to think and construct responses.

5. *Ask clear, purposeful, brief, and sequenced questions.* Avoid being vague. Focus the questions on the lesson at

What are some good teaching strategies for the effective use of questions?

hand. Plan ahead so that your questions are meaningfully tied to the topic. If your questions are long-winded, you run the risk that they will not be understood, so briefer is better. Also plan questions so that they follow a logical sequence, integrating them with previously discussed material before moving to the next topic.

6. *Monitor how you respond to students' answers.* What should you do next after a student responds to your question? Many teachers just say "Okay" or "Uh-huh" (Sadker, Sadker, & Zittleman, 2008). Usually it is wise to do more. You can use the student's response as a basis for follow-up questions and engage the student or other students in a dialogue. Provide feedback that is tailored to the student's existing level of knowledge and understanding.

7. *Be aware of when it is best to pose a question to the entire class or to a particular student.* Asking the entire class a question makes all students in the class responsible for responding. Asking a specific student a question can make other students less likely to answer it. Some reasons to ask a question to a particular student are: (a)

(continued)

BEST PRACTICES
Strategies for the Effective Use of Questions

to draw an inattentive student into the lesson, (b) to ask a follow-up question of someone who has just responded, and (c) to call on someone who rarely responds when questions are asked to the class as a whole. Don't let a small group of assertive students dominate the responses. Talk with them independently about continuing their positive responses without monopolizing class time. One strategy for giving students an equal chance to respond

is to pull names from a cookie jar or check names off a class list as students respond (Weinstein & Mignano, 2007).

8. *Encourage students to ask questions*. Praise them for good questions. Ask them "How?" and "Why?" and encourage them to ask "How?" and "Why?"

- Break the course into learning units that are aligned with instructional objectives.
- Plan instructional procedures to include corrective feedback to students if they fail to master the material at an acceptable level, such as 90 percent correct. The corrective feedback might take place through supplemental materials, tutoring, or small-group instruction.
- Give an end-of-unit or end-of-course test that evaluates whether the student has mastered all of the material at an acceptable level.

Mastery learning gets mixed reviews. Some studies indicate that mastery learning is effective in increasing the time that students spend on learning tasks (Kulik, Kulik, & Bangert-Drowns, 1990), but others find less support for mastery learning (Bangert, Kulik, & Kulik, 1983). Outcomes of mastery learning depend on the teacher's skill in planning and executing the strategy (Joyce & Weil, 2009). One context in which mastery learning might be especially beneficial is remedial reading (Schunk, 2008). A well-organized mastery learning program for remedial reading allows students to progress at their own rates based on their skills, their motivation, and the time they have to learn.

Seatwork   Seatwork refers to the practice of having all or a majority of students work independently at their seats. Teachers vary in how much they use seatwork as part of their instruction (Weinstein, 2007). Some teachers use it every day; others rarely use it. Figure 12.3 summarizes the challenges of seatwork for the teacher and the student.

Learning centers are especially good alternatives to paper-and-pencil seatwork. Figure 12.4 provides some suggestions for learning centers. A computer station can be an excellent learning center.

Homework   Another important instructional decision involves how much and what type of homework to give students (Bempechat, 2008; Marzano & Pickering, 2007; Xu, 2007). Comments by a leading researcher, Harris Cooper (2006, 2007, 2009), suggest that in the United States homework is the source of more friction between school and home than any other aspect of education. In the cross-cultural research discussed earlier that focused on Asian and American students, the time spent on homework was assessed (Chen & Stevenson, 1989). Asian students spent more time doing homework than American students did. For example, on weekends Japanese first-graders did an average of 66 minutes of homework, and American first-graders did only 18 minutes. Also, Asian students had a much more positive attitude about

For the teacher

1. Keeping track of what the rest of the class is doing
2. Keeping students on-task
3. Dealing with the varying paces at which students work ("ragged" endings)
4. Selecting or creating seatwork that is clear and meaningful
5. Matching seatwork to students' varying levels of achievement
6. Collecting, correcting, recording, and returning seatwork assignments

For the student

1. Completing assigned work on their own
2. Understanding how and when to obtain the teacher's help
3. Understanding the norms for assisting peers
4. Learning how to be effective in obtaining help from peers

FIGURE 12.3 Challenges of Seatwork for Teachers and Students

homework than American students did. And Asian parents were far more likely to help their children with their homework than American parents were.

In a recent review, Cooper and his colleagues (2006) concluded that overall research indicates there is a positive influence of homework on students' achievement. The research review also indicated that the homework-achievement link is stronger in grades 7 to 12 than kindergarten to grade 6. In one study, Cooper (1998) collected data on 709 students in grades 2 through 4 and 6 through 12. In the lower grades, there was a significant negative relation between the amount of homework assigned and students' attitudes, suggesting that elementary school children resent having to do homework. But in grades 6 and higher, the more homework students completed, the higher their achievement. It is not clear which was the cause and which the effect, though. Were really good students finishing more assignments because they were motivated and competent in academic subjects, or was completing homework assignments causing students to achieve more? Recent studies of German secondary school students support the general finding that homework assignments are linked to students' achievement gains (Trautwein, 2007; Trautwein & Ludtke, 2007).

A key aspect of the debate about whether elementary school children should be assigned homework is the type of homework assigned. What is good homework? Especially for younger children, the emphasis should be on homework that fosters a love of learning and hones study skills. Short assignments that can be quickly completed should be the goal. With young children, long assignments that go uncompleted or completed assignments that bring a great deal of stress, tears, and tantrums should be avoided. Too often teachers assign homework that duplicates without reinforcing material that is covered in class. Homework should be an opportunity for students to engage in creative, exploratory activities, such as doing an oral history of one's family or determining the ecological effects of neighborhood business. Instead of memorizing names, dates, and battles of the Civil War as a homework assignment, students might write fictional letters from Northerners to Southerners, expressing their feelings about the issues dividing the nation. The homework assignments should be linked to the next day's class activities to emphasize to students that homework has meaning and is not just a plot to make them miserable. Homework also should have a focus. Don't ask students to write an open-ended theme from a novel the class is reading. Rather, ask them to select a character and explain why he or she behaved in a particular way.

In Cooper and his colleagues' (2006) review of research, homework began to have a payoff in middle school. How can homework have little or no effect in elementary school yet be so beneficial in middle and high school? In the higher grades, it is easier to assign focused, substantive homework that requires students to integrate and apply knowledge—the type of homework that promotes learning (Corno, 1998). Also, by high school, students have resigned themselves to the routine of homework. Working hard after school and having good study skills are more accepted by middle and high school students.

Some educational psychologists argue that the main reason homework has not been effective in elementary school is that it has focused too much on subject matter and not enough on developing attitudes toward school, persistence, and responsible completion of assignments (Corno, 1998). They stress that it is not homework per se that benefits students but, rather, the opportunities it provides for the student to take responsibility. They think that teachers need to inform parents about guiding their children in these aspects of doing their homework: setting goals, managing their time, controlling their emotions, and checking their work, rather than playing avoidance games or leaving hard work for last. Teachers and parents can use homework in the early grades to help children wrestle with goal setting and follow-through.

Science

Simple experiments with lab sheets

Observations over time with recording forms

Exploring properties of objects and classifying them

Social studies

Recreating items used by different civilizations

Creating charts or graphs of population trends

Map making

Mathematics

Math "challenges" and puzzles

Manipulative activities

Art

Holiday or thematic projects

Crafts related to curriculum studies (quilting, quilling, origami, etc.)

Writing

Class story writing (e.g., add-on stories)

Rewrites of literature

Writing plays or puppet shows

Computer

Content-related programs

Simulations

Story writing

FIGURE 12.4 Suggestions for Learning Centers

Cooper and his colleagues (1989, 2006, 2007, 2009; Cooper, Robinson, & Patall, 2006; Cooper & Patell, 2007; Cooper & Valentine, 2001) also have found the following:

- Homework has more positive effects when it is distributed over a period of time rather than done all at once. For example, doing 10 math problems each night for five nights is better than doing 50 over the weekend.
- Homework effects are greater for math, reading, and English than for science and social studies.
- For middle school students, one or two hours of homework a night is optimal. High school students benefit from even more hours of homework, but it is unclear what a maximum number of hours ought to be.

What are some guidelines for assigning homework to students?

Homework can be a valuable tool for increasing learning, especially in middle and high school (Cooper, 2006, 2007, 2009). However, it is important to make homework meaningful, monitor it and give students feedback about it, and involve parents in helping their child with it. Many parents wish they knew more about teachers' learning goals for homework and teachers' suggestions for involvement strategies that will help their children learn and succeed (Hoover-Demsey & others, 2001). Also, one study found that mothers' positive affect played an important role in students' motivation to do homework (Pomerantz, Wang, & Ng, 2005).

Evaluating Teacher-Centered Instruction

Research on teacher-centered instruction has contributed many valuable suggestions for teaching, including these:

- Be an organized planner, create instructional objectives, and spend initial time orienting students to a lesson.
- Have high expectations for students' progress and ensure that students have adequate academic learning time.
- Use lecturing, explaining, and demonstrating to benefit certain aspects of students' learning.
- Engage students in learning by developing good question-asking skills and getting them involved in class discussion.
- Have students do meaningful seatwork or alternative work to allow individualized instruction with a particular student or a small group.
- Give students meaningful homework to increase their academic learning time and involve parents in students' learning.

"I don't have my homework because my little brother put a Pop-Tart® in my disk drive!"

Art Bouthillier, from *Phi Delta Kappan* (February 1997). Reprinted by permission of Art Bouthillier.

Advocates of the teacher-centered approach especially believe that it is the best strategy for teaching basic skills, which involve clearly structured knowledge and skills (such as those needed in English, reading, math, and science). Thus, in teaching basic skills, the teacher-centered approach might consist of a teacher explicitly or directly teaching grammar rules, reading vocabulary, math computations, and science facts.

Teacher-centered instruction has not been without criticism. Critics say that teacher-centered instruction often leads to passive, rote learning and inadequate opportunities to construct knowledge and understanding (McCall, 2007). They also criticize teacher-centered instruction as producing overly structured and rigid class-rooms, inadequate attention to students' socioemotional development, external rather than internal motivation to learn, too much reliance on paper-and-pencil tasks, few opportunities for real-world learning, and too little collaborative learning in small groups. Such criticisms often are leveled by advocates of learner-centered planning and instruction, which we will turn to next.

Review, Reflect, and Practice

(2) Identify important forms of teacher-centered instruction.

REVIEW

- What are some useful tools in teacher-centered lesson planning?
- What is direct instruction?
- What are some good teacher-centered instructional strategies?
- What are some pros and cons of teacher-centered instruction?

REFLECT

- As a student, have you ever wished that a teacher used more (or less) teacher-centered instruction? What lessons can you draw from this for your own work as a teacher?

PRAXIS™ PRACTICE

1. Mr. McGregor has assigned his students to write an essay explaining the impact of the use of the atomic bomb during World War II. Which cognitive level of Bloom's taxonomy is best illustrated by this assignment?
   a. analysis
   b. application
   c. comprehension
   d. knowledge

2. A math teacher works with students to solve higher-level problems. The teacher engages the students in discussions of various approaches to solving the problems. The emphasis is on understanding the processes of solving the problems, rather than on getting the correct answer. This math class is most typical of instructional methods in
   a. the United States
   b. France
   c. Japan
   d. Germany

3. Ms. Davidson is giving a lecture to introduce her students to a unit on the American Revolution. She begins with a little-known fact to pique her students' interest. She then distributes a brief outline of what her lesson will cover. She lectures from carefully prepared notes, using visual aids to help her students understand the material and keep their interest. Periodically, during the lecture, she asks questions to make sure her students are attending to, and understanding, the material. She calls on the first person to raise her hand to answer the question. If this person does not answer immediately, she supplies the answer herself, so the students do not become confused, and the lesson does not drag on. What should Ms. Davidson do differently?
   a. Allow her students more time to answer questions.
   b. Avoid asking questions during the lecture.
   c. Be more spontaneous in her class presentations.
   d. Avoid using distracting visual aids.

(continued)

Review, Reflect, and Practice

4. Ms. Bancroft likes to lecture most of the time, makes sure that her students stay on task when they are in the classroom, and has students do meaningful seatwork. Ms. Bancroft is following which of these approaches?
   a. cognitive constructivist
   b. social constructivist
   c. direct instruction
   d. individualized

   Please see the answer key at the end of the book.

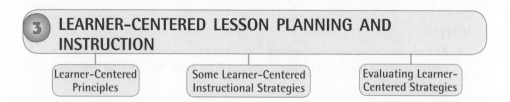

3 LEARNER–CENTERED LESSON PLANNING AND INSTRUCTION

| Learner–Centered Principles | Some Learner–Centered Instructional Strategies | Evaluating Learner–Centered Strategies |

Just as the behavioral approaches described in Chapter 7 provide the conceptual underpinnings for teacher-centered lesson planning and instruction, the information-processing and constructivist approaches discussed in Chapters 2, 8, 9, 10, and 11 form the theoretical backdrop for learner-centered lesson planning and instruction. In this section, we will explore the principles and strategies used in learner-centered instruction.

Learner–Centered Principles

Learner-centered lesson planning and instruction move the focus away from the teacher and toward the student (Bass, Contant, & Carin, 2009; Cornelius-White & Harbaugh, 2009). In one large-scale study, students' perceptions of a positive learning environment and interpersonal relationships with the teacher—factors associated with learner-centered instruction—were important in enhancing students' motivation and achievement (McCombs, 2001; McCombs & Quiat, 2001).

Increased interest in learner-centered principles of lesson planning and instruction has resulted in a set of guidelines called *Learner-Centered Psychological Principles: A Framework for School Reform and Redesign* (Presidential Task Force on Psychology and Education, 1992; Work Group of the American Psychological Association Board of Educational Affairs, 1995, 1997). The guidelines were constructed and are now periodically revised by a prestigious group of scientists and educators from a wide range of disciplines and interests. These principles have important implications for the way teachers plan and instruct, as they are based on research on the most effective ways children learn.

The Work Group of the American Psychological Association Board of Educational Affairs (1997) stresses that research in psychology relevant to education has been especially informative, including advances in our understanding of cognitive, motivational, and contextual aspects of learning. The work group states that the learner-centered psychological principles it has proposed are widely supported and are being increasingly adopted in many classrooms. The principles emphasize the

John Mahoney teaches high school math in Washington, D.C. One of his students, Nicole Williams, says, "He's not going to tell you the answer. He's going to make you think" (Briggs, 2004, p. 6D). *What are some important cognitive and metacognitive factors in learner-centered instruction?*

active, reflective nature of learning and learners. According to the work group, education will benefit when the primary focus is on the learner.

The fourteen learner-centered principles can be classified in terms of four main sets of factors: cognitive and metacognitive, motivational and emotional, developmental and social, and individual differences (Work Group of the American Psychological Association Board of Educational Affairs, 1997). Figure 12.5 describes the 14 learner-centered principles.

Some Learner-Centered Instructional Strategies

We already have discussed a number of strategies that teachers can consider in developing learner-centered lesson plans. These especially include the teaching strategies based on the theories of Piaget and Vygotsky (Chapter 2), constructivist aspects of thinking (Chapters 8 and 9), social constructivist aspects of thinking (Chapter 10), and learning and cognition in the content areas (Chapter 11). To provide you with a further sense of learner-centered strategies that you can incorporate into your lesson planning, we will examine problem-based learning, essential questions, and discovery learning.

Problem-Based Learning   Problem-based learning emphasizes real-life problem solving (Chapin, 2009; Schmidt & others, 2007). A problem-based curriculum exposes students to authentic problems like those that crop up in everyday life. Problem-based learning is a learner-centered approach that focuses on a problem to be solved through small-group efforts (Dalsgaard & Godsk, 2007; Mennin, 2007). Students identify problems or issues that they wish to explore, then locate materials and resources they need to address the issues or solve the problems. Teachers act as guides, helping students to monitor their own problem-solving efforts (Tandogan, Ozkardes, & Orhan, 2007).

One problem-based learning project involves sixth-grade students in exploring an authentic health problem in the local community: the causes, incidence, and treatment of asthma and its related conditions (Jones, Rasmussen, & Moffitt, 1997). Students learn how environmental conditions affect their health and share this understanding with others. The project

What are some learner-centered psychological principles?

Cognitive and Metacognitive Factors

1. Nature of the learning process
   The learning of complex subject matter is most effective when it is an intentional process of constructing meaning from information and experience.

2. Goals of the learning process
   The successful learner, over time and with support and instructional guidance, can create meaningful, coherent representations of knowledge.

3. Construction of knowledge
   The successful learner can link new information with existing knowledge in meaningful ways.

4. Strategic thinking
   The successful learner can create a repertoire of thinking and reasoning strategies to achieve complex goals.

5. Thinking about thinking
   Higher-order strategies for selecting and monitoring mental operations facilitate creative and critical thinking.

6. Context of learning
   Learning is influenced by environmental factors, including culture, technology, and instructional practices.

Motivational and Instructional Factors

7. Motivational and emotional influences on learning
   What and how much is learned is influenced by the learner's motivation. Motivation to learn, in turn, is influenced by the learner's emotional states, beliefs, interests, goals, and habits of thinking.

8. Intrinsic motivation to learn
   The learner's creativity, higher-order thinking, and natural curiosity all contribute to motivation to learn. Intrinsic motivation is stimulated by tasks of optimal novelty and difficulty, relevant to personal interests and providing for personal choice and control.

9. Effects of motivation on effort
   Acquisition of complex knowledge and skills requires extended learner effort and guided practice. Without learners' motivation to learn, the willingness to exert this effort is unlikely without coercion.

Developmental and Social Factors

10. Developmental influences on learning
    As individuals develop, there are different opportunities and constraints for learning. Learning is most effective when development within and across physical, cognitive, and socioemotional domains is taken into account.

11. Social influences on learning
    Learning is influenced by social interactions, interpersonal relations, and communication with others.

Individual Difference Factors

12. Individual differences in learning
    Learners have different strategies, approaches, and capabilities for learning that are a function of prior experience and heredity.

13. Learning and diversity
    Learning is most effective when differences in learners' linguistic, cultural, and social backgrounds are taken into account.

14. Standards and assessment
    Setting appropriately high and challenging standards and assessing the learner as well as learning progress—including diagnostic, process, and outcome assessment—are integral parts of the learning process.

FIGURE 12.5 Learner–Centered Psychological Principles

What is guided discovery learning?

integrates information from many subject areas, including health, science, math, and the social sciences. In a recent study, 20 eleventh-grade chemistry students were randomly assigned to either a teacher-centered or problem-based learning experience to learn about the effects of temperature, concentration, and pressure on cell potential (Tarhan & Acar, 2007). Interviews with the students following the instruction revealed that the students in both conditions were equally effective in students' understanding of the topic, but that students in the problem-based learning condition were more motivated, self-confident, and interested in solving problems.

Essential Questions   **Essential questions** are questions that reflect the heart of the curriculum, the most important things that students should explore and learn. For example, in one lesson the initial essential question was "What flies?" Students explored the question by examining everything from birds, bees, fish, and space shuttles to the notion that time flies and ideas fly. The initial question was followed by other questions, such as "How and why do things fly in nature?" "How does flight affect humans?" and "What is the future of flight?"

Essential questions like these perplex students, cause them to think, and motivate their curiosity. Essential questions are creative choices. With just a slight change, a lackluster question such as "What was the effect of the Civil War?" can become the thought-provoking question "Is the Civil War still going on?"

Discovery Learning   **Discovery learning** is learning in which students construct an understanding on their own. Discovery learning stands in contrast to the direct-instruction approach discussed earlier, in which the teacher directly explains information to students. In discovery learning, students have to figure out things for themselves. Discovery learning meshes with the ideas of Piaget, who once commented that every time you teach a child something you keep the child from learning.

As teachers began to use discovery learning, they soon found that for it to be effective as a systematic instruction approach it needed to be modified. This led to the development of **guided discovery learning**, in which students are still encouraged to construct their understanding, but with the assistance of teacher-guided questions and directions (Chen & Honomichl, 2008; Minstrell & Kraus, 2005).

A research review indicated that guided discovery learning was superior to pure discovery learning in every case (Mayer, 2004). In this review, it also was concluded that constructivist learning is best supported by curricular focus rather than pure discovery.

essential questions Questions that reflect the heart of the curriculum, the most important things that students should explore and learn.

discovery learning Learning in which students construct an understanding on their own.

guided discovery learning Learning in which students are encouraged to construct their understanding with the assistance of teacher-guided questions and directions.

DEVELOPMENTAL FOCUS 12.2
What Are Your Most Effective Learner-Centered Strategies?

Early Childhood

Learner-centered strategies are common in my preschool classroom. For example, each morning children are given time for free play in which they play dress-up, pretend to cook in a mock kitchen, and build structures using Legos. Through these activities, children not only learn important skills, but they are also instilled with a love of school.

—Missy Dangler, *Suburban Hills School*

Elementary School: Grades K–5

I use guided discovery learning in almost all of my science classes. The children work in groups, are given guidance at the beginning of the lesson and then assigned a task to do in order to find the answer to a question. When students ask questions, I refer them to an instruction sheet I have given them or ask questions to guide their thinking. If a student asks, "Can we do this?" I reply, "Try it and see!" I also encourage students to count on other members of their group to uncover answers to questions and use phrases such as "Many heads are better than one."

—Janine Guida Poutre, *Clinton Elementary School*

Middle School: Grades 6–8

In order to master new vocabulary, I often have my students quiz each other on vocabulary words. It is a noisy activity, but the students love it and learn at the same time.

—Margaret Reardon, *Pocantico Hills School*

High School: Grades 9–12

I prefer being the "guide on the side," not the "sage on the stage," when it comes to teaching. I did a writing workshop in which I presented a short mini-lesson each day, and my students chose how to spend the rest of the period. The students set their own goals, and their grade was partly based on achievement of those goals. I conferenced one-on-one with each student daily to monitor how they were doing; students loved the freedom.

—Jennifer Heiter, *Bremen High School*

Evaluating Learner-Centered Strategies

The learner-centered approach to lesson planning and instruction is positive in many ways (Cornelius-White & Harbaugh, 2009). The fourteen learner-centered principles developed by the American Psychological Association task force can be very helpful in guiding students' learning. The principles encourage teachers to help students actively construct their understanding, set goals and plan, think deeply and creatively, monitor their learning, solve real-world problems, develop more positive self-esteem and control their emotions, be internally motivated, learn in a developmentally appropriate way, collaborate effectively with others (including diverse others), evaluate their learner preferences, and meet challenging standards.

Critics of learner-centered instruction argue that it gives too much attention to the process of learning (such as learning creatively and collaboratively) and not enough to academic content (such as the facts of history) (Hirsch, 1996). Some critics stress that learner-centered instruction works better in some subjects than in others (Feng, 1996). They say that in areas with many ill-defined problems, such as the social sciences and humanities, learner-centered instruction can be effective. However, they believe that in well-structured knowledge domains such as math and science, teacher-

BEST PRACTICES
Strategies for Using Learner-Centered Instruction

1. *Become familiar with the learner-centered psychological principles and incorporate them in your lesson planning and teaching.*

2. *Focus on the whole child.* Pay attention to motivational and affective factors, and developmental and social factors, in addition to cognitive factors.

THROUGH THE EYES OF TEACHERS
Fostering Learning, Unity, and Civic Pride

Luis Recalde, a fourth- and fifth-grade science teacher at Vincent E. Mauro Elementary School, in New Haven, Connecticut, uses every opportunity to make science fascinating and motivating for students to learn. Recalde infuses hands-on science experiences with energy and enthusiasm. To help students get a better sense of what it is like to be a scientist, he brings lab coats to the classroom for students to wear. He holds science fair workshops for teachers and often gives up his vacation time to help students with science projects. He started soccer teams and gardens to foster unity and civic pride among African American and Latino students. An immigrant

Elementary school science teacher Luis Recalde holds up a seaweed specimen in one of the hands-on, high-interest learning contexts he creates for students.

himself, he knows the importance of fostering positive relations among students from different ethnic groups.

3. *Use problem-based learning, essential questions, and guided discovery learning in your teaching.*

---

centered structure works better. Critics also say that learner-centered instruction is less effective at the beginning level of instruction in a field because students do not have the knowledge to make decisions about what and how they should learn. And critics stress that there is a gap between the theoretical level of student-centered learning and its actual application (Airasian & Walsh, 1997). The consequences of implementing learner-centered strategies in the classroom are often more challenging than anticipated.

Although we have presented teacher-centered and learner-centered planning and instruction in separate sections, don't think of them as always being either/or approaches (Schuh, 2001). Many effective teachers use some of both in making the classroom a positive learning experience for children. Research on the choice and sequencing of learning activities in the classroom indicates that the use of constructivist and direct instruction approaches are often more effective than when either approach is used alone (Darling-Hammond & others, 2005; Schwartz & others, 1999).

Consider high school history teacher Robert Bain's (2005) description of how students initially spent time in learner-centered instruction working on constructing accounts of Columbus' voyage to America and struggled with the question of how the anniversaries of the voyage were celebrated. Bain then used teacher-centered direct instruction by lecturing about leading historians' current thinking about the topic. Also, a recent study of a ninth-grade technology-enhanced classoom revealed that both student-centered and teacher-centered instruction promoted students' conceptual understanding and provided students with different opportunities to engage in learning (Wu & Huang, 2007).

Review, Reflect, and Practice

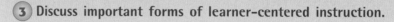

(3) **Discuss important forms of learner-centered instruction.**

REVIEW

- What is learner-centered lesson planning? Summarize the APA's fourteen learner-centered principles.
- How do problem-based learning, essential questions, and discovery learning each embody learner-centered principles?
- What are some pros and cons of learner-centered instruction?

REFLECT

- As a student, have you ever wished that a teacher would use more (or less) learner-centered instruction? What lessons can you draw from this for your own work as a teacher?

PRAXIS™ PRACTICE

1. Joan just received a *D* on her science exam. "I knew it," she states, "I've never been any good at science." Which set of factors of the APA's learner-centered principles is best exemplified by Joan's statement?
   a. cognitive and metacognitive
   b. developmental and social
   c. individual differences
   d. motivational and emotional

2. Mr. Williams wants his third-grade students to understand the purpose of blubber in marine mammals. He sets up an experiment for his students using ice water, latex gloves, and lard. First, students put their gloved hands in ice water until they cannot keep them there any longer. Other students time how long they keep their hands submerged. Then, students put their gloved hands in bags of lard and submerge their hands again. Again, other students time how long they keep their hands submerged. All of the students are able to keep their hands in the ice water longer with their hands in the lard than they can when their hands are merely gloved.

   What learner-centered instructional strategy has Mr. Williams used?
   a. discovery learning
   b. essential questions
   c. guided discovery
   d. problem-based learning

3. Ms. Flanagan, who takes a teacher-centered approach, just observed Mr. Houston's constructivist teaching in his seventh-grade math class. Ms. Flanagan is likely to be most critical of which of the following she observed?
   a. Mr. Houston assigning students homework
   b. Mr. Houston encouraging students to construct their own math problem-solving strategies
   c. Mr. Houston having high expectations for student learning
   d. Mr. Houston using technology to help students learn

Please see the answer key at the end of the book.

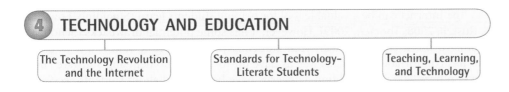

4 TECHNOLOGY AND EDUCATION

| The Technology Revolution and the Internet | Standards for Technology-Literate Students | Teaching, Learning, and Technology |

"I see what's wrong with your calcula-tor—it's the remote control to your TV."

John R. Shanks, from *Phi Delta Kappan* (June 1997). Reprinted by permission of John R. Shanks.

So far in this chapter we have described many aspects of planning and instruction. In contemporary society, technology plays important roles in planning and instruction. Three important ways that technology affects curriculum planning are: (1) as a learning goal for students to develop certain technology competencies; (2) as a resource for curriculum planning through the extensive materials that are available on the Internet; and (3) as tools that improve students' ability to learn through techniques such as simulation and visualization in science and text analysis in literature, as well as software that encourages reflection and provides models of good performances (Darling-Hammond & others, 2005).

Technology is such an important theme in education that it is woven throughout this book. In each chapter, you read a *Technology and Education* interlude related to the chapter's contents. For example, you already have studied such topics as "Technology and Children's Vocabulary Development" (Chapter 2), "Technology Connections with Students Around the World" (Chapter 5), and "Computer-Supported Intentional Learning Environments (Knowledge Forum)" (Chapter 10). Here we will explore the technology revolution and the Internet, standards for technology-literate students, and teaching and learning with technology.

The Technology Revolution and the Internet

Students today are growing up in a world that is far different technologically from the world in which their parents and grandparents were students. If students are to be adequately prepared for tomorrow's jobs, technology must become an integral part of schools and classrooms (Egbert, 2009; Kelly, McCain, & Jukes 2009).

The technology revolution is part of the information society in which we now live. People are using computers to communicate today the way people used to use pens, postage stamps, and telephones. The new information society still relies on some basic nontechnological competencies: good communication skills, the ability to solve problems, deep thinking, creative thinking, and positive attitudes. However, in today's technology-oriented world, how people pursue these competencies is being challenged and extended in ways and at a speed that few people had to cope with in previous eras (Bitter & Legacy, 2008; O'Hara & Pritchard, 2009).

The **Internet** is a system of computer networks that operates worldwide. As the core of computer-mediated communication, the Internet is playing an important role in the technology revolution, especially in schools. In many cases, the Internet has more current, up-to-date information than textbooks. By 2003, nearly 100 percent of public schools in the United States were connected to the Internet, and 93 percent of instructional classrooms had Internet-connected computers (National Center for Education Statistics, 2005).

However, the Internet did not become the common portal it is today until the introduction of the World Wide Web (the Web). The **Web** is a system for browsing Internet sites. It is named the Web because it is made of many sites linked together. The Web presents the user with documents, called Web pages, full of links to other documents or information systems. Selecting one of these links, the user can access more information about a particular topic. Web pages include text as well as multimedia (images, video, animation, and sound—all of which can be accessed by students with a click on words or images presented on a computer screen). Web indexes and search engines such as Google and Yahoo! can help students find the information they are seeking by examining and collating a variety of sources.

Internet The core of computer-mediated communication; a system of computer networks that operates worldwide.

Web A system for browsing Internet sites that refers to the World Wide Web; named the Web because it is comprised of many sites that are linked together.

A student creating a multimedia program in the Research Center for Educational Technology's AT&T classroom at Kent State University.

The Internet can be a valuable tool for helping students learn (Smaldino, Lowther, & Russell, 2008; Thorsen, 2009). However, it has some potential drawbacks (Schofield, 2006). To use it effectively with your students, you will have to know how to use it and feel comfortable with it, as well as have up-to-date equipment and software (Berson & others, 2007). In addition, concerns have been raised about students accessing pornographic material and biased Web sites, as well as the accuracy of information gleaned from the Internet. Many of these problems are solved by installing firewalls or blocking software on school servers.

When used effectively, however, the Internet expands access to a world of knowledge and people that students cannot experience in any other way (Cruz & Duplass, 2007).

Here are some effective ways that the Internet can be used in classrooms:

- *Navigating and integrating knowledge.* The Internet has huge databases of information on a vast array of topics that are organized in different ways. As students explore Internet resources, they can work on projects that integrate information from various sources that they could not otherwise access. One way to support such work is through WebQuests (http://webquest.sdsu.edu). A WebQuest is an inquiry-oriented activity designed by teachers that maximizes student learning time, emphasizes using information rather than looking for it, and stimulates thinking. WebQuests focus student efforts on doable tasks, provide a set of information resources and guidance for completing those tasks, and frame the work in an integrative context. They help introduce students to Internet searching in meaningful ways.

- *Collaborative learning.* One of the most effective ways to use the Internet in your classroom is through project-centered activities (Bruckman, 2006). Indeed, many WebQuests are designed to be collaborative, with roles and tasks assigned to different members of each group. Another collaborative use of the Internet is to have a group of students conduct a survey on a topic, put it on the Internet, and hope to obtain responses from many parts of the world. They can organize, analyze, and summarize the data they receive, and then share them with other classes around the world. Another type of collaborative learning project involves sending groups of students on Internet "scavenger hunts" to find information and/or solve a problem.

- *Computer-mediated communications (CMC).* An increasing number of innovative educational projects include the use of computer-mediated communications. For example, there are many online sites (such as www.studentsoftheworld .info, www.tesol.net/teslpnpl.html) set up for teachers and students to correspond with "pen pals" around the world. Some of these even provide safe access to more innovative CMC forms such as chats and blogs (such as www .studentsoftheworld.info). In Chapter 10, we examined Ann Brown and Joe Campione's (1996) program, Fostering a Community of Learners, in which students communicate with experts via e-mail, giving them access to a wider circle of knowledgeable people. In the Global Lab project (http://globallab.terc.edu), a yearlong, interdisciplinary science curriculum for middle school students, students conduct science investigations at their own local "study sites" and then share their findings with students around the country through an Internet discussion board.

- *Improving teachers' knowledge and understanding.* Two excellent Internet resources for teachers are the Educational Resources Information Center (ERIC at www.eric.ed.gov) and the Educators' Reference Desk (www.eduref.org), which provide free information about a wide range of educational topics. The ERIC database gives abstracts of more than 1 million journal and nonjournal educational papers going back to 1966 and the full text of over 100,000 papers from educational conferences. The Educators' Reference Desk gives easy access to over 2,000 lesson plans and over 3,000 links to online education information.

TECHNOLOGY AND EDUCATION

The GenYes Program

The goal of the GenYes program is to support the effective integration of technology in teaching and learning (GenYes, 2008). The program, created by Dennis Harper at the Northwest Regional Educational Laboratory, emphasizes that teachers and students are partners in creating lessons that use technology in ways students find meaningful and relevant. GenYes is available for both elementary and secondary school students, who learn about technology by cocreating lessons with teachers and their teachers learn about technology from the students. Instead of teaching technology skills to teachers with the hope that they will use those skills in teaching students, GenYes works with students to help them form productive technology partnerships with their teachers. Students and their teacher-partners learn how to use telecommunication devices, the Internet, presentation tools, and other emerging technologies.

Among the technology units that GenYes students and teachers collaborate on are:

- *Online communications,* such as safety, e-mail, forums, blogs, messaging, and collaborative projects
- *Digital media,* such as graphics, animation, and video
- *Digital authoring,* including planning, creating, and delivering multimedia projects
- *Web publishing,* such as how to design and construct Web pages
- *Student leadership and community service*

In addition, a number of mini-units, such as podcasting, digital storytelling, handhelds, and video tutorials can be incorporated in the GenYes class or used by students when they are working on technology projects.

GenYes students are paired, either individually or in teams, with a partner-teacher. Initial meetings are held to determine a curriculum focus that could be enriched by an infusion of technology. The GenYes students are responsible for the nuts and bolts of the technology, and the teacher provides content accuracy and pedagogical strategies.

The GenYes program was initiated in Olympia, Washington, in 1996 and is now used in a number of classrooms across the United States. Teachers and students have consistently reported that GenYes has provided them with an excellent opportunity to improve their technology skills. The GenYes program reflects the learner-centered strategies we discussed earlier in this chapter and the social constructivist approach described in Chapter 10.

Other excellent Internet resources for teachers include TappedIn (http://tappedin.org/tappedin), an online site that brings educators together in learning communities to discuss educational issues and work on collaborative projects, and the PBS TeacherLine (http://teacherline.pbs.org/teacherline), which provides both links to teaching resources and online professional development courses for teachers.

To read further about a technology program that is increasingly used in schools, see the *Technology and Education* interlude.

Standards for Technology–Literate Students

Students today are growing up in a world that is far different technologically from the world in which their parents and grandparents were students. If students are to be adequately prepared for tomorrow's jobs, schools must take an active role in ensuring students become technologically literate. Most national standards recognize this. For example, the National Council of Teachers of English/International Reading Association Standards for the English Language Arts (NCTE/IRA, 1996) include the following: "Students use a variety of technological and information resources (such as libraries, databases, computer networks, and video) to gather and synthesize information and to create and communicate knowledge," and a major theme in the National Council for the Social Studies, Curriculum Standards for the Social Studies (NCSS, 1994) is "Science, Technology, and Society."

The International Society for Technology in Education (ISTE, 2007, p. 9) has developed six technology standards for students to achieve technology literacy:

Students at Christopher Maddox High School in Park City, Utah, present a daily, live TV broadcast to more than 1,200 peers and 80 adults. The students create a program that highlights school news and events and have full responsibility for writing scripts, operating cameras, directing segments, and other aspects of a producing a TV broadcast.

1. *Creativity and innovation.* Students show creative thinking, construct knowledge, and develop innovative products using technology.

2. *Communication and collaboration.* Students use digital media and contexts to work collaboratively, including at a distance, to improve learning.

3. *Research and information fluency.* Students apply digital tools to gather, evaluate, and use information.

4. *Critical thinking, problem solving, and decision making.* Students engage in critical thinking to plan and carry out research, manage projects, solve problems, and make effective decisions using appropriate technology.

5. *Digital citizenship.* Students improve their understanding of human, societal, and cultural issues involving technology and demonstrate ethical behavior.

6. *Technology operations and concepts.* Students understand technology operations and concepts.

In addition, ISTE provides performance indicators for achieving these standards at four levels: prekindergarten through second grade, grades 3 through 5, grades 6 through 8, and grades 9 through 12. ISTE also includes examples and scenarios to illustrate how technology literacy can be integrated across the curriculum at each of these levels.

For example, a curriculum example that effectively uses technology at the first level focuses on animals and their sounds. In Sharon Fontenot's class at Prien Lake Elementary School, students learn to identify polar bears, lions, and other wild animals through images, video clips, and sounds on the *World of Animals* CD-ROM. The teacher models the effective use of technology by creating a tape recording based on information from the CD-ROM and incorporating her own voice to fit the needs of the class. Students practice reading and listening skills by answering questions that encourage them to think about both the science and social living issues related to these animals. Students create their own stories about what they learned using *Kid Pix,* a software program that lets them make their own pictures of the animals, turn them into slide shows, and print out their own books to share with family and friends.

At the second level (grades 3 through 5), a teacher might make extensive use of Internet resources. She could use the Exploring the Environment Web site (www .cotf.edu/ete) to access class-tested problem-based learning modules or the Global Learning and Observations for a Better Environment (GLOBE) Web site (www.globe .gov) to engage students in making environmental observations around the school, reporting the data to a processing facility through GLOBE, and using global images created from their data to examine local environmental issues.

Population growth and urban planning are the focus of a social studies technology-based learning activity in grades 9 through 12. The activity challenges students to find sources online and elsewhere that describe real-world population dilemmas. The activity can be altered to address different cities and regions worldwide. In small groups in class, students can discuss problems that may occur as a result of a city being heavily populated. They can be asked to project what problems a city such as Tokyo is likely to face in terms of population growth in the year 2050.

ISTE (2007) has created a profile of what characterizes a technology-literate student at prekindergarten through second grade, grades 3–5, grades 6–8, and grades 9–12. Figure 12.6 shows a sampling of these profiles.

These scenarios capture most aspects of the ways in which the Partnership for 21st Century Skills (2003) suggests technology can help teachers and schools look beyond the requirements of the No Child Left Behind legislation to help students develop the knowledge, skills, and attitudes they will need in the coming era. They advocate emphasizing core subjects and learning skills, using twenty-first-century tools to develop learning skills, teaching and learning twenty-first-century content in a twenty-first-century context, and using twenty-first-century assessments that measure twenty-first-century skills.

Teaching, Learning, and Technology

A special concern is how technology can be used to improve teaching and learning (Jonassen & others, 2008; Kelly, McCain, & Jukes, 2009). The Partnership for 21st Century Skills (2008) argues that there is a huge gap between the technology knowledge and skills most students learn in school and the technology knowledge and skills they need in the twenty-first-century workplace. The Partnership emphasizes that schools need to move beyond the emphasis on core content required by the No Child Left Behind legislation and focus more on twenty-first-century themes, including media and technology literacy.

In line with the thesis of the Partnership for 21st Century Skills (2008), over the last two decades at the Educational Technology Center at Harvard University, a number of educators have worked on ways to use technology to improve students' understanding. Martha Stone Wiske has especially been instrumental in creating ways to incorporate technology into classroom contexts that transform student learning. Stone Wiske and her colleagues (2005) recently described how to more effectively use technology to teach for understanding by considering (1) the topics that are worth understanding, (2) what students should understand about such topics, (3) how students develop and demonstrate understanding, (4) how students and teachers assess understanding, and (5) how students and teachers learn together. These five aspects of understanding are based on ideas developed at Harvard by David Perkins, Howard Gardner, and Vito Perrone. Following are Stone Wiske and her colleagues' (2005) views of how to use technology for understanding:

1. *Evaluate which topics are worth understanding.* Technology is especially appropriate for generating worthwhile and interesting learning topics. The Internet provides a wealth of information about virtually every topic imaginable that

Prekindergarten–Grade 2

1. Illustrate and communicate original ideas and stories using digital tools and media-rich resources.

2. Identify, research, and collect data on an environmental issue using digital resources and propose a developmentally appropriate solution.

3. Engage in learning activities with learners from multiple cultures through e-mail and other electronic means.

4. In collaborative group work, use a variety of technologies to produce a digital solution or product in a curriculum area.

5. Find and evaluate information related to a current or historical person or event using digital resources.

Grades 3–5

1. Produce a media-rich digital story about a local event based on first-person interviews.

2. Use digital-imaging technology to modify or create works of art for use in a digital presentation.

3. Recognize bias in digital resources while researching an environmental issue with guidance from the teacher.

4. Select and apply digital tools to collect, organize, and analyze data to evaluate theories or hypotheses.

5. Identify and investigate a global issue and generate possible solutions using digital tools and resources.

Grades 6–8

1. Describe and illustrate a content-related concept using a model, simulation, or concept-mapping software.

2. Create original animations or videos documenting school, community, or local events.

3. Gather data, examine patterns, and apply information for decision making using digital tools and resources.

4. Participate in a cooperative learning project in an online learning community.

5. Evaluate digital resources to determine the credibility of the author and publisher and the timelines and accuracy of the information.

Grades 9–12

1. Design, develop, and test a digital learning game to demonstrate knowledge and skills related to curriculum content.

2. Create and publish an online art gallery with examples and commentaries that demonstrate an understanding of different historical periods, cultures, and countries.

3. Select digital tools or resources to use for a real-world task and justify the selection based on their efficiency and effectiveness.

4. Employ curriculum-specific simulations to practice critical thinking.

5. Identify a complex global issue, develop a systematic plan of investigation, and present innovative sustainable solutions.

FIGURE 12.6 A Sampling of ISTE's (2007) Profiles for Technology-Literate Students at Different Grade Levels

DEVELOPMENTAL FOCUS 12.3

How Do You Use Technology to Help Children Learn?

Early Childhood

Technology helps preschoolers learn music—in addition to listening to music to learn a song, they can also see the written words projected on a screen along with appropriate clip art.

—Connie Christy, *Aynor Elementary School (Preschool Program)*

Elementary School: Grades K–5

I often have my fifth-grade students research topics using Google and have them sift through the information. We discuss valid sources and try to determine ones that are questionable.

—Craig Jensen, *Cooper Mountain Elementary School*

Middle School: Grades 6–8

As a Spanish language teacher, I devised a plan with a teacher from Chile in which my students e-mailed her students in Spanish. In turn, her students e-mailed mine in English. This bilingual process helped both groups of students learn the respective languages of each country.

—Margaret Reardon, *Pocantico Hills School*

High School: Grades 9–12

Because kids love technology so much, I like to display notes using PowerPoint slides instead of simply lecturing. Video clips and connection to the Internet are available, so it is easy to display visuals to reinforce topics. I also encourage my students to purchase a flash drive so that their work can be portable and all in one place.

—Jennifer Heiter, *Bremen High School*

can be mined to generate new topics or expand what students are studying as part of the curriculum. (Bruckman, 2006; Cunningham & Billingsley, 2006). The wide range of information provided by the Internet allows students to learn more about their own interests and ideas and carve a unique pathway in learning about a topic, instead of following cookie-cutter steps in a traditional textbook or workbook (Roblyer, 2006).

Wiske and her colleagues (2005) also recommend that technology can often be used effectively to teach where problem spots emerge every year. "Examples include heat and temperature or weight and density in science, ratios in mathematics, and stereotypes in history and social studies classes" (p. 28). These topics, which many students struggle to understand, are central to the subject matter and are frequently more easily understood through the use of technology.

2. *Think about what students should understand about a topic.* When teachers consider using technology in the classroom, it is important for them to think about the learning goals they have for their students. Goals might include learning a new concept or applying a key concept to relevant situations. A goal related to technology might be to understand how to find and critically examine information on the Internet that is relevant to a classroom topic. Generating goals in this manner reminds the teacher that "surfing the Web" is "not an end in itself" but rather a way to use "technology to accomplish meaningful work" (Wiske, Franz, & Breit, 2005, p. 44).

3. *Pay attention to how students develop and demonstrate understanding.* Use technology to help students "stretch their minds" and understand something in

High school students creating a PowerPoint presentation in a math class.

A student creating a bar graph on a computer.

ways that they never did before. In improving students' understanding, Stone Wiske and her colleagues (2005) recommend that teachers use technology when it can "enhance and enrich their performances of understanding. . . . Word processors, digital audio and video technologies for creating Web sites allow students to express their understanding in a rich variety of media. These technologies also capture student work in forms that can be easily revised, combined, and distributed" (Wiske, Franz, & Breit, 2005, pp. 65–66).

4. *Consider how students and teachers assess learning.* Use ongoing assessment instead of only using a final assessment (Means, 2006). During ongoing assessment, you might guide students in understanding what quality work involves or use peer collaboration to help students analyze and improve their work. A helpful strategy is to also encourage students to assess their own learning progress and to monitor how effectively they are learning. Technology can be used in several ways to effectively assess learning.

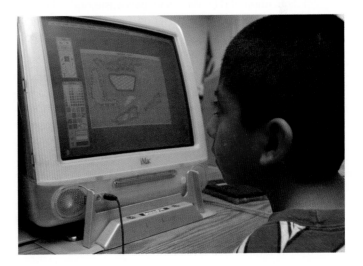

A student creating shapes and patterns on a computer in a Los Angeles elementary school.

> Digital technologies, including audio and video recorders and computers, can capture student work in forms that are easy to review. Interactive workspaces and software with multiple windows can help to keep assessment guidelines in view and even offer prompts and reminders. . . . Using networked technologies, students may post their work online where it can be readily reviewed and annotated by multiple advisors, including distant teachers and peers who cannot meet face-to-face. Technologies also provide easy means of preserving digital archives of student work. These may allow teachers and students to create individual portfolios to demonstrate and evaluate a student's work over time. (Wiske, Franz, & Breit, 2005, pp. 84–85)

We will have much more to say about technology and ongoing assessment in Chapter 16, "Classroom Assessment and Grading."

BEST PRACTICES
Strategies for Choosing and Using Technology in the Classroom

Technology will be a part of your classroom. Here are some guidelines for choosing and using it:

1. *Choose technology with an eye toward how it can help students actively explore, construct, and restructure information.* Look for software that lets students directly manipulate the information. One review found that students' learning improved when information was presented in a multimedia fashion that stimulated them to actively select, organize, and integrate visual and verbal information (Mayer, 1997). You might want to consult with a school or district media specialist for the software that best reflects these characteristics. Two excellent technology resources for teachers that emphasize the use of technology to improve students' learning and understanding are the Education with New Technologies (ENT) Web site (http://learnweb.harvard.edu/ent/home/index.cfm) and the International Society for Technology in Education (ISTE) Web site (www.iste.org). The ENT Web site is especially designed to help you integrate technology into your own classroom. Software catalogs and journals also are good sources.

2. *Look for ways to use technology as part of collaborative and real-world learning.* In Ann Brown and Joe Campione's (1996) words, education should be about "fostering a community of learners." Students often learn better when they work together to solve challenging problems and construct innovative projects (Hiltz & Goldman, 2005). Think of technologies such as the Web and e-mail as tools for providing students with opportunities to engage in collaborative learning, reaching outside the classroom to include the real world and the entire world and communicating with people in locations that otherwise would be inaccessible to them.

3. *Choose technology that presents positive models for students.* When you invite someone from the community to

talk with your class, you likely will consider the person's values and the type of role model that he or she presents. Keep in mind our earlier comments about monitoring technology for equity in ethnicity and culture. Be sure that the models that students associate with technology are diverse individuals who serve as positive role models.

4. *Your teaching skills are critical, regardless of the technology you use.* You don't have to worry that technology will replace you as a teacher. Technology becomes effective in the classroom only when you know how to use it, demonstrate it, guide and monitor its use, and incorporate it into a larger effort to develop students who are motivated to learn, actively learn, and communicate effectively. Even the most sophisticated hypermedia will not benefit students much unless you appropriately orient students to it, ask them good questions about the material, orchestrate its use, and tailor it to their needs.

5. *Continue to learn about technology yourself and increase your technological competence.* Digital technology is still changing at an amazing pace. Make it a personal goal to be open to new technology, keep up with technological advances by reading educational journals, and take courses in educational computing to increase your skills. You will be an important model for your students in terms of your attitude toward technology, your ability to use it effectively yourself, and your ability to communicate how to use it effectively to your students. In a study of computers and education in many countries, the main determinants of effective use of information technology in classrooms were the teacher's competence in using technology and the teacher's positive attitude toward technology (Collis & others, 1996).

5. *Reflect on how students and teachers can learn together.* "Networked technologies provide multiple advantages for connecting learners with reflective, collaborative communities. . . ." For example,

> E-mail permits users to send and receive many-to-many messages and to do so quickly. Students can share information and work with many other students all over the world, exchanging multiple rounds of reflective dialogue. The Web, with digital images, video and audio recordings, and videoconferencing, also allows students and their teachers to publish and collaborate on work, opening up the possibility of communicating with a wide range of audiences outside the classroom. (Wiske, Franz, & Breit, 2005, pp. 100, 102)

To evaluate your technology skills and attitudes, complete *Self-Assessment 12.1.*

SELF-ASSESSMENT 12.1

Evaluating My Technology Skills and Attitudes

How good are your technology skills? How positive are your attitudes about using technology and incorporating it into your classroom? For these items, consider the grade and subject(s) you are most likely to teach. Rate yourself from 1 to 5, with 1 = Not like me at all and 5 = Very much like me.

	1	2	3	4	5

1. I'm reasonably proficient at using a computer and installing and uninstalling software.

2. I have become comfortable with using a word-processing program.

3. I know when and how to use technology to improve students' understanding.

4. I have ideas for using word processing together with other language learning resources in the classroom.

5. I know how to search efficiently and thoroughly for information that interests me on the Internet.

6. I have ideas about how to use the Internet in my classroom.

7. I'm proficient at using e-mail.

8. I know how to use PowerPoint.

9. I have been part of collaborative learning exercises that involve technology.

10. I can see how collaborative learning can be used with technology in my classroom.

11. I am aware of the sociocultural issues involved in technology and education.

12. I know some good Web sites, journals, and software catalogs that can help me learn how to use technology more effectively in the classroom.

Scoring and Interpretation

Look at your scores for each item and evaluate your technology strengths and weaknesses. By the time you step into your classroom for your first day of teaching, make it a goal to be able to confidently rate yourself on each of these items at the level of 4 or 5. On items on which you rated yourself 1, 2, and 3, try to take technology courses at your local college that will improve your knowledge and skills in those areas.

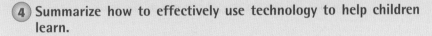

Review, Reflect, and Practice

(4) Summarize how to effectively use technology to help children learn.

REVIEW

- What characterizes the technology revolution and the Internet?
- What are some standards for technology-literate students?
- What are five things that teachers need to ask when considering the use of technology in the classroom to improve students' understanding?

(continued)

Review, Reflect, and Practice

REFLECT

- Would one or more of the ways that computers can be used to support learning and instruction be useful to the subject and grade level you plan to teach? How?

PRAXIS™ PRACTICE

1. Ms. Carlson has her students enrolled in an online history course. This type of distance learning is referred to as
   a. e-mail.
   b. virtual school.
   c. tutorial.
   d. Web enhancement.

2. Mr. Muhammad's eighth-grade history class corresponds via an Internet blog with an eighth-grade class in Spain. They discuss their viewpoints of various aspects of world history. For instance, right now they are discussing the cultural change that occurred in South America as a result of Spanish exploration and conquest. Which answer best describes this activity?
   a. collaborative learning
   b. computer-mediated communication
   c. database searching
   d. WebQuest

3. Mr. Wilson's students are examining various Web sites about world problems. As they examine each one, they are looking at the quality of the information contained on the site, including any forms of cultural, sexual, or political bias. Students will then compile a report of their findings. If Mr. Wilson is following the International Society for Technology in Education Standards, what grades does he most likely teach?
   a. PK–2
   b. 3–5
   c. 6–8
   d. 9–12

4. Which of the following examples best reflects the effective use of technology to promote student understanding?
   a. Roberto is using a classroom computer game to help him learn his multiplication facts. The game presents a fact; he types in an answer. Each correct answer earns points.
   b. Patricia is using her computer's word-processing program to type a paper for her English class after having written it out longhand.
   c. Deshawn is immersed in a computer simulation of the desert ecosystem.
   d. Carmine is texting his best friend during class regarding their plans for the evening.

Please see the answer key at the end of the book.

CRACK THE CASE
The Case of the Big Debate

Mrs. Rumer was new to teaching third grade at Hillside Elementary School. Before the school year began, she met with other new teachers and their mentors for planning sessions. The administration appeared to be aware of just how much planning was necessary for successful teaching. Mrs. Rumer openly shared her ideas with her mentor, Mrs. Humbolt, and the rest of the group.

"I really want to have a learner-centered classroom," she said. "I'd like to use aspects of problem-based learning, essential questions, and guided discovery. I think the students will learn so much more that way than if I use teacher-centered instruction."

Mrs. Humbolt smiled and said, "Well, they'd probably have more fun, but I doubt that their test scores would reflect much learning at all. We really need to prepare our students to meet state standards, Mrs. Rumer. To do that, you'd better throw in some good old-fashioned direct instruction." Several other teachers readily agreed. One commented, "That constructivist stuff is too much fluff; I want my students to be serious and learn what I teach them." Another said, "I use the computers in the classroom for drilling students to memorize material for the state tests they have to take, sort of like giving them electronic flash cards. I guess that wouldn't fit your scheme."

The other teachers' comments surprised Mrs. Rumer. She had learned in her education courses that learner-centered instruction is supposed to be the best way to teach children. She wanted her students to actively construct their knowledge, not merely have her pour information into their minds. The principal assured her that if she wanted to use a learner-centered approach, she would have that freedom.

With this assurance, Mrs. Rumer began making lists of everything she would have to plan for in order to have an effective learner-centered classroom. She began by going through the district's curriculum guide for third grade. She made lists of all the objectives. Then she went through the learner-centered psychological principles from the APA. After doing this, she realized her job was going to be a daunting one.

1. What are the issues in this case?

2. Where should Mrs. Rumer go from here?

3. How can she take a curriculum that has been taught in a teacher-centered manner and convert it to a learner-centered curriculum? Should she? Why or why not?

4. How can she incorporate technology into the curriculum so that the computers don't become mere electronic flashcards?

5. Which of the following is an activity that would most likely appeal to Mrs. Rumer?
   a. The students will master their basic multiplication facts by completing a worksheet covering them each day.
   b. The students will master their basic multiplication facts by playing multiplication baseball.
   c. The students will master their basic multiplication facts by taking daily timed tests covering them.
   d. The students will master their basic multiplication facts by writing out their multiplication tables repeatedly.

6. Which of the following is an activity that would most likely appeal to Mrs. Rumer's colleagues?
   a. The students will learn the scientific process by completing several experiments.
   b. The students will learn the scientific process by focusing on essential questions in science.
   c. The students will learn the scientific process by reading about it in their science texts and listening to lectures.
   d. The students will learn the scientific process by testing the water in a nearby creek.

Reach Your Learning Goals
Planning, Instruction, and Technology

---

(1) PLANNING: Explain what is involved in classroom planning.

Instructional Planning

Instructional planning involves developing a systematic, organized strategy for lessons. Planning is critically important to being a competent teacher, and instructional planning may be mandated by schools.

Time Frames and Planning

Teachers need to make plans for different time frames, ranging from yearly planning to daily planning. Yinger identified five time frames of teacher planning: yearly, term, unit, weekly, and daily.

---

(2) TEACHER-CENTERED LESSON PLANNING AND INSTRUCTION: Identify important forms of teacher-centered instruction.

Teacher-Centered Lesson Planning

Teacher-centered lesson planning includes creating behavioral objectives, analyzing tasks, and developing instructional taxonomies (classifications). Behavioral objectives are statements that propose changes in students' behavior to reach desired performance levels. Task analysis focuses on breaking down a complex task that students are to learn into its component parts. Bloom's taxonomy classifies educational objectives into cognitive, affective, and psychomotor domains and is used by many teachers to create goals and objectives in lesson planning.

Direct Instruction

Direct instruction is a structured, teacher-centered approach that involves teacher direction and control, high expectations for students' progress, maximum time spent by students on academic tasks, and efforts by the teacher to keep negative affect to a minimum. The teacher chooses students' learning tasks and directs students' learning of those tasks. The use of nonacademic materials is deemphasized, as is nonacademically oriented teacher-student interaction.

Teacher-Centered Instructional Strategies

Teacher-centered instructional strategies include orienting students to new material; lecturing, explaining, and demonstrating; questioning and discussing; mastery learning (learning one topic or concept thoroughly before moving on to a more difficult one); seatwork (having students work independently at their seats); and homework.

Evaluating Teacher-Centered Instruction

Teacher-centered instruction includes useful techniques, and its advocates especially believe it is the best strategy for teaching basic skills such as math computations, grammar rules, and reading vocabulary. Critics of teacher-centered instruction say that by itself it tends to lead to passive rote learning, overly rigid and structured classrooms, inadequate attention to socioemotional development, external rather than internal motivation, excessive use of paper-and-pencil tasks, too few opportunities for real-world learning, and too little collaborative learning in small groups.

3 LEARNER-CENTERED LESSON PLANNING AND INSTRUCTION: Discuss important forms of learner-centered instruction.

Learner-Centered Principles

Learner-centered lesson planning and instruction moves the focus away from the teacher and toward the student. The APA's learner-centered psychological principles emphasize the active, reflective nature of learning and learners. The fourteen principles involve cognitive and metacognitive factors (the nature of the learning process, goals of the learning process, the construction of knowledge, strategic thinking, thinking about thinking, and the context of learning); motivational and emotional factors (motivational and emotional influences on learning, intrinsic motivation to learn, and effects of motivation on effort); developmental and social factors (developmental influences on learning and social influences on learning); and individual difference factors (individual differences in learning, learning and diversity, and standards and assessments).

Some Learner-Centered Instructional Strategies

Problem-based learning emphasizes real-world problem solving. A problem-based curriculum exposes students to authentic problems. Problem-based learning focuses on small-group discussion rather than lecture. Students identify issues they wish to explore, and teachers act as guides, helping students monitor their problem-solving efforts. *Essential questions* are questions that engagingly reflect the heart of the curriculum, cause students to think, and motivate their curiosity. Discovery learning is learning in which students construct an understanding on their own. Most discovery-learning approaches today involve guided discovery, in which students are encouraged to construct their understanding with the assistance of teacher-guided questions and directions.

Evaluating Learner-Centered Strategies

The learner-centered model of planning and instruction has many positive features. The fourteen APA learner-centered principles are guidelines that can help teachers develop strategies that benefit student learning (such as encouraging students to actively construct knowledge, think deeply and creatively, be internally motivated, solve real-world problems, and collaboratively learn). Critics argue that learner-centered planning and instruction focuses too much on the process of learning and not enough on academic content; is more appropriate for social sciences and humanities than science and math; is not appropriate for beginning instruction when students have little or no knowledge about the topic; and is more challenging to implement than most teachers envision. Keep in mind that although we presented teacher-centered and learner-centered approaches separately, many teachers use aspects of both approaches.

4 TECHNOLOGY AND EDUCATION: Technology and Education: Summarize how to effectively use technology to help children learn.

The Technology Revolution and the Internet

The technology revolution is part of the information society in which we now live, and students will increasingly need to have technological skills. Today's technologies can be remarkable tools for motivating students and guiding their learning. The Internet is the core of computer-mediated communication. The Web is a system for browsing Internet sites. The Internet can be an important learning tool in many classrooms. Cautions about Internet use need to be observed.

Standards for Technology-Literate Students

The International Society for Technology in Education (ISTE) has established technology standards for students that include using digital technologies to support creativity and innovation, communication and collaboration, problem solving and decision making, and digital citizenship. In addition, ISTE provides performance indicators for achieving these standards at different grade levels.

Five things teachers need to ask regarding using technology more effectively in the classroom to improve students' learning include considering: (1) which topics are worth understanding, (2) what students should understand about such topics, (3) how students develop and demonstrate understanding, (4) how students and teachers assess understanding, and (5) how students and teachers learn together.

KEY TERMS

instructional planning 420	direct instruction 427	comparative advance	discovery learning 439
behavioral objectives 424	advance organizers 429	organizers 429	guided discovery learning 439
task analysis 425	expository advance	mastery learning 430	Internet 443
taxonomy 425	organizers 429	essential questions 439	Web 443
Bloom's taxonomy 425			

PORTFOLIO ACTIVITIES

Now that you have a good understanding of this chapter, complete these exercises to expand your thinking.

Independent Reflection

Developing a Classroom Technology Plan. Create a written plan for how you might use computers for the subject(s) and grade level you plan to teach. How will you adapt your plan for students with little or no experience with computers? How can your classroom benefit from students with advanced technology skills? (INTASC: Principles *1, 2, 4*)

Collaborative Work

Evaluating Teacher-Centered and Learner-Centered Classrooms. With three other students in the class, divide up the work of observing an early childhood, an elementary, a middle school, and a high school classroom. Reconvene after each of you has

observed a classroom, and discuss the aspects of teacher-centered and learner-centered approaches the teachers were using. Evaluate how effective the approaches were. Write a comparative analysis. (INTASC: Principles *1, 2, 3, 4, 5, 6, 7, 8, 9*)

Research/Field Experience

Instructional Planning in Action. Ask a teacher at the grade level you plan to teach to show you the materials he or she uses in planning lessons, units, the term, and the yearly curriculum for one or more subjects. Create samples for your own later use based on what the teacher shows you. Discuss the importance of planning at each of these levels. (INTASC: Principles *7, 9*)

Go to the Online Learning Center for downloadable portfolio templates.

TAKING IT TO THE NET

- List the primary components of a good lesson plan. Dissect an online lesson plan and assess its component parts. Describe the quality of your chosen lesson and how you think it could be improved. Why is it so critical to develop clear objectives? Why is it good practice to think about your method of assessment prior to conducting the lesson? www.eduref.org/Virtual/Lessons/index.shtml

- Using the selected Web site on the Online Learning Center or a site of your own choice, review an exemplary model of educational technology in action. Why is your selected program or project so successful? Reflect on your own technology skills, and note your strengths and weaknesses. Develop a pro-

fessional development action plan to enhance your educational technology skills. www.ncrel.org/sdrs/areas/issues/methods/technlgy/te800.htm

- Evaluate an online, interactive activity, such as a WebQuest. How does it measure up in these areas: academic rigor, student interest and motivation, user interface and navigability, relevance to real-world issues, and accessibility to students/teachers? http:// webquest.sdsu.edu

Connect to the Online Learning Center to explore possible answers.

STUDY, PRACTICE, AND SUCCEED

Visit www.mhhe.com/santedu4e to review the chapter with self-grading quizzes and self-assessments, to apply the chapter material to two more Crack the Case studies, and for suggested activities to develop your teaching portfolio.

CHAPTER 13

Motivation, Teaching, and Learning

The art of teaching is the art of awakening the curiosity of young minds.

—Anatole France
French Novelist and Poet, 20th Century

Learning Goals

1 Define motivation and compare the behavioral, humanistic, cognitive, and social perspectives on motivation.

2 Discuss the important processes in motivation to achieve.

3 Explain how relationships and sociocultural contexts can support or undercut motivation.

4 Recommend how to help students with achievement problems.

TEACHING STORIES Jaime Escalante

An immigrant from Bolivia named Jaime Escalante became a math teacher at Garfield High School in East Los Angeles, a school largely populated by Latino students from low-income families. When he began teaching at Garfield, many of the students had little confidence in their math abilities, and most of the teachers had low expectations for the students' success. Escalante took it as a special challenge to improve the students' math skills, even enable them to perform well on the Educational Testing Service Advanced Placement (AP) calculus exam.

The first year was difficult. Escalante's calculus class began at 8 A.M. He told the students the doors would be open at 7 A.M. and that instruction would begin at 7:30 A.M. He also worked with them after school and on weekends. He put together lots of handouts, told the students to take extensive notes, and required them to keep a folder. He gave them a five-minute quiz each morning and a test every Friday. He started with fourteen students, but in two weeks the number was cut in half. Only five students lasted through the spring. One of the boys who quit said, "I don't want to come at 7 o'clock. Why should I?"

When Escalante was teaching, on the 5-point AP calculus test (with 5 highest, 1 lowest), a 3 or better meant that a student was performing at a college level and would receive credit for the course at most major universities. The AP calculus scores for Escalante's first five students were two 4's, two 2's, and one 1. This was better than the school had done in the past, but Escalante resolved to do better.

Three years later, the AP calculus test scores for Escalante's class of 15 students were one 5, four 4's, nine 3's, and one 2. Ten years after Escalante's first class, 151 students were taking calculus in the East Los Angeles high school.

Jaime Escalante in a classroom teaching math.

Escalante's persistent, challenging, and inspiring teaching raised Garfield High, a school plagued by poor funding, violence, and inferior working conditions, to seventh place among U.S. schools in calculus. Escalante's commitment and motivation were transferred to his students, many of whom no one had believed in before Escalante came along. Escalante's contributions were portrayed in the film *Stand and Deliver.* Escalante, his students, and celebrity guests also introduce basic math concepts for sixth- to twelfth-grade students on *Futures 1 and 2 with Jaime Escalante,* a PBS series. Escalante has now retired from teaching but continues to work in a consulting role to help improve students' motivation to do well in math and improve their math skills. Escalante's story is testimony to how one teacher can make a major difference in students' motivation and achievement.

Preview

In Chapter 12, you learned that motivation is a key component of the American Psychological Association's learner-centered psychological principles. Indeed, motivation is a critical aspect of teaching and learning. Unmotivated students won't expend the necessary effort to learn. As Jaime Escalante's Teaching Story shows, highly motivated students are eager to come to school and are absorbed in the learning process.

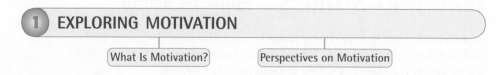

1 EXPLORING MOTIVATION

What Is Motivation?   Perspectives on Motivation

A young Canadian, Terry Fox, did one of the great long-distance runs in history (McNally, 1990). Averaging a marathon (26.2 miles) a day for five months, he ran 3,359 miles across most of Canada. What makes his grueling feat truly remarkable is that Terry Fox had lost a leg to cancer before the run, so he was running with the aid of a prosthetic limb. Terry Fox clearly was a motivated person, but exactly what does it mean to be motivated?

What Is Motivation?

Motivation involves the processes that energize, direct, and sustain behavior. That is, motivated behavior is behavior that is energized, directed, and sustained. Why did Terry Fox do this run? When Terry was hospitalized with cancer, he told himself that if he survived he would do something to help fund cancer research. Thus, the motivation for his run was to give purpose to his life by helping other people with cancer.

Terry Fox's behavior was energized, directed, and sustained. Running across most of Canada, he encountered unforeseen hurdles: severe headwinds, heavy rain, snow, and icy roads. Because of these conditions, he averaged only eight miles a day after the first month, far below what he had planned. But he kept going and picked up the pace in the second month until he was back on track. His example stands as a testimonial to how motivation can help each of us prevail.

Terry Fox's story is portrayed in a good classroom film, *The Power of Purpose.* One sixth-grade teacher showed the film to her class and then asked her students to write down what they learned from it. One student wrote, "I learned that even if something bad happens to you, you have to keep going, keep trying. Even if your body gets hurt, it can't take away your spirit."

Lance Armstrong after winning his seventh Tour de France in a row.

Let's look at another example of motivation. Lance Armstrong was an accomplished cyclist when he was diagnosed with testicular cancer in 1996. Chances of his recovery were estimated at less than 50 percent when he began chemotherapy. However, Lance did recover from the cancer and set a goal of winning the three-week, 2,000-plus-mile Tour de France, the world's premier bicycle race and one of the great tests of human motivation in sports. Day after day, Lance trained intensely, keeping the goal of winning the Tour de France in mind. Lance won the Tour de France not once but seven years in a row from 1999 through 2005.

As with Terry Fox's marathon run and Lance Armstrong's winning of the Tour de France, motivation in the classroom involves why students are behaving in a particular way and the extent to which their behavior is energized, directed, and sustained. If students don't complete an assignment because they are bored, lack of motivation is involved. If students encounter challenges in researching and writing a paper, but persist and overcome hurdles, motivation is involved.

Perspectives on Motivation

Different psychological perspectives explain motivation in different ways. Let's explore four of these perspectives: behavioral, humanistic, cognitive, and social.

The Behavioral Perspective The behavioral perspective emphasizes external rewards and punishments as keys in determining a student's motivation. **Incentives** are positive or negative stimuli or events that can motivate a student's behavior. Advocates of the use of incentives emphasize that they add interest or excitement to the class and direct attention toward appropriate behavior and away from inappropriate behavior (Emmer & Evertson, 2009).

motivation The processes that energize, direct, and sustain behavior.

incentives Positive or negative stimuli or events that can motivate a student's behavior.

Incentives that classroom teachers use include numerical scores and letter grades, which provide feedback about the quality of the student's work, and checkmarks or stars for competently completing work. Other incentives include giving students recognition—for example, by displaying their work, giving them a certificate of achievement, placing them on the honor roll, and verbally mentioning their accomplishments. Another type of incentive focuses on allowing students to do something special—such as playing computer games or going on a field trip—as a reward for good work. Shortly, in our discussion of intrinsic and extrinsic motivation, we will look more closely at the issue of whether incentives are a good idea.

The Humanistic Perspective The **humanistic perspective** stresses students' capacity for personal growth, freedom to choose their destiny, and positive qualities (such as being sensitive to others). This perspective is closely associated with Abraham Maslow's (1954, 1971) belief that certain basic needs must be met before higher needs can be satisfied. According to Maslow's **hierarchy of needs**, individuals' needs must be satisfied in this sequence (see Figure 13.1):

- *Physiological:* Hunger, thirst, sleep
- *Safety:* Ensuring survival, such as protection from war and crime
- *Love and belongingness:* Security, affection, and attention from others
- *Esteem:* Feeling good about oneself
- *Self-actualization:* Realization of one's potential

Thus, in Maslow's view, students must satisfy their need for food before they can achieve. His view also provides an explanation of why children who come from poor or abusive homes are less likely to achieve in school than children whose basic needs are met.

Self-actualization, the highest and most elusive of Maslow's needs, is the motivation to develop one's full potential as a human being. In Maslow's view, self-actualization is possible only after the lower needs have been met. Maslow cautions that most people stop maturing after they have developed a high level of esteem and therefore never become self-actualized. Some characteristics of self-actualized individuals include being spontaneous, problem-centered rather than self-centered, and creative.

The idea that human needs are hierarchically arranged is appealing. However, not everyone agrees with Maslow's ordering of motives. For example, for some students cognitive needs might be more fundamental than esteem needs. Other students might meet their cognitive needs even though they have not experienced love and belongingness.

The Cognitive Perspective According to the cognitive perspective on motivation, students' thoughts guide their motivation. In recent years, there has been a tremendous surge of interest in the cognitive perspective on motivation (Meece & Eccles, 2009; Schunk, Pintrich, & Meece, 2008). This interest focuses on such ideas as students' internal motivation to achieve, their attributions (perceptions about the causes of success or failure, especially the perception that effort is an important factor in

FIGURE 13.1 Maslow's Hierarchy of Needs

Abraham Maslow developed the hierarchy of human needs to show how we have to satisfy certain basic needs before we can satisfy higher needs. In the diagram, lower-level needs are shown toward the base of the pyramid, higher-level needs toward the peak.

humanistic perspective A view that stresses students' capacity for personal growth, freedom to choose their destiny, and positive qualities.

hierarchy of needs Maslow's concept that individual needs must be satisfied in this sequence: physiological, safety, love and belongingness, esteem, and self-actualization.

self-actualization The highest and most elusive of Maslow's needs; the motivation to develop one's full potential as a human being.

achievement), and their beliefs that they can effectively control their environment. The cognitive perspective also stresses the importance of goal setting, planning, and monitoring progress toward a goal (Schunk, 2008).

Thus, whereas the behavioral perspective sees the student's motivation as a consequence of external incentives, the cognitive perspective argues that external pressures should be deemphasized. The cognitive perspective recommends that students should be given more opportunities and responsibility for controlling their own achievement outcomes (Patall, Cooper, & Robinson, 2008).

The cognitive perspective on motivation fits with the ideas of R. W. White (1959), who proposed the concept of **competence motivation**, the idea that people are motivated to deal effectively with their environment, to master their world, and to process information efficiently. White said that people do these things because they are internally motivated to interact effectively with the environment. The concept of competence motivation explains why humans are motivated to achieve scientific and technological innovation.

The Social Perspective   Are you the kind of person who is motivated to be around people a lot? Or would you rather stay home and read a book? The **need for affiliation or relatedness** is the motive to be securely connected with other people. This involves establishing, maintaining, and restoring warm, close personal relationships. Students' need for affiliation or relatedness is reflected in their motivation to spend time with peers, their close friendships, their attachment to their parents, and their desire to have a positive relationship with their teachers.

Students in schools with caring and supportive interpersonal relationships have more positive academic attitudes and values and are more satisfied with school (Noddings, 2007). One study revealed that a key factor in students' motivation and achievement was their perception of whether they had a positive relationship with the teacher (McCombs, 2001). In other research, the value that middle school students assigned to math increased when they had a teacher whom they perceived to be high in support (Eccles, 1993).

As you think about the perspectives on motivation, realize that you don't have to adopt just one perspective. All of the perspectives provide information that is relevant to children's education.

competence motivation The idea that people are motivated to deal effectively with their environment, to master their world, and to process information efficiently.

need for affiliation or relatedness The motive to be securely connected with other people.

Review, Reflect, and Practice

(1) **Define motivation and compare the behavioral, humanistic, cognitive, and social perspectives on motivation.**

REVIEW

- What is motivated behavior?
- How would you briefly summarize the four main perspectives on motivation?

REFLECT

- Recall a situation in which you were highly motivated to accomplish something. How would you describe your motivation in terms of each of the four perspectives?

PRAXIS™ PRACTICE

1. Which of the following best exemplifies what motivation is?
   a. Robbie is emotional about the upcoming school year and wants to do well.
   b. Sherrie is energized, sets a high goal for doing well in her English class, persists with considerable effort, and makes an *A* in the class.

Review, Reflect, and Practice

    c. Carmello is good at directing his attention to what he wants to accomplish.

    d. Latisha works hard, experiences positive feelings about her academic work, and enjoys working with others.

2. Which of the following best exemplifies the cognitive perspective of motivation?

    a. Mr. Davidson gives his students tickets when he "catches them being good" so that they will continue to behave appropriately.

    b. Mr. McRoberts wants his students to believe they can be successful in anything if they try, so he ensures success for those students who work hard.

    c. Ms. Boeteng believes that her students will be more motivated in school if they establish good relationships with both her and with their classmates, so she provides emotional support.

    d. Ms. Pocius keeps a supply of cereal in her desk drawer so that if one of her students is hungry, she can provide food.

Please see the answer key at the end of the book.

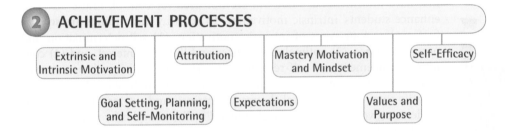

The current interest in motivation in school has been fueled by the cognitive perspective and an emphasis on discovering the most important processes involved in students' achievement. In this section, we will study a number of effective cognitive strategies for improving students' motivation to achieve. We'll begin by exploring a crucial distinction between extrinsic (external) and intrinsic (internal) motivation. That will lead us to examine several other important cognitive insights about motivation. Then, we will study the role of expectations in students' motivation.

Extrinsic and Intrinsic Motivation

Extrinsic motivation involves doing something to obtain something else (a means to an end). Extrinsic motivation is often influenced by external incentives such as rewards and punishments. For example, a student may study hard for a test in order to obtain a good grade in the course.

The behavioral perspective emphasizes the importance of extrinsic motivation in achievement; the humanistic and cognitive approaches stress the importance of intrinsic motivation in achievement. **Intrinsic motivation** involves the internal motivation to do something for its own sake (an end in itself). For example, a student may study hard for a test because he or she enjoys the content of the course.

Current evidence strongly favors establishing a classroom climate in which students are intrinsically motivated to learn (Wigfield & others, 2006). For example, one recent study of third- to eighth-grade students found that intrinsic motivation was

extrinsic motivation The external motivation to do something to obtain something else (a means to an end).

intrinsic motivation The internal motivation to do something for its own sake (an end in itself).

BEST PRACTICES
Strategies for Student Self-Determination and Choice

Here are some ways you can promote self-determination and choice in your classroom (Brophy, 2004; Deci & Ryan, 1994):

1. *Take the time* to talk with students and explain why a learning activity is important.

2. *Be attentive* to students' feelings when they are being asked to do something they don't want to do.

3. *Manage the classroom effectively, in a way that lets students make personal choices.* Let students select topics for book reports, writing assignments, and research

projects and decide how they want to report their work (for instance, to you or to the class as a whole, individually or with a partner).

4. *Establish learning centers* where students can work individually or collaboratively with other students on different projects and can select their activities from a menu that you have developed.

5. *Create self-selected interest groups* and let students work on relevant research projects.

These students were given an opportunity to write and perform their own play. These kinds of self-determining opportunities can enhance students' motivation to achieve.

positively linked with grades and standardized test scores, whereas extrinsic motivation was negatively related to achievement outcomes (Lepper, Corpus, & Iyengar, 2005).

Students are more motivated to learn when they are given choices, become absorbed in challenges that match their skills, and receive rewards that have informational value but are not used for control. Praise also can enhance students' intrinsic motivation. To see why these things are so, let's first explore four types of intrinsic motivation: (1) self-determination and personal choice, (2) optimal experiences and flow, (3) interest, and (4) cognitive engagement and self-responsibility. Then we'll discuss how extrinsic rewards can either enhance or undermine intrinsic motivation. Next we will identify some developmental changes in intrinsic and extrinsic motivation as students move up the educational ladder. Finally, we will offer some concluding thoughts about intrinsic and extrinsic motivation.

Self-Determination and Personal Choice One view of intrinsic motivation emphasizes self-determination (Deci, Koestner, & Ryan, 2001). In this view, students want to believe that they are doing something because of their own will, not because of external success or rewards.

Researchers have found that students' internal motivation and intrinsic interest in school tasks increase when students have some choice and some opportunities to take personal responsibility for their learning (Grolnick & others, 2002). For example, in one study, high school science students who were encouraged to organize their own experiments demonstrated more care and interest in laboratory work than did their counterparts who had to follow detailed instructions and directions (Rainey, 1965).

In another study, which included mainly African American students from low-income backgrounds, teachers were encouraged to give the students more responsibility for their school programs (deCharms, 1984)—in particular, opportunities to set their own goals, plan how to reach the goals, and monitor their progress toward the goals. Students were given some choice in the activities they wanted to engage in and when they would do them. They also were encouraged to take personal responsibility for their behavior, including reaching the goals that they had set. Compared with a control group, students in this intrinsic motivation/self-determination group had higher achievement gains and were more likely to graduate from high school.

Optimal Experiences and Flow Mihaly Csikszentmihalyi (2000; Rathunde & Csikszentmihalyi, 2006) also has developed ideas that are relevant to understanding

BEST PRACTICES
Strategies for Helping Students Achieve Flow

How can you encourage students to achieve flow? Here are some strategies (Csikszentmihalyi, Rathunde, & Whalen, 1993):

1. *Be competent and motivated.* Become an expert about the subject matter, show enthusiasm when you teach, and present yourself as a model who is intrinsically motivated.

THROUGH THE EYES OF TEACHERS
Turning the Classroom into an Egyptian Tomb, New York City, and Mount Olympus

Rhonda Nachamkin, who teaches first grade at River Eves Elementary School in Roswell, Georgia, has a high-energy style and approaches each unit as if it were a Hollywood production. She turns the classroom into an Egyptian tomb, New York City, and Mount Olympus. She sends parents scurrying to learn who Anubis (Egyptian god) and Prometheus (Greek Titan who stole fire) were so they can converse about these topics with their 6-year-olds. Rhonda likes to use multiple versions of fairy tales to teach reading, spelling, and analytical concepts. (Source: *USA Today*, 1999)

Rhonda Nachamkin helps one of her students, Patrick Drones, with his work.

2. *Create an optimal match.* A good strategy is to develop and maintain an optimal match between what you challenge students to do and what their skills are. That is, encourage students to achieve challenging but reasonable goals.

3. *Remove distractions from the classroom.* It is difficult for students to get into a "flow" state if there are a lot of distractions.

4. *Raise confidence.* Provide students with both instructional and emotional support that encourages them to tackle learning with confidence and a minimum of anxiety. As you will see next, Alan Haskitz, a middle school social studies teacher, describes how he does this by finding a topic that students find intrinsically interesting.

THROUGH THE EYES OF TEACHERS
Achieving Flow in a Math Class by Appraising Car Values

Most middle and high school students like cars, so I use the National Automobile Dealers Association (NADA) appraisal guides that provide an estimated value for new and used vehicles to make math more interesting for students. NADA makes the guides available without charge (www.nada.com). The students are exposed to the basic math concepts from lectures and using the textbook. However, that does not achieve flow. To acquire that level of motivation, the students design their own lessons to teach others the concepts using the NADA guidebooks for the values they are going to use in their work. I teach them how to write a multiple-choice question with stems and distracters and then stand back and watch the flow start. I hear students shuffling through the books shouting out figures, vehicle names, and "I want this car" and "Look at how much this costs." They see the lesson as important to them because they want to own a car—but more importantly, they want to be a knowledgeable buyer. They use the data to apply real-world statistics to creating problems that teach such fundamental, and sometimes difficult to grasp, concepts as percentages, depreciation, and graphing. Using these books is especially a powerful tool for remediation as it appeals to those students with difficulty graphing abstract reasoning.

intrinsic motivation. He has studied the optimal experiences of people for more than two decades. People report that these optimal experiences involve feelings of deep enjoyment and happiness. Csikszentmihalyi uses the term *flow* to describe optimal experiences in life. He has found that flow occurs most often when people develop a sense of mastery and are absorbed in a state of concentration while they engage in an activity. He argues that flow occurs when individuals are engaged in challenges they find neither too difficult nor too easy. For example, flow is occurring when a student is deeply absorbed in working on a science project that her teacher has structured at a challenging level but not beyond the student's capability.

TECHNOLOGY AND EDUCATION
Technology Integration, Authentic Tasks, Curiosity, and Interest

Authentic tasks approximate the real world or real life as closely as possible, and they can spark students' interest and curiosity. Students often perceive technology-based learning experiences as real-world activities (Cognition and Technology Group at Vanderbilt, 1997).

Integrating technology into the classroom has clearly been found to increase students' motivation to learn and engagement in learning, especially when it is used to foster authentic learning. For example, researchers have documented improved motivation (Swan & others, 2005), engagement (Silvernail & Lane, 2004), behavior (Apple Computer, 1995), and school attendance (Apple Computer, 1995) among students involved in technology-rich initiatives. In addition, research indicates that such students are better organized and more independent learners (Zucker & McGhee, 2005). Also, research reveals that special needs students can achieve at the same levels

Second-grade students in the Research Center for Educational Technology's AT&T classroom at Kent State University engaged in writing activities on mobile computers they can take with them and work on anywhere and anytime.

as regular students in some situations when using technology (Swan & others, 2006).

Serious games are software applications developed using gaming technology and design principles whose primary purpose is for something other than pure entertainment, usually for training or education. The serious games movement in education takes as its framework situated and authentic learning. One example of serious games is *Quest Atlantis* (2008), a National Science Foundation–funded project that uses a three-dimensional multiuser environment to immerse 9- to 12-year-old children in educational tasks. Currently, thousands of registered users from five continents use *Quest Atlantis* in schools. Researchers have found that students who use *Quest Atlantis* improve their learning over time in science, social studies, and sense of academic efficacy (Barab & others, 2008).

Perceived levels of challenge and skill can result in different outcomes (see Figure 13.2) (Brophy, 1998). Flow is most likely to occur in areas in which students are challenged and perceive themselves as having a high degree of skill. When students' skills are high but the activity provides little challenge, the result is boredom. When both the challenge and skill levels are low, students feel apathy. And when students face a challenging task that they don't believe they have adequate skills to master, they experience anxiety.

Interest Educational psychologists also have examined the concept of *interest*, which has been proposed as more specific than intrinsic motivation (Blumenfeld, Kempler, & Krajcik, 2006). A distinction has been made between individual interest, which is thought to be relatively stable, and situational interest, which is believed to be generated by specific aspects of a task activity. Research on interest has focused mainly on how interest is related to learning. Interest is especially linked to measures of deep learning, such as recall of main ideas and responses to more difficult comprehension questions, than to surface learning, such as responses to simple questions and verbatim recall of text (Wigfield & others, 2006). To read further about ways to stimulate students' interest, see the *Technology and Education* interlude.

Cognitive Engagement and Self-Responsibility Phyllis Blumenfeld and her colleagues (2006) proposed another variation on intrinsic motivation. They emphasize the importance of creating learning environments that encourage students to become cognitively engaged and take responsibility for their learning. The goal is to get students to become motivated to expend the effort to persist and master ideas rather than simply doing enough work to just get by and make passing grades. Especially important is to embed subject matter content

FIGURE 13.2 Outcomes of Perceived Levels of Challenge and Skill

	Students' perceived level of their own skill	
	Low	High
Students' perceived level of challenge — Low	Apathy	Boredom
Students' perceived level of challenge — High	Anxiety	Flow

and skills learning within meaningful contexts, especially real-world situations that mesh with students' interests (Perry, Turner, & Meyer, 2006).

Extrinsic Rewards and Intrinsic Motivation   Now that we have discussed a number of views of intrinsic motivation, let's examine whether classroom rewards might be useful in some situations and whether certain types of rewards might actually increase intrinsic motivation. As we saw in Chapter 7, external rewards can be useful in changing behavior. However, in some situations rewards can undermine learning. In a classic study, students who already had a strong interest in art and did not expect a reward spent more time drawing than did students who also had a strong interest in art but knew they would be rewarded for drawing (Lepper, Greene, & Nisbett, 1973).

However, classroom rewards can be useful (Cameron, 2001; Cameron & Pierce, 2008; Reeve, 2006). Two uses are (1) as an incentive to engage in tasks, in which case the goal is to control the student's behavior; and (2) to convey information about mastery (Bandura, 1982; Deci, 1975). When rewards are offered that convey information about mastery, students' feelings of competence are likely to be enhanced. It is not the reward itself that causes the effect but, rather, the offer or expectation of the reward (Schunk, 2008). Rewards used as incentives lead to perceptions that the student's behavior was caused by the external reward, and not by the student's own motivation to be competent.

To better understand the difference between using rewards to control students' behavior and using them to provide information about mastery, consider this example (Schunk, 2008): A teacher puts a reward system in place in which the more work students accomplish, the more points they will earn. Students will be motivated to work to earn points because they are told that the points can be exchanged for privileges. However, the points also provide information about their capabilities. That is, the more points students earn, the more work they have accomplished. As they accumulate points, students are more likely to feel competent. In contrast, if points are provided simply for spending time on a task, the task might be perceived as a means to an end. In this case, because the points don't convey anything about capabilities, students are likely to perceive the rewards as controlling their behavior.

What conclusions can be reached about the use of rewards in the classroom?

Thus, rewards that convey information about students' mastery can increase intrinsic motivation by increasing their sense of competence (Cameron & Pierce, 2008; Reeve, 2006). However, negative feedback, such as criticism, that carries information that students are incompetent can undermine intrinsic motivation, especially if students doubt their ability to become competent (Stipek, 2002).

Judy Cameron (2001) argues that rewards do not always decrease a student's intrinsic motivation. In her analysis of approximately a hundred studies, she found that verbal rewards (praise and positive feedback) can be used to enhance students' intrinsic motivation. She also concluded that when tangible rewards (such as gold stars and money) were offered contingent on task performance or given unexpectedly, intrinsic motivation was maintained. Some critics argue that Cameron's analysis is flawed—for instance, that it does not adequately detect some of the negative effects of rewards on motivation (Deci, Koestner, & Ryan, 2001).

In summary, it is important to examine what rewards convey about competence (Reeve, 2006). When rewards are tied to competence, they tend to promote motivation and interest. When they are not, they are unlikely to raise motivation or may diminish it once the rewards are withdrawn (Schunk, 2008).

Developmental Shifts in Intrinsic and Extrinsic Motivation   Many psychologists and educators stress that it is important for children to develop greater internalization and intrinsic motivation as they grow older (Wigfield, Byrnes, & Eccles, 2006; Wigfield & others, 2006). However, researchers have found that as students move from the early elementary school years to the high school years, their intrinsic motivation decreases

DEVELOPMENTAL FOCUS 13.1
What Are Some Strategies You Use to Help Students Achieve?

Early Childhood

Our preschoolers are given goals to achieve throughout the year. For example, weekly goals are to identify and write a new letter each week. To motivate children to achieve this goal, we ask them to bring in a special object from home that begins with the letter of the week and share it with the class. The children enjoy the weekly responsibility of bringing in special objects and feel involved in the learning process.

—Missy Dangler, *Suburban Hills School*

Elementary School: Grades K–5

I begin the school year by sharing my teaching goals with the students. After that, I ask the children to come up with a list of their goals for the year, and we display them next to the child's self-portrait. These goals and self-portraits are on display all year, so that we are all reminded of what is important. We also work on classroom rules that support the students and my goals.

—Yvonne Wilson, *North Elementary School*

Middle School: Grades 6–8

In this age of testing, it's important to motivate students to learn for learning's sake (not just to do well on a test). With that in mind, I intentionally identify material that will *not* be included in the assessment process. This material is usually high interest, trivia, or sometimes a wonderful story relevant to the material. Although this material won't be on the test, my students look forward to learning it.

—Mark Fodness, *Bemidji Middle School*

High School: Grades 9–12

My high school art students respond best to praise. Everyone loves to hear, "Wow, that looks fantastic; good job!" Another motivator for my students is that artworks that are well done may be entered in one of the many contests, shows, and exhibits we enter each year. Having a reward dangling out there is a great motivational tool.

—Dennis Peterson, *Deer River High School*

(Anderman & Mueller, 2009; Eccles, 2007; Meece & Eccles, 2009). In one research study, the biggest drop in intrinsic motivation and increase in extrinsic motivation occurred between sixth grade and seventh grade (Harter, 1981). In another study, as students moved from sixth through eighth grade, they increasingly said school was boring and irrelevant (Harter, 1996). In this study, however, students who were intrinsically motivated did much better academically than those who were extrinsically motivated.

Why the shift toward extrinsic motivation as children move to higher grades? One explanation is that school grading practices reinforce an external motivation orientation. That is, as students get older, they lock into the increasing emphasis on grades, and their internal motivation drops.

Jacquelynne Eccles and her colleagues (Eccles, 2004, 2007; Eccles & Wigfield, 2002; Wigfield, Byrnes, & Eccles, 2006) identified some specific changes in the school context that help to explain the decline in intrinsic motivation. Middle and junior high schools are more impersonal, more formal, more evaluative, and more competitive than elementary schools. Students compare themselves more with other students because they increasingly are graded in terms of their relative performance on assignments and standardized tests.

According to Jacquelynne Eccles and her colleagues, too many middle and junior high schools do not reflect an adequate person-environment fit. *What do they mean by that concept?*

Proposing the concept of *person-environment fit,* Eccles (2004, 2007) argues that a lack of fit between the middle school/junior high environment and the needs of young adolescents produces increasingly negative self-evaluations and attitudes toward school. Her research has revealed that teachers became more controlling just at the time when adolescents are seeking more autonomy, and the teacher-student relationship becomes more impersonal at a time when students are seeking more independence from their parents and need more support from other adults. At a time when adolescents are becoming more self-conscious, an increased emphasis on grades and other competitive comparisons only makes things worse.

Although there is less research on the transition to high school, the existing research suggests that, like the transition to middle school, it can produce similar problems (Eccles, Wigfield, & Schiefele, 1998). High schools often are even larger and more bureaucratic than middle schools. In such schools, a sense of community usually is undermined, with little opportunity for students and teachers to get to know each other (Bryk, Lee, & Smith, 1989). As a consequence, distrust between students and teachers develops easily and there is little communication about students' goals and values. Such contexts can especially harm the motivation of students who are not doing well academically.

What lessons can be drawn from this discussion? Perhaps the single most important lesson is that middle school and junior high school students benefit when teachers think of ways to make their school settings more personal, less formal, and more intrinsically challenging.

Some Final Thoughts About Intrinsic and Extrinsic Motivation An overwhelming conclusion of motivation research is that teachers should encourage students to become intrinsically motivated. Similarly, teachers should create learning environments that promote students' cognitive engagement and self-responsibility for learning (Blumenfeld, Kempler, & Krajcik, 2006). That said, the real world includes both intrinsic and extrinsic motivation, and too often intrinsic and extrinsic motivation have been pitted against each other as polar opposites. In many aspects of students' lives, both intrinsic and extrinsic motivation are at work (Cameron & Pierce, 2008). Further, both intrinsic and extrinsic motivation can operate simultaneously. Thus, a student may work hard in a course because she enjoys the content and likes learning about it (intrinsic) and to earn a good grade (extrinsic) (Schunk, 2008). Keep in mind, though, that many educational psychologists recommend that extrinsic motivation by itself is not a good strategy.

Our discussion of extrinsic and intrinsic motivation sets the stage for introducing other cognitive processes involved in motivating students to learn. As we explore five

Combination of causal attributions	Reason students give for failure
Internal-stable-uncontrollable	Low aptitude
Internal-stable-controllable	Never study
Internal-unstable-uncontrollable	Sick the day of the test
Internal-unstable-controllable	Did not study for this particular test
External-stable-uncontrollable	School has tough requirements
External-stable-controllable	The instructor is biased
External-unstable-uncontrollable	Bad luck
External-unstable-controllable	Friends failed to help

FIGURE 13.3 Combinations of Causal Attributions and Explanations for Failure

When students fail or do poorly on a test or an assignment, they attribute the outcome to certain causes. The explanation reflects eight combinations of Weiner's three main categories of attributions: locus (internal-external), stability (stable-unstable), and controllability (controllable-uncontrollable).

additional cognitive processes, notice how intrinsic and extrinsic motivation continue to be important. The five processes are (1) attribution, (2) mastery motivation and mindset; (3) self-efficacy; (4) goal setting, planning, and self-monitoring; and (5) expectations.

Attribution

Attribution theory states that individuals are motivated to discover the underlying causes of their own performance and behavior. Attributions are perceived causes of outcomes. In a way, attribution theorists say, students are like intuitive scientists, seeking to explain the cause behind what happens (Weiner, 2005). For example, a secondary school student asks, "Why am I not doing well in this class?" or "Did I get a good grade because I studied hard or the teacher made up an easy test, or both?" The search for a cause or explanation is most likely to be initiated when unexpected and important events end in failure, such as when a good student gets a low grade. Some of the most frequently inferred causes of success and failure are ability, effort, task ease or difficulty, luck, mood, and help or hindrance from others.

Bernard Weiner (1986, 1992) identified three dimensions of causal attributions: (1) *locus*, whether the cause is internal or external to the actor; (2) *stability*, the extent to which the cause remains the same or changes; and (3) *controllability*, the extent to which the individual can control the cause. For example, a student might perceive his aptitude as located internally, stable, and uncontrollable. The student also might perceive chance or luck as external to himself, variable, and uncontrollable. Figure 13.3 lists eight possible combinations of locus, stability, and controllability and how they match up with various common explanations of failure.

To see how attributions affect subsequent achievement strivings, consider two students, Jane and Susan. Both students fail a math test, but each attributes this negative outcome to a different set of causes (Graham & Weiner, 1996, p. 72):

> When Jane flunks her math test, she searches for the reasons for the failure. Her analysis leads her to attribute the failure to herself, not blaming her teacher or bad luck. She also attributes the failure to an unstable factor—lack of preparation and study time. Thus, she perceives that her failure was due to internal, unstable, and also controllable factors. Because the factors are unstable, Jane has a reasonable expectation that she can still succeed in the future. And because the factors are controllable, she also feels guilty. Her expectations for success enable her to overcome her deflated sense of self-esteem. Her hope for the future results in renewed goal setting and increased motivation to do well on the next test. As a result, Jane seeks tutoring and increases her study time.

> When Susan fails the test, she also searches for reasons for the failure. As it happens, her analysis leads her to attribute her failure to internal (lack of ability), stable, and uncontrollable factors. Because Susan perceives the cause of her failure to be internal, her self-esteem suffers. Because it is stable, she sees failure in her future and has a helpless feeling that she can't do anything about her situation. And because it is uncontrollable, she feels ashamed and humiliated. In addition, her parents and teacher tell her that they feel sorry for her but don't provide any recommendations or strategies for success, furthering her belief that she is incompetent. With low expectations of success, low self-esteem, and a depressed mood, Susan decides to drop out of school instead of studying harder.

What are the best strategies for teachers to use in helping students like Susan change their attributions? Educational psychologists often recommend providing stu-

attribution theory The theory that individuals are motivated to discover the underlying causes of their own behavior and performance.

The student

- Says, "I can't"
- Doesn't pay attention to teacher's instructions
- Doesn't ask for help, even when it is needed
- Does nothing (for example, stares out the window)
- Guesses or answers randomly without really trying
- Is unresponsive to teacher's exhortations to try
- Is easily discouraged
- Doesn't volunteer answers to teacher's questions
- Maneuvers to get out of or to avoid work (for example, has to go to the nurse's office)

FIGURE 13.4 Behaviors That Suggest Learned Helplessness

From Deborah Stipek, *Motivation to Learn: Integrating Theory and Practice*, 4th ed. Published by Allyn and Bacon, Boston, MA. Copyright © 2002 by Pearson Education. Reprinted by permission of the publisher.

dents with a planned series of achievement experiences in which modeling, information about strategies, practice, and feedback are used to help them (1) concentrate on the task at hand rather than worrying about failing, (2) cope with failures by retracing their steps to discover their mistake or by analyzing the problem to discover another approach, and (3) attribute their failures to a lack of effort rather than lack of ability (Boekaerts, 2006; Brophy, 2004; Dweck & Elliott, 1983).

The current strategy is not to expose students to models who handle tasks with ease and demonstrate success but rather to expose them to models who struggle to overcome mistakes before finally succeeding (Brophy, 2004). In this way, students learn how to deal with frustration, persist in the face of difficulties, and constructively cope with failure.

Mastery Motivation and Mindset

Becoming cognitively engaged and self-motivated to improve are reflected in adolescents with a mastery motivation. These children also have a growth mindset that they can produce positive outcomes if they put forth the effort.

Mastery Motivation   Developmental psychologists Valanne Henderson and Carol Dweck (1990) have found that children often show two distinct responses to difficult or challenging circumstances. Children who display **mastery motivation** are task-oriented; instead of focusing on their ability, they concentrate on learning strategies and the process of achievement rather than the outcome. Those with a **helpless orientation** seem trapped by the experience of difficulty and they attribute their difficulty to lack of ability. They frequently say such things as "I'm not very good at this," even though they might earlier have demonstrated their ability through many successes. And, once they view their behavior as failure, they often feel anxious, and their performance worsens even further. Figure 13.4 describes some behaviors that might reflect helplessness (Stipek, 2002).

In contrast, mastery-oriented children often instruct themselves to pay attention, to think carefully, and to remember strategies that have worked for them in previous situations. They frequently report feeling challenged and excited by difficult tasks, rather than being threatened by them (Anderman & Wolters, 2006). A recent study revealed that seventh- to eleventh-grade students' mastery goals were linked to how much effort they put forth in mathematics (Chouinard, Karsenti, & Roy, 2007).

Another issue in motivation involves whether to adopt a mastery or a performance orientation. Children with a **performance orientation** are focused on winning, rather than on achievement outcome; and believe that success results from winning. Does this mean that mastery-oriented children do not like to win and that performance-oriented children are not motivated to experience the self-efficacy that comes from being able to take credit for one's accomplishments? No. A matter of emphasis or degree is involved, though. For mastery-oriented individuals, winning isn't everything; for performance-oriented individuals, skill development and self-efficacy take a backseat to winning. One recent study of seventh-grade students found that girls

mastery orientation A task-oriented response to difficult or challenging circumstances that focuses on learning strategies and the process of achievement rather than the outcome.

helpless orientation A response to challenges and difficulties in which the individual feels trapped by the difficulty and attributes the difficulty to a lack of ability.

performance orientation A focus on winning rather than achievement outcome; success is believed to result from winning.

Patricia Miranda (in blue) winning the bronze medal in the 2004 Olympics. *What characterizes her growth mindset, and how is it different from someone with a fixed mindset?*

were more likely than boys to have mastery than performance goals in their approach to math achievement (Kenny-Benson & others, 2006).

Recall that the No Child Left Behind (NCLB) Act emphasizes testing and accountability. Although NCLB may motivate some teachers and students to work harder, motivation experts worry that it encourages a performance rather than a mastery motivational orientation on the part of students (Meece, Anderman, & Anderman, 2006).

A final point needs to be made about mastery and performance goals: They are not always mutually exclusive. Students can be both mastery- and performance-oriented, and researchers have found that mastery goals combined with performance goals often benefit students' success (Schunk, Pintrich, & Meece, 2008).

Mindset Carol Dweck's (2006, 2007) most recent analysis of motivation for achievement stresses the importance of children developing a **mindset**, which she defines as the cognitive view individuals develop for themselves. She concludes that individuals have one of two mindsets: (1) *fixed mindset,* in which they believe that their qualities are carved in stone and cannot change; or (2) *growth mindset*, in which they believe their qualities can change and improve through their effort. A fixed mindset is similar to a helpless orientation; a growth mindset is much like having mastery motivation.

In her recent book, *Mindset,* Dweck (2006) argued that individuals' mindsets influence whether they will be optimistic or pessimistic, shape their goals and how hard they will strive to reach those goals, and affect many aspect of their lives, including achievement and success in school and sports. Dweck says that mindsets begin to be shaped as children interact with parents, teachers, and coaches, who themselves have either a fixed mindset or a growth mindset. She described the growth mindset of Patricia Miranda:

[She] was a chubby, unathletic school kid who wanted to wrestle. After a bad beating on the mat, she was told, "You're a joke." First she cried, then she felt: "That really set my resolve . . . I had to keep going and had to know if effort and focus and belief and training could somehow legitimize me as a wrestler." Where did she get this resolve? Miranda was raised in a life devoid of challenge. But when her mother died of an aneurysm at age forty, ten-year-old Miranda . . . [thought] "If you only go through life doing stuff that's easy, shame on you." So when wrestling presented a challenge, she was ready to take it on.

Her effort paid off. At twenty-four, Miranda was having the last laugh. She won a spot on the U.S. Olympic team and came home from Athens with a bronze medal. And what was next? Yale Law School. People urged her to stay where she was already on top, but Miranda felt it was more exciting to start at the bottom again and see what she could grow into this time." (Dweck, 2006, pp. 22–23)

Consider also the powerful role second-grade Chicago teacher Marva Collins has in creating a growth mindset in her students. She tells her students, many of whom are repeating the second grade,

I know most of you can't spell your name. You don't know the alphabet, you don't know how to read, you don't know homonyms or how to syllabicate. I promise you that you will. None of you has ever failed. School may have failed you. Well, goodbye to failure children. Welcome to success. You will read hard books in here and understand what you read. You will write every day. . . . But you must help me to help you. If you don't give anything, don't expect anything. Success is not coming to you, you must come to it. (Dweck, 2006, pp. 188–189)

mindset Dweck's concept that refers to the cognitive view individuals develop for themselves; individuals have one of two mindsets: (1) fixed, or (2) growth.

Her second-grade students usually have to start off with the lowest level of reader available, but by the end of the school year, most of the students are reading at the fifth-grade level. Collins takes inner-city children living in low-income, often poverty, circumstances and challenges them to be all they can be. She won't accept failure by her students and teaches students to be responsible for their behavior every day of their lives. Collins tells students that being excellent at something is not a one-time thing but a habit, that determination and persistence are what move the world, and that thinking others will make you successful is a sure way to fail.

Self-Efficacy

In Chapter 7, "Behavioral and Social Cognitive Approaches," we introduced Albert Bandura's concept of **self-efficacy**, the belief that one can master a situation and produce positive outcomes. Bandura (1997, 2001, 2006, 2007a, b, 2008, 2009) emphasizes that self-efficacy is a critical factor in whether or not students achieve. Self-efficacy has much in common with mastery motivation and intrinsic motivation. Self-efficacy is the belief that "I can"; helplessness is the belief that "I cannot." Students with high self-efficacy agree with such statements as "I know that I will be able to learn the material in this class" and "I expect to be able to do well at this activity."

Dale Schunk (2008) has applied the concept of self-efficacy to many aspects of students' achievement. In his view, self-efficacy influences a student's choice of activities. Students with low self-efficacy for learning might avoid many learning tasks, especially those that are challenging, whereas students with high self-efficacy eagerly approach these learning tasks. Students with high self-efficacy are more likely to persist with effort at a learning task than are students with low self-efficacy. A recent study revealed that high-self-efficacy adolescents had higher academic aspirations, spent more time doing homework, and were more likely to associate learning activities with optimal experience than their low-self-efficacy counterparts (Bassi & others, 2007).

What characterizes students, teachers, and schools with high self-efficacy?

Your self-efficacy as a teacher will have a major impact on the quality of learning that your students experience (Skaalvik & Skaalvik, 2007). Students learn much more from teachers with a sense of high self-efficacy than from those beset by self-doubts. Teachers with low self-efficacy often become mired in classroom problems and are inclined to say that low student ability is the reason their students are not learning. Low-self-efficacy teachers don't have confidence in their ability to manage their classrooms, become stressed and angered at students' misbehavior, are pessimistic about students' ability to improve, take a custodial view of their job, often resort to restrictive and punitive modes of discipline, and say that if they had it to do all over again they would not choose teaching as a profession.

The ability to transmit subject matter is one aspect of instructional self-efficacy, but instructional self-efficacy also includes the belief that one can maintain an orderly classroom that is an exciting place to learn and the belief that it is possible to enlist resources and get parents positively involved in children's learning (Bandura, 1997).

Bandura (1997) also addressed the characteristics of efficacious schools. School leaders seek ways to improve instruction. They figure out ways to work around stifling policies and regulations that impede academic innovations. Masterful academic leadership by the principal builds teachers' sense of instructional efficacy; in low-achieving schools, principals function more as administrators and disciplinarians (Coladarci, 1992).

Efficacious schools are pervaded by high expectations and standards for achievement (Walsh, 2008). Teachers regard their students as capable of high academic achievement, set challenging academic standards for them, and provide support to help them reach these high standards. In contrast, in low-achieving schools not much is expected academically of students, teachers spend less time actively teaching and monitoring students' academic progress, and tend to write off a high percentage of

self-efficacy The belief that one can master a situation and produce positive outcomes.

BEST PRACTICES
Strategies for Improving Students' Self-Efficacy

Here are some good strategies for improving students' self-efficacy (Stipek, 2002):

1. *Teach specific strategies.* Teach students specific strategies, such as outlining and summarizing, that can improve their ability to focus on their tasks.

2. *Guide students in setting goals.* Help them create short-term goals after they have made long-term goals. Short-term goals especially help students to judge their progress.

3. *Consider mastery.* Give students performance-contingent rewards, which are more likely to signal mastery, rather than rewards, for merely engaging in a task.

4. *Combine strategy training with goals.* Schunk and his colleagues (Schunk, 2001; Schunk & Rice, 1989; Schunk & Swartz, 1993) have found that a combination of strategy training and goal setting can enhance students' self-efficacy and skill development. Give feedback to students on how their learning strategies relate to their performance.

5. *Provide students with support.* Positive support can come from teachers, parents, and peers. Sometimes a teacher just needs to tell a student, "You can do this."

Next, Joanna Smith, a high school English teacher, describes how she helps students who struggle with "failure syndrome."

THROUGH THE EYES OF TEACHERS
Helping Students Who Feel Like
Failures Gain Confidence

I believe that encouragement can help students overcome "failure syndrome." Students with failure syndrome give up immediately when they sense any difficulty whatsoever. It is easy to feel frustrated when facing these students, but I have found success when I truly reach them. The only way for me to reach individual students is to get to know them and their families by giving journal assignments, choices about books they read, opportunities to tell me about themselves, and by opening myself up to them. These students also need a lot of encouragement. They need to know that you have noticed and are not happy with their failure, and then they need to know you believe in them. Only then will students with failure syndrome perform.

students as unteachable (Brookover & others, 1979). Not surprisingly, students in such schools have low self-efficacy and a sense of academic futility.

Goal Setting, Planning, and Self-Monitoring

Goal setting is increasingly recognized as a key aspect of achievement (Witkow & Fuligni, 2007). Researchers have found that self-efficacy and achievement improve when students set goals that are specific, proximal, and challenging (Bandura, 1997; Schunk, 2008; Schunk, Pintrich, & Meece, 2008). A nonspecific, fuzzy goal is "I want to be successful." A more concrete, specific goal is "I want to make the honor roll by the end of the semester."

Students can set both long-term (distal) and short-term (proximal) goals. It is okay to let students set some long-term goals, such as "I want to graduate from high school" or "I want to go to college," but if you do, make sure that they also create short-term goals as steps along the way. "Getting an *A* on the next math test" is an example of a short-term, proximal goal. So is "Doing all of my homework by 4 P.M. Sunday." As mentioned earlier, attention should focus mainly on short-term goals, which help students judge their progress better than do long-term goals. David McNally (1990), author of *Even Eagles Need a Push*, advises that when students set goals and plan, they should be reminded to live their lives one day at a time. Have them make their commitments in bite-size chunks. As McNally says, a house is built one brick at a time, a cathedral one stone at a time. The artist paints one stroke at a time. The student should also work in small increments.

Another good strategy is to encourage students to set challenging goals. A challenging goal is a commitment to self-improvement. Strong interest and involvement

What changes in middle school characterize modifications in students' goals? What might middle school teachers do to improve their students' goal orientation?

in activities is sparked by challenges. Goals that are easy to reach generate little interest or effort. However, goals should be optimally matched to the student's skill level. If goals are unrealistically high, the result will be repeated failures that lower the student's self-efficacy.

Unfortunately, many of the changes involved in the transition to middle schools are likely to increase students' motivation to achieve performance goals rather than mastery goals (Eccles, 2004, 2007; Meece & Eccles, 2009; Wigfield & others, 2006). Consider that these often include a drop in grades, a lack of support for autonomy, whole-class task organization and between-class ability groupings that likely increase social comparison, concerns about evaluation, and competitiveness.

In one research study, both teachers and students reported that performance-focused goals were more common and task-focused goals less common in middle school than in elementary school classrooms (Midgley, Anderman, & Hicks, 1995). In addition, the elementary school teachers reported using task-focused goals more than middle school teachers did. At both grades, the extent to which the teachers were task-focused was linked with the students' and the teachers' sense of personal efficacy. Not unexpectedly, personal efficacy was lower for the middle school than elementary school participants. Thus, middle school teachers especially need to increasingly include task-focused goals in their instruction (Anderman, Austin, & Johnson, 2002).

In Chapter 12, we described the importance of planning for teachers. Planning is also important for students. It is not enough just to get students to set goals. It also is important to encourage them to plan how they will reach their goals. Being a good planner means managing time effectively, setting priorities, and being organized. Give students, especially at the middle school and high school levels, practice at managing their time, setting priorities, and being organized.

Expectations

Expectations can exert a powerful influence on students' motivation. Let's examine student expectations and teacher expectations.

Students' Expectations   How hard students will work can depend on how much they expect to accomplish. If they expect to succeed, they are more likely to work hard to reach a goal than if they expect to fail. Jacquelynne Eccles (1987, 1993) defined expectations for students' success as "beliefs about how well they will do on upcoming

A student and teacher at Langston Hughes Elementary School in Chicago, a school whose teachers have high expectations for students. *How do teachers' expectations influence students' achievement?*

tasks, either in the immediate or long-term future" (Wigfield & others, 2006). Three aspects of ability beliefs, according to Eccles, are students' beliefs about how good they are at a particular activity, how good they are in comparison to other individuals, and how good they are in relation to their performance in other activities.

How hard students work also depends on the value they place on the goal (Wigfield, Hoa, & Klauda, 2008). Indeed, the combination of expectancy and value has been the focus of a number of efforts to better understand students' achievement motivation for many decades (Atkinson, 1957; Eccles, 1993, 2007; Feather, 1966). In Jacquelynne Eccles' (1993, 2007) model, "expectancies and values are assumed to directly influence performance, persistence, and task choice. Expectancies and values are . . . influenced by perceptions of competence, perceptions of the difficulty of different tasks, and individuals' goals" (Wigfield & others, 2006, pp. 938–939). In Eccles' view, the culture's achievement orientation also plays a role in influencing students' expectations.

Teachers' Expectations Teachers' expectations influence students' motivation and performance (Pressley & others, 2007a, b). "When teachers hold high generalized expectations for student achievement and students perceive these expectations, students achieve more, experience a greater sense of self-esteem and competence as learners, and resist involvement in problem behaviors both during childhood and adolescence" (Wigfield & others, 2006, p. 976). In a recent observational study of twelve classrooms, teachers with high expecations spent more time providing a framework for students' learning, asked higher-level questions, and were more effective in managing students' behavior than teachers with average and low expectations (Rubie-Davis, 2007).

In thinking about teachers' expectations, it also is important to examine these expecations in concert with parents' expectations. For example, a recent study revealed that mothers' and teachers' high expectations had a positive effect on urban youths' achievement outcomes, and further that mothers' high achievement expectations for their youth had a buffering effect in the face of low teacher expectations (Benner & Mistry, 2007). Interestingly, in another recent study, teachers' positive expectations for students' achievement tended to protect students' from the negative influence of low parental expectations (Wood, Kaplan, & McLoyd, 2007).

Teachers often have more positive expectations for high-ability than for low-ability students, and these expectations are likely to influence their behavior toward them. For example, teachers require high-ability students to work harder, wait longer for them to respond to questions, respond to them with more information and in a more elaborate fashion, criticize them less often, praise them more often, are more friendly to them, call on them more often, seat them closer to the teachers' desks, and are more likely to give them the benefit of the doubt on close calls in grading than they are for students with low ability (Brophy, 2004). An important teaching strategy is to monitor your expectations and be sure to have positive expectations for students with low abilities. Fortunately, researchers have found that with support teachers can adapt and raise their expectations for students with low abilities (Weinstein, Madison, & Kuklinski, 1995).

Values and Purpose

In the discussion of expectations, we indicated that how hard students work is influenced by the value they place on the goal they have set. We also indicated that the culture's achievement orientation influences students' values. Just what are "values"? *Values* are beliefs and attitudes about the way we think things should be. They involve what is important to individuals. Values can be attached to all sorts of things, such as religion, money, sex, helping others, family, friends, self-discipline, cheating, education, career, and so on. In Chapter 3, "Social Contexts and Socioemotional Development," we described two moral education approaches that emphasize the importance of values in students' development: character education and values clarification.

Here we further examine the importance of values in students' development with a special emphasis on the importance of helping students find a path to purpose and discover their calling in life. These words reflect the title of a recent book by William Damon (2008): *The Path to Purpose: Helping Our Children Find Their Calling in Life.* For Damon, *purpose* is an intention to accomplish something meaningful to one's self and contribute something to the world beyond the self. Finding purpose involves answering such questions as "*Why* am I doing this? *Why* does it matter? *Why* is it important for me and the world beyond me? *Why* do I strive to accomplish this end?" (Damon, 2008, pp. 33–34).

In interviews with 12- to 22-year-olds, Damon found that only about 20 percent had a clear vision of where they want to go in life, what they want to achieve, and why. The largest percentage—about 60 percent—had engaged in some potentially purposeful activities, such as service learning or fruitful discussions with a career counselor—but still did not have a real commitment or any reasonable plans for reaching their goals. And slightly more than 20 percent expressed no aspirations and in some instances said they didn't see any reason to have aspirations.

Damon concludes that most teachers and parents communicate the importance of such goals as studying hard and getting good grades, but rarely discuss what the goals might lead to—the purpose for studying hard and getting good grades. Damon emphasizes that too often students focus only on short-term goals and don't explore the big, long-term picture of what they want to do with their life. These interview questions Damon (2008, p. 135) has used in his research are good springboards for getting students to reflect on their purpose:

What's most important to you in your life?

Why do you care about those things?

Do you have any long-term goals?

Why are these goals important to you?

What does it mean to have a good life?

What does it mean to be a good person?

If you were looking back on your life now, how would you like to be remembered?

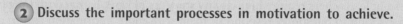

Review, Reflect, and Practice

(2) Discuss the important processes in motivation to achieve.

REVIEW

- What are extrinsic and intrinsic motivation? How are they involved in students' achievement?
- What characterizes attribution theory and an attribution approach to students' achievement?
- How does a mastery orientation compare with a helpless orientation and a performance orientation? Why is a growth mindset important in students' achievement?
- What is self-efficacy? What types of instructional strategies benefit students' self-efficacy?
- How are goal setting, planning, and self-monitoring important in improving students' motivation to achieve?
- How can students' and teachers' expectations affect students' motivation?
- What do values and purpose mean? How can the importance of students developing a purpose be summarized?

REFLECT

- Sean and Dave both get cut from the basketball team. The next year, Sean tries out again but Dave does not. What causal attributions (and their effects) could explain the behaviors of these two students?

PRAXIS™ PRACTICE

1. Which of the following is the best example of someone who is intrinsically motivated?
   a. Eric is reading the latest Harry Potter book because he wants to become a better reader.
   b. Jordan is reading the latest Harry Potter book because he can't wait to see what happens to Harry and his friends.
   c. Josh is reading the latest Harry Potter book so that he will have read enough pages to qualify for the class pizza party at the end of the month.
   d. Martynas is reading the latest Harry Potter book because his teacher assigned it and he wants to please his teacher.

2. Joan just failed a science test. "I knew it," she says, "I have never been any good at science, and I never will be." Which of the following best characterizes Joan's attribution for her failure?
   a. external-stable-controllable
   b. external-unstable-uncontrollable
   c. internal-stable-controllable
   d. internal-stable-uncontrollable

3. Which of the following is the best example of a performance goal orientation?
   a. Alicia competes with her best friend to see who can get the higher grade on every test, taking delight in receiving the high score.
   b. Cassandra hates math, does not believe that she can be successful, and gives up at the first sign of struggling.
   c. Ed struggles in math, but wants very much to learn the material, so when he gets stuck on a problem, he asks for help.
   d. Martin does his work as requested and does a fair job on it, but he doesn't really care about his grades or about how much he learns.

Review, Reflect, and Practice

4. Jacob is struggling in algebra and as a result is experiencing low self-efficacy. Which of the following students would provide the best role model?
   a. David, a local engineer, who tells the class how useful math will be in their futures
   b. Jamal, a fellow student, who has also struggled in the course but is now grasping the concepts
   c. Mrs. Jackson, Jacob's algebra teacher, who has always loved math
   d. Suzanne, a fellow student, who is getting an *A* with minimal effort

5. Which student has the least appropriate goal?
   a. As Mark is choosing courses for his senior year in high school, he decides to take the more challenging of the two courses his counselor suggested to him.
   b. Sam is taking geometry in his senior year of high school, because he has always struggled in math.
   c. Sylvia decides to take advanced placement calculus in her senior year, although she knows it is a difficult course.
   d. Zelda is a capable math student, but she chooses an easy math course in which she is almost certain to get an *A*.

6. Ms. Martin teaches eighth-grade history to an academically diverse class. DeMarcus is a gifted student who has always earned high marks. Joe has a learning disability. Ms. Martin does not believe it would be fair to expect the same performance from Joe as from DeMarcus. However, she knows that Joe can learn the material with proper scaffolding. Because of this, she seats Joe near her desk, praises him when he does something well, and gives him constructive criticism when needed.

   How are her expectations and behavior likely to affect the achievement of these students?
   a. Her expectations are likely to result in similar achievement from both students.
   b. Her expectations are likely to result in high achievement from DeMarcus and fairly high achievement from Joe.
   c. Her expectations are likely to result in high achievement from Joe and low achievement from DeMarcus.
   d. Her expectations are likely to result in low achievement from both students.

7. Which of the following questions that a teacher poses to Chase, a student in her eleventh-grade class, best reflects an inquiry about his purpose?
   a Why did you not study harder for your test this week?
   b. What's most important to you in your life?
   c. What can you do the rest of the year to get a good grade in this course?
   d. How are you going to improve your chances of becoming a school leader?

   Please see the answer key at the end of the book.

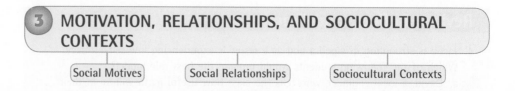

Social Motives

Childrens' social concerns influence their lives at school (Anderman & Wolters, 2006; Wentzel, 2006). Every school day, students work at establishing and maintaining social relationships. Researchers have found that students who display socially competent behavior are more likely to excel academically than those who do not (Wentzel, 1996). Overall, though, researchers have given too little attention to how students' social worlds are related to their motivation in the classroom.

Social motives are needs and desires that are learned through experiences with the social world. Students' social needs are reflected in their desires to be popular with peers and have close friends and the powerful attraction they feel to someone they love. Though each student has a need for affiliation or relatedness, some students have a stronger need than others. Some students like to be surrounded by lots of friends. In middle and high school, some students feel something is drastically missing from their lives if they don't have a girlfriend or boyfriend to date regularly. Others don't have such strong needs for affiliation. They don't fall apart if they don't have several close friends around all day and don't sit in class in an anxious state if they don't have a romantic partner.

Both teacher approval and peer approval are important social motives for most students. In the elementary school years, students are motivated to please their parents more than their peers (Berndt, 1979). By the end of elementary school, parent approval and peer approval are about equal in most students' motive systems. By eighth or ninth grade, peer conformity outstrips conformity to parents. By twelfth grade, conformity to peers drops off somewhat as students become more autonomous and make more decisions on their own.

Adolescence can be an especially important juncture in achievement motivation and social motivation (Anderman & Mueller, 2009; Eccles, 2007; Meece & Eccles, 2009). New academic and social pressures force adolescents toward new roles that involve more responsibility. As adolescents experience more intense achievement demands, their social interests might cut into the time they need for academic matters. Or ambitions in one area can undermine the attainment of goals in another area, as when academic achievement leads to social disapproval. In early adolescence, students face a choice between whether they will spend more of their time pursuing social goals or academic goals. The results of this decision have long-term consequences in terms of how far adolescents will go in their education and the careers they will pursue.

Social Relationships

Students' relationships with parents, peers, and friends have a tremendous impact on their lives. Their interactions with teachers, mentors, and others also can profoundly affect their achievement and social motivation.

Parents Research has been conducted on links between parenting and students' motivation. Studies have examined family demographic characteristics, child-rearing practices, and provision of specific experiences at home (Eccles, Wigfield, & Schiefele, 1998).

social motives Needs and desires that are learned through experiences with the social world.

Demographic Characteristics   Parents with more education are more likely than less-educated parents to believe that their involvement in their child's education is important, to be active participants in their child's education, and to have intellectually stimulating materials at home (Schneider & Coleman, 1993). When parents' time and energy are largely consumed by other concerns or people other than the child, the child's motivation can suffer. Living in a single-parent family, having parents who are consumed by their work, and living in a large family can undercut children's achievement.

Child-Rearing Practices   Even though demographic factors can affect students' motivation, more important are the parents' child-rearing practices (Wigfield & others, 2006). Here are some positive parenting practices that result in improved motivation and achievement:

- Knowing enough about the child to provide the right amount of challenge and the right amount of support
- Providing a positive emotional climate, which motivates children to internalize their parents' values and goals
- Modeling motivated achievement behavior—working hard and persisting with effort at challenging tasks

What are some good strategies parents can adopt to guide students' achievement?

Provision of Specific Experiences at Home   In addition to general child-rearing practices, parents provide various activities or resources at home that may influence students' interest and motivation to pursue various activities over time (Wigfield & others, 2006). For example, reading to one's preschool children and providing reading materials in the home are positively related to students' later reading achievement and motivation (Wigfield & Asher, 1984). Indeed, researchers have found that children's skills and work habits when they enter kindergarten are among the best predictors of academic motivation and performance in both elementary and secondary school (Entwisle & Alexander, 1993). The extent to which parents emphasize academic achievement or sports and provide opportunities and resources for their children to participate in these activities in the elementary school years influence whether the children are likely to continue to choose course work and extracurricular activities consistent with these activities in adolescence (Simpkins & others, 2004).

Peers   Peers can affect a student's motivation through social comparison, social competence and motivation, peer co-learning, and peer-group influences (Wigfield & others, 2006).

Students often compare themselves with their peers on where they stand academically and socially. Adolescents are more likely than younger children to engage in social comparison, although adolescents are prone to deny that they ever compare themselves with others (Harter, 1990, 2006). Younger children engage in social comparison (for example, bigger, faster), whereas older children and adolescents use more inference when engaging in social comparison, such as focusing on ability underlying an overt behavior. For example, in social comparison, one adolescent might learn that another adolescent did not do well on a test in school and think, "I'm smarter than him." Positive social comparisons usually result in higher self-esteem, negative comparisons in lower self-esteem. Students are most likely to compare themselves with others who are most similar to them in age, ability, and interests.

Students who are more accepted by their peers and who have good social skills often do better in school and have positive academic achievement motivation (Rubin, Bukowski, & Parker, 2006). In contrast, rejected students, especially those who are highly aggressive, are at risk for a number of achievement problems, including getting low grades and dropping out of school (Dodge, Coie, & Lynam, 2006).

How might peer relations contribute to students' achievement?

Teachers   Teachers play an important role in students' achievement (Patrick, Ryan, & Kaplan, 2007). When researchers have observed classrooms, they have found that effective, engaging teachers provide support for them to make good progress, but encourage students to become self-regulated achievers (Pressley & others, 2007a, b). The encouragement takes place in a very positive environment, one in which students are constantly being guided to become motivated to try hard and develop self-efficacy. A recent study revealed that instructional and socioemotional support (as exemplifed in attending to students' interest and initiative, providing appropriately challenging learning opportunities, and creating positive social relationships) were linked to first-grade students' achievement (as reflected in meeting reading and math academic standards) (Perry, Donohue, & Weinstein, 2007).

Many children who do not do well in school consistently have negative interactions with their teachers (Stipek, 2002). They are frequently in trouble for not completing assignments, not paying attention, goofing off, or acting out. In many cases, they deserve to be criticized and disciplined, but too often the classroom becomes a highly unpleasant place for them.

Nel Noddings (2001, 2007) stresses that students are most likely to develop into competent human beings when they feel cared for. This requires teachers to get to know students fairly well. She says that this is difficult in large schools with large numbers of students in each class. She would have teachers remain with the same students for two to three years (voluntarily on the part of the teacher and the pupil) so that teachers would be better positioned to attend to the interests and capacities of each student.

Researchers have found that students who feel they have supportive, caring teachers are more strongly motivated to engage in academic work than students with unsupportive, uncaring teachers (McCombs, 2001; Perry, Turner, & Meyer, 2006). One researcher examined students' views of the qualities of good relationships with a teacher by asking middle school students questions such as how they knew a teacher cared about them (Wentzel, 1997). As shown in Figure 13.5, students had favorable impressions of teachers who were attentive to them as human beings. Interestingly, students also considered teachers' instructional behaviors in evaluating how much their teachers cared about them. The students said that teachers convey that they care about their students when they make serious efforts to promote learning and have appropriately high standards.

Students' motivation is optimized when teachers provide them with challenging tasks in a mastery-oriented environment that includes good emotional and cognitive support, meaningful and interesting material to learn and master, and sufficient support for autonomy and initiative (Blumenfeld, Kempler, & Krajcik, 2006; Wigfield & others, 2006). Many researchers conclude that when academic work is meaningful,

FIGURE 13.5 Students' Descriptions of Teachers Who Care

	Teachers who care	Teachers who do not care
Teaching behaviors	Makes an effort to make class interesting; teaches in a special way	Teaches in a boring way, gets off-task, teaches while students aren't paying attention
Communication style	Talks to me, pays attention, asks questions, listens	Ignores, interrupts, screams, yells
Equitable treatment and respect	Is honest and fair, keeps promises, trusts me, tells the truth	Embarrasses, insults
Concern about individuals	Asks what's wrong, talks to me about my problems, acts as a friend, asks when I need help, takes time to make sure I understand, calls on me	Forgets name, does nothing when I do something wrong, doesn't explain things or answer questions, doesn't try to help me

it sustains students' attention and interest, engages them in learning, and reduces the likelihood that students will feel alienated from school (Blumenfeld, Krajcik, & Kempler, 2006). Also, as we saw in our earlier discussion of Bandura's ideas on self-efficacy (Chapter 7), the motivation and achievement climate of the entire school affects students' motivation. Schools with high expectations and academic standards, as well as academic and emotional support for students, often have students who are motivated to achieve (Reksten, 2009).

Teachers and Parents   In the past, schools have given little attention to how teachers can enlist parents as partners with them in providing opportunities for students to achieve. Currently there is considerable interest in how to accomplish this partnership (Epstein, 2009; Grant & Ray, 2009). When teachers systematically and frequently inform parents of their children's progress and get involved in their children's learning, children often reach higher levels of academic achievement (Agnew-Tally, & others, 2009; Studer, 2009).

Sociocultural Contexts

In this section, we will focus on how socioeconomic status and ethnicity can influence motivation and achievement. A special focus is diversity.

Socioeconomic Status and Ethnicity   The diversity within ethnic minority groups that we discussed in Chapter 5 also is evident in their achievement (Cushner, McClelland, & Safford, 2009; Manning & Baruth, 2009). For example, many Asian American students have a strong academic achievement orientation, but some do not (Lee & Wong, 2009).

In addition to recognizing the diversity that exists within every cultural group in terms of their achievement, it also is important to distinguish between difference and deficiency. Too often, the achievements of ethnic minority students—especially African American, Latino, and Native American—have been interpreted in terms of middle-socioeconomic-status White standards as deficits when these students simply are culturally different and distinct.

However, achievement differences are more closely related to socioeconomic status than to ethnicity (Ballentine & Roberts, 2009; Gollnick & Chinn, 2009). Many studies have found that socioeconomic status predicts achievement better than ethnicity. Regardless of their ethnic background, students from middle- and upper-income families fare better than their counterparts from low-income backgrounds in a host of achievement situations—expectations for success, achievement aspirations, and recognition of the importance of effort, for example. An especially important factor in the lower achievement of students from low-income families is lack of adequate resources, such as an up-to-date computer in the home (or even a computer at all) to support students' learning (Schunk, Pintrich, & Meece, 2008).

Sandra Graham (1986, 1990) has conducted a number of studies that reveal not only a stronger role of socioeconomic status than of ethnicity in achievement but also the importance of studying ethnic minority student motivation in the context of general motivational theory. Her inquiries fall within the framework of attribution theory and focus on the causes African American students identify for their achievement orientation, such as why they succeed or fail. Graham has found that middle-income African American students, like their

THROUGH THE EYES OF STUDENTS

"You Always Manage to Cheer Us Up"

I know our science class sometimes is obnoxious and negative but we really appreciate you. You always manage to cheer us up and treat us like your kids. That shows how much you care about us. If you hadn't been there for me like you were, I probably wouldn't be where I am now. Good luck with all of your other students and I hope they learn as much as I have. I'll miss you next year. Hope to see you around.

Letter from Jennifer to William Williford, Her Middle School Science Teacher, Perry, Georgia

UCLA educational psychologist Sandra Graham is shown talking with adolescent boys about motivation. She has conducted a number of studies which reveal that middle-socioeconomic-status African American students—like their White counterparts—have high achievement expectations and attribute success to internal factors such as effort rather than external factors such as luck.

White middle-income counterparts, have high achievement expectations and understand that failure is usually due to a lack of effort rather than bad luck.

A special challenge for many ethnic minority students, especially those living in poverty, is dealing with racial prejudice, conflict between the values of their group and the majority group, and a lack of high-achieving adults in their cultural group who can serve as positive role models (Bentley, Adams, & Stevenson, 2009; Murrell, 2009). The lack of high-achieving role models relates to the discussion in Chapter 7, "Behavioral and Social Cognitive Approaches," in which we described the importance of increasing the number of mentors in these students' lives. A recent longitudinal study of African American middle school students found that the experiences of everyday racial discrimination at school from teachers and peers were linked to declines in grades and academic task values (Eccles, Wong, & Peck, 2006).

It is important to further consider the nature of the schools that primarily serve ethnic minority students (Wigfield & others, 2006). More than one-third of African American and almost one-third of Latino students attend schools in the 47 largest city school districts in the United States, compared with only 5 percent of White and 22 percent of Asian American students. Many of these ethnic minority students come from low-income families (more than half are eligible for free or reduced-cost lunches). These inner-city schools are less likely than other schools to serve more-advantaged populations or to offer high-quality academic support services, advanced courses, and courses that challenge students' active thinking skills. Even students who are motivated to learn and achieve can find it difficult to perform effectively in such contexts (Hudley, 2009). The *Diversity and Education* interlude focuses on one individual who has become an important role model for African American students.

Review, Reflect, and Practice

(3) Explain how relationships and sociocultural contexts can support or undercut motivation.

REVIEW

- What are social motives and the need for affiliation?
- In what ways are students' school performances linked to relationships with parents, peers, friends, and teachers?
- How do ethnicity and socioeconomic status influence motivation to achieve at school?

REFLECT

- Suppose several children from low-income families in your elementary school classroom are struggling with achieving their potential. How would you work with them to improve their chances of being successful in school?

PRAXIS™ PRACTICE

1. Which of the following students is most likely to conform to peer expectations for academic achievement?
   a. Patrick, who is in second grade
   b. Ross, who is in fifth grade
   c. Sheldon, who is in eighth grade
   d. Rose, who is a senior in high school

2. Which classroom is likely to have the most positive impact on student motivation?
   a. Ms. Davidson is only concerned about her students' academic performance, not their personal lives. Her class is very challenging, though not terribly interesting.

DIVERSITY AND EDUCATION
Henry Gaskins

A special concern among educators is to find ways to support the achievement efforts of ethnic minority students, many of whom come from low-income backgrounds (Hudley, 2009). In the *Teaching Stories* segment that opened this chapter, you read about Jaime Escalante, who made a major difference in the motivation of Latino students to learn and excel at math in East Los Angeles. Another individual has been exceptional in supporting the motivation of African American students in Washington, D.C.

Henry Gaskins, a physician, began an after-school tutoring program for ethnic minority students. For four hours every weeknight and all day on Saturdays, 80 students receive study assistance from Gaskins, his wife, two adult volunteers, and academically talented peers. Those who can afford

Dr. Henry Gaskins, here talking with three high school students, began an after-school tutorial program for ethnic minority students in 1983 in Washington, D.C. Volunteers like Dr. Gaskins can be especially helpful in developing a stronger sense of the importance of education in ethnic minority adolescents.

it contribute $5 to cover the cost of school supplies. In addition to tutoring them in various school subjects, Gaskins helps the tutees learn how to set academic goals and plan how to achieve these goals. Gaskins also encourages students to self-monitor their progress toward the goals. Many of the students being tutored have parents who are high school dropouts and either can't or aren't motivated to help their sons and daughters achieve.

Every community has people like Henry Gaskins who can help provide much-needed mentoring and tutoring for students from low socioeconomic backgrounds whose parents cannot help them achieve academically. Many of these potential mentors and tutors from the community have not been contacted by school personnel. If the need exists among your students, make a commitment to scour the community for talented, motivated, and concerned adults like Gaskins, who might only need to be asked to provide mentoring and tutoring support for disadvantaged students.

Review, Reflect, and Practice

b. Mr. Nelson works hard to get to know his students on a personal as well as an academic basis. Because he cares so much for them, he makes sure that his class is easy enough for all of his students to do well.

c. Ms. Pagliuca works hard to get to know her students on a personal as well as an academic basis. She gives her students work that is challenging and interesting.

d. Mr. Williams' class is very challenging and competitive. His students compete on a daily basis for points.

(continued)

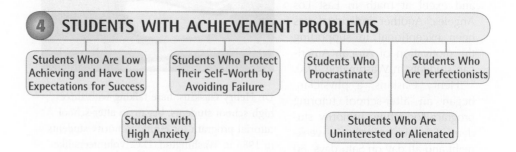

4 **STUDENTS WITH ACHIEVEMENT PROBLEMS**

Achievement problems can surface when students don't set goals, don't plan how to reach them, and don't adequately monitor their progress toward the goals. They also can arise when students are low achievers and have low expectations for success, try to protect their self-worth by avoiding failure, procrastinate, are perfectionists, become overwhelmed by anxiety, or become uninterested or alienated from school. Many of these obstacles to achievement surface during elementary school and then become more pronounced during middle school or high school. We will discuss a number of strategies that teachers, counselors, mentors, and parents can use to help students overcome obstacles to their achievement.

Students Who Are Low Achieving and Have Low Expectations for Success

Jere Brophy (1998) provided the following description of low-achieving students with low expectations for success: These students need to be consistently reassured that they can meet the goals and challenges you have set for them and that you will give them the help and support they need to succeed. However, they need to be reminded that you will accept their progress only as long as they make a real effort. They might require individualized instructional materials or activities to provide an optimal challenge for their skill level. Help them set learning goals and give them support for reaching these goals. Require these students to put forth considerable effort and make progress, even though they might not have the ability to perform at the level of the class as a whole.

Failure syndrome refers to having low expectations for success and giving up at the first sign of difficulty. Failure syndrome students are different from low-achieving students, who fail despite putting forth their best effort. Failure syndrome students don't put forth enough effort, often beginning tasks in a halfhearted manner and giving up quickly at the first hint of a challenge. Failure syndrome students often have low self-efficacy and a fixed mindset.

A number of strategies can be used to increase the motivation of students who display failure syndrome. Especially beneficial are cognitive retraining methods, such as efficacy retraining and strategy training, which are described in Figure 13.6.

failure syndrome Having low expectations for success and giving up at the first sign of difficulty.

Training method	Primary emphasis	Main goals
Efficacy training	Improve students' self-efficacy perceptions	Teach students to set and strive to reach specific, proximal, and challenging goals. Monitor students' progress and frequently support students by saying things like "I know you can do it." Use adult and peer modeling effectively. Individualize instruction and tailor it to the student's knowledge and skills. Keep social comparison to a minimum. Be an efficacious teacher and have confidence in your abilities. View students with a failure syndrome as challenges rather than losers.
Strategy training	Improve students' domain- and task-specific skills and strategies	Help students to acquire and self-regulate their use of effective learning and problem-solving strategies. Teach students what to do, how to do it, and when and why to do it.

FIGURE 13.6 Cognitive Retraining Methods for Increasing the Motivation of Students Who Display Failure Syndrome

Students Who Protect Their Self-Worth by Avoiding Failure

Some individuals are so interested in protecting their self-worth and avoiding failure that they become distracted from pursuing goals and engage in ineffective strategies. These strategies include (Covington & Dray, 2002):

- *Nonperformance.* The most obvious strategy for avoiding failure is to not try. In the classroom, nonperformance tactics include appearing eager to answer a teacher's question but hoping the teacher will call on another student, sliding down in the seat to avoid being seen by the teacher, and avoiding eye contact. These can seem like minor deceptions, but they might portend other, more chronic forms of noninvolvement such as dropping out and excessive absences.
- *Procrastination.* Individuals who postpone studying for a test until the last minute can blame failure on poor time management, thus deflecting attention away from the possibility that they are incompetent. A variation on this theme is to take on so many responsibilities that you have an excuse for not doing any one of them in a highly competent manner.
- *Setting unreachable goals.* By setting goals so high that success is virtually impossible, individuals can avoid the implication that they are incompetent, because virtually anyone would fail to reach this goal.

Efforts to avoid failure often involve *self-handicapping strategies* (Leondari & Gonida, 2007). That is, some individuals deliberately handicap themselves by not making an effort, by putting off a project until the last minute, by fooling around the night before a test, and so on so that if their subsequent performance is at a low level, these circumstances, rather than lack of ability, will be seen as the cause. A recent study revealed that self-regulatory and in-depth learning strategies were negatively linked to students' use of self-handicapping and that surface-learning and test anxiety were positively related to their use of self-handicapping (Thomas & Gadbois, 2007).

Here are a few strategies to help students reduce preoccupation with protecting self-worth and avoiding failure (Covington & Teel, 2002):

- Guide students in setting challenging but realistic goals.
- Help students strengthen the link between their effort and self-worth. Tell them to take pride in their effort and minimize social comparison.
- Encourage students to have positive beliefs about their abilities.

Students Who Procrastinate

Another way that students can fail to reach their potential is to regularly engage in procrastination (Schraw, Wadkins, & Olafson, 2007). A recent meta-analysis of research studies revealed that procrastination is linked to low self-efficacy, low conscientiousness, distractibility, and low achievement motivation (Steel, 2007). Other

BEST PRACTICES
Strategies for Helping Students Conquer Procrastination

Here are some good strategies for helping students reduce or eliminate procrastination:

1. *Get them to acknowledge that procrastination is a problem.* Too often, procrastinators don't face up to their problem. When students admit that they procrastinate, this can sometimes get them to begin thinking about how to solve the problem.

2. *Encourage them to identify their values and goals.* Get them to think about how procrastination can undermine their values and goals.

3. *Help them manage their time more effectively.* Have students make yearly (or term), monthly, weekly, and daily plans. Then help them monitor how they use their time and find ways to use it more wisely.

4. *Have them divide the task into smaller parts.* Sometimes students procrastinate because they view the task as so large and overwhelming that they will never be able to finish it. When this is the case, get them to divide the task into smaller units and set subgoals for completing one unit at a time. This strategy can often make what seems to be a completely unmanageable task manageable.

5. *Teach them to use behavioral strategies.* Have them identify the diversions that might be keeping them from focusing on the most important tasks and activities. Get them to note when and where they engage in these diversions. Then have them plan how to diminish and control their use. Another behavioral strategy is to have students make a contract with you, their parents, or a mentor. Yet another behavioral strategy is to have students build in a reward for themselves, which gives them an incentive to complete all or part of the task. For example, students might say to themselves that if they get all of their math problems completed, they will treat themselves to a movie when they finish them.

6. *Help them learn how to use cognitive strategies.* Encourage students to watch for mental self-seductions that can lead to behavioral diversions, such as "I will do it tomorrow," "What's the problem with watching an hour or two of TV now?" and "I can't do it." Help them learn how to dispute mental diversions. For example, get them to tell themselves, "I really don't have much time left and other things are sure to come up later," or "If I get this done, I'll be able to enjoy my time better."

reasons students procrastinate include (University of Buffalo Counseling Services, 2005) poor time management, difficulty concentrating, fear and anxiety (being overwhelmed by the task and afraid of getting a bad grade, for example), negative beliefs, personal problems (financial problems, problems with a boyfriend or girlfriend, and so on), boredom, unrealistic expectations and perfectionism (believing you must read everything written on a subject before you begin to write a paper, for example), and fear of failure (thinking that if you don't get an *A*, you are a failure, for example).

Procrastination can take many forms, including these (University of Illinois Counseling Center, 1996):

- Ignoring the task with the hope that it will go away
- Underestimating the work involved in the task or overestimating one's abilities and resources
- Spending endless hours on computer games and surfing the Internet
- Substituting a worthy but lower-priority activity, such as cleaning one's room instead of studying
- Believing that repeated minor delays won't hurt
- Persevering on only part of the task, such as writing and rewriting the first paragraph of a paper but never getting to the body of it
- Becoming paralyzed when having to choose between two alternatives—for example, agonizing over doing biology homework or English homework first with the outcome that neither is done

Students Who Are Perfectionists

As mentioned earlier, perfectionism is sometimes the underlying reason for procrastinating. Perfectionists think that mistakes are never acceptable, that the highest

DEVELOPMENTAL FOCUS 13.2

How Do You Help Unmotivated Students Get Motivated?

Early Childhood

Sometimes children become unmotivated because they fear that they will do something wrong or not live up to the teacher's expectations. To combat this issue, we lavish our preschoolers with praise for any and all efforts.

—Missy Dangler, *Suburban Hills School*

Elementary School: Grades K–5

Unmotivated students are usually motivated by something that holds their interest. I once had a student who was withdrawn and would not participate in group discussions. I later found out about his interest in boats, specifically the *Titanic*. I then incorporated his interests into a few different activities, and he became a different learner. He was more involved in discussions, and his confidence in the group increased as he learned of other students in class who also shared his interests.

—Heather Zoldak, *Ridge Wood Elementary School*

Middle School: Grades 6–8

An important aspect of motivation is to provide challenges for students. For example, I begin my Civil War unit by telling students that we'll be using this topic as an opportunity to see what it would be like to take a college freshman history course. Even though the material is extensive and more difficult than other units, the average grades on the final exam are higher than any other unit because students are motivated by the challenge of doing college-level work.

—Mark Fodness, *Bemidji Middle School*

High School: Grades 9–12

Building relationships with students based on their interests is a key to improving their motivation. For example, I recently talked with a student who didn't show much interest in class but loves clothes. I asked her about an outfit she had on with a cat on it (since I love cats). She explained that the outfit was Baby Phat and brought me all kinds of information on the clothing line and is even trying to get me to wear some of the clothes. More importantly, this student, who showed little interest in class, now participates and turns in assignments that are above average.

—Sandy Swanson, *Menomonee Falls High School*

 BEST PRACTICES
Strategies for Helping Students Overcome Their Perfectionist Tendencies

Here are some good strategies for guiding students in reducing or eliminating perfectionist tendencies (University of Texas at Austin Counseling and Mental Health Center, 1999):

1. *Have students list the advantages and disadvantages of trying to be perfect.* When students do this, they may discover that the cost of trying to be perfect is too great.

2. *Guide students in becoming more aware of the self-critical nature of all-or-none thinking.* Help students learn how to substitute more realistic, reasonable thoughts for their habitual overly self-critical ones.

3. *Help students become realistic about what they can achieve.* By getting students to set more realistic goals, they will gradually see that "imperfect" outcomes don't lead to the negative consequences they expect and fear.

4. *Talk with students about learning to accept criticism.* Perfectionists frequently view criticism as a personal attack and respond defensively to it. Guide students to become more objective about the criticism and about themselves.

BEST PRACTICES
Strategies to Reach the Uninterested or Alienated

Here are some ways you might be able to reach students who are uninterested or alienated (Brophy, 1998):

1. *Work on developing a positive relationship with the student.* If the uninterested or alienated student doesn't like you, it is hard to get the student to work toward any achievement goals. Show patience, but be determined to help the student and push for steady progress in spite of setbacks or resistance.

2. *Make school more intrinsically interesting.* To make school more intrinsically interesting for this type of student, find

out the student's interests and if possible include those interests in assignments that you make.

3. *Teach strategies for making academic work more enjoyable.* Help students understand that they are causing their own problems, and find ways to guide them in taking pride in their work.

4. *Consider a mentor.* Think about enlisting the aid of a mentor in the community or an older student you believe the uninterested or alienated student will respect.

FIGURE 13.7 Differences Between Perfectionists and Healthy Strivers

Perfectionist
Sets standards beyond reach and reason
Is never satisfied by anything less than perfection
Becomes dysfuntionally depressed when experiences failure and disappointment
Is preoccupied with fear of failure and disapproval—this can deplete energy levels
Sees mistakes as evidence of unworthiness
Becomes overly defensive when criticized

Healthy striver
Sets high standards, but just beyond reach
Enjoys process as well as outcome
Bounces back from failure and disappointment quickly and with energy
Keeps normal anxiety and fear of failure and disapproval within bounds—uses them to create energy
Sees mistakes as opportunities for growth and learning
Reacts positively to helpful criticism

standards of performance always have to be achieved. As indicated in Figure 13.7, healthy achievement and perfectionism differ in a number of ways. Perfectionists are vulnerable to decreased productivity, impaired health, relationship problems, and low self-esteem (Haring, Hewitt, & Flett, 2003). Depression, anxiety, and eating disorders are common outcomes of perfectionism (Rice & others, 2007).

Students with High Anxiety

Anxiety is a vague, highly unpleasant feeling of fear and apprehension. It is normal for students to be concerned or worried when they face school challenges, such as doing well on a test. Indeed, researchers have found that many successful students have moderate levels of anxiety (Bandura, 1997). However, some students have high levels of anxiety and worry constantly, which can significantly impair their ability to achieve (Burge & Heath, 2008; Lowe & Raad, 2008).

Some students' high anxiety levels are the result of parents' unrealistic achievement expectations and pressure (Wigfield & others, 2006). For many students, anxiety increases across the school years as they "face more frequent evaluation, social comparison, and (for some) experiences of failure" (Eccles, Wigfield, & Schiefele, 1998, p. 1043). When schools create such circumstances, they likely increase students' anxiety.

A number of intervention programs have been created to reduce high anxiety levels (Wigfield & others, 2006). Some intervention programs emphasize relaxation techniques. These programs often are effective at reducing anxiety but do not always lead to improved achievement. Anxiety intervention programs linked to worrying emphasize modifying the negative, self-damaging thoughts of anxious students by getting them to engage in more positive, task-focused thoughts (Meichenbaum & Butler, 1980). These programs have been more effective than the relaxation programs in improving students' achievement (Wigfield & others, 2006).

Students Who Are Uninterested or Alienated

Brophy (1998) argues that the most difficult motivation problem involves students who are apathetic, uninterested in learning, or alienated from school learning. Achieving in school is not an important value for them. To reach apathetic students requires sustained efforts to resocialize their attitudes toward school achievement (Murdock, 1999).

This chapter has focused on student motivation. It also is important for you to be motivated as a teacher as well. To evaluate your motivation, complete *Self-Assessment 13.1.*

SELF-ASSESSMENT 13.1

Evaluating My Motivation

Here are 18 statements you can use to analyze your motivational makeup. Rate yourself from 1 (not like me at all) to 5 (very much like me) on each of the statements.

1	2	3	4	5

1. I am aware of the hierarchy of motives in my life and which ones are the most important for me.

2. I am intrinsically motivated.

3. I have high expectations and standards for success.

4. My life has many moments of flow.

5. I am aware of the people in my life who have motivated me the most and what it is they did that motivated me.

6. I make achievement-related attributions that emphasize effort.

7. I have a mastery motivation orientation rather than a helpless or performance orientation.

8. I am motivated to learn and succeed because of my success aspirations, not because I want to protect my self-worth or avoid failure.

9. I have high self-efficacy in general.

10. I have high instructional self-efficacy in terms of my ability as a teacher and in terms of managing my classroom effectively.

11. I regularly set goals, plan how to reach those goals, and systematically monitor my progress toward the goals.

12. I set specific, proximal, and challenging goals.

13. I am a good time manager, regularly doing weekly plans, monitoring my use of time, and making to-do lists.

14. I am good at learning from my mistakes to improve my future success.

15. I don't let anxiety or other emotions get in the way of my motivation.

16. I have a good support system for my motivation and have positive, close relationships with people who can help me sustain my motivation.

17. I do tasks in a timely manner and I don't procrastinate.

18. I'm not a perfectionist.

Scoring and Interpretation

Examine the pattern of your responses. If you rated yourself 4 or 5 on each of the items, you likely are getting your motivation to work to your advantage, and you likely will be a positive motivational model for your students. However, for any items on which you rated yourself 3 or below, spend some time thinking about how you can improve those aspects of your motivational life.

Review, Reflect, and Practice

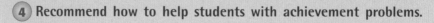

④ Recommend how to help students with achievement problems.

REVIEW

- How can low-achieving students with low achievement expectations be described and how can teachers help them?
- What are some strategies students use to protect their self-worth to avoid failure? How can these students be helped?
- What characterizes students who procrastinate and what are some strategies to help them?
- What characterizes students who are perfectionists and how can teachers help students with these tendencies?
- What is anxiety, how does high anxiety interfere with achievement, and what type of programs can benefit students with high anxiety?
- How can teachers help students who are uninterested or alienated?

REFLECT

- Think about several of your own past schoolmates who showed low motivation in school. Why do you think they behaved the way they did? What teaching strategies might have helped them?

PRAXIS™ PRACTICE

1. Which of the following students is the best example of failure syndrome?
   a. Andrea, who does not do well in school and rarely tries anymore
   b. Marcy, who works very hard and manages to earn C's
   c. Samantha, who does very well in school but does not try very hard
   d. Vivi, who is never satisfied with her own performance

2. Scott slides down in his seat to avoid being called on by the teacher. His behavior reflects which of the following in an effort to protect his self-worth by avoiding failure?
   a. failure syndrome
   b. nonperformance
   c. procrastination
   d. setting unreachable goals

3. Which teaching strategy is most likely to help students overcome procrastination?
   a. assigning a large project to be done in parts, with each part due at a different time
   b. assigning many large projects in a semester to ensure that students will have to learn to manage their time
   c. assigning no work that must be done outside of class
   d. assigning students to list all of the things they would rather do than their homework

4. Becky gets very upset when she does not receive full credit on an assignment. She takes particular offense at any critical remarks that are made of her work. Which of the following strategies is most likely to help Becky overcome her perfectionism?
   a. Give Becky lots of constructive feedback, both positive and negative, and allow her to revise her work.
   b. Make sure that Becky is capable of earning full credit on every assignment you give her.
   c. Make sure that Becky is not capable of earning full credit on any assignments you give her so she will get used to it.

Review, Reflect, and Practice

   d. Never give Becky any kind of feedback other than a grade, so you don't upset her.

5. Carmella has a great deal of anxiety about school, and it is interfering with her ability to concentrate in school. Which of the following is most likely to help her reduce her anxiety?
   a. helping her to replace her negative, self-damaging thoughts with more positive, task-focused thoughts
   b. encouraging her to set higher goals
   c. guiding her to reduce procrastination
   d. getting her to face the reality of concentrating better

6. Which of the following is most likely to help a teacher get an uninterested or alienated student to become more motivated to do well in school?
   a. Stress how important going to college is.
   b. Find out the student's interests and include those in the student's assignments.
   c. Compare the student with other students who are more motivated.
   d. Describe some strategies for reducing perfectionism.

7. Which of the following questions is most likely to get students to reflect on their purpose?
   a. What can you do to get good grades?
   b. What's most important to you in your life?
   c. How can you set better short-term goals?
   d. How can you organize your life better to find more time to study?

Please see the answer key at the end of the book.

CRACK THE CASE
The Case of the Reading Incentive Program

Catherine teaches second grade in an economically disadvantaged elementary school. Many of her students read below grade level. Some of her students have had little exposure to reading outside of school, and most do not choose to read during their free time at school. Knowing that reading skills are important to future success in school, Catherine is justifiably concerned.

In an effort to entice her students to read more, Catherine develops a reading incentive program. She places a large chart on the classroom wall to track student progress. Each time a student completes a book, he or she tells Catherine, who then places a star next to the student's name on the chart. Each student who reads five books per month receives a small prize from the class prize box. The student who reads the most books in any given month receives a larger prize. When Catherine tells her students about the new incentive program, they are very excited.

"This is great!" says Joey. "I'm gonna get the most stars!"

"No, you won't," says Peter. "Sami will. She's always got her nose stuck in a book. She's the best reader in the class."

Sami is a very good reader. She is reading well above grade level and generally favors novels from the young adult section of the library. These books are rather lengthy and take her quite some time to finish. However, she really enjoys them. Catherine has brought her several from her own collection as well, since none of her classroom books seem to interest Sami.

The first week of the program is quite exciting. Every day students tell Catherine about the books they have read. The chart begins to fill with stars. By the end of the week, all the students have at least one star next to their name except Sami. During the last week of the month, many students choose reading as a free-time activity. The students are anxious to ensure that they will earn at least one prize, and many

are devouring books in anticipation of being the month's "top reader." At the end of the month, 23 of Catherine's 25 students have 5 stars on the chart. The only exceptions are Sami, who has only 1 star, and Michael, who had chicken pox during the month. True to his word, Joey receives the most stars—15. The students excitedly choose their prizes.

The following month, the reading frenzy continues. This time Sami joins her classmates in their accumulation of stars and receives 30, making her the top reader. Joey is right behind her with 25. Every student in the class earns at least 5 stars, entitling all to a prize. Because they are all reading so much, Catherine gives them a Friday afternoon party, at which they watch an animated movie and eat popcorn.

A similar pattern is repeated over the next several months. The star chart fills quickly. Catherine believes that the students are reading enough that they will do quite well on the annual state achievement test. She is thrilled with their progress. She decides that after the test, she will drop the incentive program and just quietly keep track of how much her students read. After doing this, she notices that once again very few students are reading during their free time. Even Sami is no longer reading when she is finished with her other work. Now she draws instead.

1. What are the issues in this case?

2. Analyze the case from the perspective of extrinsic and intrinsic motivation.

3. Analyze the case from a goal-orientation perspective.

4. Why do you think Sami went from receiving 1 star the first month to receiving 30 stars the next? Why does she no longer read in her free time at school?

5. What are the problems with this type of incentive program? How might an incentive program be developed that does not undermine students' motivation to read?

Reach Your Learning Goals
Motivation, Teaching, and Learning

(1) EXPLORING MOTIVATION: Define motivation and compare the behavioral, humanistic, cognitive, and social perspectives on motivation.

What Is Motivation?

Motivated behavior is behavior that is energized, directed, and sustained.

Perspectives on Motivation

The behavioral perspective on motivation emphasizes that external rewards and punishments are the key factors that determine a student's motivation. Incentives are positive or negative stimuli or events that can motivate a student's behavior. The humanistic perspective stresses our capacity for personal growth, freedom to choose our own destiny, and our positive qualities. According to Maslow's hierarchy of needs, individuals' needs must be satisfied in this sequence: physiological, safety, love and belongness, esteem, and self-actualization. Self-actualization, the highest and most elusive of the needs Maslow describes, involves the motivation to develop one's full potential as a human being. In the cognitive perspective on motivation, students' thoughts guide their motivation. The cognitive perspective focuses on the internal motivation to achieve; attributions; students' beliefs that they can effectively control their environment; and goal setting, planning, and monitoring progress toward a goal. The cognitive perspective meshes with R. W. White's concept of competence motivation. The social perspective emphasizes the need for affiliation, which is reflected in students' motivation to spend time with peers, their close friendships, attachment to parents, and their desire to have a positive relationship with teachers.

(2) ACHIEVEMENT PROCESSES: Discuss the important processes in motivation to achieve.

Extrinsic and Intrinsic Motivation

Extrinsic motivation involves doing something to obtain something else (a means to an end) or to avoid an unpleasant consequence. Intrinsic motivation involves the internal motivation of doing something for its own sake (an end in itself). Overall, most experts recommend that teachers create a classroom atmosphere in which students are intrinsically motivated to learn. One view of intrinsic motivation emphasizes its self-determining characteristics. Giving students some choice and providing opportunities for personal responsibility increase intrinsic motivation. Csikszentmihalyi uses the term flow to describe life's optimal experiences, which involve a sense of mastery and absorbed concentration in an activity. Flow is most likely to occur in areas in which students are engaged in challenges that are neither too difficult nor too easy. Interest is conceptualized as more specific than intrinsic motivation, and interest is positively linked to deep learning. It is important for teachers to create learning environments that encourage students to become cognitively engaged and develop a responsibility for their learning. In some situations, rewards can actually undermine learning. When rewards are used, they should convey information about task mastery rather than external control. Researchers have found that as students move from the early elementary school years to high school, their intrinsic motivation drops, especially during the middle school years. The concept of person-environment fit calls attention to the lack of fit between adolescents' increasing interest in autonomy and schools' increasing control, which results in students' negative self-evaluations and attitudes toward school. Overall, the overwhelming conclusion is that it is a wise strategy to create learning environments that encourage students to become intrinsically motivated. However, in many real-world situations, both intrinsic and extrinsic motivation are involved, and too often intrinsic and extrinsic motivation have been pitted against each other as polar opposites.

| Attribution | Attribution theory states that individuals are motivated to discover the underlying causes of their own performance and behavior. Weiner identified three dimensions of causal attributions: (1) locus, (2) stability, and (3) controllability. Combinations of these dimensions produce different explanations of failure and success. |

| Mastery Motivation and Mindset | Students with a mastery orientation are challenged and excited by difficult tasks, and concentrate on learning strategies and the achievement process instead of on performance outcome. Students with a helpless orientation feel trapped by difficult tasks, are anxious, and feel they lack ability. Students with a performance orientation are focused on winning, not on achievement outcome. A mastery orientation is preferred over helpless or performance orientations in achievement situations. Mindset is the cognitive view, either fixed or growth, that individuals develop for themselves. Dweck argues that a key aspect of adolescents' development is to guide them in developing a growth mindset. Students with a growth mindset believe they can improve through effort. |

| Self-Efficacy | Self-efficacy is the belief that one can master a situation and produce positive outcomes. Bandura stresses that self-efficacy is a critical factor in whether students will achieve. Schunk argues that self-efficacy influences a student's choice of tasks and that low-self-efficacy students avoid many learning tasks, especially those that are challenging. Instructional strategies that emphasize "I can do it" benefit students. Low-self-efficacy teachers become mired in classroom problems. Setting specific, proximal (short-term), and challenging goals benefits students' self-efficacy and achievement. |

| Goal Setting, Planning, and Self-Monitoring | Researchers have found that self-efficacy and achievement increase when students set goals that are specific, proximal, and challenging. Being a good planner helps students manage time effectively, set priorities, and be organized. Giving students opportunities to develop their time management skills likely will benefit their learning and achievement. Self-monitoring is a key aspect of learning and achievement. |

| Expectations | Students' expectations for success and the value they place on what they want to achieve influence their motivation. The combination of expectancy and value have been the focus of a number of models of achievement motivation. Teachers' expectations can have a powerful influence on students' motivation and achievement. Teachers often have higher expectations for high-ability students than low-ability students. It is important for teachers to monitor their expectations and to have high expectations for all students. |

| Values and Purpose | Values are beliefs and attitudes about the way we think things should be—what is important to an individual. Purpose is an intention to accomplish something meaningful to one's self and contribute something to the world beyond the self. Damon has found that far too few students engage in purposeful reflection about what they want to do with their lives and concludes that parents and teachers need to ask students more questions, especially "Why" questions to encourage them to think more deeply about what their purpose is. |

(3) MOTIVATION, RELATIONSHIPS, AND SOCIOCULTURAL CONTEXTS: Explain how relationships and sociocultural contexts can support or undercut motivation.

| Social Motives | Social motives are needs and desires that are learned through experiences with the social world. The need for affiliation or relatedness involves the motive to be securely connected with people. Students vary in their need for affiliation—some like to be surrounded by many friends and date regularly; others do not have such strong needs. |

| Social Relationships | In terms of achievement and social motivation, teacher, peer, friend, and parental approval are important. Peer conformity peaks in early adolescence, a time of important decisions about whether to pursue academic or social motives. Understanding the parent's role in students' motivation focuses on demographic characteristics (such as education level, time spent at work, and family structure), child-rearing practices (such as providing the right amount of challenge and support), and provision of specific experiences at home (such as providing reading materials). Peers can affect students' motivation through social comparison, social competence, peer co-learning, and peer-group influences. Research shows that a teacher's support and caring can play a powerful role in students' motivation. A teacher's instructional style and socioemotional support also can play a role in a student's achievement. An important aspect of student motivation is enlisting parents as partners with you in educating the student. |

| Sociocultural Contexts | Teachers should recognize and value diversity within any cultural group and should be careful to distinguish the influences of socioeconomic status from those of ethnicity. Differences in achievement are more closely linked to socioeconomic status than to ethnicity. The quality of schools for many socioeconomically impoverished students is lower than for their middle-income counterparts. Everyday racial discrimination at school from teachers and peers is linked to a decline in African American middle school students' grades. |

4 STUDENTS WITH ACHIEVEMENT PROBLEMS: Recommend how to help students with achievement problems.

| Students Who Are Low Achieving and Have Low Expectations for Success | A student with low ability and low expectations for success often needs reassurance and support but also needs to be reminded that progress will be acceptable only when considerable effort is put forth. A student with failure syndrome (who has low expectations for success and gives up easily) likely will benefit from cognitive retraining methods such as efficacy training and strategy training. |

| Students Who Protect Their Self-Worth by Avoiding Failure | Students motivated to protect self-worth and avoid failure often engage in one or more of these ineffective strategies: nonperformance, procrastination, or setting unreachable goals. These students likely need guidance in setting challenging but realistic goals, need the link between their effort and self-worth strengthened, and benefit from developing positive beliefs about their abilities. |

| Students Who Procrastinate | Procrastination can take many forms, including ignoring a task with the hope it will go away, underestimating the amount of work a task requires, spending endless hours on distracting activities, and substituting worthwhile but lower-priority activities. Strategies for helping students overcome procrastination include acknowledging they have a procrastination problem, encouraging them to identify their values and goals, helping them manage time more effectively, having them divide the task into smaller parts, and teaching them to use behavioral and cognitive strategies. |

| Students Who Are Perfectionists | Perfectionists think that mistakes are never acceptable and that the highest standards of performance always have to be achieved. Perfectionists are vulnerable to a number of physical and mental health problems. Teachers can help students with perfectionist tendencies by having them list the advantages and disadvantages of trying to be perfect, guiding students to become more aware of the self-critical nature of their all-or-none thinking, helping them become more realistic about what they can achieve, and helping them learn how to accept criticism. |

| Students with High Anxiety | Anxiety is a vague, highly unpleasant feeling of fear and apprehension. High anxiety can result from unrealistic parental expectations. Students' anxiety increases as they get older and face more evaluation, social comparison, and failure (for some students). Cognitive programs that replace students' self-damaging thoughts with positive, constructive thoughts have been more effective than relaxation programs in benefiting student achievement. |
| Students Who Are Uninterested or Alienated | Strategies for helping an uninterested or alienated student include establishing a positive relationship with the student, making school more intrinsically interesting, using teaching strategies for making academic work more enjoyable, and considering a mentor in the community or an older student as a support person for the student. |

KEY TERMS

motivation 460	competence motivation 462	attribution theory 470	mindset 472
incentives 460	need for affiliation or	mastery orientation 471	self-efficacy 473
humanistic perspective 461	relatedness 462	helpless orientation 471	social motives 480
hierarchy of needs 461	extrinsic motivation 463	performance orientation 471	failure syndrome 486
self-actualization 461	intrinsic motivation 463		

PORTFOLIO ACTIVITIES

Now that you have a good understanding of this chapter, complete these exercises to expand your thinking.

Independent Reflection

Motivate, Invigorate, and Innovate Your Students. Design a motivationally rich classroom. What materials would be available? Describe your classroom walls and learning centers. How would teaching proceed? What types of activities would students participate in? Write up your classroom design. (INTASC: Principle 5)

Collaborative Work

Case Studies in Motivation. With three other students in the class, create a plan to improve the motivation of these students: (1) 7-year-old Tanya, who has low ability and low expectations for success; (2) 10-year-old Samuel, who works overtime to keep his self-worth at a high level but has a strong fear of failure; (3) 13-year-old Sandra, who is quiet in the classroom and underestimates her skills; and (4) 16-year-old Robert, who shows little interest in school and currently lives with his aunt (you have been unable to contact his parents). (INTASC: Principles 2, 3, 5)

Research/Field Experience

The Face of Student Motivation. Observe a teacher at the grade level you plan to teach and note the strategies he or she uses to motivate the students. Which strategies are most effective? Least effective? Why do you think this is so? Which students seem particularly difficult to motivate? Why do you think this is so? What would you do differently to foster student motivation in the classroom? (INTASC: Principles 5, 7, 9)

Go to the Online Learning Center for downloadable portfolio templates.

TAKING IT TO THE NET

- A student tells you that she lacks the ability to succeed in class. How do you respond? How would you describe your student's locus of control and attribution style? Take an online self-assessment to discover your own locus of control and attribution style. How could your style affect the way you teach and interact with students? http://discoveryhealth.queendom.com/lc_short_access.html

- Reflect on your teaching goals and what you hope to accomplish in the classroom. Take yourself through the online process of setting a goal. Design a goal-setting activity that you could integrate into your regular curriculum. Why are goals an important element of a student's learning experience? www.mygoals.com

- At-risk students are typically characterized as unmotivated and underachieving and often are placed in classes that emphasize remediation. What are some successful alternatives? Find an exemplary model for teaching at-risk students on the Web, and summarize its program components. Illustrate why students in the program become motivated to achieve at higher levels than their counterparts in remedial programs. www.ncrel.org/sdrs/areas/issues/students/atrisk/at700.htm

Connect to the Online Learning Center to explore possible answers.

STUDY, PRACTICE, AND SUCCEED

Visit www.mhhe.com/santedu4e to review the chapter with self-grading quizzes and self-assessments, to apply the chapter material to two more Crack the Case studies, and for suggested activities to develop your teaching portfolio.

CHAPTER 14

Managing the Classroom

*Precision in communication is more important
than ever in our era of hair-trigger balances,
when a false or misunderstood word may create as
much disaster as a sudden thoughtless act.*

—James Thurber
American Essayist and Humorist, 20th Century

TEACHING STORIES   Adriane Lonzarich

Adriane Lonzarich owns and operates Heartwood, a small preschool in San Mateo, California. In the afternoons, she also holds art classes for 5- to 12-year-old children. She talks about her ideas for managing the classroom:

> The most valuable advice I ever received for managing the classroom is to approach a problem or area of difficulty with three questions in this order: (1) Is it the environment? (2) Is it the teacher? (3) Is it the child? For example, if the issue of concern is unfocused energy of the group, I would first ask myself, Is it the environment? Is it overstimulating? Is there not enough to do? Do I need to rearrange the classroom and create more intimate spaces for quiet activity, or do I need to let them have more time outside, and so on? In many cases, I don't need to go on to the next two questions.
>
> Is it the teacher? Am I tired? Nervous? Uninspiring? Have I not taken the time to demonstrate the activities? Have I not been consistent in presenting, monitoring, and enforcing basic classroom rules? Have I not paid enough attention to their needs that day?
>
> Is it the child? If I've addressed all the other possibilities and I'm convinced that the problem is the child's problem, not the environment's or the teacher's, I explore what might be going on. Is anything happening in the child's home that might be causing his or her problems? Is it time for a parent conference? Does the child need help in bonding with a friend? Is the child afraid of failure and avoiding meaningful learning for that reason?
>
> This approach is empowering because it is much easier to change the environment or oneself than to change someone else's behavior. It also is effective because it does not zero in on the problem as the child's until all other avenues have been explored.

Preview

In educational circles, it is commonly said that no one pays any attention to good classroom management until it is missing. When classrooms are effectively managed, they run smoothly and students are actively engaged in learning. When they are poorly managed, they can become chaotic settings in which learning is a foreign activity. Our coverage begins by examining why classrooms need to be managed effectively, followed by strategies for designing the classroom's physical environment. Then we discuss the importance of creating a positive environment for learning and ways to be an effective communicator. The chapter concludes with information about what to do when students engage in problem behavior.

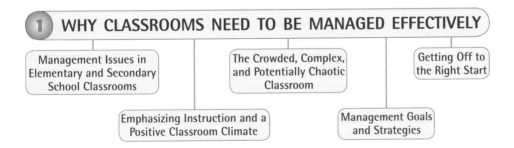

Effective classroom management maximizes children's learning opportunities (Evertson & Emmer, 2009; Larrivee, 2009). Experts in classroom management report that

Carmella Williams Scott, a middle school English and law teacher at Fairmont Alternative School in Newman, Georgia, created Juvenile Video Court TV, a student-run judicial system, so that students could experience the "other side of the bench" as a judge, lawyer, bailiff, and camera operator. She especially targeted gang leaders for inclusion in the system because they ran the school. Carmella likes to use meaningful questions to guide students' critical thinking. She believes that mutual respect is a key factor in her success as a teacher and the lack of discipline problems she has in her classes (Wong Briggs, 1999).

there has been a change in thinking about the best way to manage classrooms. The older view emphasized creating and applying rules to control students' behavior. The newer view focuses more on students' needs for nurturing relationships and opportunities for self-regulation (Noddings, 2007). Classroom management that orients students toward passivity and compliance with rigid rules can undermine their engagement in active learning, higher-order thinking, and the social construction of knowledge (Charles, 2008a, b). The new trend in classroom management places more emphasis on guiding students toward self-discipline and less on externally controlling the student (Emmer & Evertson, 2009). Historically in classroom management, the teacher was thought of as a director. In the current learner-centered trend in classroom management, the teacher is more of a guide, coordinator, and facilitator (Emmer & Evertson, 2009). The new classroom management model does not mean slipping into a permissive mode. Emphasizing caring and students' self-regulation does not mean that the teacher abdicates responsibility for what happens in the classroom (Bondy & others, 2007; Larrivee, 2009).

As you explore various aspects of managing the classroom, realize the importance of consulting and working with other staff members on management issues (Levin & Nolan, 2007). Also recognize that your class is part of the broader context of school culture and that in such areas as discipline and conflict management your policies will need to reflect and be consistent with the policies of the school and other teachers in the school. We will begin our tour of effective classroom management by exploring how management issues sometimes differ in elementary and secondary classrooms.

Management Issues in Elementary and Secondary School Classrooms

Elementary and secondary school classrooms have many similar management issues. At all levels of education, good managers design classrooms for optimal learning, create positive environments for learning, establish and maintain rules, get students to cooperate, effectively deal with problems, and use good communication strategies.

However, the same classroom management principles sometimes are applied differently in elementary and secondary schools because these two types of schools are structured differently (Evertson & Emmer 2009; Weinstein, 2007). In many elementary schools, teachers face the challenge of managing the same 20 to 25 children for the entire day. In middle and high schools, teachers face the challenge of managing five or six different groups of 20 to 25 adolescents for about 50 minutes each day. Compared with secondary school students, elementary school students spend much more time with the same students in the small space of a single classroom, and having to interact with the same people all day can breed feelings of confinement and boredom and other problems. However, with 100 to 150 students, secondary school teachers are more likely to be confronted with a wider range of problems than elementary school teachers. Also, because secondary school teachers spend less time seeing students in the classroom, it can be more difficult for them to establish personal relationships with students. And secondary school teachers have to get the classroom lesson moving quickly and manage time effectively, because class periods are so short.

Secondary school students' problems can be more long-standing and more deeply ingrained, and therefore more difficult to modify, than those of elementary school students. Also in secondary schools, discipline problems are frequently more severe, the students being potentially more unruly and even dangerous. Because most secondary school students have more advanced reasoning skills than elementary school students, they might demand more elaborate and logical explanations of rules and discipline. And in secondary schools, hallway socializing can carry into the classroom. Every hour there is another "settling down" process. Keep in mind these dif-

What are some different management issues in teaching elementary and secondary school students?

ferences between elementary and secondary schools as we further explore how to effectively manage the classroom. As we see next, at both elementary and secondary school levels, classrooms can be crowded, complex, and potentially chaotic.

The Crowded, Complex, and Potentially Chaotic Classroom

Carol Weinstein and Andrew Mignano (2007) used the title of this section, "The Crowded, Complex, and Potentially Chaotic Classroom," as an alert for potential problems and highlighted Walter Doyle's (1986, 2006) six characteristics that reflect a classroom's complexity and potential for problems:

- *Classrooms are multidimensional.* Classrooms are the setting for many activities, ranging from academic activities, such as reading, writing, and math, to social activities, such as playing games, communicating with friends, and arguing. Teachers have to keep records and keep students on a schedule. Work has to be assigned, monitored, collected, and evaluated. Students have individual needs that are more likely to be met when the teacher takes them into account.

- *Activities occur simultaneously.* Many classroom activities occur simultaneously. One cluster of students might be writing at their desks, another might be discussing a story with the teacher, one student might be picking on another, others might be talking about what they are going to do after school, and so on.

- *Things happen quickly.* Events often occur rapidly in classrooms and frequently require an immediate response. For example, two students suddenly argue about the ownership of a notebook, a student complains that another student is copying her answers, a student speaks out of turn, a student marks on another student's arm with a felt-tip pen, two students abruptly start bullying another student, or a student is rude to you.

- *Events are often unpredictable.* Even though you might carefully plan the day's activities and be highly organized, events will occur that you never expect: A fire alarm goes off; a student gets sick; two students get into a fight; a computer won't work; a previously unannounced assembly takes place; the heat goes off in the middle of the winter; and so on.

- *There is little privacy.* Classrooms are public places where students observe how the teacher handles discipline problems, unexpected events, and frustrating circumstances. Some teachers report that they feel like they are in a "fishbowl," or constantly onstage. Much of what happens to one student is observed by other

BEST PRACTICES
Strategies for a Good Beginning of the School Year

Here are some good teaching strategies for the beginning of the school year (Emmer & Evertson, 2009):

1. *Establish expectations for behavior and resolve student uncertainties.* At the beginning of the school year, students will not be sure what to expect in your classroom. They might have expectations, based on their experiences with other teachers, that are different from what your classroom will be like. In the first few days of school, lay out your expectations for students' work and behavior. Don't focus just on course content in the first few days and weeks of school. Be sure to take the time to clearly and concretely spell out class rules, procedures, and requirements so that students know what to expect in your class. Next, middle school history teacher Chuck Rawls describes what he does at the beginning of the school year.

THROUGH THE EYES OF TEACHERS
Establish Yourself in a Positive Manner

My first few days and weeks are highly structured—desks in straight rows, and daily assignments starting with Day One. I try to make the initial environment as business-like, straightforward, and structured as I possibly can. The games and easy give-and-take come later, after it is firmly established who is in charge of the class, and also if the kids are capable of doing that. Sometimes they aren't.

I'm not saying to scare the kids—they still need to feel safe and comfortable. The main thing is to establish yourself, at least in the minds of the kids, as an organized, confident, firm but fair subject-matter expert.

Someone said the lasting impression is made in the first 15 or 45 seconds of the first introduction. This is true.

2. *Make sure that students experience success.* In the first week of school, content activities and assignments should be designed to ensure that students succeed. This helps students develop a positive attitude and provides them with confidence to tackle more difficult tasks later.

3. *Be available and visible.* Show your students that they can approach you when they need information. During seatwork or group work, make yourself available instead of going to your desk and completing paperwork. Move around the room, monitor students' progress, and provide assistance when needed.

4. *Be in charge.* Even if you have stated your class rules and expectations clearly, some students will forget and others will test you to see if you are willing to enforce the rules, especially in the first several weeks of school. Continue to consistently establish the boundaries between what is acceptable and what is not acceptable in your classroom.

THROUGH THE EYES OF STUDENTS

First Week of School

Sept. 8: (First Day of Class)

Well now that I know what my teacher is like, I wish I didn't. My best friend Annie got the good teacher, Ms Hartwell. I got the witch Ms. Birdsong. The first thing she did was to read all of her rules to us. It must have taken half an hour. We will never get to do anything fun. Fifth grade is ruined.

Sept. 12: Ms. Birdsong is still strict but I'm starting to like her better. And she even is beginning to be a little funny sometimes. I guess she's just serious about wanting us to learn.

Brooke
Fifth-Grade Student
St. Louis, Missouri

students, and students make attributions about what is occurring. In one case, they might perceive that the teacher is being unfair in the way she disciplines a student. In another, they might appreciate her sensitivity to a student's feelings.

• *Classrooms have histories.* Students have memories of what happened earlier in their classroom. They remember how the teacher handled a discipline problem earlier in the year, which students have gotten more privileges than others, and whether the teacher abides by her promises. Because the past affects the future, it is important for teachers to manage the classroom today in a way that will support rather than undermine learning tomorrow. This means that the first several weeks of the school year are critical for establishing effective management principles.

The crowded, complex nature of the classroom can lead to problems if the classroom is not managed effectively. Indeed, such problems are a major public concern about schools. Year after year, the Gallup Poll has asked the public what they perceive to be the main problems schools face. In the 2004 poll (Gallup Organization, 2004), lack of discipline was rated as the second most important problem, after lack of financial support.

Getting Off to the Right Start

One key to managing the complexity of the classroom is to make careful use of the first few days and weeks of school. You will want to use this time to (1) communicate your rules and procedures to the class and get student cooperation in following them, and (2) get students to engage effectively in all learning activities.

Taking the time in the first week of school to establish these expectations, rules, and routines will help your class run smoothly and set the tone for developing a positive classroom environment.

Emphasizing Instruction and a Positive Classroom Climate

Despite the public's belief that a lack of discipline is the number one problem in schools, educational psychology emphasizes ways to develop and maintain a positive classroom environment that supports learning (Evertson & Emmer, 2009; Williams, 2009). This involves using preventive, proactive strategies rather than becoming immersed in reactive disciplinary tactics.

In a classic study, Jacob Kounin (1970) was interested in discovering how teachers responded to student misbehaviors. Kounin was surprised to find that effective and ineffective classroom managers responded in very similar ways to the misbehaviors. What the effective managers did far better than the ineffective managers was manage the group's activities. Researchers in educational psychology consistently find that teachers who competently guide and structure classroom activities are more effective than teachers who emphasize their disciplinary role (Brophy, 1996).

Throughout this book we emphasize a vision of students as active learners engaged in meaningful tasks, who think reflectively and critically and often interact with other students in collaborative learning experiences. Historically, the effectively managed classroom has been described as a "well-oiled machine," but a more appropriate metaphor for today's effectively managed classroom is a "beehive of activity" (see Figure 14.1) (Randolph & Evertson, 1995). This does not imply that classrooms should be wildly noisy and chaotic. Rather, students should be actively learning and busily engaged in tasks that they are motivated to do rather than quietly and passively sitting in their seats. Often they will be interacting with each other and the teacher as they construct their knowledge and understanding.

Management Goals and Strategies

Effective classroom management has two main goals: to help students spend more time on learning and less time on non-goal-directed activity, and to prevent students from developing academic and emotional problems.

Help Students Spend More Time on Learning and Less Time on Non–Goal-Directed Activity In Chapters 12 and 13, we discussed the importance, for both teachers and students, of being a good time manager. Effective classroom management will help you maximize your instructional time and your students' learning time. Carol Weinstein (2007) described the amount of time available for various classroom activities in a typical 42-minute secondary school class over the course of a school year. Actual yearly learning time is only about 62 hours, which is approximately half of the mandated school time for a typical class. Although her time figures are only estimates, they suggest that the hours available for learning are far less than would appear. And as we underscored in Chapter 12, "Planning, Instruction, and Technology," learning takes time.

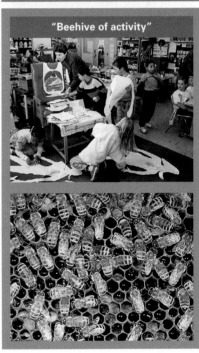

FIGURE 14.1 The Effectively Managed Classroom

"Well-oiled machine" or "beehive of activity"?

DEVELOPMENTAL FOCUS 14.1
How Do You Create a Positive Classroom Environment?

Early Childhood

We create positive classrooms for our preschoolers by frequently praising children, speaking with calm voices, following daily schedules, and setting clear rules that are expected to be followed.

—Missy Dangler, *Suburban Hills School*

Elementary School: Grades K–5

To create a positive classroom for my second-graders, I have a banner stretched across one of the walls of my classroom that reads: "This Is a Positive Learning Area"; this statement is the foundation for everything I do. On the first day of class, I tell the students that they will learn from me, learn from each other, and I will learn from them. I work with them to establish our classroom as a community of learners in order to build feelings of trust, respect, and understanding. With these values in place, academic learning can begin.

—Elizabeth Frascella, *Clinton Elementary School*

Middle School: Grades 6–8

One of the best ways to create a positive environment for my sixth-graders is to monitor classroom seating arrangements. I recognize who can sit next to each other and who can't. In middle school, when social cliques often form, I change seating arrangements every three weeks or so.

—Margaret Reardon, *Pocantico Hills School*

High School: Grades 9–12

I create a positive environment by keeping expectations high and consistently enforced. For example, I expect students to turn in their homework on time. No late work is accepted—however, I do tell students that if they are up late and overwhelmed by an assignment, they can come to me and ask for an extension. I ask that these extensions be the exception, not the rule. My high school students respond well to clear rules and expectations.

—Joseph Maley, *South Burlington High School*

Prevent Students from Developing Problems A well-managed classroom not only fosters meaningful learning but also helps prevent academic and emotional problems from developing (Bloom, 2009). Well-managed classrooms keep students busy with active, appropriately challenging tasks, have activities in which students become absorbed and motivated to learn, and establish clear rules and regulations students must abide by. In such classrooms, students are less likely to develop academic and emotional problems. By contrast, in poorly managed classrooms, students' academic and emotional problems are more likely to fester. The academically unmotivated student becomes even less motivated. The shy student becomes more reclusive. The bully becomes meaner.

Technology is increasingly being used in classroom management. To read about automating classroom management, see the *Technology and Education* interlude.

BEST PRACTICES
Strategies for Increasing Academic Learning Time

Strategies for increasing academic learning time include maintaining activity flow, minimizing transition time, and holding students accountable (Weinstein, 2007):

1. *Maintain activity flow.* In an analysis of classrooms, Jacob Kounin (1970) studied teachers' ability to initiate and maintain the flow of activity. Then he searched for links between activity flow and students' engagement and misbehavior. He found that some ineffective managers engaged in "flip-flopping"—terminating an activity, starting another, and then returning to the first one. Other ineffective managers were distracted from an ongoing activity by a small event that really did not need attention. For example, in one situation a teacher who was explaining a math problem at the board noticed a student leaning on his left elbow while working on the problem. The teacher went over to the student and told him to sit up straight, interrupting the flow of the class. Some ineffective managers "overdwell" on something that students already understand or go on at length about appropriate behavior. All of these situations—flip-flopping, respond-

ing to distractions, and overdwelling—can interrupt the classroom's flow.

2. *Minimize transition time.* In transitions from one activity to another, there is more room for disruptive behavior to occur. Teachers can decrease the potential for disruption during transitions by preparing students for forthcoming transitions, establishing transition routines, and clearly defining the boundaries of lessons.

3. *Hold students accountable.* If students know they will be held accountable for their work, they are more likely to make good use of class time. Clearly communicating assignments and requirements encourages student accountability. Explain to students what they will be doing and why, how long they will be working on the activity, how to obtain help if they need it, and what to do when they are finished. Helping students establish goals, plan, and monitor their progress also increases students' accountability. And maintaining good records can help you hold students accountable for their performance.

Review, Reflect, and Practice

1 Explain why classroom management is both challenging and necessary.

REVIEW

- Why must management principles be applied differently to elementary and secondary school classrooms?
- What are six reasons that classrooms are crowded, complex, and potentially chaotic?
- What strategies are most likely to get a school year off to the right start for a teacher?
- What do experts say should be the basic approach to classroom management? What did Kounin find that effective teachers did differently than ineffective teachers did in managing the classroom?
- What are the two main goals of effective classroom management?

REFLECT

- Which would probably be easier for you to manage—an elementary school classroom or a high school classroom? Why?

(continued)

TECHNOLOGY AND EDUCATION
Automating Classroom Management with Student Response Systems

Classroom management involves not only managing student behaviors but also managing instruction. Ideally, the two go hand in hand—students who are engaged in learning tasks are less likely to develop behavior problems. Another aspect of classroom management is record keeping. A new, relatively simple and inexpensive technology can help.

Recent years have seen a rise in popularity of classroom response systems. These systems traditionally consist of each of the following: a set of networked, low-cost handheld devices (which may be as simple as a keypad), a computer that is used as a central hub to aggregate student responses, and a whole-class display that shows questions posed to the class and the aggregation of student responses. Each of these components has a key role as teachers pose questions to students, who indicate an answer on their own devices. All answers then appear on the whole-class display in aggregated form, typically as a histogram.

Using student response systems, teachers have the ability to pose questions and give practice to whole classes of students, and to gather instant data on all of their students, which can be used to quickly assess comprehension. This true, formative assessment enables the teacher to identify students' misconceptions and errors and then correct them immediately. In addition, it encourages active student participation and helps students explore what they know and don't know—and hence take control of their own learning. Most student response systems also produce records of student responses, which can be automatically entered as grades.

Numerous studies show that these relatively simple systems can be effective classroom management tools (Swan & others, 2007; Vahey, Roschell, & Tatar, 2006). Common outcomes include increases in student engagement, teacher awareness of student knowledge, and student understanding of content matter.

A number of companies offer student response systems. Some of the more popular ones are InterWrite's Personal Response System (www.gtcocalcomp.com/interwriteprs.htm), TurningPoint's Audience Response System (www.turningtechnologies.com/highereducation.htm), and Quizdom's Student Response System (www.qwizdom.com/education_ solutions_ applications.htm).

Review, Reflect, and Practice

PRAXIS™ PRACTICE

1. Which characteristic of classrooms is best exemplified in the following scenario? Holly and Alex are having a conflict. Holly takes a black, permanent marker and makes a large mark on Alex's shirt. Mr. Bronson witnesses the incident and does nothing. Two weeks later, during another conflict, Alex makes a mark on the back of Holly's shirt with a pen. This time Mr. Bronson gives Alex a detention. Alex becomes upset at what he perceives as unfair treatment.
   a. Classrooms are multidimensional.
   b. Classrooms have histories.
   c. There is little privacy.
   d. Things happen quickly.

2. Mr. McClure wants to be certain that his students understand that he has high expectations for them. Therefore, he gives a very difficult exam during the first week of school. Which principle of getting off to the right start did Mr. McClure ignore?
   a. Be available and visible.
   b. Be in charge.
   c. Establish expectations for behavior and resolve student uncertainties.
   d. Make sure that students experience success.

Review, Reflect, and Practice

3. Which teacher is most likely to have classroom management problems?
   a. Mr. Knight, who, in an effort to keep students from being bored, has numerous activities during the period, all of which require transitional time
   b. Mr. Quinn, whose students know that they have to accomplish a significant amount of work during the period, which will be collected at the end
   c. Ms. Leifeit, whose students are always actively engaged in activities that require students to work together
   d. Ms. Jefferson, who establishes rules and procedures early in the school year and consistently enforces them

4. Which of the following teachers is likely to be most effective in maximizing academic learning time?
   a. Ms. Chang, who focuses on classroom discipline. Her students are reprimanded each and every time she notices what she perceives to be off-task behavior.
   b. Ms. George, who regularly starts one activity, stops it in favor of another, then returns to the first activity.
   c. Ms. Lange, who informs her students how long they will have to complete an activity, then warns them when there are five minutes left and then plays a certain piece of music during transition time. At the end of the music, the students are to be ready for the next activity.
   d. Ms. Purdy, who requires her students to sit up straight, with both feet on the floor as a means of gaining their attention.

Please see the answer key at the end of the book.

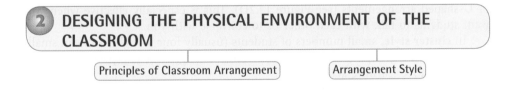

2   DESIGNING THE PHYSICAL ENVIRONMENT OF THE CLASSROOM

Principles of Classroom Arrangement   Arrangement Style

When thinking about effectively managing the classroom, inexperienced teachers sometimes overlook the physical environment. As you will see in this section, designing the physical environment of the classroom involves far more than arranging a few items on a bulletin board.

Principles of Classroom Arrangement

Here are four basic principles that you can use when arranging your classroom (Evertson & Emmer, 2009):

- *Reduce congestion in high-traffic areas.* Distraction and disruption can often occur in high-traffic areas. These include group work areas, students' desks, the teacher's desk, the pencil sharpener, bookshelves, computer stations, and storage locations. Separate these areas from each other as much as possible and make sure they are easily accessible.

- *Make sure that you can easily see all students.* An important management task is to carefully monitor students. To do this, you will need to be able to see all students at all times. Make sure there is a clear line of sight between your desk, instructional locations, students' desks, and all student work areas. Stand in different parts of the room to check for blind spots.

- *Make often-used teaching materials and student supplies easily accessible.* This minimizes preparation and cleanup time, as well as slowdowns and breaks in activity flow.

- *Make sure that students can easily observe whole-class presentations.* Establish where you and your students will be located when whole-class presentations take place. For these activities, students should not have to move their chairs or stretch their necks. To find out how well your students can see from their locations, sit in their seats in different parts of the room.

Arrangement Style

In thinking about how you will organize the classroom's physical space, you should ask yourself what type of instructional activity students will mainly be engaged in (whole-class, small-group, individual assignments, and so on). Consider the physical arrangements that will best support that type of activity (Weinstein, 2007).

Standard Classroom Arrangements Figure 14.2 shows a number of classroom arrangement styles: auditorium, face-to-face, off-set, seminar, and cluster (Renne, 1997). In traditional **auditorium style**, all students sit facing the teacher (see Figure 14.2A). This arrangement inhibits face-to-face student contacts, and the teacher is free to move anywhere in the room. Auditorium style often is used when the teacher lectures or someone is making a presentation to the entire class.

In **face-to-face style**, students sit facing each other (see Figure 14.2B). Distraction from other students is higher in this arrangement than in the auditorium style.

In **off-set style**, small numbers of students (usually three or four) sit at tables but do not sit directly across from one another (see Figure 14.2C). This produces less distraction than face-to-face style and can be effective for cooperative learning activities.

In **seminar style**, larger numbers of students (ten or more) sit in circular, square, or U-shaped arrangements (see Figure 14.2D). This is especially effective when you want students to talk with each other or to converse with you.

In **cluster style**, small numbers of students (usually four to eight) work in small, closely bunched groups (see Figure 14.2E). This arrangement is especially effective for collaborative learning activities.

Clustering desks encourages social interaction among students. In contrast, rows of desks reduce social interaction among students and direct students' attention toward the teacher. Arranging desks in rows can benefit students when they are working on individual assignments, whereas clustered desks facilitate cooperative learning. In classrooms in which seats are organized in rows, the teacher is most likely to interact with students seated in the front and center of the classroom (Adams & Biddle, 1970) (see Figure 14.3). This area has been called the "action zone" because students in the front and center locations interact the most with the teacher. For example, they most often ask questions and are most likely to initiate discussion. If you use a row arrangement, move around the room when possible, establish eye contact with students seated outside the "action zone," direct comments to students in the peripheral seats, and periodically have students change seats so that all students have an equal opportunity of being in the front and center seats.

auditorium style A classroom arrangement style in which all students sit facing the teacher.

face-to-face style A classroom arrangement style in which students sit facing each other.

off-set style A classroom arrangement style in which small numbers of students (usually three or four) sit at tables but do not sit directly across from one another.

seminar style A classroom arrangement style in which large numbers of students (ten or more) sit in circular, square, or U-shaped arrangements.

cluster style A classroom arrangement style in which small numbers of students (usually four to eight) work in small, closely bunched groups.

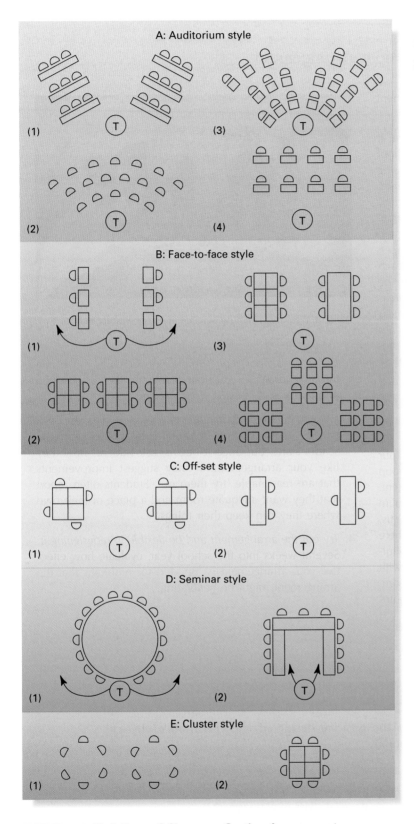

FIGURE 14.2 **Variations of Classroom Seating Arrangements**

Personalizing the Classroom According to classroom management experts Carol Weinstein and Andrew Mignano (2007), classrooms too often resemble motel rooms—pleasant but impersonal, revealing nothing about the people who use the space. Such anonymity is especially true of secondary school classrooms, where six or seven different classes might use the space in a single day. To personalize classrooms, post students' photographs, artwork, written projects, charts that list birthdays (of early childhood and elementary school students), and other positive expressions of students' identities. A bulletin board can be set aside for the "student of the week" or be used to display each student's best work of the week, personally chosen by each student.

None of the classrooms we have described will exactly match yours. However, keeping in mind the basic principles we have described should help you create an optimal classroom arrangement for learning.

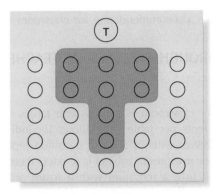

FIGURE 14.3 **The Action Zone**

"Action zone" refers to the seats in the front and center of row arrangement. Students in these seats are more likely to interact with the teacher, ask questions, and initiate discussion than students seated in more peripheral locations.

BEST PRACTICES
Strategies for Designing a Classroom Arrangement

Follow these steps in designing a classroom arrangement (Weinstein, 2007; Weinstein & Mignano, 2007):

1. *Consider what activities students will be engaging in.* If you will be teaching kindergarten or elementary school students, you might need to create settings for reading aloud, small-group reading instruction, sharing time, group math instruction, and arts and crafts. A secondary school science teacher might have to accommodate whole-group instruction, "hands-on" lab activities, and media presentations. On the left side of a sheet of paper, list the activities your students will perform. Next to each activity, list any special arrangements that need to be taken into account—for instance, art and science areas need to be near a sink, and computers need to be near an electrical outlet. Next, William Williford, who teaches science at Perry Middle School in Perry, Georgia, provides a recommendation for classroom arrangement.

THROUGH THE EYES OF TEACHERS
Hissing Cockroaches and Minicams

My classroom is set up with tables with about four students per table. This allows for individual or group activities without a lot of transition time or movement. Since my current subject is science, there is an aquarium with fish, a terrarium with a lizard or praying mantis, and a cage with Madagascar hissing cockroaches. There is a table with gadgets and mini-experiments. A Mini-cam may be focused on an earthworm or a spider with the image on the TV as students enter the classroom. The idea is to arrange the classroom so that it promotes inquiry, questioning, and thinking about science.

William Willford, teaching science at Perry Middle School.

2. *Draw up a floor plan.* Before you actually move any furniture, draw several floor plans and then choose the one that you think will work the best.

3. *Involve students in planning the classroom layout.* You can do most of your environmental planning before school starts, but once it begins, ask students how they like your arrangement. If they suggest improvements that are reasonable, try them out. Students often report that they want adequate room and a place of their own where they can keep their things.

4. *Try out the arrangement and be flexible in redesigning it.* Several weeks into the school year, evaluate how effective your arrangement is. Be alert for problems that the arrangement might be generating.

Review, Reflect, and Practice

(2) **Describe the positive design of the classroom's physical environment.**

REVIEW
- What are some basic principles of classroom design and arrangement?
- What are some standard styles of arrangement?

REFLECT
- How would you design and arrange your ideal classroom? How would you personalize it?

Review, Reflect, and Practice

PRAXIS™ PRACTICE

1. Ms. Craig likes her students to work in small groups. Therefore, she arranges her students' desks in small circles or clusters. What is the problem with this arrangement for whole-class presentations?
   a. Ms. Craig will be unable to see all of her students.
   b. Some students will have to turn their chairs to see.
   c. The classroom will be too congested.
   d. There will be blind spots.

2. Mr. James wants his students to be able to talk to each other as well as to him. What type of classroom arrangement is best suited to his needs?
   a. auditorium style
   b. cluster style
   c. offset style
   d. seminar style

Please see the answer key at the end of the book.

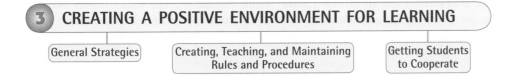

3 CREATING A POSITIVE ENVIRONMENT FOR LEARNING

General Strategies   Creating, Teaching, and Maintaining Rules and Procedures   Getting Students to Cooperate

Students need a positive environment for learning. We will discuss some general classroom management strategies for providing this environment, ways to effectively establish and maintain rules, and positive strategies for getting students to cooperate.

General Strategies

General strategies include using an authoritative style and effectively managing classroom activities.

The **authoritative classroom management style** is derived from Diana Baumrind's (1971, 1996) parenting styles, which were discussed in Chapter 3, "Social Contexts and Socioemotional Development." Like authoritative parents, authoritative teachers have students who tend to be self-reliant, delay gratification, get along well with their peers, and show high self-esteem. An authoritative strategy of classroom management encourages students to be independent thinkers and doers but still involves effective monitoring. Authoritative teachers engage students in considerable verbal give-and-take and show a caring attitude toward them. However, they still declare limits when necessary. Authoritative teachers clarify rules and regulations, establishing these standards with input from students.

The authoritative style contrasts with two ineffective strategies: authoritarian and permissive. The **authoritarian classroom management style** is restrictive and punitive. The focus is mainly on keeping order in the classroom rather than on instruction and learning. Authoritarian teachers place firm limits and controls on students and have little verbal exchange with them. Students in authoritarian classrooms tend to be passive learners, fail to initiate activities, express anxiety about social comparison,

authoritative classroom management style A management style that encourages students to be independent thinkers and doers but still provides effective monitoring. Authoritative teachers engage students in considerable verbal give-and-take and show a caring attitude toward them. However, they still set limits when necessary.

authoritarian classroom management style A management style that is restrictive and punitive, with the focus mainly on keeping order in the classroom rather than instruction or learning.

What characterizes an authoritative teaching style?

and have poor communication skills. The **permissive classroom management style** offers students considerable autonomy but provides them with little support for developing learning skills or managing their behavior. Not surprisingly, students in permissive classrooms tend to have inadequate academic skills and low self-control.

Overall, an authoritative style will benefit your students more than authoritarian or permissive styles. An authoritative style will help your students become active, self-regulated learners.

Classroom Management and Diversity The growing diversity of students makes classroom management more challenging (Lindberg, Flasch Ziegler, & Barcyzk, 2009; Scarlett, Ponte, & Singh, 2009). Children of color, especially African American and Latino children, and children from low-income backgrounds constitute a disproportionate number of referrals for discipline problems in schools (Fenning & Rose, 2007; Gay, 2006). A number of scholars argue that miscommunication between teachers and students and teachers' lack of sensitivity to cultural and socioeconomic variations in students contribute to this disproportionate number of referrals (Milner, 2006). Cultural mismatches especially are likely to appear in schools where the teachers are overwhelmingly from non-Latino White, middle-income backgrounds and the majority of the students are children of color from low-income backgrounds.

Geneva Gay (2006, p. 364) recently described such cultural mismatches and how they might be reduced:

> The commonly held belief that African Americans are disciplined more often and more severely because they commit more serious behavior infractions is not supported by research findings. Instead, they are punished more harshly for relatively minor misconduct (such as defiance, disrespect, rudeness, and disobedience) that falls within the purview of the interpretive judgments of teachers. This subjective discipline often stems from cultural misunderstandings and conflicting expectations about how students are supposed to behave in relation to each other, and in teaching-learning situations. For example, teachers may consider explicit comments from students that their teaching is boring and irrelevant as rude, insulting, and disrespectful. They may be particularly incensed by the way some students convey these sentiments. Rather than accepting them as useful feedback for improving the quality of instruction, teachers may see them as challenges to their authority that merit chastisement or even stronger disciplinary action. These tensions can be minimized by both teachers and students being more knowledgeable of each others' cultural styles of communicating, valuing, learning, and relating.

Engaging in such culturally responsive teaching and demonstrating sensitivity to cultural and socioeconomic variations in students can help teachers to reduce discipline problems in their classroom (Gollnick & Chinn, 2009). An increasing number of programs reveal that showing greater cultural sensitivity to socioculturally diverse students benefits these students when they are at risk for academic and emotional problems (Milner, 2006). To read about one program that has been successful in intervening in the lives of high-risk students from low-income, ethnic minority backgrounds, see the *Diversity and Education* interlude.

In addition to interacting with students using an authoritative style and being sensitive to ethnic and socioeconomic variations in students, there are other aspects of being an effective classroom manager. The following *Best Practices* interlude discusses strategies for being an effective classroom manager.

permissive classroom management style A management style that allows students considerable autonomy but provides them with little support for developing learning skills or managing their behavior.

DIVERSITY AND EDUCATION
The New Haven Social Development Project

Effectively intervening in the lives of high-risk students often consists of providing not only individualized attention but also community-wide collaboration for support and guidance. One program that focuses on community-wide collaboration was described by Roger Weissberg and Mark Greenberg (1998, pp. 920–921). It is called the New Haven Social Development Project and involves a high percentage of students from low-income, ethnic minority backgrounds (Kasprow & others, 1993; Schwab-Stone & others, 1995).

In this project, the superintendent and board of education for the New Haven schools established a comprehensive K–12 social development curriculum. The program consists of 25 to 50 hours of classroom-based instruction at each grade level. "The curriculum emphasized self-monitoring, problem solving, conflict resolution, and communication skills; values such as personal responsibility and respect for self and others; and content about health, culture, interpersonal relationships, and careers." The program also involves "educational, recreational, and health-promotion opportunities at the school and community levels to reinforce classroom-based instruction. These included programs such as mentoring, peer mediation, leadership groups, an Extended Day Academy with after-school clubs, health center services, and an outdoor adventure class." In addition, a school-based mental health planning team focuses attention on developing a positive climate for learning in the school. Teachers reported that the program improved the social skills and frustration tolerance of more than 80 percent of the students in grades K–3. Also, secondary school students decreased their participation in fights, felt safer at school and in the neighborhood, and felt more positive about the future as the program progressed.

Creating, Teaching, and Maintaining Rules and Procedures

To function smoothly, classrooms need clearly defined rules and procedures. Students need to know specifically how you want them to behave. Without clearly defined classroom rules and procedures, the inevitable misunderstandings can breed chaos. For example, consider these procedures or routines: When students enter the classroom, are they supposed to go directly to their seats or may they socialize for a few minutes until you tell them to be seated? When students want to go to the library, do they need a pass? When students are working at their seats, may they help each other or are they required to work individually?

What are some good strategies for establishing rules and procedures?

Both rules and procedures are stated expectations about behavior (Evertson & Emmer, 2009). *Rules* focus on general or specific expectations or standards for behavior. An example of a general rule is "Respect other persons." An example of a more specific rule is "Cell phones must always be turned off when you are in this classroom." *Procedures*, or routines, also communicate expectations about behavior, but they usually are applied to a specific activity, and their aim is to accomplish something instead of prohibit a behavior or define a general standard (Evertson & Emmer, 2009). You might establish procedures for collecting homework assignments, turning in work late, using the

BEST PRACTICES
Strategies for Being an Effective Classroom Manager

Effective classroom managers:

1. *Show how they are "with it."* Jacob Kounin (1970), whose views were discussed earlier, used the term **withitness** to describe a management strategy in which teachers show students that they are aware of what is happening. These teachers closely monitor students on a regular basis. This allows them to detect inappropriate behavior early, before it gets out of hand. Teachers who are not "with it" are likely to not notice such misbehaviors until they gain momentum and spread.

2. *Cope effectively with overlapping situations.* Kounin observed that some teachers seem to have one-track minds, dealing with only one thing at a time. This ineffective strategy often led to frequent interruptions in the flow of the class. For example, one teacher was working with a reading group when she observed two boys on the other side of the room hitting each other. She immediately got up, went over to the other side of the room, harshly criticized them, and then returned to the reading group. However, by the time she returned to the reading group, the students in the reading group had become bored and were starting to misbehave themselves. In contrast, effective managers were able to deal with overlapping situations in less disruptive ways. For example, in the reading group situation, they quickly responded to students from outside the group who came to ask questions but not in a way that significantly altered the flow of the reading group's activity. When moving around the room and checking each student's seatwork, they kept a roving eye on the rest of the class.

3. *Maintain smoothness and continuity in lessons.* Effective managers keep the flow of a lesson moving smoothly, maintaining students' interest and not giving them opportunities to be easily distracted. Earlier in the chapter, we mentioned some ineffective practices of teachers that can disrupt the flow of a lesson, including flip-flopping and overdwelling. Another teacher action that disrupts the lesson's flow is called "fragmentation," in which the teacher breaks an activity into components even though the activity could be performed as an entire unit. For example, a teacher might individually ask six students to do something, such as get out their art supplies, when all six could be asked to do this as a group.

4. *Engage students in a variety of challenging activities.* Kounin also found that effective classroom managers engage students in a variety of challenging but not overly hard activities. The students frequently worked independently rather than being directly supervised by a teacher who hovered over them. Next, Mark Fodness, an award-wining seventh-grade social studies teacher in Bemidji, Minnesota, gives this advice on managing the classroom.

THROUGH THE EYES OF TEACHERS
Great Teachers Have Few Discipline Problems

The single best method of decreasing undesirable behaviors among students is by increasing the effectiveness of teaching methods. The best teachers have very

Mark Fodness, teaching students in his middle social studies classroom.

withitness A management style described by Kounin in which teachers show students that they are aware of what is happening. Such teachers closely monitor students on a regular basis and detect inappropriate behavior early, before it gets out of hand.

pencil sharpener, or using equipment. You can develop procedures for beginning the day (for example, a procedure for "settling in" to the classroom—maybe a social item such as a riddle or brief note about school events), leaving the room (for example, to go to the bathroom), returning to the room (such as after lunchtime), and ending the day (for example, clearing off desks and leaving on time).

Rules tend not to change because they address fundamental ways we deal with others, ourselves, and our work, such as having respect for others and their property, and keeping our hands and our feet to ourselves. On the other hand, procedures may change because routines and activities in classrooms change.

BEST PRACTICES
Strategies for Being an Effective Classroom Manager

few discipline problems, not because they are great disciplinarians, but because they are great teachers. To emphasize this point with one of my student teachers, I had her follow our class out the door and into their next classes. She later returned, amazed at what she had seen. Students who she had thought were very well behaved had been off-task or disruptive in other classrooms. In one room, where a substitute teacher was doing his best to fill in, she described students' behavior as "shocking." Yet in another class, where the teacher was presenting a riveting lesson on a novel,

the same students once again were well behaved even though the teacher did not seem to be using any specific discipline strategy.

Many first-year teachers, and veterans alike, identify discipline as their number one teaching challenge. However, the best solution is to use exemplary teaching strategies. I asked my seventh-grade students to identify the characteristics of teachers who had well-behaved classes. Here is a sample of their responses: well prepared, interesting, funny, organized, fair, caring, nice, and energetic.

Teaching Rules and Procedures   What is the best way to get students to learn about rules and procedures? Should the teacher make the rules and procedures, then inform the class about them? Should students be allowed to participate in generating rules and procedures?

Some teachers like to include students in setting rules in the hope that this will encourage them to take more responsibility for their own behavior (Emmer & Evertson, 2009). Student involvement can take many different forms, including a discussion of the reason for having rules and the meaning of particular rules. The teacher might begin by having students discuss why rules are needed and then move on to a number of individual rules. The teacher can clarify the rule by describing, or asking students to describe, the general area of behavior it involves. Students usually can contribute concrete examples of the rule.

Some teachers start off with a whole-class discussion of classroom rules. During the discussion, the teacher and the students suggest possible rules for the classroom, and the teacher records these on an overhead projector, a chalkboard, or a large piece of chart paper. Then, the teacher and students arrange them into broad categories and develop titles for the categories. In some classrooms, this activity is followed by having students role-play each of the rules.

In some schools, students are allowed to participate in setting rules for the entire school. In some cases, student representatives from each room or grade level participate in generating school-wide rules with guidance from teachers and school administrators. However, within individual classrooms, especially in elementary schools, it is uncommon for students to participate in creating rules. Most teachers prefer to create and present their rules, although as indicated earlier, they may encourage discussion of the rules. In secondary schools, especially high schools, greater student contribution to rule setting is possible because of their more-advanced cognitive and socioemotional knowledge and skills.

Many effective classroom teachers clearly present their rules to students and give explanations and examples of them. Teachers who set reasonable rules, provide understandable rationales for them, and enforce them consistently usually find that the majority of the class will abide by them.

Getting Students to Cooperate

You want your students to cooperate with you and abide by classroom rules without always having to resort to discipline to maintain order. How can you get your

BEST PRACTICES
Strategies for Establishing Classroom Rules and Procedures

Here are four principles to keep in mind when you establish rules and procedures for your classroom (Weinstein, 2007, pp. 99–102):

1. *Rules and procedures should be reasonable and necessary.* Ask yourself if the rules and procedures you are establishing are appropriate for this grade level. Also ask yourself if there is a good reason for the rule or procedure. For example, one secondary school teacher has a rule that students must come to class on time. Students are clearly told that if they are late, they will get a detention even on the first violation. She explains the rule to the students at the beginning of the school year and tells them the reason for the rule: If they are late, they might miss important material.

2. *Rules and procedures should be clear and comprehensible.* If you have general rules, make sure that you clearly specify what they mean. For example, one teacher has the rule "Be prepared." Instead of leaving the rule at this general level, the teacher specifies what it means to be prepared and describes specific procedures involving the rule: having your homework, notebook, pen or pencil, and textbook with you every day.

   As mentioned earlier, one issue that crops up when establishing classroom rules is whether to let students

participate in making them. Involving students in generating classroom rules can increase students' sense of responsibility to abide by them, especially in secondary schools. Some students will suggest ridiculous rules, which you can simply veto. Some teachers will establish general rules and then ask students to generate specific examples of the rules.

3. *Rules and procedures should be consistent with instructional and learning goals.* Make sure that rules and procedures do not interfere with learning. Some teachers become so concerned about having an orderly, quiet classroom that they restrict students from interacting with each other and from engaging in collaborative learning activities.

4. *Classroom rules should be consistent with school rules.* Know what the school's rules are, such as whether particular behaviors are required in the halls, in the cafeteria, and so on. Many schools have a handbook that spells out what is acceptable and what is not. Familiarize yourself with the handbook. Some teachers go over the handbook with students at the beginning of the school year so that students clearly understand the school's rules regarding absenteeism, truancy, fighting, smoking, substance abuse, abusive language, and so on.

students to cooperate? There are three main strategies: Develop a positive relationship with students, get students to share and assume responsibility, and reward appropriate behavior.

Develop a Positive Relationship with Students When most of us think of our favorite teacher, we think of someone who cared about whether or not we learned. Showing that you genuinely care about students as individuals apart from their academic work helps to gain their cooperation (Pianta, 2006). It is easy to get caught up in the pressing demands of academic achievement and classroom business and ignore the socioemotional needs of students.

One study found that in addition to having effective rules and procedures, successful classroom managers also showed a caring attitude toward students (Emmer, Evertson, Anderson, 1980). This caring was evidenced in part by a classroom environment in which students felt safe and secure and were treated fairly. The teachers were sensitive to their needs and anxieties (for example, they created enjoyable activities the first several days of the school year rather than giving them diagnostic tests) and had good communication skills (including listening skills), and they effectively expressed their feelings to students. The classroom atmosphere was relaxed and pleasant. For example, the focus was on academic work but teachers gave students breaks and allowed them free time to read, use the computer, or draw. Figure 14.4 presents some teaching guidelines for developing a positive relationship with students.

Get Students to Share and Assume Responsibility   Earlier in this chapter, we discussed the importance of developing an authoritative atmosphere in the classroom and the issue of whether students should be allowed to participate in establishing class rules. Some experts on classroom management argue that sharing responsibility with students for making classroom decisions increases the students' commitment to the decisions (Blumenfeld, Kempler, & Krajcik, 2006).

Reward Appropriate Behavior   We have discussed rewards extensively in Chapter 7, "Behavioral and Social Cognitive Approaches." You might want to read the discussion of rewards in that chapter again, especially the section "Applied Behavior Analysis in Education," and think about how rewards can be used in effectively managing the classroom. The discussion of rewards in Chapter 13, "Motivation, Teaching, and Learning," also is relevant to classroom management, especially the information about rewards and intrinsic motivation. Following are some guidelines for using rewards in managing the classroom.

Choose Effective Reinforcers   Find out which reinforcers work best with which students and individualize reinforcement. For one student, the most effective reward might be praise; for another, it might be getting to do a favorite activity. Remember that pleasurable activities often are especially valuable in gaining students' cooperation. You might tell a student, "When you complete your math problems, you can go to the media area and play a computer game."

Use Prompts and Shaping Effectively   Remember that if you wait for students to perform perfectly, they might never do so. A good strategy is to use prompts and shape students' behavior by rewarding improvement. Some prompts come in the form of hints or reminders, such as "Remember the rule about lining up." Recall from Chapter 7 that shaping involves rewarding a student for successive approximations to a specified target behavior. Thus, you might initially reward a student for getting 60 percent of her math problems right, then for 70 percent the next time, and so on.

Use Rewards to Provide Information About Mastery, Not to Control Students' Behavior   Rewards that impart information about students' mastery can increase their intrinsic motivation and sense of responsibility. However, rewards that are used to control students' behavior are less likely to promote self-regulation and responsibility. For example, a student's learning might benefit from the student being selected as student of the week because the student engaged in a number of highly productive, competent activities. However, the student likely will not benefit from being given a reward for sitting still at a desk; such a reward is an effort by the teacher to control the student, and students in heavily controlled learning environments tend to act like "pawns."

1. Give a student a friendly "hello" at the door.

2. Have a brief one-on-one conversation about things that are happening in the student's life.

3. Write a brief note of encouragement to the student.

4. Use students' names in class more.

5. Show enthusiasm about being with students (even late in the day, week, or year).

6. Risk more personal self-disclosures, which help students see you as a real person. However, don't cross the line and go too far. Always take into account children's level of understanding and emotional vulnerability in disclosing information about yourself to them.

7. Be an active listener who carefully attends to what the student is saying, even if it is something trivial.

8. Let students know that you are there to support and help them.

9. Keep in mind that developing positive, trusting relationships takes time. This especially is the case for students from high-risk environments who might not initially trust your motives.

FIGURE 14.4 Guidelines for Establishing Positive Relationships with Students

What are some guidelines for the effective use of rewards in the classroom?

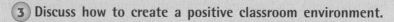

BEST PRACTICES
Strategies for Guiding Students to Share and Assume Responsibility

Here are some guidelines for getting students to share and assume responsibility in the classroom (Fitzpatrick, 1993):

1. *Involve students in the planning and implementation of school and classroom initiatives.* This participation helps to satisfy students' needs for self-confidence and belonging.

2. *Encourage students to judge their own behavior.* Rather than pass judgment on students' behavior, ask questions that motivate students to evaluate their own behavior. For example, you might ask, "Does your behavior reflect the class rules?" or "What's the rule?" Such questions place responsibility on the student. Initially, some students try to blame others or change the subject. In such situations, stay focused and guide the student toward accepting responsibility.

3. *Don't accept excuses.* Excuses just pass on or avoid responsibility. Don't even entertain a discussion about excuses. Rather, ask students what they can do the next time a similar situation develops.

4. *Give the self-responsibility strategy time to work.* Students don't develop responsibility overnight. Many student misbehaviors are ingrained habits that take a long time to break. One strategy is to be patient one more time than the student expects—difficult to do, but good advice.

5. *Let students participate in decision making by holding class meetings.* In his book *Schools Without Failure,* William Glasser (1969) argued that class meetings can be used to deal with student behavior problems or virtually any issue that is of concern to teachers and students.

Review, Reflect, and Practice

(3) Discuss how to create a positive classroom environment.

REVIEW

- What are some general strategies for creating a positive environment for learning?
- What are some hallmarks of good classroom rules?
- What are the best approaches in getting students to cooperate?

REFLECT

- In your classroom, what standards of "good" behavior would be nonnegotiable? Would you be flexible about some things? Explain.

PRAXIS™ PRACTICE

1. Ms. Rockefeller has high expectations for her students' behavior. She is rather harsh with punishments when they do not live up to these expectations and accepts no explanations for noncompliance. Her standard response to excuses is, "I don't want to hear it. You broke the rules. You know the consequences." Which management style does Ms. Rockefeller exemplify?
   a. authoritative
   b. authoritarian
   c. permissive
   d. neglectful

2. Which of the following is the best example of a clearly stated classroom procedure?
   a. Keep your hands to yourself.
   b. Put all homework in the homework folder when you come in.
   c. Respect other people's property.
   d. Stay in your seat unless you have permission to get up.

Review, Reflect, and Practice

3. Which teacher is most likely to gain the cooperation of students in following classroom rules and procedures?
   a. Ms. Benes and her students developed a list of rules and procedures at the beginning of the school year; however, she does not enforce the rules and procedures she has established. There are no reinforcements for proper behavior and no consequences for inappropriate behavior.
   b. Ms. Costanza wants her classroom to be very orderly. As a result, she punishes students for the slightest infractions.
   c. Ms. Kramer's students participated in the development of classroom rules. They all agreed that each rule was necessary and that the procedures would make things run more smoothly. When students disobey a rule, she asks them if their behavior is appropriate.
   d. Ms. Peterman has a long list of rules and procedures for students to follow. For instance, when they come in the classroom, they are to first put their homework in the proper folder, then change into their P.E. shoes. If students do these things in the opposite order, they are reprimanded.

Please see the answer key at the end of the book.

4 BEING A GOOD COMMUNICATOR

Speaking Skills   Listening Skills   Nonverbal Communication

Managing classrooms and constructively resolving conflicts require good communication skills (Engleberg & Wynn, 2008; Seiler & Beall, 2008). Three key aspects of communication are speaking skills, listening skills, and nonverbal communication.

Speaking Skills

You and your students will benefit considerably if you have effective speaking skills and you work with your students on developing their speaking skills. Let's first explore some strategies for speaking with your class.

Speaking with the Class and Students   In speaking with your class and students, one of the most important things to keep in mind is to clearly communicate information (Hogan & others, 2008; Zarefsky, 2008). *Clarity* in speaking is essential to good teaching.

Some good strategies for speaking clearly with your class include (Florez, 1999):

1. Selecting vocabulary that is understandable and appropriate for the level of your students
2. Speaking at an appropriate pace, neither too rapidly nor too slowly
3. Being precise in your communication and avoiding being vague
4. Using good planning and logical thinking skills as underpinnings of speaking clearly with your class

What are some barriers to effective verbal communication?

Barriers to Effective Verbal Communication   Barriers to effective verbal communication include (Gordon, 1970):

- *Criticizing.* Harsh, negative evaluations of another person generally reduce communication. An example of criticizing is telling a student, "It's your fault you flunked the test; you should have studied." Instead of criticizing, you can ask students to evaluate why they did not do well on a test and try to get them to arrive at an attribution that reflects lack of effort as the reason for the poor grade.
- *Name-calling and labeling.* These are ways of putting down the other person. Students engage in a lot of name-calling and labeling. They might say to another student, "You are a loser," or "You are stupid." Monitor students' use of such name-calling and labeling. When you hear this type of statement, intervene and talk with them about considering other students' feelings.
- *Advising.* Advising is talking down to others while giving them a solution to a problem. For example, a teacher might say, "That's so easy to solve. I can't understand why . . ."
- *Ordering.* Commanding another person to do what you want is often not effective because it creates resistance. For example, a teacher might yell at a student, "Clean up this space, right now!" Instead, a calm, firm reminder such as "Remember the rule of cleaning things up when we are finished" works better.
- *Threatening.* Threats are intended to control the other person by verbal force. For example, a teacher might say, "If you don't listen to me, I'm going to make your life miserable here." A better strategy is to approach the student more calmly and talk with the student about listening better.
- *Moralizing.* This means preaching to the other person about what he or she should do. For example, a teacher might say, "You know you should have turned your homework in on time. You ought to feel bad about this." Moralizing increases students' guilt and anxiety. A better strategy in this case is not to use words such as *should* and *ought* but, instead, to talk with the student in a less condemning way about why the homework was not turned in on time.

Giving students opportunities to practice their speaking skills is a vastly underutilized aspect of elementary and secondary education. Fear of speaking in front of a group is consistently listed as the number one fear of adults. *How do you think you can help your students become more effective speakers?*

Giving an Effective Speech   Not only will you be speaking in your class every day to your students in both formal and informal ways, but you also will have opportunities to give talks at educational and community meetings. Knowing some good strategies for giving a speech can significantly reduce your anxiety and help you deliver an effective speech (Gregory, 2008; Nelson, Titsworth, & Pearson, 2009).

Also, as most of us reflect on our experiences as students, we can remember few opportunities to give talks in class unless we took a specific class in speech. But not only can students be given speaking opportunities through formal presentations, but they also can participate in panel discussions and debates. All these activities give students opportunities to improve their speaking, organizational, and thinking skills (Hogan & others, 2008; Lucas, 2007).

Here are some guidelines for delivering a speech, which can benefit students as well as teachers (Alverno College, 1995):

- *Connect with the audience.* Talk directly to the audience; don't just read your notes or recite a memorized script.
- *State your purpose.* Keep this focus throughout the talk.
- *Effectively deliver the speech.* Use eye contact, supportive gestures, and effective voice control.

THROUGH THE EYES OF STUDENTS

Forensics Teacher Tommie Lindsey's Students

Tommie Lindsey teaches competitive forensics (public speaking and debate) at Logan High School in Union City, California. Forensics classes in most U.S. schools are mainly in affluent areas, but most of Lindsey's students come from impoverished or at-risk backgrounds. His students have won many public speaking honors.

The following comments by his students reflect Lindsey's outstanding teaching skills:

> He's one of the few teachers I know who cares so much. . . . He spends hours and hours, evenings, and weekends, working with us.
> —Justin Hinojoza, 17

> I was going through a tough time. . . . Mr. Lindsey helped me out. I asked how I could pay back and and he said, "Just help someone the way I helped you."
> —Robert Hawkins, 21

> This amazing opportunity is here for us students and it wouldn't be if Mr. Lindsey didn't create it.
> —Michael Joshi, 17

As a ninth-grade student, Tommie Lindsey became a public speaker. He says that his English teacher doubted his ability, and he wanted to show her how good he could be at public speaking, preparing a speech that received a standing ovation. Lindsey remembers, "She was expecting me to fail, and I turned the tables on her. . . . And we do

Tommie Lindsey, working with his students on improving their public speaking and debate skills.

that with our forensic program. When we started, a lot of people didn't believe our kids could do the things they do."

For his outstanding teaching efforts, Tommie Lindsey was awarded a prestigious McArthur Fellowship in 2005. (Source: Seligson, 2005)

- *Use media effectively.* This can help the audience grasp key ideas and varies the pace of the talk.

Listening Skills

Effectively managing your classroom will be easier if you and your students have good listening skills. Listening is a critical skill for making and keeping relationships (Gamble & Gamble, 2008; Hybels & Weaver, 2009). If you are a good listener,

PEANUTS © United Features Syndicates, Inc.

How would you describe the nonverbal behaviors of the teachers and the students in these two photographs?

students, parents, other teachers, and administrators will be drawn to you. If your students are good listeners, they will benefit more from your instruction and will have better social relationships. Poor listeners "hog" conversations. They talk "to" rather than "with" someone. Good listeners actively listen. They don't just passively absorb information. **Active listening** means giving full attention to the speaker, focusing on both the intellectual and the emotional content of the message.

Some good active listening strategies follow:

- Pay careful attention to the person who is talking, including maintaining eye contact.
- Paraphrase.
- Synthesize themes and patterns.
- Give feedback in a competent manner.

Nonverbal Communication

In addition to what you say, you also communicate by how you fold your arms, cast your eyes, move your mouth, cross your legs, or touch another person. Indeed, many communication experts maintain that most interpersonal communication is nonverbal (Richmond, McCroskey, & Hickson, 2008; Stewart, 2009). Even a person sitting in a corner, silently reading, is nonverbally communicating something, perhaps that he or she wants to be left alone. And when you notice your students blankly staring out the window, it likely indicates that they are bored. It is hard to mask nonverbal communication. Recognize that it can tell you how you and others really feel.

Let's further explore nonverbal communication by examining facial expressions, personal space, and silence. People's faces disclose emotions and telegraph what really matters to them (Adams & Galanes, 2009; Leathers & Eaves, 2008). A smile, a frown, a puzzled look all communicate.

Each of us has a personal space that at times we don't want others to invade. Not surprisingly, given the crowdedness of the classroom, students report that having their own space where they can put their materials and belongings is important

active listening A listening style that gives full attention to the speaker and notes both the intellectual and emotional content of the message.

DEVELOPMENTAL FOCUS 14.2
What Are Some Effective Communication Skills Used in the Classroom?

Early Childhood

At our preschool, we communicate in such a way that children know what they *can do,* not what they can't. For example, instead of telling children to "keep quiet," we tell them to "use their listening ears."

—Heidi Kaufman, *MetroWest YMCA Child Care and Educational Program*

Elementary School: Grades K–5

I use a lot of call and response methods to get my second-graders' attention. For example, I say, "One, two, three, eyes on me," and the children respond, "One, two, eyes on you." On the first day of school, they are taught to stop what they are doing when they hear me say this and turn to me for new instructions or information.

—Janine Guida Poutre, *Clinton Elementary School*

Middle School: Grades 6–8

One of the keys to communicating effectively is good listening skills. I teach my students to have respect for speakers by having them clear their desk of everything on it whenever someone, teacher or student, is presenting. This strategy assures that the class is listening and respecting the person making a presentation rather than doodling in notebooks or reading.

—Mark Fodness, *Bemidji Middle School*

High School: Grades 9–12

I show my students the importance of being an effective communicator by giving them a complicated set of directions verbally (such as how to properly fold a dinner napkin) and then asking them to do the task without talking to anyone or asking questions. After this activity, I hold a discussion on why it was impossible to do the task given the ineffective communication of instructions. This activity quickly shows students the value of communicating effectively.

—Sandy Swanson, *Menomonee Falls High School*

to them. Make sure that all students have their own desks or spaces. Tell students that they are entitled to have this individual space, and that they should courteously respect other students' space.

In our fast-paced, modern culture we often act as if there is something wrong with anyone who remains silent for more than a second or two after something is said to them. In Chapter 10, we indicated that after asking a question of students, many teachers rarely remain silent long enough for students to think reflectively before giving an answer. By being silent, a good listener can observe the speaker's eyes, facial expressions, posture, and gestures for communication; think about what the other person is communicating; and consider what the most appropriate response is. Of course, silence can be overdone and is sometimes inappropriate (Richmond, McCrosky, & Hickson, 2008). It is rarely wise to listen for an excessive length of time without making some verbal response.

We have discussed a number of communication skills that will help you manage your classroom effectively. To evaluate your communication skills, complete *Self-Assessment 14.1.*

SELF-ASSESSMENT 14.1
Evaluating My Communication Skills

Good communication skills are critical for effectively managing a classroom. Read each of the statements and rate them on a scale from 1 (very much unlike me) to 5 (very much like me).

	1	2	3	4	5
1. I know the characteristics of being a good speaker in class and with students.					
2. I am good at public speaking.					
3. I do not tend to dominate conversations.					
4. I talk "with" people, not "to" people.					
5. I don't criticize people very much.					
6. I don't talk down to people or put them down.					
7. I don't moralize when I talk with people.					
8. I'm good at giving my full attention to someone when they are talking with me.					
9. I maintain eye contact when I talk with people.					
10. I smile a lot when I interact with people.					
11. I know the value of silence in communication and how to practice it effectively.					

Scoring and Interpretation

Look over your self-ratings. For any items on which you did not give yourself a 4 or 5, work on improving these aspects of your communication skills. Both you and your students will benefit.

Review, Reflect, and Practice

(4) Identify some good approaches to communication for both students and teachers.

REVIEW

- What are some barriers to effective speech? What are some principles of good speech?
- What is active listening and what can teachers and students do to develop active listening skills?
- What are some important aspects of nonverbal communication for teachers to understand?

REFLECT

- What are your own communication strengths and weaknesses? What might you do to improve them?

PRAXIS™ PRACTICE

1. Ms. Carmichael is upset with Zack, one of her fifth-grade students, because he has not turned in his homework for the third time in the past week. She is discussing

Review, Reflect, and Practice

the situation with him, trying to express the importance of turning in assignments on time. Which of the following is likely to be her best response to the situation?

a. "Okay, Zack, you may turn it in tomorrow."

b. "What is wrong with you, Zack? This is the third time in a week! I know you can do the work. Are you just plain lazy? Is that it? This is getting ridiculous. Do you want to fail?"

c. "Zack, I know you can do the work. Are you trying to make things more difficult for me by not turning it in?"

d. "Zack, I can't possibly assess your understanding of the material when you don't turn in your work. This can't continue. Please get it to me by the end of the day, and no more late work."

2. Edward and James are having a discussion about the best way to engage their students' interest in American history. Which of the following best exemplifies active listening?

a. As Edward speaks about the importance of integrating electronic media into their courses, James interrupts with an argument that primary sources are much more useful and accurate.

b. As Edward speaks about the importance of integrating electronic media into their courses, James makes a rude noise and tells him that is a bunch of nonsense.

c. As Edward speaks, James maintains eye contact and nods occasionally. However, James is really planning how he will counter Edward's assertion that electronic media will engage the students.

d. As Edward speaks, James maintains eye contact, nods his head occasionally, and leans forward. When Edward has finished, James says, "So what you're saying is that if we used more electronic media, the kids would be more interested, right?"

3. As Edward is speaking about the importance of integrating electronic media into their American history courses, James checks his watch, looks toward the door, and drums his fingers on the desk. What message is James communicating?

a. interest

b. disdain

c. anxiety

d. boredom

Please see the answer key at the end of the book.

5 DEALING WITH PROBLEM BEHAVIORS

Management Strategies   Dealing with Aggression

No matter how well you have planned and created a positive classroom environment, problem behaviors will emerge. It is important that you deal with them in a timely, effective manner.

Carolyn Evertson (*center* in red in a COMP classroom), a leading expert on classroom management, created COMP, a classroom management program, with Evelyn Harris. COMP includes many of the themes we have emphasized in developing a positive environment for learning. COMP emphasizes supporting students' learning and guiding students in taking responsibility for their own decisions, behavior, and learning. COMP also includes strategies for problem prevention, management and instruction integration, student involvement, and professional collaboration among teachers. The program is implemented through training workshops, classroom application, and collaborative reflection. Research has revealed that COMP results in positive changes in teacher and student behavior (Evertson & Harris, 1999).

Management Strategies

Classroom management experts Carolyn Evertson and Edward Emmer (2009) distinguish between minor and moderate interventions for problem behaviors. The following discussion describes their approach.

Minor Interventions   Some problems require only minor interventions. These problems involve behaviors that, if infrequent, usually don't disrupt class activities and learning. For example, students might call out to the teacher out of turn, leave their seats without permission, engage in social talk when it is not allowed, or eat candy in class. When only minor interventions are needed for problem behaviors, these strategies can be effective (Evertson & Emmer, 2009, pp. 188–190):

- *"Use nonverbal cues.* Make eye contact with the student and give a signal such as a finger to the lips, a head shake, or a hand signal to issue a desist."

- *Keep the activity moving.* Sometimes transitions between activities take too long, or a break in activity occurs when students have nothing to do. In these situations, students might leave their seats, socialize, crack jokes, and begin to get out of control. A good strategy is not to correct students' minor misbehaviors in these situations but rather start the next activity in a more timely fashion. By effectively planning the day, you should be able to eliminate these long transitions and gaps in activity.

- *Move closer to students.* When a student starts misbehaving, simply moving near the student will often cause the misbehavior to stop.

- *"Redirect the behavior."* If students get off-task, let them know what they are supposed to be doing. You might say, "Okay, remember, everybody is supposed to be working on math problems."

- *"Provide needed instruction."* Sometimes students engage in minor misbehaviors when they haven't understood how to do the task they have been assigned. Unable to effectively do the activity, they fill the time by misbehaving. Solving this problem involves carefully monitoring students' work and providing guidance when needed.

- *Directly and assertively tell the student to stop.* Establish direct eye contact with the student, be assertive, and tell the student to stop the behavior. "Keep your comments brief and monitor the situation until the student complies. Combine this strategy with redirection to encourage desirable behavior."

- *"Give the student a choice."* Place responsibility in the student's hands by saying that he or she has a choice of either behaving appropriately or receiving a negative consequence. Be sure to tell the student what the appropriate behavior is and what the consequence is for not performing it.

Moderate Interventions   Some misbehaviors require a stronger intervention than those just described—for example, when students abuse privileges, disrupt an activity, goof off, or interfere with your instruction or other students' work. Here are some moderate interventions for dealing with these types of problems (Evertson, Emmer, & Worsham, 2009, pp. 177–178):

- *"Withhold a privilege or a desired activity."* Inevitably, you will have students who abuse privileges they have been given, such as being able to move around the classroom or to work on a project with friends. In these cases, you can revoke the privilege.

- *"Isolate or remove students."* In Chapter 7, we also discussed the time-out, which involves removing a student from positive reinforcement. If you choose to use a time-out, you have several options. You can (1) keep the student in the classroom, but deny the student access to positive reinforcement; (2) take the student outside the activity area or out of the classroom; or (3) place the student in a time-out room designated by the school. If you use a time-out, be sure to clearly identify the student's behavior that resulted in the time-out, such as "You are being placed in time-out for 30 minutes because you punched Derrick." If the misbehavior occurs again, reidentify it and place the student in time-out again. After the time-out, don't comment on how well the student behaved during the time-out; just return the student to the activity that was interrupted.

- *Impose a penalty.* A small amount of repetitious work can be used as a penalty for misbehavior. In writing, a student might have to write an extra page; in math, a student might have to do extra problems; in physical education, a student might have to run an extra lap. The problem with penalties is that they can harm the student's attitude toward the subject matter.

Students also can be made to serve a detention for their misbehaviors, at lunch, during recess, before school, or after school. Teachers commonly assign detentions for goofing off, wasting time, repeating rule violations, not completing assignments, and disrupting the class. Some detentions are served in the classroom; some schools have a detention hall where students can be sent. If the detention occurs in your classroom, you will have to supervise it. The length of the detention should initially be short, on the order of 10 to 15 minutes, if the misbehavior is not severe. As when using the time-out, you will need to keep a record of the detention.

Using Others as Resources   Among the people who can help you get students to engage in more-appropriate behavior are peers, parents, the principal or counselor, and mentors.

Peer Mediation   Peers sometimes can be very effective at getting students to behave more appropriately. Peer mediators can be trained to help students resolve quarrels and change undesirable behaviors. For example, if two students have started to argue with each other, an assigned peer mediator can help to mediate the dispute, as described later in the chapter when we discuss conflict resolution.

Parent-Teacher Conference   You can telephone the student's parents or confer with them in a face-to-face conference. Just informing them can sometimes get the student to improve behavior. Don't put the parents on the defensive or suggest that you are blaming them for their child's misbehavior in school. Just briefly describe the problem and say that you would appreciate any support that they can give you.

Enlist the Help of the Principal or Counselor   Many schools have prescribed consequences for particular problem behaviors. If you have tried unsuccessfully to deal with the behavior, consider asking the school's administration for help. This might involve referring the student to the principal or a counselor, which may result in a detention or warning to the student, as well as a parent conference with the principal. Letting the principal or counselor handle the problem can save you time. However, such help is not always practical on a regular basis in many schools.

Find a Mentor   Earlier we underscored the importance of students having at least one person in their life who cares about them and supports their development. Some students, especially those from high-risk impoverished backgrounds, do not have

"How come when you say we have a problem, I'm always the one who has the problem?"

George Abbott from *Phi Delta Kappan*, vol. 74, no. 2 (October 1992), p. 171. Reprinted by permission of George Abbott.

DEVELOPMENTAL FOCUS 14.3

How Do You Handle Student Misbehavior in the Classroom?

Early Childhood

We teach our preschoolers that misbehavior always brings a consequence. We first speak to students about why the behavior is wrong and ways to conduct themselves next time. We also send notes home to parents when misbehavior occurs. A student will be placed in time-out as a last resort.

—Missy Dangler, *Suburban Hills School*

Elementary School: Grades K–5

I make it a point to call every parent during the first month of school to establish a nonthreatening rapport and to have a good-natured telephone call be the first communication of the year between us. During the call, I introduce myself, say something positive about his or her child, and ask the parent if he or she has any questions for me. If and when there is a call to be made to a parent for student misbehavior, I have already made positive contact with the parent, and the parent may be more willing to help with the problem.

—Janine Guida Poutre, *Clinton Elementary School*

Middle School: Grades 6–8

If a student presents a problem that may cause harm to other classmates, either remove that student or remove the entire class. Students look to adults for safety.

—Felicia Peterson, *Pocantico Hills School*

High School: Grades 9–12

I treat all of my students with respect, even the ones that are misbehaving. For example, when I see signs of misbehavior, I meet with the student individually outside of class and say something like "I get distracted when you talk to Sally while I'm speaking. Could you work on that for me? I don't want to stop class, because I think that would be embarrassing for you." Most students are receptive to the respect that I give them in these situations.

—Joseph Maley, *South Burlington High School*

". . . and suddenly there were teachers all over the place!"

From *Classroom Chuckles* by Bill Knowlton. Copyright © by Bill Knowlton. Reprinted by permission of Scholastic Inc.

that one person. A mentor can provide such students with the guidance they need to reduce problem behaviors (Lindley, 2009; Rowley, 2009). Look around the community for potential mentors for students in high-risk, low-income circumstances.

Dealing with Aggression

Violence in schools is a major, escalating concern. In many schools, it now is common for students to fight, bully other students, or threaten each other and teachers verbally or with a weapon. These behaviors can arouse your anxiety and anger, but it is important to be prepared for their occurrence and handle them calmly (Kottler & Kottler, 2009). Avoiding an argument or emotional confrontation will help you to solve the conflict.

Fighting   Classroom management experts Carolyn Evertson and Edward Emmer (2009) recommend the following in dealing with students who are fighting. In elementary school, you can usually stop a fight without risking injury to yourself. If for some reason you cannot intervene, immediately get help from other teachers or administrators. When you intervene, give a loud verbal command: "Stop!" Separate the fighters, and as you keep them separated, tell other students to leave or return to what they are doing. If you intervene in a fight that involves secondary school students, you will probably need the help of one or two other adults. Your school likely will have a policy regarding fighting. If so, you should carry it out and involve the principal and/or parents if necessary.

Generally, it is best to let the fighters have a cooling-off period so that they will calm down. Then meet with the fighters and get their points of view on what precipitated the fight. Question witnesses if necessary. Have a conference with the fighters, emphasizing the inappropriateness of fighting, the importance of taking each other's perspective, and the importance of cooperation.

Bullying   Significant numbers of students are victimized by bullies (Green, 2008; Kaiser & Rasminsky, 2009; Pepler & others, 2008). In a national survey of more than 15,000 sixth- through tenth-grade students, nearly one of every three students said that they had experienced occasional or frequent involvement as a victim or perpetrator in bullying (Nansel & others, 2001). In this study, bullying was defined as verbal or physical behavior intended to disturb someone less powerful. As shown in Figure 14.5, being belittled about looks or speech was the most frequent type of bullying. A recent study revealed that bullying decreased as students went from the fall of the sixth grade (20 percent were bullied extensively) through the spring of the eighth grade (6 percent were bullied extensively) (Nylund & others, 2007).

Who is likely to be bullied? In the study just described, boys and younger middle school students were most likely to be affected (Nansel & others, 2001). Children who said they were bullied reported more loneliness and difficulty in making friends, while those who did the bullying were more likely to have low grades and to smoke and drink alcohol. Researchers have found that anxious, socially withdrawn, and aggressive children are often the victims of bullying (Hannish & Guerra, 2004). Anxious and socially withdrawn children may be victimized because they are non-threatening and unlikely to retaliate if bullied, whereas aggressive children may be the targets of bullying because their behavior is irritating to bullies (Rubin, Bukowski, & Parker, 2006).

What are the outcomes of bullying? Bullies and victims are characterized by a number of negative developmental outcomes (Arseneault & others, 2008; Beaty & Alexeyev, 2008; Peter, Roberts, & Buzdugan, 2008). A recent study indicated that bullies and their victims in adolescence were more likely to experience depression and engage in suicide ideation and attempt suicide than their counterparts who were not involved in bullying (Brunstein & others, 2007). Another recent study revealed that bullies, victims, or those who were both bullies and victims had more health problems (such as headaches, dizziness, sleep problems, and anxiety) than their counterparts who were not involved in bullying (Srabstein & others, 2006).

School climate may play a role in bullying, although few research studies have been conducted on this topic (Espelage & Swearer, 2004). A school climate in which adults and peers accept bullying fosters bullying. One study revealed that schools with high academic standards, high parental involvement, and effective discipline had less bullying (Ma, 2002).

An increasing number of prevention/intervention programs have been developed to reduce bullying (Bowes & others, 2008; Breakstone, Dreiblatt, & Dreiblatt, 2009). How can bullying be reduced? A recent research review revealed mixed results for school-based intervention (Vreeman & Carroll, 2007). School-based interventions vary greatly, ranging from involving the whole school in an antibullying campaign to individualized social-skills training. Following are two of the most promising school-based bullying intervention programs and where you can obtain information about them:

- *Olweus Bullying Prevention.* Created by Dan Olweus, this program focuses on 6- to 15-year-olds, with the goal of decreasing opportunities and rewards for bullying. School staff are instructed in ways to improve peer relations and

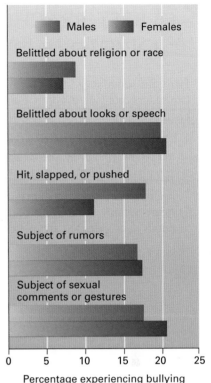

FIGURE 14.5 Bullying Behaviors Among U.S. Youth

This graph shows the types of bullying most often experienced by U.S. youth. The percentages reflect the extent to which bullied students said that they had experienced a particular type of bullying. In terms of gender, note that when they were bullied, boys were more likely to be hit, slapped, or pushed than girls were.

BEST PRACTICES
Strategies for Reducing Bullying

Here are some suggestions for how teachers and schools can reduce bullying (Cohn & Canter, 2003; Hyman & others, 2006; Limber, 1997, 2004; Milsom & Gallo, 2006):

1. *Get older peers to serve as monitors for bullying and intervene when they see it taking place.*

2. *Be aware that bullying often occurs outside the classroom, so you may not actually see it taking place. Also, many victims of bullying don't report the bullying to adults. Unsupervised areas such as the playground, bus,*

and school corridors are common places where students are bullied.

3. *If you observe bullying in your classroom or in other locations, you will need to make a decision about whether it is serious enough to report to school authorities or parents.*

4. *Get together with other teachers and the school administration to develop school-wide rules and sanctions against bullying and post them throughout the school.*

What are some strategies for reducing bullying?

make schools safer. A large study with 2,500 students in 42 schools in Norway found that the Olweus program was effective in reducing bullying (Olweus, 1994). Information on how to implement the program can be obtained from the Center for the Study and Prevention of Violence at the University of Colorado (www.colorado.edu/cspv/blueprints).

- *Bully-Proofing Your School.* This program is tailored for students in kindergarten through the eighth grade and offers a school-wide approach and a teacher curriculum for reducing bullying. It emphasizes how to recognize bullying behavior and quickly respond to it and how to develop students' communication skills in conflict situations. Intervention methods are provided, school posters related to bullying are available, and a parent's guide helps involve parents in effective ways to reduce bullying. Recent research indicates that this program is effective in reducing bullying (Beran & Tutty, 2002; Plog, Epstein, & Porter, 2004). Information about the Bully-Proofing Your School program is available at www.sopriswest.com.

There is increasing concern about *cyberbullying*, which occurs when a child or adolescent is tormented, threatened, harassed, or humiliated by another child or adolescent on the Internet (Aricak & others, 2008; Hinduja & Patchin, 2009; Smith & others, 2008). To learn more about helping students prevent cyberbullying, see the Web site of Stop Cyberbullying (2008) (www.stopcyberbullying.org/).

Defiance or Hostility Toward the Teacher Edmund Emmer and Carolyn Evertson (2009) discussed the following strategies for dealing with students who defy you or are hostile toward you. If students get away with this type of behavior, it likely will continue and even spread. Therefore, try to defuse the event by keeping it private and handling the student individually, if possible. If the defiance or hostility is not extreme and occurs during a lesson, try to depersonalize it and say that you will deal with it in a few minutes to avoid a power struggle. At an appropriate later time, meet with the student and spell out any consequence the misbehavior might merit.

In extreme and rare cases, students will be completely uncooperative, in which case you should send another student to the office for help. In most instances, though, if you stay calm and don't get into a power struggle with the student, the student will calm down, and you can talk with the student about the problem.

Review, Reflect, and Practice

(5) Formulate some effective approaches that teachers can use to deal with problem behaviors.

REVIEW

- What are some minor and moderate interventions for managing problem behaviors in the classroom environment? Who else can help?
- What can the teacher do about fighting, bullying, and defiance? What are some effective school-based bullying intervention programs?

REFLECT

- How worried are you about problem behaviors among the students you plan to teach? In view of your own current skills, personality, and values, what steps could you begin to take to prepare yourself for dealing with them?

PRAXIS™ PRACTICE

1. Mr. Martin is telling his students how to complete their assignment for tomorrow. While he talks, Sally and Shelly are discussing their after-school plans. Mr. Martin should
   a. interrupt his instruction to say, "Listen up, girls or you'll be spending your after school hours with me."
   b. interrupt his instructions to ask, "Is there something that you would like to share with the class, girls?"
   c. keep talking, but look directly at Sally and Shelly; if that doesn't work, slowly approach them.
   d. stop his instructions and wait silently for the girls to stop talking, while looking directly at them, then say, "Thank you, ladies."

2. Ken is a fifth-grade student who is not well liked by his peers. They tease him about the way he looks, the way he dresses, his lack of coordination, and his lack of emotional self-regulation. The bulk of this takes place on the playground during recess. The teasing often reduces Ken to tears, which seems to add fuel to the fire. Which of the following is most likely to reduce this bullying behavior?
   a. in-school suspensions for the bullies
   b. isolating Ken from his peers so he does not have to deal with the bullying
   c. removing the bullies' recess privileges
   d. social-skills training for both the bullies and Ken

Please see the answer key at the end of the book.

CRACK THE CASE
The Case of the Chatty Student

Mrs. Welch was a new middle school language-arts teacher. Prior to beginning her new position, she developed a classroom management plan that mirrored the code of conduct for the school. She expected the students to behave respectfully toward her and toward their classmates. She also expected them to respect school property and the learning environment. In addition, she expected them to keep their hands, feet, and possessions to themselves. Minor behavioral infractions were to result in a verbal warning. Further infractions would net more severe consequences in steps: a detention, a referral to the office, and a call to the students' parents. Mrs. Welch was pleased with her management plan. She distributed it to students on the first day of class. She also distributed it to parents at the annual Back-to-School Night during the first week of school.

Darius, a student in one of Mrs. Welch's seventh-grade classes, was what Mrs. Welch termed "chatty." He was very social and spent much of his class time talking to other students rather than working. Mrs. Welch tried moving him to different parts of the room and tried seating him next to students to whom she had never seen him talk, neither of which decreased his chattiness. He simply made new friends and continued chatting, sometimes disrupting the class in the process. She tried seating him next to girls, and this seemed to make things even worse.

Darius was very bright in addition to being very social. Although he was only in seventh grade, he was taking algebra with a group of mathematically advanced eighth-grade students. This was something of an anomaly in this school; in fact, it had never been done previously. The algebra teacher, Mrs. Zaccinelli, and Darius had a good relationship. He never disrupted her class or misbehaved in any way in her class. Mrs. Zaccinelli was amazed to hear that Darius did not always behave appropriately in his other classes.

Mrs. Zaccinelli served as Mrs. Welch's mentor. She had helped Mrs. Welch to write her classroom management plan and served as a sounding board when she had difficulties. At one point when Mrs. Welch was discussing her eighth-grade classes, Mrs. Zaccinelli referred to inclusion in the eighth-grade algebra class as "a privilege, not a right." She further told Mrs. Welch that she expected her students to behave appropriately at all times.

The next day, Darius was especially talkative in class. Mrs. Welch asked him to stop talking. He did, but he resumed his chatter within five minutes. When he began talking again, Mrs. Welch took him aside and told him loudly, "That's it,

Darius. I'm going to have you removed from algebra class. You know taking that class is a privilege, not a right."

Darius was stunned. He sat quietly for the rest of the period but did not participate. He made no eye contact with Mrs. Welch or any other students. The rest of the day was something of a blur to him. He had no idea how he would explain this to his parents.

When Darius told his mother he was going to be removed from algebra for his behavior in language arts, she immediately went to see Mrs. Welch. She tried to tell Mrs. Welch that to remove Darius from algebra would be to deny him the free and appropriate public education to which he (and all other students) was entitled. Mrs. Welch held her ground and insisted that she could and would have his placement altered.

1. What are the issues in this case?

2. Is removal from algebra class an appropriate consequence for Darius? Why or why not?

3. Do you think removal from algebra class would have a positive effect on Darius's behavior? Why or why not?

4. What impact do you think this would have on his motivation in school?

5. How do you think this situation will impact the relationship between Mrs. Welch and Darius?

6. What do you think Darius's mother will do now?

7. How do you think Mrs. Zaccinelli will react when she hears about the situation?

8. How do you think the principal will react?

9. What should Mrs. Welch do?

10. How would Mrs. Welch's strategy of moving Darius to quiet him be characterized?
    a. This is an example of a minor intervention.
    b. This is an example of a moderate intervention.
    c. This is an example of a severe intervention.
    d. This is an example of an effective intervention.

11. Which of the following is likely to be the most effective way for Mrs. Welch to deal with Darius's chatty behavior?
    a. Make Darius write out a page of the dictionary.
    b. Put tape over Darius's mouth.
    c. Isolate Darius from his peers for the remainder of the period.
    d. Send Darius to the office for the principal to discipline.

Reach Your Learning Goals
Managing the Classroom

(1) WHY CLASSROOMS NEED TO BE MANAGED EFFECTIVELY: Explain why classroom management is both challenging and necessary.

Management Issues in Elementary and Secondary School Classrooms

Many management issues are similar across elementary and secondary school classrooms. However, these differences in elementary and secondary classrooms have meaning for the way classrooms need to be managed: Elementary school teachers often see the same 20 to 25 students all day long; secondary school teachers see 100 to 150 students about 50 minutes a day. Confinement, boredom, and interaction with the same people all day in elementary school can create problems. Secondary school teachers have to get the lesson moving quickly. They also might see a greater range of problems, and their students can have more long-standing problems that are more difficult to modify. These problems can be more severe than those of elementary school students. Secondary school students might demand more elaborate and logical explanations of rules and discipline.

The Crowded, Complex, and Potentially Chaotic Classroom

Six reasons that classrooms are crowded, complex, and potentially chaotic are (1) multidimensionality, (2) simultaneous activities going on, (3) events occurring at a rapid pace, (4) often unpredictable events, (5) lack of privacy, and (6) classroom histories.

Getting Off to the Right Start

Good strategies for getting off to the right start are to (1) establish expectations for behavior and resolve student uncertainties, (2) make sure that students experience success, (3) be available and visible, and (4) be in charge.

Emphasizing Instruction and a Positive Classroom Climate

The focus in educational psychology used to be on discipline. Today it is on developing and maintaining a positive classroom environment that supports learning. This involves using proactive management strategies rather than being immersed in reactive discipline tactics. Historically, the well-managed classroom was conceptualized as a "well-oiled machine," but today it is more often viewed as a "beehive of activity." Kounin found that good classroom managers effectively manage the group's activities.

Management Goals and Strategies

Goals and strategies include (1) helping students spend more time on learning and less time on non-goal-directed activity (maintain activity flow, minimize transition times, and hold students accountable) and (2) preventing students from developing academic and emotional problems.

(2) DESIGNING THE PHYSICAL ENVIRONMENT OF THE CLASSROOM: Describe the positive design of the classroom's physical environment.

Principles of Classroom Arrangement

Basic principles of effective design of the classroom's physical environment include (1) reducing congestion in high-traffic areas, (2) making sure that you can easily see all students, (3) making often-used teaching materials and student supplies easily accessible, and (4) making sure that all students can see whole-class presentations.

Arrangement Style

Classroom arrangement styles include auditorium, face-to-face, off-set, seminar, and cluster. It is important to personalize the classroom and become an environmental designer who considers what activities students will be engaging in, draw up a floor plan, involve students in classroom design, and try out the arrangement and be flexible in redesigning it.

535

3 **CREATING A POSITIVE ENVIRONMENT FOR LEARNING:** Discuss how to create a positive classroom environment.

General Strategies

Use an authoritative style of classroom management rather than an authoritarian or permissive style. The authoritative style involves considerable verbal give-and-take with students, a caring attitude toward students, and limits on student behavior when necessary. Authoritative teaching is linked with competent student behavior. Also, being sensitive to ethnic and socioeconomic variations in students is an important aspect of managing the classroom effectively. Kounin's work revealed other characteristics that were associated with effective classroom management: exhibiting withitness, coping with overlapping situations, maintaining smoothness and continuity in lessons, and engaging students in a variety of challenging activities.

Creating, Teaching, and Maintaining Rules and Procedures

Distinguish between rules and procedures and consider the appropriateness of including students in the discussion and generation of rules. Classroom rules should be (1) reasonable and necessary, (2) clear and comprehensible, (3) consistent with instructional and learning goals, and (4) consistent with school rules.

Getting Students to Cooperate

Getting students to cooperate involves (1) developing a positive relationship with students; (2) getting students to share and assume responsibility (involve students in the planning and implementation of school and classroom initiatives, encourage students to judge their own behavior, don't accept excuses, and give the self-responsibility strategy time to work); and (3) rewarding appropriate behavior (choose effective reinforcers, use prompts and shaping effectively, and use rewards to provide information about mastery).

4 **BEING A GOOD COMMUNICATOR:** Identify some good approaches to communication for both students and teachers.

Speaking Skills

Some barriers to effective speech include being imprecise and vague, using poor grammar, using vocabulary inappropriate for the students' level, and speaking too quickly or too slowly. You and your students will benefit considerably if you have effective speaking skills and you work with your students on developing their speaking skills. Speaking effectively with the class and students involves being a clear communicator, connecting with the audience, using media effectively, and avoiding barriers to verbal communication such as criticizing, name-calling, ordering, and threatening. Both teachers and students can benefit from knowing how to give speeches effectively.

Listening Skills

Active listening occurs when a person gives full attention to the speaker, focusing on both the intellectual and the emotional content of the message. Some good active listening strategies are to (1) pay careful attention to the person who is talking, including maintaining eye contact; (2) paraphrase; (3) synthesize themes and patterns; and (4) give feedback in a competent manner.

Nonverbal Communication

A number of communication experts stress that the majority of communication is nonverbal rather than verbal. It is hard to mask nonverbal communication, so a good strategy is to recognize that nonverbal communication usually reflects how a person really feels. Nonverbal communication involves facial expressions and eye communication, touch, space, and silence.

5 DEALING WITH PROBLEM BEHAVIORS: Formulate some effective approaches that teachers can use to deal with problem behaviors.

Management Strategies

Interventions can be characterized as minor or moderate. Minor interventions involve using nonverbal cues, keeping the activity moving, moving closer to students, redirecting the behavior, giving needed instruction, directly and assertively telling the student to stop the behavior, and giving the student a choice. Moderate interventions include withholding a privilege or a desired activity, isolating or removing students, and imposing a penalty or detention. A good management strategy is to have supportive resources. These include using peers as mediators, calling on parents for support, enlisting the help of a principal or counselor, and finding a mentor for the student.

Dealing with Aggression

Violence is a major, escalating concern in schools. Be prepared for aggressive actions on the part of students so that you can calmly cope with them. Try to avoid an argument or emotional confrontation. Helpful guidelines for dealing with fighting, bullying, and defiance or hostility toward the teacher include developing and posting school-wide rules and sanctions against bullying, defusing the hostile event by keeping it private and handling the student individually, and if needed sending another student to the office for help. Two school-based bullying intervention programs are Olweas Bullying Prevention and Bully-Proofing Your School.

 KEY TERMS

auditorium style 510	cluster style 510	authoritarian classroom	withitness 516
face-to-face style 510	authoritative classroom	management style 513	active listening 524
off-set style 510	management style 513	permissive classroom	
seminar style 510		management style 514	

 PORTFOLIO ACTIVITIES

Now that you have a good understanding of this chapter, complete these exercises to expand your thinking.

Independent Reflection

Cultivating Respectful Student-Teacher Relationships. How self-disclosing and open should teachers be with students? It is important for teachers to develop positive relationships with students, but is there a point at which teachers become too close with their students? Write a personal reflection on this issue, incorporating thoughts about how it might relate to your future work as a teacher. (INTASC: Principle 6)

Collaborative Work

Creating Classroom Rules. List the rules you feel your students must follow. Describe how you might react when students break

these rules. Then get together with three or four of your classmates and discuss each other's lists. Revise your rules based on their feedback. (INTASC: Principle 5)

Research/Field Experience

Researching School Discipline Policies. Interview school counselors at an elementary, a middle, or a high school. Ask them to describe the discipline policies at their schools and to evaluate how well they work. Also ask them to describe the most difficult student problem they have ever dealt with. Write up that problem as a case study. (INTASC: Principles 5, 9)

Go to the Online Learning Center for downloadable portfolio templates.

TAKING IT TO THE NET

- A classroom's organization, physical space, and design highly influence the overall learning environment. List several descriptors that depict your ideal classroom environment. Anticipate challenges, and discuss how you could compensate for a classroom lacking storage space, natural light, or special areas for computer or group work. www.teachervision.com/lesson-plans/lesson-5803.html

- Make a list of rules for your classroom. Review the list and think about these questions: Are the rules worded in a positive manner? Are they appropriate and understandable for your target grade level? Did you consider involving your students in creating the rules? Design a class project for developing rules together as a collaborative group. www.educationworld.com/a_lesson/lesson/lesson274.shtml

- A student continually is disruptive in your class and has difficulty staying on task. You have lost your temper occasionally and have also sent the student to the office, all with no effect on the student's behavior. Develop a new discipline strategy for this student. What do you think the student needs in order to successfully participate in class? www.honorlevel.com

Connect to the Online Learning Center to explore possible answers.

STUDY, PRACTICE, AND SUCCEED

Visit www.mhhe.com/santedu4e to review the chapter with self-grading quizzes and self-assessments, to apply the chapter material to two more Crack the Case studies, and for suggested activities to develop your teaching portfolio.

CHAPTER 15

Standardized Tests and Teaching

People do not have equal talents. But all individuals should have an equal opportunity to develop their talents.

—John F. Kennedy
U.S. President, 20th Century

Chapter Outline

Learning Goals

1 Discuss the nature and purpose of standardized tests as well as the criteria for evaluating them.

2 Compare aptitude and achievement tests and describe different types of achievement tests as well as some issues involved in these tests.

3 Identify the teacher's roles in standardized testing.

4 Evaluate some key issues in standardized testing.

TEACHING STORIES   Barbara Berry

Barbara Berry teaches French and humanities at Ypsilanti High School in Ypsilanti, Michigan, where she also is chairperson of the foreign languages department. She offers this story related to standardized tests:

I had a fourth-year French student who was a wonderful student and clearly had a gift for languages. A minority student, she had been recruited by a major state university and offered a "full-ride" scholarship, provided she met certain requirements on the Scholastic Assessment Test (SAT). She took the test and did well on the verbal part but not well enough on the math part to meet the scholarship requirements. She was taking her fourth year of math classes and receiving above-average grades but said she just didn't like math and didn't understand it.

Although I was teaching French at the time, I knew that I enjoyed math and had done well in school and on standard-

ized tests. I knew that the SAT math section includes a lot of algebra. I offered to tutor her before she retook the SAT. She accepted the offer. I obtained some algebra materials from the math department to help work with her. Mostly, though, she worked on her own, reading the book and doing problems, only coming to me when she encountered problems. We met about once a week. About six weeks later, she retook the test and improved her math SAT score by 110 points. She got the scholarship.

I did not teach this student much math, although I did help her work through some of the more difficult problems. What I did most to help her were two things: (1) I communicated my own enthusiasm for math and expressed confidence in her ability to do it, and (2) I focused her efforts on the material that the test assesses. Since we related so well with each other in my French class, I felt that I could help her feel better about her ability to do math.

Preview

As Barbara Berry's story shows, standardized tests can have a major impact on students' lives. They are widely used to evaluate students' learning and achievement. Although they are increasingly used to compare students' performance in different schools, districts, states, and countries, they are not without controversy. We begin our discussion in this chapter by examining some basic ideas about standardized tests and then distinguish aptitude and achievement tests. Then we explore what your role as a teacher is likely to be in regard to standardized testing and conclude the chapter by describing several important issues in standardized testing.

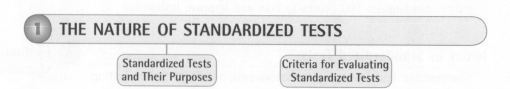

1   THE NATURE OF STANDARDIZED TESTS

| Standardized Tests and Their Purposes | Criteria for Evaluating Standardized Tests |

Chances are, you have taken a number of standardized tests. In kindergarten, you may have taken a school readiness test, in elementary school some basic skills or achievement tests, and in high school the SAT or ACT test for college admission. But what does it mean to say that a test is "standardized"? And what purpose is served by standardized testing?

Standardized Tests and Their Purposes

Standardized tests have uniform procedures for administration and scoring and often allow a student's performance to be compared with the performance of other students at the same age or grade level on a national basis. Standardized tests can serve a number of purposes:

- *Provide information about students' progress.* Standardized tests are a source of information about how well students are performing. Students in one class might get *A*'s but perform at a mediocre level on a nationally standardized test, and students in another class might get *B*'s and do extremely well on the same nationally standardized test. Without an external, objective marker such as a standardized test, individual classroom teachers have difficulty knowing how well their students are performing compared with students elsewhere in the state or nation.

- *Diagnose students' strengths and weaknesses.* Standardized tests also can provide information about a student's learning strengths or weaknesses (Popham, 2008; Taylor & Nolen, 2008). For example, a student who is not doing well in reading might be given one or more standardized tests to pinpoint the student's learning weaknesses. When standardized tests are given for diagnostic purposes, they usually are given individually rather than to a group of students.

- *Provide evidence for placement of students in specific programs.* Standardized tests can be used to make decisions about whether a student should be allowed to enter a specific program. In elementary school, a standardized test might be used to provide information for placing students in different reading groups. In high school, a standardized test might be used to determine which math classes a student should take. In some cases, standardized tests are used along with other information to evaluate whether a student might be allowed to skip a grade or to graduate. Students also might take standardized tests to determine their suitability for particular careers.

- *Provide information for planning and improving instruction.* In conjunction with other information about students, scores from standardized tests can be used by teachers in making decisions about instruction. For example, students' scores on a standardized test of reading skills administered at the start of the school year can help teachers determine the level at which they need to gear their reading instruction. Students' scores on a standardized test at the end of the year might inform teachers about how effective their reading instruction has been, information that could be used to continue similar instruction or modify it accordingly.

- *Contribute to accountability.* Schools and teachers are increasingly being held accountable for students' learning (Stover, 2007). Although this is controversial, standardized tests are being used to determine how effectively schools are using tax dollars (Yell & Drasgow, 2009). In Texas, principals can lose their jobs if their school's standardized test scores don't measure up. In Maryland, schools that don't do well forfeit thousands of dollars in reward money. Interest in accountability has led to the creation of **standards-based tests**, which assess skills that students are expected to have mastered before they can be promoted to the next grade or permitted to graduate (Kingston, 2008a). Schools that use standards-based tests often require students who do not pass the tests to attend special programs in the summer that will help them reach the minimum level of competency required by the school system. **High-stakes testing** is using tests in a way that will have important consequences for the student, affecting decisions such as whether the student will be promoted to the next grade or be allowed to graduate. Later in the chapter, we will discuss state-mandated tests, which are increasingly being used to make such "high-stakes" decisions.

What are some of the most important purposes of standardized tests?

standardized tests Tests that have uniform procedures for administration and scoring and often allow a student's performance to be compared with the performance of other students at the same age or grade level on a national basis.

standards-based tests Tests that assess skills that students are expected to have mastered before they can be promoted to the next grade or permitted to graduate.

high-stakes testing Using tests in a way that will have important consequences for the student, affecting such decisions as whether the student will be promoted or be allowed to graduate.

For now, though, note that an important theme throughout this chapter is that a standardized test should not be the only method for evaluating a student's learning. Nor should standardized tests by themselves be considered sufficient information in holding schools accountable for students' learning (Brookhart, 2008; Popham, 2008).

Criteria for Evaluating Standardized Tests

Among the ways to evaluate standardized tests are to understand whether the test is norm-referenced or criteria-referenced, and the extent to which the test is valid, reliable, and fair. Let's begin our discussion by examining norm-referenced and criterion-referenced tests.

Norm-Referenced and Criterion-Referenced Tests Standardized tests can be norm-referenced or criterion-referenced. A **norm group** is the group of individuals previously tested that provides a basis for interpreting a test score. Thus, in **norm-referenced tests** a student's score is interpreted by comparing it with how others (the norm group) performed (Kingston, 2008b).

The norm-referenced test is said to be based on *national norms* when the norm group consists of a nationally representative group of students. For example, a standardized test for fourth-grade science knowledge and skills might be given to a national sample of fourth-grade students. The scores of the representative sample of thousands of fourth-grade students become the basis for comparison. This norm group should include students from urban, suburban, and rural areas; different geographical regions; private and public schools; boys and girls; and different ethnic groups. Based on an individual student's score on the standardized science test, the teacher can determine whether a student is performing above, on a level with, or below a national norm (Gregory, 2007; Gronlund & Waugh, 2009). The teacher also can see how the class as a whole is performing in relation to the general population of students.

Unlike norm-referenced tests, **criterion-referenced tests** are standardized tests in which the student's performance is compared with established criteria (McMillan, 2007). State standardized tests are typically criteria-referenced tests that do not use norms. For example, criterion-referenced tests might assess whether a student has attained a level of achievement termed "proficient," or reached a certain percentage level, such answering 80 percent of the items correctly. Criterion-referenced tests are designed to assess students' skills and knowledge in specific areas, such as English, math, and science.

Validity, Reliability, and Fairness Whether the standardized test is norm-referenced or criterion-referenced, three important ways to evaluate the test is whether it is valid, reliable, and fair. Let's examine a standardized test's validity first.

Validity Traditionally, validity has been defined as the extent to which a test measures what it is intended to measure. However, an increasing number of assessment experts in education argue that not just the characteristics of the test itself are valid or invalid—rather, it also is important to consider the inferences that are made about the test scores (Leighton, 2008; McMillan, 2007; Suen, 2008). Thus, **validity** involves the extent to which a test measures what it is intended to measure and whether inferences about test scores are accurate.

In terms of the test characteristics themselves—the substance of the test—three types of validity can be described: content validity, criterion validity, and construct validity. A valid standardized test should have good **content validity**, which is the test's ability to sample the content that is to be measured. This concept is similar to "content-related evidence." For example, if a standardized fourth-grade science test purports to assess both content information and problem-solving skills, then the test should include items that measure content information about science and items that measure problem-solving skills.

norm group The group of individuals previously tested that provides a basis for interpreting a test score.

norm-referenced tests Standardized tests in which a student's score is interpreted by comparing it with how others (the norm group) performed.

criterion-referenced tests Standardized tests in which the student's performance is compared with established criteria.

validity The extent to which a test measures what it is intended to measure and whether inferences about the test scores are accurate.

content validity A test's ability to sample the content that is to be measured.

Another form of validity is **criterion validity**, which is the test's ability to predict a student's performance as measured by other assessments or criteria (Parke, 2008). How might criterion validity be assessed for the standardized science test? One method is to get a representative sample of fourth-grade teachers to evaluate the competence of the students in their science classes and then compare those competence ratings with the students' scores on the standardized tests. Another method is to compare the scores of students on the standardized test with the scores of the same students on a different test that was designed to test the same material.

Criterion validity can be either concurrent or predictive (Oosterhof, 2009). **Concurrent validity** is the relation between the test's scores and other criteria that are currently (concurrently) available. For example, does the standardized fourth-grade science test correspond to students' grades in science this semester? If it does, we say that test has high concurrent validity. **Predictive validity** is the relation between test scores and the student's future performance. For example, scores on the fourth-grade science test might be used to predict how many science classes different students will take in high school, whether middle school girls are interested in pursuing a science career, or whether students will win an award in science at some point in the future.

A third type of validity is *construct validity*. A *construct* is an unobservable trait or characteristic of a person, such as intelligence, creativity, learning style, personality, or anxiety. **Construct validity** is the extent to which there is evidence that a test measures a particular construct. Construct validity is the broadest of the types of validity we have discussed and can include evidence from concurrent and predictive validity (Kraska, 2008). Judgments about construct validity might also rely on a description of the development of the test, the pattern of the relations between the test and other significant factors (such as high correlations with similar tests and low correlations with tests measuring different constructs), and any other type of evidence that contributes to understanding the meaning of test scores. Because a construct typically is abstract, a variety of evidence may be needed to determine whether a test validly measures a particular construct.

Earlier we indicated that we should consider not only the substance of the test in determining validity but also whether inferences about the test scores are accurate (McMillan, 2007). Let's look at an example of how this might work. A school superintendent decides to use test scores from a standardized test given to students each spring as an indicator of teacher competence. In other words, the test scores are being used to *infer* whether teachers are competent. These are the validity questions in this situation: How reasonable is it to use standardized test scores to measure teacher competence? Is it actually true (accurate) that teachers whose students score high are more competent than teachers whose students score low?

Reliability **Reliability** is the extent to which a test produces a consistent, reproducible score. To be called reliable, scores must be stable, dependable, and relatively free from errors of measurement (Miller, 2008; Popham, 2008). Reliability can be measured in several ways, including test-retest reliability, alternate-forms reliability, and split-half reliability.

Test-retest reliability is the extent to which a test yields the same performance when a student is given the same test on two occasions. Thus, if the standardized fourth-grade science test is given to a group of students today and then given to them again a month later, the test would be considered reliable if the students' scores were consistent across the two testings. There are two negative features of test-retest reliability: Students sometimes do better the second time they take the test because of their familiarity with it, and some students may have learned information in the time between the first test and the second test that changes their performance.

Alternate-forms reliability is determined by giving different forms of the same test on two different occasions to the same group of students and observing how consistent the scores are. The test items on the two forms are similar but not identical. This strategy eliminates the likelihood that students will perform better on the

---

criterion validity A test's ability to predict a student's performance as measured by other assessments or criteria.

concurrent validity The relation between a test's scores and other criteria that are currently (concurrently) available.

predictive validity The relation between test scores and the student's future performance.

construct validity The extent to which there is evidence that a test measures a particular construct. A construct is an unobservable trait or characteristic of a person, such as intelligence, learning style, personality, or anxiety.

reliability The extent to which a test produces a consistent, reproducible score.

test-retest reliability The extent to which a test yields the same performance when a student is given the same test on two occasions.

alternate-forms reliability Reliability judged by giving different forms of the same test on two different occasions to the same group of students to determine how consistent their scores are.

If it is stated that a test is valid and reliable, what does that mean? What are some different types of validity and reliability?

second test administration due to their familiarity with the items, but it does not eliminate a student's increase in knowledge and increased familiarity with the testing procedures and strategies.

Split-half reliability involves dividing the test items into two halves, such as the odd-numbered and even-numbered items. The scores on the two sets of items are compared to determine how consistently the students performed across each set. When split-half reliability is high, we say that the test is *internally consistent*. For example, on the standardized fourth-grade science test, the students' scores on the odd-numbered and even-numbered items could be compared. If they scored similarly on the two sets of items, we could conclude that the science test had high split-half reliability.

Reliability is influenced by a number of errors in measurement. A student can have adequate knowledge and skill, yet still not perform consistently across several tests because of a number of internal and external factors. Internal factors include health, motivation, and anxiety. External factors include inadequate directions given by the examiner, ambiguously created items, poor sampling of information, and inefficient scoring. When students perform inconsistently across the same or similar tests of their knowledge and skill, careful analysis should be made of internal and external factors that may have contributed to the inconsistency.

Validity and reliability are related (Gregory, 2007). A test that is valid is reliable, but a test that is reliable is not necessarily valid. People can respond consistently on a test, but the test might not be measuring what it purports to measure. To understand this, imagine that you have three darts to throw. If all three fall close together, you have reliability. However, you have validity only if all three hit the bull's-eye.

Fairness and Bias Fair tests are unbiased and nondiscriminatory (McMillan, 2007). They are not influenced by factors such as gender, ethnicity, or subjective factors such as the bias of a scorer. When tests are fair, students have the opportunity to demonstrate their learning so that their performance is not affected by their gender, ethnicity, disability, or other factors unrelated to the purpose of the test.

An unfair test is a test that puts a particular group of students at a disadvantage (Bolt, 2008; Popham, 2008). This often occurs when there is something about the test

split-half reliability Reliability judged by dividing the test items into two halves, such as the odd-numbered and even-numbered items. The scores on the two sets of items are compared to determine how consistently the students performed across each set.

that makes it more difficult for students with certain characteristics. For instance, suppose a test that is supposed to assess writing skills asks students to write a short story about a boy who practices very hard to be good in football and makes the team. Clearly, this type of item will be easier for boys than girls because boys are generally more familiar with football, so the test will be unfair to girls as an assessment of their writing skills. Consider also an item that might be used to assess reading comprehension. The reading passage is about a sailing experience. Thus, students who have had experience in sailing are likely to have an easier time reading and understanding the passage than those who have not. It is impossible to completely eliminate all unfair aspects of a test for every student, but test-makers can do much to create tests that are as fair as possible.

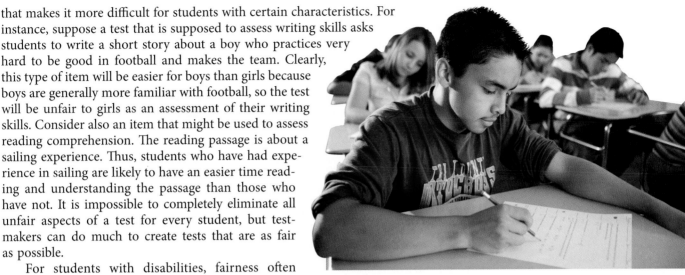

What are some characteristics of fair and unfair tests?

For students with disabilities, fairness often requires adaptations in administering the test (Friend, 2008). Many of the adaptations depend on the particular disability. The goal is to lessen the negative influence of the disability on the trait being tested. For example, for students with a hearing disability, be sure that the directions are written; for students with a visual problem, be sure that directions are given orally.

Review, Reflect, and Practice

(1) **Discuss the nature and purpose of standardized tests as well as the criteria for evaluating them.**

REVIEW

- What is meant by standardized test? What are the uses of standardized tests?
- What are norm-referenced and criterion-referenced tests? Why are validity, reliability, and fairness important in judging the quality of a standardized test?

REFLECT

- Can a test be valid but not reliable? Reliable but not valid? Explain in your own words.

PRAXIS™ PRACTICE

1. Which of the following is the best example of using the results of a standardized test to provide information for planning and improving instruction?
   a. At Lincoln Elementary School, students take a standardized achievement test each year to help determine who is in need of specialized services.
   b. At Jefferson Elementary School, teacher salary increases are based in part on student performance on the state-mandated standardized test.
   c. Mr. Whitney uses the results of the social studies portion of the state-mandated standardized achievement test to help him to see how well his instruction is working to help his students meet state standards in history.
   d. Ms. Walker uses the results of a standardized reading test to place her students into small instructional reading groups. She gives the same test several times throughout the school year to gauge progress and regroup students.

(continued)

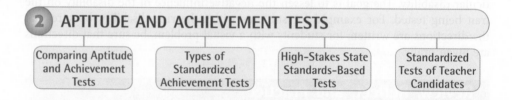

2 APTITUDE AND ACHIEVEMENT TESTS

| Comparing Aptitude and Achievement Tests | Types of Standardized Achievement Tests | High-Stakes State Standards-Based Tests | Standardized Tests of Teacher Candidates |

There are two main types of standardized tests: aptitude tests and achievement tests. First, we will define and compare these types of tests, then examine different types of achievement tests. Next, we'll describe high-stakes state standards-based tests, as well as standardized tests of teacher candidates.

Comparing Aptitude and Achievement Tests

An **aptitude test** is designed to predict a student's ability to learn a skill or accomplish something with further education and training. Aptitude tests include general mental ability tests such as the intelligence tests (Stanford-Binet, Wechsler scales, and so on) that we described in Chapter 4, "Individual Variations." They also include tests used to predict success in specific academic subjects or occupational areas. For example, one aptitude test might be given to students to predict their future success in math, whereas another might be given to predict whether an individual is likely to do well in sales or medicine.

An **achievement test** is intended to measure what the student has learned or what skills the student has mastered (Gronlund & Waugh, 2009). However, the distinction between aptitude and achievement tests is sometimes blurred. Both types of tests assess a student's current status, the questions they use are often quite similar, and usually the results of the two kinds of tests are highly correlated.

The SAT that you may have taken as part of your admission to college is usually described as an aptitude test, but the SAT can be an aptitude test or an achievement test, depending on the purpose for which it is used. If it is used to predict your success in college, it is an aptitude test. If it is used to determine what you have learned (such as vocabulary, reading comprehension, and math skills), it is an achievement test.

Types of Standardized Achievement Tests

There are numerous types of standardized achievement tests. One common way to classify them is as survey batteries, specific subject tests, or diagnostic tests.

aptitude test A type of test that is used to predict a student's ability to learn a skill or accomplish something with further education and training.

achievement test A test that measures what the student has learned or what skills the student has mastered.

Survey Batteries   A *survey battery* is a group of individual subject-matter tests that is designed for a particular level of students. Survey batteries are the most widely used national norm-referenced standardized tests (McMillan, 2004). Some common batteries are the California Achievement Tests, Iowa Tests of Basic Skills, Metropolitan Achievement Tests, and Stanford Achievement Test Series.

Many survey batteries also contain a number of subtests within a subject area. For example, the Metropolitan Achievement Tests include reading as one of the subject areas at each level. The reading subtests on the Metropolitan Tests include vocabulary, word recognition, and reading comprehension.

In their early years, survey batteries consisted of multiple-choice items to assess the student's content knowledge. However, recent editions have increasingly included open-ended items that evaluate the student's thinking and reasoning skills.

Tests for Specific Subjects   Some standardized achievement tests assess skills in a particular area such as reading or mathematics. Because they focus on a specific area, they usually assess the skill in a more detailed, extensive way than a survey battery. Two examples of specific area tests that involve reading are the Woodcock Reading Mastery Tests and the Gates-McKillop-Horowitz Reading Diagnostic Test. Some standardized subject-area tests cover such topics as chemistry, psychology, or computer science that are not included in survey batteries.

Diagnostic Tests   As we said earlier, diagnosis is an important function of standardized testing. *Diagnostic testing* consists of a relatively in-depth evaluation of a specific area of learning. Its purpose is to determine the specific learning needs of a student so that those needs can be met through regular or remedial instruction. Reading and mathematics are the two areas in which standardized tests are often used for diagnosis.

Test publishers of all national norm-referenced standardized achievement tests claim that their tests can be used for diagnosis (McMillan, 2004). However, for a test to be effective in diagnosis it should have several test items for each skill or objective that is measured, and many of these national tests fall short in this regard.

High-Stakes State Standards-Based Tests

As the public and government have demanded increased accountability of how effectively schools are educating our nation's children, state standards-based tests have taken on a more powerful role (Popham, 2008).

States have mandated tests for many years, but their emphasis has recently changed (Airasian & Russell, 2008). Prior to the 1990s, their content was not closely linked with what was actually taught and learned in the classroom. The early state-mandated assessments simply provided an overall view of how students in a state were performing in certain subject areas, especially reading and mathematics.

In the 1990s, efforts began to connect state-mandated testing to state-endorsed instructional objectives. Most states already have identified or are in the process of identifying objectives that every student in the state is expected to achieve. These objectives form the basis not only for these mandated standards-based tests but also for such activities as teacher education and curriculum decisions. Teachers are strongly encouraged to incorporate these objectives into their classroom planning and instruction. In many states, the objectives are reflected in the achievement tests that are given to every student in the state.

The Format of State Standards-Based Tests   From a constructivist point of view, state standards-based tests have the wrong format, consisting mainly of multiple-choice items. When construction-based assessments are included, they typically involve short-answer items or writing prompts. Very few states include a portfolio as part of their assessment. Almost all states use criterion-referenced scoring, which means that the student's score is evaluated against predetermined standards.

Possible Advantages and Uses of High-Stakes Testing A number of policy-makers argue that high-stakes state standards-based testing will have a number of positive effects:

- Improved student performance
- More time teaching the subjects tested
- High expectations for all students
- Identification of poorly performing schools, teachers, and administrators
- Improved confidence in schools as test scores increase

The widest uses of these tests for guiding the progress of individual students have to do with decisions regarding remediation, promotion, and graduation. Remediation consists of assigning students who do not do well on the tests to special classes. Such remediation usually occurs after school, on Saturday, or during the summer. Currently, thirteen states require and fund remediation strategies to help low-performing students reach state standards.

Many endorsers of state standards-based tests argue that students should not be promoted to the next grade without reaching a certain standard of performance on the tests. In this regard, the goal is to end social promotion (promotion based on the idea that students should not be left behind their age-mates). Currently, test-based promotion policies have been instituted in nine states.

State standards-based tests are also being used to determine whether a student should be allowed to graduate from high school in twenty-four states. Such a decision can have a major impact on a youth's future (McNergney & McNergney, 2007).

In addition, state standards-based tests are used to make decisions about school and staff accountability. Holding schools accountable means using test scores to place the schools in designated categories, such as watch/warning (which is publicly reported and implies that improvement is expected); probation (which usually requires the school to submit a comprehensive reform plan); failing/in crisis (which requires serious outside assistance in developing an improvement plan); accredited, accredited with warning, and nonaccredited.

Criticism of State Standards-Based Tests Critics of the state standards-based tests argue that state-mandated tests lead to these negative consequences (McMillan, 2002):

- *Dumbing down the curriculum with greater emphasis on rote memorization than on problem-solving and critical-thinking skills.* In one analysis, most state tests focused on less-demanding knowledge and skills rather than more-complex cognitive skills (Quality Counts, 2001). This narrows the curriculum and focuses it more on lower-order cognitive skills. Adhering to a test-driven curriculum often means superficial coverage of topics.
- *Teaching to the test.* Teachers increasingly teach knowledge and skills that are to be covered on the state tests (Stiggins, 2008). They spend inordinate amounts of time on testlike activities and practice tests, with less time for actual teaching of important content and skills. In one survey, more than six of ten public school teachers said that state standards-based testing has led to teaching that focuses too much on state tests (Quality Counts, 2001). About two-thirds indicated that state standards-based testing was forcing them to concentrate too much on information that would be tested, to the detriment of other important areas.
- *Discrimination against low-socioeconomic-status (SES) and ethnic minority children.* This results when disproportionate percentages of these children do not meet the state standards, while higher-SES and non-Latino White students do. Researchers have found that students who are placed in the lowest tracks or remedial programs—disproportionately low-income and minority students—are most likely to experience subsequent inferior teaching and reduced achieve-

What are some criticisms of state standards-based tests?

ment (Cooper & Sherk, 1989; Oakes, 1990). There is evidence that high-stakes state standards-based testing that rewards or sanctions schools based on average student scores can create incentives for pushing low-scorers into special education, holding them back a grade, and encouraging them to drop out of school so that the schools' average scores will look better (Darling-Hammond, 2001).

For these reasons and others, the American Psychological Association, the American Educational Research Association, and the National Council on Measurement in Education have issued standards for the use of tests, noting that test scores are too limited and unstable to be used as the sole source of information for any major decision about student placement or promotion. Test scores should always be used in combination with other sources of information about student achievement when making important decisions about students (National Research Council, 2001).

Because high-stakes state standards-based testing is relatively new, there is little systematic research on its consequences (McMillan, 2007). However, there are some serious concerns about the way high-stakes testing currently is structured. One concern involves the validity of the inferences that can be drawn from the results (National Research Council, 2001). Just documenting higher test scores does not mean that education has improved. Indeed, if the tests are assessing the wrong skills or are flawed, it could mean just the opposite. As yet, we do not know if the high-stakes testing is causing students to be better prepared for college and the workplace.

Yet another concern is the extent to which high-stakes testing is useful for improving teaching and learning—the ultimate goal of educational reforms (National Research Council, 2001; Stiggins, 2008). Most current high-stakes tests provide very limited information for teachers and administrators about why students do not perform well or how they can modify instruction to improve student achievement. Most of the high-stakes tests provide only general information about where a student stands relative to peers (such as scoring at the 63rd percentile) or whether the students have not performed well in certain domains (such as performing below the basic level in mathematics). Such tests do not provide information about whether students are using misguided strategies to solve problems or which concepts in a domain students do not understand. In sum, most current high-stakes tests do not provide information about the types of interventions that would improve students' performance or even yield information about their strengths and weaknesses.

THROUGH THE EYES OF STUDENTS

"It's as if a Test Score Is All There Is to a Person"

"Spend enough time in school and you start to think that standardized tests are the only things that matter in life. My standardized test scores are disappointing but I take pride in being in the top four percent of my class. I have a 4.0 GPA. If I can pull off those kinds of grades in tough classes—including three Advanced Placement courses—I'm forced to wonder, what do these tests really prove?

"It's as if a test score is all there is to a person. I enjoy all kinds of creative writing, and I spend long nights trying to *understand* school subjects, rather than just memorize formulas. But none of this matters for standardized tests" (Garcia, 2001).

Tania Garcia
Twelfth-Grade Student
Oakland High School
Oakland, California

We also know that it is not a good strategy to rely solely on a single test when making important decisions about students or evaluating schools (Brookhart & Nitko, 2007). Multiple indicators—including grades, attendance, performance assessments, and percentage of students who go to college—also need to be considered. We also know that if state standards-based tests continue to be used, they need to be changed to better reflect higher-order thinking skills, not encourage teachers to teach to the test, and not penalize students from low-income and minority backgrounds (Stiggins, 2008). Later in the chapter, we will further discuss problems with the formats of high-stakes testing.

No Child Left Behind In Chapter 1, we described the No Child Left Behind (NCLB) Act, the federal government's legislation that was signed into law in 2002. NCLB is the U.S. government's effort to hold schools and school districts accountable for the success or failure of their students. The legislation shifts responsibility to the states, with states being required to create their own standards for students' achievement in mathematics, English/language arts, and science. Reading and math assessments in grades 3 to 8 were required through 2006, then beginning in the 2007–2008 school year, science assessments were made in elementary, middle, and high schools. The goal by 2014 is that every U.S. student will test to proficiency in core math and literacy skills (Gleibermann, 2007; Shaul, 2007).

States are required to create an accountability system that ensures students are making adequate annual progress in the subject areas just mentioned (Yell, 2008; Yell & Drasgow, 2009). Schools that fail to make *adequate yearly progress (AYP)* for two consecutive years are labeled "underperforming." Underperforming schools are to be given special help, but they must give parents the option of moving their children to a better-performing school (Sadker, Sadker, & Zittleman, 2008). If underperforming schools don't improve after four years, states are required to implement major staff and curriculum changes in the schools, and if progress is not made after five years, states must close the schools. A difficulty in achieving AYP is that it must be achieved not only for the entire school but certain subgroups of students as well, including those who are economically disadvantaged, students from ethnic minority groups, students with disabilities, and students with limited English proficiency (Hallahan, Kauffman, & Pullen, 2009; Tileston & Darling, 2008).

Also as part of the No Child Left Behind legislation, states and districts are required to provide report cards that show a school's performance level, so that the public is aware of which schools are underperforming. Another aspect of the No Child Left Behind legislation is that all teachers now are required to be "highly qualified," which means being licensed and having an academic major in the field in which they are teaching. Schools are required to notify parents if a teacher is not "highly qualified." A recent analysis revealed considerable variability across states in what constitutes a highly qualified teacher (Birman & others, 2007). The percentage of teachers who fell into the "not highly qualified category" was higher for special education teachers, teachers of limited proficiency English students, middle school teachers, and teachers in high-poverty and high ethnic minority schools.

Each state is allowed to have different criteria for what constitutes passing or failing grades on tests designated for NCLB inclusion. An analysis of NCLB data indicated that almost every fourth-grade student in Mississippi knows how to read but only half of Masschusetts's students do (King, 2007). Clearly, Mississippi's standard for passing the reading test are far below that of Massachusetts. In the recent analysis of state-by-state comparisons, many states have taken the safe route and are keeping the passing bar low. Thus, while one of NCLB's goals was to raise standards for achievement in U.S. schools, apparently allowing states to set their own standards likely has lowered achievement.

A number of criticisms of No Child Left Behind have been made. Some critics argue that the NCLB legislation will do more harm than good (Connors, 2007; Lewis, 2007). In a recent book, leading educator Nel Noddings (2007) criticized virtually every aspect of NCLB, arguing that it does not provide educationally justifiable interpretations of accountability, standards, and testing. Another leading educator, Michael Pressley (2007), commented that there is too much testing in today's schools and that teachers are spending way too much time preparing for standardized tests.

One widely adopted criticism stresses that using a single score from a test as the sole indicator of students' and teachers' progress and competence represents a very narrow aspect of students' and teachers' skills. This criticism is similar to the one leveled at IQ testing, described in Chapter 4. To more accurately assess student progress and achievement, many psychologists and educators argue that a number of measures should be used—including tests, quizzes, projects, portfolios, and classroom observations—rather than a single score on a single test. Also, the tests schools are using to assess achievement and progress as part of NCLB don't measure such important skills as creativity, motivation, persistence, flexible thinking, and social skills (Goldberg, 2005). Critics point out that teachers and schools are spending far too much class time "teaching only to the test" by drilling students and having them memorize isolated facts at the expense of more student-centered constructivist teaching that focuses on higher-level thinking skills, which students need for success in life (Neil, 2006).

Another criticism is that the increased cost of carrying out standardized testing on a state-wide basis, including creating tests, administering them, scoring them, and reporting their results to the federal government, comes at a time when most states are facing budget crunches (Lewis, 2005). Having to spend so much more money on testing means that some existing resources and programs in other areas will have to be trimmed or eliminated (Kubick & McLoughlin, 2005).

One goal of NCLB is to close the ethnic achievement gap that characterizes lower achievement by African American and Latino students and higher achievement by Asian American and non-Latino White students. However, leading expert Linda Darling-Hammond (2007) recently concluded that NCLB has failed to reach this goal. She criticizes NCLB for inappropriate assessment of English language learners and students with special needs, strong incentives to exclude low-achieving students from school to achieve test score targets, and the continued shortage of highly qualified teachers in high-need schools.

Other criticisms of NCLB were described in Chapter 6, "Learners Who Are Exceptional," and Chapter 9, "Complex Cognitive Processes." Recall that some individuals are concerned that in the era of No Child Left Behind policy there is a neglect of students who are gifted in the effort to raise the achievement level of students who are not doing well (Clark, 2008; Cloud, 2007). So too is there mounting concern that No Child Left Behind legislation has harmed the development of students' creative thinking by focusing attention on the memorization of content (Beghetto & Kaufman, 2009; Sternberg, 2009).

Despite such criticisms, the U.S. Department of Education is committed to implementing No Child Left Behind, and schools are making accommodations to meet the requirement of this law (Hirsch, 2007; Stover, 2007). Indeed, most educators support the importance of high expectations and high standards of excellence for students and teachers. At issue, however, is whether the tests and procedures mandated by NCLB are the best ones for achieving these high standards (Campbell, 2007; Kauffman & Konold, 2007).

Educators are increasingly interested in ways that technology can be used effectively in conjunction with standardized tests, such as those required by No Child Left Behind. To read about how this was accomplished in an early literacy program in New Mexico, see the *Technology and Education* interlude.

DEVELOPMENTAL FOCUS 15.1

What Is Your Opinion of the No Child Left Behind Act?

Early Childhood

Our preschool receives state funding so that financially disadvantaged children receive a quality preschool experience that their parents would not otherwise be able to afford. The No Child Left Behind Act is controversial and continues to be hotly debated; however, no matter what your opinion is, unless educational opportunities are created for the least financially able, the American educational system will never be equal for all. Everyone deserves a chance to shine, and a quality preschool education is a start.

—Valarie Gorham, *Kiddie Quarters, Inc.*

Elementary School: Grades K–5

The NCLB Act is an idealistic approach to measuring student growth and teacher effectiveness. Just as no one program works in every classroom, we cannot expect all children to meet the same standards regardless of their background or experiences. The stress of having to meet state benchmarks and increase scores on state and/or national tests has taken a toll on veteran teachers. For us, teaching is no longer fun—we are now required to teach so many test-specific skills that we are unable to instill a lifelong love of learning in our students.

—Karen Perry, *Cooper Mountain Elementary School*

Middle School: Grades 6–8

NCLB is a typical example of how the education "pendulum" swings too far in any given direction. Although testing is important, NCLB makes testing the ultimate measuring tool. Many students who do not excel at reading or math (or who struggle with standardized tests) are seen as failures, as are the schools they attend. Ironically, these students and schools spend so much time trying to remediate for the tests that they are not allowed to explore other options in which the student might thrive.

—Mark Fodness, *Bemidji Middle School*

High School: Grades 9–12

I find it somewhat ridiculous that teachers are graded by how well their students do. Are dentists judged by how many patients have zero cavities? On the other hand, NCLB does hold teachers accountable and raises the bar. In that sense, it is beneficial.

—Jennifer Heiter, *Bremen High School*

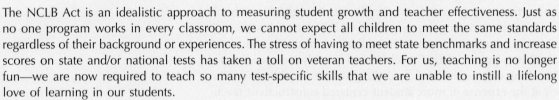

Standardized Tests of Teacher Candidates

Not only do students have to take standardized tests, but as you are likely aware, so do teacher candidates (Darling-Hammond, 2006; Pecheone & Chung, 2006). Many teacher candidates are required to take some version of the PRAXIS™ tests or a test created by an individual state.

The PRAXIS™ Tests and State Tests for Teachers   Most states now require teacher candidates to take a licensing exam. In some cases, this involves one or more PRAXIS™ tests published by Educational Testing Service or a test that is used only by a particular state. A recent count indicated that 43 states now use PRAXIS™ tests (Hack, 2008). The tests used by states for licensing of teacher candidates assess (1) basic skills or general academic ability; (2) subject-matter knowledge (such as math, English, science, or social studies); and/or (3) pedagogical knowledge. In many cases, there is little consistency across states in which specific tests are used.

TECHNOLOGY AND EDUCATION
Standardized Testing, Data-Driven Decision Making, and Handheld Computers

The growing emphasis on accountability and data-driven decision making occasioned by the No Child Left Behind legislation has prompted educators to think differently about how standardized assessments and resulting data can inform classroom instruction, and ultimately affect student achievement. Educators across the country, therefore, are working hard to develop strategies that provide standardized test data to stakeholders at all levels of the educational system and offer teachers technical assistance to administer assessments and use results effectively. Increasingly, districts and schools are turning to technology-based applications.

A good example is the state of New Mexico's early literacy program. A recipient of a federal Department of Education Reading First grant, the state recognized that Reading First offered them not only a unique opportunity to support literacy instruction, but also a way to collect and use data in

A New Mexico teacher using a handheld computer in student assessment.

a standardized fashion. State education officials contracted with Wireless Generation, a company that provides mobile software for early literacy assessments and that allows teachers to use handheld computers to administer assessments, record student data, and then upload that assessment data to a desktop computer and to a Web site where it is immediately made available in graphic form. This lets teachers view a student's assessment results, as well as individual student data in relation to previous assessments or assessment data from other students in the same classroom. While several

assessments reside on the handhelds, the state required that the participating teachers administer the Dynamic Indicators of Basic Early Literacy Skills, also known as the DIBELS (Good & Kaminski, 2003) to all of their students during three assessment windows throughout the school year—fall, winter, and spring.

Researchers found many benefits for the handheld computers in the program (Hupert & Heinze, 2006). Teachers reported that the use of handhelds was much more efficient. They said it was much easier to bring the handheld around with them to administer the DIBELS. Also the results were instantly uploaded in contrast to having to reenter pencil and paper data. This led to a second benefit, instantaneous feedback—teachers immediately saw results in a variety of formats for both individual students and their entire class. These first two benefits, in turn, led to several others, including shaping professional development opportunities to address perceived problems, strengthening home-school communications in that teachers could immediately report on student achievement, and enhancing the use of data to drive instruction.

The success of New Mexico's Reading First project has led several other states (Florida, Oklahoma, and Ohio), the Bureau of Indian Affairs, and school districts, such as those of Chicago and New York City, to contract with Wireless Generation to supply participating teachers with handhelds to administer the DIBELS.

The PRAXIS™ tests consist of PRAXIS I™, PRAXIS II™, and PRAXIS III™. The *PRAXIS I*™ test is a preliminary screening of basic skills that is often taken early in an undergraduate program or before a student is formally admitted to a teacher certification program.

PRAXIS II™ tests are essentially exit exams that typically are taken in the junior or senior year of undergraduate school to ensure that students know their specialty content areas and/or effective pedagogy before being awarded a preliminary teaching certificate (Shorall, 2009). The PRAXIS II™ tests cover four main categories: (1) organizing content knowledge for student learning, (2) creating an environment for student learning, (3) teaching for student learning, and (4) teacher professionalism. They use a case-study approach to measure students' pedagogical knowledge. The PRAXIS II™ tests are oriented toward specific age groups (elementary school—K–6; middle school—grades 5–9; and secondary school—grades 7–12).

PRAXIS III™ tests are assessments of classroom teaching performance. They are typically administered during the first year of teaching and can be used as part of

DEVELOPMENTAL FOCUS 15.2

What Were Your Experiences with the Teachers' Standardized Test?

Early Childhood

Preschool teachers do not need to pass state-standardized tests. There are, however, certificate programs for those who choose to teach young children.

—Valarie Gorham, *Kiddie Quarters, Inc.*

Elementary School: Grades K–5

I honestly don't remember much about the test I took because it was over 19 years ago. What I do remember was that it was rigorous, and that I reviewed all I could think of in math, reading, and writing before the test. I also thought about and reflected on my education and what kind of philosophy I wanted to adopt as a teacher.

—Craig Jensen, *Cooper Mountain Elementary School*

Middle School: Grades 6–8

Taking the PRAXIS™ test was an extremely intense and stressful time for me. For the PRAXIS™ II, I bought a study guide. I worked with the guide for about two weeks before the test, which prepared me—however, the test was still difficult because either you know the information or you don't.

—Casey Maass, *Edison Middle School*

High School: Grades 9–12

When taking these types of tests, it is important to be able to write with a clock blinking on the computer screen. I practiced for this particular scenario by playing video games so I got used to performing under the pressure of a blinking clock.

—Sandy Swanson, *Menomonee Falls High School*

a licensing decision. PRAXIS III™ tests include essays, oral response tests, listening tasks, portfolio reviews, video stimuli, and in-class observation.

Criticisms of the current PRAXIS™ and state licensure tests for teacher candidates have been made. Three such criticisms follow (Darling-Hammond & Baratz-Snowden, 2005, pp. 61–62):

- *Tests assess "low-level or marginally relevant knowledge and skills" rather than "deep knowledge of subject matter and actual teaching skills."*
- *The cutoff scores for the tests sometimes are low or not enforced.* If states are experiencing a shortage of teachers, "they often waive the testing requirement" and hire individuals who have failed the test.
- *There is a lack of consistency across states that has restricted teacher mobility.* This is especially a problem because some states have teacher surpluses, others teacher shortages.

The Call for a National Test for Teacher Candidates   Currently, no national test is required for teacher candidates, but recently the call for one was made (Wineburg, 2006). The National Academy of Education, which is made up of a distinguished group of educators, prepared *A Good Teacher in Every Classroom* (Darling-Hammond & Baratz-Snowden, 2005). The report states that the national test should assess a common core of knowledge for professional preparation, including how to create learning opportunities that make subjects accessible to all students. The National Academy of Education also recommended that the test results should be incorporated into state licensing requirements:

Such a test, like those used to certify doctors, lawyers, and architects, should demonstrate not only what teachers *know* about their subjects and how to teach them but also what they can *do* in the classroom; for example, whether they can plan and implement lessons to teach standards, evaluate students' needs and design instruction to meet them, use a variety of teaching strategies, and maintain a purposeful, productive classroom. Fortunately, assessments that use videotapes of teaching and teachers' and students' work samples to evaluate what teachers actually do in the classroom have been developed by the National Board for Professional Teaching Standards (for use in certifying veteran accomplished teachers) and by states such as Connecticut for use in licensing beginning teachers. (Darling-Hammond & Baratz-Snowden, 2005, pp. 62–63)

Review, Reflect, and Practice

(2) Compare aptitude and achievement tests and describe different types of achievement tests as well as some issues involved in these tests.

REVIEW

- How can aptitude and achievement tests be compared?
- What are survey batteries, specific subject tests, and diagnostic tests?
- What are some possible advantages to high-stakes state standards-based testing and what are some ways their results are being used? What are some criticisms of high-stakes state standards-based testing?
- How can standardized tests of teachers be characterized?

REFLECT

- What value do you see in the No Child Left Behind legislation? What problems? Should No Child Left Behind legislation be abolished or retained? Explain.

PRAXIS™ PRACTICE

1. Which of the following would be an appropriate use of an aptitude test?
   a. Josh takes a standardized test to help determine whether he is likely to be successful in medical school.
   b. Pete takes a standardized test to help determine what he has learned in his teacher preparation program.
   c. Stan takes a standardized test to determine to what degree he has met state mathematics standards.
   d. Penelope takes a standardized test to determine if she can graduate from high school.

2. Ms. Jerovitz is reviewing the results of a standardized achievement test her students have taken. She carefully examines and charts the scores on each of the subtests included in the test. She has scores in mathematical reasoning, computation, vocabulary, reading comprehension, spelling, science, and social studies. What type of test did her students most likely take?
   a. diagnostic test
   b. aptitude test
   c. intelligence test
   d. survey battery

3. Ms. Comer is frustrated by the state standards-based tests she must give to her third-grade students. State funding for the district is now tied to performance on these tests. As a result, Ms. Comer and other teachers are under pressure from

(continued)

Review, Reflect, and Practice

the administration and board of education to ensure that all students meet state standards. Which of the following is the most likely outcome of this scenario?

a. Ms. Comer and other teachers will become better teachers so that their students will achieve at higher levels.

b. Ms. Comer and other teachers will begin to teach only the things that will be covered on the state standards-based test, thus narrowing the curriculum and student learning opportunities.

c. Ms. Comer and other teachers will ignore the pressure from administrators and the board of education, continue to teach as they always have, and hope for the best.

d. Ms. Comer and other teachers will spend more time enriching their curriculum so that students will achieve at higher levels.

4. Sally is nervous about the test she will be taking as part of the teacher certification process. The test will cover information regarding educational psychology and child development. Which test is Sally most likely taking?

a. PRAXIS I™

b. PRAXIS II™

c. PRAXIS III™

d. National Teacher Certification Test

Please see the answer key at the end of the book.

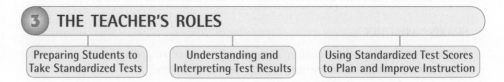

3 | THE TEACHER'S ROLES

| Preparing Students to Take Standardized Tests | Understanding and Interpreting Test Results | Using Standardized Test Scores to Plan and Improve Instruction |

The teacher's roles in standardized testing include preparing students for the test, understanding and interpreting test results, and communicating test results to parents. Teachers also use test scores to plan and improve instruction.

Preparing Students to Take Standardized Tests

All students need the opportunity to do their best. One way to do this is to make sure that students have good test-taking skills (McMillan, 2007; Tileston & Darling, 2008). You should communicate a positive attitude about the test to students. Explain the test's nature and purpose and describe it as an opportunity and a challenge rather than an ordeal. Avoid saying anything that can cause students to get nervous about the test. If you observe that anxiety in some students may hinder their performance, consider having a counselor talk with them about ways to reduce their test anxiety.

Some don'ts regarding teachers preparing students for standardized tests include (McMillan, 2002): don't teach to the test, don't use the standardized test format for classroom tests, don't describe tests as a burden, don't tell students that important decisions will be made solely on the results of a single test, don't use previous forms of the same test to prepare students, and don't convey a negative attitude about the test.

DEVELOPMENTAL FOCUS 15.3
How Do You Prepare Your Students for Standardized Tests?

Early Childhood

A standard test is administered to our preschool children twice per school year. In September, it measures how much they know; in the spring, it measures how much they have learned. The test is hands-on; children manipulate materials and answer questions aloud. There is no preparation for this test.

—Valarie Gorham, *Kiddie Quarters, Inc.*

Elementary School: Grades K–5

We practice on sample tests, discussing the kinds of questions that will appear on the test, strategies for answers, and general good attitudes for test taking (for example, don't rush, read the whole question). We also reorganize the desks so that students get used to the testing configuration. I have students stretch, take deep breaths, and wriggle their fingers in order to warm up for the test. I also make a few cheerful comments before the test to relax them.

—Keren Abra, *Convent of the Sacred Heart Elementary School*

Middle School: Grades 6–8

As a social studies teacher, I assist the language-arts and reading teachers in preparing students for the standardized exam by helping students build their writing skills. I assign essays after each unit and teach students to prepare the essays in the same way that they will need to do on the state test. The social studies department in my district meets monthly with the language-arts department so that we can work together to raise test scores.

—Casey Maass, *Edison Middle School*

High School: Grades 9–12

In addition to going over the standard test-taking strategies, we also stress the importance of eating a filling breakfast the day of the test and getting a good night's sleep the night before the test.

—Jennifer Heiter, *Bremen High School*

Understanding and Interpreting Test Results

Knowledge of some basic descriptive statistics will help you interpret standardized tests. Your ability to understand and interpret standardized tests will come in handy when you have parent-teacher conferences regarding children in your class. We will discuss these basic statistics as well as some ways that test results are commonly reported.

Understanding Descriptive Statistics Our primary focus here is on **descriptive statistics**, which are mathematical procedures used to describe and summarize data (information) in a meaningful way. We will study frequency distributions, measures of central tendency, measures of variability, and the normal distribution.

Frequency Distributions The first step in organizing data involves creating a **frequency distribution**, a listing of scores, usually from highest to lowest, along with the number of times each score appears. Imagine that a test was given and 21 students received the following scores on the test: 96, 95, 94, 92, 88, 88, 86, 86, 86, 86, 84, 83, 82, 82, 82, 78, 75, 75, 72, 68, and 62. Figure 15.1a shows a frequency distribution for these scores. Frequency distributions often are presented graphically. For example, a **histogram** is a frequency distribution in the form of a graph. Vertical bars represent the frequency of scores per category. Figure 15.1b shows a histogram for the

descriptive statistics Mathematical procedures that are used to describe and summarize data (information) in a meaningful way.

frequency distribution A listing of scores, usually from highest to lowest, along with the number of times each score appears.

histogram A frequency distribution in the form of a graph.

(a) Frequency Distribution

Score	Frequency
96	1
95	1
94	1
92	1
88	2
86	4
84	1
83	1
82	3
78	1
75	2
72	1
68	1
62	1

(b) Histogram

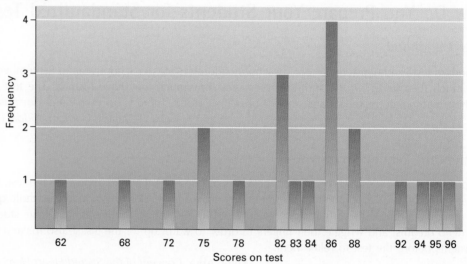

FIGURE 15.1 A Frequency Distribution and Histogram

MISS PEACH. By permission of Mell Lazarus and Creators Syndicate, Inc.

21 scores. A histogram often is called a *bar graph*. Notice in the histogram that the horizontal axis (the *x*-axis) indicates the obtained scores and the vertical axis (the *y*-axis) indicates how often each score occurs.

Although representing a group of scores graphically can provide insight about students' performance, so can some statistical techniques that represent scores numerically. These techniques involve the concepts of central tendency and variability, each of which we will discuss.

Measures of Central Tendency   A measure of **central tendency** is a number that provides information about the average, or typical, score in a set of data. There are three measures of central tendency: mean, median, and mode. The **mean** is the numerical average of a group of scores, commonly labeled as X or M by statisticians. The mean is computed by adding all the scores and then dividing the sum by the number of scores. Thus, the mean for the 21 students' test scores above is 1,740/21 = 82.86. The mean often is a good indicator of the central tendency of a group of scores.

The **median** is the score that falls exactly in the middle of a distribution of scores after they have been arranged (or ranked) from highest to lowest. In our example of 21 test scores, the median is the 11th ranked score (10 above, 10 below it), so the median is 84.

The **mode** is the score that occurs most often. The mode can be determined easily by looking at the frequency distribution or histogram. In our example of 21 scores, the mode is 86 (the score occurring most often—four times). The mode is most revealing when its value is much more frequent than the other values or scores. For example, in the 21 scores in our example, if 15 of the 21 scores had been the same, then the mode probably would be the best measure of central tendency for the data. In this case, the mean and median would be less meaningful.

central tendency A number that provides information about the average, or typical, score in a set of data.

mean The numerical average of a group of scores.

median The score that falls exactly in the middle of a distribution of scores after they have been arranged (or ranked) from highest to lowest.

mode The score that occurs most often.

BEST PRACTICES
Strategies for Improving Students' Test-Taking Skills

Here are some important test-taking skills that you might want to discuss with your students (Gronlund, 2006):

1. *Read the instructions carefully.*

2. *Read the items carefully.*

3. *Keep track of the time and work quickly enough to finish the test.*

4. *Skip difficult items and return to them later.*

5. *Make informed guesses instead of omitting items, if scoring favors doing so.*

6. *Eliminate as many items as possible on multiple-choice items.*

7. *Follow directions carefully in marking the answer (such as darkening the entire space).* Make sure students know how to do this

8. *Check to be sure that the appropriate response was marked on the answer sheet.*

9. *Go back and check answers if time permits.* Next, Marlene Wendler, a fourth-grade teacher in New Ulm, Minnesota, describes her experiences with standardized tests that her students take.

Through the Eyes of Teachers
*Make Sure You Evaluate Your Students
on More than Just Tests*

Standardized tests are just one very small, isolated picture of a child. A much fuller "video" comes from daily observations. Do not unfairly label a child based on a test. Rarely or never during the school year do my students encounter fill-in-the-oval items like those on standardized tests. Therefore, to be fair, before standardized testing I give them examples similar to the format of the test. If adults take a test with a special format, they prepare themselves by practicing in that format. Why should it be any different for children?

A set of scores may have more than one mode. For example, in our example of 21 students taking a test, if four students had scored 86 and four students had scored 75, then the set of scores would have two modes (86 and 75). A set of scores with two modes is called a *bimodal distribution.* It is possible for a set of scores to have more than two modes, in which case it is called a *multimodal distribution.*

Measures of Variability   In addition to obtaining information about the central tendency of a set of scores, it also is important to know about their variability. **Measures of variability** tell us how much the scores vary from one another. Two measures of variability are range and standard deviation.

The **range** is the distance between the highest and lowest scores. The range of the 21 students' test scores in our example is 34 points ($96 - 62 = 34$). The range is a rather simple measure of variability and it is not used often. The most commonly used measure of variability is the standard deviation.

The **standard deviation** is a measure of how much a set of scores varies on the average around the mean of the scores. In other words, it reveals how closely scores cluster around the mean (Frey, 2005). The smaller the standard deviation, the less the scores tend to vary from the mean. The greater the standard deviation, the more the scores tend to spread out from the mean. Calculating a standard deviation is not very difficult, especially if you have a calculator that computes square roots. To calculate a standard deviation, follow these four steps:

1. Find the mean of the scores.
2. From each score, subtract the mean and then square the difference between the score and the mean. (Squaring the scores will eliminate any minus signs that result from subtracting the mean.)
3. Add the squares and then divide that sum by the number of scores.
4. Compute the square root of the value obtained in step 3. This is the standard deviation.

measures of variability Measures that tell how much scores vary from one another.

range The distance between the highest and lowest scores.

standard deviation A measure of how much a set of scores varies on the average around the mean of the scores.

The formula for these four steps is

$$\sqrt{\frac{\Sigma(\chi - \overline{\chi})^2}{N}}$$

where χ = the individual score and $\overline{\chi}$ the mean, N = the number of scores, and Σ means "the sum of."

Applying this formula to the test scores of the 21 students,

1. We already computed the mean of the scores and found that it was 82.86.

2. Subtract 82.86 from the first score: 96 − 82.86 = 13.14. Square 13.14 to get 172.66. Save the value and go on to do the same for the second score, the third score, and so on.

3. Add the 21 scores to get 1,543.28. Divide the sum by 21: 1,543.28/21 = 73.49.

4. Find the square root of 73.49. The result is 8.57, the standard deviation.

Calculators are very helpful in computing a standard deviation. To evaluate your knowledge of and skills in computing the various measures of central tendency and variability we have described, complete *Self-Assessment 15.1*. Mastering these kinds of descriptive statistics is useful not only for classroom work but also for understanding research results. The standard deviation is a better measure of variability than the range because the range represents information about only two bits of data (the highest and lowest scores), whereas the standard deviation represents combined information about all the data. It also usually is more helpful to know how much test scores are spread out or clustered together than to know the highest and lowest scores. If a teacher gives a test and the standard deviation turns out to be very low, it means the scores tend to cluster around the same value. That could mean that everyone in the class learned the material equally well, but it more likely suggests that the test was too easy and is not discriminating very effectively between students who mastered the material and those who did not.

The Normal Distribution In a **normal distribution**, most of the scores cluster around the mean. The farther above or below the mean we travel, the less frequently each score occurs. A normal distribution also is called a *normal curve, bell-shaped*

"Tonight, we're going to let the statistics speak for themselves."

© The New Yorker Collection 1974 Edward Koren from cartoonbank.com. All Rights Reserved.

normal distribution A "bell-shaped curve" in which most of the scores are clustered around the mean; the farther above or below the mean that we travel, the less frequently each score occurs.

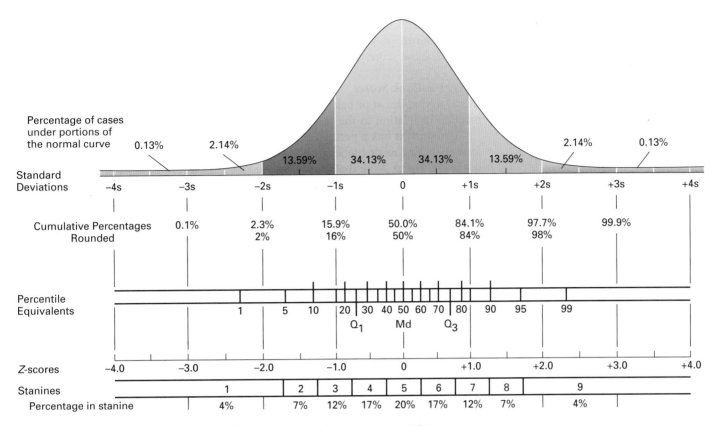

FIGURE 15.2 Some Commonly Reported Test Scores Based on the Normal Curve

Source: "Methods of Assessing Test Scores" adapted from *Test Service Bulletin* No. 48. Copyright © 1955 by NCS Pearson, Inc. Reproduced with permission. All right reserved.

curve, or *bell curve.* Many characteristics, such as human intelligence measured by intelligence tests, athletic ability, weight, and height, follow or approximate a normal distribution. Normal distributions are useful to know about because when testing a large number of students with a good standardized test, the graph of resulting scores will tend to resemble a normal curve (Bart & Kato, 2008).

We presented the normal distribution for standardized testing of intelligence in Chapter 4. Here we provide a more detailed description of the normal distribution, including some important characteristics (see Figure 15.2). First, the normal distribution is symmetrical. Because of this symmetry, the mean, median, and mode are identical in a normal distribution. Second, its bell shape shows that the most common scores are near the middle. The scores become less frequent the farther away from the middle they appear (that is, as they become more extreme). Third, the normal distribution incorporates information about both the mean and the standard deviation. The area on the normal curve that is 1 standard deviation above the mean and 1 standard deviation below it represents 68.26 percent of the scores. At 2 standard deviations above and below the mean, 95.42 percent of the scores are represented. Finally, at 3 standard deviations above and below the mean, 99.74 percent of the scores are included. If we apply this information to the normal distribution of IQ scores in the population, 68 percent of the population has an IQ between 85 and 115, 95 percent an IQ between 70 and 130, and 99 percent between 55 and 145.

Interpreting Test Results   Understanding descriptive statistics provides the foundation for effectively interpreting test results (Aiken & Groth-Marnat, 2006). About four to eight weeks after a standardized test has been administered, test results are returned to the school. A **raw score** is the number of items the student answered correctly on the test. Raw scores, by themselves, are not very useful because they don't provide information about how easy or difficult the test was or how the student fared

raw score The number of items the student answered correctly on the test.

Stanine Score	Percentile Rank Score
9	96 or Higher
8	89–95
7	77–88
6	60–76
5	40–59
4	23–39
3	11–22
2	4–10
1	Below 4

FIGURE 15.3 The Relation Between Stanine Score and Percentile-Rank Score

compared with other students. Test publishers usually provide teachers with many different kinds of scores that go beyond raw scores. These include percentile-rank scores, stanine scores, grade-equivalent scores, and standard scores.

Percentile-Rank Scores A **percentile-rank score** reveals the percentage of the distribution that lies at or below the score. It also provides information about the score's position in relation to the rest of the scores. Percentile ranks range from 1 to 99.

If a student has a percentile rank of 81 on a test, it means that the student performed as well as or higher on the test than 81 percent of the sample who made up the norm group. Note that percentiles do not refer to percentages of items answered correctly on the test. Percentile rank for standardized tests is determined by comparison with the norm group distribution. Different comparison groups may be used in computing percentile ranks, such as urban norms or suburban norms.

Stanine Scores A **stanine score** describes a student's test performance on a 9-point scale ranging from 1 to 9. Scores of 1, 2, and 3 are usually considered to be below average; 4, 5, and 6 average; and 7, 8, and 9 above average. As in the case of a student's percentile rank score, a stanine score in one subject area (such as science) can be compared with the student's stanine score in other areas (such as math, reading, and social studies).

A stanine refers to a specific percentage of the normal curve's area. The correspondence between a stanine score and a percentile-rank score is shown in Figure 15.3. A stanine score provides a more general index of a student's performance, whereas a percentile rank score yields a more precise estimation.

Grade-Equivalent Scores A **grade-equivalent score** indicates a student's performance in relation to grade level and months of the school year, assuming a 10-month school year (Tollefson, 2005). Thus, a grade-equivalent score of 4.5 refers to fourth grade, fifth month in school. A grade equivalent of 6.0 stands for the beginning of the sixth grade. In some test reports, a decimal is omitted so that 45 is the same as 4.5 and 60 is the same as 6.0.

Grade-equivalent scores should be used only to interpret a student's progress, not for grade placement. Many educators point out that because grade-equivalent scores are often misleading and misinterpreted, other types of scores, such as standard scores, are more appropriate to use.

Standard Scores A **standard score** is expressed as a deviation from the mean, which involves the concept of standard deviation that we discussed earlier. The term *standard* as used in *standard score* does not refer to a specific level of performance or expectation but rather to the standard normal curve (McMillan, 2002). Scores on state standards-based tests that we discussed earlier in our coverage of high-stakes testing are standard scores derived from raw score distributions, and they are unique to each state. For example, in Virginia, the standard score ranges from 0 to 600 with a score of 400 designated as "proficient."

Actually, the stanine scores and grade-equivalent scores we already have profiled are standard scores. Two additional standard scores we will evaluate here are *z*-scores and *T*-scores (Peyton, 2005).

A **z-score** provides information about how many standard deviations a raw score is above or below the mean. Calculation of a *z*-score is done using this formula:

$$z\text{-score} = \frac{\chi - \bar{\chi}}{SD}$$

where χ = any raw score, $\bar{\chi}$ mean of the raw scores, and SD equals the standard deviation of the raw score distribution.

percentile-rank score The percentage of a distribution that lies at or below the score.

stanine score A 9-point scale that describes a student's performance.

grade-equivalent score A score that indicates a student's performance in relation to grade level and months of the school year, assuming a 10-month school year.

standard score A score expressed as a deviation from the mean; involves the standard deviation.

z-score A score that provides information about how many standard deviations a raw score is above or below the mean.

Consider again our example of 21 students taking a test. What would a student's *z*-score be if the student's raw score were 86? Using the formula just shown it would be

$$\frac{86 - 82.6}{8.57} = .37$$

Thus, the raw score of 86 is .37 of a standard deviation above the mean. The *z*-score mean is 0 and the standard deviation is 1.

In addition to showing a student's relative placement on a test, standard scores also allow for comparisons across different types of tests (Powell, 2002). For example, a student may score 1 standard deviation above the mean on a math test and 1 standard deviation below the mean on a reading test. Comparisons of raw scores don't always allow for such comparisons.

Don't Overinterpret Test Results   Use caution in interpreting small differences in test scores, especially percentile rank and grade-equivalent test scores. All tests have some degree of error.

A good strategy is to think of a score not as a single number but as a location in a band or general range. Small differences in test scores are usually not meaningful.

Some test reports include percentile bands, a range of scores (rather than a single score) expressed in percentiles, such as 75th to 85th percentile for an obtained score of 80. The Metropolitan Achievement Tests use percentile bands in reporting scores. A percentile rank of 6 to 8 points or a two- to five-month grade-equivalence difference between two students rarely indicates any meaningful difference in achievement.

When considering information from a standardized test, don't evaluate it in isolation (Neukrug & Fawcett, 2006). Evaluate it in conjunction with other information you know about the student and your classroom instruction. Most manuals that accompany standardized tests warn against overinterpretation.

Using Standardized Test Scores to Plan and Improve Instruction

Teachers can use standardized test scores from the end of the previous year in planning their instruction for the next year and as a way to evaluate the effectiveness of instruction after content and skills have been taught (McMillan, 2007). Any use of standardized test results should be made in conjunction with information from other sources.

Prior to instruction, standardized test results may provide an indication of the general ability of the students in the class. This can help the teacher select the appropriate level of instruction and materials to begin the school year. A standardized test should not be used to develop a very low or very high expectation for a student or the entire class. Expectations should be appropriate and reasonable. If the results of a reading readiness test suggest that the class overall lacks appropriate reading skills, the teacher needs to carefully select reading materials that the students will be able to understand.

A very recent development involves test publishers developing items that correspond to the standards in state tests, then allowing schools or teachers to pull from an item bank to "test" progress toward meeting the standard (McMillan, 2007). The intent is to provide an evaluation of student learning that can be used to plan subsequent teaching weekly or monthly. Usually the tests are online, and information about them can be found on the Web sites of major testing companies, such as Educational Testing Service.

What are some effective ways teachers can use standardized test results to plan and improve instruction?

BEST PRACTICES
Strategies for Communicating Test Results to Parents

Here are some good strategies for communicating test results to parents (McMillan, 1997):

1. *Don't report the test scores in isolation.* Report the scores in the context of the student's overall work and performance on other classroom assessments. This will help keep parents from placing too much importance on a score from a single standardized test.

2. *Try to use easy-to-understand language when you describe the students' test results to parents.* Don't get caught up in using obscure test language. Be able to report the information in your own words.

3. *Let parents know that the scores are approximate rather than absolute.* You might say something about how various internal and external factors can affect students' test scores.

4. *Recognize that percentile scores or bands are the easiest set of scores for parents to understand.*

5. *Prior to the conference, spend some time familiarizing yourself with the student's test report.* Make sure you know how to interpret each score you report to parents. It is not a good idea just to show parents the numbers on a test report. You will need to summarize what the scores mean.

6. *Be ready to answer questions that parents might have about their child's strengths, weaknesses, and progress.*

7. *Rather than talking "to" or lecturing parents, talk "with" them in a discussion format.* After you have described a test result, invite them to ask questions that will help you to further clarify for them what the test results mean.

THROUGH THE EYES OF TEACHERS
The Importance of Parents' Support

Vicky Stone, a middle school language-arts teacher in Huntington, West Virginia, says that parental support is also vital to the success of her strategy. She holds parent conferences to inform and enable parents to be partners in the student's educational program for the year. They discuss the student's strengths and weaknesses. Based on the SAT (Stanford Achievement Test) and the parental input, her lesson plans take into account the students' weaknesses, including outcome for correction.

Standardized tests are sometimes used in grouping students. In cooperative learning, it is common to group students so that a wide range of abilities is reflected in the group. However, a single test score or single test should not be used by itself for any instructional purpose. It always should be used in conjunction with other information.

The subscales of tests (such as in reading and math) can be used to pinpoint strengths and weaknesses of incoming students in particular subject areas. This can help teachers to determine the amount of instruction to give in different areas. If students' achievement is considerably lower than what is expected on the basis of ability testing, they may need further testing, special attention, or counseling.

Standardized tests administered after instruction can be used to evaluate the effectiveness of instruction and the curriculum. Students should score well in the areas that have been emphasized in instruction. If they do not, then both the test itself and the instruction need to be analyzed to determine why this is the case.

In using standardized tests to plan and improve instruction, we underscore again, it is important not to use a single test or test score to make decisions. This is especially relevant in placement decisions, which should be made on the basis of information from multiple sources, including prior teachers' comments, grades, systematic observations, and further assessments. It also is very important to guard against using a single test to develop an expectation for a student's ability and to make sure that the student's test scores reflect a fair assessment.

Review, Reflect, and Practice

3 **Identify the teacher's roles in standardized testing.**

REVIEW

- What are effective ways to prepare students for standardized tests?
- What roles do frequency distributions, measures of central tendency and variability, and normal distributions play in describing standardized test results? What are some different types of scores? How should scores be evaluated?
- How can standardized tests be used in planning and improving instruction?

REFLECT

- Considering the grade level and subject(s) that you plan to teach, how might standardized test results be useful to you in your instructional planning?

PRAXIS™ PRACTICE

1. Mark, Jenny, Nicole, and Chris are all taking the SAT this year. Which student is preparing the most wisely?
   a. Chris, who has taken a test-taking skills test every year throughout high school
   b. Jenny, who has consistently taken relatively easy high school courses, and has gotten straight *A*'s
   c. Mark, who has enrolled in a specialized, expensive SAT preparation program
   d. Nicole, who has taken a rigorous high school program of studies, and has reviewed some of the math she took in her early high school years

2. Ms. Scott has just received the standardized test scores for her class. As she reviews each of them, she notices that Pete scored at the 98th percentile on the reading portion of this nationally normed test. What does this mean?
   a. Pete did better than all but 2 percent of the norm group on the test.
   b. Pete's score is 1 standard deviation above the mean score of the norm group.
   c. Pete got 98 percent of the answers correct on the reading portion of the test.
   d. Pete's score is 3 standard deviations above the mean score of the norm group.

3. Which of the following is an example of best practices in using the results of standardized tests to plan and improve instruction?
   a. Ms. Carter uses her students' standardized test scores to determine their placement in her class.
   b. Mr. Peabody decides that the standardized test scores are invalid when his students do not do well in an area he emphasized in class.
   c. Mr. Lemhert looks at the standardized test scores of each student and uses the information to help him identify relative strengths and weaknesses.
   d. Ms. Ziegler uses her students' standardized test scores to explain their classroom performance to their parents.

Please see the answer key at the end of the book.

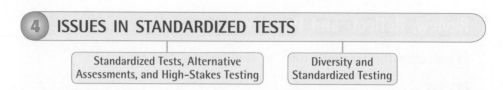

4 ISSUES IN STANDARDIZED TESTS

Standardized Tests, Alternative
Assessments, and High–Stakes Testing

Diversity and
Standardized Testing

As we have already mentioned, standardized testing is controversial. One debate concerns how standardized tests stack up against alternative methods of assessment, especially in high-stakes state standards-based testing. Another is about whether standardized tests discriminate against ethnic minority students and students from low-income backgrounds.

Standardized Tests, Alternative Assessments, and High–Stakes Testing

As we will explain in greater detail in Chapter 16, alternative assessments include assessments of student performance, such as assessments of oral presentations, real-world problems, projects, and portfolios (systematic and organized collections of the student's work that demonstrate the student's skills and accomplishments). Which is the best way to assess student performance—standardized tests that mainly rely on multiple-choice questions, or alternative assessments?

Assessment expert Grant Wiggins (1992) argues that performance tests should be used, either instead of standardized tests that mainly include multiple-choice questions or at least as part of the student's total assessment. He concludes that performance assessment is more meaningful, involves higher-level thinking skills, and fits better with current educational reform that emphasizes constructivist and social constructivist learning. In Kentucky and Vermont, the inclusion of problem solving in mathematics and the written communication of mathematical ideas on state-mandated tests led teachers to work more on these areas in their math instruction.

Some states—such as Arizona, California, Kentucky, and Wisconsin—have pulled back from earlier, more ambitious efforts to include alternative assessments in state-mandated tests. In part, that was because early studies indicated that the alternative assessments did not yield results that were as consistent as multiple-choice tests.

Blaine Worthen and Vicki Spandel (1991) argue that when used correctly, standardized tests do have value. However, they provide only partial assessment and, thus, have limits. Worthen and Spandel stress that standardized tests are especially helpful in providing information about comparability from a "big picture" perspective. Comparing their class with the one down the hall won't give teachers the information they need about where their students stand compared with the broader population of students. Standardized tests can provide better information about "big picture" questions: Are my fourth-grade students learning basic math? Can my seventh-grade students read at a predefined level of competency?

At the same time, Worthen and Spandel urge teachers to scrupulously avoid any misuses of tests or test results and to educate themselves about tests so that they understand their capabilities and limitations, not asking tests to do more than they can or are intended to do. They also say a standardized test should be only one of a number of assessments used to evaluate students.

Diversity and Standardized Testing

Earlier in the chapter, we raised the issue of fairness in standardized testing (McMillan, 2007). And in Chapter 4, "Individual Variations," we discussed issues related to diversity and assessment. A special concern is cultural bias in tests and the importance of creating culturally responsive tests for diagnostic and instructional purposes (Banks, 2008). Because of the potential for cultural bias in standardized tests, it is

How might standardized tests discriminate against ethnic minority students?

DIVERSITY AND EDUCATION
Mirror, Mirror on the Wall, Which Is the Fairest Test of All?

The title above was used to introduce a discussion of whether portfolio assessment is more equitable than standardized tests for ethnic minority students, students from impoverished backgrounds, and females (Supovitz & Brennan, 1997). The researchers compared the traditional standardized test results and portfolio assessment performance of first- and second-grade students in a medium-size urban setting. They analyzed the relative contribution of students' background characteristics to their performance. If the portfolio assessments are more equitable than standardized tests, the gap in scores between high-income non-Latino White students and low-income minority students should be reduced.

At both grade levels, the gap in performance between African American and non-Latino White students was reduced by about half in portfolio assessment when compared with scores on standardized tests. Thus, portfolio assessment significantly reduced the gap between African American and non-Latino White students' performance but did not eliminate it. Interestingly, a gender gap appeared, with girls outperforming boys by a larger margin on portfolio assessment than on assessment with standardized tests. Portfolio assessment had no detectable impact, on the average, on the relative performance of students from low-income backgrounds or students in the English-language-learning program. These students performed consistently worse than their counterparts on both portfolio assessment and standardized tests.

In sum, portfolio assessment holds considerable promise by focusing instruction on higher-level thinking skills, providing useful feedback to teachers about students' thinking skills, and emphasizing real-world problem solving. However, in this study, portfolio assessment had mixed effects on equalizing the differences in performance of students with different backgrounds and experience.

important to assess students using a variety of methods. As indicated earlier, many assessment experts consider that performance and portfolio assessments reduce some of the inequity that characterizes standardized tests for ethnic minority students and students from low-income backgrounds (Stiggins, 2008). To read further about whether portfolio assessment is more equitable for students from ethnic minority and other backgrounds, read the *Diversity and Education* interlude.

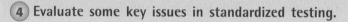

Review, Reflect, and Practice

4 Evaluate some key issues in standardized testing.

REVIEW

- Why is it argued that performance assessments should accompany standardized tests in high-stakes testing?
- What has changed when different ethnic groups have been compared using performance assessments instead of standardized tests?

REFLECT

- In what situations would you rather be tested with standardized testing? With performance assessments? Why?

PRAXIS™ PRACTICE

1. Which of the following is the best example of a performance test used to issue a driver's license?
   a. a road test
   b. a written test covering the rules of the road
   c. a vision test
   d. a computerized test covering the meaning of road signs
2. What is a good test strategy to avoid cultural bias?
   a. Use a single, good standardized test to control for extraneous influences.
   b. Assess students using a variety of methods.
   c. Assume that ethnic differences are due to heredity.
   d. Avoid using portfolios for assessment purposes.

Please see the answer key at the end of the book.

CRACK THE CASE
The Case of the Standardized Test Pressure

Ms. Pryor teaches third grade at Pulaski Elementary School in Steelton. In her state, third grade is the first grade at which students are tested using the state-wide standardized test. The test, given in March of each year, is supposed to measure how well the school is doing at meeting state standards in math, science, reading, writing, and social studies. This test yields individual, classroom, school, and district scores, and compares these to state averages. The state uses district-level scores to address school funding. Schools that have a large percentage of students who do not meet or exceed state standards run the risk of losing a portion of their funding. In recent years, the Steelton School District has broadened the purpose of the state-mandated tests to include how well an individual teacher is doing at helping the students to meet state standards. Student scores have become part of the teacher evaluation process. Steelton teachers receive merit points based on the percentage of their class that meets or exceeds state standards. Those with more merit points are given greater consideration if they request an in-district transfer, reimbursement for attending conferences, or release time for other development activities. Ms. Pryor has always received merit points for her students' performance on this test.

In addition to the state test, the district uses a nationally normed test to assess achievement. This test yields individual scores as they relate to national norms. These scores are reported as percentile-rank scores and grade-equivalent scores. This test is generally given near the beginning of the school year. The district uses the results of these tests to identify students in need of special education services or enrichment programs.

Ms. Pryor is not thrilled about giving her students so many standardized tests. She says, "Sometimes it seems all we do is prepare for these tests and take them." However, she makes sure she has taught her students appropriate test-taking strategies. She also tries to give her students some experiences that mirror the standardized tests, such as filling in bubbles on answer sheets, and having limited time in which to complete tests. She carefully goes over tests from previous years and uses them to write lesson plans. She is certain to have covered everything covered on previous state tests prior to the test in March, leaving the "fun stuff" for the end of the school year. The week before state testing, Ms. Pryor sends notes home to parents asking them to ensure that their children get adequate sleep and eat breakfast during testing weeks. After all, student performance on these tests impacts how the school is perceived and whether or not Ms. Pryor will receive merit points.

In the past, some groups of students have been excused from state testing. These students included those with learning disabilities and those who were not proficient at English. However, this year the rules have changed. The state now mandates that all students be tested regardless of ability or primary language. This concerns Ms. Pryor. If these students are included in the state testing, it is rather unlikely that her class will all meet or exceed state standards, resulting in no merit points for Ms. Pryor.

After receiving the results of the nationally normed tests, Ms. Pryor devises a strategy to ensure that more of her students will meet or exceed state standards on the state test in the spring. She begins by looking at her students' national percentile scores. She separates the students into three groups—those who scored above the 60th percentile, those who scored between the 40th and 60th percentiles, and those who scored below the 40th percentile. Her rea-

soning is that those who scored above the 60th percentile will meet state standards with no problem. In fact, many of them probably already have met state standards for third grade, given their grade-equivalent scores on the national test. She needn't worry about this group. Those who scored below the 40th percentile are not likely to meet state standards no matter what she does. Some may come close, but the return on her effort is not likely to be great. That leaves the middle group. She reasons that if she works intensively with this group, she has a chance of helping them to meet state standards—and that if they do, she will meet her goal in terms of merit points.

1. What testing issues are evident in this case?

2. What does Ms. Pryor do correctly in terms of preparing her students to take standardized tests?

3. What does Ms. Pryor do incorrectly in terms of preparing her students to take standardized tests?

4. What does it mean if a student's national percentile-rank score is 60?
   a. The student got 60% of the items correct.
   b. The student scored as well as or better than 60% of the students in the norm group.
   c. The student scored as well as or worse than 60% of the students in the norm group.
   d. The student scored as well as or better than 60% of the students in his class.

5. When Ms. Pryor uses percentile-rank scores on the nationally normed achievement test to evaluate likely performance on the state-mandated test, what is she likely expecting from the nationally normed test?
   a. She expects the nationally normed test to have predictive ability for the state-mandated test.
   b. She expects the nationally normed test to have concurrent validity.
   c. She expects the nationally normed test to have test-retest reliability.
   d. She expects the nationally normed test to have split-half reliability.

6. In what ways is it evident that the state-mandated test is a high-stakes test?

7. Why do you think Ms. Pryor decided only to concentrate her efforts at the middle of her class?

8. To what extent do you agree with her strategy? Why?

Reach Your Learning Goals

Standardized Tests and Teaching

---

(1) THE NATURE OF STANDARDIZED TESTS: Discuss the nature and purpose of standardized tests as well as the criteria for evaluating them.

Standardized Tests and Their Purposes

Standardized tests have uniform procedures for administration and scoring. Many standardized tests allow a student's performance to be compared with the performance of other students at the same age or grade level on a national basis. The purposes of standardized tests include providing information about students' progress, diagnosing students' strengths and weaknesses, providing evidence for placement of students in specific programs, providing information for planning and improving instruction, and contributing to accountability. Interest in accountability has led to the creation of standards-based tests and high-stakes testing. Important decisions about students should be made not on the basis of a single standardized test but rather on the basis of information from a variety of assessments.

Criteria for Evaluating Standardized Tests

The most important ways to evaluate standardized tests involve whether they are norm-referenced or criterion-referenced, and the extent to which they are valid, reliable, and fair. Norm-referenced tests involve comparing a student's performance with a group of individuals previously tested that provides a basis for interpreting the student's score. National norms are based on a nationally representative group of students. Criterion-referenced tests are standardized tests in which the student's performance is compared to established criteria rather than norms. State standardized tests are typically criterion-referenced, and criterion-referenced tests are designed to assess skills and knowledge in specific areas, such as English, math, and science. Validity is the extent to which a test measures what it is intended to measure and the extent to which inferences about test scores are accurate. Three important types of validity are content validity, criterion validity (which can be either concurrent or predictive), and construct validity. Reliability is the extent to which a test produces a consistent, reproducible measure of performance. Reliable measures are stable, dependable, and relatively free from errors of measurement. Reliability can be measured in several ways, including test-retest reliability, alternate-forms reliability, and split-half reliability. Fair tests are unbiased and nondiscriminatory, uninfluenced by irrelevant factors such as gender, ethnicity, or bias on the part of the scorer.

---

(2) APTITUDE AND ACHIEVEMENT TESTS: Compare aptitude and achievement tests and describe different types of achievement tests as well as some issues involved in these tests.

Comparing Aptitude and Achievement Tests

An aptitude test predicts a student's ability to learn, or what the student can accomplish with further education and training. An achievement test measures what the student has learned, or the skills the student has mastered. Aptitude tests include general mental ability tests, such as intelligence tests, and specific tests used to predict success in an academic subject or occupational area. The SAT test can be used as an aptitude test or as an achievement test.

Types of Standardized Achievement Tests

Standardized achievement tests include survey batteries (individual subject matter tests that are designed for a particular level of students), specific subject tests (assess a skill in a more detailed, extensive way than a survey battery), and diagnostic tests (given to students to pinpoint specific learning needs so those needs can be met with regular or remedial instruction).

High-Stakes State Standards-Based Tests	Some possible advantages of high-stakes state standards-based testing: improved student performance; more time teaching subjects being tested; high expectations for all students; identification of poorly performing schools, teachers, and administrators; and improved confidence in schools as test scores improve. High-stakes state standards-based tests are being used in decisions about remediation, promotion, and graduation. High-stakes state standards-based tests are criticized for dumbing down the curriculum, promoting rote memorization, encouraging teachers to teach to the test, and discriminating against students from low-income and minority backgrounds.
Standardized Tests of Teacher Candidates	Most teacher candidates have to take one or more standardized tests as part of licensure to teach in a particular state. Many states use one or more of the PRAXIS™ tests created by Educational Testing Service, although some states create their own test. Criticisms of the current tests of teacher candidates have been made, and a call for a national test of teacher candidates has been made.

3) THE TEACHER'S ROLES: Identify the teacher's roles in standardized testing.

Preparing Students to Take Standardized Tests	Make sure that students have good test-taking skills; communicate a positive attitude about the test to students; describe the test as an opportunity, not an ordeal; and avoid saying anything to raise students' anxiety.
Understanding and Interpreting Test Results	Descriptive statistics are math procedures used to describe and summarize data in a meaningful way. A frequency distribution is a listing of scores, usually from highest to lowest, along with the number of times each score appears. A histogram is one way that frequency distribution information can be presented. Measures of central tendency include the mean, median, and mode. Measures of variability tell how much scores vary and include the range and standard deviation. The normal distribution is also called a bell-shaped curve in which most scores cluster around the mean. A normal distribution is symmetrical and incorporates information about both the mean and the standard deviation. A raw score is the number of items a student gets right on a test, which typically is not as useful as many other types of scores. Percentile-rank scores reveal the percentage of the distribution that lies at or below the particular score. Stanine scores describe a student's performance on a 9-point scale ranging from 1 to 9. Grade-equivalent scores indicate a student's performance in relation to grade level and months of the school year. Standard scores are expressed as a deviation from the mean and involve the concept of standard deviation (z-scores are examples of standard scores). Avoid overinterpreting test results. A good strategy is to think of a score not as a single score but as being located in a band or general range. Don't evaluate standardized test results in isolation from other information about the student, such as classroom performance and the nature of instruction.
Using Standardized Test Scores to Plan and Improve Instruction	Standardized test scores can be used to plan and improve instruction either prior to instruction or after instruction. Standardized tests sometimes are used in grouping students, but it is important to guard against unrealistic expectations for students based on test scores. The subscales of tests can be used to pinpoint students' strengths and weaknesses in particular subject areas, which can help teachers determine the amount of instruction to give in different areas. Standardized tests should always be used in conjunction with other information about students and the appropriateness and fairness of the tests evaluated.

Standardized Tests, Alternative Assessments, and High-Stakes Testing

There is disagreement about the value of standardized tests versus alternative assessments such as performance tests and portfolio assessments. When used correctly, standardized tests have value but provide only part of the assessment picture and do have limits. Some assessment experts and teachers believe that high-stakes state standards-based testing should include more alternative assessments.

Diversity and Standardized Testing

African American, Latino, and Native American students perform more poorly than non-Latino White students on many standardized tests. Cultural bias is of special concern in standardized testing. This gap in performance was cut in about half between African American and non-Latino White students when portfolio assessment was used and compared with standardized test scores. Some assessment experts believe that performance assessments have the potential to reduce bias in testing.

KEY TERMS

standardized tests 541	concurrent validity 543	achievement test 546	range 559
standards-based tests 541	predictive validity 543	descriptive statistics 557	standard deviation 559
high-stakes testing 541	construct validity 543	frequency distribution 557	normal distribution 560
norm group 542	reliability 544	histogram 557	raw score 561
norm-referenced tests 542	test-retest reliability 543	central tendency 558	percentile-rank score 562
criterion-referenced tests 542	alternate-forms	mean 558	stanine score 562
validity 542	reliability 543	median 558	grade-equivalent score 562
content validity 542	split-half reliability 544	mode 558	standard score 562
criterion validity 543	aptitude test 546	measures of variability 559	z-score 562

PORTFOLIO ACTIVITIES

Now that you have a good understanding of this chapter, complete these exercises to expand your thinking.

Independent Reflection

Find a Frequency Distribution. Create a frequency distribution and histogram for the following scores: 98, 96, 94, 94, 92, 90, 90, 88, 86, 86, 86, 82, 80, 80, 80, 80, 80, 78, 76, 72, 70, 68, 64. (INTASC: Principle 8)

Collaborative Work

Calculate and Interpret Test Results. With a partner in your class, calculate the mean, median, and mode of the 23 scores just listed. Compute the range and standard deviation for these scores. What do these figures mean? (INTASC: Principle 8)

Research/Field Experience

What Do the Critics Say About Standardized Testing? In a short essay, evaluate each of the following criticisms of standardized tests. State whether you agree with the criticism and then explain your reasoning. (1) High-stakes multiple-choice tests will lead to a "dumbing down" of teaching and learning. (2) Establishing national tests will undermine new educational programs at the state and local levels. (INTASC: Principle 8)

Go to the Online Learning Center for downloadable portfolio templates.

TAKING IT TO THE NET

- A current trend in assessment is returning to traditional testing formats, such as true/false and multiple-choice. Discuss how these items can be written so that students' higher-level, critical-thinking skills are evaluated. Provide several examples of multiple-choice items that utilize students' analytical skills rather than recognition and recall. **http://cit.necc.mass.edu/ atlt/TestCritThink.htm**

- Standardized tests that were designed to measure student achievement are now being used to assess the quality of a student's education, including the teacher, principal, school, and school system. Is this use of standardized achievement test scores valid? Why or why not? **www.familyeducation .com/article/0,1120,1-6219,00.html**

- One criticism of high-stakes standardized testing is that teachers spend too much time "teaching to the test." Examine this criticism and brainstorm ways that teachers can implement a standards-based curriculum without sacrificing creativity and differentiated instruction. **www.ascd.org/ed_topics/el200009_ tomlinson.html**

Connect to the Online Learning Center to explore possible answers.

 ## STUDY, PRACTICE, AND SUCCEED

Visit **www.mhhe.com/santedu4e** to review the chapter with self-grading quizzes and self-assessments, to apply the chapter material to two more Crack the Case studies, and for suggested activities to develop your teaching portfolio.

CHAPTER 16

Classroom Assessment

I call my tests "opportunities" to give students a different way of thinking about them.

—**Bert Moore**
Contemporary American Psychologist

Chapter Outline

Learning Goals

1 Discuss the classroom as an assessment context.

2 Provide some guidelines for constructing traditional tests.

3 Describe some types of alternative assessments.

4 Construct a sound approach to grading.

TEACHING STORIES Vicky Farrow

Vicky Farrow is a former high school teacher who currently teaches educational psychology at Lamar University in Beaumont, Texas. She reflects on the ongoing process of assessment in the classroom and what to do and what not to do in constructing tests:

Assessment is an ongoing process. It is more than giving tests or assigning grades. It is everything a teacher does to determine if his or her students are learning. It may be asking students questions, monitoring their understanding as you circulate through the room during an activity, and noticing the frown on the face of a student who is confused or the smile of a student who has grasped the concept. Without this ongoing assessment, a teacher can never know if instruction is effective or needs to be modified. Done effectively, assessment provides a teacher with valuable information for providing an optimal learning experience for every child.

When you do give tests, every item on a test should relate back to the objectives. This helps the teacher avoid "gotcha" questions—those questions that may be trivial or unimpor-

tant to the intended learning outcomes. If it is not important enough to spend valuable class time on, it probably is not important enough to test the student over.

Be careful that test items are written at an appropriate level. The test should be testing students' understanding of the unit content, not their reading skills (unless, of course, it is reading skills that are being tested). I remember as a student taking an analogies test that was intended to assess my ability to identify relationships between concepts. However, the vocabulary was so difficult that I missed some items because the words were too difficult for that level of schooling.

If an essay question is on an examination, write a model answer *before* grading the exam. Would you make your answer key for a multiple-choice test from a student's paper, wrong answers and all? Of course not! It does not make any more sense to do that with an essay item. If an essay item is well written and a model answer is constructed in advance, the grade a student receives will more accurately reflect the level of that student's understanding of the material being tested.

Preview

Assessment of students' learning has recently generated considerable interest in educational circles. This interest has focused on such issues as the extent to which teachers should incorporate state standards into their teaching and assessment, as well as the degree to which teachers should use traditional tests or alternative assessments. Our coverage of classroom assessments begins with an examination of the varied features of the classroom as an assessment context. Then we contrast traditional tests and alternative assessments, followed by discussion of the role of grading in education.

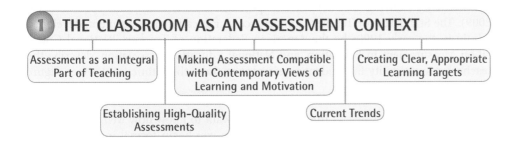

1 THE CLASSROOM AS AN ASSESSMENT CONTEXT

- Assessment as an Integral Part of Teaching
- Making Assessment Compatible with Contemporary Views of Learning and Motivation
- Creating Clear, Appropriate Learning Targets
- Establishing High-Quality Assessments
- Current Trends

When you think of assessment, what comes to mind? Probably tests. However, as we discuss the classroom as a context for assessment, you will discover that contemporary assessment strategies involve far more than testing.

FIGURE 16.1 Teacher Decision Making Before, During, and After Instruction

These are questions a teacher can answer to improve assessment before, during, and after instruction.

Preinstruction	During instruction	Postinstruction
Do my students have the prerequisite knowledge and skills to be successful?	Are students paying attention to me?	How much have my students learned?
What will interest my students?	Are students understanding the material?	What should I do next?
What will motivate my students?	To which students should I direct questions?	Do I need to review anything the class didn't understand?
How long should I plan to cover each unit?	What type of questions should I ask?	What grades should I give?
What teaching strategies should I use?	How should I respond to student questions?	What should I tell my students?
How should I grade students?	When should I stop lecturing?	How should I change my instruction next time?
What type of group learning should I use?	Which students need extra help?	Do the test scores really reflect what my students know and can do?
What are my learning objectives or targets?	Which students should be left alone?	Is there anything that students misunderstood?

Assessment as an Integral Part of Teaching

Teachers spend more time in assessment than you might imagine. In one analysis, they spent 20 to 30 percent of their professional time dealing with assessment matters (Stiggins, 2001). And that time allocation for assessment was made before the introduction of No Child Left Behind legislation in 2002 (discussed in Chapter 15), which mandates states to test students' achievement to determine if they are making adequate yearly progress. The high-stakes testing required by No Child Left Behind has meant that teachers have to integrate this testing in their assessment planning (Musial & others, 2009; Yell & Drasgow, 2009). For example, many teachers spend considerable time prepping students for such tests.

With so much time spent on assessment, it should be done well (Liu, 2009; Marzano, 2008). Assessment expert James McMillan (2007, 2008) stresses that competent teachers frequently evaluate their students in relation to learning goals and adapt their instruction accordingly. Assessment not only documents what students know and can do but also affects their learning and motivation. These ideas represent a change in the way assessment is viewed, away from the concept that assessment is an isolated outcome done only after instruction is finished and toward the concept of integrating assessment with instruction (Otero, 2006).

Think of integrating instruction and assessment in terms of three time frames: preinstruction, during instruction, and postinstruction (McMillan, 2008; O'Shea, 2009). The Standards for Teacher Competence in Educational Assessment, developed jointly in the early 1990s by the American Federation of Teachers, National Council on Measurement in Education, and National Education Association, describe the teacher's responsibility for student assessment in these three time frames (see Figure 16.1).

Preinstruction Assessment Imagine that you want to know how well your students can solve a certain level of math problem before you begin formal instruction on a more advanced level. You might look at your students' prior grades and their scores on standardized math tests, as well as observe your students for several days to see how well they perform. These assessments are designed to answer this question: What math skills are my students able to demonstrate? If the results of your assessment

What is formative assessment? Why is it such as important aspect of assessment?

indicate that students lack prerequisite knowledge and skills, you will decide to begin with materials that are less difficult for them. If they do extremely well on your preinstruction assessment, you will move your level of instruction to a higher plane. Without this preinstructional assessment, you run the risk of having a class that is overwhelmed (if your instruction level is too advanced) or bored (if your instruction level is too low).

Much of preinstructional assessment is informal observation (Taylor & Nolen, 2008). In the first several weeks of school, you will have numerous opportunities to observe students' characteristics and behavior. Be sensitive to whether a student is shy or outgoing, has a good or weak vocabulary, speaks and listens effectively, is considerate of others or is egocentric, engages in appropriate or inappropriate behavior, and so on. Also focus on the student's nonverbal behavior for cues that might reveal nervousness, boredom, frustration, or a lack of understanding.

In preinstructional assessments, guard against developing expectations that will distort your perception of a student. It is virtually impossible not to have expectations about students. Because teacher expectations are potentially powerful influences on student learning, some teachers don't even want to look at a student's prior grades or standardized test scores. Whether you do or do not examine such assessment information, work on making your expectations realistic. If you err, err in the direction of having overly positive expectations for students.

A good strategy is to treat your initial impressions of students as hypotheses to be confirmed or modified by subsequent observation and information. Some of your initial observations will be accurate; others will need to be revised. As you try to get a sense of what your students are like, refrain from believing hearsay information, from making enduring judgments based on only one or two observations, and from labeling the student (Airasian & Russell, 2008).

Some teachers also administer diagnostic pretests in subject areas to examine a student's level of knowledge and skill. And many schools are increasingly collecting samples of students' work in portfolios, which can accompany a student from grade to grade. The portfolios provide teachers with a far more concrete, less biased set of information to evaluate than other teachers' hearsay comments. We will describe portfolios in much greater depth later in the chapter.

Assessment During Instruction   One of the most significant trends in classroom assessment is the increasing use of **formative assessment**, which is assessment during

formative assessment Assessment during the course of instruction rather than after it is completed.

DEVELOPMENTAL FOCUS 16.1

What Are Your Thoughts on Effective and Ineffective Assessment of Students?

Early Childhood

Effective assessments at the preschool level occur when you look at the individual child and the progress that child has made. If teachers compare one child's progress with another's, then ineffective assessment takes place because children learn at different paces during early childhood.

—Missy Dangler, *Suburban Hills School*

Elementary School: Grades K–5

I find it effective to ask my students to demonstrate understanding and interpretation of the concepts taught to them. I get more useful assessment from an explanatory or analytical paragraph or essay than from a long test comprised of short answers. I also assess effort, observing students in discussions, as they process their work, and how they research tasks.

—Keren Abra, *Convent of the Sacred Heart Elementary School*

Middle School: Grades 6–8

Since not all students are good test takers, I vary how I assess them. For example, I like to ask questions while they are working and when they finish an assignment to see how much they learned from the beginning of a lesson. I give students a grade for positive participation if they ask good questions.

—Casey Maass, *Edison Middle School*

High School: Grades 9–12

A pen-and-paper test or a Scantron is a low-level test in which students can memorize material and forget it soon after. Effective assessment involves the student's demonstration of thorough knowledge and understanding with a project, paper, or portfolio.

—Sandy Swanson, *Menomonee Falls High School*

the course of instruction rather than after it is completed. Formative assessment has become a buzzword with its emphasis on assessment for learning rather than assessment of learning (Keeley, 2008; O'Shea, 2009; Stiggins, 2008). An important aspect of being an effective teacher is assessing students' understanding—formative assessment is extremely important in this regard. Your ongoing observation and monitoring of students' learning while you teach informs you about what to do next (Careless, 2008; Liu, 2009). Assessment during instruction helps you set your teaching at a level that challenges students and stretches their thinking. It also helps you to detect which students need your individual attention.

Assessment during instruction takes place at the same time as you make many other decisions about what to do, say, or ask next to keep the classroom running smoothly and help students actively learn (Airasian & Russell, 2008). It requires listening to student answers, observing other students for indications of understanding or confusion, framing the next question, and looking around the class for misbehavior (Gallavan, 2009; Hammerman, 2009). Simultaneously, the teacher needs to monitor the pace of the activity, which students to call on, answer quality, and the sequence of content. With small groups, the teacher might need to be aware of several different activities simultaneously.

Oral questions are an especially important aspect of assessment during instruction. Some teachers ask as many as 300 to 400 questions a day, not only to stimulate students' thinking and inquiry but also to assess their knowledge and skill level.

When you ask questions, remember to avoid overly broad, general questions; involve the whole class in questioning instead of calling on the same students all of the time; allow sufficient "wait time" after asking a question; probe students' responses with follow-up questions; and highly value students' own questions (Airasian & Russell, 2008).

An increasing trend in formative assessment is to get students to assess their own progress on a day-to-day basis (McMillan & Hearn, 2008). An important goal of student self-assessment is for students to become deeply involved in evaluating their schoolwork so they can more quickly determine how they are progressing. Encouraging students to assess their own progress also can increase their self-confidence and motivation to learn. Getting students to be reflective and monitor their progress is a key aspect of student self-assessment. Self-monitoring relates to our discussion of self-regulation in Chapter 7, "Behavioral and Social Cognitive Approaches," and our coverage of metacognition in Chapter 8, "The Information-Processing Approach." One of the biggest challenges in incorporating student self-assessment in classroom assessment is getting students used to doing it (McMillan, 2007, 2008). A good teaching strategy is to create student self-assessment worksheets, checklists, and other prepared material to facilitate their evaluation of their progress.

Feedback is an important aspect of formative assessment (Keeley, 2008; Tierney & Charland, 2007). The idea is to not only continually assess students as they learn but to provide informative feedback so that students' focus is appropriate. Researchers have found that positive feedback during formative assessment increases students' self-regulation of learning (Davis & McGowen, 2007). As part of providing feedback in formative assessment, instructional "correctives" are used to help students make progress. The idea is that there is assessment, feedback, and then more instruction (McMillan, 2007, 2008). Figure 16.2 describes some dos and don'ts in giving praise as a part of feedback.

Postinstruction Assessment   **Summative assessment** (or formal assessment) is assessment after instruction is finished with the purpose of documenting student performance. Assessment after instruction provides information about how well your students have mastered the material, whether students are ready for the next unit, what grades they should be given, what comments you should make to parents, and how you should adapt your instruction (McMillan, 2007, 2008).

Making Assessment Compatible with Contemporary Views of Learning and Motivation

Throughout this book, we have encouraged you to view students as active learners who discover and construct meaning; set goals, plan, and reach goals; associate and link new information with existing knowledge in meaningful ways; think reflectively, critically, and creatively; develop self-monitoring skills; have positive expectations for learning and confidence in their skills; are enthusiastically and internally motivated to learn; apply what they learn to real-world situations; and communicate effectively.

Assessment plays an important role in effort, engagement, and performance (Hammerman, 2009). Your informal observations can provide information about how motivated students are to study a subject. If you have a good relationship with the student, direct oral questioning in a private conversation can often produce valuable insight about the student's motivation. In thinking about how assessment and motivation are linked, ask yourself if your assessments will encourage students to become more meaningfully involved in the subject matter and more intrinsically motivated to study the topic (Butler & McMunn, 2006; Chang, 2007). Assessments that are challenging but fair should increase students' enthusiasm for learning. Assessments that are too difficult will lower students' self-esteem and self-efficacy, as well as raise their anxiety. Assessing students with measures that are too easy will bore them and not motivate them to study hard enough.

Do
Focus on specific accomplishments.
Attribute success to effort and ability.
Praise spontaneously.
Refer to prior achievement.
Individualize and use variety.
Give praise immediately.
Praise correct strategies leading to success.
Praise accurately with credibility.
Praise privately.
Focus on progress.

Don't
Focus on general or global achievement.
Attribute success to luck or other's help.
Praise predictably.
Ignore prior achievement.
Give the same praise to all students.
Give praise much later.
Ignore strategies and focus only on outcomes.
Praise for undeserving performance.
Praise publicly.
Focus solely on current performance.

FIGURE 16.2 Do's and Don'ts of Using Praise When Giving Feedback during Formative Assessment

From McMillan, J.H., *Classroom Assessment: Principles and Practice for Effective Standards-Based Instruction*, 4/e. Published by Allyn and Bacon, Boston, MA. Copyright © 2007 by Pearson Education. Reprinted by permission of the publisher.

summative assessment Assessment after instruction is finished to document student performance; also called formal assessment.

FIGURE 16.3 Examples of Unit Learning Targets

Students will be able to explain how various cultures are different and how cultures influence people's beliefs and lives by answering orally a comprehensive set of questions about cultural differences and their effects.

Students will demonstrate their knowledge of the parts of a plant by filling in words or a diagram for all parts studied.

Students will demonstrate their understanding of citizenship by correctly identifying whether previously unread statements about citizenship are true or false. A large number of items is used to sample most of the content learned.

Students will be able to explain why the American Constitution is important by writing an essay that indicates what would happen if we abolished our Constitution. The papers would be graded holistically, looking for evidence of reasons, knowledge of the Constitution, and organization.

Students will show that they know the difference between components of sentences by correctly identifying verbs, adverbs, adjectives, nouns, and pronouns in seven of eight long, complex sentences.

Students will be able to multiply fractions by correctly computing eight of ten fraction problems. The problems are new to the students; some are similar to "challenge" questions in the book.

Students will be able to use their knowledge of addition, subtraction, division, and multiplication to solve word problems that are similar to those used in the sixth-grade standardized test.

Students will demonstrate their understanding of how visual art conveys ideas and feelings by correctly indicating, orally, how examples of art communicate ideas and feelings.

Susan Brookhart (1997, 2002, 2004, 2008) developed a model of how classroom assessment helps motivate students. She argues that every classroom environment hosts a series of repeated assessment events. In each assessment event, the teacher communicates with the students through assignments, activities, and feedback about performance. Students respond according to their perceptions of these learning opportunities and how well they think they will be able to perform. Brookhart argues that this view of classroom assessment suggests that teachers should evaluate students using a variety of performances, especially performances that are meaningful to students.

Similarly, many other classroom assessment experts emphasize that if you think motivated, active learning is an important goal of instruction, you should create alternative assessments that are quite different from traditional tests, which don't evaluate how students construct knowledge and understanding, set and reach goals, and think critically and creatively (Brookhart, 2008; McMillan, 2007; Stiggins, 2008). Later in the chapter, we will explore how alternative assessments can be used to examine these aspects of students' learning and motivation.

Creating Clear, Appropriate Learning Targets

Tying assessment to current views on learning and motivation also involves developing clear, appropriate learning goals, or targets (Marzano, 2008). A *learning target* consists of what students should know and be able to do. You should establish criteria for judging whether students have attained the learning target (McMillan, 2007). Figure 16.3 provides some examples of unit learning targets.

Establishing High-Quality Assessments

Another important goal for the classroom as an assessment context is achieving high-quality assessment. Assessment reaches a high level of quality when it yields reliable and valid information about students' performance. High-quality assessments also are fair (McMillan, 2007, 2008). Validity and reliability are concerned with the consistency and accuracy of the inferences teachers make about students from assessment information.

Validity   *Validity* refers to the extent to which assessment measures what it is intended to measure. In the context of classroom assessment, validity also includes how accurate and useful a teacher's inferences are about the assessment (Leighton; 2008; McMillan, 2008). *Inferences* are conclusions that individuals draw from information.

You can't obtain information about everything a student learns. Thus, your assessment of a student will necessarily be a sample of the student's learning. The most important source of information for validity in your classroom will be *content-related evidence,* the extent to which the assessment reflects what you have been teaching (McMillan, 2007).

Adequately sampling content is clearly an important goal of valid assessment. Use your best professional judgment when sampling content. Thus, you wouldn't want to use just one multiple-choice question to assess a student's knowledge of a chapter on geography. An increasing trend is to use multiple methods of assessment, which can provide a more comprehensive sampling of content. Thus, the teacher might assess students' knowledge of the geography chapter with some multiple-choice questions, several essay questions, and a project to complete. Always ask yourself whether your assessments of students are adequate samples of their performance. For example, is the completed science project all that you will use to grade the student, or will you include information about the student's mastery of the general course content, the student's effort, and his or her class participation in your grading?

Linking instruction and assessment in the classroom leads to the concept of **instructional validity**: the extent to which the assessment is a reasonable sample of what actually went on in the classroom (McMillan, 2007, 2008). For example, a classroom assessment should reflect both what the teacher taught and students' opportunity to learn the material. Consider a math class in which the teacher gives students a test on their ability to solve multiplication problems. For instructional validity, it is important that the teacher competently instructed students in how to solve the problems and gave students adequate opportunities to practice this skill.

An important strategy for validity in classroom assessment is to systematically link learning targets, content, instruction, and assessment (McMillan, 2007, 2008). Imagine that you are a science teacher and that one of your learning targets is to get students to think more critically and creatively in designing science projects. Ask yourself what content is important to achieve this learning target. For instance, will it help students to read biographies of famous scientists that include information about how they came up with their ideas? Also ask yourself what learning targets you will emphasize in instruction. For your target regarding students' science projects, it will be important for you to carry through in your instruction on the theme of helping students to think critically and creatively about science.

Reliability   *Reliability* is the extent to which a test produces consistent, reproducible scores. Reliable scores are stable, dependable, and relatively free from errors of measurement (Miller, 2008). Consistency depends on circumstances involved in taking the test and student factors that vary from one test to another (McMillan, 2007).

Reliability is not about the appropriateness of the assessment information but is about determining how consistently an assessment measures what it is measuring (Sven, 2008). If a teacher gives students the same test in a math class on two occasions and the students perform in a consistent manner on the tests, this indicates that the test was reliable. However, the consistency in students' performance (with high-scorers being high both times the test was given, middle-scorers performing similarly across the two assessments, and low-scorers doing poorly on both assessments) says nothing about

instructional validity The extent to which the assessment is a reasonable sample of what went on in the classroom.

whether the test actually measured what it was designed to measure (for example, being an accurate, representative sample of questions that measured the math content that had been taught). Thus, reliable assessments are not necessarily valid.

Reliability is reduced by errors in measurement. A student can have adequate knowledge and skill and still not perform consistently across several tests because of a number of factors. Internal factors can include health, motivation, and anxiety. External factors can include inadequate directions given by the teacher, ambiguously created items, poor sampling of information, and inefficient scoring of the student's responses. For example, a student might perform extremely well on the first test a teacher gives to assess the student's reading comprehension but considerably lower on the second test in this domain. The student's lack of knowledge and skill could be the reason for the low reliability across the two assessments, but the low reliability also could be due to any number of measurement errors.

Fairness High-quality classroom assessment is not only valid and reliable but also fair (McMillan, 2007, 2008; Popham, 2008). Assessment is fair when all students have an equal opportunity to learn and demonstrate their knowledge and skill (Yung, 2001). Assessment is fair when teachers have developed appropriate learning targets, provided competent content and instruction to match those targets, and chosen assessments that reflect the targets, content, and instruction.

Assessment bias includes offensiveness and unfair penalization (Popham, 2008). An assessment is biased if it is offensive to a subgroup of students. This occurs when negative stereotypes of particular subgroups are included in the test. For example, consider a test in which the items portray males in high-paying and prestigious jobs (doctors and business executives) and females in low-paying and less prestigious jobs (clerks and secretaries). Because some females taking the test likely will be offended by this gender inequality, and appropriately so, the stress this creates may produce a less-successful outcome for females on the test.

An assessment also may be biased if it unfairly penalizes a student based on the student's group membership, such as ethnicity, socioeconomic status, gender, religion, and disability (Hargis, 2006). For example, consider an assessment that focuses on information that students from affluent families are far more likely to be familiar with than students from low-income families (Popham, 2008). A teacher decides to see how well students can collaboratively solve problems in groups. The content of the problem to be discussed is a series of locally presented operas and symphonies likely to have been attended only by those who can afford the high ticket prices. Even if the affluent students didn't attend these musical events themselves, they may have heard their parents talk about them. Thus, students from low-income families might perform less effectively on the collaborative problem-solving exercise pertaining to musical events not because they are less skilled at such problem solving but because they are unfamiliar with the events.

Some assessment experts believe it is important to create a philosophy of *pluralistic assessment,* which includes being responsive to cultural diversity in the classroom and at school (Payne, 1997). This usually includes performance assessments during instruction and after instruction. To learn more about culturally responsive strategies in assessing students, read the *Diversity and Education* interlude.

Current Trends

Here are some current trends in classroom assessment (Hambleton, 1996; McMillan, 2007; National Research Council, 2001):

- *Using at least some performance-based assessment.* Historically, classroom assessment has emphasized the use of **objective tests**, such as multiple-choice, which have relatively clear, unambiguous scoring criteria. In contrast, **performance assessments** require students to create answers or products that dem-

objective tests Tests that have relatively clear, unambiguous scoring criteria, usually multiple-choice tests

performance assessment Assessment that requires creating answers or products that demonstrate knowledge and skill; examples include writing an essay, conducting an experiment, carrying out a project, solving a real-world problem, and creating a portfolio.

DIVERSITY AND EDUCATION
Culturally Responsive Strategies for Assessing Students

Geneva Gay (1997, pp. 215–216, 218) evaluated the role of ethnicity and culture in assessment and recommended a number of culturally responsive strategies in assessing students. She advocates (1) modifying the Eurocentric nature of current U.S. instruction and achievement assessments, (2) using a wider variety of assessment methods that take into account the cultural styles of students of color, (3) evaluating students against their own records, and (4) assessing students in ways that serve culturally appropriate diagnostic and developmental functions.

Achievement assessments "are designed to determine what students know. Presumably they reflect what has been taught in schools." Gay argues that "although progress has been made in the last three decades to make school curricula more inclusive of ethnic and cultural diversity, most of the knowledge

What are some culturally responsive strategies for assessing students?

taught, and consequently the achievement tests, continue to be Eurocentric." She points out that even mastery of skills tends to be "transmitted through Eurocentric contexts. For instance, achievement tests may embed skills in scenarios that are not relevant to the cultural backgrounds and life experiences of students of color," as when a teacher asks "immigrant students from the Caribbean who have never experienced snow to engage in problem solving" by evaluating the challenges and dilemmas presented by a blizzard—the students might have the problem-solving skill to respond to this request, but their unfamiliarity with cold winters can interfere with their ability to perform the task effectively.

This does not mean that students of color should not be assessed or that they should not be expected to meet high achievement standards. They should. However, "to avoid perpetuating educational inequality through assessment procedures, these students should not always be expected to demonstrate" knowledge and skills in terms of contexts with which they are not familiar. A good strategy is to use a variety of assessment methods to ensure that no single method gives an advantage to one ethnic group or another. These methods should include socioemotional measures as well as measures of academic content. Teachers also should carefully observe and monitor students' performance for verbal and non-verbal information in the assessment context.

Gay further argues that norm-referenced traditional assessments should be used only in conjunction with performance assessments. More emphasis should be given to evaluating students against their own records, with the focus being on improvement, rather than on comparisons with other students.

Gay also stresses that assessment should always "serve diagnostic and developmental functions and be culturally responsible. . . . Narrative reports, developmental profiles, student-teacher-parent conferences, and anecdotal records should always be included in reporting students' progress."

onstrate their knowledge or skill. Examples of performance assessment include writing an essay, conducting an experiment, carrying out a project, solving a real-world problem, and creating a portfolio (Stiggins, 2008).

DEVELOPMENTAL FOCUS 16.2
How Do You Use Performance Assessment in the Classroom?

Early Childhood

Most of the assessments in early childhood classrooms are based on a performance assessment model. Teachers observe and record information that the child presents as part of play and participation in classroom activities. For example, a teacher might date a paper that a child used to write her full phone number for the first time, demonstrating the knowledge of identity, ability to write the specific numbers, sequencing, memory, and more. This piece of information would be kept in the child's portfolio record to be shared with the family as part of the assessment process.

—Heidi Kaufman, *Metro West YMCA Child Care and Educational Program*

Elementary School: Grades K–5

I set up an assignment that students prepare in class and for homework. For example, they can memorize and perform a poem or write and perform a speech about a human rights activist. I assess the student's performance, research, content, language, effort, and care.

—Keren Abra, *Convent of the Sacred Heart Elementary School*

Middle School: Grades 6–8

One project I give my students is a decades project. The students get to choose a decade that interests them and present their findings to the class. They can do this like a news report and dress up like people from that decade. They can also bring in music from their decade and mementoes as well. This is a lot of fun and a great learning experience for students.

—Casey Maass, *Edison Middle School*

High School: Grades 9–12

In sophomore English, students give four speeches. One demonstrates a method, one uses PowerPoint as a visual aid, one shares a personal story, and one is videotaped and reflected on formally. We also do extemporaneous speeches where a student will choose a topic and speak for two minutes. Speeches are often very stressful for many high school students, but I usually see growth with each speech.

—Jennifer Heiter, *Bremen High School*

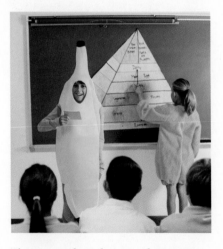

The two students here are demonstrating their knowledge and understanding of nutrition. *What are some other examples of performance assessment?*

- *Examining higher-level cognitive skills.* Rather than assess only content knowledge, as many objective tests do, a current trend is to evaluate a student's higher-level cognitive skills, such as problem solving, critical thinking, decision making, drawing of inferences, and strategic thinking.
- *Using multiple assessment methods.* In the past, assessment meant using a test—often a multiple-choice test—as the sole means of assessing a student. A current trend is to use multiple methods to assess students. Thus, a teacher might use any number of these methods: a multiple-choice test, an essay, an interview, a project, a portfolio, and student evaluations of themselves. Multiple assessments provide a broader view of the child's learning and achievement than a single measure.
- *Using more multiple-choice items to prepare students for taking high-stakes state standards-based tests.* Just when a trend in assessment that was more compatible with cognitive, constructivist, and motivational approaches (performance assessment, use of portfolios, and student self-assessment) had developed, teachers returned to using objective formats for assessment, in many cases more than before. In assessment expert James McMillan's (2007, p. 19) view, many teachers need to balance the demands of tests mandated by No Child

TECHNOLOGY AND EDUCATION
Web-Based Assessment

Many school systems are turning to *Web-based assessment—* assessment available on the Internet—because of its potential for greater accuracy and cost reduction. A number of testing firms, including Educational Testing Service, are developing tests to be administered on computers in the classroom, school, or district, but those are not Web-based assessments. If an assessment is Web-based, students use a computer and the assessment takes place on the Internet (Smaldino, Lowther, & Russell, 2008; Wang, 2007).

Some of the best Web-based assessments can be easily adapted to the curriculum you use in your classroom. Some of the assessments focus on recording and evaluating student behavior, some involve academic progress, and others include all of these areas. The best Web-based assessments let teachers "develop their own tests or forms and usually include a databank of questions or other assessment tools. Most are aligned with various state and national standards," or No Child Left Behind (Doe, 2004).

Left Behind "with what they know about best practices of teaching and assessment that maximize student learning and motivation. Clearly, classroom assessment must be considered in the current climate that emphasizes high-stakes testing."

- *Having high performance standards.* Another trend is the demand for high performance standards, even world-class performance standards, for interpreting educational results. Some experts say that world-class performance standards are driving contemporary classroom assessment by providing goals, or targets, to attain (Taylor, 1994). However, questions arise about who should set these standards and whether they should be set at all.

- *Using computers as part of assessment.* Traditionally, computers have been used to score tests, analyze test results, and report scores. Today, computers increasingly are being used to construct and administer tests, as well as to present different assessment formats to students in a multimedia environment (Musial & others, 2009). With coming advances in technology, assessment practices are likely to be very different from traditional paper-and-pencil tests. To read further about an increasing way computers are being used in assessment, see the *Technology and Education* interlude.

Trends in assessment also include emphasizing integrated rather than isolated skills, involving students in all aspects of assessment, giving students more feedback, and making standards and criteria public rather than private and secretive.

What are some ways that computers are being used in the assessment of students?

Review, Reflect, and Practice

(1) Discuss the classroom as an assessment context.

REVIEW

- Describe assessment before, after, and during instruction.
- How can assessment be brought into line with contemporary views of learning and motivation?
- What are learning targets?
- What standards can be used to judge the quality of classroom assessments?
- What are some current trends in assessing students' learning?

REFLECT

- Think of one of the better teachers that you had as a K–12 student. In retrospect, how would you describe the teacher's classroom as an "assessment context"?

PRAXIS™ PRACTICE

1. Which of the following is the best example of formative assessment?
   a. Mr. Harrison's students write a paper at the conclusion of a unit of instruction. This allows him to assess to what degree his students understand the content of the unit.
   b. Mr. Shockey asks his students open-ended questions during instruction. This way he can determine to what degree his students understand the content of his lesson.
   c. Ms. Manning plays a game of *Jeopardy!* at the end of her unit of instruction to assess student understanding of the content of the unit.
   d. Ms. Walker gives her students a brief assessment prior to beginning a unit of instruction, so she knows what her students are already capable of doing. This allows her to gear her instruction to her students' zones of proximal development.

2. Which of the following assessments will most likely enhance student motivation to study and learn?
   a. Mr. Ditka assigns his students a project that requires knowledge from the unit of instruction to complete successfully.
   b. Mr. Payton gives periodic tests that are easy enough for all of his students to earn high scores if they have attended class.
   c. Mr. Rivera puts two or three tricky questions in each test so he can determine which of his students read the items carefully before responding.
   d. Mr. Singletary constructs very challenging exams to ensure that only those students who have studied the material carefully will be successful.

3. Ms. Ramirez has assigned her students to analyze the water in a nearby stream, determine the level of pollution in the stream, and develop a solution to the pollution problem. What type of learning target has she created?
   a. affect
   b. knowledge
   c. product
   d. reasoning

4. Ms. Vick has created an assessment to measure the degree to which her students have mastered the content of her unit on the U.S. Constitution. Included in the test are items about the Bill of Rights, other constitutional amendments,

Review, Reflect, and Practice

the American Revolution, and World War II. What is the best description of this assessment?

a. It is likely to yield both valid and reliable scores.
b. The scores are unlikely to be valid or reliable.
c. While the scores may be reliable, they will not be valid.
d. While the scores may be valid, they will not be reliable.

5. Ms. Krzyzewski is teaching a science unit on anatomy. Students have been studying the anatomy of various animals. Which of the following is the best example of a performance assessment of this material?

a. Students answer oral questions regarding the structures present in different animals.
b. Students write an essay comparing and contrasting the anatomy of frogs and pigs.
c. Students dissect animals and identify their anatomical parts.
d. Students take a multiple-choice test covering the material in the unit.

Please see the answer key at the end of the book.

(2) TRADITIONAL TESTS

Selected-Response Items   Constructed-Response Items

Traditional tests are typically paper-and-pencil tests in which students select from choices, calculate numbers, construct short responses, or write essays. Our coverage of traditional tests focuses on two main types of item formats in assessment: (1) selected-response items and (2) constructed-response items.

Selected-Response Items

Selected-response items have an objective format that allows students' responses to be scored quickly. A scoring key for correct responses is created and can be applied by an examiner or by a computer. Multiple-choice; true/false, and matching items are the most widely used types of items in selected-response tests.

Multiple-Choice Items   A **multiple-choice item** consists of two parts: the stem plus a set of possible responses (McMorris & Tan, 2008). The stem is a question or statement. Incorrect alternatives are called *distractors*. The student's task is to select the correct choice from among the distractors—for example:

What is the capital of Vermont? (Stem)
   a. Portland (Distractor)
   b. Montpelier (Answer)
   c. Boston (Distractor)
   d. Weston (Distractor)

Students below the fourth grade probably should answer questions on the test page rather than on a separate answer sheet. Young elementary school students tend

selected-response items Test items with an objective format in which student responses can be scored quickly. A scoring guide for correct responses is created and can be applied by an examiner or a computer.

multiple-choice item An objective test item consisting of two parts: a stem plus a set of possible responses.

BEST PRACTICES
Strategies for Writing Multiple-Choice Items

Some good strategies for writing high-quality multiple-choice items include the following (Gronlund & Waugh, 2009; Haladyna, 2002; McMillan, 2007; Sax, 1997):

1. *Write the stem as a question.*

2. *Give three or four possible alternatives from which to choose.*

3. *State items and options positively when possible.* Elementary school students especially find negatives confusing. If you use the word *not* in the stem, *italicize* or <u>underline</u> it—for example:

   Which of the following cities is *not* in New England?
   a. Boston
   b. Chicago
   c. Montpelier
   d. Providence

4. *Include as much of the item as possible in the stem, thus making the stem relatively long and the alternatives relatively short*—for example:

   Which U.S. president wrote the Gettysburg Address?
   a. Thomas Jefferson
   b. Abraham Lincoln
   c. James Madison
   d. Woodrow Wilson

5. *Alternatives should grammatically match the stem so that no answers are grammatically wrong.* For example, the first item is better than the second:

   Orville and Wilbur Wright became famous because of which type of transportation?
   a. airplane
   b. automobile
   c. boat
   d. train
   Orville and Wilbur Wright became famous because of an
   a. airplane
   b. automobile
   c. boat
   d. train

6. *Write items that have a clearly defensible correct or best option.* Unless you give alternative directions, students will assume that there is only one correct or best answer to an item.

7. *Vary the placement of the correct option.* Students who are unsure of an answer tend to select the middle options and avoid the extreme options. Alphabetizing response choices (by the first letters in the response) will help to vary the placement of the correct option.

8. *Beware of cues in the length of the options.* Correct answers tend to be longer than incorrect ones because of the need to include specifications and qualifications that make it true. Lengthen the distractors (incorrect responses) to approximately the same length as the correct answer.

9. *Don't expect students to make narrow distinctions among answer choices.* For example, the first item is better than the second:

   The freezing point of water is
   a. 25°F
   b. 32°F
   c. 39°F
   d. 46°F
   The freezing point of water is
   a. 30°F
   b. 31°F
   c. 32°F
   d. 33°F

10. *Do not overuse "None of the above" and "All of the above."* Also avoid using variations of "a. and b." or "c. and d. but not a."

11. *Don't use the exact wording in a textbook when writing a question.* Weak students might recognize the correct answer but not really understand its meaning.

12. *Write at least some items that encourage students to engage in higher-level thinking.* As we indicated earlier in the chapter, a current trend is to use more multiple-choice items in classroom assessment because of the demands imposed on teachers by high-stakes state standards-based tests. An important issue in the return to using more multiple-choice items is the cognitive level demanded by the items. Many teachers report that they use "higher-level" test items, but in reality they mainly are lower-level recall and recognition items (McMillan, 2007).

    Here are some recommendations for writing higher-level thinking multiple-choice items (Center for Instructional Technology, 2006):

    • Don't write more than three or four items a day that involve higher-level thinking because they are more difficult to write and take more time than more simple, straightforward items.

    • Write one or two items after a class (a good idea for writing any test items) and then simply assemble them at a later time when making up a test.

BEST PRACTICES
Strategies for Writing Multiple-Choice Items

- Use some analogy-based items (see the discussion of analogies in Chapter 9, Complex Cognitive Processes"). An example of a multiple-choice item using an analogy is:

  Bandura is to social cognitive theory as _____ is to social constructivist theory:
  - a. Piaget
  - b. Siegler
  - c. Vygotsky
  - d. Skinner

- Write some case-study items. You already have encountered many of these in this textbook. Many of the PRAXIS™ Practice features at the end of main sections in a chapter and all of the *Crack the Case* multiple-choice items at the end of chapters involve case studies.
- Write items in which students have to select what is missing or needs to be changed in a scenario you provide.

to respond slowly and lose their place easily when they have to use a separate answer sheet (Sax, 1997). Using a separate answer sheet with older students often reduces scoring time because the answers usually can fit on only one page. Many school districts have commercially printed answer sheets that teachers can order for their classes. If you hand-score multiple-choice tests, consider preparing a scoring stencil by cutting or punching holes in the answer sheet in the locations of the correct answers.

For most classroom requirements, simply count the number of answers marked correctly. Some teachers penalize students for guessing by deducting for wrong answers, but assessment experts say that this probably is not worth the extra bother and frequently leads to mistakes in scoring (Sax, 1997).

Strengths and limitations of multiple-choice items are listed in Figure 16.4.

True/False Items   A true/false item asks a student to mark whether a statement is true or false—for example:

Montpelier is the capital of Vermont.   True   False

The ease with which true/false items can be constructed has a potential drawback. Teachers sometimes take statements directly from a text or modify them slightly when making up true/false items. Avoid this practice, because it tends to encourage rote memorization with little understanding of the material.

The strengths and limitations of true/false items are described in Figure 16.5.

Matching Items   Used by many teachers with younger students, matching requires students to connect one group of stimuli correctly with a second group of stimuli (Hambleton, 1996). Matching is especially well suited for assessing associations or links between two sets of information. In a typical matching format, a teacher places a list of terms on the left side of the page and a description or definition of the terms on the right side of the page. The student's task is to draw lines between the columns that correctly link terms with their definitions or descriptions. In another format, a space is left blank next to each term, in which the student writes the correct number or letter of the description/definition. When using matching, limit the number of items to be matched to no more than eight or ten. Using no more than five or six items per set is a good strategy.

Matching tests are convenient for teachers in that (Popham, 2008) (1) their compact form requires little space, thus making it easy to assess quite a lot of information efficiently, and (2) they can be easily scored by using a correct-answer template.

But matching tests may tend to ask students to connect trivial information. Also, most matching tasks require students to connect information they have simply memorized, although items can be constructed that measure more complex cognitive skills (Sax, 1997).

Strengths

1. Both simple and complex learning outcomes can be measured.
2. The task is highly structured and clear.
3. A broad sample of achievement can be measured.
4. Incorrect alternatives provide diagnostic information.
5. Scores are less influenced by guessing than true/false items.
6. Scoring is easy, objective, and reliable.

Limitations

1. Constructing good items is time consuming.
2. It is frequently difficult to find plausible distractors.
3. The multiple-choice format is ineffective for measuring some types of problem solving and the ability to organize and express ideas.
4. Score can be influenced by reading ability.

FIGURE 16.4 Strengths and Limitations of Multiple-Choice Items

From Norman E. Gronland, *Assessment of Student Achievement*, 6th edition. Published by Allyn and Bacon, Boston, MA. Copyright © 1998 by Pearson Education. Reprinted by permission of the publisher.

Strengths

1. The item is useful for outcomes where there are only two possible alternatives (for example, fact or opinion, valid or invalid).
2. Less demand is placed on reading ability than in multiple-choice items.
3. A relatively large number of items can be answered in a typical testing period.
4. Scoring is easy, objective, and reliable.

Limitations

1. It is difficult to write items at a high level of knowledge and thinking that are free from ambiguity.
2. When a statement indicates correctly that a statement is false, that response provides no evidence that the student knows what is correct.
3. No diagnostic information is provided by the incorrect answers.
4. Scores are more influenced by guessing than with any other item type.

FIGURE 16.5 Strengths and Limitations of True/False Items

From Norman E. Gronland, *Assessment of Student Achievement*, 6th edition. Published by Allyn and Bacon, Boston, MA. Copyright © 1998 by Pearson Education. Reprinted by permission of the publisher.

Constructed-Response Items

Constructed-response items require students to write out information rather than select a response from a menu. Short-answer and essay items are the most commonly used forms of traditional constructed-response items. In scoring, many constructed-response items require judgment on the part of the examiner (Reynolds, Livingston, & Willson, 2006).

Short-Answer Items A **short-answer item** is a constructed-response format in which students are required to write a word, a short phrase, or several sentences in response to a task. For example, a student might be asked, "Who discovered penicillin?" The short-answer format allows recall and could provide a problem-solving assessment of a wide range of material. The disadvantages of short-answer questions are that they can require judgment to be scored and typically measure rote learning.

Sentence completion is a variation of the short-answer item, in which students express their knowledge and skill by completing a sentence. For example, a student might be asked to complete this sentence stem: The name of the person who discovered penicillin is _____.

Essays **Essay items** allow students more freedom of response to questions but require more writing than other formats (Fowles & Odendahl, 2008). Essay items are especially good for assessing students' understanding of material, higher-level thinking skills, ability to organize information, and writing skills. Here are some examples of high school essay questions:

What are the strengths and weaknesses of a democratic approach to government?

Describe the main themes of the novel you just read.

Argue that the United States is a gender-biased nation.

Essay items can require students to write anything from a few sentences to several pages. In some cases, teachers ask all students to answer the same essay question(s). In others, teachers let students select from a group of items the item(s) they want to write about, a strategy that makes it more difficult to compare different students' responses.

Suggestions for writing good essay items include these (Sax, 1997):

- *Specify limitations.* Be sure to specify the length of the desired answer and the weight that will be given to each item in determining scores or judgments.

- *Structure and clarify the task.* Make clear what they are supposed to write about. A poorly worded item is "Who was George Washington?" This could be answered in six words: "First president of the United States." In cases like this, ask yourself what more you want the student to tell. This more-structured essay item requires more thinking on the part of the student:

Discuss several events in the life of George Washington that confirm or disprove the claim that "he never told a lie." Use the events to support a claim of your own about how truthful Washington was.

- *Ask questions in a direct way.* Don't get too tricky. You might hear the term *rubric* used in regard to scoring students' responses on essays and other tests. In this context, rubric simply means a scoring system. Figure 16.6 lists some strengths and limitations of essay questions.

constructed-response items Items that require students to write out information rather than select a response from a menu.

short-answer item A constructed-response format in which students are required to write a word, a short phrase, or several sentences in response to a task.

essay items Items that require more writing than other formats but allow more freedom of response to questions.

BEST PRACTICES
Strategies for Scoring Essay Questions

Here are some good strategies for scoring essays (Sax, 1997):

1. *Outline a plan for what constitutes a good or acceptable answer prior to administering or scoring students' responses* (McMillan, 2007). Essays can be scored holistically or analytically. *Holistic scoring* means making an overall judgment about the student's answer and giving it a single number or letter. You might make this judgment based on your overall impression of the essay or base it on several criteria that you have generated. Holistic scoring is often used when essays are long. *Analytic scoring* means scoring various criteria separately, then adding up the points to produce an overall score for the essay. Analytic scoring can be time consuming, so avoid having more than three or four criteria for an essay.

2. *Devise a method by which you can score the essays without knowing which students wrote them.* You might do this by having students write their name beside a number on a separate sheet, then write only their number on the essay. When you record the grade, you can match up the student's number and name. This reduces the chance that your positive or negative expectations for the student will enter into your evaluation of the responses.

3. *Evaluate all answers to the same questions together.* Read and score all students' responses to one item before moving on to the next item. It is easier for you to remember the criteria for evaluating an answer to a single essay item than to remember the criteria for all essay items. Also, if you read all of one student's responses together, your evaluation of the first few items will tend to influence your evaluation of the remaining items.

4. *Decide on a policy for handling irrelevant or incorrect responses.* Some students try to bluff their way through essays. Other students write everything they know about a topic without taking the time to zero in on what the item is asking for. Still other students might use poor grammar, misspell words, or write illegibly. Decide ahead of time whether and how much you will penalize such responses.

5. *If possible, reread papers before handing them back to students.* This helps you guard against any flaws or oversights in your scoring.

6. *Write comments on the paper.* An essay, especially a long one, with only a number or letter grade on it does not give adequate feedback to a student. And if you only circle or correct spelling errors and grammar, you are not giving students insight about the content of their essay responses. A good strategy is to write a number of brief comments at appropriate places throughout the essay, such as "Expand this idea more," "Unclear," or "Needs an example," in addition to making overall comments about the essay at its beginning or end. It is better to write comments throughout the essay than to make one or two minor comments in one part of the essay.

Strengths

1. The highest level of learning outcomes (analysis, synthesis, evaluation) can be measured.
2. The integration and application of ideas can be emphasized.
3. Preparation time is usually less than for selection-type formats.

Limitations

1. Achievement may not be adequately sampled due to the time needed to answer each question.
2. It can be difficult to relate essay responses to intended learning outcomes because of freedom to select, organize, and express ideas.
3. Scores are raised by writing skill and bluffing, and lowered by poor handwriting, misspelling, and grammatical errors.
4. Scoring is time consuming, subjective, and possibly unreliable.

FIGURE 16.6 Strengths and Limitations of Essay Questions

From Norman E. Gronland, *Assessment of Student Achievement,* 6th edition. Published by Allyn and Bacon, Boston, MA. Copyright © 1998 by Pearson Education. Reprinted by permission of the publisher.

Review, Reflect, and Practice

(2) **Provide some guidelines for constructing traditional tests.**

REVIEW

- What are some important ideas to remember when creating multiple-choice, true/false, and matching items?
- What are constructed-response items and how do short-answer items differ from essay items?

REFLECT

- Why do you think traditional testing has survived so long in K–12 classrooms?

PRAXIS™ PRACTICE

1. Mr. Brown, a college instructor, includes the following item in a test about the impact of the family on children: What parenting style does Homer Simpson exhibit? Mr. Brown's possible answers are authoritative, authoritarian, neglectful, and permissive. Which of the following is the most appropriate criticism of Mr. Brown's question and answers?
   a. It is too easy to eliminate options because they are not all parenting styles.
   b. Parenting style has nothing to do with the impact of family on children.
   c. The question is biased in favor of people who watch *The Simpsons*.
   d. There is more than one clearly correct response.

2. Mr. Dent has just returned Marcia's graded essay to her. Notations of spelling and grammar errors, and the grade, 42/50—*B*, are all he has written on the test. What is the most appropriate criticism of this assessment?
   a. An essay should never be worth this many points on a test.
   b. Essays should not be graded numerically.
   c. There are no comments to help Marsha see where she did well and where she lost points.
   d. Spelling and grammar errors should not be marked on an essay.

Please see the answer key at the end of the book.

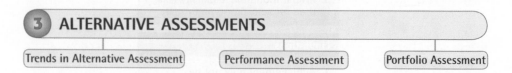

(3) **ALTERNATIVE ASSESSMENTS**

Trends in Alternative Assessment   Performance Assessment   Portfolio Assessment

There are alternatives to the traditional assessments that we just discussed (McMillan, 2007, 2008; Musial & others, 2009; Stiggins, 2008). Let's examine some trends in this regard.

Trends in Alternative Assessment

One current trend is to require students to solve some type of authentic problem or to perform in terms of completing a project or demonstrating other skills outside the context of a test or an essay (Gallavan, 2009; Gronlund & Waugh, 2009). Another

Middle Ages option model

Directions:
Make a model of a creature or character from the Middle Ages. Write a one-half to one page description of your character (tell who or what it is and its importance in the Middle Ages). Your model must portray the creature or character through the use of appropriate costume, props, or other attributes.

Scoring Guide
25   Model portrays the character or creature and time period through the use of attire, props, and other attributes
10   Artistic quality
15   Model shows evidence of effort
50   A one-half to 1 page written description of the character is included

Family history option: family tree poster

Directions:
Make a poster of your family tree, going back at least three generations. Provide as much information about the family members as possible, including, but not limited to, birthdate, death date (if not living), occupation, place of birth, accomplishments, and so on. In addition, provide at least two anecdotes about your family's history (for example, how they came to live in our town, special notoriety, honors, awards, medals). You must *write out* your family tree! (You may not make a copy of a commercially prepared family tree and paste it on the poster.) Make your poster attractive and neat!

Scoring Guide
25   Family tree includes at least three generations prior to you
25   In addition to names, most entries include information such as birth, death, and place of birth
25   Poster includes at least two anecdotes about interesting or well-known family members
15   Poster is neatly and attractively typed or written by you
10   Mechanics, spelling, usage

FIGURE 16.7 Examples of Alternative Assessment in a Middle School Language–Arts Class

trend is to have students create a learning portfolio to demonstrate what they have learned (Belgrad, 2008; Kingore, 2008). Such alternative assessments are needed to make instruction compatible with contemporary views of learning and motivation (Stiggins, 2008).

Alternative assessments offer students more choices than they would have in taking a test or writing an essay (Hammerman, 2009; Oosterhof, 2009). Consider several alternative assessments that a middle school language-arts teacher devised (Combs, 1997). She gave students a menu of options to choose from that included book reports, artwork, videos, and models. For example, in a unit on mystery, students might choose to write a report on an author of mystery stories, write an original mystery, make a children's mystery book, or conduct an interview with a private investigator. Each of these options came with a detailed set of instructions and a scoring guide for quality control. Figure 16.7 shows the directions and scoring guide for alternative assessments that focus on the Middle Ages and family history.

Authentic assessment means evaluating a student's knowledge or skill in a context that approximates the real world or real life as closely as possible. Traditional assessment has involved the use of paper-and-pencil tests that are often far removed from real-world contexts. An increasing trend is to assess students with items that more closely reflect reality (Fiene & McMahon, 2007). In some circles, the terms *performance assessment* and *authentic assessment* have been used interchangeably. However, not all performance assessments are authentic (McMillan, 2008).

Critics of authentic assessment argue that such assessments are not necessarily superior to more conventional assessments, such as multiple-choice and essay tests (Terwilliger, 1997). They say that the proponents of authentic assessment rarely

authentic assessment Evaluating a student's knowledge or skill in a context that approximates the real world or real life as closely as possible.

(a) The equipment consists of a spinning Earth globe inside a carton box, three sticky towers, and a flashlight; the students stick Towers A and B at two specific U.S. locations on the globe and are told what Tower C's shadow looks like when it is noon for Towers A and B. They have to find out where in the U.S. Tower C is. The solution requires modeling the sunlight by using the flashlight to project the towers' shadows onto the globe.

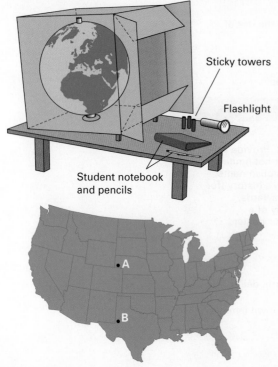

Sticky towers

Flashlight

Student notebook and pencils

(b) Draw a dot on this map to show where you think Tower C is. How did you figure out where Tower C is?

(c)

Observation/results	score
Tower C is in eastern United States	1
Tower C is in northeastern United States	1
Tower C is somewhere between Pennsylvania and Maine	1

Data gathering/modeling		score
Flashlight Position	Points flashlight at Equator	2
Flashlight Motion	Moves flashlight from E to W	2
Globe Rotation	Rotates globe Rotates globe from W to E	1 2
Towers	Moves Tower C around on the map/globe until shadow is matched	1
	Moves Tower C around on the map/globe in the E/NE region until shadow is matched	2
Shadows	Uses shadows of Towers A and B as reference	1

(b) The response format involves having students record in notebooks their solutions, the actions they carried out, and the reasoning behind their actions.

(c) Students' performances are scored for the accuracy of their results and the accuracy of their modeling, reasoning, and observations.

FIGURE 16.8 A Performance-Based Assessment in Science: Daytime Astronomy

present data in support of the validity of authentic assessments (Braden, 2005). They also point out that authentic assessments don't adequately examine knowledge and basic skills.

Performance Assessment

Moving from traditional assessment with objective tests to performance assessment has been described as going from "knowing" to "showing" (Burz & Marshall, 1996). Performance assessments include what is commonly thought of as students' actual performances (such as in dance, music, art, and physical education), as well as papers, projects, oral presentations, experiments, and portfolios (Gallavan, 2009; Gronlund & Waugh, 2009). Figure 16.8 shows an example of a performance assessment in science (Solano-Flores & Shavelson, 1997).

Some disciplines, such as art, music, and physical education, have been using performance assessments for many years. The major change in performance assessment has involved introducing these forms of assessment into the traditional "academic areas."

Features of Performance Assessment Performance assessments often include an emphasis on "doing" open-ended activities for which there is no correct, objective answer and that may assess higher-level thinking. Performance assessment tasks sometimes also are realistic. Evaluating performance often includes direct methods of evaluation, self-assessment, assessment of group performance as well as individual performance, and an extended period of time for assessment (Hambleton, 1996).

Traditional tests emphasize what students know. Performance assessments are designed to evaluate what students know and can do. In many cases, there is no correct, objective answer. For example, there is no one "correct answer" when a student gives a talk in class, creates a painting, performs a gymnastic routine, or designs a science project. Many performance assessments give students considerable freedom to construct their own responses rather than narrowing their range of answers. Although this makes scoring more difficult, it provides a context for evaluating students' higher-level thinking skills, such as the ability to think deeply about an issue or a topic (Stiggins, 2008).

Performance assessments use direct methods of evaluation, such as evaluating writing samples to assess writing skills and oral presentations to assess speaking and judging oral presentations to assess speaking skills (Gallavan, 2009; Oosterhof, 2009). Observing a student give an oral presentation is a more direct assessment than asking the student a series of questions about speaking skills on a paper-and-pencil test.

Some performance assessments also involve having students evaluate their own performance. This emphasis shifts responsibility away from teachers and places it more squarely on the student's shoulders. Rubrics are useful aids to students in conducting self-assessments. For example, students might be required to evaluate a scrapbook that they have created (Goodrich, 1997). One criterion for evaluation might be "Gives enough details?" with the following possible responses: excellent ("Yes, I put enough details to give the reader a sense of time, place, and events"), good ("Yes, I put in some details, but some key details are missing"), minimal ("No, I did not put in enough details but did include a few"), and inadequate ("No, I had almost no details").

Some performance assessments evaluate how effectively a group of students perform, not just how the students perform individually. Thus, a group of students might be assigned to create a science project rather than having each student do a project individually. Evaluation of the student can include both the individual's contribution and the group's product. Group projects are often complex and allow for the assessment of cooperative skills, communication skills, and leadership skills.

Finally, as we noted, performance assessments may take place over an extended period of time (Gallavan, 2009). In traditional assessment, assessment occurs in a single time frame. For example, a teacher gives a multiple-choice test and students are allowed an hour to take it. By contrast, it is not unusual for performance assessments to involve sustained work over days, weeks, and even months. For example, a student might be evaluated once a month on the progress the student is making on a science project, then receive a final evaluation when the project is completed (Hammerman, 2009; Liu, 2009).

Guidelines for Performance Assessment Guidelines for using performance assessments cover four general issues (Airasian & Russell, 2008): (1) establishing a clear purpose, (2) identifying observable criteria, (3) providing an appropriate setting, and (4) judging or scoring the performance.

Make sure that any performance assessment has a clear purpose and that a clear decision can be made from the assessment. The purposes can be diverse: to assign a grade, to evaluate a student's progress, to recognize the important steps in a performance, to generate products to be included in a learning portfolio, to provide concrete examples of students' work for admission to college or other programs, and so forth.

Performance criteria are specific behaviors that students need to perform effectively as part of the assessment. Establishing performance criteria helps the teacher to go beyond general descriptions (such as "Do an oral presentation" or "Complete a science project") in specifying what the student needs to do (Easton, 2007). Performance criteria help you make your observations more systematic and focused. As guidelines, they direct your observations. Without such criteria, your observations can be unsystematic and haphazard. Communicating these performance criteria to students at the beginning of instruction lets students know how to focus their learning.

performance criteria Specific behaviors that students need to perform effectively as part of an assessment.

Once you have clearly outlined the performance criteria, it is important to specify the setting in which you will observe the performance or product. You may want to observe behaviors directly in the regular flow of classroom activity, in a special context you create in the classroom, or in a context outside the classroom. As a rule of thumb it is a good idea to observe the student on more than one occasion, because a single performance might not fairly represent the student's knowledge or skill.

Finally, you will need to score or rate the performance. *Scoring rubrics* involve the criteria that are used to judge performance, what the range in the quality of the performance should look like, what score should be given and what that score means, and how the different levels of quality should be described and differentiated from one another (Depka, 2007; Educational Testing Service, Arter, & Cappius, 2008; Fitzgerald, 2007; Larkin, 2008).

In preparing a rubric, you may want to (Re: Learning by Design, 2000):

1. *Include a scale of possible points to be assigned in scoring work.* High numbers usually are assigned to the best work. Scales typically use 4, 5, or 6 as the highest score, down to 1 or 0 for the lowest score.

2. *Provide descriptors for each performance criteria to increase reliability and avoid biased scoring.*

3. *Decide whether the rubric will be generic, genre-specific, or task-specific.* If generic, the rubric can be used to judge a broad performance, such as communication or problem solving. If genre-specific, the rubric applies to a more specific type of performance, such as an essay, a speech, or a narrative as a form of communication; open-ended or closed-end problems as kinds of problems solved. A task-specific rubric is unique to a single task, such as a single math problem or a speech on a specific topic.

4. *Decide whether the rubric should be longitudinal.* This type of rubric assesses progress over time toward mastery of educational objectives. One strategy for developing rubrics is to work backward from *exemplars*—examples of student work (McMillan, 1997, p. 218). "These exemplars can be analyzed to determine what descriptors distinguish them. The examples can also be used as *anchor* papers for making judgments, and can be given to students to illustrate the dimensions." An *anchor* is a sample of work or performance used to set the specific performance standard for a rubric level. Thus, attached to a paragraph describing a six-level performance in writing might be two or three samples of writing to illustrate several levels (Re: Learning by Design, 2000). Figure 16.9

FIGURE 16.9 Scoring Rubric for a Report on an Invention

Note: A teacher might assign each of the columns a score and/or label, such as column 1: 4 (Excellent), column 2: 3 (Good), column 3: 2 (Minimal), and column 4: 1 (Inadequate).

Criteria	Quality			
Purposes	The report explains the key purposes of the invention and also points out less obvious ones.	The report explains all of the key purposes of the invention.	The report explains some of the purposes of the invention but misses key purposes.	The report does not refer to the purposes of the invention.
Features	The report details both key and hidden features of the invention and explains how they serve several purposes.	The report details the key features of the invention and explains the purposes they serve.	The report neglects some of the features of the invention or the purposes they serve.	The report does not detail the features of the invention or the purposes they serve.
Critique	The report discusses the strengths and weaknesses of the invention, and suggests ways that it can be improved.	The report discusses the strengths and weaknesses of the invention.	The report discusses either the strengths or weaknesses of the invention, but not both.	The report does not mention the strengths or weaknesses of the invention.
Connections	The report makes appropriate connections between the purposes and features of the invention and many different kinds of phenomena.	The report makes appropriate connections between the purposes and features of the invention and one or two phenomena.	The report makes unclear or inappropriate connections between the invention and other phenomena.	The report makes no connections between the invention and other things.

BEST PRACTICES
Strategies for Developing Scoring Rubrics

Here are some good strategies for incorporating scoring rubrics in performance assessments (Goodrich, 1997; McMillan, 2007; Re: Learning by Design, 2000):

1. *Match the type of rating with the purpose of the assessment.* If your purpose is global and you need a general judgment, use a holistic scale. If your purpose is to provide specific feedback on different aspects of a performance, use a more analytical approach.

2. *Share the criteria with students prior to instruction.* This encourages students to incorporate the descriptions as standards to guide their work.

3. *Build your rubrics from the top, starting from a description of an exemplary performance.* Even if no student can perform at an exemplary level, the rubric should be built from a picture of excellence to establish an anchor for scoring. A good strategy is to use two or three examples of excellence rather than a single example so that students are not limited in their thinking about what an excellent performance is. After you have described the best level of quality, describe the worst; then fill in the middle levels.

4. *Carefully construct the rubric language for each criterion or score.* Use words such as excellent and good, and carefully describe what each term means. Typically, you will have a paragraph for each criterion or score that includes concrete indicators of when the criterion or score has been met.

5. *Make rubrics more authentic.* Criteria should validly, not arbitrarily, distinguish different degrees of performance. Here are some criteria that are often used in assessing writing in large-scale performance tests: organization, usage/word choice, focus, sentence construction, mechanics, and voice. However, the following criteria are more authentic in that they relate more clearly to the impact of the writing (and they include the previously mentioned criteria without restricting the writer to conventions and rules): clarity, memorability, persuasiveness, and enticingness.

6. *Show students models.* Let students examine examples of good and not-so-good work. Identify what's good or bad about the models.

7. *Take appropriate steps to minimize scoring error.* A scoring system should be objective and consistent. Some types of errors, in particular, should be avoided in scoring rubrics. The most common errors involve personal bias and halo effects of the person making the judgment. Personal bias occurs when teachers tend to give students higher scores (such as mostly 5 and 6 on a 1- to 6-point scale), lower scores (give mostly 1 or 2), or scores in the middle (give mostly 3 or 4). A halo effect occurs when a teacher's general impression of the student influences the score given on a particular performance.

shows a scoring rubric for scoring a report on an invention. Figure 16.10 indicates the importance of clarity in creating rubrics.

Evaluating Performance Assessment   Many educational psychologists support the increased use of performance-based assessment (Gallavan, 2009; Stiggins, 2008). They contend that performance assessments involve students more in their learning, encourage higher-level thinking skills, can measure what is really important in the curriculum, and can tie assessment more to real-world, real-life experiences.

Criterion: gains audience's attention
Quality

(a)	Creative beginning	Boring beginning	No beginning
(b)	Gives details or an amusing fact, a series of questions, a short demonstration, a colorful visual or a personal reason for why they picked the topic	Gives a one- or two-sentence introduction, then starts the speech	Does not attempt to gain the audience's attention, just starts the speech

FIGURE 16.10 Creating Clarity in a Rubric for One Dimension of an Oral Presentation

The descriptions in (a) are rather vague and do not clearly specify what students need to do to be evaluated very positively on the criterion. The descriptions in (b) provide more detailed specifications of how the criterion will be rated, a recommended strategy.

Traditional tests	Portfolios
• Separate learning, testing, and teaching	• Link assessment and teaching to learning
• Fail to assess the impact of prior knowledge on learning by using short passages that are often isolated and unfamiliar	• Address the importance of the student's prior knowledge as a critical determinant to learning by using authentic assessment activities
• Rely on materials requesting only literal information	• Provide opportunities to demonstrate inferential and critical thinking that are essential for constructing meaning
• Prohibit collaboration during the assessment process	
• Often treat skills in isolated contexts to determine achievement for reporting purposes	• Represent a collaborative approach to assessment involving both students and teachers
• Assess students across a limited range of assignments that may not match what students do in classrooms	• Use multifaceted activities while recognizing that learning requires integration and coordination of communication skills
• Assess students in a predetermined situation where the content is fixed	• Represent the full range of instructional activities that students are doing in their classrooms
• Assess all students on the same dimensions	• Can measure the student's ability to perform appropriately in unanticipated situations
• Address only achievement	• Measure each student's achievements while allowing individual differences
• Seldom provide vehicles for assessing students' abilities to monitor their own learning	• Address improvement, effort, and achievement
• Are mechanically scored or scored by teachers who have little input into the assessment	• Implement self-assessment by having students monitor their learning
• Rarely include items that assess emotional responses to learning	• Engage students in assessing their progress and/or accomplishments and establishing on-going learning goals
	• Provide opportunities to reflect upon feelings about learning

FIGURE 16.11 Contrasting Traditional Tests and Portfolios

However, "although support for performance-based assessment is high in many parts of the United States and Canada, effective implementation" faces several hurdles (Hambleton, 1996, p. 903). Performance assessments often "take considerably more time to construct, administer, and score than objective tests." Also, many performance tests do not meet the standards of validity and reliability advocated by many educational psychologists. Moreover, the research base for performance tests is not well established.

Still, even the strongest supporters of traditional tests acknowledge that these tests do not measure all of what schools expect students to learn (Hambleton, 1996). Although planning, constructing, and scoring performance tests is challenging, teachers should make every effort to include performance assessments as an important aspect of their teaching (Stiggins, 2008).

Portfolio Assessment

Interest in portfolio assessment has increased dramatically in recent years (Oosterhof, 2009). Portfolios represent a significant departure from traditional tests of learning (Glazer, 2007; Kingore, 2008). Figure 16.11 summarizes the contrast between portfolios and traditional testing.

A **portfolio** consists of a systematic and organized collection of a student's work that demonstrates the student's skills and accomplishments. A portfolio is a purposeful collection of work that tells the story of the student's progress and achievements (Belgrad, 2008). It is much more than a compilation of student papers stuffed into a manila folder or a collection of memorabilia pasted into a scrapbook. To qualify for inclusion in a portfolio, each piece of work should be created and organized in

portfolio A systematic and organized collection of a student's work that demonstrates the student's skills and accomplishments.

a way that demonstrates progress and purpose. Portfolios can include many different types of work, such as writing samples, journal entries, videotapes, art, teacher comments, posters, interviews, poetry, test results, problem solutions, recordings of foreign language communication, self-assessments, and any other expression of the student that the teacher believes demonstrates the student's skills and accomplishments (Kingore, 2008). Portfolios can be collected on paper, in photographs, and on audiotape, videotape, computer disk, or CD-ROM. Assessment expert Joan Herman (1996) says that portfolio assessment has become increasingly popular because it is a natural way to integrate instruction and assessment.

Four classes of evidence that can be placed in students' portfolios are artifacts, reproductions, attestations, and productions (Barton & Collins, 1997). *Artifacts* are documents or products, such as student papers and homework, that are produced during normal academic work in the classroom. *Reproductions* consist of documentation of a student's work outside the classroom, such as special projects and interviews. For example, a student's description of an interview with a local scientist in the community about the scientist's work is a reproduction. *Attestations* represent the teacher's or other responsible persons' documentation of the student's progress. For example, a teacher might write evaluative notes about a student's oral presentation and place them in the student's portfolio. *Productions* are documents the student prepares especially for the portfolio. Productions consist of three types of materials: goal statements, reflections, and captions. Students generate goal statements about what they want to accomplish with their portfolio, write down their reflections about their work and describe their progress, and create captions that describe each piece of work in the portfolio and its importance.

Using Portfolios Effectively   Effective use of portfolios for assessment requires (1) establishing the portfolio's purpose, (2) involving the student in decisions about it, (3) reviewing the portfolio with the student, (4) setting criteria for evaluation, and (5) scoring and judging the portfolio.

Establishing Purpose   Portfolios can be used for different purposes (Belgrad, 2008; Van Tartwijk & others, 2007). Two broad types of purpose are to document growth and to show best work. A **growth portfolio** consists of the student's work over an extended time frame (throughout the school year or even longer) to reveal the student's progress in meeting learning targets. Growth portfolios also are sometimes referred to as "developmental portfolios." Growth portfolios are especially helpful in providing concrete evidence of how much a student has changed or learned over time. As students examine their portfolios, they can see for themselves how much they have improved. One example of a growth portfolio is the Integrated Language Arts Portfolio used in the elementary school grades in Juneau, Alaska (Arter, 1995). It is designed to replace report cards and grades as a way to demonstrate growth and accomplishments. Growth is tracked along a developmental continuum for levels of skills in reading, writing, speaking, and listening. A student's status on the continuum is marked at several designated times during the year. Samples of the student's work are used as the basis for judgments about the student's developmental level.

A **best-work portfolio** showcases the student's most outstanding work. Sometimes it even is called a "showcase portfolio." Best-work portfolios are more selective than developmental portfolios and often include the student's latest product. Best-work portfolios are especially useful for parent-teacher conferences, students' future teachers, and admission to higher education levels.

"Passportfolios," or "proficiency portfolios," are sometimes used to demonstrate competence and readiness to move on to a new level of work (Lankes, 1995). For example, the Science Portfolio is an optional aspect of the Golden State Evaluation in California (California State Department of Education, 1994). It is produced during a year of science and contains a problem-solving investigation, a creative expression (presenting a scientific idea in a unique and original manner), a "growth through

growth portfolio A portfolio of work over an extended time frame (throughout the school year or longer) to reveal the student's progress in meeting learning targets.

best-work portfolio A portfolio that showcases the student's most outstanding work.

DEVELOPMENTAL FOCUS 16.3
How Do You Use Portfolios in Your Classroom?

Early Childhood

We use portfolios to collect specific work done by our children—such as sample writing and pictures—three times during the year. We arrange these portfolios similarly so that we can assess and compare the child's development over the year. Parents are shown the portfolios during conferences to demonstrate how their child has progressed. We also use portfolios as a tool to assess possible developmental delays.

—Valarie Gorham, *Kiddie Quarters, Inc.*

Elementary School: Grades K–5

My fourth-graders do a "Best Work" writing portfolio and a "Draft" writing portfolio. The process of gathering materials for both of these portfolios takes roughly five weeks, with writing lessons mixed in. By the end of the year, students see their writing progress by examining both their Draft and Best Work portfolios.

—Shane Schwarz, *Clinton Elementary School*

Middle School: Grades 6–8

I have my students keep portfolios with their tests, quizzes, reports, projects, essays, and other important assignments. A key part of the portfolio process is when I instruct students to take their portfolios home, evaluate their work with their parents or guardians, and then come back to school with a set of goals to improve their work in class.

—Casey Maass, *Edison Middle School*

High School: Grades 9–12

I use portfolios for my work-experience students. Four times a year, they include evaluations from supervisors at their job assignments, their own reflections on the job itself, completed job applications, and feedback on interviews that they have gone on. I encourage students to assemble their portfolios professionally for use when seeking their next job.

—Sandy Swanson, *Menomonee Falls High School*

writing" section that demonstrates progress over time in understanding a concept, and self-reflection. The Central Park East Secondary School in New York City uses portfolios to determine graduation eligibility. Students are required to complete fourteen portfolios that demonstrate their competence in areas such as science and technology, ethics and social issues, community service, and history (Gold & Lanzoni, 1993).

Involving Students in Selecting Portfolio Materials Many teachers let students make at least some of the decisions about the portfolio's contents. When students are allowed to choose the contents for their own portfolios, a good strategy is to encourage self-reflection by having them write a brief description of why they chose each piece of work (Airasian & Russell, 2008).

Reviewing with Students Explain to students at the beginning of the year what portfolios are and how they will be used. You also should have a number of student-teacher conferences throughout the year to review the student's progress and help the student to plan future work for the portfolio (McMillan, 2007).

Setting Criteria for Evaluation   Clear and systematic performance criteria are essential for effectively using portfolios (Tillema & Smith, 2007). Clear learning targets for students make developing performance criteria much easier. Ask yourself what knowledge and skills you want your students to have. This should be the focus of your teaching and your performance criteria.

Scoring and Judging   It takes considerable time to score and judge portfolios (Airasian & Russell, 2008). Teachers must evaluate not only each individual item but also the portfolio as a whole. When the portfolio's purpose is to provide descriptive information about the student for the teacher at the next grade level, no scoring or summarizing of the portfolio might be necessary. However, when its purpose is to diagnose, reflect improvement, provide evidence for effective instruction, motivate students to reflect on their work, or give grades to students, summary scoring and judgments are needed. Checklists and rating scales are commonly used for this purpose. As with other aspects of portfolio assessment, some teachers give students the opportunity to evaluate and critique their own work.

Evaluating the Role of Portfolios in Assessment   Learning portfolios have several strengths: Their comprehensive nature captures the complexity and completeness of the student's work and accomplishments. They provide opportunities for encouraging student decision making and self-reflection. They motivate students to think critically and deeply. And they provide an excellent mechanism for evaluating student progress and improvement (Musial & others, 2009).

Learning portfolios also have several weaknesses: They take considerable time to coordinate and evaluate. Their complexity and uniqueness make them difficult to evaluate, and their reliability is often much lower than that of traditional tests. And their use in large-scale assessments (such as statewide evaluation) is expensive. However, even with these weaknesses in mind, most educational psychology experts and educational organizations, such as the National Education Association, support the use of portfolios.

Now that you've read about many types of assessment, this is a good time to think about what your classroom assessment philosophy will be. *Self-Assessment 16.1* gives you this opportunity.

Review, Reflect, and Practice

(3) Describe some types of alternative assessments.

REVIEW

- What makes an assessment "authentic"? What are some criticisms of authentic assessments?
- What are some of the features of performance assessment? What are some guidelines for using them?
- What is a portfolio and how can portfolios be used in assessment? What are some strengths and weaknesses of portfolios?

REFLECT

- Suppose that you were teaching this course in educational psychology. How would you go about creating rubrics for assessing answers to the preceding three items?

(continued)

SELF-ASSESSMENT 16.1
Planning My Classroom Assessment Practices

With the subject matter and grade level at which you plan to teach in mind, examine the following list of assessments that we have discussed in this chapter. Rate each of the assessments on this scale: 1 = I don't plan to use this at all, 2 = I plan to use this occasionally, 3 = I plan to use this moderately, 4 = I plan to use this often, and 5 = This will be one of the most important assessments I will use.

	1	2	3	4	5
1. Informal observations in preinstructional assessment					
2. Structured exercises in preinstructional assessment					
3. Observation during instruction					
4. Questions during instruction					
5. Student self-assessment					
6. Assessments of students' motivation, effort, and participation					
7. True/false items					
8. Multiple-choice items					
9. Matching					
10. Short-answer items					
11. Essays					
12. Authentic assessment					
13. Experiments					
14. Projects					
15. Oral presentations					
16. Interviews					
17. Performances					
18. Exhibitions					
19. Portfolios					

Look back through your responses and then use this information to help you formulate your classroom assessment philosophy here. If you need more space, do this outside the book or on the student Web site.

_____

_____

_____

Review, Reflect, and Practice

PRAXIS™ PRACTICE

1. Nicole has just been told that as part of her teacher certification process, there will be a performance assessment. Which of the following is the best performance assessment of Nicole's teaching skills?
   a. a multiple-choice exam
   b. an essay exam

Review, Reflect, and Practice

    c. an exam based on case studies

    d. direct observation of classroom teaching

2. Kyle is working on his portfolio for journalism class. Included in the portfolio are his teacher's evaluation notes regarding articles he has written for the school newspaper. These notes are examples of which of the following:

    a. artifacts

    b. attestations

    c. productions

    d. reproductions

Please see the answer key at the end of the book.

4 GRADING AND REPORTING PERFORMANCE

| The Purposes of Grading | The Components of a Grading System | Reporting Students' Progress and Grades to Parents | Some Issues in Grading |

"Your grading curve and my learning curve don't intersect."

Dave Carpenter from *Phi Delta Kappan* (1997). Reprinted with permission of Dave Carpenter.

Grading means translating descriptive assessment information into letters, numbers, or other marks that indicate the quality of a student's learning or performance.

The Purposes of Grading

Grading is carried out to communicate meaningful information about a student's learning and achievement (Anderson, 2008; Oosterhof, 2009; Taylor & Nolen, 2008). In this process, grades serve four basic purposes (Airasian & Russell, 2008):

- *Administrative.* Grades help determine students' class rank, credits for graduation, and whether a student should be promoted to the next grade.
- *Informational.* Grades can be used to communicate with students, parents, and others (such as admissions officers for subsequent schooling) about a student's work. A grade represents the teacher's overall conclusion about how well a student has met instructional objectives and learning targets.
- *Motivational.* Many students work harder because they are extrinsically motivated by a desire for high grades and a fear of low grades.
- *Guidance.* Grades help students, parents, and counselors to select appropriate courses and levels of work for students. They provide information about which students might require special services and what levels of future education students will likely be able to handle.

The Components of a Grading System

Grades reflect teachers' judgments. Three main types of teacher judgments underlie a teacher's grading system (Airasian & Russell, 2008): (1) What standard of comparison will I use for grading? (2) What aspects of students' performance will I use to establish grades? and (3) How will I weight different kinds of evidence in giving grades?

Standards of Comparison A student's performance can be graded by comparing it with the performance of other students or to predefined standards of performance.

grading Translating descriptive assessment information into letters, numbers, or other marks that indicate the quality of a student's learning or performance.

Comparing Performance Across Students **Norm-referenced grading** is a grading system based on comparison of a student's performance with that of other students in the class or of other classes and other students. In such a system, students get high grades for performing better than most of their classmates, and students get low grades for performing worse. Norm-referenced grading is commonly referred to as *grading on the curve*. In norm-referenced grading, the grading scale determines what percentages of students get particular grades. In most instances, the scale is created so that the largest percentage of students get *C*s.

This is a typical breakdown of grades: 15 percent *A*'s, 25 percent *B*'s, 40 percent *C*'s, 15 percent *D*'s, and 5 percent *F*'s. In assigning grades, instructors often look for gaps in the range of scores. If six students score 92 to 100 and ten students score 81 to 88, and there are no scores between 88 and 92, the teacher would assign a grade of *A* to the 92 to 100 scores and a *B* to the 81 to 88 scores. Norm-referenced grading has been criticized for reducing students' motivation, increasing their anxiety, increasing negative interactions among students, and hindering learning.

Comparing Performance with a Predetermined Standard **Criterion-referenced grading** is being used when students receive a certain grade for a certain level of performance, regardless of any comparison with the work of other students. Sometimes criterion-referenced grading is called *absolute grading*. Typically, criterion-referenced grading is based on the proportion of points attained on a test or the level of mastery reached in a performance skill, such as giving an oral presentation and meeting all the predetermined criteria. Criterion-referenced grading is recommended over norm-referenced grading.

In theory, the standard established is supposed to be absolute, but in practice it doesn't always work out that way (McMillan, 2007). For example, a school system often develops a grading system that goes something like this: *A* = 94 to 100 percent correct, *B* = 87 to 93 percent, *C* = 77 to 86 percent, *D* = 70 to 76 percent, and *F* = below 70 percent. Although this system is absolute in the sense that every student must get 94 points to get an *A* and every student who does not get at least 70 points gets an *F*, teachers and classrooms vary enormously in what constitutes mastery of material to get a 94, an 87, a 77, or a 70. One teacher might give very hard tests, another very easy tests.

Many teachers use different cutoff scores than the ones just mentioned. Some teachers argue that low grades discourage student motivation and refuse to give *D*'s or *F*'s; others won't fail students unless their scores fall below 50.

Standards-based grading is a recent development based on criterion-referenced grading. It involves basing grading on standards that students are expected to achieve in a course (O'Shea, 2009). In some cases, national associations, such as the National Council of Teachers of Mathematics (NCTM), have developed standards that students should achieve. Thus, in one form of standards-based grading, a mathematics teacher might tie students' grades to how well they meet these national standards.

Aspects of Performance Over the course of a grading period, students will likely have created many products that can be evaluated and used as a basis for grading. These can include test and quiz results, as well as various alternative assessments such as oral reports, projects, interviews, and homework. Increasingly, portfolios are used as the complete collection of materials to be graded or a portion of the work on which an overall grade is based. Some educators argue that grades should be based only on academic performance. In the view of other educators, grades should be based mainly on academic performance, but teacher ratings of motivation, effort, and participation can be factored in as well.

Many teachers use tests as the main, or even sole, basis for assigning grades. However, many assessment experts recommend basing an overall grade on a series of tests and other types of assessments (McMillan, 2007). Thus, a semester grade in geography might be based on two major tests and a final, eight quizzes, homework, two oral reports, and a project. Basing a grade on a series of tests and different types

norm-referenced grading A grading system based on a comparison of a student's performance with that of other students in the class or of other classes and other students.

criterion-referenced grading A grading system based on a certain grade for a certain level of performance regardless of any comparison with the work of other students.

of assessment helps to balance out students' strengths and weaknesses, as well as compensate for a poor performance or two because of internal and external sources of measurement error.

Some educators advocate factoring characteristics such as motivation, effort, and participation into grades, especially by giving borderline students a plus or minus. Thus, a teacher might convert a student's B to a B+ if the student was highly motivated, put forth considerable effort, and actively participated in the class—or to a B–, if the student was poorly motivated, made little effort, and did not actively participate. However, some educators stress that grades should be based only on academic performance. One of the problems with including factors such as effort in grades is the difficulty in determining the reliability and validity of effort. Measures of effort or improvement can be made more systematic and reliable by developing scoring rubrics and examples (McMillan, 2007).

Weighting Different Kinds of Evidence   You will need to determine how much weight to give the different components of a student's grade. For example, the teacher might arrive at a weighting system that looks something like this:

Major tests (2):	20 percent
Final test:	25 percent
Quizzes:	20 percent
Homework:	5 percent
Oral report:	10 percent
Project:	20 percent

Many teachers don't use homework as a component for a grade. One reason for this is that when a student's grade depends on homework or other work done outside class, parents might be tempted to do their child's work to ensure a high grade. Another reason is that including homework as a component of grading favors students from better home environments. As with other aspects of classroom assessment, your judgment is involved in how you synthesize information to arrive at a student's grade. If a student fails to turn in a certain number of homework assignments, some teachers lower the student's grade.

Reporting Students' Progress and Grades to Parents

Grades are the most common method of informing parents about a child's progress and performance in the classroom (Airasian & Russell, 2008). However, grades by themselves provide limited information, are usually given infrequently, communicate little in the way of specific information about how the student is learning, and rarely include information about the student's motivation, cooperation, and classroom behavior. Because of these limitations, more than grades are needed to give parents a full portrait of the student (Durham, 2006).

The Report Card   The report card is a standard method of reporting students' progress and grades to parents. The form of judgments on report cards varies from one school system to another, and, in many cases, from one grade level to another. Some report cards convey letter grades (typically *A, B, C, D,* and *F,* sometimes also allowing pluses and minuses). Some report cards convey numerical scores (such as 91 in math, 85 in English, and so on). Other report cards have a pass/fail category in one or more subjects. Yet other report cards have checklists indicating skills or objectives the student has attained. Some report cards have categories for affective characteristics, such as effort, cooperation, and other appropriate and inappropriate behaviors.

THROUGH THE EYES OF STUDENTS

Accepting Responsibility

Our teacher tells us that our grades are our responsibility. Nobody else's. "Don't blame anybody else but yourself if you don't make good grades," she says. At the beginning of the year, she said she would help us every way she could to help us make good grades and she has been good about that.

Cassandra
Middle School Student
Atlanta, Georgia

"How much to shred a report card?"

© Martha F. Campbell. Reprinted by permission.

BEST PRACTICES
Strategies for Parent-Teacher Conferences Related to Grades and Assessment

Here are some good strategies for meeting with parents about their child's progress and grades (Payne, 1997):

1. *Be prepared.* Review the student's performance prior to the meeting with parents. Think about what you are going to say to the parents.

2. *Be positive.* Even if the student has performed poorly, try to find at least some areas to discuss in which the student has performed well. This does not mean glossing over and ignoring a student's lack of achievement; it means including positive areas in addition to the negative ones.

3. *Be objective.* Even though you want to look for positive aspects of the student's record to communicate to parents, be objective and honest. Don't give parents false hopes if the student has low ability in a particular subject area.

4. *Practice good communication skills.* Good communication means being an active listener and giving parents adequate opportunities to contribute to the conversation. Make sure that parents and students understand your grading criteria. Next, Lynn Ayres, an English teacher at East Middle School, Ypsilanti, Michigan, provides her thoughts about this topic.

THROUGH THE EYES OF TEACHERS
Some Grading Strategies

I think it is extremely important that parents and students clearly know what is expected of students if they are to succeed in my class. I try to help students understand that they are in control of the grade they get. If students think a grading system is capricious or unknowable, it creates frustration, anxiety, and is of little use in motivating students. By getting them to see that their grades are in their own hands, I move to the position of "facilitator" in the classroom. The students see me as someone who is there to *help* them achieve rather than someone who sits in judgment of their work and gives them a grade.

5. *Don't talk about other students.* The focus of the parent-teacher conference should be on the parent's child. Don't compare the child with other students.

"I don't know why you're so surprised by his poor grades. Every day you asked him what he did at school, and every day he answered, 'Nothing.'"

© Art Bouthiller. Reprinted with permission.

Checklists of skills and objectives are mainly used in elementary schools or kindergartens. In the higher elementary school grade levels and secondary schools, letter grades are mainly used, although these might be accompanied by other information such as written comments.

Written Progress Reports Another reporting strategy is to provide parents with a weekly, biweekly, or monthly report of the student's progress and achievement (McMillan, 2007). These written reports can include the student's performance on tests and quizzes, projects, oral reports, and so on. They also can include information about the student's motivation, cooperation, and behavior, as well as suggestions for how parents can help students improve their performance.

Parent-Teacher Conferences Parent-teacher conferences are another way to communicate information about grades and assessment. Such conferences are both a responsibility and an opportunity (Durham, 2006). Parents have a right to know how their child is doing in school and how their child might improve. Conferences provide an opportunity for giving parents helpful information about how they can be partners with you in helping the child learn more effectively.

Some Issues in Grading

Should a zero be given to a missed assignment or paper? Should teachers go strictly by the numbers when assigning a grade? Should grading be abolished? Is there too much grade inflation? These are important issues that concern many educators today.

Should a Missed Assignment or Paper Receive a Zero?   One grading issue is whether a student should be given a zero or at least some points for a missed assignment or paper. Including a zero with other scores badly skews the mean of the scores. Many experts on assessment recommend not using a zero in this manner because it weights the assignment or paper more than what was intended because the interval between 0 and 65 or 70 is more than the intervals between the scores for other grades (McMillan, 2007). Using a score of 60 for a missed assignment or paper is considered more reasonable.

Should Teachers Go Strictly by the Numbers in Grading?   A concern in making out grades is that too many teachers engage in "mindless" number crunching, which is now more likely to occur with grading software available. No matter how objective the process is for averaging scores and grades, grading is a matter of professional judgment (Durham, 2006). Going strictly by the numbers can result in a grade that is not consistent with the actual knowledge and skill of the student, especially if pulled down by minor assignments and homework, or a later paper. In the end, it is important for teachers to be confident that the grade they give reflects what the student knows, understands, and is able to do in relation to standards of performance (McMillan, 2007).

Should Grading Be Abolished?   Occasionally there are calls to abandon grades, usually based on the belief that evaluation of students is necessary but that competitive grading deemphasizes learning in favor of judging. Critics argue that grading discourages the vast majority of students, especially those who receive below-average grades. The critics often call for more constructive evaluation that encourages students to engage in maximum effort by underscoring their strengths, identifying concrete ways to improve, and providing positive feedback (Culbertson & Jalongo, 1999). Critics also point out that grading often motivates students to study only the material that will be on the test.

What are some issues in grading?

As classroom assessment experts Peter Airasian and Michael Russell (2008) concluded, grades are powerful symbols in our society that are taken seriously by students, teachers, and the public. Regardless of whether you like the way grading is currently conducted or think it should be drastically changed, in the foreseeable future it is important for you to take grading your students seriously and do it in a way that is fair to your students. Never use grades to reward or punish students because you like them or don't like them. Always base students' grades on how well they have learned the subject matter, based on objective evidence of learning.

Is There Too Much Grade Inflation?   Some teachers do not like to give low grades because they point out that they diminish the student's motivation to learn. However, some critics argue that grade inflation, especially in the form of giving high grades for mediocre performance, provides students a false belief that they are learning and achieving more than they actually are. The result is that many students discover that they can perform well below their ability and still achieve high grades (Guskey, 2001). A rising tide of grade inflation has occurred (Sraiheen & Lesisko, 2006). In 2003, 42 percent of U.S. college-bound seniors had an *A* average compared with 28 percent in 1989, but the average scores of the students on college admissions tests in 2003 were lower than in 1989 (College Board, 2004).

Review, Reflect, and Practice

(4) **Construct a sound approach to grading.**

REVIEW

- What are the purposes of grading?
- What types of judgments underlie a teacher's grading system? Comment about each type.
- What are some choices in reporting students' progress to parents?
- What are some issues in grading?

REFLECT

- What criteria would you adopt for deciding whether a teacher is doing an excellent job in grading?

PRAXIS™ PRACTICE

1. Amaal brings home her school report card. On the card are letter grades indicating that Amaal has earned an *A* in math, reading, and social studies, and a *B* in science and P.E. Her parents look over her grades, sign the card, and return it to the school. What purpose did these grades serve?
   a. administrative
   b. guidance
   c. informational
   d. motivational

2. Mr. Walker teaches algebra. On the first day of class, he tells students that of the 25 students in the class, 5 would receive *A*'s, 6 would receive *B*'s, 7 would receive *C*'s, 4 would receive *D*'s, and 3 would receive *F*'s. What type of grading system is Mr. Walker using?
   a. criterion referenced
   b. norm referenced
   c. standards-based
   d. weighted

3. Isabella brings home her quarterly school report card. On the card are letter grades indicating that Isabella has earned an *A* in math, language arts, and social studies, and a *B* in science and P.E. Which of the following is a valid criticism of such a grading system?
   a. It gives parents too much information about the student's performance.
   b. It is too specific.
   c. Letter grades are unfair.
   d. It does not provide enough information to allow parents to evaluate their child's performance.

4. Ms. Gregory and Ms. Templeton are discussing grading issues. Which of the following comments made by Ms. Gregory and Ms. Templeton is the *least* likely to be supported by educational psychologists?
   a. Many students are being rewarded with high grades for mediocre performance.
   b. In the last several decades, grades have been increasing, while SAT scores have been going down.
   c. Some teachers don't like to give low grades because they believe the low grades decreased students' motivation.
   d. Grades should be abolished.

Please see the answer key at the end of the book.

CRACK THE CASE
The Case of the Project

Mr. Andrews generally was using traditional, multiple-choice tests in his sixth-grade class on ancient history, but the students seemed bored with studying for these tests and with his lectures. Therefore, for the unit on ancient Mesopotamia, he decided to allow the students to complete a project instead of taking a test. He gave these choices:

- Construct a test covering the chapter on Mesopotamia.
- Create a game about Mesopotamia.
- Create a diorama about Mesopotamia.
- Write a play about life in Mesopotamia.
- Create artifacts from Mesopotamia that an archaeologist might find.

Mr. Andrews' co-teacher, Ms. Benjamin, told the children that they could not use a computer to complete their projects.

Sally decided to write a test for her project. She carefully read the chapter and constructed questions as she went along. She used short-answer questions because she was worried about constructing good multiple-choice questions. It had been her experience that the distractors used in these questions were often confusing. She felt the same way about true/false questions. She wanted to make her questions as clear as possible because she didn't want her classmates mad at her when they took her test.

Sally carefully printed each question because of the ban on using a computer. She then created a key, which she intended to use to grade her classmates' tests. The final product consisted of 25 short-answer questions. She was very proud of her work the day she turned it in.

Mr. Andrews looked at her test and told her, "This isn't acceptable. Why didn't you type it?"

"Ms. Benjamin told us we couldn't use computers."

"That isn't what she meant. She meant you couldn't use the Internet," responded Mr. Andrews. "Take it home and type it. Turn it in tomorrow."

Sally left the room, very upset. She took her test home and carefully typed both the test and the key. She turned them in the next day. Three days later, Sally received these marks:

Content: **B** Did not include a question on religion (actually Sally did have a question regarding polytheism). Should have included a variety of question types, such as multiple-choice, matching, and true/false.

Mechanics: **A**   Nicely typed. Correct spelling used.

Accuracy: **B**

Effort: **C**

Overall Grade C

Sally was upset with her grade. "A C for effort?! I worked really hard on this! I even had to do it twice, 'cause of stupid Ms. Benjamin!" She took her grade sheet and test home and showed it to her mother. Sally's mother was equally upset, particularly about the low grade for effort. She called Mr. Andrews, asking to see the guidelines for the project and the grading rubric. Mr. Andrews was unable to provide either. She asked him the difference between content and accuracy. He could not tell her. She also asked him how he had measured effort, to which he responded, "I consider what I expect from students and then what they give me."

"So you're telling me that you graded content three times. Once you gave her a B, once a B, and once a C, right?"

Mr. Andrews did not know how to respond to her question.

1. What are the issues involved in this situation?
2. What did Mr. Andrews do wrong?
3. How should he have gone about developing his alternative assessments?
4. How should he have developed his grading guide?
5. What do you think of the practice of including an effort grade on students' projects? Why?

Reach Your Learning Goals
Classroom Assessment

---

(1) THE CLASSROOM AS AN ASSESSMENT CONTEXT: Discuss the classroom as an assessment context.

Assessment as an Integral Part of Teaching

Preinstruction assessment, assessment during instruction, and postinstruction assessment should be integral to teaching. Much of preinstruction assessment involves informal observations, which require interpretation. In informal observations, watch for nonverbal cues that give insights about the student. Structured exercises also can be used in preinstruction assessment. Guard against expectations that will distort your perception of a student. Treat your initial perceptions as hypotheses to be confirmed or modified by subsequent observation and information. Some teachers also administer pretests in subject areas. An increasing trend is to examine students' learning portfolios from previous grades. Formative assessment is assessment during instruction with an emphasis on assessment for learning instead of assessment of learning. An increasing trend is to have students engage in self-assessment of their progress on a day-to-day basis as part of formative assessment. Summative assessment, or formal assessment, is assessment after instruction is finished in order to document student mastery of the material, whether students are ready for the next unit, how your teaching should be adapted, and what grades the students should get.

Making Assessment Compatible with Contemporary Views of Learning and Motivation

To bring assessment into line with contemporary views of motivation and learning, it is important to focus on the following: active learning and constructing meaning; the use of planning and goal setting; reflective, critical, and creative thinking; positive student expectations for learning and confidence in skills; degree of motivation; the ability to apply what is learned to real-world situations; and effective communication. Consider the role that assessment (especially alternative assessment) plays in effort, engagement, and performance.

Creating Clear, Appropriate Learning Targets

A learning target, much like an instructional objective, consists of what students should know and be able to do.

Establishing High-Quality Assessments

High-quality assessments are valid, reliable, and fair. Validity is the extent to which an assessment measures what it is intended to measure, as well as how accurate and useful a teacher's inferences are. Reliability is the extent to which assessments produce consistent, reproducible scores. Assessment is fair when all students have an equal opportunity to learn and demonstrate their knowledge and skills. A pluralistic assessment philosophy, including being sensitive to cultural diversity, also contributes to fairness.

Current Trends

Current trends in assessment include using at least some performance-based assessments, examining higher-level skills, using multiple assessment methods, having high performance standards, and using computers as a part of assessment. Other trends focus on assessing an integration of skills, giving students considerable feedback, and making standards and criteria public.

---

(2) TRADITIONAL TESTS: Provide some guidelines for constructing traditional tests.

Selected-Response Items

A multiple-choice item has two parts: a stem and a number of possible options or alternatives. Incorrect alternatives are called distractors. True/false items can seem easy to construct but can encourage rote memorization. Matching items often are used with younger students.

| Constructed-Response Items | Constructed-response items require students to write out information rather than select it from a menu. Short-answer and essay items are the most commonly used constructed-response items. Short-answer items require students to write a word, a short phrase, or several sentences in response to a task and often encourage rote memorization. Essay questions allow students more freedom of response than the other item formats. Essay questions are especially good for assessing students' understanding, higher-level thinking skills, organizational skills, and writing skills. |

(3) ALTERNATIVE ASSESSMENTS: Describe some types of alternative assessments.

| Trends in Alternative Assessment | Authentic assessment is evaluating a student's knowledge or skill in a context that approximates the real world or real life as closely as possible. Critics argue that authentic assessments are not necessarily better than more conventional assessments, that there are few data to support their validity, and that they don't adequately examine knowledge and basic skills. |

| Performance Assessment | Performance assessments of higher-level thinking often emphasize "doing," open-ended activities for which there is no one correct answer. The tasks are sometimes realistic, and many, but not all, performance assessments are authentic (approximate the real world or real life). Evaluating performance often includes direct methods of evaluation, self-assessment, assessment of group performance as well as individual performance, and an extended period of time. There are four main guidelines in using performance assessments: (1) establishing a clear purpose, (2) identifying observable criteria, (3) providing an appropriate setting, and (4) judging or scoring the performance. |

| Portfolio Assessment | A portfolio is a systematic and organized collection of a student's work to demonstrate skills and accomplishments. Four classes of evidence can be included: artifacts, reproductions, attestations, and productions. Using a portfolio for assessment requires (1) establishing the portfolio's purpose, (2) involving the student in decisions about it, (3) reviewing the portfolio with the student, (4) setting criteria for evaluation, and (5) scoring and judging the portfolio. Two broad types of purposes of portfolios are to document growth through a growth portfolio and to showcase the student's most outstanding work through a best-work portfolio. Learning portfolios have strengths—such as capturing the complexity and completeness of the student's work and accomplishments, as well as encouraging student decision making and self-reflection—and weaknesses—such as the time required to coordinate and evaluate them and the difficulty in evaluating them. |

(4) GRADING AND REPORTING PERFORMANCE: Construct a sound approach to grading.

| The Purposes of Grading | Grading purposes include administrative (help determine students' class rank, credits); informational (communicate with parents, teachers, students); motivational (students' desire for higher grades); and guidance (select appropriate courses and levels for students). |

| The Components of a Grading System | Three main types of teacher judgments underlie a grading system: (1) standard of comparison to use for grading (norm-referenced or criterion-referenced—criterion-referenced grading is recommended over norm-referenced); (2) aspects of students' performance (a good strategy is to base an overall grade on a series of assessments, including tests and other assessments); and (3) weighting of different kinds of evidence (judgment is involved in how teachers synthesize information to arrive at a student's grade). |

611

| Reporting Students' Progress and Grades to Parents | Report cards are the standard method of reporting. Checklists of skills and objectives are sometimes used in kindergarten and elementary school. Letter grades are standard in the higher elementary grades and secondary schools. Reporting also includes written progress reports and parent-teacher conferences. |

| Some Issues in Grading | Issues in grading include (1) whether teachers should assign a zero for a missed assignment or paper; (2) whether teachers should go strictly by the numbers in grading; (3) whether grading should be abolished (although the form of grading might change in the future, judgments about students' performance will still be made and communicated to students, parents, and others); and (4) whether grade inflation is a problem. |

 KEY TERMS

formative assessment 577	multiple-choice item 587	authentic assessment 593	grading 603
summative assessment 579	constructed-response	performance criteria 595	norm-referenced
instructional validity 581	items 590	portfolio 598	grading 604
objective tests 582	short-answer item 590	growth portfolio 599	criterion-referenced
performance assessment 582	essay items 590	best-work portfolio 599	grading 604
selected-response items 587			

 PORTFOLIO ACTIVITIES

Now that you have a good understanding of this chapter, complete these exercises to expand your thinking.

Independent Reflection

State Your Views on Assessment. Think about the following statements and decide whether you agree or disagree with each. (1) Multiple-choice tests should not be used to assess students' learning. (2) A teacher should never use a single measure to assess learning. (3) Performance-based assessment is too subjective. (INTASC: Principle 8) Explain your position.

Collaborative Work

Develop an Assessment Plan. Get together with a classmate who plans to teach the same subject(s) and grade level. Select a sub-

ject and construct a plan for assessment throughout the course. (INTASC: Principles 1, 8)

Research/Field Experience

Balancing Traditional and Alternative Assessments. Consider a course you took in grade school or high school in which your performance was assessed using traditional methods. In a brief position statement, explain how students could have been evaluated using alternative assessments or some combination of traditional and alternative assessments. What would have been gained (or lost) by using alternative assessments? (INTASC: Principle 8)

Go to the Online Learning Center for downloadable portfolio templates.

TAKING IT TO THE NET

- The Coalition of Essential Schools (CES) is a national network of schools that uses alternative assessments and culminating exhibitions to evaluate their students. Read one or more CES articles. What is your analysis? Discuss the effectiveness of CES assessment strategies. To what degree do you believe the CES approach is replicable across schools? **www.essentialschools.org/cs/resources/view/ces_res/223**

- Your fifth-grade science students are engaged in a one-week collaborative project. They are constructing models of world habitats and will conduct oral presentations of their finished projects. Design a scoring rubric and outline the criteria you will use to measure student performance. Will students be graded as a group, independently, or both? Will they conduct self- or peer-assessments? **www.school.discovery.com/ schrockguide/ assess.html**

- Browse the Web to locate examples of K–12 electronic student portfolios. What are typically the main components of a digital portfolio? Discuss the benefits of using electronic portfolios to showcase and archive student work. Include benefits to students, families, teachers, and schools in your response. **www .education-world.com/a_tech/tech111.shtml**

Connect to the Online Learning Center to explore possible answers.

STUDY, PRACTICE, AND SUCCEED

Visit **www.mhhe.com/santedu4e** to review the chapter with self-grading quizzes and self-assessments, to apply the chapter material to two more Crack the Case studies, and for suggested activities to develop your teaching portfolio.

Glossary

A

accommodation Piagetian concept of adjusting schemas to fit new information and experiences.

achievement test A test that measures what the student has learned or what skills the student has mastered.

action research Research used to solve a specific classroom or school problem, improve teaching and other educational strategies, or make a decision at a specific level.

active listening A listening style that gives full attention to the speaker and notes both the intellectual and emotional content of the message.

advance organizers Teaching activities and techniques that establish a framework and orient students to material before it is presented.

algorithms Strategies that guarantee a solution to a problem.

alternate-forms reliability Reliability judged by giving different forms of the same test on two different occasions to the same group of students to determine how consistent their scores are.

amygdala The seat of emotions in the brain.

analogy A correspondence in some respects between otherwise dissimilar things.

androgyny The presence of positive masculine and feminine characteristics in the same individual.

applied behavior analysis Application of the principles of operant conditioning to change human behavior.

aptitude test A type of test that is used to predict a student's ability to learn a skill or accomplish something with further education and training.

articulation disorders Problems in pronouncing sounds correctly.

Asperger syndrome A relatively mild autism spectrum disorder in which the child has relatively good verbal language, milder nonverbal language problems, a restricted range of interests and relationships, and often engages in repetitive routines.

assimilation Piagetian concept of the incorporation of new information into existing knowledge (schemas).

associative learning Learning that two events are connected (associated).

Atkinson-Shiffrin model A model of memory that involves a sequence of three stages: sensory memory, short-term memory, and long-term memory.

attention The focusing of mental resources.

attention deficit hyperactivity disorder (ADHD) A disability in which children consistently show one or more of the following characteristics over a period of time: (1) inattention, (2) hyperactivity, and (3) impulsivity.

attribution theory The theory that individuals are motivated to discover the underlying causes of their own behavior and performance.

auditorium style A classroom arrangement style in which all students sit facing the teacher.

authentic assessment Evaluating a student's knowledge or skill in a context that approximates the real world or real life as closely as possible.

authoritarian classroom management style A management style that is restrictive and punitive, with the focus mainly on keeping order in the classroom rather than instruction or learning.

authoritarian parenting A restrictive and punitive parenting style in which there is little verbal exchange between parents and children; associated with children's social incompetence.

authoritative classroom management style A management style that encourages students to be independent thinkers and doers but still provides effective monitoring. Authoritative teachers engage students in considerable verbal give-and-take and show a caring attitude toward them. However, they still set limits when necessary.

authoritative parenting A positive parenting style that encourages children to be independent but still places limits and controls on their actions; extensive verbal give-and-take is allowed; associated with children's social competence.

autism spectrum disorders (ASD) Also called pervasive developmental disorders, they range from the severe disorder labeled autistic disorder to the milder disorder called Asperger syndrome. Children with these disorders are characterized by problems in social interaction, verbal and nonverbal communication, and repetitive behaviors.

autistic disorder A severe developmental autism spectrum disorder that has its onset in the first three years of life and includes deficiencies in social relationships, abnormalities in communication, and restricted, repetitive, and stereotyped patterns of behavior

automaticity The ability to process information with little or no effort.

B

backward-reaching transfer Occurs when the individual looks back to a previous situation for information to solve a problem in a new context.

behavioral objectives Statements that communicate proposed changes in students' behavior to reach desired levels of performance.

behaviorism The view that behavior should be explained by observable experiences, not by mental processes.

belief perseverance The tendency to hold on to a belief in the face of contradictory evidence.

best-work portfolio A portfolio that showcases the student's most outstanding work.

between-class ability grouping (tracking) Grouping students based on their ability or achievement.

Big Five factors of personality Openness, conscientiousness, extraversion, agreeableness, and neuroticism (emotional stability).

Bloom's taxonomy Developed by Benjamin Bloom and colleagues; classifies educational objectives into three domains—cognitive, affective, and psychomotor.

C

care perspective A moral perspective that focuses on connectedness and relationships among people; Gilligan's approach reflects a care perspective.

case study An in-depth look at an individual.

categories They group objects, events, and characteristics on the basis of common properties.

central tendency A number that provides information about the average, or typical, score in a set of data.

centration Focusing, or centering, attention on one characteristic to the exclusion of all others; characteristic of preoperational thinking.

cerebral palsy A disorder that involves a lack of muscle coordination, shaking, or unclear speech.

character education A direct approach to moral education that involves teaching students basic moral literacy to prevent them from engaging in immoral behavior and doing harm to themselves or others.

children who are gifted Children with above-average intelligence (usually defined as an IQ of 130 or higher) and/or superior talent in some domain such as art, music, or mathematics.

chunking Grouping, or "packing," information into "higher-order" units that can be remembered as single units.

classical conditioning A form of associative learning in which a neutral stimulus becomes associated with a meaningful stimulus and acquires the capacity to elicit a similar response.

cluster style A classroom arrangement style in which small numbers of students (usually four to eight) work in small, closely bunched groups.

cognitive apprenticeship A relationship in which an expert stretches and supports a novice's understanding and use of a culture's skills.

cognitive behavior approaches Changing behavior by getting individuals to monitor, manage, and regulate their own behavior rather than letting it be controlled by external factors.

cognitive moral education An approach to moral education based on the belief that students should value things such as democracy and justice as their moral reasoning develops; Kohlberg's theory has served as the foundation for many cognitive moral education programs.

collectivism A set of values that support the group.

comparative advance organizers Organizers that introduce new material by connecting it with the students' prior knowledge.

competence motivation The idea that people are motivated to deal effectively with their environment, to master their world, and to process information efficiently.

concept map A visual presentation of a concept's connections and hierarchical organization.

concepts Ideas about what categories represent, or said another way, the sort of thing we think category members are.

concrete operational stage Piaget's third cognitive developmental stage, lasting from about 7 to 11 years of age. At this stage, the child thinks operationally, and logical reasoning replaces intuitive thought but only in concrete situations; classification skills are present, but abstract problems present difficulties.

concurrent validity The relation between a test's scores and other criteria that are currently (concurrently) available.

confirmation bias The tendency to search for and use information that supports our ideas rather than refutes them.

conservation The idea that some characteristic of an object stays the same even though the object might change in appearance; a cognitive ability that develops in the concrete operational stage, according to Piaget.

constructed-response items Items that require students to write out information rather than select a response from a menu.

constructivist approach A learner-centered approach to learning that emphasizes the importance of individuals actively constructing knowledge and understanding with guidance from the teacher.

construct validity The extent to which there is evidence that a test measures a particular construct. A construct is an unobservable trait or characteristic of a person, such as intelligence, learning style, personality, or anxiety.

content validity A test's ability to sample the content that is to be measured.

continuity-discontinuity issue The issue regarding whether development involves gradual, cumulative change (continuity) or distinct stages (discontinuity).

contracting Putting reinforcement contingencies into writing.

control group In an experiment, a group whose experience is treated in every way like the experimental group except for the manipulated factor.

conventional reasoning In Kohlberg's theory, the middle level of moral development; at this level, internalization is intermediate in the sense that individuals abide by certain standards (internal), but these essentially are the standards of others (external).

convergent thinking Thinking with the aim of producing one correct answer. This is usually the type of thinking required on conventional intelligence tests.

cooperative learning Learning that occurs when students work in small groups to help each other learn.

corpus callosum Where fibers connect the brain's left and right hemispheres.

correlational research Research that describes the strength of the relation between two or more events or characteristics.

creativity The ability to think about something in novel and unusual ways and come up with unique solutions to problems.

criterion-referenced grading A grading system based on a certain grade for a certain level of performance regardless of any comparison with the work of other students.

criterion-referenced tests Standardized tests in which the student's performance is compared with established criteria.

criterion validity A test's ability to predict a student's performance as measured by other assessments or criteria.

critical thinking Thinking reflectively and productively and evaluating the evidence.

cross-cultural studies Studies that compare what happens in one culture with what happens in one or more other cultures; they provide information about the degree to which people are similar and to what degree behaviors are specific to certain cultures.

cue-dependent forgetting Retrieval failure caused by a lack of effective retrieval cues.

culture-fair tests Tests of intelligence that are intended to be free of cultural bias.

culture The behavior patterns, beliefs, and all other products of a particular group of people that are passed on from generation to generation.

D

decay theory The theory that new learning involves the creation of a neurochemical "memory trace," which will eventually disintegrate. Thus, decay theory suggests that the passage of time is responsible for forgetting.

decision making Evaluating alternatives and making choices among them.

declarative memory The conscious recollection of information, such as specific facts or events that can be verbally communicated.

deductive reasoning Reasoning from the general to the specific.

deep/surface styles Involve the extent to which students approach learning materials in a way that helps them understand the meaning of the materials (deep style) or as simply what needs to be learned (surface style).

dependent variable The factor that is measured in an experiment.

descriptive statistics Mathematical procedures that are used to describe and summarize data (information) in a meaningful way.

development The pattern of biological, cognitive, and socioemotional processes that begins at conception and continues through the life span. Most development involves growth, although it also eventually involves decay (dying).

developmentally appropriate education Education based on knowledge of the typical development of children within an age span (age-appropriateness) as well as the uniqueness of the child (individual-appropriateness).

differentiated instruction Involves recognizing individual variations in students' knowledge, readiness, interests, and other characteristics, and taking these differences into account when planning curriculum and engaging in instruction.

difficult child A temperament style in which the child tends to react negatively, cries frequently, engages in irregular routines, and is slow to accept new experiences.

direct instruction approach A structured, teacher-centered approach characterized by teacher direction and control, high teacher expectations for students' progress, maximum time spent by students on academic tasks, and efforts by the teacher to keep negative affect to a minimum.

direct instruction Structured, teacher-centered approach focused on academic activity; characterized by teacher direction and control, high teacher expectations for student progress, and keeping negative affect to a minimum.

discovery learning Learning in which students construct an understanding on their own.

divergent thinking Thinking with the aim of producing many answers to the same question. This is characteristic of creativity.

divided attention Concentrating on more than one activity at a time.

Down syndrome A genetically transmitted form of mental retardation due to an extra (47th) chromosome.

dyscalculia Also known as developmental arithmetic disorder, this learning disability involves difficulty in math computation.

dysgraphia A learning disability that involves difficulty in handwriting.

dyslexia A severe impairment in the ability to read and spell.

E

early-later experience issue The issue of the degree to which early experiences (especially infancy) or later experiences are the key determinants of the child's development.

easy child A temperament style in which the child is generally in a positive mood, quickly establishes regular routines, and easily adapts to new experiences.

ecological theory Bronfenbrenner's theory that consists of five environmental systems: microsystem, mesosystem, exosystem, macrosystem, and chronosystem.

educational psychology The branch of psychology that specializes in understand-

ing teaching and learning in educational settings.

elaboration The extensiveness of information processing involved in encoding.

emotional and behavioral disorders Serious, persistent problems that involve relationships, aggression, depression, fears associated with personal or school matters, and other inappropriate socioemotional characteristics.

emotional intelligence The ability to perceive and express emotion accurately and adaptively, to understand emotion and emotional knowledge, to monitor one's own and others' emotions and feelings, to discriminate among them, and to use this information to guide one's thinking and action

empowerment Providing people with intellectual and coping skills to succeed and make this a more just world.

encoding The process by which information gets into memory.

encoding specificity principle The principle that associations formed at the time of encoding or learning tend to be effective retrieval cues.

English as a second language (ESL) A widely used term for bilingual education programs and classes that teach English to students whose native language is not English.

epilepsy A neurological disorder characterized by recurring sensorimotor attacks or movement convulsions.

episodic memory The retention of information about the where and when of life's happenings.

equilibration A mechanism that Piaget proposed to explain how children shift from one stage of thought to the next. The shift occurs as children experience cognitive conflict, or disequilibrium, in trying to understand the world. Eventually, they resolve the conflict and reach a balance, or equilibrium, of thought.

essay items Items that require more writing than other formats but allow more freedom of response to questions.

essential questions Questions that reflect the heart of the curriculum, the most important things that students should explore and learn.

ethnicity A shared pattern of characteristics such as cultural heritage, nationality, race, religion, and language.

ethnographic study In-depth description and interpretation of behavior in an ethnic or a cultural group that includes direct involvement with the participants.

executive attention Involves action planning, allocating attention to goals, error detection and compensation, monitoring

progress on tasks, and dealing with novel or difficult circumstances.

experimental group The group whose experience is manipulated in an experiment.

experimental research Research that allows the determination of the causes of behavior; involves conducting an experiment, which is a carefully regulated procedure in which one or more of the factors believed to influence the behavior being studied is manipulated and all others are held constant.

expert knowledge Also called *subject matter knowledge*; means excellent knowledge about the content of a particular discipline.

expository advance organizers Organizers that provide students with new knowledge that will orient them to the upcoming lesson.

expressive language The ability to use language to express one's thoughts and communicate with others.

extrinsic motivation The external motivation to do something to obtain something else (a means to an end).

F

face-to-face style A classroom arrangement style in which students sit facing each other.

failure syndrome Having low expectations for success and giving up at the first sign of difficulty.

far transfer The transfer of learning to a situation that is very different from the one in which the initial learning took place.

fixation Using a prior strategy and thereby failing to examine a problem from a fresh, new perspective.

fluency disorders Disorders that often involve what is commonly referred to as "stuttering."

formal operational stage Piaget's fourth cognitive developmental stage, which emerges between about 11 and 15 years of age; thought is more abstract, idealistic, and logical in this stage.

formative assessment Assessment during the course of instruction rather than after it is completed.

forward-reaching transfer Occurs when the individual looks to apply learned information to a future situation.

Fostering a Community of Learners (FCL) A social constructivist program that focuses on literacy development and biology. FCL encourages reflection and discussion through the use of adults as role models, children teaching children, and online computer consultation.

frequency distribution A listing of scores, usually from highest to lowest, along with the number of times each score appears.

fuzzy trace theory States that memory is best understood by considering two types of memory representations: (1) verbatim memory trace and (2) fuzzy trace, or gist. In this theory, older children's better memory is attributed to the fuzzy traces created by extracting the gist of information.

G

gender The characteristics of people as males and females.

gender role The set of expectations that prescribe how males and females should think, act, and feel.

gender schema theory States that gender-typing emerges as children gradually develop gender schemas of what is gender-appropriate and gender-inappropriate in their culture.

gender stereotypes Broad categories that reflect impressions and beliefs about what behavior is appropriate for females and males.

gender-typing The process by which children acquire the thoughts, feelings, and behaviors that are considered appropriate for their gender in a particular culture.

grade-equivalent score A score that indicates a student's performance in relation to grade level and months of the school year, assuming a 10-month school year.

grading Translating descriptive assessment information into letters, numbers, or other marks that indicate the quality of a student's learning or performance.

growth portfolio A portfolio of work over an extended time frame (throughout the school year or longer) to reveal the student's progress in meeting learning targets.

guided discovery learning Learning in which students are encouraged to construct their understanding with the assistance of teacher-guided questions and directions.

H

helpless orientation A response to challenges and difficulties in which the individual feels trapped by the difficulty and attributes the difficulty to a lack of ability.

heuristics Strategies or rules of thumb that can suggest a solution to a problem but don't ensure that it will work.

hidden curriculum Dewey's concept that every school has a pervasive moral atmosphere, even if it does not have a specific program of moral education.

hierarchy of needs Maslow's concept that individual needs must be satisfied in this sequence: physiological, safety, love and belongingness, esteem, and self-actualization.

high-road transfer The transfer of learning from one situation to another that is conscious and effortful.

high-stakes testing Using tests in a way that will have important consequences for the student, affecting such decisions as whether the student will be promoted or be allowed to graduate.

hindsight bias The tendency to falsely report, after the fact, that we accurately predicted an event.

histogram A frequency distribution in the form of a graph.

hostile environment sexual harassment Occurs when students are subjected to unwelcome sexual conduct that is so severe, persistent, or pervasive that it limits the students' ability to benefit from their education.

humanistic perspective A view that stresses students' capacity for personal growth, freedom to choose their destiny, and positive qualities.

hypothetical-deductive reasoning Piaget's formal operational concept that adolescents can develop hypotheses to solve problems and systematically reach (deduce) a conclusion.

I

identity achievement The identity status in which individuals have explored meaningful alternatives and made a commitment.

identity diffusion The identity status in which individuals have neither explored meaningful alternatives nor made a commitment.

identity foreclosure The identity status in which individuals have made a commitment but have not explored meaningful alternatives.

identity moratorium The identity status in which individuals are in the midst of exploring alternatives but their commitments are absent or vaguely defined.

impulsive/reflective styles Also referred to as *conceptual tempo*, they involve a student's tendency either to act quickly and impulsively or to take more time to respond and reflect on the accuracy of the answer.

incentives Positive or negative stimuli or events that can motivate a student's behavior.

inclusion Educating children with special education needs full-time in the regular classroom.

independent variable The manipulated, influential, experimental factor in an experiment.

individualism A set of values that give priority to personal rather than to group goals.

Individuals with Disabilities Education Act (IDEA) This act spells out broad mandates for services to all children with disabilities, including evaluation and determination of eligibility, appropriate education and an individualized education plan (IEP), and education in the least restrictive environment (LRE).

individualized education plan (IEP) A written statement that spells out a program specifically tailored for the student with a disability.

inductive reasoning Reasoning from the specific to the general.

indulgent parenting A parenting style of involvement but few limits or restrictions on children's behavior; linked with children's social incompetence.

information-processing approach A cognitive approach in which children manipulate information, monitor it, and strategize about it. Central to this approach are the cognitive processes of memory and thinking.

instructional planning A systematic, organized strategy for planning lessons.

instructional validity The extent to which the assessment is a reasonable sample of what went on in the classroom.

intelligence Problem-solving skills and the ability to adapt to and learn from experiences.

intelligence quotient (IQ) A person's mental age (MA) divided by chronological age (CA), multiplied by 100.

interference theory The theory that we forget not because we actually lose memories from storage but because other information gets in the way of what we are trying to remember.

Internet The core of computer-mediated communication; a system of computer networks that operates worldwide.

intrinsic motivation The internal motivation to do something for its own sake (an end in itself).

intuitive thought substage The second substage of preoperational thought, lasting from about 4 to 7 years of age. Children begin to use primitive reasoning and want to know the answer to all sorts of questions. They seem so sure about their knowledge in this substage but are unaware of how they know what they know.

J

jigsaw classroom A classroom in which students from different cultural backgrounds cooperate by doing different parts of a project to reach a common goal.

Joplin plan A standard nongraded program for instruction in reading.

justice perspective A moral perspective that focuses on the rights of the individual; Kohlberg's theory is a justice perspective.

L

laboratory A controlled setting from which many of the complex factors of the real world have been removed.

language disorders Significant impairments in a child's receptive or expressive language.

language A form of communication, whether spoken, written, or signed, that is based on a system of symbols.

lateralization The specialization of functions in each hemisphere of the brain.

learning A relatively permanent influence on behavior, knowledge, and thinking skills, which comes about through experience.

learning and thinking styles Individuals' preferences in how they use their abilities.

learning disability A child with a learning disability has difficulty in learning that involves understanding or using spoken or written language and the difficulty can appear in listening, thinking, reading, writing, and spelling. A learning disability also may involve difficulty in doing mathematics. To be classified as a learning disability, the learning problem is not primarily the result of visual, hearing, or motor disabilities; mental retardation; emotional disorders; or due to environmental, cultural, or economic disadvantage.

least restrictive environment (LRE) A setting that is as similar as possible to the one in which children who do not have a disability are educated.

levels of processing theory The theory that processing of memory occurs on a continuum from shallow to deep, with deeper processing producing better memory.

long-term memory A type of memory that holds enormous amounts of information for a long period of time in a relatively permanent fashion.

low-road transfer The automatic, often unconscious, transfer of learning to another situation.

M

mastery learning Involves learning one topic or concept thoroughly before moving on to a more difficult one.

mastery orientation A task-oriented response to difficult or challenging circumstances that focuses on learning strategies and the process of achievement rather than the outcome.

means-end analysis A heuristic in which one identifies the goal (end) of a problem, assesses the current situation, and evaluates what needs to be done (means) to decrease the difference between the two conditions.

mean The numerical average of a group of scores.

measures of variability Measures that tell how much scores vary from one another.

median The score that falls exactly in the middle of a distribution of scores after they have been arranged (or ranked) from highest to lowest.

memory span The number of digits an individual can report back without error in a single presentation.

memory The retention of information over time, which involves encoding, storage, and retrieval.

mental age (MA) An individual's level of mental development relative to others.

mental processes Thoughts, feelings, and motives that cannot be observed by others.

mental retardation A condition with an onset before age 18 that involves low intelligence (usually below 70 on a traditional individually administered intelligence test) and difficulty in adapting to everyday life.

mental set A type of fixation in which an individual tries to solve a problem in a particular way that has worked in the past.

metacognition Cognition about cognition, or "knowing about knowing."

metalinguistic awareness Knowledge about language, such as knowing what a preposition is.

mindfulness Means being alert, mentally present, and cognitively flexible while going through life's everyday activities and tasks. Mindful students maintain an active awareness of the circumstances in their lives.

mindset Dweck's concept that refers to the cognitive view individuals develop for themselves; individuals have one of two mindsets: (1) fixed, or (2) growth.

mode The score that occurs most often.

Montessori approach An educational philosophy in which children are given considerable freedom and spontaneity in choosing activities and are allowed to move from one activity to another as they desire.

moral development Development with respect to the rules and conventions of just interactions between people.

morphology Refers to the units of meaning involved in word formation.

motivation The processes that energize, direct, and sustain behavior.

multicultural education Education that values diversity and includes the perspectives of a variety of cultural groups on a regular basis.

multiple-choice item An objective test item consisting of two parts: a stem plus a set of possible responses.

myelination The process of encasing many cells in the brain with a myelin sheath, increasing the speed at which information travels through the nervous system.

N

naturalistic observation Observation outside of a laboratory in the real world.

nature-nurture issue Issue that involves the debate about whether development is primarily influenced by nature (an organism's biological inheritance) or nurture (environmental experiences).

nature-nurture issue The issue regarding whether development is influenced primarily by nature (an organism's biological inheritance) or by nurture (an organism's environmental experiences). The "nature" proponents claim biological inheritance is the most important influence on development; the "nurture" proponents claim environmental experiences are the most important.

near transfer The transfer of learning to a situation that is similar to the one in which the initial learning took place.

need for affiliation or relatedness The motive to be securely connected with other people.

negative reinforcement Reinforcement based on the principle that the frequency of a response increases because an aversive (unpleasant) stimulus is removed.

neglectful parenting A parenting style of uninvolvement in which parents spend little time with their children; associated with children's social incompetence.

neo-Piagetians Developmental psychologists who argue that Piaget got some things right but that his theory needs considerable revision; emphasize how to process information through attention, memory, and strategies.

network theories Theories that describe how information in memory is organized and connected; they emphasize nodes in the memory network.

nongraded (cross-age) program A variation of between-class ability grouping in which students are grouped by their ability in particular subjects, regardless of their age or grade level.

norm-referenced grading A grading system based on a comparison of a student's performance with that of other students in the class or of other classes and other students.

norm-referenced tests Standardized tests in which a student's score is interpreted by comparing it with how others (the norm group) performed.

normal distribution A symmetrical distribution, with a majority of scores falling in the middle of the possible range of scores and few scores appearing toward the extremes of the range.

norm group The group of individuals previously tested that provides a basis for interpreting a test score.

objective tests Tests that have relatively clear, unambiguous scoring criteria, usually multiple-choice tests

observational learning Learning that involves acquiring skills, strategies, and beliefs by observing others.

off-set style A classroom arrangement style in which small numbers of students (usually three or four) sit at tables but do not sit directly across from one another.

operant conditioning Also called instrumental conditioning, this is a form of learning in which the consequences of behavior produce changes in the probability that the behavior will occur.

organization Piaget's concept of grouping isolated behaviors into a higher-order, more smoothly functioning cognitive system; the grouping or arranging of items into categories.

orthopedic impairments Restricted movements or lack of control of movements, due to muscle, bone, or joint problems.

overconfidence bias The tendency to have more confidence in judgment and decisions than we should based on probability or past experience.

participant observation Observation in which the observer-researcher is actively involved as a participant in the activity or setting.

pedagogical content knowledge Knowledge about how to effectively teach a particular discipline.

percentile-rank score The percentage of a distribution that lies at or below the score.

performance assessment Assessment that requires creating answers or products that demonstrate knowledge and skill; examples include writing an essay, conducting an experiment, carrying out a project, solving a real-world problem, and creating a portfolio.

performance criteria Specific behaviors that students need to perform effectively as part of an assessment.

performance orientation A focus on winning rather than achievement outcome; success is believed to result from winning.

permissive classroom management style A management style that allows students

considerable autonomy but provides them with little support for developing learning skills or managing their behavior.

person-situation interaction The view that the best way to conceptualize personality is not in terms of personal traits or characteristics alone, but also in terms of the situation involved.

personality Distinctive thoughts, emotions, and behaviors that characterize the way an individual adapts to the world.

phonics approach An approach that emphasizes that reading instruction should teach phonics and its basic rules for translating written symbols into sounds; early reading instruction should use simplified materials.

phonology A language's sound system.

portfolio A systematic and organized collection of a student's work that demonstrates the student's skills and accomplishments.

positive reinforcement Reinforcement based on the principle that the frequency of a response increases because it is followed by a rewarding stimulus.

postconventional reasoning In Kohlberg's theory, the highest level of moral development; at this level, moral development is internalized and not based on external standards.

pragmatics The use of appropriate language in different contexts.

preconventional reasoning In Kohlberg's theory, the lowest level of moral development; at this level, the child shows no internalization of moral values, and moral reasoning is controlled by external rewards and punishments.

predictive validity The relation between test scores and the student's future performance.

prefrontal cortex The highest level in the frontal lobes that is involved in reasoning, decision making, and self-control.

prejudice An unjustified negative attitude toward an individual because of the individual's membership in a group.

Premack principle The principle that a high-probability activity can serve as a reinforcer for a low-probability activity.

preoperational stage The second Piagetian stage, lasting from about 2 to 7 years of age; symbolic thought increases but operational thought is not yet present.

problem-based learning Learning that emphasizes authentic problems like those that occur in daily life.

problem solving Finding an appropriate way to attain a goal.

procedural memory Nondeclarative knowledge in the form of skills and cognitive operations. Procedural memory cannot be

consciously recollected, at least not in the form of specific events or facts.

program evaluation research Research designed to make decisions about the effectiveness of a particular program.

project-based learning Students work on real, meaningful problems and create tangible products.

prompt An added stimulus or cue that is given just before a response that increases the likelihood the response will occur.

prototype matching Deciding if an item is a member of a category by comparing it with the most typical item(s) of the category.

Public Law 94-142 The Education for All Handicapped Children Act, which required that all students with disabilities be given a free, appropriate public education and which provided the funding to help implement this education.

punishment A consequence that decreases the probability that a behavior will occur.

quid pro quo sexual harassment Occurs when a school employee threatens to base an educational decision (such as a grade) on a student's submission to unwelcome sexual conduct.

random assignment In experimental research, the assignment of participants to experimental and control groups by chance.

range The distance between the highest and lowest scores.

rapport talk The language of conversation and a way of establishing connections and negotiating relationships; more characteristic of females than males.

raw score The number of items the student answered correctly on the test.

receptive language The reception and understanding of language.

reciprocal teaching A learning arrangement in which students take turns leading a small-group discussion; can also involve teacher-scaffolded instruction.

reciprocal teaching A learning arrangement used by FCL in which students take turns leading a small-group discussion.

rehearsal The conscious repetition of information over time to increase the length of time information stays in memory.

reinforcement (reward) A consequence that increases the probability that a behavior will occur.

reliability The extent to which a test produces a consistent, reproducible score.

report talk Talk that gives information; more characteristic of males than females.

response cost Taking a positive reinforcer away from an individual.

S

scaffolding A technique that involves changing the level of support for learning. A teacher or more-advanced peer adjusts the amount of guidance to fit the student's current performance.

schedules of reinforcement Partial reinforcement timetables that determine when a response will be reinforced.

schema Information—concepts, knowledge, information about events—that already exists in a person's mind.

schema theories Theories that when we construct information, we fit it into information that already exists in our mind.

schemas In Piaget's theory, actions or mental representations that organize knowledge.

Schools for Thought (SFT) A social constructivist program that combines aspects of The Jasper Project, Fostering a Community of Learners, and CSILE.

script A schema for an event.

selected-response items Test items with an objective format in which student responses can be scored quickly. A scoring guide for correct responses is created and can be applied by an examiner or a computer.

selective attention Focusing on a specific aspect of experience that is relevant while ignoring others that are irrelevant.

self-actualization The highest and most elusive of Maslow's needs; the motivation to develop one's full potential as a human being.

self-efficacy The belief that one can master a situation and produce positive outcomes.

self-esteem Also called self-image and self-worth, the individual's overall conception of himself or herself.

self-instructional methods Cognitive behavior techniques aimed at teaching individuals to modify their own behavior.

self-regulatory learning The self-generation and self-monitoring of thoughts, feelings, and behaviors in order to reach a goal.

semantic memory An individual's general knowledge about the world, independent of the individual's identity with the past.

semantics The meaning of words and sentences.

seminar style A classroom arrangement style in which large numbers of students (ten or more) sit in circular, square, or U-shaped arrangements.

sensorimotor stage The first Piagetian stage, lasting from birth to about 2 years of age, in which infants construct an understanding of the world by coordinating sensory experiences with motor actions.

sensory memory Memory that holds information from the world in its original form for only an instant.

serial position effect The principle that recall is better for items at the beginning and the end of a list than for items in the middle.

seriation A concrete operation that involves ordering stimuli along some quantitative dimension.

service learning A form of education that promotes social responsibility and service to the community.

sexism Prejudice and discrimination against an individual because of the person's sex.

shaping Teaching new behaviors by reinforcing successive approximations to a specified target behavior.

short-answer item A constructed-response format in which students are required to write a word, a short phrase, or several sentences in response to a task.

short-term memory A limited-capacity memory system in which information is retained for as long as 30 seconds, unless the information is rehearsed, in which case it can be retained longer.

situated cognition The idea that thinking is located (situated) in social and physical contexts, not within an individual's mind.

slow-to-warm-up child A temperament style in which the child has a low activity level, is somewhat negative, and displays a low intensity of mood.

social cognitive theory Bandura's theory that social and cognitive factors, as well as behavior, play important roles in learning.

social constructivist approach Approach that emphasizes the social contexts of learning and that knowledge is mutually built and constructed.

social constructivist approach Emphasizes the social contexts of learning and that knowledge is mutually built and constructed; Vygotsky's theory exemplifies this approach.

social motives Needs and desires that are learned through experiences with the social world.

social studies The field that seeks to promote civic competence with the goal of helping students make informed and reasoned decisions for the public good as citizens of a culturally diverse, democratic society in an interdependent world.

socioeconomic status (SES) A grouping of people with similar occupational, educational, and economic characteristics.

specific language impairment (SLI) Involves problems in language development that are not accompanied by other obvious physical, sensory, or emotional problems; in some cases, the disorder is called developmental language disorder.

speech and language disorders A number of speech problems (such as articulation disorders, voice disorders, and fluency disorders) and language problems (difficulties in receiving information and expressing language).

splintered development The circumstances in which development is uneven across domains.

split-half reliability Reliability judged by dividing the test items into two halves, such as the odd-numbered and even-numbered items. The scores on the two sets of items are compared to determine how consistently the students performed across each set.

standard deviation A measure of how much a set of scores varies on the average around the mean of the scores.

standardized tests Tests that have uniform procedures for administration and scoring and often allow a student's performance to be compared with the performance of other students at the same age or grade level on a national basis.

standards-based tests Tests that assess skills that students are expected to have mastered before they can be promoted to the next grade or permitted to graduate.

standard score A score expressed as a deviation from the mean; involves the standard deviation.

stanine score A 9-point scale that describes a student's performance.

stereotype threat The anxiety that one's behavior might confirm a negative stereotype about one's group.

strategy construction Creation of a new procedure for processing information.

subgoaling The process of setting intermediate goals that place students in a better position to reach the final goal or solution.

summative assessment Assessment after instruction is finished to document student performance; also called formal assessment.

sustained attention Maintaining attention over an extended period of time; also called vigilance.

symbolic function substage The first substage of preoperational thought, occurring between about 2 to 4 years of age; the ability to represent an object not present develops and symbolic thinking increases; egocentrism is present.

syntax The ways words are combined to form acceptable phrases and sentences.

systematic desensitization A method based on classical conditioning that reduces anxiety by getting the individual to associate deep relaxation with successive visualizations of increasingly anxiety-provoking situations.

task analysis Breaking down a complex task that students are to learn into its component parts.

taxonomy A classification system.

teacher-as-researcher Also called teacher-researcher, this concept involves classroom teachers conducting their own studies to improve their teaching practice.

temperament A person's behavioral style and characteristic ways of responding.

test-retest reliability The extent to which a test yields the same performance when a student is given the same test on two occasions.

theory of mind Awareness of one's own mental processes and the mental processes of others.

thinking Manipulating and transforming information in memory, which often is done to form concepts, reason, think critically, make decisions, think creatively, and solve problems.

time-out Removing an individual from positive reinforcement.

transactional strategy instruction approach A cognitive approach to reading that emphasizes instruction in strategies, especially metacognitive strategies.

transfer Applying previous experiences and knowledge to learning or problem solving in a new situation.

transitivity The ability to reason and logically combine relationships.

triarchic theory of intelligence Sternberg's view that intelligence comes in three main forms: analytical, creative, and practical.

validity The extent to which a test measures what it is intended to measure and whether inferences about the test scores are accurate.

values clarification An approach to moral education that emphasizes helping people clarify what their lives are for and what is worth working for; students are encouraged to define their own values and understand the values of others.

voice disorders Disorders producing speech that is hoarse, harsh, too loud, too high-pitched, or too low-pitched.

Web A system for browsing Internet sites that refers to the World Wide Web; named the Web because it is comprised of many sites that are linked together.

whole-language approach An approach that stresses that reading instruction should parallel children's natural language learning. Reading materials should be whole and meaningful.

within-class ability grouping Placing students in two or three groups within a class to take into account differences in students' abilities.

withitness A management style described by Kounin in which teachers show students that they are aware of what is happening. Such teachers closely monitor students on a regular basis and detect inappropriate behavior early, before it gets out of hand.

working memory A three-part system that holds information temporarily as a person performs a task. A kind of "mental workbench" that lets individuals manipulate, assemble, and construct information when they make decisions, solve problems, and comprehend written and spoken language.

Z

z-score A score that provides information about how many standard deviations a raw score is above or below the mean.

zone of proximal development (ZPD) Vygotsky's term for the range of tasks that are too difficult for children to master alone but that can be mastered with guidance and assistance from adults or more-skilled children.

PRAXIS™ Answer Key

CHAPTER 1

Historical Background
1. b
2. c

Effective Teaching
1. d
2. b

Research in Educational Psychology
1. a
2. d
3. c

CHAPTER 2

An Overview of Child Development
1. d   3. a
2. c   4. d

Cognitive Development
1. b
2. d
3. c

Language Development
1. a
2. b
3. b

CHAPTER 3

Contemporary Theories
1. b
2. c

Social Contexts of Development
1. b
2. d
3. a

Socioemotional Development
1. c
2. b

CHAPTER 4

Intelligence
1. c   3. d
2. b   4. b

Learning and Thinking Styles
1. a
2. d

Personality and Temperament
1. b
2. b

CHAPTER 5

Culture and Ethnicity
1. c   3. a
2. c   4. c

Multicultural Education
1. d   3. a
2. d   4. a

Gender
1. c   4. a
2. c   5. a
3. b

CHAPTER 6

Who Are Children with Disabilities?
1. c   5. c
2. b   6. b
3. a   7. b
4. b   8. d

Educational Issues Involving Children with Disabilities
1. b
2. c

Children Who Are Gifted
1. a
2. a
3. b

CHAPTER 7

What Is Learning?
1. b
2. b

Behavioral Approaches to Learning
1. d
2. b

Applied Behavior Analysis in Education
1. a   3. d
2. a   4. d

Social Cognitive Approaches to Learning
1. b   3. a
2. a   4. d

CHAPTER 8

The Nature of the Information-Processing Approach
1. b
2. a
3. a

Attention
1. a
2. a

Memory
1. a   3. a
2. b   4. d

Expertise
1. b
2. a
3. b

Metacognition
1. d
2. c
3. a

CHAPTER 9

Conceptual Understanding
1. b
2. c

Thinking
1. d   3. a
2. c   4. a

Problem Solving
1. b   3. b
2. a   4. a

Transfer
1. b
2. c

CHAPTER 10

Social Constructivist Approaches to Teaching
1. a
2. b

Teachers and Peers as Joint Contributors to Students' Learning
1. b   3. a
2. b   4. a

Structuring Small-Group Work
1. b
2. d
3. d

Social Constructivist Programs
1. b
2. a

CHAPTER 11

Expert Knowledge and Pedagogical Content Knowledge
1. b

Reading
1. c   4. c
2. c   5. b
3. b

Writing
1. c
2. b
3. b

Mathematics
1. a   4. b
2. b   5. d
3. c

Science
1. d
2. c

Social Studies
1. a
2. d

CHAPTER 12

Planning
1. b
2. d

Teacher-Centered Lesson Planning and Instruction
1. a   3. a
2. c   4. c

Learner-Centered Lesson Planning and Instruction
1. d
2. c
3. b

Technology and Education
1. b   3. c
2. b   4. a

CHAPTER 13

Exploring Motivation
1. b
2. b

Achievement Processes
1. b   5. d
2. d   6. b
3. a   7. b
4. b

Motivation, Relationships, and Sociocultural Contexts
1. c
2. c
3. d

Students with Achievement Problems
1. a   5. a
2. b   6. b
3. a   7. b
4. a

CHAPTER 14

Why Classrooms Need to Be Managed Effectively
1. b   3. a
2. d   4. c

Designing the Physical Environment of the Classroom
1. b
2. d

Creating a Positive Environment for Learning
1. b
2. b
3. c

Being a Good Communicator
1. d
2. d
3. d

Dealing with Problem Behaviors
1. c
2. d

CHAPTER 15

The Nature of Standardized Tests
1. b
2. a

Aptitude and Achievement Tests
1. a   3. b
2. d   4. b

The Teacher's Roles
1. d
2. a
3. c

Issues in Standardized Tests
1. a
2. b

CHAPTER 16

The Classroom as an Assessment Context
1. b   4. c
2. a   5. c
3. d

Traditional Tests
1. c
2. c

Alternative Assessments
1. d
2. b

Grading and Reporting Performance
1. c   3. d
2. b   4. d

References

A

Aartson, M. J., Martin, M., & Zimprich, D. (2003). Gender differences in level and change in cognitive functioning: Results from the longitudinal aging study in Amsterdam. *Gerontology, 50,* 35–38.

ABC News. (2005). *Larry Paige and Sergey Brin.* Retrieved December 12, 2005, from http://abcnews.go.com?Entertainment/12/8/05

Academic Software. (1996). *Adaptive Device Locator System* [computer program]. Lexington, KY: Author.

Achieve, Inc. (2005). *Rising to the challenge: Are high school graduates prepared for college and work?* Washington, DC: Author.

Adams, A., Carnine, D., & Gersten, R. (1982). Instructional strategies for studying content area texts in the intermediate grades. *Reading Research Quarterly, 18,* 27–53.

Adams, G. R. (2008). Erikson's theory of psychosocial development. In N. J. Salkind (Ed.), *Encyclopedia of educational psychology.* Thousand Oaks, CA: Sage.

Adams, K. L., & Galanes, G. J. (2009). *Communicating in groups* (7th ed.). New York: McGraw-Hill.

Adams, R., & Biddle, B. (1970). *Realities of teaching.* New York: Holt, Rinehart & Winston.

Adi-Japha, E., Landau, Y. E., Frenkel, L., Ticher, M., Gross-Tsur, V., & Shalev, R. S. (2007). ADHD and dysgraphia: Underlying mechanisms. *Cortex, 43,* 700–709.

Agnew-Tally, J., Mott, D., Brooks, S., & Thornburg, K. (2009). Teacher as a family resource and advocate. In K. B. Grant & J. A. Ray (Eds.), *Home, school, and community collaboration.* Thousand Oaks, CA: Sage.

Ahrons, C. (2007). Introduction to the special issue on divorce and its aftermath. *Family Process, 46,* 3–6.

Aiken, L. R., & Groth-Marnat, G. (2006). *Psychological testing and assessment* (12th ed.). Boston: Allyn & Bacon.

Airasian, P. W., & Russell, M. K. (2008). *Classroom assessment* (6th ed.). New York: McGraw-Hill.

Airasian, P. W., & Walsh, M. E. (1997, February). Constructivist cautions. *Phi Delta Kappan,* pp. 444–450.

Alberto, P. A., & Troutman, A. C. (2006). *Applied analysis for teachers* (7th ed.). Upper Saddle River, NJ: Prentice Hall.

Alexander, P. A. (2003). The development of expertise. *Educational Researcher, 32* (8), 10–14.

Allen, B. (2008). Head Start. In N. J. Salkind (Ed.), *Encyclopedia of educational psychology.* Thousand Oaks, CA: Sage.

Allen, J. P., & Antonishak, J. (2008). Adolescent peer influences: Beyond the dark side. In M. J. Prinstein & K. A. Dodge (Eds.), *Understanding peer influence in children and adolescents.* New York: Guilford.

Allington, R. L. (2009). *What really matters in fluency.* Boston: Allyn & Bacon.

All Kinds of Minds. (2005). *Learning Base: Self-regulating and learning.* Retrieved July 16, 2005, from www.allkindsofminds.org/learning

Alverno College. (1995). *Writing and speaking criteria.* Milwaukee, WI: Alverno Productions.

Alyahri, A., & Goodman, R. (2008, in press). Harsh corporal punishment of Yemeni children: Occurrence, type, and associations. *Child Abuse and Neglect.*

Amabile, T. M. (1993). (Commentary). In D. Goleman, P. Kaufman, & M. Ray, (Eds.), *The creative spirit.* New York: Plume.

Amabile, T. M., & Hennesey, B. A. (1992). The motivation for creativity in children. In A. K. Boggiano & T. S. Pittman (Eds.), *Achievement and motivation.* New York: Cambridge University Press.

Amato, P. R. (2006). Marital discord, divorce, and children's well-being: Results from a 20-year longitudinal study of two generations. In A. Clarke-Stewart & J. Dunn (Eds.), *Families count.* New York: Cambridge University Press.

American Association of University Women. (1993). *Hostile hallways.* Washington, DC: Author.

American Association of University Women. (2006). *Drawing the line: Sexual harassment on campus.* Washington, DC: Author.

American Association on Mental Retardation, Ad Hoc Committee on Terminology and Classification. (1992). *Mental retardation* (9th ed.). Washington, DC: Author.

Anastasi, A., & Urbino, S. (1997). *Psychological testing* (11th ed.). Upper Saddle River, NJ: Prentice Hall.

Anderman, E. M., Austin, C. C., & Johnson, D. M. (2002). The development of goal orientation. In A. Wigfield & J. S. Eccles (Eds.), *Development of achievement motivation.* San Diego: Academic Press.

Anderman, E. M., & Mueller, C. (2009). Middle school transitions and adolescent development: Disentangling psychological, social, and biological effects. In J. Meece & J. Eccles (Eds.), *Handbook of research on schools, schooling, and human development.* Clifton, NJ: Psychology Press.

Anderman, E. M., & Murdock, T. B. (Eds.). (2007). *Psychology of academic cheating.* San Diego: Academic Press.

Anderman, E. M., & Wolters, C. A. (2006). Goals, values, and affect: Influences on student motivation. In P. A. Alexander & P. H. Winne (Eds.), *Handbook of educational psychology* (2nd ed.). Mahwah, NJ: Erlbaum.

Anderson, D. R., Lorch, E. P., Field, D. E., Collins, P. A., & Nathan, J. G. (1985, April). *Television viewing at home: Age trends in visual attention and time with TV.* Paper presented at the biennial meeting of the Society for Research in Child Development, Toronto.

Anderson, E., Greene, S. M., Hetherington, E. M., & Clingempeel, W. G. (1999). The dynamics of parental remarriage. In E. M. Hetherington (Ed.), *Coping with divorce, single parenting, and remarriage.* Mahwah, NJ: Erlbaum.

Anderson, J. R. (2009). Context theory of classification learning. In D. Shanks (Ed.), *Psychology of learning.* Thousand Oaks, CA: Sage.

Anderson, K. G., Tapert, S. F., Moadab, I., Crowley, T. J., & Brown, S. A. (2007). Personality risk profile for conduct disorder and substance use disorders in youth. *Addictive Behaviors, 32,* 2377–2382.

Anderson, L. B. (2007). A special kind of tutor. *Teaching Pre K–8, 37* (No.5), 56–57.

Anderson, L. W., & Krathwohl, D. R. (Eds.). (2001). *A taxonomy for learning, teaching, and assessing.* New York: Longman.

Anderson, V., Jacobs, R., & Harvey, A. H. (2005). Prefrontal lesions and attentional skills in childhood. *Journal of the International Neuropsychological Society, 11,* 817–831.

Anderson, V. J. (2008). Grading. In N. J. Salkind (Ed.), *Encyclopedia of educational psychology.* Thousand Oaks. CA: Sage.

Andersson, U., & Lyxell, B. (2007). Working memory deficit in children with mathematical difficulties: A general or specific deficit? *Journal of Experimental Child Psychology, 96,* 197–228.

Anguiano, R.P.V. (2004). Families and schools: The effect of parental involvement on high school completion. *Journal of Family Issues, 25,* 61–85.

Applebee, A. & Langer, J. (2006). The partnership for literacy: A study of professional development, instructional change and student growth. Retrieved August 5, 2008, from http://cela.albany.edu/publication/IRAResearch.

Apple Computer. (1995). Changing the conversation about teaching, learning and technology: A report on 10 years of ACOT research. Retrieved April 8, 2005, from http://images.apple.com/education/k12/leadership/acot/pdf/10yr.pdf

Aricak, T. & others. (2008). Cyberbullying among Turkish adolescents. *Cyberpsychology and Bullying, 11,* 253–261.

Aronson, E. E. (1986, August). *Teaching students things they think they already know about: The case of prejudice and desegregation.* Paper presented at the meeting of the American Psychological Association, Washington, DC.

Aronson, E. E., Blaney, N., Sephan, C., Sikes, J., & Snapp, M. (1978). *The jigsaw classroom.* Beverly Hills, CA: Sage.

Aronson, E. E., & Patnoe, S. (1997). *The jigsaw classroom* (2nd ed.). Boston: Addison-Wesley.

Aronson, J. (2002). Stereotype threat: Contending and coping with Unnerving Expectations. *Improving academic achievement.* San Diego: Academic Press.

Arseneault, L. Milne, B. J., Taylor, A., Adams, F., Delgado, K., Caspi, A., & Moffit, T. E. (2008). Being bullied as an environmentally mediated contributing factor to children's internalizing problems: A study of twins discordant for victimization. *Archives of Pediatric and Adolescent Medicine, 162,* 145–150.

Arter, J. (1995). *Portfolios for assessment and instruction.* ERIC Document Reproduction Service No. ED388890.

Arthur, J. (2008). Traditional approaches to character education in Britain and America. In L. Nucci & D. Narvàez (Eds.), *Handbook of moral and character education.* Clifton, NJ: Psychology Press.

Asa, I. K., & Wiley, J. (2008). Hindsight bias in insight and mathematical problem solving: Evidence of different reconstruction mechanisms for metacognitive versus situational judgments. *Memory and Cognition, 36,* 822–837.

ACSD. (2009). *Classroom management that works.* Upper Saddle River, NJ: Prentice Hall.

Astrom, R. L., Wadsworth, S. J., & DeFries, J. C. (2007). Etiology of the stability of reading difficulties: The longitudinal twin study of reading disabilities. *Twin Research and Human Genetics, 10,* 434–439.

Atkinson, J. W. (1957). Motivational determinants of risk-taking behavior. *Psychological Review, 64,* 359–372.

Atkinson, R. C., & Shiffrin, R. M. (1968). Human memory: A proposed system and its control processes. In K. W. Spence & J. T. Spence (Eds.), *The psychology of learning and motivation* (Vol. 2). San Diego: Academic Press.

Aucoin, K. J., Frick, P. J., & Bodin, S. D. (2006). Corporal punishment and child adjustment. *Journal of Applied Developmental Psychology, 27,* 527–541.

August, P. (2002, September 26). They all look alike. *San Francisco Chronicle,* p. A29.

B

Babbie, E. R. (2005). *The basics of social research* (3rd ed.). Belmont, CA: Wadsworth.

Baddeley, A. (1993). Working memory and conscious awareness. In A. P. Collins, S. E. Gatherhole, M. A. Conway, & P. E. Morris (Eds.), *Theories of memory.* Mahwah, NJ: Erlbaum.

Baddeley, A. (2000). Short-term and working memory. In E. Tulving & F. I. M. Craik (Eds.), *The Oxford handbook of memory.* New York: Oxford University Press.

Baddeley, A. D. (2006) Working memory: An overview. In S. Pickering (Ed.), *Working Memory and Education.* New York: Academic Press.

Baddeley, A. D. (2007a). *Working memory, thought and action.* New York: Oxford University Press.

Baddeley, A. D. (2007b). Working memory: Multiple models, multiple mechanisms. In H. L. Roediger, Y. Dudai, S. M. Fitzpatrick (Eds.), *Science of memory: Concepts.* New York: Oxford University Press.

Bain, R. B. (2005). "They thought the world was flat?": Applying the principles of *How people learn* in teaching high school history. In M. S. Donovan & J. D. Bransford (Eds.), *How students learn.* Washington, DC: National Research Council.

Ballentine, J. H., & Hammock, J. H. (2009). *The sociology of education* (6th ed.). Upper Saddle River, NJ: Prentice Hall.

Ballentine, J. H., & Roberts, K. A. (2009). *Our social world* (2nd ed.). Thousand Oaks, CA: Sage.

Bandura, A. (1965). Influence of models' reinforcement contingencies on the acquisition of imitative responses. *Journal of Personality and Social Psychology, 1,* 589–596.

Bandura, A. (1982). Self-efficacy mechanism in human agency. *American Psychologist, 37,* 122–147.

Bandura, A. (1986). *Social foundations of thought and action.* Englewood Cliffs, NJ: Prentice Hall.

Bandura, A. (1997). *Self-efficacy: The exercise of control.* New York: W. H. Freeman.

Bandura, A. (2001). Social cognitive theory. *Annual Review of Psychology.* Palo Alto, CA: Annual Reviews.

Bandura, A. (2006). Toward a psychology of human agency. *Perspectives on Psychological Science, 1,* 164–180.

Bandura, A. (2007a). Self-efficacy. In S. Clegg & J. Bailey (Eds.), *International encyclopedia of organization studies.* Thousand Oaks, CA: Sage.

Bandura, A. (2007b). Social cognitive theory. In W. Donsbach (Ed.), *International encyclopedia of communication.* Thousand Oaks, CA: Sage.

Bandura, A. (2008). Reconstrual of "free will" form the agentic perspective of social cognitive theory. In J. Baer, J. C. Kaufman, & R. F. Bau-

meister (Eds.), *Are we free?: Psychology and free will.* Oxford, UK: Oxford University Press.

Bandura, A. (2009a). Social and policy impact of social cognitive theory. In M. Mark, S. Donaldson, & B. Campbell (Eds.), *Social psychology and program/policy evaluation.* New York: Guilford.

Bandura, A. (2009b). Vicarious learning. In D. Matsumoto (Ed.), *Cambridge dictionary of psychology.* New York: Cambridge University Press.

Bandura, A. (2009c). Agency. In D. Carr (Ed.), *Encyclopedia of life course and human development.* New York: Macmillan.

Banerjee, T. D., Middleton, F., & Faraone, S. V. (2007). Environmental risk factors for attention-deficit hyperactivity disorder. *Acta Pediatrica, 96,* 1269–1274.

Bangert, K., Kulik, J., & Kulik, C. (1983). Individualized systems of instruction in secondary schools. *Review of Educational Research, 53,* 143–158.

Banks, J. A. (1995). *Multicultural education: Its effects on student's racial and gender role attitudes.* In J. A. Banks & C. A. M. Banks (Eds.), *Handbook of research on multicultural education.* New York: Macmillan.

Banks, J. A. (1997). *Teaching strategies for ethnic studies* (6th ed.). Boston: Allyn & Bacon.

Banks, J. A. (2003). *Teaching strategies for ethnic studies* (7th ed.). Boston: Allyn & Bacon.

Banks, J. A. (2006). *Cultural diversity and education* (5th ed.). Boston: Allyn & Bacon.

Banks, J. A. (2008). *Introduction to multicultural education* (4th ed.). Boston: Allyn & Bacon.

Banks, J. A., Cochran-Smith, M., Moll, L., Richert, A., Zeichner, K., LePage, P., Darling-Hammond, L., Duffy, H., & McDonald, M. (2005). Teaching diverse learners. In L. Darling-Hammond & J. Bransford (Eds.), *Preparing teachers for a changing world.* San Francisco: Jossey-Bass.

Barab, S. A., Thomas, M., Dodge, T., Carteaux, R., & Tuzun, H. (2008, in press). Making learning fun: Quest Atlantis, a game without guns. *Educational Technology Research and Development.*

Barbaresi, W. J., Katusic, S. K., Colligan, R. C., Weaver, A. L., Leibson, C. L., & Jacobsen, S. J. (2006). Long-term stimulant medication treatment of attention-deficit/hyperactivity disorder: Results from a population-based study. *Journal of Developmental and Behavioral Pediatrics, 27,* 1–10.

Bart, W. M. (2008). Bloom's taxonomy of educational objectives. In N. J. Salkind (Ed.), *Encyclopedia of educational psychology.* Thousand Oaks, CA: Sage.

Bart, W. M., & Kato, K. (2008). Normal curve. In N. J. Salkind (Ed.), *Encyclopedia of educational psychology.* Thousand Oaks, CA: Sage.

Bart, W. M., & Peterson, D. P. (2008). Stanford-Binet test. In N. J. Salkind (Ed.), *Encyclopedia of educational psychology.* Thousand Oaks, CA: Sage.

Bartlett, J. (July 2008). *Personal conversation.* Richardson, TX: Department of Psychology, University of Texas at Dallas.

Barton, J., & Collins, A. (1997). Starting Out: Designing your portfolio. In J. Batton & A. Collins (Eds.), *Portfolio assessment: A handbook for educators.* Boston: Addison-Wesley.

Bass, J. E., Contant, T. L., & Carin, A. A. (2009). *Activities for teaching science as inquiry* (7th ed.). Boston: Allyn & Bacon.

Bassi, M., Steca, P., Della Fave, A., & Caprara, G. V. (2007). Academic self-efficacy beliefs and quality of experience on learning. *Journal of Youth and Adolescence, 36,* 301–312.

Battistich, V. A. (2008). The Child Development Project: Creating caring school communities. In L. Nucci & D. Narvàez (Eds.), *Handbook of moral and character education.* Clifton, NJ: Psychology Press.

Bauer, P. J. (2006). Event memory. In W. Damon & R. Lerner (Eds.), *Handbook of child psychology* (6th ed.). New York: Wiley.

Bauer, P. J. (2008, in press). Learning and memory: Like a horse and carriage. In A. Needham & A. Woodward (Eds.), *Learning and the infant mind.* New York: Oxford University Press.

Bauerlein, M. (2008). *The dumbest generation: How the digital age stupefies young Americans and jeopardizes our future (or, don't trust anyone under 30).* New York: Tarcher.

Baumeister, R. F., Campbell, J. D., Krueger, J. L., & Vohs, K. D. (2003). Does high self-esteem cause better performance, interpersonal success, happiness, or healthier lifestyles? *Psychological Science in the Public Interest, 4* (No. 1), 1–44.

Baumgartner, E., & Zabin, C. J. (2008). A case study of project-based instruction in the ninth grade: A semester-long study of intertidal diversity. *Environmental Education Research, 14,* 97–114.

Baumrind, D. (1971). Current patterns of parental authority. *Developmental Psychology Monographs, 4* (1, Part 2).

Baumrind, D. (1996, April). Unpublished review of J. W. Santrock's *Children,* 5th ed. (New York: McGraw-Hill).

Beal, C. M., Mason-Bolick, C. H., & Martorella, P. H. (2009). *Teaching social studies in middle and secondary schools* (5th ed.). Boston: Allyn & Bacon.

Beatty, B. (1998). From laws of learning to a science of values: Efficiency and morality in Thorndike's educational psychology. *American Psychologist, 53,* 1145–1152.

Beaty, J. J. (2009). *50 early childhood literacy strategies* (2nd ed.). Boston: Allyn & Bacon.

Beaty, L. A., & Alexeyev, E. B. (2008 Spring). The problem of school bullies: What the research tells us. *Adolescence, 43,* 1–11.

Beck, I. I., McKeown, G. M., Sinatra, K. B., & Loxterman, J. A. (1991). Revising social studies texts from a text-processing perspective: Evidence of improved comprehensibility. *Reading Research Quarterly, 26,* 251–276.

Bednar, R. L., Wells, M. G., & Peterson, S. R. (1995). *Self-esteem* (2nd ed.). Washington, DC: American Psychological Association.

Beghetto, R. A., & Kaufman, J. C. (Eds.). (2009). *Nurturing creating in the classroom.* New York: Cambridge University Press.

Begley, S., & Interlandi, J. (2008, June 2). The dumbest generation? Don't be dumb. *Newsweek.* Retrieved July 22, 2008, from www.newsweek.com/id/13855336/

Beilock, S. L., Rydell, R. J., & McConnell, A. R. (2007). Stereotype threat and working memory: Mechanisms, alleviation, and spillover. *Journal of Experimental Psychology: General, 136,* 256–276.

Beins, B. (2004). *Research methods.* Boston: Allyn & Bacon.

Beirne-Smith, M., Patton, J. R., & Kim, S. H. (2006). *Mental retardation* (7th ed.). Upper Saddle River, NJ: Prentice Hall.

Belgrad, S. (2008). *The portfolio connection* (3rd ed.). Thousand Oaks, CA: Corwin.

Belland, B. R., Glazewski, K. D., & Richardson, J. C. (2008). A scaffolding framework to support the construction of evidence-based arguments among middle school students. *Educational Technology Research and Development, 56,* 401–422.

Bem, S. L. (1977). On the utility of alternative procedures for assessing psychological androgyny. *Journal of Consulting and Clinical Psychology, 45,* 196–205.

Bempechat, J. (2008). Homework. In N. J. Salkind (Ed.), *Encyclopedia of educational psychology.* Thousand Oaks, CA: Sage.

Bender, H. L., Allen, J. P., McElhaney, K. B., Antonishak, J., Moore, C. M., Kello, H. O., & Davis, S. M. (2007). Use of harsh physical discipline and developmental outcomes in adolescence. *Development and Psychopathology, 19,* 227–242.

Bender, W. N. (2008). *Learning disabilities* (6th ed.). Boston: Allyn & Bacon.

Benner, A. D., & Mistry, R. S. (2007). Congruence of mother and teacher educational expectations and low-income youth's academic competence. *Journal of Educational Psychology, 99*, 140–153.

Bennett, T., Szatmari, P., Bryson, S., Volden, J., Zwaigenbaum, L., Vaccarella, L., Duku, E., & Boyle, M. (2008). Differentiating autism and Asperger syndrome on the basis of language delay or impairment. *Journal of Autism and Developmental Disorders, 38*, 616–625.

Benson, P. L., Sales, P. C., Hamilton, S. F., & Gesma, A. (2006). Positive youth development. In W. Damon, & R. Lerner (Eds.), *Handbook of child psychology* (6th Ed.). New York: Wiley.

Bentley, K. L., Adams, V. N., & Stevenson, H. C. (2009). Racial socialization: Roots, processes, and outcomes. In H. A. Neville, B. M. Tynes, & S. O. Utley (Eds.), *Handbook of African American psychology.* Thousand Oaks, CA: Sage.

Beran, T. N., & Tutty, L. (2002). *An evaluation of the Bully Proofing Your School Program.* Unpublished manuscript, Calgary: RESOLVE, Alberta, CAN.

Berecz, J. M. (2009). *Theories of personality.* Boston: Allyn & Bacon.

Bereiter, C., & Scardamalia, M. (2006). Education for the knowledge age: Design-centered models of teaching and instruction. In P. A. Alexander & P. H. Winne (Eds.), *Handbook of educational psychology* (2nd ed.). Mahwah, NJ: Erlbaum.

Berg, B. L. (2007). *Qualitative methods for the social sciences* (6th Ed.). Boston: Allyn & Bacon.

Berk, L. E. (1994). Why children talk to themselves. *Scientific American, 271* (5), 78–83.

Berk, L. E., & Spuhl, S. T. (1995). Maternal interaction, private speech, and task performance in preschool children. *Early Childhood Research Quarterly, 10*, 145–169.

Berko, J. (1958). The child's learning of English morphology. *Word, 14*, 150–177.

Berko Gleason, J. (2004). Unpublished review of J. W. Santrock's *Life-span development,* 9th ed. (New York: McGraw-Hill).

Berko Gleason, J. (2005). The development of language: An overview and a preview. In J. Berko Gleason (Ed.), *The development of language* (6th ed.). Boston: Allyn & Bacon.

Berko Gleason, J. (2009). The development of language: An overview. In J. Berko Gleason & N. Ratner (Eds.), *The development of language* (7th ed.). Boston: Allyn & Bacon.

Berko Gleason, J., & Ratner, N. (Eds.). (2009). *The development of language* (7th ed.). Boston: Allyn & Bacon.

Berkowitz, M. W., Battistich, V. A., & Bier, M. (2008). What works in character education: What is known and what needs to be known. In L. Nucci & D. Narvàez (Eds.), *Handbook of moral and character education.* Clifton, NJ: Psychology Press.

Berliner, D. (2006). Educational psychology: Searching for essence throughout a century of influence. In P. A. Alexander & P. H. Winne (Eds.), *Handbook of educational psychology* (2nd ed.). Mahwah, NJ: Erlbaum.

Bernard, R. H., Cahng, D., Abrami, P. C., Sicoly, F., Borokhovski, E., & Surkes, M. A. (2008). Exploring the structure of the Watson-Glaser critical thinking appraisal: One scale or many subscales? *Thinking Skills and Creativity, 3*, 15–22.

Berndt, T. J. (1979). Developmental changes in conformity to peers and parents. *Developmental Psychology, 15*, 608–616.

Berninger, V. W. (2006). A developmental approach to learning disabilities. In W. Damon & R. Lerner (Eds.), *Handbook of child psychology* (6th ed.). New York: Wiley.

Berninger, V. W., & Abbott, R. (2005, April). *Paths leading to reading comprehension in at-risk and normally developing second-grade readers.* Paper presented at the meeting of the Society for Research in Child Development, Atlanta.

Berson, M. J., Cruz, B. C., Duplass, J. A., & Johnston, J. H. (2007). *Social studies on the Internet* (3rd ed.). Upper Saddle River, NJ: Prentice Hall.

Betts, J., McKay, J., Maruff, P., & Anderson, V. (2006). The development of sustained attention in children: The effect of age and task load. *Child Neuropsychology, 12*, 205–221.

Bhatara, V. S., & Aparasu, R. R. (2007). Pharmacotherapy with atomoxetine for U.S. children and adolescents. *Annals of Clinical Psychiatry, 19*, 175–180.

Bialystok, E. (1997). Effects of bilingualism and biliteracy on children's emerging concepts of print. *Developmental Psychology, 33*, 429–440.

Bialystok, E. (1999). Cognitive complexity and attentional control in the bilingual mind. *Child Development, 70*, 537–804.

Bialystok, E. (2001). Metalinguistic aspects of bilingual processing. *Annual Review of Applied Linguistics, 21*, 169–181.

Bialystok, E. (2007). Acquisition of literacy in preschool children: A framework for research. *Language Learning, 57*, 45–77.

Bianco, I. H., Carl, M., Russell, C., Clarke, J. D., & Wilson, S. W. (2008). Brain asymmetry is encoded at the level of axon terminal morphology. *Neural Development, 3*, 9.

Biederman, J. (2007). Advances in the neurobiology of ADHD. *CNS Spectrums, 12* (Suppl. 4), S6–S7.

Bilalic, M., McLeod, P., & Gobet, F. (2008, in press). Why good thoughts block better ones: The mechanism of the pernicious Einstellung (set) effect. *Cognition.*

Bill and Melinda Gates Foundation. (2006). *The silent epidemic: Perspectives on high school dropouts.* Seattle: Author.

Bill and Melinda Gates Foundation. (2008). *Report gives voice to dropouts.* Retrieved July 5, 2008, from www.gatesfoundation.org/United States/Education/TransformingHighSchools/Related

Birman, B. F., Le Floch, K. C., Klekotka, A., Ludwig, M., Taylor, J., Walters, K., Wayne, A., & Yoon, K-S. (2007). *State and local implementation of the "No Child Left Behind Act." Volume II—Teacher quality under "NCLB": Interim report.* Jessup, MD: U.S. Department of Education.

Birren, J. E. (Ed.) (2007). *Encyclopedia of gerontology* (2nd ed.). San Diego: Academic Press.

Bitter, G. G., & Legacy, J. M. (2008). *Using technology in the classroom* (7th ed.). Boston: Allyn & Bacon.

Bjorklund, D. F. (2005). *Children's thinking* (4th ed.). Belmont, CA: Wadsworth.

Bjorklund, D. F., Dukes, C., & Brown, R. D. (2009). The development of memory strategies. In M. Courage & N. Cowan (Eds.), *The development of memory in infancy and childhood.* Clifton, NJ: Psychology Press.

Bjorklund, D. F., & Rosenbaum, K. (2000). Middle childhood: Cognitive development. In A. Kazdin (Ed.), *Encyclopedia of psychology.* Washington, DC, & New York: American Psychological Association and Oxford University Press.

Blackhurst, A. E. (1997, May/June). Perspectives on technology in special education. *Teaching Exceptional Children,* pp. 41–47.

Blair, C., & Razza, R. P. (2007). Relating effortful control, executive function, and false belief understanding to emerging math and literacy ability in kindergarten. *Child Development, 78*, 647–663.

Blair, T. R., Rupley, W. H., & Nichols, W. D. (2007). The effective teacher of reading: Considering the "what" and "how" of instruction. *Reading Teacher, 60*, 432–438.

Blakemore, J. E. O., Berenbaum, S. A., & Liben, L. S. (2009). *Gender development.* Clifton, NJ: Psychology Press.

Blakemore, S-J., & Choudhury, S. (2006). Brain development during puberty: State of the science. *Developmental Science, 9*, 11–14.

Blank, H., Nestler, S., von Collani, G., & Fischer, V. (2008). How many hindsight biases are there? *Cognition, 106*, 1408–1440.

Block, J. H., & Block, J. (1980). The role of ego-control and ego-resiliency in the organization of behavior. In W. A. Collins (Ed.), *Minnesota symposium on child psychology* (Vol. 13). Minneapolis: University of Minnesota Press.

Bloom, B., & Dey, A. N. (2006). Summary health statistics for U.S. children: National Health Interview survey, 2004. *Vital Health Statistics, 227*, 1–85.

Bloom, B. S. (1971). Mastering learning. In J. H. Block (Ed.), *Mastery learning.* New York: Holt, Rinehart & Winston.

Bloom, B. S. (Ed.). (1985). *Developing talent in young people.* New York: Ballantine.

Bloom, B. S., & Krathwohl, D. (Eds.). (1956). *Taxonomy of education objectives: Handbook 1. Cognitive domain.* New York: Longman, Green.

Bloom, B. S., Engelhart, M. D., Frost, E. J., Hill, W. H., & Krathwohl, D. R. (1956). *Taxonomy of educational objectives.* New York: David McKay.

Bloom, L. (1998). Language acquisition in its developmental context. In W. Damon (Ed.). *Handbook of child psychology* (5th ed., Vol. 2). New York: Wiley.

Bloom, L. A. (2009). *Classroom management.* Upper Saddle River, NJ: Prentice Hall.

Blumenfeld, P., Kempler, T. M., & Krajcik, J. S. (2006). Motivation and cognitive engagement in learning environments. In R. K. Sawyer (Ed.), *Cambridge handbook of learning sciences.* New York: Cambridge University Press.

Blumenfeld, P. C., Krajcik, J., & Kempler, T. (2006). Motivation in the classroom. In W. Damon & R. Lerner (Eds.), *Handbook of child psychology* (6th ed.). New York: Wiley.

Blumenfeld, P. C., Pintrich, P. R., Wessles, K., & Meece, J. (1981, April). *Age and sex differences in the impact of classroom experiences on self-perceptions.* Paper presented at the biennial meeting of the Society for Research in Child Development, Boston.

Bodrova, E., & Leong, D. J. (2007). *Tools of the mind* (2nd ed.). Upper Saddle River, NJ: Prentice Hall.

Boekaerts, M. (2006). Self-regulation and effort investment. In W. Damon & R. Lerner (Eds.), *Handbook of child psychology* (6th ed.). New York: Wiley.

Bohannon, J. N., & Bonvillian, J. D. (2009). Theoretical approaches to language acquisition. In J. Berko Gleason & N. B. Ratner (Eds.), *The development of language.* Boston: Allyn & Bacon.

Bolt, S. (2008). Testing. In N. J. Salkind (Ed.), *Encyclopedia of educational psychology.* Thousand Oaks, CA: Sage.

Bondy, E., Ross, D. D., Gallingane, C., & Hambacher, E. (2007). Creating environments of success and resilience: Culturally responsive classroom management and more. *Urban Education, 42*, 326–348.

Bookhart, S. M. (1997). A theoretical framework for the role of classroom assessment in motivating student effort and achievement. *Applied Measurement in Education, 10*, 161–180.

Borman, K. M., Cahill, S. E., & Cotner, B. A. (2007). *The Praeger handbook of American high schools.* Oxford, UK: Praeger.

Bornstein, M. H., & Zlotnik, D. (2008). Parenting styles and their effects. In M. M. Haith & J. B. Benson (Eds.), *Encyclopedia of infant and early childhood development.* Oxford, UK: Elsevier.

Bouchen, J. (2009). *The artistic spectrum.* Thousand Oaks, CA: Sage

Boucher, J. (2009). *The Autistic spectrum.* Thousand Oaks, CA: Sage.

Bowes, D., Marquis, M., Young, W., Holowaty, P., & Issac, W. (2008, in press). Process evaluation of a school-based intervention to increase physical activity and reduce bullying. *Health Promotion Practice.*

Bowles, T. (1999). Focusing on time orientation to explain adolescent self concept and academic achievement: Part II. Testing a model. *Journal of Applied Health Behaviour, 1,* 1–8.

Boyles, N. S., & Contadino, D. (1997). *The learning differences sourcebook.* Los Angeles: Lowell House.

Braden, J. P. (2005). Performance-based assessment. In S. W. Lee (Ed.), *Encyclopedia of school psychology.* Thousand Oaks, CA: Sage.

Brahier, D. J. (2009). *Teaching secondary and middle school mathematics* (3rd ed.). Boston: Allyn & Bacon.

Brainerd, C. J., Forrest, T. J., Karibian, D., & Reyna, V. F. (2006). Fuzzy-trace theory and memory development. *Developmental Psychology, 42,* 962–979.

Brainerd, C. J., & Gordon, L. L. (1994). Development of verbatim and gist memory for numbers. *Developmental Psychology, 30,* 163–177.

Brainerd, C. J., & Reyna, V. F. (2004). Fuzzy-trace theory and memory development. *Developmental Review, 24,* 396–439.

Bransford, J., Barron, B., Pea, R., Meltzoff, A., Kuhl, P., Bell, P., Stevens, R., Schwartz, D., Vye, N., Rcevos, B., Roschelle, J., & Subelli, N. (2006). Foundations and opportunities for an interdisciplinary science. In R. R. Sawyer (Ed.), *The Cambridge handbook of the learning sciences.* New York: Cambridge University Press.

Bransford, J., Darling-Hammond, L., & LePage, P. (2005). Introduction. In L. Darling-Hammond & J. Bransford (Eds.), *Preparing teachers for a changing world.* New York: Jossey-Bass.

Bransford, J., Derry, S., Berliner, D., Hammerness, K., & Beckett, K. I. (2005). Theories of learning and their role in teaching. In I. Darling-Hammond & J. Bransford (Eds.), *Preparing teachers for a changing world.* San Francisco: Jossey-Bass.

Bransford, J., & Donovan, M. S. (2005). Scientific inquiry and *How people learn.* In M. S. Donovan & J. D. Bransford (Eds.), *How students learn.* Washington, D.C: National Academies Press.

Bransford, J., Stevens, R., Schwartz, D., Meltzoff, A., Pea, R., Roschelle, J., Vye, N., Kuhl, P., Bell, P., Barron, B., Reeves, B., & Sabelli, N. (2006). Learning theories and education: Toward a decade of synergy. In P. A. Alexander & P. H. Winne (Eds.)

Bransford, J. D., & Stein, B. S. (1993). *The IDEAL problem solver.* New York: W. H. Freeman.

Breakstore, S., Dreiblatt, M., & Dreiblatt, K. (2009). *How to stop bullying and social aggression.* Thousand Oaks, CA: Corwin.

Bredekamp, S., & Copple, C. (Eds.) (1997). *Developmentally appropriate practice in early childhood programs* (rev. ed.). Washington, DC: National Association for the Education of Young Children.

Brewer, M. (2007). The social psychology of intergroup relations: Social categorization, in group bias, and outgroup prejudice. In A. W. Kruglanski & E. T. Higgins (Eds.), *Social psychology: Handbook of basic principles* (2nd ed.). New York: Guilford.

Brewer, M. B., & Campbell, D. I. (1976). *Ethnocentrism and intergroup attitudes.* New York: Wiley.

Brewer, W. F. (2009). Implicit learning and tacit knowledge. In D. Shanks (Ed.), *Psychology of learning.* Thousand Oaks, CA: Sage.

Briggs, T. W. (1999, October 14). Honorees find keys to unlocking kids' minds. Retrieved March 10, 2000, from www.usatoday.com/education

Briggs, T. W. (2004, October 14). Students embrace vitality of USA Today's top 20 teachers. *USA Today,* p. 70.

Briggs, T. W. (2005, October 13). *USA Today's* 2005 All-USA Teacher Team. *USA Today,* p. 6D.

Brody, N. (2000). Intelligence. In A. Kazdin (Ed.), *Encyclopedia of psychology.* Washington, DC, & New York: American Psychological Association and Oxford University Press.

Brody, N. (2007). Does education influence intelligence? In P. C. Kyllonen, R. D. Roberts, & L. Stankov (Eds.), *Extending intelligence.* Mahwah, NJ: Erlbaum.

Bronfenbrenner, U. (1995). Developmental ecology through space and time: A future perspective. In P. Moen, G.H. Elder, & K. Luscher (Eds.), *Examining lives in context.* Washington, DC: American Psychological Association.

Bronfenbrenner, U. (2004). *Making human beings human.* Thousand Oaks, CA: Sage.

Bronfenbrenner, U., & Morris, M.A. (1998). The ecology of developmental processes. In W. Damon (ed.), *Handbook of child psychology* (5th ed., Vol. 1). New York: Wiley.

Bronfenbrenner, U., & Morris, M.A. (2006). The ecology of developmental processes. In W. Damon & R. Lerner (Eds.), *Handbook of child psychology* (6th ed.). New York: Wiley.

Bronstein, P. (2006). The family environment: Where gender socialization begins. In J. Worell & C. D. Goodheart (Eds.), *Handbook of girls' and women's psychological health.* New York: Oxford University Press.

Brookhart, S. M. (2002). What will teachers know about assessment, and how will that improve instruction? In R. W. Kissitz & W. D. Schafer (Eds.), *Assessment in educational reform: Both means and ends.* Boston: Allyn & Bacon.

Brookhart, S. M. (2004). *Grading.* Upper Saddle River, NJ: Prentice Hall.

Brookhart, S. M. (2008). *Assessment and grading in classrooms.* Upper Saddle River, NJ: Prentice Hall.

Brookhart, S. M., Nitko, A. J. (2007). *Educational assessment of students* (5th ed.). Upper Saddle River, NJ: Prentice Hall.

Brookhart, S. M., & Nitko, A. J. (2008). *Assessment and grading in classrooms.* Upper Saddle River, NJ: Prentice Hall.

Brookover, W. B., Beady, C., Flood, P., Schweitzer, U., & Wisenbaker, J. (1979). *School social systems and student achievement: Schools make a difference.* New York: Praeger.

Brooks, J. G., & Brooks, M. G. (1993). *The case for constructivist classrooms.* Alexandria, VA: Association for Supervision and Curriculum Development.

Brooks, J. G., & Brooks, M. G. (2001). *In search of understanding: The case for constructivist classrooms.* Upper Saddle River, NJ: Merrill.

Brophy, J. (1996). *Teaching problem students.* New York: Guilford.

Brophy, J. (1998). *Motivating students to learn.* New York: McGraw-Hill.

Brophy, J. (2004). *Motivating students to learn* (2nd ed.). Mahwah, NJ: Erlbaum.

Brown, A. L. (1997). Transforming schools into communities of thinking and learning about serious matters. *American Psychologist, 52,* 399–413.

Brown, A. L., & Campione, J. C. (1996). Psychological learning theory and the design of innovative environments. In L. Schauble & R. Glaser (Eds.), *Contributions of instructional innovation to understanding learning.* Mahwah, NJ: Erlbaum.

Brown, B. B., Bakken, J. P., Ameringer, S. W., & Mahon, S. D. (2008). A comprehensive conceptualization of the peer influence process in adolescence. In M. J. Prinstein & K. A. Dodge (Eds.), *Understanding peer influence in children and adolescents.* New York: Guilford.

Brown, P. L., & Jenkins, H. M. (2009). On the law of effect. In D. Shanks (Ed.), *Psychology of learning.* Thousand Oaks, CA: Sage.

Brown, R. P., & Day, E. A. (2006). The difference isn't black and white: Stereotype threat and the race gap on Raven's Advanced Progressive Matrices. *Journal of Applied Psychology, 91,* 979–985.

Bruckman, A. (2006). Learning in online communities. In R. K. Sawyer (Ed.), *The Cambridge handbook of the learning sciences.* New York: Cambridge University Press.

Bruer, J. (1993) *Schools for Thought.* Cambridge, MA: MIT University Press.

Bruner, J. (1996). *Toward a theory of instruction.* Cambridge, MA: Harvard University Press.

Bruning, R., & Horn, C. (2001). Developing motivation to write. *Educational Psychologist, 35,* 25–37.

Brunstein Klomek, A., Marrocco, F., Kleinman, M., Schofeld, I. S., & Gould, M. S. (2007). Bullying, depression, and suicidality in adolescents. *Journal of the American Academy of Child and Adolescent Psychiatry, 46,* 40–49.

Bryant, D. P., Smith, D. D., & Bryant, B. R. (2008). *Teaching students with special needs in inclusive classrooms.* Boston: Allyn & Bacon.

Bryant, J. A. (Ed.). (2007). *The children's television community.* Mahwah, NJ: Erlbaum.

Bryant, J. B. (2009). Language in social contexts: Communication competence in the preschool years. In J. Berko Gleason & N. Ratner (Eds.), *The development of language* (7th ed.). Boston: Allyn & Bacon.

Bryk, A. S., Lee, V. E., Smith, J. B. (1989, May). *High school organization and its effects on teachers and students: An interpretive summary of the research.* Paper presented at the conference on Choice and Control in American Education, University of Wisconsin, Madison.

Bukowski, W. M., Brendgen, M., & Vitaro, F. (2007). Peers and socialization: Effects on externalizing and internalizing problems. In J. E. Grusec & P. D. Hastings (Eds.), *Handbook of socialization.* New York: Guilford.

Burchinal, M., Nelson, L., Carlson, M., & Brooks-Gunn, J. (2008, in press). Neighborhood characteristics and child care type and quality. *Early Education and Development.*

Burge, P. L., & Filer, K. (2008). Gender. In N. J. Salkind (Ed.), *Encyclopedia of educational psychology.* Thousand Oaks, CA: Sage.

Burge, P. L., & Heath, E. V. (2008). Test anxiety. In N. J. Salkind (Ed.), *Encyclopedia of educational psychology.* Thousand Oaks, CA: Sage.

Burger, J. M. (2008). *Personality* (7th ed.). Belmont, CA: Wadsworth.

Burke, K. (2006). *From standards to rubrics in six steps.* Thousand Oaks, CA: Corwin.

Burke-Adams, A. (2007). The benefits of equalizing standards and creativity: Discovering a balance in instruction. *Gifted Child Quarterly, 30,* 58–63.

Burkham, D. T., Lee, V. E., & Smerdon, B. A. (1997). Gender and science learning early in high school: Subject matter and laboratory experiences. *American Educational Research Journal, 34,* 297–331.

Burnette, J. (1998). Reducing the disproportionate representation of minority students in special education. *ERIC/OSEP Digest, No. E566.*

Bursuck, W. D., & Damer, M. (2007). *Reading instruction for students who are at risk or have disabilities.* Boston: Allyn & Bacon.

Burz, H. L., & Marshall, K. (1996). *Performance-based curriculum for mathematics.* ERIC Document Reproduction Service No. ED400194.

Buss, D. M. (2008). *Evolutionary psychology* (3rd ed.). Boston: Allyn & Bacon.

Butler, S. M., & McMunn, N. D. (2006). *A teacher's guide to classroom assessment.* Thousand Oaks, CA: Corwin.

Bybee, R. W., Powell, J. C., & Trowbridge, L. W. (2008). *Teaching secondary science* (9th ed.). Upper Saddle River, NJ: Prentice Hall.

Byrnes, J. P. (2008). *Cognitive development and learning in instructional contexts* (3rd ed.). Boston: Allyn & Bacon.

C

Cahill, L., Raier, R. J., White, N. S., Fallon, J., Kilparaick, L., Lawrence, C., Potkin, S. G., & Alkire, M. T. (2001). Sex-related differences in amygdale activity during emotionally influenced memory storage. *Neurobiology of Learning and Memory, 75,* 1–9.

California State Department of Education. (1994). *Golden State examination science portfolio.* Sacramento: Author.

Cameron, J. R. (2001). Negative effects of reward on intrinsic motivation—a limited phenomenon. *Review of Educational Research, 71,* 29–42.

Cameron, J. R., Hansen, R., & Rosen, D. (1989). Preventing behavioral problems in infancy through temperament assessment and parental support programs. In W. B. Carey & S. C. McDevitt (Eds.), *Clinical and educational applications of temperament research.* Amsterdam: Sets & Zeitlinger.

Cameron, J. R., & Pierce, D. (2008). Intrinsic versus extrinsic motivation. In N. J. Salkind (Ed.), *Encyclopedia of educational psychology.* Thousand Oaks, CA: Sage.

Camilleri, B. (2005). Dynamic assessment and intervention: Improving children's narrative abilities. *International Journal of Language and Communication Disorders, 40,* 240–242.

Campbell, B. (2008). *Handbook of differentiated instruction using the multiple intelligences: Lesson plans and more.* Boston: Allyn & Bacon.

Campbell, C. Y. (1988, August 24). Group raps depiction of teenagers. *Boston Globe,* p. 44.

Campbell, D. T., & LeVine, D. T. (1968). Ethnocentrism and intergroup relations. In R. Abelson & others (Eds.), *Theories of cognitive consistency.* Chicago: Rand McNally.

Campbell, F. A. (2007). The malleability of the cognitive development of children of low-income African American families: Intellectual test performance over twenty-one years. In P. C. Kyllonen, R. D. Roberts, & L. Stankov (Eds.), *Extending intelligence.* Mahwah, NJ: Erlbaum.

Campbell, L., Campbell, B., & Dickinson, D. (2004). *Teaching and learning through multiple intelligence* (3rd ed.). Boston: Allyn & Bacon.

Campbell, P. (2007). Edison is the symptom, NCLB is the disease, *Phi Delta Kappan International, 88,* 438–443.

Campione, J. (2001, April). *Fostering a Community of Learners.* Paper presented at the meeting of the American Educational Research Association, Seattle.

Cano, M. A. (2008). Multicultural education. In N. J. Salkind (Ed.), *Encyclopedia of educational psychology.* Thousand Oaks, CA: Sage.

Cardelle-Elawar, M. (1992). Effects of teaching metacognitive skills to students with low mathematics ability. *Teaching and Teacher Education, 8,* 109–121.

Carnegie Council on Adolescent Development. (1995). *Great transitions.* New York: Carnegie Foundation.

Carnegie Foundation. (1989). *Turning points: Preparing youth for the 21st century.* New York: Author.

Carpendale, J. I., & Chandler, M. J. (1996). On the distinction between false belief understanding and subscribing to an interpretive theory of mind. *Child Development. 67,* 1686–1706.

Carpendale, J. I. M., Muller, U., & Bibok, M. B. (2008). Piaget's theory of cognitive development. In N. J. Salkind (Ed.), *Encyclopedia of educational psychology.* Thousand Oaks, CA: Sage.

Carr, D. (2008). Character education as the cultivation of virtue. In L. Nucci & D. Narvàez (Eds.), *Handbook of moral and character education.* Clifton, NJ: Psychology Press.

Carrell, S. E., Malmstrom, F. V., & West, J. E. (2008). Peer effects in academic cheating. *Journal of Human Resources, 43,* 173–207.

Carroll, J. (1993). *Human cognitive abilities.* Cambridge, UK: Cambridge University Press.

Carroll, J. B. (1963). A model of school learning. *Teachers College Record, 64,* 723–733.

Carter, N., Prater, M. A., & Dyches, T. T. (2009). *What every teacher should know about: Adaptations and accommodations for students with mild to moderate disabilities.* Upper Saddle River, NJ: Prentice Hall.

Casbergue, R. M., & Harris, K. (1996). Listening and literacy: Audiobooks in the reading program. *Reading Horizons, 37,* 48–59.

Case, R. (2000). Conceptual structures. In M. Bennett (Ed.), *Developmental psychology.* Philadelphia: Psychology Press.

Casey, B. J., Getz, S., & Galvan, A. (2008). The adolescent brain. *Developmental Review, 28,* 62–77.

Casey, B. J., Jones, R. M., & Hare, T. A. (2008). The adolescent brain. *Annals of the New York Academy of Sciences, 1124,* 111–126.

Catalano, R. F., Hawkins, J. D., & Toumbourou, J. W. (2008). Positive youth development in the United States: History, efficacy, and links to moral and character education. In L. Nucci & D. Narvàez (Eds.), *Handbook of moral and character education.* Clifton, NJ: Psychology Press.

Cave, R. K. (2002, August). *Early adolescent language: A content analysis of child development and educational psychology textbooks.* Unpublished doctoral dissertation, University of Nevada–Reno, Reno.

Caviness, L. B. (2008). Brain-relevant education. In N. J. Salkind (Ed.), *Encyclopedia of educational psychology.* Thousand Oaks, CA: Sage.

Ceci, S. J., & Gilstrap, L. L. (2000). Determinants of intelligence: Schooling and intelligence. In A. Kazdin (Ed.), *Encyclopedia of psychology.* Washington, DC, & New York: American Psychological Association and Oxford University Press.

Ceci, S. J., & Williams, W. M. (1997). Schooling, intelligence, and income. *American Psychologist, 52,* 1051–1058.

Center for Instructional Technology. (2006). *Writing multiple-choice questions that demand critical thinking.* Retrieved January 12, 2006, from http://cit.necc.mass.edu/atlt/TestCritThink.htm

Chall, J. S. (1979). The great debate: Ten years later with a modest proposal for reading stages. In L. B. Resnick & P. A. Weaver (Eds.), *Theory and practice of early reading.* Mahwah, NJ: Erlbaum.

Chan, D. W. (2008). Emotional intelligence, self-efficacy, and coping among Chinese prospective and in-service teachers in Hong Kong. *Educational Psychology, 28,* 397–408.

Chang, M.-M. (2007). Enhancing web-based language learning through self-assessment. *Journal of Computer Assisted Leaning, 23,* 187–196.

ChanLin, J-J., & Chan, K-C. (2007). Integrating inter-disciplinary expert for supporting problem-based learning. *Innovations in Education and Teaching, 44,* 211–224.

ChanLin, L-J. (2008). Technology integration applied to project-based learning in science. *Innovations in Education and Teaching International, 45,* 55–65.

Chao, R. K. (2005, April). *The importance of guan in describing the parental control of immigrant Chinese.* Paper presented at the meeting of the Society for Research in Child Development, Atlanta.

Chao, R. K. (2007, March). *Research with Asian Americans: Looking back, moving forward.* Paper presented at the meeting of the Society for Research in Child Development, Boston.

Chapin, J. R. (2009). *Elementary social studies* (7th ed.). Boston: Allyn & Bacon.

Chapman, J. W., Tunmer, W. E., & Prochnow, J. E. (2001). Does success in the Reading Recovery program depend on developing proficiency in phonological-processing skills? A longitudinal study in the whole language instructional context. *Scientific Studies of Reading, 15,* 141–176.

Chapman, O. L. (2000). Learning science involves language, experience, and modeling. *Journal of Applied Developmental Psychology, 21,* 97–108.

Charles, C. M. (2008a). *Building classroom discipline* (8th ed.). Boston: Allyn & Bacon.

Charles, C. M. (2008b). *Today's best classroom management strategies.* Boston: Allyn & Bacon.

Charles, C. M., & Senter, G. W. (2008). *Elementary classroom management* (5th ed.). Boston: Allyn & Bacon.

Charney, J., Hmelo-Silver, C. E., Sofer, W., Neigeborn, L., Coletta, S., & Nemeroff, M. (2007). Cognitive apprenticeship in science through immersion in laboratory practices. *International Journal of Science Education, 29,* 195–213.

Charney, R. S. (2005). *Exploring the first "R": To reinforce.* Retrieved October 20, 2006, from www.nca.org/classmanagement/ifc050201.html

Chart, H., Grigorenko, E. L., & Sternberg, R. J. (2008). The Aurora battery: Toward better identification of giftedness. In C. Callahan & J. Plucker (Eds.), *What the research says about: An encyclopedia of research on gifted education.* Waco, TX: Prufrock Press.

Chavous, T. M., Rivas-Drake, D., Smalls, C., Griffin, T., & Cogburn, C. (2008). Gender matters, too: The influences of school discrimination and racial identity on academic engagement among African American adolescent boys and girls. *Developmental Psychology, 44* (3), 637–654.

Chen, C., & Stevenson, H. W. (1989). Homework: A cross-cultural comparison. *Child Development, 60,* 551–561.

Chen, Z., & Honomichl, R. (2008). Discovery learning. In N. J. Salkind (Ed.), *Encyclopedia of educational psychology.* Thousand Oaks, CA: Sage.

Chess, S., & Thomas, A. (1977). Temperamental individuality from childhood to adolescence. *Journal of Child Psychiatry, 16,* 218–226.

Chi, M. T. H. (1978). Knowledge structures and memory development. In R. S. Siegler (Ed.), *Children's thinking.* Mahwah, NJ: Erlbaum.

Chi, M. T. H. (2000). Self-explaining: The dual processes of generating inference and repairing mental models. In R. Glaser (Ed.), *Advances in instructional psychology: Educational design and cognitive science.* (Vol. 5), pp. 161–238.

Chi, M. T. H. (2008). Three types of conceptual change: belief revision, mental model transformation, and categorical shift. In S. Vosniadou (Ed.), *International handbook of research on conceptual change.* Clifton, NJ: Psychology Press.

Chi, M. T. H., Bassok, M., Lewis, M. W., Reimann, P., & Glaser, R. (1989). Self-explanations: How students study and use examples in learning to solve problems. *Cognitive Science, 13,* 145–182.

Chi, M. T. H., Roy, M., & Hausmann, R. G. M. (2008). Observing tutorial dialogues collaboratively: Insights about human tutoring effectiveness from vicarious learning. *Cognitive Science, 32,* 301–341.

Chiappe, D., & MacDonald, K. (2005). The evolution of domain-general mechanisms in intelligence and learning. *Journal of General Psychology, 132,* 5–40.

Children's Defense Fund. (1992). *The state of America's children.* Washington, DC: Author.

Children's Defense Fund. (2008). *Child welfare and mental health.* Retrieved July 28, 2008, from www.childrensdefense.org.

Chiu, C., & Hong, Y. (2007). Cultural processes: Basic principles. In A. W. Kruglanski & E. T. Higgins (Eds.), *Social psychology: Handbook of basic principles* (2nd ed.). New York: Guilford.

Chiu, M-H., Chorng-Jee, G., & Treagust, D. F. (2007). Assessing students' conceptual understanding in science: An introduction about a national project in Taiwan. *International Journal of Science Education, 29,* 379–390.

Chiu, M. M. (2007). Families, economies, cultures, and science achievement in 41 countries: Country-, school-, and student-level analyses. *Journal of Family Psychology, 21,* 510–519.

Chomsky, N. (1957). *Syntactic structures.* The Hague: Mouton.

Chouinard, R., Karsenti, T., & Roy, N. (2007). Relations among competence beliefs, utility value, achievement goals, and effort in mathematics. *British Journal of Educational Psychology, 77,* 501–517.

Christ, T. T., & Thorndike, R. M. (2008). Intelligence tests. In N. J. Salkind (Ed.), *Encyclopedia of educational psychology.* Thousand Oaks, CA: Sage.

Christenson, S. L., & Thurlow, M. L. (2004). School dropouts: Prevention considerations, interventions, and challenges. *Current Directions in Psychological Science, 13,* 36–39.

Chronis, A. M., Chacko, A., Fabiano, G. A., Wymbs, B. T., & Pelham, W. E. (2004). Enhancements to the behavioral parent training paradigm for families of children with ADHD: Review and future directions. *Clinical Child and Family Psychology Review, 7,* 1–27

Clark, B. (2008). *Growing up gifted* (7th ed.). Upper Saddle River, NJ: Prentice Hall.

Clark, K. B., & Clark, M. P. (1939). The development of the self and the emergence of racial identification in Negro preschool children. *Journal of Social Psychology, 10,* 591–599.

Clark, L. (Ed.). (1993). *Faculty and student challenges in facing cultural and linguistic diversity.* Springfield, IL: Charles C. Thomas.

Clarke-Stewart, K. A. (2006). What have we learned? Proof that families matter, policies for families and children, prospects for future research. In A. Clarke-Stewart & J. Dunn (Eds.), *Families count:* New York: Cambridge University Press.

Clerkin, C. (2008). Gender bias. In N. J. Salkind (Ed.), *Encyclopedia of educational psychology.* Thousand Oaks, CA: Sage.

Cloud, J. (2007, August 27). Failing our geniuses. *Time,* 40–47.

Cochran-Smith, M. (1995). Color blindness and basket making are not the answers: Confronting the dilemmas of race, culture, and language diversity in teacher education. *American Educational Research Journal, 32,* 493–522.

Cognition and Technology Group at Vanderbilt. (1997). *The Jasper Project.* Mahwah, NJ: Erlbaum.

Cohn, A., & Canter, A. (2003). *Bullying: Facts for schools and parents.* Washington, DC: National Association of School Psychologists.

Coie, J. (2004). The impact of negative social experiences on the development of antisocial behavior. In J. B. Kupersmidt & K. A. Dodge (Eds.), *Children's peer relations: From development to intervention.* Washington, DC: American Psychological Association.

Coladarci, T. (1992). Teachers' sense of efficacy and commitment to teaching. *Journal of Experimental Education, 60,* 323–337.

Colangelo, N., & Davis, G. A. (2003). *Handbook of gifted education* (3rd ed.). Boston: Allyn & Bacon.

Colangelo, N. C., Assouline, S. G., & Gross, M. U. M. (2004). *A nation deceived: How schools hold back America's brightest students.* Retrieved October 16, 2006, From http://nationdeceived.org/

Colby, A., Kohlberg, L., Gibbs, J., & Lieberman, M. (1983). A longitudinal study of moral judgment. *Monograph: the Society for Research in Child Development, 48* (21, Serial No. 201).

Cole, C. F., Arafat, C., Tidhar, C., Tafesh, W. Z., Fox, N. A., Killen, M., Ardila-Rey, A. Leavitt, L. A., Lesser, G., Richman, B. A., & Yung, F. (2003). The educational impact of Rechov Sumsum/Shar's Simsim: A *Sesame Street* television series to promote respect and understanding among children living in Israel, the West Bank, and Gaza. *International Journal of Behavioural Development, 27,* 409–423.

Cole, M. (2006). Culture and cognitive development in phylogenetic, historical, and ontogenetic perspective. In W. Damon & R. Lerner (Eds.), *Handbook of child psychology* (6th ed.). New York: Wiley.

Cole, M., & Gajdamaschko, N. (2007). Vygotsky and culture. In H. Daniels, J. Wertsch, & M. Cole (Eds.), *The Cambridge companion to Vygotsky.* New York: Cambridge University Press.

Coley, R. (2001). *Differences in the gender gap: Comparisons across/racial/ethnic groups in the United States.* Princeton, NJ: Educational Testing Service.

College Board. (2004). *2003 college-bound seniors tables and related items.* Princeton, NJ: Author.

Collins, M. (1996, Winter). The job outlook for '96 grads. *Journal of Career Planning,* pp. 51–54.

Collins, W. A., & Steinberg, L. (2006). Adolescent development in interpersonal context. In W. Damon & R. Lerner (Eds.), *Handbook of child psychology* (6th ed.). New York: Wiley.

Collins, W. A., & van Dulmen, M. (2006). The significance of middle childhood peer competence for work and relationship in early childhood. In A. C. Huston & M. N. Ripke (Eds.), *Developmental contexts in middle childhood.* New York: Cambridge University Press.

Collis, B. A., Knezek, G. A., Lai, K. W., Miyashita, K. T., Pelgrum, W. J., Plomp, T., & Sakamoto, T. (1996). *Children and computers in school.* Mahwah, NJ: Erlbaum.

Colom, R., & Flores-Mendoza, C. E. (2007). Intelligence predicts scholastic achievement irrespective of SES factors: Evidence from Brazil. *Intelligence, 35,* 243–251.

Colombo, J., McCardle, P., & Freund, L. (Eds.). (2009). *Infant pathways to language.* Clifton, NJ: Psychology Press.

Coltrane, S. L., Parke, R. D., Schofield, T. H., Tsuha, J., Chavez, M., & Lio, S. (2008). Mexican American families and poverty. In D. R. Crane & T. B. Heaton (Eds.), *Handbook of families and poverty.* Thousand Oaks, CA: Sage.

Combs, D. (1997, September). Using alternative assessment to provide options for student success. *Middle School Journal,* pp. 3–8.

Comer, J. P. (1988). Educating poor minority children. *Scientific American, 259,* 42–48.

Comer, J. P. (2004). *Leave no child behind.* New Haven, CT: Yale University Press.

Comer, J. P. (2005). Child and adolescent development: The critical missing focus in school reform. *Phi Delta Kappan, 86,* 757–763.

Comstock, G., & Scharrer, E. (2006). Media and popular culture. In W. Damon & R. Lerner (Eds.), *Handbook of child psychology* (6th ed.). New York: Wiley.

Conger, R., & Conger, K. J. (2008). Understanding the processes through which economic hardship influences rural families and children. InD. R. Crane & T. B. Heaton (Eds.), *Handbook of families and poverty.* Thousand Oaks, CA: Sage.

Conley, M. W. (2008). *Content area literacy: Learners in context.* Boston: Allyn & Bacon.

Constantinos, C., & Papageorgiou, E. (2007). A framework of mathematics inductive reasoning. *Learning and Instruction, 17,* 55–66.

Conti-Ramsden, G. (2008). Heterogeneity of specific language impairment. In C. Norbury, B. Tomblin, & D. Bishop (Eds.), *Understanding developmental language disorders in children.* Milton Park, UK: Routledge.

Cook, P. J., MacCoun, R., Muschkin, C., & Vigdor, J. (2008). The negative impacts of starting middle school in the sixth grade. *Journal of Policy Analysis and Management, 27,* 104–121.

Cook, T. D., Deng, Y., & Morgano, E. (2007). Friendship influences during early adolescence: The special role of friends' grade point average. *Journal of Research on Adolescence, 17,* 325–356.

Cooper, C. R. (1995, March). *Multiple selves, multiple worlds.* Paper presented at the meeting of the Society for Research in Child Development, Indianapolis.

Cooper, E. (2008). Realities and responsibilities in the education village. In L. C. Tillman (Ed.), *The SAGE handbook of African American education.* Thousand Oaks, CA: Sage.

Cooper, E., & Sherk, J. (1989). Addressing urban school reform: Issues and alliances, *Journal of Negro Education, 58,* 315–331.

Cooper, H. (1989). Synthesis of research on homework. *Educational Leadership, 47* (3), 85–91.

Cooper, H. (1998, April). *Family, student, and assignment characteristics of positive homework experiences.* Paper presented at the meeting of the American Educational Research Association, San Diego.

Cooper, H. (2007). *The battle over homework: Common ground for administrators, teachers, and parents* (3rd ed.). Thousand Oaks, CA: Corwin.

Cooper, H. (2009, in press). Homework. In T. Bidell (Ed.), *Chicago companion to the child.* Chicago: University of Chicago Press.

Cooper, H., & Patall, E. A. (2007). Homework. In S. Mathison & E. W. Ross (Eds.), *Battleground schools* (pp. 319–326). Westport, CT: Greenwood press.

Cooper, H., Robinson, J. C., & Patall, E. A. (2006). Does homework improve academic achievement? A synthesis of research, 1987–2003. *Review of Educational Research, 76,* 1–62.

Cooper, H., & Valentine, J. C. (2001). Using research to answer practical questions about homework. *Educational Psychologist, 36,* 143–153.

Cooper, J. E., Horn, S., & Strahan, D. B. (2005). "If only they would do their homework": Promoting self-regulation in high school English classes. *High School Journal, 88,* 10–25.

Cooper, R., & Huh, C. R. (2008). Improving academic possibilities of students of color during the middle school to high school transition: Conceptual and strategic considerations in a U.S. context. In K. Asamen, M. L. Ellis, & G. L. Berry (Eds.), *The SAGE*

Cooper, S. M., & McLoyd, V. C. (2008, in press). Race-related socialization and the well-being of African American adolescents: The moderating role of mother-adolescent relationship. *Journal of Research on Adolescence.*

Cooper, S. M., McLoyd, V., Wood, D., & Hardaway, C. (2008). The mental health consequences of racial discrimination for African American adolescents. In S. Quintana and C. McKown (Eds.), *Handbook of race, racism and the developing child*. New York: Wiley.

Copeland, L. (2003, December). Science teacher just wanted to do some good, and he has. *USA Today*. Retrieved January 15, 2005, from www.usatoday.com/news/education/2003–12–30-laster-usual_x.htm

Copeland, S. R., & Luckasson, R. (2008). Mental retardation. In N. J. Salkind (Ed.), *Encyclopedia of educational psychology*. Thousand Oaks, CA: Sage.

Cornelivs-White, J. H., & Harbaugh, A. P. (2009). *Learner-centered instruction*. Thousand Oaks, CA: Sage.

Corno, L. (1998, March 30). Commentary. *Newsweek*, p. 51.

Cossentino, J. (2008). Montessori schools. In N. J. Salkind (Ed.), *Encyclopedia of educational psychology*. Thousand Oaks, CA: Sage.

Council for Exceptional Children. (1998). *CEC's comments on the proposed IDEA regulations*. Washington, DC: Author.

Council of Chief State School Officers (2005). *Marilyn Jachetti Whirry*. Retrieved October 19, 2006, from www.ccsso.org/

Courage, M. L., & Richards, J. E. (2008). Attention. In M. M. Haith & J. B. Benson (Eds.), *Encyclopedia of infant and early childhood development*. Oxford, UK: Elsevier.

Covington, M. V., & Dray, E. (2002). The development course of achievement motivation: A need-based approach. In A. Wigfield & J. S. Eccles (Eds.), *Development of achievement motivation*. San Diego: Academic Press.

Covington, M. V., & Teel, K. T. (1996). *Overcoming student failure*. Washington, DC: American Psychological Association.

Cowan, N., & Alloway, T. (2009). The development of working memory in childhood. In M. Courage & N. Cowan (Eds.), *The development of memory in infancy and childhood*. Clifton, NJ: Psychology Press.

Cox, J. E., & Nelson, D. (2008). The relationship between thinking patterns and emotional skills. *Journal of Humanistic Counseling, Education, and Development, 47,* (1) 1–9.

Cox, M. J., Neilbron, N., Mills-Koonce, W. R., Pressel, A., Oppenheimer, C. W., & Szwedo, D. E. (2008). Marital relationship. In M. M. Haith & J. B. Benson (Eds.), *Encyclopedia of infant and early childhood development*. Oxford, UK: Elsevier.

Coyne, S. M., Archer, J., Eslea, M., & Liechty, T. (2008, in press). Adolescent perceptions of indirect forms of relational aggression: Sex of perpetrator effects. *Aggressive Behavior*.

Craik, F. I. M., & Lockhart, R. S. (1972). Levels of processing: A framework for memory research. *Journal of Verbal Learning and Verbal Behavior, 11,* 671–684.

Crane, D. R., & Heaton, T. B. (Eds.). (2008). *Handbook of families and poverty*. Thousand Oaks, CA: Sage.

Crawford, M., & Unger, R. (2004). *Women and gender* (4th ed.) New York: McGraw-Hill.

Creswell, J. W. (2008). *Educational research* (3rd ed.). Upper Saddle River, NJ: Prentice Hall.

Crick, N. R., Ostrov, J. F., & Kawabata, Y. (2007). Relational aggression and gender: An overview. In D. J. Flannery, A. T. Vazsonyi, & I. D. Waldman (Eds.), *The Cambridge handbook of violent behavior and aggression*. New York: Cambridge University Press.

Crimmins, D., Farrell, A. F., Smith, P. W., & Bailey, A. (2007). *Positive strategies for students with behavior problems*. Baltimore: Brookes.

Crosnoe, R., Riegle-Crumb, C., Field, S., Frank, K., & Muller, C. (2008). Peer group contexts of girls' and boys' academic experiences. *Child Development, 79,* 139–155.

Crouter, A. C. (2006). Mothers and fathers at work. In A. Clarke-Stewart & J. Dunn (Eds.), *Families count*. New York: Cambridge University Press.

Crouter, A. C., & McHale, S. (2005). The long arm of the job revisited: Parenting in dual-earner families. In T. Luster & L. Okagaki (Eds.), *Parenting*. Mahwah, NJ: Erlbaum.

Crowley, K., Callahan, M. A., Tenenbaum, H. R., & Allen, E. (2001). Parents explain more to boys than to girls during shared scientific thinking. *Psychological Science, 12,* 258–261.

Cruickshank, D. R., Metcalf, K. M., & Jenkins, D. B. (2009). *The act of teaching* (5th ed.). Boston: Allyn & Bacon.

Cruz, B. C., & Duplass, J. A. (2007). *The elementary teacher's guide to the best Internet resources*. Upper Saddle River, NJ: Prentice Hall.

Csapo, B. (2007). Research into learning to learn through the assessment of quality and organization of learning outcomes. *Curriculum Journal, 18,* 195–210.

Csikszentmihalyi, M. (1996). *Creativity*. New York: HarperCollins.

Csikszentmihalyi, M. (2000). Creativity: An overview. In A. Kazdin (Ed.), *Encyclopedia of psychology*. Washington, DC, & New York: American Psychological Association and Oxford University Press.

Csikszentmihalyi, M., Rathunde, K., & Whalen, S. (1993). *Talented teenagers: The roots of success and failure*. Cambridge, UK: Cambridge University Press.

Culbertson, L. D., & Jalongo, M. R. (1999). "But what's wrong with letter grades?" Responding to parents' questions about alternative assessments. *Childhood Education, 75,* 130–135.

Cunningham, C. A., & Billingsley, M. (2006). *Curriculum web* (2nd ed.). Boston: Allyn & Bacon.

Cunningham, P. M. (2009). *Phonics they use* (5th ed.). Boston: Allyn & Bacon.

Cunningham, P. M., & Hall, D. P. (2009). *Making words first grade*. Boston: Allyn & Bacon.

Curran, K., DuCette, J., Eisenstein, J., & Hyman, I. A. (2001, August). *Statistical analysis of the cross-cultural data: The third year*. Paper presented at the meeting of the American Psychological Association, San Francisco.

Curtis, M. E., & Longo, A. M. (2001, November). Teaching vocabulary development to adolescents to improve comprehension. Retrieved February 8, 2004, from www.readingonline.org/articles/curtis/

Cushner, K. H. (2006). *Human diversity in action* (2nd ed.). Boston: McGraw-Hill.

Cushner, K. H., McClelland, A., & Safford, P. (2009). *Human diversity in education* (6th ed.). New York: McGraw-Hill.

D

D'Onofrio, B. M. (2008). Nature vs. nurture. In M. M. Haith & J. B. Benson (Eds.), *Encyclopedia of infancy and early childhood development*. Oxford, UK: Elsevier.

Dahl, R. E. (2004). Adolescent brain development: A period of vulnerabilities and opportunities. *Annals of the New York Academy of Sciences, 1021,* 1–22.

Dai, D. Y. (2008). Intelligence and intellectual development. In N. J. Salkind (Ed.), *Encyclopedia of educational psychology*. Thousand Oaks, CA: Sage.

Dakes, J., & Lipton, M. (2007). *Teaching to change the world* (3rd ed.). New York: McGraw-Hill.

Daley, D. (2006). Attention deficit hyperactivity disorder: A review of the essential facts. *Child: Care, Health, and Development, 32,* 193–204.

Dalsgaard, C., & Godsk, M. (2007). Transforming traditional lectures into problem-based blended learning: Challenges and experiences. *Open Learning, 22,* 29–42.

Damon, W. (2008). *The path to purpose: Helping our children find their calling in life*. New York: Free Press.

Daniels, H. (2007). Pedagogy. In H. Daniels, J. Wertsch, & M. Cole (Eds.), *The Cambridge companion to Vygotsky*. New York: Cambridge University Press.

Dansereau, D. F. (1988). Cooperative learning strategies. In C. E. Weinstein, E. T. Goetz, & P. A. Alexander (Eds.), *Learning and study strategies*. Orlando, FL: Academic Press.

Darling-Hammond, L. (2001, August). *What's at stake in high-stakes testing?* Paper presented at the meeting of the American Psychological Association, San Francisco.

Darling-Hammond, L. (2006). Assessing teacher education. *Journal of Teacher Education, 57,* 120–138.

Darling-Hammond, L. (2007). Race, inequality, and educational accountability: The irony of "No Child Left Behind." *Race, Ethnicity, and Education, 10,* 245–260.

Darling-Hammond, L., Banks, J., Zumswalt, K., Gomez, L., Sherin, M. G., Griesdorn, J., & Finn, L-E. (2005). Educational goals and purposes: Developing a curricular vision for education. In L. Darling-Hammond & J. Bransford (Eds.), *Preparing teachers for a changing world*. San Francisco: Jossey-Bass.

Darling-Hammond, L., & Baratz-Snowden, J. (Eds.). (2005). *A good teacher in every classroom: Preparing the highly qualified teachers our children deserve*. San Francisco: Jossey-Bass.

Darling-Hammond, L., & Bransford, J. (Eds.). (2005). *Preparing teachers for a changing world*. San Francisco: Jossey-Bass.

Davidson, D. (1996). The effects of decision characteristics on children's selective search of predecisional information. *Acta Psychologica, 92,* 263–281.

Davidson, G. C., & Neale, J. M. (2007). *Abnormal psychology* (10th ed.). New York: Wiley.

Davidson, J., & Davidson, B. (2004). *Genius denied: How to stop wasting our brightest young minds*. New York: Simon & Schuster.

Davidson, M., Lickona, T., & Khmelkov, V. (2008). A new paradigm for high school character education. In L. Nucci & D. Narvàez (Eds.), *Handbook of moral and character education*. Clifton, NJ: Psychology Press.

Davies, J., & Brember, I. (1999). Reading and mathematics attainments and self-esteem in years 2 and 6—an eight-year cross-sectional study. *Educational Studies, 25,* 145–157.

Davis, G. E., & McGowen, M. A. (2007). Formative feedback and the mindful teaching of mathematics. *Australian Senior Mathematics Journal, 21,* 19–29.

Davis, M. J. (2008). Identity development. In N. J. Salkind (Ed.), *Encyclopedia of educational psychology*. Thousand Oaks, CA: Sage.

Davis, O. S. P., Arden, R., & Plomin, R. (2008). g in middle childhood: Moderate and genetic and shared environmental influence using diverse measures of cognitive ability at 7, 9, and 10 years in a large population sample of twins. *Intelligence, 36,* 68–80.

Deary, I. J., Strand, S., Smith, P., & Fernandes, C. (2007). Intelligence and educational achievement. *Intelligence, 35,* 13–21.

deCharms, R. (1984). Motivation enhancement in educational settings. In R. Ames & C. Ames (Eds.), *Research on motivation in education* (Vol. 1). Orlando: Academic Press.

Deci, E. I., Koestner, R., & Ryan, R. M. (2001). Extrinsic rewards and intrinsic motivation in education: Reconsidered once again. *Review of Educational Research, 71*, 1–28.

Deci, E. L. (1975). *Intrinsic motivation.* New York: Plenum.

Deci, E. L., & Ryan, R. (1994). Promoting self-determined education. *Scandinavian Journal of Educational Research, 38*, 3–14.

De Corte, E., & Verschaffel, L. (2006). Mathematical thinking and learning. In W. Damon & R. Lerner (Eds.), *Handbook of child psychology* (6th ed.). New York: Wiley.

DeGarmo, D. S., & Martinez, C. R. (2006). A culturally informed model of academic well-being for Latino youth: The importance of discriminatory experiences and social support. *Family Relations, 55*, 267–278.

de Haan, M., & Martinos, M. (2008). Brain function. In M. M. Haith & J. B. Benson (Eds.), *Encyclopedia of infant and early childhood development.* Oxford, UK: Elsevier.

Delisle, J. R. (1987). *Gifted kids speak out.* Minneapolis: Free Spirit Publishing.

DeLoache, J. S., Simcock, G., & Macari, S. (2007). Places, trains, and automobiles—and tea sets. *Developmental Psychology, 43*, 1579–1586.

Demaree, H. A., Everhart, D. E., Youngstrom, E. A., & Harrison, D. W. (2005). Brain lateralization of emotional processing: Historical roots and a future incorporating dominance. *Behavioral and Cognitive Neuroscience Reviews, 4*, 3–20.

Demetriou, A., Christou, C., Spanoudis, G., & Platsidou, M. (2002). The development of mental processing: Efficiency, working memory, and thinking. *Monographs of the Society for Research in Child Development*, Serial No. 268, 67, 1.

Dempster, F. N. (1981). Memory span: Sources of individual and developmental differences. *Psychological Bulletin, 89*, 63–100.

Denzine, G. M. (2008). Social learning theory. In N. J. Salkind (Ed.), *Encyclopedia of educational psychology.* Thousand Oaks, CA: Sage.

Depka, E. (2007). *Designing assessment for mathematics.* Thousand Oaks, CA: Corwin.

Derman-Sparks, L., & the Anti-Bias Curriculum Task Force. (1989). *Anti-bias curriculum.* Washington, DC: National Association for the Education of Young Children.

DeRosier, M. E., & Marcus, S. R. (2005). Building friendships and combating bullying: Effectiveness of S.S.GRIN at one-year follow-up. *Journal of Clinical Child and Adolescent Psychology, 34*, 140–150.

Deshler, D. D., & Hock, M. F. (2007). Adolescent literacy: Where we are, where we need to go. In M. Pressley, A. K. Billman, K. H. Perry, K. E. Reffitt, & J. M. Reynolds (Eds.), *Shaping literacy achievement.* New York: Guilford.

Dewey, J. (1993). *How we think.* Lexington, MA: D.C. Health.

DeZolt, D. M., & Hull, S. H. (2001). Classroom and school climate. In J. Worell (Ed.), *Encyclopedia of women and gender.* San Diego: Academic Press.

de Zoysa, P., Newcombe, P. A., & Rajapakse, L. (2008). Consequences of parental corporal punishments on 12-year-old children in the Colombo district. *Ceylon Medical Journal, 53*, 7–9.

Diaz, C. (1997). Unpublished review of J. W. Santrock's *Educational psychology* (I). New York: McGraw-Hill).

Diaz, C. (2005). Unpublished review of J. W. Santrock's *Educational psychology* (3rd ed.). New York: McGraw-Hill.

Diaz-Rico, L. T. (2008a). *A course for teaching English learners.* Boston: Allyn & Bacon.

Diaz-Rico, L. T. (2008b). *Strategies for teaching English learners* (2nd ed.). Boston: Allyn & Bacon.

Dickinson, D. (1998). *How technology enhances Howard Gardner's eight intelligences.* Retrieved February 15, 2002, from www.america-tomorrow.com/ati/nhl80402.htm

Dingus, J. E. (2008). "I'm learning the trade": Mentoring networks of Black women teachers. *Urban Education, 43*, 361–377.

Dishion, T. J., Piehler, T. F., & Myers, M. W. (2008). Dynamics and ecology of adolescent peer influence. In M. J. Prinstein & K. A. Dodge (Eds.), *Understanding peer influence in children and adolescents.* New York: Guilford.

Dixon, S. V., Graber, J. A., & Brooks-Gunn, J. (2008). The roles of respect for parental authority and parenting practices in parent-child conflict among African American, Latino, and European American families. *Journal of Family Psychology, 22*, 1–10.

Dodge, K. A., Coie, J. D., & Lynam, D. R. (2006). Aggression and antisocial behavior in youth. In W. Damon & R. Lerner (Eds.), *Handbook of child psychology* (6th ed.). New York: Wiley.

Doe, C. G. (2004). A look at... Web-based assessment. *Multimedia Schools, 11 (2)*, 1–6.

Doherty, M. (2009). *Theory of mind.* Clifton, NJ: Psychology Press.

Donahue, J. W. (2008). Operant conditioning. In N. J. Salkind (Ed.), *Encyclopedia of educational psychology.* Thousand Oaks, CA: Sage.

Dowker, A. (2006). What can functional brain imaging studies tell us about typical and atypical cognitive development in children. *Journal of Physiology, Paris, 99*, 333–341.

Doyle, W. (1986). Classroom organization and management. In M. C. Wittrock (Ed.), *Handbook of research on teaching* (3rd ed.). New York: Macmillan.

Doyle, W. (2006). Ecological approaches to classroom management. In C. M. Evertson & C. S. Weinstein (Eds.), *Handbook of classroom management.* Mahwah, NJ: Erlbaum.

Drake, F. D., & Nelson, L. R. (2009). *Engagement in teaching history* (2nd ed.). Boston: Allyn & Bacon.

Drefs, M. A., & Saklofske, D. H. (2008). Intelligent quotient (IQ). In N. J. Salkind (Ed.), *Encyclopedia of educational psychology.* Thousand Oaks, CA: Sage.

Driscoll, A., & Nagel, N. G. (2008). *Early childhood education* (4th ed.). Boston: Allyn & Bacon.

Dubois, D. L., & Karcher, M. J. (Eds.). (2006). *Handbook of youth mentoring.* Thousand Oaks, CA: Sage.

Dubois, J., & others. (2008). Microstructural correlates of infant functional development: Example of the visual pathways. *Journal of Neuroscience, 28.* 1943–1948.

Dubow, E. F., Huesmann, L. R., & Greenwood, D. (2007). Media and youth socialization. InJ. E. Grusec & P. D. Hastings (Eds.), *Handbook of socialization.* New York: Guilford.

Dunkelberger, M. (2008). Speech disabilities. In N. J. Salkind (Ed.), *Encyclopedia of educational psychology.* Thousand Oaks, CA: Sage.

Dunlosky, J., & Metcalfe, J. (2009). *Metacognition.* Thousand Oaks, CA: Sage.

Dunning, D. (2008). Learning style. In N. J. Salkind (Ed.), *Encyclopedia of educational psychology.* Thousand Oaks, CA: Sage.

Durham, Q. (2006). *The realities of classroom testing and grading.* Lanham, MD: Rowman & Littlefield.

Durrant, J. E. (2008). Physical punishment, culture, and rights: Current issues for professionals. *Journal of Developmental and Behavioral Pediatrics, 29*, 55–66.

Durston, S., & Casey, B. J. (2006). What have we learned about cognitive development from neuroimaging. *Neuropsychologia, 44*, 2149–2157.

Durston, S., Davidson, M. C., Tottenham, N. T., Galvan, A., Spicer, J., Fossella, J. A., & Casey, B. J. (2006). A shift from diffuse to focal cortical activity with development. *Developmental Science, 9*, 1–8.

Dweck, C. S. (2006). *Mindset.* New York: Random House.

Dweck, C. S. (2007). Boosting achievement with messages that motivate. *Education Canada, 47*, 6–10.

Dweck, C. S., & Elliott, E. (1983). Achievement motivation. In P. Mussen (Ed.), *Handbook of child psychology* (4th ed., Vol. 4). New York: Wiley.

E

Eagle, J. W. (2008). Behavior modification. In N. J. Salkind (Ed.), *Encyclopedia of educational psychology.* Thousand Oaks, CA: Sage.

Eagle, J. W., & Oeth, J. (2008). Parent-teacher conferences. In N. J. Salkind (Ed.), *Encyclopedia of educational psychology.* Thousand Oaks, CA: Sage.

Eagly, A. H. (2001). Social role theory of sex differences and similarities. In J. Worell (Ed.), *Encyclopedia of women and gender.* San Diego: Academic Press.

Eagly, A. H. (2008, in press). Gender roles. In J. Levine & M. Hogg (Eds.), *Encyclopedia of group processes and intergroup relations.* Thousand Oaks, CA: Sage.

Eagly, A. H., & Crowley, M. (1986). Gender and helping behavior: A meta-analytic review of the social psychological literature. *Psychological Bulletin, 100*, 283–308.

Eagly, A. H., & Steffen, V. J. (1986). Gender and aggressive behavior: A meta-analytic review of the social psychological literature. *Psychological Bulletin, 100*, 309–330.

Easton, L. B. (2007). Walking our walk about standards. *Phi Delta Kappan, 88*, 391–394.

Eby, J. W., Herrell, A. L., & Jordan, M. L. (2009). *Teaching in elementary school: A reflective approach* (5th ed.). Boston: Allyn & Bacon.

Eccles, J. S. (1987). Gender roles and women's achievement-related decisions. *Psychology of Women Quarterly, 11*, 135–172.

Eccles, J. S. (1993). School and family effectson the ontogeny of children's interests, self-perceptions, and activity choice. In J. Jacobs (Ed.), *Nebraska symposium on motivation.* Lincoln: University of Nebraska Press.

Eccles, J. S. (2004). School, academic motivation, and stage-environment fit. In R. Lerner & L. Steinberg (Eds.), *Handbook of adolescent psychology* (2nd ed.). New York: Wiley.

Eccles, J. S. (2007). Families, schools, and developing achievement-related motivations and engagement. In J. E. Grusec & P. D. Hastings (Eds.), *Handbook of socialization.* New York: Guilford.

Eccles, J. S., & Wigfield, A. (2002). Motivational beliefs, values, and goals. *Annual Review of Psychology* (Vol. 53). Palo Alto, CA: Annual Reviews.

Eccles, J. S., Wigfield, A., & Schiefele, U. (1998). Motivation to succeed. In W. Damon (Ed.), *Handbook of child psychology* (5th ed., Vol. 3). New York: Wiley.

Eccles, J. S., Wong, C. A., & Peck, S. C. (2006). Ethnicity as a social context for the development of African-American adolescents. *Journal of School Psychology, 44*, 407–426.

Echevarria, J., Vogt, M., & Short, D. J. (2008). *Making content comprehensible for English learners* (3rd ed.). Boston: Allyn & Bacon.

Educational Cyber Playground. (2006). *Ringleader Alan Haskvitz.* Retrieved July 1, 2006, from http://www.edu-cyberpg.com/ringleaders/al.html

Educational Testing Service. (2002). *Differences in the gender gap.* Princeton: Author.

Educational Testing Service, Arter, J. A., & Cappius, J. (2008). *Creating and recognizing quality rubrics.* Upper Saddle River, NJ: Prentice Hall.

Edwards, R., & Hamilton, M. A. (2004). You need to understand my gender role: An empirical test of Tannen's model of gender and communication. *Sex Roles, 50,* 491–504.

Egbert, J. L. (2009). *Supporting learning with technology.* Boston: Allyn & Bacon.

Ehri, L., Nunes, S., Stahl, S., & Willows, D. (2001). Systematic phonics instruction helps students learn to read: Evidence from the National Reading Panel's meta-analysis. *Review of Educational Research, 71,* 393–447.

Eisenberg, N. (1986). *Altruistic emotion, cognition, and behavior.* Hillsdale, NJ: Erlbaum.

Eisenberg, N., & Morris, A. S. (2004). Moral cognitions and prosocial responding in adolescence. In R. Lerner & L. Steinberg (Eds.), *Handbook of adolescent psychology* (2nd ed.). New York: Wiley.

Eisenberg, N., Martin, C. L., & Fabes, R. A. (1996). Gender development and gender effects. In D. C. Berliner & R. C. Calfee (Eds.), *Handbook of educational psychology.* New York: Macmillan.

Eisenberg, N., Spinrad, T. L., & Smith, C. L. (2004). Emotion-related regulation: Its conceptualization, relations to social functioning, and socialization. In P. Philippot & R. S. Feldman (Eds.), *The regulation of emotion.* Mahwah, NJ: Erlbaum.

Eisenberger, R. (2009). Commitment, choice, and self-control. In D. Shanks (Ed.), *Psychology of learning.* Thousand Oaks, CA: Sage.

Eisenhower Foundation. (2008). *Quantum Opportunities program.* Retrieved July 29, 2008, from http://www.eisenhowerfoundation.org/qop.php

Eisner, E. W. (1999, May). The uses and limits of performance assessment. *Phi Delta Kappan, 80,* 658–661.

Elkind, D. (1976). *Child development and education: A Piagetian perspective.* New York: Oxford University Press.

Elkind, D. (1978). Understanding the young adolescent. *Adolescence, 13,* 127–134.

Elliott, C. H., & Chandler, T. (2008). Schemas. In N. J. Salkind (Ed.), *Encyclopedia of educational psychology.* Thousand Oaks, CA: Sage.

Ellis, S., Klahr, D., & Siegler, R. S. (1994, April). *The birth, life, and sometimes death of good ideas in collaborative problem-solving.* Paper presented at the meeting of the American Education Research Association, New Orleans.

Emmer, E. T., & Everston, C. (2009). *Classroom management for middle and secondary teachers* (8th ed.). Boston: Allyn & Bacon.

Emmer, E. T., Evertson, C. M., & Anderson, L. M. (1980). Effective classroom management at the beginning of the school year. *Elementary School Journal, 80,* 219–231.

Enfield, A., & Collins, D. (2008). The relationship of service-learning, social justice, multicultural competence, and civic engagement. *Journal of College Student Development, 49,* 95–109.

Engle, P. L., & Black, M. M. (2008). The effect of poverty on child development and educational outcomes. *Annals of the New York Academy of Sciences, 1136,* 243–256.

Engleberg, I. A., & Wynn, D. R. (2008). *Challenge of communicating.* Boston: Allyn & Bacon.

Engler, B. (2009). *Personality theories* (8th ed.). Belmont, CA: Wadsworth.

Entwisle, D. R., & Alexander, K. L. (1993). Entry into the school: The beginning school transition and educational stratification in the United States. *Annual Review of Sociology, 19,* 401–423.

Epstein, J. L. (1983). Longitudinal effects offamily-school-person interactions on student outcomes.

Research in Sociology and Education and Socialization, 4, 101–127.

Epstein, J. L. (1998, April). *Interactive homework: Effective strategies to connect home and school.* Paper presented at the meeting of the American Educational Research Association, San Diego.

Epstein, J. L. (2001). *School, family, and community partnerships.* Boulder, CO: Westview Press.

Epstein, J. L. (2005). Results of the Partnership School-CSR model for student achievement over three years. *Elementary School Journal, 106,* 151–170.

Epstein, J. L. (2007a). Family and community involvement. In K. Borman, S. Cahill, & B. Cotner (Eds.), *American high school: An encyclopedia.* Westport, CT: Greenwood

Epstein, J. L. (2007b). Homework. In K. Borman, S. Cahill, & B. Cotner (Eds.), *American high school: An encyclopedia.* Westport, CT: Greenwood

Epstein, J. L. (2009). *School, family, and community partnerships* (3rd ed.). Thousand Oaks, CA: Corwin.

Ericsson, K. A. (2006). The influence of experience and deliberate practice on the development of superior expert performance. In K. A. Ericsson, N. Charness, P. J. Feltovich, & R. R. Hoffman (Eds.), *The Cambridge handbook of expertise and expert performance.* New York: Cambridge University Press.

Ericsson, K. A., Krampe, R. T., & Tesch-Romer, C. (1993). The role of deliberate practice in the acquisition of expert performance. *Psychological Review, 100,* 363–406.

Ericsson, K. A., Krampe, R. T., & Tesch-Romer, C. (2009). Three aspects of cognitive development. In D. Shanks (Ed.), *Psychology of learning.* Thousand Oaks, CA: Sage.

Erikson, E. H. (1968). *Identity: Youth and crisis.* New York: W.W. Norton.

Evans, G. W. (2004). The environment of childhood poverty. *American Psychologist, 59,* 77–92.

Evans, G. W., & English, K. (2002). The environment of poverty: Multiple stressor exposure, psychophysiological stress, and socioemotional adjustment. *Child Development, 73,* 1238–1248.

Evans, G. W., & Kim, P. (2007). Childhood poverty and health: Cumulative risk exposure and stress dysregulation. *Psychological Science, 18,* 953–957.

Evertson, C. M., & Emmer, E. T. (2009). *Classroom management for elementary teachers* (8th ed.). Boston: Allyn & Bacon.

Evertson, C. M., & Harris, A. H. (1999). Support for managing learning-centered classrooms: The classroom organization and management program. In H. J. Freiberg (Ed.), *Beyond behaviorism: Changing the classroom management paradigm.* Boston: Allyn & Bacon.

Exploratorium. (2008). Retrieved January 16, 2008, from www.exploratorium.edu/educate/index.html

F

Fair, D., & Schlaggar, B. L. (2008). Brain development. In M. M. Haith & J. B. Benson (Eds.), *Encyclopedia of infant and early childhood development.* Oxford, UK: Elsevier.

Faraone, S. V. (2007). Stimulant therapy in the management of ADHD: Mixed amphetamine salts (extended release). *Expert Opinion on Pharmacotherapy, 8,* 2127–2134.

Farkas, G. (2001). *Poverty and children's vocabulary development.* Unpublished manuscript, Pennsylvania State University.

Feather, N. T. (1966). Effects of prior success and failure on expectations of success and subsequent

performance. *Journal of Personality and Social Psychology, 3,* 287–298.

Federal Interagency Forum on Child and Family Statistics. (2008). *America's children in brief: Key national indicators of well-being, 2008.* Washington, DC: Author.

Feinberg, M. E., & Kan, M. L. (2008). Establishing family foundations: Intervention effects on coparenting, parent/infant well-being, and parent-child relations. *Journal of Family Psychology, 22,* 253–263.

Feng, Y. (1996). Some thoughts about applying constructivist theories to guide instruction. *Computers in the Schools, 12,* 71–84.

Fenning, P., & Rose, J. (2007). Overrepresentation of African American students in exclusionary discipline: The role of school policy. *Urban Education, 42,* 536–559.

Fenzel, L. M., Blyth, D. A., & Simmons, R. G. (1991). School transitions, secondary. In R. M. Lerner, A. C. Petersen, & J. Brooks-Gunn (Eds.), *Encyclopedia of Adolescence* (Vol. 2). New York: Garland.

Fielding, L. G., Wilson, P. T., & Anderson, R. C. (1986). A new focus on free reading: The role of tradebooks in reading instruction. In T. Raphael (Ed.), *The contexts of school-based literacy.* New York: Random House.

Fiese, B. H., Eckert, T., & Spagnola, M. (2006). Family context in early childhood: A look at practices and beliefs that promote early learning. In B. Spodak & O. N. Sarancho (Eds.), *Handbook of research on the education of young children* (2nd ed.). Mahwah

Finn, B. (2008). Framing effects on metacognitive monitoring and control. *Memory and Cognition, 36,* 813–821.

Fischer, K. W., & Immordino-Yang, M. H. (2008, in press). The fundamental importance of the brain and learning for education. In *The Jossey-Bass reader on the brain and learning.* San Francisco: Jossey-Bass.

Fisher, D., Frey, N., & Berkin, A. (2009). *Good habits, great readers.* Boston: Allyn & Bacon.

Fitzgerald, M. (2007). Write right! Owner's manual project develops communication skills. *Tech Directions, 66,* 14–18.

Fitzpatrick, J. (1993). *Developing responsible behavior in schools.* South Burlington, VT: Fitzpatrick Associates.

Fivush, R. (2009). Sociocultural perspectives on autobiographical memory. In M. Courage & N. Cowan (Eds.), *The development of memory in infancy and childhood.* Clifton, NJ: Psychology Press.

Flake, C., Kuhs, T., Donnelly, A., & Ebert, C. (1995). Teacher as researcher: Reinventing the role of teacher. *Phi Delta Kappan, 76,* 405–407.

Flavell, J. H. (1999). Cognitive development. *Annual Review of Psychology* (Vol. 50). Palo Alto, CA: Annual Reviews.

Flavell, J. H. (2004). Theory-of-mind development: Retrospect and prospect. *Merrill-Palmer Quarterly. 50,* 274–290.

Flavell, J. H., Fredrichs, A., & Hoyt, J. (1970). Developmental changes in memorization processes. *Cognitive Psychology. 1,* 324–340.

Flavell, J. H., Green, F. L., & Flavell, E. R. (1995). Young children's knowledge about thinking. *Monographs of the Society for Research in Child Development.* 60 (1, Serial No. 243).

Flavell, J. H., Green, F. L., & Flavell, E. R. (1998). The mind has a mind of its own: Developing knowledge about mental uncontrollability. *Cognitive Development, 13,* 127–138.

Flavell, J. H., Miller, P. H., & Miller, S. (2002). *Cognitive development* (4th ed.). Upper Saddle River, NJ: Prentice Hall.

Florez, M. A. C. (1999). Improving adult English language learners' speaking skills. *ERIC Digest,* EDO–LE–99–01, 1–5.

Flower, L. S., & Hayes, J. R. (1981). Problem-solving and the cognitive processes in writing. In C. Frederiksen & J. F. Dominic (Eds.), *Writing: The nature, development, and teaching of written communication.* Mahwah, NJ: Erlbaum.

Flynn, J. R. (1999). Searching for justice: The discovery of IQ gains over time. *American Psychologist, 54,* 5–20.

Flynn, J. R. (2007a). The history of the American mind in the 20th century: A scenario to explain gains over time and a case for the irrelevance of *g.* In P. C. Kyllonen, R. D. Roberts, & L. Stankov (Eds.), *Extending intelligence.* Mahwah, NJ: Erlbaum.

Flynn, J. R. (2007b). *What is intelligence? Beyond the Flynn effect.* New York: Cambridge University Press.

Fogarty, R. (Ed.). (1993). *The multiage classroom.* Palatine, IL: IRI/Skylight.

Forcier, R. C., & Descy, D. E. (2008). *The computer as an educational tool: Productivity and problem solving.* (5th ed.). Upper Saddle River, NJ: Prentice Hall.

Fowles, M. E., & Odendahl, N. V. (2008). Essay tests. In N. J. Salkind (Ed.), *Encyclopedia of educational psychology.* Thousand Oaks. CA: Sage.

Frankenberg, E. & Orfield, G. (Eds.). (2007). *Lessons in integration.* Charlottesville, VA: University of Virginia Press.

Frederkse, M., Lu, A., Aylward, E., Barta, P., Sharma, T., & Perlsons, G. (2000). Sex differences in inferior lobule volume in schizophrenia. *American Journal of Psychiatry, 157,* 422–427.

Fredricks, J. A. (2008). Extracurricular activities. In N. J. Salkind (Ed.), *Encyclopedia of educational psychology.* Thousand Oaks, CA: Sage.

Fredricks, J. A., & Eccles, J. S. (2006). Is extracurricular participation associated with beneficial outcomes? Concurrent and longitudinal relations. *Developmental Psychology, 42,* 698–713.

Frey, B. (2005). Standard deviation. In S. W. Lee (Ed.), *Encyclopedia of school psychology.* Thousand Oaks, CA: Sage.

Friedman, N. P., Haberstick, B. C., Willcutt, E. G., Miyake, A., Young, S. E., Corley, R. P., & Hewitt, J. K. (2007). Greater attention problems during childhood predict poorer executive functioning in late adolescence. *Psychological Science, 18,* 893–900.

Friend, M. (2008). *Special education* (2nd ed.). Boston: Allyn & Bacon.

Fritschmann, N. S., & Solari, E. J. (2008). Learning disabilities. In N. J. Salkind (Ed.), *Encyclopedia of educational psychology.* Thousand Oaks, CA: Sage.

Frydenberg, E. (2008). *Adolescent coping.* Clifton, NJ: Psychology Press.

Frye, D. (1999). Development of intention: The relation of executive function to theory of mind. In P. D. Zelazo, J. W. Astington, & D. R. Olson (Eds.), *Developing theories of intention: Social understanding and self-control.* Mahwah, NJ: Erlbaum.

Frye, D. (2004). Unpublished review of J. W. Santrock's *Child Development,* 11th ed. (New York: McGraw-Hill).

Fuchs, D., Fuchs, L. S., & Burish, P. (2000). Peer-assisted strategies: An empirically-supported practice to promote reading. *Learning Disabilities Research and Practice, 9,* 203–212.

Fuchs, D., Fuchs, L. S., Mathes, P. G., & Simmons, D. C. (1997). Peer-assisted learning strategies: Making classrooms more responsive to diversity. *American Educational Research Journal, 34,* 174–206.

Fuligni, A. J., & Fuligni, A. S. (2007). Immigrant families and the educational achievement of their children. In J. E. Lansford, K. Deater-Deckhard, & M. H. Bornstein (Eds.), *Immigrant families in contemporary society.* New York: Guilford.

Fund, Z. (2007). The effects of scaffolded computerized science problem-solving on achievement outcomes: A comparative study of support programs. *Journal of Computer Assisted Learning, 23,* 410–424.

Furth, H. G., & Wachs, H. (1975). *Thinking goes to school.* New York: Oxford University Press.

Fusaro, M., & Nelson, C. A. (2009, in press). Developmental cognitive neuroscience and education practice. In O. A. Barbarin, P. Frome, & D. Marie-Winn (Eds.), *The handbook of developmental science and early schooling: Translating basic research into practice.* New York: Guilford.

Fuson, K. C., Kalchman, M., & Bransford, J. D. (2005). Mathematical understanding: An introduction. In M. S. Donovan & J. D. Bransford (Eds.), *How students learn.* Washington, DC: National Academies Press.

G

Gabriele, A. J., & Montecinos, C. (2001). Collaborating with a skilled peer: The influence of achievement goals and perceptions of partners' competence on the participation and learning of low-achieving students. *Journal of Experimental Education, 69,* 152–178.

Galambos, N. L., Krahn, H. J., & Barker, E. T. (2006). Depression, self-esteem, and anger in emerging adulthood: Seven-year trajectories. *Developmental Psychology, 42,* 350–365.

Gall, M. D., Gall, J. P., & Brog, W. R. (2007). *Educational research* (8th ed.). Boston: Allyn & Bacon.

Gallagher, J. J. (2007). *Teaching science for understanding.* Upper Saddle River, NJ: Prentice Hall.

Gallavan, N. P. (2009). *Developing performance-based assessments: Middle and secondary.* Thousand Oaks, CA: Corwin Press.

Gallup Organization. (2004). *Gallup Poll: The public's attitudes toward schools.* Princeton, NJ: Author.

Galotti, K. M. (2008). *Cognitive psychology in and out of the laboratory* (4th ed.). Belmont, CA: Wadsworth.

Gamaron, A. (1990, April). *The consequences of track-related instructional differences for student achievement.* Paper presented at the meeting of American Educational Research Association, Boston.

Gamble, T. K., & Gamble, M. (2008). *Communication works* (9th ed.). New York: McGraw-Hill.

Gambrell, L. B., Malloy, J. A., & Anders-Mazzoni, S. (2007). Evidence-based best practices for comprehensive literacy instruction. In L. B. Gambrell, L. M. Morrow, & M. Presley (Eds.), *Best practices in literacy instruction.* New York: Guilford.

Gambrell, L. B., Morrow, L. M., & Pressley, M. (Eds.). (2007). *Best practices in literacy instruction.* New York: Guilford.

Gandara, P. (2002). *Peer group influence and academic aspirations across cultural/ethnic groups of high school students.* Santa Cruz, University of California, Center for Research on Education, Diversity and Excellence.

GarageBand. (2008). Retrieved January 16, 2008, from www.apple.com/ilife/garageband/

Garcia, G. E., & Willis, A. I. (2001). Frameworks for understanding multicultural literacies. In P. R. Schmidt & P. B. Mosenthal (Eds.), *Reconceptualizing literacy in the new age of multiculturalism and pluralism.* Greenwich, CT: IAP.

Garcia, T. (2001, May 1). Testing and other measures of life. *San Francisco Chronicle,* pp. D3, 4.

Gardner, H. (1983). *Frames of mind.* New York: Basic Books.

Gardner, H. (1993). *Multiple intelligences.* New York: Basic Books.

Gardner, H. (1998). Multiple intelligences: Myths and messages. In A. Woolfolk (Ed.), *Readings in educational psychology* (2nd ed.). Boston: Allyn & Bacon.

Gardner, H. (2002). The pursuit of excellence through education. In M. Ferrari (Ed.), *Learning from extraordinary minds.* Mahwah, NJ: Erlbaum.

Gargiulo, R. M. (2009). *Special education in contemporary society.* Thousand Oaks, CA: Sage.

Garmon, A., Nystrand, M., Berends, M., & LePore, P. C. (1995). An organizational analysis of the effects of ability grouping. *American Educational Research Journal, 32,* 687–715.

Garner, H. (1993). *Multiple intelligences.* New York: Basic Books.

Gauvain, M. (2008). Vygotsky's sociocultural theory. In M. M. Haith & J. B. Benson (Eds.), *Encyclopedia of infant and early childhood development.* Oxford, UK: Elsevier.

Gauvain, M., & Perez, S. M. (2007). The socialization of cognition. In J. E. Grusec & P. D. Hastings (Eds.), *Handbook of socialization.* New York: Guilford.

Gay, G. (1997). Educational equality for students of color. In J. A. Banks & C. M. Banks (Eds.), *Multicultural Education* (3rd ed.). Boston: Allyn & Bacon.

Gay, G. (2006). Connections between classroom management and culturally responsive teaching. In C. M. Evertson & C. S. Weinstein (Eds.), *Handbook of classroom management.* Mahwah, NJ: Erlbaum.

Gay, L. R., Mills, G., & Airasian, P. W. (2009). *Educational research* (9th ed.). Upper Saddle River, NJ: Prentice Hall.

Gelman, R. (1969). Conservation acquisition: A problem of learning to attend to relevant attributes. *Journal of Experimental Child Psychology, 7,* 67–87.

Gelman, S. A., & Opfer, J. E. (2004). Development of the animate-inanimate distinction. In U. Goswami (Ed.), *Blackwell handbook of childhood cognitive development.* Malden, MA: Blackwell.

GenYes. (2008). Retrieved on February 10, 2008, from *http://genyes.com/*

Gerrard, M., Gibbons, F. X., Houlihan, A. E., Stock, M. L., & Pomery, E. A. (2008). A dual-process approach to health risk decision-making: The prototype-willingness model. *Developmental Review, 28,* 29–61.

Gerstorf, D., Herlitz, A., & Smith, J. (2006). Stability of sex differences in cognition in advanced old age: The role of education and attrition. *Journals of Gerontology B: Psychological Sciences, 61,* 245–249.

Ghee, A. C., & Johnson, C. S. (2008). Emotional intelligence: A moderator of perceived alcohol peer norms and alcohol use. *Journal of Drug Education, 38,* 71–83.

Gibson, V., & Hasbrouck, J. (2008). *Differentiated instruction.* New York: McGraw-Hill.

Giedd, J. N. (2008). The teen brain: Insights from neuroimaging. *Journal of Adolescent Health, 42,* 335–343.

Giedd, J. N., & others. (2006). Puberty-related influences on brain development. *Molecular and Cellular Endocrinology, 25,* 154–162.

Giedd, J. N., Lenroott, R. K., Shaw, P., Lalonde, F., Celano, M., White, S., Tossell, J., Addington, A., & Gogtay, N. (2008). Trajectories of anatomic brain development as a phenotype. *Novartis Foundation Symposium, 289,* 101–118, 193–195.

Gil-Olarte Marquez, P., Palomera, M. R., & Brackett, M. A. (2007). Relating emotional intelligence to social competence and academic achievement in high school students. *Psicothema, 18* (Suppl.), S118–S123.

Gill, D. L. (2001). Sports and athletics. In J. Worell (Ed.), *Encyclopedia of women and gender.* San Diego: Academic Press.

Gill, J. (1997, July). Personal conversation. Richardson: University of Texas at Dallas.

Gillies, R. M. (2007). *Cooperative learning: Integrating theory and practice.* Thousand Oaks, CA: Sage.

Gilligan, C. (1982). *In a different voice.* Cambridge, MA: Harvard University Press.

Gilligan, C. (1996). The centrality of relationships in psychological development: A puzzle, some evidence, and a theory. In G. G. Noam & K. W. Fischer (Eds.), *Development and vulnerability in close relationships.* Hillsdale, NJ: Erlbaum.

Gilligan, C. (1998). *Minding women: Reshaping the education realm.* Cambridge, MA: Harvard University Press.

Ginorio, A., & Huston, M. (2000). *Si Puede! Yes, we can: Latinas in school.* Washington, DC: American Association of University Women.

Ginsburg-Block, M. (2005). Peer tutoring. In S. W. Lee (Ed.), *Encyclopedia of school psychology.* Thousand Oaks, CA: Sage.

Given, L. M. (2008). Qualitative research methods. In N. J. Salkind (Ed.), *Encyclopedia of educational psychology.* Thousand Oaks, CA: Sage.

Glaser, C., & Brunstein, G. C. (2007). Improving fourth-grade students' composition skills: Effects of strategy instruction and self-regulation procedures. *Journal of Educational Psychology, 99* (2), 297–310.

Glasgow, N. A., & Hicks, C. D. (2009). *What successful teachers do.* Thousand Oaks, CA: Sage.

Glasser, W. (1969). *Schools without failure.* New York: Harper & Row.

Glassman, M. (2001). Dewey and Vygotsky: Society, experience, and inquiry in educational practice. *Educational Researcher, 30* (4), 3–14.

Glazer, S. M. (2007). A classroom portfolio system. In J. R. Paratore & R. L. McCormack (Eds.), *Classroom literacy assessment.* New York: Guilford.

Gleibermann, E. (2007). Nothing will leave No Child Behind. *Education Digest, 72,* 19–25.

Glesne, C. (2007). *Becoming qualitative researchers* (3rd ed.). Boston: Allyn & Bacon.

Gluck, M. A. & Bower, G. H. (2009). Automatic and effortful processes in memory. In D. Shanks (Ed.), *Psychology of learning.* Thousand Oaks, CA: Sage.

Glynn, S. (2007). The teaching-with-analogies model: Build conceptual bridges with mental models. *Science and Children, 44,* 52–55.

Goffin, S. G., & Wilson, C. S. (2001). *Curriculum models and early childhood education.* Upper Saddle River, NJ: Prentice Hall.

Gold, J., & Lanzoni, M. (Eds.). (1993). [Video] *Graduation by portfolio—Central Park East Secondary School.* New York: Post Production, 29th St. Video, Inc.

Goldberg, M. (2005, January). Test mess 2: Are we doing better a year later? *Phi Delta Kappan, 86,* 389–395.

Goldfield, B. A., & Snow, C. A. (2009). Individual differences in language development. In J. Berko Gleason & N. Ratner (Eds.), *The development of language* (7th ed.). Boston: Allyn & Bacon.

Goldman-Rakic, P. (1996). *Bridging the gap.* Presentation at the workshop sponsored by the Education Commission of the States and the Charles A. Dana Foundation, Denver.

Goleman, D. (1995). *Emotional intelligence.* New York: Basic Books.

Goleman, D., Kaufman, P., & Ray, M. (1993). *The creative spirit.* New York: Plume.

Gollnick, D. M., & Chinn, P. C. (2009). *Multicultural education in a pluralistic society* (8th ed.). Boston: Allyn & Bacon.

Gonsalves, L., & Leonard, J. (2007). *New hope for urban high schools.* Oxford, UK: Praeger.

Gonzales, N. A., Dumka, L. E., Muaricio, A. M., & German, M. (2007). Building bridges: Strategies to promote academic and psychological resilience for adolescents of Mexican origin. In J. E. Lansford, K. Deater Deckhard, & M. H. Bornstein (Eds.), *Immigrant families in contemporary society.* New York: Guilford.

González, J. M. (Ed.). (2009). *Encyclopedia of bilingual education.* Thousand Oaks, CA: Sage.

González, N., & Moll, L. C., & Amanti, C. (Eds.). (2005). *Funds of knowledge: Theorizing practices in households, communities, and classrooms.* Mahwah, NJ: Erlbaum.

Good, R. H., & Kaminski, R. A. (2003). *Dynamic indicators of basic early literacy skills* (6th ed.). Longmont, CO: Sopris West Educational Services.

Goodlad, S., & Hirst, B. (1989). *Peer tutoring: A guide to learning by teaching.* New York: Nichols.

Goodman, N. D., Tenenbaum, J. B., Feldman, J., & Griffiths, T. L. (2008). A rational analysis for rule-based concept learning. *Cognitive Science, 32,* 108–154.

Goodrich, H. (1997). Understanding rubrics. *Educational Leadership, 54,* 14–17.

Goos, L. M., Ezzatian, P., & Schachar, R. (2007). Parent-of-origin effects in attention-deficit hyperactivity disorder. *Psychiatry Research, 149,* 1–9.

Gordon, T. (1970). *Parent effectiveness training.* New York: McGraw-Hill.

Gort, M. (2008). Bilingualism. In N. J. Salkind (Ed.), *Encyclopedia of educational psychology.* Thousand Oaks, CA: Sage.

Gortmaker, V. J., Daly, E. J., McCurdy, M., Persampieri, M. J., & Hergenrader, M. (2007). Improving reading outcomes for children with learning disabilities: Using brief experimental analysis to develop parent-tutoring interventions. *Journal of Applied Behavior Analysis, 40,* 203–221.

Gottlieb, G. (2007). Probabilistic epigenesis. *Developmental Science, 10,* 1–11.

Gracia, E., & Herrero, J. (2008). Is it considered violence? The acceptability of physical punishment of children in Europe. *Journal of Marriage and the Family, 70,* 210–217.

Graham, S. (1986, August). *Can attribution theory tell us something about motivation in Blacks?* Paper presented at the meeting of the American Psychological Association, Washington, DC.

Graham, S. (1990). Motivation in African Americans. In G. L. Berry & J. K. Asamen (Eds.), *Black students.* Newbury Park, CA: Sage.

Graham, S. (2005, February 16). Commentary in *USA Today,* p. 2D.

Graham, S. (2008, in press). Teaching writing. P. Hogan (Ed.), *Cambridge encyclopedia of language sciences.* Cambridge, UK: Cambridge University Press.

Graham, S., & Harris, K. R. (2008, in press). Evidence-based writing practices: Drawing recommendations from multiple sources. *British Journal of Educational Psychology* (monograph series).

Graham, S., & Olinghouse, N. (2009, in press). Learning and teaching writing. In E. Anderman & L. Anderman (Eds.), *Psychology of classroom learning.* Farmington Hills, MI: Thomas Gale.

Graham, S., & Perin, D. (2007). A meta-analysis of writing instruction for adolescent students. *Journal of Educational Psychology, 99,* 445–476.

Graham, S., & Weiner, B. (1996). Theories and principles of motivation. In D. C. Berliner & R. C. Calfee (Eds.), *Handbook of educational psychology.* New York: Macmillan.

Grant, K. B., & Ray, J. A. (Eds.). (2009). *Home, school, and community collaboration.* Thousand Oaks, CA: Sage.

Gratz, R. R., & Bouton, P.J. (1996). Erikson and early childhood educators. *Young Children, 51,* 74–78.

Graves, D. A., & Graves, S. B. (2008). Multicultural issues in the lives of developing children in the 21st century. In K. Asamen, M. L. Ellis, & G. L. Berry (Eds.), *The SAGE handbook of child development, multiculturism, and media.* Thousand Oaks, CA: Sage.

Gray, J. (1992). *Men are from Mars, women are from Venus.* New York: HarperCollins.

Gray, T., & Madson, L. (2007). Ten easy ways to engage your students. *College Teaching, 55,* 83–87.

Gredler, M. E. (2008). Vygotsky's cultural-historical theory of development. In N. J. Salkind (Ed.), *Encyclopedia of educational psychology.* Thousand Oaks, CA: Sage.

Gredler, M. E. (2009). *Learning and instruction* (6th ed.). Upper Saddle River, NJ: Prentice Hall.

Gredler, M. E., & Shields, C. C. (2007). *Vygotsky's legacy.* New York: Guilford.

Green, V. A. (2008). Bullying. In N. J. Salkind (Ed.), *Encyclopedia of educational psychology.* Thousand Oaks, CA: Sage.

Greenfield, P. P. M., Suzuki, L. K., & Rothstein-Fisch, C. (2006). Cultural pathways through human development. In W. Damon & R. Lerner (Eds.), *Handbook of child psychology* (6th ed.). New York: Wiley.

Greeno, J. G. (1993). For research to reform education and cognitive science. In L. A. Penner, G. M. Batche, H. M. Knoff, & D. L. Nelson (Eds.), *The challenge in mathematics and science education: Psychology's response.* Washington, DC: American Psychological Association.

Greeno, J. S. (2006). Learning in activity. In R. K. Sawyer (Ed.), *The Cambridge handbook of learning sciences.* New York: Oxford University Press.

Greenough, W. T. (1997, April 21). Commentary in article, "Politics of biology." *U.S. News & World Report,* p. 79.

Greenough, W. T. (2000). Brain development. In A. Kazdin (Ed.), *Encyclopedia of psychology.* Washington, DC, & New York: American Psychological Association and Oxford University Press.

Gregory, H. (2008). *Public speaking for college and career* (8th ed.). New York: McGraw-Hill.

Gregory, R. J. (2007). *Psychological testing* (5th ed.). Boston: Allyn & Bacon.

Greydanus, D. E., Pratt, H. D., & Patel, D. R. (2007). Attention deficit hyperactivity disorder across the lifespan: The child, adolescent, and adult. *Disease-A-Month, 53,* 70–131.

Grigg, W. S., Lauko, M. A., and Brockway, D. M. (2006). *The nation's report card: Science 2005* (NCES 2006–466). U.S. Department of Education, National Center for Education Statistics. Washington, DC: U.S. Government Printing Office.

Grigorenko, E. L., Jarvin, L., Tan, M., & Sternberg, R. J. (2008). Something new in the garden: Assessing creativity in academic domains. *Psychology Science Quarterly.*

Grindstaff, K., & Richmond, G. (2008). Learners' perceptions of the roles of peers in a research experience: Implications for the apprenticeship process, scientific inquiry, and collaborative work. *Journal of Research in Science Teaching, 45,* 251–272.

Grolnick, W. S., Gurland, S. T., Jacob, K. F., & Decourcey, W. (2002). The development of self-determination in middle childhood and adolescence. In A. Wigfield & J. S. Eccles (Eds.), *Development of achievement motivation.* San Diego: Academic Press.

Gronlund, N. E. (2006). *Assessment of student achievement* (8th ed.). Boston: Allyn & Bacon.

Gronlund, N. E., & Waugh, C. K. (2009). *Assessment of student achievement* (9th ed.). Upper Saddle River, NJ: Prentice Hall.

Grossman, P., Schoenfeld, A., & Lee, C. (2005). Teaching subject matter. In L. Darling-Hammond & J. Bransford (Eds.), *Preparing teachers for a changing world.* New York: Jossey-Bass.

Guastello, D. D., & Guastello, S. J. (2003). Androgyny, gender role behavior, and emotional intelligence among college students and their parents. *Sex Roles, 49,* 663–673.

Guilford, J. P. (1967). *The structure of intellect.* New York: McGraw-Hill.

Guillaume, A. M. (2008). *K–12 classroom teaching* (3rd ed.). Upper Saddle River, NJ: Prentice Hall.

Guillem, F., Mograss, M. (2005). Gender differences in memory processing: Evidence from event-related potentials to faces. *Brain and Cognition, 57,* 84–92.

Gulbahar, Y. (2007). Technology planning: A roadmap to successful technology integration in schools. *Computers & Education, 49,* 943–056.

Gunning, T. G. (2000). *Creating literacy instruction for all children* (3rd ed.). Boston: Allyn & Bacon.

Gunning, T. G. (2008). *Creating literacy instruction for all students in grades 4 to 8* (2nd ed.). Boston: Allyn & Bacon.

Gupta, A., Thornton, J. W., & Huston, A. C. (2008). Working families should not be poor—the New Hope project. In D. R. Crane & T. B. Heaton (Eds.), *Handbook of families and poverty.* Thousand Oaks, CA: Sage.

Gur, R. C., Mozley, L. H., Mozley, P. D., Resnick, S. M., Karp, J. S., Alavi, A., Arnold, S. E., & Gur, R. E. (1995). Sex differences in regional cerebral glucose metabolism during a resting state. *Science, 267,* 528–531.

Gurwitch, R. H., Silovksy, J. F., Schultz, S., Kees, M., & Burlingame, S. (2001). *Reactions and guidelines for children following trauma/disaster.* Norman, OK: Department of Pediatrics, University of Oklahoma Health Science Center.

Guskey, T. R. (2001). Fixing grading policies that undermine standards. *The Education Digest, 66* (7), 16–21.

Gustafsson, J-E. (2007). Schooling and intelligence: Effects of track of study on level and profile of cognitive abilities. In P. C. Kyllonen, R. D. Roberts, & L. Stankov (Eds.), *Extending intelligence.* Mahwah, NJ: Erlbaum.

Guthrie, J. T., Wigfield, A., Barbosa, P., Perencevich, K. C., Taboada, A., Davis, M. H., Scafiddi, N., & Tonks, S. (2004). Increasing reading comprehension and engagement through Concept Oriented Reading Instruction. *Journal of Educational Psychology, 96,*

H

Hack, T. (2008). PRAXIS. In N. J. Salkind (Ed.), *Encyclopedia of educational psychology.* Thousand Oaks, CA: Sage.

Hacker, D., Dunlosky, J., & Graesser, A. (Eds.). (2009). *Handbook of metacognition in education.* Clifton, NJ: Psychology Press.

Hadwin, J., & Perner, J. (1991). Pleased and surprised: Children's cognitive theory of emotion. *British Journal of Developmental Psychology, 9,* 215–234.

Hagen, J. W., & Lamb-Parker, F. G. (2008). Head Start. In M. M. Haith & J. B. Benson (Eds.), *Encyclopedia of infant and early childhood development.* Oxford, UK: Elsevier.

Hakuta, K. (2000). Bilingualism, In A. Kazdin (Ed.). *Encyclopedia of psychology.* Washington, DC, and New York: American Psychological Association and Oxford University Press.

Hakuta, K. (2001, April 5). *Key policy milestones and directions in the education of English language learners.* Paper prepared for the Rockefeller Foundation Symposium, Leveraging change: An emerging framework for educational equity, Washington, DC.

Hakuta, K. (2005, April). *Bilingualism at the intersection of research and public policy.* Paper presented at the meeting of the Society for Research in Child Development, Atlanta.

Hakuta, K., Butler, Y. G., & Witt, D. (2000). *How long does it take English learners to attain proficiency?* Berkeley, CA: The University of California Linguistic Minority Research Institute Policy Report 2000–1.

Haladyna, T. M. (2002). *Essentials of standardized achievement testing: Validity and accountability.* Boston: Allyn & Bacon.

Hale, S. (1990). A global developmental trend in cognitive processing speed. *Child Development, 61,* 653–663.

Hale-Benson, J. E. (1982). *Black children: Their roots, culture, and learning styles.* Baltimore: The Johns Hopkins University Press.

Halford, G. S. (2008). Cognitive developmental theories. In M. M. Haith & J. B. Benson (Eds.), *Encyclopedia of infant and early childhood development.* Oxford, UK: Elsevier.

Hall, D. P., & Cunningham, P. M. (2009). *Making words kindergarten.* Boston: Allyn & Bacon.

Hall, G. E., Quinn, L. F., & Gollnick, D. M. (2008). *Joy of teaching.* Boston: Allyn & Bacon.

Hall, L. J. (2009). *Autism spectrum disorders: From therapy to practice.* Boston: Allyn & Bacon.

Hallahan, D. P., & Kauffman, J. M. (2006). *Exceptional learners* (10th ed.). Boston, Allyn & Bacon.

Hallahan, D. P., Kauffman, J. M., & Pullen, P. C. (2009). *Exceptional learners* (11th ed.). Boston: Allyn & Bacon.

Hallinan, M. (2003). Ability grouping and student learning. In D. Ravitch (Ed.), *Brookings' papers on educational policy, 2003.* Washington, DC: Brookings Institution.

Halonen, J. (2008). Express yourself. In J. W. Santrock & J. Halonen, *Your guide to college success* (5th ed.). Belmont, CA: Wadsworth.

Halpern, D. F. (2006). Girls and academic success: Changing patterns of academic achievement. In J. Worell & C. D. Goodheart (Eds.), *Handbook of girls and women's psychological health.* New York: Oxford University Press.

Halpern, D. F., Benbow, C. P., Geary, D. C., Gur, R. C., & Hyde, J. S. (2007). The science of sex differences in science and mathematics. *Psychological Science in the Public Interest, 8,* 1–51.

Hambleton, R. K. (1996). Advances in assessment models, methods, and practices. In D. C. Berliner & R. C. Calfee (Eds.), *Handbook of educational psychology.* New York: Macmillan.

Hamilton, S. F., & Hamilton, M. A. (2004). Contexts for mentoring: Adolescent-adult relationships in workplaces and communities. In R. Lerner & L. Steinberg (Eds.), *Handbook of adolescent psychology* (2nd ed.). New York: Wiley.

Hammerman, E. (2009). *Formative assessment strategies for enhanced learning in science, K–8.* Thousand Oaks, CA: Corwin.

Hammerness, K., Darling-Hammond, L., Grossman, P., Rust, F., & Shulman, L. (2005). How teachers learn and develop. In L. Darling-Hammond & J. Bransford (Eds.), *Preparing teachers for a changing world.* San Francisco: Jossey-Bass.

Hanna, W. (2007). The new Bloom's taxonomy: Implications for music education. *Arts Education Policy Review, 108,* 7–16.

Hannish, L. D., & Guerra, N. G. (2004). Aggressive victims, passive victims, and bullies: Development continuity or developmental change? *Merrill-Palmer Quarterly, 50,* 17–38.

Harada, V. H., Kirio, C., & Yamamoto, S. (2008). Project-based learning: Rigor and relevance in high schools. *Library Media Connection, 26* (No. 6), 4–16, 18, 20.

Hargis, C. H. (2006). *Teaching low achieving and disadvantaged students* (3rd ed.). Springfield, IL: Charles C Thomas.

Haring, M., Hewitt, P. L., & Flett, G. L. (2003). Perfectionism and quality of intimate relationships. *Journal of Marriage and the Family, 65,* 143–158.

Harris, K. R., & Graham, S. (2008, in press). Self-regulated strategy development in writing: Premises, evolution, and the future. *British Journal of Educational Psychology* (monograph series).

Harris, K. R., Graham, S., Brindle, M., & Sandmel, K. (2009, in press). Metacognition and children's writing. In D. Hacker, J. Dunlosky, & A. Graesser (Eds.), *Handbook of metacognition in education.* Clifton, NJ: Psychology Press.

Harris, K. R., Graham, S., & Mason, L. (2008). *Powerful writing strategies for all students.* Baltimore, MD: Brookes Publishing.

Harris, K. R., Graham, S., Mason, L., & Friedlander, B. (2008). *Powerful writing strategies for all students.* Baltimore, MD: Brookes.

Harris, P. L. (2006). Social cognition. In W. Damon & R. Lerner (Eds.), *Handbook of child psychology* (6th ed.). New York: Wiley.

Harris, R. J., Schoen, L. M., & Elensley, D. L., (1992). A cross-cultural study of story memory. *Journal of Cross-Cultural Psychology, 23,* 133–147.

Harris, Y. R., & Graham, J. A. (2007). *The African American child.* New York: Springer.

Hart, B., & Risley, T. R. (1995). *Meaningful differences in the everyday experiences of young Americans.* Baltimore: Paul H. Brooks.

Hart, C. H., Charlesworth, R., Durland, M. A., Burts, D. C., DeWolf, M., & Fleege, P.O. (1996). *Developmentally appropriate practice in preschool classrooms.* Unpublished manuscript, Brigham Young University, Provo, Utah.

Hart, C. H., Yang, C., Charlesworth, R., & Burts, D. C. (2003, April). *Early childhood teachers' curriculum beliefs, classroom practices, and children's outcomes: What are the connections?* Paper presented at the biennial meeting of the Society for Research in Child Development, Tampa, FL.

Hart, D., Atkins, R., & Donnelly, T. M. (2006). Community service and moral development. In M. Killen & J. Smetana (Eds.), *Handbook of moral development.* Mahwah, NJ: Erlbaum.

Hart, D., Matsuba, M. K. & Atkins, R. (2008). The moral and civic effects of learning to serve. In L. Nucci & D. Narvàez (Eds.), *Handbook of moral and character education.* Clifton, NJ: Psychology Press.

Harter, S. (1981). A new self-report scale of intrinsic versus extrinsic orientation in the classroom: Motivational and informational components. *Developmental Psychology, 17,* 300–312.

Harter, S. (1990). Self and identity development. In S. S. Feldman & G. R. Elliott (Eds.), *At the threshold. The developing adolescent.* Cambridge, MA: Harvard University Press.

Harter, S. (1996). Teacher and classmate influences on scholastic motivation, self-esteem, and level of voice in adolescents. In J. Juvonen & K. R. Wentzel (Eds.), *Social motivation.* New York: Cambridge University Press.

Harter, S. (1999). *The construction of the self*. New York: Guilford.

Harter, S. (2006). The self. In W. Damon & R. Lerner (Eds.), *Handbook of child psychology* (6th ed.). New York: Wiley.

Hartshorne, H., & May, M. S. (1928–1930). *Moral studies in the nature of character: studies in deceit* (Vol. 1); *Studies in self-control* (Vol. 2); *Studies in the organization of character* (Vol. 3). New York: Macmillan.

Hartup, W. W. (1983). The peer system. In P. H. Mussen (Ed.), *Handbook of child psychology* (4th ed., Vol. 4). New York: Wiley.

Hasirci, D., & Demirkan, H. (2003). Creativity in learning environments: The case of two sixth grade art rooms. *Journal of Creative Behavior, 37*, 17–41.

Hastings, P. D., Utendale, W. T., & Sullivan, C. (2007). The socialization of prosocial development. In J. E. Grusec & P. D. Hastings (eds.), *Handbook of socialization*. New York: Guilford.

Hatano, G., & Oura, Y. (2003). Commentary: Reconceptualizing school learning using insight from expertise research. *Educational Researcher, 32*, 26–29.

Hayashino, D., & Chopra, S. B. (2009). Parenting and raising families. In N. Tewari & A. Alvarez (Eds.), *Asian American psychology*. Clifton, NJ: Psychology Press.

Hayes, J. R., & Flower, L. S. (1986). Writing research and the writer. *American Psychologist, 41*, 1106–1113.

Haynes, R. L., Folkerth, R. D., Szweda, L. I., Volpe, J. J., & Kinney, H. C. (2006). Lipid peroxidation during cerebral myelination. *Journal of Neuropathology and Experimental Neurology, 65*, 894–904.

Healey, J. F. (2009). *Race, ethnicity, and class* (5th ed.). Thousand Oaks, CA: Sage.

Heath, S. B. (1989). Oral and literate traditions among Black Americans living in poverty. *American Psychologist, 44*, 367–373.

Heaven, P. C., & Ciarrochi, J. (2008). Parental styles, conscientiousness, and academic performance in high school: A three-wave longitudinal study. *Personality and Social Psychology Bulletin, 34*, 451–461.

Heiphetz, L., & Vescio, T. K. (2008). Discrimination. In N. J. Salkind (Ed.), *Encyclopedia of educational psychology*. Thousand Oaks, CA: Sage.

Heit, E. (2008). Properties of inductive reasoning. In J. E. Adler & L. J. Rips (Eds.), *Reasoning*. New York: Cambridge University Press.

Heller, C., & Hawkins, J. (1994, Spring). Teaching tolerance. *Teachers College Record*, p. 2.

Heller, K. W., Forney, P. E., Alberto, P. A., Bet, S. E., & Schwartzman, M. N. (2009). *Understanding physical, health, and multiple disabilities* (2nd ed.). Boston: Allyn & Bacon.

Henderson, V. L., & Dweck, C. S. (1990). Motivation and achievement. In S. S. Feldman & G. R. Elliott (Eds.), *At the threshold: The developing adolescent*. Cambridge, MA: Harvard University Press.

Hendricks, C. C. (2009). *Improving schools through action research*. Upper Saddle River, NJ: Prentice Hall.

Hendriks, A. A., Kuyper, H., Offringa, G. J., & Van der Werf, M. P. (2008, in press). Assessing young adolescents' personality with the Five-Factor Personality Inventory. *Assessment*.

Henninger, M. L. (2009). *Teaching young children* (4th ed.). Upper Saddler River, NJ: Prentice Hall.

Henson, K. (1988). *Methods and strategies for teaching in secondary and middle schools*. New York: Longman.

Hergenhahn, B. R., & Olson, M. H. (2009). *Introduction to theories of learning* (8th ed.). Upper Saddle River, NJ: Prentice Hall.

Herman, G. E., Henninger, N., Ratliff-Schaub, K., Pastore, M., Fitzgerald, S., & McBride, K. L. (2007). Genetic testing in autism: How much is enough? *Genetics in Medicine, 9*, 268–274.

Herman, J. (1996). Commentary in "The latest on student portfolios." *NEA Today, 15* (4), 17.

Hernandez, D. J., Denton, N. A., & McCartney, S. E. (2007). Family circumstances of children in immigrant families. In J. E. Lansford, K. Deater-Deckhard, & M. H. Bornstein (Eds.), *Immigrant families in contemporary society*. New York: Guilford.

Hertzog, N. B. (1998, January/February). Gifted education specialist. *Teaching Exceptional Children*, pp. 39–43.

Hetherington, E. M. (1995, March). *The changing American family and the well-being of others*. Paper presented at the meeting of the Society for Research in Child Development, Indianapolis.

Hetherington, E. M. (2006). The influence of conflict, marital problem solving, and parenting on children's adjustment in nondivorced, divorced, and remarried families. In A. Clarke-Stewart & J. Dunn (Eds.), *Families count*. New York: Cambridge University Press.

Hetherington, E. M., & Kelly, J. (2002). *For better or for worse: Divorce reconsidered*. New York: Norton.

Hick, P., & Thomas, G. (Eds.). (2009). *Inclusion and diversity in education*. Thousand Oaks, CA: Sage.

Hiebert, E. H., & Raphael, T. E. (1996). Psychological perspectives to literacy and extensions to educational practice. In D. C. Berliner & R. C. Calfee (Eds.), *Handbook of educational psychology*. New York: Macmillan.

Higgins, A., Power, C., & Kohlberg, L. (1983, April). *Moral atmosphere and moral judgment*. Paper presented at the biennial meeting of the Society for Research in Child Development, Detroit.

Hilgard, E. R. (1996). History of educational psychology. In D. C. Berliner & R. C. Calfee (Eds.), *Handbook of educational psychology*. New York: Macmillan.

Hiltz, S. R., & Goldman, R. (Eds.). (2005). *Learning together online*. Mahwah, NJ: Erlbaum.

Hinduja, S., & Patchin, S. (2009). *Bullying beyond the Schoolyard*. Thousand Oaks, CA: Corwin.

Hirsch, E. D. (1996). *The schools we need: And why we don't have them*. New York: Doubleday.

Hirsch, E. D. (2007). Using tests productively. *Educational Horizons, 85*, 97–110.

Hirsh, R. (2004). *Early childhood curriculum: Incorporating multiple intelligences, developmentally appropriate practices, and play*. Boston: Allyn & Bacon.

Hirt, E. R., & Reilly, T. S. (2008). Reciprocal determinism. In N. J. Salkind (Ed.), *Encyclopedia of educational psychology*. Thousand Oaks, CA: Sage.

Hocutt, A. M. (1996). Effectiveness of special education: Is placement the critical factor? *Future of Children, 6*(1), 77–102.

Hodapp, R. M., & Dykens, E. M. (2006). Mental retardation. In W. Damon & R. Lerner (Eds.), *Handbook of child psychology* (6th ed.). New York: Wiley.

Hofer, A., Siedentopf, C. M., Ischebeck, A., Rettenbacher, M. A., Verius, M., Felber, S., & Fleischhacker, W. (2007a). Sex differences in brain activation patterns during processing of positively and negatively balanced emotional stimuli. *Psychological Medicine, 37*, 109–119.

Hofer, A., Seidentopf, C. M., Ischebeck, A., Rettenbacher, M. A., Verius, M., Felber, S., & Fleischhacker, W. (2007b). Gender differences in regional cerebral activity during the perception of emotion: A functional MRI study. *Neuroimage, 132*, 854–862.

Hogan, J. M., Andrews, P. H., Andrews, J. R., & Williams, G. (2008). *Public speaking and civic engagement*. Boston: Allyn & Bacon.

Holberg, C. (1995). Technology in special education. *Technology and Learning, 14*, 18–21.

Hollingsworth, J., & Ybarra, S. (2009). *Explicit direct instruction (EDI)*. Thousand Oaks, CA: Sage.

Hollingworth, L. S. (1916). Sex differences in mental tests. *Psychological Bulletin, 13*, 377–383.

Hollis-Sawyer, L. A., & Sawyer, T. P. (2008). Potential stereotype threat and face validity effects on cognitive-based test performance in the classroom. *Educational Psychology, 28*, 291–304.

Holly, M. L., Arhar, J., & Kasten, W. C. (2009). *Action Research for teachers* (3rd ed.). Upper Saddle River, NJ: Prentice Hall.

Holter, A., & Narvàez, D. (2008, in press). Moral education. In E. Anderman & L. Anderman (Eds.), *Psychology of classroom learning: An encyclopedia*. Farmington Hills, MI: Thomson Gale.

Holtzman, L. (2009). *Vygotsky at work and play*. Oxford, UK: Routledge.

Homa, D. (2008). Long-term memory. In N. J. Salkind (Ed.), *Encyclopedia of educational psychology*. Thousand Oaks, CA: Sage.

Hooper, S., Ward, T. J., Hannafin, M. J., & Clark, H. T. (1989). The effects of aptitude composition on achievement during small group learning. *Journal of Computer-Based Instruction, 16*, 102–109.

Hoover-Dempsey, K. V., Battiato, C., Walker, J. M. T., Reed, R. P., Dejong, J. M., & Jones, K. P. (2001). Parental involvement in homework. *Educational Psychologist, 36*, 195–209.

Horn, J. (2007). Spearman, g, expertise, and the nature of human cognitive capacity. In P. C. Kyllonen, R. D. Roberts, & L. Stankov (Eds.), *Extending intelligence*. Mahwah, NJ: Erlbaum.

Horowitz, F. D., Darling-Hammond, L., Bransford, J., Comer, J., Rosebrock, K., Austin, K., & Rust, F. (2005). Educating teachers for developmentally appropriate practice. In L. Darling-Hammond & J. Bransford (Eds.), *Preparing teachers for a changing world*.

Horwitz, E. K. (2008). *Becoming a language teacher*. Boston: Allyn & Bacon.

Howe, M. J. A., Davidson, J. W., Moore, D. G., & Sloboda, J. A. (1995). Are there early childhood signs of musical ability? *Psychology of Music, 23*, 162–176.

Hudley, C. (2009). Academic motivation and achievement of African American youth. In H. A. Neville, B. M. Tynes, & S. O. Utley (Eds.), *Handbook of African American psychology*. Thousand Oaks, CA: Sage.

Huesmann, L. R., Dubow, E. F., Eron, L. D., & Boxer, P. (2006). Middle childhood family—contextual and personal factors as predictors of adult outcomes. In A. C. Huston & M. N. Ripke (Eds.), *Developmental contexts in middle childhood: Bridges to adolescenc*

Huetinck, L., & Munshin, S. N. (2008). *Teaching mathematics in the 21st century* (3rd ed.). Boston: Allyn & Bacon.

Hult, R. E. (2008). Kohlberg's stages of moral development. In N. J. Salkind (Ed.), *Encyclopedia of educational psychology*. Thousand Oaks, CA: Sage.

Humphrey, N., Curran, A., Morris, E., Farrell, P., & Woods, K. (2007). Emotional intelligence and education: A critical review. *Educational Psychology, 27*, 235–254.

Hunt, E. (2006). Expertise, talent, and social encouragement. In K. A. Ericsson, K. Charness, P. J. Feltovich, & R. R. Hoffman (Eds.), *The Cambridge handbook of expertise and expert performance*. New York: Cambridge University Press.

Hunt, E. B. (1995). *Will we be smart enough? A cognitive analysis of the coming work force*. New York: Russell Sage.

Hunt, R. R., & Ellis, H. C. (2004). *Fundamentals of cognitive psychology* (7th ed.), New York: McGraw-Hill.

Hunt, R. R., & Kelly, R. E. S. (1996). Accessing the particular from the general: The power of distinctiveness in the context of organization. *Memory and Cognition, 24*, 217–225.

Hupert, N., & Heinze, J. (2006). Results in the Palms of their hands: Using handheld computers for data-driven decision making in the classroom. In M. van't Hooft & K. Swan (Eds.), *Ubiquitous computing in education: Invisible technology, visible results.* Mahwah, NJ: Erlbaum.

Huston, A. C., Epps, S. R., Shim, M. S., Duncan, G. J., Crosby, D. A., & Ripke, M. N. (2006). Effects of a family poverty intervention program last from middle childhood to adolescence. In A. C. Huston & M. N. Ripke (Eds.), *Developmental contexts in middle childhood.* New York: Cambridge University Press.

Huston, A. C., & Ripke, M. N. (2006). Experiences in middle childhood and children's development. In A. C. Huston & M. N. Ripke (Eds.), *Developmental contexts in middle childhood.* New York: Cambridge University Press.

Hutson, R. A. (2008). Poverty. In N. J. Salkind (Ed.), *Encyclopedia of educational psychology.* Thousand Oaks, CA: Sage.

Huttenlocher, J., Haight, W., Bruk, A., Seltzer, M., & Lyons, T. (1991). Early vocabulary growth: Relation to language input and gender. *Developmental Psychology, 27*, 236–248.

Huttenlocher, P. R., & Dabholkar, A. S. (1997). Regional differences in synaptogenesis in human cerebral cortex. *Journal of Comparative Neurology, 37* (2), 167–178.

Huurre, T., Junkkari, H., & Aro, H. (2006). Long-term psychosocial effects of parental divorce: A follow-up study from adolescence to adulthood. *European Archives of Psychiatry and Clinical Neuroscience, 256*, 256–263.

Hybels, S., & Weaver, R. L. (2009). *Communicating effectively* (9th ed.). New York: McGraw-Hill.

Hyde, J. S. (2005). The gender similarities hypothesis. *American Psychologist, 60*, 581–592.

Hyde, J. S. (2007). *Half the human experience* (7th ed.). Boston: Houghton Mifflin.

Hyde, J. S., Lindberg, S. M., Linn, M. C., Ellis, A. B., & Williams, C. C. (2008). Gender similarities characterize math performance. *Science, 321*, 494–495.

Hyman, I., Eisenstein, J., Amidon, A., & Kay, B. (2001, August 28). An update on the cross-cultural study of corporal punishment and abuse. In F. Farley (Chair), *Cross-cultural aspects of corporal punishment and abuse: A research update.* Symposium presented at the 2001 Annual Convention of the American Psychological Association, San Francisco.

Hyman, I., Kay, B., Tabori, A., Weber, M., Mahon, M., & Cohen, I. (2006). Bullying: Theory, research, and interventions. In C. M. Evertson, & C. S. Weinstein (Eds.), *Handbook of classroom management: Research, practice, and contemporary issues.* Mahwah, NJ: Erlbaum.

Hyson, M. (2007). Curriculum. In R. New & M. Cochran (Eds.), *Early childhood education: An international encyclopedia of early childhood education.* New York: Greenwood.

Hyson, M., Copple, C., & Jones, J. (2006). Early childhood development and education. In K. A. Renninger & I. E. Sigel (Eds.), *Handbook of child psychology* (6th ed.). New York: Wiley.

I

IBM. (2006). Valuing diversity. Retrieved January 15, 2006, from http://www.306.ibm.com/employment/us/diverse/camps

IDRA. (2008). *Coca-Cola Valued Youth program.* Retrieved August 4, 2008, from www.idra.org/Coca-Cola_Valued_Youth_Program.html/

"I Have a Dream" Foundation. (2008). *About us.* Retrieved July 5, 2008, from http://www.ihad.org

Imada, T., Zhang, Y., Cheour, M., Taulu, S., Ahonen, A., & Kuhl, P. K. (2007). Infant speech perception activates Broca's area: A developmental magnetoencephalography study. *Neuroreport, 17*, 957–962.

Imbo, I., & Vandierendonck, A. (2007). The development of strategy use in elementary school children: Working memory and individual differences. *Journal of Experimental Child Psychology, 96*, 284–309.

Impett, E. A., Schoolder, D., Tolman, L., Sorsoli, L., & Henson, J. M. (2008). Girls' relationship authenticity and self-esteem across adolescence. *Developmental Psychology, 44*, 722–733.

International Montessori Council. (2006). *Much of their success on prime-time television.* Retrieved March 24, 2006, from www.Montessori.org/enews/barbara walters.html

International Society for Technology in Education (ISTE). (2001). *National educational technology standards for teachers—Preparing teachers to use technology.* Eugene, OR: Author.

International Society for Technology in Education (ISTE). (2007). *National educational technology standards for students.* Eugene, OR: Author.

Irvin, J. L., Buehl, D. R., & Kiemp, R. M. (2007). *Reading and the high school student* (2nd ed.). Boston: Allyn & Bacon.

Irvine, J.J. (1990). *Black students and school failure.* New York: Greenwood.

J

Jalongo, M. R. (2007). *Early childhood language arts* (4th ed.). Boston: Allyn & Bacon.

James, W. (1890). *Principles of psychology.* New York: Dover.

James, W. (1899/1993). *Talks to teachers.* New York: W. W. Norton.

Jarvin, L., Newman, T., Randi, J., Sternberg, R. J., & Grigorenko, E. L. (2008). Matching instruction and assessment in the education of gifted children: An illustration with teaching for successful intelligence. In C. Callahan & J. Plucker (Eds.), *What the research says about: An encyclopedia of research on gifted education.* Waco, TX: Prufrock Press.

Jenkins, J., & Jenkins, L. (1987). Making peer tutoring work. *Educational Leadership, 44*, 68–68.

Jenkins, J. M., & Astington, J. W. (1996). Cognitive factors and family structure associated with theory of mind development in young children. *Developmental Psychology, 32*, 70–78.

Jensen, A. R. (2008). Book review. *Intelligence, 36*, 96–97.

Jensen, P. S., & others. (2007). 3-year follow-up of the NIMH MTA study. *Journal of the American Academy of Child and Adolescent Psychiatry, 46*, 989–1002.

Jenson-Campbell, L. A., & Malcolm, K. T. (2007). The importance of conscientiousness in adolescent interpersonal relationships. *Personality and Social Psychology Bulletin, 33*, 368–383.

John-Steiner, V. (2007). Vygotsky on thinking and speaking. In H. Daniels, J. Wertsch, & M. Cole (Eds.), *The Cambridge companion to Vygotsky.* New York: Cambridge University Press.

Johnsen, S. (2005). Within-class acceleration. *Gifted Child Today, 28*, 5.

Johnson, A. P. (2008). *Short guide to action research* (3rd ed.). Boston: Allyn & Bacon.

Johnson, D. R., & Johnson, F. P. (2009). *Joining together* (10th ed.). Upper Saddle River, NJ: Prentice Hall.

Johnson, D. W., & Johnson, R. T. (1994). *Learning together and alone* (4th ed.). Boston: Allyn & Bacon.

Johnson, D. W., & Johnson, R. T. (2002). *Multicultural and human relations.* Allyn & Bacon.

Johnson, J. S., & Newport, E. L. (1991). Critical period effects on universal properties of language: The status of subjacency in the acquisition of a second language. *Cognition, 39*, 215–258.

Johnson, K., & Street, E. M. (2008). Direct instruction. In N. J. Salkind (Ed.), *Encyclopedia of educational psychology.* Thousand Oaks, CA: Sage.

Johnson, W., te Nijenhuis, J., & Bouchard, T. J. (2008). Still just 1 *g*: Consistent results from five test batteries. *Intelligence, 36*, 81–95.

Johnson-Laird, P. N. (2008). Mental models and deductive reasoning. In J. E. Adler & L. J. Rips (Eds.), *Reasoning.* New York: Cambridge University Press.

Jonassen, D. H. (1996). *Computers in the classroom: Mindtools for critical thinking.* Columbus, OH: Merrill/Prentice Hall.

Jonassen, D. H. (2007). On the role of concepts in learning and instructional design. *Educational Technology Research and Development, 54*, 177–196.

Jonassen, D. H., & Grabowski, B. L. (1993). *Handbook of individual differences, learning, and instruction.* Mahwah, NJ: Erlbaum.

Jonassen, D. H., Howland, J., Marra, R. M., & Crismond, D. (2008). *Meaningful learning with technology* (3rd ed.). Upper Saddle River, NJ: Prentice Hall.

Jones, B. F., Rasmussen C. M., & Moffitt, M. C. (1997). *Real-life problem solving.* Washington, DC: American Psychological Association.

Jones, M. D., & Galliher, R. V. (2007). Ethnic identity and psychological functioning in Navajo adolescents. *Journal of Research on Adolescence, 17*, 683–696.

Josephson Institute of Ethics. (2006). *2006 Josephson Institute report card on the ethics of American youth: Part one—integrity.* Los Angeles: Author.

Joyce, B. R., & Weil, M. (2009). *Models of teaching* (8th ed.). Boston: Allyn & Bacon.

Jurecic, A. (2006). Mindblindness: Autism, writing, and the problem of empathy. *Literature and Medicine, 25*, 1–23.

K

Kagan, J. (1965). Reflection-impulsivity and reading development in primary *grade children. Child Development, 36*, 609–628.

Kagan, J. (2002). Behavioral inhibition as a temperamental category. In R. J. Davidson, K. R. Scherer, & H. H. Goldsmith (Eds.), *Handbook of affective sciences.* New York: Oxford University Press.

Kagan, J. (2008). Fear and wariness. In M. M. Haith & J. B. Benson (Eds.), *Encyclopedia of infant and early childhood development.* Oxford, UK: Elsevier.

Kagan, J. & Fox, N. A. (2006). Biology, culture, and temperamental bias. In W. Damon & R. Lerner (Eds.), *Handbook of child psychology* (6th ed.). New York: Wiley.

Kagan, S. (1992). *Cooperative learning.* San Juan Capistrano, CA: Resources for Teachers.

Kagan, S. L., & Scott-Little, C. (2004). Early learning standards. *Phi Delta Kappan, 82*, 388–395.

Kagitcibasi, C. (2007). *Family, self, and human development across cultures.* Mahwah, NJ: Erlbaum.

Kahneman, D., & Tversky, A. (1995). Conflict resolution: A cognitive perspective. In K. Arrow, R. H. Mnookin, L. Ross, A. Tversky, & R. Wilson (Eds.), *Barriers to conflict resolution.* New York: Norton.

Kail, R. (2002). Developmental change in proactive interference. *Child Development, 73* (6), 1703–1714.

Kail, R. V. (2007). Longitudinal evidence that increases in processing speed and working memory enhance children's reasoning. *Psychological Science, 18,* 312–313.

Kaiser, B., & Rasminsky, J. (2009). *Challenging behavior in elementary and middle school.* Upper Saddle River, NJ: Prentice Hall.

Kamii, C. (1985). *Young children reinvent arithmetic: Implications of Piaget's theory.* New York: Teachers College Press.

Kamii, C. (1989). *Young children continue to reinvent arithmetic.* New York: Teachers College Press.

Kamps, D. M., & others. (2008). The efficacy of ClassWide Peer Tutoring in middle schools. *Education and Treatment of Children, 31,* 119–152.

Kane, M. J., Poole, B. J., Toolkit, S. W., & Engle, R. W. (2007). Working memory capacity and top-down control of visual search: Exploring the boundaries of "executive attention." *Journal of Experimental Psychology: Learning, 32,* 749–777.

Kapur, M., Volklis, J., & Kinzer, C. K. (2008). Sensitivities to early exchange in synchronous computer-supported collaborative learning (CSCL) groups. *Computers and Education, 51,* 54–66.

Karnes, F. A., & Stephens, K. R. (2008). *Achieving excellence: Educating the gifted and talented.* Upper Saddle River, NJ: Prentice Hall.

Karniol, R., Grosz, E., & Schorr, I. (2003). Caring, gender-role orientation, and volunteering. *Sex Roles, 49,* 11–19.

Karpov, Y. V. (2006). *The neo-Vygotskian approach to child development.* New York: Cambridge University Press.

Karreman, A., van Tuijl, C. van Aken, M. A. G., & Dekovic, M. (2008). Parenting, coparenting, and effortful control in preschoolers. *Journal of Family Psychology, 22,* 30–40.

Kasprow, W. J., & others. (1993). *New Haven Schools Social Development Project: 1992.* New Haven, CT: New Haven Public Schools.

Katz, L. (1999). Curriculum disputes in early childhood education. *ERIC Clearinghouse on Elementary and Early Childhood Education,* Document EDO-PS-99-13.

Katzov, H. (2007). New insights into autism from a comprehensive genetic map. *Clinical Genetics, 72,* 186–187.

Kauffman, J. M., & Hallahan, D. P. (2005). *Special education: what it is and why we need it.* Boston: Allyn & Bacon.

Kauffman, J. M., & Konold, T. R. (2007). Making sense in education: Pretence (including No Child Left Behind) and realities in rhetoric and policy about schools and schooling. *Exceptionality, 15,* 75–96.

Kauffman, J. M., & Landrum, T. J. (2009). *Characteristics of emotional and behavioral disorders of children and youth* (9th ed.). Boston: Allyn & Bacon.

Kauffman, J. M., McGee, K., & Brigham, M. (2004). Enabling or disabling? Observations on changes in special education. *Phi Delta Kappan, 85,* 613–620.

Kaufman, S. B., & Sternberg, R. J. (2007). Giftedness in the Euro-American culture. In S. N. Phillipson & M. McCann (Eds.), *Conceptions of giftedness: Socio-cultural perspectives.* Mahwah, NJ: Erlbaum.

Kaufman, S. B., & Sternberg, R. J. (2008). Conceptions of giftedness. In S. I. Pfeiffer (Ed.), *Handbook of giftedness in children.* New York: Springer.

Kazdin, A. E. (2008). Time-out. In N. J. Salkind (Ed.), *Encyclopedia of educational psychology.* Thousand Oaks, CA: Sage.

Keating, D. P. (1990). Adolescent thinking. In S. S. Feldman & G. R. Elliott (Eds.), *At the threshold: The developing adolescent.* Cambridge, MA: Harvard University Press.

Keeley, P. (2008). *Science formative assessment.* Thousand Oaks, CA: Corwin.

Kellogg, R. T. (1994). *The psychology of writing.* New York: Oxford University Press.

Kellough, R. D., & Carjuzaa, J. D. (2009). *Teaching in the middle and secondary schools* (9th ed.). Boston: Allyn & Bacon.

Kellough, R. D., & Jarolimek, J. D. (2008). *Teaching and learning K–8* (9th ed.). Boston: Allyn & Bacon.

Kellow, J. T., & & Jones, B. D. (2008). The effects of stereotypes on the achievement gap: Reexamining the academic performance of African American high school students. *Journal of Black Psychology, 34,* 94–120.

Kelly, F. S., McCain, T., & Jukes, I. (2009). *Teaching the digital generation.* Thousand Oaks, CA: Sage.

Kelly, J. B. (2007). Children's living arrangements following separation and divorce: Insights from empirical and clinical research. *Family Process, 46,* 35–52.

Kelly, M. M., & Forsyth, J. P. (2007). Observational fear conditioning in the acquisition and extinction of attentional bias for threat: An experimental evaluation. *Emotion, 7,* 324–335.

Kelly, S. (2008). Tracking. In N. J. Salkind (Ed.), *Encyclopedia of educational psychology.* Thousand Oaks, CA: Sage.

Kenny-Benson, G. A., Pomerantz, E. M., Ryan, A. M., & Patrick, H. (2006). Sex differences in math performance: The role of children's approach to schoolwork. *Developmental Psychology, 42,* 11–26.

Keogh, B. K. (2003). *Temperament in the classroom.* Baltimore: Brookes.

Kerr, M. M., & Nelson, C. M. (2006). *Strategies for assessing behavior problems in the classroom* (5th ed.). Upper Saddle River, NJ: Prentice Hall.

Kerschreiter, R., Schulz-Hardt, S., Mojzisch, A., & Frey, D. (2008). Biased information search in homogeneous groups: Confidence as a moderator for the effect of anticipated task requirements. *Personality and Social Psychology Bulletin, 34,* 679–691.

Keys, C. B., McDonald, K. E., Myrick, S., & Williams, T. T. (2008). Disabilities. In N. J. Salkind (Ed.), *Encyclopedia of educational psychology.* Thousand Oaks, CA: Sage.

Kilburg, G. M., & Hancock, T. (2007). Assessing sources of collateral damage in four mentoring programs. *Teachers College Record, 108,* 132–138.

Kim, S.Y., Su, J., Yankura, L., & Yee, B. (2009). Asian American and Pacific Islander families. In N. Tewari & A. Alvarez (Eds.), *Asian American psychology.* Clifton, NJ: Psychology Press.

King, L. (2007, June 7). The standards complaint. *USA Today,* p. 11D.

King, P. E., & Behnke, R. R. (2005). Problems associated with evaluating student performance in groups. *College Teaching, 53,* 57–61.

King, S. H., & Cardwell, N. M. (2008). Creating a new model of education for African-American children: Mobilizing stakeholder partners in service to sustained academic success. In L. C. Tillman (Ed.), *The SAGE handbook of African American education.* Thousand Oaks, CA: Sage.

Kingore, B. (2008). *Developing portfolios for authentic assessment, PreK–3.* Thousand Oaks, CA: Corwin.

Kingston, E. (2008). Emotional competence and drop-out rates in higher education. *Education and Training, 50,* 128–1389.

Kingston, N. (2008a). Standardized scores. In N. J. Salkind (Ed.), *Encyclopedia of educational psychology.* Thousand Oaks, CA: Sage.

Kingston, N. (2008b). Norm-referenced tests. In N. J. Salkind (Ed.), *Encyclopedia of educational psychology.* Thousand Oaks, CA: Sage.

Kinshuk, T. L., & McNab, P. (2006). Cognitive trait modeling: The case of inductive reasoning ability. *Innovations in Education and Teaching, 43,* 151–161.

Kitayama, S., & Cohen, D. (Eds.). (2007). *Handbook of cultural psychology.* New York: Guilford.

Kivel, P. (1995). *Uprooting racism: How White people can work for racial justice.* Philadelphia: New Society.

Klaczynski, P. A., & Narasimham, G. (1998). Development of scientific reasoning biases: Cognitive versus ego-protective explanations. *Developmental Psychology, 34,* 175–187.

Klausmeier, H. J. (2004). Conceptual learning and development. In W. E. Craighead & C. B. Nemeroff (Eds.), *The concise Corsini encyclopedia of psychology and behavioral sciences.* New York: Wiley.

Klein, S. B. (2009). *Learning* (5th ed.). Thousand Oaks, CA: Sage.

Kling, K. C., Hyde, J. S., Showers, C. J., & Buswell, B. N. (1999). Gender differences in self-esteem: A meta-analysis. *Psychological Bulletin, 125,* 470–500.

Klingman, A. (2006). Children and war trauma. In W. Damon & R. Lerner (Eds.), *Handbook of child psychology* (6th ed.). New York: Wiley.

Klingner, J. K., Blanchett, W. J., & Harry, B. (2007). Race, culture, and developmental disabilities. In S. L. Odom, R. H. Horner, M. E. Snell, & J. Blacher (Eds.), *Handbook of developmental disabilities.* New York: Guilford.

Knecht, S., Draeger, B., Floeel, A., Lohmann, H., Breitenstein, C., Henningson, H., & Ringelstein, E. (2001). Behavioral relevance of atypical language lateralization in healthy subjects. *Brain, 124,* 1657–1665.

Knowledge Forum. (2008). Retrieved January 16, 2008, from www.knowledgeforum.com/

Knudsen, E. (2007). Mechanisms of attention. *Annual Review of Neuroscience,* (Vol. 30). Palo Alto, CA: Annual Reviews.

Kohen, D. E., Leventhal, T., Dahinten, V. S., & McIntosh, C. N. (2008). Neighborhood disadvantage: Pathways of effects for young children. *Child Development, 79,* 156–169.

Kohlberg, L. (1976). Moral stages and moralization: The cognitive-developmental approach. In T. Lickona (Ed), *Moral development and behavior.* New York: Holt, Rinehart & Winston.

Kohlberg, L. (1986). A current statement of some theoretical issues. In S. Modgil & C. Modgil (Eds.), *Lawrence Kohlberg.* Philadelphia: Falmer.

Koppelman, K., & Goodhart, L. (2008). *Understanding human differences* (2nd ed.). Boston: Allyn & Bacon.

Kottler, J. A., & Kottler, E. (2009). *Students who drive you crazy.* Thousand Oaks, CA: Corwin.

Kounin, J. S. (1970). *Discipline and management in classrooms.* New York: Holt, Rinehart & Winston.

Kozol, J. (1991). *Savage inequalities.* New York: Crown.

Kozol, J. (2005). *The shame of the nation.* New York: Crown.

Krajcik, J. S., & Blumenfeld, P. C. (2006). Project-based learning. In R. K. Sawyer (Ed.), *The Cambridge handbook of learning sciences.* New York: Oxford University Press.

Kraska, M. (2007). Assessment. In N. J. Salkind (Ed.), *Encyclopedia of educational psychology.* Thousand Oaks, CA: Sage.

Kraska, M. (2008). Quantitative research methods. In N. J. Salkind (Ed.), *Encyclopedia of* *educational psychology*. Thousand Oaks, CA: Sage.

Krathwohl, D. R., Bloom, B. S., & Masia, B. B. (1964). *Taxonomy of educational objectives. Handbook II: Affective domain.* New York: David McKay.

Kretuzer, L. C., & Flavell, J. H. (1975). An interview study of children's knowledge about memory. *Monographs of the Society for Research in Child Development, 40* (1, Serial No. 159).

Kroger, J. (2007). *Identity development: Adolescence through adulthood.* Thousand Oaks, CA: Sage.

Kubick, R. J., & McLoughlin, C. S. (2005). No Child Left Behind Act of 2001. In S. W. Lee (Ed.). *Encyclopedia of school psychology,* Thousand Oaks, CA: Sage.

Kuder, S. J. (2009). *Teaching students with language and communication disabilities* (3rd ed.). Boston: Allyn & Bacon.

Kuhn, D. (1999). Metacognitive development. In L. Balter & S. Tamis-Lemodnda (Eds.), *Child psychology: A handbook of contemporary issues.* Philadelphia: Psychology Press.

Kuhn, D. (2008a). The skills of argument. In J. E. Adler & L. J. Rips (Eds.), *Reasoning.* New York: Cambridge University Press.

Kuhn, D. (2008b). Formal operations from a twenty-first-century perspective. *Human Development, 51,* 48–55.

Kuhn, D., Garcia-Mila, M., Zohar, Z., & Anderson, C. (1995). Strategies for knowledge acquisition. *Monographs of the Society for Research in Child Development, 60* (4, Serial No. 245), 1–127.

Kuhn, D., & Franklin, S. (2006). The second decade: What develops (and how)? In W. Damon & R. Lerner (Eds.), *Handbook of child psychology* (6th ed.). New York: Wiley.

Kuhn, D., Katz, J., & Dean, D. (2004). Developing reason. *Thinking & Reasoning, 10* (2), 197–219.

Kuhn, D., Weinstock, M., & Flaton, R. (1994). How well do jurors reason? Competence dimensions of individual variation in a juror reasoning task. *Psychological Science, 5,* 289–296.

Kuhn, M. R. (2009). *The hows and whys of fluency instruction.* Boston: Allyn & Bacon.

Kulik, C. L., Kulik, J. A., & Bangert-Drowns, R. L. (1990). Effectiveness of mastery learning programs: A meta-analysis. *Review of Educational Research, 60,* 265–299.

Kulik, J. A. (1992). An analysis of the research on ability grouping. *Monograph of the National Research Center on the Gifted and Talented* (No. 9204). Storrs: University of Connecticut.

Kunzmann, R. (2003). From teacher to student: The value of teacher education for experienced teachers. *Journal of Teacher Education, 54,* 241–253.

L

Lainhart, J. E. (2006). Advances in autism neuroimaging research for the clinician and geneticist. *American Journal of Medical Genetics, C: Seminars in Medical Genetics, 142,* 33–39.

Laird, R. D., Criss, M. M., Pettit, G. S., Dodge, K. A., & Bates, J. E. (2008, in press). Parents' monitoring knowledge attenuates the link between antisocial friends and adolescent delinquent behavior. *Journal of Abnormal Child Psychology.*

Lajoie, S. P., & Azevedo, R. (2006). Teaching and learning in technology-rich environments. In P. A. Alexander & P. H. Winne (Eds.), *Handbook of educational psychology* (2nd ed.). Mahwah, NJ: Erlbaum.

Lamb, M. E., Bornstein, M., & Teti, D. (2002). *Development in infancy* (4th ed.). Mahwah, NJ: Erlbaum.

Lammers, W. J., & Badia, P. (2005). *Fundamentals of behavioral research.* Belmont, CA: Wadsworth.

Lamon, M., Secules, T., Petrosino, A. J., Hackett, R., Bransford, J. D., & Goldman, S. R. (1996). Schools for thought. In L. Schauble & R. Glaser (Eds.), *Innovations in learning.* Mahwah, NJ: Erlbaum.

Landa, S. (2000, Fall). If you can't make waves, make ripples. *Intelligence Connections Newsletter of the ASCD, X* (No. 1), 6–8.

Langer, E. J. (1997). *The power of mindful learning.* Reading, MA: Addison-Wesley.

Langer, E. J. (2000). Mindful learning. *Current Directions in Psychological Science, 9,* 220–223.

Langer, E. J. (2005). *On becoming an artist.* New York: Ballantine.

Lankes, A. M. D. (1995). *Electronic portfolios: A new idea in assessment.* ERIC Document Reproduction Service No. ED390377.

Lapsley, D. (2008). Moral self-identity as the aim of education. In L. Nucci & D. Narvàez (Eds.), *Handbook of moral and character education.* Clifton, NJ: Psychology Press.

Lara, L. E. (2006, April). *Young Latinas and their relation to the new technologies.* Paper presented at the meeting of the American Educational Research Association, San Francisco.

Larkin, M. J. (2008). Rubrics. In N. J. Salkind (2008), *Encyclopedia of educational psychology.* Thousand Oaks, CA: Sage.

Larrivee, B. (2009). *Authentic classroom management.* Upper Saddler River, NJ: Prentice Hall.

Larson, R., & Sheeber, L. (2008, in press). The daily emotional experience of adolescence. In N. Allen & L. Sheeber (Eds.), *Adolescent emotional development and the emergence of depressive disorders.* New York: Cambridge University Press.

Larson, R. W. (2001). How U.S. children and adolescents spend their time: What it does (and doesn't) tell us about their development. *Current Directions in Psychological Science, 10,* 160–164.

Larson, R. W. (2007). Development of the capacity for teamwork in youth development. In R. K. Silbereisen & R. M. Lerner (Eds.), *Approaches to positive youth development.* Thousand Oaks, CA: Sage.

Larson, R. W., & Verma, S. (1999). How children and adolescents spend time across the world: Work, play, and developmental opportunities. *Psychological Bulletin, 125,* 701–736.

Larson, R. W., & Wilson, S. (2004). Adolescence across place and time: Globalization and the changing pathways to adulthood. In R. Lerner & L. Steinberg (Eds.), *Handbook of adolescent psychology.* New York: Wiley.

Lasky-Su, J., Biderman, J., Laird, N., Tsuang, M., Doyle, A. E., Smoller, J. W., Lange, C., & Faraone, S. V. (2007). Evidence for an association of the dopamine D5 receptor gene on age at onset of attention deficit hyperactivity disorder. *Annals of Human Genetics, 71,* 648–659.

Lazar, L., & others. (1982). Lasting effects of early education. *Monographs of the Society for Research in Child Development, 47.*

Lazarus, P. J., & Benson, N. (2008). Emotional intelligence. In N. J. Salkind (Ed.), *Encyclopedia of educational psychology.* Thousand Oaks, CA: Sage.

Leaper, C., & Brown, C. S. (2008). Perceived experiences with sexism among adolescent girls. *Child Development, 79,* 685–704.

Leaper, C., & Smith, T. E. (2004). A meta-analytic review of gender variations in children's language USE: Talkativeness, affiliative speech, and assertive speed. *Developmental Psychology, 40,* 993–1027.

Leary, M. R. (2008). *Introduction to behavioral research* (5th ed.). Upper Saddle River, NJ: Pearson.

Leathers, D., & Eaves, M. H. (2008). *Successful nonverbal communication* (4th ed.). Boston: Allyn & Bacon.

Lee, C. D., & Slaughter-Defoe, D. (1995). Historical and sociocultural influences of African American education. In J. A. Banks, & C. M. Banks (Eds.), *Handbook of research on multicultural education.* New York: Macmillan.

Lee, S. J., & Wong, A. N. (2009). The model minority and the perceptual foreigner: Stereotypes of Asian Americans. In N. Tewari & A. Alvarez (Eds.), *Asian American psychology.* Clifton, NJ: Psychology Press.

Lee, V. E., Croninger, R. G., Linn, E., & Chen, X. (1995, March). *The culture of sexual harassment in secondary schools.* Paper presented at the meeting of the Society for Research in Child Development, Indianapolis.

Lehr, C. A., Hanson, A., Sinclair, M. F., & Christensen, S. L. (2003). Moving beyond dropout prevention towards school completion. *School Psychology Review, 32,* 342–364.

Lehrer, R., & Schauble, L. (2006). Scientific thinking and science literacy: Supporting developmental change in learning contexts. In W. Damon & R. Lerner (Eds.), *Handbook of child psychology* (6th ed.). New York: Wiley.

Leighton, J. P. (2008). Validity. In N. J. Salkind (Ed.), *Encyclopedia of educational psychology.* Thousand Oaks, CA: Sage.

Leonard, L. B. (2007). Processing limitations and the grammatical profile of children with specific language impairment. *Advances in Child Development and Behavior, 35,* 135–171.

Leondari, A., & Gonida, E. (2007). Predicting academic self-handicapping in different age groups: The role of personal achievement goals and social goals. *British Journal of Educational Psychology, 77,* 595–611.

Lepper, M. R., Corpus, J. H., & Iyengar, S. S. (2005). Intrinsic and extrinsic orientations in the classroom: Age differences and academic correlates. *Journal of Educational Psychology, 97,* 184–196.

Lepper, M. R., Greene, D., & Nisbett, R. (1973). Undermining children's intrinsic interest with intrinsic rewards: A test of the overjustification hypothesis. *Journal of Personality and Social Psychology, 28,* 129–137.

Lerner, R. M., Boyd, M., & Du, D. (2008). Adolescent development. In I. B. Wiener &C. B. Craighead (Eds.), *Encyclopedia of psychology.* Thousand Oaks, CA: Sage.

Lesaux, N., & Siegel, L. (2003). The development of reading in children who speak English as a second language. *Developmental Psychology, 39,* 1005–1019.

Lesser, G. (1972). Learning, teaching, and television production for children: The experience of *Sesame Street. Harvard Educational Review, 42,* 232–272.

Lessow-Hurley, J. (2009). *The foundations of dual language instruction* (5th ed.). Boston: Allyn & Bacon.

Leventhal, T., Brooks-Gunn, J., & Kamerman, S. B. (2008). Communities as place, face and space: Provision of services to poor, urban children and their families. In J. DeFilippis & S. Saegert (Eds.), *The community development reader.* New York: Routledge.

Lever-Duffy, J., & McDonald, J. B. (2008). *Teaching and learning with technology* (3rd ed.). Boston: Allyn & Bacon.

Levin, J. (1980). *The mnemonics '80s: Keywords in the classroom.* Theoretical paper No. 86. Wisconsin Research and Development Center for Individualized Schooling, Madison.

Levin, J., & Nolan, J. (2007). *Principles of classroom management* (5th ed.). Boston: Allyn & Bacon.

Levine, L. N., & McCloskey, M. L. (2009). *Teaching learners of English in mainstream classrooms.* Boston: Allyn & Bacon.

Levykh, M. G. (2008). The affective establishment and maintenance of Vygotsky's zone of proximal development. *Educational Theory, 58,* 83–101.

Lewis, A. C. (2005, January). States feel the crunch of NCLB. *Phi Delta Kappan, 86,* 339–340.

Lewis, A. C. (2007). Looking beyond NCLB. *Phi Delta Kappan, 88,* 483–484.

Lewis, F. M., Murdoch, B. E., & Woodyatt, G. C. (2007). Communicative competence and metalinguistic ability: Performance by children and adults with autism spectrum disorder. *Journal of Autism and Developmental Disorders, 37,* 1525–1538.

Liben, L. S. (1995). Psychology meets geography: Exploring the gender gap on the national geography bee. *Psychological Science Agenda, 8,* 8–9.

Liederman, J., Kantrowitz, L., & Flannery, K. (2005). Male vulnerability to reading disability is not likely to be a myth: A call for new data. *Journal of Learning Disabilities, 38,* 109–129.

Liegeois, F., Connelly, A., Baldeweg, T., &Vargha-Khadem, F. (2008, in press). Speaking with a single cerebral hemisphere: fMRI language organization after hemispherectomy in childhood. *Brain and Language.*

Limber, S. P. (1997). Preventing violence among school children. *Family Futures, 1,* 27–28.

Limber, S. P. (2004). Implementation of the Olweus Bullying Prevention Program in American schools: Lessons learned from the field. In D. L. Espelage & S. M. Swearer (Eds.), *Bullying in American schools.* Mahwah, NJ: Erlbaum.

Lindberg, J., Flasch Ziegler, M., & Barcyzk, L. (2009). *Common-Sense classroom management techniques for working with students with significant disabilities.* Thousand Oaks, CA: Corwin.

Lindley, F. (2009). *The portable mentor* (2nd ed.). Thousand Oaks, CA: Corwin.

Lindsey, E. W., & Stopp, H. (2008). Friendship. In N. J. Salkind (Ed.), *Encyclopedia of educational psychology.* Thousand Oaks, CA: Sage.

Lippman, L. G. (2008). Classical conditioning. In N. J. Salkind (Ed.), *Encyclopedia of educational psychology.* Thousand Oaks, CA: Sage.

Lipsitz, J. (1984). *Successful schools for young adolescents.* New Brunswick, NJ: Transaction Books.

Litt, J., Taylor, H. G., Klein, N., & Hack, M. (2005). Learning disabilities in children with very low birth weight: Prevalence, neuropsychological correlates, and educational interventions. *Journal of Learning Disabilities, 38,* 130–141.

Litton, E. F. (1999). Learning in America: The Filipino-American sociocultural perspective. In C. Park & M. M. Chi (Eds.), *Asian-American education: Prospects and challenges.* Westport, CT: Bergin & Garvey.

Liu, C. H., Murakami, J., Eap, S., & Nagayama Hall, G. C. (2009). Who are Asian Americans? An overview of history, immigration, and communities. In N. Tewari & A. Alvarez (Eds.), *Asian American psychology.* Clifton, NJ: Psychology Press.

Liu, W. M., & Hernandez, J. (2008). Social class and classism. In N. J. Salkind (Ed.), *Encyclopedia of educational psychology.* Thousand Oaks, CA: Sage.

Liu, X. (2009). *Essentials of science classroom assessment.* Thousand Oaks, CA: Corwin.

Local Initiatives Support Corp. (LISC). (2005, August). LISC/NEF and One Economy launch $1 billion initiative to bridge the digital divide. Retrieved January 10, 2006, from http://www.lisc.org/whatsnew/press/releases/2005.08.08.0.shtml

Lockl, K., & Schneider, W. (2007). Knowledge about the mind: Links between theory of mind and later metamemory. *Child Development, 78,* 148–167.

Logan, J. (1997). *Teaching stories.* New York: Kodansha International.

Lord, T., & Baviskar, S. (2007). Moving students from information recitation to information understanding: Exploiting Bloom's taxonomy in creating science questions. *Journal of College Science Teaching, 36,* 40–44.

Loukas, A., Suizzo, M-A., & Prelow, H. M. (2007). Examining resource and protective factors in the adjustment of Latino youth in low income families: What role does maternal acculturation play? *Journal of Youth and Adolescence, 36,* 489–501.

Lowe, P. A., & Raad, J. M. (2008). Anxiety. In N. J. Salkind (Ed.), *Encyclopedia of educational psychology.* Thousand Oaks, CA: Sage.

Lubinski, D. (2000). Measures of intelligence: Intelligence tests. In A. Kazdin (Ed.), *Encyclopedia of Psychology.* Washington, DC, & New York: American Psychological Association and Oxford University Press.

Lucas, S. E. (2007). *The art of public speaking* (9th ed.). New York: McGraw-Hill.

Luders, E., Natr, K. L., Thompson, P. M., Rex, D. E., Jancke, L., Steinmetz, H., & Toga, A. W. (2004). Gender differences in cortical complexity. *Native Neuroscience, 1,* 799–800.

Luna, B., Garver, K., Urban, T., Lazar, N., & Sweeney, J. (2004). Maturation of cognitive processes from late childhood to adulthood. *Child Development, 75*(5), 1357–1372.

Luria, A., & Herzog, E. (1985, April). *Gender segregation across and within settings.* Paper presented at the biennial meeting of the Society for Research in Child Development, Toronto.

Lynn, R. (1996). Racial and ethnic differences in intelligence in the U.S. on the Differential Ability Scale. *Personality and Individual Differences, 26,* 271–273.

Lyon, T. D., & Rovell, J. H. (1993). Young children's understanding of forgetting over time. *Child Development, 64,* 789–800.

M

Ma, X. (2002). Bullying in middle school: Individual and school characteristics of victims and offenders. *School Effectivness and School Improvement, 13,* 63–89.

Maag, J. W. (2001). Rewarded by punishment: Reflections on the disuse of positive reinforcement in schools. *Exceptional Children, 67,* 173–186.

Mabbott, D. J., Noseworthy, M., Bouffet, E., Laughlin, S., & Rockel, C. (2006). White matter growth as a mechanism of cognitive development in children. *Neuroimage, 33,* 936–946.

Maccoby, E. E. (1998). *The two sexes: Growing up apart, coming together.* Cambridge, MA: Harvard University Press.

Maccoby, E. E. (2002). Gender and group processes: *Current Directions in Psychological Science, 11,* 54–58.

Maccoby, E. E. (2007). Historical overview of socialization research and theory. In J. E. Grusec & P. D. Hastings (Eds.), *Handbook of socialization.* New York: Guilford.

Maccoby, E. E., & Jacklin, C. N. (1974). *The psychology of sex differences.* Palo Alto, CA: Stanford University Press.

MacGeorge, E. L. (2004). The myth of gender cultures: Similarities outweigh differences in men's and women's provisions of and responses to supportive communication. *Sex Roles, 50,* 143–175.

Madle, R. A. (2008). Applied behavior analysis. In N. J. Salkind (Ed.), *Encyclopedia of educational psychology.* Thousand Oaks, CA: Sage.

Madrid, L. D., Canas, M., & Ortega-Medina, M. (2007). Effects of team competition versus team cooperation in classwide peer tutoring. *Journal of Educational Research, 100,* 155–160.

Mael, F. A. (1998). Single-sex and coeducational schooling: Relationships to socioemotional and academic development. *Review of Educational Research, 68*(2), 101–129.

Mager, R. (1962). *Preparing instructional objectives* (2nd ed.). Palo Alto, CA: Fearon.

Maggio, R. (1987). *The non-sexist word finder: A dictionary of gender-free usage.* Phoenix: Oryx.

Magliano, J. P., & Perry, P. J. (2008). Individual differences. In N. J. Salkind (Ed.), *Encyclopedia of educational psychology.* Thousand Oaks, CA: Sage.

Magnusson, S. J., & Palincsar, A. S. (2005). Teaching to promote the development of scientific knowledge and reasoning about light at the elementary school level. In M. S. Donovan & J. D. Bransford (Eds.), *How students learn.* Washington, DC: National Academies Press.

Maier, S. F., & Seligman, M. E. P. (2009). Fears, phobias, and preparedness: Toward an evolved module of fear and fear learning. In D. Shanks (Ed.), *Psychology of learning.* Thousand Oaks, CA: Sage.

Major, B., Barr, L., Zubek, J., & Babey, S. H. (1999). Gender and self-esteem: A meta-analysis. In W. Swann & J. Langlois (Eds.), *Sexism and stereotypes in modern society: The gender science of Janet Tayler Spence.* Washington, DC: American Psychological Association.

Makel, M. C., & Plucker, J. A. (2008). Creativity. In S. I. Pfeiffer (Ed.), *Handbook of giftedness in children.* New York: Springer.

Malik, N.M., & Furman, W. (1993). Practitioner review: Problems in children's peer relations; What can the clinician do? *Journal of Child Psychology and Psychiatry, 34,* 1303–1326.

Mandara, J. (2006). The impact of family functioning on African American males' academic achievement: A review and clarification of the empirical literature. *Teachers College Record, 108,* 206–233.

Mandler, G. (1980). Recognizing: The judgment of previous occurrence. *Psychological Review, 87,* 252–271.

Mandler, J. M. (2004). *The origins of mind.* New York: Oxford University Press.

Manis, F. R., Keating, D. P., & Morrison, F. J. (1980). Developmental differences in the allocation of processing capacity. *Journal of Experimental Child Psychology, 29,* 156–169.

Manning, M. L., & Baruth, L. G. (2009). *Multicultural education of children and adolescents* (5th ed.). Boston: Allyn & Bacon.

Marcia, J. E. (1980). Identity in adolescence. In J. Adelson (Ed.), *Handbook of adolescent psychology.* New York: Wiley.

Marcia, J. E. (1998). Optimal development from an Eriksonian perspective. In H. S. Friedman (Ed.), *Encyclopedia of mental health* (Vol. 2). San Diego: Academic Press.

Marcovitch, H. (2004). Use of stimulants for attention deficit hyperactivity disorder: AGAINST. *British Medical Journal, 329,* 908–909.

Marinis, T., & van der Lely, H. K. (2007). On-line processing of wh- questions in children with G-SLI and typically developing children. *International Journal of Language and Communication Disorders, 42,* 557–582.

Marklein, M. B. (1998, November 24). An eye-level meeting of the minds. *USA Today,* p. 9D.

Martin, G. L., & Pear, J. (2007). *Behavior modification* (8th ed.). Upper Saddle River, NJ: Prentice Hall.

Martin, J. L. (2008). Peer sexual harassment: Finding voice, changing culture—an intervention strategy for adolescent females. *Violence Against Women, 14,* 100–124.

Martin, L. R., Friedman, H. S., & Schwartz, J. E. (2007). Personality and mortality risk across the life span: The importance of conscientiousness as a biopsychosocial attribute. *Health Psychology, 26,* 428–436.

Martin, R., Sexton, C., Franklin, T., Gerlovich, J., & McElroy, D. (2009). *Teaching science for all children* (5th ed.). Boston: Allyn & Bacon.

Marton, F., Hounsell, D. J., & Entwistle, N. J. (1984). *The experience of learning.* Edinburgh: Scottish Academic Press.

Marx, D. M., & Stapel, D. A. (2006). Distinguishing stereotype threat from priming effects: On the role of the social self and threat-based concerns. *Journal of Personality and Social Psychology, 91,* 243–254.

Marzano, R. (2008). *Designing and assessing educational objectives.* Thousand Oaks, CA: Corwin.

Marzano, R. J., & Pickering, D. J. (2007). Special topic: The case for and against homework. *Educational Leadership, 64,* 74–79.

Maslow, A. H. (1954). *Motivation and personality.* New York: Harper & Row.

Maslow, A. H. (1971). *The farther reaches of human nature.* New York: Viking Press.

Massa, N. M. (2008). Problem-based learning (PBL): A real-world antidote to the standards and testing regime. *New England Journal of Higher Education, 22* (No. 4), 19–20.

Mastropieri, M. A., & Scruggs, T. E. (2007). *Inclusive classroom* (3rd ed). Upper Saddle River, NJ: Prentice Hall.

Mathematica. (2008). Retrieved January 16, 2008, from www.wolfram.com/products/mathematica/index.html

Mathes, P. G., & Fletcher, J. M. (2008). Dyslexia. In N. J. Salkind (Ed.), *Encyclopedia of educational psychology.* Thousand Oaks, CA: Sage.

Mathes, P. G., Torgesen, J. K., & Allor, J. H. (2001). The effects of peer-assisted literacy strategies for first-grade readers with and without additional computer-assisted instruction in phonological awareness. *American Educational Research Journal, 38,* 371–410.

Matlin, M. W. (2005). *Cognition* (6th Ed.). New York: Wiley.

Matlin, M. W. (2008). *Psychology of women* (6th ed.). Belmont, CA: Wadsworth.

Matsumoto, D., & Huang, L. (2008). *Culture and psychology.* Belmont, CA: Wadsworth.

Matusov, E., Bell, N., & Rogoff, B. (2001). *Schooling as a cultural process: Working together and guidance by children from schools differing in collaborative practices.* Unpublished manuscript, Department of Psychology, University of California at Santa Cruz.

May, M. (2001, November 21). San Leandro kids lap up their lessons. *San Francisco Chronicle,* pp. A1, 24.

Mayer, J. D., Salovey, D. R., & Caruso, D. R. (2007). What is emotional intelligence and what does it predict? In P. C. Kyllonen, R. D. Roberts, & L. Stankov (Eds.), *Extending intelligence.* Mahwah, NJ: Erlbaum.

Mayer, J. D., Salovey, P., & Caruso, D. R. (2002). *Mayer–Salovey–Caruso Emotional Intelligence Test (MSCEIT): User's manual.* Toronto, Ontario: Multi-Health Systems.

Mayer, J. D., Salovey, P., & Caruso, D. R. (2004). Emotional intelligence: Theory, findings, and implications. *Psychological Inquiry, 15,* 197–215.

Mayer, M. J., Van Acker, R., Lochman, J. E., & Gresham, F. M. (Eds.). (2009). *Cognitive-behavioral interventions for emotional and behavioral disorders: School-based practice.* New York: Guilford.

Mayer, R. E. (1997). Multimedia learning: Are we asking the right questions? *Educational Psychologist, 32,* 1–19.

Mayer, R. E. (2004). Should there be a three-strike rule against pure discovery learning? *American Psychologist, 59,* 14–19.

Mayer, R. E. (2004). Teaching of subject matter. *Annual Review of Psychology, 55.* Palo Alto, CA: Annual Review, 5.

Mayer, R. E. (2008). *Learning and instruction* (2nd ed.). Upper Saddle River, NJ: Prentice Hall.

Mayhew, M. J., & King, P. (2008). How curricular content and pedagogical strategies affect moral reasoning development in college students. *Journal of Moral Education, 37,* 17–40.

Maynard, A. E. (2008). What we thought we knew and how we came to know it: Four decades of cross-cultural research from a Piagetian point of view. *Human Development, 51,* 56–65.

Mazurek, K., Winzer, M. A., & Majorek, C. (2000). *Education in a global society.* Boston: Allyn & Bacon.

McAdoo, H. P., & Younge, S. N. (2009). Black families. In H. A. Neville, B. M. Tynes, & S. O. Utley (Eds.), *Handbook of African American psychology.* Thousand Oaks, CA: Sage.

McAnarney, E. R. (2008). Editorial: Adolescent brain development: Forging new links? *Journal of Adolescent Health, 42,* 321–323.

McBurney, D. H., & White, T. L. (2007). *Research methods* (7th ed.). Belmont, CA: Wadsworth.

McCall, A. (2007). Supporting exemplary social studies teaching in elementary schools. *Social Studies, 97,* 161–167.

McCarthy, J. (2007). Children with autism spectrum disorders and intellectual disability. *Current Opinion in Psychiatry, 20,* 472–476.

McClelland, M. M., Cameron, C. E., Connor, C. M., Farris, C. L., Jewkes, A. M., & Morrison, F. J. (2007). Links between behavioral regulation and preschoolers' literacy, vocabulary, and math skills. *Developmental Psychology, 43,* 947–959.

McCombs, B. L. (2001, April). *What do we know about learners and learning? The learner-centered framework.* Paper presented at the meeting of the American Educational Research Association, Seattle.

McCombs, B. L., & Quiat, M. A. (2001). *Development and validation of norms and rubrics for the Grades K-5 assessment of learner-centered principles (ALCP) surveys.* Unpublished manuscript, University of Denver Research Institute, Denver.

McCormick, C. B., & Pressley, M. (1997). *Educational psychology.* New York: Longman.

McCrae, R. R., & Costa, P. T. (2006). Cross-cultural perspectives on adult personality trait development. In D. K. Mroczek & T. D. Little (Eds.), *Handbook of personality development.* Mahwah, NJ: Erlbaum.

McDonald, B. A., Larson, C. D., Dansereau, D. I., & Spurlin, J. E. (1985). Cooperative dyads: Impact on text learning and transfer. *Contemporary Educational Psychology, 10,* 369–377.

McElhaney, K. B., Antonishak, J., & Allen, J. P. (2008). "They like me, they like me not": Popularity and adolescents' perceptions of acceptance predicting social functioning over time. *Child Development, 79,* 720–731.

McGee, L. M., & Richgels, D. J. (2008). *Literacy's beginnings: Supporting young readers and writers* (5th ed.). Boston: Allyn & Bacon.

McGoey, K. E., & Rezzetano, K. (2008). Token reinforcement programs. In N. J. Salkind (Ed.), *Encyclopedia of educational psychology.* Thousand Oaks, CA: Sage.

McKay, R. (2008), Multiple intelligences. In N. J. Salkind (Ed.), *Encyclopedia of educational psychology.* Thousand Oaks, CA: Sage.

McKeough, A., Palmer, J., Jarvey, M., & Bird, S. (2007). Best narrative writing practices when teaching from a developmental perspective. In S. Graham, C. A. MacArthur, & J. Fitzgerald (Eds.), *Best practices in writing instruction.* New York: Guilford.

McLoyd, V. C., Aikens, N. L., & Burton, L. M. (2006). Childhood poverty, policy, and practice. In W. Damon & R. Lerner (Eds.), *Handbook of child psychology* (6th ed.). New York: Wiley.

McLoyd, V. C., & Smith, J. (2002). Physical discipline and behavior problems in African American, European American, and Hispanic children: Emotional support as a moderator. *Journal of Marriage and the Family, 64,* 40–53.

McMillan, J. H. (1997). *Classroom assessment.* Boston: Allyn & Bacon.

McMillan, J. H. (2002). *Essential assessment concepts for teachers and administrators.* Thousand Oaks, CA: Corwin.

McMillan, J. H. (2004). *Educational research* (4th ed.). Boston: Allyn & Bacon.

McMillan, J. H. (2007). *Classroom assessment* (4th ed.). Boston: Allyn & Bacon.

McMillan, J. H. (2008). *Assessment essentials for standards-based education* (2nd ed.). Thousand Oaks, CA: Corwin.

McMillan, J. H. (2008). *Educational research* (5th ed.). Boston: Allyn & Bacon.

McMillan, J. H., & Hearn, J. (2008). *Student self-assessment: A path to enhance student motivation and achievement.* Unpublished manuscript, Virginia Commonwealth University, Richmond, VA.

McMorris, R. F., & Tan, X. (2008). Multiple-choice tests. In N. J. Salkind (Ed.), *Encyclopedia of educational psychology.* Thousand Oaks, CA: Sage.

McNally, D. (1990). *Even eagles need a push.* New York: Dell.

McNergney, R. F., & McNergney, J. M. (2007). *Education: The practice and profession of teaching* (5th ed.). Boston: Allyn & Bacon.

Md-Yunus, S. (2007). How parents can encourage creativity in children. *Childhood Education, 83,* 236.

Means, B. (2006). Prospects for transforming schools with technology-supported assessment. In R. K. Sawyer (Ed.), *The Cambridge handbook of the learning sciences.* New York: Cambridge University Press.

Meece, J. L., Anderman, E. M., & Anderman, L. H. (2006). Classroom goal structure, student motivation, and academic achievement. *Annual Review of Psychology, 57* (Vol. 57). Palo Alto, CA: Annual Reviews.

Meece, J. L., & Eccles, J. (Eds.). (2009). *Handbook of research on schools, schooling and human development.* Clifton, NJ: Psychology Press.

Meece, J. L., & Kurtz-Costes, B. (2001). Introduction: The schooling of ethnic minority children. *Educational Psychologist, 36,* 57–66.

Meichenbaum, D., & Butler, L. (1980). Toward a conceptual model of the treatment of test anxiety: Implications for research and treatment. In I. G. Sarason (Ed.), *Test anxiety.* Mahwah, NJ: Erlbaum.

Meichenbaum, D., Turk, D., & Burstein, S. (1975). The nature of coping with stress. In I. Sarason & C. Spielberger (Eds.), *Stress and anxiety.* Washington, DC: Hemisphere.

Meltzoff, A. N., & Brooks, R. (2009). Social cognition: The role of gaze following in early word learning. In J. Colombo, P. McCardle, & L. Freund (Eds.), *Infant pathways to language.* Clifton, NJ: Psychology Press.

Melzi, G., & Ely, R. (2009). Language development in the school years. In J. Berko Gleason & N. Ratner (Eds.), *The development of language.* Boston: Allyn & Bacon.

Menn, L., & Stoel Gammon, C. (2009). Phonological development: Learning words and sound patterns. In J. Berko Gleason & N. B. Ratner (Eds.), *The psychology of language* (7th ed.). Boston: Allyn & Bacon.

Mennin, S. (2007). Small-group problem-based learning as a complex adaptive system. *Teaching and Teacher Education: An International Journal of Research and Studies, 23,* 303–313.

Merali, N. (2008). Immigration. In N. J. Salkind (Ed.), *Encyclopedia of educational psychology.* Thousand Oaks, CA: Sage.

Mercer, N. (2008). Talk and the development of reasoning and understanding. *Human Development, 51,* 90–100.

Merenda, P. (2004). Cross-cultural adaptation of educational and psychological testing. In R. K. Hambleton, P. F. Merenda, & C. D. Spielberger (Eds.), *Adapting educational and psychological tests for cross-cultural assessment.* Mahwah, NJ: Erlbaum.

Merrell, K. W., Carrizales, D., Feuerborn, L., Gueldner, B. A., & Tran, O. K. (2007). *Strong kids—grades 6–8: A social and emotional learning curriculum.* Baltimore: Brookes.

Merrell, K. W., Parisi, D., & Whitcomb, S. A. (2007). *Strong start—grades K–2: A social and emotional learning curriculum.* Baltimore: Brookes.

Mertler, C. A., & Charles, C. M. (2008). *Introduction to educational research* (6th ed.). Boston: Allyn & Bacon.

Metzger, M. (1996, January). Maintaining a life, *Phi Delta Kappan, 77,* 346–351.

Mezzacappa, E. (2004). Alerting, orienting, and executive attention: Developmental properties and socioeconomic correlates in an epidemiological sample of young, urban children. *Child Development, 75,* 1373–1386.

Michaels, S. (1986). Narrative presentations: An oral preparation for literacy with first graders. In J. Cook-Gumperz (Ed.), *The social construction of literacy.* New York: Cambridge University Press.

Middleton, J., & Goepfert, P. (1996). *Inventive strategies for teaching mathematics.* Washington, DC: American Psychological Association.

Midgley, C., Anderman, E., & Hicks, L. (1995). Differences between elementary school and middle school teachers and students: A goal theory approach. *Journal of early adolescence, 15,* 90–113.

Miller, C. F., Lurye, L., Zosuls, K., & Ruble, D. N. (2008). *Developmental changes in the accessibility of gender stereotypes.* Unpublished manuscript, Department of Psychology, Princeton, NJ.

Miller, G. A. (1956). The magical number seven, plus or minus two: Some limits on our capacity for information processing. *Psychological Review, 48,* 337–442.

Miller, J. E. (2008). Gifted and talented education. In N. J. Salkind (Ed.), *Encyclopedia of educational psychology.* Thousand Oaks, CA: Sage.

Miller, J. W. (2001). *Using educational technologies to promote vocabulary development among heterogeneously-grouped fifth graders.* Unpublished manuscript, Harvard University, Boston.

Miller, K. F. (2000). Representational tools and conceptual change: The young scientist's tool kit. *Journal of Applied Developmental Psychology, 21,* 21–25.

Miller, L. K. (2006). *Principles of everyday behavior analysis* (4th ed.), Belmont, CA: Wadsworth.

Miller, M. D. (2008). Reliability. In N. J. Salkind (Ed.), *Encyclopedia of educational psychology.* Thousand Oaks, CA: Sage.

Miller, P. H. (2000). How best to utilize a deficiency: A commentary on Water's "Memory strategy development." *Child Development, 71,* 1013–1017.

Miller, T. W., Nigg, J. T., & Faraone, S. V. (2007). Axis I and II comorbidity in adults with ADHD. *Journal of Abnormal Psychology, 116,* 519–528.

Miller-Jones, D. (1989). Culture and testing. *American Psychologist, 44,* 360–366.

Mills, D., & Mills, C. (2000). *Hungarian kindergarten curriculum translation.* London: Mills Production.

Milner, H. R. (2006). Preservice teachers' learning about cultural and racial diversity. *Urban Education, 41 (4),* 343–375.

Milner-Bolotin, M., Kotlicki, A., & Rieger, G. (2007). Can students learn from lecture demonstration?: The role and place of interactive lecture experiments in large introduction science courses. *Journal of College Science, 36,* 45–49.

Milsom, A., & Gallo, L. L. (2006). Bullying in middle schools: Prevention and intervention. *Middle School Journal, 37,* 12–19.

Miltenberger, R. G. (2008). *Behavior modification* (4th ed.). Belmont, CA: Wadsworth.

Minstrell, J., & Kraus, P. (2005). Guided inquiry in the science classroom. In M. S. Donovan & J. D. Bransford (Eds.), *How students learn.* Washington, DC: National Research Council.

Minuchin, P. P., & Shapiro, E. K. (1983). The school as a context for social development. In P. H. Mussen (Ed.), *Handbook of child psychology* (4th ed., Vol. 4). New York: Wiley.

Mitchell, M. L., & Jolley, J. M. (2007). *Research designs explained* (6th ed.). Belmont, CA: Wadsworth.

Moll, L. C., & González, N. (2004). Engaging life: A funds of knowledge approach to multicultural education. In J. A. Banks & C. A. M. Banks (Eds.), *Handbook of research on multicultural education* (2nd ed.). San Francisco: Jossey-Bass.

Monaco, T. (2008). The application of molecular genetics to the study of specific language impairment. In C. Norbury, B. Tomblin, & D. Bishop (Eds.), *Understanding developmental language disorders in children.* Milton Park, UK: Routledge.

Montero-Sieburth, M., & Meléndez, E. (2007). *Latinos in a changing society.* Westport, CT: Prager.

Moon, S. M. (2008). Personal and social development. In K. A. Karnes & K. R. Stephens (Eds.), *Achieving excellence: Educating the gifted and talented.* Upper Saddle River, NJ: Prentice Hall.

Moran, S., & Gardner, H. (2006). Extraordinary achievements. In W. Damon & R. Lerner (Eds.). *Handbook of child psychology,* (6th ed.). New York: Wiley.

Morra, S., Gobbo, C., Marini, Z., & Sheese, R. (2007). *Cognitive development: Neo-Piagetian perspectives.* Mahwah, NJ: Erlbaum.

Morris, P., & Kalil, A. (2006). Out of school time use during middle childhood in a low-income sample: Do combinations of activities affect achievement and behavior? In A. Huston & M. Ripke (Eds.), *Middle childhood: Contexts of development.* New York: Cambridge University Press.

Morrison, G. S. (2009). *Early childhood education today* (11th ed.). Upper Saddle River, NJ: Prentice Hall.

Morrow, L. (2009). *Literacy development in the early years* (7th ed.). Boston: Allyn & Bacon.

Morse, D., & Jutras, F. (2008). Implementing concept-based learning in a large undergraduate classroom. *CBE Life Science Education, 7,* 243–253.

Moyer, J. R., & Dardig, J. C. (1978). Practical task analysis for teachers. *Teaching Exceptional Children, 11,* 16–18.

Mraz, M., Podak, N. D., & Rasinski, T. V. (2008). *Evidence-based instruction in reading: A professional development guide to phonemic awareness.* Boston: Allyn & Bacon.

Munkata, Y. (2006). Information processing: Approaches to development. In W. Damon & R. Lerner (Eds.), *Handbook of educational psychology.* New York: Wiley.

Murdock, T. B. (1999). The social context of risk: Status and motivational predictors of alienation in middle school. *Journal of Educational Psychology, 91,* 62–75.

Murdock, T. B., Miller, A., & Kohylardt, J. (2004). Effects of classroom context variables on high school students' judgments of the acceptability and likelihood of cheating. *Journal of Educational Psychology, 96,* 765–777.

Murrell, P. C. (2009). Identity, agency, and culture: Black achievement and educational attainment. In L. C. Tillman (Ed.), *The SAGE handbook of African American education.* Thousand Oaks, CA: Sage.

Musial, D., Nieminen, G., Thomas, J., & Burke, K. (2009). *Foundations of meaningful educational assessment.* New York: McGraw-Hill.

Myerson, J., Rank, M. R., Raines, F. Q., & Schnitzler, M. A. (1998). Race and general cognitive ability: The myth of diminishing returns in education. *Psychological Science, 9,* 139–142.

N

NAASP. (1997, May/June). Students say: What makes a good teacher? *Schools in the Middle,* pp. 15–17.

NAEYC. (2002). *Early learning standards: Creating the conditions for success.* Washington, DC: Author.

Nagy, W. E., & Scott, J. A. (2000). Vocabulary processes. In M. L. Kamil, P. B. Mosenthal, P. D. Pearson, & R. Barr (Eds.), *Handbook of reading research* (Vol. 3). Mahwah, NJ: Erlbaum.

Nansel, T. R., Overpeck, M., Pilla, R. S., Ruan, W. J., Simons-Morton, B., & Scheidt, P. (2001). Bullying behaviors among U.S. youth: Prevalence and association with psychosocial adjustment. *Journal of the American Medical Association, 285,* 2094–2100.

Narvàez, D. (2006). Integrative moral education. In M. Killen & J. Smetana (Eds.), *Handbook of moral development.* Mahwah, NJ: Erlbaum.

Narvàez, D. (2008). Four component model. In F. C. Power, R. J. Nuzzi, D, Narvàez, D. K. Lapsley, & T. C. Hunt (Eds.), *Moral education: A handbook.* Westport, CT: Greenwood.

Narvàez, D., Lynchard, N., Vavdich. J., & Mattan, B. (2008, March). *Cheating: Explicit recognition, implicit evaluation, moral judgment and honor code training.* Paper presented at the annual meeting of the Society for Research in Adolescence Chicago.

Nash, J. M. (1997, February 3). Fertile minds. *Time,* pp. 50–54.

Nathan, M. J., & Petrosino, A. J. (2003). Expert blind spot among preservice teachers. *American Educational Research Journal, 40(4),* 905–928.

National Assessment of Educational Progress. (2002). *The nation's report card.* Washington, DC: National Center for Education Statistics.

National Assessment of Educational Progress. (2005). *The Nation's report card 2005.* Washington, DC: U.S. Department of Education.

National Assessment of Educational Progress. (2007). *The nation's report card.* Washington, DC: National Center for Education Statistics.

National Assessment of Reading Progress. (2000). *Reading achievement.* Washington, DC: National Center for Education Statistics.

National Association for the Education of Young Children. (1996). NAEYC position statement: Responding to linguistic and cultural diversity—Recommendations for effective early childhood education. *Young Children, 51,* 4–12.

National Center for Education Statistics. (1997). *School-family linkages.* Washington, DC: U.S. Department of Education.

National Center for Education Statistics. (2003). Digest of Education Statistics, Table 52. Washington, DC: Author.

National Center for Education Statistics. (2005). *Internet access in U.S. public schools.* Washington, DC: U.S. Department of Education.

National Center for Education Statistics. (2006). *Children with disabilities in public schools.* Washington, DC: U.S. Department of Education.

National Center for Education Statistics. (2006). *Contexts of elementary and secondary education.* Washington, DC: Author.

National Center for Education Statistics (2007). *The condition of education 2007.* Washington, DC: U.S. Department of Education.

National Center for Education Statistics. (2008). *Children and youth with disabilities in public Schools.* Washington, DC: U.S. Department of Education.

National Center for Education Statistics. (2008). *The condition of education 2008. School dropout rates.* Washington, DC: U.S. Department of Education.

National Center for Learning Disabilities. (2006). *Learning disabilities.* Retrieved March 6, 2006, from http://www.ncld.org/

National Council for the Social Sciences. (2000). *National standards for social studies teachers.* Baltimore: Author.

National Council for the Social Studies (NCSS). (1994). *Expectations of excellence: Curriculum standards for social studies.* Waldorf, MD: Author.

National Council of Teachers of English/International Reading Association (NCTE/IRA). (1996). *Standards for the English Language Arts.* Urbana, IL: National Council of Teachers of English.

National Institutes of Health. (1993). *Learning disabilities* NIH publication No. 93–3611). Bethesda, MD: Author.

National Reading Panel. (2000). *Teaching children to read.* Washington, DC: National Institute of Child Health and Human Development.

National Research Council. (2000). *How people learn.* Washington, DC: National Academy Press.

National Research Council. (2001). *Knowing what students know.* Washington, DC: National Academic Press.

National Research Council. (2005). *How students learn.* Washington, DC: National Academies Press.

NCTM. (2000). *Principles and standards for school mathematics.* Reston, VA: Author.

NCTM. (2007a). *Navigating through number & operations in grades 3–5.* Reston, VA: Author.

NCTM. (2007b). *Making sense of mathematics: Children sharing and comparing solutions to challenging problems.* Reston, VA: Author.

NCTM. (2007c). *Mathematics teaching today: Professional standards for teaching mathematics, revision.* Reston, VA: Author.

Neil, M. (2006). Preparing teachers to beat the agonies of NCLB. Retrieved August 3, 2006, from www.eddigest.com

Neisser, U., Boodoo, G., Bouchard, T. J., Boykin, A. W., Brody, N., Ceci, S. J., Halpern, D. F., Loehlin, J. C., Perloff, R., Sternberg, R. J., & Urbina, S. (1996). Intelligence: Knowns and unknowns. *American Psychologist, 51*, 77–101.

Nelson, C. A. (2003). Neural development and lifelong plasticity. In R. M. Lerner, F. Jacobs, & D. Wertlieb (Eds.), *Handbook of applied developmental science* (Vol. I). Thousand Oaks, CA: Sage.

Nelson, C. A. (2009, in press). Brain development and behavior. In A. M. Rudolph, C. Rudolph, L.

First, G. Lister, & A. A. Gersohon (Eds.), *Rudolph's pediatrics* (22nd ed.). New York: McGraw-Hill.

Nelson, C. A., Thomas, K. M., & De Haan, M. (2006). Neural bases of cognitive development. In W. Damon & R. Lerner (Eds.), *Handbook of child psychology* (6th ed.). New York: Wiley.

Nelson, J. A., & Eckstein, D. (2008). A service-learning model for at-risk adolescents. *Education and Treatment of Children, 31*, 223–237.

Nelson, K. (2006). Development of representation in childhood. In E. Bialystok & F. I. M. Craik (Eds.), *Lifespan cognition.* New York: Oxford University Press.

Nelson, P. E., Titsworth, S., & Pearson, J. C. (2009). *ispeak: Public speaking for contemporary life.* New York: McGraw-Hill.

Nesbit, J. C., & Hadwin, A. F. (2006). Methodological issues in educational psychology. In P. A. Alexander & P. H. Winne (Eds.), *Handbook of educational psychology* (2nd ed.). Mahwah, NJ: Erlbaum.

Neugarten, B. L. (1988). *Policy issues for an aging society.* Paper presented at the meeting of the American Psychological Association, Atlanta.

Neukrug, E. S., & Fawcett, R. C. (2006). *Essentials of testing and assessment* (Belmont, CA: Wadsworth.

Neuman, R. J., Lobos, E., Reich, W., Henderson, C. A., Sun, L. W., & Todd, R. D. (2007). Prenatal smoking exposure and dopaminergic genotypes interact to cause a severe ADHD subtype. *Biological Psychiatry, 61*, 1320–1328.

Neville, H. J. (2006). Different profiles of plasticity within human cognition. In Y. Munakata & M. H. Johnson (Eds.), *Attention and performance XXI: Processes of change in brain and cognitive development.* Oxford. UK: Oxford University Press.

New, R. (2005). The Reggio Emilia approach: Provocations and partnerships with U.S. early childhood educators. In J. I. Roopnarine & J. E. Johnson (Eds.), *Approaches to early childhood education* (4th ed.). Columbus, OH: Merrill/Prentice Hall.

New, R. (2007). Reggio Emilia as cultural activity. *Theory into Practice, 46*, 5–13.

Newton, E., Padak, N. D., & Rasinski, T. V. (2008). *Evidence-based instruction in reading: A professional development guide to vocabulary.* Boston: Allyn & Bacon.

NICHD Early Child Care Research Network. (2005). Predicting individual differences in attention, memory, and planning in first graders from experiences at home, child care, and school. *Developmental Psychology, 41*, 99–114.

Nichols, J. D., & Miller, R. B. (1994). Cooperative learning and student motivation. *Contemporary Educational Psychology, 19*, 167–178.

Nieto, A. M., & Saiz, C. (2008). Evaluation of Halpern's "structural component" for improving critical thinking. *Spanish Journal of Psychology, 11*, 266–274.

Nieto, S. (2005). *Why we teach.* New York: Teachers College Press.

Nieto, S., & Bode, P. (2008). *Affirming diversity* (5th ed.). Boston: Allyn & Bacon.

Nikola-Lisa, W., & Burnaford, G. E. (1994). A mosaic: Contemporary schoolchildren's images of teachers. In P. B. Joseph & G. E. Burnaford (Eds.), *Image of schoolteachers in twentieth century America.* New York: St. Martin's Press.

Nintendo Wii. (2008). Retrieved January 16, 2008, from http://www.nintendo.com/wii

Nisbett, R. E., & Ross, L. (1980). *Human inference.* Upper Saddle River, NJ: Prentice Hall.

Nissman, B. S. (2009). *What every teacher should know about teacher-tested classroom management strategies* (3rd ed.). Upper Saddle River, NJ: Prentice Hall.

Noddings, N. (2001). The care tradition: Beyond "add women and stir." *Theory into Practice, 40*, 29–34.

Noddings, N. (2007). *When school reform goes wrong.* New York: Teachers College Press.

Noddings, N. (2008). All our students thinking. *Educational Leadership, 65*, 8–13.

Noddings, N. (2008). Caring and moral education. In L. Nucci & D. Narvàez (Ed.), *Handbook of moral and character education.* Clifton, NJ: Psychology Press.

Noftie, E. E., & Robins, R. W. (2007). Personality predictors of academic outcomes: Big five correlates of GPA and SAT scores. *Journal of Personality and Social Psychology, 93*, 116–130.

Nokelainen, P., & Flint, J. (2002). Genetic effects on human cognition: Lessons from the study of mental retardation syndromes. *Journal of Neurology, Neurosurgery, and Psychiatry, 43*, 287–296.

Nokes, J. D., Dole, J. A., & Hacker, D. J. (2007). Teaching high school students to use heuristics while reading historical texts. *Journal of Educational Psychology, 99*, 492–504.

Nolen-Hoeksema, S. (2007). *Abnormal psychology* (4th ed.). New York: McGraw-Hill.

Norbury, C., Tomblin, B., & Bishop, D. (Eds.), (2008). *Understanding developmental language disorders in children.* Milton Park, UK: Routledge.

Nucci, L. (2006). Education for moral development. In M. Killen & J. Smetana (Eds.), *Handbook of moral development.* Mahwah, NJ: Erlbaum.

Nucci, L., & Narvàez, D. (2008). Introduction and overview. In L. Nucci & D. Narvàez (Eds.), *Handbook of moral and character education.* Clifton, NJ: Psychology Press.

Nylund, K., Bellmore, A., Nishina, A., & Graham, S. (2007). Subtypes, severity, and structural stability of peer victimization: What does latent class analysis say? *Child Development, 78*, 1706–1722.

O'Donnell, A. M. (2006). The role of peers and group learning. In P. A. Alexander & P. H. Winne (Eds.), *Handbook of educational psychology* (2nd ed.). Mahwah, NJ: Erlbaum.

O'Donnell, A.M., & Levin, J. R. (2001). Educational psychology's healthy growing pains. *Educational Psychologist, 36*, 73–82.

O'Hara, S., & Pritchard, R. (2009). *Teaching vocabulary with hypermedia, 6–12.* Boston: Allyn & Bacon.

O'Shea, M. (2009). *Pathways through teaching series: Assessment throughout the year.* Upper Saddle River, NJ: Prentice Hall.

O'Toole, A. (2007, April). Personal communication. Richardson, TX: Department of Psychology, University of Texas at Dallas.

Oakes, J. (1990). *Multiplying inequalities: The effects of race, social class, and tracking on opportunities to learn mathematics and science.* Santa Monica: The RAND Corporation.

Oakes, J., & Lipton, M. (2007). *Teaching to change the world* (3rd ed.). New York: McGraw-Hill.

Oakes, J., Saunders, M. (2002). *Access to textbooks, instructional materials, equipment, and technology: Inadequacy of California's schools.* Los Angeles: Department of Education, UCLA.

Oakes, L. M. (2008). Categorization skills and concepts. In M. M. Haith & J. B. Benson (Eds.), *Encyclopedia of infant and early childhood development.* Oxford, UK: Elsevier.

Ogbu, J. U. (1989, April). *Academic socialization of Black children: An inoculation against future failure?* Paper presented at the meeting of the Society for Research in Child Development, Kansas City.

Ogbu, J. U., & Stern, P. (2001). Caste status and intellectual development. In R. J. Sternberg & E. L. Grigorenko (Eds.), *Environmental effects on cognitive abilities.* Mahwah, NJ: Erlbaum.

Ogle, D., & Beers, J. W. (2009). *Engaging in the language arts.* Boston: Allyn & Bacon.

Okagki, L. (2006). Ethnicity. In P. A. Alexander & P. H. Winne (Eds.), *Handbook of educational psychology* (2nd ed.). Mahwah, NJ: Erlbaum.

Oldehinkel, A. J., Ormel, J., Veenstra, R., De Winter, A., & Verhulst, F. C. (2008). Parental divorce and offspring depressive symptoms: Dutch developmental trends during early adolescence. *Journal of Marriage and the Family, 70,* 284–293.

Oliva, J. M., Azcarate, P., & Navarrete, A. (2007). Teaching models in the use of analogies as a resource in the science classroom. *International Journal of Science Education, 29,* 45–66.

Olson, M., & Hergenhahn, B. R. (2009). *Introduction to theories of learning* (8th ed.). Upper Saddle River, NJ: Prentice Hall.

One Community. (2008). Retrieved January 16, 2008, from www.onecleveland.org/

Oosterhof, A. (2009). *Developing and using classroom assessments* (4th ed.). Upper Saddle River, NJ: Prentice Hall.

Ormerod, A. J., Collinsworth, L. L., & Perry, L. A. (2008). Critical climate: Relations among sexual harassment, climate, and outcomes for high school girls and boys. *Psychology of Women Quarterly, 32,* 113–125.

Ornstein, P. A., Haden, C. A., & Elischberges, H. B. (2006). Children's memory development. In E. Bialystok & E. L. M. Craik (Eds.), *Lifespan cognition.* New Mark: Oxford University Press.

Orth, U., Robins, R. W., & Roberts, B. W. (2008, in press). Low self-esteem prospectively predicts depression in adolescence and young adulthood. *Journal of Personality and Social Psychology.*

Osofsky, J. D. (Ed.). (2007). *Young children and trauma.* New York: Guilford.

Otero, V. K. (2006). Moving beyond the "get it or don't" conception of formative assessment. *Journal of Teacher Education, 57,* 247–255.

Otten, L. J., Henson, R. N., & Rugg, M. D. (2001). Depth of processing effects on neural correlates of memory encoding, *Brain, 124,* 399–412.

Ostrov, J. M., Keating, C. F., & Ostrov, J. M. (2004). Gender difference in preschool aggression during free play and structured interactions: An observational study. *Social Development, 13,* 255–277.

P

Paivio, A. (1971). *Imagery and verbal processes.* Fort Worth, TX: Harcourt Brace.

Paivio, A. (1986). *Mental representations: A dual coding approach.* New York: Oxford University Press.

Palincsar, A. S., & Brown, A. L. (1984). Reciprocal teaching of comprehension-fostering and comprehension-monitoring activities. *Cognition and Instruction, 1,* 117–175.

Palmer, P. J. (2008). *The courage to teach* (10th anniversary ed.). San Francisco: Jossey-Bass.

Pan, B. A., & Uccelli, P. (2009). Semantic development. In J. Berko Gleason & N. Ratner (Eds.), *The development of language* (7th ed.). Boston: Allyn & Bacon.

Pan, B. A., Rowe, M. L., Singer, J. D., & Snow, C. E. (2005). Maternal correlates of growth in toddler vocabulary production in low-income families. *Child Development, 76,* 763–782.

Pang, V. O. (2005). *Multicultural education.* (3rd ed.). New York: McGraw-Hill.

Parente, M. E., & Mahoney, J. L. (2008, in press). Activity participation in childhood and adolescence. Invited chapter to appear in D. Carr (Ed.), *Encyclopedia of the life course and human development.* Farmington Hills, MI: Gale Research.

Paris, S. G., & Paris, A. H. (2006). Assessments of early reading. In W. Damon & R. Lerner (Eds.), *Handbook of child psychology* (6th ed.). New York: Wiley.

Park, C. (1997). Learning style preferences of Asian American (Chinese, Filipino, Korean, and Vietnamese) students in secondary schools. *Equity and Excellence in Education, 30* (2), 68–77.

Park, E., & King, K. (2003). Cultural diversity in language socialization in the early years. *ERIC Digest,* EDO-FL-03-13, pp. 1–2.

Park, S. H., & Ertmer, P. A. (2008). Examining barriers in technology-enhanced problem-based learning: Using a performance support systems approach. *British Journal of Educational Psychology, 39,* 631–643.

Parke, C. S. (2008). Criterion-referenced testing. In N. J. Salkind (Ed.), *Encyclopedia of educational psychology.* Thousand Oaks, CA: Sage.

Parke, R. D., & Buriel, R. (2006). Socialization in the family: Ethnic and ecological perspectives. In W. Damon & R. Lerner (Eds.), *Handbook of child psychology* (6th ed.). New York: Wiley.

Parke, R. D., Leidy, M. S., Schofield, T. J., Miller, M. A., & Morris, K. L. (2008). Socialization. In M. M. Haith & J. B. Benson (Eds.), *Encyclopedia of infant and early childhood development.* Oxford, UK: Elsevier.

Parker, W. (2009). *Social studies in elementary education* (13th ed.). Boston: Allyn & Bacon.

Partnership for 21st Century Skills. (2003). Learning for the 21st century, Washington. DC: Author. Retrieved January 30, 2006, from http://www.21stcenturyskills.org/images/stories/otherdocs/P21_Report.pdf

Partnership for 21st Century Skills. (2008). Retrieved January 16, 2008, from www.21stcenturyskills.org/

Patall, E. A., Cooper, H. & Robinson, J. C. (2008, in press). The effects of choice on intrinsic motivation and related outcomes: A meta-analysis of research findings. *Psychological Bulletin.*

Patrick, H., Ryan, A. M., & Kaplan, A. (2007). Early adolescents' perceptions of the classroom social environment, motivational beliefs, and engagement. *Journal of Educational Psychology, 99,* 83–98.

Patterson, C. J., & Hastings, P. D. (2007). Socialization in the context of family diversity. In J. E. Grusec & P. D. Hastings (Eds.), *Handbook of socialization.* New York: Guilford.

Paus, T., Toro, R., Lerner, J. V., Lerner, R. M., Perron, M., Pike, G. B., Richer, L., Steinberg, L., Veillete, S., & Pausova, Z. (2008, in press). Morphological properties of action-observation cortical network in adolescents with low and high resistance to peer influence. *Social Neuroscience.*

Pavlov, I. P. (1927). *Conditioned reflexes.* New York: Dover.

Pawan, F. (2008). Content-area teachers and scaffolded instruction for English language learners. *Teaching and Teacher Education: An International Journal of Research and Studies, 24,* 1450–1462.

Payne, D. A. (1997). *Applied educational assessment.* Belmont, CA: Wadsworth.

Payne, K. T. (2008). Cultural diversity. In N. J. Salkind (Ed.), *Encyclopedia of educational psychology.* Thousand Oaks, CA: Sage.

Pearce, J. M., & Hall, G. (2009). A model for stimulus generalization: Pavlovian conditioning. In D. Shanks (Ed.), *Psychology of learning.* Thousand Oaks, CA: Sage.

Pecheone, R. L., & Chung, R. R. (2006). Evidence in teacher education. *Journal of Teacher Education, 57,* 22–36.

Pena, E., & Bedore, J. A. (2009). Bilingualism. In R. G. Schwartz (Ed.), *Handbook of child language disorders.* Clifton, NJ: Psychology Press.

Pennington, B. F., & Bishop, D. V. M. (2009). Relations among speech, language, and reading disorders. *Annual Review of Psychology* (Vol. 60). Palo Alto, CA: Annual Reviews.

Pepler, D., Jiang, D. Craig, W., & Connolly, J. (2008). *Developmental trajectories of bullying and associated factors. Child Development, 79,* 325–338.

Peregoy, S. F., & Boyle, O. F. (2009). *Reading, writing, and learning in ESL* (5th ed.). Boston: Allyn & Bacon.

Perin, D. (2007). Best practices in teaching writing to adolescents. In S. Graham, C. A. MacArthur, & J. Fitzgerald (Eds.), *Best practices in writing instruction.* New York: Guilford.

Perret-Clermont, A-N., & Barrelet, J-M. (Eds.). (2008). *Jean Piaget and Neuchatel: The learner and the scholar.* Philadelphia: The Psychology Press.

Perry, K. E., Donohue, K. M., & Weinstein, R. S. (2007). Teaching practices and the promotion of achievement and adjustment in first grade. *Journal of School Psychology, 45,* 269–292.

Perry, N. E., Turner, J. C., & Meyer, D. K. (2006). Classrooms as contexts for motivating learning. In P. A. Alexander & P. H. Winne (Eds.), *Handbook of educational psychology* (2nd ed.). Mahwah, NJ: Erlbaum.

Persky, H. R., Daane, M. C., & Jin, Y. (2003). *The nation's report card: Writing 2002.* Washington, DC: U.S. Department of Education.

Peter, T., Roberts, L. W., & Buzdugan, R. (2008). Suicidal ideation among Canadian youth: A multivariate analysis. *Archives of Suicide Research, 12,* 263–275.

Peterson, G. B. (2008). Shaping. In N. J. Salkind (Ed.), *Encyclopedia of educational psychology.* Thousand Oaks, CA: Sage.

Peterson, R. L., McGrath, L. M., Smith, S. D., & Pennington, B. F. (2007). Neuropsychology and genetics of speech, language, and literacy disorders. *Pediatric Clinics of North America, 54,* 543–561.

Peyton, V. (2005). Standard score. In S. W. Lee (Ed.), *Encyclopedia of school psychology.* Thousand Oaks, CA: Sage.

Pfeiffer, S. I., & Blei, S. (2008). Gifted identification beyond the IQ test: Rating scales and other assessment procedures. In S. I. Pfeiffer (Ed.), *Handbook of giftedness in children.* New York: Springer.

Pham, A. V., & Carlson, J. S. (2008). Family influences. In N. J. Salkind (Ed.), *Encyclopedia of educational psychology.* Thousand Oaks, CA: Sage.

Philipsen, N. M., Johnson, A. D., & Brooks-Gunn, J. (2009, in press). Poverty, effects on social and emotional development. *International encyclopedia of education* (3rd ed.). St. Louis, MO: Elsevier.

Phinney, J. S. (2006). Ethnic identity exploration in emerging adulthood. In J. J. Arnett & J. L. Tanner (Eds.), *Emerging adults in America.* Washington, DC: American Psychological Association.

Phinney, J. S., & Ong, A. D. (2007). New directions for ethnic identity research in immigrant families. In J. Lansford, K. Deater-Deckard, & M. Bornstein (Eds.), *Immigrant families in contemporary society.* New York: Guilford.

Phye, G. D. (1990). Inductive problem solving: Schema inducement and memory-based transfer. *Journal of Educational Psychology, 82,* 826–831.

Phye, G. D., & Sanders, C. E. (1994). Advice and feedback: Elements of practice for problem solving. *Contemporary Educational Psychology, 19,* 286–301.

Piaget, J. (1954). *The construction of reality in the child.* New York: Basic Books.

Piaget, J., & Inhelder, B. (1969). *The child's conception of space*. New York: Norton.

Pianta, R. C. (2006). Classroom management and relationships between children and teachers: Implications for practice. In C. M. Evertson & C. S. Weinstein (Eds.), *Handbook of classroom management*. Mahwah, NJ: Erlbaum.

Piggott, J. (2007). Cultivating creativity. *Mathematics Incorporating Micromath, 202*, 3–6.

Pleiss, M. K., & Feldhusen, J. F. (1995). Mentors, role models, and heroes in the lives of gifted children. *Educational Psychologist 30*, 159–169.

Pliszka, S. R. (2007). Pharmacologic treatment of attention deficit hyperactivity disorder: Efficacy, safety, and mechanisms of action. *Neuropsychology Review, 17*, 61–72.

Plog, A., Epstein, L., & Porter, W. (2004, April). *Implementation fidelity: Lessons learned from the Bully-Proofing Your School Program*. Paper presented at the meeting of the National School Psychologists Association, Dallas.

Plomin, R., DeFries, J. C., & Fulker, D. W. (2007). *Nature and nurture during infancy and early childhood*. New York: Cambridge University Press.

Plucker, J. A., & Beghetto, R. A. (2008). Creativity. In N. J. Salkind (Ed.), *Encyclopedia of educational psychology*. Thousand Oaks, CA: Sage.

Pollack, W. (1999). *Real boys*. New York: Owl Books.

Polson, D. (2001). Helping children learn to make responsible choices. In B. Rogoff, C. G. Turkanis & L. Bartlett (Eds.), *Learning together: Children and adults in a school community*. New York: Oxford University Press.

Pomerantz, E. M., Wang, Q., & Ng, F. (2005). Mothers' affect in the homework context: The importance of staying positive. *Developmental Psychology, 41*, 414–427.

Popham, W. J. (2008). *Classroom assessment* (8th ed.). Boston: Allyn & Bacon.

Portals. (2008). Retrieved January 16, 2008, from www.newgrounds.com/portal/view/404612

Posada, G. (2008). Attachment. In M. M. Haith & J. B. Benson (Eds.), *Encyclopedia of infancy and early childhood development*. Oxford, UK: Elsevier.

Posavac, E. J., & Carey, R. (2007). *Program evaluation* (7th ed.). Upper Saddle River, NJ: Prentice Hall.

Posner, G. J., & Rudnitsky, A. N. (2006). *Course design: A guide to curriculum development for teachers* (7th ed.). Boston: Allyn & Bacon.

Posner, M. I., & Rothbart, M. K. (2007). *Educating the human brain*. Washington, DC: American Psychological Association.

Poulin, F., & Pedersen, S. (2007). Developmental changes in gender composition of friendship networks in adolescent girls and boys. *Developmental Psychology, 43*, 1484–1496.

Powell, B. (2002). Unpublished review of J. W. Santrock's *Educational psychology*, 2nd ed. New York: McGraw-Hill.

Power, F. C., & Higgins-D'Alessandro, A. (2008). The Just Community Approach to moral education and moral atmosphere of the school. In L. Nucci & D. Narvàez (Eds.), *Handbook of moral and character education*. Clifton, NJ: Psychology Press.

Power, F. C., Narvàez, D., Nuzzi, R., Lapsley, D. & Hunt, T. (Eds.). (2008). *Moral education: A handbook*. Westport, CT: Greenwood.

Prawat, R. S. (2008). Constructivism. In N. J. Salkind (Ed.), *Encyclopedia of educational psychology*. Thousand Oaks, CA: Sage.

Preiss, D., & Sternberg, R. J. (Eds.). (2009, in press). *From genes to context: New discoveries about learning from educational research and their applications*. New York: Springer.

Presidential Task Force on Psychology and Education. (1992). *Learner-centered psychological principles: Guidelines for school redesign and reform* (Draft). Washington, DC: American Psychological Association.

Pressley, M. (1983). Making meaningful materials easier to learn. In M. Pressley & J. R. Levin (Eds.), *Cognitive strategy research: Educational applications*. New York: Springer-Verlag.

Pressley, M. (2007). Achieving best practices. In L. B. Gambrell, L. M. Morrow, & M. Pressley (Eds.), *Best practices in literacy instruction*. New York: Guilford.

Pressley, M. (2007). An interview with Michael Pressley by Terri Flowerday and Michael Shaughnessy. *Educational Psychology Review, 19*, 1–12.

Pressley, M., Allington, R., Wharton-McDonald, R., Block, C. C., & Morrow, L. M. (2001). *Learning to read: Lessons from exemplary first grades*. New York: Guilford.

Pressley, M., Borkowski, J. G., & Schneider, W. (1989). Good information processing: What it is and what education can do to promote it. *International Journal of Educational Research, 13*, 857–867.

Pressley, M., Cariligia-Bull, T., Deane, S., & Schneider, W. (1987). Short-term memory, verbal competence, and age as predictors of imagery instructional effectiveness. *Journal of Experimental Child Psychology, 43*, 194–211.

Pressley, M., Dolezal, S. E., Raphael, L. M., Welsh, L. M., Bogner, K., & Roehrig, A. D. (2003). *Motivating primary-grades teachers*. New York: Guilford.

Pressley, M., & Harris, K. R. (2006). Cognitive strategies instruction: From basic research to classroom instruction. In P. A. Alexander & P. H. Winne (Eds.), *Handbook of educational psychology* (2nd ed.). Mahwah, NJ: Erlbaum.

Pressley, M., & Hilden, K. (2006). Cognitive strategies. In W. Damon & R. Lerner (Eds.), *Handbook of child psychology* (6th ed.). New York: Wiley.

Pressley, M., Levin, J. R., & McCormick, C. B. (1980). Young children's learning of a foreign language vocabulary: A sentence variation of the keyword. *Contemporary Educational Psychology, 5*, 22–29.

Pressley, M., & McCormick, C. B. (2007). *Child and adolescent development for educators*. New York: Guilford.

Pressley, M., Mohan, L., Raphael, L. M., & Fingeret, L. (2007a). How does Bennett Woods Elementary School produce such high reading and writing achievement? *Journal of Educational Psychology, 99*, 221–240.

Pressley, M., Mohan, L., Fingeret, L., Reffitt, K., & Raphael-Bogaert, L. R. (2007b). Writing instruction in engaging and effective elementary settings. In S. Graham, C. A. MacArthur, & J. Fitzgerald (Eds.), *Best practices in writing instruction*. New York:

Pressley, M., Raphael, L., Gallagher, D., & DiBella, J. (2004). Providence–St. Mel School: How a school that works for African-American students works. *Journal of Educational Psychology, 96*, 216–235.

Pressley, M., Schuder, T., SAIL Faculty and Administration, German, J., & El-Dinary, P. B. (1992). A researcher-educator collaborative interview study of transactional comprehension strategies instruction. *Journal of Educational Psychology, 84*, 231–246.

Pressley, M., Wharto-McDonald, R., Allington, R., Block, C. C., Morrow, H. L., Tracey, D., Baker, K., Brooks, G., Cronin, J., Nelson, E., & Woo, D. (2001). A study of effective first grade literacy instruction. *Scientific Studies of Reading, 15*, 35–58.

Pretz, J. E. (2008). Intuition versus analysis: Strategy and experience in complex everyday problem solving. *Memory and Cognition, 36*, 554–566.

Prinsen, F. R., Volman, M. L. L., & Terwel, J. (2007). Gender-related differences in computer-mediated communication and computer-supported collaborative learning. *Journal of Computer Assisted Learning, 23*, 393–409.

Proctor-Williams, K., & Fey, M. E. (2007). Recast density and acquisition of novel irregular past tense verbs. *Journal of Speech, Language, and Hearing Research, 50*, 1029–1047.

Pryor, J. H., Hurtado, S., Sharkness, J., & Korn, W. S. (2007). *The American freshman: National norms for fall 2007*. Los Angeles: Higher Education Research Institute, UCLA.

PSU. (2006). Anchored instruction. Retrieved January 6, 2006, from http://www.ed.psu.edu/nasa/achrtxt.html

Pueschel, S. M., Scola, P. S., Weidenman, L. E., & Bernier, J. C. (1995). *The special child*. Baltimore: Paul H. Brookes.

Putallaz, M., Grimes, C. L., Foster, K. J., Kupersmidt, J., & Coie, J. D. (2007). Overt and relational aggression and victimization: Multiple perspectives within the school setting. *Journal of School Psychology, 45*, 459–586.

Quality counts. (2001). *A better balance: Standards, tests, and the tools to succeed*. Bethesda, MD: Education Week on the Web.

Quest Atlantis. (2008). Retrieved January 16, 2008, from www.crit.indiana.edu/research/qa.html

Quiamzade, A., Mugny, G., & Darnon, C. (2008, in press). The coordination of problem solving strategies: When low competence sources exert more influence on task processing than high competence sources. *British Journal of Social Psychology*.

Quijada, P. D. (2008). Culture. In N. J. Salkind (Ed.), *Encyclopedia of educational psychology*. Thousand Oaks, CA: Sage.

Quinn, P. C., Bhatt, R. S., & Hayden, A. (2008, in press). What goes with what: Development of perceptual grouping in infancy. In B. Ross (Ed.), *Motivation* (Vol. 49). Oxford, UK: Elsevier.

Quiocho, A. L., & Ulanoff, S. H. (2009). *Differentiated literacy instruction for English language learners*. Boston: Allyn & Bacon.

R

Raffaelli, M., & Ontai, L. L. (2004). Gender socialization in Latino/a families: Results from two retrospective studies. *Sex Roles, 50*, 287–299.

Rainey, R. (1965). The effects of directed vs. non-directed laboratory work on high school chemistry achievement. *Journal of Research in Science Teaching, 3*, 286–292.

Rakoczy, H., Warneken, F., & Tomasello, M. (2007). "This way!", "No! That way!"—3 year-olds know that two people can have mutually incompatible desires. *Cognitive Development, 22*, 47–68.

Ramey, C. T., Bryant, D. M., Campbell, F. A., Sparling, J. J., & Wasik, B. H. (1988). Early intervention for high-risk children. The Carolina Early Intervention Program. In R. H. Price, E. L. Cowen, R. P. Lorion, & J. Ramos-McKay (Eds.), *14 ounces of prevention*. Washington, DC: American Psychological Association.

Ramey, C. T., Ramey, S. L., & Lanzi, R. G. (2001). Intelligence and experience. In R. J. Sternberg & E. L. Grigorenko (Eds.), *Environmental effects on cognitive abilities*. Mahwah, NJ: Erlbaum.

Ramey, C. T., Ramey, S. L., & Lanzi, R. G. (2006). Children's health and education. In W. Damon & R. Lerner (Eds.), *Handbook of child psychology* (6th ed.). New York: Wiley.

Ramphal, C. (1962). *A study of three current problems in education.* Unpublished doctoral dissertation, University of Natal, India.

Randolph, C. H., & Evertson, C. M. (1995). Managing for learning: Rules, roles, and meanings in a writing class. *Journal of Classroom Instruction, 30,* 17–25.

Randolph, K. A., & Johnson, J. L. (2008). School-based mentoring programs: A review of the research. *Children and Schools, 30,* 177–185.

Rapee, R. M., Hudson, J. L., & Schiering, C. A. (2009). Anxiety disorders during childhood and adolescence: Origins and treatment. *Annual Review of Clinical Psychology* (Vol. 5). Palo Alto, CA: Annual Reviews.

Rasinski, T. V., & Padak, N. D. (2008). *From phonics to fluency: The teaching of decoding and reading fluency in elementary school* (2nd ed.). Boston: Allyn & Bacon.

Rathunde, K., & Csikszentmihalyi, M. (2006). The developing person: An experiential perspective. In W. Damon & R. Lerner (Eds.), *Handbook of child psychology* (6th ed.). New York: Wiley.

Ratner, N. B. (2005). Atypical language development. In J. B. Gleason (Ed.), *The development of language.* Boston: Allyn & Bacon.

Ratner, N. B. (2009). Atypical language development. In J. Berko Gleason (Ed.), *The development of language* (7th ed.). Boston: Allyn & Bacon.

Rauscher, K. J. (2008). Workplace violence against adolescent workers in the U.S. *American Journal of Industrial Medicine, 51,* 539–544.

Re: Learning by Design. (2000). *Design resource center.* Re: Learning by Design. Retrieved July 16, 2002. From, http://www.relearning.org.

Redelmeier, D. A. (2005). Improving patient care: The cognitive psychology of missed diagnoses. *Annals of Internal Medicine, 142,* 115–120.

Reeb, B. C., Fox, N. A., Nelson, C. A., & Zeanah, C. H. (2008, in press). The effects of early institutionalization on social behavior and underlying neural correlates. In M. de Haan & M. Gunnar (Eds.), *Handbook of social developmental neuroscience.* Malden, MA: Blackwell.

Reeve, C. L., & Lam, H. (2007). Consideration of *g* as a common antecedent for cognitive ability test performance, test motivation, and perceived fairness. *Intelligence, 35,* 347–358.

Reeve, J. (2006). Extrinsic rewards and inner motivation. In C. M. Evertson & C. S. Weinstein (Eds.), *Handbook of classroom management.* Mahwah, NJ: Erlbaum.

Regalado, M., Sareen, H., Inkelas, M., Wissow, L. S., & Halfon, N. (2004). Parents' discipline of young children: Results from the National Survey of Early Childhood Health. *Pediatrics, 113* (Suppl.), 1952–1958.

Reid, G., Fawcett, A., Manis, F., & Siegel, L. (2009). *The SAGE handbook of dyslexia.* Thousand Oaks, CA: Sage.

Reinders, H., & Youniss, J. (2006). School-based required community service and civic development in adolescence. *Applied Developmental Science, 10,* 2–12.

Reksten, L. E. (2009). *Sustaining extraordinary student achievement.* Thousand Oaks, CA: Corwin.

Renne, C. H. (1997). *Excellent classroom management.* Belmont, CA: Wadsworth.

Renzulli, J. S. (1998). A rising tide lifts all ships: Developing the gifts and talents of all students. *Phi Delta Kappan, 80,* 1–15.

Renzulli, J. S., & Reis, S. M. (1997). The schoolwide enrichment model. In N. Colangelo & G. A. Davis (Eds.), *Handbook of gifted education.* Boston: Allyn & Bacon.

Rescorla, R. A. (2009). A theory of Pavlovian conditioning: Variations in the effectiveness of reinforcement and nonreinforcement. In D. Shanks (Ed.), *Psychology of learning.* Thousand Oaks, CA: Sage

Reutzel, D. R., & Cooter, R. B. (2009). *Essentials of teaching to read* (2nd ed.). Boston: Allyn & Bacon.

Reyna, V. F. (2004). How people make decisions that involve risk: A dual-process approach. *Current Directions in Psychological Science, 13,* 60–66.

Reyna, V. F., & Rivers, S. E. (2008). Current theories of risk and national decision making. *Developmental Review, 78,* 1–11.

Reynolds, C. R., Livingston, R., & Wilson, V. (2006). *Measurement and assessment in education.* Boston: Allyn & Bacon.

Reysen, M. (2008). Memory. In N. J. Salkind (Ed.), *Encyclopedia of educational psychology.* Thousand Oaks, CA: Sage.

Ricco, R. B. (2007). Individual differences in the analysis of informal reasoning fallacies. *Contemporary Educational Psychology, 32,* 459–484.

Rice, K. G., Leever, B. A., Noggle, C. A., & Lapsley, D. A. (2007). Perfectionism and depressive symptoms in early adolescence. *Psychology in the Schools, 44,* 139–156.

Richards, R. (Ed.). (2007). *Everyday creativity and new views of human nature: Psychological, social, and spiritual perspectives.* Washington, DC: American Psychological Association.

Richmond, V. P., McCroskey, J. C., & Hickson, M. L. (2008). *Nonverbal behavior in interpersonal relations* (6th ed.). Boston: Allyn & Bacon.

Rico, S. A., & Shulman, J. H. (2004). Invertebrates and organ systems: Science instruction "Fostering a Community of Learners." *Journal of Curriculum Studies, 36,* 159–182.

Rips, L. J. (2008). Logical approaches to human deductive reasoning. In J. E. Adler & L. J. Rips (Eds.), *Reasoning.* New York: Cambridge University Press.

Rittle-Johnson, B. (2006). Promoting transfer: Effects of self-explanation and direct instruction. *Child Development, 77,* 1–15.

Rivas-Drake, D., Hughes, D., & Way, N. (2008). A closer look at peer discrimination, ethnic identity, and psychological well-being among urban Chinese American sixth graders. *Journal of Youth and Adolescence, 37*(1), 12–21.

Roberts, B. W., Jackson, J. J., Fayard, J. V., Edmonds. G., & Meints, J. (2009, in press). Conscientiousness. In M. Leary & R. Hoyle (Eds.), *Handbook of individual differences in social behavior.* New York, NY: Guilford.

Roberts, B. W. & Mroczek, D. K. (2008). Personality trait stability and change. *Current Directions in Psychological Science, 17,* 31–35.

Roberts, D. F. & Foehr, U. G. (2008). Trends in media use. *Future of Children, 18* (No. 1), 11–37.

Robins, R. W., Trzesniewski, K. H., Tracey, J. L., Potter, J., & Gosling, S. D. (2002). Age differences in self-esteem from age 9 to 90. *Psychology and Aging, 17,* 423–434.

Robinson, N. M. (2008). The social world of gifted children and youth. In S. I. Pfeiffer (Ed.), *Handbook of giftedness in children.* New York: Springer.

Robinson-Riegler, G. L., & Robinson-Riegler, B. (2008). *Cognitive psychology.* Boston: Allyn & Bacon.

Roblyer, M. D. (2006). *Integrating educational technology into teaching* (4th ed.). Upper Saddle River, NJ: Prentice Hall.

Roblyer, M. D., Edwards, J., & Havriluk, M. A. (1997). *Integrating educational technology into education.* Upper Saddle River, NJ: Merrill/Prentice Hall.

Rodriquez-Galindo, C. A. (2006, April). *What's left behind: Home and school understandings of*

literacy. Paper presented at the meeting of the American Educational Research Association, San Francisco.

Rogoff, B. (1990). *Apprenticeship in thinking.* New York: Oxford University Press.

Rogoff, B. (2003). *The cultural nature of human development.* New York: Oxford University Press.

Rogoff, B., Moore, L., Najafi, B., Dexter, A., Correa-Chavez, M., & Solis, J. (2007). Children's development of cultural repertoires through participation in everyday routines and practices. In J. E. Grusec & P. D. Hastings (Eds.), *Handbook of socialization.* New York: Guilford.

Rogoff, B., Turkanis, C. G., & Barlett, L. (Eds.). (2001). *Learning together. Children and adults in a school community.* New York: Oxford University Press.

Rohrbeck, C. A., Ginsburg-Block, M. D., Fantuzzo, J. W., & Miller, T. R. (2003). Peer-assisted learning interventions with elementary school students: A meta-analytic review. *Journal of Educational Psychology, 95,* 240–257.

Rosch, E. H. (1973). On the internal structure of perceptual and semantic categories. In T. E. Moore (Ed.), *Cognition and the acquisition of language.* New York: Academic Press.

Roscoe, R. D., & Chi, M. T. H. (2008). Tutor learning: The role of explaining and responding to questions. *Instructional Science, 36,* 321–350.

Rosenberg, M. S., Westling, D. L., & McLeskey, J. (2008). *Special education for today's teachers.* Upper Saddle River, NJ: Prentice Hall.

Rosenshine, B. (1971). *Teaching behaviors and student achievement.* London: National Foundation for Educational Research.

Rosenweig, M. R. & Bennett, E. L. (2009). The role of deliberate practice in the acquisition of expert performance. In D. Shanks (Ed.), *Psychology of Learning.* Thousand Oaks, CA: Sage.

Rosnow, R. L., & Rosenthal, R. (2008). *Beginning behavioral research* (6th ed.). Upper Saddle River, NJ: Prentice Hall.

Roth, W-M. (2007). Situating situated cognition. In J. L. Kincheloe, H. A. Raymond, & S. R. Steinberg (Eds.), *The Praeger handbook of education and psychology* (Vol. 4). Westport, CT: Praeger.

Rothbart, M. K. (2004). Temperament and the pursuit of an integrated developmental psychology. *Merrill-Palmer Quarterly, 50,* 492–505.

Rothbart, M. K. (2007). Temperament, development, and personality. *Current Directions in Psychological Science, 16,* 207–212.

Rothbart, M. K., & Bates, J. E. (2006). Temperament. In W. Damon & R. Lerner (Eds.), *Handbook of child psychology* (6th ed.). New York: Wiley.

Rothbart, M. K., & Garstein, M. A. (2008). Temperament. In M. M. Haith & J. B. Benson (Eds.), *Encyclopedia of infant and early childhood development.* Oxford, UK: Elsevier.

Rowe, M. (1986). Wait time: Slowing down may be a way of speeding up! *Journal of Teacher Education, 37,* 43–50.

Rowe, R. J. (Ed.). (1994). *Preschoolers as authors: Literacy learning in the social world of the classroom.* Cresskill, NJ: Hampton Press.

Rowley, J. B. (2009). *Becoming a high performance mentor.* Thousand Oaks, CA: Corwin.

Rowley, S. R., Kurtz-Costes, B., & Cooper, S. M. (2009, in press). The role of schooling in ethnic minority achievement and attainment. In J. Meece and J. Eccles (Eds), *Handbook of research on schools, schooling, and human development.*

Rubie-Davies, C. M. (2007). Classroom interactions: Exploring the practices of high- and low-expectation teachers. *British Journal of Educational Psychology, 77,* 289–306.

Rubin, K. H., Fredstrom, B., & Bowker, J. (2008, in press). Future directions in . . . friendship in childhood and early adolescence. *Social Development.*

Rubin, K. H., Bukowski, W., & Parker, J. (2006). Peer interactions, relationships, and groups. In W. Damon & R. Lerner (Eds.), *Handbook of child psychology* (6th ed.). New York: Wiley.

Ruble, D. N., Martin, C. L., & Berenbaum, S. A. (2006). Gender development. In W. Damon & R. Lerner (Eds.), *Handbook of child psychology* (6th ed.). New York: Wiley.

Rueda, R., & Yaden, D. B. (2006). The literacy education of linguistically and culturally diverse young children: An overview of outcomes, assessment, and large-scale interventions. In B. Spodek & O. N. Saracho (Eds.), *Handbook of research on the education of young children*. Mahwah, NJ: Erlbaum.

Rumberger, R. W. (1995). Dropping out of middle school: A multilevel analysis of students and schools. *American Education Research Journal, 3,* 583–625.

Rummell, N., & Spada, H. (2005). Learning to collaborate: An instructional approach to promoting collaborative problem solving in computer-mediated settings. *Journal of Learning Sciences, 14,* 201–241.

Runco, M. (2007). Human nature and personal creativity: An epistemological perspective. In R. Richards (Ed.), *Everyday creativity and new views of human nature: Psychological, social, and spiritual perspectives*. Washington, DC: American Psychological Association.

Rutter, M. (2007). Gene-environment interdependence. *Developmental Science, 10,* 12–18.

Rutter, M., & Schopler, E. (1987). Autism and pervasive developmental disorders: Concepts and diagnostic issues. *Journal of Autism and Pervasive Developmental Disorders, 17,* 159–186.

Rutter, T. (2005). *What separates problem readers from proficient ones? Virginia Mann focuses on three elements.* Retrieved April 20, 2005, from www.brainconnection.com/

S

Saarni, C. (1999). *The development of emotional competence*. New York: Guilford.

Saarni, C., Campos, J., Camras, L. A., & Witherington, D. (2006). Emotional development. In W. Damon & R. Lerner (Eds.), *Handbook of child psychology* (6th ed.). New York: Wiley.

Sabers, D. S., Cushing, K. J. & Berliner, D. C. (1991). Differences among teachers in a task characterized by simultaneity, multidimensionality, and immediacy. *American Educational Research Journal, 28,* 63–88.

Sachs, J. (2009). Communication development in infancy. In J. Berko Gleason & N. B. Ratner (Eds.), *The development of language* (7th ed.). Boston: Allyn & Bacon.

Sackett, P. R. Hardison, C. M., & Cullen, M. J. (2004). On interpreting stereotype threat as accounting for African American–White differences in cognitive tests. *American Psychologist, 59,* 7–13.

Sackett, P. R., Hardison, C. M., & Cullen, M. J. (2005). On interpreting research on stereotype threat and test performance. *American Psychologist, 60,* 271–272.

Sadker, D. M., Sadker, M. P., & Zittleman, K. R. (2008). *Teachers, schools, and society* (8th ed.). New York: McGraw-Hill

Sadker, D. M., & Sadker, M. P. (2005). *Teachers, schools, and society* (7th ed.). New York: McGraw-Hill.

Sadker, M. P., & Sadker, D. M. (1994). *Failing at fairness: How America's schools cheat girls*. New York: Scribners.

Saenz, L. M., Fuchs, L. S., & Fuchs, D. (2005). Peer-assisted learning strategies for English language learners with learning disabilities. *Exceptional Children, 71,* 231–247.

Salomon, G., & Perkins, D. (1989). Rocky roads to transfer: Rethinking mechanisms of a neglected phenomenon. *Educational Psychologist, 24,* 113–142.

Salovey, P., & Mayer, J. D. (1990). Emotional intelligence. *Imagination, Cognition, and Personality, 9,* 185–211.

Saltzstein, H. D. (2008). Moral development. In N. J. Salkind (Ed.), *Encyclopedia of educational psychology*. Thousand Oaks, CA: Sage.

Sanger, M. N. (2008). What we need to prepare teachers for the moral nature of their work. *Journal of Curriculum Studies, 40,* 169–185.

Sanson, A. V., & Rothbart, M. K. (1995). Child temperament and parenting. In M. H. Bornstein (Ed.), *Handbook of parenting* (Vol. 4). Hillsdale, NJ: Erlbaum.

Sanson, A. V., & Rothbart, M. K. (2002). Child temperament and parenting. In M. H. Bornstein (Ed.), *Handbook of parenting*. Mahwah, NJ: Erlbaum.

Santiago-Delefosse, M. J., & Delefosse, J. M. O. (2002). Three positions on child thought and language. *Theory and Psychology, 12,* 723–747.

Santrock, J. W., & Halonen, J. A. (2009). *Your guide to college success* (6th ed.). Belmont, CA: Wadsworth.

Savage, T. V., & Armstrong, D. G. (2008). *Effective teaching in elementary social studies* (6th ed.). Upper Saddle River, NJ: Prentice Hall.

Sax, G. (1997). *Principles of educational and psychological measurement and evaluation* (4th ed.). Belmont, CA: Wadsworth.

Scardamalia, M., & Bereiter, C. (1994). Computer support for knowledge-building communities. *Journal of the Learning Sciences, 3 (3),* 265–283.

Scardamalia, M., & Bereiter, C. (2006). Knowledge building: Theory, pedagogy, and technology. In R. K. Sawyer (Ed.), *Cambridge handbook of learning sciences*. New York: Oxford University Press.

Scardamalia, M., Bereiter, C., & Lamon, M. (1994). The CSILE Project: Trying to bring the classroom into the world. In K. McGilly (Ed.), *Classroom lessons*. Cambridge, MA: MIT Press.

Scarlett, W. G., Ponte, I. C., & Singh, J. P. (2009). *Approaches to behavior and classroom management*. Thousand Oaks, CA: Sage

Scarr, S., & Weinberg, R. A. (1983). The Minnesota Adoption Studies: Genetic differences and malleability. *Child Development, 54,* 253–259.

Schacter, D. L. (2000). Memory systems. In A. Kazdin (Ed.), *Encyclopedia of psychology*. Washington, DC, & New York: American Psychological Association and Oxford University Press.

Schacter, D. L. (2001). *The seven deadly sins of memory*. Boston: Houghton Mifflin.

Schader, R. (2008). Parenting. In N. J. Salking (Ed.), *Encyclopedia of educational psychology*. Thousand Oaks, CA: Sage.

Schaie, K. W. (2007). Generational differences: Age-period-cohort. In J. E. Birren (Ed.), *Encyclopedia of gerontology* (2nd ed.). San Diego: Academic Press.

Schauble, L., Beane, D. B., Coates, G. D., Martin, L. M. W., & Sterling, P. V. (1996). Outside classroom walls: Learning in informal environments. In L. Schauble & R. Glaser (Eds.), *Innovations in learning*. Mahwah, NJ: Erlbaum.

Schick, B., de Villiers, P., de Villiers, J., & Hoffmeister, R. (2007). Language and theory of mind: A study of deaf children. *Child Development, 78,* 376–396.

Schmidt, H. G., Loyens, S. M. M., Van Gog, T., & Paas, F. (2007). Problem-based learning is compatible with human cognitive architecture: Commentary on Kirschner, Sweller, and Clark (2006). *Educational Psychologist, 42,* 91–97.

Schmidt, J. A., Shumow, L., & Kacar, H. (2007). Adolescents' participation in service activities and its impact on academic, behavioral, and civic outcomes. *Journal of Youth and Adolescence, 36,* 127–140.

Schmidt, M. E., & Vandewater, E. A. (2008). Media and attention, cognition, and school achievement. *Future of Children, 18* (No. 1), 64–85.

Schneider, B., & Coleman, J. S. (1993). *Parents, their children, and schools*. Boulder, CO: Westview.

Schneider, W. (2004). Memory development in childhood. In U. Goswami (Ed.), *Blackwell handbook of childhood cognitive development*. Malden, MA: Blackwell.

Schneider, W., & Bjorklund, D. F. (1998). Memory. In W. Damon (Ed.), *Handbook of child psychology* (5th Ed.). New York: Wiley.

Schneider, W., & Pressley, M. (1997). *Memory development between 2 and 20* (2nd ed.). Mahwah, NJ: Erlbaum.

Schoenfeld, A. H. (2004). Multiple learning communities: Students, teachers, instructional designers, and researchers. *Journal of Curriculum Studies, 36,* 237–255.

Schoenfeld, A. H. (2006). Mathematics teaching and learning. In P. A. Alexander and P. H. Winne (Eds.), *Handbook of educational psychology* (2nd ed.). Mahwah, NJ: Erlbaum.

Schofield, J. W. (2006). Internet use in the schools: Promise and problems. In R. K. Sawyer (Ed.), *The Cambridge handbook of the learning sciences*. New York: Cambridge University Press.

Schofield, W. (2003). The colorblind perspective in school: Causes and consequences. In J. A. Banks & C. A. M. Banks (Eds.), *Multicultural education* (updated 4th ed.). New York: Wiley.

Schoon, I., Parsons, S., & Sacker, A. (2004). Socioeconomic adversity, educational resilience, and subsequent levels of adult adaptation. *Journal of Adolescent Research, 19,* 383–404.

Schraw, G. (2006). Knowledge structures and processes. In P. A. Alexander & P. H. Winne (Eds.), *Handbook of educational psychology* (2nd ed.), Mahwah, NJ: Erlbaum.

Schraw, G., Wadkins, T., & Olafson, L. (2007). Doing the things we do: A grounded theory of academic procrastination. *Journal of Educational Psychology, 99,* 12–25.

Schrum, L., & Berenfeld, B. (1997). *Teaching and learning in the information age: A guide to telecommunications*. Boston: Allyn & Bacon.

Schuh, K. (2001, April). *Teacher-centered and learner-centered: What's the relationship?* Paper presented at the meeting of the American Educational Research Association, Seattle.

Schultz, D. P., & Schultz, S. E. (2009). *Theories of personality* (9th ed.). Belmont, CA: Wadsworth.

Schunk, D. H. (2001). Social cognitive theory and self-regulated learning. In B. J. Zimmerman & D. H. Schunk (Eds.), *Self-regulated learning and achievement* (2nd ed.). Mahwah, NJ: Erlbaum.

Schunk, D. H. (2008). *Learning theories: An educational perspective* (5th ed.). Upper Saddle River, NJ: Prentice Hall.

Schunk, D. H., Pintrich, P. R., & Meece, J. L. (2008). *Motivation in education: Theory, research, and applications* (3rd ed.). Upper Saddle River, NJ: Prentice Hall.

Schunk, D. H., & Rice, J. M. (1989). Learning goals and children's reading comprehension. *Journal of Reading Behavior, 23,* 351–364.

Schunk, D. H., & Swartz, C. W. (1993). Goals and progressive feedback: Effects on self-efficacy and writing achievement. *Contemporary Educational Psychology, 18,* 337–354.

Schunk, D. H., & Zimmerman, B. J. (2006). Competence and control beliefs: Distinguishing the means and ends. In P. A. Alexander & P. H. Winne (Eds.), *Handbook of educational psychology* (2nd ed.). Mahwah, NJ: Erlbaum.

Schwab-Stone, M., & others. (1995). *New Haven Schools Social Development Project: 1994.* New Haven, CT: New Haven Public Schools.

Schwartz, D. L., Bransford, J. D., & Sears, D. (2005). Efficiency and innovation in transfer. In J. Mestre (Ed.), *Transfer of learning: Research and perspectives.* Greenwich, CT: Information Age Publishing.

Schwartz, D. L., Lin, X., Brophy, J., & Bransford, J. D. (1999). Toward the development of flexibly adaptive instructional designs. In C. M. Reigelut (Ed.), *Instructional design theories and models* (Vol. II). Mahwah, NJ: Erlbaum.

Schwartz, D. L., Varma, S., & Martin, L. (2008). Dynamic transfer and innovation. In S. Vosniadou (Ed.), *Handbook of conceptual change.* Clifton, NJ: Psychology Press.

Schwartz, J. E. (2008). *Elementary mathematics pedagogical content knowledge.* Boston: Allyn & Bacon.

Schweinhart, L. J. (1999, April). *Generalizing from High/Scope longitudinal studies.* Paper presented at the meeting of the Society for Research in Child Development, Albuquerque.

Sciutto, M. J., & Eisenberg, M. (2007). Evaluating the evidence for and against an overdiagnosis of ADHD. *Journal of Attention Disorders, 11,* 106–113.

Sears, D. A. (2006, June). Effects of innovation versus efficiency tasks on recall and transfer in individual and collaborative learning contexts. In *Proceedings of the 7th International Conference on Learning Sciences,* p. 681–687.

Sears, D. A. (2008). Unpublished review of J. W. Santrock's, *Educational psychology* (4th ed.). (New York: McGraw-Hill).

Segal, J. W. (1996). Foreword. In L. Schauble & R. Glaser (Eds.), *Innovations in learning.* Mahwah, NJ: Erlbaum.

Seiler, W. J., & Beall, M. (2008). *Communication* (7th ed.). Boston: Allyn & Bacon.

Seligson, T. (2005, February 20). They speak for success. *Parade Magazine.*

Sellers, R. M., Copeland-Linder, N., Martin, P. P., & Lewis, R. L. (2006). Racial identity matters: The relationship between racial discrimination and psychological functioning in African American adolescents. *Journal of Research on Adolescence, 16,* 187–216.

Sensenbaugh, R. (1995). Reading Recovery. *ERIC Clearinghouse on Reading, English, and Communication Digest, No. 106.*

Shah, A. K., & Oppenheimer, D. M. (2008). Heuristics made easy: An effort-reduction framework. *Psychological Bulletin, 134,* 207–222.

Shalev, R. S. (2004). Developmental dyscalculia. *Journal of Child Neurology, 19,* 765–771.

Shanks, D. (Ed.), (2009). *Psychology of learning.* Thousand Oaks, CA: Sage.

Sharan, S. (1990). Cooperative learning and helping behavior in the multi-ethnic classroom. In H. C. Foot, M. J. Morgan, & R. H. Shute (Eds.), *Children helping children.* New York: Wiley.

Sharan, S., & Sharan, S. (1992). *Expanding cooperative learning through group investigation.* New York: Teachers College Press.

Sharan, S., & Shaulov, A. (1990). Cooperative learning, motivation to learn, and academic achievement. In S. Sharan (Ed.), *Cooperative learning.* New York: Praeger.

Shastry, B. S. (2007). Developmental dyslexia: An update. *Journal of Human Genetics, 52,* 104–109.

Shaul, M. S. (2007). *No Child Left Behind Act: States face challenges measuring academic growth that education's initiatives may help address.* Washington, DC: Government Accountability Office.

Shaw, P., & others. (2008). Neurodevelopmental trajectories of the human cerebral cortex. *Journal of Neuroscience, 28,* 3586–3594.

Shaw, P., Eckstrand, K., Sharp, W., Blumenthal, J., Lerch, J. P., Greenstein, D., Clasen, L., Evans, A., Giedd, J., & Rapoport, J. L. (2007). Attention-deficit/hyperactivity disorder is characterized by a delay in cortical maturation. *Proceedings of the National Academy of Sciences, 104* (No. 49). 19649–19654.

Shaywitz, B. A., Lyon, G. R., & Shaywitz, S. E. (2006). The role of functional magnetic resonance imaging in understanding reading and dyslexia. *Developmental Neuropsychology, 30,* 613–632.

Shaywitz, S. E., Gruen, J. R., & Shaywitz, B. A. (2007). Management of dyslexia, its rationale, and underlying neurobiology. *Pediatric Clinics of North America, 54,* 609–623.

Shaywitz, S. E., Morris, R., & Shaywitz, B. A. (2008). The education of dyslexic children from childhood to young adulthood. *Annual Review of Psychology* (Vol. 59). Palo Alto, CA: Annual Reviews.

Shea, S. E., & Coyne, L. W. (2008). Parenting styles. In N. J. Salkind (Ed.), *Encyclopedia of educational psychology.* Thousand Oaks, CA: Sage.

Sheldon, S. B., & Epstein, J. L. (2005). School programs of family and community involvement to support children's reading and literacy involvement across the grades. In J. Flood & P. Anders (Eds.), *Literacy development of students in urban schools.* Newark

Shen, J., Poppink, S., Cui, Y., & Fan, G. (2007). Lesson planning: A practice of professional responsibility and development. *Educational Horizons, 85,* 248–258.

Shen, J., Zhen, J., & Poppink, S. (2007). Open lessons: A practice to develop a learning community for teachers. *Educational Horizons, 85,* 181–191.

Sherblom, S. (2008). The legacy of the "care challenge": Re-envisioning the outcome of the justice-care debate. *Journal of Moral Education, 37,* 81–98.

Sherin, M. G., Mendez, E. P., & Louis, D. A. (2004). A discipline apart: The challenges of "Fostering a Community of Learners" in a mathematics classroom. *Journal of Curriculum Studies, 36,* 207–232.

Sherman, C. W., & Mueller, D. P. (1996, June). *Developmentally appropriate practice and student achievement in inner-city elementary schools.* Paper presented at Head Start's Third National Research Conference, Washington, DC.

Shields, P. M., & others. (2001). *The status of the teaching profession 2001.* Santa Cruz, CA: The Center for the Future of Teaching and Learning.

Shields, S. A. (1991). Gender in the psychology of emotion: A selective research review. In K. T. Strongman (Ed.), *International review of studies on emotion* (Vol. 1). New York: Wiley.

Shiraev, E., & Levy, D. A. (2007). *Cross-cultural psychology* (3rd ed.). Boston: Allyn & Bacon.

Shirts, R. G. (1997). *BAFA, BAFA, a cross-cultural simulation.* Del Mar, CA: SIMILE II.

Shorall, C. (2009). *What every teacher should know about the Praxis II test* (3rd ed.). Upper Saddle River, NJ: Prentice Hall.

Shulman, L. S., & Shulman, J. H. (2004). How and what teachers learn: A shifting perspective. *Journal of Curriculum Studies, 36,* 257–274.

Siegel, L. S. (2003). Learning disabilities. In I. B. Weiner (Ed.), *Handbook of psychology* (Vol. 7). New York: Wiley.

Siegler, R.S. (1998). *Children's thinking* (3rd ed.). Upper Saddle River, NJ: Prentice Hall.

Siegler, R. S. (2002). Microgenetic studies of self-explanation. In N. Garnott & J. Parziale (Eds.), *Microdevelopment: A process-oriented perspective for studying development and learning.* New York: Cambridge University Press.

Siegler, R. S. (2006). Microgenetic analysis of learning. In W. Damon & R. Lerner (Eds.), *Handbook of child psychology* (6th ed.). New York: Wiley.

Siegler, R. S. (2007). Cognitive variability. *Developmental Science 10,* 104–109.

Siegler, R. S., & Alibali, M. W. (2005). *Children's thinking* (4th ed.). Upper Saddle River, NJ: Prentice Hall.

Siegler, R. S., & Chen, Z. (2008). Differentiation and integration: Guiding principles for analyzing cognitive change. *Developmental Science, 11,* 433–438.

Siegler, R. S., & Robinson, M. (1982). The development of numerical understanding. InH. W. Reese & L. P. Litsitt (Eds.), *Advances in child development and behavior* (Vol. 12). New York: Academic Press.

Silva, C. (2005, October 31). When teen dynamo talks, city listens. *Boston Globe,* pp. B1, B4.

Silvernail, D. L., & Lane, D. M. M. (2004). *The impact of Maine's one-to-one laptop program on middle school teachers and students.* (Report #1). Gorham, ME: Maine Education Policy Research Institute, University of Southern Maine Office.

Sim, T. N., & Ong, L. P. (2005). Parent punishment and child aggression in a Singapore Chinese preschool sample. *Journal of Marriage and the Family, 67,* 85–99.

Simons, J., Finlay, B., & Yang, A. (1991). *The adolescent and young adult fact book.* Washington, DC: Children's Defense Fund.

Simos, P. G., Fletcher, J. M., Sarkari, S., Billingsley, R. L., Denton, C., & Papanicolaou, A. C. (2007). Altering the brain circuits for reading through intervention: A magnetic source imaging study. *Neuropsychology, 21,* 485–496.

Simpkins, S. D., Fredricks, J. A., Davis-Kean, P. E., & Eccles, J. S. (2006). Healthy mind, healthy habits: The influence of activity involvement in middle childhood. In A. C. Huston and M. N. Ripke (Eds.), *Developmental context in middle childhood.* New York: Cambridge University Press.

Simpson, R. L., & LaCava, P. G. (2008). Autism spectrum disorders. In N. J. Salkind (Ed.), *Encyclopedia of educational psychology.* Thousand Oaks, CA: Sage.

Singer, D. G., & Singer, J. L. (1987). Practical suggestions for controlling television. *Journal of Early Adolescence, 7,* 365–369.

Skaalvik, E. M., & Skaalvik, S. (2007). Dimensions of teacher self-efficacy and its relations to strain factors, perceived collective teacher self-efficacy, and teacher burnout. *Journal of Educational Psychology, 99,* 611–625.

Skarakis-Doyle, E. (2008). Language disorders. In N. J. Salkind (Ed.), *Encyclopedia of educational psychology.* Thousand Oaks, CA: Sage.

Skidmore, D. (2009). Race and special education. In P. Hick & G. Thomas (Eds.), *Inclusion and diversity in education.* Thousand Oaks, CA: Sage.

Skinner, B. F. (1938). *The behavior of organisms.* New York: Appleton-Century-Crofts.

Skinner, B. F. (1954). The science of learning and the art of teaching. *Harvard Educational Review, 24*, 86–97.

Skinner, B. F. (1957). *Verbal behavior.* New York: Appleton-Century-Crofts.

Skinner, B. F. (1958). Teaching machines. *Science, 128*, 969–977.

Slade, E. P., & Wissow, L. S. (2004). Spanking in early childhood and later behavior problems: A prospective study. *Pediatrics, 113*, 1321–1330.

Slavin, R. E. (1990). Achievement effects of ability grouping in secondary schools: A best-evidence synthesis. *Review of Educational Research, 60*, 471–500.

Slavin, R. E. (1995). *Cooperative learning: Theory, research, and practic* (2nd ed.). Boston: Allyn & Bacon.

Slavin, R. E., Daniels, C., & Madden, N. A. (2005). "Success for All" middle schools add content to middle grades reform. *Middle School Journal, 36* (5), 1–8.

Slavin, R. E., Madden, N. A., Chambers, B., & Haxby, B. (2009). *2 million children* (2nd ed.). Thousand Oaks, CA: Sage.

Slavin, R. E., Madden, N. A., Dolan, L. J., & Wasik, B. A. (1996). *Every child, every school: Success for all.* Newbury Park, CA: Corwin Press.

Slotta, J. D., & Chi, M. T. H. (2008). The impact of ontology training on conceptual change: Helping students understand the challenging topics in science. *Cognition and Instruction.*

Smaldino, S. E., Lowther, D. L., & Russell, J. D. (2008). *Instructional technology and media for learning* (9th ed.). Upper Saddle River, NJ: Prentice Hall.

Smalls, C., White, R., Chavous, T., & Sellers, R. (2007). Racial ideological beliefs and racial discrimination experiences as predictors of academic engagement among African American adolescents. Manuscript accepted for publication in *Journal of Black Psychology, 33*, 299–330.

Smith, P. K., Mahdavi, J., Carvalho, M., Fisher, S., Russell, S., & Tippett, N. (2008). Cyberbullying: Its nature and impact in secondary school pupils. *Journal of Child Psychology and Psychiatry, 49*, 376–385.

Smith, S. D., & Bulman-Fleming, M. B. (2005). An examination of the right-hemisphere hypothesis of the lateralization of emotion. *Brain and Cognition, 57*, 210–213.

Smith, S. S. (2006). *Early childhood mathematics* (3rd ed.). Boston: Allyn & Bacon.

Smith, T. E. C., Polloway, E. A., Patton, J. R., & Dowdy, C. A. (2008). *Teaching students with special needs in inclusive settings* (5th ed.). Boston: Allyn & Bacon.

Smoll, F. L., & Schutz, R. W. (1990). Quantifying gender differences in physical performance: A developmental perspective. *Developmental Psychology, 26*, 360–369.

Smyth, M. M., Collins, A. F., Morris, P. E., & Levy, P. (1994). *Cognition in action* (2nd ed.). Hove, UK: Erlbaum.

Snell, M. E., & Janney, R. E. (2005). *Practices for inclusive schools: Collaborative teaming* (2nd ed.). Baltimore: Brookes.

Snow, C. E. & Kang, J. Y. (2006). Becoming bilingual, biliterate, and bicultural. In W. Damon & R. Lerner (Eds.), *Handbook of child psychology* (6th ed.). New York: Wiley.

Snow, R. E., Como, L., & Jackson, D. (1996). Individual differences in affective and cognitive functions. In D. C. Berliner & R. C. Calfee (Eds.), *Handbook of educational psychology.* New York: Macmillan.

Snowling, M. (2008). Reading intervention for children with specific language impairment. In C. Norbury, B. Tomblin, & D. Bishop (Eds.), *Understanding developmental language disorders in children.* Milton Park, UK: Routledge.

Soares, D., & Vannest, K. J. (2008). Cognitive behavior modification. In N. J. Salkind (Ed.), *Encyclopedia of educational psychology.* Thousand Oaks, CA: Sage.

Soderman, A. K., & Farrell, P. (2008). *Creating literacy-rich preschools and kindergartens.* Boston: Allyn & Bacon.

Soenens, B., Vansteenkiste, M., Goosens, L., Duriez, B., & Niemiec, C. P. (2008). The intervening role of relational aggression between psychological control and friendship quality. *Social Development, 17*, 661–681.

Solano-Flores, G., & Shavelson, R. J. (1997). Using interactive lecture demonstration to create an active learning environment. *American Journal of Physics, 64*, 338–352.

Solimeno, A., Mebane, M. E., Tomai, M., & Francescato, D. (2008). The influence of students' and teachers' characteristics on the efficacy of face-to-face and computer-supported collaborative learning. *Computers and Education, 51*, 109–128.

Solomon, D., Watson, M. S., & Battistich, V. A. (2002). Teaching and school effects on moral/prosocial development. In V. Richardson (Ed.), *Handbook for research on teaching.* Washington, DC: American Educational Research Association.

Solso, R. L., MacLin, O. H., & MacLin, M. K. (2008). *Cognitive psychology* (8th ed.). Boston: Allyn & Bacon.

Soltesz, F., Szucs, D., Dekany, J., Markus, A., & Csepe, V. (2007). A combined event-related potential and neuropsychological investigation of developmental dyscalculia. *Neuroscience Letters, 417*, 181–186.

Song, S. Y., & Siegel, N. M. (2008). Peer influences. In N. J. Salkind (Ed.), *Encyclopedia of educational psychology.* Thousand Oaks, CA: Sage.

Soto, C. J., John, O. P., Gosling, S. D., & Potter, J. (2008). The development of psychometrics of big five reports: Acquiescence, factor structure, coherence, and differentiation from ages 10 to 20. *Journal of Personality and Social Psychology, 94*, 718–73

Soukup, M., & Feinstein, S. (2007). Identification, assessment, and intervention strategies for deaf and hard of hearing students with learning disabilities. *American Annals of the Deaf, 152*, 56–62.

Sousa, D. A. (1995). *How the brain learns: A classroom teacher's guide.* Reston, VA: National Association of Secondary School Principals.

South, M., Ozonoff, S., & McMahon, W. M. (2005). Repetitive behavior profiles in Asperger syndrome and high-functioning autism. *Journal of Autism and Developmental Disorders, 35*, 145–158.

Sowell, E. R., Thompson, P. M., Leonard, C. M., Welcome, S. E., Kan, E., & Toga, A. W. (2004). Longitudinal mapping of cortical thickness and brain growth in children. *Journal of Neuroscience, 24*, 8223–8231.

Spear, L. P. (2007). Brain development and adolescent behavior. In D. Coch, K. W. Fischer, & G. Dawson (Eds.), *Human behavior: Learning and the developing brain.* New York: Guilford.

Spence, J. T., & Buckner, C. E. (2000). Instrumental and expressive traits, trait stereotypes, and sexist attitudes: What do they signify? *Psychology of Women Quarterly, 24*, 44–62.

Spence, J. T., & Helmreich, R. (1978). *Masculinity and feminity: Their psychological dimensions.* Austin: University of Texas Press.

Spencer, M. B. (2006). Phenomenology and ecological systems theory. In W. Damon & R. Lerner (Eds.), *Handbook of child psychology* (6th ed.). New York: Wiley.

Spencer, R. (2007). "It's not what you expected": A qualitative study of youth mentoring relationship failures. *Journal of Adolescent Research, 22*, 331–354.

Spironelli, C., & Angrilli, A. (2008, in press). Developmental aspects of automatic word processing: Language lateralization of early ERP components in children, young adults, and middle-aged adults. *Biological Psychology.*

Spring, J. (2008). *American education* (13th ed.). New York: McGraw-Hill.

Squire, L. (1987). *Memory and brain.* New York: Oxford University Press.

Srabstein, J. C., McCarter, R. J., Shao, C., & Huang, Z. J. (2006). Morbidities associated with bullying behaviors in adolescents: School based study of American adolescents. *International Journal of Adolescent Medicine and Health, 18*, 587–596.

Sraiheen, A., & Lesisko, L. J. (2006). Grade inflation: An elementary and secondary perspective. *ERIC Documents, ED490038.*

Sroufe, L. A. (2007). Commentary: The place of development in developmental psychology. In A. Masten (Ed.), *Multilevel dynamics in developmental psychology.* Mahwah, NJ: Erlbaum.

Sroufe, L. A., Cooper, R. G., DeHart, G., and Bronfenbrenner, U. (1992). *Child development: Its nature and course* (2nd ed.). New York: McGraw-Hill.

Stahl, S. (2002, January). *Effective reading instruction in the first grade.* Paper presented at the Michigan Reading Recovery conference, Dearborn, MI.

Stalnaker, R. C. (2008). The problem of deduction. In J. E. Adler & L. J. Rips (Eds.), *Reasoning.* New York: Cambridge University Press.

Stanovich, K. (2007). *How to think straight about psychology* (8th ed.). Boston: Allyn & Bacon.

Stanovich, K. E. (1994). Romance and reality. *Reading Teacher, 47*, 280–291.

Stanovich, K. E., & West, R. F. (2008). On the relative independence of thinking biases and cognitive ability. *Journal of Personality and Social Psychology, 94*, 672–695.

Steel, P. (2007). The nature of procrastination: A meta-analytic and theoretical review of quintessential self-regulatory failure. *Psychological Bulletin, 133*, 65–94.

Steele, C. M., & Aronson, J. A. (2004). Stereotype threat does not live by Steele and Aronson (1995) alone. *American Psychologist, 59*, 47–48.

Stein, D. J., Fan, J., Fossella, J., & Russell, V. A. (2007). Inattention and hyperactivity-impulsivity: Psychobiological and evolutionary underpinnings. *CNS Spectrum, 12*, 190–196.

Steinberg, L. (2004). Risk taking in adolescence: What changes, and why? *Annals of the New York Academy of Sciences, 1021*, 59–60.

Steinberg, L. (2007). Risk-taking in adolescence: New perspectives from brain and behavioral science. *Current Directions in Psychological Science, 16*, 55–59.

Steinberg, L. (2008). A social neuroscience perspective on adolescent risk-taking. *Developmental Review, 28*, 78–106.

Stephens, J. M. (2008). Cheating. In N. J. Salkind (Ed.), *Encyclopedia of educational psychology.* Thousand Oaks, CA: Sage.

Sternberg, R. J. (1986). *Intelligence applied.* Fort Worth, TX: Harcourt Brace.

Sternberg, R. J. (1993). *Sternberg Triarchic Abilities Test (STAT).* Unpublished test, Department of Psychology, Yale University, New Haven, CT.

Sternberg, R. J. (1997). *Thinking styles.* New York: Cambridge University Press.

Sternberg, R. J. (2002). Intelligence: The triarchic theory of intelligence. In J. W. Gutherie (Ed.), *Encyclopedia of education* (2nd ed.). New York: Macmillan.

Sternberg, R. J. (2006). *Cognitive psychology* (4th ed.). Belmont, CA: Wadsworth.

Sternberg, R. J. (2007a). g, g's, or jeez: Which is the best model for developing abilities, competencies, and expertise? In P. C. Kyllonen, R. D. Roberts, & L. Stankov (Eds.), *Extending intelligence: Enhancement and new constructs* (pp. 250–265). Mahwah, NJ: Lawrence Erlbaum Associates.

Sternberg, R. J. (2007b). Finding students who are wise, practical, and creative. *The Chronicle of Higher Education, 53* (44), B11.

Sternberg, R. J. (2008a). The triarchic theory of successful intelligence. In N. Salkind (Ed.), *Encyclopedia of educational psychology.* Thousand Oaks, CA: Sage.

Sternberg, R. J. (2008b). The triarchic theory of successful intelligence. In B. Kerr (Ed.), *Encyclopedia of giftedness, creativity, and talent.* Thousand Oaks, CA: Sage.

Sternberg, R. J. (2008c). Schools should nurture wisdom. In B. Z. Presseisen (Ed.), *Teaching for intelligence* (2nd ed., pp. 61–88). Thousand Oaks, CA: Corwin.

Sternberg, R. J. (2008d, in press). Wisdom, intelligence, creativity, synthesized: A model of giftedness. In T. Balchin, B. Hymer, & D. Matthews (Eds.), *International Companion to Gifted Education.* London: Routledge Falmer.

Sternberg, R. J. (2008e, in press). Successful intelligence as a framework for understanding cultural adaptation. In S. Ang & L. Van Dyne (Eds.), *Handbook on cultural intelligence.* New York: M. E. Sharpe.

Sternberg, R. J. (2009a). *Cognitive psychology* (5th ed.). Belmont, CA: Wadsworth.

Sternberg, R. J. (2009b). The triarchic theory of successful intelligence. In B. Kerr (Ed.), *Encyclopedia of giftedness, creativity, and talent.* Thousand Oaks, CA: Sage.

Sternberg, R. J. (2009b). Wisdom. In S. J. Lopez (Ed.) *Encyclopedia of Positive Psychology.* Blackwell Publishing.

Sternberg, R. J. (2009c). Teaching for creativity. In R. A. Beghetto & J. C. Kaufman (Eds.), *Nurturing creativity in the classroom.* New York: Cambridge University Press.

Sternberg, R. J., & Ben-Zeev, T. (2001). *Complex cognitive processes.* New York: Oxford University Press.

Sternberg, R. J., Castejon, J. L., Prieto, M. D., Hautamäki, J., & Grigorenko, E. L. (2001a). Confirmatory factory analysis of the Sternberg triarchic abilities test in three international samples: An empirical test of the triarchic theory of intelligence.

Sternberg, R. J., & Clinkenbeard, P. R. (1995, May/June). The triarchic model applied to identifying, teaching, and assessing gifted children. *Roeper Review,* 255–260.

Sternberg, R. J., & Grigorenko, E. L. (2007). *Teaching for successful intelligence* (2nd ed.). Thousand Oaks, CA: Corwin Press.

Sternberg, R. J., & Grigorenko, E. L. (2008). Ability testing across cultures. In L. Suzuki (Ed.), *Handbook of multicultural assessment* (3rd ed.). New York: Jossey-Bass

Sternberg, R. J., Jarvin, L. & Reznitskaya, A. (2009). Teaching for wisdom through history: Infusing wise thinking skills in the school curriculum. In M. Ferrari (Ed.), *Teaching for Wisdom.* Amsterdam: Springer.

Sternberg, R. J., Jarvin, L., & Grigorenko, E. L. (2009). *Teaching for intelligence, creativity, and success.* Thousand Oaks, CA: Corwin.

Sternberg, R. J., Kaufman, J., & Grigorenko, E. L. (2008). *Applied intelligence.* New York: Cambridge University Press.

Sternberg, R. J., & Spear-Swerling, P. (1996). *Teaching for thinking.* Washington, DC: American Psychological Association.

Sternberg, R. J., & the Rainbow Project Collaborators. (2006). The Rainbow Project: Enhancing the SAT through assessments of analytical, practical, and creative skills. *Intelligence, 34,* 321–350.

Sternberg, R. J., & Williams, W. M. (1996). *How to develop student creativity.* Alexandria, VA: ASCD.

Stevens, R. J. (2008). Cooperative learning. In N. J. Salkind (Ed.), *Encyclopedia of educational psychology.* Thousand Oaks, CA: Sage.

Stevenson, H. W. (1992, December). Learning from Asian schools. *Scientific American,* pp. 6, 70–76.

Stevenson, H. W. (1995). Mathematics achievement of American students: First in the world by 2000? In C. A. Nelson (Ed) *Basic and applied perspectives in learning, cognition, and development.* Minneapolis: University of Minnesota Press.

Stevenson, H. W. (2000). Middle childhood: Education and schooling. In A. Kazdin (Ed.), *Encyclopedia of psychology.* Washington, DC, & New York: American Psychological Association and Oxford University Press.

Stevenson, H. W. (2001). *Commentary on NCTM standards.* Department of Psychology, University of Michigan, Ann Arbor.

Stevenson, H. W., & Hofer, B. K. (1999). Education policy in the United States and abroad: What we can learn from each other. In G. J. Cizek (Ed.), *Handbook of educational policy.* San Diego: Academic Press.

Stevenson, H. W., Lee, S., Chen, C., Stigler, J. W., Hsu, C., & Kitamura, S. (1990). Contexts of achievement. *Monographs of the Society for Research in Development, 55* (Serial No. 221).

Stevenson, H. W., Lee, S., & Stigler, J. W. (1986). Mathematics achievement of Chinese, Japanese, and American children. *Science, 231,* 693–699.

Stewart, J. (2009). *Bridges not walls: A book about interpersonal communication* (10th ed.). New York: McGraw-Hill.

Stiggins, R. J. (2001). *Student-involved classroom assessment* (3rd ed.). Upper Saddle River, NJ: Prentice Hall .

Stiggins, R. J. (2008). *Introduction to student-involved assessment for learning* (5th ed.). Upper Saddle River, NJ: Prentice Hall.

Stipek, D. J. (2002). *Motivation to learn* (4th ed.). Boston: Allyn & Bacon.

Stipek, D. J. (2005, February 16). Commentary in *USA Today,* p. 1D.

Stipek, D. J., Feiler, R., Daniels, D., & Milburn, S. (1995). Effects of different instructional approaches on young children's achievement and motivation. *Child Development, 66,* 209–223.

Stop Cyberbullying. (2008). Retrieved January 16, 2008, from www.stopcyberbullying.com/

Stover, D. (2007). The big fixes now needed for "No Child Left Behind." *Education Digest, 72,* 4–11.

Strasburger, V. C., Wilson, B. J., & Jordan, A. (2008). *Children, adolescents, and the media.* Thousand Oaks, CA: Sage.

Straus, M. A. (1991). Discipline and deviance: Physical punishment of children and violence and other crimes in adulthood. *Social Problems, 38,* 133–154.

Strenze, T. (2007). Intelligence and socioeconomic success: A meta-analytic review of longitudinal research. *Intelligence, 35,* 401–426.

Stringer, E. (2008). *Action research in education* (2nd ed.). Upper Saddle River, NJ: Prentice Hall.

Strong-Wilson, T., & Ellis, J. (2007). Children and place: Reggio Emilia's environment as third teacher. *Theory into Practice, 46,* 40–47.

Struckman, A. (2005). Classwide peer tutoring. In S. W. Lee (Ed.), *Encyclopedia of school psychology.* Thousand Oaks, CA: Sage.

Studer, J. (2009). Teacher as family communication facilitator. In K. B. Grant & J. A. Ray (Eds.), *Home, school, and community collaboration.* Thousand Oaks, CA: Corwin.

Suen, H. K. (2008). Measurement. In N. J. Salkind (Ed.), *Encyclopedia of educational psychology.* Thousand Oaks, CA: Sage.

Sunal, C. S., & Haas, M. E. (2008). *Social studies for the elementary and middle grades: A constructivist approach* (3rd ed.). Boston: Allyn & Bacon.

Supovitz, J. A., & Brennan, R. T. (1997, Fall). Mirror, mirror on the wall, which is the fairest test of all? An examination of the equality of portfolio assessment relative to standardized tests. *Harvard Educational Review, 67* (3), 472–501.

Suthers, D., Weiner, A., Connelly, J., & Paolucci, M. (1995, August). *Engaging students in critical discussion of science and public policy issues.* Paper presented at the 7th World Conference on Artificial Intelligence, Washington, DC.

Suyemoto, K. L. (2009). Multiracial Asian Americans. In N. Tewari & A. Alvarez (Eds.), *Asian American psychology.* Clifton, NJ: Psychology Press.

Swan, K., Cook, D., Kratcoski, A., Lin, Y., Schenker, J., & van't Hooft, M. (2006). Ubiquitous computing: Rethinking teaching, learning and technology integration. In S. Tettegah & R. Hunter (Eds.), *Educational and technology: Issues and applications, policy, and administration.* New York: Elsevier.

Swan, K., Kratcoski, A., van't Hooft, M., Campbell, D., & Miller, D. (2007). *Technology support for whole group engagement: A pilot study. Advanced Technologies for Learning, 4* (2), 68–73.

Swan, K., van't Hooft, M., Kratcoski, A., & Unger, D. (2005). Uses and effects of mobile computing devices in K–8 classrooms: a preliminary study. *Journal of Research on Technology and Education, 38* (1), 99–112.

Swanson, H. L. (1999). What develops in working memory? A life-span perspective. *Developmental Psychology, 35,* 986–1000.

Swanson, L., & Kim, K. (2007). Working memory, short-term memory, and naming speed as predictors of children's mathematical performance. *Intelligence, 35,* 151–168.

Sykes, C. J. (1995). *Dumbing down our kids: Why American children feel good about themselves but can't read, write, or add.* New York: St. Martin's Press.

Szucs, D., & Goswami, U. (2008, in press). Educational neuroscience: Defining a new discipline for the study of mental representations. *Mind, Brain, and Education.*

T

Tager-Flusberg, H. (2005). Putting words together: Morphology and syntax. In J. Berko Gleason (Ed.), *The development of language* (6th ed.). Boston: Allyn & Bacon.

Tager-Flusberg, H., & Zukowski, A. (2009). Putting words together: Morphology and syntax in the preschool years. In J. Berko Gleason & N. Ratner (Eds.), *The development of language* (7th ed.). Boston: Allyn & Bacon.

Tamis-LeMonda, C. S., Way, N., Hughes, D., Yoshikawa, H., Kallman, R. K., & Niwa, E. Y. (2008). Parents' goals for children: The dynamic coexistence of individualism and collectivism in cultures and individuals. *Social Development, 17,* 183–209.

Tandogan, R. O., & Ozkardes, R., & Orhan, A. (2007). The effects of problem-based active learning in science education on students' academic achievement, attitude, and concept learning. *Eurasia Journal of Mathematics, Science, and Technology, 3,* 71–81.

Tannen, D. (1990). *You just don't understand!* New York: Ballantine.

Tanner, J. M. (1978). *Fetus into man.* Cambridge, MA: Harvard University Press.

Tarhan, L., & Acar, B. (2007). Problem-based learning in an eleventh grade chemistry class: "Factors affecting cell potential." *Research in Science & Technological Education, 25,* 351–369.

Tartaglia, N. R., Hansen, R. L., & Hagerman, R. J. (2007). Advances in genetics. In S. L. Odom, R. H. Horner, M. E. Snell, & J. Blacher (Eds.), *Handbook of developmental disabilities.* New York: Guilford.

Tassell-Baska, J., & Stambaugh, T. (2006). *Comprehensive curriculum for gifted learners* (3rd ed.). Boston: Allyn & Bacon.

Taylor, C. (1994). Assessment of measurement or standards: The peril and the promise of large-scale assessment reform. *American Educational Research Journal, 32,* 231–262.

Taylor, C., & Nolen, S. B. (2008). *Classroom assessment* (2nd ed.). Upper Saddle River, NJ: Prentice Hall.

Taylor, L. S., & Whittaker, C. R. (2009). *Bridging multiple worlds* (2nd ed.). Boston: Allyn & Bacon.

Taylor, R. D., & Lopez, E. I. (2005). Family management practice, school achievement, and problem behavior in African American adolescents: Mediating processes. *Applied Developmental Psychology, 26,* 39–49.

Taylor, R. L., Brady, M., & Richards, S. B. (2005). *Mental retardation.* Boston: Allyn & Bacon.

Taylor, R. L., Smiley, L., & Richards, S. B. (2009). *Exceptional students.* New York: McGraw-Hill.

Taylor, S. E., & Stanton, A. L. (2007). Coping resources, coping processes, and mental health. *Annual Review of Clinical Psychology* (Vol. 3). Palo Alto, CA: Annual Reviews.

Tenenbaum, H. R., Callahan, M., Alba-Speyer, C., & Sandoval, L. (2002). Parent-child science conversations in Mexican descent families: Educational background, activity, and past experience as moderators. *Hispanic Journal of Behavioral Science, 24,* 225–248.

Tennyson, R., & Cocchiarella, M. (1986). An empirically based instructional design theory for teaching concepts. *Review of Educational Research, 56,* 40–71.

Terman, D. L., Larner, M. B., Stevenson, C. S., & Behrman, R. E. (1996). Special education for students with disabilities: Analysis and recommendations. *Future of Children, 6* (1), 4–24.

Terry, W. S. (2006). *Learning and memory* (3rd ed.). Boston: Allyn & Bacon.

Terwilliger, J. (1997). Semantics, psychometrics, and assessment reform: A close look at "authentic" assessments. *Educational Researcher, 26,* 24–27.

Tewari, N., & Alvarez, A. (Eds.). (2009). *Asian American psychology.* Clifton, NJ: Psychology Press.

Thomas, A., & Chess, S. (1991). Temperament in adolescence and its functional significance. In R. M. Lerner, A. C. Petersen, & J. Brooks-Gunn (Eds.), *Encyclopedia of adolescence* (Vol. 2). New York: Garland.

Thomas, C. R., & Gadbois, S. A. (2007). Academic self-handicapping: The role of self-concept clarity and students' learning strategies. *British Journal of Educational Psychology, 77,* 109–119.

Thomas, J. R., & Thomas, K. T. (1988). Developmental gender differences in physical activity. *Quest, 40,* 219–229.

Thomas, M. S. C., & Johnson, M. H. (2008). New advances in understanding sensitive periods in brain development. *Current Directions in Psychological Science, 17,* 1–5.

Thomas, R. M. (2005). *Teachers doing research.* Boston: Allyn & Bacon.

Thomas, V., Ray, K., & Moon, S. M. (2007). Counseling gifted individuals and their families: A systems perspective. In S. Mendaglio & J. Peterson (Eds.), *Counseling the gifted.* Waco, TX: Prufrock Press.

Thompson, J. G. (2008). *First year teacher's survival guide* (2nd ed.). San Francisco: Jossey-Bass.

Thompson, P. M., Giedd, J. N., Woods, R. P., MacDonald, D., Evans, A. C., & Toga, A. W. (2000). Growth patterns in the developing brain detected by using continuum mechanical tensor maps. *Nature, 404,* 190–193.

Thompson, R. A. (2008). Unpublished review of J. W. Santrock's Life-span development, 12th ed. (New York: McGraw-Hill).

Thompson, R. A., Meyer, S. C., & Jochem, R. (2008). Emotion regulation. In M. M. Haith & J. B. Benson (Eds.), *Encyclopedia of infant and early childhood development.* Oxford, UK: Elsevier.

Thompson, T., Moore, T., & Symons, F. (2007). Psychotherapeutic medications and positive behavior support. In S. L. Odom, R. H. Horner, M. E. Snell, & J. Blacher (Eds.), *Handbook of developmental disabilities.* New York: Guilford.

Thornton, C. D., & Goldstein, L. S. (2006). Feminist issues in early childhood scholarship. In B. Spodek & O. N. Saracho (Eds.), *Handbook of research on the education of young children.* Mahwah, NJ: Erlbaum.

Thorsen, C. (2009). *Techtactics.* Boston: Allyn & Bacon.

Thurgood, S. (2001). Inside home visits: Response from the Early Head Start program director. *Early Childhood Research Quarterly, 16,* 73–75.

Tierney, R., & Charland, J. (2007, April). *Stocks and prospects: Research on formative assessment in secondary classrooms.* Paper presented at the meeting of the American Educational Research Association, Chicago.

Tileston, D., & Darling, S. (2008). *Teaching strategies that prepare students for high-stakes tests.* Thousand Oaks, CA: Corwin.

Tillema, H., & Smith, K. (2007). Portfolio appraisal: In search of criteria. *Teaching and Teacher Education, 23,* 442–456.

Toga, A. W., Thompson, P. M., & Sowell, E. R. (2006). Mapping brain maturation. *Trends in Neurosciences, 29,* 148–159.

Tolchinsky, L. (2002). *The child's path to writing and numbers.* Mahwah, NJ: Erlbaum.

Tollefson, N. (2005). Grade-equivalent scores. In S. W. Lee (Ed.), *Encyclopedia of school psychology.* Thousand Oaks, CA: Sage.

Tomlinson, C. A. (2006). *An educator's guide to differentiating instruction.* Boston: Houghton Mifflin.

Tompkins, G. E. (2009). *Language arts* (7th ed.). Boston: Allyn & Bacon.

Tong, S., Baghurst, P., Vimpani, G., & McMichael, A. (2007). Socioeconomic position, maternal IQ, home environment, and cognitive development. *Journal of Pediatrics, 151,* 284–288.

Toulmin, S. E. (2008). The layout of arguments. In J. E. Adler & L. J. Rips (Eds.), *Reasoning.* New York: Cambridge University Press.

Trautwein, U. (2007). The homework–achievement relation reconsidered: Differentiating homework time, homework frequency, and homework effort. *Learning and Instruction, 17,* 372–388.

Trautwein, U., & Ludtke, O. (2007). Students' self-reported effort and time on homework in six school subjects: Between-students differences and within-students differences. *Journal of Educational Psychology, 99,* 432–444.

Triandis, H. C. (2007). Culture and psychology. In S. Kitayama & D. Cohen (Eds.), *Handbook of cultural psychology.* New York: Guilford.

Trzesniewski, K. H., Donnellan, M. B., Moffit, T. E. Robins, R. W., Poulton, R., & Caspi, A. (2006). Low self-esteem during adolescence predicts poor health, criminal behavior, and limited income prospects during adulthood. *Developmental Psychology, 42,* 38.

Tsal, Y., Shaler, L., & Mevorach, C. (2005). The diversity of attention deficits in ADHD. *Journal of Learning Disabilities, 38,* 142–157.

Tsang, C. L. (1989). Bilingual minorities and language issues in writing. *Written Communication, 9* (1), 1–15.

Tulving, E. (1972). Episodic and semantic memory. In E. Tulving & W. Donaldson (Eds.), *Origins of memory.* San Diego: Academic Press.

Tulving, E. (2000). Concepts of memory. In E. Tulving & F. I. M. Craik (Eds.), *The Oxford handbook of memory.* New York: Oxford University Press.

Tunteler, E., & Resing, W. C. M. (2007). Effects of prior assistance in using analogies on young children's unprompted analogical problem-solving over time: A microgenetic study. *British Journal of Educational Psychology, 77,* 43–68.

Turkeltaub, P. E., Gareau, L., Flowers, D. L., Zeffiro, T. A., & Eden, G. F. (2003). Development of neural mechanisms for reading. *Nature Neuroscience,16,* 765–780.

Turnbull, H. R., Huerta, N., & Stowe, M. (2009). *What every teacher should know about: The Individuals with Disabilities Education Act as amended in 2004* (2nd ed.). Upper Saddle River, NJ: Prentice Hall.

U.S. Department of Education. (2000). *To assure a free and appropriate public education of all children with disabilities.* Washington, DC: U.S. Office of Education.

U.S. Department of Education. (2006). *Teaching our youngest.* Washington, DC: Author.

U.S. Office for Civil Rights. (2008). *Sexual harassment.* Retrieved July 30, 2008, from www.ed.gov/about/offices/list/ocr/qa-sexharass.html

U.S. Office of Education. (1998). *The Benchmark Study.* Washington, DC: Office of Education & Minority Affairs.

U.S. Office of Education. (1999). *Elementary and secondary school compliance reports.* Washington, DC: U.S. Government Printing Office.

Ullman, J. G. (2005). *Making technology work for learners with special needs.* Boston: Allyn & Bacon.

Umana-Taylor, A. J. (2006, March). *Ethnic identity, acculturation, and enculturation: Considerations in methodology and theory.* Paper presented at the meeting of the Society for Research on Adolescence, San Francisco.

Umbreil, J., Ferro, J., Liaupsin, C. J., & Lane, K. I. (2007). *Functional behavioral assessment and function-based intervention.* Upper Saddle River, NJ: Prentice Hall.

University of Buffalo Counseling Services. (2005). *Procrastination.* Buffalo, NY: Author.

University of Illinois Counseling Center. (1996). *Overcoming procrastination.* Urbana-Champaign, Il.: Department of Student Affairs.

University of Texas at Austin Counseling and Mental Health Center. (1999). *Coping with perfectionism.* Austin, TX: Author.

Upfront. (2001, January 1). Cheating hall of shame (Vol. 133, No. 9), 12–14.

USA Today. (1999). All-USA TODAY Teacher Team. Retrieved January 15, 2004, from www.usatoday.com/news/education/1999

USA Today. (2000, October 10). All-USA first teacher team. Retrieved November 15, 2004, from http://www.usatoday.com/life/teacher/teach/htm

USA Today. (2001, October 10). All-USA first teacher term. Retrieved November 20, 2004, from http://www.usatoday.com/news/education2001

USA Today. (2003, October 15). From kindergarten to high school, they make the grade. Retrieved April 22, 2006 from www.usatoday.com/news/education/2003-10-15-2003-winners

Vacca, J. A., Vacca, R. T., Gove, M. K., Burkey, L. C., Lenhart, L. A., & McKeon, C. A. (2009). *Reading and learning to read* (7th ed.). Boston: Allyn & Bacon.

Vahey, P., Roschelle, J., & Tatar, D. (2006). Moving between the private and the public in the mathematics classroom with handheld technology. In M. van't Hooft & K. Swan (Eds.), *Ubiquitous computing: Invisible technology, visible impact.* Mahwah, NJ: Erlbaum.

Vallone, R. P., Griffin, D. W., Lin, S., & Ross, L. (1990). Overconfident prediction of future actions and outcomes by self and others. *Journal of Personality and Social Psychology, 58,* 582–592.

Van Buren, E., & Graham, S. (2003). *Redefining ethnic identity: Its relationship to positive and negative school adjustment outcomes for minority youth.* Paper presented at the meeting of the Society for Research in Child Development, Tampa.

Van de Walle, J. (2007). *Elementary and middle school mathematics* (6th ed.). Boston: Allyn & Bacon.

Van de Walle, J. A., & Lovin, L. A. H. (2006). *Teaching student-centered mathematics: Grades 3–5.* Boston: Allyn & Bacon.

Van Houten, R., Nau, P., Mackenzie-Keating, S., Sumeoto, D., & Colavecchia, B. (1982). An analysis of some variables influencing the effectiveness of reprimands. *Journal of Applied Behavior Analysis, 15,* 65–83.

Van Tartwijk, J., Driessen, E., Van Der Vleuten, C., & Stokking, K. (2007). Factors influencing the successful introduction of portfolios. *Quality in Higher Education, 13,* 69–79.

VanTassel-Baska, J., & Stambaugh, T. (2008). Curriculum and instructional considerations in programs for the gifted. In S. I. Pfeiffer (Ed.), *Handbook of giftedness in children.* New York: Springer.

Varzi, A. C. (2008). Patterns, rules, and inferences. In J. E. Adler & L. J. Rips (Eds.), *Reasoning.* New York: Cambridge University Press.

Vaslie, A. J. (2008). *Speak with confidence* (10th ed.). Boston: Allyn & Bacon.

Verbeemen, T., Vanpaemel, W., Pattyn, S., Storms, G., & Verguts, T. (2007). Beyond exemplars and prototypes as memory representations of natural concepts: A clustering approach. *Journal of Memory and Language, 56,* 357–554.

Vogt, W. P. (2007). *Quantitative research methods for professionals in education and other fields.* Boston: Allyn & Bacon.

Vosniadou, S. (2007). The cognitive-situative divide and the problem of conceptual change. *Educational Psychologist, 42,* 55–66.

Vreeman, R.C., & Carroll, A.E. (2007). A systematic review of school-based interventions to prevent bullying. *Archives of Pediatric and Adolescent Medicine, 161,* 78–88.

Vukelich, C., Christie, J. F., & Enz, B. J. (2008). *Helping children learn language and literacy: Birth through kindergarten* (2nd ed.). Boston: Allyn & Bacon.

Vygotsky, L. S. (1962). *Thought and language.* Cambridge, MA: MIT Press.

W

Wagner, R. K., & Sternberg, R. J. (1986). Tacit knowledge and intelligence in the everyday world. In R. J. Sternberg & R. K. Wagner (Eds.), *Practical intelligence.* Cambridge, UK: Cambridge University Press.

Wallerstein, J. S. (2008). Divorce. In M. M. Haith & J. B. Benson (Eds.), *Encyclopedia of infant and early childhood development.* Oxford, UK: Elsevier.

Walsh, J. (2008). Self-efficacy. In N. J. Salkind (Ed.), *Encyclopedia of educational psychology.* Thousand Oaks, CA: Sage.

Wang, C. X., & Dwyer, F. M. (2007). Instructional effects of three concept mapping strategies in facilitating student achievement. *International Journal of Instructional Media, 33,* 135.

Wang, T.-H. (2007). What strategies are effective for formative assessment in an E-learning environment. *Journal of Computer Assisted Learning, 23,* 171–186.

Warrington, M., & Younger, M. (2003). "We decided to give it a twirl": Single-sex teaching in English comprehensive schools. *Gender and Education, 15,* 339–350.

Watson, D. L., & Tharp, R. G. (2007). *Self-directed behavior* (9th ed.). Belmont, CA: Wadsworth.

Webb, J. T., Gore, J. L., Mend, E. R., & DeVries, A. R. (2007). *A parent's guide to gifted children.* Scottsdale, AZ: Great Potential Press.

Webb, N. M. (1994). Sex differences in interaction and achievement in cooperative small groups. *Journal of Educational Psychology, 76,* 33–34.

Webb, N. M., & Palincsar, A. S. (1996). Group processes in the classroom. In D. C. Berliner &R. C. Calfee (Eds.), *Handbook of educational psychology.* New York: Macmillan.

Weber, E. (2005). *MI strategies in the classroom and beyond.* Boston: Allyn & Bacon.

Webster, N. S., & Worrell, F. C. (2008). Academically-talented adolescents' attitudes toward service in the community. *Gifted Child Quarterly, 52,* 170–179.

Weiler, J. (1998). Success for All. *ERIC/CUE Digest, No.* 139.

Weiner, B. (1986). *An attributional theory of motivation and emotion.* New York: Springer.

Weiner, B. (1992). *Human motivation: Metaphors, theories, and research.* Newbury Park, CA: Sage.

Weiner, B. (2005). *Social motivation, justice, and the moral emotions.* Mahwah, NJ: Erlbaum.

Weingartner, C. (2009). *Principal mentoring.* Thousand Oaks, CA: Sage.

Weinstein, C. E., & Acee, T. W. (2008). Cognitive view of learning. In N. J. Salkind (Ed.), *Encyclopedia of educational psychology.* Thousand Oaks, CA: Sage.

Weinstein, C. S. (2007). *Middle and secondary classroom management* (3rd ed.). Boston: McGraw-Hill.

Weinstein, C. S., & Mignano, A. (2007). *Elementary classroom management* (4th ed.). Boston: McGraw-Hill.

Weinstein, R. S. (2004). *Reaching higher: The power of expectations in schooling* (paperback ed.). Cambridge, MA: Harvard University Press.

Weinstein, R. S., Madison, S. M., & Kuklinski, M. R. (1995). Raising expectations in schooling: Obstacles and opportunities for change. *American Educational Research Journal, 32*(1), 121–159.

Weiss, L. A., & others. (2008). Association between microdeletion and microduplication at 16p11.2 and autism. *New England Journal of Medicine, 358,* 667–675.

Weiss, S. J. (2008). Stimulus control. In N. J. Salkind (Ed.), *Encyclopedia of educational psychology.* Thousand Oaks, CA: Sage.

Weissberg, R. P., & Greenberg, M. T. (1998). School and community competence-enhancement prevention programs. In W. Damon (Ed.), *Handbook of child psychology* (Vol. 4). New York: Wiley.

Wellhousen, K. (1996, Fall). Do's and don'ts for eliminating hidden bias. *Childhood Education,* pp. 36–39.

Wellman, H. M. (2004). Understanding the psychological world: Developing a theory of mind. In U. Goswami (Ed.), *Blackwell handbook of childhood cognitive development.* Malden, MA: Blackwell.

Wellman, H. M., Cross, D., & Watson, J. (2001). Meta-analysis of theory-of-mind development: The truth about false belief. *Child Development, 72,* 655–684.

Wellman, H. M., & Woolley, J. D. (1990). From simple desires to ordinary beliefs: The early development of everyday psychology. *Cognition, 35,* 245–275.

Welshman, D. (2000). *Social studies resources.* St. Johns, Newfoundland: Leary Brooks Jr. High School.

Wenglinsky, H. (2002). The link between teacher classroom practices and student academic performance. *Education Policy Analysis Archives, 10,* 12.

Wentzel, K. R. (1996). Social goals and social relationships as motivators of school adjustment. In J. Juvonen & R. Wentzel (Eds.), *Social motivation.* New York: Cambridge University Press.

Wentzel, K. R. (1997). Student motivation in middle school: The role of perceived pedagogical caring. *Journal of Educational Psychology, 89,* 411–419.

Wentzel, K. R. (2006). A social motivation perspective for classroom management. In C. M. Evertson & C. S. Weinstein (Eds.), *Handbook of classroom management.* Mahwah, NJ: Erlbaum.

Wentzel, K. R., Barry, C. M., & Caldwell, K. A. (2004). Friendships in middle school: Influences on motivation and school adjustments. *Journal of Educational Psychology, 96,* 195–203.

Wentzel, K.R., & Erdley, C.A. (1993). Strategies for making friends: Relations to social behavior and peer acceptance in early adolescence. *Developmental Psychology, 29,* 819–826.

Werker, J. E. & Tees, R. C. (2005). Speech perception as a window for understanding plasticity and commitment in language systems of the brain. *Developmental Psychobiology, 46,* 223–251.

Wertsch, J. (2008). From social interaction to higher psychological processes. *Human Development, 51,* 66–79.

Wertsch, J. V. (2007). Mediation. In H. Daniels, J. Wertsch, & M. Cole (Eds.), *The Cambridge companion to Vygotsky*. New York: Cambridge University Press.

What Works Clearinghouse. (2007). *Elementary school math.* Rockville, MD: Author.

What Works Clearinghouse. (2007a). *Reading Recovery.* Rockville, MD: Author.

What Works Clearinghouse. (2007b). *Success for All.* Rockville, MD: Author.

What Works Clearinghouse. (2007c). *Peer-assisted learning strategies.* Rockville, MD: Author.

Wheelock, A. (1992). *Crossing the tracks: How "untracking" can save American's schools.* New York: New Press.

Whitcomb, J. A. (2004). Dilemmas of design and predicaments of practice: Adapting the "Fostering a Community of Learners" model in secondary school English language arts. *Journal of Curriculum Studies, 36,* 183–206.

White, R. W. (1959). Motivation reconsidered: The concept of confidence. *Psychological Review, 66,* 297–333.

Whitescarver, K. (2006, April). *Montessori rising: Montessori education in the United States, 1955–present.* Paper presented at the meeting of the American Education Research Association, San Francisco.

Whittle, S., Yap, M. B., Yucel, M., Fornito, A., Simmons, J. G., Sheeber, L., & Allen N. B. (2008). Prefrontal and amygdala volumes are related to adolescents' affective behaviors during parent-adolescent interactions. *Proceedings of the National Academy of Sciences USA, 105,* 3652–3657.

Wiersman, W., & Jurs, S. G. (2009). *Research methods in education* (9th ed.). Upper Saddle River, NJ: Prentice Hall.

Wigfield, A., & Asher, S. R. (1984). Social and motivational influences on reading. In P. D. Pearson, R. Barr, M. L. Kamil, & P. Mosenthal (Eds.), *Handbook of reading research.* New York: Longman.

Wigfield, A., Byrnes, J. P., & Eccles, J. S. (2006). Developing during early adolescence. In P. A. Alexander & P. H. Winne (Eds.), *Handbook of educational psychology* (2nd ed.). Mahwah, NJ: Erlbaum.

Wigfield, A., Eccles, J. S., Schiefele, U., Roeser, R., & Davis-Kean, P. (2006). Development of achievement motivation. In W. Damon & R. Lerner (Eds.), *Handbook of child psychology* (6th ed.). New York: Wiley.

Wigfield, A., Hoa, L. W., & Klauda, S. L. (2008). The role of achievement values in the self-regulation of achievement behaviors. In D. H. Schunk & B. J. Zimmerman (Eds.), *Motivation and self-regulated learning: Theory, research, and applications.* Mahwah, NJ: Erlbaum.

Wiggins, G. (1992, May). *Creating tests worth taking. Educational Leadership,* pp. 26–33.

Wildman, T. M. (2008). Learning. In N. J. Salkind (Ed.), *Encyclopedia of educational psychology.* Thousand Oaks, CA: Sage.

Wiles, J. (2009). *Leading curriculum development.* Thousand Oaks, CA: Sage.

Wilkins, E. A., & Clift, R. T. (2007). Building a network of support for teachers. *Action in Teacher Education, 28,* 25–35.

Williams, K. C. (2009). *Elementary classroom management.* Thousand Oaks, CA: Sage.

Williams, R. B. (2007). *Cooperative learning: A standard for high achievement.* Thousand Oaks, CA: Corwin.

Willingham, D. T. (2008). Critical thinking: Why is it so hard to teach? *Arts Education Policy Review, 109,* (No. 4), 21–29.

Wineburg, M. S. (2006). Evidence in teacher preparation. *Journal of Teacher Education, 57,* 51–64.

Winn, I. J. (2004). The high cost of uncritical teaching. *Phi Delta Kappan, 85,* 496–497.

Winne, P. H. (2001). Self-regulated learning viewed from models of information processing. In B. J. Zimmerman & D. H. Schunk (Eds.), *Self-regulated learning and academic achievement.* Mahwah, NJ: Erlbaum.

Winne, P. H. (2005). Key issues in modeling and applying research on self-regulated learning. *Applied Psychology: An International Review, 54,* 232–238.

Winner, E. (1986, August). Where pelicans kiss seals. *Psychology Today,* pp. 24–35.

Winner, E. (1996). *Gifted children: Myths and realities.* New York: Basic Books.

Winner, E. (1997). Exceptionally high intelligence and schooling. *American Psychologist, 52,* 1070–1081.

Winner, E. (2000). The origins and ends of giftedness. *American Psychologist, 55,* 159–169.

Winner, E. (2006). Development in the arts: Drawing and music. In W. Damon & R. Lerner (Eds.), *Handbook of child psychology* (6th ed.). New York: Wiley.

Winsler, A., Carlton, M. P., & Barry, M. J. (2000). Age-related changes in preschool children's systematic use of private speech in a natural setting. *Journal of Child Language, 27,* 665–687.

Winsler, A., Diaz, R. M., & Montero, I. (1997). The role of private speech in the transition from collaborative to independent task performance in young children. *Early Childhood Research Quarterly, 12,* 59–79.

Wiske, S., Franz, K. R., & Breit, L. (2005). *Teaching for understanding with technology.* New York: Wiley.

Witkow, M. R., & Fuligni, A. J. (2007). Achievement goals and daily school experiences among adolescents with Asian, Latino, and European American backgrounds. *Journal of Educational Psychology, 99,* 584–596.

Wittrock, M. C., & Lumsdaine, A. A. (1977). Instructional psychology. *Annual Review of Psychology, 28,* 417–459.

Wolsey, T. D., & Fisher, D. (2009). *Learning to predict and predicting to learn.* Upper Saddle River, NJ: Prentice Hall.

Wong, T. B. (2004, October 14). *USA Today's 2004 all-USA team. USA Today,* p. 6D.

Wong Briggs, T. (1999, October 14). *Honorees find keys to unlocking kids' minds.* Retrieved March 10, 2000, from www.usatoday.com/education

Wong Briggs, T. (2007, October 18). An early start for learning. *USA Today,* p. 6D.

Wong Briggs, T. W. (2004, October 14). Students embrace vitality of *USA Today's* top 20 teachers. *USA Today,* p. 7D.

Wong Briggs, T. W. (2005). Math teacher resets the learning curve. Retrieved March 6, 2006, from www.usatoday.com/news/education/2005-04-05-math-teacher_x.htm

Wood, D., Kaplan, R., & McLoyd, V. C. (2007). Gender differences in educational expectations of urban, low-income African American youth: The role of parents and schools. *Journal of Youth and Adolescence, 36,* 417–427.

Wood, J. (2001). Can software support children's vocabulary development? *Language Learning and Technology, 5,* 166–201.

Wood, J., & Duke, N. K. (1997). Inside "Reading Rainbow": A spectrum of strategies for promoting literacy. *Language Arts, 74,* 95–106.

Work Group of the American Psychological Association Board of Educational Affairs. (1995). *Learner-centered psychological principles: A framework for school redesign and reform* (Draft). Washington, DC: American Psychological Association.

Work Group of the American Psychological Association Board of Educational Affairs. (1997). *Learner-centered psychological principles: A framework for school reform and redesign.* Washington, DC: American Psychological Association.

Worthen, B. R., & Spandel, V. (1991, February). Putting the standardized test debate in perspective. *Educational Leadership,* pp. 65–69.

Wright Group. (2004). *Everyday math* (2nd ed.). New York: McGraw-Hill.

Wright Group. (2007). *Everyday math* (3rd ed.). New York: McGraw-Hill.

Write:Outloud. (2008). Retrieved January 16, 2008, from www.donjohnston.com/products/write_outloud/index.html

Wu, H-K., & Huang, Y-L. (2007). Ninth-grade student engagement in teacher-centered andstudent-centered technology-enhanced learning environments. *Science Education, 91,* 727–749.

Xu, J. (2007). Middle-school homework management: More than just gender and family involvement. *Educational Psychology, 27,* 173–189.

Yang, S. C., & Liu, S. F. (2005). The study of interactions and attitudes of third-grade students' learning information technology via a cooperative approach. *Computers in Human Behavior, 21,* 45–72.

Yasnitsky, A., & Ferrari, M. (2008). From Vygotsky to Vygotskian psychology: Introduction to the history of the Kharkov School. *Journal of the History of the Behavioral Sciences, 44,* 119–145.

Yell, M. (2008). No Child Left Behind. In N. J. Salkind (Ed.), *Encyclopedia of educational psychology.* Thousand Oaks, CA: Sage.

Yell, M. L., & Drasgow, E. (2009). *What every teacher should know about No Child Left Behind.* (2nd ed.). Upper Saddle River, NJ: Prentice Hall.

Yen, S-C. (2008). Short-term memory. In N. J. Salkind (Ed.), *Encyclopedia of educational psychology.* Thousand Oaks, CA: Sage.

Yinger, R. J. (1980). Study of teacher planning. *Elementary School Journal, 80,* 107–127.

Young, E. L., Boye, A. E., & Nelson, D. A. (2006). Relational aggression: Understanding, identifying, and responding in schools. *Psychology in the Schools, 43,* 297–312.

Yung, B. H. W. (2001). Three views of fairness in a school-based assessment scheme of practical work in biology. *International Journal of Science Education, 23,* 985–1005.

Zabrucky, K. M., & Agler, L-M. L. (2008). Metacognition and learning. In N. J. Salkind (Ed.), *Encyclopedia of educational psychology.* Thousand Oaks, CA: Sage.

Zagorsky, J. L. (2007). Do you have to be smart to be rich? The impact of IQ on wealth, income, and financial distress. *Intelligence, 35,* 489–501.

Zalc, B. (2006). The acquisition of myelin: A success story. *Novartis Foundation Symposium, 276,* 15–21.

Zarefsky, D. (2008). *Public speaking* (5th ed.). Boston: Allyn & Bacon.

Zarrillo, J. (2008). *Teaching elementary social studies* (3rd ed.). Upper Saddle River, NJ: Prentice Hall.

Zelazo, P. D., & Müller, U. (2004). Executive function in typical and atypical development. In U. Goswami (Ed.), *Blackwell handbook of cognitive development.* Malden, MA: Blackwell.

Zentall, S. S. (2006). *ADHD and education.* Upper Saddle River, NJ: Prentice Hall.

Zhang, L. F., & Sternberg, R. J. (2008a). Learning in a cross-cultural perspective. In T. Husén & T. N. Postlethwaite (Eds.), *International encyclopedia of education* (3rd ed.), *Learning and cognition.* Oxford: Elsevier.

Zhang, L. F., & Sternberg, R. J. (2008b). Intellectual styles and creativity. *In Routledge companion to creativity.*

Zigler, E. F., & Finn-Stevenson, M. (1999). Applied developmental psychology. In M. H. Bornstein & M. E. Lamb (Eds.), *Developmental psychology* (4th ed.). Mahwah, NJ: Erlbaum.

Zimmerman, B. J., Bonner, S., & Kovach, R. (1996). *Developing self-regulated learners.* Washington, DC: American Psychological Association.

Zoo Cams Worldwide. (2008). Retrieved January 16, 2008, from www.zoos-worldwide.de/zoocams. html

Zosuls, K. M., Lurye, L. E., & Ruble, D. N. (2008). Gender: Awareness, identity, and stereotyping. In M. M. Haith & J. B. Benson (Eds.), *Encyclopedia of infant and early childhood development.* Oxford, UK: Elsevier.

Zucker, A. A., & McGhee, R. (2005). A study of one-to-one computer use in mathematics and science instruction at the secondary level in Henrico County Public Schools. Washington, DC: SRI International.

Credits

TEXT AND LINE ART

Chapter 1

p. 2 Teaching Stories, Margaret Metzger: From Margaret Metzger, "Maintaining a Life," *Phi Delta Kappan,* vol. 77 (January 1996), pp. 346–351. Reprinted by permission of the author. Figure 1.1, Student's Images of Their Best and Worst Teachers: From "Students say: What makes a good teacher?" in *Schools in the Middle,* vol. 6, no. 5 (May/June 1997). Copyright © 1997 National Association of Secondary School Principals. Reprinted by permission. For more information on NASSP products and services to promote excellence in middle level and high school leadership, visit www.principals.org. Figure 1.2, Parents' Explanations of Science to Sons and Daughters at a Science Museum: Adapted from "Parents explain more to boys than girls during shared scientific thinking" by Kevin Crowley, Maureen A. Callanan, Harriet R. Tenenbaum, and Elizabeth Allen, in *Psychological Science, 12* (2001), pp. 258–261, Figure 1. Used by permission of Blackwell Publishing and Kevin Crowley. Figure 1.3, Possible Explanations for Correctional Data: From John W. Santrock, *Life-Span Development,* 10th ed., Figure 2.9, p. 62. Copyright © 2006 by The McGraw-Hill Companies, Inc. Reprinted with permission.

Chapter 2

Figure 2.1, Periods and Processes of Development: From John W. Santrock, *Life-Span Development,* 10th ed., p. 20. Copyright © 2006 by The McGraw-Hill Companies, Inc. Reprinted with permission. Figure 2.5, Changes in the Adolescent Brain: From John Santrock, *Essentials of Life-Span Development,* 1st ed., Figure 9.3. Copyright © 2008 by The McGraw-Hill Companies, Inc. Reprinted with permission. pp. 38–40 Excerpts from Fischer & Immordino-Yang, 2008: From "The fundamental importance of the brain and learning in education" by K.W. Fischer and M.H. Immordino Yang in *The Jossey-Bass Reader on the Brain and Learning.* Copyright © 2008 by John Wiley & Sons, Inc. Figure 2.10 a&b, Developmental Changes in Children's Drawings: From *The Symbolic Drawings of Young Children.* Reprinted by permission of Dr. Dennie Palmer Wolf. Figure 2.11, The Three Mountain Task: From John W. Santrock, *Psychology,* 7th ed. Copyright © 2003 by The McGraw-Hill Companies, Inc. Reprinted with permission. Figure 2.13, Piaget's Conservation Task: From John Santrock, *Essentials of Life-Span Development,* 1st ed., Figure 9.3. Copyright © 2008 by The McGraw-Hill Companies, Inc. Reprinted with permission. Figure 2.16, Writing Process of a 5-Year-Old Boy: From Bodrova, E. and Leong, D.J. (2001, 2007) *Tools of the Mind,* Geneva, Switzerland: International Bureau of Education, UNESCO. Figure 2.18, Stimuli in Berko's Study of Young Children's Understanding of Morphological Rules: From "The Child's Learning of English Morphology" by Jean Berko in *Word,* vol. 14 (1958), p. 154. Reprinted by permission of Jean Burko Gleason.

Chapter 3

Figure 3.1, Bronfenbrenner's Ecological Theory of Development: From *Child: Development in a Social Context* by Claire B. Kopp and Joanne B. Krakow, eds., p. 648. Copyright © 1982 by Addison-Wesley Publishing Company, Inc. Published by Pearson Education, Inc., Glenview, IL. p. 82 Excerpts from *Are America's Schools Leaving Latinas Behind?* From *¡Si, Se Puede! Yes, We Can: Latinas in School* by Angela Ginorio and Michelle Huston. Washington, DC: American Association of University Women Educational Fund, 2000, pp. 1–2. Reprinted with permission of American Association of University Women. Figure 3.3, Single-Parent Families in Various Countries: From John W. Santrock, *Life-Span Development,* 10th ed.,

Figure 9.8. Copyright © 2006 by The McGraw-Hill Companies, Inc. Reprinted with permission. Figure 3.4, Trends in High School Dropout Rates: National Center for Education Statistics, 2007. Figure 3.5, The Decline in Self-Esteem in Adolescence: From "Global Self-Esteem Across the Life Span" by R.W. Robins, K.H. Trzesniewski, J.L. Tracy, S.D. Gosling, and J. Potter, in *Psychology and Aging, 17,* 423–434 (Figure 1., p. 428). Copyright © 2002 by the American Psychological Association. Figure 3.6, Marcia's Four Identity Statuses: From John W. Santrock, *Life-Span Development,* 10th ed. Copyright © 2006 by The McGraw-Hill Companies, Inc. Reprinted with permission.

Chapter 4

p. 116 Teaching Stories, Shiffy Landa: From "If You Can't Make Waves, Make Ripples" by Shiffy Landa in *Intelligence Connections: Newsletter of the ASCD,* Vol.X, No. 1 (Fall 2000), pp. 6–8. Reprinted by permission of Thomas R. Hoerr, Ph.D., Head of School., New City School, St. Louis, www.newcityschool .org. Figure 4.1, The Normal Curve and Standard-Binet IQ Scores: From John W. Santrock, *Life-Span Development,* 10th ed. Figure 10.6. Copyright © 2006 by The McGraw-Hill Companies, Inc. Reprinted with permission. Technology and Education: Technology and Multiple Intelligences: Excerpts from *How Technology Enhances Howard Gardner's Eight Intelligences* by Dee Dickinson, pp. 1–3, at www.america-tomorrow .com/ati/nh180402.htm. Copyright © 1998 New Horizons for Learning. Reprinted with permission. Figure 4.4, The Increase in IQ Scores from 1932 to 1997: From "The Increase in IQ Scores from 1932–1997" by Ulric Neisser. Reprinted by permission of the author.

Chapter 5

Figure 5.2, Actual and Projected Number of U.S. Adolescents Aged 10–15, 2000–2100: After data presented by the U.S. Census Bureau (2002). National Population Projections I Summary Files. Washington, D.C. U.S. Census Bureau. Figure 5.3, African American Adolescents' Reports of Racial Hassles in the Past Year: After Table 1 from "Racial Identity Matters: The Relationship Between Racial Discrimination and Psychological Functioning in African American Adolescents" by R.M. Sellers et al., in *Journal of Research on Adolescence, 16* (2): 187–216. Copyright © 2006. Reprinted by permission of Blackwell Publishing Ltd. p. 162 Best Practices: Strategies for Working with Linguistically and Culturally Diverse Children: Recommendations excerpted from "Responding to Linguistic and Cultural Diversity: Recommendations for Effective Early Childhood Education" in *Young Children, 51* (2), pp. 4–12. A Position Statement of the National Association for the Education of Young Children (NAEYC), adopted 1995. Reprinted with permission. p. 184 Through the Eyes of Teachers: From *Teaching Stories* by Judy Logan. Copyright © 1997 by Judy Logan. Reprinted by permission of Kodansha America, Inc. Figure 5.4, National Science Scores for Boys and Girls: National Assessment of Educational Progress (2005).

Chapter 6

Figure 6.4, Classification of Mental Retardation Based on IQ: From *Mental Retardation: Definition, Classification, and Systems of Supports,* p. 26. Copyright © 1992 by American Association on Mental Retardation (AAMR). Reproduced with permission of American Association on Mental Retardation (AAMR) via Copyright Clearance Center. Figure 6.6, Percentage of U.S. Students with Disabilities 6 to 21 Years of Age Receiving Special Services: Data for 2004–2005 School Year: National Center for Education Statistics, 2007.

Chapter 7

p. 230 Teaching Stories: Ruth Sidney Charney: From "Using Language to Encourage and Empower Children, Part 2: Exploring the First 'R': To Reinforce" by Ruth Sidney Charney in *Education World* (2005). Reprinted with permission of Ruth S. Charney and Education World, www.educationworld.com. Figure 7.5, Schedules of Reinforcement and Different Patterns of Responding: From John W. Santrock, *Psychology,* 7th ed., Fig. 7.9. Copyright © 2003 by The McGraw-Hill Companies, Inc. Reprinted with permission. Figure 7.6, Attitudes about Corporal Punishment in Different Countries: After *Statistical Analysis of the Cross-Cultural Data: The Third Year* by Irwin Hyman. Paper presented at the meeting of the American Psychological Association, San Francisco, 2001. Reprinted by permission of Irwin Hyman. Figure 7.7, Bandura's Social Cognitive Theory: From John W. Santrock, *Psychology,* 7th ed., Fig. 12.6, p. 487. Copyright © 2003 by The McGraw-Hill Companies, Inc. Reprinted with permission. Figure 7.11, A Model of Self-Regulatory Learning: From *Developing Self-Regulated Learners: Beyond Achievement to Self-Efficacy* by B.J. Zimmerman, S. Bonner, and R. Kovach. Washington, DC: American Psychological Association (Figure 1, p. 11). Copyright © 1996 by the American Psychological Association.

Chapter 8

Figure 8.1, Processing Information in Memory: From John W. Santrock, *Psychology,* 7th ed. Copyright © 2003 by The McGraw-Hill Companies, Inc. Reprinted with permission. Figure 8.2, Verbal Elaboration and Memory: From "Young Children's Learning of a Foreign Language Vocabulary: A Sentence Variation of the Keyword Method" by M. Pressley, J.R. Levin, and C. B. McCormick in *Contemporary Educational Psychology,* vol. 5 pp. 22–29. Copyright © 1980, with permission from Elsevier. Figure 8.3, Imagery and Memory of Verbal Information: From "Short-Term Memory, Verbal Competence, and Age as Predictors of Imagery Instructional Effectiveness" by M. Pressley, T. Cariligia-Bull, S. Deane, and W. Schneider in *Journal of Experimental Child Psychology,* vol. 43, pp. 194–211. Copyright © 1987, with permission from Elsevier. Figure 8.5, Working

Memory: From John W. Santrock, *Psychology,* 7th ed. Figure 8.8, p. 314. Copyright © 2003 by The McGraw-Hill Companies, Inc. Reprinted with permission. Figure 8.6, Developmental Changes in Working Memory: Adapted from "What Develops in Working Memory? A Life Span Perspective" by H.L. Swanson in *Developmental Psychology,* 35, 986–1000 (Table 1, p. 990). Copyright © 1999 by the American Psychological Association. Figure 8.7, Atkinson and Shiffrin's Theory of Memory: From John W. Santrock, *Psychology,* 7th ed. Figure 8.5, p. 312. Copyright © 2003 by The McGraw-Hill Companies, Inc. Reprinted with permission. Figure 8.8, Classification of Long-Term Memory's Contents: From John W. Santrock, *Psychology,* 7th ed. Figure 8.9, p. 316. Copyright © 2003 by The McGraw-Hill Companies, Inc. Reprinted with permission. Figure 8.9, The Serial Position Effect: Adapted from *Human Memory: Theory and Data* by Bennet B. Murdock, Jr. Potomac, MD: Lawrence Erlbaum Associates, 1974. Figure 8.10, The Keyword Method: From John W. Santrock, *Life-Span Development,* 6th ed. Copyright © 1997 by The McGraw-Hill Companies, Inc. Reprinted with permission. Figure 8.11, Memory for Numbers and Chess Pieces: From "Knowledge Structures and Memory Development" by M.T.H. Chi in *Children's Thinking,* edited by R. S. Siegler. Copyright © 1978 by Lawrence Erlbaum, Inc. Permission conveyed via Copyright Clearance Center and the author. Figure 8.12, An Example of How Information Is Organized in the Mind of an Expert and a Novice: From "Cognitive Mechanisms Facilitating Human Problem Solving in a Realistic Domain: The Example of Physics" by Frederick Reif. Printed at the University of California at Berkeley, October 19, 1979. Reprinted by permission of the author. Figure 8.13, Developmental Changes in False-Belief Performance: From John W. Santrock, *Life-Span Development,* 10th ed. Figure 8.15, p. 244. Copyright © 2006 by The McGraw-Hill Companies, Inc. Reprinted with permission.

Chapter 9

p. 311 Teaching Stories: Marilyn Whirry: Council of Chief State School Officers. (2000). Description of 2000 National Teacher of the Year Marilyn Jachetti

Whirry. Washington, DC: Author. http://www.ccsso.org/Projects/national_teacher_of_the_year/national_teachers/156.cfm. Used by permission of the Council of Chief State School Officers. Figure 9.2, Example of a Concept Map for the Concept of Reptile: From John W. Santrock, *Educational Psychology,* 2nd ed., Figure 9.1. Copyright © 2006 by The McGraw-Hill Companies, Inc. Reprinted with permission. Figure 9.3, Getting Students to Generate Hypotheses about a Concept: From John W. Santrock, *Psychology,* 5th ed. Copyright © 1997 by The McGraw-Hill Companies, Inc. Reprinted with permission.

Chapter 11

Figure 11.2, A Sample Timetable for a Writing Deadline: From *Your Guide to College Success: Strategies for Achieving Your Goals,* Media Edition, 2nd Edition by Santrock and Halonen. Copyright © 2002 Wadsworth, a part of Cengage Learning, Inc: Reproduced by permission. www.cengage.com/permissions. pp. 408–409 Ten themes that should be emphasized in courses in the social sciences: From National Council for the Social Sciences, *National Standards for Social Studies Teachers* (2000). Copyright © National Council for the Social Studies. Reprinted by permission.

Chapter 12

Figure 12.1, Five Time Spans of Teacher Planning and Their Occurrence over the School Year: From "A Study of Teaching Planning" by R.J. Yinger in *The Elementary School Journal,* Vol. 80, No. 3 (January 1980), p. 113. Copyright © 1980 by The University of Chicago. Reprinted by permission of the University of Chicago Press, via the Copyright Clearance Center. Figure 12.3, Challenges of Seatwork for Teachers and Students: From Carol Simon Weinstein and Andrew J. Mignano, Jr., *Elementary Classroom Management,* 2nd ed. Copyright © 1997 by The McGraw-Hill Companies, Inc. Reprinted with permission. Figure 12.4, Suggestions for Learning Centers: From Carol Simon Weinstein and Andrew J. Mignano, Jr., *Elementary Classroom Management,* 2nd ed. Copyright © 1997 by The McGraw-Hill Companies, Inc. Reprinted with permission. Figure 12.5 a&b, Learner-Centered Psychological

Principles: From John W. Santrock, *Child Development,* 3rd edition. Figure 17.1. Copyright © by The McGraw-Hill Companies, Inc. Reprinted with permission. Figure 12.6 a&b, A Sampling of ISTE's (2007) Profiles for Technology-Literate Students at Different Grade Levels: Reprinted with permission from *National Educational Technology Standards for Students, Second Edition,* © 2007, ISTE® (International Society for Technology in Education), www.iste.org. All rights reserved. pp. 447–450 Excerpts from Martha Stone Wiske, with Kristi Rennebohm Franz and Lisa Breit, *Teaching for Understanding with Understanding:* From *Teaching for Understanding with Technology* by Martha Stone Wiske, with Kristi Rennebohm Franz and Lisa Breit. Copyright © 2005 by John Wiley & Sons, Inc. Reprinted with permission of John Wiley & Sons, Inc.

Chapter 13

Figure 13.2, Outcomes of Perceived Levels of Challenge and Skill: From Jere Brophy, *Motivating Students to Learn.* Copyright © 1998 by The McGraw-Hill Companies, Inc. Reprinted with permission. Figure 13.3, Combinations of Causal Attributions and Explanations for Failure: From *Human Motivation: Metaphors, Theories, and Research,* by Bernard Weiner, Table 6.4, p. 253. Copyright © 1992 by Sage Publications, Inc. Reprinted by permission of Sage Publications, Inc. Figure 13.6, Cognitive Retaining Methods for Increasing the Motivation of Students Who Display Failure Syndrome: From Jere Brophy, *Motivating Students to Learn.* Copyright © 1998 by The McGraw-Hill Companies, Inc. Reprinted with permission.

Chapter 14

Figure 14.3, The Action Zone: From *Excellent Classroom Management,* 1st edition by Carl H. Rinne. Copyright © 1997 Wadsworth, a part of Cengage Learning, Inc. Reproduced by permission. www.cengage.com/permissions. p. 514 Excerpts from Geneva Gay, 2006: From "Culturally Responsive Teaching" in *Handbook of Classroom Management,* C.M. Everton and C.S. Weinstein, eds. Copyright © 2006 by Lawrence Erlbaum, Inc. Permission conveyed via Copyright Clearance Center. Figure 14.4, Guidelines for Establishing Positive Relationships with

Students: From Carol Simon Weinstein, *Secondary Classroom Management*, 1st Ed. Copyright © 1996 by The McGraw-Hill Companies, Inc. Reprinted with permission. Figure 14.5, Bullying Behaviors among U.S. Youth: From "Bullying Behaviors among U.S. Youths: Prevalence and Association with Psychosocial Adjustment" by Tonja R. Nansel et al. in *Journal of the American Medical Association,* Vol. 285 (2001), pp. 2094–2100.

Chapter 16

Figure 16.1, Teacher Decision Making Before, During and After Instruction: From *Essential Assessment Concepts for Teachers and Administrators* by James H. McMillan, Figure 1.1, p. 3. Copyright © 2001 by Corwin Press, Inc. Reprinted by permission of Corwin Press, Inc. Figure 16.7, Examples of Alternative Assessment in a Middle School Language Arts Class: From "Using Alternative Assessment to Provide Options for Student Success" by Dorie Combs in *Middle School Journal,* September 1997. Copyright © 1997 National Association of Secondary School Principals. Reprinted by permission. For more information on NASSP products and services to promote excellence in middle level and high school leadership, visit www.principals.org. Figure 16.8, A Performance-Based Assessment in Science Daytime Astronomy: From "Development of Performance Assessments in Science" by G. Solano-Flores and R.J. Shavelson in *Educational Measurement,* September 1997, Figure 1, p. 17. Reprinted by permission of the National Council on Measurement in Education. Figure 16.9, Scoring Rubric for a Report on an Invention: From "Understanding Rubrics" by Heidi Goodrich in *Educational Leadership,* Vol. 54, No. 4 (1997), Figure 1. Reprinted by permission of the author. Figure 16.10, Creating Clarity in a Rubric for One Dimension of an Oral Presentation: From "Understanding Rubrics" by Heidi Goodrich in *Educational Leadership,* Vol. 54, No. 4 (1997), Figure 1. Reprinted by permission of the author. Figure 16.11, Contrasting Traditional Tests and Portfolios: From *Portfolios: Clarifying, Constructing, and Enhancing* by Nancy Jean Johnson and Leonie Marie Rose. Copyright © 1997 by Technomic Publishing Company, Inc. Reprinted by permission of the publisher.

PHOTOS

Chapter 1

Opener: © Steve Chenn/Corbis; p. 3 (top): © Brown Brothers; p. 3 (middle): Columbia University Archives, Columbia University in the City of New York; p. 3 (bottom): © Archives of the History of American Psychology, University of Akron; p. 4 (left): Prints and Photographs Collection CN10383, Center for American History, University of Texas at Austin.; p. 4 (middle): Courtesy of Kenneth Clark; p. 4 (right): © Archives of the History of American Psychology, University of Akron; p. 5: © 2007, USA TODAY. Reprinted with permission; p. 7: © Ariel Skelley/Corbis; p. 8 (top): © Corbis RF; p. 8 (bottom): © Davis Turner; p. 9: © Ariel Skelley/Corbis; p. 10: Courtesy of Valerie Pang; p. 11 (top): © Gabe Palmer/Corbis; p. 11 (bottom): © LWA-JDC/Corbis; p. 12: Courtesy Donald L. Mccoy, Program Manager, IBM Multicultural People in Technology; p. 15: © Alan Marler; p. 19: Courtesy of Steven and Cindi Binder; p. 20: © LWA-Dann Tardif/Corbis; p. 22: © Gabe Palmer/Corbis

Chapter 2

Opener: © Jose Luis Pelaez/Corbis; 2.1 (Infancy): John Santrock; 2.1 (Early childhood): © Joe Sohm/The Image Works; 2.1 (Middle childhood): © Corbis website; 2.1 (Adolescence): © James L. Shaffer; p. 33 (top): © David Young-Wolff/Photo Edit; p. 33 (bottom): © Jose Luis Pelaez/Corbis; 2.2: © Photo Researchers; 2.6: © A. Glaubman/Photo Researchers; 2.7 (top): © David Grubin Productions Inc. Reprinted by permission; 2.7 (bottom): Courtesy of Dana Boatman, Ph.D., Department of Neurology, John Hopkins University. Reprinted with permission from *The Secret Life of the Brain,* © 2001 by the National Academy of Sciences, the National Academies Press, Washington, D.C.; p. 39 (top): © Jim Craigmyle/Corbis; p. 39 (bottom): © Chase Jarvis/Corbis RF; 2.13: © Paul Fusco/Magnum Photos; p. 46: © David Young-Wolff/Photo Edit; p. 47: © Stewart Cohen/Stone/Getty Images; p. 49 (left): © Archives Jean Piaget, Universite De Geneve, Switzerland; p. 49 (right): © M & E Bernheim/Woodfin Camp; p. 50: © Billy Calzada; 2.15: © Elizabeth Crews/The Image Works; p. 53: © James Wertsch/Washington University at St. Louis; p. 54: © 2005, USA Today. Reprinted with permis-

sion; 2.16 a&b: Images courtesy of E. Bodrova and D.J. Leong, from *Tools of the Mind,* 2007; 2.17 (left): A.R. Lauria/Dr. Michael Cole, Laboratory of Human Cognition, University of California, San Diego; 2.17 (right): © 1999 Yves deBraine/Black Star p. 59: © Anne Rippy/The Image Bank/Getty Images; p. 60: © David Pollack/Corbis; p. 63: Reading Rainbow © GPN/University of Nebraska; p. 65: © Tim Pannell/Corbis

Chapter 3

Opener: © Comstock Select/Corbis RF; p. 74: Courtesy of Urie Bronfenbrenner; p. 76: © Sarah Putnam/Index Stock/Photolibrary; p. 80: © Ariel Skelley/CORBIS; p. 81: © Jose Luis Pelaez/CORBIS; p. 82: © Michael Newman/Photo Edit; p. 83: © PunchStock RF; p. 84: © Robert E. Daemmrich/Stone/Getty; p. 87: © Elizabeth Crews; p. 88: © Corbis RF; p. 89: © Eric Anderson/Stock Boston; p. 91: From "Open Window" © 1994 Municipality of Reggio Emilia Infant-toddler Centers and Preschools Published by Reggio Children; p. 92 (top): © AP/Wide World Photos; p. 92 (bottom): © Ronnie Kaufman/The Stock Market/Corbis; p. 94: © Big Cheese Photo/SuperStock RF; p. 95: Courtesy of "I Have a Dream," Houston, TX; p. 96: © istock; p. 102: © 1997 USA Today Photo Library, photo by Robert Deutsch; p. 104: © Keith Carter; p. 105: © Thinkstock/Corbis RF; p. 107: © Matthew J. Lee, The Boston Globe; p. 108 (top): © Reuters/NewMedia Inc./Corbis; p. 108 (bottom): © AP/Wide World Photos

Chapter 4

Opener: © Will Hart/Photo Edit; p. 117: National Library of Medicine; p. 120: Courtesy of Robert Sternberg; p. 122: © Jay Gardner, 1998; p. 123: © Joe McNally; p. 129: © Owen Franken/Corbis; p. 130: © Nathan Benn/Corbis; p. 131: © Will & Deni McIntyre/Corbis; p. 133 (top): © David Austin/Stock Boston; p. 133 (bottom): © Ben Simmons/The Stock Market/Corbis; p. 134: © AVID Center, San Diego CA; p. 140: © Jonathan Cavendish/Corbis; p. 142: © Gabe Palmer/zefa/Corbis

Chapter 5

Opener: © David Young-Wolff/Stone/Getty Images; p. 151 (top): © Bloomimage/Corbis RF; p. 151 (bottom): © Charles Gupton/Corbis; p. 152: © Getty RF; p. 153: Courtesy Vonnie McLoyd; p. 154 (top):

© Michael Conroy/AP Wide World Photos; p. 154 (bottom): © Joseph Sohm/ChromoSohm Inc./Corbis; p. 155: © 2004, USA Today. Reprinted with permission; p. 157: Courtesy Quantum Opportunities Program at the Carver Center in Washington, D.C.; p. 158 (top): © Alison Wright/Corbis; p. 158 (bottom): "Bookjacket," from THE SHAME OF THE NATION by Jonathan Kozol, copyright © 2005 by Jonathan Kozol. Used by permission of Crown Publishers, a division of Random House, Inc,; p. 161: © Elizabeth Crews; p. 168: © Renee C. Byer/Sacramento Bee/ZUMA Press; p. 169: © Jose Luis Pelaez, Inc./Corbis; p. 170 (top): Courtesy Rod Chlysta, Research Center for Educational Technology, Kent State University; p. 170 (bottom): © Ellis Herwig/Stock Boston; p. 171: © James Ransome; p. 173: © John S. Abbott; p. 175 (top): © BigStock Photos; p. 175 (bottom): © O'Brien Productions/Corbis; p. 179: © Roy McMahon/Corbis; p. 180: © AFP/Getty; p. 182: © Jim Cummins/Corbis; p. 184: © Judy Logan

Chapter 6

Opener: © Tony Freeman/Photo Edit; 6.2: © AP/Wide World Photos; p. 197: © Spencer Tirey; p. 198: © David Young-Wolff/Photo Edit; p. 201: © Jill Cannefax/EKM Nepenthe; p. 203: Courtesy of Angie Erickson; p. 205: Courtesy of Charla Peltier; p. 206: © AP/Wide World Photos; p. 207 (top): © LWA-Dann Tardif/Corbis; p. 207 (bottom): © PunchStock RF; p. 212: © Richard Hutchings/Photo Researchers; p. 216 (left): Bob Daemmrich/Stock Boston; p. 216 (right): Used by permission of Don Johnston Inc.; p. 217: © Koichi Kamoshida/Newsmakers/Getty Images; p. 220: © Doug Wilson/Corbis; p. 221: © 2007, USA TODAY. Reprinted with permission

Chapter 7

Opener: © Tony Freeman/Photo Edit; p. 232: © Ron Chapple Stock/Corbis RF; p. 233: © Sovfoto; 2.3: © Elizabeth Crews; p. 235: © Rob Meinychuk/Brand X/Corbis RF; p. 236: Nina Leen, Life Magazine, Time, Inc./Getty Images; 7.4 (left): © Bob Daemmrich/Stock Boston; 7.4 (middle): © Michael Newman/Photo Edit; 7.4 (right): © David Young-Wolff/Photo Edit; p. 242: © B. Daemmrich/The Image Works; p. 246: © Corbis RF; p. 248: Courtesy of Albert Bandura;

7.8: © Jeffry W. Myers/Corbis; 7.9 (top & bottom): Courtesy of Albert Bandura; p. 251: © Owen Franken/Corbis; p. 253: © Irwin Thompson/The Dallas Morning News; p. 256: © 2006 Sesame Workshop, New York, New York. Photograph by Richard Termine. All Rights Reserved

Chapter 8

Opener: © Ariel Skelley/Corbis; p. 271: © LWA-JDC/Corbis; p. 273: © Yellow Dog Productions/Getty; p. 274 (top): © Michael Prince/Corbis; p. 274 (bottom): © Paul Conklin/Photo Edit; p. 288: © David Butow/SABA/Corbis; p. 294: © Gill Ross/Corbis; p. 295: © Color Day Productions/The Image Bank/Getty Images; p. 296: © S.Lauterwasser/Lebrecht/The Image Works; p. 297: © Yellow Dog Productions/The Image Bank/Getty Images; p. 299: © Joe Baker, Images.com/Corbis; p. 302: © Royalty-Free/Corbis

Chapter 9

Opener: © Ellen Senis/The Image Works; p. 314 (left): © Digital Vision RF; p. 314 (middle): © D. Robert & Lorri Franz/Corbis; p. 314 (right): © DLILLC/Corbis RF; p. 319 (top): © Anthony Harve/Getty Rf; p. 319 (bottom): © Elizabeth Crews; p. 321 (left & right): Courtesy Rod Chlysta, Research Center for Educational Technology, Kent State University; p. 322: © Copyright 1999, USA Today Photo Library, photo by Robert Hanashiro; p. 326 (top): © Francisco Cruz/SuperStock; p. 326 (bottom): © Paul A. Souders/Corbis; p. 332: © AFP/Corbis; p. 334: © Gabe Palmer/Corbis; p. 341: © USA Today Photo Library, photo by Michael A. Schwarz

Chapter 10

Opener: Courtesy of Compton-Drew Investigative Learning Center Middle School, St. Louis, MO; p. 349: © Spencer Grant/Photo Edit; p. 352: © David Young-Wolff/Photo Edit; p. 353: Courtesy Robert Slavin, Success For All; p. 355: © PALS Tutoring Program, Vanderbilt Kennedy Center, Vanderbilt University, photographer Larry Wilson; p. 356: Courtesy of Coca-Cola Valued Youth Program; p. 357: © S.E. McKee/AP/Wide World; p. 364: © Tony Freeman/Photo Edit; p. 365: © Todd Lillard Photography; p. 369: Courtesy of Joe Campione, University of Berkeley, School of Education.; p. 370 (top & bottom): © Cognition & Technology Group,

LTC, Peabody College, Vanderbilt University; p. 371: Courtesy of Compton-Drew Investigative Learning Center Middle School, St. Louis, MO

Chapter 11

Opener: © David Young-Wolff/Photo Edit; p. 380: © LWS-Sharie Kennedy/Corbis; p. 381: © Comstock/Punchstock RF; p. 382 (left): © Tom & Dee Ann McCarthy/Corbis; p. 382 (right): © Gabe Palmer/Corbis; p. 383: © Gideon Mendel/Corbis; p. 388: © Michael Keller/Corbis; p. 396: © Jim Graham; p. 398: © Tom & Dee Ann McCarthy/Corbis; p. 399: © Richard T. Nowitz/Corbis; p. 401: © Paul S. Howell; p. 402: © Andrew Itkoff; p. 405: © Dale Sparks; p. 406: © Patty Wood; p. 409: © Image 100/Corbis RF; p. 411: © Teacher's Curriculum Institute

Chapter 12

Opener: © Francisco Cruz/SuperStock; p. 423: © Michael S. Yamashita/Corbis; p. 426 (top): © SW Productions/Brand X/Corbis RF; p. 426 (middle): © Mooboard/Corbis RF; p. 426 (bottom): © Bill Aaron/Photo Edit; p. 427: © John Henley/Corbis; p. 428: © Robert Isaacs/Photo Researchers; p. 429: © Tom & Dee Ann McCarthy/Corbis; p. 431: © Bob Daemmrich/The Image Works; p. 434: © Anna Palma; p. 437 (top): © 2004, USA Today. Reprinted with permission; p. 437 (bottom): © William Hart/Photo Edit; p. 439: © Tom & Dee Ann McCarthy/Corbis; p. 441: © Stan Godlewski Photography; p. 444: Courtesy Rod Chlysta, Research Center for Educational Technology, Kent State University; p. 446: © Rene Mansi/iStock photo; p. 449 (top left): © Michael Newman/Photo Edit; p. 449 (top right): © Bill Aron/Photo Edit; p. 449 (bottom): © Michael Newman/Photo Edit

Chapter 13

Opener: © Cleve Bryant/Photo Edit; p. 459: © Michael Tweed/AP/Wide World Photos; p. 460: © Oliver Hoslet/Corbis; 13.1 (family): © Lawrence Migdale; 13.1 (crossing): © David Young-Wolff/Stone/Getty Images; 13.1 (teens): © Tessa Codrington/Stone/Getty Images; 13.1 (mirror): © Rhoda Sidney; 13.1 (flute): © Lonnie Duka/Stone/Getty Images; p. 464: © Elizabeth Crews/The Image Works; p. 465: © Michael A. Schwarz Photography; p. 466: Courtesy Rod Chlysta, Research

Center for Educational Technology, Kent State University; p. 467: © LWA-Sharie Kennedy/Corbis; p. 469: © M. Antman/The Image Works; p. 472: © AP/Wide World Photos; p. 473: © Ariel Skelley/Blend Images/Corbis RF; p. 475: © Gabe Palmer/Corbis; p. 476: © Ralf-Finn Hestoft/Corbis; p. 481 (top): © Bill Stanton; p. 481 (bottom): © Michael Keller/Corbis; p. 483: Courtesy of Sandra Graham; p. 485: © Joan Marcus

Chapter 14

Opener: © Todd Pearson/Corbis; p. 502: Michael A. Schwarz Photography; p. 503 (left): © PunchStock RF; p. 503 (right): © Royalty-Free/Corbis; 14.1 (top): © Spencer Grant/Photo Edit; 14.1 (middle 1): © David Young-Wolff/Photo Edit; 14.1 (middle 2): © Elizabeth Crews; 14.1 (bottom): © Rick Raymond/Stone/Getty Images; p. 512: © William Williford, Perry Middle School, Perry, GA; p. 514: © Royalty-Free/Corbis; p. 515: O'Brien Productions/Corbis; p. 516: © Mark Fodness; p. 519: © LWA-Dann Tardif/zefa/Corbis; p. 522 (top): © Gabe Palmer/Corbis; p. 522 (bottom): © Tom Stewart/Corbis; p. 523: © Tommie Lindsey; p. 524 (left): © Royalty-Free/Corbis; p. 524 (right): © Gabe Palmer/Corbis; p. 528: Courtesy of Department of Teaching and Learning, Peabody College, Vanderbilt University; p. 532: © Don Hammond/Design Pics/Corbis RF

Chapter 15

Opener: © Bill Aron/Photo Edit; p. 541: © Bob Daemmrich/The Image Works; p. 543: © Will & Deni McIntyre/Corbis; p. 545: © Will & Deni McIntyre/Corbis; P. 549: © Charles Gupton/Corbis; p. 553: Photos courtesy Martha McArthur, Reading First Program, NM; p. 563 & 566: © Will & Deni McIntyre/Corbis

Chapter 16

Opener: © David Young-Wolff/Photo Edit; p. 577: © First Light/Corbis; p. 583: © Will & Deni McIntyre/Corbis; p. 584: © Randy Faris/Corbis RF; p. 585: © Superstock RF; p. 607: © Gabe Palmer/Corbis

Name Index

Subject Index

A

Ability, heterogeneous, for small-group work, 363
Ability grouping
between-class, 133–134
within-class, 134–135
Absolute grading, 604
Abstraction in language development, 62
Accommodation in Piaget's theory, 40
Accountability, standardized tests and, 19, 541
Achievement, 463–479
attribution and, 470–471
ethnicity and, 483–484
expectations and, 475–477
extrinsic and intrinsic motivation and, 463–470
goal setting, planning, and self-monitoring and, 474–475
high anxiety and, 490
mastery motivation and, 470–471
mindset and, 472–473
perfectionism and, 488–490
procrastination and, 487–488
reciprocal determinism model and, 248
self-efficacy and, 473–474
socioeconomic status and, 483–484
students who are low achieving and have low expectations for success and, 486–487
students who are uninterested or alienated and, 490
students who protect their self-worth by avoiding failure and, 487
values and purpose and, 477
Achievement tests, 546
standards-based, 547–551
types of, 546–547
Action research, 22
Active listening, 524
Adaptive expertise, 293–294
Adolescence, 31
brain development in, 37
critical thinking in, 320
language development in, 65–66
metacognition in, 301
schooling in, 93–96
time use in, cross-cultural studies of, 152
Advancement Via Individual Determination (AVID) program, 134
Advance organizers, 429
Affective domain in Bloom's taxonomy, 425–426
Affiliation, need for, 462

African Americans. *See also* Diversity; Ethnicity
achievement of, 483–484
intrinsic motivation and, 464
motivation and, 483–484
parenting styles of, 81
parents as monitors and, 84
Age. *See also specific age groups*
mental, 117
Aggression
gender differences in, 178–179
managing, 530–533
Agressive behaviors, 206–207
Algorithms, problem solving and, 331–332
Alienation, achievement and, 490
Alphabetic principle, 62
Alternate-forms reliability, 544
Alternative assessments, 566, 592–603.
See also Classroom assessment
authentic assessment for, 593–594
performance assessment for, 594–598
portfolio assessment for, 598–601
trends in, 592–594
Amygdala, 37
Analogies, 318
Analytical intelligence, 120
Anchor papers, 596
Androgyny, 179
Anxiety, 207
achievement and, 490
Applied behavior analysis, 238–247
contracting and, 240–241
decreasing undesirable behaviors and, 242–246
differential reinforcement and, 242
evaluation of, 246
extinction and, 242
increasing desirable behaviors and, 239–242
negative reinforcement and, 241
presenting aversive stimuli and, 244–246
prompts and, 241
reinforcement schedule and, 239–240
reinforcers and, 239
removing desirable stimuli and, 242
response cost and, 243–244
shaping and, 241–242
time-out and, 243
Apprenticeship, cognitive, 351–352
Aptitude tests, 546
standards-based, 547–551
Articulation disorders, 204–205
Artifacts, 599
Asperger syndrome, 205, 206
Assessment

alternative. *See* Alternative assessments
authentic, 593–594
classroom. *See* Classroom assessment
pluralistic, 581
in Schools for Thought, 372
tests for. *See* High-stakes testing; Standardized tests; Traditional tests
Web-based, 585
Assessment skills, 10–11
Assimilation in Piaget's theory, 40
Assistive technology, 215, 216
Associative learning, 231
Athletics, eliminating gender bias and, 182
Atkinson-Shiffrin model, 282–283
Attention, 273–277
definition of, 273
developmental changes in, 274–275
divided, 273
executive, 273
helping students pay, 276
observational learning and, 249
selective, 273
sustained, 273
Attention deficit hyperactivity disorder (ADHD), 198–200
causes and treatment of, 198–200
characteristics of, 198
diagnosis and developmental status and, 198
Attestations, 599
Attribution theory, 470–471
Authentic assessment, 593–594
performance assessment compared with, 593
Authoritarian classroom management style, 513–514
Authoritarian parenting, 80
Authoritative classroom management style, 513
Authoritative parenting, 80
Autism spectrum disorders (ASIs), 205–206
Autistic disorder, 205, 206
Automaticity, 271
Autonomy versus shame and doubt stage, 75
Average children, 88

B

Babbling, 61
Backward-reaching transfer, 340
Bar graphs, 557–558
Behavioral approach, 3–4
Behavioral disorders, 206–207

Behavioral objectives, 424–425
Behavioral perspective on motivation, 460–461
Behaviorism, 231
Beliefs
false, 301
perseverance of, 324
Bell-shaped curve, 560–561
Belvedere computer technology system, 298
Best-work portfolios, 599
Between-class ability grouping (tracking), 133–134
Bias
in classroom assessment, 581
confirmation, 324
cultural, intelligence tests and, 130–133
ethnic, 159
gender, eliminating, 180–185
hindsight, 324
overconfidence, 324
reducing, in multicultural education, 171
referral, 194
in tests, 544–545
Big Brothers and Big Sisters, 353
"Big Five" factors of personality, 140
Bilingual education, 161, 163
Bilingualism, 160–162
learning a second language and, 160
Binet tests, 117–118
Biological influences on language development, 59–61
Biological processes, 30
Blending, phonological awareness and, 385
Bloom's taxonomy, 425–427
Bodily-kinesthetic skills, in Gardner's theory, 122, 124, 125
Boys and Girls Clubs of America, 353
Brain, 35–40
gender differences in, 176–177
lateralization and, 37–38
Brain damage, mental retardation due to, 202
Brain development
in adolescence, 37
children's education and, 38–40
in middle and late childhood, 36
neuron and brain region development and, 35–36
plasticity and, 38
Brain scans, learning disabilities and, 195–196
Brainstorming, 327
Bronfenbrenner's ecological theory, 74–75
Bullying, 531–533
Bully-Proofing Your School, 532